PIONEERS
OF THE
GAME

The Evolution of
Men's Professional Tennis

MARSHALL HAPPER

ISBN: 978-1937559953

Published by New Chapter Press
1175 York Ave
Suite #3s
New York, NY 10065
www.NewChapterMedia.com
@NewChapterMedia

Distributed by IPG
www.IPGBook.com

For my wonderful wife, Karen Scott Happer, who put up with the loss of my time with her during the years I was writing this book,

and thanks to:

Randy Walker of New Chapter Press, Inc., my editor and publisher,

and

The International Tennis Federation, the ATP Tour, the United States Tennis Association, the International Tennis Hall of Fame, the All England Lawn Tennis Club and the Wimbledon Museum for sharing their historical records

and thanks also to some wonderful and very helpful friends:

Roy L. Reardon, Jim McManus, Mike Davies, Christopher Davies, Christopher Stokes, Warren F. Kimball, Weller Evans, Greg Sharko, John Barrett, Robert McNicol, Meredith Miller Richards, Sarah Frandsen, Bill Babcock and Richard H. Adams.

WHAT THEY ARE SAYING ABOUT "PIONEERS OF THE GAME"

<u>Jimmy Connors, Former World No. 1</u>

"This is about the development of men's tennis from the beginning. The Pioneers molded the game, but did those involved have their own agendas? Marshall Happer had to deal with all the 'players' - those on the court and those behind the scenes. This is a story that needs to be told - to understand how tennis has gotten to where it is now. Many questions will be answered, and maybe, just maybe, a few more will be asked."

<u>Ivan Lendl, Former World No. 1</u>

"I was opposed to many of the rules that Marshall held us to and we fought all the time, but looking back he had an impossible job which he tried to manage in the fairest way possible."

<u>Craig Tiley, Tennis Australia CEO</u>

"Success is optimised by having respect and a better understanding of the past. Marshall's book will help everyone in tennis reflect and gain greater knowledge of what came before them. The Pioneers of the Game have given us all much to be thankful for. We have the most enduring and exciting sport in the world, but at the same time today have challenges with the narrative. We can learn from the lessons of the past through Marshall's account and use this history to continue to improve our truly global sport. Thank you, Marshall, for your efforts in bringing to life this account. You are leading the way today, just like you did then."

<u>Cliff Drysdale, Member of WCT "Handsome Eight" as a Pro, First President of ATP, Men's Tennis Council Player Representative, ESPN Television Commentator</u>

"There were so many moving parts to this interesting story. At that time tennis organizations and players in this drama were staking their claim to a place at the table. Marshall Happer was in the right place then, and he led the game thru its formative stage when there was no clear end in sight. He steered the discussion forcefully but gently through those turbulent times. Indeed, for a long while he was the lead pioneer. Marshall has done diligent research so this book is a definitive historical account. It is a great trip down memory lane and a fascinating tale of the birth of pro tennis."

"Men's professional tennis today owes a huge thank you to Marshall Happer who was the Administrator for the Men's Tennis Council, the first and only unified governing body for men's professional tennis. In his role, Marshall professionalized the administration of men's tennis and curtailed the rampant player misconduct with the enforcement of the Code of Conduct while leading the development of professional officiating for tennis. Professional tennis needed someone with Marshall's passion for tennis and legal background to build the foundation for the sport we enjoy today."

"The game of tennis is so much poorer when someone of Marshall Happer's administrative skills, integrity and unequaled code of ethics, is sitting on the sidelines."

"As a founding member of the ATP and later a member of the Men's Tennis Council representing the North American Tournaments, I had the privilege of spending many hours in meeting rooms with Marshall. Marshall Happer was without question one of the most, if not the most, visionary and influential leader during one of the most momentous and critical periods in tennis history after the beginning of 'The Open Era.' Much of the success that tennis has achieved is due to some sound fundamentals that were established under Marshall's leadership then. This book tells the accurate historical story of that period. It is a must read for Tennis fans, and should be mandatory reading for all Players, Tournament Directors and Tennis Officials."

"Marshall Happer's Pioneers of the Game includes all of the years of my career in tennis. As a member of the Men's Tennis Council, I had the task in 1980-1981 of leading the worldwide search with Arthur Ashe and Philippe Chatrier for a full time Administrator to set up an office in New York City to provide independent professional administration for men's tennis for the first time. That search culminated with Marshall's employment who served in that capacity from 1981 until the Men's Tennis Council was dissolved after 1989. Marshall's Pioneers of the Game details the evolution of men's professional tennis from a mostly amateur sport into the professional sport of today along with for the first time the trials and tribulations of the inside competition among the insiders of the game he calls the "Pioneers of the Game" as tennis became a true professional sport. The players and administrators of today all are benefiting from the work of the Pioneers and this important history should be helpful to all of them."

<u>Weller Evans, Former Men's Tennis Council Player Representative and Longtime ATP Staff Professional in the Job that Was Closest to the Players</u>

"In any endeavor, it is essential to know from where you have come in order to have a clearer understanding of the possibilities that lie ahead. Pioneers of the Game begins with the birth of Open Tennis and details the tumultuous and at times tempestuous evolution of the men's professional game through what many consider the golden age of tennis. Not only was it important to accurately chronicle these historical events but also provide a reference for those in who's hands the game rests today and in the future. Marshall, having lived it, has done just that."

<u>Micky Den Tuinder Lawler, President of WTA Women's Tennis Association, Tour Liaison for Men's Tennis Council 1986-1988</u>

"Pioneers of the Game provides the reader with a unique and inside personal insight into the fascinating world of tennis. This game is as competitive and intense behind the scenes as it is on the court. The thick plots that evolved on the international stage rival any adventure in Ian Fleming's James Bond series. In 1986, my first job in professional tennis was traveling the world as a Tour Liaison for the Men's Tennis Council led by Marshall Happer to provide the players and the tournaments with communication services. As a young woman on Marshall's team, I revered his keen ability to lead with an optimal balance of authority, respect, and compassion. I still do. The Men's Tennis Council was the first and last unified governing body for men's professional tournaments with representatives of the players, tournaments and the International Tennis Federation. Marshall tried unsuccessfully to save the MTC, but it was dissolved in 1990, when the ATP Tour began and the Grand Slams became independent. If everyone involved in men's and women's professional tennis reads Pioneers of the Game, I wonder if the unification of governance might be considered again."

<u>Brian Tobin, President of Tennis Australia, Both an ITF Representative and a Tournament Representative on the Men's Tennis Council and Later President of the ITF</u>

"This book provides a detailed history of the development which occurred in the organisation of the major men's professional tennis tour in the period 1970s-1990s. This was a turbulent period in the Game, highlighted by a series of lawsuits. The MIPTC was fortunate to have as it COO at the time, Marshall Happer, an experienced and qualified lawyer."

<u>David Hill, Former Chairman and CEO Fox Sports Media Group</u>

"Cast your mind back to the most epic struggle you have witnessed in a tennis match. Where two great champions, neither of whom would give an inch, battled right to the very last gasp. That match pales into insignificance when you compare it to the battles which birthed today's men's tennis world. A must for anyone who calls themselves a tennis lover, Marshall Happer's meticulously researched and erudite book – for the very first time – spells out the bloody, bruising and lawsuit filled dawn of the modern tennis era. With more twists and turns than a John Le Carre novel – no one's tennis library is complete without Happer's Pioneers of the Game."

Ken Solomon, Tennis Channel, President and Executive Producer, "Barnstormers - The Birth of Open Tennis"

"Marshall Happer has written the definitive history of one of the most unlikely and least understood origin stories of any major sport, chronicling the tumultuous 40 year birth of men's, and eventually all, professional tennis. As the strong yet understated leader, Happer served as the game's first and only true Commissioner/COO, presiding over a colorful and brilliant band of iconic and legendary tennis pioneers who together laid the framework for what today is the world's most ubiquitous professional sports tour. Pioneers of the Game reveals in riveting, page turning detail how the game's founders threaded many a needle in organizing and delivering to the world a professional game which today represents the most broadly attended and most universal global events, featuring the world's highest paid and best known athletes. Commissioner Happer's meticulous, fascinating and thoroughly entertaining narrative has never before been told, and is a must read for any tennis fan or player seeking the unique origins of the professional game."

Jerry Solomon, Former President of ProServ Management Company

"When Marshall Happer arrived on the scene he was essentially tasked by the Men's Pro Council to tame what was the loosely regulated world of men's pro tennis. Marshall introduced rules and disciplines and doctrines that none of us-players, agents and tournament directors-were interested in being bound by so we spent a lot of time trying to find loopholes that would enable us to undo what he was doing. It resulted in a lot of friction but also some pretty good laughs and a weird kind of camaraderie amidst the threatened lawsuits and boycotts. We were working on a blank canvas. I don't think we realized it would get as big as it has become."

Reg Lansberry, Former MTC Director of Media Relations 1984-1989

"For the record, I have always been justifiably proud of the fact that I was one of those who "went down with the ship" on December 31, 1989. While I have never harbored any illusions that the Men's Tennis Council has ever garnered (or ever will) the credit that it rightfully deserved in the years since then, perhaps your book will help to draw attention to its many accomplishments. Among scores of the departed, in my mind's eye, I continue to believe that if Arthur Ashe, Gene Scott, David Gray, Ron Bookman and so many others, were still alive today, they would all rightfully trumpet that long list."

Contents

Preface

It took a number of years for tennis to mature as a professional sport and in lots of ways it is still maturing as it competes with all the other sports for talented athletes and fans. I have written this book to provide the so far unwritten or incomplete history of the inside struggles and conflicts of the relatively small group of pioneers and visionaries who led and shaped the development and professionalism of the business, administration and governance of professional tennis for men prior to 1990.

This is not a book about great players and great tennis matches. It is about the competition and struggles of the important people I call the Pioneers of the Game who were responsible for the development and maturing of tennis as a professional sport, the curtailment of player misconduct and the development of professional tennis officiating prior to 1990. The great players included are because of their impact on the governance and development of the sport. The leaders of men's professional tennis today are standing on their shoulders.

Prior to 1974, the International Tennis Federation (ITF) was the governing body of men's tennis. From 1974 – 1989, the Men's Tennis Council (MTC) was the first and the only unified governing body for men's professional tennis with representatives of the ITF, the players and the tournaments. From 1974-1980, the MTC operated without any permanent administration and in 1981, I was honored to be selected to be the first (and as fate would have it the only) Administrator for the MTC, leaving my law practice in Raleigh, North Carolina, to move to New York City to develop the first full time professional administration for men's tennis. I served as the MTC Administrator until the MTC ceased operations on December 31, 1989, when the ITF, Tournament and Player constituents of the MTC split. January 1, 1990, thus marked the end of the unified governance for men's professional tennis under the MTC, the end of the ATP as a pure player association, the creation the ATP Tour as a joint venture between the ATP and the non-Grand Slam tournaments, and the creation of the Grand Slam Committee, now called the Grand Slam Board, for the newly independent Grand Slam tournaments, the Australian Open, French Open, Wimbledon and the U.S. Open, while the ITF continued to manage the Davis Cup team competition.

Between 1974 and 1989, there were only 30 members of the MTC. In 2021, 14 are deceased and 16 are still with us (two ITF Representatives, six Tournament Representatives, eight Player Representatives). Each of the MTC representatives had competing interests and agendas (many even within their own constituencies) which in large part provided their support for me as the Administrator to act as I was independent of each constituency and obligated to serve all of them.

After I finally retired in 2009 from the practice of law and had time to focus on preserving the history of the MTC and the small group of visionaries who I call the Pioneers of the Game, I quickly realized that the history of the MTC and the accomplishments of its 30 volunteer members and the others who worked with them could not be told or understood without understanding what happened before 1974 with the earlier Pioneers that caused the MTC to be created. This led me back to the 40+ year struggle between amateur and professional tennis and the struggle for the opening of tennis to all professionals in 1968, all of which involved the important Pioneers of the Game. I discovered that this history was scattered in the minutes and records of the 90 international governance meetings of the MTC over its 16 years of existence, the archives of the ITF and the ATP Tour, numerous articles in the *London Times, New York Times, Tennis Week, International Tennis Weekly,* the annual World of *Tennis series* (1968-2001), *World Tennis Magazine, Tennis Magazine,* the annual *USTA Yearbooks,* plus numerous other books and publications and retained in the memories of many of the living participants. As a result, it has taken me several years to study and assimilate that material and conduct interviews with many of the living participants for this book. My presentations of the annual tennis calendars of sanctioned tournaments and important special events for these formulative years are more complete than the records of the ITF and the ATP Tour. I have also provided my outsider's analysis of what happened between 1990 and 2021.

I am keenly aware that many of today's tennis leaders and fans may not have been born during the period of the MTC governance between 1974 and 1989 and that none of the leading players of today were around then as Roger Federer, the oldest leading player of today, was not born until 1981. Nevertheless, I hope today's leaders, players and fans will all be interested to learn how our wonderful sport was developed and my analysis of what is happening today. You will note that many of the problems faced by the Pioneers are having to be faced again by today's leaders.

Let me hasten to add, this book is about men's professional tennis, not women's professional tennis. The struggles the women had occurred to some extent simultaneously with the men's struggles and would provide an interesting book of its own.

I am proud that I had the opportunity to meet and work for and with many of the Pioneers of the Game. I wish I had known all of this history when I was privileged to be involved in men's professional tennis.

Marshall Happer
2021

Foreword – Steve Flink

The history of professional tennis has never been fully understood by even the most erudite of the game's ardent followers. The pro game has flourished despite a multitude of intricacies making governance an arduous task for all of the entities. After the arrival of "Open Tennis" in 1968, when all of the best players—pros and amateurs—were permitted at last to compete against each other in the major championships, the sport exploded with popularity in the public eye.

But establishing a coherent political structure for the game of tennis and raising the level of professionalization across the board and through the decades was a monumental task for all of the indispensable leaders who stepped into the arena behind the scenes to make it happen. It is a fascinating story in so many ways. Estimable individuals of considerable stature and enduring importance stepped forward and propelled professional tennis into a new sphere. They guided the game with skill, dedication and clarity into uncharted territory. These distinguished power brokers broke new ground despite suffering the inevitable growing pains along the way.

In this compelling and immensely significant book, Marshall Happer—a central figure in the evolution of pro tennis and one of its most crucial citizens— writes the definitive historical account of how it all transpired, of those who contributed most mightily to the growth and wellbeing of the sport, of why the many challenges confronted by the those in and around the establishment were ultimately successful in their quest to turn the men's game into a place of growing prominence along the landscape of sports.

Happer sweepingly examines the breadth and scope of professional tennis in this far reaching book, going back to its roots in the 1920's, showing how it has evolved ever since.

No one but the industrious and enterprising Happer could have written this comprehensive account. He was singularly qualified to take on such a substantial and daunting task. Happer was a passionate tennis participant in his younger years. Growing up in North Carolina, he played high school tennis. From 1957-60, he played for the ACC champion North Carolina Tar Heels. In 1966 and 1967, he took the North Carolina State Doubles Championships with different partners. The following year, he was the founder and President of the Raleigh Racquet Club. Later, Happer enhanced his growing reputation for leadership as President of the North Carolina and Southern Tennis Associations.

Over the course of the 1970's, Happer staged tournaments in Raleigh as part of the Southern Prize Money circuit within the USTA. As that decade closed, Happer organized the USTA's national secondary prize money circuits. Meanwhile, Happer believed the Association of Tennis Professionals (ATP)— which was born in 1972 and introduced computer rankings the following year— was failing to meet the needs of emerging players struggling to make a living. He negotiated and gained approval for ATP Ranking points in 1976 at satellite tournaments although the larger breakthrough and acceleration was in 1978 and 1979 with the emergence of $25,000 American Express satellite events. Happer's persistence was instrumental in opening up a critical pathway for players to compete on the international Grand Prix circuit.

But it was in 1981 that Happer moved into another realm of the sport in a position of wide ranging authority. He was named as the independent administrator for the Men's Tennis Council, the international governing body for men's professional tennis. He did not wear the official label of "commissioner" of the men's game but that essentially is what he was. He was responsible for the administration of the worldwide Grand Prix of tennis. He remained in that enormously influential post until the end of 1989 when the MTC disbanded. During his productive tenure, the Code of conduct was implemented, the first pro tennis officials were employed by his organization, and drug testing for the players was introduced.

Renowned *New York Times* columnist Dave Anderson wrote in 1983 that Happer was "the most important person in tennis... the closest thing to a commissioner that this fragmented and footloose sport has had."

In "Pioneers of the Game", Happer always understates his own lofty contributions to both the MTC and even what he did from 1990-95 as COO of the USTA. He reserves his richest praise for the likes of Jack Kramer, Philippe Chatrier, Lamar Hunt, Herman David, Donald Dell, Judge Robert J. Kelleher, Mike Davies, Cliff Drysdale, Arthur Ashe, Owen Williams and others who played massive roles in advancing the sport. He takes us through the trials, tribulations and intermingling of the ITF and ATP, WCT and the Grand Prix, the growing influence of the agents, the rising stock of the players, the cross currents and complexities of critical decision making, and the extraordinary dedication of the sport's administrative hierarchy.

To be sure, the most absorbing material in the book surrounds the MTC, which was established in 1974 but became increasingly significant as the chief governing body of the game during the years when Happer was in charge for most of the eighties. That was a time when tennis seemed to have found order amidst the chaos. The Council was comprised of three players, three tournament directors and three ITF representatives. The balance of power in men's tennis was fundamentally fair. The presence of Happer presiding as the leader of that organization was reassuring to all of the powers that be who realized they needed a clear-eyed, level-headed, highly principled and unfailingly dispassionate individual in charge and willing to hear all sides of a debate.

In this remarkable book, Happer draws on his prodigious collection of material from the MTC years, and those chapters are filled with information and anecdotes only he could have gathered. He not only writes about what happened and why it occurred, but sprinkles those pages with the interactions of various leaders who inevitably clashed with their different personalities, priorities and outlooks. Happer explains how he tried to resolve any disputes as diplomatically as possible for the betterment of the Council.

In my view, Happer was the ultimate diplomat, a man enormously respected by everyone in any position of authority, a fellow of unimpeachable integrity, a figure who defined himself through his fundamental decency and unshakable transparency.

He was also—and very definitely remains— a workhorse. This book was years in the making because he left no stone unturned, exhaustively researching every fact he could, spending endless hours in libraries, contacting his many friends in the tennis universe, digging out detail after detail until, ultimately, the job was done. As I followed his progress in email exchanges and occasional conversations, I was reminded of a magazine piece I once did on him. In that article, I wrote, "If there were 36 hours in a day, it wouldn't be enough for Marshall Happer."

That was in 1979. Nothing has changed. And that is why this book fills such a critical void in tennis journalism. Some of the books done on pro tennis thus far have touched on the administrative side of the game and those in the decision making forefront, but most were superficial. None of those books has been nearly as comprehensive as this one regarding the inner workings of the pro game, the people behind the scenes who have mattered the most, and the developments that took place which colored the landscape and shaped the universe. Happer thematically demonstrates ably across 39 chapters the complexities faced by those who have been charged with keeping the international tennis ship afloat over the past half century. He not only lays out the facts painstakingly with simplicity, but also interprets history with unmistakable lucidity.

Happer's work in the 1980's and nineties allowed him to tap into his vast reservoir of knowledge from that time when he played such a pivotal role the hierarchy of tennis leadership. I assumed correctly that the chapters from that period would be standouts. And yet, the rest of the book is no less informative, entertaining or all encompassing. Happer traces pro tennis back to its early days in the 1920's, delves deeply into the groundbreaking years in the 1960's leading up to Open Tennis, and writes powerfully about the embryonic stages of the Open Era when the sport was spiraling, when authorities needed to figure out the right set of guidelines, and when the winds of change were blowing ferociously all through the corridors of the game.

Happer then concludes with some penetrating writing on the evolution of men's tennis since the Men's Tennis Council ended at the end of the eighties and the ATP Tour commenced the following year. He covers that span with the same unswerving commitment to accuracy and clarity that he delivers in the rest of a book that will be regarded by historians like myself as a treasure.

In closing, I will add only this: having spent my life in tennis as a journalist for nearly fifty years, I have met no one in the world of tennis who has been as unwaveringly scrupulous as Marshall Happer. Above all else, this book is a clear reflection of his character.

Steve Flink
2017 International Tennis Hall of Fame Inductee

CHAPTER 1:

BEFORE 1968: AMATEUR SPORT VS. PROFESSIONAL SPORT

In the beginning, there was only amateur tennis and men's tennis was controlled by the national associations of each country and the International Lawn Tennis Federation (ILTF). The ILTF was founded in 1913, with 15 nations: Australia, Austria, Belgium, Denmark, France, Germany, Great Britain, Hungary, Italy, Netherlands, Russia, South Africa, Spain, Sweden and Switzerland. The ILTF name was changed in 1977 to the International Tennis Federation (ITF). The United States Lawn Tennis Association (USLTA) refused to join because the ILTF had agreed that Great Britain could in perpetuity stage the "World Championships." In 1923, the USLTA joined the ILTF upon the agreement that the "World Championships" would be dropped and the ILTF would recognize four official championships: the official championships of Great Britain (Wimbledon, founded 1877), United States (founded 1881), France (founded 1891) and Australia (founded 1905), todays' four Grand Slams. Eventually, all national associations annually staged an amateur national championship. All tournaments were knock-out competitions, except that prior to 1912 for the U.S. Nationals and prior to 1922 for Wimbledon, the players competed for the right to challenge last year's champion.

Davis Cup

In addition to the amateur national championships, the Davis Cup was the recognized official amateur international team competition. It began in 1900 originally between the United States and Great Britain, and in 1905 was enlarged to include France, Austria, Belgium and Australia. By the 1920s there were over 20 nations involved. The Davis Cup competition was originally owned by the Davis Cup Nations. It was transferred to the ITF in 1979. Prior to 1972, teams competed for the right to challenge last year's champion nation in a "Challenge Round." The Challenge Round format was changed in 1972 to a straight knockout competition with all nations competing.

Shamateur Tennis

The ILTF and the national tennis associations wanted and needed the best amateur tennis players for their Davis Cup teams and for their national and international tournaments to justify the sale of tickets and sponsorships. To become one of the best amateur tennis players, required a tennis player to commit to play year-round in international competition and travel to tournaments scheduled in the spring and early summer in Europe, in the summer in the United States and Canada, and in the winter in South America and Australia. As a result, full-time employment outside of tennis was not possible and tennis players had to seek (or beg for) funding of their expenses from the national associations and the tournaments in which they competed. The rules were adamant that tennis players could only receive travel and living expenses and could not make any profit at all. Apparently, almost everyone violated this untenable rule, so its enforcement was mostly non-existent and amateur tennis became "shamateur tennis." However, none of those amateur players became wealthy from tennis. Many good tennis athletes dropped out of tennis after completing junior or college tennis because professional tennis as a viable career simply did not exist before 1968.

Owen Williams, The "Potato Peeler for Wimbledon"

Owen Williams of Johannesburg, South Africa, became a "tennis bum" "shamateur" in 1951. Owen earned his way to Wimbledon by peeling potatoes on the *Pretoria Castle* sailing from Port Elizabeth to Southhampton via Cape Town as one of 23 third assistant cooks. Owen wrote in his book *Ahead of the Game*[1]: "Before leaving South Africa, I had sold my old battered Hudson Terraplane for 30 quid (English pounds) and, added to my wages for peeling potatoes I now had 40 pounds sterling between me and starvation. No friends, no relatives, and more definitive, no return ticket to South Africa. I was never more lost in my life. Did I ever think of turning back? Not on your Nelly!"

When Owen's story hit the British press, he was recognized on the streets of London immediately. Owen was accepted in the 1951 Wimbledon qualifying where he was brutally introduced to serve and volley play on grass. He received no expense money. However, when he earned the No. 1 ranking in South Africa he was paid £200 Pounds which had to cover travel plus three weeks in London. He considered it a "very satisfactory sum."

Owen, who was always one of the smartest tennis professionals, described "shamateurism" in *Ahead of the Game*[2]: "Attaining the highest amount for expenses was quite a talent in and of itself. The Americans, unless they absconded to Europe, were confined very much to the U.S. circuits and the ironclad rule of 25 U.S. dollars a day.

For the rest of us it was a case of '*catch as catch can*' and having the nerve to push your asking price to the limit. I learned very early on to think outside the box! Most of the negotiating took place at Wimbledon. All the world's players were there, and it was easy for tournaments to send a representative. Bear in mind that these people were sent there to break the rules, but they were nevertheless leading officials of their home Associations! As I have said, I called it cheating fairly…Nothing could be committed to paper! The irony – it was a *gentleman's agreement!*"

Williams retired from shamateur tennis at the end of 1956 and returned to Johannesburg. He returned with $20,000 as the self-proclaimed "highest paid player in the world." By 1969, he would be recognized as the most famous professional tournament director in the world as he promoted the South African Open in Johannesburg and also the U.S. Open in New York.

Owen Williams

In *Open Tennis*[3], Richard Evans recalled his two-page spread in *The Sunday Times* in 1967, as follows: "Accurately depicting the players' tea-room at Wimbledon during The Championship as an open market with tournament directors from around the world bartering for the services of 'amateur' players, the article offered up the next best thing to a ranking list of the day. From the bottom up, it listed such players as Britain's Mike Sangster, the great bearded Dane Torben Ulrich and Australia's Owen Davidson as being in the $300-$400-a-week class for under-the-counter payments. (Nikki) Pilic, Wilhelm Bungert of West Germany, Thomas Koch of Brazil and Marty Mulligan, the Italian-based Australian, were said to be worth up to $500 a week. A select quartet comprising (John) Newcombe, (Tony) Roche, Sweden's lanky Jan-Erik Lundquist and Rafael Osuna, the delightful Mexican who was later killed in an air crash, were named as $700-a-week players. Roy Emerson and Cliff Drysdale were listed at $900, with Manolo Santana, the Wimbledon champion of 1966 and winner of both the French and the Forest Hills titles, top of the heap at $1,000. That was the shady world of tennis "shamateurism' as laid out for all to see in *The Sunday Times*.

Actually, the figures were a little conservative. 'Emmo and I were getting 15 hundred a week,' Santana told me (Evans). 'We had come to an agreement between ourselves to ask for that and most of the tournaments could easily afford it. Some just wouldn't pay, of course. When I went to Australia in '65 to play the Davis Cup finals, the Australian LTA wanted me to play in their Championships. But when I told them the price, they refused. So, I didn't play. When Emmo played in Spain he got paid. For a couple of years, it was simply better for us to remain amateur because all the other top players had turned pro. If I had turned (pro), I would have gone to MacCall, but in the end I stayed with the 'shamateur' system, embarrassing as it was. I was relieved when Open Tennis came in. It ended all that hyprocrisy for everyone.'"

First Professional Tour:
Charles "Cash & Carry" Pyle and Suzanne Lenglen

Suzanne Lenglen won the French Championships in 1925 and 1926 and Wimbledon in 1919, 1920, 1921, 1922, 1923, 1925, had a career record of 341-7 with 81 titles and was the No. 1 player in the world for many years. The first professional tour promoter I found was Charles C. "Cash & Carry" Pyle who in 1926 paid Suzanne Lenglen $50,000 to turn professional and play in a tour in the United States, Canada, Cuba and Mexico during which she defeated Mary K. Brown, the first U.S. professional female 38-0.

Billie Jean King wrote in her 1988 book *We Have Come A Long Way*[4], "Suzanne was widely criticized within the tennis community and in France for her decision to turn professional. The All England Club revoked her honorary membership. One British publication, *Lawn Tennis and Badminton*, went so far as to say her retirement was good for the game, because 'her unbridled temperament was always making for difficulties.'

Suzanne had no difficulty making the decision. Her family's fortune had withered away, she was in need of money, and she had no wish to continue filling promoters' pockets at the expense of her own. She once described the act of turning professional as 'an escape from bondage and slavery.'

In an article that appears in her tour's program, Suzanne wrote, 'In the twelve years I have been champion, I have earned literally millions of francs for tennis and have paid thousands of francs in entrance fees to be allowed to do so.... I have worked as hard at my career as any man or woman has worked at any career. And in my whole lifetime I have not earned $5,000 – not one cent of that by my specialty, my life study – tennis...' 'I am twenty-seven and not wealthy – should I embark on any other career and leave the one for which I have what people call genius? Or should I smile at the prospect of actual poverty and continue to earn a fortune – for whom?'"

"Suzanne's criticism of tennis went beyond self-serving arguments. She saw how the amateur system hurt others, too. 'Under these absurd and antiquated amateur rulings, only a wealthy person can compete, and the fact of the matter is that only wealthy people *do* compete,' she complained. 'Is that fair? Does it advance the sport? Does it make tennis more popular – or does it tend to suppress and hinder an enormous amount of tennis talent lying dormant in the bodies of young men and women whose names are not in the social register?' Thus, Suzanne Lenglen was an early leader in the fight against the establishment's stranglehold on tennis – a battle that took players forty years to win."

On July 4, 1938, Suzanne died at age 39 of pernicious anemia so, Suzanne Lenglen, France's greatest female player did not live to see Open Tennis in 1968, or to witness the international success of tennis as a profession. Today, however, she is honored with "Court Suzanne Lenglen" which is the No. 2 feature court at Roland-Garros, the home of the French Open.

Frank Shields Ordered to Default Wimbledon Final

Bud Collins reported in *The Bud Collins, History of Tennis*[5] that in 1931, Frank Shields of the United States twisted his ankle while defeating top-seeded Jean Borotra of France in the semifinals of Wimbledon and was scheduled to play Sidney Wood in the final. The USLTA Davis Cup Committee demonstrated its tight control over American amateurs by ordering Shields to default to Wood, his teammate, "in order to recuperate for the Davis Cup semifinal against Great Britain the following weekend in Paris." Can you imagine the insult to Wimbledon and to Shields? In that Davis Cup semifinal, Shields defeated Fred Perry, but the United States lost 3-2.

Small Group As Pros

Only a small group of players were able to make a living as professionals prior to 1968 and they were pretty much marginalized by the amateur game controlled by the ILTF. According to Jack Kramer in *The Game*[6], Vic Seixas, Neal Fraser and Chuck McKinley were the only three players who won Wimbledon and the U.S. Championships who never turned pro. Once a player turned pro, he was barred from all amateur tournaments including the Grand Slams and the Davis Cup.

Important Early Pros

The important early pros who sought to make a living as professional tennis players were: Karel Koželuh, Prague (pro before 1912), Hans Nüsslein, Nuremburg, (pro 1926), Vinnie Richards, Yonkers, N.Y., (Pro 1927), Bill Tilden, Philadelphia (pro 1931), Ellsworth Vines, Los Angeles (pro 1934), George Lott, Springfield, Ill., (pro 1934), Fred Perry, Portwood, Stockport Britain, (pro 1936), Don Budge, Oakland (pro 1938), Bobby Riggs, Los Angeles, (pro 1941), Jack Kramer, Las Vegas, (pro 1947), Pancho Segura, Guayaquil, Ecuador, (pro 1947), Pancho Gonzales, Los Angeles (pro 1949), Frank Sedgman, Mount Albert, Australia, (pro 1953), Tony Trabert, Cincinnati (pro 1955), Ken Rosewall, Sydney, Australia, (pro 1956), Lew Hoad, Glebe Australia, (pro 1957), Mal Anderson, Theodore, Australia, (pro 1958) and Ashley Cooper, Melbourne Australia, (pro 1959). All of them have been inducted into the International Tennis Hall of Fame.

1919-1959 Pro Events

Before 1968, there were only a few small prize money tournaments for pros, the most important of which were the U.S. Pro Championships in Boston which began in 1927, the French Pro which began in 1930 and the London Indoor at Wembley which began in 1934. There were also a few professional "barnstorming" tours consisting mainly of one-night stands, usually consisting of a headline challenge match with or without an "undercard" match as an opener, plus a doubles match.

Jack Harris, American Promoter

Max Robertson wrote in *The Encyclopedia of Tennis*[7]: "Immediately after World War II, however, some of the tours did command considerable public interest. American Jack Harris, promoter of prewar tours with such players as Ellsworth Vines v. Don Budge and Fred Perry v. Budge, contracted Bobby Riggs to play a tour against Budge in 1946-7. Riggs, the 1939 Wimbledon champion just out of military service, was to oppose the acknowledged pro champion, Budge. It was a relatively short tour, Riggs winning 23 matches to 21. That led Harris to sign the top amateur, Jack Kramer, to challenge Riggs in 1947-8. He also signed Pancho Segura (Ecuador), and Dinny Pails (Australia), to play a companion match on the nightly odyssey. This tour was extremely well received, and the opener (Riggs v. Kramer) at Madison Square Garden in New York drew 15,114 people – one of the largest tennis crowds ever – despite the fact that New York was paralyzed by a raging blizzard. Kramer won that tour by 69-20 in matches and became the pro king. He made $85,000, Riggs $50,000."

Bobby Riggs, Promoter

"In 1949, Harris withdrew from promotion and Riggs got his baptism as a promoter, staging the next tour by enticing Pancho Gonzales into a series against Kramer. This was the longest head-to-head tour, extending from October 1949 to May 1950, Kramer emphasizing his dominance, 96-27. Both he and Gonzales made $72,000. Frank Parker was also involved, having signed to face Segura."

Jack Kramer, Promoter

In 1951, Jack Kramer assumed the role as promoter and player for his new Kramer Tour. He tried to induce Frank Sedgman, the most famous Aussie Davis Cup player, who had won the Australian Championships in 1949 and 1950 and the U.S, Championships in 1951, to turn pro. Harry Hopman, the Australian Davis Cup captain used his column in the newspaper, *The Melbourne Herald*, to launch a fund to keep Sedgman as an amateur. Joe McCauley wrote in *The History of Professional Tennis*[8]: "A considerable amount of money was collected ($50,000) and used to purchase a petrol station which was then registered in the name of his future bride (Jean Spence). For some reasons, the pious Hopman, a strong opponent of the paid game, did not regard that as an infringement on Sedgman's amateur status." Sedgman married Jean on January 31, 1952, won Wimbledon and the U.S. Championships in 1952, and then turned pro anyway.

Max Robertson further reported in *The Encyclopedia of Tennis*[9] that in the 1953 Kramer Tour, Kramer defeated Sedgman 54-41, but Sedgman made $102,000 and was the first pro to exceed $100,000. "That was Kramer's last tour as a principal, an arthritic back causing him to retire except for occasional appearances. He continued as promoter and put together a 1954 round-robin tour of Gonzalez, Segura, Sedgman and Don Budge, with others filling in from time to time. For the first time, a tour loser (Gonzales) was invited back as a principal, and he demonstrated his coming of age by winning the tour. He was to remain on top for nearly a decade, and, remarkably, a player to reckon with into the 1970s. A string of amateur champions joined up to challenge Gonzales – unsuccessfully: Tony Trabert (1956), 74-27; Ken Rosewall (1957), 50-26; Lew Hoad (1958), 51-36; Ashley Cooper, Mal Anderson and Hoad in a round-robin tour (1959); Alex Olmedo, Rosewall and Segura (1960); Andrés Gimeno, Olmedo, Buchholz, Barry MacKay, Hoad, Sedgman, Trabert, Cooper (1961)."

Gonzalez and Hoad

The impact of the rivalry between Pancho Gonzales and Lew Hoad had a very important impact on professional and amateur tennis and if it had continued, it could have hastened the approval for Open Tennis simply because they were the very best players in the world and each of their matches was legendary.

In 1958, Pancho Gonzales was 30 years old and was the best tennis player in the world. Think about it: Gonzales was the best player in the world and he was not included in the world rankings because he was a professional. Lew Hoad was born in Glebe, New South Wales, Australia, on November 23, 1934, and as an amateur, Lew won the Australian Championships in 1956, the French Championships in 1956, and Wimbledon in 1956 and 1957. In 1956, he lost in the finals of the U.S. Championships to Ken Rosewall in four sets, just missing the Grand Slam. Lew turned pro and joined the Kramer Tour in 1957 at age 23. In 1958, Lew was 24 years old.

Hoad Challenges Gonzales for Best in the World

Jack Kramer wrote in his book *The Game*[10]: "We opened in Brisbane in early in 1958. It was a smash hit. The ground shook everywhere we played. We had 13 dates in Australia and New Zealand and set attendance records with ten of them. Hoad-Gonzales was such a duel that, looking back, I know it is what sealed my doom with the amateurs. It blew amateur tennis off the map. Would you pay to see Ashley Cooper vs. Mal Anderson for the championship of Australian amateurs or Hoad vs. Gonzales for the championship of the world?

They really fought each other. In Adelaide, Gonzales played with bleeding fingers, in Sydney with an aching forearm muscle. Neither would quit. For once in his life, Lew Hoad cared. The thing was so exciting that even he got swept along. We started off playing five sets, and invariably it went five sets. We had to kill the doubles finale, the programs went so long. Then I cut the feature back to best-of-three because I was afraid that I was going to kill them both if they had to go five every day.

And what made it so exciting was that Hoad was staying with him. Gonzales was up 5-4, but then Lew really got rolling and own the last four matches Down Under, and when we flew to the States, he was up 8-5. The first night, in San Francisco, Hoad won 6-4, 20-18 to go up 9-5. I thought he would blow Gorgo out right there, and the next match, in Los Angeles, Hoad won the first set 6-3, and then they fell into another marathon. This one went even longer than the Frisco set, 24-22, but this one Gorgo won, and then the match, 6-1 in the third. He was only down 9-6 instead of 10-5. We flew to New York the next day and drew 15,237, up till then the largest tennis crowd in the U.S. history. They played best-of-five here, but after Hoad won a 9-7 set, Gonzales played like a demon and swept three in a row at love, four and four.

So that made it 9-7, and it looked like Gonzales was coming back. But no. After those back-to-back wins in L.A. and New York, Hoad took full command. He won nine of the next eleven matches. The tide had turned for him – no question. You see, most of the matches remained close, three sets. And Gonzales was playing well. Some nights he was playing as well as he had ever played in his life. They raised each other's games. But that was Gorgo's problem. He was playing beautifully, and he was getting beat. Near the end of February, they flew out to the Coast again for some matches, and I went out to the L.A. airport to touch base with them. When Gorgo got off the plane, I could see in his eyes he was a beaten man. I'd seen it before when I beat him on tour.

As I said before, when you go one-on-one night after night, one player takes charge. Hoad could serve with Gonzales, and he was every bit as quick. But he was much stronger. He could flick deep topspin shots with his wrist that Gonzales couldn't believe a human being could hit. Hoad also had a tougher overhead, and he had better groundstrokes. They both knew all this by now. The longer they played, the more certain it was that Hoad would win. I had a new champion – and he was blond and handsome and popular, and very cooperative too. If Lew Hoad could whip Pancho Gonzales, so too could he bring amateur tennis to its senses and force open tennis.

A few days after they came back to California, they moved out to Palm Springs to play at The Tennis Club. It was the height of the tourist season, and the word was out that there was a new champion in the making. By now, Hoad was up eighteen matches to nine. The demand for tickets was so high, I remember that we had to stick Sinatra way up in the back – and he was damned glad to get in the gate. Lana Turner was there with Fernando Lamas. Elizabeth Taylor was there with Mike Todd; it was just a couple of months before his plane went down. It was a little chillier in Palm Springs, outdoors with the sun down. Gonzales beat Hoad. Then the next morning, Lew work up with a stiff back. The long drive to Phoenix didn't help, and he lost there. And the same thing the next night in Albuquerque, then El Paso. He just couldn't get loose with his back. We tried everything, but the only thing that helped at all was three or four days of rest – and we were playing every night. As Hoad went down physically, Gorgo's confidence rose and the assurance came back to his eyes. In about three weeks, he had caught him. The matches were still close, and every now and then Hoad was his old self. But too often he was tight. We could never be sure of the back. After a while, I had to start letting the promoters work off a percentage of the gross to a percentage of the net because on some nights Hoad couldn't even play. Gonzales began to pull away. From 9-18, he went 42-18, and won the tour 51-36."

Gonzales on Hoad

Pancho Gonzales wrote in his book *Man with a Racket*[11]: "The Hoad" tour was the worst strain I ever went through; frankly, I'm not too anxious to play him again. Even when my lead widened, I couldn't afford to relax. I'd replay every match in my mind hours after it was over. Especially those I lost. I'd be mean for days, even scowling at waitresses and strangers on the street. A scowl didn't have much effect on Lew. It's hard to see across the court."

Importance of Gonzales vs. Hoad Rivalry

If the extremely exciting Gonzales vs. Hoad rivalry had continued for a couple more years with such great crowds, the ILTF may have voted for Open Tennis in 1960 instead of 1968. Many of the great players of this era and later, will tell you that Lew Hoad was their favorite and most respected professional idol. Just wait for Fred

Stolle's description of the last match between his personal hero, Lew Hoad, and Pancho Gonzales in 1967 at Wimbledon, Hoad's last great competitive match.

1960 Vote for Open Tennis Failed

As reported by David Gray in *Shades of Gray*, and by Jack Kramer in *The* Game[12], in 1960, there was a big push to get the ILTF to vote for Open Tennis, but it failed by five votes at the annual meeting of the ILTF in Paris. After the vote failed, Kramer signed Mike Davies of Britain, Kurt Nielsen of Denmark, Robert Haillet of France, Andrés Gimeno of Spain, Alex Olmedo of Peru, Butch Buchholz of St. Louis, Barry MacKay of Cincinnati, and Luis Ayala of Santiago Chile in an effort to change from his "king of the hill" format to more of a tournament format.

Kramer, Chatrier & Dell

Jack Kramer and Philippe Chatrier became life-long personal friends in the 1950s and they began to work and dream together for the creation of Open Tennis and the restructuring of men's professional tennis. Kramer later involved his protégé, Donald Dell, in their close relationship. The collective and individual impact of Kramer, Chatrier and Dell on the structure of men's professional tennis was enormous and not many people, even insiders in the game, knew how close they were personally and professionally as they worked for different constituencies that often were at odds with each other and with them. Chatrier, Kramer and Dell spent a lot of time together as they debated and planned the structure and restructure of men's professional tennis through the years. The influence of these three men as up-front leaders and behind the scenes instigators was enormous and was critical for the early development and success of Open Tennis.

Kramer wrote in *The Game*[13], "I grew more and more frustrated as I watched the finest carryover sport in the world being strangled of its natural popularity by a bunch of hypocritical idiots who ran the amateurs. The last thing I wanted was to run all of tennis. I just wanted to make a living out of it. I couldn't have run tennis even if I wanted to. If the last decade has taught us nothing else, it is that no one man can run even a nickel's worth of tennis. That's the problem; no one can gain sufficient control to bring fair order to the game. On the other hand, it was indisputable that I did run pro tennis. (Donald Dell and some of the other kids still call me 'The Czar' in honor of those days.) I don't suppose any one man ever so controlled a professional sport as I did. But if I ran it, I didn't run it into the ground."

Upon the recommendation of his friend Chatrier, Kramer closed his Kramer professional tour in November of 1962. Kramer said in *The Game*:[14] "I volunteered to leave the sport to free pro tennis of Jack Kramer so that amateur tennis couldn't hold me up as the bogeyman anymore....I had tried everything: star tours, round-robins, traditional tournaments, different rules, different scoring, different serves...I've got to get out or we'll never see an open game."

IPTPA Tour

After 1962, Frank Sedgman and Tony Trabert led the former Kramer pros via the first players' association, the International Professional Tennis Players Association (IPTPA), to keep pro tennis alive. The new players joining the Kramer Tour players who turned pro after 1962 were Rod Laver of Rockhampton Australia (pro 1963), Pierre Barthès of Béziers, France (pro 1966), Fred Stolle of Hornsby, Australia, (pro 1967) and Dennis Ralston of Bakersfield, California, (pro 1967). In order to get Laver, who won the 1962 amateur Grand Slam, to turn pro in 1963, Rosewall and Hoad agreed to guarantee him $125,000 in 1963. Butch Buchholz told me all the other players joined to assure their commitment to continue in professional tennis. Their goal became to try to create 16-draw real tournaments with 14 pros and two locals.

In 1964, Ken Rosewall was still No. 1, but Rod Laver was No. 2. In 1965, Rod Laver became No. 1 and Ken Rosewall slipped to No. 2. Hoad was out much of the year with foot and back problems. In 1966, Laver continued as No.1 and the IPTPA hired Wally Dill to take over from Tony Trabert to manage the IPTPA tour.

At the end of 1966, leading amateurs Manolo Santana, Roy Emerson, John Newcombe and Tony Roche refused to turn pro and elected to remain as "shamateurs." Joe McCauley wrote in *The History of Professional Tennis*[15]: "Emmo was quoted as saying he declined because, 'he couldn't afford to take a pay cut!' Nevertheless, the amateur game continued on "a gradual descent to a basic level of mediocrity," wrote Mike Davies in the *Tennis Rebel*[16]. Kramer wrote in *The Game*[17]: "The Aussies couldn't come close to selling the 12,000 permanent seats. In the early rounds of the French and Australian championships the crowds sometimes numbered in the hundreds. For the finals at Forest Hills, the stadium would be half-filled, and some of the press would leave the marquee, go up into the stands and sunbathe as they watched the championships...The networks could not find a sponsor for the matches at Forest Hills – not even the finals. Naturally, in the face of this disastrous turn, the amateur officials never considered that they might be doing something wrong."

1967 Governing Bodies

The ILTF was the governing body for men's professional tennis, except for the new World Championship Tennis (WCT), the new National Tennis League (NTL) and Davis Cup. Davis Cup was governed by the Davis Cup Nations, which was an organization separate from the ILTF.

1967 Significant Tennis Leaders	
ILTF President:	Giorgio de Stefani (Italy)
USLTA President:	Bob Kelleher
Australian LTA President:	C.A. Edwards
British LTA President:	Sir Carl Aarvold
French FFT President:	Roger Cirotteau
French FFT Vice President:	Jean Borotra
Chairman of Wimbledon:	Herman David
WCT Owners:	Dave Dixon, Lamar Hunt and Al Hill, Jr.
WCT Executive Director:	Bob Briner
NTL Owner:	George MacCall

Proposed Wimbledon Pro Test Event

At 1966 Wimbledon, Herman David, Chairman of Wimbledon, agreed with the BBC to test the viability of professional tennis for 1968 Wimbledon by staging an eight-draw professional tennis test event after 1967 Wimbledon with $35,000 in singles prize money and $10,000 in doubles prize money, the largest prize money tournament in history. Kramer was asked to procure the players.

WCT and NTL Founded

In early 1967, Dave Dixon who had been a professional golfer, was the chairman of a proposed new Superdome in New Orleans and he was on the hunt for sports that could be played there. Dixon traveled to an IPTPA event at the Racquet and Riding Club in Binghamton, New York, and became hooked on men's professional tennis. Dixon contacted his old friend, Lamar Hunt, who became his partner in a new professional tour known as World Championship Tennis (WCT). Almost simultaneously, George MacCall, the U.S. Davis Cup captain in 1965-1967, created his own professional tour, the National Tennis League (NTL).   •

Wimbledon Test Event

The 1967 amateur Wimbledon finished on July 7, 1967, with John Newcombe defeating Wilhelm Bungert in the final 6-3, 6-1, 6-1 in a dull three sets. The Wimbledon Experimental Pro Tournament was staged August 25-28, 1967, with eight professionals: Pancho Gonzales, Rod Laver, Ken Rosewall, Dennis Ralston, Andres Gimeno, Butch Buchholz, Fred Stolle and Lew Hoad.

The Match All The Pros Wanted To See

There are all kinds of tennis matches by exceptionally talented professionals. Once in a while, there is a match that all the professional players want to see. The first-round Gonzales v. Hoad match in the 1967 pro event at Wimbledon was such a match. I wish I could have been there. Stolle described the match in *Tennis Down Under*[18]: "Coming back to Wimbledon also brought me back to witness one of the most glorious matches I have ever seen. Lew Hoad versus Pancho Gonzalez. Hoad had been my hero and my idol for twelve or fifteen years, and Pancho had taught me some important

Pancho Gonzales   Lew Hoad

lessons about mental preparation on the court. He had pulled me aside on many occasions pointing out that the pros would pick on my weakness until I learned how to get over it. Pancho always preached mental strength, then like a good teacher, he himself would try to tear down my defenses. But when it came down to a head-to-head confrontation, my heart was still with Lew Hoad. By this time, Lew Hoad's back was killing him. It was well known around the circuit that Hoad could play one great match, but would then be barely able to walk on the following day. Lew Hoad had tried everything known to medical science, but still could not come back after a hard, long match. Lew never lost his physical strength or his tremendous disposition, his fierce desire to win, so the Hoad versus Gonzalez match was one I wanted to see for myself. I was rooting for Hoad the way you root for a schoolboy hero when he had past his prime. As an adult, you have a mental picture of how your idol used to be. You never wanted him to change or get old, and in a sense you never believed that he would get old. I wanted Hoad to play well and win, but I knew that Gonzalez would try to smash and humiliate him. More than anything, I did not want to see Lew Hoad lose or fall on his face. Lots of us became very emotional. It was the last dance for the old pro. Here we were, back at Wimbledon, centre court. In the first match, Laver disposed of me quickly. I ran into the shower, dressed as quickly as I could and ran up the Players' Box. By the time I arrived, Gonzalez had won the first set. He played his dink game. He hit short and low. He dropped shots. He made Lew run and move and stop short. He tried to break Hoad's back. I could hardly bring myself to watch. Lew Hoad was out on the grass, with tennis shoes still stained red from the clay courts in Spain where he had played just before Wimbledon, trying to muster up one more surge of passion to go out strong against Pancho. It was one of those rare moments when you could see the spirit taking over the body. Out of sheer will and determination, Lew Hoad fought back. It was as if that pain in his own back did not matter anymore. He flipped into a zone that is very difficult to describe to one who does not play top-flight athletics. There is a moment where the restrictions of the past and the limitations of the body seem to evaporate. It's the same kind of zone where a mother can lift a wrecked car off an unconscious child. At certain times in tennis, you can see a man have super vision. He can anticipate and respond in milliseconds. His mind is so tuned into the moment that there is a feeling of the supernatural. Experiencing this moment is one thing but, watching it can be even more moving and meaningful. I can remember that feeling watching Lew Hoad battling Pancho Gonzalez in that match at Wimbledon. You could sense that Lew had shifted into another gear. He won the second set. It was heavy artillery against heavy artillery. These two great players went at it as if this were the last tennis match of all time. It had the feeling of a judgment day, both gave it everything they had. Each one wanted to win more than anything else in the world. Gonzalez went to match point in the third set. Hoad saved it. They both had the look of fire in their eyes. The match went to seven all. The tension was unbelievable. Hoad was relaxed and controlled, hitting for the lines. He held his serve with four straight cannon shots that Gonzalez could not return. Leading 7-6 in the third set, Hoad found himself having a match point with Gonzalez serving. Pancho showed neither fear nor trepidation. He slammed a patented, pinpoint serve down the middle which made Hoad stretch and reach, and maybe pop his back. Lew made a decent return on a forehand lunge. Pancho was in great position to volley. He hit a great shot. All Lew could do was lob it on the run. He was lucky to get his racket on the ball. It was one of those high, arching, spinning lobs that take hours to come down. Pancho took one look at it, saw it was going way out and did not even turn to make a run or a play at the ball. He started to walk back to the service line, expecting to be serving at deuce, meaning that the advantage was back on his side. Hoad could not take much more of this pounding. Hoad would fall sooner or later. It did not matter to Pancho. The wind held the ball up. Some say the wind brought the ball back after Pancho had determined not to make a play on the shot. It was almost as if the baselines had feelings and a magnetic pull, because somehow the ball died and died and landed exactly on the baseline. No doubt about it. The ball was in. The match was over. Lew Hoad won 8-6 in the third set. He had come back to Wimbledon. Pancho Gonzalez then hit the longest tennis ball that I have ever seen hit in my life. He took the remaining ball he had in his hand and smashed it out of the stadium, at the far end. Not the end where The Royal Box was, but the far end of the stadium out into the adjoining courts. Pancho was very upset and disappointed. Lew's arms shot up in the air because he was so excited. He looked up at the Players' Box where he knew his Australian mates were standing and he pumped his arm in the air once more. It was a salute, a gesture of recognition and appreciation. It was as if this miracle was all for us. It was possible to have *one more great moment*. The next day, Lew Hoad could hardly get out of bed, much less dress and stand on the court. But he showed up, hobbling, bent over in pain to meet his long-time friend and traveling companion, Ken Rosewall, in the second round. Kenny took pity and took Lew out of his misery, 6-2, 6-3. Lew Hoad never really played a competitive match again."

Seeing a match like that is incredibly special lifetime experience and reading about it is not bad either. Whenever you notice that professional players are watching a match, get there as soon as you can because it is going to be interesting.

The results of the Wimbledon Test Event were as follows: First Round: Laver d. Stolle 6-4, 6-2, Gimeno d. Ralston 6-1, 6-2, Rosewall d. Buchholz 5-7, 6-2, 6-3, Hoad d. Gonzales 3-6, 11-9, 8-6. Semifinals: Laver d. Gimeno 6-3, 6-4, Rosewall d. Hoad 6-2, 6-3. Final: Laver d. Rosewall 6-2, 6-2, 12-10. Doubles Final: Gonzales/Gimeno d. Laver/Stolle 6-4, 14-12. Kramer wrote in *The Game*[19]: "The event was an absolute smash. The matches sold out every day and the BBC ratings were high."

Shamateur Tennis Denounced

A few weeks later, Herman David publicly denounced that shamateur tennis was "a living lie" and with the full backing of the Wimbledon Committee he stated publicly that in 1968, Wimbledon would "be open to all categories of players, amateur and professional alike."[20]

NTL and WCT Make Offers

During the Wimbledon Test Event, Dave Dixon of WCT and George MacCall of NTL began making offers to the players consisting of guarantees against prize money plus traveling expenses. The amateur U.S. Championships finished on September 9, 1967. In the semifinals, Clarke Graebner defeated Jan Leschly and John Newcombe defeated Gene Scott. In the final, Newcombe defeated Graebner 6-4, 6-4, 8-6. By the end of the 1967 US Championships, the players had decided to sign with the promoters and to close the ITPTA. For the NTL, MacCall signed Rod Laver, Ken Rosewall, Pancho Gonzales, Fred Stolle, Andres Gimeno and Roy Emerson, along with Billie Jean King, Ann Jones, Francoise Durr and Rosie Casals. For WCT, Dixon signed John Newcombe, Tony Roche, Cliff Drysdale, Roger Taylor, Niki Pilic, Dennis Ralston and Butch Buchholz, who were immediately marketed as the "Handsome Eight." Owen Davidson also turned pro in 1967 and became Wimbledon's resident pro.

Bob Briner, the Executive Director of the new WCT was quoted in *The Bud Collins, History of Tennis*[21]: "We had in one fell swoop taken all the stars out of the game. If anyone was ever going to see them again at Wimbledon and Forest Hills, the ILTF had to make an accommodation." "Open tennis came about so fast after that it was pitiful."

LTA Votes to Remove the Sham and Hypocrisy

Following Herman David's decision to open 1968 Wimbledon in October of 1967, the British LTA voted by an overwhelming majority for Open Tennis beginning in 1968. Derek Penman, the Chairman of the LTA Rules Committee was quoted by David Gray in *Shades of Gray*[22]: "the main object was not that they should have an Open Wimbledon but that they should remove sham and hypocrisy from the game…For too long, we have been governed by a set of amateur rules which are quite unenforceable. We know that so-called amateur players bargain for payments grossly in excess of what they are entitled to but without which they cannot live. We know that tournament committees connive at this, otherwise there would be no players at their tournaments. We feel we owe it not only to ourselves but to our players to release them from this humiliating and hypocritical situation and to make it possible for them to earn openly and honestly the rewards to which their skill entitles them." *The ILTF did not appreciate or support the rebellion of Wimbledon and the LTA.*

Amateur Grand Slams

Date	Grand Slams	Singles Winner	Turned Pro	Singles #2	Turned Pro
1918	US Championships	R. Lindley Murray		William Tilden	
1919	Australian Championships	Algernon Kingacote		Eric Pockley	
1919	US Championships	Bill Johnston		William Tilden	
1919	Wimbledon	Gerald Patterson		Algernon Kingscote	
1920	Australian Championships	Pat O'Hara Wood		Ronald Thomas	
1920	US Championships	William Tilden		Bill Johnston	
1920	Wimbledon	William Tilden		Zenzo Shimidzu	
1921	Australian Championships	Rhys Gemmell		Alf Hedeman	
1921	US Championships	William Tilden		Wallace Johnson	
1921	Wimbledon	Brian Norton		Manuel Alonso	
1922	Australian Championships	James Anderson		Gerald Patterson	
1922	US Championships	William Tilden		Bill Johnston	
1922	Wimbledon	Gerald Patterson		Randolph Lycett	
1923	Australian Championships	Pat O'Hara Wood		Bert St. John	
1923	US Championships	William Tilden		Bill Johnston	
1923	Wimbledon	Bill Johnston		Frank Hunter	
1924	Australian Championships	James Anderson		Richard Schlesinger	
1924	US Championships	William Tilden		Bill Johnston	
1924	Wimbledon	Jean Borotra		Rene Lacoste	
1925	Australian Championships	James Anderson		Gerald Patterson	
1925	French Championships	Rene Lacoste		Jean Borotra	
1925	US Championships	William Tilden		Bill Johnston	
1925	Wimbledon	Rene Lacoste		Jean Borotra	
1926	Australian Championships	John Hawkes		James Willard	
1926	French Championships	Henri Cochet		Rene Lacoste	

Year	Tournament	Winner		Runner-up
1926	US Championships	Rene Lacoste		Jean Borotra
1926	Wimbledon	Jean Borotra		Howard Kinsey
1927	Australian Championships	Gerald Patterson		John Hawkes
1927	French Championships	Rene Lacoste		William Tilden
1927	US Championships	Rene Lacoste		William Tilden
1927	Wimbledon	Henry Cochet		Jean Borotra
1928	Australian Championships	Jean Borotra		Ronald Cummings
1928	French Championships	Henri Cochet		Rene Lacoste
1928	US Championships	Henri Cochet		Frank Hunter
1928	Wimbledon	Rene Lacoste		Henry Cochet
1929	Australian Championships	Colin Gregory		Richard Schlesinger
1929	French Championships	Rene Lacoste		Jean Borotra
1929	US Championships	William Tilden		Frank Hunter
1929	Wimbledon	Henri Cochet		Jean Borotra
1930	Australian Championships	Edgar Moon		Harry Hopman
1930	French Championships	Henri Cochet		William Tilden
1930	US Championships	John Doeg		Frank Shields
1930	Wimbledon	William Tilden	1931	Wilmer Allison
1931	Australian Championships	Jack Crawford		Harry Hopman
1931	French Championships	Jean Borotra		Christian Boussus
1931	US Championships	Ellsworth Vines		George Lott
1931	Wimbledon	Sydney Wood		Frank Shields
1932	Australian Championships	Jack Crawford		Harry Hopman
1932	French Championships	Henri Cochet		Giorgio De Stefani
1932	US Championships	Ellsworth Vines		Henri Cochet
1932	Wimbledon	Ellsworth Vines	1934	Henry W. Austin
1933	Australian Championships	Jack Crawford		Keith Gledhill
1933	French Championships	Jack Crawford		Henri Cochet
1933	US Championships	Fred Perry		Jack Crawford
1933	Wimbledon	Jack Crawford		Ellsworth Vines
1934	Australian Championships	Fred Perry		Jack Crawford

1934	French Championships	Gottfried Von Cramm		Jack Crawford
1934	US Championships	Fred Perry		Wilmer Allison
1934	Wimbledon	Fred Perry		Jack Crawford
1935	Australian Championships	Jack Crawford		Fred Perry
1935	French Championships	Fred Perry		Gottfried Von Cramm
1935	US Championships	Wilmer Allison		Sidney Wood, Jr.
1935	Wimbledon	Fred Perry		Gottfried Von Cramm
1936	Australian Championships	Adrian Quist		Jack Crawford
1936	French Championships	Gottfried Von Cramm		Fred Perry
1936	US Championships	Fred Perry		Don Budge
1936	Wimbledon	Fred Perry	1936	Gottfried Von Cramm
1937	Australian Championships	Vivian McGrath		John Bromwich
1937	French Championships	Henner Jenkel		Henry W. Austin
1937	US Championships	Don Budge		Gottfried Von Cramm
1937	Wimbledon	Don Budge		Gottfried Von Cramm
1938	Australian Championships	Don Budge		John Bromwich
1938	French Championships	Don Budge		Roderick Menzel
1938	US Championships	Don Budge		Gene Mako
1938	Wimbledon	Don Budge	1938	Henry W. Austin
1939	Australian Championships	John Bromwich		Adrian Quist
1939	French Championships	Don McNeill		Bobby Riggs
1939	US Championships	Bobby Riggs		Welby Van Horn
1939	Wimbledon	Bobby Riggs		Elwood Cooke
1940	Australian Championships	Adrian Quist		Jack Crawford
1940	Australian Championships	Adrian Quist		Jack Crawford
1940	US Championships	Don McNeill		Bobby Riggs

PIONEERS OF THE GAME

1941	US Championships	Bobby Riggs	1941	Francis Kovacs
1942	US Championships	Ted Schroeder		Frank Parker
1943	US Championships	Joseph Reuben Hunt		Jack Kramer
1944	US Championships	Frank Parker		Bill Talbert
1945	US Championships	Frank Parker		Bill Talbert
1946	Australian Championships	John Bromwich		Dinny Pails
1946	French Championships	Marcel Bernard		Jaroslav Drobny
1946	US Championships	Jack Kramer		Tom Brown
1946	US Championships	Jack Kramer		Tom Brown
1946	Wimbledon	Yvon Petra		Geoff Brown
1947	Australian Championships	Dinny Pails	1947	John Bromwich
1947	French Championships	Jozef Asboth		Eric Sturgess
1947	US Championships	Jack Kramer	1947	Frank Parker
1947	Wimbledon	Jack Kramer		Tom Brown
1948	Australian Championships	Adrian Quist		John Bromwich
1948	French Championships	Frank Parker		Jaroslav Drobny
1948	US Championships	Pancho Gonzales		Eric Sturgess
1948	Wimbledon	Bob Falkenberg		John Bromwich
1949	Australian Championships	Frank Sedgman		John Bromwich
1949	French Championships	Frank Parker		Budge Patty
1949	US Championships	Pancho Gonzales	1949	Ted Schroeder
1949	Wimbledon	Ted Schroeder		Jaroslav Drobny
1950	Australian Championships	Frank Sedgman		Ken McGregor
1950	French Championships	Budge Patty		Jaroslav Drobny
1950	US Championships	Art Larsen		Herb Flam
1950	Wimbledon	Budge Patty		Frank Sedgeman
1951	Australian Championships	Dick Savitt		Ken McGregor
1951	French Championships	Jaroslav Drobny		Eric Sturgess
1951	US Championships	Frank Sedgman		Vic Sexias
1951	Wimbledon	Dick Savitt		Ken McGregor
1952	Australian Championships	Ken McGregor		Frank Sedgeman

20

Year	Tournament	Winner		Runner-up	
1952	French Championships	Jaroslav Drobny		Frank Sedgeman	
1952	US Championships	Frank Sedgman	1953	Gardnar Malloy	
1952	Wimbledon	Frank Sedgman		Jaroslav Drobny	
1953	Australian Championships	Ken Rosewall		Mervyn Rose	
1953	French Championships	Ken Rosewall		Vic Sexias	
1953	US Championships	Tony Trabert		Vic Sexias	
1953	Wimbledon	Vic Sexias		Kurt Nielsen	
1954	Australian Championships	Mervyn Rose		Rex Hartwig	
1954	French Championships	Tony Trabert		Art Larsen	
1954	US Championships	Vic Sexias		Rex Hartwig	
1954	Wimbledon	Jaroslav Drobny		Ken Rosewall	
1955	Australian Championships	Ken Rosewall		Lew Hoad	
1955	French Championships	Tony Trabert		Sven Davidson	
1955	US Championships	Tony Trabert	1955	Ken Rosewall	
1955	Wimbledon	Tony Trabert		Kurt Nielsen	1960
1956	Australian Championships	Lew Hoad		Ken Rosewall	
1956	French Championships	Lew Hoad		Sven Davidson	
1956	US Championships	Ken Rosewall	1956	Lew Hoad	
1956	Wimbledon	Lew Hoad		Ken Rosewall	
1957	Australian Championships	Ashley Cooper		Neale Frazer	
1957	French Championships	Sven Davidson		Herb Flam	
1957	US Championships	Mal Anderson	1958	Ashley Cooper	
1957	Wimbledon	Lew Hoad	1957	Ashley Cooper	
1958	Australian Championships	Ashley Cooper		Mal Anderson	
1958	French Championships	Mervyn Rose		Luis Ayala	
1958	US Championships	Ashley Cooper	1959	Mal Anderson	
1958	Wimbledon	Ashley Cooper		Neale Fraser	
1959	Australian Championships	Alexandro Olmedo		Neale Fraser	
1959	French Championships	Nicola Pietrangeli		Ian Vermaak	
1959	US Championships	Neale Fraser		Alexandro Olmedo	
1959	Wimbledon	Alexandro Olmedo	1960	Rod Laver	

Year	Tournament	Winner		Runner-up	
1960	Australian Championships	Rod Laver		Neale Fraser	
1960	French Championships	Nicola Pietrangeli		Luis Ayala	1962
1960	US Championships	Neale Fraser		Rod Laver	
1960	Wimbledon	Neale Fraser		Rod Laver	
1961	Australian Championships	Roy Emerson		Rod Laver	
1961	French Championships	Manuel Santana		Nicola Pietrangeli	
1961	US Championships	Roy Emerson		Rod Laver	
1961	Wimbledon	Rod Laver		Chuck McKinley	
1962	Australian Open	Rod Laver		Roy Emerson	
1962	French Championships	Rod Laver		Roy Emerson	
1962	US Championships	Rod Laver	1963	Roy Emerson	
1962	Wimbledon	Rod Laver		Marty Mulligan	
1963	Australian Championships	Roy Emerson		Ken Fletcher	
1963	French Championships	Roy Emerson		Pierre Darmon	
1963	US Championships	Rafael Osuna		Frank Froehling III	
1963	Wimbledon	Chuck McKinley		Fred Stolle	
1964	Australian Championships	Roy Emerson		Fred Stolle	
1964	French Championships	Manuel Santana		Nicola Pietrangeli	
1964	US Championships	Roy Emerson		Fred Stolle	
1964	Wimbledon	Roy Emerson		Fred Stolle	
1965	Australian Championships	Roy Emerson		Fred Stolle	
1965	French Championships	Fred Stolle		Tony Roche	
1965	US Championships	Manuel Santana		Cliff Drysdale	
1965	Wimbledon	Roy Emerson		Fred Stolle	
1966	Australian Championships	Roy Emerson		Arthur Ashe	
1966	French Championships	Tony Roche	1967	Istvan Gulyas	
1966	US Championships	Fred Stolle	1967	John Newcombe	
1966	Wimbledon	Manuel Santana		Dennis Ralston	
1967	Australian Championships	Roy Emerson		Arthur Ashe	
1967	French Championships	Roy Emerson	1968	Tony Roche	
1967	US Championships	John Newcombe	1967	Clark Graebner	
1967	Wimbledon	John Newcombe		Wilhelm Bungert	

Amateur World Rankings

1919

1	Gerald Patterson (AU)
1	Bill Johnston (US)
3	Andre Gobert (FR)
4	Bill Tilden (US)
5	Norman Brookes (AU)
6	Algernon Kingscote (GB)
7	Dick Williams (US)
8	Percival Davson (GB)
9	Will Davis (US)
10	William Laurentz (FR)

1920

1	Bill Tilden (US)
2	Bill Johnston (US)
3	Algernon Kingscote (GB)
4	Jim Cecil Parke (IE)
5	Andre Gobert (FR)
6	Norman Brookes (AU)
7	Dick Williams (US)
8	William Laaurentz (FR)
9	Zenzo Shimidzu (JP)
10	Gerald Patterson (AU)

1921

1	Bill Tilden (US)
2	Bill Johnston (US)
3	Vinnie Richards (US)
4	Zenzo Shimidzu (JP)
5	Gerald Patterson (AU)
6	James Anderson (AU)
7	Brian Norton (ZA)
8	Manuel Alonso (ES)
9	Dick Williams (US)
10	Andre Gobert (FR)

1922

1	Bill Tilden (US)
2	Bill Johnston (US)
3	Gerald Patterson (AU)
4	Vinnie Richards (US)
5	Jim Anderson (AU)
6	Henri Cochet (FR)
7	Pat O'Hara Wood (AU)
8	Dick Williams (US)
9	Algernon Kingscote (GB)
10	Andre Gobert (FR)

1923

1	Bill Tilden (US)
2	Bill Johnston (US)
3	Jim Anderson (AU)
4	Dick Williams (US)
5	Frank Hunter (US)
6	Vinnie Richards (US)
7	Brian Norton (ZA)
8	Manuel Alonso (ES)
9	Jean Washer (BE)
10	Henri Cochet (FR)

1924

1	Bill Tilden (US)
2	Vinnie Richards (US)
3	Jim Anderson (AU)
4	Bill Johnston (US)
5	Rene Lacosta (FR)
6	Jean Borotra (FR)
7	Howard Kinsey (US)
8	Gerald Patterson (US)
9	Henry Cochet (FR)
10	Manuel Alonso (ES)

1925

1	Bill Tilden (US)
2	Bill Johnston (US)
3	Vinnie Richards (US)
4	Rene Lacoste (FR)
5	Dick Williams (US)
6	Jean Borotra (FR)
7	Gerald Patterson (AU)

1926

1	Rene Lacoste (FR)
2	Jean Borotra (FR)
3	Henri Cochet (FR)
4	Bill Johnston (US)
5	Bill Tilden (US)
6	Vinnie Richards (US)
7	Takeichi Harada (JP)

1927

1	Rene Lacoste (FR)
2	Bill Tilden (US)
3	Henri Cochet (FR)
4	Jean Borotra (FR)
5	Manuel Alonso (ES)
6	Frank Hunter (US)
7	George Lott (US)

8	Manuel Alonso (ES)	8	Manuel Alonso (ES)	8	John Hennessey (US)
9	Brian Norton (ZA)	9	Howard Kinsey (US)	9	Jacques Brugnon (FR)
10	Takeichi Harada (JP)	10	Jacques Brugnon (FR)	10	Jan Kozeluh (CZ)

1928		1929		1930	
1	Henri Cochet (FR)	1	Henri Cochet (FR)	1	Henri Cochet (FR)
2	Rene Lacoste (FR)	2	Rene Lacoste (FR)	2	Bill Tilden (US)
3	Bill Tilden (US)	3	Jean Borotra (FR)	3	Jean Borotra (FR)
4	Frank Hunter (US)	4	Bill Tilden (US)	4	John Doeg (US)
5	Jean Borotra (FR)	5	Frank Hunter (US)	5	Frank Shields (US)
6	George Lott (US)	6	George Lott (US)	6	Wilmer Allison (US)
7	Bunny Austin (GB)	7	John Doeg (US)	7	George Lott (US)
8	John Hennessey (US)	8	John Van Ryn (US)	8	Umberto de Morpurgo (IT)
9	Umberto de Morpurgo (IT)	9	Bunny Austin (GB)	9	Christian Boussus (FR)
10	John Hawkes (AU)	10	Umberto de Morpurgo (IT)	10	Bunny Austin (GB)

1931		1932		1933	
1	Henri Cochet (FR)	1	Ellsworth Vines (US)	1	Jack Crawford (AU)
2	Bunny Austin (GB)	2	Henri Cochet (FR)	2	Fred Perry (GB)
3	Ellsworth Vines (US)	3	Jean Borotra (FR)	3	Jiro Satoh (JP)
4	Fred Perry (GB)	4	Wilmer Allison (US)	4	Bunny Austin (GB)
5	Frank Shields (US)	5	Cliff Sutter (US)	5	Ellsworth Vines (US)
6	Sidney Wood (US)	6	Daniel Prenn (DE)	6	Henry Cochet (FR)
7	Jean Borotra (FR)	7	Fred Perry (GB)	7	Frank Shields (US)
8	George Lott (US)	8	Gottfried von Cramm (DE)	8	Sidney Wood (US)
9	Jiro Satoh (JP)	9	Bunny Austin (GB)	9	Gottfried von Cramm (DE)
10	John Van Ryn (US)	10	Jack Crawford (AU)	10	Lester Stoefen (US)

1934		1935		1936	
1	Fred Perry (GB)	1	Fred Perry (GB)	1	Fred Perry (GB)
2	Jack Crawford (AU)	2	Jack Crawford (AU)	2	Gottfried von Cramm (DE)
3	Gottfried von Cramm (DE)	3	Gottfried von Cramm (DE)	3	Don Budge (US)
4	Bunny Austin (GB)	4	Wilmer Allison (US)	4	Adrian Quist (AU)
5	Wilmer Allison (US)	5	Bunny Austin (GB)	5	Bunny Austin (GB)

6	Sidney Wood (US)	6	Don Budge (US)	6	Jack Crawford (AU)
7	Roderich Menzel (CZ)	7	Frank Shields (US)	7	Wilmer Allison (US)
8	Frank Shields (US)	8	Viv McGrath (AU)	8	Bryan Grant (US)
9	Giogio de Stefani (IT)	9	Christian Boussus (FR)	9	Henner Henkel (DE)
10	Christian Boussus (FR)	10	Sidney Woods (US)	10	Viv McGrath (AU)

1937		1938		1939	
1 Don Budge (US)	1	Don Budge (US)	1	Bobby Riggs (US)
2 Gottfried von Cramm (DE)	2	Bunny Austin (GB)	2	John Bromwich (AU)
3 Henner Henkel (DE)	3	John Bromwich (AU)	3	Adrian Quist (AU)
4 Bunny Austin (GB)	4	Bobby Riggs (US)	4	Franjo Puncec (RS)
5 Bobby Riggs (US)	5	Sidney Wood (US)	5	Frank Parker (US)
6 Bryan Grant (US)	6	Adrian Quist (AU)	6	Henner Henkel (DE)
7 Jack Crawford (AU)	7	Roderich Menzel (CZ)	7	Don McNeill (US
8 Roderich Menzel (CZ)	8	Jiro Yamagishi (JP)	8	Elwood Cooke (US)
9 Frank Parker (US)	9	Gene Mako (US)	9	Welby Van Horn (US)
10 Charlie Hare (GB)	10	Franjo Puncec (RS)	10	Joe Hunt (US)

1946		1947		1948	
1 Jack Kramer (US)	1	Jack Kramer (US)	1	Frank Parker (US)
2 Ted Schroeder (US)	2	Ted Schroeder (US)	2	Ted Schroeder (US)
3 Jaroslav Drobny (CZ)	3	Frank Parker (US)	3	Pancho Gonzalez (US)
4 Yvon Petra (FR)	4	John Bromwich (AU)	4	John Bromwich (AU)
5 Marcel Bernard (FR)	5	Jaroslav Drobny (CZ)	5	Jaroslave Drobny (CZ)
6 John Bromwich (AU)	6	Dinny Pails (AU)	6	Eric Sturgess (ZA)
7 Tom Brown (US)	7	Tom Brown (US)	7	Bob Falkenburg (US)
8 Gardnar Mulloy (US)	8	Budge Patty (US)	8	Joszef Asboth (HU)
9 Frank Parker (US)	9	Joszef Asboth (HU)	9	Lennart Bergelin (SE)
10 Geoff Brown (AU)	10	Gardnar Mulloy (US)	10	Adrian Quist (AU)

1949		1950		1951	
1 Pancho Gonzalez (US)	1	Budge Patty (US)	1	Frank Sedgman (AU)
2 Ted Schroeder (US)	2	Frank Sedgman (AU)	2	Dick Savitt (US)
3 Bill Talbert (US)	3	Art Larsen (US)	3	Jaroslav Drobny (EG)
4 Frank Sedgman (AU)	4	Jaroslav Drobny (EG)	4	Vic Seixas (US)

5	Frank Parker (US)	5	Herbie Flam (US)	5	Tony Trabert (US)
6	Eric Sturgess (ZA)	6	Ted Schroeder (US)	6	Ted Schroeder (US)
7	Jaroslav Drobny (CZ)	7	Vic Seixas (US)	7	Ken McGregor (AU)
8	Budge Patty (US)	8	Ken McGregor (AU)	8	Herbie Flam (US)
9	Gardnar Mulloy (US)	9	Bill Talbert (US)	9	Art Larsen (US)
10	Billy Sidwell (AU)	10	Eric Sturgess (ZA)	10	Mervyn Rose (AU)

	1952		1953		1954
1	Frank Sedgman (AU)	1	Tony Trabert (US)	1	Jaroslav Drobny (EG)
2	Jaroslav Drobny (EG)	2	Ken Rosewall (AUS)	2	Tony Trabert (US}
3	Ken McGregor (AU)	3	Vic Seixas (US)	3	Ken Rosewall (AU)
4	Mervyn Rose (AU)	4	Jaroslav Drobny (EG)	4	Vic Seixas (US)
5	Vic Seixas (US)	5	Lew Hoad (AU)	5	Rex Hartwig (AU)
6	Herbie Flam (US)	6	Mervyn Rose (AU)	6	Mervyn Rose (AU)
7	Gardnar Mulloy (US)	7	Kurt Nielsen (DK)	7	Lew Hoad (AU)
8	Eric Sturgess (ZA)	8	Budge Patty (US)	8	Budge Patty (US)
9	Dick Savitt (US)	9	Sven Davidson (SE)	9	Art Larsen (US)
10	Ken Rosewall (AU)	10	Enrique Morea (AR)	10	Enrique Morea (AR)
				10	Ham Riochardson (US)
				10	Sven Davidson (SE)

	1955		1956		1957
1	Tony Trabert (US)	1	Lew Hoad (AU)	1	Ashley Cooper (AU)
2	Ken Rosewall (AU)	2	Ken Rosewall (AUS)	2	Mal Anderson (AU)
3	Lew Hoad (AU)	3	Ham Richardson (US)	3	Sven Davidson (SE)
4	Vic Seixas (US)	4	Vic Seixas (US)	4	Herbie Flam (US)
5	Rex Hartwig (AU)	5	Sven Davidson (SE)	5	Neale Fraser (AU)
6	Budge Patty (US)	6	Neale Fraser (AU)	6	Mervyn Rose (AU)
7	Ham Richardson (US)	7	Ashley Cooper (AU)	7	Vic Seixas (USA)
8	Kurt Nielsen (DK)	8	Dick Savitt (US)	8	Budge Patty (US)
9	Jaroslav Drobny (EG)	9	Herbie Flam (US)	9	Nicola Pietrangeli (IT)
10	Sven Davidson (SE)	10	Budge Patty (US)	10	Dick Savitt (US)
10	Mervyn Rose (AU)	10	Nicola Pietrangeli (IT)		

	1958		1959		1960
1	Ashley Cooper (AU)	1	Neale Fraser (AU)	1	Neale Fraser (AU)
2	Mal Anderson (AU)	2	Alex Olmedo (PE)	2	Rod Laver (AU)
3	Mervyn Rose (AU)	3	Nicola Pietrangeli (IT)	3	Nicola Piertrangeli (IT)
4	Neale Fraser (AU)	4	Barry MacKay (US)	4	Barry MacKay (US)
5	Luis Ayala (CL)	5	Rod Laver (AU)	5	Butch Buchholz, Jr. (US)
6	Ham Richardson (US)	6	Luis Ayala (CL)	6	Roy Emerson (AU)
7	Nicola Pietrangeli (IT)	7	Roy Emerson (AU)	7	Luis Ayala (CL)
8	Ulf Schmidt (SE)	8	Bernard Bartzen (US)	8	Ramanathan Krishnan (IN)
9	Barry MacKay (US)	9	Ramanathan Krishnan (IN)	9	Jan-Erik Lundquist (SE)
10	Sven Davidson (SE)	10	Ian Vermaak (ZA)	10	Dennis Ralston (US)

	1961		1962		1963
1	Rod Laver (AU)	1	Rod Laver (AU)	1	Rafael Osuna (MX)
2	Roy Emerson (AU)	2	Roy Emerson (AU)	2	Chuck McKinley (US)
3	Manolo Santana (ES)	3	Manolo Santana (ES)	3	Roy Emerson (AU)
4	Nicola Pietrangeli (IT)	4	Neal Fraser (AU)	4	Manolo Santana (ES)
5	Chuck McKinley (US)	5	Chuck McKinley (US)	5	Fred Stolle (AU)
6	Ramanathan Krishnan (IN)	6	Rafael Osuna (MX)	6	Frank Froehling III (US)
7	Luis Ayala (CL)	7	Marty Mulligan (AU)	7	Dennis Ralston (US)
8	Neal Fraser (AU)	8	Bob Hewitt (AU)	8	Boro Jovanovic (SR)
9	Jan-Erik Lundquist (SE)	9	Ramanathan Krishnan (IN)	9	Mike Sangster (GB)
10	Ulf Schmidt (SE)	10	Wilhelm Bungert (DE)	10	Marty Mulligan (AU)

	1964		1965		1966
1	Roy Emerson (AU)	1	Roy Emerson (AU)	1	Manolo Santana (ES)
2	Fred Stolle (AU)	2	Manolo Santana (ES)	2	Fred Stolle (AU)
3	Jan-Erik Lundquist (SE)	3	Fred Stolle (AU)	3	Roy Emerson (AU)
4	Wilhelm Bungert (DE)	4	Cliff Drysdale (ZA)	4	Tony Roche (AU)
5	Chuck McKinley (US)	5	Marty Mulligan (AU)	5	Dennis Ralston (US)
6	Manolo Santana (ES)	6	Jan-Erik Lundquist (SE)	6	John Newcombe (AU)
7	Nicola Pietrangeli (IT)	7	Tony Roche (AU)	7	Arthur Ashe (US)
8	Christian Kuhnke (DE)	8	John Newcombe (AU)	8	Istvan Gulyas (HU)
9	Dennis Ralston (US)	9	Dennis Ralston (US)	9	Cliff Drysdale (ZA)
10	Rafael Osuna (MX)	10	Arthur Ashe (US)	10	Ken Fletcher (AU)

1967

1	John Newcombe (AU)
2	Roy Emerson (AU)
3	Manolo Santana (ES)
4	Marty Mulligan (AU)
5	Tony Roche (AU)
6	Bob Hewitt (ZA)
7	Nikki Pilic (YU)
8	Clark Graebner (US)
9	Arthur Ashe (US)
10	Jan Leschy (DK)
	Wilhelm Bungert (DE)
	Cliff Drysdale (ZA)

1967 Pro Tennis Calendar

Dates	Tournaments	Winner	Finalist	Scores
1/31/1967	Toowoomba	Fred Stolle	Dennis Ralston	6-3, 10-8
1/31/1967	Toowoomba	Rod Laver	Pancho Gonzales	4-6, 6-3, 6-4
2/5/1967	Sydney	Dennis Ralston	Fred Stolle	7-9, 6-3,6-2
2/5/1967	Sydney	Pancho Gonzales	Ken Rosewall	3-6, 6-4, 6-4
2/5/1967	Sydney	P. Gonzales - D. Ralston	K. Rosewall - F. Stolle	6-2, 15-13
2/5/1967	Sydney	Dennis Ralston	Ken Rosewall	6-3, 8-6
2/5/1967	Sydney	Pancho Gonzales	Fred Stolle	6-3, 8-6
2/5/1967	Sydney	K. Rosewall - F. Stolle	P. Gonzales - D. Ralston	6-3, 6-4
2/6/1967	Rockhampton	Dennis Ralston	Fred Stolle	6-3, 5-7, 9-7
2/6/1967	Rockhampton	Rod Laver	Pancho Gonzales	6-3, 8-10, 7-5
2/8/1967	Brisbane	Rod Laver	Dennis Ralston	12-10, 0-6, 6-2
2/8/1967	Brisbane	Pancho Gonzales	Fred Stolle	6-4, 6-8, 6-3
2/8/1967	Brisbane	Fred Stolle	Dennis Ralston	6-3, 6-8, 8-6
2/8/1967	Brisbane	Rod Laver	Pancho Gonzales	6-2, 5-7, 9-7
2/11/1967	Adelaide	Dennis Ralston	Ken Rosewall	13-11, 6-1
2/11/1967	Adelaide	Pancho Gonzales	Fred Stolle	10-8, 6-4
2/11/1967	Adelaide	P. Gonzales - D. Ralston	K. Rosewall - F. Stolle	11-9, 6-4
2/11/1967	Adelaide	Dennis Ralston	Fred Stolle	6-4, 6-2
2/11/1967	Adelaide	Ken Rosewall	Pancho Gonzales	6-4, 8-6
2/11/1967	Adelaide	K. Rosewall - F. Stolle	P. Gonzales - D. Ralston	9-7, 9-7
2/14/1967	Shepparton	Fred Stolle	Dennis Ralston	7-5, 1-6, 6-1
2/14/1967	Shepparton	Pancho Gonzales	Ken Rosewall	6-4, 4-6, 6-4
2/14/1967	Shepparton	P. Gonzales - D. Ralston	K. Rosewall - F. Stolle	10-8,
2/19/1967	Melbourne	Pancho Gonzales	Rod Laver	6-2, 6-4
2/19/1967	Melbourne	Dennis Ralston	Fred Stolle	9-7, 6-3
2/21/1967	Christc+B69hurch	Fred Stolle	Pancho Gonzales	6-3, 8-6
2/21/1967	Christchurch	Rod Laver	Dennis Ralston	13-11, 6-4
2/22/1967	Dunedin	Fred Stolle	Pancho Gonzales	6-3, 8-6

2/22/1967	Dunedin	Rod Laver	Pancho Gonzales	6-0, 7-9, 13-11
2/24/1967	Auckland	Dennis Ralston	Fred Stolle	6-3, 11-9
2/24/1967	Auckland	Rod Laver	Pancho Gonzales	6-0, 6-3
2/26/1967	Auckland	Fred Stolle	Dennis Ralston	7-5, 4-6, 6-3
2/26/1967	Auckland	Pancho Gonzales	Rod Laver	8-6, 4-6, 7-5
2/26/1967	Sewanee	Earl Baumgardner	Del Sylvia	1-6, 6-4, 6-3
3/5/1967	New York	Rod Laver	Pancho Gonzales	7-5, 14-16, 7-5, 6-2
3/12/1967	San Juan	Rod Laver	Andres Gimeno	6-4, 3-6, 6-1
3/12/1967	San Juan	Butch Buchholz	Luis Ayala	10-5,
3/19/1967	Orlando	Rod Laver	Pancho Gonzales	6-4, 2-6, 6-0
3/19/1967	Orlando	Dennis Ralston	Andres Gimeno	8-3,
3/26/1967	Miami Beach	Rod Laver	Andres Gimeno	6-3, 6-3
3/26/1967	Miami Beach	Dennis Ralston	Fred Stolle	8-5,
4/2/1967	Boston	Rod Laver	Ken Rosewall	6-4, 6-0
4/5/1967	London	Ken Rosewall	Dennis Ralston	6-4, 6-2
4/9/1967	Paris	Rod Laver	Ken Rosewall	6-0, 10-8, 10-8
4/9/1967	Paris	Dennis Ralston	Fred Stolle	6-1, 8-6
4/15/1967	Brussels	Fred Stolle	Dennis Ralston	6-3, 6-4
4/15/1967	Brussels	Pierre Barthes	Rod Laver	6-4, 4-6, 6-4
4/15/1967	Lille	Dennis Ralston	Fred Stolle	9-7, 12-10
4/15/1967	Lille	Rod Laver	Pierre Barthes	6-3, 9-11, 6-4
4/15/1967	Besanqon	Rod Laver	Pierre Barthes	4-6, 6-4, 8-6
4/15/1967	Besanqon	Dennis Ralston	Fred Stolle	7-5, 6-4
4/15/1967	Strasbourg	Dennis Ralston	Pierre Barthes	6-3, 6-1
4/15/1967	Strasbourg	Rod Laver	Fred Stolle	6-4, 9-7
4/15/1967	Lyon	Fred Stolle	Rod Laver	6-1, 3-6, 6-4
4/15/1967	Lyon	Dennis Ralston	Pierre Barthes	6-2, 6-3
4/15/1967	Marseille	Rod Laver	Dennis Ralston	6-4, 6-3
4/15/1967	Marseille	Pierre Barthes	Fred Stolle	6-4, 3-6, 7-5
4/15/1967	Toulouse	Rod Laver	Pierre Barthes	6-1, 6-4
4/15/1967	Toulouse	Dennis Ralston	Fred Stolle	10-8, 11-9
4/15/1967	Bordeaux	Dennis Ralston	Pierre Barthes	6-1, 6-4
4/15/1967	Bordeaux	Rod Laver	Fred Stolle	4-6, 7-5, 6-1
4/15/1967	Remmes	Fred Stolle	Pierre Barthes	6-4, 6-3
4/15/1967	Remmes	Rod Laver	Dennis Ralston	q2-6, 6-3, 10-8

5/7/1967	Birmingham	Pancho Gonzales	Alan Mills	6-4, 6-2
5/7/1967	Birmingham	Sammy Giammalva	Mike Davies	6-4, 8-6
5/14/1967	San Diego	Rod Laver	Dennis Ralston	6-4, 12-10
5/14/1967	San Diego	Butch Buchholz	Mike Davies	6-2, 7-5
5/28/1967	Los Angeles	Ken Rosewall	Rod Laver	6-2, 2-6, 7-5
5/28/1967	Los Angeles	Dennis Ralston	Butch Buchholz	3-6, 6-4, 7-5
6/4/1967	San Francisco	Ken Rosewall	Rod Laver	4-6, 6-2, 8-6
6/4/1967	San Francisco	Andres Gimeno	Alex Olmedo	WO
6/9/1967	New York	Rod Laver	Ken Rosewall	6-4, 6-4
6/18/1967	St. Louis	Ken Rosewall	Andres Gimeno	6-3, 6-4
6/18/1967	St. Louis	Dennis Ralston	Fred Stolle	21-19 VASS
6/25/1967	Newport Beach	Ken Rosewall	Rod Laver	6-3, 6-3
7/4/1967	Oklahoma City	Rod Laver	Ken Rosewall	6-2, 3-6, 6-4
7/4/1967	Oklahoma City	Dennis Ralston	Andres Gimeno	10-8, 7-9, 8-6
7/9/1967	Cincinnati	Andres Gimeno	Ken Rosewall	6-4, 6-3
7/9/1967	Cincinnati	Rod Laver	Dennis Ralston	6-1, 7-5
7/16/1967	Boston	Rod Laver	Andres Gimeno	4-6, 6-4, 6-3, 7-5
7/16/1967	Boston	Ken Rosewall	Fred Stolle	10-5,
7/23/1967	Newport VASS	Rod Laver 93	Andres Gimeno 83	Ken Rosewall 82
7/30/1967	Binghampton	Rod Laver	Andres Gimeno	6-1, 6-3
7/30/1967	Binghampton	Fred Stolle	Barry MacKay	6-1, 6-0
8/12/1967	Eastbourne	John Horne	Charles Applewhaite	3-6, 3-6, 6-3, 9-7, 6-4
8/13/1967	Fort Worth	Rod Laver	Dennis Ralston	8-6, 6-9
8/13/1967	Fort Worth	Pancho Gonzales	Fred Stolle	2-6, 6-2, 6-2
8/28/1967	Wimbledon	Rod Laver	Ken Rosewall	6-2, 6-2, 12-10
8/28/1967	Wimbledon #3	Andres Gimeno	Lew Hoad	6-3, 6-3
9/6/1967	Pretoriaet al.	Fred Stolle	Andres Gimeno	6-1, 6-2
9/6/1967	Pretoria et al.	Ken Rosewall	Rod Laver	6-3, 6-2
9/4/1967	Johannesburg	Keith Diepraam	Pierre Barthes	4-6, 6-1, 6-2
9/4/1967	Johannesburg	Ken Rosewall	Andres Gimeno	6-4, 6-2
9/4/1967	Johannesburg	Fred Stolle	Rod Laver	2-6, 6-3, 7-5
9/10/1967	Durban	Ken Rosewall	Fred Stolle	6-4, 6-2
9/10/1967	Durban	Rod Laver	Andres Gimeno	6-3, 6-3
9/11/1967	East London	Andres Gimeno	Fred Stolle	6-3,

9/11/1967	East London	Rod Laver	Ken Rosewall	8-5,
9/12/1967	Port Elizabeth	Andres Gimeno	Ken Rosewall	10-0,
9/12/1967	Port Elizabeth	Rod Laver	Fred Stolle	
9/16/1967	Cape Town	Ken Rosewall	Fred Stolle	6-1, 3-6, 6-3
9/16/1967	Cape Town	Rod Laver	Butch Buchholz	
9/23/1967	Johannesburg	Rod Laver	Andres Gimeno	6-1, 8-6
9/23/1967	Johannesburg	Ken Rosewall	Butch Buchholz	6-3, 6-4
9/24/1967	Mbabane	Fred Stolle	Andre Gimeno	6-3, 6-4
9/24/1967	Mbabane	Ken Rosewall	Rod Laver	6-2, 8-6
10/1/1967	Lecco	G. Balierini		
10/1/1967	Paris	J. Mateo	M. Belkhodja	4-6, 6-3, 6-2, 6-1
10/2/1967	Fresno	Dennis Ralston	Alex Olmedo	7-5, 6-2
10/2/1967	Fresno	Ian Crookenden	L. Huebner	6-1, 6-1
10/8/1967	Marseille	Pierre Barthes	Fred Stolle	2-6, 9-7, 11-9
10/8/1967	Marseille	Andres Gimeno	Ken Rosewall	11-9, 6-3
10/16/1967	Paris	Rod Laver	Andres Gimeno	6-4, 8-6, 4-6, 6-2
10/16/1967	Paris	Ken Rosewall	Fred Stolle	6-2, 6-4
10/18/1967	Prague	Dennis Ralston	Rod Laver	7-5, 6-1
10/18/1967	Prague	Butch Buchholz	Fred Stolle	6-4, 7-5
10/28/1967	London	Rod Laver	Ken Rosewall	2-6, 6-1, 1-6, 8-6, 6-2
10/28/1967	London	Andres Gimeno	Owen Davidson	6-2, 6-1
11/26/1967	Boca Raton	Sammy Giammalva	W. Woodcock	6-2, 4-6, 6-3

The History of Professional Tennis, Joe McCauley (Great Britian 2000, 2003), 244-250.

CHAPTER 2:

1968: OPEN TENNIS AT LAST, NTL AND WCT CONTRACT PROS, CRISIS NO. 1

1968 Governing Bodies

The ILTF was the governing body for men's professional tennis in 1968, except for WCT events, the NTL events and Davis Cup. The Davis Cup was governed by the Davis Cup Nations, which was an organization separate from the ILTF.

1968 Significant Tennis Leaders

ILTF President:	Giorgio de Stefani (Italy)
USLTA President:	Bob Kelleher
Australian LTA President:	C.A. Edwards
British LTA President:	Sir Carl Aarvold
French FFT President:	Marcel Benard
French FFT Vice President:	Jean Borotra
Chairman of Wimbledon:	Herman David
WCT Owners:	Dave Dixon, Lamar Hunt and Al Hill, Jr.
WCT Executive Director:	Bob Briner
NTL Owner:	George MacCall

British LTA Out On A Very Long Limb

In early 1968, the British LTA was "out on a very long limb." Giorgio de Stefani, who had been a pre-war star of the Italian Davis Cup team was the President of the ILTF and he was adamantly opposed to Open Tennis. In January, de Stefani announced on behalf of the ILTF that "because of its anti-democratic and illegal unilateral decision to admit professionals, Britain would be excluded from all international events." Stefani was embarrassed when on January 11, Richard Evans reported in the *Evening News* that de Stefani had on behalf of the Italian Federation paid Nikki Pietrangeli, the hero of Italy after twice winning the French Championships, to keep him as an "amateur"[23]. *Tennis logic was great wasn't? Let's pay the amateurs to keep them as amateurs.*

Robert J. Kelleher (a California attorney in 1968, who in 1970 would be appointed by President Nixon as a United States Federal Judge) was president of the USLTA in 1967 and 1968. Kelleher was a lifelong close friend of fellow Californian, Jack Kramer, and through Kramer also a close friend of Donald Dell. Don't forget that Philippe Chatrier of France, also a close friend of Kramer and Dell, was also in the mix, advocating for Open Tennis.

At the USLTA Annual Meeting at the Del Coronado Hotel in San Diego in February of 1968, after what was described as "five days of tortuous maneuvering and lobbying," Kelleher skillfully led the USLTA to support Open Tennis with the final vote being with 16 USLTA Sections voting in favor and only the Middle States Section of Pennsylvania, Delaware and parts of New Jersey voting against.[24]

On March 30, the battle moved to the ILTF Emergency General Meeting at the Automobile Club on the Place de la Concorde in Paris where Kelleher joined with Derek Hardwick, Derek Penman and Jean Borotra, one of the famous French Musketeers, to support Open Tennis against de Stefani and others who opposed Open Tennis. In order to obtain approval for Open Tennis, Kelleher eventually agreed, in addition to the categories of amateur and contract professionals for NTL and WCT pros, to accept the creation of a new "authorized player" category for players not under contract with the NTL or the WCT who could accept prize money at Open Tournaments and continue to play in the Davis Cup. The British LTA complained that "the authorized player is the quintessence of hypocrisy. It is no cure for shamateurism as we shall still get players who are not authorized but are still receiving money under the table." However, the LTA eventually agreed to the creation of the "authorized player" category for those nations who wanted to use it. Richard Evans wrote in *Open Tennis*[25], "No one was defeated. Honour was satisfied – but only fools failed to realize that the game had been irrevocably changed."

The USLTA did not approve the "authorized/registered player" category to allow American non-contract pros to compete for prize money in open tournaments until February 8, 1969. The British LTA elected to just have "Players" and never considered having the "authorized/registered" player category.[26]

Condemnation of Shamateurism

Jack Kramer made his final condemnation on Shamateurism in *The Game:*[27] "In the shamateur days, we were only athletic gigolos – which is what Tilden called us – and the system was immoral and evil. I mean to be harsh. Tennis has changed so much in the last decade that it will not be long before the shamateur days are forgotten or looked upon fondly, all quaint nostalgia. I don't want the truth forgotten…overall the system was rotten and so were most of the people who ran it…I hope the amateur officials who were guilty and who are still alive from that era feel terrible about what they continued for so long, because they have been proven wrong and they deserve rebuke." The Richard Evans summary of shamateurism in *Open* Tennis[28] was just as condemning. "We talk blithely of the good old days, but although they did indeed have redeeming features that the modern age has lost, they were also great days for racists, snobs and blinkered buffoons."

Four Competitions

In 1968, the first year of Open Tennis, there were four organized competitions for men: ILTF Open tournaments (beginning in May), NTL events, WCT events and Davis Cup. There were 12 Open ILTF sanctioned tournaments, open to amateurs, teaching professionals, contract pros under contract with WCT and NTL and "registered/ authorized/independent" quasi professionals. The NTL had 31 NTL tournaments and events competed in by the NTL contract pros and WCT had 36 tournaments and events competed in by the WCT contract pros. They competed in some of the 12 ILTF Open Tournaments and in some other pro tournaments. Sometimes both the WCT pros and the NTL pros played in the same tournaments. Davis Cup was limited to amateurs and "registered/authorized" quasi professionals while WCT and NTL contract pros were barred. The Davis Cup Challenge Round format continued whereby all of the participating nations competed with each other for the right to "challenge" last year's winner in the final. I found 66 additional events staged in 1968.

ILTF's 12 Open Tournaments in 1968

[AM = Amateur; RP = Registered Player]

Bournemouth $14,000 +NTL	Ken Rosewall (NTL) d. Rod Laver (NTL)
French Open $? +NTL	Ken Rosewall (NTL) d. Rod Laver (NTL)
Beckingham $? +NTL and WCT	Fred Stolle (NTL) d. Roy Emerson (NTL)
Queens $? +NTL and WCT	Clark Graebner (AM) d. Tom Okker (RP)
Wimbledon $ 63,000 + NTL and WCT	Rod Laver (NTL) d. Tony Roche (WCT)
Dublin $? +NTL	Tom Okker (RP) d. Lew Hoad (NTL)

Gstaad $? + WCT	Cliff Drysdale (WCT) d. Tom Okker (RP)
Hilversum Dutch Open	Bob Maud (AM/RP) d. Istvan Gulyas (AM/RP)
Hamburg $? + WCT	John Newcombe (WCT) d. Cliff Drysdale (WCT)
U.S. Open $100,000 + NTL and WCT	Arthur Ashe (AM) d. Tom Okker (RP)
Los Angeles $ 30,000 +NTL	Rod Laver (NTL) d. Ken Rosewall (NTL)
Buenos Aires $? +NTL	Roy Emerson (NTL) d. Rod Laver (NTL)

Contract Pros vs. Independents

While the contract pros did very well in the 12 Open tournaments of 1968, they did not, as Jack Kramer and lots of people in tennis had predicted, completely dominate the amateurs and the "authorized/registered players." After recognizing that Laver (NTL) defeated Roche (WCT) in the final at Wimbledon, Gene Scott commented in the *New York Times*[29] that "the professional idols fell like dominoes" at Wimbledon. Pilic (WCT) lost to amateur Herb Fitzgibbon (#15 in US), Drysdale (WCT) lost to amateur Tom Edlefson (#12 US), Gimeno (WCT) lost to Ray Moore (#4 South Africa), Emerson (NTL) lost to Tom Okker (#1 Netherlands) , Newcombe (WCT) lost to amateur Arthur Ashe (#2 US), Stolle (NTL) lost to amateur Clark Graebner (#4 US).

Later in 1968, when Arthur Ashe as an amateur defeated Tom Okker, a "registered player," in the final of the U.S. Open, which included all the contract pros, it was clear that there were many more great players than the eight WCT contract pros and the six NTL contract pros. The emergence of Ashe, Okker and Graebner, who were not contract pros, was significant and they were ranked among the 1968 Top Ten.

Davis Cup Bars Contract Pros

The national associations who voted unanimously on March 30 at the ILTF meeting for Open Tennis to open the door for the talented professionals to compete in Open tournaments voted 24-8 in July for just the opposite – to ban contract pros from playing Davis Cup[30]. *Go figure!* Soon they would discover that it took a 2/3 majority to undo this ridiculous decision and permit contract pros to play in the Davis Cup. Later, they would also find it difficult to get any professional tennis players to play Davis Cup for no compensation. Contract pros continued to be banned from the Davis Cup in 1968, 1969, 1970, 1971 and 1972. The loss of Australia's contract pros, Stolle, Newcombe, Roche and Emerson, who had won the Davis Cup for Australia in 1964, 1965, 1966 and 1967, opened the way for the new

U.S. Captain, Donald Dell, to win the Davis Cup with amateurs Ashe, Graebner, Smith, Lutz and Pasarell in 1968.

WCT

When Dave Dixon created World Championships Tennis, Inc., in 1967, he owned 50 percent, Lamar Hunt owned 25 percent and Hunt's cousin, Al Hill, Jr., owned 25 percent. Lamar Hunt had founded the American Football League in 1959. Bob Briner was hired as WCT's Executive Director and Ron Bookman was hired as the first WCT public relations professional. Dixon, Briner, Hunt and Hill had no experience in the staging of tennis tournaments or the complicated tennis politics of the ILTF and the national associations.[31]

The WCT headliners were Newcombe, who had just won Wimbledon and the U.S. Championships in 1967, the 1966 French champion Roche and Dennis Ralston, America's No. 1 player. Ralston was guaranteed $50,000, Newcombe $45,000, Roche $40,000 and the others at least $25,000 each. Briner said: "We lost $300,000 the first year, but only $15,000 of that went to players who fell short of their guarantees." The WCT plan was to play five sessions in every town and hit two towns a week, estimating a minimum of 20,000 spectators a week with a $17,000 profit every week. That soon became wishful thinking as two events per week in different cities was way too grueling for the players. Mike Davies, who was then retired and living in California, was summoned by Butch Buchholz to come in and try to stem the flood. Rich Koster reported in *The Tennis Bubble*[32]: "When Davies arrived, the first question he asked Dixon was how the whole setup worked. 'It's easy, Mike,' Dave said. 'We run the whole show. We rent the arena, put up the prize money, promote the tournament, advertise it, pay for the officials, transportation, and we…'" 'I see your whole problem, Dave,' Mike interjected. 'You pay *them*. Before, they always paid *us*'. And that was what turned it around." Briner said: "'Operating from that simple premise, we never again lost on a tournament.' Throughout their disastrous beginning, the Handsome Eight had not only been providing the talent and energy, but also taking the financial risk. Dixon had, in effect, been his own sponsor as well as promoter. After Davies entered the picture, the pros stopped sponsoring themselves, stopped taking all the financial risks. They began 'selling' their services; thereafter, the money lost was not theirs, it was the sponsors' in the particular towns and arenas where they played…"

Dave Dixon Departs

Soon, Dixon telephoned Hunt and told him he was in over his head, so Hunt and Hill took over WCT and Dixon departed. WCT's headquarters was moved from New Orleans to Dallas. The WCT format was changed so that week-long tournaments replaced the three-night programs. Briner hired Mike Davies as a tournament liaison man to go to cities in advance to develop a relationship with the tennis people and with sponsors.[33]

Crisis No. 1: Travel Expenses/Corporate Fees for Contract Pros for 1969

Now just in case you thought since Open Tennis was approved that peace was here, now we begin Crisis No.1. The NTL and WCT had an agreement with each of their contract pros providing for a minimum cash guarantee against prize money winnings plus their traveling expenses. Consequently, they demanded reimbursement of traveling expenses (plus corporate fees) for their contract pros, who played in Open ILTF tournaments and naturally the ILTF objected since other players in those tournaments were not also getting prize money plus expense reimbursement and fees. This Crisis No. 1 began with Open Tennis in 1968 and was boiling at the beginning of 1969 as the NTL and WCT were threatening to boycott all the ILTF open tournaments, including the Grand Slams.[34]

1968 Grand Slams

The Australian Championships was amateur in January of 1968 before Open Tennis and none of the NTL or WCT contract pros participated. At the open French Open, the NTL pros participated, but the WCT pros did not. Both the NTL contract pros and the WCT contract pros participated in the open Wimbledon and the open U.S. Open. The $100,000 in U.S. Open prize money was the largest in the history of tennis.

Australian Championships (Amateur)

William W. Bowrey d. Juan Gisbert, Sr. 7-5, 2-6, 9-7, 6-4.
Dick Crealy-Allen Stone d. Terry Addison-Ray Keldie 10-8, 6-4, 6-3.

French Open

Ken Rosewall d. Rod Laver 6-3, 6-1, 2-6, 6-2.
Ken Rosewall-Fred Stolle d. Roy Emerson-Rod Laver 6-3, 6-4, 6-3.

Wimbledon

Rod Laver d. Tony Roche 6-3, 6-4, 6-2.
John Newcombe-Tony Roche d. Ken Rosewall-Fred Stolle 3-6, 8-6, 5-7, 14-12, 6-3.

U.S. Open

Arthur Ashe d. Tom Okker 14-12, 5-7, 6-3, 3-6, 6-3.
Bob Lutz-Stan Smith d. Bob Hewitt-Ray Moore 6-4, 6-4, 9-7.
Since Arthur Ashe was in the U.S. Army when he won the 1968 U.S. Open,
he was an amateur and could not receive the prize money. Tom Okker,
who was runner-up to Ashe, was a Netherlands "Registered Player" and was entitled
to accept prize money.

Davis Cup Challenge Round Final

United States d. Australia 4-1 (Adelaide - Grass)

Clark Graebner (US) d. Bill Bowrey, (AU) 8-10, 6-4, 8-6, 3-6, 6-1.
Arthur Ashe (US) d. Ray Ruffels (AU) 6-8, 7-5, 6-3, 6-3.
B. Lutz-S. Smith (US) d. J. Alexander - R. Ruffels (AU) 6-4, 6-4, 6-2.
Clark Graebner (US) d. Ray Ruffels (AU) 3-6, 8-6, 2-6, 6-3, 6-1.
Bill Bowrey (AU) d. Arthur Ashe, (US) 2-6, 6-3, 11-9, 8-6.

1968 World Rankings[35]

[RP = Independent Pro; IND = Independent Pro]

	Bud Collins			Lance Tingay	
1.	Rod Laver	NTL	1.	Rod Laver	NTL
2.	Arthur Ashe	RP	2.	Arthur Ashe	RP
3.	Ken Rosewall	NTL	3.	Ken Rosewall	NTL
4.	Tony Roche	WCT	4.	Tom Okker	WCT
5.	Tom Okker	IND	5.	Tony Roche	WCT
6.	John Newcombe	WCT	6.	John Newcombe	WCT
7.	Clark Graebner	RP	7.	Clark Graebner	RP
8.	Dennis Ralston	WCT	8.	Dennis Ralston	WCT
9.	Cliff Drysdale	WCT	9.	Cliff Drysdale	WCT
10.	Pancho Gonzales	NTL	10.	Pancho Gonzales	NTL

1968 Prize Money Top 10[36]

1.	Tony Roche	$63,504	6.	Butch Buchholz	$31,786
2.	John Newcombe	$57,011	7.	Roger Taylor	$29,523
3.	Cliff Drysdale	$37,880	8.	Pierre Barthes	$26,516
4.	Dennis Ralston	$34,626	9.	Marty Riessen	$14,985
5.	Nikki Pilic	$32,846	10.	Ray Moore	$ 6,000

1968 Tournament Calendar

Date	Tournaments	Singles Winner	Singles #2	Doubles Winners	Doubles #2
10/12/1967	Melbourne Pro WCT	Tony Roche	John Newcombe	J. Newcombe - T. Roche	R. Keldie - B. Kearney
11/19/1967	Brisbane Pro NTL/WCT	Roy Emerson	John Newcombe	J. Newcombe - T. Roche	R. Emerson - B. Bowery
11/26/1967	Sydney Open +NTL/WCT	Tony Roche	Roy Emerson	B. Bowrey - R. Emerson	J. Leschly - T. Ulrich
12/3/1967	Melbourne	Tony Roche	Bill Bowery	R. Emerson - T. Roche	J. Leschly - T. Ulrich
12/16/1967	Adelaide Pro WCT	John Newcombe	Tony Roche	J. Newcombe - T. Roche	B. Bowrey - R. Emerson
1/7/1968	Perth	Bill Bowrey	Ray Ruffels	P. Curtis - G. Stilwell	B. Bowrey - R. Ruffles
1/13/1968	Auckland	Colin Stubs	Brian Fairlie	B. Fairlie - C. Stubs	K. Parum - O. Woolcott
1/14/1968	Hobart	Ray Ruffles	Graham Stilwell	R. Ruffles - A. Stone	P. Curtis - G. Stilwell
1/19/1968	Australian Championships Melbourne AM	Bill Bowrey	Juan Gisbert	D. Crealy - A. Stone	T. Addison - R. Keldie
1/22/1968	Sydney VASS Pro WCT	Tony Roche #1	Nikki Pilic #2	Cliff Drysdale #3	Roger Taylor #4
1/22/1968	Sydney VASS Pro WCT	Pierre Barthes #5	John Newcombe #6	Dennis Ralston #7	Butch Buchholz #8
1/28/1968	Richmond Amateur	Arthur Ashe	Chuck McKinley		
2/4/1968	Copenhagen	Jan Leschly	Alex Metreveli	O. Bengtson - K. Anderson	J. Leschly - T. Ulrich
2/6/1968	Tulsa Amateur	Peter Van Lingen	Joaquin Loyo-Mayo	J. Fillol - H. Richardson	J. Loyo-Mayo - V. Zarazua
2/7/1968	Kansas City VASS Pro WCT	Tony Roche	Butch Buchholz		
2/8/1968	Philadelphia Amateur	Manolo Santana	Jan Leschly	A. Ashe - C. Pasarell	T. Koch - T. Ulrich
2/11/1968	Pittsburgh Amateur	Mark Cox	Bob Lutz	B. Lutz - S. Smith	M. Cox - R. Holmberg
2/11/1968	Miami VASS Pro WCT	Butch Buchholz	Tony Roche	C. Drysdale - R. Taylor	J. Newcombe - T. Roche
2/11/1968	Buffalo	Clark Graebner	Marty Riessen	C. Graebner - M. Riessen	M. Sangster - B. Wilson

2/18/1968	Salisbury Amateur	Cliff Richey	Clark Graebner	T. Koch - T. Okker	B. Lutz - S. Smith
2/20/1968	Macon Amateur	Jan Leschly	Mike Sangster		
2/28/1968	LaJolla Doubles Amateur			B. Lutz - S. Smith	A. Ashe - R. Emerson
3/3/1968	Kiamesha Lake Amateur	Arthur Ashe	Jan Leschly	R. Osuna - M. Riessen	A. Ashe - R. Holmberg
3/3/1968	Kingston	Tom Okker	Manuel Orantes	I. Buding - J. Osborne	T. Okker - A.R. Russell
3/10/1968	Barranquilla Amateur	Tom Okker	Marty Riessen	T. Okker - M. Riessen	M. Cox - M. Sangster
3/15/1968	St. Louis VASS Pro WCT	Dennis Ralston	John Newcombe		
3/15/1968	Houston VASS Pro WCT	Pierre Barthes	John Newcombe		
3/15/1968	New Orleans VASS Pro WCT	Cliff Drysdale	Tony Roche		
3/15/1968	Orlando VASS Pro WCT	Cliff Drysdale	Tony Roche		
3/17/1968	Caracas Amateur	Marty Riessen	Cliff Richey	T. Okker - M. Riessen	J. Arilla - M. Orantes
3/17/1968	Phoenix Amateur	Stan Smith	Bob Lutz	B. Lutz - S. Smith	M. Lara - J. Loyo-Mayo
3/18/1968	Mexico City Amateur	Manuel Osuna	Joaquin Loyo-Mayo		
3/22/1968	San Diego Pro WCT	Butch Buchholz	Dennis Ralston		
3/24/1968	Curacao	Marty Riessen	Tom Okker	T. Okker - M. Riessen	J. Kodes - J. Kukal
3/25/1968	Buenos Aires Pro NTL	Rod Laver	Pancho Gonzales		
3/31/1968	NY Amateur	Arthur Ashe	Roy Emerson		
4/1/1968	Bogota Pro NTL	Andres Gimeno	Fred Stolle	R. Laver - F. Stolle	A. Gimeno - P. Gonzales
4/1/1968	Los Altos Hills Pro WCT	Nikki Pilic	Dennis Ralston	B. Buchholz - D. Ralston	J. Newcombe - T. Roche
4/3/1968	Bakersfield Pro WCT	John Newcombe	Cliff Drysdale	D. Ralston - R. Taylor	N. Pilic - T. Roche
4/7/1968	San Juan Amateur	Mark Cox	Allen Fox	B. Bowrey - R. Ruffels	M. Cox - M. Sangster
4/7/1968	Nice	Alex Metreveli	Barry Phillips-Moore	S. Likhachev - A. Metreveli	G. Battrick - P.R. Hutchins

4/8/1968	Fresno Pro WCT	Butch Buchholz	Tony Roche	C. Drysdale - R. Taylor	J. Newcombe - T. Roche
4/14/1968	St. Petersburg Amateur	Mike Belkin	Jaime Fillol	P. Cramer - J. Fillol	M. Belkin - A. Fox
4/14/1968	Tampa Amateur	Manolo Santana	Istvan Gulyas	M. Cox - R. Ruffels	Z. Franulovic - I. Gulyas
4/14/1968	Hollywood Pro NTL	Roy Emerson	Ken Rosewall	R. Emerson - R. Laver	P. Gonzales - K. Rosewall
4/15/1968	Cannes Pro NTL	Andres Gimeno	Fred Stolle		
4/15/1968	Cannes Pro NTL	Billie Jean King	Rosie Casals		
4/15/1968	Johannesburg	Tom Okker	Marty Riessen	T. Okker - M. Riessen	B. Hewitt - F. McMillan
4/15/1968	Catania	Marty Mulligan	Ian Tiriac		
4/15/1968	Monte Carlo	Nicola Pietrangeli	Alex Metreveli	S. Likhachev - A. Metreveli	P. Beust - D. Contet
4/18/1968	London Pro +NTL	Rod Laver	Ken Rosewall		
4/19/1968	Paris Pro NTL	Ken Rosewall	Andres Gimeno		
4/19/1968	Paris Pro NTL	Billie Jean King	Ann Hayden Jones		
4/21/1968	Charlotte Amateur	Arthur Ashe	Ron Holmberg	A. Ashe - R. Holmberg	B. Bowrey - V. Sexias
4/21/1968	Houston Amateur	Cliff Richey	Boro Jovanovic	J. Loyo-Mayo - R. Osuna	C. Graebner - C. Richey
4/21/1968	Evanston Pro WCT	John Newcombe	Nikki Pilic		
4/21/1968	Palermo	Ian Tiriac	Marty Riessen		
4/22/1968	Bournemouth $14k Open +NTL	Ken Rosewall	Rod Laver	R. Emerson - R. Laver	A. Gimeno - P. Gonzales
4/25/1968	Ojai Amateur	Joaquin Loyo-Mayo	Jim Hobson	D. Leach - B. Potthast	M. Lara - J. Loyo-Mayo
4/28/1968	Corpus Christi Amateur	Peter Van Lingen	Ray Ruffels	P. Guzman - R. Ruffels	R. Fisher - J. Parker
4/28/1968	Paris	Bob Carmichael	Pierre Darmon	T. Koch - J. Mandarino	J. Barclay - G. Goven
4/28/1968	Naples	Marty Mulligan	Nicola Pietrangeli		
4/29/1968	Atlanta Amateur	Bill Bowrey	Ron Holmberg	R. Holmberg - R. Ruffels	
5/4/1968	Portola Valley Amateur	Jim McManus	Jeff Borowiak	D. Jacobus - J. McManus	B. Hill - E. Van Dillen
5/5/1968	Los Angeles Amateur	Stan Smith	Dick Leach	B. Lutz - S. Smith	J. McManus - J. Osborne

5/5/1968	Minneapolis Pro WCT	Dennis Ralston	John Newcombe	J. Newcombe - T. Roche	B. Buchholz - D. Ralston
5/6/1968	London Pro NTL	Billie Jean King	Ann Hayden Jones		
5/6/1968	London Pro NTL	Rod Laver	Ken Rosewall	R. Emerson - R. Laver	A. Gimeno - P. Gonzales
5/12/1968	Buffalo Pro WCT	Butch Buchholz	Dennis Ralston		
5/18/1968	NY US Pro NTL	Rod Laver	Ken Rosewall		
5/18/1968	NY Pro NTL	Ann Hayden Jones	Billie Jean King		
5/19/1968	Rome Amateur	Tom Okker	Bob Hewitt	T. Okker - M. Riessen	N. Kalogeropoulos - A. Stone
5/27/1968	French Open Open +NTL	Ken Rosewall	Rod Laver	K. Rosewall - F. Stolle	R. Emerson - R. Laver
5/29/1968	Sacramento Amateur	Clark Graebner	Stan Smith	B. Lutz - S. Smith	A. Ashe - C. Pasarell
6/2/1968	Baltimore Pro WCT	Dennis Ralston	Tony Roche	C. Drysdale - R. Taylor	P. Barthes - N. Pilic
6/9/1968	Montgomery Amateur	Joaquin Loyo-Mayo	Vicente Zarazua	J. Loyo-Mayo - V. Zarazua	J. Pickens - B. Seewagen
6/10/1968	LaJolla Amateur	Stan Smith	Roy Barth	D. Leach - R. Osuna	M. Lara - J. Loyo-Mayo
6/15/1968	Beckenham Open +NTL	Fred Stolle	Roy Emerson	R. Emerson - F. Stolle	J. Barrett - B. Howe
6/15/1968	Bristol	Arthur Ashe	Clark Graebner	B. Hewitt - F. McMillan	C. Graebner - J. Osborne
6/16/1968	Birmingham Amateur	Peter Van Lingen	Zan Guerry	J. Loyo-Mayo - P. Van Lingen	B. Conti - R. Hernando
6/16/1968	Chestnut Hills Pro +NT/WCT	Rod Laver	John Newcombe		
6/16/1968	Lugano Open + WCT	Ian Tiriac	Tom Okker	T. Okker - M. Riessen	B. Bowrey - R. Ruffles
6/20/1968	Eastbourne	Mark Cox	Owen Davidson	M. Cox - O. Davidson	P. Curtis - Lumsden
6/22/1968	London Open +NTL/WCT	Clark Graebner	Tom Okker [Rain]	Rain	Rain
6/24/1968	Wimbledon $63K Open +NTL/WCT	Rod Laver	Tony Roche	J. Newcombe - T. Roche	K. Rosewall - F. Stolle
7/5/1968	Indianapolis Amateur	Jaime Fillol	Cliff Richey	B. Lutz - S. Smith	J. McManus - J. Osborne
7/7/1968	Cincinnati Amateur	Bill Harris	Tom Gorman	B. Brown - R. Goldman	J. Loyo-Mayo - J. Fillol

7/13/1968	Dublin Open +NTL	Tom Okker	Lew Hoad	M. Cox - K. Fletcher	L. Hoad - T. Okker
7/14/1968	Gstaad Open +WCT	Cliff Drysdale	Tom Okker	J. Newcombe - D. Ralston	M. Anderson - T. Okker
7/15/1968	Paris Pro NTL/ WCT	Rod Laver	John Newcombe	R. Emerson - R. Laver	K. Rosewall - F. Stolle
7/21/1968	Milwaukee Amateur	Clark Graebner	Stan Smith	B. Lutz - S. Smith	T. Mozur - M. Riessen
7/21/1968	Hilversum Open	Bob Maud	Istvan Gulyas	J. Kodes - J. Kukal	I. Buding - H. Elschenbroich
7/28/1968	Copenhagen	Jan Leschly	Marty Mulligan		
7/28/1968	Philadelphia Amateur	Arthur Ashe	Marty Riessen	C. Graebner - C. Pasarell	A. Ashe - M. Riessen unfinished
8/1/1968	Bastad Pro WCT	Dennis Ralston	Nikki Pilic	John Newcombe	Roger Taylor
8/2/1968	Maribor Pro WCT	Nikki Pilic	Cliff Drysdale	Roger Taylor	Tony Roche
8/3/1968	Cannes Pro WCT	John Newcombe	Marty Riessen		
8/4/1968	South Orange Amateur	Charles Pasarell	Clark Graebner	C. Graebner - C. Pasarell	B. Lutz - S. Smith
8/5/1968	Danish Nationals	Jan Leschly	Torben Ulrich		
8/9/1968	Kansas City Amateur	Jim Parker	Ingo Buding	J. Parker - R. Susman	McKenna - P. Van Lingen
8/9/1968	Pensacola Amateur	Armistead Neely	Jaime Fillol	T. Edlefsen - A. Neely	A. Stone - C. Stubbs
8/11/1968	Binghamton Pro NTL	Andres Gimeno	Fred Stolle	R. Laver - F. Stolle	R. Emerson - A. Gimeno
8/11/1968	Binghamton Pro NTL	Billie Jean King	Rosie Casals	R. Emerson - B.J. King	A. Gimeno - R. Casals
8/11/1968	Southhampton Amateur	Ron Holmberg	Gene Scott	B. Hewitt - R. Moore	C. Steele III - P. Sullivan
8/12/1968	Toronto Amateur	Ramanathan Krishnan	Torben Ulrich	H. Fauquier - J. Sharpe	M. Lara - J. Singh
8/13/1968	Hamburg Open +WCT	John Newcombe	Cliff Drysdale	T. Okker - M. Riessen	J. Newcombe - T. Roche
8/15/1968	Los Angeles Pro NTL	Pancho Gonzales	Rod Laver		
8/15/1968	Oakland Pro NTL	Fred Stolle	Pancho Gonzales		
8/18/1968	Baltimore Amateur	Bob Hewitt	Colin Stubs	B. Hewitt - R. Holmberg	P. Cornejo - J. Fillol

8/18/1968	Fort Worth Pro NTL	Ken Rosewall	Andres Gimeno		
8/18/1968	Fort Worth Pro NTL	Ann Hayden Jones	Billie Jean King		
8/18/1968	Knokke-le Zoute Amateur	Mark Cox	Ray Ruffels		
8/18/1968	Newport Pro VASS WCT	Marty Riessen	Cliff Drysdale		
8/25/1968	Boston Amateur	Arthur Ashe	Bob Lutz	B. Lutz - S. Smith	B. Hewitt - R. Moore
8/29/1968	US Open $100K Open +NTL/ WCT	Arthur Ashe	Tom Okker	B. Lutz - S. Smith	A. Ashe - A. Gimeno
9/14/1968	Los Angeles $30k Open +NTL	Rod Laver	Ken Rosewall	K. Rosewall - F. Stolle	C. Drysdale - R. Taylor
9/19/1968	Dallas Amateur	Ray Moore	Alan Stone		
9/30/1968	Benoni et al.Pro WCT	John Newcombe	Tony Roche	B. Buchholz - M. Riessen	J. Newcombe - T. Roche
10/1/1968	Midland Pro NTL	Pancho Gonzales	Roy Emerson		
10/1/1968	Milan	Nicola Pietrangeli	E. Castigliano	N. Pietrangeli - S. Tacchini	M Di Domenico - Di Matteo
10/2/1968	Nareberth Pro	R. Kaufman	A. Chassard	R. Kaufman - E. Muehlbauer	W. Kenney - D. Richardson
10/6/1968	Johannesburg Pro WCT	Tony Roche	Butch Buchholz	C. Drysdale - R. Taylor	P. Barthes - R. Moore
10/6/1968	San Francisco Amateur	Stan Smith	Jim McManus	B. Lutz - S. Smith	J. McManus - J. Osborne
10/6/1968	La Jolla Amateur	Stan Smith	Roy Barth	R. Leach - R. Osuna	M. Lara - J. Loyo-Mayo
10/7/1968	Corpus Christi Pro NTL	Rod Laver	Andres Gimeno	R. Emerson - R. Laver	A. Gimeno - P. Segura
10/7/1968	Corpus Christi Pro NTL	Ann Hayden Jones	Rosie Casals		
10/9/1968	Durban Pro WCT	John Newcombe	Tony Roche	C. Drysdale - R. Taylor	J. Newcombe - T. Roche
10/10/1968	Lanunceston Amateur	Phil Dent	Bob Giltinan	J. Alexander - P. Dent	R. Brent - W. Lloyd
10/13/1968	Fresno Pro NTL	Fred Stolle	Barry MacKay	B. Mackay - P. Segura	A. Olmedo - F. Stolle
10/13/1968	Sydney	Phil Dent	Bob Giltinan	J. Alexander - P. Dent	Brent - W. Lloyd
10/15/1968	Lecco Pro	G. Bologna	G. Ballerini		

10/15/1968	Cape Town Pro WCT	Tony Roche	Cliff Drysdale	J. Newcombe - T. Roche	C. Drysdale - R. Taylor
10/15/1968	East London Pro WCT	John Newcombe	Cliff Drysdale		
10/15/1968	Kimberley Pro WCT	John Newcombe	Tony Roche		
10/15/1968	Port Elizabeth Pro WCT	Roger Taylor	Tony Roche		
10/15/1968	Kroonstad Pro WCT	Cliff Drysdale	Ray Moore		
10/15/1968	Johannesburg Pro WCT	Marty Riessen	Butch Buchholz	C. Drysdale - R. Taylor	P. Barthes - N. Pilic
10/19/1968	Stalybridge Dewar Cup	Bob Hewitt	Gerald Battrick	M. Cox - P. Curtis	G. Stilwell - K. Woodbridge
10/22/1968	Porto Alegre	Jorge Paulo Lemann	Thomas Koch		
10/26/1968	Perth Dewar Cup	Mark Cox	Bob Hewitt	O. Davidson - B. Howe	G. Battrick - P.R. Hutchins
11/2/1968	Aberavon Dewar Cup	Bob Hewitt	Owen Davidson	B. Hewitt - F. McMillan	O. Davidson - T. Okker
11/3/1968	Phoenix Amateur	Stan Smith	Bob Lutz	B. Lutz - S. Smith	M. Lara - J. Loyo-Mayo
11/7/1968	Marseille Pro NTL	Pancho Gonzales	Ken Rosewall		
11/9/1968	Torquay Dewar Cup	Bob Hewitt	Owen Davidson	O. Davidson - B. Hewitt	G. Stilwell - K. Woodbridge
11/11/1968	Lyon Pro NTL	Ken Rosewall	Pancho Gonzales		
11/11/1968	Lyon Pro NTL	Francoise Durr	Lise Buding		
11/11/1968	Buenos Open +NTL	Roy Emerson	Rod Laver	A. Gimeno - F. Stolle	R. Emerson - R. Laver
11/15/1968	Sao Paulo Pro NTL	Rod Laver	Andres Gimeno	Fred Stolle	Roy Emerson
11/15/1968	La Paz Pro NTL	Rod Laver	Andres Gimeno	Fred Stolle	Roy Emerson
11/15/1968	Lima Pro NTL	Fred Stolle	Andres Gimeno	Roy Emerson	Rod Laver
11/16/1968	London Dewar Cup	Bob Hewitt	Bob Lutz	Bob Lutz - S. Smith	B. Howe - M. Sangster
11/21/1968	London Pro + NTL & WCT	Ken Rosewall	John Newcombe	J. Newcombe - T. Roche	P. Gonzales - A. Gimeno
11/23/1968	Adelaide Amateur	Bill Bowrey	Allen Stone		
11/23/1968	London Dewar Cup	Stan Smith	Mark Cox	O. Davidson - B. Hewitt	B. Lutz - S. Smith

12/1/1968	NY Madison Pro NTL/WCT	Tony Roche	Pancho Gonzales		
12/1/1968	Brisbane Amateur	Arthur Ashe	Stan Smith	B. Lutz - S. Smith	T. Addison - R. Keldie
12/22/1968	New Orleans Amateur	Cliff Richey	Ron Holmberg	R. Holmberg - J. McManus	T. Edlefsen - C. Richey

http://www.atpworldtour.com/en/scores/results-archive.

http://www.itftennis.com/procircuit/tournaments/men's-calendar.aspx?tour=&reg=&nat=&sur=&cate=AL&iod=& fromDate=01-01-1968&toDate=29-12-1974.

Tennis History, Jim McManus (Canada 2010).

1970 USLTA Yearbook.

Official 1989 MTC Media Guide, (MTC 1989).

World of Tennis '69, Edited by John Barrett, compiled by Lance Tingay, (London 1969).

CHAPTER 3:

1969: CONTRACT PROS, EMERGENCE OF INDEPENDENT PROS, CRISIS NO. 2

1969 Governing Bodies

The ILTF was the governing body for men's professional tennis in 1969, except for WCT, the NTL and Davis Cup. Davis Cup was still governed by the Davis Cup Nations.

1969 Significant Tennis Leaders	
ILTF President:	Giorgio de Stefani (Italy) until July
ILTF President:	Ben Barnett (Australia) beginning in July
USLTA President:	Alastair Martin
Australian LTA President:	Wayne Reid
British LTA President:	Sir Carl Aarvold
French FFT President:	Marcel Bernard
French FFT Vice President:	Philippe Chatrier
Chairman of Wimbledon:	Herman David
WCT Owners:	Lamar Hunt and Al Hill, Jr.
WCT Executive Director:	Bob Briner until September
WCT Executive Director:	Mike Davies beginning in September
NTL Owners:	George MacCall and Fred Podesta

Five Competitions

In 1969, the second year of Open Tennis, there were five organized competitions for men: ILTF Open Tournaments, Non-Open Prize Money Tournaments, NTL, WCT and Davis Cup. There were 72 ILTF authorized Open tournaments (up from 12 in 1968), open to amateurs, teaching pros, contract pros under contract with WCT and NTL and registered players. In addition, there were 38 NTL tournaments and events and 38 WCT tournaments and events, which included some of the ILTF Open tournaments and some other pro tournaments. Sometimes both the WCT pros and the NTL pros played in the same tournaments. In 1969, the WCT contract pros were enlarged from eight to 14, with the addition of Ray Moore, Owen Davidson, Tom Okker, Mal Anderson, Ron Holmberg and Marty Riessen. Davis Cup was limited to amateurs and "registered players." The Davis Cup Challenge Round continued. WCT and NTL contract pros were barred[37].

Crisis No.1: Competition for Registered Players; Corporate Fees Demanded

As the NTL and the WCT moved to add the top registered players as contract pros, an intense competition began with the ILTF and the national associations who wanted to keep them from becoming contract pros so they could play Davis Cup. The NTL and WCT continued to demand travel expenses and corporate fees from the ILTF Open tournaments, including the Grand Slams. The new USLTA president Alastair Martin, like Kelleher, had a larger vision for the future of tennis than most of their predecessors. Martin told Neil Amdur of the *New York Times*[38]: "The professional managers did a service to tennis by playing in the opens last year." "I don't think the International Lawn Tennis Federation people feel this way, but I think the professionals should be recompensed for this." After a lot of discussions, the ILTF and the Grand Slams reluctantly agreed to make expense reimbursements for the contract pros for 1969 only in an agreement with Bob Briner of WCT and George MacCall of the NTL. "From a spectator's point of view, the game has been saved for 1969," said Philippe Chatrier, vice president of the French Federation, to Fred Tupper of the *New York Times*[39].

Arthur Ashe, who had won the 1968 U.S. Open and was now out of the Army, was the one major star not under contract with the NTL or WCT. Both of them attempted to buy Ashe for $400,000-$450,000 per year, a huge sum in 1969. Kramer said in *The Game*[40] that WCT's failure to sign Ashe at any price was the "single biggest mistake of Hunt's sports career." If they had been successful in obtaining Ashe in 1969, they would have had all of the current stars. That would have given them control of men's professional tennis and the ILTF and the Grand Slams would have been at their mercy to obtain any of their contract pros. However, Ashe was now represented by Donald Dell who had signed him with enough commercial contracts so he did not need the NTL or WCT money and he liked the idea of being independent. Soon, when Stan Smith got out of the Army, he joined Ashe and Dell and they led the development of a group of great independent players including Clark Graebner, Bob Lutz, Charlie Pasarell, Ilie Nastase, etc. Representation of Ashe, Smith, Lutz and Pasarell made Donald Dell an important force in the game. "Dell was planning a complete restructuring of the old amateur game before most people understood what he was talking about," Richard Evans wrote in *Open Tennis*[41].

On February 8, 1969, the USLTA created the "Player" ("Registered Player") category which permitted the independent players to play for prize money in Open tournaments and still be treated like amateurs so as to be eligible for the Davis Cup. The overriding emerging consensus among the upcoming independent (Registered Players) pros was *treat us as professionals by putting all the money up in prize money so we can compete for it and we will pay our own expenses as independent business men*[42]. The emergence of the independent pros was strong evidence that no one could probably ever buy tennis because there would always be new players coming up every year. To accommodate the independent pros, the USLTA "invented" a new category of Non-Open prize money tournaments that were not open to the WCT and NTL contract pros. The eight Non-Open prize money tournaments in the United States in 1969 were:

Indianapolis $25,000	Zeljko Franulovic d. Arthur Ashe
Washington $25,000	Thomas Koch d. Arthur Ashe
Cincinnati $25,000	Cliff Richey d. Allen Stone
Orange $23,000	Stan Smith d. Clark Graebner
Southampton $12,000	Clark Graebner d. Bob Lutz
Philadelphia $15,000	Cliff Richey d. Bob Carmichael
Boston $25,000	Stan Smith d. Bob Lutz
San Francisco $20,100	Stan Smith d. Cliff Richey

Tennis Champions Acquires NTL

In 1969, the NTL contract pros were still the original six men and four women. Apparently, George MacCall needed additional financial backing so in June of 1969, the NTL was acquired by Tennis Champions, Inc., led by Fred J. Podesta, formerly with Madison Square Garden for 25 years and the tournament director of the 1968 U.S. Open. Reports suggest that Podesta and MacCall each owned 50 percent of the NTL/Tennis Champions going forward. Soon after the acquisition of the NTL, Podesta, announced for 1970 the new "Tennis Champions $200,000 Classic" to begin in February of 1970 consisting of "winner-take-all" challenge matches beginning with 10 weekends of $10,000 challenge matches, followed by two semifinals for $25,000 each and concluding on the 13th week with a $50,000 final. Said Podesta to Neil Amdur of the *New York Times*[43]: "From the surveys we've taken and people we've talked with, this is the most interesting format ever tried for tennis. We think it can become the most successful."

Newcombe's ITPA

The first players' association, the IPTPA, founded by the pros in 1963 after Jack Kramer ceased the Kramer Tour in 1962, was disbanded after the pros signed with the NTL and WCT in 1967. In 1969, the International Tennis Players' Association (ITPA), the second players' association, was founded and was led by John Newcombe. The problem for the ITPA was that Newcombe was a contract pro with WCT and now there were a number of independent professionals (like Ashe, Smith, etc.) who had not signed with either WCT or the NTL and who had their own different agendas. As a result, the ITPA would not last long[44].

In September of 1969, Bob Briner resigned as Executive Director of WCT and Mike Davies, age 34, was appointed to succeed him. It was no surprise as Mike had demonstrated that he had one of the best business minds in the sport[45]. Briner apparently left WCT in a financial mess and thankfully Lamar Hunt had the money necessary to clean it up[46]. Rex Bellamy of the *London Times*[47] wrote that Mike Davies *"is probably at 34 the single most powerful man in the world game.* Yet Davies earned his first money by picking potatoes, arrived in the United States six years ago without a job, and twice decided to go into business because he could not earn a living from professional tennis. Instead he has decisively made it."

Alastair Martin, Joe Cullman, Owen Williams and Mike Gibson

Alastair Martin (President of the USLTA 1969-1970), acting more like a professional businessman than an amateur tennis administrator, made three interesting appointments for the 1969 U.S. Open. First, he appointed Joe Cullman (Joseph F. Cullman 3rd) Chief Executive of Phillip Morris as Tournament Chairman and increased the prize money from $100,000 to $125,000. Then, he and Cullman appointed Owen Williams of Johannesburg as the U.S. Open Tournament Director and Mike Gibson of Wimbledon as the U.S. Open Referee. Williams was considered the most successful tennis promoter in the world and Gibson was considered the best tennis referee in the world.[48] In spite of lots of rain for the 1969 U.S. Open, the innovations made by Williams made the tournament a huge success. The "patrons club" he promoted was the predecessor to the now famous U.S. Open Club. Just like sponges, all tournament promoters whenever they hear about a good idea, they immediately begin to copy and implement it at their own events. Nevertheless, the USLTA volunteers did not like it that a "foreigner" had been hired as a paid professional to direct the U.S. Open and Billy Talbert was appointed to succeed him in 1970[49].

Crisis No. 2: Travel Expenses/Corporate Fees for Contract Pros for 1970

Throughout 1969, threats, discussions, negotiations continued between the NTL, WCT, the ILTF and the national associations with respect to the demands of the NTL and WCT for expenses and appearance money for their contract pros from the 1970 Open tournaments. NTL and WCT continued to try to sign more "independent pros" and the national associations continued to try to entice signed contract pros to terminate their contracts and become eligible for the Davis Cup. No resolution was found during 1969, so 1970 started with Crisis No. 2 boiling.[50]

1969 Grand Slam Winners

This was Laver's second Grand Slam Year after his first in 1962 as an amateur.

Australian Open

Rod Laver d. Andres Gimeno 6-3, 6-4, 7-5.
Roy Emerson-Rod Laver d. Ken Rosewall-Fred Stolle 7-9, 6-3, 6-8, 14-12, 12-10.

French Open

Rod Laver d. Ken Rosewall 6-4, 6-3, 6-4.

John Newcombe-Tony Roche d. Tom Okker-Marty Riessen 6-4, 7-5, 7-5.

Wimbledon

Rod Laver d. John Newcombe 6-3, 5-7, 6-4, 6-4.
John Newcombe-Tony Roche d. Tom Okker-Marty Riessen 7-5, 11-9, 6-3.

U.S. Open

Rod Laver d. Tony Roche 7-9, 6-1, 6-3, 6-3.
Ken Rosewall-Fred Stolle d. Charles Pasarell-Dennis Ralston 2-6, 7-5, 13-11, 6-3.

1969 Davis Cup Challenge Round Finals

United States d. Romania 5-0 (Cleveland –Hard)

Arthur Ashe (US) d. Ilie Nastase (RO) 6-2, 15-13, 7-5.
Stan Smith (US) d. Ion Tiriac (RO) 6-8, 6-3, 5-7, 6-4, 6-4.
Bob Lutz-Stan Smith (US) d. Ilie Nastase-Ion Tiriac (RO) 8-6, 6-2, 11-9.
Stan Smith (US) d. Ilie Nastase (RO) 4-6, 4-6, 6-4, 6-1, 11-9.
Arthur Ashe (US) d. Ion Tiriac (RO) 6-3, 8-6, 3-6, 4-0 (default).

1969 World Rankings[51]
(RP= Registered Player)

	Bud Collins			Lance Tingay	
1.	Rod Laver	NTL	1.	Rod Laver	NTL
2.	Tony Roche	WCT	2.	Tony Roche	WCT
3.	John Newcombe	WCT	3.	John Newcombe	WCT
4.	Ken Rosewall	NTL	4.	Tom Okker	WCT
5.	Tom Okker	WCT	5.	Ken Rosewall	NTL
6.	Pancho Gonzalez	NTL	6.	Arthur Ashe	RP
7.	Stan Smith	RP	7.	Cliff Drysdale	WCT
8.	Arthur Ashe	RP	8.	Pancho Gonzales	NTL
9.	Cliff Drysdale	WCT	9.	Andres Gimeno	NTL
10.	Andres Gimeno	NTL	10.	Fred Stolle	NTL

1969 Official Earnings Top 10[52]

1. Rod Laver (NTL)	$123,405		6. Ken Rosewall (NTL)	$ 46,800
2. Tony Roche (WCT)	$ 75,045		7. Pancho Gonzales (NTL)	$ 46,320
3. Tom Okker (WCT)	$ 65,451		8. Marty Riessen (WCT)	$ 43,441
4. Roy Emerson (NTL)	$ 62,655		9. Fred Stolle (NTL)	$ 43,115
5. John Newcombe (WCT)	$ 52,610		10. Arthur Ashe (RP)	$ 42,030

1969 Tournament Calendar

Dates	Tournaments	Singles Winner	Singles #2	Doubles Winners	Doubles #2
12/31/1968	Perth $5,000 Open +NTL	Marty Riessen	Ken Rosewall	M. Riessen - K. Rosewall	J. Alexander - P. Dent
1/5/1969	Hobart $5K Open +NTL & WCT	Fred Stolle	Tony Roche	M. Anderson - R. Taylor	T. Roche - F. Stolle
1/6/1969	Melbourne Open	Stan Smith	Arthur Ashe	D. Crealy - A. Stone	B. Bowrey - R. Ruffels
1/6/1969	Tulsa Open	Tom Koch	Vicente Zarazua	H. Hose - V. Zarazua	J. Borowiak - P. Van Lingen
1/19/1969	Sydney $25K Open + NTL/WCT	Tony Roche	Rod Laver	R. Emerson - R. Laver	J. Newcombe - T. Roche
1/20/1969	Australian Open $25k Open + NTL	Rod Laver	Andres Gimeno	R. Emerson - R. Laver	K. Rosewall - F. Stolle
1/23/1969	Salt Lake City Open	Jim McManus	Tom Gorman	J. McManus - J. Osborne	R. Barth - S. Tidball
1/26/1969	Ft. Lauderdale Open	Pat Cramer	Jaime Fillol	P. Cramer - L. Garcia	M. Belkin - F. Tutvin
2/1/1969	Auckland $10k Open +NTL/WCT	Tony Roche	Rod Laver	R. Moore - R. Taylor	M. Anderson - T. Lejus
2/2/1969	Miami Open	Jaime Fillol	Pancho Guzman	G. Mulloy - E. Rubinoff	P. Guzman - N. Kalogetopoulus
2/2/1969	Richmond Open	Clark Graebner	Tom Koch	C. Graebner - C. Richey	T. Koch - T. Ulrich
2/3/1969	Pittsburg Open	Jan Kodes	Herb Fitzgibbon		
2/5/1969	Philadelphia $30k Open +NTL & WCT	Rod Laver	Tony Roche	T. Okker - M. Riessen	J. Newcombe - T. Roche
2/13/1969	Hollywood Pro NTL/WCT	Tony Roche	Rod Laver	J. Newcombe - T. Roche	B. Buchholz - D. Ralston
2/15/1969	London Open	Jan Leschly	Manuel Orantes	J. Leschly - T. Ulrich	G. Battrick - M. Sangster
2/16/1969	Cowra Open	Dick Crealy	Ray Ruffels		
2/16/1969	Salisbury Open	Stan Smith	Ismail El Shafei	B. Lutz - S. Smith	R. Holmberg - C. Pasarell

2/18/1969	Buffalo Open	Clark Graebner	Mark Cox	M. Cox - T. Edlefsen	C. Graebner - C. McKinley
2/23/1969	Macon Open	Manolo Orantes	Mark Cox	J. Kodes - J. Kukal	M. Cox - P. Curtis
2/27/1969	Oakland Pro NTL/WCT	Tony Roche	Rod Laver	J. Newcombe - T. Roche	R. Emerson - R. Laver
2/27/1969	Oakland OK US Pro NTL	Billie Jean King	Ann Hayden Jones		
2/28/1969	Portland Pro NTL	Rod Laver	Pancho Gonzales		
2/28/1969	Portland Pro NTL	Billie Jean King	Ann Hayden Jones		
3/8/1969	Los Angeles Pro NTL	Billie Jean King	Ann Hayden Jones		
3/8/1969	Los Angeles Pro NTL/WCT	Rod Laver	Marty Riessen	R. Emerson - R. Laver	J. Newcombe - T. Roche
3/8/1969	Phoenix Amateur	Cliff Richey	Manuel Santana	R. Barth - S. Tidball	J. Osborne - C. Richey
3/9/1969	La Jolla Doubles Amateur			R. Barth - Steve Tidball	M. Lara - J. Loyo-Mayo
3/15/1969	Barranquilla Amateur	Ilie Nastase	Jan Kodes	T. Koch - E. Mandarino	Z. Franulovic - I. Nastase
3/15/1969	St. Petersburg Open	Zeljko Franulovic	Jaime Fillol	Z. Franulovic - I. Nastase	M. Belkin - J.E. Mandarino
3/18/1969	New Rochelle Amateur	Clark Graebner	Charlie Pasarell	S. Stockton - N. Weld	B. Seewagen - J. Subirats
3/24/1969	Caracas Open	Thomas Koch	Mark Cox	J. Kodes - J. Kukal	J. McManus - J. Osborne
3/28/1969	NY Open + NTL/WCT	Andres Gimeno	Arthur Ashe		
3/31/1969	Jo'burg $3k Open + NTL & WCT	Rod Laver	Tom Okker	P. Gonzales - R. Moore	B. Hewitt - F. McMillan
3/31/1969	Norfolk Open	Hans Plotz	Jan Kukal	G. Battrick - M. Holecek	B. Bowrey - R. Ruffels
4/6/1969	Jacksonville Amateur	Pancho Guzman	Mike Belkin	P. Cramer - S. Ginman	B. Marcher - H. Rapp
4/7/1969	San Juan Open	Arthur Ashe	Charles Pasarell	J. Alexander - P. Dent	M. Cox - P. Curtis
4/13/1969	Mexico City Amateur	Thomas Koch	Manuel Osuna	M. Osuna - R. Ruffels	T. Koch - E. Mandarino
4/14/1969	Charlotte Amateur	Mark Cox	Jan Kodes	J. Alexander - P. Dent	Z. Franulovic - N. Spear

4/14/1969	Durban $8,000 Open +WCT	Robert Maud	Julian Krinsky	K. Diepraam - C. Drysdale	B. Hewitt - F. McMillan
4/15/1969	Monte Carlo $10k Open + NTL/WCT	Tom Okker	John Newcombe	O. Davidson - J. Newcombe	P. Gonzales - D. Ralston
4/22/1969	Houston Amateur	Zeljko Franulovic	R. H. Osuna	C. Graebner - R. Osuna	T. Edlefsen - S. Smith
4/27/1969	Dallas Amateur	Stan Smith	Tom Koch	T. Edlefsen - S. Smith	J. Alexander - P. Dent
4/27/1969	Ojai Valley Amateur	Haroun Rahim	Jeff Borowiak	D. Leach - B. Potthast	R. Cornell - S. Cornell
4/28/1969	Bournemouth $15k Open + WCT	John Newcombe	Bob Hewitt	B. Hewitt - F. McMillan	J.C. Barclay - R. Wilson
5/1/1969	Atlanta Open	Tom Koch	Bill Bowrey	B. Bowery - R. Ruffels	T. Kock - E. Mandarino
5/1/1969	San Francisco Amateur	Tom Brown	Erik Van Dillen	G. Cantin - C Meinhardt	L. Dodge - W. Reed
5/2/1969	Hamburg $16,500 Open	Tony Roche	Tom Okker	T. Okker - M. Riessen	J. Barclay - J. Fassbender
5/4/1969	London Pro +NTL	Rod Laver	Ken Rosewall		
5/4/1969	Portola Valley Amateur	Erik Van Dillen	Paul Gerken	J. McManus - J. Osborne	H.Kamakana - D. Kierbow
5/9/1969	Tokyo Pro NTL/ WCT	Tom Okker	Roy Emerson		
5/11/1969	Madrid Amateur	Manuel Santana	Arthur Ashe	M. Orantes - M. Santana	A. Ashe - C. Pasarell
5/12/1969	Berlin $10k Open +WCT	Ray Moore	Cliff Drysdale	B. Hewitt - F. McMillan	R. Moore - M. Riessen
5/12/1969	Brussels $10,000 Open + WCT	Tom Okker	Zeljko Franulovic	J. Newcombe - T. Okker	B. Hewitt - F. McMillan
5/12/1969	London	Brian Fairlie	Graham Stillwell		
5/12/1969	Los Angeles Amateur	Stan Smith	Bob Lutz	A. Olmedo - S. Smith	B. Bond - D. Leach
5/17/1969	NY Pro NTL	Rod Laver	Roy Emerson		
5/18/1969	Barcelona Amateur	Manuel Orantes	Manuel Santana	M. Orantes - P. Rodriguez	T. Addison - R. Keldie
5/18/1969	Overland Park Amateur	Clark Graebner	Tom Edlefsen	D. Leach - B. Potthast	M. Davies - R. Susman
5/21/1969	Rome $16,000 Open + WCT	John Newcombe	Tony Roche	J. Newcombe - T. Roche	T. Okker - M. Riessen

5/24/1969	Amsterdam Pro WCT	Tom Okker	Andres Gimeno		
5/24/1969	London	Allen Stone	John Cooper	T. Addison - B. Giltinan	B. Carmichael K. Fletcher
5/29/1969	French Open $35k + NTL/ WCT	Rod Laver	Ken Rosewall	J. Newcombe - T. Roche	R. Emerson - R. Laver
5/31/1969	Surbiton	Gerald Battrick	John Cooper	T. Addison - J. Cooper	G. Battrick - K. Fletcher
6/2/1969	Sacramento Open	Clark Graebner	Eric Van Dillen	B. Lutz - E. Van Dillen	M. Lara - J. Loyo-Mayo
6/7/1969	Manchester Open	Clark Graebner	Graham Stillwell	L. Ayala - C. Graebner	P. Curtis - G. Stillwell
6/9/1969	Bristol $20k Open + NTL/ WCT	Ken Rosewall	Pierre Barthes	J. Newcombe - M. Riessen	C. Drysdale - R. Taylor
6/14/1969	Nottingham Amateur	John Cooper	Geoff Masters	S. Matthews - T. Ryan	J. Bartlett - G. Masters
6/15/1969	Beckenham Open	Ove Bengston	Tom Gorman	J. Alexander - P. Dent	B. Bowrey - K. Fletcher
6/15/1969	Mobile Amateur	Mike Belkin	Peter Van Lingen	J. Medonos - P. Van Lingen	R. Reid - R. Tanner
6/21/1969	Chattanooga Amateur	Joaquin Loyo-Mayo	Zan Guerry	S. Faulk - H. Hose	M. Estep - Z. Guerry
6/21/1969	London $2,400 Open	Fred Stolle	John Newcombe	O. Davidson - D. Ralston	O. Bengston - T. Koch
6/23/1969	Wimbledon $75k +NTL/WCT	Rod Laver	John Newcombe	J. Newcombe - T. Roche	T. Okker - M. Riessen
7/1/1969	Birmingham Amateur	Turner Howard	Jamie Pressly	S. Faulk - J. Medonos	P. Gerken - F.D. Robbins
7/7/1969	Dublin $10,000 Open +WCT	Bob Hewitt	Nikki Pilic	B. Hewitt - F. McMillan	N. Pilic - R. Taylor
7/7/1969	Newport Wales Open	Mark Cox	Graham Stillwell	M. Cox - P. Curtis	J. Cooper - R. Power
7/12/1969	Dusseldorf Open	Wilhelm Bungert	Christian Kuhnke	M. Holecek - H. Plotz	H. Elschenbroich - J. Gisbert Sr.
7/13/1969	Bastad Open	Manuel Santana	Ion Tiriac	I. Nastase - I. Tiriac	M. Orantes - M. Santana
7/13/1969	Washington $25k Non-Open	Thomas Koch	Arthur Ashe	P. Cornejo - J. Fillol	B. Lutz - S. Smith
7/14/1969	Aix-en-Provence $7k Open + NTL/ WCT	Roy Emerson	Harold Elschenbroich	M. Anderson - R. Emerson	C. Drysdale - R. Taylor

7/15/1969	Boston $33k Pro +NTL/WCT	Rod Laver	John Newcombe	P. Gonzales - R. Laver	J. Newcombe - T. Roche
7/19/1969	Eastbourne Open	C. Kuhnke	Jeff Borowiak	I Buding - C. Kuhnke	S. Ball - B. Giltinan
7/20/1969	Hoylake Open	Ray Ruffels	Brian Fairlie	K. Fletcher - R. Ruffels	M. Santana - T. Ulrich
7/20/1969	Milwaukee Pro WCT	Tom Okker	Marty Riessen	J. Newcombe - T. Roche	T. Okker - M. Riessen
7/27/1969	Gstaad $12,000 Open + NTL	Roy Emerson	Tom Okker	T. Okker - M. Riessen	O. Davidson - Stolle
8/1/1969	Indianapolis $25k Non-Open	Zeljko Franulovic	Arthur Ashe	W. Bowrey - C. Graebner	R. Crealy - A. Stone
8/3/1969	Hilversum $5k Open +WCT	Tom Okker	Roger Taylor	T. Okker - R. Taylor	J. Kodes - J. Kukal
8/3/1969	Minneapolis Open	Tom Edlefsen	Mike Davies	C. Henry - N. Neely	T. Edlefsen - C. McKinley
8/3/1969	Portschach Pro NTL/WCT	Roy Emerson	Cliff Drysdale	R. Holmberg - M. Riessen	M. Anderson - R. Emerson
8/4/1969	Cincinnati $17.5k Non-Open	Cliff Richey	Allen Stone	B. Lutz - S. Smith	A. Ashe - C. PaZArell
8/6/1969	Orange $23,000 Non-Open	Stan Smith	Clark Graebner	B. Lutz - S. Smith	A. Ashe - C. Graebner
8/6/1969	St. Louis Pro NTL	Rod Laver	Fred Stolle	A. Olmedo - F. Stolle	R. Laver - P. Segura
8/6/1969	St. Louis Pro NTL	Billie Jean King	Rosie Casals	F. Stolle - B.J. King	R. Laver - A. H. Jones
8/9/1969	Toronto $7.5k Open + NTL/WCT	Cliff Richey	Butch Buchholz	R. Holmberg - J. Newcombe	B. Buchholz - R. Moore
8/10/1969	Binghamton Pro NTL	Rod Laver	Pancho Gonzales		
8/10/1969	Binghamton NTL	Billie Jean King	Ann Hayden Jones		
8/10/1969	Southampton $12k Non-Open	Clark Graebner	Bob Lutz	C. Graebner - B. Lutz	O. Parun - A. Stone
8/17/1969	Fort Worth Pro NTL/WCT	Rod Laver	Ken Rosewall	B. Buchholz - R. Moore	T. Okker - T. Roche
8/17/1969	Philadelphia $15k Non-Open	Cliff Richey	Bob Carmichael	B. Bowery - J. Osborne	D. Crealy - A. Stone
8/18/1969	Kitzbuhel Open	Manuel Santana	Manuel Orantes	M. Orantes - M. Santana	B. Hewitt - M. Mulligan
8/18/1969	Malaga Pro NTL/WCT	Roy Emerson	Cliff Drysdale		

8/24/1969	Boston $25,000 Non-Open	Stan Smith	Bob Lutz	D. Crealy - A. Stone	B. Bowrey - C. PaZArell
8/24/1969	Newport VASSS Pro WCT	Tom Okker	Dennis Ralston	T. Okker - M. Riessen	D. Ralston - R. Taylor
8/24/1969	Rochester Amateur	Butch Seewagen	Zan Guerry	T. Leonard - E. Van Dillen	B. McKinley - D. Stockton
8/25/1969	Istanbul TR Turkey Open	Bob Hewitt	Bob Maud	J. Kodes - J. Kukal	B. Hewitt - B. Maud
8/27/1969	US Open $137,000 + NTL/WCT	Rod Laver	Tony Roche	K. Rosewall - F. Stolle	C. Pasarell - D. Ralston
9/7/1969	Kansas City Open	Gerald Battrick	Bill Bowrey	B. Bowrey - M. Cox	G. Battrick - G. Stillwell
9/11/1969	Chicago Pro WCT	Ken Rosewall	Butch Buchholz	T. Okker - M. Riessen	B. Buchholz - R. Moore
9/11/1969	Evanston Pro NTL	Ken Rosewall	Butch Buchholz	T. Okker - M. Riessen	B. Buchholz - R. Moore
9/14/1969	Atlanta Pro WCT	Butch Buchholz	John Newcombe	T. Okker - M. Riessen	J. Newcombe - T. Roche
9/14/1969	Incline Village Pro NTL	Billie Jean King	Rosie Casals		
9/14/1969	Incline Village Pro NTL	Fred Stolle	Ken Rosewall	F. Stolle - K. Rosewall	A. Gimeno - P. Gonzales
9/15/1969	Carlsbad Open	Bob Carmichael	Tom Edlefsen	T. Addison - R. Keldie	R. Barth - S. Tidball
9/15/1969	San Francisco $20.1k Non-Open	Stan Smith	Cliff Richey	T. Koch - S. Smith	T. Addison - R. Keldie
9/20/1969	Los Angeles $30k Open + NTL/WCT	Pancho Gonzales	Cliff Richey	P. Gonzales - R. Holmberg	J. McManus - J. Osborne
9/21/1969	Oviedo Open	Manuel Orantes	Manuel Santana		
10/5/1969	Tucson Pro NTL/WCT	Tony Roche	Tom Okker	T. Okker - M. Riessen	T. Roche - R. Taylor
10/12/1969	Las Vegas Open	Nancy Richey	Billie Jean King		
10/12/1969	Las Vegas Open +NTL	Pancho Gonzales	Arthur Ashe		
10/18/1969	Perth Dewar Cup Open	Ismail EL Shafei	Mark Cox	M. Cox - P. Curtis	J. Clifton - D. Lloyd
10/19/1969	Madrid Open	Manuel Santana	Juan Gisbert	B. Hewitt - M. Mulligan	J. Gisbert - M. Orantes
10/20/1969	NY US Pro NTL/WCT	Rod Laver	Roy Emerson		

10/25/1969	Stalybridge Dewar Cup Open	Mark Cox	Bob Hewitt	M. Cox - P. Curtis	P. Hutchins - S. Matthews
10/26/1969	Sydney	Ray Ruffels	Ian Fletcher		
10/28/1969	Dakar Pro WCT	Tony Roche	Marty Riessen		
10/29/1969	Cologne $20k Pro NTL/WCT	Andres Gimeno	Roy Emerson	P. Barthes - T. Roche	A. Gimeno - K. Rosewall
11/1/1969	Aberavon Dewar Cup Open	Lew Hoad	Bob Hewitt	M. Cox - P. Curtis	L. Hoad - R. Howe
11/1/1969	Stockholm $25K Open + NTL & WCT	Nikki Pilic	Ilie Nastase	R. Emerson - R. Laver	A. Gimeno - F. Stolle
11/2/1969	Casablanca ro WCT	Tony Roche	Tom Okker		
11/5/1969	Midland Pro NTL	Ken Rosewall	Pancho Gonzales		
11/5/1969	Midland Pro NTL	Billie Jean King	Rosie Casals		
11/5/1969	Paris Open + WCT	Tom Okker	Butch Buchholz	J. Newcombe - T. Roche	T. Okker - M. Riessen
11/8/1969	Torquay Dewar Cup Open	Mark Cox	J. G. Clifton	G. Battrick - G. Stillwell	M. Cox - P. Curtis
11/9/1969	Barcelona Pro NTL	Andres Gimeno	Rod Laver		
11/11/1969	Buenos Aires Open	Francios Jauffret	Zeljko Franulovic	P. Cornejo - J. Fillol	R. Emerson - F. McMillan
11/11/1969	Rockdale Amateur	Ray Ruffels	Ian Fletcher	R. Keldie - R. Ruffels	S. Ball - B. Giltinan
11/13/1969	London Dewar Cup Open	Mark Cox	Bob Hewitt	B. Hewitt - L. Hoad	C Pasarell - S. Smith
11/17/1969	Brisbane Amateur	Ray Ruffels	Allen Stone	R. Ruffels - A. Stone	J. Bartlett - G. Masters
11/17/1969	London $46.2k Open +NTL/ WCT	Rod Laver	Tony Roche	R. Emerson - R. Laver	P. Gonzales - B. Hewitt
12/1/1969	Santiago Open	Jan Kodes	M. Holecek	M. Holecek - J. Kodes	F. Cornejo - J. Fillol
12/3/1969	Madrid Pro NTL/WCT	Rod Laver	Roger Taylor		
12/27/1969	East London Open	Bob Maud	Bob Hewitt	K. Diepraam - C. Drysdale	B. Hewitt - F. McMillan

12/28/1969	New Orleans $4,200 Open	Cliff Richey	Jim Osborne	R. Barth - J. Osborne	S. Faulk - T. Mozur

http://www.atpworldtour.com/en/scores/results-archive.

http://www.itftennis.com/procircuit/tournaments/men's-calendar.aspx?tour=&reg=&nat=&sur=&cate=AL&iod=& fromDate=01-01-1968&toDate=29-12-1974.

Tennis History, Jim McManus, (Canada 2010).

1970 USLTA Yearbook.

Official 1989 MTC Media Guide, (MTC 1989).

BP Year Book of World Tennis 1970, Edited by John Barrett, Compiled by Lance Tingay, (London 1970).

CHAPTER 4:

1970: PEPSI GRAND PRIX BEGINS VS. NTL AND WCT PRO TOURS, CRISES NOS. 2, 3

1970 Governing Bodies

The ILTF was the governing body for men's professional tennis in 1970, except for WCT, NTL and Davis Cup. Davis Cup was still governed by the Davis Cup Nations.

1970 Significant Tennis Leaders

ILTF President:	Ben Barnett (Australia)
USLTA President:	Alastair Martin
Australian LTA President:	Wayne Reid
British LTA President:	Sir Carl Aarvold
French FFT President:	Marcel Benard
French FFT Vice President:	Philippe Chatrier
Chairman of Wimbledon:	Herman David
WCT Owners:	Lamar Hunt and Al Hill, Jr.
WCT Executive Director:	Mike Davies
NTL Owners:	George MacCall and Fred Podesta

Six Competitions

In 1970, the third year of Open Tennis, there were six organized competitions for men: USLTA-IPA Indoor Circuit, NTL Tennis Champions Classics, WCT, Pepsi Grand Prix and Davis Cup. The USLTA sanctioned seven USLTA Indoor Tournaments promoted by Bill Riordan. The NTL staged 16 "Tennis Champions Classics" best-of-five set challenge matches for $10,000 "winner-take-all" in prize money, plus two semifinal challenge matches for $25,000 in prize money and the final for $50,000 in prize money. WCT staged 15 professional tournaments and events. Note that when other publications have listed WCT with 16 tournaments in 1970, they have added the 1970 Louisville Grand Prix tournament to the 15 pro WCT tournaments. Actually, the WCT pros played in many more Grand Prix Open tournaments. I counted 34 additional Open tournaments in which some of the WCT and NTL contract pros competed. In addition, WCT promoted the World Cup in Boston won by Australia over the United States 5-2.

Creation of Grand Prix

In February, an ILTF subcommittee agreed to submit for approval by the ILTF in July, Jack Kramer's proposed "Grand Prix of Tennis" for up to 30 ILTF Open tournaments in 1971. The plan was to have each tournament contribute 10 percent of its prize money into a Bonus Pool to be used as an incentive for the players to commit to participate in the circuit tournaments. *You have to love the people in tennis. Prior to 1968, Jack Kramer was the "enemy of the ILTF" as he promoted professional tennis and advocated for the approval of Open Tennis. Now that the ILTF and the national associations have Open Tennis and are in a competition with the NTL and the WCT for the best players, most of whom are contract pros, they have called on Kramer to help save them.*

As a result of the refusal of the NTL and WCT contract pros to agree to compete in the 1970 ILTF Open tournaments, especially the French Open, the ILTF moved quickly in April, to approve the experimental Grand Prix of Tennis to begin in 1970, instead of waiting for 1971. Kramer was called and he quickly obtained Pepsico to become the sponsor of the 1970 Pepsi Grand Prix for $75,000. The new Grand Prix was published by the ILTF as "an experimental scheme" for April – December of 1970 under the general direction and control of the International Calendar Committee which was responsible to the Committee of Management of the I.L.T.F.[53]

Tournaments were to be open to all categories of players. Players had to be accepted on the basis of ability, with qualifying competitions if necessary. Seeding had to be on merit as decided by the local committee. Before the ATP Computer rankings, the "system of merit" was determined by local committees' evaluations of entry applications and player records submitted by players along with the national association rankings – a very imprecise and a sometimes blatantly unfair method often with a little "home cookin." Each tournament had to contribute at least 10 percent of its total advertised prize money to a Bonus Pool which would be supplemented by Pepsico's sponsor contribution for bonuses for the top 20 players. Players had to play for advertised prize money only. No additional payments could be made to anyone competing, directly or indirectly. The ILTF was adamant against the payment of appearance fees for contract professionals. The USLTA did not agree until August to join the new 1970 Pepsi Grand Prix.

The ILTF sanctioned 21 Pepsi Grand Prix prize money tournaments beginning in May in Bournemouth, open to all, including the year-end Pepsi Masters in Tokyo. Cliff Richey a "registered pro" accumulated the most Pepsi Grand Prix points, but declined to play in the year-end Pepsi Masters event in Tokyo. The six Pepsi Masters players were Stan Smith, Arthur Ashe, Jan Kodes, Zeljko Franulovic, Rod Laver (NTL/WCT) and Ken Rosewall (NTL/WCT) and it was won by Stan Smith with a 4-1 round robin record. Rod Laver (NTL-WCT) was second with also a 4-1 round robin record. In addition to the Pepsi Grand Prix, there were other non-Grand Prix Open tournaments.

Davis Cup

Davis Cup continued to be limited to amateurs and "Players" or "Registered Players." WCT and NTL contract pros were barred. The Challenge Round was continued. In July, the Davis Cup nations again rejected a proposal that Davis Cup be opened to all classes of players. *Illogic: we need all the contract pros to play in the Davis Cup, but we just have to continue to reject them; that will teach them!*

Crisis No. 2: Fees for 1970

In February, WCT and the NTL rejected the USLTA's proposal for participation in the U.S. Open tournaments in 1970 mainly because there was no agreement to pay travel expenses and corporate fees for the participation of the contract pros. "If they want to know what war is like, they'll find out fast," Mike Davies said to Neil Amdur of the *New York Times*. "They've really let themselves in for a lot of trouble…If it means war, I'm not going to worry about scheduling…If they're out to hurt us or kill us, this is war. We just may decide to schedule a major pro tournament in New York around the time of the United States Open."[54]

Subsequent to the USLTA annual meeting in Tucson in February, the USLTA met with the ILTF, LTA and other national associations in Europe and they apparently decided that none of them would pay "corporate fees" or "guarantees" to the pro groups in 1970. As you might guess, they all did not abide by that decision. So, Crisis No. 2 continued in 1970 with this seemingly impossible dilemma. The independent pros paid their own travel expenses and had no guaranteed income – only the prize money they won. They objected to the payment of travel expenses and fees for the contract pros and not for them. However, many of the Open tournaments made their own arrangements with the pro groups for the participation of contract pros in their tournaments. Only a few of those deals were reported publicly. The ILTF Open tournaments in Monaco, Rome, Bournemouth and Johannesburg all made direct deals with WCT for the participation of some of its contract pros. The WCT and NTL pros competed in some Open tournaments, presumably for "fees" and did not compete in others, which apparently declined to pay.

The Australian Open had WCT pros, but no NTL pros and was won by Arthur Ashe, a "Registered Player" or "independent pro." The French Open had no WCT and no NTL pros and was won by independent pro Jan Kodes. Wimbledon had WCT pros and NTL pros and was won by WCT pro John Newcombe. The U.S. Open had WCT pros and NTL pros and was won by NTL/WCT pro Ken Rosewall. *Having made it through 1968, 1969 and most of 1970, the fun was about to begin with a new Crisis No. 3 for 1971 to test everyone's stamina.*

Laver Foregoes Grand Slam

Rod Laver, who had won the Grand Slam in 1969, elected not to enter the January 1970 Australian Open which offered only $14,000 in prize money, thus foregoing the opportunity to win a third Grand Slam. Instead, as a NTL contract pro, he competed in the NTL's new event, the "$200,000 Tennis Champions Classic". On January 23, Gonzales defeated Laver 7-5, 3-6, 2-6, 6-3, 6-2 before a crowd of 14,761 at Madison Square Garden in the first $10,000 winner-take-all challenge match of the 1970 Tennis Championships Classic.[55]

ITPA Championships - Philadelphia

On behalf of the NTL and WCT contract pros, John Newcombe as president of the ITPA (the 2nd players' association) had convinced Ed and Marilyn Fernberger to stage their Philadelphia indoor tournament, which was the first United States Open tournament of 1970 as the "ITPA Championships". The Fernbergers proposed to pay $5,000 in fees to both the NTL and the WCT. Stan Smith and Arthur Ashe were the leading "independent" or "Registered Players" in the United States. Smith threated a boycott of Philadelphia over the reduction in prize money from $50,000 to $40,000 to pay "fees" to the NTL and WCT. "Fees" were not available to the independent pros. Apparently, the Fernbergers solved this issue for the 1970 Philadelphia indoors with the independent pros by increasing the prize money to $60,000. There was never another IPTA Championship as the IPTA could never represent all the players because it did not have the independent pros.

Riordan's AITP or IPA

In March, Bill Riordan claimed to have "32 international tennis stars" announce the formation of the third players' association, the "Association of Independent Professionals" (AITP or IPA) to counteract the bargaining strength of the contract professionals." No one would ever actually see a membership roster for Bill Riordan's IPA.[56]

Dell Becomes Agent

In May, it was formally announced that Donald Dell had become the manager of Arthur Ashe, Bob Lutz, Stan Smith and Charlie Pasarell. Thus, began the ProServ management company, which would become one of the most powerful influences in the Game.[57]

Sudden Death Tiebreaker

In July, the new nine-point "experimental" tiebreaker was agreed for use at the 1970 U.S. Open. Jimmy Van Alen, the creator/inventor was delighted! The nine-point tiebreaker came to be known as "Sudden Death" but it would soon lose out to the Wimbledon 12-point tiebreaker which was favored by Wimbledon and the players.[58]

Contract Pros

The NTL and WCT began 1970 with 24 contract pros.

	WCT Contract Pros	Year Signed		NTL Contract Pros	Year Signed
1.	Butch Buchholz	1967	1.	Ken Rosewall	1967
2.	Pierre Barthes	1967	2.	Pancho Gonzales	1967
3.	Cliff Drysdale	1967	3.	Andres Gimeno	1967
4.	Roger Taylor	1967	4.	Rod Laver	1967
5.	John Newcombe	1967	5.	Fred Stolle	1967
6.	Tony Roche	1967	6.	Roy Emerson	1967
7.	Nikola Pilic	1967			
8.	Dennis Ralston	1967			
9.	Ray Moore	1969			

10.	Owen Davidson	1969
11.	Tom Okker	1969
12.	Ron Holmberg	1969
13.	Marty Riessen	1969
14.	Mal Anderson	1969
15.	Ismael El Shafei	1970
16.	Graham Stillwell	1970
17.	Mark Cox	1970
18.	Zeljko Franulovic	1970

In July, WCT acquired the contracts of the six NTL contract pros for about $350,000 per year, which expanded WCT to 24 pros.

19.	Ken Rosewall	1970
20.	Pancho Gonzales	1970
21.	Andres Gimeno	1970
22.	Rod Laver	1970
23.	Fred Stolle	1970
24.	Roy Emerson	1970

As of July, the NTL Tennis Champions Classics was over for 1970 and was planned again for promotion by the NTL in 1971, but all the contract pros were under contract with WCT. Mike Davies said to Neil Amdur of the *New York Times*[59], "It's been very unwieldly for the two groups coordinating schedules, trading players, for tournaments, expenses and overhead….World Championship Tennis plans to be around for a long time and we want to have the best players…With the quality of players we have under contract now, I definitely envision a strong pro tour for next year. How successful, money-wise, it will depend on how successful I am in selling it. But my job should be considerably easier with everybody under one roof."

1971 WCT Million Dollar Tour Announced

During the 1970 U.S. Open, WCT announced that in 1971, it would promote a million dollar tour consisting of 20 $50,000 tournaments for the top 32 professionals, with the top eight qualifying for a $100,000 final tour event. The *New York Times*[60] reported:

"Reaction to the announcement was mixed. Alastair B. Martin, the president of the United States Lawn Tennis Association said the concept was 'terrific,' and should help tennis."

Ashe Joins WCT

Notwithstanding the success of the 1970 Pepsi Grand Prix, later in September, Dell finally negotiated an agreement for Arthur Ashe to join WCT in 1971, along with Bob Lutz and Charles Pasarell. The cost was said to exceed a million for Ashe, but it gave WCT all the top stars for 1971, except for the up and coming Ilie Nastase and a few other independent pros. Stan Smith was still in the Army, but he was added later. The promise of the new 1971 WCT million dollar tour also kept the existing WCT contract pros from leaving WCT. Ashe told Neil Amdur of the *New York* Times[61]: "I appreciate everything the U.S.L.T.A. has done for me…But they just move too slowly for me." "They make bad appointments; their hands are tied by antiquated rules and they don't want to assume a role of leadership." Ashe (and Dell) had been upset that Bob Kelleher had not been given a more prominent position with the ILTF.

Six more players were then added to the WCT contract pro list:

25.	Arthur Ashe	1970	28.	Brian Fairlie	1970
26.	Bob Lutz	1970	29	Ray Ruffels	1970
27.	Charles Pasarell	1970	30.	Bob Carmichael	1970

Crisis No. 3: Ban Contract Pros in 1971

In November, out of fear of the proposed 20-city $1 million WCT tour in 1971, Alastair Martin proposed to ban all contract pros in 1971 from all sanctioned Open tournaments. This became Crisis No. 3. In my research, I have been impressed by the sound judgment provided by Alastair Martin in trying to find a way to work with the contract pros and keep them in the U.S. Open and the other American tournaments. But to seek to have a U.S. Open without the top 32 men in the world was a stupid goal and any such ban would certainly have been successfully challenged under the U.S. antitrust laws. Apparently, some common sense emerged at the November annual meeting of the USLTA when the proposal to ban all the male and female pros was "put off." The delegates must have realized that if the Australian Open, French Open and Wimbledon all had the contract pros and the U.S. Open and the U.S. tournaments did not, it would be a disaster for American tennis. So, negotiations began again with WCT, but who can facilitate any negotiations to seek a solution to Crisis No. 3?[62]

Ted Tinling

Everyone needs to know about Ted Tinling of Great Britain (1910-1990, Hall of Fame 1986). I was privileged to meet Ted late in life and he was great personal friend to my wife, Karen, and just about everyone else in the game. Ted was bald and was 6'5" in height. He was witty, literate and had been a lieutenant colonel in British intelligence during World War II. Ted made beautiful as well as avant-garde costumes for many female players, including Maureen Connolly, Maria Bueno, Billie Jean King, Rosie Casals, Margaret Court, Evonne Goolagong, Chris Evert and Tracy Austin. Ted was also a personal friend of Mike Davies who was also from Great Britain.[63]

So, when the ILTF and the national associations were so unprofessional and distrusted by Lamar Hunt and Mike Davies of WCT, Ted Tinling was, perhaps, the only knowledgeable possible intermediary and he was selected to chair secret talks between the ILTF and WCT upon the principle that the two organizations should cooperate in working towards a single worldwide competition. The ILTF was represented by the ILTF Emergency Committee comprised of Robert Colwell, first vice president of the USLTA, Robert Abdesselam of France, Allan Heyman of Denmark and Ben Barnett of Australia. ILTF President Ben Barnett said to the *New York Times*[64], "We agree with the basic sentiments, but we are not dictators, nor will we be dictated to. The I.L.T.F. has responsibility to lawn tennis all over the world and we are not going to sell our birthright to a millionaire in America."

The secret Ted Tinling Committee recommendations to the ILTF Emergency Committee resulted in the appointment of Derek Hardwick of England, Robert Abdesselam of France and Robert Colwell of Seattle to go to Dallas to negotiate with WCT. The Australian Open was not represented since it had already made a separate deal with WCT for the January 1971 Australian Open. After five days of meetings during December in Dallas, the Grand Slam representatives adjourned to consider a proposed agreement. On December 8, an agreement was announced.[65]

Presumably, the terms of the "deal" were secret or at least they were not announced publicly anywhere that I could find them. However, take a look at the 1971 Pepsi Grand Prix Rules. Remember how the 1970 Rule No.3 prohibited all "additional payments … directly or indirectly, in respect of the participation of any lawn tennis player." The 1971 Pepsi Grand Prix Rules provided that 20-25 percent of the available prize money shall be used for travel allowances, "available to all players and touring professionals without discrimination" and "must be paid to the organization under whose authority the competitor is entered." It looks like the changes in the 1971 Grand Prix Rules confirm that travel expenses would be paid to WCT for the WCT pros and that travel expenses would also be paid to all the other "independent" players. That presumably settled the demand for "corporate" or "participation" fees by WCT for 1971 and provided that the fees for the independent pros would be paid to their national associations in 1971. This concluded Crisis No. 3 for 1971, but, do not fear. I will continue numbering the Crises in men's professional tennis and this is only Crisis No. 3. Try to guess how many there will be through 1989? Maybe 32?

1970 Grand Slam Winners

Australian Open

Arthur Ashe d. Dick Crealy 6-4, 9-7, 6-2.
Bob Lutz-Stan Smith d. John Alexander-Phil Dent 8-6, 6-3, 6-4.

French Open

Jan Kodes d. Zeljko Franulovic 6-2, 6-4, 6-0.
Ilie Nastase-Ion Tiriac d. Arthur Ashe-Charles Pasarell 6-2, 6-4, 6-3.

Wimbledon

John Newcombe d. Ken Rosewall 5-7, 6-3, 6-2, 3-6, 6-1.
John Newcombe-Tony Roche d. Ken Rosewall-Fred Stolle 10-8, 6-3, 6-1.

U.S. Open

Ken Rosewall d. Tony Roche 2-6, 6-4, 7-6, 6-3.
Pierre Barthes-Nikki Pilic d. Roy Emerson-Rod Laver 6-3, 7-6, 4-6, 7-6.

Davis Cup

1970 Challenge Round Finals

United States d. West Germany 5-0
(Cleveland – Hard)

Arthur Ashe (US) d. Wilhelm Bungert (DE) 6-2, 10-8, 6-2.
Cliff Richey (US) d. Christian Kuhnke (DE) 6-1, 6-4, 6-2.
Bob Lutz-Stan Smith (US) d. Christian Kuhnke-Wilhelm Bungert (DE) 6-3, 7-5, 6-4.
Cliff Richey (US) d. Wilhelm Bungert (DE) 6-4, 6-4, 7-5.
Arthur Ashe (US) d. Christian Kuhnke (DE) 6-8, 10-12, 9-7, 13-11, 6-4.

1970 World Rankings[66]

	Bud Collins			Lance Tingay	
1.	John Newcombe	WCT	1.	John Newcombe	WCT
2.	Ken Rosewall	NTL	2.	Ken Rosewall	NTL
3.	Tony Roche	WCT	3.	Rod Laver	NTL
4.	Rod Laver	NTL	4.	Tony Roche	WCT
5.	Ilie Nastase	RP	5.	Tom Okker	WCT
6.	Tom Okker	WCT	6.	Ilie Nastase	RP
7.	Cliff Richey	RP	7.	Cliff Richey	RP
8.	Stan Smith	RP	8.	Arthur Ashe	RP/WCT
9.	Arthur Ashe	RP/WCT	9.	Andres Gimeno	NTL
			9.	Niki Pilic	WCT
10.	Andres Gimeno	NTL	10.	Dennis Ralston	WCT
			10.	Roger Taylor	WCT

1970 Pepsi Grand Prix Singles Bonus Pool Top 10
(1st Bonus Pool)[67]

1. Cliff Richey (US)	$25,000		6. Zeljko Franulovic (RS)	$ 9,500
2. Arthur Ashe (US)	$17,000		7. John Newcombe (AU)	$ 8,500
3. Ken Rosewall (AU)	$15,000		8. Jan Kodes (CZ)	$ 7,500
4. Rod Laver (AU)	$12,000		9. Tony Roche (AU)	$ 6,500
5. Stan Smith (US)	$10,500		10. Bob Carmichael (AU)	$ 6,000

The only contract pros earning a part of the 1970 Pepsi Grand Prix Bonus Pool were: Ken Rosewall (NTL/WCT), Rod Laver (NTL/WCT), John Newcombe (WCT), Tony Roche (WCT), Dennis Ralston (WCT), Cliff Drysdale (WCT) and Roy Emerson (NTL/WCT).

1970 Official Earnings Top 10[68]

1.	Rod Laver	$201,453	6.	Stan Smith	$ 95,251
2.	Arthur Ashe	$141,018	7.	John Newcombe	$ 78,251
3.	Ken Rosewall	$140,455	8.	Pancho Gonzalez	$ 77,365
4.	Cliff Richey	$ 97,000	9.	Clark Graebner	$ 68,000
5.	Roy Emerson	$ 96,485	10.	Tony Roche	$ 67,232

1970 NTL Tennis Champions Classic

Date	Tournaments	Singles Winner	Singles #2	Scores
1/23/1970	New York City $10,000 WTA	Pancho Gonzales	Rod Laver	7-5, 3-6, 2-6, 6-3, 6-2
1/31/1970	Detroit $10,000 WTA	Pancho Gonzales	John Newcombe	6-4, 6-4, 6-2
2/15/1970	Miami Beach $10,000 WTA	Roy Emerson	Pancho Gonzales	6-3, 6-2, 6-0
3/2/1970	Los Angeles $10,000 WTA	Roy Emerson	Ken Rosewall	7-5, 4-6, 7-5, 6-4
4/3/1970	Brisbane $10,000 WTA	Roy Emerson	Andres Gimeno	9-7, 1-6, 4-6, 6-3, 6-2
5/1/1970	Dayton $10,000 WTA	Roy Emerson	Fred Stolle	7-5, 7-5, 6-4
5/21/1970	West Orange Feed-in	Ken Rosewall	John Newcombe	5-7, 7-5, 6-1, 6-2
5/21/1970	West Orange Feed-in	Rod Laver	Andres Gimeno	4-6, 4-6, 6-1, 6-1, 6-2
5/22/1970	Los Angeles $10,000 WTA	Tom Okker	Fred Stolle	6-3, 6-3, 2-6, 6-1
5/23/1970	West Orange $10,000 WTA	Rod Laver	Tony Roche	6-2, 6-4, 6-2
6/1/1970	New York $10,000 WTA	Ken Rosewall	Fred Stolle	5-7, 6-0, 6-4, 6-1
6/1/1970	New York $10,000 WTA	Tom Okker	Tony Roche	6-3, 3-6, 7-5, 3-6, 6-4
6/2/1970	New York $10,000 WTA	Ken Rosewall	Tom Okker	6-2, 6-4, 6-2
6/2/1970	New York $25,000 Semis WTA	Rod Laver	Pancho Gonzales	6-3, 6-3, 6-1
6/5/1970	New York $25,000 Semis WTA	Ken Rosewall	Roy Emerson	4-6, 6-1, 6-4, 4-6, 7-5
7/16/1970	New York $35,000 Final WTA	Rod Laver	Ken Rosewall	6-4, 6-3, 6-3

1970 Tournament Calendar

Date	Tournament	Singles Winner	Singles #2	Doubles Winners	Doubles #2
1/1/1970	Perth	Allan Stone	Phil Dent	G. Battrick - G. Russell	R. Paul - M. Werren
1/1/1970	Valencia	Manuel Santana	Manuel Orantes		
1/3/1970	Port Elizabeth	Bob Hewitt	Mark Cox	B. Hewitt - F. McMillan	J. Saul - D. Matthews
1/10/1970	Blomfontein	Bob Hewitt	Mark Cox	B. Hewitt - F. McMillan	M. Cox - G. Stilwell
1/10/1970	Hobart	Jim McManus	Bob Carmichael	S. Smith - B. Lutz	A. Stone - D. Crealy
1/17/1970	Cape Town	Bob Maud	Bob Hewitt	B. Hewitt - F. McMillan	B. Maud - A. Wolpert
1/18/1970	Orlando	Frank Froehling	Mike Belkin	P. Guzman - B. Parrot	F. Froehling - Waters
1/19/1970	Australian Open $14,000 +WCT	Arthur Ashe	Dick Crealy	S. Smith - B. Lutz	J. Alexander - P. Dent
1/23/1970	Auckland $15,000	Roger Taylor	Tom Okker	D. Crealy - R. Ruffels	J. Alexander - P. Dent
1/23/1970	NY $10,000 NTL TCC WTA	Pancho Gonzales	Rod Laver	7-5, 3-6, 2-6, 6-3, 6-2	Tennis Champions Classic
1/28/1970	Ft. Lauderdale $2.5k Non-Open	Cliff Richey	Clark Graebner	F. Froehling - C. Graebner	B. Higgins - G. Mulloy
1/31/1970	Detroit $10,000 NTL TCC WTA	Pancho Gonzales	John Newcombe	6-4, 6-4, 6-2	Tennis Champions Classic
2/1/1970	Omaha $10,000 Open USLTA	Stan Smith	Jim Osborne	B. Lutz - S. Smith	I. Nastase - I. Tiriac
2/1/1970	San Diego	Roy Barth	Tito Vasquez	R. Barth - T. Vasquez	B. Brown - D. Leach
2/2/1970	Philly $60K USLTA +NTL/ WCT	Rod Laver	Tony Roche	I. Nastase - I. Tiriac	A. Ashe - D. Ralston
2/14/1970	North Miami Beach WCT	Ken Rosewall	Andres Gimeno		
2/15/1970	Buffalo Open USLTA	Clark Graebner	Bob Lutz	C. Graebner - G. Scott	C. McKinley - D. Stockton
2/15/1970	Hackensack	Herb Fitzgibbon	Peter Fishbach		
2/15/1970	Miami Beach $10k TCC WTA	Roy Emerson	Pancho Gonzales	6-3, 6-2, 6-3	Tennis Champions Classic

2/15/1970	Richmond $12,500 Open USLTA	Arthur Ashe	Stan Smith	A. Ashe - C. Pasarell	J. McManus - S. Smith
2/15/1970	Salisbury $50k Open +NTL/ WCT	Ilie Nastase	Cliff Richey	A. Ashe - S. Smith	B. Farley - O. Parun
2/20/1970	Corpus Christi WCT	Ken Rosewall	John Newcombe	J. Newcombe - D. Ralston	B. Buchholz - R. Moore
2/23/1970	Macon $15.000 Open USLTA	Cliff Richey	Arthur Ashe	T. Addison - B. Carmichael	I. Nastase - I. Tiriac
2/25/1970	Los Angeles WCT	Dennis Ralston	Rod Laver		
3/2/1970	Los Angeles $10,000 TCC WTA	Roy Emerson	Ken Rosewall	7-5, 4-6, 7-5, 6-4	Tennis Champions Classic
3/2/1970	Hampton Non-Open	Stan Smith	Cliff Richey	A. Ashe - S. Smith	I. Nastase - I. Tiriac
3/4/1970	London $24,000 +WCT	Marty Riessen	Ken Rosewall	T. Okker - M. Riessen	O. Davidson - R. Laver
3/8/1970	London	Stan Smith	Thomas Koch	S. Smith - A. Ashe	I. Nastase - I. Tiriac
3/9/1970	Boston $20,000 WCT WC	Australia	United States	5-2	
3/9/1970	Boston $20,000 WCT WC	Cliff Richey	John Newcombe	6-4, 3-6, 6-4	
3/9/1970	Boston $20,000 WCT WC	Fred Stolle	Arthur Ashe	6-3, 6-2	
3/9/1970	Boston $20,000 WCT WC	John Newcombe	Stan Smith	7-5, 6-3	
3/9/1970	Boston $20,000 WCT WC		8-6, 4-6, 10-8	J. Newcombe - F. Stolle	A. Ashe - C. Graebner
3/9/1970	Boston $20,000 WCT WC	Cliff Richey	Fred Stolle	4-6, 6-2, 6-4	
3/9/1970	Boston $20,000 WCT WC	John Newcombe	Stan Smith	6-3, 6-3	
3/9/1970	Boston $20,000 WCT WC		6-3, 2-6,7-5	J. Newcombe - F. Stolle	A. Ashe - S. Smith
3/15/1970	LaJolla Doubles			M. Lara - E. Van Dillen	R. Barth - S. Tidball
3/15/1970	Cairo $7,000 Open	Manuel Santana	Alex Metreveli	I. El Shafei - J Kukal	V. Korotkov - A. Metreveli
3/15/1970	Caracas	Tom Gorman	Gerald Battrick	T. Gorman - R. Keldie	G. Battrick - P. Curtis

3/15/1970	Curacao	Gerald Battrick	J. Gisbert	T. Koch - J.E. Mandarino	J. McManus - J. Osborne
3/15/1970	Rochester	Herb Fitzgibbon	Joaquin Loyo-Mayo	A. Palafox - J. Loyo-Mayo	S. Stockton - N. Weld
3/22/1970	Barranquilla	Zeljko Franulovic	Nikola Spear	J. McManus - J. Osborne	I. Molina - J. Velasco
3/22/1970	Sydney $25k Open +WCT/ NTL	Rod Laver	Ken Rosewall	K. Rosewall - F. Stolle	B. Bowrey - R. Taylor
3/24/1970	Johannesburg $45k +NTL/ WCT	Rod Laver	Frew McMillan	B. Hewitt - F. McMillan	C. Drysdale - R. Taylor
3/29/1970	Jacksonville $10,000 Open	Arthur Ashe	Brian Fairlie	R. Keldie - H. Ploetz	R. Barth - C. Steele
3/30/1970	San Juan	Arthur Ashe	Cliff Richey	T. Addison - B. Carmichael	A. Ashe - C. Pasarell
4/3/1970	Brisbane $10k TCC WTA	Roy Emerson	Andres Gimeno	9-7, 1-6, 4-6, 6-3, 6-2	Tennis Champions Classic
4/6/1970	Durban Open +NTL/WCT	Bob Hewitt	Cliff Drysdale	B. Hewitt - F. McMillan	M. Cox - G. Stilwell
4/6/1970	St. Petersburg $10,000 Open	Jan Kodes	Joaquin Loyo-Mayo	S. Baranyi - P. Szoke	S. Beeland - A. Neely
4/13/1970	Monte Carlo $20,275 +NTL/ WCT	Zeljko Franulovic	Manual Orantes	M. Riessen - R. Taylor	P. Barthes - N. Pilic
4/15/1970	Hamilton Round Robin	Arthur Ashe	Zelko Franulovic		
4/15/1970	Catania	Ion Tiriac	I. Gulyas	I. Nastase - I. Tiriac	E. Drossart - A. Panatta
4/15/1970	Charlotte Open	Cliff Richey	Bob Carmichael	M. Santana - C. Graebner	J. McManus - J. Osborne
4/15/1970	Kingston	C. Kuhnke	Gerald Battrick	I. Buding - C. Kuhnke	T. Addison - B. Carmichael
4/15/1970	Palermo	I. Gulyas	Ilie Nastase	I. Nastase - I. Tiriac	J.G. Clifton - D. Lloyd
4/20/1970	Rome $30,000 GP +WCT	Ilie Nastase	Jan Kodes	I. Nastase - I. Tiriac	B. Bowrey - O. Davidson
4/21/1970	Dallas $25,000 WCT	Andres Gimeno	Roy Emerson	R. Emerson - W. Jacques	K. Rosewall - F. Stolle
4/21/1970	Houston $25,000 Open	Clark Graebner	Cliff Richey	T. Addison - B. Carmichael	M. Santana - C. Graebner
4/27/1970	Bournemouth $35k GP-2 + WCT	Mark Cox	Bob Hewitt	T. Okker-T. Roche	B. Bowrey - O. Davidson

5/1/1970	Dayton $10k NTL TCC WTA	Roy Emerson	Fred Stolle	7-5, 7-5, 6-4	Tennis Champions Classic
5/1/1970	Ojai Open	Jeff Austin	Jimmy Connors	J. Austin - D. Smith	T. Neudecker - J. Rombeau
5/3/1970	Kansas City $10,000 Open	Arthur Ashe	Clark Graebner	A. Ashe - B. Lutz	T. Addison - C. Graebner
5/4/1970	Atlanta Open	Cliff Richey	Frank Froehling	T. Howard - L. Schloss	C. Henry - J. Skogstad
5/7/1970	London WCT	Marty Riessen	Ken Rosewall	T. Okker - M. Riessen	O. Davidson - R. Laver
5/8/1970	Atlanta $25,000 WCT/NTL	Tom Okker	Dennis Ralston	T. Okker - M. Riessen	R. Emerson - P. Segura
5/10/1970	Los Angeles Open	Erik Van Dillen	Allen Fox	M. Lara - E. Van Dillen	D. Bohrnstedt - F. Gentil
5/10/1970	Sacramento Open	Arthur Ashe	Barry MacKay	A. Ashe - B. Lutz	J. McManus - J. Osborne
5/11/1970	Brussels $15,300 Open +WCT	Tom Okker	Ilie Nastase	I. Nastase - I. Tiriac	B. Bowrey - M. Riessen
5/11/1970	West Berlin Open	G. Govern	C. Kuhnke	T. Addison - B. Carmichael	O. Davidson - H. Elschenbroich
5/15/1970	Columbus	Clark Graebner	Gene Scott		
5/15/1970	Madrid	Manuel Santana	Lew Hoad	A. Munoz - M. Orantes	J. Gisbert - M. Santana
5/15/1970	Naples	Ilie Nastase	Marty Mulligan	I. Nastase - F. Pala	N.Kalogeropoulos - M. Mulligan
5/17/1970	Las Vegas $50,000 +NTL/WCT	Pancho Gonzalez	Rod Laver	R. Laver - R. Emerson	C. Drysdale - R. Taylor
5/21/1970	West Orange NTL TCC Feed-in	Ken Rosewall	John Newcombe	5-7, 7-5, 6-1, 6-2	Tennis Champions Classic
5/21/1970	West OrangeNTL TCC Feed-in	Rod Laver	Andres Gimeno	4-6, 4-6, 6-1, 6-1, 6-2	Tennis Champions Classic
5/22/1970	Los Angeles $10k TCC WTA	Tom Okker	Fred Stolle	6-3, 6-3, 2-6, 6-1	Tennis Champions Classic
5/23/1970	Portola Valley $3,000 Open	Barry MacKay	Allen Fox	D. Leach - B. Potthast	R. Rippnet - R. Tanner
5/23/1970	West Orange $10k TCC WTA	Rod Laver	Tony Roche	6-2, 6-4, 6-2	Tennis Champions Classic
5/25/1970	French Open $100,000 GS-A	Jan Kodes	Zelko Franulovic	I. Nastase - I. Tiriac	A. Ashe - C. Pasarell
5/25/1970	Surbiton	Bob Maud	Frew McMillan	F. McMillan- B. Maud	S. Ball - R. Giltinan

6/1/1970	St. Louis $30,000 WCT/NTL	Rod Laver	Ken Rosewall	A. Gimeno - J. Newcombe	R. Emerson - R. Laver
6/1/1970	Manchester	Bob Lutz	Tom Gorman	F. McMillan- B. Maud	P. Marzano - A. Panatta
6/1/1970	New York $10k TCC WTA	Ken Rosewall	Fred Stolle	5-7, 6-0, 6-4, 6-1	Tennis Champions Classic
6/1/1970	New York $10k TCC WTA	Tom Okker	Tony Roche	6-3, 3-6, 7-5, 3-6, 6-4	Tennis Champions Classic
6/1/1970	Tulsa	Brian Fairlie	Tom Edlefsen	B. McKinley - D. Stockton	B. Fairlie - O. Parun
6/2/1970	New York $10k TCC WTA	Ken Rosewall	Tom Okker	6-2, 6-4, 6-2	Tennis Champions Classic
6/2/1970	New York $25k NTC TCC WTA	Rod Laver	Pancho Gonzales	6-3, 6-3, 6-1	Tennis Champions Classic
6/5/1970	New York $25k NTL TCC WTA	Ken Rosewall	Roy Emerson	4-6, 6-1, 6-4, 4-6, 7-5	Tennis Champions Classic
6/7/1970	Casablanca $25,000 WCT	John Newcombe	Andres Gimeno	M. Cox - G. Stilwell	R. Taylor - M. Riessen
6/7/1970	Little Rock	Zan Guerry	Vicente Zarzua		
6/8/1970	Beckenham Open	Clark Graebner	Robert Maud	C. Graebner - F. McMillan	D. Crealy - A. Stone
6/8/1970	Bristol $29,336 Open +NTL/WCT	Nikki Pilic	Rod Laver	R. Laver - D. Ralston	T. Okker - M. Riessen
6/8/1970	Nottingham Open	Stan Smith	Chauncey Steele III	B. Hewitt - B. Lutz	A. Ashe - S. Smith
6/14/1970	Montgomery Amateur	Peter Van Lingen	Paul Gerken	M. Lara - V. Zarazua	P. Gerken - M. Machette
6/15/1970	Eastbourne $9,860 +NTL/WCT	Ken Rosewall	Bob Hewitt	K. Rosewall - F. Stolle	R. Maud - A. Stone
6/15/1970	London $9,288 +NTL/WCT	Rod Laver	John Newcombe	T. Okker - M. Riessen	A. Ashe - C. Pasarell
6/21/1970	Columbus	Frank Froehling	Armistead Neely		
6/22/1970	Wimbledon $100.8k GS +NTL/WCT	John Newcombe	Ken Rosewall	J. Newcombe - T. Roche	K. Rosewall - F. Stolle
6/28/1970	Birmingham Amateur	Zan Guerry	Charlie Owens	T. Howard - T. Mozur	B. Siska - S. Stefanki
7/2/1970	Bastad $33,000 Open GP-1	Dick Crealy	Georges Goven	D. Crealy - A. Stone	J. Kodes - Z. Franulovic
7/5/1970	Newport Wales +NTL/WCT	Ken Rosewall	John Newcombe	O. Davidson - J. Newcombe	N. Pilic - K. Rosewall

Date	Tournament	Winner	Finalist	Doubles Winners	Doubles Finalists
7/6/1970	Dublin $11,448 +NTL/WCT	Tony Roche	Rod Laver	R. Laver - T. Roche	T. Okker - M. Riessen
7/6/1970	Dusseldorf	Wilhelm Bungert	Christian Kuhnke		
7/6/1970	Felixstowe	Robert Giltinan	R. Dowdeswell	S. Ball - R. Giltinan	R. Dowdeswell - H. Irvin
7/6/1970	Malvern	Frew McMillan	Andrew Pattison	S. Matthews - F. McMillan	P. Doerner -A. Pattison
7/12/1970	Chattanooga Amateur	Paul Gerken	Jeff Borowiak	J. Gardner - Z Guerry	B. Goeltz - F. McNair
7/12/1970	Kansas City	Frank Froehling v	Terry Addison	B. Alloo - J. Parker Rain	T. Addison - J. Cooper Rain
7/13/1970	Hoylake $12,792 Open +WCT	John Newcombe	Owen Davidson	B. Bowrey - O. Davidson	J. Newcombe - I. El Sharei
7/13/1970	Washington $35,000 GP-2	Cliff Richey	Arthur Ashe	B. Hewitt - F. McMillan	I. Nastase - I. Tiriac
7/16/1970	New York $35k NTL TCC WTA	Rod Laver	Ken Rosewall	6-4, 6-3, 6-3	Tennis Champions Classic
7/18/1970	Gstaad $17,000 +WCT	Tony Roche	Tom Okker	C. Drysdale - R. Taylor	T. Okker - M. Riessen
7/20/1970	Cincinnati $25,000 GP-2 + NTL	Ken Rosewall	Cliff Richey	I. Nastase - I. Tiriac	B. Hewitt - F. McMillan
7/25/1970	Leicester $5,566 Open +WCT	Tom Okker	Roger Taylor	C. Drysdale - R. Taylor	B. Bowrey - O. Davidson
7/27/1970	Indianapolis $50,000 GP-1 Open	Cliff Richey	Stan Smith	C. Graebner - A. Ashe	I. Nastase - I. Tiriac
8/2/1970	Louisville $25,000 WCT & GP-2	Rod Laver	Ken Rosewall	J. Newcombe - T. Roche	R. Emerson - R. Laver
8/2/1970	Hilversum $10,000 Open +WCT	Tom Okker	Roger Taylor	O. Davidson - B. Bowrey	J. Alexander - P. Dent
8/3/1970	Boston $50,000 GP-1 +NTL/WCT	Tony Roche	Rod Laver	R. Emerson - R. Laver	T. Ulrich - El Shafei
8/4/1970	Rochester Amateur	Roscoe Tanner	Haroon Rahim	L. Alvarez - T. Vasquez	B. McKinley - D. Stockton
8/9/1970	Kitzbuhel	Zeljko Franulovic	John Alexander	J. Alexander - P. Dent	Z. Franulovic - J. Kodes
8/10/1970	Hamburg $23,050 +WCT	Tom Okker	Ilie Nastase	B. Hewitt - F. McMillan	T. Okker - N. Pilic
8/10/1970	Munich GP-2 +WCT	Ian Tiriac	Nikola Pilic	O. Davidson - N. Pilic	B. Hewitt - F. McMillan

8/12/1970	Toronto $22,000 +NTL/WCT	Rod Laver	Roger Taylor	B. Bowrey - M. Riessen	C. Drysdale - F. Stolle
8/16/1970	Columbus $12,000	Bob Lutz	Tom Gorman	B. Lutz - S. Smith	T. Gorman - R. Ruffels
8/17/1970	Philadelphia $15,000 GP-2	Ray Ruffels	Jaime Fillol	B. Bowrey - R. Ruffels	J. Osborn - J. McManus
8/17/1970	Southhampton Amateur Grass	Haroon Rahim	John Gardner	B. McKinley - D. Stockton	J. Borowiak - H. Rahim
8/23/1970	Fort Worth $15,000 WCT	Rod Laver	Roy Emerson	R. Emerson - R. Laver	R. Moore - J. Newcombe
8/24/1970	Istanbul	Bob Hewitt	Zelko Franulovic	B. Hewitt - J.E. Mandarino	J. Alexander - P. Dent
8/30/1970	Newport VASSS $10,000 WCT	Marty Riessen	5-1 Round Robin		
9/1/1970	Orange $25k GP-2 +NTL/WCT	Rod Laver	Bob Carmichael	P. Cornejo - J. Fillol Susp.	A. Gimeno - R. Laver Susp.
9/2/1970	US Open $176,000 GS-A +NTL/WCT	Ken Rosewall	Tony Roche	N. Pilic - P. Barthes	R. Laver - R. Emerson
9/6/1970	Charlotte	Cliff Richey	Erik Van Dillen	B. Lutz - S. Smith	C. Rickey - E. Van Dillen
9/15/1970	Belgrade	Zeljko Franulovic	N. Spear	P. Hutka - V. Zednik	
9/19/1970	Los Angeles $60k GP-1 +NTL/WCT	Rod Laver	John Newcombe	T. Okker - M. Riessen	S. Smith - B. Lutz
9/28/1970	San Francisco $35,000 Open GP-2	Arthur Ashe	Cliff Richey	S. Smith - B. Lutz	T. Gorman - R. Barth
10/6/1970	Vancouver $40,000 WCT	Rod Laver	Roy Emerson	R. Emerson - R. Laver	P. Barthes - N. Pilic
10/11/1970	Midland $10,000 WCT	Roger Taylor	John Newcombe	O. Davidson - J. Newcombe	M. Cox - G. Stilwell
10/13/1970	Edinburgh Dewars Cup	Tom Gorman	J.G. Paish	I. Tiriac - V. Zednik	J. Alexander - T. Gorman
10/15/1970	Madrid	Manuel Orantes	Manuel Santana	H. Eischenbroich - E. Mandarino	L. Hoad - M. Santana
10/15/1970	Pensacola	Dick Crealy	Bob Carmichael	D. Crealy - A. Stone	R. Russell - L. Schloss
10/15/1970	Salvador	J.E. Mandarino	Thomas Koch	J.P. Lemann - I. Ribeiro	T.Koch - J.E. Mandarino

10/18/1970	Tucson $15,000 WCT	Marty Riessen	Roy Emerson	P. Gonzalez - R. Emerson	D. Ralston - M. Riessen
10/18/1970	Denver	Arthur Ashe	Charlie Pasarell	J. Kodes - J. Osborne	A. Ashe - M. Riessen
10/18/1970	Phoenix $25,000 GP-2	Stan Smith	Jim Osborne	D. Crealy - R. Ruffels	J. Kodes - C. Pasarell
10/20/1970	Manchester Dewars Cup	Ion Tiriac	John Alexander	B. Howe - H. Zahr	J. Alexander - T. Gorman
10/25/1970	Barcelona $28,800 Open +WCT	Manuel Santana	Rod Laver	L. Hoad - M. Santana	A. Gimeno - R. Laver
10/27/1970	Aberavon Dewars Cup	Gerald Battrick	V. Zednik	J.G. Clifton - P. Hutchins	I. Nastase - I. Tiriac
10/31/1970	Buenos Aires $30,000 GP-1	Zeljko Franulovic	Manuel Orantes	B. Carmichael - R. Ruffels	Z. Franulovic - J. Kodes
11/2/1970	Torquay Dewars Cup	V. Zednik	P. Hutchins	J. Alexander - T. Gorman	I. Nastase - I. Tiriac
11/9/1970	Paris $34,000 GP-2 +WCT/NTL	Arthur Ashe	Marty Riessen	K. Rosewall - P. Gonzalez	T. Okker - M. Riessen
11/12/1970	London Dewars Cup Final	John Alexander	Tom Gorman	J. Alexander - T. Gorman	J.G. Clifton - P. Hutchins
11/16/1970	London $35,680 GP-1 +WCT/NTL	Rod Laver	Cliff Richey	K. Rosewall - S. Smith	I. Nastase - I. Tiriac
11/22/1970	Stockholm $36,500 GP-2 +WCT	Stan Smith	Arthur Ashe	S. Smith - A. Ashe	B. Carmichael - O. Davidson
12/9/1970	Tokyo Pepsi Masters GP +WCT/NTL	Stan Smith	Rod Laver	S. Smith - A. Ashe	R. Laver - J. Kodes

http://www.atpworldtour.com/en/scores/results-archive.

http://www.itftennis.com/procircuit/tournaments/men's-calendar.aspx?tour=&reg=&nat=&sur=&cate=AL&iod=&fromDate=01-01-1968&toDate=29-12-1974.

Tennis History, Jim McManus (Canada 2010).

1971 USLTA Yearbook.

Official 1989 MTC Media Guide, (MTC 1989).

World of Tennis '71, Edited by John Barrett and Compiled by Lance Tingay, (London, 1971).

CHAPTER 5:

1971: PEPSI GRAND PRIX VS. WCT MILLION DOLLAR TOUR, PROS BANNED AGAIN, CRISIS NO. 4

1971 Governing Bodies

The ILTF was the governing body for men's professional tennis in 1971, except for the WCT, NTL and Davis Cup. Davis Cup continued to be governed by the Davis Cup Nations.

1971 Significant Tennis Leaders

ILTF President:	Allan Heyman (Denmark)
USLTA President:	Bob Colwell
Australian LTA President:	Wayne Reid
British LTA President:	Sir Carl Aarvold
French FFT President:	Marcel Benard
French FFT Vice President:	Philippe Chatrier
Chairman of Wimbledon:	Herman David
WCT Owners:	Lamar Hunt and Al Hill, Jr.
WCT Executive Director:	Mike Davies
NTL Owners:	George MacCall and Fred Podesta

Five Competitions

In 1971, the fourth year of Open Tennis, there were five organized competitions for men: USLTA-IPA Indoor Circuit, Pepsi Grand Prix, NTL Tennis Champions Classics, WCT and Davis Cup, plus a few additional individual events. There were seven USLTA

Indoor Tournaments promoted by Bill Riordan (a USLTA official and the "CEO or President" of the Association of Independent Tennis Players "AITP" or "IPA"). The Pepsi Grand Prix consisted of 33 prize money tournaments, open to all, including the year-end Pepsi Masters in Paris for the top seven players with a $150,000 Bonus Pool. Ilie Nastase won the round robin Pepsi Masters with a 6-0 record for the $15,000 first prize. Stan Smith was second with a 4-1 record. John Newcombe and Ken Rosewall qualified for the Masters, but declined to participate since they had not played in enough Grand Prix tournaments to qualify for the Bonus Pool.

The NTL staged 18 "Tennis Champions Classics" best-of-five set challenge matches for $10,000 in prize money, plus two semifinal challenge matches for $25,000 in prize money and the finals for $50,000 in prize money won for a second year in a row by Rod Laver. As a matter of fact, Laver won every challenge match. This was limited to WCT contract pros.

The WCT "Million Dollar" tour consisted of 17 WCT $50,000 professional tournaments open only to 32 WCT contract pros, plus three tournaments that were also part of the Pepsi Grand Prix: Australian Open, Washington DC and San Francisco. Philadelphia, Rome and Bristol were part of the WCT Tour and not part of the Grand Prix. The Tour culminated with the year-end $100,000 "World Championship of Tennis" for the top eight players with a first prize of $50,000, the largest single payoff for any tennis event ever. The quarterfinals and semifinals were staged in Houston and the final was staged in Dallas. Rosewall defeated Laver in the WCT Finals for the $50,000 first prize 6-4, 1-6, 7-6, 7-6.

Rex Bellamy described the WCT Finals[69]: "Famous names gathered in Dallas, among them Tony Trabert (referee), that loyal supporter Charlton Heston, and the first man on the moon, Neil Armstrong, who presented the prizes after the finals. Players and camp followers were housed in one of America's most luxurious hotels. We saw some thrilling tennis of the highest quality. Yet, the most lasting impression of those ten days was their effect on the heart. That sense of occasion kept coming through. The exclusively professional game had found a stage worthy of its actors. Houston and Dallas amount to much more than the climax of the inaugural WCT circuit. They were also a bridge between the hard times and a golden future. At the climax it seemed entirely appropriate that Laver and Rosewall should be on court and Trabert beside it. They had been through it all. Said Rod, 'This event will stand out in my memory for many, many years'. And 'I'm very fortunate,' said Rosewall, 'that I'm still around. Many great players have been unable to stay in the game long enough to see all this work come through. I'll remember this match and circuit for the rest of my life.' For WCT, everything except Wimbledon had paled beside the competition for places in this tournament. It was the fulfillment of a dream, for WCT and for the professional game as a whole."

In addition to the 20 WCT series tournaments, plus the Houston/Dallas finals on the "Million Dollar Tour", WCT promoted two special events: the World Cup in Boston won by the United States over Australia 4-3, and the CBS Tournament of Champions in Hilton Head won by Rod Laver over John Newcombe 6-2, 7-5.

Davis Cup

Davis Cup was again limited to amateurs and "Registered Players". WCT and NTL contract pros were barred. The United States brought Frank Froehling out of retirement to replace Cliff Richey at the last moment and defeated Romania 3-2 in Charlotte NC's Olde Providence Tennis Club, the site for the last Challenge Round, which was abolished beginning in 1972.

Rules

The 1971 Pepsi Grand Prix was controlled by the Grand Prix Committee of the ILTF instead of the ILTF Calendar Committee. Tournaments had to have minimum 32 draws, with four wild cards and four qualifying spots and a minimum of £8,300 in prize money with 20 percent of the prize money to be used for travel allowances available to all players.

Tournaments contributed 10 percent of their prize money to the Bonus Pool to provide, with Pepsico's contribution, for Bonus Pool Awards for the top 20 men who played in a minimum of nine tournaments. The Pepsi Masters was to include the top seven players selected by the ILTF. In a throwback to the old days, an additional rule stated: "The Organising Committee of the Grand Prix may direct that the entry of a lawn tennis player in any Grand Prix event be refused if, in their opinion, acceptance of the entry would not be in the best interests of the Game."[70] *I call this the "nightmare boycott rule." Fortunately, it was not used in 1971.*

WCT and the ILTF seemed to be satisfied with the settlement deal made to end Crisis No. 3, whereby each Pepsi Grand Prix tournament was required to pay travel expenses to all players in addition to prize money. So, Pepsi Grand Prix tournaments were open in 1971 to Registered Players/independent pros and WCT contract pros. WCT tournaments were open only to the 32 WCT contract pros. *Guess whether that peace agreement continued into 1972?*

12-Point Tiebreaker

Wimbledon announced that in 1971, the 12-point tiebreaker would be used for the first time at 8-8 in each set, except the final set. Goodbye to Jimmy Van Alen's nine-point "Sudden Death" tiebreaker.[71]

USLTA Rankings

For the first time the USLTA issued two sets of rankings for 1970. The contract pros were included for the first time in its "All-American" rankings and not included in the USLTA rankings[72].

1970 All-American Men's Rankings by the USLTA

1. Cliff Richey, San Angelo, TX (IND)
2. Stan Smith, Pasadena, CA (IND)
3. Marty Riessen, Evanston, IL (contract pro)
4. Arthur Ashe, Gum Spring, VA (contract pro)
5. Dennis Ralston, Bakersfield, CA (contract pro)
6. Pancho Gonzales, Los Angeles, CA (contract pro)
7. Clark Graebner, New York, NY (IND)
8. Robert Lutz, Los Angeles, CA (contract pro)
9. Tom Gorman, Seattle, WA (IND)
10. Butch Buchholz, St. Louis, MO (contract pro)

1970 USLTA Rankings

1. Cliff Richey, San Angelo, TX (IND)
2. Stan Smith, Pasadena, CA (IND)
3. Arthur Ashe, Gum Springs, VA (IND) (contract pro in September of 1970)
4. Clark Graebner, New York, NY (IND)
5. Bob Lutz, Los Angeles, CA (IND) (contract pro in September of 1970)
6. Tom Gorman, Seattle, WA (IND)
7. Jim Osborne, Honolulu, HI (IND)
8. Jim McManus, Berkeley, CA (IND)
9. Barry MacKay, San Francisco, CA (IND) (Reinstated as independent in 1969)

10.   Charles Pasarell, Puerto Rico, (IND) (contract pro in September of 1970)

11.   Erik van Dillen, San Mateo, CA (IND)

12.   Tom Edlefsen, Los Angeles, CA (IND)

13.   Allen Fox, Los Angeles, CA (IND)

14.   James Connors, Belleville, IL (IND)

15.   Roy Barth, San Diego, CA (IND)

16.   Jeff Borowiak, Berkeley, CA (IND)

17.   Paul Gerken, Norwalk, CT (IND)

18.   Frank Froehling 2nd, Miami, FL (IND)

19.   Tom Leonard, Arcadia, CA (IND)

20.   Roscoe Tanner, Lookout Mountain, TN (IND)

WCT TV in 1972

In November, NBC and WCT announced that eight of 25 WCT tournaments in 1972 would be broadcast on national television.[73] The NBC deal was masterminded by Mike Davies, WCT Executive Director, who sold $1 million in advertising for NBC to seal the agreement. *This was one of the most important developments in the history of men's professional tennis!* No matter what the on-site seating capacity for a tennis tournament was, the potential television audience was much, much greater and Mike and Lamar knew and understood this more than anyone else in the game. Lamar Hunt said: "As it has done for other sports in North America, we feel television will greatly publicize and popularize professional tennis on this continent."[74]

Pepsico to Withdraw

In November, the ILTF announced that Pepsi-Cola had withdrawn its sponsorship of the Grand Prix circuit at the end of 1971 claiming that it had not received sufficient publicity for the capital outlay. The capital outlay was only $75,000![75]

Crisis No. 4: Ban of Contract Pros for 1972

On July 3, the ILTF and WCT began Crisis No. 4 when they issued a joint statement saying they had failed to reach agreement on WCT's demand for travel and other fees for the participation of the WCT contract pros in the 1972 Grand Prix and Grand Slams. The ILTF Committee of Management announced that it would recommend that all WCT contract pros be banned from all 1972 ILTF sanctioned tournaments. On July 7, in Stresa,

Italy, the ILTF voted, apparently unanimously, to sever relations with WCT and ban the WCT contract pros in 1972. "'It was either them or us', a federation delegate said after the vote to sever relations with WCT," wrote Charles Friedman in the *New York Times*. "'Things couldn't have gone on this way.'"[76]

U.S. Open Withdrawals

Laver, Rosewall, Stolle, Emerson, Roche, Gimeno and Drysdale all withdrew from the 1971 U.S. Open. It was not clear to what extent the announced 1972 ban was involved. In September, Joe Cullman sent a letter to CBS demanding a renegotiation of the Philip Morris sponsorship of the U.S. Open television on account of the withdrawal of those top players.[77]

Crisis No. 4 Continued

USLTA President Robert B. Colwell and the USLTA delegates to the ILTF obviously supported and participated in the decision in July at the ILTF Annual Meeting to ban all WCT contract pros from all ILTF sanctioned tournaments, including Grand Prix tournaments and the Grand Slams, beginning in 1972. The ban also included banning any use of tennis facilities of clubs affiliated with the national associations. Then in November, Colwell said he would present a plan to the ILTF to try to avert the split. Colwell actually suggested that the USLTA may pull out of the ILTF if the ban (which he supported and voted for) was implemented.[78] *Consistency is elusive in tennis.*

Lamar Hunt announced that as a result of the ban of its contract pros in 1972, WCT would schedule an increasing number of events in the United States. "This is not WCT's plan; however, it is the reality of what will happen because WCT does not intend to try to force the best players, and the most competitive level of tennis play, on any country which does not want to see it," Hunt said as reported by John Barrett.[79] Crisis No. 4 was really boiling at the start of 1972!

1971 Grand Slam Winners

Australian Open

Ken Rosewall d. Arthur Ashe 6-1, 7-5, 6-3.
John Newcombe-Tony Roche d. Tom Okker-Marty Riessen 6-2, 7-6.

French Open

Jan Kodes d. Ilie Nastase 8-6, 6-2, 2-6, 7-5.
Arthur Ashe-Marty Riessen d. Tom Gorman-Stan Smith 6-8, 4-6, 6-3, 6-4, 11-9.

Wimbledon

John Newcombe d. Stan Smith 6-3, 5-7, 2-6, 6-4, 6-4.
Roy Emerson-Rod Laver d. Arthur Ashe-Dennis Ralston 4-6, 9-7, 6-8, 6-4, 6-4.

U.S. Open

Stan Smith d. Jan Kodes 3-6, 6-3, 6-2, 7-6.
John Newcombe-Roger Taylor d. Stan Smith-Eric Van Dillen 6-7, 7-6, 4-6, 7-6.

1971 Challenge Round Finals

United States d. Romania 3-2 (Charlotte – Clay)

Stan Smith (US) d. Ilie Nastase (RO) 7-5, 6-3, 6-1.
Frank Froehling (US) d. Ion Tiriac (RO) 3-6, 1-6, 6-1, 6-3, 8-6.
Ilie Nastase – Ion Tiriac (RO) d. Stan Smith – Erik Van Dillen (US) 7-5, 6-4, 8-6.
Stan Smith (US) d. Ion Tiriac (RO) 8-6, 6-3, 6-0.
Ilie Nastase (RO) d. Frank Froehling (US) 6-3, 6-1, 4-6, 6-4.

1971 World Rankings[80]

	Bud Collins			Lance Tingay	
1.	John Newcombe	WCT	1.	John Newcombe	WCT
2.	Stan Smith	RP	2.	Stan Smith	RP
3.	Ken Rosewall	WCT	3.	Rod Laver	WCT
4.	Rod Laver	WCT	4.	Ken Rosewall	WCT
5.	Jan Kodes	RP	5.	Jan Kodes	RP
6.	Arthur Ashe	WCT	6.	Arthur Ashe	WCT
7.	Ilie Nastase	RP	7.	Tom Okker	WCT
8.	Tom Okker	WCT	8.	Cliff Drysdale	WCT
9.	Cliff Drysdale	WCT	9.	Marty Riessen	WCT
10.	Marty Riessen	WCT	10.	Ilie Nastase	RP

1971 Pepsi Grand Prix Singles Bonus Pool Top 10 (2nd Bonus Pool)[81]

1.	Stan Smith	$25,000	6.	John Newcombe	$*
2.	Ilie Nastase	$17,000	7.	Pierre Barthes	$ 9,500
3.	Zeljko Franulovic	$15,000	8.	Ken Rosewall	$*
4.	Jan Kodes	$12,000	9.	Clark Graebner	$ 8,500
5.	Cliff Richey	$10,500	10.	Tom Gorman	$ 7,500

*Did not compete in the required 9 Grand Prix Tournaments.

1971 Official Earnings Top 10[82]

1.	Rod Laver	$292,453	6.	Stan Smith	$103,806
2.	Ken Rosewall	$138,371	7.	John Newcombe	$101,514
3.	Tom Okker	$120,465	8.	Marty Riessen	$ 81,301
4.	Ilie Nastase	$114,000	9.	Clark Graebner	$ 75,400
5.	Arthur Ashe	$104,642	10.	Cliff Richey	$ 75,000

1971 NTL Tennis Champions Classic

Date	Challenge Matches	Singles Winner	Singles Loser	Score
1/2/1971	New York City $10,000	Rod Laver	Ken Rosewall	6-3, 6-2, 7-5
1/9/1971	Rochester $10,000	Rod Laver	John Newcombe	6-4, 6-2, 4-6, 5-7, 6-4
1/13/1971	Boston $10,000	Rod Laver	Tony Roche	7-5, 4-6, 3-6, 7-5, 6-1
1/16/1971	Philadelphia $10,000	Rod Laver	Roy Emerson	6-2, 6-3, 7-5
1/21/1971	New York $10,000	Rod Laver	Arthur Ashe	7-5, 6-4, 7-5
1/23/1971	Detroit $10,000	Rod Laver	Tom Okker	5-7, 5-7, 6-2, 6-2, 6-2
1/28/1971	New York City $10,000	Rod Laver	Arthur Ashe	3-6, 6-3, 6-3, 6-4
1/28/1971	New York City $5k Losers Bracket	Tom Okker	John Newcombe	6-4, 6-2, 1-6, 6-3
2/3/1971	Los Angeles $10,000	Rod Laver	Roger Taylor	6-3, 7-5, 6-2
2/3/1971	Los Angeles $5k Losers Bracket	Dennis Ralston	Tony Roche	6-2, 7-5, 7-5
2/6/1971	New York City $10,000	Rod Laver	Tom Okker	6-1, 6-4, 6-3
2/6/1971	New York City $5k Losers Bracket	Roy Emerson	Roger Taylor	4-6, 6-1, 6-3, 7-5
2/17/1971	New York City $10,000	Rod Laver	Dennis Ralston	3-6, 6-1, 6-4, 6-3
2/19/1971	New Haven $10,000	Rod Laver	Roy Emerson	6-3, 5-7, 6-3, 3-6, 6-3
2/22/1971	New York City Playoff	Dennis Ralston	Arthur Ashe	6-2, 4-6, 7-6
3/18/1971	New York City Semis $15k - $5k	Rod Laver	Dennis Ralston	6-2, 6-4, 7-5
3/18/1971	New York City Semis $15k- $5k	Tom Okker	Roy Emerson	6-4, 2-6, 4-6,, 6-3, 6-4
3/19/1971	New York City Finals $35,000	Rod Laver	Tom Okker	7-5, 6-2, 6-1

1971 Tournament Calendar

Date	Tournaments	Singles Winner	Singles #2	Doubles Winners	Doubles #2
1/2/1971	New York $10,000 WTA TCC	Rod Laver	Ken Rosewall	6-3, 6-2, 7-5	
1/9/1971	Rochester $10,000 WTA TCC	Rod Laver	John Newcombe	6-4, 6-2, 4-6, 5-7, 6-4	
1/10/1971	Hobart	Alex Metreveli	John Alexander	J. Alexander - P. Dent	V. Zednik - M. Holecek
1/13/1971	Boston $10,000 WTA TCC	Rod Laver	Tony Roche	7-5, 4-6, 3-6, 7-5, 6-1	
1/15/1971	FT. Lauderdale	Cliff Richey	Pat Cramer	P. Cramer - R. Mandelstam	B. Gottfried - H. Solomon
1/15/1971	Melbourne	Alex Metreveli	Phil Dent		
1/15/1971	New Orleans	Erik Van Dillen	Haroon Rahim	T. Gorman - B. Lutz	D. Crealy - R. Russell
1/15/1971	Orlando	Miguel Olvera	Mike Belkin	K. Watanabe - S. Yoshil	R. Barth - F. Froehling
1/15/1971	Washington	Jaime Fillol	Tom Koch		
1/18/1971	Sydney	Phil Dent	John Alexander	J. Alexander - P. Dent	A. Metreveli - M. Anderson
1/21/1971	New York $10,000 WTA TCC	Rod Laver	Arthur Ashe	7-5, 6-4, 7-5	
1/23/1971	Detroit $10,000 WTA TCC	Rod Laver	Tom Okker	5-7, 5-7, 6-2, 6-2, 6-2	
1/28/1971	New York $10,000 WTA TCC	Rod Laver	Arthur Ashe	3-6, 6-3, 6-3, 6-4	
1/28/1971	New York TCC	Tom Okker	John Newcombe	6-4, 6-2, 1-6, 6-3	
1/31/1971	Omaha $15,000 USLTA	Ilie Nastase	Cliff Richey	C. Graebner - T. Koch	J. McManus - J. Osborne
2/3/1971	Los Angeles $10,000 WTA TCC	Rod Laver	Roger Taylor	6-3, 7-5, 6-2	
2/3/1971	Los Angeles $5,000 WTA TCC	Dennis Ralston	Tony Roche	6-2, 7-5, 7-5	
2/6/1971	New York $10,000 WTA TCC	Rod Laver	Tom Okker	6-1, 6-4, 6-3	

2/6/1971	New York TCC	Roy Emerson	Roger Taylor	4-6, 6-1, 6-3, 7-5	
2/7/1971	Des Moines $15,000 USLTA	Cliff Richey	Vladimir Zednik	M. Holecek - V. Zednik	T. Edlefsen - F. Froehling
2/7/1971	Richmond $20,000	Ilie Nastase	Arthur Ashe	A. Ashe - D. Ralston	J. Newcombe - K. Rosewall
2/9/1971	Philadelphia $10,000 WTA TCC	Rod Laver	Roy Emerson	6-2, 6-3, 7-5	
2/14/1971	New York $25,000 USLTA	Zeljko Franulovic	Clark Graebner	J. Gisbert - M. Orantes	J. Connors - H. Rahim
2/14/1971	Philadelphia $50,000 WCT	John Newcombe	Rod Laver	unfinished	
2/15/1971	Buffalo USLTA	Tom Gorman	Peter Curtis	T. Gorman - J. McManus	B. McKinley - D. Stockton
2/15/1971	Miami	Eddie Dibbs	Dan Bleckinger	P. Cramer - R. Mandelstam	M. Olvera - E. Zuleta
2/15/1971	Miami	Manuel Orantes	Eddie Dibbs	E. Mandarino - M. Orantes	E. Dibbs - L. Garcia
2/15/1971	Salt Lake City Amateur	Roscoe Tanner	Jeff Borowiak	A. Mayer - R. Tanner	J. Borowiak - L. Alvarez
2/17/1971	New York $10,000 WTA TCC	Rod Laver	Dennis Ralston	3-6, 6-1, 6-4, 6-3	
2/19/1971	New Haven $10,000 WTA TCC	Rod Laver	Roy Emerson	6-3, 5-7, 6-3, 3-6, 6-3	
2/21/1971	Salisbury $50,000 USLTA	Clark Graebner	Cliff Richey	M. Orantes - J. Gisbert	C. Graebner - T. Koch
2/22/1971	New York Playoff TCC	Dennis Ralston	Arthur Ashe	6-2, 4-6, 7-6	
3/1/1971	Macon $20,000 USLTA	Zeljko Franulovic	Ilie Nastase	C. Graebner - T. Koch	Z. Franulovic - J. Kodes
3/2/1971	London $30,000	Rod Laver	Nikki Pilic	R. Emerson - R. Laver	A. Gimeno - R. Taylor
3/7/1971	Auckland $16,000	Bob Carmichael	Allen Stone	B. Carmichael - R. Ruffels	B. Fairlie - R. Moore
3/7/1971	Hampton $34,600 USLTA	Ilie Nastase	Clark Graebner	I. Nastase - I. Tiriac	C. Graebner - T. Koch
3/14/1971	Australian Open $59,060 +WCT	Ken Rosewall	Arthur Ashe	J. Newcombe - T. Roche	T. Okker - M. Riessen
3/15/1971	Cairo EG Egyptian Open $5,000	Alex Metreveli	Ismail El Shafei	P. Barthes - J. Chanfreau	B. Fairlie - I. El Shafei

3/15/1971	Jacksonville $15,000	Tom Edlefsen	Clark Graebner	T. Edlefsen - C. Graebner	M. Holecek - O. Parun
3/15/1971	LaJolla Doubles			J. Borowiak - H. Rahim	J. Austin - J. Connors
3/15/1971	West Palm Beach	Frank Froehling	Pat Cramer	M. Olvera - E. Zuleta	R. Smith - S. Turner
3/18/1971	New York $15,000 TCC	Rod Laver	Dennis Ralston	6-2, 6-4, 7-5	
3/18/1971	New York $15,000 TCC	Tom Okker	Roy Emerson	6-4, 2-6, 4-6,, 6-3, 6-4	
3/19/1971	New York $30,000 TCC Finals	Rod Laver	Tom Okker	7-5, 6-2, 6-1	
3/21/1971	Caracas	Thomas Koch	Manuel Orantes	T. Koch - E. Mandarino	G. Battrick - P. Curtis
3/28/1971	Chicago $50,000 WCT	John Newcombe	Arthur Ashe	T. Okker - M. Riessen	J. Newcombe - T. Roche
4/4/1971	Durban	Bob Hewitt	Manuel Santana	B. Hewitt - M. Santana	C. Diederichs - D Phillips
4/4/1971	Miami $50,000 WCT	Cliff Drysdale	Rod Laver	J. Newcombe - T. Roche	R. Emerson - R. Laver
4/4/1971	Nice GP-D	Ilie Nastase	Jan Kodes	I. Nastase - I. Tiriac	P. Barthes - F. Jauffret
4/5/1971	Monte Carlo $20,000 GP-C	Ilie Nastase	Tom Okker	I. Nastase - I. Tiriac	R. Taylor - T. Okker
4/5/1971	San Juan $25,000	Stan Smith	Cliff Richey	E. Van Dillon - S. Smith	O. Parun - N. Spear
4/12/1971	Denver $17,500	Ken Rosewall	Cliff Drysdale	C. Drysdale - C. Pasarell	J. Alexander - K. Rosewall
4/15/1971	St. Petersburg $25,000	Mike Belkin	Harald Eidchenbroich	E. Dibbs - L. Garcia	M. Belkin - P. Burwash
4/17/1971	Johannesburg $51,000	Ken Rosewall	Fred Stolle	K. Rosewall - F. Stolle	B. Hewitt - F. McMillan
4/18/1971	Charlotte $25,000 GP-C	Arthur Ashe	Stan Smith	M. Riessen - T. Roche	A. Ashe - D. Ralston
4/18/1971	Palermo GP-C	Roger Taylor	Pierre Barthes	P. Barthes - G. Goven	I. Nastase - I. Tiriac
4/25/1971	Boston $30,000 WC SP	USA	AUS	4-3	
4/25/1971	Boston $30,000 WC SP	Arthur Ashe	Roy Emerson	6-4, 7-5	
4/25/1971	Boston $30,000 WC SP	John Newcombe	Dennis Ralston	6-3, 3-6, 6-4	

4/25/1971	Boston $30,000 WC SP	Marty Riessen	Tony Roche	6-3, 6-4	
4/25/1971	Boston $30,000 WC SP		7-6, 6-7, 6-1	A. Ashe - D. Ralston	J. Newcombe - T. Roche
4/25/1971	Boston $30,000 WC SP	John Newcombe	Arthur Ashe	6-4. 3-6, 6-3	
4/25/1971	Boston $30,000 WC SP	Dennis Ralston	Roy Emerson	6-1, 6-7, 7-6	
4/25/1971	Boston $30,000 WC SP		6-4, 5-7, 6-2	R. Emerson - F. Stolle	B. Lutz - M. Riessen
4/25/1971	Catania IT GP-C	Jan Kodes	Georges Goven	P. Bartes - F. Jauffret	J. Kodes - J. Kulcal
4/25/1971	Houston $25,000 GP-C	Cliff Richey	Clark Graebner	O. Parun - M. Holecek	T. Edlefsen - F. Froehling
5/2/1971	Dallas $50,000 WCT	John Newcombe	Arthur Ashe	T. Okker - M. Riessen	B. Lutz - C. Pasarell
5/2/1971	Paris GP-C	Stan Smith	Francois Jauffret	S. Smith - T. Gorman	P. Barthes - F. Jauffret
5/9/1971	Madrid	Ian Tiriac	Ilie Nastase	I. Nastase - I. Tiriac	T. Koch - J. Mandarino
5/10/1971	Rome $50,000 WCT	Rod Laver	Jan Kodes	J. Newcombe - T. Roche	A. Gimeno - R. Taylor
5/15/1971	Kansas City	Cliff Richey	Alex Olmedo	C. Graebner - E. Van Dillen	T. Edlefsen - F. Froehling
5/15/1971	Ojai	Raul Ramirez	Mike Machette	J. Hobson - R. Ramirez	J. Andrews - M. Machette
5/15/1971	Portola Valley	Jim McManus	Tom Leonard	J. Borowiak - T. Vasquez	A. Mayer - R. Tanner
5/16/1971	Tehran $50,000 WCT	Marty Riessen	John Alexander	J. Newcombe - T. Roche	B. Carmichael - R. Ruffels
5/22/1971	Bournemouth $36,000 GP-B	Gerald Battrick	Zeijko Franulovic	B. Bowrey - O. Davidson	J. Fillol - P. Cornejo
5/23/1971	Brussels GP-B	Cliff Drysdale	Ilie Nastase	T. Okker - M. Riessen	I. Nastase - I. Tiriac Unfinished
5/23/1971	Hamburg $20,000 GP-B	Andres Gimeno	Peter Szoke	J. Alexander - A. Gimeno	D. Crealy - A. Stone
5/24/1971	French Open $100,000 GS-A	Jan Kodes	Ilie Nastase	A. Ashe - M. Riessen	T. Gorman - S. Smith
6/5/1971	Manchester	Colin Dibley	Bob Hewitt	B. Hewitt - R. Keldie	A. Gardiner - G. Perkins
6/12/1971	Beckenham	Stan Smith	Premjit Lail	S. Ball - G. Masters	T. Addison - R. Keldie

6/12/1971	Bristol $50,000 WCT	Unfinished		Unfinished	
6/12/1971	Nottingham	Jaime Fillol	G. Perkins	R. Case - C. Dibley	P. Cornejo - J. Fillol
6/14/1971	Eastbourne GP-D	Unfinished		Unfinished	
6/14/1971	Montgomery	Humphrey Hose	Mike Belkin		
6/15/1971	Birmingham	Dick Dell	John Gardner	B. Gottfried - H. Solomon	J. Austin - F.D. Robbins
6/15/1971	Columbus	Mike Belkin	Tom Edlefsen	S. Fault - A. Neely	P. Guzman - M, Kreiss
6/15/1971	Tulsa	Harold Solomon	Zan Guerry	B. McKinley - D. Stockton	P. Guzman - J. Osborne
6/19/1971	London GP-D	Stan Smith	John Newcombe	T. Okker - M. Riessen	S. Smith - E. Van Dillon
6/21/1971	Wimbledon $90,696 GS-A	John Newcombe	Stan Smith	R. Laver - R. Emerson	A. Ashe - D. Ralston
7/10/1971	Newport Wales $19,200 GP-C	Ken Rosewall	Roger Taylor	K. Rosewall - R. Taylor	J. Clifton - J. Paish
7/11/1971	Bastad $33,000 GP-B	Ilie Nastase	Jan Leschly	I. Nastase - I. Tiriac	B. Seewagen - J. Pinto-Bravo
7/11/1971	Chattanooga Amateur	Harold Solomon	Charles Owens	A. Mayer - R. Tanner	J. Austin - F. McNair
7/11/1971	Gstaad $20,000 GP-B	John Newcombe	Tom Okker	J. Alexander - P. Dent	J. Newcombe - T. Okker
7/12/1971	Dublin $30,000	Cliff Drysdale	Clark Graebner	B. Bowrey - O. Davidson	P. Cornejo - J. Fillol
7/15/1971	Belgrade	Zeljko Franulovic	Manuel Orantes	J. Gisbert - M. Orantes	Z. Franulovic - B. Jovanovic
7/18/1971	Washington $50,000 +WCT GP-B	Ken Rosewall	Marty Riessen	T. Okker - M. Riessen	R. Ruffels - B. Carmichael
7/24/1971	Leicester	Syd Ball	Bob Hewitt	H. Irvine - A. Pattison	B. Hewitt - R. Keldie
7/25/1971	Kitzbuhel	Clark Graebner	Manuel Orantes	C. Graebner - I. Tiriac v	J. Fassbender - H. Pohmann
7/25/1971	Louisville $50,000 WCT	Tom Okker vs.	Cliff Drysdale	R. Emerson - Rod Laver v	K. Rosewall - F. Stolle
7/25/1971	Winston-Salem GP-C	Jaime Fillol	Zeljko Franulovic	J. McManus - J. Osborne	J. Austin - J. Connors
8/1/1971	Columbus $30,000 GP-D	Tom Gorman	Jimmy Connors	J. McManus - J. Osborne	J. Connors - R. Tanner
8/1/1971	Quebec $50,000 WCT	Tom Okker	Rod Laver	R. Emerson - Rod Laver	T. Okker - M. Riessen

8/2/1971	Cincinnati $30,000 GP-C	Stan Smith	Juan Gisbert	S. Smith - E. Van Dillon	S. Mayer - R. Tanner
8/3/1971	Dusseldorf	Christian Kuhnke	Toshiro Sakai		
8/3/1971	Hilversum	Gerald Battrick	Ross Case	J. Barclay - D. Contet	J. Cooper - C. Dibley
8/8/1971	Boston $50,000 WCT	Ken Rosewall	Cliff Drysdale	R. Emerson - Rod Laver	T. Okker - M. Riessen
8/8/1971	Senigallia GP-D	Adriana Panatta	Marty Mulligan	G. Widjojo - A. Widjojo	E. Di Matteo - A. Zugarelli
8/9/1971	Indianapolis $50,000 GP-B	Zeijko Franulovic	Cliff Richey	J. Kodes - Z. Franulovic	E. Van Dillon - C. Graebner
8/9/1971	Istanbul	Ilie Nastase	A. Pattison	I. Nastase - I. Tiriac	B. Hewitt - A. Pattison
8/15/1971	Southampton Amateur	John Gardner	Raul Ramirez	V. Gerulaitis - G. Scott	S. Mott - B. Teacher
8/15/1971	Toronto $70,000 WCT	John Newcombe	Tom Okker	T. Okker - M. Riessen	A. Ashe - D. Ralston
8/22/1971	Philadelphia $15,000 GP-D	Clark Graebner	Dick Stockton	C. Graebner - J. Osborne	C. McKinley - D. Stockton
8/22/1971	Fort Worth $50,000 WCT	Rod Laver	Marty Riessen	R. Emerson - R. Laver	T. Okker - M. Riessen
8/28/1971	Hilton Head $15,000 CBS TC SP	Rod Laver	John Newcombe	6-2, 7-5	
8/29/1971	Orange $25,000 GP-C	Clark Graebner	Pierre Barthes	B. Carmichael - T. Leonard	C. Graebner - E. Van Dillon
9/1/1971	US Open $160,000 GS-A	Stan Smith	Jan Kodes	J. Newcombe - R. Taylor	S. Smith - E. Van Dillon
9/13/1971	Sacramento $28,000 GP-C	Bob Lutz	Alex Olmedo	J. McManus - J. Osborne	F. McMillan - B. Maud
9/20/1971	Los Angeles $52,500 GP-B	Pancho Gonzales	Jimmy Connors	J. Alexander - P. Dent	F. Froehling/ C. Graebner
10/3/1971	San Francisco $50,000 +WCT GP-C	Rod Laver	Ken Rosewall	R. Laver - R. Emerson	K. Rosewall/ F. Stolle
10/10/1971	Vancouver $50,000 WCT	Ken Rosewall	Tom Okker	R. Emerson - R. Laver	J. Alexander - P. Dent
10/15/1971	Pensacola	Milan Holocek	Nikki Spear	T. Addison - R. Keldie	T. Edlefsen - F. Froehling
10/16/1971	Edinburgh Dewar Cup	Bob Hewitt	Gerald Battrick	B. Hewitt - R. Seegers	J. Fillol - R. Moore
10/17/1971	Cologne $50,000 WCT	Bob Lutz	Jeff Borowiak	T. Okker - M. Riessen	R. Emerson - R. Laver

10/23/1971	Billingham Dewar Cup	Jaime Fillol	Gerald Battrick	G. Battrick - I. Tiriac	J. Fillol - R. Moore
10/24/1971	Barcelona $50,000 WCT	Manuel Orantes	Bob Lutz	Z. Franulovic - J. Gisbert	C. Drysdale - A. Gimeno
11/1/1971	London $55,000 GP-B	Ilie Nastase	Rod Laver	B. Hewitt - F. McMillan	B. Bowrey - O. Davidson
11/6/1971	Aberavon Dewar Cup	Bob Hewitt	Gerald Battrick	B. Hewitt - R. Seegers	J.G. Clifton - J. G. Paish
11/7/1971	Stockholm $50,000 WCT	Arthur Ashe	Jan Kodes	T. Gorman - S. Smith	A. Ashe - B. Lutz
11/14/1971	Bologna $50,000 WCT	Rod Laver	Arthur Ashe	K. Rosewall - F. Stolle	F. McMillan - R. Maud
11/15/1971	Casablanca	Ion Tiriac	F. Jauffret		
11/20/1971	London	Gerald Battrick	Bob Hewitt	B. Hewitt - R. Seegers	G. Battrick - J.G. Paish
11/26/1971	Dallas WCT Finals	Ken Rosewall	Rod Laver	6-4, 1-6, 7-6, 7-6	
12/1/1971	Buenos Aires GP-B	Zeijko Franulovic	Ilie Nastase	Z. Franulovic - I. Nastase	J. Fillol - P. Cornejo
12/12/2012	Paris Pepsi Masters	Ilie Nastase	Stan Smith	5-7, 7-6, 6-3	

http://www.atpworldtour.com/en/scores/results-archive.

http://www.itftennis.com/procircuit/tournaments/men's-calendar.aspx?tour=&reg=&nat=&sur=&cate=AL&iod=& fromDate=01-01-1968&toDate=29-12-1974.

Tennis History, Jim McManus (Canada 2010).

1972 USLTA Yearbook.

Official 1989 MTC Media Guide, (MTC 1989).

World of Tennis '72 , Edited by John Barrett and compiled by Lance Tingay, (London 1972).

CHAPTER 6:

1972: COMMERCIAL UNION GRAND PRIX BEGINS, PEACE AGREEMENT, ATP BEGINS, CRISES NOS. 4, 5

1972 Governing Bodies

The ILTF was the governing body for men's professional tennis in 1972, except for WCT and Davis Cup. The Davis Cup was still governed by the Davis Cup Nations. The NTL was gone.

1972 Significant Tennis Leaders

ILTF President:	Allan Heyman (Denmark)
USLTA President:	Bob Colwell
Australian LTA President:	Wayne Reid
British LTA President:	Sir Carl Aarvold
French FFT President:	Marcel Benard
French FFT Vice President:	Philippe Chatrier
Chairman of Wimbledon:	Herman David
WCT Owners:	Lamar Hunt and Al Hill, Jr.
WCT Executive Director:	Mike Davies

Four Competitions

In 1972, the fifth year of Open Tennis, Commercial Union replaced Pepsico as the sponsor of the Grand Prix and there were four organized competitions for men: USLTA-IPA Indoor Circuit, Commercial Union Grand Prix, WCT and the Davis Cup. The USLTA – IPA Indoor Circuit consisted of 12 U.S. indoor tournaments organized by Bill Riordan for the USLTA and marketed as the Boise Cascade Classic with a $50,000 bonus pool. Ilie Nastase won the first prize of $15,000 and Jimmy Connors won the second prize of $9,000. Four of those tournaments, Salisbury, New York, Hampton and Washington were also in the Commercial Union Grand Prix and the other eight were prize money tournaments outside of the Commercial Union Grand Prix.

The 1972 Commercial Union Grand Prix consisted of 35 Open prize money tournaments, including the year-end Commercial Union Masters in Barcelona with $50,000 in prize money for the top eight players and a $250,000 Bonus Pool. Ilie Nastase defeated Stan Smith 6-3, 6-2, 3-6, 2-6, 6-3, to win the Commercial Union Masters event. Nastase won first prize in the Bonus Pool of $50,000 and Stan Smith won the $35,000 second prize.

The 1972 WCT circuit consisted of 22 WCT $50,000 professional tournaments open only to 32 WCT contract pros, plus the Dallas $100,000 "World Championship of Tennis" in May for the top eight players again with a first prize of $50,000 and with a new $50,000 Fall Final in Rome. This was again marketed as the "Million Dollar Tour."

NBC Preempts: Tennis Becomes Popular with General Public

NBC preempted its sacred 6:00 PM Sunday news broadcast and two following programs to cover the dramatic marathon fifth-set tiebreaker match won by Ken Rosewall over Rod Laver in the WCT Finals in Dallas for the $50,000 first prize 4-6, 6-0, 6-3, 6-7, 7-6. Twenty-three million people watched what many said was the greatest match of

all time.[83] Steve Tignor wrote on Tennis.com in 2015 that one writer described the match as "The kind of match that one waits a lifetime to see — a nerve-wracking, blood-tingling epic." *That match and that television exposure made professional tennis instantly popular with the general public.* Mike Davies told tennis journalist Paul Fein[84]: "Nothing in the history of communications can compare with it (television). It is quite possible for a player to play one match on national television before more people than he would ever play live to in his whole career."

Ken Rosewall   Rod Laver

Ashe defeated Lutz in the WCT Fall Final in Rome. WCT also promoted a special made-for-television tournament, the "CBS Tennis Classic" in Hilton Head, SC, featuring the top 16 players in the WCT Tour. The individual matches were shown on CBS between March and August, often in weeks in which Grand Prix tournaments were being played, which certainly irritated the Grand Prix tournaments, the ILTF and the USLTA. Ken Rosewall defeated John Newcombe in the CBS final. In addition, WCT promoted the Aetna World Cup in Hartford won by Australia over the United States 6-1.

Davis Cup

Davis Cup was limited to amateurs and "professionals" who were not WCT contract pros. WCT contract pros continued to be barred. This was the first year after the deletion of the Challenge Round. In January, the Davis Cup Committee (of the Davis Cup Nations, not the ILTF) announced that South Africa which had been barred from the Davis Cup for the previous two years would be reinstated for 1972. The USLTA objected to the reinstatement and in April there was a vote to exclude South Africa from the 1972 Davis Cup competition, with a recommendation for reinstatement for 1973, but with South Africa playing in the South American Zone instead of the European Zone. South Africa's Apartheid was a bigger problem with European governments.

Rules

The 1972 Grand Prix rules were the same as in 1971, except the minimum prize money was increased to £12,000. The Bonus Pool required 12 tournaments and had 20 awards. The 1971 provisions for the payment of travel allowances to WCT for the contract pros and to the National Associations for the independent pros were deleted. There was to be no payment of travel expenses or corporate fees to WCT. *Instead of simply refusing to pay WCT travel expenses/corporate fees, the ILTF and the Grand Slams banned the contract pros from playing altogether.*[85] *Brilliant!*

Crisis No. 4: Continued:
Ban of Contract Pros for 1972

The ban of the WCT Contract Pros for 1972 became Crisis No. 4. It also originally included a ban on the use of the facilities of any member clubs of the USLTA and the other national associations. However, under threat of the American anti-trust laws, the ban on the use of member club facilities was deleted early. Said Arthur Ashe in the *New York Times*[86]: "'Let them try to ban me...I'm a lifetime member of the U.S.L.T.A. and a former United States Open champion." Ashe said he was prepared to "test his case in court."

The USTA expressed some concern over the ILTF ban for 1972 at its Annual Meeting in February in Houston and voted to try to make a deal with WCT. The officers of the USLTA were voting members of the ILTF so they had obviously voted for the 1972 ban. It is amusing that there was now a clamor to reconsider the issue as if they had no involvement in the decision to ban the pros in 1972 in the first place. *There was no need to ban the WCT contract pros.* All they had to do was refuse to pay "fees" to the WCT. If they had not banned them, the contract pros could and probably would have insisted on entering at least some of the Grand Slams in 1972, no matter what Hunt and WCT said. In Europe, there were no anti-trust laws, so the ILTF and the European Federations were accustomed to banning. However, once the ILTF Grand Prix circuit included tournaments in the United States, it became subject to the U.S. antitrust laws and Arthur Ashe's threat of litigation if his entry to the U.S. Open was denied in 1972 was a very valid threat.

Kramer "speaking for the USLTA" said to Neil Amdur of the *New York Times*[87]: "They don't need us…and for sure, we don't need them." *Who would have guessed that Jack Kramer was now a "spokesman" for the USLTA in February; in August, he would go on to help create the ATP and become its first Executive Director.*

In March, the ILTF and WCT met for three days in London and again failed to find any agreeable settlement to their dispute. Since the WCT contract pros were all banned from competing in 1972 Wimbledon, Mike Davies scheduled the Holton Classic $50,000 WCT tournament in St. Louis, MO, during 1972 Wimbledon. *Why not?* Lamar Hunt agreed to cancel St. Louis so the contract pros could play Wimbledon, if and only if an agreement could be reached by March 15. The door remained open to seek a solution, but who was going to do it? There was no mention of Teddy Tinling this time.

But then Jack Kramer and Donald Dell came to the rescue. In April, it was announced that the USLTA would present a "Peace Plan" at the upcoming ILTF meeting in Copenhagen, Denmark. Undisclosed were extensive efforts of Kramer and Dell behind the scenes working for a solution for the ILTF, USLTA and WCT. Again, the ILTF and the USLTA had called on Kramer (and his protégé Dell) to help save it. The proposed Peace Plan was announced on April 15 by Walter Elcock, USLTA First Vice President. The major proposals were: (i) WCT would have exclusivity for the first four months of each year (after the Australian Open) and the ILTF Grand Prix would have exclusivity for the last eight months of each year, (ii) WCT would not sign any more contract pro agreements and would let all the existing contracts expire and (iii) All pros, contract pros and independent pros would be eligible to play in all WCT and Grand Prix tournaments. Unsolved was the status of the USLTA-IPA indoor circuit scheduled during the first four months of each year promoted by Bill Riordan. However, when the ILTF Committee of Management met in April in Copenhagen, an agreement could not be reached. Allan Heyman, ILTF President told the *New York Times*[88] that "the discussions had proved more difficult than expected by some members."

Finally, on April 26, it was announced in London that the ILTF and WCT had reached a "Peace Agreement," signed by Allan Heyman, President of the ILTF and Lamar Hunt, owner of WCT, subject to the approval of the 96 nations of the ILTF at its annual general meeting in Helsinki, Finland in July. Fred Tupper reported in the *New York Times*[89]: "This agreement would not have been signed by me unless I was assured of wholehearted support," said Heyman. "The war is over."

Since the agreement was not completed by March 15, WCT could not cancel its St. Louis tournament against Wimbledon, so the WCT contract pros could not play in 1972 Wimbledon. As a matter of fact, the pros could not play at Wimbledon at all prior to 1968 and most of them would not play in 1973 on account of the ATP Boycott. To provide enough player jobs in the first four months of each year, WCT agreed to promote two circuits of 11 tournaments each leading to the Dallas Finals, each with a 32-draw open to all players. WCT would have three additional "specials" for a total of 26 tournaments, at least 11 of which were to be outside of the United States. Fred Tupper further reported in the *New York Times*:[90] *"Who made peace possible? A former tennis promoter, Jack Kramer, and a former United States Davis Cup Captain, Donald Dell.* Allan Heyman and Lamar Hunt acknowledged the contributions of Jack Kramer and Donald Dell to the development of the Peace Plan. *"They spent a tremendous number of hours to put this thing together,' said Hunt. 'The tower of strength,' said Heyman."* Kramer later wrote in his book *The Game*[91], "Before I raised hell, they were going to let him (Hunt) schedule forty tournaments." WCT was limited to 26 tournaments in the Peace Agreement.

On April 29, the USLTA announced in the *New York Times*[92]: "that it would support the 'peace' agreement" and Philip Morris informed CBS that it would continue its sponsorship of the U.S. Open telecast. On July 12, in Helsinki, Finland, the ILTF announced that the Peace Agreement "had been ratified by an overwhelming margin 232-15."[93] As a result of the ban, the WCT contract pros were banned prior to July 12, so the 1972 Australian Open, 1972 French Open and 1972 Wimbledon did not have any of them. However, they could play in the 1972 U.S. Open in August-September.

So, Peace at Last, Peace at Last or Is It and Will it Last? The questionable legality of the actual historical WCT-ILTF Peace Agreement was never challenged and it would last for 1973-1975-6 and would be completely forgotten in 1977.

Froehling, Addison and Richey Sign With WCT

U.S. Davis Cup player Frank Froehling and Australia's Terry Addison signed with WCT in January and were scheduled to join the WCT tour in Richmond on February 2-6. They replaced Andres Gimeno and Frew McMillan who elected not to renew their agreements with WCT. In April, Cliff Richey signed a four-year contract with WCT said to guarantee $100,000 per year to become the 33rd WCT contract pro. "I think Lamar has done more for the game as an individual than anyone," said Richey to Neil Amdur of the *New York Times*[94]: "He's proved that professional tennis can be put on in a big-league way. I'm not saying this in detriment to the independent game, but a guy like Lamar has proved you can do it up first-class."

Jimmy Connors

Jimmy Connors of Belleville, Illinois won the NCAA singles championship in 1971. After one year at UCLA, he turned pro in 1972 and in his first event as a pro in January of 1972, Connors won the USLTA Indoor Circuit tournament in Jacksonville, Florida, by defeating Clark Graebner 7-5, 6-4. Connors was raised by his mother, Gloria Connors and his grandmother, "Two-Mom" in Bellevue Illinois. At Gloria Connors' request, Bill Riordan became Connor's exclusive agent and Riordan always claimed the Connors was a member of his IPA – maybe the only member? Connors never would join the ATP.[95]

Mike Davies Innovations

During his tenure as Executive Director of WCT from 1969-1981, Mike Davies was responsible for many innovations and rule changes in the game, such as: (i) first professional circuit to incorporate the tie-breaker, (ii) first to insist on colored clothing on the players, (iii) introduction of a colored tennis ball (first orange, then yellow) in 1972, (iv) 30 seconds between points and 90 seconds between change-overs (to accommodate television commercials), (v) first to place chairs on the court for the players during change-overs, (vi) first to have a player representative and a trainer travel with the players to each tournament, (vii) first to permit overrules by the chair umpire and experiment with electronic line calling in 1972, (viii) first to complete a television deal with a major network (NBC) for the *World Championship of Tennis Series*, culminating in the Dallas finals, (ix) first to syndicate television coverage of tournaments in the United States to individual television stations and (x) first to sign a contract (with ESPN) before the network ever came on the air.[96]

ILTF Approves Yellow Balls (Not Wimbledon Yet)

Following WCT's lead, the ILTF at its 1972 Annual General Meeting in Helsinki, Finland approved yellow balls. However, Wimbledon still continued white tennis balls on its grass. *In 1975, Wimbledon finally and very reluctantly added chairs for the players during changeovers. Wimbledon's television coverage also had commercials.*

Creation of Association of Tennis Professionals (ATP)
Players' Association No. 4

At 1972 Wimbledon and 1972 WCT St. Louis (scheduled opposite Wimbledon) guidelines were submitted to the players for the creation of the Association of Tennis Professionals, ATP, the fourth players' association. "The players are the ultimate reservoir of what's good in spectator tennis," said Bob Briner, the former tennis executive, who was among a group of officials asked to help draw the guidelines."[97]

The ATP was founded in September with Cliff Drysdale as the first president and Jack Kramer as the first Executive Director without pay. Kramer said in his book *The Game*[98]: "I felt that would help convince people that I wasn't taking the position just for power. I felt that if Kramer were a pro's volunteer, then an amateurs' volunteer like Herman David, the working chairman of Wimbledon, would be more inclined to accept me and my organization."

Rex Bellamy wrote in the *London Times*[99] of the new ATP: "Playing conditions, tournament organization, seedings, the work of umpires and line judges, and a clarification of some obscure ILTF rules are among other subjects the ATP are studying. They are potentially powerful. But their painstakingly constructive approach is cooperative rather than militant; and it represents the considered views and proposed deeds of men who know their business better than anyone else does. It is to be hoped that the game's 'Establishment' recognize the value of their formidable new allies."

1973 USLTA-IPA Indoor Circuit

Bill Riordan announced[100] that his USLTA-IPA Indoor Circuit in the United States in 1973 would have more than $300,000 in prize money and would include Ilie Nastase, John Newcombe, Manuel Orantes of Spain and Jimmy Connors. Newcombe was said to have joined the independents after stopping his WCT pro contract. Obviously, Lamar Hunt did not like this competition and obviously, Bill Riordan hated to have to compete with WCT.

Crisis No. 5: Peace Agreement Conflict With USLTA Indoor Circuit

Crisis No. 5 was caused by the ILTF-WCT Peace Agreement, which beginning in 1973, gave WCT exclusivity in the first four months of each year for 22 tournaments with $50,000 each in that time period leading to its Dallas Finals. The USLTA-IPA indoor circuit promoted by Bill Riordan was scheduled in the same time period against the WCT tournaments. In the Peace Agreement, the ILTF (and the USLTA) agreed that while the USLTA National Indoor Championships in Salisbury promoted by Bill Riordan, could have the same prize money as the WCT tournaments ($50,000), no other tournament against the WCT tournaments could have more than 40 percent of the WCT prize money or a maximum of $20,000. This was a huge competitive advantage for WCT over Riordan's USLTA-IPA indoor circuit tournaments. *So, did letting Salisbury have $50,000 in prize money settle Crisis No.5?[101] Stay tuned!*

1972 Grand Slam Winners

Australian Open

Ken Rosewall d. Mal Anderson 7-6, 6-3, 7-5.
Ken Rosewall-Owen Davidson d. Ross Case-Geoff Masters 3-6, 7-6, 6-2.

French Open

Andres Gimeno d. Patrick Proisy 4-6, 6-3, 6-1, 6-1.
Bob Hewitt-Frew McMillan d. Patricio Cornejo-Jaime Fillol, Sr. 6-3, 8-6, 3-6, 6-1.

Wimbledon

Stan Smith d. Ilie Nastase 4-6, 6-3, 6-3, 4-6, 7-5.
Bob Hewitt-Frew McMillan d. Stan Smith-Eric Van Dillen 6-2, 6-2, 9-7.

U.S. Open

Ilie Nastase d. Arthur Ashe 3-6, 6-3, 6-7, 6-4, 6-3.
Cliff Drysdale-Roger Taylor d. Owen Davidson-John Newcombe 6-4, 7-6, 6-3.

1972 Final Round

United States d. Romania 3-2 (Bucharest – Clay)

Stan Smith (US) d. Ilie Nastase (RO) 11-9, 6-2, 6-3.
Ion Tiriac (RO) d. Tom Gorman (US) 4-6, 2-6, 6-4, 6-3 6-2.
Stan Smith – Erik Van Dillen (US) d. Ilie Nastase – Ion Tiriac (RO) 6-2, 6-0, 6-3.
Stan Smith (US) d. Ion Tiriac (RO) 4-6, 6-2, 6-4, 2-6, 6-0.
Ilie Nastase (RO) d. Tom Gorman (US) 6-1, 6-2, 5-7, 10-8.

1972 World Rankings[102]

	Bud Collins			Lance Tingay	
1.	Stan Smith	IND	1.	Stan Smith	IND
2.	Ken Rosewall	WCT	2.	Ilie Nastase	IND
3.	Ilie Nastase	IND	3.	Ken Rosewall	WCT
4.	Rod Laver	WCT	4.	Rod Laver	WCT
5.	Arthur Ashe	WCT	5.	Arthur Ashe	WCT
6.	John Newcombe	WCT	6.	John Newcombe	WCT
7.	Bob Lutz	WCT	7.	Cliff Richey	WCT
8.	Tom Okker	WCT	8.	Manuel Orantes	IND
9.	Marty Riessen	WCT	9.	Andres Gimeno	IND
10.	Andres Gimeno	IND	10.	Jan Kodes (CZ)	IND

Stan Smith was never No.1 on the ATP Computer, because it did not begin until 1973.

1972 Commercial Union Grand Prix Singles Bonus Pool Top 10 (3rd Bonus Pool)[103]

[Remember the WCT Pros were barred until the U.S. Open]

1.	Ilie Nastase	$50,000	6.	Bob Hewitt	$13,000
2.	Stan Smith	$35,000	7.	Jimmy Connors	$12,000
3.	Manuel Orantes	$25,000	8.	Tom Gorman	$11,000
4.	Jan Kodes	$20,000	9.	Andrew Pattison	$10,000
5.	Andres Gimeno	$16,000	10.	Patrick Proisy	$ 9,000

1972 Official Earnings Top 10[104]

1.	Ilie Nastase	$176,000	6.	Rod Laver	$100,200
2.	Stan Smith	$142,300	7.	Tom Okker	$ 90,004
3.	Ken Rosewall	$132,950	8.	Jimmy Connors	$ 90,000
4.	John Newcombe	$120,600	9.	Marty Riessen	$ 74,436
5.	Arthur Ashe	$119,775	10.	Cliff Drysdale	$ 68,433

1972 Tournament Calendar

Date	Tournament	Singles Winner	Singles #2	Doubles Winners	Doubles #2
1/5/1972	Australian Open A	Ken Rosewall	Mal Anderson	K. Rosewall - O. Davidson	R. Case - G. Masters
1/9/1972	Baltimore $7,500 USLTA	Ilie Nastase	Jimmy Connors	J. Connors - H. Rahim	P. Barthes - C. Graebner
1/9/1972	Sydney	Alex Metreveli	Patrice Dominguez	R. Case - J. Cooper	P. Dominguez - P. Proisy
1/15/1972	Ft. Lauderdale	Brian Gottfried	Pat Cornejo	M. Olvera - E. Zuelta	R. Benavides - O. Chirella
1/16/1972	Hobart	Alex Metreveli	Wanaro N'Godrella	J. Cooper - C. Dibley	P. Dominguez - P. Proisy
1/16/1972	Jacksonville USLTA	Jimmy Connors	Clark Graebner	J. McManus - J. Osborne	V. Zednik - F. Froehling
1/22/1972	London	Cliff Richey	Clark Graebner	C. Graebner - T. Gorman	B. Hewitt - F. McMillan
1/23/1972	Adelaide	Alex Metreveli	Kim Warwick	J. Cooper - C. Dibley	R. Case - A. Metreveli
1/23/1972	Auckland	Onny Parun	Steve Faulk	O. Parun - R. Simpson	I. Beverly- D. Knight
1/23/1972	Roanoke USLTA	Jimmy Connors	Vladimir Zednik	J. Connors - H. Rahim	V. Zednik - I. Crookenden
1/29/1972	Copenhagen	Jan Leschly	Ray Moore	J. Hrebec -F. Pala	J. Leschly - T. Ulrich
1/30/1972	Cleveland $6,000 USLTA	Vladimir Zednik	Haroon Rahim	G. Battrick - O. Parun	V. Zednik - O. Bengtson
1/30/1972	Omaha $15,000 USLTA	Ilie Nastase	Ian Tiriac	I. Nastase - I. Tiriac	A. Gimeno - M. Orantes
2/6/1972	Des Moines $15,000 USLTA	Pancho Gonzales	Georges Govern	J. McManus - J. Osborne	G. Govern - T. Koch
2/6/1972	Kansas City $15,000 USLTA	Tom Edlefsen	Erik Van Dillon	I. Nastase - I. Tiriac	A. Gimeno - M. Orantes
2/6/1972	Perth	Alex Metreveli	John Cooper	R. Case - G. Masters	J. Cooper - C. Dibley
2/6/1972	Richmond $50,000 WCT	Rod Laver	Cliff Drysdale	T. Okker - M. Riessen	J. Newcombe - T. Roche
2/13/1972	Philadelphia $50,000 WCT	Rod Laver	Ken Rosewall	A. Ashe - B. Lutz	J. Newcombe - T. Roche
2/14/1972	Los Angeles $25,000 GP-C	Andres Gimeno	Pierre Barthes	J. McManus - J. Osborne	I. Nastase - I. Tiriac

2/20/1972	Salisbury 50,000 USLTA & GP-B	Stan Smith	Ilie Nastase	A. Gimeno - M. Orantes	V. Zednik - J. Gisbert
2/20/1972	Toronto $50,000 WCT	Rod Laver	Ken Rosewall	B. Carmichael - R. Ruffels	R. Emerson - R. Laver
2/28/1972	New York $50,000 GP-C	Stan Smith	Juan Gisbert		
3/3/1972	Miami $50,000 WCT	Ken Rosewall	Cliff Drysdale	T. Okker - M. Riessen	J. Newcombe - T. Roche
3/5/1972	Hampton $35,000 USLTA & GP-C	Stan Smith	Ilie Nastase	I. Nastase - I. Tiriac	M. Orantes - A. Gimeno
3/12/1972	Hartford WC WCT SP	Australia	USA	6-1	
3/12/1972	Hartford WC WCT SP	John Newcombe	Arthur Ashe	4-6, 6-4, 7-5	
3/12/1972	Hartford WC WCT SP	Rod Laver	Charles Pasarell	4-6,, 6-4, 7-6	
3/12/1972	Hartford WC WCT SP	Roy Emerson	Bob Lutz	3-6,7-6, 6-4	
3/12/1972	Hartford WC WCT SP	Charles Pasarell	John Newcombe	4-6, 7-6. 6-3	
3/12/1972	Hartford WC WCT SP	Rod Laver	Arthur Ashe	6-2, 3-6, 6-4	
3/12/1972	Hartford WC WCT SP		6-3, 6-4	R. Emerson - R. Laver	A. Ashe - B. Lutz
3/12/1972	Hartford WC WCT SP		6-2, 3-6, 6-4	J. Newcombe - T. Roche	B. Lutz - M. Riessen
3/12/1972	Washington $25,000 GP-C	Stan Smith	Jimmy Connors	C. Richey - T. Edlefsen	T. Koch - C. Graebner
3/15/1972	La Jolla Doubles			M. Lara - R. Ramirez	A. Mayer - R. Tanner
3/15/1972	Los Angeles	Pancho Gonzales	Alex Olmedo	A. Olmedo - S. Tidball	L. Alvarez - S. Krulevitz
3/15/1972	Portola Valley	Alex Mayer	Roscoe Tanner	A. Mayer - R. Tanner	D. Knight - W. Reed
3/15/1972	Mountain View	Alex Mayer	Roscoe Tanner	A. Mayer - R. Tanner	H. kamakana - G. Shephard
3/17/1972	Caracas	Manuel Orantes	Haroon Rahim	J. Fillol - P. Cornejo	J. McManus - M. Orantes
3/19/1972	Chicago $50,000 WCT	Tom Okker	Arthur Ashe	T. Okker - M. Riessen	R. Emerson - R. Laver
3/26/1972	Hilton Head $40k CBS WCT SP	Ken Rosewall	John Newcombe	7-5, 6-3	

3/27/1972	Monte Carlo $20,000 GP-D	Ilie Nastase	Frantisek Pala	P. Beust - D. Contet	J. Hrebec - F. Pala
4/2/1972	Macon $25,000 WCT	Mark Cox	Roy Emerson	R. Emerson - T. Okker	M. Cox - G. Stilwell
4/3/1972	Hong Kong	Mal Anderson	Pancho Gonzales	M. Anderson - G. Masters	J. Kamiwazumi - T. Sakai
4/8/1972	Johannesburg $50,000 GP-A	Cliff Richey	Manuel Orantes	B. Hewitt - F. McMillan	G. Govern - R. Moore
4/9/1972	Houston $50,000 WCT	Rod Laver	Ken Rosewall	R. Emerson - R. Laver	K. Rosewall - F. Stolle
4/16/1972	Madrid GP-B	Ilie Nastase	Frantisek Pala	I. Nastase - S. Smith	M. Orantes - A. Gimeno
4/16/1972	Quebec $50,000 WCT	Marty Riessen	Rod Laver	B. Carmichael - R. Ruffels	T. Addison - J. Alexander
4/23/1972	Charlotte $50,000 WCT	Ken Rosewall	Cliff Richey	T. Okker - M. Riessen	J. Newcombe - T. Roche
4/23/1972	Nice $30,000 GP-D	Ilie Nastase	Jan Kodes	J. Kodes - S. Smith	F. McMillan - I. Nastase
4/26/1972	Rome IT $56,000 GP-A	Manuel Orantes	Jan Kodes	I. Nastase - I. Tiriac	L. Hoad - F. McMillan
4/30/1972	Denver $50,000 WCT	Rod Laver	Marty Riessen	R. Emerson - R. Laver	C. Drysdale - R. Taylor
5/6/1972	Birmingham	Pat Cramer	Guillermo Vilas	S. Ball - K. Fletcher	M. Farrell - J. Lloyd
5/7/1972	Las Vegas $50,000 WCT	John Newcombe	Cliff Drysdale	R. Emerson - R. Laver	J. Newcombe - T. Roche
5/13/1972	Bournemouth GP-C	Bob Hewitt	Pierre Barthes	B. Hewitt - F. McMillan	I. Nastase - I. Tiriac
5/14/1972	Brussels $26,650 GP-C	Manuel Orantes	Andres Gimeno	M. Orantes - J. Gisbert	J. Fillol - P. Cornejo
5/14/1972	Dallas $100,000 WCT Finals	Ken Rosewall	Rod Laver	4-6, 6-0, 6-3, 6-7, 7-6	
6/3/1972	Surbiton	Premjit Lall	Ross Case	J. de Mendoza - K. Weatherley	P. Doerner - R. Keldie Rain
6/4/1972	French Open $100,000 GS AA	Andres Gimeno	Patrick Proisy	B. Hewitt - F. McMillan	J. Fillol - P. Cornejo
6/10/1972	Nottingham	Jimmy Connors	Colin Dibley		
6/11/1972	Hamburg GP-B	Manuel Orantes	Adriano Panatta	J. Kodes - I. Nastase	B. Hewitt - I. Tiriac
6/17/1972	Beckenham	Alex Metreveli	Anand Amritraj	R. Gonzales - T. Ulrich	S. Likhachev - A. Metreveli
6/17/1972	Bristol GP-C	Bob Hewitt	Alex Olmedo	B. Hewitt - F. McMillan	C. Graebner - L. Hoad

6/24/1972	Eastbourne	Andres Gimeno	Pierre Barthes	J. Gisbert - M. Orantes	N. Kalogeropoulos - A. Pattison
6/24/1972	London	Jimmy Connors	John Paish	J. McManus - J. Osborne	J. Fassbender - K. Meiler
7/2/1972	Raleigh	Raz Reid	Charles Owens	J. Delaney - C. Hagey	A. Neely - J. Oescher
7/2/1972	St. Louis $50,000 WCT	John Newcombe	Nikki Pilic	J. Newcombe - T. Roche	J. Alexander - P. Dent
7/2/1972	Raleigh Southern Championships	Raz Reid	Charles Owens	J. Delaney - C. Hagey	A. Neely - J. Oescher
7/8/1972	Wimbledon GS AA	Stan Smith	Ilie Nastase	B. Hewitt - F. McMillan	S. Smith - E. Van Dillon
7/9/1972	Bretton Woods $25,000 WCT	Cliff Richey	Jeff Borowiak	J. Alexander - F. Stolle	N. Pilic - C. Richey
7/16/1972	Bastad $30,000 GP-C	Manuel Orantes	Ilie Nastase	M. Orantes - J. Gisbert	N. Fraser - I. Nastase
7/16/1972	Gstaad GP-C	Andres Gimeno	Adriano Panatta	A. Gimeno - A. Munoz	A. Panatta - I. Tiriac
7/23/1972	Columbus $30,000 GP-D	Jimmy Connors	Andrew Pattison	J. Connors - P. Gonzales	D. Stockton - C. McKinley
7/23/1972	Kitzbuhel GP-D	Colin Dibley	Dick Crealy	J. Fassbender - H. Pohmann	M. Anderson - G. Masters
7/23/1972	Washington $50,000 WCT	Tony Roche	Marty Riessen	T. Okker - M. Riessen	J. Newcombe - T. Roche
7/30/1972	Louisville $50,000 WCT	Arthur Ashe	Mark Cox	A. Ashe - B. Lutz	J. Alexander - P. Dent
7/30/1972	Winston-Salem $30,000 GP-D	Bob Hewitt	Andrew Pattison	B. Hewitt - A. Pattison	I. Fletcher - S. Faulk
7/31/1972	Cincinnati $42,500 GP-C	Jimmy Connors	Guillermo Vilas	B. Hewitt - F. McMillan	P. Gerken - H. Hose
8/1/1972	Dusseldorf	Ilie Nastase	Jurgen Fassbender	I. Nastase - F. McMillan	M. Mulligan - I. Tiriac
8/1/1972	Hilversum	John Cooper	Hans Kary	R. Case - G. Masters	J. Cooper - C. Dibley
8/6/1972	Boston $50,000 WCT	Bob Lutz	Tom Okker	J. Newcombe - T. Roche	A. Ashe - B. Lutz
8/13/1972	Cleveland $50,000 WCT	Mark Cox	Ray Ruffles	C. Drysdale - R. Taylor	F. Froehling - C. Pasarell
8/13/1972	Indianapolis $60,000 GP-A	Bob Hewitt	Jimmy Connors	B. Hewitt - F. McMillan	J. Fillol - P. Cornejo
8/15/1972	Ocean City	Jimmy Connors	Herb Fitzgibbon		
8/20/1972	Fort Worth $50,000 WCT	John Newcombe	Ken Rosewall	T. Okker - M. Riessen	K. Rosewall - F. Stolle

8/20/1972	Toronto $70,000 GP-A	Ilie Nastase	Andrew Pattison	I. Nastase - I. Tiriac	J. Kodes - J. Kukal
8/27/1972	Orange	Ilie Nastase	Manuel Orantes	P. Gonzales - C. Graebner	S. Mayer - R. Tanner
8/27/1972	Philadelphia $15,000	Roger Taylor	Mal Anderson	R. Case - G. Masters	J. Austin - M. Estep
8/30/1972	US Open $160,000 GS-AA	Ilie Nastase	Arthur Ashe	C. Drysdale - R. Taylor	J. Newcomb - O. Davidson
9/17/1972	Montreal $50,000 WCT	Arthur Ashe	Roy Emerson	T. Okker - M. Riessen	R. Maud - K. Rosewall
9/17/1972	Sacramento $25,000 GP-C	Stan Smith	Colin Dibley	S. Smith - E. Van Dillon	P. Dominguez - P. Proisy
9/17/1972	Seattle $25,000 GP-C	Ilie Nastase	Tom Gorman	R. Case - G. Masters	J. Chanfreau - W. N'Godrella
9/24/1972	Los Angeles $60,000 GP-A	Stan Smith	Roscoe Tanner	J. Connors - P. Gonzales	I. El Shafei - B. Fairlie
10/1/1972	Alamo $50,000 WCT	John Newcombe	Cliff Drysdale	T. Okker - M. Riessen	I. El Shafei - B. Fairlie
10/1/1972	San Francisco $34,000 GP-C	Jimmy Connors	Roscoe Tanner	B. Hewitt - F. McMillan	L. Bengtson - B. Borg
10/7/1972	Tokyo $33,222 WCT	Ken Rosewall	Fred Stolle	J. Newcombe - F. Stolle	J. Alexander - K. Rosewall
10/8/1972	Midland	Brian Fairlie	Haroon Rahim	B. Carmichael - H. Rahim	M. Cox - G. Battrick
10/21/1972	Billingham Dewar's Cup	John Lloyd	Pat Cramer	P. Cramer - J. Fassbender	D. Fletcher - J. Zabrodsky
10/22/1972	Barcelona GP-A	Jan Kodes	Manuel Orantes	M. Orantes - J. Gisbert	I. Nastase - F. McMillan
10/22/1972	Vancouver $50,000 WCT	John Newcombe	Marty Riessen	J. Newcombe - F. Stolle	C. Drysdale - A. Stone
10/24/1972	Edinburgh Dewar's Cup	Ray Moore	Pat Cramer	R. Howe - I. Nastase	J. Feaver - S. Warboys
10/29/1972	Essen $50,000 WCT	Nikki Pilic	Bob Lutz	T. Okker - M. Riessen	T. Addison - B. Carmichael
10/30/1972	Paris $50,000 GP-B	Stan Smith	Andres Gimeno	P. Barthes - F. Jauffret	A. Gimeno - J. Gisbert
10/31/1972	Aberavon Dewar's Cup	Jurgen Fassbender	Clark Graebner	M. Farrell -J. Lloyd	P. Cramer - J. Fassbender
11/5/1972	Gothenburg $50.000 WCT	John Newcombe	Roy Emerson	T. Okker - M. Riessen	I. El Shafei - B. Fairlie
11/6/1972	Torquay Dewar's Cup	Ray Moore	Pat Cramer	J. Clifton - S. Matthews	I. Fletcher - J. Zabrodsky
11/12/1972	Stockholm $63,500 GP-A	Stan Smith	Tom Okker	T. Okker - M. Riessen	R. Emerson - C. Dibley

11/18/1972	London Dewar Cup GP-C	Ilie Nastase	Tom Gorman		
11/18/1972	Rotterdam $50,000 WCT	Arthur Ashe	Tom Okker	R. Emerson - J. Newcombe	A. Ashe - B. Lutz
11/26/1972	Melbourne	Geoff Masters	Mal Anderson	J. Cooper - C. Dibley	K. Rosewall - M. Anderson
11/26/1972	Rome $50,000 WCT Winter Finals	Arthur Ashe	Bob Lutz		
11/27/1972	Brisbane	Ken Rosewall	Geoff Masters	R. Case - G. Masters	G. Goven - W. N'Godrella
12/1/1972	Buenos Aires	Karl Meiler	Guillermo Vilas	J. Fillol - J. Pinto-Bravo	I. Molina - B. Phillips-Moore
12/2/1972	Barcelona $50,000 CU Masters GP	Ilie Nastase	Stan Smith	6-3, 6-2, 3-6, 2-6, 6-3	
12/2/1972	Brisbane	Ken Rosewall	Geoff Masters	R. Case - G. Masters	G. Govern - W. N'Godrella
12/2/1972	Johannesburg	John Newcombe	John Alexander	J. Newcombe - F. Stolle	J. Alexander - K. Rosewall
12/9/1972	Perth	Patrick Proisy	Colin Dibley	R. Case - G. Masters	J. Cooper - S. Meed
12/10/1972	New York $75,000 USLTA	Charles Pasarell	Pancho Gonzales	C. Graebner - F. McMillan	B. Gottfried - D. Stockton
12/17/1972	Adelaide	Alex Metreveli	Colin Dibley	R. Case - G. Masters	A. Metreveli - T. Kakulia
12/24/1972	Hobart	John Cooper	Patrice Dominguez	Mal Anderson	Unfinished

http://www.atpworldtour.com/en/scores/results-archive.

http://www.itftennis.com/procircuit/tournaments/men's-calendar.aspx?tour=&reg=&nat=&sur=&cate=AL&iod=&fromDate=01-01-1968&toDate=29-12-1974.

Tennis History, Jim McManus, (Canada 2010).

1973 USLTA Yearbook.

Official 1989 MTC Media Guide, (MTC 1989).

World of Tennis '73, Edited by John Barret and compiled by Lance Tingay, (London 1973).

CHAPTER 7:

1973: BATTLE OF SEXES, BOYCOTT OF WIMBLEDON, ATP RANKINGS BEGIN, CRISES NOS. 6, 7, 8, 9

It looked like the ILTF, WCT and the USLTA marched into 1973 with peace at hand.

1973 Governing Bodies

The ILTF was the governing body for men's professional tennis in 1973, except for WCT and Davis Cup. Davis Cup was still governed by the Davis Cup Nations.

1973 Significant Tennis Leaders	
ILTF President:	Allan Heyman (Denmark)
USLTA President:	Walter Elcock
Australian LTA President:	Wayne Reid
British LTA President:	Sir Carl Aarvold
French FFT President:	Philippe Chatrier
Chairman of Wimbledon:	Herman David
ATP President:	Cliff Drysdale
ATP Executive Director:	Jack Kramer
ATP Legal Counsel:	Donald Dell
WCT Owners:	Lamar Hunt and Al Hill, Jr.
WCT Executive Director:	Mike Davies

Four Competitions

In 1973, the sixth year of Open Tennis, there were four organized competitions for men: USLTA-IPA/Riordan Indoor Circuit, WCT, Commercial Union Grand Prix and Davis Cup. There were 13 U.S. indoor tournaments known as the USLTA Indoor Circuit organized by Bill Riordan outside of the Commercial Union Grand Prix and in competition with WCT. Remember that the Peace Agreement permitted the U.S. Indoor Championships in Salisbury, Maryland staged by Riordan to have $50,000 in prize money, but prohibited all other tournaments during the WCT "monopoly" to have more than $20,000 in prize money. Nevertheless, Riordan was able to attract Ilie Nastase and Jimmy Connors (both represented by Riordan) to headline his USLTA Indoor Circuit along with Jurgen Fassbender, Clark Graebner and other independent pros.

WCT staged 26 WCT Tournaments. The WCT circuit consisted of 11 $50,000 32-draw professional tournaments open to all players in "Group A-Laver" and 11 $50,000 32-draw professional tournaments open to all players in "Group B-Rosewall", plus the Dallas Finals for a $100,000 "World Championship of Tennis" in May for the top eight singles players again with a first prize of $50,000. For the first time, a new $80,000 World Doubles Championship in Montreal was staged for the top eight doubles teams. Stan Smith defeated Arthur Ashe 6-3, 6-3, 4-6, 6-4 in Dallas and Bob Lutz and Stan Smith defeated Tom Okker and Marty Riessen 6-2, 7-6, 6-0 in Montreal. In addition to the 24 WCT "circuit" tournaments, WCT staged two special events: CBS Tennis Classic in Hilton Head won by Rod Laver over Stan Smith and the Aetna World Cup in Hartford won by Australia over the United States 5-2.

There were 52 Commercial Union Grand Prix Open prize money tournaments, including the year-end Commercial Union Masters in Boston with $50,000 in prize money for the top eight players and a $375,000 Bonus Pool. Ilie Nastase defeated Tom Okker 6-3, 7-5, 4-6, 6-3 to win the Commercial Union Masters event.

Davis Cup was opened to all players whose WCT contracts had expired or been released. So, for the first time since 1967, Davis Cup was open to the former contract pros. The Challenge Round had been discontinued in 1972.

There were 24 additional prize money tournaments, outside of the Commercial Union Grand Prix, in addition to the 13 USLTA indoor tournaments promoted by Bill Riordan. In May, Alan King staged the first "Alan King Caesar's Palace" $150,000 tournament for ATP members only as a fundraiser for the ATP which was not in the Commercial Union Grand Prix. This was the largest prize money ever for a 32-draw men's tournament. Brian Gottfried defeated Arthur Ashe 6-1, 6-3 in the finals for the $30,000 first prize.[105]

Rules

The 1973 rules of the ILTF Commercial Union Grand Prix were generally the same as in 1972, with only a few changes. The Commercial Union Masters was to have eight players. If none of the top eight were from the host country the, eighth player would be the highest Bonus Points player from the host country.[106]

Nastase Misconduct Again

On February 23, Ilie Nastase lost to Brian Gottfried, 6-2, 6-1 at the U.S. Indoors in Salisbury promoted by Bill Riordan (Nastase's agent). Nastase "stopped trying after  some early line calls went against him." Bill Riordan announced a $500 fine by his IPA. I doubt Riordan ever sought to collect the fine as he was promoting Salisbury and representing Nastase.[107]

In August in Cincinnati during a match with Orantes, Nastase cursed Referee Jim Meakin and called him a "dummy." Nastase told Gerald Eskenazi of the *New York Times*: "I called the official a dummy because he was a dummy. I was right." Since there was no Code of Conduct yet, Meakin withheld Nastase's $9,000 in prize money and filed a complaint with the USLTA which fined Nastase $4,500.[108]

Ilie Nastase

ATP Singles Computer Rankings

On August 23, 1973, the ATP issued its first ATP Computer Rankings list, which would eventually become the objective system of merit for the selection of entries in all men's professional tournaments. The first ranking listed 185 players. This meant that only 185 players had a computer ranking and all other up-and-coming players had no computer ranking and no reasonable pathway to obtain one except via wild cards into Grand Prix tournaments, after which the points earned would be divided by 12 to obtain a ranking average. This provided the 185 initially ranked players with a sort of monopoly for a few years. Nastase was #1 on the 1st year-end ATP Computer Ranking for 1973.

Crisis No. 6: Boycott of Wimbledon

The 1973 year was to be a year of "peace in our time" but the Crisis No.7 relating to WTT was percolating when the ATP boycott of Wimbledon became Crisis No. 6. Remember that Nikki Pilic of Yugoslavia signed with WCT in 1967 and was a member of the WCT "Handsome Eight." As a contract pro he was barred by the Davis Cup nations from playing Davis Cup in 1967, 1968, 1969, 1970, 1971 and 1972. Players like Pilic whose WCT contracts expired or were terminated became "reinstated" by their national associations and eligible to play in the 1973 Davis Cup. The Yugoslavs were scheduled to play New Zealand at Zagreb on clay in a third round Davis Cup tie in May of 1973, and they were favored to win. However, Pilic was playing the 1973 WCT tour and he and his doubles partner, Allen Stone of Australia, were close to qualifying for the WCT Doubles Championships in Montreal. If qualified, Pilic and Stone would lose money if they did not compete in Montreal, which was scheduled in the same week as the Davis Cup tie with New Zealand.

Pilic claimed that he gave the Yugoslav federation, which was headed, incidentally, by the uncle of Pilic's wife, a conditional yes, indicating that he would only play if he and Stone did not qualify for the WCT doubles championship. Pilic ended up qualifying to play in Montreal. The Yugoslav federation ordered him to play in the Davis Cup tie with New Zealand but Pilic declined to do so. In that tie, New Zealand defeated Yugoslavia 3-2. The Yugoslav national association claimed that Pilic had agreed to play and that he was obligated to play Davis Cup since he had been selected by his national association. Pilic's contract with WCT or his obligation to his partner, Alan Stone, were not important to the Yugoslavs. The Yugoslavs issued a nine-month international ban against Pilic for his failure to play in the Davis Cup tie. There were no anti-trust laws in Europe to prevent these kind of bans.[109]

Philippe Chatrier called his friend Jack Kramer, who is now the ATP Executive Director, to alert him to the situation. Kramer called Allan Heyman, ILTF President, and got the suspension delayed until a hearing could be held by the ILTF Emergency Committee on the matter and that delay permitted Pilic to play in the 1973 French Open. Kramer and Dell (ATP Legal Counsel) were permitted to attend the hearing at which the Yugoslav Davis Cup captain claimed that Pilic had assured him over the telephone that he would definitely play. Pilic denied that.[110]

Nikki Pilic

Pilic lost in the French Open final to Nastase 6-3, 6-3, 6-0. Apparently the ILTF Emergency Committee decided on June 2, during the French Open, to uphold the Yugoslav ban, but not announce it until after Pilic completed the French Open. Soon after Pilic lost to Nastase, the ILTF announced that it had upheld the ban, but had reduced the ban from nine months to approximately one month until June 30 which meant Pilic was now banned from the Italian Championships, Queens and Wimbledon. Just for good measure, on June 13, the Yugoslav Tennis Federation banned Nikki Pilic for life from the national tennis team.[111]

As he describes in *The Game*[112], Kramer flew from Paris to Rome to meet with the Board of the ATP and several top players, the day before the Italian Open was to begin without Pilic. He met with Cliff Drysdale, the first ATP President, Arthur Ashe, Stan Smith and John Newcombe. Kramer advised them that "you can't let them get away with it...Cave in here just because Wimbledon is involved, and it'll pop up again next year somewhere else." The Italians accepted Pilic's entry into the Italian Open and paid a small fine quietly months later. The ILTF did not mind because they believed that Wimbledon was the best place to have a war with the players. The president of the ILTF was Allan Heyman, a famous Queens Counsel (QC) Barrister.

To put it mildly, Allan Heyman and the leaders of the ILTF and Wimbledon grossly miscalculated the resolve of Kramer, Dell and the ATP players. Heyman knew that the top players had been banned from Wimbledon in 1972 and were anxious to play in 1973 [they had also been banned prior to 1968]. Heyman knew that Kramer was the long-time television commentator for the BBC for Wimbledon and he believed that Kramer would at the end of the day not let the players boycott Wimbledon.[113]

Pilic Was Unpopular

Kramer wrote in *The Game*[114] that no player was more unpopular with the other players than Pilic: "He was stubborn and argumentative on the court, sure that everything he hit went in and that everything his opponent hit went out. Only the linesmen and umpires disliked him more than the players. Also, ironically, he was a political reactionary who was very much opposed to the concept of unions. The thought that Nikki Pilic would be saved by the other players banding together on his behalf was too much to expect. But, of course. that is just what happened."

At Kramer's suggestion, Cliff Drysdale, President of ATP, asked Allan Heyman to meet with him. Heyman refused so Drysdale got the support of the ATP Board of Directors to start circulating petitions to the players to boycott Wimbledon if Pilic was refused entry. Virtually, all the players in Rome supported and signed the petition. Soon thereafter Kramer flew to London to meet with Heyman and Herman David, but they would not "give an inch."[115]

Allan Heyman said to the *London Times*[116]: "No responsible national or international sports organization can allow itself to be intimidated by threats of a walk-out, which seems so much in vogue at the present time. It is a great pity that the world's premier tennis tournament may suffer as a result of the ATP action. But it would be an even greater pity if threats of a strike were to rule the game of lawn tennis in the future, especially after a dispute has been adjudicated upon by a tribunal accepted by both sides of the dispute."

When Allan Heyman said the ILTF Emergency Committee, comprised totally of ILTF members, was "a tribunal accepted by both sides of the dispute," he was engaging in wishful thinking. I would compare this to claiming that a defendant in a criminal case would agree to have a committee appointed by the prosecutor to determine guilt.

On behalf of Pilic, the ATP filed an application for an interim injunction on the ground of restraint of trade in the Queen's Bench Division against the ILTF and

Wimbledon. Kramer asked that they only wanted proof the suspension was justified.[117] Kramer said in *The Game*[118]: *"The judge declared firmly that he had no jurisdiction in the matter, and therefore the ban on Pilic had to stand and he charged the ATP with all the $18,000 of legal costs of the proceeding."* "The ruling did not surprise us, but unfortunately the British press and public took the no-decision ruling as a decision against us. Some of the very press who had been urging us to take this stand now turned on us. Since I was identified as the Number 1 villain, I took the most heat. It was a player's issue and I thought it best that a player be speaking for us so more and more, Drysdale stood up front. Besides, Cliff is especially articulate. In all my years of tennis, I never met a player as smooth as Drysdale. He is as clever as he is handsome, the finest politician I ever saw in the game."

Kramer continued: "Drysdale was the champion of the boycott. In the whole affair there were a lot of kids who reacted in fascinating ways – Newcombe, Ashe, Smith, Nastase, Rosewall – but none of them was more intriguing than Drysdale. The night after we received the court's decision – Wednesday, June 20, five days before the start of the tournament – Drysdale convened the full board of the ATP and we thrashed things out till two in the morning. The board voted to boycott."

Included on the board were Mark Cox, Arthur Ashe, Stan Smith, Jim McManus, Ismail El Shafei, Pilic himself, who was on the board, and Drysdale among the players, plus Pierre Darmon and Kramer. Afterwards Drysdale told the press: "These are the hardest words I'll ever utter, but the ATP Board of Directors have voted to urge its members not to play in the 1973 Wimbledon championships." The next day Drysdale assembled the whole ATP membership. The vote was unanimous. The boycott was on. Kramer said the decision was taken with "deep regret".[119]

Ken Rosewall and Stan Smith (who would have been seeded No. 1) wanted to search one last time for a way to avoid the boycott and save Wimbledon. Drysdale called another meeting of the ATP Executive Council. On the motion to call for another membership vote, McManus, Ashe and Kramer voted against and Smith, Cox and (John) Barrett voted in favor. Kramer wrote in *The Game*[120]: "Three-to-Three. We all looked down at President Drysdale. He paused. At last he said: 'I abstain.' Brilliant! I almost fell off the chair. The vote was a tie. There would be no changes, but Drysdale had escaped being charged with being the one man who ruined Wimbledon. Did I tell you he was the slickest? It really was a master move." John Barrett, a non-player member of the ATP Board, resigned soon thereafter saying: 'I am fully in sympathy with A.T.P. and all it is fighting for, but I don't agree with the methods of some of its members.".[121]

Drysdale said publicly: "The position is now final and irrevocable." *Kramer's friend Philippe Chatrier, who was then the French Davis Cup Captain and Vice President of the French FFT, was the one high official who supported him and the boycott "all the way".*[122]

Later, Pilic felt guilty and came to Kramer to then offer to withdraw from Wimbledon, which would completely undermine the boycott. Kramer wrote:[123], "I was thunderstruck. I got that crazy sonuvabitch on the next plane back to Yugoslavia before he could confess to anybody else."

After the boycott withdrawals, the eight seeds in the men's singles draw were (there were only 8 seeds at the Grand Slams in 1973):

1. Ilie Nastase, Romania, ATP member.

2. Jan Kodes, Czechoslovakia, Non-ATP Member.

3. Roger Taylor, UK, ATP member.

4. Alex Metreveli, Soviet Union, Non-ATP Member.

5. Jimmy Connors, (age 20) USA, Non-ATP Member.

6. Bjorn Borg, (age 17) Sweden, Non-ATP Member (1972 Junior Wimbledon winner).

7. Owen Davidson, Australia, Non-ATP Member (former UK National Coach).

8. Jurgen Fassbender, West Germany, Non-ATP Member

Roger Taylor and Ilie Nastase Defied Boycott

Roger Taylor was the only British player to defy the boycott and play Wimbledon. He told Rex Bellamy of the *London Times*[124]: "It was a very hard decision. I was tormented by it for days. The easiest thing would have been to follow the other players. But I felt I should support Wimbledon. I am playing solely to support the tournament." Taylor decided that any prize money he won was to go to ATP. Ilie Nastase and Roger Taylor, both ATP members who defied the boycott, were given standing ovations at Wimbledon.[125]

Jan Kodes, the No. 2 seed from Czechoslovakia, defeated Alex Metreveli, the No. 4 seed from the Soviet Union 6-1, 9-8 (7-5), 6-3 to win 1973 Wimbledon. Billie Jean King defeated Chris Evert 6-0, 7-5 to win the women's singles. Unseeded American Sandy Mayer upset top seed Ilie Nastase in the fourth round 6-4, 8-6, 6-8, 6-4. Unseeded Vijay Amritraj of India upset No. 7 seed Owen Davidson in the fourth round 7-5, 8-9, 6-3, 6-4. In the quarterfinals, Mayer upset No. 8 Jurgen Fassbender, Metreveli defeated No. 5 Connors, Taylor defeated No. 6 Borg and Kodes defeated Amritraj. In the semifinals, Metreveli defeated Mayer and Kodes defeated Taylor. Connors and Nastase defeated John Cooper and Neale Fraser 3-6, 6-3, 6-4, 8-9, 6-1 in the men's doubles final. Rosie Casals and Billie Jean King defeated Francoise Durr and Betty Stove 6-1, 4-6, 7-5 in the women's doubles finals. Billie Jean King and Owen Davidson defeated Janet Newberry and Raul Ramirez 6-3, 6-2 in the mixed doubles final. At the Wimbledon Ball, Kodes "urged both sides to join together and make peace in tennis."[126]

Players Suspended

The Italian Federation suspended its players Adriano Panatta and Paolo Bertolucci for three months for participating in the boycott which doomed its Davis Cup tie against Spain. The British LTA banned Mark Cox, Graham Stillwell and Gerald Battrick from taking part in any British tournaments until further notice. In September, the British ban was lifted. The Spanish Federation suspended Manuel Orantes, Andres Gimeno and Antonio Munoz from Davis Cup play against Italy.[127]

Nastase Fined by ATP

In September, Nastase was fined $5,000 by the ATP for defying the boycott of Wimbledon. Initially, Nastase refused to pay the fine claiming he was ordered by his national federation to play Wimbledon, but Tiriac blew the whistle on Nastase and said that was a lie.[128]

Kramer's Final Reflection

Jack Kramer documented his final reflection on the boycott of Wimbledon in his book *The Game*[129]: "Looking back, my only satisfaction is that I think many people – the press particularly – who were so cruel to me and the players now realize that one man only was responsible for the boycott: Allan Heyman. He is as astute as he is egotistical, and he could see power flowing from his ILTF to the players' ATP, and the argument between Nikki Pilic and the Yugoslav Federation came as a godsend. So, he used Wimbledon as his weapon to screw up our growth. Not then, not now do I blame Wimbledon or Mr. David (Herman David, Chairman of Wimbledon). They had no choice but to do Heyman's bidding." Herman David died on February 25, 1974, age 68, so the 1973 Wimbledon was his last one.

Pilic and Djokovic

Just to show you how interconnected the tennis world is. Novak Djokovic was born May 22, 1987, in Serbia and as a youngster, he showed great talent for tennis. In September of 1999, his parents sent him to Nikki Pilic's Tennis Academy in Oberschleish, Germany near Munich, for four years to complete his development as a junior and prepare him for professional tennis.[130]

Solution is Sought

Kramer wrote in *The Game*[131]: "When it was all over, we (Kramer and Chatrier) began working together to form a committee of equal support among players, tournament directors, and federations officials, who could run the game more wisely and fairly. Immediately after Wimbledon the ILTF directed its ILTF Committee of Management to try to find a solution, if possible, with the ATP, provided the ILTF had to have ultimate control. In July, after the Wimbledon boycott, both the ATP and the ILTF proposed that "solely on an experimental basis" a new committee be created to govern men's professional tennis. Ultimately, they agreed on a seven-person ILTF Grand Prix Committee comprised of three ILTF members and three ATP members with the ILTF President as Chairman with the casting vote. The ILTF considered that it still had "ultimate control."[132]

Crisis No. 7: World Team Tennis Panic

The 1973 year began with the ILTF and WCT apparently stable and happy with the division of the year under the Peace Agreement, subject to Bill Riordan's unhappiness with the marginalization of his USLTA-IPA indoor circuit competing against WCT. Then in February, from seemingly nowhere, came the bombshell announcement of the founding of World Team Tennis (WTT) which became Crisis No. 7. The creators were accomplished and well-funded sports entrepreneurs: Dennis Murphy, Jordan Kaiser and Larry King. Murphy (WTT President) was a founder of the American Basketball Association (ABA) and the World Hockey Association (WHA) and was then president of the Los Angeles Sharks of the WHA. Kaiser (Executive Vice President) was a Windy City construction executive and was owner of the WHA Chicago Cougars. Larry King (WTT Vice President and Chief Administrator) was the husband of Billie Jean King, who had helped organize the Virginia Slims Tennis Circuit for women with Gladys Heldman and Joe Cullman of Phillip Morris. The original concept for the WTT was to have 12 team franchises for sale at $50,000 each with league matches for men and women pros from May to August of each year competing against all Commercial Union Grand Prix Tournaments except for Wimbledon in that time period.[133]

In May, WTT sold 16 team franchises for $50,000 each, plus a $10,000 assessment:

New York	New York Sets
Boston	Boston Lobsters
Philadelphia	Philadelphia Freedoms

Detroit	Detroit Loves
Florida	Florida Flamingos
Pittsburgh	Pittsburgh Triangles
Cleveland	Cleveland Nets
Toronto-Buffalo	Toronto-Buffalo Royals
Chicago	Chicago Aces
Houston	Houston EZ Riders
Denver moved to Phoenix	Phoenix Racquets
Minnesota	Minnesota Buckskins
San Diego sold to Hawaii	Hawaii Leis
Phoenix sold to Baltimore	Baltimore Banners
Los Angeles	Los Angeles Strings
San Francisco-Oakland	Golden Gaters

Lamar Hunt was present at the bidding, but elected not to purchase a franchise. "In April 1973, Kramer issued a call to arms to the ILTF, USLTA, foreign federations, and righteous thinking tennis players everywhere," wrote Greg Hoffman in The Art of World Team Tennis[134]. "Characterizing WTT as a blatant 'attempt by rich American businessmen to take over the sport,' he called for a united effort to quash the new league before it could get established. Failure to do so, Kramer hinted darkly, would be an open invitation to disaster."

The ATP's original constitution provided that players would compete "solely for prize money" so salaries were prohibited. However, during the July boycott of Wimbledon, the WTT recruiters signed Owen Davidson, Kerry Melville and Clark Graebner, who were not members of the ATP.

WTT applied for sanctions from the USLTA and the ILTF who soon recognized that the American anti-trust laws would probably require that they be granted. Nevertheless, in the ILTF meeting in Warsaw in July of 1973, a rule was approved authorizing the ILTF Management Committee and the national federations to ban or fine players who signed contracts with WTT.[135]

In August, it was announced that 10 players had already signed with WTT, the most notable of which were Billie Jean King ($100,000+-year) and John Newcombe ($75,000+-year) to five-year contracts. WTT declined to identify the other players who had signed, but Linda Tuero and Jimmy Connors reportedly had also signed. Throughout the Fall of 1973, Allan Heyman, the ILTF president, continued to threaten the banning of players who signed with WTT. In September, Kramer asked the ATP Board to "boot Newk" out of the ATP for signing with WTT. The ATP Board refused. In January of 1974, ATP officially assumed a position of neutrality by modifying its bylaws to enable members to sign WTT contracts. ATP President, Cliff Drysdale, instantly signed with the Florida franchise and others followed suit.[136] In addition, despite the proposed ban, more and more players signed with WTT, e.g., Evonne Goolagong, Kerry Melville, Rosie Casals, Vitas Gerulaitis, Isabel Fernandez, Ken Rosewall, John Alexander, etc.[137]

When the WTT offered to pay sanction fees to the USLTA and to the ILTF, there was no way that the sanctioning of WTT could continue to be refused. In March of 1974, it was finally agreed on a $48,000 sanction fee to the ILTF and a $96,000 sanction fee to the USLTA with the added agreement that WTT players would be released to play in the Italian Open and the French Open[138].

However, Kramer and Chatrier continued to oppose the WTT. The French FFT sent a letter to all ATP players informing them that if they signed with WTT, their entries into the French Open would be rejected.[139] A meeting of 24 European national associations was called for February of 1974.[140] As you might guess, Philippe Chatrier's best friend Jack Kramer was supporting Chatrier's plan for a European tournament ban of WTT signed players without regard to the ILTF sanction. WTT Commissioner George MacCall said there were "plenty of fine players" for WTT and for the European tournaments. However, no tournament wants "some fine players". Every tournament wants "all of the fine players".[141]

Crisis No. 8: ILTF Sanctioning Authority

Bill Riordan was still irritated that the WCT-ITLF "Peace Agreement" limited his USLTA-IPA circuit tournaments, which were in competition with WCT, to 40 percent of the WCT tournament prize money and that all major prize money tournament sanctions were controlled by the ILTF. On July 11, the ILTF enacted a rule over the objection of the USLTA that required all tournaments with $12,500 or more in prize money to be sanctioned by the ILTF.[142]

Riordan sought to get the USLTA to defy the ILTF and if necessary withdraw from the ILTF because of this new rule. Riordan instigated a Special Membership Meeting of the USLTA in New York City on September 7, 1973, to consider a Resolution rejecting the ILTF rule and in essence threating to withdraw from the ILTF. As then the Second Vice President of the USTA's Southern Section, I attended this meeting. Since this was my first USLTA meeting, I was astounded that all of a sudden, the USLTA was going to be voting on maybe departing the ILTF. There was a total of 194,000 USLTA membership votes available and for the Resolution to pass, 97,000 votes were needed for a majority. The total vote tally in favor of the Resolution was 89,997 so, the Resolution lost by a narrow margin of 7,003 votes. I still remember that the Southern Section (20 percent) vote which was cast near the end of the voting could have provided the needed majority, but in fact sealed the defeat of the Resolution. Bill Riordan was obviously disappointed and upset but the sanctioning of professional tournaments worldwide needed to be done by the ILTF as the international authority. The significance was that the USLTA did not take the dangerous step of confronting the ILTF and the other national associations and either withdrawing or being forced to withdraw as part of the international governing body. While we often think that the USLTA is completely separate from the ILTF, we forget that the USLTA's officers were an active part of the leadership of the ILTF and at this moment Walter Elcock, the President of the USLTA, was a member of the important ILTF Emergency Committee and Committee of Management and in line to succeed Allan Heyman as President of the ILTF in 1974.

Crisis No. 9: ATP Proposes Annual Two-Week Davis Cup Format and Threatens ILTF

In July, after the Wimbledon boycott, the ATP proposed a change in format for the Davis Cup to a two-week event with 16 countries made up of eight seeded teams and eight teams determined from the qualifying. Dave Anderson reported in the *New York Times*[143]: Ashe foresaw a "high publicity" event with satellite television and the construction where necessary, of a major tennis facility that would be available for future tennis events. "'Last year the Davis Cup nations wouldn't consider any new proposals,' Ashe said. 'If they don't do it this year, with the unity among the players that we have now, there may not be a Davis Cup for a while.'"

Jack Kramer warned that without some such change a new competition might be launched.[144] The Davis Cup Nations declined to consolidate the various Davis Cup rounds at one venue in 1973 and apparently the ATP did not further seek to force the issue in 1973. However, in 1975, the ATP created its own country against country cup event known as the "Nations Cup." The ILTF hated it. To ease tensions with the ILTF a bit, ATP Executive Director Butch Buchholz changed its name to World Team Cup in 1982. The World Team Cup was discontinued after 2011. The ILTF did not change the Davis Cup to a "World Group" format of 16 nations until 1981 and the consolidation into a two-week event did not begin until 2019. The ATP World Team Cup was revived as the ATP Cup in 2020.

Battle of the Sexes

In 1939, Bobby Riggs won the men's singles, doubles and mixed doubles at Wimbledon and the men's singles at the U.S. Championships and following Don Budge, the 1938 Grand Slam champion, as one of the best players in the world. In 1973, at age 55, Bobby Riggs was not the best 50 and over senior player in the United States. However, he was long known as the biggest "hustler" in the history of tennis, willing to bet and gamble on just about anything and everything.

In 1973, Margaret Court, had won 13 of her last 14 tournaments. Riggs challenged Mrs. Court and heightened the interest for this unusual happening with his continuous putdown of women's tennis. Riggs rubbed it in by claiming that he was better than all of them. Court accepted Riggs' challenge "to determine whether women can play tennis on a level with men." The best of three-set match for $10,000 "winner-take-all" was originally scheduled for April 28 at the San Diego Country Estates on clay, but played on Mother's Day, May 13 at a real estate development in Ramona, California. Billy Talbert, Carole Caldwell Graebner, Harry Hopman, Sarah Palfrey Danzig, Sidney Wood, Gene Scott, Allison Danzig, Jack Stahr and Fred Perry all predicted that Riggs would win. Margaret Court choked and Riggs won in 57 minutes 6-2, 6-1.[145]

As soon as the match was over Riggs began baiting Billie Jean King for a match. He told Neil Amdur of the *New York Times*[146]: "I want her, she's the Women's Libber leader," Riggs said of King, who initially turned down the first Riggs challenge. Court's embarrassing defeat forced King to accept the Riggs challenge in a $100,000 winner-take-all match. Riggs claimed that "after he defeated her, women's lib will be set back 20 years."[147]

"The match will provide the greatest payoff in tennis history," wrote Gerald Eskenazi in the *New York Times*[148]: "It is likely that each will make more money than any other athlete, except fighters, previously received for one appearance. In addition to the $100,000 prize to the winner, each is guaranteed $100,000 in ancillary rights – TV, radio, films. Thus, the winner will earn at least $200,000." ABC paid $700,000 for the television rights for the match scheduled for prime time on September 20 in the Houston Astrodome. The 46,000 Astrodome seats available for the match were priced on a scale from $10 to $100 each. In August, Jimmy (The Greek) Snyder, the famous Law Vegas oddsmaker, made Bobby Riggs a 5-2 favorite.

Billie Jean Wins

Billie Jean defeated Bobby 6-4, 6-3, 6-3. There were 30,492 spectators and a prime time television audience of 48 million. Riggs politely said "She was too good." Senators

Hugh Scott of Pennsylvania and Mike Mansfield of Montana acclaimed Billie Jean's victory. Billie Jean declined any rematch saying: "Margaret went and opened the door and I hope I shut it." Court also declined a proposed rematch in Australia.[149]

1973 Grand Slam Winners

Australian Open

John Newcombe d. Onny Parun 6-3, 6-7, 7-5, 6-1.
Mal Anderson-John Newcombe d. John Alexander-Phil Dent 6-3, 6-4, 7-6.

French Open

Ilie Nastase d. Nikki Pilic 6-3, 6-3, 6-0.
John Newcombe-Tom Okker d. Jimmy Connors-Ilie Nastase 6-1, 3-6, 6-3, 5-7, 6-4.

Wimbledon (ATP Boycott Year)

Jan Kodes d. Alex Metreveli 6-1, 9-8, 6-3.
Jimmy Connors-Ilie Nastase d. John Cooper-Neale Fraser 3-6, 6-3, 6-4, 8-9, 6-1.

U.S. Open

John Newcombe d. Jan Kodes 6-4, 1-6, 4-6, 6-2, 6-2.
Owen Davidson-John Newcombe d. Rod Laver-Ken Rosewall 7-5, 2-6, 7-5, 7-5.

1973 Davis Cup Finals

Australia d. USA 5-0 (Cleveland - Indoor)

John Newcombe (AU) d. Stan Smith (US) 6-1, 3-6, 6-3, 3-6, 6-4.
Rod Laver (AU) d. Tom Gorman (US) 8-10, 8-6, 6-8, 6-3, 6-1.
Rod Laver-John Newcombe (AU) d. Stan Smith-Eric Van Dillen (US) 6-1, 6-2, 6-4.
John Newcombe (AU) d. Tom Gorman (US) 6-2, 6-1, 6-3.
Rod Laver (AU) d. Stan Smith (US) 6-3, 6-4, 3-6, 6-2.

Laver and Newcombe were no longer WCT contract pros so they were eligible for Davis Cup again.

1973 World Rankings[150]

	Bud Collins				Lance Tingay	
1.	Ilie Nastase	IND		1.	John Newcombe	WCT
2.	John Newcombe	WCT		2.	Stan Smith	IND
3.	Jimmy Connors	IND		3.	Ilie Nastase	IND
4.	Tom Okker	WCT		4.	Jan Kodes	IND
5.	Stan Smith	IND		5.	Arthur Ashe	WCT
6.	Ken Rosewall	WCT		6.	Ken Rosewall	WCT
7.	Manuel Orantes	IND		7.	Rod Laver	WCT
8.	Rod Laver	WCT		8.	Tom Gorman	IND
9.	Jan Kodes	IND		9.	Jimmy Connors	IND
10.	Arthur Ashe	WCT		10.	Tom Okker	WCT

ATP Year-End Rankings[151]

1.	Ilie Nastase		6.	Ken Rosewall
2.	John Newcombe		7.	Manuel Orantes
3.	Jimmy Connors		8.	Rod Laver
4.	Tom Okker		9.	Jan Kodes
5.	Stan Smith		10.	Arthur Ashe

1973 Commercial Union Grand Prix Singles Bonus Pool Top 10 (4th Bonus Pool)[152]

1.	Ilie Nastase	$55,000		6.	Jan Kodes	$16,750
2.	John Newcombe	$37,500		7.	Stan Smith	$15,250
3.	Tom Okker	$27,500		8.	Tom Gorman	$13,750
4.	Jimmy Connors	$22,500		9.	Bjorn Borg	$12,750
5.	Manuel Orantes	$18,750		10.	Arthur Ashe	$11,750

1973 Official Earnings Top 10[153]

1.	Ilie Nastase	$228,750	6.	Arthur Ashe	$127,850
2.	Stan Smith	$204,225	7.	Rod Laver	$120,125
3.	Tom Okker	$173,500	8.	Ken Rosewall	$110,950
4.	Jimmy Connors	$156,400	9.	Manuel Orantes	$ 97,175
5.	John Newcombe	$133,050	10.	Brian Gottfried	$ 87,850

FIRST ATP COMPUTER RANKINGS, AUGUST 23, 1973, 185 PLAYERS

1. Ilie Nastase	25. Dick Stockton	49. Andres Gimeno	73. Corrado Barrazutti
2. Manuel Orantes	26. Jiri Hrebec	50. Raul Ramirez	73. Bernard Mignot
3. Stan Smith	27. Guillermo Vilas	51. Ove Bengtson	73. Jaime Pinto-Bravo
4. Arthur Ashe	28. Brian Fairlie	51. Leif Johannsson	73. Stephen Warboys
5. Rod Laver	29. Bjorn Borg	51. Buster Mottram	77. Robert Maud
6. Ken Rosewall	30. Hans Pohmann	51. Marty Mulligan	78. Antonio Munoz
7. John Newcombe	31. Jurgen Fasbender	55. Geoff Masters	79. Andrew Pattison
8. Adriano Panatta	32. John Alexander	56. Georges Goven	80. Marcelo Lara
9. Tom Okker	32. Francois Jauffret	57. Onny Parun	81. Wanaro Godrella
10. Jimmy Connors	34. Alex Metreveli	58. Clark Graebner	82. Barry Phillips-Moore
11. Jan Kodes	35. Paul Gerkin	59. Mike Estep	83. Jeff Austin
12. Paolo Bertolucci	36. Patrice Dominguez	60. Phil Dent	84. Jim Delaney
13. Roger Taylor	37. Bob Lutz	60. Billy Martin	85. John Lloyd
14. Marty Riessen	38. Erik Van Dillen	62. Ross Case	86. John Paish
15. Tom Gorman	39. Eddie Dibbs	63. Harold Solomon	87. Jean Chanfreau
16. Nikki Pilic	40. Cliff Drysdale	64. Charlie Pasarell	87. Milan Holecek
17. Cliff Richey	41. Antonio Zugarelli	65. Gerald Battrick	87. Ismail El Shafei
18. Mark Cox	42. Fred Stolle	66. Juan Gisbert	87. Ian Fletcher
19. Roy Emerson	43. Vijay Amritraj	67. Bob Carmichael	87. Atilla Korpas
20. Karl Meiler	44. Colin Dibley	68. John Cooper	87. Charlie Owens
21. Brian Gottfried	44. Sandy Mayer	69. Frank Froehling	87. Harlon Kahim
22. Roscoe Tanner	46. Dick Crealy	70. Allan Stone	87. Ion Tiriac
23. Patrick Proisy	47. Peter Szoke	71. Frew McMillan	87. Pierre Barthes
24. Jaime Fillol	48. Ray Moore	72. Boro Jovanovic	96. Vladimir Zednik

97. Patricio Cornejo	115. Dennis Ralston	145. Victor Amaya	169. Syd Ball
98. Szaboles Baranyi	122. Graham Stilwell	146. Wilhelm Bungert	170. Janos Benyik
98. Zeljko Franulovic	123. Jun Kamiwazumi	147. Jose Castanon	171. Hans Engert
100. Hans Kary	124. Nicholas Kalogeropoulos	148. EugenioCastigliano	172. Frank Gerbert
101. Jim McManus	125. Vitas Gerulaitis	149. Tom Christensen	173. Zan Guerry
102. Robert Machan	126. Gene Scott	150. B. Csoknyl	174. Richard Lewis
102. Ivan Molina	127. Vladimir Korotkov	151. Ezio Di Matteo	175. Piero Toci
102. Tito Vazquez	128. Herb Fitzgibbon	152. Frank Falderbaum	176. Pat DuPre
105. Tom Edlefsen	129. Pancho Gonzalez	153. Rudy Hernando	177. Toshiro Sakai
106. Edison Mandarino	130. Jeff Simpson	154. Jan Hordijk	178. Premjit Lall
106. Butch Seewagen	131. Owen Davidson	155. Rudy Hoskowetz	179. Roy Barth
108. Terry Addison	132 Harald Elschenbrdich	156. Teimuraz Kakdulia	180. Julian Ganzabal
109. John Feaver	133. Bob Giltinan	157. Freddie McNair	181. Humphrey Hose
109. Terry Ryan	134. Colin Dowdeswell	158. Bernie Mitton	182. F.D. Robbins
111. Pat Cramer	135. Jadip Mukerjea	159. Terry Moor	183. David Lloyd
112. John Bartlett	136. Dick Dell	160. Pancho Musalem	184. Nicola Spear
112. Tom Leonard	137. Peter Kanderal	161. Ulrich Pinner	185. Kim Warwick.
114. Torben Ulrich	138. Tadeusz Nowicki	162. Bellus Prajoux	
115. Jeff Borowiak	139. Ray Ruffels	163. Jasjit Singh	
115. Byron Bertram	140. Richard Russell	164. Shamil Tarpishev	
115. Billy Higgins	141. Brian Teacher	165. Anatoli Volkov	
115. Jan Kukai	142. John Whitlinger	166. Lito Alvarez	
115. Joaquin Loyo-Mayo	143. Jean-Loup Rouyer	167. Dick Bohrnstedt	
115. Frantisek Pala	144. J.L. Halliett	168. Sherwood Stewart	

1973 Tournament Calendar

Date	Tournament	Singles Winner	Singles #2	Doubles Winners	Doubles #2
1/1/1973	Australian Open $74.5k A	John Newcombe	Onny Parun	J. Newcombe - M. Anderson	J. Alexander - P. Dent
1/7/1973	Baltimore $15k USLTA	Jimmy Connors	Sandy Mayer	J. Connors - C. Graebner	P. Gerken - S. Mayer
1/9/1973	Auckland $18.5k	Onny Parun	Patrick Proisy	B. Fairlie - A. Stone	R. Carmichael - R. Crealy
1/15/1973	Miami $50k WCT A	Rod Laver	Dick Stockton	R. Emerson - R. Laver	T. Addison - C. Dibley
1/16/1973	Jacksonville USLTA	Jimmy Connors	Clark Graebner	G. Battrick - J. Fillol	O. Bengtson - H. Rahim
1/18/1973	London $50k WCT B	Brian Fairlie	Mark Cox	T. Okker - M. Riessen	A. Ashe - R. Tanner
1/20/1973	Birm'hm $15k USLTA	Sandy Mayer	Charlie Owens	P. Cramer - J. Fassbender	C. Graebner - I. Tiriac
1/21/1973	Roanoke $7.5k USLTA	Jimmy Connors	Ian Fletcher	J. Connors - J. Gisbert	I. Fletcher - B. Seewagon
1/22/1973	San Diego $50k WCT A	Colin Dibley	Stan Smith	R. Emerson - R. Laver	N. Pilic - A. Stone
1/28/1973	Omaha $17k USLTA	Ilie Nastase	Jimmy Connors	B. Brown - M. Estep	J. Connors - J. Gisbert
1/29/1973	Milan $50k WCT B	Marty Riessen	Roscoe Tanner	T. Okker - M. Riessen	K. Rosewall - F. Stolle
1/30/1973	Richmond $50k WCT A	Rod Laver	Roy Emerson	R. Emerson - R. Laver	T. Addison - C. Dibley
2/4/1973	Des Moines USLTA	Clark Graebner	N. Kalogeropoulos	J. Hrebec - J. Kukal	J. Gisbert - I. Tiriac
2/5/1973	Philadelphia $50k WCT A	Stan Smith	Bob Lutz	B. Gottfried - D. Stockton	R. Emerson - R. Laver
2/11/1973	Salt Lake City $17.5k USLTA	Jimmy Connors	Paul Gerken	M. Estep - R. Ramirez	J. Hrebec - J. Kukal
2/11/1973	Toronto $50,000 Laver A	Rod Laver	Roy Emerson	J. Alexander - P. Dent	R. Emerson - R. Laver
2/11/1973	Copenhagen $50,000 Rosewall B	Roger Taylor	Marty Riessen	T. Gorman - E. Van Dillon	M. Cox - G. Stilwell
2/17/1973	Calgary $17,500 USLTA	Ilie Nastase	Paul Gerken	M. Estep - I. Nastase	S. Baranyi - P. Szoke
2/19/1973	Cologne $50,000 Rosewall B	Jan Kodes	Brian Fairlie	M. Cox - G. Stilwell	T. Okker - M. Riessen

2/24/1973	Salisbury $50,000 USLTA	Jimmy Connors	Karl Meiler	J. Fassbender - J. Gisbert	C. Graebner - I. Nastase
2/26/1973	Chicago $50,000 Rosewall B	Arthur Ashe	Roger Taylor	K. Rosewall - F. Stolle	I. El Shafei - B. Fairlie
3/3/1973	Hampton $35,000 USLTA	Jimmy Connors	Ilie Nastase	C. Graebner - I. Nastase	J. Connors - I. Tiriac
3/10/1973	Paramus $15,000 USLTA	Jimmy Connors	Clark Graebner	J. Gisbert - I. Nastase	S. Siegel - I. Tiriac
3/10/1973	San Juan USLTA	Alex Metreveli	Roger Taylor	F. Jauffret - O. Parun	P. Cornejo - J. Fillol
3/12/1973	Charleston $15,000 USLTA	Jergen Fassbender	Clark Graebner	C. Graebner - I. Nastase	J. Fassbender - J. Gisbert
3/12/1973	Hilton Head CBS Classic SP	Rod Laver	Stan Smith	6-2, 6-4	
3/14/1973	Caracas $15,000	Tom Gorman	Francois Jauffret	J. Fillol - T. Koch	T. Gorman - E. Van Dillon
3/19/1973	Atlanta $50,000 Laver A	Stan Smith	Rod Laver	R. Emerson - R. Laver	R. Maud - A. Pattison
3/19/1973	Washington $50,000 Rosewall B	Tom Okker	Arthur Ashe	T. Okker - M. Riessen	A. Ashe - R. Tanner
3/24/1973	Washington $20,000 USLTA	Ilie Nastase	Jimmy Connors	J. Fassbender - K. Meiler	J. Connors - Ilie Nastase
3/25/1973	Jackson $10,000 USLTA	Eddie Dibbs	Frew McMillan	Z. Guerry - F. McMillan	J. Fassbender - T. Vasquez
3/25/1973	Vancouver $50,000 Rosewall B	Tom Gorman	Jan Kodes	P. Barthes - R. Taylor	T. Gorman - E. Van Dillon
3/26/1973	St. Louis $50,000 Laver A	Stan Smith	Rod Laver	O. Bengtson - J. McManus	T. Addison - C. Dibley
3/26/1973	Valencia	Manuel Orantes	Adriano Panatta	M. Estep - I. Tiriac	P. Hombergen - B. Mignot
4/2/1973	Munich $50,000 Laver A	Stan Smith	Cliff Richey	N. Pilic - A. Stone	C. Drysdale - C. Richey
4/2/1973	Houston $50,000 Rosewall B	Ken Rosewall	Fred Stolle	T. Okker - M. Riessen	A. Ashe - R. Tanner
4/2/1973	Barcelona	Ilie Nastase	Adriano Panatta	J. Gisbert - M. Orantes	M. Estep - I. Tiriac
4/8/1973	Brussels $50,000 Laver A	Stan Smith	Rod Laver	B. Lutz - S. Smith	J. Alexander - P. Dent
4/9/1973	Cleveland $50,000 Rosewall B	Ken Rosewall	Roger Taylor	K. Rosewall - F. Stolle	I. El Shafei - B. Fairlie
4/9/1973	Nice	Manuel Orantes	Adriano Panatta	J. Gisbert - M. Orantes	P. Beust - D. Contet

4/14/1973	Johannesburg $50,000 Laver A	Brian Gottfried	Jaime Fillol	B. Lutz - S. Smith	F. McMillan - A. Stone
4/16/1973	Monte Carlo $15,000	Ilie Nastase	Bjorn Borg	J. Gisbert - I. Nastase	G. Goven - P. Proisy
4/17/1973	Charlotte $50,000 Rosewall B	Ken Rosewall	Arthur Ashe	T. Okker - M. Riessen	T. Gorman - E. Van Dillon
4/23/1973	Gothenburg Laver A	Stan Smith	John Alexander	R. Emerson - R. Laver	N. Pilic - A. Stone
4/23/1973	Denver $50,000 Rosewall B	Mark Cox	Arthur Ashe	A. Ashe - R. Tanner	T. Okker - M. Riessen
4/23/1973	Madrid	Ilie Nastase	Adriano Panatta	I. Nastase - R. Norberg	J. Gisbert - M. Orantes
4/30/1973	Florence	Ilie Nastase	Adriano Panatta	P. Bertolucci - A. Panatta	J. Gisbert - I. Nastase
5/3/1973	Montreal $80,000 WCT Doubles			B. Lutz - S. Smith	T. Okker - M. Riessen
5/6/1973	Kansas City $15,000	Charles Pasarell	Tony Roche	H. Rahim - J. Borowiak	F. Froehling - C. Pasarell
5/7/1973	Bournemouth $67,500 B	Adriano Panatta	Illie Nastase	I. Nastase - J. Gilbert	A. Panatta - I. Tiriac
5/7/1973	Dallas $100,000 WCT Finals	Stan Smith	Arthur Ashe	6-3, 6-3, 4-6, 6-4	
5/8/1973	Hartford $33,000 WC WCT SP	Australia 5	USA 2		
5/8/1973	Hartford $33,000 WC WCT SP	Stan Smith	John Newcombe		
5/8/1973	Hartford $33,000 WC WCT SP	Roy Emerson	Arthur Ashe		
5/8/1973	Hartford $33,000 WC WCT SP	Ken Rosewall	Marty Riessen		
5/8/1973	Hartford $33,000 WC WCT SP	Marty Riessen	John Newcombe		
5/8/1973	Hartford $33,000 WC WCT SP	Ken Rosewall	Stan Smith		
5/8/1973	Hartford $33,000 WC WCT SP			J. Alexander - K. Rosewall	R. Lutz - S. Smith
5/8/1973	Hartford $33,000 WC WCT SP			R. Emerson - J. Newcombe	A. Ashe - M. Riessen
5/12/1973	Las Vegas $75,000 ATP #1	Brian Gottfried	Arthur Ashe	B. Gottfried - D. Stockton	K. Rosewall - F. Stolle
5/21/1973	Clingford	Owen Davidson	Colin Dowdeswell	R. Buwalda - B. Mitton	D. Crawford - J. Fort
5/21/1973	French Open $137K GS AA	Ilie Nastase	Nikki Pilic	J. Newcombe - T. Okker	J. Connors - Ilie Nastase

6/2/1973	Surbiton	Owen Davidson	Tony Roche	O. Davidson - T. Roche	S. Ball - B. Giltinan
6/2/1973	Rome $128,828 A	Ilie Nastase	Manuel Orantes	J. Newcombe - T. Okker	R. Case - G. Masters
6/4/1973	Berlin C	Hans Pohmann	Karl Meiler	J. Fassbender - H. Pohmann	R. Ramirez - J. Loyo-Mayo
6/9/1973	Chichester	Vijay Amritraj	Doug Crawford	J. James - M. Phillips	D. Joubert - J. Yuill
6/11/1973	Nottingham $75,000 B	Eric Van Dillon	Frew McMillan	T. Gorman - E. Van Dillon	B. Carmichael - F. McMillan
6/11/1973	Beckenham	Alex Metreveli	Bjorn Borg	O. Davidson - T. Roche	S. Likhachev - A. Metreveli
6/11/1973	Hamburg B	Eddie Dibbs	Karl Meiler	J. Fassbender - H. Pohmann	M. Orantes - I. Tiriac
6/18/1973	London C	Ilie Nastase	Roger Taylor	T. Okker - M. Riessen	R. Keldie - R. Moore
6/18/1973	Eastbourne C	Mark Cox	Patrice Dominguez	O. Bengtson - J. McManus	M. Orantes - I. Tiriac
6/25/1973	Wimbledon $132,000 GS AA	Jan Kodes	Alex Metreveli	J. Connors - I. Nastase	N. Fraser - J. Cooper
7/1/1973	Raleigh $5,000 Southern Chps.	Tom Edlefsen	Fred McNair	G. Amaya - J. Amaya	F. McNair - R. Reid
7/8/1973	Bastad $75,000 B	Stan Smith	Manuel Orantes	S. Smith - N. Pilic	B. Carmichael - F. McMillan
7/9/1973	Newport Wales C	Roger Taylor	Bob Giltinan	B. Bertram - B. Lloyd	B. Giltinan - R. Keldie
7/9/1973	Dusseldorf	Hans-J. Pohmann	Jurgen Fassbender	H. Elschenbroich -U. Pinner	W. Bungert - A. Korpas
7/9/1973	Gstaad B	Ilie Nastase	Roy Emerson	K. Meiler - P. Proisy	T. Okker - S. Mayer
7/16/1973	Hoylake	Bob Giltiman	Owen Davidson	B. Mitton - G.W. Perkins	P. McNamee - R. Simpson
7/16/1973	Boston $60,000 B	Jimmy Connors	Arthur Ashe	S. Smith - E. Van Dillon	I. El Shafei - M. Riessen
7/16/1973	Kitzbuhel C	Manuel Orantes	Raul Ramirez	J. McManus - R. Ramirez	E. Mandarino - T. Vasquez
7/16/1973	Hilversum C	Tom Okker	Andres Gimeno	I. Molina - A. Stone	A. Gimeno - A. Munoz
7/23/1973	Washington $75,000 A	Arthur Ashe	Tom Okker	R. Case - G. Masters	D. Crealy - A. Pattison
7/23/1973	Bretton Woods $25,000 C	Vijay Amritraj	Jimmy Connors	R. Laver - F. Stolle	B. Carmichael - F. McMillan
7/30/1973	Louisville $75,000 A	Manuel Orantes	John Newcombe	M. Orantes - I. Tiriac	C. Graebner - J. Newcombe

7/30/1973	Columbus $25,000 C	Jimmy Connors	Charlie Pasarell	G. Battrick - G. Stilwell	C. Dibley - C. Pasarell
8/6/1973	Cincinnati $75,000 B	Ilie Nastase	Manuel Orantes	J. Alexander - P. Dent	B. Gottfried - R. Ramirez
8/6/1973	Winston-Salem $25,000 C	Jaime Fillol	Gerald Battrick	B. Carmichael - F. McMillan	B. Fairlie - I. El Shafei
8/13/1973	Indianapolis $90,000 B	Manuel Orantes	Georges Govern	B. Carmichael - F. McMillan	I. Tiriac - M. Orantes
8/13/1973	Philadelphia $25,000 C	Mike Estep	Gene Scott	C. Dibley - A. Stone	J. Austin - F. McNair
8/20/1973	Toronto $100,000 A	Tom Okker	Manuel Orantes	R. Laver - K. Rosewall	O. Davidson - J. Newcombe
8/20/1973	Orange $30,000 C	Colin Dibley	Vijay Amritraj	J. Connors - I. Nastase	T. Gorman - P. Gonzales
8/27/1973	US Open $227,200 GS AA	John Newcombe	Jan Kodes	O. Davidson - J. Newcombe	R. Emerson - R. Laver
9/10/1973	Aptos $37,500 C	Jeff Austin	Onny Parun	J. Austin - F. McNair	R. Moore - O. Parun
9/10/1973	Seattle $37,500 C	Tom Okker	John Alexander	T. Gorman - T. Okker	B. Carmichael - F. McMillan
9/17/1973	Los Angeles $75,000 A	Jimmy Connors	Tom Okker	J. Kodes - V. Zednek	J. Connors - Ilie Nastase
9/19/1973	Columbia $23,000	John Newcombe	Dick Stockton	J.Newcombe - O. Davidson	D. Dell - S. Stewart
9/24/1973	San Francisco $50,000 B	Roy Emerson	Bjorn Borg	R. Emerson - S. Smith	O. Bengsten - J. McManus
9/24/1973	Chicago $50,000 B	Tom Okker	John Newcombe	O. Davidson - J. Newcombe	G. Battrick - G. Stilwell
10/2/1973	Quebec $50,000 B	Jimmy Connors	Marty Riessen	B. Carmichael - F. McMillan	J. Connors - M. Riessen
10/2/1973	Fort Worth $50,000 B	Eddie Dibbs	Brian Gottfried	B. Gottfried - D. Stockton	O. Davidson - J. Newcombe
10/2/1973	Osaka $25,000 C	Ken Rosewall	Toshiro Sakai	J. Borowiak - T. Gorman	J. Kamiwazumi - K. Rosewall
10/8/1973	Tokyo $60,000 B	Ken Rosewall	John Newcombe	M. Anderson - K. Rosewall	A. Dibley - A. Stone
10/14/1973	Barcelona A	Ilie Nastase	Manuel Orantes	I. Nastase - T. Okker	A. Munoz - M. Orantes
10/15/1973	Madrid A	Tom Okker	Jaime Fillol	I. Nastase - T. Okker	B. Carmichael - F. McMillan
10/15/1973	Manila C	Ross Case	Geoff Masters	M. Lara - S. Stewart	J. Fassbender - H. Pohlman
10/15/1973	New Delhi B	Vijay Amritraj	Mal Anderson	J. McManus - R. Ramirez	V. Amritraj - An. Amritraj

10/22/1973	Aberavon Dewar's Cup	Mark Cox	Owen Davidson	M. Cox - O. Davidson	D. Lloyd - J. Paish
10/24/1973	Tehran A	Raul Ramirez	John Newcombe	R. Laver - J. Newcombe	R. Case - G. Masters
10/24/1973	Prague C	Jiri Hrebec	Jan Kodes	J. Kodes - V. Zednek	R. Machan - B. Tarcozy
10/29/1973	Paris B	Ilie Nastase	Stan Smith	J. Gisbert - I. Nastase	A. Ashe - R. Tanner
10/29/1973	Hong Kong $25,000 C	Rod Laver	Charlie Pasarell	C. Dibley - R. Laver	P. Gerken - B. Gottfried
10/29/1973	Djkarta $25,000 C	John Newcombe	Ross Case	M. Estep - I. Fletcher	J. Newcombe - A. Stone
10/30/1973	Edinburgh Dewer's Cup	Roger Taylor	John Feaver	O. Davidson - R. Taylor	D. Lloyd - J. Paish
11/4/1973	Sydney $50,000 B	Rod Laver	John Newcombe	R. Laver - J. Newcombe	M. Anderson - K. Rosewall
11/5/1973	Stockholm $75,000 A	Tom Gorman	Bjorn Borg	J. Connors - I. Nastase	B. Carmichael - F. McMillan
11/6/1973	Billingham Dewar's Cup	Roger Taylor	Raz Reid	C. Dowdeswell - J. Hordijk	D. Lloyd - J. Paish
11/11/1973	Notingham	Tom Gorman	Eric van Dillen	T. Gorman - E. van Dillen	B. Carmichael - F. McMillan
11/12/1973	Dewar Cup B	Tom Okker	Ilie Nastase	M. Cox - O. Davidson	G. Battrick - G. Stilwell
11/12/1973	Christ Church C	Fred Stolle	Brian Gottfried	An. Amritraj - F. McNair	J. Fassbender - J. Simpson
11/14/1973	Johannesburg $60,000 A	Jimmy Connors	Arthur Ashe	A. Ashe - T. Okker	L. Hoad - R. Maud
11/19/1973	Buenos Aires $40,000 B	Guillermo Vilas	Bjorn Borg	E. Dibbs - I. Molina	Z. Franulovic - I. Tiriac
11/27/1973	Adelaide	Jiri Hrebec	Robert Giltiman	S. Ball - R. Giltiman	
12/8/1973	Boston $50,000 CU Masters	Ilie Nastase	Tom Okker	6-3, 7-5. 4-6, 6-3	

http://www.atpworldtour.com/en/scores/results-archive.

http://www.itftennis.com/procircuit/tournaments/men's-calendar.aspx?tour=&reg=&nat=&sur=&cate=AL&iod=& fromDate=01-01-1968&toDate=29-12-1974.

Tennis History, Jim McManus, (London 2010).

1974 USLTA Yearbook

Official 1989 MTC Media Guide, (MTC 1989).

World of Tennis '74, Edited by John Barrett and compiled by Lance Tingay, (London 1974).

CHAPTER 8:

1974: MIPTC FOUNDED, WORLD TEAM TENNIS BEGINS, CONNORS BANNED, CRISES NOS. 10, 11, 12, 13

The ILTF, WCT, ATP and the USLTA marched into 1974, relatively at peace with each other, but there was the pending battle with WTT.

1974 Governing Bodies

The Grand Prix Committee of the ILTF was the governing body of men's professional tennis until September 4, 1974, when it became the independent Men's International Professional Tennis Council (MIPTC), except for WCT, WTT and Davis Cup. The Davis Cup Nations were still the governing body for Davis Cup.

1974 Significant Tennis Leaders	
ILTF President:	Allan Heyman (Denmark) until July
ILTF President:	Walter Elcock (United States) beginning in July
USLTA President:	Stan Malless (succeeding Elcock)
Australian LTA President:	Wayne Reid
British LTA President:	Sir Carl Aarvold
French FFT President:	Philippe Chatrier
Chairman of Wimbledon:	Sir Brian Burnett (succeeding Herman David)
ATP President:	Cliff Drysdale until June
ATP President:	Arthur Ashe beginning June
ATP Executive Director:	Jack Kramer
WCT Owners:	Lamar Hunt and Al Hill, Jr.
WCT Executive Director:	Mike Davies

Five Competitions

In 1974, the seventh year of Open Tennis, there were five organized competitions for men: USLTA – IPA Indoor Circuit, WCT, Commercial Union Grand Prix, Davis Cup and WTT. There were 14 U.S. indoor tournaments known as the USLTA Indoor Circuit, organized by Bill Riordan in competition with the WCT time period in the first four months of the year. WCT promoted 27 open professional tournaments and two special events. The WCT circuit tournaments were: Philadelphia ($100,000) plus eight Red Group, eight Blue Group and eight Green Group tournaments each with $50,000 in prize money. Its tour featured 28 WCT pros plus four new pros and leading to the WCT Finals in Dallas ($100,000) and WCT Rothman's World Doubles Finals in Montreal ($80,000). The WCT special events were: CBS Classic at Lakeway, Texas, and the Aetna World Cup in Hartford, Connecticut. The field for the Dallas Finals was the strongest in history and included John Newcombe, Tom Okker, Rod Laver, Stan Smith, Bjorn Borg, Arthur Ashe, Jan Kodes and Ilie Nastase. Record crowds exceeded the stadium's capacity and electronic aid in calling the service line was a new innovation. Borg was a month short of his 18th birthday. Mike Davies was quoted as saying: "I have wine that's older than he is."[154]

Newcombe defeated Borg 4-6, 6-3, 6-3, 6-2 in Dallas and Bob Hewitt and Frew McMillan defeated Owen Davidson and John Newcombe 6-2, 6-7, 6-1, 6-2 in Montreal. Cliff Richey defeated John Alexander 7-6, 6-1 to win the CBS Classic and Australia defeated the United States 5-2 to win the Aetna World Cup.

The Commercial Union Grand Prix consisted of 47 Open professional tournaments. The Commercial Union Masters was staged in Melbourne, Australia, in December and was won by Guillermo Vilas over Ilie Nastase 7-6, 6-2, 6-3, 3-6, 6-4.

Davis Cup was open to all players whose WCT contracts had expired or been released. WTT with franchises in 16 U.S. cities promoted matches from May through August in conflict with the European spring tournaments (Italian Open, French Open, etc.) and the American summer tournaments.

There were additional prize money tournaments outside of the Commercial Union Grand Prix and outside of the USLTA Indoor Circuit tournaments promoted by Bill Riordan which included two ATP fundraisers: Alan King Caesar's Palace Classic in Las Vegas and the American Airlines Games in Tucson. In Las Vegas, Rod Laver defeated Marty Riessen 6-2, 6-2 in singles and Roy Emerson and Rod Laver defeated Frew McMillan and John Newcombe 6-7, 6-4, 6-4 in doubles. In Tucson, John Newcombe defeated Arthur Ashe 6-3, 7-6 in singles and Charles Pasarell and Sherwood Stewart defeated Tom Edlefsen and Manuel Orantes 6-4, 6-4 in doubles.

Rules

The minimum prize money for Grand Prix tournaments was increased to at least £25,000 and the tournament classifications were Triple Crown, AA, A, B and C. The tournaments classified as Group "Triple Crown" were the French Open, Wimbledon and the U.S. Open. The Australian Open, as the weakest of the Grand Slams, was not included in the Triple Crown category and was listed in the Group B category. Players were required to play in a total of 10 tournaments to qualify for a Bonus Pool Award, seven of which had to be Triple Crown or AA category tournaments. Grand Prix tournaments could not also be in the WCT circuit.[155]

Interestingly, the 1974 Grand Prix Rules *did not prohibit* the type of discrimination used to bar Nikki Pilic from Wimbledon in 1973. The bad part of the rule required "good standing with the National Association of the country in which the tournament is held." *That just about permitted the host national association to do anything, including invite another boycott.*

Elcock ILTF President

In July, at the ILTF Annual General Meeting in Amsterdam, Walter Elcock, President of the USLTA, was elected to also be the President of the ILTF succeeding Allan Heyman. *It was obviously helpful that the USLTA hadn't withdrawn from the ILTF as proposed by Bill Riordan.*

Arthur Ashe Second ATP President

Complementing the ATP tournament bureaus in Los Angeles and Paris, a third office was opened in Dallas by Bob Briner, an original ATP Board member who was the ATP Secretary to the MIPTC. Pierre Darmon resigned from the Paris Bureau and Richard Evans succeeded him. At the ATP annual meeting during Wimbledon, Arthur Ashe was elected to succeed Cliff Drysdale as the second President of the ATP. Thus, the new ATP Officers and Board of Directors were: Arthur Ashe (President), John Newcombe (Vice President), Jack Kramer (Executive Director), Jim McManus (Treasurer), Jaime Fillol (Secretary), Pierre Darmon, Bob Briner, Richard Evans, Cliff Drysdale, Stan Smith, Ray Moore, Ion Tiriac, Ove Bengtson and Dick Dell. Donald Dell was legal counsel.

ILTF Grand Prix Committee

Finally, and for the first time, the ILTF agreed to share the governance of men's professional tennis with representatives of the players. The model of a joint management council consisting of players and the ILTF as contrasted with a player union and a collective bargaining agreement made more sense for professional tennis in which everyone, players, tournaments and national federations were all independent contractors. The Pioneers of the Game worked hard to make joint governance work even while aggressively pursuing their competing agendas.

The 1974 Grand Prix Rules established the seven-person Grand Prix Committee of the ILTF as the governing body of the 1974 Commercial Union Grand Prix consisting of: Chairman – The President of the I.L.T.F. or designate (Allan Heyman, then Walter Elcock), three representatives of the ILTF: Philippe Chatrier, Derek Hardwick and Stan Malless, plus three representatives of ATP: Jack Kramer, Donald Dell and the President of ATP or designate. [Cliff Drysdale was President of the ATP].[156]

MIPTC

The Grand Prix Committee met five times during 1974: Paris in February, Tucson in March, Rome in May, London in June and New York in September. In New York on September 4, the Grand Prix Committee became the *independent* Men's International Professional Tennis Council (MIPTC). The ILTF members were Walter Elcock (US), President of the ILTF as Chairman, Derek N. Hardwick (GB), Philippe Chatrier (FR) and Stan Malless (US) with S. Basil Reay as ILTF Secretary. The ATP members were Jack Kramer (US), Pierre Darmon (FR) and Arthur Ashe (US), with Bob Briner as ATP Secretary and with Donald Dell as ATP Legal Counsel.

The new MIPTC met September 4 in New York, October 31-November 1, in Paris and December 12-13 in Melbourne. In New York in September, the Council concurred with the decisions taken by the Grand Prix Committee, recognized and confirmed that: (i) the ILTF-WCT Peace Agreement was approved, (ii) the Council was the governing authority for the sanctioning of tournaments with £7,500 and over in prize money, (iii) the Council was the governing body for the organization of the Grand Prix, Grand Prix Rules, Tournament Calendar, and (iv) it was responsible for the discipline of players with the ATP, etc. In the beginning there was no written Code of Conduct and no uniformity of penalties. Ashe also made it clear that he and the ATP members did not support the contention that national associations could suspend their own players in their own countries, e.g., no more Pilic-type suspensions.[157]

In October in Paris, it was agreed that so long as Wimbledon retained its traditional date, the week following Wimbledon would be exclusive to Europe, and that the week after that would be shared between Europe and the United States after which the American tournaments would have exclusivity. This division of the calendar worked for many years. In addition, it was agreed that ATP could have up to six fund raising events per year to raise money for financing ATP's operations. The ATP had two "member-only" tournaments in 1974 (Las Vegas and Tucson), which were outside of the Grand Prix. The original concept was that the ATP would be self-supporting and would not be looking for money from the ILTF or the tournaments. *Guess how long that lasted?*[158]

In Melbourne in December, the suggestion that there should be events during the second week of the French Open, Wimbledon and/or the U.S. Open was rejected. In December, the Council approved the planned $100,000 challenge match in January of 1975 between Jimmy Connors and Rod Laver. This would be the first of Connors' agent, Bill Riordan's "World Heavy Weight Championship of Tennis Winner-Take-All" promotions.[159]

WTT

After Dennis Murphy resigned as the first president of WTT in the final days of 1973, WTT entered 1974 with Jordan Kaiser as its second president with Larry King as Vice President, George MacCall (formerly of the NTL) as Commissioner and 16 team franchises. WTT played matches from May to August. The original format with each match comprised of a men's singles, a women's singles and a mixed doubles was later changed to a set each of women's singles, men's singles, women's doubles, men's doubles, and mixed doubles.

EASTERN DIVISION

Team	Won	Lost	Players
Philadelphia Freedoms	39	5	Billie Jean King, Fred Stolle, Brian Fairlie, Buster Mottram, Julie Anthony.
Pittsburgh Triangles	30	14	Ken Rosewall, Vitas Gerulaitis, Evonne Goolagong, Isabel Fernandez.
Detroit Loves	30	14	Phil Dent, Allan Stone, Butch Seewagen, Rosemary Casals, Kerry Harris.

Cleveland Nets	21	23	Cliff Richey, Ray Moore, Nancy Gunter, Peaches Bartkowicz, Laura DuPont.
Boston Lobsters	19	25	Roger Taylor, Raz Reid, Kerry Melville, Janet Newberry, Pat Bostrom, Frances Taylor.
New York Sets	15	29	Manuel Santana, Charles Owens, Sandy Mayer, Nikki Pilic, Pam Teeguarden, Sharon Walsh, Virginia Wade.
Baltimore Banners	16	28	Jimmy Connors, Bob Carmichael, Byron Bertram, Betty Stove, Joyce Hume, Kathy Kuykendall
Toronto-Buffalo Royals	13	31	Tom Okker, Ian Fletcher, Mike Estep, Wendy Overton, Laura Rossouw.

WESTERN DIVISION

Team	Won	Lost	Players
Denver Racquets	30	14	Andrew Pattison, Tony Roche, Francoise Durr, Kris Kemmer.
Minnesota Buckskins	27	17	Bob Hewitt, Owen Davidson, David Lloyd, Ann Jones, Mona Schallan.
Houston EZ Riders	24	19	John Newcombe, Dick Stockton, Karen Krantzcke, Lesley Bowrey, Helen Gourlay.
Golden Gators	23	21	Roy Emerson, Dick Bohrnstedt, Frew McMillan, Lesley Hunt, Ilana Kloss, Barbara Downs.
Florida Flamingos	19	25	Cliff Drysdale, Mark Cox, Frank Froehling, Mike Belkin, Maria Bueno, Laura Fleming, Nancy Epstein, Betty Grubb.
Los Angeles Strings	16	28	John Alexander, Geoff Masters, John Fort, Van Linge, Marita Redondo, Kathy Harter.

| Chicago Aces | 15 | 29 | Ray Ruffels, Graham Stilwell, Kim Warwick, Butch Buchholz, Sue Stap, Janet Young, Marcie Louie. |
| Hawaii Leis | 14 | 29 | Ross Case, Dennis Ralston, Valerie Ziegenfuss, Ann Kiyomura, Kristy Pigeon, Brigitte Cuypers. |

In the WTT Finals, the Denver Racquets defeated the Philadelphia Freedoms 2-0 (27-21, 28-24).

The original concept for WTT was to have 16 teams at $50,000 per franchise, pay players the $30,000 to $40,000 they could expect to earn from prize money tournaments during the WTT timeframe and draw a break-even attendance of 3,500 per match. In bidding for as many top players as they could, the WTT franchises foolishly contracted to pay much, much more for players, e.g., $1.8 million for Billie Jean King for five years, $75,000 per year for John Newcombe, $135,000 per year for Tom Okker, etc. Obviously, there was even more for Ilie Nastase and Jimmy Connors. Average attendance was only around 1,750 per match. "To say that WTT took a financial beating during the first season would be an understatement," wrote Greg Hoffman in *The Art of World Team Tennis*. "Collectively, the 16 franchises had dropped nearly eight million dollars, more than three times the amount originally projected, and several teams were in serious trouble."[160]

WTT paid the $96,000 USLTA sanction fee with WTT tickets, but it refused to pay anything on the agreed ILTF sanction fee on account of the banning of its players from the Italian Open and the French Open.

Default Precedent Established

The precedent for defaulting of players was established in 1974. At the Italian Open in Rome, Jan Kodes was defaulted for trying to push the tournament referee off the stadium court three times. At the USLTA National Clay Court Championships in Indianapolis, Ilie Nastase was defaulted for "stalling and foul language" by 74-year old Bill Macassin, who had been a "tennis umpire for 50 years."[161]

U.S. Open to Clay in 1975

In October, the USLTA and the West Side Tennis Club agreed to convert 11 of its 23 grass courts to Har-Tru (clay) for the 1975 U.S. Open.[162]

Crisis No. 10: WCT and USLTA

Lamar Hunt

In January, Lamar Hunt told the Tennis Writers Association in Philadelphia that WCT was considering declaring independence of its operations in the United States. "WCT has come to question whether there is justification for an amateur body (the USLTA) attempting to exert nationwide control of professional tennis," he said to the *New York Times*.[163]

Fred Tupper reported the USLTA's response in the *New York Times*[164]: "'Our position is a simple one,' countered USLTA President, Walter Elcock. 'If Mr. Hunt seeks no sanctioning, he will receive none and the USLTA and ILTF rules relevant to such events will be applied. I can only say that the USLTA has been the governing body of tennis long before he had an interest in it, and we are not in it for profit. I would like to put Mr. Hunt, WCT and team tennis on notice that the USLTA will not desert the many professionals and amateurs who look to us for leadership…We are prepared to work with the WCT and WTT, but we are not prepared to be dominated or bullied by them.' 'We may well be on a crash course with WCT,' said Allan Heyman, the ILTF president." *There was no resolution of this Crisis No. 10. It just continued to linger.*

Kramer, Chatrier and Dell Oppose WTT

Kramer, Chatrier and Dell opposed the creation of WTT on account of its conflict with the Grand Prix tournaments staged between May and August notwithstanding WTT's sanctions by the ILTF and the USLTA in February and the change in ATP Bylaws to "give each member complete freedom of choice to pursue his career in any sphere of the professional game."[165]

Bill Riordan Would Not Play by "Their Rules"

Bill Riordan

Bill Riordan challenged the rules and sanctioning power of the USLTA, ILTF, MIPTC and fought constantly against them. He also hated Jack Kramer and Donald Dell and he considered their involvement with the ATP to be an attempt to control the game. They all likewise hated Riordan, but he represented Jimmy Connors and he was the promoter of the USLTA Indoor Circuit, his IPA independent player association, and his "World Heavyweight Championship of Tennis" events. Rich Koster wrote in *The Tennis*

Bubble[166]: "It has been said of William F. Riordan. 'If you rolled up his sleeves, I'll bet you'd find a dozen wrist watches.' As apt as that may be, it only begins to scrape the personality of the most unsettling force in tennis. Riordan is unquestionably a flimflam artist, but he is also a revolutionary and a genius at promotion, a combination of many paradoxes and images. Like the reformed drinker he is, he is also a reformed establishmentarian." "Jack Kramer, Donald Dell, the ministers of the ILTF, and virtually every other rival in tennis are almost irrational on the subject of Bill Riordan. He has not played by the rules; by *their* rules. He has refused to abide by their agreements, and he is blind to their vision of the game. It's impossible to deal with him; but it is also difficult to deal effectively without him. He is an ominous presence, a single man with a second-rate circuit who has managed to jam the machinery of alliance, of peace, and of monopoly."

Crisis No. 11: Banned from Italian Open and French Open

Jimmy Connors

Evonne Goolagong and Jimmy Connors won the 1974 Australian Open, the first leg of the 1974 calendar year Grand Slam. They both signed contracts and played for WTT, but each reserved the right to pull out of WTT matches to enter the Italian Open and the French Open. Their entries were rejected because they had signed with WTT.[167]

Jimmy Connors

The banning of Connors from the French Open led to six lawsuits, mostly initiated by Bill Riordan, Jimmy Connors' agent: (1) May 30, 1974: Goolagong and Connors vs. French Tennis Federation for an Emergency Court mandatory entry into the 1974 French Open, (2) July 3, 1974: Connors vs. Kramer, Dell and Commercial Union for injunction and damages relating to 1974 French Open ban and various anti-trust issues, (3) September 4, 1974: Goolagong and Connors vs. French Tennis Federation for damages for the banning of their entries into the 1974 French Open, (4) April 10, 1975: Kramer vs. Riordan and Connors for defamation, (5) June 21, 1975: Connors vs. Ashe for defamation and (6) June 21, 1975: Riordan vs. Ashe, Kramer, Dell and Briner for defamation.

Crisis No 12: Lawsuit Against French Open

In May, Philippe Chatrier, speaking of the threat of the American anti-trust laws, said it would be a good thing to test in court if the American anti-trust laws could be applied outside of the United States.[168] On May 30, Evonne Goolagong and Jimmy

Connors sued the French Tennis Federation in a civil action to seek a mandatory entry into the 1974 French Open in the Emergency Court of France. The French Judge Pierre Regnault ruled there were no grounds for an emergency ruling and suggested that the players could sue for damages in an ordinary civil court.[169] Jimmy Connors wrote in his 2013 book *The Outsider* that he thought "that was the end of the dispute, as far as I was concerned. I wasn't bitter. I was disappointed...Back to business."[170] However, on approximately September 4, Googalong and Connors did indeed sue, presumably with the support of WTT, the French Tennis Federation for $200,000 each in damages for their ban from the 1974 French Open in the Civil Court of France.[171]

Crisis No. 13: Connors vs. Kramer et al.

In June, WTT announced it intended to file a $10-million damage suit against Kramer, Dell, the ATP and Commercial Union, the sponsor of the Grand Prix for the denial of the entry of Connors and Goolagong into the French Open and "for conspiring to destroy" WTT. The ATP voted to support Kramer and Dell and that probably stopped WTT from actually filing a lawsuit since WTT had lots of ATP members signed.[172]

However, on July 3, a lawsuit, presumably supported by WTT and obviously instigated by Bill Riordan, was filed with Jimmy Connors as Plaintiff against Jack Kramer, Donald Dell and Commercial Union in the Southern District of New York. On December 20, an Amended and Supplemental Complaint was filed alleging that the defendants "have monopolized, conspired to monopolize and have attempted to monopolize the supply of professional male tennis players and the business of professional tennis in violation of Section 2 of the Sherman Act" etc., and requested preliminary and permanent injunctions, plus actual money damages of $1,000,000 and additional damages and punitive damages in excess of $10 million, trebled.[173]

It is difficult not to note that Bill Riordan, Connors' agent, who filed this lawsuit without Connors' knowledge, was using Connors to seek several things important to him: destruction of the ATP, which would be beneficial to his IPA, destruction of the 1972 ILTF-WCT Peace Agreement which was detrimental to his USLTA-IPA Indoor Circuit and revenge for his personal animosity against Kramer and Dell.

The ATP was probably indemnifying Kramer and Dell on the lawsuit and it was clearly of the opinion that if it lost the lawsuit brought on behalf of Connors there would be no Council because there would be no ATP and no ATP Representatives. The ATP contended that the Connors lawsuit was an attack on the very fabric of the game and was a potentially destructive suit to international tennis and was an attempt to destroy the ILTF and all orderly international regulation of professional tennis. ATP requested that the ILTF and the National Associations join in the defense of the lawsuit. I have found no evidence that any of them did or did not come to the aid of the ATP's legal defense.

New Rule for 1975 Prohibits Banning for WTT Players

In November of 1974, the new MIPTC, which included Kramer and Chatrier, attempted to settle the matter by requiring all sanctioned tournaments in 1975 to accept all WTT players who applied for entry and met the ranking requirements. Thus, the WTT ban was prohibited beginning in 1975. Chatrier, as a member of the Council, reluctantly agreed.[174]

All lawsuits and especially antitrust lawsuits are time consuming and expensive for all parties. The Connors lawsuit really scared Kramer, Dell and the ATP players, none of whom had any insurance for anti-trust claims. So, going into 1975, this expensive and very bitter lawsuit continued along with the Goolagong - Connors lawsuit in France against the French Tennis Federation. For at least the moment, WCT, ILTF, MIPTC and WTT seemed to be at peace with each other, but not with Riordan and Connors. *Connors was mostly unaware of what Riordan was doing.*

1974 Grand Slam Winners

Australian Open

Jimmy Connors d. Phil Dent 7-6, 6-4, 4-6, 6-3.
Syd Ball- Ross Case d. Bob Giltinan-Geoff Masters 6-7, 6-3, 6-4.

French Open

Bjorn Borg d. Manuel Orantes 2-6, 6-7, 6-0, 6-1, 6-1.
Dick Crealy-Stan Smith d. Bob Lutz-Onny Parun 6-3, 6-3, 3-6, 5-7, 6-4.

Connors Could Have Won the 1974 Grand Slam

Jimmy Connors was denied entry into the 1974 French Open by the French Tennis Federation because he had signed and was playing for WTT, so Borg won the French Open without any challenge from Connors. However, on August 14, 1974, Connors defeated Borg 5-7, 6-3, 6-4 to win the U.S. National Clay Court Championships in Indianapolis. This was a fairly good indication that if Connors had been allowed to enter the French

Open, he could have won it and would have become a winner of the Grand Slam in 1974. Connors also defeated Borg in straight sets in the semifinals of the 1975 U.S. Open on clay.

Wimbledon

Jimmy Connors d. Ken Rosewall 6-1, 6-1, 6-4.
Bob Lutz-John Newcombe d. Tony Roche-Stan Smith 8-6, 6-4, 6-4.

U.S. Open

Jimmy Connors d. Ken Rosewall 6-1, 6-0, 6-1.
Patricio Cornejo-Bob Lutz d. Jaime Fillol-Stan Smith 6-3, 6-3.

1974 Davis Cup

On January 13, the United States was defeated 4-1 by Colombia in the first round of the 1974 Davis Cup competition in Bogota (elevation 8,740 feet). Erik Van Dillen and Harold Solomon lost both singles to Jairo Velasco and Ivan Molina with the only point won being the doubles by Van Dillen and Charles Pasarell.

Davis Cup Final Round

India vs. South Africa

Indian Team: Vijay Amritraj, Anand Amritraj, Jasjit Singh and Sashi Menon. South African Team: Bob Hewitt, Frew McMillan, Ray Moore and Rob Maud. India defaulted under order of the Indian government as a protest against the South African government's policy of Apartheid.

1974 World Rankings[175]

Bud Collins	Lance Tingay	ATP Year-End Rankings
1. Jimmy Connors	1. Jimmy Connors	1. Jimmy Connors
2. John Newcombe	2. Ken Rosewall	2. John Newcombe

3. Bjorn Borg		3. John Newcombe		3. Bjorn Borg	
4. Rod Laver		4. Bjorn Borg		4 Rod Laver	
5. Guillermo Vilas		5. Ilie Nastase		5. Guillermo Vilas	
6. Tom Okker		6. Stan Smith		6. Tom Okker	
7. Arthur Ashe		7. Rod Laver		7. Arthur Ashe	
8. Ken Rosewall		8. Manuel Orantes		8. Ken Rosewall	
9. Stan Smith		9. Alex Metreveli		9. Stan Smith	
10. Ilie Nastase		10. Guillermo Vilas		10. Ilie Nastase	

1974 Commercial Union Grand Prix Singles Bonus Pool Top 10 (5th Bonus Pool)[176]

1.	Guillermo Vilas	$100,000	6.	Ilie Nastase	$19,750
2.	Jimmy Connors	$ 50,000	7.	Onny Parun	$17,750
3.	Manuel Orantes	$ 37,500	8.	Harold Solomon	$16,000
4.	Bjorn Borg	$ 27,500	9.	Arthur Ashe	$15,000
5.	Raul Ramirez	$ 22,500	10.	Stan Smith	$14,000

1974 Official Earnings Top 10[177]

1.	Jimmy Connors	$285,490	6.	Arthur Ashe	$151,760
2.	Guillermo Vilas	$266,210	7.	Stan Smith	$138,500
3.	John Newcombe	$258,230	8.	Raul Ramirez	$135,185
4.	Bjorn Borg	$206,160	9.	Rod Laver	$117,450
5.	Ilie Nastase	$172,805	10.	Tom Okker	$116,285

1974 Tournament Calendar

Date	Tournaments	Singles Winner	Singles #2	Doubles Winners	Doubles #2
12/16/1973	Perth	Colin Dibley	Bob Giltinan		
12/17/1973	Hobart	Colin Dibley	Jaz Singh	T. Bernasconi - J. Haillet	W. N'Godrella - J.P. Meyer
1/1/1974	Australian Open $74,500 B	Jimmy Connors	Phil Dent	R. Case - G. Masters	S. Ball - B. Giltinan
1/6/1974	Sydney NSW	Geoff Masters	Colin Dibley	B. Borg - C. Dibley	J. Marks - G. Pollard
1/6/1974	Dallas $60,000 Mxd			B.J. King - O. Davidson	R. Casals - M. Riessen
1/13/1974	Auckland	John Lloyd	Mark Farrell	R. Hawks - R. Simpson	J. P. Meyer - W. N'Godrella
1/20/1974	Lakeaway CBS WCT SP	Cliff Richey	John Alexander		
1/20/1974	Roanoke $20,000 USLTA	Jimmy Connors	Karl Meiler	V. Gerulaitis - S. Mayer	I. Crookenden - J. Simpson
1/20/1974	Auckland	Bjorn Borg	Onny Parun		
1/27/1974	Philadephiia $100,000 WCT SP	Rod Laver	Arthur Ashe	P. Cramer - M. Estep	J. Chartreau - G. Goven
1/27/1974	Omaha $20,000 USLTA	Karl Meiler	Jimmy Connors	J. Fassbender - K. Meiler	I. Fletcher - K. Warwick
1/29/1974	Richmond $50,000 Red	Ilie Nastase	Tom Gorman	N. Pilic - A. Stone	J. Alexander - P. Dent
2/2/1974	Oslo	Bjorn Borg	Ray Moore	B. Borg _ K. Johansson	D. Palm - J. Zabrodsky
2/3/1974	Baltimore $20k USLTA	Sandy Mayer	Clark Graebner	J. Fassbender - K. Meiler	O. Davidson - C. Graebner
2/3/1974	Dayton $25,000 USLTA	Raul Ramirez	Brian Gottfried	R. Case - G. Masters	B. Gottfried - D. Stockton
2/3/1974	Modena	Adrino Panatta	Antonio Zugarelli		
2/4/1974	St. Pete. $50,000 Blue	John Newcombe	Alex Metreveli	O. Davidson - J. Newcombe	C. Graebner - C. Pasarell
2/10/1974	Little Rock $20k USLTA	Jimmy Connors	Karl Meiler	J. Fassbender - K. Meiler	V. Gerulaitis - B. Hewitt
2/11/1974	Bologna $50,000 Green	Arthur Ashe	Mark Cox	O. Bengtson - B. Borg	A. Ashe - R. Tanner
2/17/1974	Toronto $50,000 Red	Tom Okker	Ilie Nastase	R. Ramirez - T. Roche	T. Okker - M. Riessen

2/17/1974	Birm'ham $25k USLTA	Jimmy Connors	Sandy Mayer	I. Fletcher - S. Mayer	N. Kalogeropoulos - I. Molina
2/18/1974	Hempstead $50,000 Blue	Stan Smith	John Newcombe	J. Borowiak - D. Crealy	R. Case - G. Masters
2/18/1974	London $50,000 Green	Bjorn Borg	Mark Cox	O. Bengtson - B. Borg	M. Farnell - J. Lloyd
2/24/1974	Salisbury $50k USLTA	Jimmy Connors	Frew McMillan	J. Connors - F. McMillan	B. Bertram - A. Pattison
3/3/1974	Miami $50,000 Red	Cliff Drysdale	Tom Gorman	J. Alexander - P. Dent	T. Okker - M. Riessen
3/3/1974	San Diego $50k Blue	John Newcombe	Stan Smith	C. Graebner - C. Pasarell	R. Emerson - D. Ralston
3/3/1974	Barcelona $50,000 Green	Arthur Ashe	Bjorn Borg	A. Ashe - R. Tanner	T. Edelfsen - T. Leonard
3/3/1974	Paramus $20,000 USLTA	Sandy Mayer	Jurgen Fassbender		
3/10/1974	Hampton $35k USLTA	Jimmy Connors	Ilie Nastase	Z. Franulovic - N. Pilic	P. Cramer - M. Estep
3/11/1974	Hartford WC SP	Australia 5	USA 2		
3/11/1974	Hartford WC SP	Rod Laver	Stan Smith	7-5, 6-2	
3/11/1974	Hartford WC SP	Tom Gorman	Ken Rosewall	6-4, 6-4	
3/11/1974	Hartford WC SP	John Newcombe	Arthur Ashe	6-2, 5-7, 6-4	
3/11/1974	Hartford WC SP	Arthur Ashe	Rod Laver	6-3, 6-3	
3/11/1974	Hartford WC SP		6-7, 6-4, 6-4	J. Newcombe - T. Roche	A. Ashe - S. Smith
3/11/1974	Hartford WC SP	John Newcombe	Stan Smith	6-3, 6-4	
3/11/1974	Hartford WC SP		6-2, 1-6, 6-2	R. Laver - K. Rosewall	D. Ralston - M. Riessen
3/11/1974	Caracas	Charles Pasarell	Eddie Dibbs		
3/17/1974	Washington $50,000 Red	Ilie Nastase	Tom Okker	B. Hewitt - F. McMillan	T. Okker - M. Riessen
3/17/1974	Sao Paulo $50,000 Green	Bjorn Borg	Arthur Ashe	A. Panatta - I. Tiriac	O. Bengtsen - B. Borg
3/17/1974	Calgary $25,000	Karl Meiler	Byron Bertram	B. Bertram - J. Fassbender	I. Molina - J. Velasco
3/18/1974	Salt Lake $20k USLTA	Jimmy Connors	Vitas Gerulaitis	J. Connors - V. Gerulaitis	I. Molina - J. Velasco
3/24/1974	Jackson $20,000 USLTA	Sandy Mayer	Karl Meiler	F. McNair - R. Reid	B. Bertram - J. Fassbender
3/25/1974	Rotterdam $50,000 Red	Tom Okker	Tom Gorman	B. Hewitt - F. McMillan	P. Barthes - I. Nastase
3/27/1974	Tempe $20,000 USLTA	Jimmy Connors	Vijay Amritraz	J. Fassbender - K. Meiler	I. Fletcher - K. Warwick

3/31/1974	Atlanta $50,000 Blue	Dick Stockton	Jiri Hrebec	B. Lutz - S. Smith	B. Gottfried - D. Stockton
3/31/1974	Palm Desert $50k Green	Rod Laver	Roscoe Tanner	J. Kodes - V. Zednik	R. Moore - O. Parun
3/31/1974	Tucson $150,000 ATP	John Newcombe	Arthur Ashe	C. Pasarell - S. Stewart	T. Edelfsen - M. Orantes
4/7/1974	Munich $50,000 Red	Frew McMillan	Nikki Pilic	B. Hewitt - F. McMillan	P. Barthes - I. Nastase
4/7/1974	New Orleans $50k Blue	John Newcombe	Jeff Borowiak	B. Lutz - S. Smith	O. Davidson - J. Newcombe
4/7/1974	Wash'ton $20k USLTA	Vijay Amritraz	Karl Meiler	I. Fletcher - G. Russo	I. Crookenden - F. Drilling
4/8/1974	Monte Carlo $50,000 Red	Andrew Pattison	Ilie Nastase	J. Alexander - P. Dent	M. Orantes - T. Roche
4/8/1974	Orlando $50,000 Blue	John Newcombe	Jaime Fillol	O. Davidson - J. Newcombe	B. Gottfried - D. Stockton
4/8/1974	Tokyo $50,000 Green	Rod Laver	Juan Gisbert	R. Moore - O. Parun	J. Gisbert - R. Taylor
4/15/1974	Johannesburg $50k Red	Andrew Pattison	John Alexander	B. Hewitt - F. McMillan	J. McManus - A. Pattison
4/15/1974	Charlotte $50k Blue	Jeff Borowiak	Dick Stockton	B. Mottram - R. Ramirez	O. Davidson - J. Newcombe
4/15/1974	Houston $50,000 Green	Rod Laver	Bjorn Borg	C. Dibley - R. Laver	A. Ashe - R. Tanner
4/22/1974	St. Louis $50,000 Blue	Stan Smith	Alex Metreveli	I. El Shafei - B. Fairlie	R. Case - G. Masters
4/22/1974	Denver $50,000 Green	Roscoe Tanner	Arthur Ashe	A. Ashe - R. Tanner	M. Cox - J. Kamiwazumi
4/28/1974	Florence $25,000 C	Adriano Panatta	Paolo Bertolucci	P. Bertolucci - A. Panatta	R. Machan - B. Taroczy
5/5/1974	Montreal $80k WCT Dbls.		6-2, 6-7,6-1, 6-2	B. Hewitt - F. McMillan	O. Davidson - J. Newcombe
5/5/1974	Columbus $16,500	Jeff Borowiak	Ken Rosewall		
5/6/1974	Portland $15,000	Ilie Nastase	Roger Taylor		
5/8/1974	Dallas WCT Finals	John Newcombe	Bjorn Borg	4-6, 6-3, 6-3, 6-2	
5/12/1974	Portola Valley	Jim McManus	Chico Hagey		
5/13/1974	Las Vegas $150,000	Rod Laver	Marty Riessen	R. Emerson - R. Laver	F. McMillan - J. Newcombe
5/19/1974	Munich $25,000 C	Jurgen Fassbender	Francois Jauffret	A. Munoz - M. Orantes	J. Fassbender - H. Pohlman
5/26/1974	Hamburg $50,000 B	Eddie Dibbs	Hans Plotz	J. Fassbender - H. Pohlman	B. Gottfried - R. Ramirez

5/26/1974	Bournmouth $50,000 B	Ilie Nastase	Paulo Bertolucci	J. Gisbert - I. Nastase	Z. Barazzutti - P. Bertolucci
6/1/1974	Surbiton	Bob Giltinan	Syd Ball	J. Paish - S. Warboys	R. Keldie - P. Walthall
6/2/1974	Rome $128,100 AA	Bjorn Borg	Ilie Nastase	B. Gottfried - R. Ramirez	J. Gisbert - I. Nastase
6/8/1974	Manchester	Jimmy Connors	Michael Collins	S. Ball - B. Giltinan	W. Perkins - P. Walthall
6/15/1974	Beckenham	Vijay Amritraz	Tom Gorman	D. Dell - S. Stewart	C. Kachel - G. Thomson
6/16/1974	French Open 407k FF GS	Bjorn Borg	Manuel Orantes	D. Crealy - O. Parun	B. Lutz - S. Smith
6/22/1974	Nottingham $100k AA	Stan Smith	Alex Metreveli	C. Pasarell - E. Van Dillon	B. Lutz - S. Smith
7/7/1974	Wimbledon £97,100 GS	Jimmy Connors	Ken Rosewall	John Newcombe - T. Roche	B. Lutz - S. Smith
7/9/1974	Dussledorf	Bernard Mignot	Jiri Hrebec		
7/13/1974	Newport Wales	Armisteed Neely	Michael Collins	B. Giltiman - Lall	R. Simpson - F. Van Der Merwe
7/14/1974	Bastad $50,000 B	Bjorn Borg	Adriano Panatta	P. Bertolucci - A. Panatta	O. Bengtsen - B. Borg
7/14/1974	Gstaad $50,000 B	Guillermo Vilas	Manuel Orantes	J. Higueras - M. Orantes	R. Emerson - T. Koch
7/14/1974	Dublin $50,000 B	Sherwood Stewart	Colon Dowdeswell	C. Dowdeswell - J. Yuill	J. Andrew - L. Alvarez
7/14/1974	Raleigh $5,000 Southern Chps.	Trey Waltke	Mike Cahill	B. Teacher - S. Mott	M. Cahill - T. Moor
7/21/1974	Kitzbuhel $50,000 B	Balazs Taroczy	Onny Parun	I. Molina - J. Velasco Rain	B. Raroczy - F. Pata Rain
7/21/1974	Hilversum $25,000 C	Guillermo Vilas	Barry Phillips-Moore	T. Vasquez - G. Vilas	L. Alvarez - J. Gonzales
7/21/1974	Chicago $50,000 C	Stan Smith	Marty Riessen	T. Gorman - M. Riessen	B. Gottfried - R. Ramirez
7/29/1974	Washington $100k AA	Harold Solomon	Guillermo Vilas	T. Gorman - M. Riessen	P. Cornejo - J. Fillol
8/4/1974	Cincinnati $25,000 C	Marty Riessen	Bob Lutz	D. Dell - S. Stewart	J. Delaney - J. Whitlinger
8/4/1974	Louisville $100,000 AA	Guillermo Vilas	Jaime Fillol	C. Pasarell - E. Van Dillon	J. Fassbender - H. Pohlman
8/11/1974	Indianapolis $130k AA	Jimmy Connors	Bjorn Borg	J. Connors - I. Nastase	J. Fassbender - H. Pohlman
8/11/1974	Bretton Woods $50k B	Rod Laver	Harold Solomon	J. Borowiak - R. Laver	G. Goven - F. Jaufret

154

8/18/1974	Toronto $130,000 AA	Guillermo Vilas	Manuel Orantes	M. Orantes - G. Vilas	J. Fassbender - H. Pohlman
8/18/1974	Columbus $50,000 B	Raul Ramirez	Roscoe Tanner	V. Amritraz - An. Amritraz	T. Gorman - B. Lutz
8/25/1974	Boston $100,000 AA	Bjorn Borg	Tom Okker	B. Lutz - S. Smith	H. Pohlman - M. Riessen
8/25/1974	South Orange $50,000 B	Alex Metreveli w.o.	Jimmy Connors	B. Gottfried - R. Ramirez	V. Amritraz - An. Amritraz
8/25/1974	Philadelphia $25,000 C	John Lloyd	John Whitlinger	R. Barth - H. Hose	M. Machette - F. McNair
9/9/1974	US Open $271,720 GS	Jimmy Connors	Ken Rosewall	B. Lutz - S. Smith	P. Cornejo - J. Fillol
9/15/1974	Cedar Grove $50,000 B	Ilie Nastase	Juan Gisbert	S. Siegel - K. Warwick	D. Crealy - B. Tanis
9/22/1974	Los Angeles $100k AA	Jimmy Connors	Harold Solomon	R. Case - G. Masters	B. Gottfried - R. Ramirez
9/30/1974	San Francisco $100k AA	Ross Case	Arthur Ashe	B. Lutz - S. Smith	J. Alexander - S. Ball
10/6/1974	Honolulu $50,000 B	John Newcombe	Roscoe Tanner	D. Stockton - R. Tanner	O. Davidson - J. Newcombe
10/13/1974	Madrid $75,000 A	Ilie Nastase	Bjorn Borg	P. Dominguez - A. Munoz	B. Gottfried - R. Ramirez
10/13/1974	Tokyo $75,000 A	John Newcombe	Ken Rosewall	Rain	Rain
10/20/1974	Barcelona $76,000 A	Ilie Nastase	Manuel Orantes	J. Gisbert - I. Nastase	M. Orantes - G. Vilas
10/20/1974	Sydney A	John Newcombe	Cliff Richey	R. Case - G. Masters	J. Newcombe - T. Roche
10/27/1974	Tehran $100,000 AA	Guillermo Vilas	Raul Ramirez	M. Orantes - G. Vilas	B. Gottfried - R. Ramirez
10/27/1974	ChristChurch C	Roscoe Tanner	Ray Ruffels	I. El Shafei - R. Tanner	S. Ball - R. Ruffels
10/27/1974	Melbourne $25,000 C	Dick Stockton	Geoff Masters	A. Stone - R. Reid	M. Estep - P. Kronk
11/1/1974	Hilton Head $135,000 SP	Ilie Nastase	Bjorn Borg	B. Borg - R. Laver	I. Nastase - S. Smith
11/2/1974	Cardiff Dewar Cup	Mark Cox	Zelijko Franulovic	D. Lloyd - S. A. Warboys	M. Coz - Z. Franulovic
11/3/1974	Paris $50,000 B	Brian Gottfried	Eddie Dibbs	P. Dominguez - F. Jaufret	B. Gottfried - R. Ramirez
11/3/1974	Vienna $25,000 C	Vitas Gerulatis	Andrew Pattison	R. Moore - A. Pattison	B. Hewitt - F. McMillan
11/3/1974	Jakarta B	Onny Parun	Kim Warwick	I. El Shafei - R. Tanner	J. Fassbender - H. Pohlman

11/9/1974	Edinburgh Dewar Cup	Mark Cox	R.A. Lewis	D. Lloyd - S. A. Warboys	R.A. Lewis - P. Siviter
11/10/1974	Stockholm $100,000 AA	Arthur Ashe	Tom Okker	T. Okker - M. Riessen	B. Hewitt - F. McMillan
11/10/1974	Hong Kong $50,000 B	Unfinished			
11/16/1974	Dewar Cup $75,000 A	Jimmy Connors	Brian Gottfried	J. Connors - I. Nastase	B. Gottfried - R. Ramirez
11/17/1974	Bombay $50,000 B	Onny Parun	Tony Roche	A. Amritraj - V. Amritraj	
11/17/1974	Manila $50,000 B	Ismail El Shafei	Hans-Jurgen Pohmann	S. Ball - R. Case	
11/17/1974	Oslo $25,000 C	Jeff Borowiak	Karl Meiler	K. Meiler - H. Rahim	J. Borowiak - V. Geruliatis
11/24/1974	Buenos Aires $50,000 A	Guillermo Vilas	Manuel Orantes	M. Orantes - G. Vilas	P. Cornejo - J. Fillol
11/26/1974	Johannesburg $130k AA	Jimmy Connors	Arthur Ashe	B. Hewitt - F. McMillan	T. Okker - M. Riessen
11/30/1974	Brisbane	Bob Giltinan	U. Marten	B. Giltiman - G. Thomson	R. Gehring - U. Pinner
12/7/1974	Adelaide	Bjorn Borg	Onny Parun		
12/7/1974	Hobart	Geoff Masters	Toshiro Sakai	R. Case - G. Masters	K. Hirai - T. Sakai
12/14/1974	Bloemfontein	Pat Cramer	Armistead Neely	W. Bocker - L. Merry	W. Prinsloo - D. Schneider
12/15/1974	Melbourne $100k CU Masters	Guillermo Vilas	Ilie Nastase	7-6, 6-2, 6-3, 3-6, 6-4	
12/15/1974	Perth	Ross Case	Geoff Masters	M. Anderson - C. Dibley	R. Case - G. Masters
12/15/1974	Durbin	Bob Hewitt	J. Yuill	P. Cramer - D. Phillips	Michau - G. Rhodes
12/15/1974	East London	Armisteed Neely	Barry Phillips-Moore	W. Prinsloo - D. Schneider	P. Cramer - C. Dowdeswell
12/15/1974	Port Elizabeth	Bob Hewitt	Pat Cramer	P. Cramer - C. Dowdeswell	W. Prinsloo - D. Schneider
12/22/1974	Sydney NSW	Tony Roche	Phil Dent	S. Ball - B. Carmichael	J. Alexander - P. Dent
12/23/1974	Caracas	Arthur Ashe	Tom Gorman		

http://www.atpworldtour.com/en/scores/results-archive.

http://www.itftennis.com/procircuit/tournaments/men's-calendar.aspx?tour=&reg=&nat=&sur=&cate=AL&iod=& fromDate=01-01-1968&toDate=29-12-1974.

Tennis History, Jim McManus, (Canada 2010).

1975 USLTA Yearbook.

Official 1989 MTC Media Guide,(MTC 1989).

World of Tennis '75, Edited by John Barrett and compiled by Lance Tingay, (London 1975).

CHAPTER 9:

1975: WCT PEACE AGREEMENT ENDS, RIORDAN-CONNORS LAWSUITS, CRISES NOS. 14, 15, 16

1975 Governing Bodies

The MIPTC was the governing body for men's professional tennis in 1975, except for WCT, WTT and the Davis Cup. Davis Cup was still governed by the Davis Cup Nations.

1975 Significant Tennis Leaders

ILTF President:	Walter Elcock (United States) until July
ILTF President:	Derek Hardwick (Great Britain) beginning in July
USLTA/USTA President:	Stan Malless
Australian LTA President:	Wayne Reid
British LTA President:	Sir Carl Aarvold
French FFT President:	Philippe Chatrier
Chairman of Wimbledon:	Sir Brian Burnett
ATP President:	Arthur Ashe
ATP Executive Director:	Jack Kramer
WCT Owners:	Lamar Hunt and Al Hill, Jr.
WCT Executive Director:	Mike Davies

1975 MIPTC

ILTF: Walter Elcock, (ILTF President) Chairman, Derek Hardwick

Philippe Chatrier and Stan Malless, with Basil Reay as Joint

Secretary. In August, Hardwick succeeded Elcock as Chairman and Paolo Angeli succeeded Hardwick.

ATP: Jack Kramer, Pierre Darmon and Arthur Ashe with Bob Briner as Joint Secretary.

USLTA to USTA

With the change from grass to clay at the U.S. Open at Forest Hills in 1975, it did not make much sense to continue with the word "Lawn" in its name so in February at its annual meeting in Amelia Island Florida, the USLTA became the USTA.[178]

Five Competitions

In 1975, the eighth year of Open Tennis, there were five organized competitions for men: the USLTA – IPA Indoor Circuit, WCT, Commercial Union Grand Prix, Davis Cup and WTT. There were 13 USLTA indoor tournaments organized by Bill Riordan in competition with the WCT time period in the first four months of the year. Prize money was limited to $20,000 except for Riordan's U.S. Indoors in Salisbury.

WCT promoted 31 professional tournaments and events. The 27 tournament WCT circuit was comprised of Philadelphia ($115,000) plus eight Red Group, eight Blue Group and eight Green Group ($60,000) tournaments, the WCT Finals ($100,000) in Dallas and the WCT Doubles Finals ($90,000) in Mexico City. Philadelphia always received the players from all the WCT Groups at the beginning of each year. Arthur Ashe defeated Bjorn Borg 3-6, 6-4, 6-4, 6-0 in Dallas and Brian Gottfried and Raul Ramirez defeated Mark Cox and Cliff Drysdale 7-6, 6-7, 7-6 in Mexico City. The four special events were: CBS Classic in Puerto Rico ($60,000) won by Rod Laver over Arthur Ashe 6-3, 7-5, Aetna World Cup ($37,500) won by USA 4-2 over Australia, London Rothmans Indoor ($60,000) won by Mark Cox over Brian Fairlie 6-1, 7-5 and a WCT Doubles Challenge ($35,000) in Dallas won by Brian Gottfried and Raul Ramirez over Bob Hewitt and Frew McMillan 7-5, 6-3, 4-6, 2-6, 7-5. WCT was only permitted under the Peace Agreement to have 26 events so WCT exceeded the limit by five events.

There were 43 Commercial Union Grand Prix Open prize money tournaments, including the year-end Commercial Union Masters in Melbourne won by Ilie Nastase over Bjorn Borg 6-2, 6-2, 6-1. For the Masters doubles, Juan Gisbert and Manuel Orantes defeated Jurgen Fassbender and Hans-Jurgen Pohmann 7-5, 6-1. The 1975 year was the first year of the Doubles Masters for four doubles teams.

The Davis Cup was open to all players whose WCT contracts had expired or been released. World Team Tennis with franchises in 10 United States cities staged matches from May through August in conflict with the European Spring tournaments (Italian Open, French Open, etc.) and the American summer tournaments. ATP fundraiser events included the Alan King Caesar's Palace Classic in Las Vegas ($150,000) won by Roscoe Tanner over Ross Case 5-7, 7-5, 7-6 in singles and by John Alexander and Phil Dent over Bob Carmichael and Cliff Drysdale 6-1, 6-4 in doubles, the American Airlines Games ($175,000) in Tucson won by John Alexander over Ilie Nastase 7-5, 6-2 in singles and Raul Ramirez and William Brown over Ray Moore and Dennis Ralston 2-6, 7-6, 6-4 in doubles and the new ATP Nations Cup ($100,000) in Kingston, Jamaica, won by the USA over Great Britain 2-1. *This was the first year of the Nations Cup which the ATP commenced because the ILTF would not make changes to the Davis Cup.*[179]

[A bit if Trivia: In the finals of the Alan King Caesars Palace Classic, unseeded Aussie Ross Case had 3 match points before losing to Roscoe Tanner 11-9 in the exciting final set tiebreaker for the $30,000 winner's prize. Caesar's Palace was so pleased with the match that it increased Ross's 2nd prize from $15,000 to $30,000.[180] Ross's Aussie mates gave Ross the nickname "Snake" which sticks with him even today. Ross claims it was because of his good luck in Las Vegas. All the Aussie players have nicknames. See if you can identify them: "Rocket", "Muscles", "Fiery", "Emmo", "Davo", "Newk", "JA", "Nails", "Maca", "Rusty", "Wild Thing", "Woodies", etc.].

Rules

The minimum prize money required for 1975 Grand Prix tournaments was increased from $25,000 to $50,000. The Triple Crown category still did not include the Australian Open and had a minimum prize money level of $150,000 plus a Bonus Pool contribution of $18,500 and an ILTF fee of $2,380. The Australian Open was not a Triple Crown, not a Category AA or a Category A as it only qualified for a Category B which had minimum prize money of $43,750. Instead of having to compete in 10 tournaments in 1974, the 1975 participation requirement only specified a minimum of two $50,000 prize money tournaments, presumably upon the assumption that the players would play the Triple Crown, 'AA' and 'A' category tournaments anyway. The rule requiring "good standing with the national association of the country" upon which WTT players had been discriminated against (Connors and Goolagong) was deleted. With the Chairman casting the tie-breaking vote, by a vote of 4-3, a new rule was added to prohibit tournaments from paying appearance guarantees to players and for disqualification and fines against tournaments and players who violated the rules. The MIPTC was now finally in existence and was trying to consolidate the governance of men's professional tennis.[181]

As an Appendix to the 1975 Grand Prix Rules, the MIPTC promulgated the first set of Tournament Regulations for use worldwide. Previously, the tournaments used a variety of tournament regulations issued by various national associations. The ATP Computer Rankings were adopted as the official system of merit, "until such time as the Council advise tournament organisers otherwise." This was the first time that the ATP Computer Ranking System, which began in 1973, was specifically mentioned in the Grand Prix Rules. All tournament draws were required to be made by the official referee and open to the public with only one seeding list (earlier there was a home seeding list and a foreign seeding list). The number of players to be seeded was standardized to be as follows:

32 competitors	8 seeds
48 competitors	8 seeds
64 competitors	16 seeds
98 competitors	16 seeds
128 competitors	16 seeds

In 1973, the Grand Slams only had eight seeds. Here in 1975, there would be 16 seeds. It would be a while before the Grand Slams would have 32 seeds. Finally, players were allowed to sit during the changeovers and chairs were therefore to be provided. For the first time, we had uniform international Tournament Regulations for men's professional tennis. Finally, we were accommodating television commercials during the 90-second changeovers and providing some place for the players to sit, per a Mike Davies innovation.[182]

All Grand Prix tournaments were required to be played under the ILTF *Rules of the Game*. Those Rules were amended in 1974 to require beginning in 1975 the 12-point (Wimbledon) tiebreaker and not the Jimmy Van Alan five-of-nine Sudden Death Tiebreaker.[183] There was no overrule in 1975, so the calls of a linesman were final and could not be changed by the chair umpire. However, the Brits were testing out the overrule anyway.[184]

MIPTC Meetings

In 1975, the MIPTC held five meetings: February 7-9 in Bermuda, June 19 in London, August 31-September 2 in New York, November 2-5 in Paris and December 3-7 in Stockholm.

Letter from Connors/Riordan Attorney

In a letter dated November 1, 1974, from J. Edward Meyer III, attorney for Jimmy Connors and Bill Riordan to Stan Malless, President of the USLTA (and a member of the MIPTC), Meyer stated on behalf of Jimmy Connors and Bill Riordan, they "strongly" requested Malless to withdraw from the MIPTC and stated that "The composition of the Council is so inherently replete with conflicts of interests and with restrictive European influences that the judgments and decisions can never be deemed objective." The Meyer letter was part of Kramer's claim in his subsequent lawsuit against Connors and Riordan for defamation.[185]

In Bermuda in February, the ILTF claimed that tournaments had to be sanctioned by a national association before being sanctioned by the MIPTC. The ATP claimed that the sanctioning and scheduling power of the MIPTC was absolute and not subject to any other bodies. This issue was not resolved here. The MIPTC would never agree to be bound by national association sanctioning, but would sometimes use national association sanctioning as an additional condition for MIPTC sanctioning.

Collection from U.S. Tournaments

A motion was made that all Bonus Pool contributions and ILTF authorization fees in respect of U.S. tournaments be collected by the USTA and for the remainder of the world to be collected by the ILTF. The vote on this motion was 4-3 with the Chairman (ILTF President) breaking the tie. So, this began the disagreement between the ATP and the ILTF as to who would collect from national association tournaments and who would collect from independent tournaments.[186]

In London in June, it was noted that instead of paying their Bonus Pool deposits to the USTA, Chicago, Washington, Louisville, Cincinnati, Toronto, Columbus, Orange, Houston, Los Angeles and San Francisco all sent their deposits to the ATP, who agreed to forward them to the ILTF for the Bonus Pool. This was a little defiance by the American tournaments! At this meeting, the MIPTC agreed to recommend to the ILTF and the ATP that the MIPTC should continue for a further experimental period of one year. *Nobody was agreeing to anything for the long term.*[187] [Years later Christopher Stokes, the ILTF Finance Officer, told me that the accounting firm that provided the annual audit for the MIPTC could never obtain a full and accurate accounting of all the MIPTC funds that went through the ATP checking account for the MIPTC].

Expansion of Council

In New York in August-September, the MIPTC agreed on the formation of a new expanded Council beginning in 1976, composed of three player representatives, three ILTF representatives, three tournament representatives and a chairman appointed by the ILTF with no vote. It was agreed that the ILTF would elect the ILTF representatives and appoint the non-voting chairman and the top 150 ranked players, regardless of their status (as a member or non-member of the ATP) would nominate and elect the three player representatives. The three tournament representatives would be a North American Representative, a European Representative and a "Rest of the World" Representative elected by the tournaments in their respective geographical areas. The terms of office would be two years.[188]

End of WCT-ILTF Peace Agreement

WCT was only permitted under the Peace Agreement to promote 22 circuit tournaments and four special events, but in 1975, WCT had 25 circuit tournaments and six special events, which exceeded the limit by five events. The Peace Agreement was executed in 1972 and began in 1973 and had an original term of eight years with the right of either party to terminate on three years notice after December 25, 1977. However, the Peace Agreement required WCT to have 32 minimum draws in the WCT tournaments with the option to have 64 players if two tournament groups were promoted. The obvious purpose of this provision was to require a minimum of 32 player jobs since WCT was going to have a sort of monopoly. On March 20, 1975, WCT sent a letter to the ILTF proposing that in 1976, WCT planned to reduce from three groups to two groups and each circuit tournament would have prize money of $100,000 and a draw of 16 except for Philadelphia which would have $115,000 in prize money and a 32 draw and be part of both groups. In addition, WCT proposed to have a new special event series of "head-to-head" matches. At the April 18-19, 1975, meeting of the ILTF Committee of Management, the ILTF decided that if WCT went forward with its proposal, it would be a breach of the Peace Agreement requiring the ILTF to terminate the Peace Agreement and by letter dated April 19, 1975, WCT was notified of the possible termination by the ILTF. The ILTF requested WCT to respond by May 5, 1975.[189]

At the July 2-4, 1975, meeting of the ILTF Management Committee, it was reported that WCT intended to go ahead with its plans for 1976, in breach of the Peace Agreement and therefore the ILTF had terminated the Peace Agreement. The President reported that the 1976 WCT events would continue to be sanctioned by the ILTF and would be paying the ILTF sanction fees, but "there would be no 'WCT protected period.'"[190]

WCT had apparently concluded that the protections of the Peace Agreement were not worth being forced to continue with 32-draw minimums and being prohibited from going forward with its new "head-to-head" special events. WCT also knew or hoped that the U.S. Antitrust laws would prevent the ILTF and the MIPTC from using monopoly power to put WCT out of business.[191]

Since the WCT-ILTF Peace Agreement had been terminated, the MIPTC could have scheduled the 1976 Grand Prix to begin in January in competition with the WCT tournaments. However, the MIPTC did not begin scheduling the Grand Prix to begin in January until 1977; since WCT reduced its tournament schedule in 1976, a player unemployment problem was created.[192]

Player Unemployment Problem

In Stockholm in December, to help with the unemployment problem created by WCT's reduction from 32 draws to 16 draws in 1976, the MIPTC approved eight 1976 tournaments for a "European Spring Circuit" outside the Grand Prix:

March 8-14	Cologne	$25,000
March 15-21	Basel	$30,000
March 22-28	Valencia	$30,000
March 29-April 4	Barcelona	$30,000
April 5-11	Nice	$30,000
April 12-18	Majorca	$30,000
April 19-25	Florence	$30,000
April 26 – May 2	Madrid	$30,000

ATP

In 1975, Jack Kramer continued as ATP Executive Director, but Bob Briner was appointed as ATP's Chief Administrative Officer and the ATP offices were moved from Los Angeles to the new World Trade Center in Dallas in January of 1976. Dennis Spencer was hired to assist Briner. Arthur Ashe continued as ATP President, with John Newcombe as Vice President and Jim McManus as Secretary/Treasurer. Donald Dell continued as legal counsel. Richard Evans was the Director of the European Tournament Bureau and Pierre Darmon continued with Kramer and Briner as non-player Directors on the ATP Board. The new ATP newspaper, *International Tennis Weekly* was scheduled to commence in January of 1976 with Dennis Spencer as its first editor.[193]

First ATP Awards Dinner

The first ATP Awards Dinner was instigated by Bob Briner and was staged on September 8, 1975, in Dallas with Alan King as the Master of Ceremonies. Awards were given to:

Player of the Year	Arthur Ashe
ATP Lifetime Award	Philippe Chatrier
Newcomer of the Year	Vitas Gerulaitis
Doubles Team of the Year	Brian Gottfried – Raul Ramirez
Tennis Writer of the Year	Rex Bellamy
Tennis Broadcaster of the Year	Bud Collins
ATP Dr. Johnson Children's Award	Vic Braden
ATP Grand Master Award	Pancho Gonzales
ATP Service Award	Jim McManus
Court Officials of the Year	Flo and Mike Blanchard
President's Award	Jack Kramer

WTT

Larry King continued to be the President of WTT. The average match attendance in 1975 was 3,050, but all the owners lost money again.[194]

EASTERN DIVISION

Team	Won	Lost	Players
Pittsburgh Triangles	36	8	Mark Cox, Evonne Goolagong, Vitas Gerulaitis, Kim Warwick, Rayni Fox, Nancy Gunter Richey, Peggy Michael.
New York Sets	34	10	Coach Fred Stolle, Billie Jean King, Virginia Wade, Sandy Mayer, Charles Owens, Mona Guerrant, Betsy Nagelsen.
Boston Lobsters	20	24	Coach Ion Tiriac, Bob Hewitt, Raz Reid, Kerry Melville Reid, Greer "Cat" Stevens,

Bill Drake, Pam Teguarden, Francis Troll, Wendy Turnbull, Val Ziegenfuss.

| Indiana Loves | 18 | 26 | Coach Allen Stone, Ray Ruffels, Roy Barth, Pat Bostrom, Carrie Meyer, Wendy Overton. |
| Cleveland Nets | 16 | 28 | Marty Riessen, Ann Hayden Jones, Clark Graebner, Laura DuPont, Leslie Hunt, Sue Step, Maro Tiff, Val Ziegenfuss, Bob Giltinan. |

WESTERN DIVISION

Team	Won	Lost	Players
San Francisco/Oakland			
Golden Gators	29	15	Tom Okker, Betty Stove, Coach Frew McMillan, Dick Bohrnstedt, Whitney Reed, Ann Kiyomura, Ilana Kloss, Kate Lathan.
Phoenix Racquets	22	22	Coach Tony Roche, Francoise Durr, Andrew Pattison, Jeff Austin, Brian Fairlie, Roger Taylor, Pam Austin, Kristien Shaw, Stephanie Tolleson.
Los Angeles Strings	20	24	Rosie Casals, Ross Case, Bob Lutz, Mike Machette, Geoff Masters, Kathy Harter, Bettyann Stuart.
Hawaii Leis	14	30	John Newcombe, Butch Buchholz, Owen Davidson, Tom Edlefsen, Barry MacKay, Charles Panui, Charles Pasarell, Dick Stockton, Mary Ann Beattie, Joyce Champaigne, Margaret Court, Brigitte Cuypers, Heather Dalgren, Helen Gourlay, Mary Hamilton, Kathy Kuykendall, Kristie Pigeon Ann Kiyomura, Kristy Pigeon.

San Diego Friars   12   34   Vijay Amritraj, Anand Amritraj, John Andrews, Jeff Cowan, Tom Leonard, Mike Machette, Sashi Menon, Dennis Ralston, Bill Schoen, Ken Stuart, Brigitte Cuypers, Helen Gourlay, Leslie Hunt, Marita Redondo, Francis Troll, Janet Young.

Pittsburgh won the playoffs 4-1. Notable men players who played WTT in 1974, but did not continue in 1975 were: John Alexander, Gerald Battrick, Bill Bowrey, Jimmy Connors, Phil Dent, Cliff Drysdale, Roy Emerson, Frank Froehling, Bob McKinley, Ray Moore, Nikki Pilic, Cliff Richey, Manuel Santana, Gene Scott and Graham Stillwell.[195]

Connors vs. Laver Challenge

After Connors defeated Ken Rosewall in the 1974 U.S. Open final, Bill Riordan proposed a challenge match between the 22-year-old Connors against the 36-year-old Rod Laver at Caesars Palace for $100,000.[196] It was the largest prize money ever offered for a tennis match and it was televised by CBS. Vin Scully and Tony Trabert provided commentary and Pancho Gonzales was the referee. Coaches on the court were Pancho Segura for Connors and Roy Emerson for Laver. Linesmen were Don Budge, Ted Schroeder, Barry MacKay, Frank Parker, Billy Talbert, Hugh Stewart, Tom Brown, Gardnar Mulloy, Gene Mako, Dick Savitt and Sven Davidson.[197]

On February 2, Connors beat Laver 6-4, 6-2, 3-6, 7-5 to win the first "Winner-Take-All" "World Heavyweight Tennis Championships." CBS got a 33 share against the 28 share of ABC's *Wide World of Sports*. Blue collar America became interested in Jimmy Connors and professional tennis.[198]

Connors vs. Newcombe Challenge

After Connors won the challenge with Laver, Bill Riordan focused on a new challenge match with John Newcombe. In January of 1975, Newcombe had defeated Connors 7-5, 3-6, 6-4, 7-6 (9-7) in the final of the Australian Open before a capacity crowd of 12,500 at Kooyong Stadium in Melbourne.[199] The Connors vs. Newcombe challenge was scheduled for April 26 in Las Vegas for $250,000 "Winner-Take-All" again televised by CBS.[200] On April 26, Connors defeated Newcombe 6-3, 4-6, 6-2, 6-4 and collected nearly $500,000 while Newcombe netted about $250,000. *So much for "Winner-Take-All."*[201]

Challenge Matches Broke the Mold

Bill Riordan told Rich Koster in *The Tennis Bubble*[202]: "I've said the game was locked in a medieval vise. We freed it. Connors broke the mold. He gave it to the masses. That didn't ruin tournaments. It was the best thing ever. Tournaments are booming. If the game is going to grow and prospect, it can't be locked into just one concept."

More Nastase Misconduct

A perfect example of player misconduct and terrible officiating before the MIPTC had a Code of Conduct happened on April 5 at the ATP member-only $175,000 American Airlines Games semifinals in Tucson, Arizona. Ken Rosewall was leading Ilie Nastase 6-3, 5-4 when at 15-15, Nastase disagreed with a call and walked off the court and refused to continue play. The umpire, Boyd Morse, did nothing. Eventually, Nastase was persuaded by Richard Evans to continue. Rosewall's concentration and rhythm were then gone and he lost the match to Nastase. Nastase should have been defaulted.[203] In the final, John Alexander was leading 7-5, 4-2, when Nastase "visibly quit trying" and "flaunted his unhappiness by half-hearted waves of his racquet and soft serves."[204]

On May 16 at Bournemouth, Nastase was disqualified by chair umpire Eric Auger for "persistent arguing" during his quarterfinal match with Patrice Proisy of France. At the Italian Open, Nastase walked off the court and conceded his semifinal match to Raul Ramirez when the Mexican was leading 6-2, 5-2.[205] In Washington, Nastase was defaulted after having failed to resume play when ordered by the referee.[206] In the 1975 Canadian Open final, Nastase lost, 7-6, 6-0, 6-1, to Manuel Orantes amid charges that he had "not put forth an honest effort."[207] The MIPTC fined Nastase $8,000 for "conduct detrimental to the game" for his tanking of the finals in the Canadian Open.[208]

At the Commercial Union Masters in Stockholm, Nastase was defaulted in his first-round match against Arthur Ashe (President of ATP) for delaying play when Ashe was leading 1-6, 7-5, 4-1 and 40-15. Horst Klosterkemper, the West German Referee, issued the default after a telephone call with Derek Hardwick, President of the ILTF (and Chairman of the MIPTC). "What is important now for the good of the game is to develop a code of ethics for the players," Ashe said to the *New York Times*.[209] Ashe followed through with the 1st Code of Conduct at the MIPTC's December meeting.

First Code of Conduct: Arthur Ashe, Author

At the December meeting of the Council, the Canadian Lawn Tennis Association was the first national governing body to complain to the MIPTC concerning player behavior via a letter from Lawrence F. Strong, Vice President, dated October 30, recommending the adoption of a Code of Conduct and the development of professional officials. As promised, Arthur Ashe authored and championed the adoption of a Code of Conduct and because the Code was developed by and for the players, it was accepted by the players. After much discussion and consideration, the MIPTC adopted the first MIPTC Code of Conduct to be effective January 1, 1976, and ordered it to be distributed. Minor offenses and fines against players were authorized to be levied by the tournament committees upon report from the referee and/or a chair umpire, while major offenses were directed to a Grievance Committee. The Code specified fines for Punctuality Penalties, Court Behavior Penalties, Dress Violation Fines, Tournament Entry Fines, Tournament Offenses and Conduct Detrimental or Prejudicial to the Best Interest of Men's Professional Tennis.[210] While the first Code of Conduct was a terrific start for the MIPTC, the grievance procedure that required tournament committees, on report from the referee and a chair umpire, to issue and collect fines from players would prove to be ineffective. Every tournament committee spent every minute of every year to entice players to play in their tournaments, so they naturally had no appetite to fine or default players. Volunteer chair umpires and referees who had conflicts with players were often not invited back next year so they likewise have little appetite to fine or default players. This problem would not be solved for a number of years.

Crisis No. 14: Kramer vs. Riordan and Connors for Defamation

In response to the case filed by Jimmy Connors against Jack Kramer, Donald Dell and Commercial Union on July 3, 1974, (Crisis No. 13), Kramer filed a Complaint on April 10, 1975, against Riordan and Connors for defamation in the United States District Court for the Southern District of Indiana which became Crisis No. 14. Kramer alleged in his Complaint that Riordan and Connors "caused" the writing of a letter by his attorney that defamed Kramer when it said: "This kid [Connors] will save the game from the piranhas …. The Dells, Kramers, Hunts have weaved their web, they have reached their final act, they are blatantly illegal in trying to control tennis and all of its players;" and "ATP stands for three things – bans, boycotts and baloney. Jimmy and I have fought the monopolistic, monolithic, meanderings of those piranhas. Shotgun guys like Kramer, Dell and Hunt are like the people who promote the perfect dogfood and find out the dogs don't like it. They are strictly cold-blooded tennis propositioners who are only out for personal gain." As damages for the alleged defamation by Riordan and Connors, Kramer sought $1,000,000 in compensatory damages and $2,000,000 in punitive damages.[211] *As you might guess, Jimmy Connors had little or no knowledge of what his agent and the lawyer hired by Riordan was doing or saying, but now he was a defendant and probably paying the legal fees.*

Crises No. 15 and No. 16: Connors vs. Ashe and Riordan vs. Ashe, Kramer, Dell and Briner

On approximately June 20, 1975, just prior to 1975 Wimbledon, Riordan filed two additional lawsuits in the United States District Court for the Southern District of Indiana, Indianapolis Division. One on behalf of Jimmy Connors against Arthur Ashe, the President of ATP, for defamation in a letter he said that "Jimmy was brash, arrogant and unpatriotic." (Crisis No. 15). The other by Bill Riordan against Ashe, Kramer, Dell and Briner, for defamation for a Briner article referring to Riordan as a "nihilist" a copy of which was seen, but never actually published (Crisis No. 16).[212] Connors learned about these lawsuits two days before the beginning of Wimbledon in 1975. The lawsuits caused Connors to endure animosity from the players throughout Wimbledon which was a significant distraction for him. He ended up losing to Ashe in a four-set final.[213]

Settlement of Crises Nos. 12, 13, 14, 15 and 16

Immediately after losing to Ashe in the Wimbledon final, Connors had the lawsuit against Ashe withdrawn and in the week before the U.S. Open after hours of discussions, all the pending cases were settled. The *New York Times* reported that Connors "settled out of court for cash and a large life-insurance policy."[214]

Connors wrote in his book *The Outsider* in 2013: "I was young, I didn't understand it then, don't understand it now. Bill said that we had won, but the reality was different. The whole episode had been an incredible waste of time, energy, and money: neither side came out on top. As I recall, we ended up getting nowhere near the level of damages claimed in the press (obviously, I didn't see a penny of it), but it wasn't the outcome that really mattered. It had all been an unwelcome sideshow. All I wanted to do was play tennis."[215]

Soon thereafter, Connors finally split with Riordan. 1976 was the end of the USLTA Indoor Circuit as it was folded into the Grand Prix and Riordan lost the USTA National Indoors to Memphis in 1977. The split with Connors was the end of Riordan's IPA player "association", which maybe never had more than one member.[216]

The best I have been able to learn is that the only governance/rule issue obtained by Connors/Riordan as a result of these lawsuits was the agreement of the ATP to open its two member-only tournaments to all players in 1976, including Connors. Riordan did not get Jack Kramer to resign from the MIPTC. He did not get the USTA to resign from the ILTF. He did not get the WCT-ILTF Peace Agreement nullified although it died of its own volition after 1975. However, he did lose Jimmy and the ATP lost a lot of money on lawyers.

Riordan: "Jimmy Saved the Game"

Undaunted, Riordan told Rich Kostner in *The Bubble*[217]: "I claim that years from now, when the history of all this is written, instead of being vilified, people will say Jimmy saved the game. Every player, ten years from now will owe his tennis birthright to Jimmy Connors. Because he stood up to the establishment." Or was it just Riordan using Connors to stand up against Kramer and Dell? *Jimmy certainly never knew he was "saving the game" from the establishment.*

Kramer's Confession

In 1979 Kramer wrote in *The Game*[218]: "I'll admit it now: the French and the Italians were wrong to bar Jimmy and all the other WTT players. If the French and Italians wanted to fight WTT, fine – but they should not have used the players as weapons. My whole life, I've fought to open up the game for players, and this one time I got caught on the side that was trying to keep players out. As much, as I dislike contract players, they were the lesser of two evils in this case. It was the tournaments that violated the spirit of the Grand Prix. But I really had nothing to do with the decision, and I don't suppose it matters anyway. Bill was in a suing mood."[219]

Gloria Connors Managed Jimmy

After termination of Riordan as his manager, Jimmy Connors relied on his mother, Gloria Connors, to manage his career which included associations with Mark McCormack's IMG management company and Donald Dell's ProServ management company from time to time.

1975 Grand Slam Winners

Australian Open

John Newcombe d. Jimmy Connors 7-5, 3-6, 6-4, 7-6.
John Alexander – Phil Dent d. Bob Carmichael – Allen Stone 6-3, 7-6.

French Open

Bjorn Borg d. Guillermo Vilas 6-2, 6-3, 6-4.
Brian Gottfried – Raul Ramirez d. John Alexander – Phil Dent 6-4, 2-6, 6-2, 6-4.
[Note: Jimmy Connors refused to enter the 1975 French Open because he had been banned by the French Tennis Federation in 1974].

Wimbledon

Arthur Ashe d. Jimmy Connors 6-1, 6-1, 5-7, 6-4.
Vitas Gerulaitis – Sandy Mayer d. Colin Dowdeswell – Allen Stone 7-5, 8-6, 6-4.

U.S. Open (first year on clay)

Manuel Orantes d. Jimmy Connors 6-4, 6-3, 6-3.
Jimmy Connors – Ilie Nastase d. Tom Okker – Marty Riessen 6-4, 7-6.

1975 Davis Cup

Davis Cup Final (Stockholm - Indoors)

Sweden d. Czechoslovakia 3-2.

Bjorn Borg (SE) d. Jiri Hrebec (CZ) 6-1, 6-3, 6-0.
Jan Kodes (CZ) d. Ove Bengtson (SE) 4-6, 6-2, 7-5, 6-4.
O. Bengtson-B. Borg (SE) d J. Kodes-V. Zednik (CZ) 6-4, 6-4, 6-4.
Bjorn Borg (SE) d. Jan Kodes (CZ) 6-4, 6-2, 6-2.
Jiri Hrebec (CZ) d. Ove Bengtson (SE) 1-6, 6-3, 6-1, 6-4.

Nations Cup – Jamaica

United States d. Great Britain 2-1.

Roscoe Tanner (US) d. Roger Taylor (GB) 6-3, 2-6, 6-4.
Buster Mottram (GB) d. Arthur Ashe (US) 7-5, 5-7, 6-1.
Arthur Ashe – Roscoe Tanner (US) d. Buster Mottram – Roger Taylor (GB) 6-1, 1-6, 6-4.

1975 World Rankings[220]

Bud Collins

1.   Jimmy Connors
2.   Guillermo Vilas
3.   Bjorn Borg
4.   Arthur Ashe
5.   Manuel Orantes
6.   Ken Rosewall
7.   Ilie Nastase
8.   John Alexander
9.   Roscoe Tanner
10. Rod Laver

Lance Tingay

1.   Arthur Ashe
2.   Manuel Orantes
3.   Jimmy Connors
4.   Bjorn Borg
5.   Guillermo Vilas
6.   Ilie Nastase
7.   Raul Ramirez
8.   John Newcombe
9.   Rod Laver
10. Roscoe Tanner

Rino Tommasi

1.   Jimmy Connors
2.   Guillermo Vilas
3.   Bjorn Borg
4.   Arthur Ashe
5.   Rod Laver
6.   Manuel Orantes
7.   Ilie Nastase
8.   Ken Rosewall
9.   Tom Okker
10. Raul Ramirez

ATP Year End Rankings[221]

1.   Jimmy Connors
2.   Guillermo Vilas
3.   Bjorn Borg
4.   Arthur Ashe
5.   Manuel Orantes
6.   Ken Rosewall
7.   Ilie Nastase
8.   John Alexander
9.   Roscoe Tanner
10. Rod Laver

1975 Commercial Union Grand Prix Bonus Pool Top 10[222]

Singles (6th Bonus Pool)

1. Guillermo Vilas $100,000
2. Manuel Orantes $ 60,000

Doubles (1st Bonus Pool)

1T. Juan Gisbert $25,000
2T. Manuel Orantes $25,000

3. Bjorn Borg	$ 40,000	3. Brian Gottfried	$15,000
4. Arthur Ashe	$ 30,000	4. Raul Ramirez	$12,000
5. Ilie Nastase	$ 25,000	5. Ilie Nastase	$10,000
6. Jimmy Connors	*	6. Wojtek Fibak	$ 8,000
7. Raul Ramirez	$ 22,000	7. Hans Pohmann	$ 7,000
8. Adriano Panatta	$ 20,000	8. Jurgen Fassbender	$ 6,000
9. Harold Solomon	$ 18,000	9. Jan Kodes	$ 5,500
10. Eddie Dibbs	$ 17,000	10. Fred McNair	$ 5,000

*Did not play in enough tournaments to qualify.

1975 Official Earnings Top 10[223]

1.	Arthur Ashe	$326,750	6.	Ilie Nastase	$180,536
2.	Manuel Orantes	$269,785	7.	Brian Gottfried	$167,960
3.	Guillermo Vilas	$249,287	8.	Jimmy Connors	$163,135
4.	Bjorn Borg	$221,088	9.	Roscoe Tanner	$150,459
5.	Raul Ramirez	$211,385	10.	John Alexander	$138,050

1975 Tournament Calendar

Date	Tournaments	Singles Winner	Singles #2	Doubles Winners	Doubles #2
1/1/1975	Australian Open $70,000 B	John Newcombe	Jimmy Connors	J. Alexander - P. Dent	B. Carmichael - A. Stone
1/12/1975	Auckland	Onny Parun	Brian Fairlie	B. Carmichael - R. Ruffels	B. Fairlie - O. Parun
1/19/1975	Baltimore $50,000 USLTA	Brian Gottfried	Allen Stone	D. Crealy - R. Ruffels	F. McMillan - I. El Shafei
1/19/1975	Freeport $50,000 USLTA	Jimmy Connors	Karl Meiler		
1/19/1975	Puerto Rico $60,000 WCT CBS	Rod Laver	Arthur Ashe	6-3, 7-5	
1/26/1975	Philadelphia $115,000 WCT	Marty Riessen	Vitas Gerulaitis	B. Gottfried - R. Ramirez	D. Stockton - E. Van Dillon
1/26/1975	Birmingham $30,000 USLTA	Jimmy Connors	Billy Martin		
2/1/1975	Dayton $30,000 USLTA	Brian Gottfried	Geoff Masters		
2/2/1975	Las Vegas Challenge SP	Jimmy Connors	Rod Laver	6-4, 6-2, 3-6, 7-5	
2/2/1975	Richmond $60,000 WCT Green	Bjorn Borg	Arthur Ashe	H. Kary - F. McNair	P. Bertolucci - A. Panatta
2/2/1975	Roanoke $30,000 USLTA	Roger Taylor	Vitas Gerulaitis		
2/9/1975	St. Pete. $60,000 WCT Blue	Raul Ramirez	Roscoe Tanner	B. Gottfried - R. Ramirez	C. Pasarell - R. Tanner
2/9/1975	Little Rock $25,000 USLTA	Billy Martin	George Hardie	M. Lara - B. Phillips-Moore	J. Austin - C. Owens
2/9/1975	Basle	Jiri Hrebec	Ilie Nastase		
2/12/1975	Bologna $60,000 WCT Green	Bjorn Borg	Arthur Ashe	P. Bertolucci - A. Panatta	A. Ashe - T. Okker
2/16/1975	Toronto $60,000 WCT Red	Harold Solomon	Stan Smith	D. Stockton - E. Van Dillon	An. Amritraj - V. Amritraj
2/16/1975	Salisbury $50,000 USLTA	Jimmy Connors	Vitas Gerulaitis	J. Connors - I. Nastase	J. Kodes - R. Taylor
2/23/1975	Carlsbad $60,000 WCT Blue	Rod Laver	Allen Stone	B. Gottfried - R. Ramirez	C. Pasarell - R. Tanner

Date	Event	Winner	Finalist	Doubles Winner	Doubles Finalist
2/23/1975	Barcelona $60,000 WCT Green	Arthur Ashe	Bjorn Borg	A. Ashe - T. Okker	P. Bertolucci - A. Panatta
2/23/1975	Fort Worth $60,000 WCT Red	John Alexander	Dick Stockton	B. Lutz - S. Smith	J. Alexander - P. Dent
2/23/1975	Boca Raton $25,000 ProServ SP	Jimmy Connors	Jurgen Fassbender		
3/2/1975	Fairfield $30,900 USLTA	Roger Taylor	Sandy Mayer		
3/2/1975	San Antonio $60,000 WCT Red	Dick Stockton	Stan Smith	J. Alexander - P. Dent	M. Cox - C. Drysdale
3/2/1975	Rotterdam $60,000 WCT Green	Arthur Ashe	Tom Okker	B. Hewitt - F. McMillan	J. Higeras - B. Taroczy
3/8/1975	London WCT SP	Mark Cox	Brian Fairlie	P. Bertolucci - A. Panatta	J. Fassbender - H. Pohlman
3/9/1975	Cairo	Manuel Orantes	Francois Jauffret		
3/9/1975	Shreveport $15,000 USLTA	Juan Gisbert	Wojtek Fibak	B. Brown - J. Gisbert	J. Benyik - R. Machan
3/9/1975	Hartford $37,500 WCT WC SP	Australia	USA	4-3,	
3/9/1975	Hartford $37,500 WCT WC SP	Rod Laver	Dick Stockton	5-7. 6-4, 7-6	
3/9/1975	Hartford $37,500 WCT WC SP	John Newcombe	Arthur Ashe	6-7, 6-4, 6-2	
3/9/1975	Hartford $37,500 WCT WC SP	Stan Smith	Ken Rosewall	6-2, 7-6	
3/9/1975	Hartford $37,500 WCT WC SP	Dick Stockton	John Newcombe	4-6, 6-4, 6-2	
3/9/1975	Hartford $37,500 WCT WC SP		6-3, 2-6, 6-3	R. Laver - J. Newcombe	B. Lutz - S. Smith
3/9/1975	Hartford $37,500 WCT WC SP	Rod Laver	Arthur Ashe	6-2, 7-6	
3/9/1975	Hartford $37,500 WCT WC SP		3-6, 6-3, 7-6	A. Ashe -D. Stockton	J. Alexander - K. Rosewall
3/16/1975	Washington $60,000 WCT Red	Mark Cox	Dick Stockton	M. Estep - R. Simpson	An. Amritraj - V. Amritraj
3/16/1975	Munich $60,000 WCT Green	Arthur Ashe	Bjorn Borg	B. Hewitt - F. McMillan	C. Barazzutti - A. Zugarelli

3/16/1975	Sao Paulo $60,000 WCT Blue	Rod Laver	Charlie Pasarell	R. Case - G. Masters	B. Gottfried - R. Ramirez
3/16/1975	Hampton $35.000 USLTA	Jimmy Connors	Jan Kodes	I. Crookenden - I. Fletcher	K. Meiler - J. Pisecky
3/23/1975	Memphis $60,000 WCT Red	Harold Solomon	Jiri Hrebec	D. Stockton - E. Van Dillon	M. Cox - C. Drysdale
3/23/1975	Caracas $60,000 WCT Blue	Rod Laver	Raul Ramirez	R. Case - G. Masters	B. Gottfried - R. Ramirez
3/23/1975	New York $25,000 USLTA	Vitas Gerulatis	Jimmy Connors		
3/30/1975	Monte Carlo $60K WCT Green	Manuel Orantes	Bob Hewitt	B. Hewitt - F. McMillan	A. Ashe - T. Okker
3/30/1975	Atlanta $60,000 WCT Red	Mark Cox	John Alexander	An. Amritraj - V. Amritraj	M. Cox - C. Drysdale
3/30/1975	Orlando $60,000 WCT Blue	Rod Laver	Vitas Gerulaitis	B. Gottfried - R. Ramirez	C. Dibley - R. Ruffles
3/30/1975	Jackson $35,000 USLTA	Ken Rosewall	Butch Buchholz		
4/6/1975	Tucson $175,000 ATP	John Alexander	Ilie Nastase	B. Brown - R. Ramirez	R. Moore - D. Ralston
4/6/1975	Washington $25,000	Alex Metreveli	Haroon Rahim	V. Gerulaitis - C. Graebner	T. Kakulia - A. Metreveli
4/13/1975	St. Louis $60,000 WCT Blue	Vitas Gerulatis	Roscoe Tanner	C. Dibley - R. Ruffles	R. Case - G. Masters
4/13/1975	Barcelona	Ilie Nastase	Juan Gisbert		
4/19/1975	Johannesburg $60K WCT Green	Buster Mottram	Tom Okker	A. Ashe - T. Okker	B. Hewitt - F. McMillan
4/20/1975	Denver $60K WCT Blue	Jimmy Connors	Brian Gottfried	R. Emerson - R. Laver	B. Carmichael - A. Stone
4/20/1975	Tokyo $60,000 WCT Red	Bob Lutz	Stan Smith	B. Lutz - S. Smith	J. Alexander - P. Dent
4/20/1975	Valencia	Ilie Nastase	Manuel Orantes		
4/20/1975	Buenos Aires	Guillermo Vilas	Clark Graebner	M. Santana - G. Vilas	J. Ganzabal - C. Graebner
4/26/1975	Los Vegas $250K Challenge SP	Jimmy Connors	John Newcombe	6-3, 4-6, 6-2, 6-4	
4/27/1975	Houston $60,000 WCT Red	Ken Rosewall	Cliff Drysdale	B. Lutz - S. Smith	M. Estep - J. Simpson

Date	Tournament	Winner	Finalist	Doubles Winners	Doubles Finalists
4/27/1975	Stockholm $60,000 WCT Green	Arthur Ashe	Tom Okker	A. Ashe - T. Okker	P. Dominguez - K. Warwick
4/27/1975	Charlotte $60,000 WCT Blue	Raul Ramirez	Roscoe Tanner	P. Cornejo - J. Fillol	B. Fairlie - I. El Shafei
4/27/1975	Madrid	Ilie Nastase	Manuel Orantes		
5/4/1975	Mexico City $90,000 WCT Doubles			B. Gottfried - R. Ramirez	M. Cox - C. Drysdale
5/5/1975	Nice	Dick Crealy	Ivan Molina	M. Lara - J. Loyo-Mayo	I.. Molina - J. Velasco
5/11/1975	Munich $50,000 B	Guillermo Vilas	Karl Meiler	W. Fibak - J. Kodes	H. Elschenbroich - M. Holeoek
5/11/1975	Dallas $100,000 WCT Finals	Arthur Ashe	Bjorn Borg	3-6, 6-4, 6-4, 6-0	
5/11/1975	Florence	Paolo Bertolucci	Georges Govern		
5/12/1975	Dallas $35,000 WCT SP			B. Gottfried - R. Ramirez	B. Hewitt - F. McMillan
5/18/1975	Bournemouth $50,000 B	Manuel Orantes	Patrick Proisy	J. Gisbert - M. Orantes	S. Ball - D. Crealy
5/18/1975	Los Vegas $150,000 ATP	Roscoe Tanner	Ross Case	J. Alexander - P. Dent	B. Carmichael - C. Drysdale
5/25/1975	Hamburg $100,000 AA	Manuel Orantes	Jan Kodes	J. Gisbert - M. Orantes	W. Fibak - J. Kodes
5/31/1975	Surbiton	Peter McNamara	Steve Dockerty	G.M. Orapez - C.S. Wells	D.H. Collings - C. Robertson
6/1/1975	Dusseldorf $50,000 B	Jaime Fillol	Jan Kodes	F. Jauffret - J. Kodes	H. Elschenbroich - H. Kary
6/1/1975	Rome $120,000 AA	Raul Ramirez	Manuel Orantes	B. Gottfried - R. Ramirez	J. Connors - I. Nastase
6/7/1975	Chichester	Syd Ball	Bernie Mitten	S. Ball - B. Mottram	P. McNamara - A. Russel
6/14/1975	Beckenham	Arthur Ashe	Roscoe Tanner	F. McNair - S. Stewart	A. Ashe - R. Tanner
6/15/1975	French Open $172,000 GS	Bjorn Borg	Guillermo Vilas	B. Gottfried - R. Ramirez	J. Alexander - P. Dent
6/21/1975	Nottingham $108,000 AA	Tom Okker	Tony Roche	C. Pasarell - R. Tanner	T. Okker - M. Reissen
6/21/1975	Eastbourne	Mark Cox	Teimuraz Kakulia	A. Amritraj - M. Estep	W. Brown - T. Kakulia

7/5/1975	Wimbledon $266,000 GS	Arthur Ashe	Jimmy Connors	V. Gerulaitis - S. Mayer	C. Dowdeswell - A. Stone
7/12/1975	Dublin	Alvin Gardiner	A.G. Fawcett	W. Ewart - A.G. Fawcett	R. Farlain - H.K. Richards
7/13/1975	Gstaad $50,000 B	Ken Rosewall	Karl Meiler	J. Fassbender - H. Pohlman	C. Dowdeswell - K. Rosewall
7/13/1975	Bastad $50,000 B	Manuel Orantes	Jose Higuras	O. Bengtson - B. Borg	J. Gilbert - M. Orantes
7/13/1975	Kitzbuhel $50,000 B	Adriano Panatta	Jan Kodes	P. Bertolucci - A. Panatta	P. Dominguez - F. Jauffret
7/13/1975	Raleigh $5,000 Southern Chps.	Hank Pfister	Sashi Menon	B. Brock - T. Dixon	C. Hagey - S. Menon
7/20/1975	Hilversum $50,000 B	Guillermo Vilas	Zeljko Franulovic	W. Fibak - G. Vilas	Z. Franulovic - J. Lloyd
7/20/1975	Chicago $50,000 B	Roscoe Tanner	John Alexander	J. Alexander - P. Dent	M. Cahill - J. Whitlinger
7/20/1975	Istanbul	Colin Dowdeswell	Ferdi Taygan	C. Dibley - T. Koch	C. Dowdeswell - J. Feaver
7/27/1975	Washington $100,000 AA	Guillermo Vilas	Harold Solomon	B. Lutz - S. Smith	B. Gottfried - R. Ramirez
8/3/1975	Louisville $100,000 AA	Guillermo Vilas	Ilie Nastase	W. Fibak - G. Vilas	B. Gottfried - R. Ramirez
8/3/1975	Cincinnati $60,000 B	Tom Gorman	Sherwood Stewart	P. Dent - C. Drysdale	M. Lara - J. Loyo Mayo
8/10/1975	North Conway $50,000 B	Jimmy Connors	Ken Rosewall	E. Van Dillon - H. Rahim	J. Alexander - P. Dent
8/10/1975	Indianapolis $100,000 AA	Manuel Orantes	Arthur Ashe	J. Gisbert - M. Orantes	W. Fibak - H. Pohlmann
8/17/1975	Toronto $130,000 AA	Manuel Orantes	Ilie Nastase	C. Drysdale - R. Moore	J. Kodes - I. Nastase
8/18/1975	Columbus $50,000 B	Vjay Amritraj	Bob Lutz	B. Lutz - S. Smith	J. Fassbender - H. Pohlman
8/24/1975	Boston $100,000 AA	Bjorn Borg	Guillermo Vilas	B. Gottfried - R. Ramirez	J. Andrews - M. Estep
8/24/1975	Orange $50,000 B	Ilie Nastase	Bob Hewitt	J. Connors - I. Nastase	D. Crealy - J. Lloyd
9/7/1975	US Open $290,680 GS	Manuel Orantes	Jimmy Connors	J. Connors - I. Nastase	T. Okker - M. Reissen
9/21/1975	Los Angeles $100,000 AA	Arthur Ashe	Roscoe Tanner	An. Amritraj - V. Amritraj	C. Drysdale - M. Reissen
9/21/1975	Bermuda	Jimmy Connors	Vitas Gerulaitis		
9/28/1975	San Francisco $100,000 AA	Arthur Ashe	Guillermo Vilas	F. McNair - S. Stewart	A. Stone - K. Warwick

10/5/1975	Honolulu $50,000 B	Jimmy Connors	Sandy Mayer	F. McNair - S. Stewart	J. Borowiak - H. Rahim
10/5/1975	Aviles	Nikki Pilic	Juan Muntanola		
10/5/1975	Kingston $100,000 ATP NC	USA	Great Briain	2-1,	
10/5/1975	Kingston $100,000 ATP NC	Roscoe Tanner	Roger Taylor	6-3, 2-6, 6-4	
10/5/1975	Kingston $100,000 ATP NC	Buster Mottram	Arthur Ashe	7-5, 5-7, 6-1	
10/5/1975	Kingston $100,000 ATP NC		6-1, 1-6, 6-4	A. Ashe - R. Tanner	B. Mottram - R. Taylor
10/12/1975	Madrid $75,000 A	Jan Kodes	Adriano Panatta	J. Kodes - I. Nastase	J. Gisbert - M. Orantes
10/12/1975	Melbourne $50,000 B	Brian Gottfried	Harold Solomon	R. Case - G. Masters	B. Gottfried - R. Ramirez
10/19/1975	Barcelona $75,000 A	Bjorn Borg	Adriano Panatta	B. Borg - G. Vilas	W. Fibak - K. Meiler
10/19/1975	Sydney $100,000 AA	Stan Smith	Bob Lutz	B. Gottfried - R. Ramirez	R. Case - G. Masters
10/26/1975	Tehran $100,000 AA	Eddie Dibbs	Ivan Molina	J. Gisbert - M. Orantes	B. Hewitt - F. McMillan
10/26/1975	Perth $50,000 B	Harold Solomon	Sandy Mayer	B. Gottfried - R. Ramirez	R. Case - G. Masters
11/2/1975	Paris $50,000 B	Tom Okker	Arthur Ashe	W. Fibak - K. Meiler	I. Nastase - T. Okker
11/2/1975	Manilla $50,000 B	Ross Case	Corrado Barazzuti	R. Case - G. Masters	S. Ball - K. Warwick
11/9/1975	Tokyo $100,000 AA	Raul Ramirez	Manuel Orantes	B. Gottfried - R. Ramirez	J. Gisbert - M. Orantes
11/9/1975	Stockholm $100,000 AA	Adriano Panatta	Jimmy Connors	W. Fibak - K. Meiler	J. Connors - I. Nastase
11/15/1975	Dewar Cup $94,000 A	Eddie Dibbs	Jimmy Connors	J. Connors - I. Nastase	W. Fibak - K. Meiler
11/16/1975	Hong Kong $50,000 B	Tom Gorman	Sandy Mayer	T. Okker - K. Rosewall	B. Carmichael - S. Mayer
11/16/1975	Buenos Aires A	Guillermo Vilas	Adriano Panatta	P. Bertolucci - A. Panatta	J. Fassbender - H. Pohlman
11/23/1975	Calcutta $75,000 A	Vjay Amritraj	Manuel Orantes	J. Gisbert - M. Orantes	An. Amritraj - V. Amritraj

11/25/1975	Johannesburg $100,000 AA	Harold Solomon	Brian Gottfried	B. Hewitt - F. McMillan	K. Meiler - C. Pasarell
11/27/1975	Helsinki $15,000	Ilie Nastase	Wojtek Fibak		
12/7/1975	Stockholm $130,000 CU Masters	Ilie Nastase	Bjorn Borg	J. Gisbert - M. Orantes	J. Fassbender - H. Pohlman
12/7/1975	Adelaide	Syd Ball	John Lloyd	M. Anderson - D. Dibley	S. Ball - B. Giltinan
12/14/1975	Brisbane	Mal Anderson	Mark Edmondson		
12/14/1975	Perth	Ray Ruffels	John Lloyd	S. Ball - R. Case	C. Dibley - R. Ruffels
12/21/1975	Sydney $37,800	Ross Case	John Marks	M. Edmonson - J. Marks	C. Kachel - P. McNamara
10/24/1975	Hilton Head $135,000 SP	Ilie Nastase	Rod Laver	E. Goolagong - R. Laver Mxd	R. Casals - I. Nastase

http://www.atpworldtour.com/en/scores/results-archive.

http://www.itftennis.com/procircuit/tournaments/men's-calendar.aspx?tour=&reg=&nat=&sur=&cate=AL&iod=& fromDate=01-01-1968&toDate=29-12-1975

Tennis History, Jim McManus, (Canada 2010).

1976 USLTA Yearbook.

Official 1989 MTC Media Guide, (MTC 1989).

World of Tennis '76, Edited by John Barrett compiled by Lance Tingay, (London 1976).

CHAPTER 10:

1976: MIPTC EXPANDS, WCT ANTI-TRUST THREAT, CRISIS NO. 17

The ILTF, WCT, ATP, USTA and WTT marched into 1976, relatively at peace with each other. In 1976 the MIPTC did not schedule Commercial Union Grand Prix tournaments in the 1st 4 months of the year against WCT.

1976 Governing Bodies

The MIPTC was the governing body of men's professional tennis in 1976, except for WCT, WTT and the Davis Cup. The Davis Cup Nations still governed the Davis Cup.

1976 Significant Tennis Leaders

ILTF President:	Derek Hardwick (Great Britain)
USTA President:	Stan Malless
Australian LTA President:	Wayne Reid
British LTA President:	Sir Carl Aarvold
French FFT President:	Philippe Chatrier
Chairman of Wimbledon:	Sir Brian Burnett
ATP President:	Arthur Ashe
ATP Executive Director:	Jack Kramer until April
ATP Executive Director:	Bob Briner beginning in April
WCT Owners:	Lamar Hunt and Al Hill, Jr.
WCT Executive Director:	Mike Davies

1976 MIPTC

In the 1976 MIPTC elections, the MIPTC was expanded from 7 to 10 members, adding three Tournament Representatives beginning with the August 30-31, MIPTC meeting.

ILTF: Derek Hardwick, Chairman, Stan Malless, Paolo Angeli and Phillipe Chatrier with David Gray as Joint Secretary.

Players: Bob Briner, Arthur Ashe and Pierre Darmon with Doug Tkachuk as Joint Secretary.

Tournaments: Jack Kramer (North America), Lars Myhrman (Europe) and Owen Williams (Rest of the World).

Five Competitions

In 1976, the ninth year of Open Tennis, there were five organized competitions for men: the USTA-IPA US Indoor Circuit, WCT, Commercial Union Grand Prix, Davis Cup and WTT. There were 10 U.S. Indoor tournaments known as the USTA Indoor Circuit or the IPA/Riordan Circuit, organized by Bill Riordan in competition with the WCT time period in the first four months of the year. WCT promoted 30 WCT professional tournaments and events: The WCT point series of 27 tournaments included Philadelphia ($115,000) 32 draw, plus 24 ($100,000) 16 draw tournaments, leading to the WCT Finals in Dallas ($100,000) and the WCT Doubles Finals in Kansas City ($100,000). Bjorn Borg defeated Guillermo Vilas 1-6, 6-1, 7-5, 6-1 in Dallas and Wojtek Fibak and Karl Meiler defeated Bob Lutz and Stan Smith 6-3, 2-6, 3-6, 6-3, 6-4, in Kansas City.

WCT also staged three special events: Aetna World Cup ($70,000) in which the United States defeated Australia 6-1, Avis Challenge Cup Round Robin ($320,000) in Hawaii January 22 – May 3, and the Caesar's Palace Challenge Cup ($320,000) in Las Vegas December 12-19. Ilie Nastase defeated Arthur Ashe in the finals of the Avis Challenge Cup 6-3, 1-6, 6-7, 6-3, 6-1. Ilie Nastase defeated Jimmy Connors in the finals of the Caesar's Palace Challenge Cup 3-6, 7-6, 6-4, 7-5. The WCT-ILTF Peace Agreement had been terminated so WCT could have 16 draw qualifying tournaments instead of 32 draws and there was no restriction on the number of special events. While the MIPTC could have scheduled the Grand Prix to begin against WCT in January, it did not do so until 1977.

There were 49 Commercial Union Grand Prix Open prize money tournaments, including the year-end Commercial Union Masters in Houston won by Manuel Orantes over Wojtek Fibak 5-7, 6-2, 0-6, 7-6, 6-1. Ilie Nastase, Jimmy Connors and Bjorn Borg did not play in the Masters in 1976. Fred McNair and Sherwood Stewart defeated Brian Gottfried and Raul Ramirez 6-3, 5-7, 5-7, 6-4, 6-4 for the Doubles Masters.

WTT had franchises in 10 U.S. cities with matches from May through August, in conflict with the European Spring tournaments (Italian Open, French Open, etc.) and the American summer tournaments. Non-Grand Prix tournaments included nine European Spring $30,000 tournaments and two non-Grand Prix ATP (now open to all players, ATP members and non-ATP members, courtesy of the Connors' lawsuits) fundraiser tournaments: American Airlines Games ($200,000) in Palm Springs, won by Jimmy Connors over Roscoe Tanner 6-4, 6-4 in singles and by Colin Dibley and Sandy Mayer over Ray Moore and Erik van Dillen 6-4, 6-7, 7-6 in doubles, and the Alan King Caesar's Palace Classic ($150,000) in Las Vegas, won by Jimmy Connors over Ken Rosewall 6-1, 6-3 in singles and by Arthur Ashe and Charles Pasarell over Bob Lutz and Stan Smith 6-4, 6-2 in doubles. *Thus, the Connors' lawsuits that opened these ATP tournaments to him was fruitful.*

In addition, there were two challenge matches. In Gothenberg, Sweden ($100,000), Bjorn Borg defeated Rod Laver 6-4, 6-2, 7-5 in the first challenge match in Europe. Borg won the $100,000 while Laver received only $6,000.[224] In Las Vegas, Jimmy Connors defeated Manuel Orantes 6-2, 6-1, 6-0 and won the $250,000 prize. Both players were expected to receive an additional $200,000 from the television rights.[225] I found 18 other unaffiliated prize money tournaments.

Rules

The grouping of tournaments was changed to six groups (Triple Crown and 1, 2, 3, 4, and 5 Star tournaments). The Australian Open was a "2 Star" category tournament in 1976, while the other three Grand Slams were in the "Triple Crown" category. The 1976 Bonus Pool was $1,000,000 with $800,000 in 35 singles prizes ranging from $150,000 to $8,000 and 20 doubles prizes ranging from $40,000 to $3,000. Every player was required to play in at least three (3) 1 Star and/or 2 Star tournaments. There was no up-front tournament commitment so the tournaments would still not know who was going to enter until the new 60-day entry deadline. That was still too late for any meaningful promotional publicity.

The MIPTC Tournament Regulations were part of the Grand Prix Rules and no longer just an Appendix. The ATP Computer Rankings were again approved for the 1976 Grand Prix for all tournaments (no more preference to last year's Bonus Pool standings.) The tournament entry deadline was moved from 30 to 60 days. Singles computer rankings were given preference over new doubles computer rankings for doubles entries. The responsibility for the referee to enforce the new MIPTC Code of Conduct was added.[226] *It was never going to work to have a referee hired by the tournament issue fines against players that the tournament was recruiting like mad to get to enter the tournament every year.*

MIPTC Meetings

In 1976, the MIPTC held nine meetings: January 8-10 in the Dominican Republic, March 9-10 in London, April 12 in Majorca, May 25 in New York, June 19-20, 22, 26, 29 in New York, August 30-31 in New York, September 3 in New York, October 25-27 in London and December 8-9, 11-12 in Houston.

In the Dominican Republic in January, it was explained that Bonus Pool Points for the Davis Cup were deleted "because 100 percent of the ATP players voted against having them." Only a limited number of players could be selected for the Davis Cup each year and the rank-and-file players considered it to give them an unfair advantage for the Bonus Pool if they received Bonus Pool Points.

In connection with the establishment of the new nine-member MIPTC in 1976, it was agreed, subject to approval by the ILTF, that Derek Hardwick, the current Chairman of the MIPTC who was also the President of the ILTF until July of 1977, would continue to be MIPTC Chairman until July of 1977, with no voting rights. Thereafter, the new nine-member MIPTC would select the Chairman and if the Chairman was not one of the nine MIPTC members, the Chairman would have no vote. The ILTF Representatives assumed that Philippe Chatrier would be elected to succeed Derek Hardwick as the incoming new president of the ILTF and that he would be elected as the non-voting Chairman of the Council. *That did not quite work out!*

In addition, it was agreed that if one of the three parties, ILTF, Players or Tournaments felt that the MIPTC was not working for the benefit of professional tennis, the whole body would be dissolved and negotiations would start to form a new body. *No long-term commitments by anyone!* The MIPTC confirmed that the new nine-member MIPTC would have complete autonomy over the sanctioning of all tournaments with $17,500 or more in prize money, the discipline of players and tournaments and the administration of the Grand Prix; this ended the argument that the national associations had to also issue a sanction.[227]

In London in March, it was agreed that the 1977 Grand Prix would be scheduled from January 3, 1977, through November 27, 1977, with the Masters tournament December 5-11, 1977. This would be the first time since the ILTF-WCT Peace Agreement that the Grand Prix would be competing with WCT. *Do you think that might lead to a new lawsuit with WCT?*

In addition, it was agreed that the 150 players authorized to vote on the selection of the three player representatives for the new nine-member MIPTC would be selected from both the ATP Computer Ranking System and the new USTA Computer Ranking System. The top 130 players on each computer ranking list would be authorized and then one from each list would be added for the remaining 20 players authorized to vote. This is the first mention of the new USTA Computer Ranking System which Stan Malless was pushing for adoption by the MIPTC over the ATP Computer Ranking System.[228]

Commercial Union Withdraws

In Majorca in April, Commercial Union announced that it would not exercise its option to sponsor the 1977 and 1978 Grand Prix and that its sponsorship would end after the 1976 Masters; understandably, a panic ensued to find a new Grand Prix sponsor.[229]

Colgate Sponsorship Proposed

In New York in May, the MIPTC agreed with various provisions for a proposed new Colgate Grand Prix sponsorship agreement with Colgate Palmolive: three-year term for 1977, 1978 and 1979 with option for 1980 and 1981, Bonus Pool contributions: 1977: $600,000, 1978: $675,000, 1979: $750,000, 1980 Option: $825,000, 1981 Option: $900,000, with Masters Tournament prize money to be $250,000. Colgate was to have all rights to the Masters tournament except there was a pending issue about who would have the television rights to the Masters.[230]

In New York in June, the MIPTC objected to Colgate as the proposed sponsor of the Grand Prix as it wanted to also sponsor the women's Grand Prix and Colgate withdrew its offer of sponsorship.[231] *So, the panic for a new sponsor began again.*

MIPTC Election

In New York in August was the first meeting of the new nine-member MIPTC after its elections. Deloitte, Haskins and Sells, the accounting firm that conducted the elections of the Player Representatives and the Tournament Representatives, reported: (i) Only 54 of 150 players voted and Cliff Drysdale, Bob Briner and Pierre Darmon were elected; (ii) Only 21 of 32 European tournaments voted and Lars Myhrman was elected. Myhrman was the Tournament Director of the Swedish National Championships in Bastad and thus was aligned with the Swedish national association, a member of the ILTF; (iii) Only 22 of 37 United States tournaments voted and Jack Kramer was elected with 31 votes over Mike Davies' 29 votes; (iv) Only 16 of 23 "Rest of the World" tournaments voted and Owen Williams was elected with 22 votes over Wayne Reid's 21 votes. Wayne Reid was President of the Australian national association and thereby aligned with the ILTF. Owen Williams was the tournament director of the South African Championships, one of the "official" ILTF international championships. History showed that on many contested issues, the voting tended to be 4-4 with Lars Myhrman voting with the ILTF Representatives and Jack Kramer voting with the Player Representatives, thus leaving Owen Williams as the "swing vote."

The ILTF appointed Stan Malless, Philippe Chatrier and Paolo Angeli as its three ILTF Representatives and Derek Hardwick remained as Chairman until his term as ILTF President ended in July 1977. Chatrier hoped as the new President of the ILTF to succeed Hardwick as Chairman. David Gray was appointed as the ILTF Joint Secretary and Doug Tkachuk was appointed as the ATP Joint Secretary, so there was no consolidation of the Secretary position. The ILTF and the ATP did not trust each other very much even though they always worked together to govern the sport.

It was agreed that effective December 31, 1976, no member of the MIPTC should be allowed to serve on any international women's tennis council. Derek Hardwick had unsuccessfully argued that both the MIPTC and a women's Council should have the same chairman to assist in the coordination between the men and the women's tours. *The lack of interest by the men players and the men's tournaments in the women or their competitiveness with the women would endure.*

Up to this time, the MIPTC had devoted much of its meetings to dealing with Code of Conduct fines. At this meeting, it was agreed that in the future the Joint Secretaries would deal with the penalties imposed under the Code, with the Council to be consulted in special circumstances only. This gave the Joint Secretaries a lot of new administrative authority. It also did not work. Neither the ATP Joint Secretary or the ILTF Joint Secretary was equipped to enforce fines against players.

The tentative proposed 1977 calendar for the first half of the year was agreed. This calendar included Grand Prix tournaments throughout the "traditional" WCT period of January to May. *Sounds like a big conflict is coming with WCT in 1977!*[232]

Colgate Sponsorship

In New York in September, since Colgate had withdrawn its sponsorship offer, the MIPTC was in a panic to find a new sponsor for 1977. At this meeting, the MIPTC agreed to appoint the consortium of West and Nally and Dell, Craighill, Fentress and Benton as exclusive agents until October 23 to find a new sponsor for the 1977 Grand Prix. Dell and Briner were working behind the scenes to revive Colgate. Dell wanted to represent Colgate.[233]

In London in October, the sponsorship of Colgate Palmolive with the MIPTC for the sponsorship of the Grand Prix was resurrected and the sponsorship contract dated October 20, presented by Colgate was approved, accepted and signed by Derek Hardwick for the MIPTC. The terms as previously presented were accepted with a three-year term for 1977, 1978 and 1979, plus an option for 1980 and 1981. Bob Briner also signed to evidence approval by ATP. Notwithstanding the MIPTC's objection, Colgate also became the sponsor of the women's circuit beginning in 1977 to be known as the "Colgate Series."[234]

Colgate hired ProServ (Donald Dell) to stage the Colgate Masters and Colgate funded a Colgate promotional staff to promote its sponsorship of the Colgate Grand Prix and the Colgate Series. In 1977, a young intern named Jerry Solomon began his tennis career with Colgate. He would later become the president of ProServ. Colgate and ProServ moved the Colgate Masters into January in Madison Square Garden. The Masters would continue in January through January of 1986. This caused big problems for the Australian grass tournaments and the Australian Open since most top players were reluctant to fly to Australia in December – January to play on grass before returning to the United States to play indoors.

At this meeting a motion was approved that an administrator acceptable to the majority of the Council should be appointed as soon as possible. At this time the parties could not even agree that the MIPTC would permanently continue. This is 1976 and I was not appointed until 1981. *A slight delay.*[235]

ATP and USTA Computer Rankings

In Houston in December, the MIPTC adopted the ATP Computer Ranking system as the system of merit for the selection of players for the 1977 Grand Prix with the condition that any proposed changes be reported to the MIPTC before any amendments were made. The USTA had developed its own new USTA Computer rankings which it contended was a better ranking system than the ATP Computer ranking system since it was based on the actual strength of the fields in tournaments and not merely points per round based on prize money as in the ATP Computer Ranking system. The USTA was permitted to publish the USTA Computer rankings at frequent intervals so that, after six months, the players could evaluate the two systems and decide which list they preferred in the future.

Finally ATP Computer Points for Satellites

Between 1973 and 1975, there were several small (less than $25,000 per tournament) prize money circuits in the United States. Larry Turville and Armistead Neely were administering the Florida WATCH satellite circuit. I was administering the two Southern satellite circuits for the Southern Tennis Association and Alex Aitchison was administering the American Express satellite circuit from the Port Washington Tennis Academy. Administering the circuits required us to solicit entries, evaluate the player records and accept the entries and determine the seedings for the tournaments. None of the players on these circuits were awarded any ATP points and all of them were upset that entry into the Grand Prix tournaments and into the few tournaments with $25,000 in prize money was not available to them except as wild cards. The ATP divisor of 12 ensured that until a player earned 12 points, he still could not gain entry over an original ATP member with a one-point average and who had not won a match in an entire year. I had been having a discussion with Jack Kramer as Executive Director of ATP for several years about getting ATP points for the satellite circuits as had Turville and Neely. After Bob Briner succeeded Kramer as ATP Executive Director in 1976, and Jim McManus moved into management with the ATP, Jim became the key ATP leader who found a way to open the ATP Computer Rankings to the up-and-coming young professionals and every young player needs to know about him. When he passed away in Ponte Vedra in 2011, the ATP Tour named its headquarters building the "Jim McManus Building" in his honor.

Jim McManus and Bob Briner agreed to award ATP Computer Points in 1976 to satellite circuits on the basis that a five-tournament satellite circuit with $5,000 per tournament would be treated as one $25,000 tournament by ATP. It, of course, took five weeks of play and only the top six players received ATP points on a scale of 8, 6, 4, 3, 2, 1, in a $25,000 satellite circuit. Circuits could have more than five tournaments. Circuits with $36,000 in prize money awarded points to nine players on a scale of 14, 12, 10, 8, 6, 4, 3, 2, 1. Circuits with $56,000 in prize money awarded points to 12 players on a scale of 20, 18, 16, 14, 12, 10, 8, 6, 4, 3, 2, 1. In 1976, the first year of ATP Computer Points for satellite circuits, the Florida WATCH Circuit, the Southern Circuit and the French Satellite Circuit were included. The 10 tournament Southern Circuit that I administered had over $56,000 in prize money, so we had 12 players receive ATP Points in 1976, led by Terry Moor who earned 20 ATP points. For me to get the Southern circuits up to $56,000, Bob Briner generously contributed $9,000 on behalf of the ATP in 1976.

This was only a small opening for the new players and it was still extremely difficult to earn enough points to move ahead of enough of the 185 original ATP members in the rankings so as to gain direct entry into the big tournaments. But, at least professional tennis was finally open to new up-and-coming players some.

Experimental Point Penalty System

In addition, the Council approved an experimental point penalty system, to be used, in conjunction with the Code, for tournaments authorized by the MIPTC. This was the first new way to deal with player misconduct directly during a match instead of fines after completion of a match.[236]

WTT

The 1976 year was the third for WTT with 10 continuing franchises and Larry King continued as President. Chris Evert, Rod Laver, Ilie Nastase and Martina Navratilova were added to its already impressive roster of *overpaid* players. In March, WTT staged a series of matches with a United States WTT team against a Russian Team. Two matches in Moscow sold 25,000 tickets each and were followed by matches in Philadelphia, Cleveland and Indianapolis. The seeds were planted for the entrance of a Russian franchise into WTT in 1977.

EASTERN DIVISION

Team	Won	Lost	Players
Pittsburgh Triangles	24	20	Mark Cox, Evonne Goolagong, Vitas Gerulaitis, Bernie Mitton, Peggy Michael, Sue Stap.
New York Sets	33	10	Coach Fred Stolle, Billie Jean King, Virginia Wade, Sandy Mayer, Phil Dent, Lindsey Beaven, Linda Siegeiman.
Boston Lobsters	18	25	Coach Ion Tiriac, John Alexander, Mike Estep, Kerry Melville, Greer "Cat" Stevens, Pam Teeguarden.

Indiana Loves	19	25	Coach Allen Stone, Ray Ruffels, Syd Ball, Mona Guerrant, Ann Kiyomura, Pat Bostrom, Carrie Meyer.
Cleveland Nets	20	24	Coach Marty Riessen, Martina Navratilova, Rayni Fox, Wendy Overton, Haroon Rahim, Bob Giltinan.

WESTERN DIVISION

Team	Won	Lost	Players
San Francisco/Oakland Golden Gaters	28	16	Coach Frew McMillan, Tom Okker, Jeff Borowiak, John Lucas, Francoise Durr, Betty Stove, Racquel Giscatre.
Phoenix Racquets	30	14	Coach Tony Roche, Andrew Pattison, Butch Walts, Chris Evert, Kristien Shaw, Stephanie Tolleson.
Los Angeles Strings	22	22	Bob Lutz, Vijay Amritraj, Ashok Amritraj, Dennis Ralston, Charles Pasarell, Rosie Casals, Ann Haydon Jones, Diane Fromholtz.
Hawaii Leis	12	32	Coach Butch Buchholz, Owen Davidson, Ilie Nastase, Margaret Court, Helen Gourlay, Nancy Gunter, Sue Stap, Marcie Louie.
San Diego Friars	12	34	Coach Cliff Drysdale, Ross Case, Rod Laver, Terry Holladay, Janet Young, Bettyann Stuart.

New York won the playoffs 5-1. Finals: New York defeated Golden Gaters 3-0: 31-23, 29-27 and 31-13.

The average WTT match attendance increased to 3,850, a 26 percent increase over 1976. At the end of the 1976 WTT Season: (i) The Pittsburgh Triangles closed shop, (ii) The Hawaii Leis moved to Seattle and Oakland and became the Sea-Port Cascades, (iii) A new franchise, the Pennsylvania Keystones was introduced and then taken over by the Soviet Union via the Soviet Tennis Federation with players: Alex Metreveli, Olga Morozova, Natasha Chmyreva, Marina Kroshina, Temuraz Kakulia and Vadim Borisov, (iv) Bjorn Borg signed a three-year contract with the Cleveland Nets for $1.5 million that included his fiancée, Mariana Simionescu, (v) Butch Buchholz was named as the new WTT Commissioner and President, replacing Larry King, and he moved the WTT headquarters to St. Louis. King went off to manage the New York Sets whose name was changed to the New York Apples.

Wrote Greg Hoffman in *The Art of World Team Tennis*, "No longer is WTT just 'that American inter-city league' as the British press had sarcastically labeled it in 1974. No way. WTT is for real! Finally." *But was it? They were still losing money.*[237]

ATP

In December of 1975, Bob Briner, an original non-player member of the Board of Directors, became the Administrative Director of the ATP. In April of 1976, Kramer resigned as Executive Director of ATP and Bob Briner became the second Executive Director of the ATP. In contrast (to Kramer), Briner shunned the limelight and did not enjoy conversing with the rank and file players. Briner hired Doug Tkachuk, a fellow Texan who had worked with him during his days in professional basketball, as the No. 2 in the ATP Dallas headquarters in addition to Dennis Spencer, the first editor of *International Tennis Weekly* (ITW). By May, Philippe Chatrier's *Tennis de France* had bought the French rights to *ITW*, and immediately started printing an edition for circulation in France.

John Newcombe was elected in June as the third President of the ATP succeeding Arthur Ashe. Jamie Fillol became Vice President and Jim McManus continued as Secretary-Treasurer. New Board members elected were Lito Alvarez and Adriano Panatta to join Arthur Ashe, Cliff Drysdale, Stan Smith, Patrick Proisy, Ray Moore, Pierre Darmon, Bob Briner and Jack Kramer. When Richard Evans, the ATP European Bureau Director, put his name forward as a candidate for the MIPTC it did not go over well. "Briner was furious," Evans wrote in his book *Open Tennis*: "'None of my staff shall be allowed to run for the Council.' He decreed."[238]

Bob Briner, Pierre Darmon and Cliff Drysdale were elected to represent the players on the MIPTC after a disappointingly low vote by the players. Soon thereafter Briner fired Evans. In Europe, Paul Svehlik, an English hockey international who had worked briefly as a road manager for World Championship Tennis earlier in the year, was appointed to run the Paris Office (replacing Evans). ATP Treasurer Jim McManus took on additional duties as road manager at various tournaments, as did another board member, Lito Alvarez." After being fired, Evans at "Newcombe's invitation," became a candidate to replace Jack Kramer on the ATP Board of Directors and was elected by a narrow margin to the chagrin of Briner and Dell.

JAKS Awards Dinner

The second ATP Awards Dinner was staged on September 13 in Dallas with Alan King again as the Master of Ceremonies. The awards were now named the JAKS Awards to honor Jack Kramer and were given to:

Player of the Year	Bjorn Borg
Female Player of the Year	Chris Evert
ATP Lifetime Award	Jack Kramer
Newcomer of the Year	Wojtek Fibak
Female Newcomer of the Year	Sue Barker
Doubles Team of the Year	Brian Gottfried – Raul Ramirez
Female Doubles Team of the Year	Billie Jean King and Betty Stove
Tennis Writer of the Year	Rex Bellamy
Tennis Broadcaster of the Year	Bud Collins
ATP Dr. Johnson Children's Award	John Barrett
ATP Grand Master Award	Frank Sedgman
ATP Service Award	Jim McManus
Court Officials of the Year	Flo and Mike Blanchard
President's Award	Ed Hickey
ATP Special Awards	Ethel Kennedy, Longwood Cricket Club, New England National Merchants' Bank and Cecile Kreisberg.

Computer Rankings Systems: ATP vs. USTA

The ranking of tennis players from all over the world has always been an imprecise endeavor. Without an extensive record of head-to-head wins and losses between all players, it is not possible to perfectly rank players. Since tennis tournaments are staged all over the world and tennis players come from all over the world, there are just not enough head-to-head match ups. Prior to the creation and adoption of the ATP Computer Rankings System in 1973 as the system of merit for the selection of tennis players for acceptance into tournaments, players would submit entries to tournaments accompanied by their national rankings and their "unverified and often embellished" records of important match wins. When I ran the Southern Championships in Raleigh N.C. from 1972-1977, we had players from 20+- countries, with national rankings and no ATP points, so I had to try to evaluate the player records submitted. I was always amazed as how many players who applied for entry into the Southern Championships claimed "wins" over Arthur Ashe. It was impossible to make an accurate evaluation of a No. 2 ranked European player with a No. 4 ranked United States player or a No. 3 ranked South American player or among even lower ranked players.

ATP Computer Rankings

The ATP was founded in 1972, and in 1973, the ATP introduced the ATP Computer Rankings System for singles. The doubles rankings were added in March of 1976. The original solemn commitment and vow of the members of ATP was that the ATP Rankings System could only be used for rankings and that no kind of political or leverage for any other purpose would ever be permitted. *Well, as we shall see, that subsequently changed somewhat.* Ray Moore was the first Chairman of the ATP Computer Committee and he was followed by Victor Amaya and then Mike Estep. The first and for many years the only "political" use of the ATP Computer Rankings was adopted in the 1978 Tournament Regulations for Grand Prix Tournaments to severely penalize players for really late withdrawals after noon Friday before the beginning of the tournament by awarding a 1st round loser's "one point" to bring down a player's ranking average as a penalty.

The next significant violation of the no political leverage protection for the integrity of the ATP Computer System did not occur until sometime in the 1980s when Mike Estep was Chairman. I do not think that the ATP Computer System was used again for significant political purposes until 1990 after the ATP was dissolved and the new ATP Tour commenced.

The ATP system was more of a points system than a ranking system because it included no evaluation of the actual strength of the field in the tournaments or the relative ranking of players defeated. The ATP system just assumed the higher prize money tournaments always had the stronger fields. The ATP system provided for rating points for each round based solely on the tournament's prize money and later added some bonus computer points for wins over seeded and higher-ranked players. Grand Prix tournaments and other MIPTC sanctioned tournaments with at least $25,000 in prize money awarded ATP Computer Points. Tournaments with less than $25,000 in prize money awarded no computer points until Satellite points were finally added in 1976 to groups of five tournaments with at least $5,000 each in prize money. The 185 players ranked on the first ATP Computer Rankings issued on August 23, 1973, received a kind of monopoly for several years. ATP ranked players on their average ATP points, which was determined by dividing a player's total points by the number of tournaments played or a divisor of 12. The ATP justified the divisor of 12 on the assumption that to be a professional, a player must at least play in 12 tournaments per year. The downside of the divisor of 12 was that it prohibited a lot of new players from getting into 12 tournaments per year. The ATP awarded each first round loser one ATP point. As a result, a player who played in at least 12 tournaments and never won a round would still have a one-point average which would make him ranked above all new players who had less than 12 points or a one-point average. Remember all new players started with no points.

USTA Computer Rankings System

Dr. Leslie Jenkins of Knoxville, Tennessee, a past President of the USTA's Southern Section and a member of the USTA's Ranking Committee, was a Nuclear Physicist at Oak Ridge in Tennessee. By 1975, Dr. Jenkins developed a sophisticated computer rankings system and gave it to the USTA and the USTA tested it and adopted it for the USTA national rankings. Dr. Jenkins and his wife, Jean, entered tournament results and produced (boot-legged) the USTA Computer Rankings on the Oak Ridge computers. In 1976, I was the new President of the USTA's Southern Section. I was convinced by Dr. Jenkins that his USTA Computer Rankings System was a much better ranking system than the ATP system. The USTA system utilized a sophisticated algorithm developed after extensive testing by Dr. Jenkins that computed the strength of the fields of each tournament based on the values of the players entered and then awarded points based on the actual strength of the field and the values of the players defeated. Thus, there was no $25,000 prize money threshold for tournaments to be considered as the strength of the players in the field, not the prize money, determined the values assigned to wins in each tournament. As the value of players defeated changed during the year, the points awarded for those wins were scaled upwards or downwards. By contrast, the ATP Computer Rankings System awarded ranking points based on the amount of prize money without regard to the actual quality of the players in the tournament. In January of 1978, the USTA announced the sponsorship by Equitable Life Insurance Company of the USTA/Equitable Computer Rankings.

At the December 8-9, 11-12, 1976, meeting of the MIPTC in Houston, Stan Malless (ILTF Representative on the MIPTC and President of the USTA) proposed the adoption of the new USTA Computer Rankings System instead of the ATP Computer Rankings

System. After a long discussion, Malless told me that the MIPTC voted 5-4 to adopt the ATP Computer Ranking system as the system of merit for the selection of players for the 1977 Grand Prix with the condition that any proposed changes be reported to the MIPTC before any amendments were made. The USTA was permitted to publish the USTA Computer rankings at frequent intervals so that, after six months, the players could evaluate the two systems and decide which list they preferred in the future. While the USTA Computer Rankings system may very well have been a fairer and more accurate rankings system that could be used as the system of merit for Grand Prix tournaments, it had two fatal flaws: (i) It was not developed by the players; and (ii) Players could not understand the algorism and add up their own points.

Notwithstanding the weakness of the ATP system as a ranking system, it was simple and each player could compute his points and his average on the back of an envelope. In addition, all of the weakness of the system were readily known so when there were really weak prize money tournaments with easy points to be had, all the players could see that and thus, there was a sort of correction available to all players. A number of professional players became quite successful in finding the tournaments with the weakest fields and the easiest points. The players support for their computer rankings system has never wavered so its weaknesses as a true ranking system just have never mattered. However, it is worth noting that the women's professional tour used the USTA Computer System for women's professional tennis for a number of years, all run gratis by Les and Jean Jenkins on the Oak Ridge computers.

More Nastase Misconduct

The new MIPTC Code of Conduct debuted in 1976. On January 24 at the USLTA-IPA Indoor Circuit tournament in Baltimore there was yet more misconduct from Ilie Nastase not dealt with by the amateur tournament officials who now had the new Code of Conduct. Nastase caused five major interruptions in a match against Harold Solomon and at other times, as described by local media, he "crossed over the net, shouted at linespeople, screamed at the crowd and cursed in both Romanian and English." Tom Gorman defeated Nastase in the final.

Nastase misbehaved at the ATP's American Airlines Games in Palm Springs, the Tennis Week Open in Orange, N.J., the U.S. Open and in Hong Kong. His U.S. Open fine of $1,000 got him over the $3,000 annual maximum resulting in a 21-day suspension. The *New York Times* article on ATP's Palm Springs tournament contained a photo of Nastase with a caption saying: "Ilie Nastase spitting at a spectator as he walked off court yesterday."[239][240]

1976 Crisis No. 17: WCT vs. MIPTC et al.

In 1976, discussions were held with WCT about the possible inclusion of WCT tournaments in the 1977 Grand Prix as the MIPTC was planning to begin the 1977 Grand Prix in January of 1977, in direct competition with WCT, instead of in May as in 1973-1976.[241] *Doesn't this sound like the beginning of a possible new war with WCT?*

On April 6, WCT applied for inclusion of 25 tournaments scheduled during January – May in the 1977 Grand Prix as a "circuit within a circuit" plus its singles and doubles finals and an unspecified number of other special events. *The volunteer members of the MIPTC were terrified of a possible anti-trust lawsuit by WCT.* On June 4, Derek Hardwick, the MIPTC Chairman, sent a letter to WCT confirming WCT's inclusion in the 1977 Grand Prix which was counter-signed by Mike Davies, WCT's Executive Director.[242]

Next, WCT issued a press release announcing a new special event to be known as the WCT Tournament of Champions for 16 WCT tournament winners for $200,000 in prize money with matches to be played at different sites during the year. The members of the Council did not like the proposed Tournament of Champions as it gave an additional edge to the WCT tournaments in the Grand Prix over the regular Grand Prix tournaments and was planned to be finished after and outside of the "traditional" January to May WCT period. The members of the Council stated over and over again that all of the WCT special events would have to be sanctioned and scheduled by the MIPTC just as all other events, so WCT could not have unilateral control on their approval or scheduling.[243] On June 26, the MIPTC informed WCT that it was formally accepted into the 1977 Grand Prix on the basis of the June 4 agreement that had been countersigned by WCT for 25 WCT-Grand Prix tournaments.[244]

But, by letter dated September 10, 1976, from WCT to all members of the MIPTC, WCT declined entry into the 1977 Grand Prix and demanded that the 1977 Grand Prix be restricted so as not to interfere with WCT's 1977 tournament program. WCT threatened an anti-trust lawsuit against the MIPTC *and its individual members* and demanded that the Council: (i) limit the Grand Prix schedule of events so as to make it possible for independent circuits, including WCT, to continue to operate on a practical plane or (ii) accord Grand Prix status to independent circuits on terms which do not involve anti-competitive restraints on the conduct of non-Grand Prix events or which do not require all circuits to rigidly conform to the Council's tournament concepts (number of players, prize money, etc.). WCT demanded an answer from the Council within 10 days.[245]

The MIPTC did not have any anti-trust insurance coverage and each member was scared that they could be sued individually by WCT. By letter dated September 30, 1976, from Bob Briner, Cliff Drysdale, Jack Kramer and Stan Malless to WCT, which was endorsed by a cable dated October 4, 1976, from Paulo Angeli, Pierre Darmon, Derek

Hardwick and Lars Myhrman to WCT, the MIPTC basically caved to WCT's demands and offered WCT 11 WCT $100,000 tournaments, plus Philadelphia as a "circuit within a circuit" as 1977 Grand Prix tournaments in the "traditional" WCT period as long as its sponsor did not conflict with the Grand Prix sponsor with WCT being freely permitted to conduct its planned special events.[246]

Surprisingly, by letter dated October 26, 1976, from WCT to the Chairman of the MIPTC, WCT rejected the MIPTC offer and said it would "take whatever independent steps are necessary to function as a viable circuit in 1977 and subsequently." The threat of a lawsuit by WCT was continued, but WCT said: "We are willing to discuss relations for future operations (1978 and thereafter) but do request that such discussions be on a first-person basis with a representative or representatives who are members of the Council and who are authorized to act for the Council. In order that WCT's plans for 1978 not be delayed, we would suggest that such discussions take place within 30-45 days."[247]

When the MIPTC could not reach an agreement to include WCT in the 1977 Grand Prix, the MIPTC proceeded to revise the format of the Grand Prix to schedule Grand Prix tournaments throughout the full year of 1977 and in direct competition with WCT for the first time. The MIPTC had to provide players with the jobs being lost by WCT's reduction in the size of its tournaments.

So, WCT planned to operate independently of the 1977 Colgate Grand Prix and continue its threat of an antitrust lawsuit against the MIPTC. However, in December, a MIPTC sub-committee led by Derek Hardwick met with Lamar Hunt to discuss a proposal for WCT to join the Grand Prix in 1978.[248]

1976 Grand Slam Winners

Australian Open

Mark Edmondson d. John Newcombe 6-7, 6-3, 7-6, 6-1.
John Newcombe – Tony Roche d. Ross Case – Geoff Masters 7-6, 6-4.

French Open

Adriano Panatta d. Harold Solomon 6-1, 6-4, 4-6, 7-6.
Fred McNair – Sherwood Stewart d. Juan Gisbert Sr. – Manuel Orantes 7-6, 6-4.

[Panatta d. Borg in the semifinals 6-3, 6-3, 2-6, 7-6.]

Wimbledon

Bjorn Borg d. Ilie Nastase 6-4, 6-2, 9-7.
Brian Gottfried – Raul Ramirez d. Ross Case – Geoff Masters 3-6, 6-3, 8-6, 2-6, 7-5.

U.S. Open (second year on clay)

Jimmy Connors d. Bjorn Borg 6-4, 3-6, 7-6, 6-4.
Tom Okker – Marty Riessen d. Paul Kronk – Cliff Letcher 6-4, 6-4.

1976 Davis Cup

Davis Cup Final

Italy d. Chile 4-1 (Santiago - Clay)

Corrado Barazzutti (IT) d. Jaime Fillol (CL) 7-5, 4-6, 7-5, 6-1.
Adriano Panatta (IT) d. Patricio Cornejo (CL) 6-3, 6-1, 6-3.
Barazzutti - Panatta (IT) d. Cornejo – Fillol (CL) 3-6, 6-2, 9-7, 6-3.
Adriano Panatta (IT) d. Jaime Fillol (CL) 8-6, 6-4, 3-6, 10-8.
Belus Prajoux (CL) d. Antonio Zugarelli (IT) 6-4, 6-4, 6-2.

1976 World Rankings[249]

Bud Collins	Lance Tingay	ATP Year-End Rankings
1. Jimmy Connors	1. Jimmy Connors	1. Jimmy Connors
2. Bjorn Borg	2. Bjorn Borg	2. Bjorn Borg
3. Ilie Nastase	3. Adriano Panatta	3. Ilie Nastase
4. Manuel Orantes	4. Ilie Nastase	4. Manuel Orantes
5. Raul Ramirez	5. Guillermo Vilas	5. Raul Ramirez
6. Guillermo Vilas	6. Eddie Dibbs	6. Guillermo Vilas
7. Adriano Panatta	7. Harold Solomon	7. Adriano Panatta
8. Harold Solomon	8. Manual Orantes	8. Harold Solomon
9. Eddie Dibbs	9. Raul Ramirez	9. Eddie Dibbs
10. Brian Gottfried	10. Roscoe Tanner	10. Brian Gottfried

1976 Commercial Union Grand Prix Bonus Pool Top 10[250]

Singles (7th Bonus Pool)			Doubles (2nd Bonus Pool)		
1.	Raul Ramirez	$150,000	1.	Raul Ramirez	$40,000
2.	Manuel Orantes	$ 90,000	2.	Brian Gottfried	$25,000
3.	Jimmy Connors	*	3.	Sherwood Stewart	$20,000
4.	Eddie Dibbs	$ 60,000	4.	Fred McNair	$16,000
5.	Harold Solomon	$ 45,000	5.	Bob Hewitt	$13,000
6.	Guillermo Vilas	$ 35,000	6.	Stan Smith	$10,000
7.	Roscoe Tanner	$ 30,000	7.	Wojtek Fibak	$ 8,500
8.	Wojtek Fibak	$ 26,000	8.	Juan Gisbert	$ 8,000
9.	Brian Gottfried	$ 23,000	9.	Geoff Masters	$ 7,500
10.	Bjorn Borg	*	10.	Marty Riessen	$ 7,000

* Connors failed to play in Masters. Others did not play in two 1 Star and/or 2 Star tournaments.

1976 Official Earnings Top 10[251]

1.	Raul Ramirez	$484,343	6.	Harold Solomon	$236,690
2.	Jimmy Connors	$315,081	7.	Eddie Dibbs	$233,428
3.	Manuel Orantes	$281,880	8.	Brian Gottfried	$231,075
4.	Guillermo Vilas	$238,738	9.	Wojtek Fibak	$210,086
5.	Arthur Ashe	$236,933	10.	Roscoe Tanner	$208,710

1976 Tournament Calendar

Date	Tournaments	Singles Winner	Singles #2	Doubles Winners	Doubles #2
1/4/1976	Australian Open $103,000 2 Star	Mark Edmonson	John Newcombe	J. Newcombe - T. Roche	R. Case - G. Masters
1/11/1976	Columbus $100,000 WCT	Arthur Ashe	Andrew Pattison	B. Hewitt - F. McMillan	A. Ashe - T. Okker
1/11/1976	Monterrey $100,000 WCT	Eddie Dibbs	Harold Solomon	B. Gottfried - R. Ramirez	R. Case - G. Masters
1/11/1976	Auckland	Onny Parun	Brian Fairlie		
1/19/1976	Indianapolis $100,000 WCT	Arthur Ashe	Vitas Gerulaitis	B. Lutz - S. Smith	V. Gerulaitis - T. Gorman
1/19/1976	Atlanta $100,000 WCT	Ilie Nastase	Jeff Borowiak	J. Alexander - P. Dent	W. Fibak - K. Meiler
1/25/1976	Baltimore IPA	Tom Gorman	Ilie Nastase	B. Hewitt - F. McMillan	I. Nastase - C. Richey
1/25/1976	Birmingham $50,000 IPA	Jimmy Connors	Roscoe Tanner	J. Connors - E. Van Dillon	H. Pfister - D. Ralston
2/1/1976	Philadelphia $115,000 WCT	Jimmy Connors	Bjorn Borg	R. Laver - D. Ralston	B. Hewitt - F. McMillan
2/7/1976	Barcelona $100,000 WCT	Eddie Dibbs	Cliff Drysdale	B. Lutz - S. Smith	W. Fibak - K. Meiler
2/8/1976	Dayton $35,000 IPA	Jaime Fillol	Andrew Pattison	R. Ruffles - S. Stewart	J. Fillol - C. Pasarell
2/8/1976	Boca Raton $60,000 IPA	Butch Walts	Cliff Richey	V. Gerulaitis - C. Graebner	B. Walts - B. Manson
2/8/1976	Richmond $100,000 WCT	Arthur Ashe	Brian Gottfried	B. Gottfried - R. Ramirez	A. Ashe - T. Okker
2/15/1976	Toronto $100,000 WCT	Bjorn Borg	Vitas Gerulaitis	J. Fillol - F. McMillan	A. Metreveli - I. Nastase
2/15/1976	Lagos 100,000 WCT	Dick Stockton	Arthur Ashe		
2/22/1976	Salisbury $50,000 IPA	Ilie Nastase	Jimmy Connors	F. McNair - S. Stewart	S. Krulevitz - T. Waltke
2/22/1976	Rome $100,000 WCT	Arthur Ashe	Bob Lutz	B. Lutz - S. Smith	D. Crealy - F. McMillan
2/22/1976	St. Louis $100,000 WCT	Guillermo Vilas	Vijay Amritraj	B. Gottfried - R. Ramirez	J. Alexander - P. Dent
2/27/1976	Gothenburg $100,000 SP	Bjorn Borg	Rod Laver	6-4, 6-2, 7-5	

2/28/1976	Las Vegas $250,000 SP	Jimmy Connors	Manuel Orantes	6-2, 6-1, 6-0	
2/29/1976	Rotterdam $100,000 WCT	Arthur Ashe	Bob Lutz	R. Laver - F. McMillan	A. Ashe - T. Okker
2/29/1976	Fort Worth $100,000 WCT	Guillermo Vilas	Phil Dent	V. Gerulaitis - S. Mayer	E. Dibbs - H. Solomon
3/7/1976	Little Rock $35,000 IPA	Haroon Rahim	Colin Dibley	S. Ball - R. Ruffels	V. Pecci - H. Rahim
3/7/1976	Basle $30,000 ATP	Jan Kodes	Jiri Hrebec	F. McMillan - T. Okker	D. Crealy - K. Meiler
3/7/1976	Hartford $70,000 WC WCT SP	United States	Australia	6-1,	
3/7/1976	Hartford $70,000 WC WCT SP	Bob Lutz	John Alexander	5-7, 6-3, 6-2	
3/7/1976	Hartford $70,000 WC WCT SP	Arthur Ashe	John Newcombe	6-3, 6-4	
3/7/1976	Hartford $70,000 WC WCT SP	Jimmy Connors	Tony Roche	6-4, 7-5	
3/7/1976	Hartford $70,000 WC WCT SP	Arthur Ashe	Tony Roche	3-6, 6-2, 6-3	
3/7/1976	Hartford $70,000 WC WCT SP	Jimmy Connors	John Newcombe	6-2, 6-3	
3/7/1976	Hartford $70,000 WC WCT SP		7-6, 6-4	J. Newcombe - T. Roche	B. Lutz - S. Smith
3/7/1976	Hartford $70,000 WC WCT SP		7-6, 6-4	A. Ashe - D. Ralston	J. Alexander - P. Dent
3/14/1976	Nurenburg $30,000 ATP	Frew McMillan	Thomas Koch	F. McMillan - K. Meiler	C. Dowdeswell - P. Kronk
3/14/1976	Hampton $49,000 IPA	Jimmy Connors	Ilie Nastase		
3/14/1976	Mexico City $100,000 WCT	Raul Ramirez	Eddie Dibbs	B. Gottfried - R. Ramirez	B. Fairlie - I. El Shafei
3/14/1976	Memphis $100,000 WCT	Vijay Amritraj	Stan Smith	An. Amritraj - V. Amritraj	M. Reissen - R. Tanner
3/20/1976	San Diego $100,000 IPA	Ilie Nastase	Jimmy Connors	M. Riessen - R. Tanner	P. Fleming - S. Mayer
3/21/1976	Washington $100,000 WCT	Harold Solomon	Onny Parun	E. Dibbs - H. Solomon	M. Cox - C. Drysdale
3/21/1976	Jackson $100,000 WCT	Ken Rosewall	Raul Ramirez	B. Gottfried - R. Ramirez	R. Case - G. Masters
3/21/1976	Malta $30,000 ATP	Thomas Koch	Roger Taylor	M. Edmondson - A. Panatta	J. Lloyd - R. Taylor
3/28/1976	Palm Springs $200,000 ATP	Jimmy Connors	Roscoe Tanner	C Dibley - S. Mayer	E. Van Dillon - R. Moore

3/28/1976	Valencia $30,000 ATP	Manuel Orantes	Kjell Johansson	J. Gisbert - M. Orantes	C. Barazzutti - A. Zugarelli
4/4/1976	Towson $30,000 IPA	Vitas Gerulaitis	Sherwood Stewart	F. McNair - S. Stewart	C. Drysdale - I. Tiriac
4/4/1976	Barcelona $30,000 ATP	Paolo Bertolucci	Jun Kuki	W. Fibak - J. Niedzwiedski	C. Dowdeswell - P. Kronk
4/4/1976	Sao Paulo $100,000 WCT	Bjorn Borg	Guillermo Vilas	R. Case - G. Masters	C. Pasarell - A. Stone
4/4/1976	Caracas $100,000 WCT	Raul Ramirez	Ilie Nastase	B. Gottfried - R. Ramirez	J. Borowiak - I. Nastase
4/11/1976	Nice $30,000 ATP	Corrado Barazzutti	Jan Kodes	P. Dominguez - F. Jauffret	W. Fibak - K. Meiler
4/11/1976	Johannesburg $100,000 WCT	Onny Parun	Cliff Drysdale	M. Riessen - R. Tanner	F. McMillan - T. Okker
4/11/1976	Houston $100,000 WCT	Harold Solomon	Ken Rosewall	R. Laver - K. Rosewall	C. Pasarell - A. Stone
4/18/1976	Monte Carlo $100,000 WCT	Guillermo Vilas	Wojtek Fibak	W. Fibak - K. Meiler	B. Borg - G. Vilas
4/18/1976	Charlotte $100,000 WCT	Tony Roche	Vitas Gerulaitis	J. Newcombe - T. Roche	V. Gerulaitis - S. Mayer
4/19/1976	Palma Mallorca $30,000 ATP	Buster Mottram	Jun Kuki	J. Andrew - C. Dibley	M. Edmonson - J. Marks
4/25/1976	Sacramento $25,000 IPA	Tom Gorman	Bob Carmichael	T. Gorman - S. Stewart	M. Cahill - J. Whitlinger
4/25/1976	Madrid $30,000 ATP	Victor Pecci	Eric Deblicker	C. Kirmayr - E. Mandarino	J. Andrews - C. Dibley
4/26/1976	Stockholm $100,000 WCT	Wojtek Fibak	Ilie Nastase	A. Metreveli - I. Nastase	T. Okker - A. Panetta
4/26/1976	Denver $100,000 WCT	Jimmy Connors	Ross Case	J. Alexander - P. Dent	J. Connors - B. Martin
5/2/1976	Kansas City WCT Dbles.			W. Fibak - K. Meiler	B. Lutz - S. Smith
5/3/1976	Honolulu WCT Cup $100,000 Finals	Ilie Nastase	Arthur Ashe	6-3, 1-6, 6-7, 6-3, 6-1	
5/3/1976	Honolulu WCT Cup $50,000 Semis	Ilie Nastase	Bjorn Borg	6-1, 3-6, 0-6, 6-3, 6-4	
5/3/1976	Honolulu WCT Cup $50,000 Semis	Arthur Ashe	Ken Rosewall	2-6, 6-4, 6-2, 6-2	
5/3/1976	Honolulu WCT Cup $10,000 RR	Arthur Ashe	Raul Ramirez	6-2, 7-6, 6-1	

Date	Tournament	Winner	Runner-up	Score	Doubles Winners	Doubles Runners-up
5/3/1976	Honolulu WCT Cup $10,000 RR	Arthur Ashe	John Newcombe	3-6, 6-2, 6-3, 7-5		
5/3/1976	Honolulu WCT Cup $10,000 RR	Arthur Ashe	Bjorn Borg	6-4, 7-6, 6-3		
5/3/1976	Honolulu WCT Cup $10,000 RR	Bjorn Borg	John Newcombe	2-6, 7-5, 6-2, 6-4		
5/3/1976	Honolulu WCT Cup $10,000 RR	Bjorn Borg	Raul Ramirez	6-3, 4-6, 6-0, 3-0 Ret.		
5/3/1976	Honolulu WCT Cup $10,000 RR	John Newcombe	Raul Ramirez	6-4, 6-1, 3-6, 5-7, 3-2 Ret'd		
5/3/1976	Honolulu WCT Cup $10,000 RR	Ken Rosewall	Rod Laver	6-4, 6-1, 6-3		
5/3/1976	Honolulu WCT Cup $10,000 RR	Ken Rosewall	John Alexander	6-3, 6-4, 7-6		
5/3/1976	Honolulu WCT Cup $10,000 RR	Rod Laver	John Alexander	6-1, 1-6, 7-6, 6-2		
5/3/1976	Honolulu WCT Cup $10,000 RR	Ilie Nastase	John Alexander	6-3, 6-4, 7-6		
5/3/1976	Honolulu WCT Cup $10,000 RR	Ilie Nastase	Rod Laver	7-6, 6-1, 4-6, 6-3		
5/3/1976	Honolulu WCT Cup $10,000 RR	Ilie Nastase	Ken Rosewall	6-0, 6-2, 6-2		
5/9/1976	Florence	Paolo Bertolucci	Patrick Proisy		C. Dibley - C. Kirmayr	P. Szoke - B. Taroczy
5/9/1976	Dallas WCT Finals	Bjorn Borg	Guillermo Vilas	1-6, 6-1, 7-5, 6-1		
5/9/1976	Munich $50,000 1 Star	Manuel Orantes	Karl Meiler		J. Gisbert - M. Orantes	J. Fassbender - H. Pohlman
5/16/1976	Las Vegas $150,000 ATP	Jimmy Connors	Ken Rosewall		A. Ashe - C. Pasarell	B. Lutz - S. Smith
5/18/1976	Bournemouth $75,000 2 Star	Wojtek Fibak	Manuel Orantes		W. Fibak - F. McNair	J. Gisbert - M. Orantes
5/23/1976	Hamburg $100,000 3 Star	Eddie Dibbs	Manuel Orantes		F. McNair - S. Stewart	D. Crealy - K. Warwick
5/30/1976	Dusseldorf $75,000 2 Star	Bjorn Borg	Manuel Orantes		W. Fibak - K. Meiler	B. Carmichael - R. Moore
5/30/1976	Rome $115,200 5 Star	Adriano Panatta	Guillermo Vilas		B. Gottfried - R. Ramirez	G. Masters - J. Newcombe
6/12/1976	Beckenham	Roscoe Tanner	Jimmy Connors		D. Stockton - R. Tanner	D. Lloyd - J. Lloyd
6/13/1976	French Open 840,600 FF GS	Adriano Panatta	Harold Solomon		F. McNair - S. Stewart	B. Gottfried - R. Ramirez
6/19/1976	Nottingham $100,000 3 Star	Jimmy Connors	Ilie Nastase			Rain

6/20/1976	Berlin $50,000 1 Star	Victor Pecci	Hans Pohlman	P. Cornejo - A. Munoz	J. Fassbender - H. Pohlman
7/3/1976	Wimbledon £78,800 GS	Bjorn Borg	Ilie Nastase	B. Gottfried - R. Ramirez	R. Case - G. Masters
7/5/1976	Raleigh $10,000 Southern Chps.	Terry Moor	Mark Meyers	J. James - M. Lara	R. Fagel - F. Gonzalez
7/11/1976	Gstaad $75,000 2 Star	Raul Ramirez	Adriano Panatta	J. Fassbender - H. Pohlman	P. Bertolucci - A. Panatta
7/11/1976	Bastad $100,000 3 Star	Antonio Zugarelli	Corrado Barazzutti	F. McNair - S. Stewart	W. Fibak - J. Gisbert
7/11/1976	Myrtle Beach $150,000 SP	Ilie Nastase	Manuel Orantes	6-4, 6-3	
7/18/1976	Kitzbuhel $75,000 2 Star	Manuel Orantes	Jan Kodes	J. Hrebec - J. Kodes	J. Fassbender - H. Pohlman
7/18/1976	Hilversum $50,000 1 Star	Balazs Taroczy	Ricardo Cano	R. Cano - B. Prajoux	W. Fibak - B. Taroczy
7/18/1976	Cincinnati $100,000 3 Star	Roscoe Tanner	Eddie Dibbs	E. Van Dillon - S. Smith	E. Dibbs - H. Solomon
7/26/1976	Washington $125,000 4 Star	Jimmy Connors	Raul Ramirez	B. Gottfried - R. Ramirez	A. Ashe - J. Connors
8/2/1976	Louisville $125,000 4 Star	Harold Solomon	Wojtek Fibak	B. Bertram - P. Cramer	E. Van Dillon - S. Smith
8/8/1976	North Conway $100,000 3 Star	Jimmy Connors	Raul Ramirez	B. Gottfried - R. Ramirez	R. Cano - V. Pecci
8/8/1976	Columbus $87,500 2 Star	Roscoe Tanner	Stan Smith	B. Brown - B. Teacher	F. McNair - S. Stewart
8/16/1976	Indianapolis $157,000 5 Star	Jimmy Connors	Wojtek Fibak	B. Gottfried - R. Ramirez	F. McNair - S. Stewart
8/23/1976	Toronto $155,000 5 Star	Guillermo Vilas	Wojtek Fibak	B. Hewitt - R. Ramirez	J. Gisbert - M. Orantes
8/30/1976	South Orange $60,000 1 Star	Ilie Nastase	Roscoe Tanner	F. McNair - M. Riessen	V. Gerulaitis - I. Nastase
8/30/1976	Boston $125,000 4 Star	Bjorn Borg	Harold Solomon	R. Ruffles - A. Stone	M. Cahill - J. Whitlinger
9/12/1976	US Open $184,000 GS	Jimmy Connors	Bjorn Borg	T. Okker - M. Riessen	P. Kronk - C. Letcher
9/19/1976	Newport $37,500 SP	Vijay Amritraj	Brian Teacher		
9/19/1976	Woodlands GP Dbls. ATP			B. Gottfried - R. Ramirez	P. Dent - A. Stone
9/19/1976	Hamilton $50,000 1 Star	Cliff Richey	Gene Mayer	M. Cahill - J. Whitlinger	D. Crealy - R. Ruffles
9/27/1976	Los Angeles $125,000 4 Star	Brian Gottfried	Arthur Ashe	B. Lutz - S. Smith	A. Ashe - C. Pasarell

10/3/1976	Caracas $100,000 Nastase SP	Ilie Nastase	Jimmy Connors	6-1, 6-3	
10/4/1976	San Francisco $125,000 4 Star	Roscoe Tanner	Brian Gottfried	D. Stockton - R. Tanner	B. Gottfried - B. Hewitt
10/6/1976	Antwerp Challenge Match SP	Ilie Nastase	Bjorn Borg	6-0, 4-6, 6-2	
10/10/1976	Aviles	Zeljko Franulovic	Jan Kodes		
10/10/1976	Tehran $150,000 5 Star	Manuel Orantes	Raul Ramirez	W. Fibak - R. Ramirez	J. Gisbert - M. Orantes
10/10/1976	Soedertaelja Challenge SP	Ilie Nastase	Bjorn Borg	2-6, 7-5, 6-0, 6-4	
10/10/1976	Hawaii $100,000 3 Star	Harold Solomon	Bob Lutz	R. Moore - A. Stone	D. Stockton - R. Tanner
10/15/1976	Hilton Head $195,000 SP	Bjorn Borg	Arthur Ashe	A. Ashe - R. Laver	B. Borg - I. Nastase
10/17/1976	Oslo Challenge SP	Ilie Nastase	Bjorn Borg	2-6, 7-6, 6-0, 6-4	
10/17/1976	Madrid $100,000 3 Star	Manuel Orantes	Eddie Dibbs	W. Fibak - R. Ramirez	B. Hewitt - F. McMillan
10/17/1976	Brisbane $50,000 1 Star	Mark Edmonson	Phil Dent	S. Ball - K. Warwick	B. Fairlie - I. El Shafei
10/24/1976	Barcelona $100,000 3 Star	Manuel Orantes	Eddie Dibbs	B. Gottfried - R. Ramirez	B. Hewitt - F. McMillan
10/24/1976	Sydney $125,000 4 Star	Geoff Masters	Jim Delaney	B. Fairlie - I. El Shafei	S. Ball - K. Warwick
10/31/1976	Vienna $50,000 1 Star	Wojtek Fibak	Raul Ramirez	B. Hewitt - F. McMillan	B. Gottfried - R. Ramirez
10/31/1976	Perth $50,000 1 Star	Ray Ruffles	Phil Dent	D. Stockton - R. Tanner	B. Carmichael - I. El Shafei
10/31/1976	Paris $50,000 1 Star	Eddie Dibbs	Jaime Fillol	T. Okker - M. Riessen	F. McNair - S. Stewart
11/6/1976	Tokyo $100,000 3 Star	Roscoe Tanner	Corrado Barazzuti	B. Carmichael - K. Rosewall	B. Fairlie - I. El Shafei
11/6/1976	Cologne $50,000 1 Star	Jimmy Connors	Frew McMillan	B. Hewitt - F. McMillan	C. Dowdeswell - M. Estep
11/6/1976	London $135,000 3 Star	Raul Ramirez	Manuel Orantes	D. Lloyd - J. Lloyd	J. Feaver - J. James
11/14/1976	Stockholm $150,000 5 Star	Mark Cox	Manuel Orantes	B. Hewitt - F. McMillan	T. Okker - M. Riessen
11/14/1976	Hong Kong $75,000 2 Star	Ken Rosewall	Ilie Nastase	H. Pfister - B. Walts	An. Amritraj - I. Nastase
11/14/1976	San Jose	Charles Pasarell	Andrew Pattison		

11/21/1976	Manilla $75,000 2-Star	Brian Fairlie	Ray Ruffles	R. Case - G. Masters	An. Amritraj - C. Barazzuti
11/21/1976	Sao Paulo $50,000 1 Star	Guillermo Vilas	Jose Higueras	L. Alvarez - V. Pecci	R. Cano - B. Prajoux
11/21/1976	London £62,500 5 Star	Jimmy Connors	Roscoe Tanner	S. Smith - R. Tanner	W. Fibak - B. Gottfried
11/26/1976	Copenhagen SP	Bjorn Borg	Wojtek Fibak	7-5, 3-6, 7-6, 7-5	
11/28/1976	Buenos Aires $75,000 2 Star	Guillermo Vilas	Jaime Fillol	C. Kirmayr - T. Vasquez	R. Cano - B. Prajoux
11/28/1976	Bangalore $50,000 1 Star	Kim Warwick	Sashi Menon	B. Carmichael - R. Ruffels	B. Nunna - C. Mukerjea
11/28/1976	Johannesburg 4 Star	Harold Solomon	Brian Gottfried	B. Gottfried - S. Stewart	J. Gisbert - S. Smith
12/5/1976	Santiago	Jose Higueras	Carlos Kirmayr	P. Cornejo - H. Gildemeister	L. Alvarez - B. Prajoux
12/12/1976	Houston $130,000 CU Masters	Manuel Orantes	Wojtek Fibak	F. McNair - S. Stewart	B. Gottfried - R. Ramirez
12/19/1976	Las Vegas $100,000 WCT Cup Finals	Ilie Nastase	Jimmy Connors	3-6, 7-6, 6-4, 7-5	
12/19/1976	Las Vegas $50,000 WCT Cup Semis	Jimmy Connors	Vitas Gerulaitis	5-7, 7-6, 7-6, 6-1	
12/19/1976	Las Vegas $50,000 WCT Cup Semis	Ilie Nastase	Manuel Orantes	6-2, 2-6, 6-2, 6-1	
12/19/1976	Las Vegas WCT Cup $10,000 RR	Vitas Gerulaitis	Adriano Panatta	6-1, 6-4	
12/19/1976	Las Vegas WCT Cup $10,000 RR	Vitas Gerulaitis	Ken Rosewall	6-3, 6-0	
12/19/1976	Las Vegas WCT Cup $10,000 RR	Jimmy Connors	Ken Rosewall	6-2, 6-2	
12/19/1976	Las Vegas WCT Cup $10,000 RR	Jimmy Connors	Adriano Panatta	7-6, 6-3	
12/19/1976	Las Vegas WCT Cup $10,000 RR	Jimmy Connors	Vitas Gerulaitis	6-4, 6-4	
12/19/1976	Las Vegas WCT Cup $10,000 RR	Adriano Panatta	Ken Rosewall	7-5, 3-6, 6-3	
12/19/1976	Las Vegas WCT Cup $10,000 RR	Manuel Orantes	Harold Solomon	6-2, 2-6, 6-2	
12/19/1976	Las Vegas WCT Cup $10,000 RR	Manuel Orantes	Ilie Nastase	7-5, 3-6, 6-4	

12/19/1976	Las Vegas WCT Cup $10,000 RR	Harold Solomon	Rod Laver	6-3, 6-4	
12/19/1976	Las Vegas WCT Cup $10,000 RR	Ilie Nastase	Rod Laver	6-3,, 6-1	
12/19/1976	Las Vegas WCT Cup $10,000 RR	Rod Laver	Manuel Orantes	4-6, 7-6,7-5	
12/26/1976	Melbourne $40,000 AU vs. US	Australia	Americas	4-0,	
12/26/1976	Melbourne $40,000 AU vs. US	John Alexander	Arthur Ashe	6-3, 6-7, 6-3, 3-6, 6-1	
12/26/1976	Melbourne $40,000 AU vs. US	Ken Rosewall	Guillermo Vilas	6-2, 6-3, 6-0	
12/26/1976	Melbourne $40,000 AU vs. US	Ken Rosewall	Arthur Ashe		
12/26/1976	Melbourne $40,000 AU vs. US	John Alexander	Guillermo Vilas		

http://www.atpworldtour.com/en/scores/results-archive.

http://www.itftennis.com/procircuit/tournaments/men's-calendar.aspx?tour=&reg=&nat=&sur=&cate=AL&iod= &fromDate=01-01-1968&toDate=29-12-1976.

Tennis History, Jim McManus, (Canada 2010).

1977 USLTA Yearbook.

Official 1989 MTC Media Guide, (MTC 1989).

World of Tennis 1977, Edited by John Barrett and compiled by Lance Tingay, (London 1977)

CHAPTER 11:

1977: COLGATE GRAND PRIX BEGINS VS. WCT TOUR, ANTI-TRUST SETTLEMENT, CRISIS NO. 17 CONTINUED

The ITF, WCT, ATP, USTA and WTT marched into 1977, relatively at peace with each other, except for the conflict of the Grand Prix tournaments competing with WCT in the first four months of the year and WCT's legal claims against the MIPTC et al., which could lead to an anti-trust lawsuit or an agreement for WCT to join the Colgate Grand Prix in 1978.

1977 Governing Bodies

The MIPTC was the governing body of men's professional tennis in 1977, except for WCT, WTT and Davis Cup which was still governed by the Davis Cup Nations.

1977 Significant Tennis Leaders	
ILTF/ITF President:	Derek Hardwick (Great Britain), until July
ILTF/ITF President:	Philippe Chatrier (France) beginning in July
USTA President:	W.E. "Slew" Hester
Australian LTA President:	Brian Tobin
British LTA President:	Sir Carl Aarvold
French FFT President:	Philippe Chatrier
Chairman of Wimbledon:	Sir Brian Burnett
ATP President:	John Newcombe
ATP Executive Director:	Bob Briner
WCT Owners:	Lamar Hunt and Al Hill, Jr.
WCT Executive Director:	Mike Davies

In 1977, the name of the International Lawn Tennis Federation (ILTF) was changed to the International Tennis Federation (ITF).

1977 MIPTC

ITF:
Derek Hardwick, Chairman until July, Philippe Chatrier, Stan Malless and Paolo Angeli with David Gray as Joint Secretary. In August, Derek Hardwick replaced Philippe Chatrier and Brian Tobin replaced Paolo Angeli.

Tournaments:
Lars Myhrman (Europe), Owen Williams (Rest of World) and Jack Kramer (North America). In August, John Harris replaced Jack Kramer.

Players:
Bob Briner, Pierre Darmon and Cliff Drysdale with Doug Tkachuk as Joint Secretary. In August, Bob Briner succeeded Derek Hardwick as Chairman and the 10th member of the MIPTC was eliminated.

Four Competitions

In 1977, the 10th year of Open Tennis, there were four organized competitions for men: Colgate Grand Prix, WCT, Davis Cup and WTT.

There were 77 Colgate Grand Prix Open prize money tournaments, including the year-end Colgate Masters in Madison Square Garden. In 1977, Grand Prix tournaments were scheduled during the first part of the year against the WCT tournaments, which now had 16-draws, except for the 32-draw Philadelphia tournament. The Colgate Masters was moved into Madison Square Garden for 1977-1979 Grand Prix years and was scheduled for January 4-8, 1978, (for the 1977 Grand Prix year) with $400,000 in prize money and $100,000 to the winner. It was won by Jimmy Connors over Bjorn Borg 6-4, 1-6, 6-4. Bob Hewitt and Frew McMillan defeated Bob Lutz and Stan Smith 7-5, 7-6, 6-3 for the Doubles Masters.

The USTA - IPA Indoor Circuit tournaments, previously promoted by Bill Riordan, were folded into the 1977 Colgate Grand Prix and the U.S. National Indoors was moved from Salisbury, where it was promoted by Riordan since 1964, to the Memphis Racquet

Club in Memphis, Tennessee. Memphis had outbid Riordan, who no longer represented Connors, for the USTA sanction. So, Bill Riordan was left solely to promote his "World Heavyweight Championship of Tennis" matches and he would soon run into huge problems there.

The WCT point series of 12 tournaments included Philadelphia ($200,000) 32-draw, plus 11 ($100,000) 16-draw tournaments, leading to the WCT Finals in Dallas and the WCT Doubles Finals in Kansas City. Jimmy Connors defeated Dick Stockton 6-7, 6-1, 7-5, 6-1 in Dallas and Vijay Amritraj and Stockton defeated Vitas Gerulaitis and Adriano Panatta 7-6, 7-6, 4-6, 6-3 in Kansas City. WCT also staged four other special events: (i) Finals of 1976 Caesar's Palace Challenge Cup in Las Vegas on April 10 where Ilie Nastase defeated Jimmy Connors 3-6, 7-6, 6-4, 7-5, (ii) Aetna World Cup ($100,000) in Hartford March 10-13 where the United States defeated Australia 7-0, (iii) Caesar's Palace Challenge Cup ($320,000) in Las Vegas November 14-20 where Connors defeated Roscoe Tanner in the final 6-2, 5-6, 3-6, 6-2, 6-5, and (iv) Shakeys Tournament of Champions in Lakeway, Texas, March 10-13 and Madison Square Garden November 17, where Harold Solomon defeated Ken Rosewall 7-6, 6-2, 2-6, 0-6, 6-3.

Davis Cup was open to all players and was won 3-1 by Australia over Italy. WTT featured franchises in 10 U.S. cities with matches from May through August in conflict with the European Spring tournaments (Italian Open, French Open, etc.) and the American Summer tournaments. There were other events, not in the Colgate Grand Prix and not WCT events including: (i) One ATP tournament, the Alan King Caesar's Palace Classic ($250,000) in Las Vegas won by Jimmy Connors over Raul Ramirez 6-4, 5-7, 6-2 in singles and by Bob Lutz and Stan Smith over Bob Hewitt and Raul Ramirez 6-3, 3-6, 6-4 in doubles and (ii) The World Heavyweight of Tennis Challenge Match in Puerto Rico ($250,000) where Connors defeated Ilie Nastase 4-6, 6-3, 7-6, 6-3.

In 1977, the ATP was involved in six events: February 27: Palm Springs $225,000 ATP American Airlines Tennis Games, May 1: Las Vegas $250,000 ATP Alan King Classic at Caesar's Palace, June 12: Birmingham (GB) ATP John Player Championships, August 30: Boston $125,000 ATP U.S. Pro Championships, September 18: Woodlands $125,000 ATP-Grow World Doubles and November 20: London $125,000 ATP Benson and Hedges Championships at Wembley. All of the ATP events were in the Grand Prix, except for the Alan King Caesars Palace Classic.

Crisis No. 17 Continued: WCT vs. MIPTC et al.

In his book *The Game*[252], Jack Kramer wrote, "By 1977, he (Lamar Hunt) was down to twenty-three players, using no more than sixteen a week, which meant that the great bulk of the playing professionals would be out of work for much of the year. So, the Grand

Prix came into the WCT time period, and with its $1,000,000-bonus pool it appeared to be a much more attractive circuit. Hunt could compete only by going back to his old policy of paying contracts. It cost him, it seems, as much as $700,000 to get Connors for one season; Nastase cost about $1,500,000 for three. Moreover, the agents of the lesser players heard about these windfall payments and began to try to get more money for their boys. WCT was really taking its lumps, and there didn't appear to be any way out of the bind. That's when Lamar decided that he would like to become part of the Grand Prix."

Toronto MIPTC Meeting February 14-16

In Toronto in February, the Council met, but there are no minutes for this MIPTC meeting. The notation in the MIPTC minute book said: "Minutes of MIPTC Toronto, February 1977, (not typed as of September 77)." It was a well-known fact that the Joint Secretaries, Doug Tkachuk and David Gray, often could not agree on draft minutes for the MIPTC and sometimes no minutes were filed or the ones filed were never formally approved. Owen Williams began providing his "Rest of the World" tournaments and many others who requested them, copies of his meeting notes from the MIPTC meetings. Owen's notes were extremely popular and were often the best source of what actually happened at MIPTC meetings.

Based on the correspondence at the time, it is reasonable to assume that all nine members of the Council were present at the Toronto meeting and that WCT was represented at the meeting by Lamar Hunt, Mike Davies and with Paul Tagliabue and/ or Bill Adams as counsel for WCT. Just prior to the meeting, WCT proposed that the MIPTC create a new "Super Series" level of 40 tournaments with WCT having 11 Super Series with 32 draws at $150,000 each, plus Philadelphia as a 48 draw Super Series at $200,000. The WCT tournaments would be a "circuit within a circuit" in that they would be in the WCT circuit and also in the Grand Prix circuit. In addition, WCT would have five special events such as the Dallas singles finals, the WCT doubles finals, Aetna World Cup, Tournament of Champions and one other special event.

WCT agreed to separately honor it player appearance contracts that continued after 1977, if included in the 1978 Grand Prix, but not to enter into any additional ones. The continuing threat was that if WCT was not accommodated in the 1978 Grand Prix, antitrust litigation would ensue. WCT requested the Council to produce a firm position as to the precise 1978 format and participation of WCT in the 1978 Grand Prix by the close of the Toronto meeting on February 16. At the Toronto meeting, the MIPTC developed a consensus with respect to the proposed 1978 Grand Prix Rules and asked James W. Lillie, ITF Counsel, to prepare a draft for review by the MIPTC.

I have been unable to determine if WCT actually filed its threatened anti-trust lawsuit against the MIPTC after the end of the Toronto meeting on February 16. James Lillie, Esquire, who was counsel for the ITF at the time told me that he thought a complaint was actually filed in a United States District Court, but that it was withdrawn soon after filing. Either way the matter was settled by mutual agreement on March 23.

At the March 21-23, 1977, MIPTC meeting in Paris, the MIPTC after extensive discussions and various drafts of agreement, a final settlement draft was prepared by Paul Tagliabue for WCT, Steve Umin for ATP and James Lillie for the ITF, dated March 23, pursuant to which the MIPTC issued an invitation to WCT to join the 1978 Grand Prix which was accepted by WCT. The agreement also required the adoption of a "conflict of interest" rule by the MIPTC after which a formal release of all parties from the (threatened or actual) WCT lawsuit would be executed.[253]

At the June 15-16, 1977, MIPTC Meeting in Eastbourne, the MIPTC agreed that in 1978 WCT would have eight of 28 Grand Prix Super Series tournaments as a "circuit-in-a-circuit", plus five special events: WCT Finals in Dallas, WCT Doubles Finals in Kansas City, WCT Tournament of Champions in Las Vegas, WCT Aetna World Cup in Hartford and the WCT Challenge Cup in Montego Bay.[254]

At the June 26 MIPTC Meeting in London, all members of the Council and others attending the following meetings, were asked to provide a statement for submission, declaring any tennis conflict of interest.[255] At the August 26-28, 1977, MIPTC meeting in Boston, it was agreed that the Conflicts of Interest Policy of the MIPTC would require all persons attending a meeting of the Council to give a full conflict of interest disclosure of all tennis related interests and everyone eligible to vote in the election of the Council would have automatic access to the file of the conflict of interest disclosures. Mike Davies agreed to execute a complete general release and covenant not to sue to all parties, i.e., the MIPTC and its individual members plus Philippe Chatrier and Jack Kramer (former members), the ATP, the ITF, Commercial Union Assurance Company, the Colgate Palmolive Company, and the partnership and individual partners of the firm of Dell, Craighill, Fentress and Benton. It was understood and agreed that the release did not apply to any future acts.[256]

Thus, ended Crisis No. 17 with the MIPTC and WCT planning to live happily ever after with WCT promoting a WCT "circuit" within the Colgate Grand Prix. *Do you want to believe that this solution permanently solved all issues between WCT and the MIPTC?*

Kramer wrote in *The Game*[257], "I was on the Council at the time, but after the decision I started phasing myself out of the political picture and I resigned from the Council shortly after...As Hunt knows full well, everybody in tennis is especially vulnerable to his threats because we all have so many conflicts." John Harris replaced Kramer as Representative of the North American tournaments.

Rules

The MIPTC changed the "Triple Crown" group to the "Grand Slam" group and added the Australian Open *for the first time* with the French Open, Wimbledon and the U.S. Open with minimum prize money of $200,000. A new "6 Star" category was added for tournaments with $175,000 in prize money. Each tournament was required to contribute 12.5 percent of its prize money to the Bonus Pool and pay an ITF fee of $500. To be eligible for the Bonus Pools, players had to compete in 15 Grand Prix tournaments, including at least two 1 Star or 2 Star tournaments. Entry was by the 60-day entry deadline, so there was still no up-front promotable player commitment that could be advertised six months in advance by the tournaments. The 1977 Grand Prix Rules required that everything for the MIPTC be sent to "the Secretaries of the Council," apparently seeking to require each to receive everything and giving each authority to act on everything. *Keep in mind that there was a lack of trust between the ITF and the ATP so neither wanted the other to act unilaterally.* David Gray was the ITF Joint Secretary and Doug Tkachuk was the Player Joint Secretary and there was not much trust between them. Because the Council only met periodically, the Joint Secretaries assumed lots of power to deal with the day-to-day administration of the MIPTC, including the Code of Conduct.

The 1977 Rules eliminated the option to have a native of the location of the Colgate Masters as the eighth player and mandated that the eight players would be selected from the Bonus Point standings. Since the Colgate Masters was now located in the United States at Madison Square Garden, there was little chance that none of the top eight players would be an American.

Again, the Tournament Regulations began with "where the words 'computer ranking' are used these refer to the ATP ranking which has been approved by the Council for use in the 1977 Grand Prix." Wild cards were limited to four per year. The positive effect was to make players with high rankings apply for direct entry instead of as last-minute wild cards. The negative effect was to limit the opportunities of new players with no or extremely low computer rankings. Detailed prize money breakdowns were specified for the first time in the 1977 Tournament Regulations. The total player compensation was listed as "Prize Money" with 12.5 percent going to the Bonus Pool Contribution and 87.5 percent going to on-site prize money for distribution to the singles (70 percent) and doubles (17.5 percent) players at the tournament. The prize money breakdown was developed by the leaders of ATP with the goal of making a fair distribution of the available prize money to all the players in the draw. The prize money breakdown for the singles and doubles players for each round was specified. Contrast that with WCT which always wanted 50 percent to go to the winner. Tournament Regulation 32(d) reconfirmed that "The umpire may not overrule a linesman but must give a decision when a linesman is unsighted." Tournament Regulation 32(g) specified "a maximum of one minute shall elapse from the cessation of the previous game to the time players are ready to begin the next game."[258]

MIPTC Meetings

In 1977, the MIPTC held seven meetings: January 20-22 in Paris, February 14-16 in Toronto, March 21 in Paris, June 15-16 in Eastbourne, June 26 in London, August 26-28 in Boston and October 28-30 in London.

Council Administrator – Not Yet

In January in Paris, it was agreed that no offer should be made for a Council Administrator until the Council was on a sound financial footing. It was noted that interest by a well-known American journalist in the position had been expressed. *Perhaps, Bud Collins?*

Experimental Point Penalty System; Good Bye to USTA Computer Rankings

In addition, it was agreed that 10 tournaments in 1977 would be authorized to use the experimental Point Penalty System including Indianapolis, U.S. Open and Columbus. By a vote of 4-1 with one abstention, it was agreed that the players to vote in the 1977 MIPTC election would be the top 150 players on the ATP Computer Rankings and all references to the USTA Computer Rankings were to be deleted. *Goodbye to the USTA Computer Rankings System by the Grand Prix!*[259]

MIPTC Election

In Eastbourne in June[260], the Council received the results of the MIPTC election with the new terms to begin in August of 1977. The members elected were:

ITF: Derek Hardwick, Stan Malless and Brian Tobin with David Gray as ITF Joint Secretary. In July of 1977, Philippe Chatrier replaced Derek Hardwick as President of the ITF so they hoped that Chatrier would be elected as the non-voting Chairman of the MIPTC in August of 1977.

Players: Pierre Darmon, Cliff Drysdale and Bob Briner with Doug Tkachuk as Players' Joint Secretary.

Tournaments: John Harris (North America), Lars Myhrman, (Europe) and Owen Williams (Rest of the World). Jack Kramer had resigned in disgust over the agreement to include WCT into the 1978 Grand Prix.

Briner Elected Chairman

In Boston in August, Philippe Chatrier (ITF President) upon the invitation of Derek Hardwick attended the MIPTC meeting. Chatrier was obviously expecting to be elected as the non-voting Chairman of the MIPTC. Previously, the voting on the MIPTC usually consisted of the three ITF Representatives plus Lars Myhrman voting for the ITF leadership while the three Player Representatives and Jack Kramer voted for the player leadership with Owen Williams as the "swing vote." John Harris, who replaced Jack Kramer, was a partner with Donald Dell in the Washington Super Series tournament so he was a reliable vote with the players. Brian Tobin moved, seconded by Stan Malless, the nomination of Philippe Chatrier as a non-member, non-voting Chairman. Cliff Drysdale moved, seconded by Owen Williams, the nomination of Bob Briner for Chairman. The second by Owen Williams signaled that he had "swung" with the players in favor of Briner along with John Harris. A ballot was held and Bob Briner was elected as the new Chairman of the MIPTC. It is easy to guess that the voting was 5-4 with Drysdale, Darmon, Briner, Harris and Williams voting for Briner and with Hardwick, Malless, Tobin and Myhrman voting for Chatrier. So for the first time in history, the ITF no longer controlled the Chairmanship of the MIPTC and the 10th member of the MIPTC was deleted. More importantly, the players had a sort of reliable 5-4 voting majority on the MIPTC with Owen Williams being the so-called "swing vote." Actually, Owen Williams had not permanently "swung" in any direction. However, as a result of the vote, Philippe Chatrier would not be a member of the MIPTC for the next two years, but he would begin a long term as President of the ITF.

Disciplinary Officers

In addition at the meeting, the MIPTC designated John Harris for the United States, Lars Myhrman for Europe, and Owen Williams for the Rest of the World as Disciplinary Officers to hear and determine appeals of player misconduct fines. It was agreed that an appeal made at a tournament, where the Disciplinary Officer concerned was connected, should be heard by a Disciplinary Officer from another area. *Now, don't you just know that this was never going to work? Tournament Directors spend most of their time trying to solicit players to enter their tournaments and as a result they have absolutely no interest in penalizing any players, and they didn't.*[261]

Affidavit Against Guarantees Required for the First Time

In London in October, the MIPTC agreed that player commitments for the 1978 Grand Prix would require an affidavit from each player that he would not accept guarantees or other payments in connection with competing in a Grand Prix tournament. "This is the most significant step ever taken to clean up a practice that threatens the heart of tournament tennis, Briner said to Neil Amdur of the *New York Times*. "The rules will be strictly enforced."[262]

MIPTC Sanction Fees Replace ITF Fees and Search for Legal Counsel

Also in October, the Council began charging MIPTC sanction fees to tournaments to replace the old ITF authorization fees. In addition, the Council agreed to seek and appoint a legal counsel for the MIPTC and asked Steve Umin, Jay Lillie, Donald Dell, Frank Craighill and Paul Tagliabue, the attorneys for various parties attending MIPTC meetings, to put forward four recommendations for consideration at the next meeting. The MIPTC was advised that it should become a formal corporation, but the Council could never agree on becoming incorporated in any one country. When I was hired in 1981, I drafted and the Council adopted a constitution and bylaws, but it continued as an international unincorporated association until its liquidation in 1990. I did, however, obtain an IRS 501(c)(6) tax exemption for the MIPTC.[263]

Borg Commits to 1977 WCT Dallas Finals

Bjorn Borg won the WCT Finals in Dallas in 1976, and his agent, Bud Stanner of International Management Group (IMG) informed WCT that Borg would be playing the 1977 WCT Circuit and that WCT could advertise his participation, which WCT did. However, early in 1977, Borg informed WCT that he was now not going to play in the 1977 WCT circuit. WCT filed a lawsuit in the State District Court in Dallas for breach of contract seeking $5.7 million in damages against Bjorn Borg, IMG, Colgate, the sponsor of the Grand Prix, and Bancroft, Borg's tennis racquet manufacturer. *Welcome to conflicts of interest in tennis. IMG represents Borg and through its subsidiary TWI it represents WCT. Tennis has always been good at claiming there is a really good Chinese wall separating conflicts of interest within the same company.*[264]

Europeans Object to Americanization of Professional Tennis

The Europeans began to object to the imbalance of men's professional tennis in the United States vs. Europe and the rest of the world.[265] Rich Koster wrote in *The Tennis Bubble*[266]: "The key word for tennis in the 1970s is Americanization: American promotion, American money, and American television. Like it or not, the United States is where it is *mostly* at…Tennis is not an American game, but professional tennis is a penny-ante operation without American financing. Of the world's top players, 75% are not Americans, but that really isn't a consideration. The sport is professional, not national." (This was long before cable and satellite television or non-government owned over-the-air television was available outside of the US).

Rich Koster Analysis: The Future of Tennis, Order is Needed

In 1976, Rich Koster wrote in *The Tennis Bubble*[267]: "In reflecting back over the interviews and political positions of the major figures in tennis, it's obvious that there is no absolute right and wrong. Each faction has some merit, just as each has a right to the ground it has occupied. None has a franchise on Truth, but most contributed at least some light on progress. A solution in tennis is the grandest of dreams, and those who should be dreaming are fighting.

The line which is repeated most often is that tennis is different. Indeed it is, by virtue of its international character. For the purposes of the Game, that is, the game played by these men and women of superior talent, an audience is necessary. Certainly somebody must watch, either in the arenas, stadiums, or living rooms, if Connors and Evert and King and Ashe are to go on as millionaires.

The common denominator is the fan. Tennis must be presented so that the fan understands it, has confidence in its integrity, and can enjoy the maximum it has to offer. That is necessary because in any sports equation, the customer is No. 1 - and essential. That would seem the place to begin. For the public to understand tennis, it must recognize some pattern. There must be order, some annual, seasonal development which the sport's followers can count on.

Will there be a World Series in October? A Super Bowl in January? Stanley Cup in the spring? Certainly, there will. They have become part of the order of things; they are yearly events. If it's October and your football team is 2-2, the Super Bowl is still a distinct possibility. If it's July and your baseball team is third, eight games behind, there's still hope.

If tennis is to fulfill its potential, it would seem it needs such constraints, such precedents. It needs order. And to have order, there must be authority.

That does not mean a half-dozen conflicting authorities, all effective within their own spheres, rather, authority which is responsible to those tens of millions of spectators, authority which will guarantee that tennis is not a collection of circuses, not a spinoff of Abe Saperstein's Globetrotters, not a January-to-January barnstorm for the financial indulgence of 200, 300 or even 1,000 players, who play when they want and tank when they choose to take a few days' vacation."

"What tennis needs is not Judge Landis, it needs a conciliator who, once he makes a decision has the power to enforce it. For now, the prospect of establishing order is remote. There is too much energy left for the battle." Koster's analysis was also reprinted in the *New York Times* on March 13, 1977.[268]

Rich Koster's thoughtful analysis of the need for order in professional tennis was insightful and important when he wrote it in 1976 and it is just as insightful and important today.

Spaghetti Strung Racquets Banned

The "spaghetti" racquet which involved an unusual stringing procedure was creating surprisingly effective results in matches. The "spaghetti" racquet, which was rigged with fishing line or other bonding substances, imparted exaggerated spin to the ball. At the 1977 U.S. Open, Mike Fishbach of Great Neck, New York upset Billy Martin and Stan Smith while using it. In October, the ITF banned the use of the spaghetti racquet "until permanent rules could be written to determine the legal size, shape and composition of racquets." The USTA also banned the spaghetti racquet after it was banned by the ITF.[269]

Nastase Banned from 1978 Davis Cup

Ilie Nastase was banned from the 1978 Davis Cup by the Davis Cup Nations' Committee due to his unsportsmanlike behavior in a Davis Cup match in June between Romania and Great Britain in Bucharest. Nastase was given a right of appeal. *Misconduct by "Nasty" was his norm.*[270]

WTT

Butch Buchholz, WTT Commissioner and President

The 1977 year was the fourth year of WTT with 10 franchises. Butch Buchholz was the WTT Commissioner and President for 1977.

In 1977, each team played 44 matches and total games won determined the winner of each match. The Pittsburgh Triangles closed shop and were replaced by a new franchise, the Pennsylvania Keystones. However, the Pennsylvania Keystones subcontracted its franchise for 1977 to "The Soviets," a new franchise owned by the Russian Tennis Federation featuring all Russian players. The Russian Federation was paid $200,000 by WTT for all its "amateur" players.[271]

The Hawaii Leis moved to Seattle and Oakland and became the Sea-Port Cascades. The WTT players for 1977 included Ilie Nastase, Rod Laver, Chris Evert, Martina Navratilova, Alex Metreveli, Olga Morozova, Billie Jean King, Virginia Wade, Sandy Mayer, Ray Ruffels, Vitas Gerulaitis and Bjorn Borg.

EASTERN DIVISION

Team	Won	Lost	Players
Pennsylvania Keystones			
The Soviets	12	32	Alex Metreveli, Teuraz Kakulia, Vadim Borisov, Olga Morozova, Natasha Chmyreva, Marina Kroshina, Sergei Gruzman.
New York Apples	33	11	Coach Fred Stolle, Billie Jean King, Virginia Wade, Sandy Mayer, Ray Ruffels, Lindsey Beaven, Linda Siegelman, Anne Fritz.
Boston Lobsters	35	9	Coach Roy Emerson, Tony Roche, Martina Navratilova, Greer Stevens, Mike Estep.
Indiana Loves	21	23	Coach Allen Stone, Vitas Gerulaitis, Ann Kiyomura, Syd Ball, Sue Barker, Sue Mappin.
Cleveland Nets	15	27	Coach Marty Riessen, Bjorn Borg, Mariana Simionescu, Wendy Turnbull, Peggy Michel, Renee Richards, Bob Giltinan.

WESTERN DIVISION

Team	Won	Lost	Players
San Francisco/Oakland Golden Gaters	25	19	Coach Frew McMillan, Francoise Durr, Terry Holladay, Tom Okker.
Phoenix Racquets	28	16	Coach Ross Case, Butch Walts, Chris Evert, Kristien Shaw, John Alexander, Brian Cheney, Janet Newberry, Stephanie Tolleson.
Los Angeles Strings	11	33	Coach Dennis Ralston, Ilie Nastase, Rosie Casals, Mark Cox, Diane Fromholtz, Valerie Ziegenfuss, Charles Pasarell.
Sea-Port Cascades (formerly Hawaii Leis)	18	26	Coach Tom Gorman, Erik Van Dillen, Joanne Russell, Betty Stove, Brian Parrott (club pro substituting for Erik Van Dillen), Pat Rostrom, Steve Docherty.
San Diego Friars	21	23	Coach Cliff Drysdale, Coach Rod Laver, Julie Anthony, Raz Reid, Kerry Reid, Mona Guerrant.

EASTERN DIVISION

Semifinals:	New York d. Indiana 2-1
	Boston d. Cleveland 2-1
Final:	New York d. Boston 2-0

WESTERN DIVISION

Semi-Finals	Phoenix d. Sea-Port 2-0

Finals
San Diego d. Golden Gaters 2-0
Phoenix d. San Diego 2-1

PLAY-OFF FINALS

New York d. Phoenix 2-0

"For winning its second consecutive WTT title, the New York team divided up $36,000, far and away the largest winning share in the history of the league."[272]

[Note that the WTT Championship Play-Offs were being completed on August 27, 1977, just prior to the beginning of the 1977 U.S. Open. This means that the WTT players had been playing one set matches all Summer indoors and not on the clay surface of the Summer U.S. Grand Prix tournaments and the U.S. Open or any two-out-of-three or three-out-of-five set matches. While WTT was great for the older players who did not want to travel anymore and great for the lesser players who could not make it on the Grand Prix, it was probably a detriment for up-and-coming players who would have been able to improve more in the Grand Prix tournament competition. *One set in a WTT men's match was not much professional tennis.*

ATP

ATP President John Newcombe

The expanded 1977 ATP staff included Patricio Rodriguez, road manager, Jim McManus, road manager (after resigning form the Board) and Owen Davidson, coordinator of satellite circuits worldwide. Beginning in 1976, ATP had finally begun to offer a small number of computer points to Satellite circuits of five tournaments with $5,000 each in prize money, treating them as one $25,000 tournament for computer points. This caused the development of lots of new Satellite circuits. The ATP Officers and Board remained unchanged from 1976: John Newcombe, President, Jamie Fillol, Vice President, Bob Briner, Executive Director, Jim McManus, Secretary/Treasurer, Lito Alvarez, Arthur Ashe, Pierre Darmon, Cliff Drysdale, Richard Evans, Patrick Proisy and Stan Smith. When Jim McManus, resigned to become a full-time salaried Road Manager, he was replaced on the ATP Board by Zeljko Franulovic.[273]

1977 JAKS Awards

On September 12, at the Woodlands in Texas, the ATP held its third JAKs Awards:

Player of the Year	Bjorn Borg
ATP Lifetime Award	Roy Wilder
Newcomer of the Year	Tim Gullikson
Doubles Team of the Year	Bob Hewitt – Frew McMillan
Adidas-ATP Sportsmanship Award	Arthur Ashe
Tennis Writer of the Year	Rex Bellamy
Tennis Broadcaster of the Year	Bud Collins
ATP Dr. Johnson Children's Award	Sherry Snyder
ATP Great Player of the Past	Lew Hoad
ATP Service Award	Jaime Fillol
Court Official of the Year	Bertie Bowron
President's Award	Donald Dell
Special Awards:	
For Contribution to Pro Tennis	Dave Dixon
Special Support of ATP Activities	American Airlines
Adidas ATP Sportsmanship Award	Arthur Ashe

Slew Hester and the U.S. Open Move to Flushing Meadows

On February 7, 1977, W.E. "Slew" Hester, age 64, was elected as President of the USTA to succeed Stan Malless. Hester was the first "deep Southerner" to serve as President of the USTA. Slew was an oil well "wildcatter" who "hit winners with 85 to 90 of his 200 oil digs," as described by Neil Amdur in the *New York Times*[274]. He was awarded a Bronze Star for running part of the "Redball Express" during World War II and he had won over 500 amateur tennis trophies. He also built the River Hills Tennis Club in his hometown of Jackson, Mississippi and ran a lot of tournaments there. Amdur wrote that Slew liked to play the "good ole boy with a smile and outstretched hand and he enjoyed his cigars, long and mild, along with his sour mash Bourbon."

The U.S. Open had been held at the West Side Tennis Club in Forest Hills (Queens, New York City), since it moved from Newport, Rhode Island in 1915. The USTA wanted to expand the stadium and tournament facilities for the U.S. Open and Slew sought to purchase the club or obtain a long term extension of its agreement for the U.S. Open.[275]

David Kenneth Spector, the USTA's architect, wrote in *Tennis Week*[276]: "The West Side wanted the USTA to pay to expand their antiquated stadium, build six indoor courts, remodel and expand their clubhouse. Plus, the Club wanted to share heavily in the profits. The Club members voted to make this a 'take it or leave it' deal. To spend what was (then) estimated to be over $7 million for a two-week event, coupled with no greater control of the tournament, was unacceptable to the USTA." Warren Kimball said in *The United States Tennis Association: Raising The Game*[277]: "Hester, incredulous, responded 'Gee, you have got to be kidding.' 'Suppose we refuse it?' he asked… West Side responded: 'If you refuse this, the West Side Club would be better off without the U.S. Open.'"

Slew Hester

Subsequently, Slew got help from Lewis Rudin, a big real estate developer in New York City, found the vacant Singer Bowl stadium at Flushing Meadows - Corona Park in Queens and in record time obtained governmental approval, began and finished construction of a new U.S. Open facility just in time for the 1978 U.S. Open which would change from clay to hard courts at a cost of just under $10 million. The construction included the dividing and upfitting of the Singer Bowl stadium, into a new 20,000-seat Louis Armstrong Stadium and a new Grandstand 5,600-seat stadium, installing 16-32 outdoor tennis courts and 4-8 indoor tennis courts. There was not enough time for a formal lease which would require an act of the New York State Legislature, so Slew went forward with a one-year concession agreement subject to annual renewals. It would be 1981 before a formal lease could be obtained.

Warren Kimball further wrote[278]: "George Gowen (USTA's long-time volunteer Chief Legal Officer at the time) deftly described the risks and the results: 'When we lifted the Open from Forest Hills, we did so to gain undisputed ownership and control. We gambled every cent we had and even what we could expect from the future. It was only four miles from West Side Tennis Club, but the distance travelled by the USTA in eighteen months could not be measured in miles.'"

WCT to Stage Tournament at Forest Hills in 1978

In December, the West Side Tennis Club announced a deal with WCT for a new $200,000+ tournament beginning in 1978. It would soon become the site for the WCT Tournament of Champions and would help West Side recover from the loss of the U.S. Open. As we shall see, the early Spring weather in New York was uncertain and the staging of a clay court tournament in New York prior to the French Open, would cause a serious conflict with Monte Carlo, Hamburg and Rome that preceded the French Open.[279]

The End of the Heavyweight Championships of Tennis Challenges

Bill Riordan, having lost Jimmy Connors, having lost the USTA Indoor Championships which had moved from Salisbury to the Memphis Racquet Club and having lost the USTA Indoor Circuit as all of its tournaments were now in the Colgate Grand Prix, was left to his promotion of the "Heavyweight Championship of Tennis Winner-Take-All" challenge matches. Riordan boasted, as documented in *The Tennis Bubble* by Rich Koster[280]: "I've copyrighted the name, 'The Heavyweight Championship of Tennis.' I have complete control. If they want to play, they have to play for me. It's set for six years. I'm not looking beyond that. I have a contract with CBS-TV and Caesar's Palace. The money is obscene. The figures are ridiculous. One challenge a year, I don't care about the money. I believe money is to be thrown off freight trains. But I've out finessed my enemies. In one afternoon, they ended up with the crumbs. I won. I'm eating the cake." *To say that Riordan was colorful would be an understatement.*

Connors Beats Nastase in Challenge

On March 5, 24-year-old Jimmy Connors defeated 30-year-old Ilie Nastase 4-6, 6-3, 7-5, 6-3 before 2,400 fans at the Cerromar Beach Hotel in Dorado Beach, Puerto Rico to win the fourth Bill Riordan "Heavyweight Championship of Tennis" $250,000 "winner take-all" match. Previously, there had been three challenge matches, with Laver, Newcombe and Orantes. The Connors vs. Nastase match exceeded the three hours allotted by CBS television for millions of viewers.

Riordan admitted that television viewers were told they were watching a $250,000 winner-take-all tennis match but Connors was guaranteed $500,000, win or lose, and Nastase received $150,000. Neil Amdur reported in the *New York Times*[281]: "Bill Riordan. who promoted three of the four "Heavyweight Championship of Tennis" matches, including the Connors-Nastase pairing in Puerto Rico, said that the final score of the match, televised nationally by CBS Sports, and won by Connors in four sets, had had no effect on the financial split. There was no $250,000 prize, he added. 'The match had been set up on the basis of winner-take-all for $250,000,' Riordan said by phone last night from Louisville, Ky. 'But at the last minute I had to renegotiate the contract with CBS and Nastase.' Asked why television viewers were not informed that the match was not winner-take-all, Riordan said, "I would definitely accept the blame for that."

But what about the CBS broadcast license and the licenses of all the CBS affiliates that are under FCC supervision? The misrepresentation of those matches as "winner-take-all" was false and misleading to the public. CBS provided a 61-page report concluding that "we have found no reason to believe that there was any intentional deception of the public by CBS personnel." The report was submitted to the FCC on July 1 and filed with "communications subcommittees of the Senate and the House of Representatives, which are investigating television coverage of sports" and later released publicly."[282]

Subsequently, the FCC staff submitted a 23-page report to the members of the House subcommittee investigating the relationship between network television and sports. The report concluded that "The conduct of top CBS officials cannot be excused considering the weight of the evidence, by suggesting 'it was all a mistake.'… It appears to the subcommittee staff that, in view of facts which were in possession of responsible CBS officials and the failure of those officials to take such action to disclose those facts, CBS sought to mislead the public as to the nature of the 'Heavyweight Championship of Tennis.'"[283]

On November 4, CBS Sports President Robert Wussler admitted to a Congressional House Communications Sub-Committee that the CBS promotion of the Heavyweight Championship of Tennis as winner-take-all matches "was sloppy", but denied "any attempt to deceive" the public.[284]

In March of 1978, Wussler resigned from CBS on the eve of a scheduled Federal Communication Commission meeting at which "the agency was to decide whether and how to chastise CBS for misrepresenting a series of specially promoted tennis matches as 'winner-take-all' events."[285]

The FCC penalized CBS by imposing a short-term, license on one of the stations owned by CBS "as punishment for improprieties" with the Riordan event telecasts. *Needless to say, CBS did not thank Bill Riordan or promote any more "World Heavyweight Championship of Tennis, Winner-Take-All" matches.*[286]

At the end of 1977, Bill Riordan did not represent Ilie Nastase. He did not represent Jimmy Connors. You could not find any members of his IPA (Independent Players Association). He had lost the U.S. National Indoors. There was no Riordan USTA Indoor Circuit and all his former tournaments had been folded into the Colgate Grand Prix. And now he had lost his "Heavyweight Championship of Tennis Winner-Take-All" promotions. Alas, Bill Riordan had no money "to throw off of trains".

1977 Grand Slam Winners

Australian Open

January

Roscoe Tanner d. Guillermo Vilas 6-3, 6-3, 6-3.
Arthur Ashe – Tony Roche d. Erik Van Dillen – Charles Pasarell 6-4, 6-4.

French Open

Guillermo Vilas d. Brian Gottfried 6-0, 6-3, 6-0.
Brian Gottfried – Raul Ramirez d. Wojtek Fibak – Jan Kodes 7-6, 4-6, 6-3, 6-4.
[Borg played WTT in 1977 so he did not enter the 1977 French Open].

Wimbledon

Bjorn Borg d. Jimmy Connors 3-6, 6-2, 6-1, 5-7, 6-4.
Ross Case – Geoff Masters d. John Alexander – Phil Dent 6-3, 6-4, 3-6, 8-9, 6-4.
[John McEnroe, an amateur age 18, scheduled to become a freshman at Stanford in September won three qualifying matches to gain entry into the 128-player main draw and then advanced to the semifinals of Wimbledon as an amazing introduction to professional tennis. Connors defeated McEnroe in the semis 6-3, 6-3, 4-6, 6-4 in two hours and 37 minutes.]

U.S. Open
(third year on clay, last year at Forest Hills)

Guillermo Vilas d. Jimmy Connors 2-6, 6-3, 7-6, 6-0.
Bob Hewitt – Frew McMillan d. Brian Gottfried – Raul Ramirez 6-4, 6-0.

Australian Open

[Moved to December to accommodate move of Colgate Masters into January].

Vitas Gerulaitis d. John Lloyd 6-3, 7-6, 3-6, 6-2.
Ray Ruffels – Alan Stone d. John Alexander – Phil Dent 7-6, 7-6.

1977 Davis Cup

Davis Cup Final (Sydney – Grass)

Australia d. Italy 3-1

Tony Roche (AU) d. Adriano Panatta (IT) 6-3, 6-4, 6-4.
John Alexander (AU) d. Corrado Barazzutti (IT) 6-2, 8-6, 4-6, 6-2.
Bertolucci - Panatta (IT) d. Alexander – Dent (AU) 6-4, 6-4, 7-5.
John Alexander (AU) d. Adriano Panatta (IT) 6-4, 4-6, 2-6, 8-6, 11-9.
Tony Roche (AU) vs. Corrado Barazzutti (IT) unfinished.

1977 World Rankings[287]

Bud Collins

1. Jimmy Connors
2. Guillermo Vilas
3. Bjorn Borg
4. Vitas Gerulaitis
5. Brian Gottfried
6. Eddie Dibbs
7. Manuel Orantes
8. Raul Ramirez
9. Ilie Nastase
10. Dick Stockton

Lance Tingay

1. Bjorn Borg
2. Guillermo Vilas
3. Jimmy Connors
4. Vitas Gerulaitis
5. Brian Gottfried
6. Dick Stockton
7. Eddie Dibbs
8. Raul Ramirez
9. Harold Solomon
10. Roscoe Tanner

Rino Tomassi

1. Bjorn Borg
2. Jimmy Connors
3. Guillermo Vilas
4. Brian Gottfried
5. Vitas Gerulaitis
6. Eddie Dibbs
7. Dick Stockton
8. Ilie Nastase
9. Manuel Orantes
10. Raul Ramirez

Year-End ATP Rankings[288]

1. Jimmy Connors
2. Guillermo Vilas
3. Bjorn Borg
4. Vitas Gerulaitis
5. Brian Gottfried
6. Eddie Dibbs
7. Manuel Orantes
8. Raul Ramirez
9. Ilie Nastase
10. Dick Stockton

1977 Colgate Grand Prix Bonus Pool Top 10[289]

Singles (8th Bonus Pool)

1.	Guillermo Vilas	$300,000
2.	Brian Gottfried	$125,000
3.	Bjorn Borg	$ 75,000

Doubles (3rd Bonus Pool)

1.	Bob Hewitt	$85,000
2.	Frew McMillan	$40,000
3.	Raul Ramirez	$35,000

4.	Manuel Orantes	$ 50,000	4.	Stan Smith	$30,000
5.	Eddie Dibbs	$ 45,000	5.	Brian Gottfried	$16,000
6.	Roscoe Tanner	$ 40,000	6.	Phil Dent	$14,000
7.	Raul Ramirez	$ 35,000	7.	Bob Lutz	$12,000
8.	Jimmy Connors	*	8.	John Alexander	$10,000
9.	Vitas Gerulaitis	*	9.	Sherwood Stewart	$ 9,000
10.	Harold Solomon	$ 32,000	10.	Fred McNair	$ 8,000

* Under the required minimum tournaments.

1977 Official Earnings Top 10[290]

1.	Guillermo Vilas	$766,065	6.	Dick Stockton	$277,626
2.	Brian Gottfried	$458,791	7.	Vitas Gerulaitis	$260,883
3.	Jimmy Connors	$428,919	8.	Raul Ramirez	$244,723
4.	Bjorn Borg	$337,020	9.	Wojtek Fibak	$238,035
5.	Eddie Dibbs	$283,555	10.	Bob Hewitt	$219,163

1977 Tournament Calendar

Date	Tournaments	Singles Winner	Singles #2	Doubles Winners	Doubles #2
1/1/1977	Sydney $75,000 GP 2 Star	Tony Roche	Dick Stockton	S. Ball - K. Warwick	M. Edmonson - J. Marks
1/9/1977	Australian Open $250,000 GS	Roscoe Tanner	Guillermo Vilas	A. Ashe - T. Roche	E. Van Dillon - C. Pasarell
1/16/1977	Adelaide $75,000 GP 2 Star	Victor Amaya	Brian Teacher	D. Stockton - C. Letcher	S. Ball - K. Warwick
1/16/1977	Birmingham $100,000 WCT	Jimmy Connors	Bill Scanlon	W. Fibak - T. Okker	B. Martin - B. Scanlon
1/16/1977	Auckland $25,000	Vijay Amritraj	Tim Wilkison	C. Lewis - R. Simpson	J. Smith - P. Langsford
1/23/1977	Boco West $200,000 SP	Bjorn Borg	Jimmy Connors	6-4, 5-7, 6-3	
1/23/1977	Baltimore $100,000 3 Star	Bian Gottfried	Guillermo Vilas	G. Vilas - I. Tiriac	J. Kodes - R. Case
1/30/1977	Philadelphia $200,000 WCT	Dick Stockton	Jimmy Connors	B. Hewitt - F. McMillan	W. Fibak - T. Okker
1/31/1977	Auckland	Chris Lewis	Tim Wilkison	D. Collins - G. Snook	C. Lewis - R. Lewis
2/6/1977	No. Little Rock $50,000 1 Star	Sandy Mayer	Haroon Rahim	C. Dibley - H. Rahim	B. Hewitt - F. McMillan
2/6/1977	Dayton $50,000 1 Star	Jeff Borowiak	Buster Mottram	H. Pfister - B. Walts	J. Borowiak - A. Pattison
2/6/1977	Richmond $100,000 WCT	Tom Okker	Vitas Gerulaitis	W. Fibak - T. Okker	R. Case - T. Roche
2/6/1977	Wellington	Brian Fairlie	David Collins		
2/13/1977	Miami $50,000 1 Star	Eddie Dibbs	Raul Ramirez	B. Gottfried - R. Ramirez	P. Kronk - C. Letcher
2/13/1977	Springfield $50,000 1 Star	Guillermo Vilas	Stan Smith	B. Hewitt - F. McMillan	G. Vilas - I. Tiriac
2/13/1977	Mexico City $100,000 WCT	Ilie Nastase	Wojtek Fibak	W. Fibak - T. Okker	I. Nastase - A. Panatta
2/19/1977	Ocean City $100,000	Vitas Gerulaitis	Bob Lutz	B. Scanlon - A. Metreveli	C. Richey - J. McEnroe
2/20/1977	San Hose $50,000 1 Star	Jiri Hrebec	Sandy Mayer	B. Hewitt - F. McMillan	G. Masters - T. Gorman
2/20/1977	Toronto $100,000 WCT	Dick Stockton	Jimmy Connors	W. Fibak - T. Okker	R. Case - T. Roche
2/27/1977	Palm Springs $225,000 6 Star	Brian Gottfried	Guillermo Vilas	B. Hewitt - F. McMillan	M. Reissen - R. Tanner

3/5/1977	Puerto Rico $250,000 SP	Jimmy Connors	Ilie Nastase	4-6, 6-3, 7-6, 6-3	
3/6/1977	Memphis $175,000 6 Star	Bjorn Borg	Brian Gottfried	F. McNair - S. Stewart	S. Smith - B. Lutz
3/8/1977	Monterrey $100,000 WCT	Wojtek Fibak	Vitas Gerulaitis	R. Case - W. Fibak	B. Martin - B. Scanlon
3/13/1977	Johannesburg $175,000 6 Star	Bjorn Borg Rain	Guillermo Vilas	B, Hewitt - F. McMillan	C. Pasarell - E. Van Dillon
3/13/1977	Hampton $50,000 1 Star	Sandy Mayer	Stan Smith	S. Mayer - S. Smith	P. Kronk - C. Letcher
3/13/1977	Hartford $100,000 WC WCT	United States	Australia	7-0,	
3/13/1977	Hartford $100,000 WC WCT	Dick Stockton	Tony Roche	4-6, 7-6, 6-2,	
3/13/1977	Hartford $100,000 WC WCT	Jimmy Connors	John Alexander	6-1, 6-4	
3/13/1977	Hartford $100,000 WC WCT	Brian Gottfried	Ross Case	3-6, 6-4, 6-4	
3/13/1977	Hartford $100,000 WC WCT	Jimmy Connors	Tony Roche	6-4, 7-5	
3/13/1977	Hartford $100,000 WC WCT		6-4, 6-4	B. Gottfried - D. Stockton	R. Case - T. Roche
3/13/1977	Hartford $100,000 WC WCT	Dick Stockton	John Alexander	7-5, 7-5	
3/13/1977	Hartford $100,000 WC WCT		6-3, 6-1	M. Riessen - R.Tanner	M. Edmondson - R. Emerson
3/13/1977	Lakeway $200,000 TC WCT	Ken Rosewall	Eddie Dibbs	6-2, 6-2	
3/20/1977	Washington $100,000 3 Star	Brian Gottfried	Bob Lutz	S. Smith - B. Lutz	B. Gottfried - R. Ramirez
3/20/1977	Helsinki $50,000 1 Star	Mark Cox	Kjell Johansson	J. Hbrec - H. Kary	J. Lloyd - D. Lloyd
3/20/1977	St. Louis $100,000 WCT	Jimmy Connors	John Alexander	I. Nastase - A. Panatta	V. Amritraj - D. Stockton
3/27/1977	San Diego $100,000 3 Star	Brian Gottfried	Marty Riessen	B. Hewitt - F. McMillan	R. Ruffels - A. Stone
3/27/1977	Cairo $30,000	Francois Jauffret	Frank Gebert	J. Bartlett - J. Marks	R. Lewis - P. Dupre
3/27/1977	Rotterdam $100,000 WCT	Dick Stockton	Ilie Nastase	W. Fibak - T. Okker	V. Amritraj - D. Stockton
4/3/1977	Nice $50,000 1 Star	Bjorn Borg	Guillermo Vilas	G. Vilas - I. Tiriac	C. Kachel - C. Lewis
4/3/1977	Los Angeles $150,000 5 Star	Stan Smith	Brian Gottfried	B. Hewitt - F. McMillan	S. Smith - B. Lutz

4/3/1977	London $100,000 WCT	Eddie Dibbs	Vitas Gerulaitis	I. Nastase - A. Panatta	M. Cox - E. Dibbs
4/9/1977	Jackson $58,000	Brian Teacher	Bill Scanlon	B. Hewitt - F. McMillan	K. Rosewall - P. Dent
4/10/1977	Monte Carlo $100,000 WCT	Bjorn Borg	Corrado Barazzutti	F. Jauffret - J. Kodes	W. Fibak - T. Okker
4/10/1977	Las Vegas $100,000 SP WCT	Ilie Nastase	Jimmy Connors	3-6, 7-6, 6-4, 7-5	
4/17/1977	Murcia $50,000 1 Star	Jose Higueras	Buster Mottram	F. Jauffret - P. Donminguez	H. Guildemeister - B. Prajoux
4/17/1977	Buenos Aires	Guillermo Vilas	Wojtek Fibak	W. Fibak - I. Tiriac	G. Vilas - L. Alvarez
4/17/1977	Houston $100,000 WCT	Adriano Panatta	Vitas Gerulaitis	I. Nastase - A. Panatta	J. Alexander - P. Dent
4/23/1977	Virginia Beach	Guillermo Vilas	Ilie Nastase	R. Ruffles - P. Dominguez	F. Gonzalez - J. McEnroe
4/24/1977	Charlotte $100,000 WCT	Corrado Barazzutti	Eddie Dibbs	T. Okker - K. Rosewall	C. Barazzutti - A. Panatta
4/24/1977	Florence $30,000	Paulo Bertolucci	John Feaver	C. Lewis - R. Simpson	I. Molina - J. Velasco
4/24/1977	Denver $100,000 3 Star	Bjorn Borg	Brian Gottfried	C. Dibley - G. Masters	
5/1/1977	Munich $75,000 2 Star	Zeljko Franulovic	Victor Pecci	F. Pala - B. Taroczy	N. Spear - J. Whitlinger
5/1/1977	Las Vegas $250,000	Jimmy Connors	Raul Ramirez	S. Smith - B. Lutz	B. Hewitt - R. Ramirez
5/1/1977	Charleston	Victor Amaya	Deon Joubert	M. Lara - K. McMillan	E. Friedler - J. Karzan
5/8/1977	Kansas City $200,000 WCT			V. Amritraj - D. Stockton	V. Gerulaitis - A. Panatta
5/8/1977	Augusta	Zan Guerry	Rick Fagel	M. Cahill - T. Moor	Z. Guerry - J. James
5/15/1977	Hamburg $125,000 4 Star	Paolo Bertolucci	Manuel Orantes	B. Hewitt - K. Meiler	P. Dent - K. Warwick
5/15/1977	Dallas $200,000 WCT Finals	Jimmy Connors	Dick Stockton	6-7, 6-1, 7-5, 6-1	
5/22/1977	Dusseldorf $75,000 2 Star	Wojtek Fibak	Ray Moore	K. Meiler J. Fassbender	P. Kronk - C. Letcher
5/22/1977	Rome $150,000 5 Star	Vitas Gerulaitis	Antonio Zugareli	B. Gottfried - R. Ramirez	F. McNair - S. Stewart
6/5/1977	French Open $250,000 GS	Guillermo Vilas	Brian Gottfried	B. Gottfried - R. Ramirez	W. Fibak - J. Kodes

6/12/1977	Brussels $75,000 2 Star	Harold Solomon	Karl Meiler	N. Pilic - Z. Franulovic	F. Pala - B. Taroczy
6/12/1977	Nottingham $100,000 3 Star	Tim Gullikson	Jaime Fillol	Singles & Doubles cancelled	Rain
6/18/1977	London $100,000 3 Star	Raul Ramirez	Mark Cox	V. Amritraj - An. Amritraj	J. Lloyd - D. Lloyd
6/19/1977	Berlin $50,000 1 Star	Paolo Bertolucci	Jiri Hrebec	B. Prajoux - H. Gildemeister	V. Zednik - J. Hrebec
7/2/1977	Wimbledon £204,340 GS	Bjorn Borg	Jimmy Connors	R. Case - G. Masters	J. Alexander - P. Dent
7/2/1977	Raleigh $10,000 Southern Chps.	Terry Moore	Zan Guerry	M. Lara - A. Neely	Z. Guerry - J. James
7/10/1977	Bastad $75,000 2 Star	Corrado Barazzutti	Balazs Taroczy	M. Edmonson - J. Marks	F. Jaffret - J. Hallet
7/10/1977	Gstaad $75,000 2 Star	Jeff Borowiak	Jean Caujolle	J. Fassbender - K. Meiler	C. Dowdeswell - B. Hewitt
7/10/1977	Newport $50,000 1 Star	Tim Gullikson	Hank Pfister	I. El Shafei - B. Fairlie	T. Gullikson - T. Gullikson
7/13/1977	Lakeway $200,000 TC WCT	Harold Solomon	Dick Stockton	6-4, 6-4	
7/17/1977	Hilversum $75,000 2 Star	Patrick Proisy	Lito Alvarez	A. Munez - J. Higueras	F. Jaffret - J. Hallet
7/17/1977	Kitzbuhel $75,000 2 Star	Guillermo Vilas	Jan Kodes	B. Mottram - R. Taylor	C. Dowdeswell - C. Kachel
7/18/1977	Cincinnati $100,000 3 Star	Harold Solomon	Mark Cox	J. Alexander - P. Dent	B. Hewitt - R. Tanner
7/25/1977	Washington $125,000 4 Star	Guillermo Vilas	Brian Gottfried	J. Alexander - P. Dent	F. McNair - S. Stewart
8/1/1977	Louisville US $125,000 4 Star	Guillermo Vilas	Eddie Dibbs	J. Alexander - P. Dent	C. Letcher - C. Kachel
8/7/1977	North Conway $125,000 4 Star	John Alexander	Manuel Orantes	B. Gottfried - R. Ramirez	F. McNair - S. Stewart
8/8/1977	South Orange $75,000 2 Star	Guillermo Vilas	Roscoe Tanner	W. Fibak - C. Dibley	G. Vilas - I. Tiriac
8/14/1977	Columbus $125,000 4 Star	Guillermo Vilas	Brian Gottfried	S. Smith - B. Lutz	P. Fleming - G. Mayer
8/14/1977	Indianapolis $125,000 4 Star	Manuel Orantes	Jimmy Connors	J. Fillol - P. Cornejo	D. Crealy - C. Letcher
8/22/1977	Toronto $125,000 4 Star	Jeff Borowiak	Jaime Fillol	B. Hewitt - R. Ramirez	F. McNair - S. Stewart
8/29/1977	Rye SP	Guillermo Vilas	Ilie Nastase	6-2, 6-0	
8/30/1977	Boston $125,000 4 Star	Manuel Orantes	Eddie Dibbs	S. Smith - B. Lutz	B. Hewitt - B. Gottfried

9/10/1977	US Open $462,420 GS	Guillermo Vilas	Jimmy Connors	B. Hewitt - F. McMillan	B. Gottfried - R. Ramirez
9/17/1977	NY $200,000 TC WCT	Harold Solomon	Ken Rosewall	7-6, 6-2, 2-6, 0-6, 6-3	
9/18/1977	Woodlands $125,000 Doubles			T. Okker - M. Riessen	T. Gullikson - T. Gullikson
9/18/1977	Laguna Niguel	Andrew Pattison	Colin Dibley	B. Martin - C. Hagey	P. Fleming - T. Waltke
9/26/1977	Paris $50,000 1 Star	Guillermo Vilas	C. Roger-Vasselin	J. Thamin - C. Roger-Vasselin	I. Nastase - I. Tiriac
9/26/1977	Los Angeles $125,000 4 Star	Raul Ramirez	Brian Gottfried	F. McMillan - S. Mayer	T. Leonard - M. Machette
9/30/1977	Hilton Head $220,000 SP	Bjorn Borg	Roscoe Tanner	R. Tanner - B. Borg	V. Gerulaitis - J. Newcombe
10/2/1977	San Francisco $125,000 4 Star	Butch Walts	Brian Gottfried	M. Riessen - D. Stockton	F. McNair - S. Stewart
10/2/1977	Aix-en-Provence $50,000 1 Star	Ilie Nastase	Guillermo Vilas	I. Nastase - I. Tiriac	P. Dominguez - R. Norberg
10/9/1977	Tehran $150,000 5 Star	Guillermo Vilas	Eddie Dibbs	I. Nastase - I. Tiriac	B. Hewitt - F. McMillan
10/9/1977	Hawaii $100,000 3 Star	Jimmy Connors	Brian Gottfried	S. Smith - B. Lutz	B. Gottfried - R. Ramirez
10/9/1977	Rotterdam SP	Ilie Nastase	Vitas Gerulaitis	6-2, 6-2	
10/16/1977	Brisbane $50,000 1 Star	Vitas Gerulaitis	Tony Roche	B. Scanlon - V. Gerulaitis	M. Anderson - K. Rosewall
10/16/1977	Madrid $100,000 3 Star	Bjorn Borg	Jaime Fillol	B. Hewitt - F. McMillan	M. Orantes - A. Munoz
10/23/1977	Sydney $125,000 4 Star	Jimmy Connors	Ken Rosewall	J. Newcombe - T. Roche	R. Case - G. Masters
10/23/1977	Barcelona $100,000 3 Star	Bjorn Borg	Manuel Orantes	J. Kodes - W. Fibak	B. Hewitt - F. McMillan
10/30/1977	Vienna $50,000 1 Star	Brian Gottfried	Wojtek Fibak	B. Hewitt - F. McMillan	J. Kodes - W. Fibak
10/30/1977	Perth $50,000 1 Star	Vitas Gerulaitis	Geoff Masters	R. Ruffles - A. Stone	J. Whitlinger - N. Saviano
10/30/1977	Basle $50,000 1 Star	Bjorn Borg	John Lloyd	B. Mottram - M. Cox	J. James - J. Feaver
11/6/1977	Paris $50,000 1 Star	Corrado Barazzutti	Brian Gottfried	B. Gottfried - R. Ramirez	J. Borowiak - R. Taylor
11/6/1977	Cologne $50,000 1 Star	Bjorn Borg	Wojtek Fibak	B. Hewitt - F. McMillan	F. McNair - S. Stewart
11/6/1977	Tokyo $100,000 3 Star	Manuel Orantes	Kim Warwick	G. Masters - K. Warwick	C. Dibley - C. Sachel

11/13/1977	Stockholm $150,000 5 Star	Sandy Mayer	Ray Moore	T. Okker - W. Fibak	B. Gottfried - R. Ramirez
11/13/1977	Hong Kong $75,000 2 Star	Ken Rosewall	Tom Gorman	K. Warwick - S. Ball	M. Reissen - R. Tanner
11/13/1977	Bogota $50,000 1 Star	Guillermo Vilas	Jose Higueras	H. Gildemeister - B. Prajoux	J. Andrew - C. Kimayr
11/20/1977	London $125,000 4 Star	Bjorn Borg	John Lloyd	S. Mayer - F. McMillan	B. Gottfried - R. Ramirez
11/20/1977	Manila $75,000 2 Star	Karl Meiler	Manuel Orantes	C. Kachel - J. Marks	M. Cahill - T. Moor
11/20/1977	Santiago $50,000 1 Star	Guillermo Vilas	Jaime Fillol	J. Fillol - P. Cornejo	H. Bunis - P. McNamee
11/20/1977	Las Vegas WCT Cup $100,000	Jimmy Connors	Roscoe Tanner	6-2, 5-6, 3-6, 6-2, 6-5	
11/20/1977	Las Vegas WCT Cup $50,000	Roscoe Tanner	Dick Stockton	6-5, 6-5	
11/20/1977	Las Vegas WCT Cup $50,000	Jimmy Connors	Ilie Nastase	6-2, 6-4	
11/20/1977	Las Vegas WCT Cup $10,000	Ilie Nastase	Vitas Gerulaitis	6-6, 5-6, 6-4	
11/20/1977	Las Vegas WCT Cup $10,000	Ilie Nastase	Rod Laver	6-3, 6-4	
11/20/1977	Las Vegas WCT Cup $10,000	Ilie Nastase	Roscoe Tanner	5-6, 6-4, 6-5	
11/20/1977	Las Vegas WCT Cup $10,000	Vitas Gerulaitis	Roscoe Tanner	5-6, 6-4, 6-4	
11/20/1977	Las Vegas WCT Cup $10,000	Roscoe Tanner	Rod Laver	6-3, 6-1	
11/20/1977	Las Vegas WCT Cup $10,000	Rod Laver	Vitas Gerulaitis	2-6, 6-5, 6-5	
11/20/1977	Las Vegas WCT Cup $10,000	Jimmy Connors	John Alexander	6-2, 6-1	
11/20/1977	Las Vegas WCT Cup $10,000	Jimmy Connors	Ken Rosewall	6-0, 6-2	
11/20/1977	Las Vegas WCT Cup $10,000	Dick Stockton	Jimmy Connors	6-5, 6-5	
11/20/1977	Las Vegas WCT Cup $10,000	Dick Stockton	John Alexander	6-3, 5-6, 6-4	
11/20/1977	Las Vegas WCT Cup $10,000	Ken Rosewall	John Alexander	5-6, 6-4, 6-4	
11/20/1977	Las Vegas WCT Cup $10,000	Ken Rosewall	Dick Stockton	3-6, 6-4, 6-3	

11/26/1977	Buenos Aires $75,000 2 Star	Guillermo Vilas	Jaime Fillol	G. Vilas - I. Tiriac	R. Cano - A. Munoz
11/26/1977	Taipei $50,000 1 Star	Tim Gullikson	Ismail El Shafei	P. Dupre - J. Delaney	T. Gorman - S. Dockery
11/26/1977	Oviedo $100,000 3 Star	Eddie Dibbs	Raul Ramirez	F. McNair - S. Stewart	J. Kodes - R. Ramirez
11/26/1977	Tokyo Gunz SP	Ken Rosewall	Ilie Nastase	4-6, 7-6, 6-4	
12/4/1977	Bombay $50,000 1 Star	Vijay Amritraj	Terry Moor	M. Cahill - T. Moor	M. Lara - J. Singh
12/6/1977	Johannesburg $150,000 5 Star	Guillermo Vilas	Buster Mottram	S. Smith - B. Lutz	P. Fleming - R. Moore
12/11/1977	Adelaide $100,000 3 Star	Tim Gullikson	Chris Lewis	S. Ball - K. Warwick	J. Alexander - P. Dent
12/18/1977	Sydney $125,000 4 Star	Roscoe Tanner	Brian Teacher	J. Alexander - P. Dent	R. Ruffels - A. Stone
12/20/1977	Adelaide $50,000 Toyota SP	United States	Australia	4-0,	
12/20/1977	Adelaide $50,000 Toyota SP	Vitas Gerulaitis	Tony Roche	6-2, 3-6, 6-1	
12/20/1977	Adelaide $50,000 Toyota SP	Roscoe Tanner	John Alexander	6-4, 7-6	
12/20/1977	Adelaide $50,000 Toyota SP	Roscoe Tanner	Tony Roche	6-3, 4-6, 6-4	
12/20/1977	Adelaide $50,000 Toyota SP	Vitas Gerulaitis	John Alexander	6-2, 4-6, 6-2	
12/29/1977	Zurich $25,000	Jan Norback	Jacek Niedzwiedski	N. Pilic - R. Probst	C. R.-Vasselin - P. Hagelauer
12/31/1977	Australian Open $250,000 GS	Vitas Gerulaitis	John Lloyd	R. Ruffles - A. Stone	J. Alexander - P. Dent
1/8/1978	NY $250,000 Colgate Masters	Jimmy Connors	Bjorn Borg	B. Hewitt - F. McMillan	S. Smith - B. Lutz

http://www.atpworldtour.com/en/scores/results-archive.

http://www.itftennis.com/procircuit/tournaments/men's-calendar.aspx?tour=&reg=&nat=&sur=&cate=AL&iod=&fromDate=01-01-1968&toDate=29-12-1977.

Tennis History, Jim McManus, (Canada 2010).

1978 USLTA Yearbook.

Official 1989 MTC Media Guide, (MTC 1989).

World of Tennis 1978, Edited by John Barrett and compiled by Lance Tingay, (London 1978).

CHAPTER 12:

1978: WCT MERGED INTO COLGATE GRAND PRIX, PEACE AT LAST?

With WCT merged into the Colgate Grand Prix, with the 1978 Bonus Pool being the largest ever, with WCT's Lamar Hunt and Mike Davies participating in MIPTC meetings, and with ATP Executive Director Bob Briner as Chairman of the MIPTC, was peace and prosperity finally at hand?

1978 Governing Bodies

The MIPTC was the governing body for men's professional tennis in 1978, except for WTT and Davis Cup. WCT was merged into the Colgate Grand Prix in 1978 for the first time. Davis Cup continued to be governed by the Davis Cup Nations.

1978 Significant Tennis Leaders

ITF President:	Philippe Chatrier (France)
USTA President:	W.E. "Slew" Hester
Australian LTA President:	Brian Tobin
British LTA President:	Sir Carl Aarvold
French FFT President:	Philippe Chatrier
Chairman of Wimbledon:	Sir Brian Burnett
ATP President:	John Newcombe until July
ATP President:	Jaime Fillol beginning in July
ATP Executive Director:	Bob Briner
WCT Owners:	Lamar Hunt and Al Hill, Jr.
WCT Executive Director:	Mike Davies

1978

MIPTC

ITF: Derek Hardwick, Brian Tobin and Stan Malless with David Gray as Joint Secretary.

Tournaments: Lars Myhrman (Europe), Owen William (Rest of the World) and John Harris (North America).

Players: Bob Briner, Chairman, Pierre Darmon and Cliff Drysdale with Doug Tkachuk as Joint Secretary. Arthur Ashe replaced Pierre Darmon in October.

Legal Counsel: Roy L. Reardon, Esquire

Three Competitions

In 1978, the 11th year of Open Tennis, there were three organized competitions for men: the Colgate Grand Prix, the Davis Cup and WTT. Davis Cup was open to all players and was won 4-1 by the United States over Great Britain.

There were 87 Colgate Grand Prix Open prize money tournaments, including the year-end Colgate Masters in Madison Square Garden in New York City. Included in the 87 tournaments were the four Grand Slams and 28 Super Series tournaments with $175,000+ in prize money. The ATP's Alan King-Caesar's Palace Classic was finally added in April as part of the Colgate Grand Prix and won by Harold Solomon over Corrado Barazzutti 6-1, 3-0 Ret'd in singles and by Alvaro Fillol and Jaime Fillol over Bob Hewitt and Raul Ramirez 6-3, 7-6 in doubles. The Colgate Masters was again staged at Madison Square Garden and was won by John McEnroe over Arthur Ashe 6-7, 6-3, 7-5 in singles and by Peter Fleming and John McEnroe over Wojtek Fibak and Tom Okker 6-4, 6-2, 6-4 in doubles.

In 1978, the ATP was involved in seven events: February 19, Palm Springs, $225,000 ATP American Airlines Tennis Games, April 30, Las Vegas, $250,000 ATP Alan King Classic at Caesar's Palace, May 8, Dusseldorf, #200,000 Ambre Solaire ATP Nation's Cup (Nations Cup began in 1975 in Jamaica, but was not staged in 1976 and 1977), June 18, Birmingham (GB), ATP John Player Championships, August 28, Boston $175,000 ATP U.S. Pro Championships, September 17, Woodlands, $200,000 ATP-Lipton World

Doubles and November 19, London, $175,000 ATP Benson and Hedges Championships at Wembley. All were in the Colgate Grand Prix except for the Nations Cup.

WCT staged eight of the 28 Super Series tournaments. The eight WCT tournaments, in addition to leading as part of the 86 Grand Prix tournaments to the Colgate Grand Prix Bonus Pool and the Colgate Masters, also led as a "circuit within a circuit" to the WCT Finals in Dallas won by Vitas Gerulaitis over Eddie Dibbs 6-3, 6-2, 6-1 and the WCT Doubles Finals in Kansas City won by Wojtek Fibak and Tom Okker over Bob Lutz and Stan Smith 6-7, 6-4, 6-0, 6-3. The Dallas Finals and the Kansas City Finals were considered as WCT special events. WCT staged five other special events outside of the Colgate Grand Prix: (i) March 26, Las Vegas, $200,000 Shakeys Tournament of Champions won by Bjorn Borg over Vitas Gerulaitis 6-5, 5-6, 6-4, 6-5 (Tiebreak at 5-all), (ii) May 12, Hartford, $100,000 Aetna World Cup won by the United States over Australia 6-1, (iii) July 16, Forest Hills, $300,000 WCT Invitational won by Vitas Gerulaitis over Ilie Nastase 6-2, 6-0 in singles and by John Alexander and Phil Dent over Fred McNair and Sherwood Stewart 7-6, 7-6 in doubles, (iv) December 17, Montego Bay $320,000 WCT Challenge Cup won by Ilie Nastase over Peter Fleming 2-6, 5-6, 6-2, 6-4, 6-4 and (v) January 7, 1979, London, $200,000 WCT Braniff Airways World Doubles won by Peter Fleming and John McEnroe over Ilie Nastase and Sherwood Stewart 3-6, 6-2, 6-3, 6-1.

Another new event in Madrid was the $175,000 Copa Marlboro International Tennis Cup won by Europe over South America 4-3 during the week of March 12. This event was created in competition with the WCT Aetna World Cup between the USA and Australia.

World Team Tennis with franchises in 10 U.S. cities for 1978, staged matches from May through August in conflict with the European Spring tournaments (Italian Open, French Open, etc.) and the American Summer tournaments. It was the fifth year of WTT.

Rules

The significant changes to the 1977 Grand Prix Rules deleted the 1-6 Star categories and established three group categories for 1978: Grand Slam, Super Series and smaller tournaments, later called Regular Series and Open Week Series. Bonus Pool prizes were increased in singles from 35-50 and in doubles from 20-35. The minimum number of tournaments required for eligibility for the Bonus Pools was increased from 15 to 20, including at least four ATP designated $50,000 or $75,000 tournaments. The ATP was supposed to designate each player to a specific $50,000 or $75,000 tournament four times during the Grand Prix year. This was the first attempt to designate players to four specific small tournaments to ensure they had marketable fields to the extent possible; the 20 tournament commitment was just a condition of Bonus Pool awards. Players and tournaments were required to sign an affidavit that they would not accept or pay appearance guarantees.

Again, the Tournament Regulations began with "where the words 'computer ranking' are used these refer to the ATP singles and doubles computer ranking which has been approved by the Council for use in the 1978 Grand Prix." Entry deadlines were reduced from 60 days to 42 days for main draw and increased from 30 days to 42 days for qualifying and a new withdrawal deadline was set at 42 days.[291]

First Political Use of ATP Computer Rankings

In the first political use of the ATP Computer Rankings, a new rule specified a "one point" or first-round loss for the record of any player withdrawing within 72 hours after the draw has been made. The new rule forced the players to withdraw early for injuries rather than wait until the tournament was about to begin. Seeds were to be based on the computer ranking 7 days instead of 15 days prior to the start of a tournament. The draw only had to be remade if two or more of the top eight seeds withdrew more than 48 hours prior to the start of play. Within 48 hours, a re-draw was optional. Still, Grand Slams were to have only 16 seeds. The MIPTC eliminated any use of the singles computer ranking in the selection of doubles entries, focusing solely on the doubles computer ranking. For the first time, the MIPTC agreed that a chair umpire could overrule a linesman.

MIPTC Meetings

In 1978, the MIPTC held five meetings: January 5-7 in New York, April 17-19 in Nice, July 23-24 in London, September 1-2 in New York and October 26-28 in Tokyo.

McEnroe An Amateur

In January in New York, it was agreed that McEnroe, who was a freshman at Stanford, could participate in the 1978 Colgate Grand Prix as an amateur and that he did not have to sign a Grand Prix player commitment contract if it would jeopardize his amateur status with the NCAA. *Do you remember who won the 1978 NCAAs and the 1978 Colgate Masters?*[292]

Australian Open and Colgate Masters Dates

In April in Nice, the Australian Open dates were changed to December 26, 1978 – January 3, 1979, to accommodate the new Colgate Masters dates which were changed to January 8-14, 1979, in New York. As long as the Masters was scheduled indoors in

Madison Square Garden in January, the Australian Open had an impossible burden to solicit players to fly to Australia over Christmas and play on grass just before coming back to New York for the Masters and the following indoor tournaments. It would take until 1986 for the Masters to be moved into December so that the Australian Open could move into January.

WCT vs. Borg Lawsuit Settled

Also in April, it was disclosed that WCT had settled its lawsuit against Bjorn Borg for his failure to play in the WCT 1977 tour for a commitment by Borg to play in "X" number of WCT Grand Prix tournaments over a three-year period. The MIPTC questioned if the WCT-Borg settlement violated the prohibition against guarantees. Lamar Hunt assured the MIPTC that no guarantees were involved, just the obligation to play in some WCT tournaments. If Borg withdrew from a WCT tournament, there was no penalty, just the obligation to play in another WCT tournament.

Legal Counsel

Roy L. Reardon, Esquire, of Simpson Thacher was recommended by WCT and the ITF Representatives and the Council approved his employment as legal counsel for the MIPTC. This was one of the best decisions ever made by the Council. Roy Reardon was a very well-respected anti-trust lawyer and he was independent of all of the constituencies of the Council members. *Roy was just what the Council needed.*

Authority of the ITF and MIPTC Regarding Rules of Tennis

ITF President Philippe Chatrier attended and asked if the players were willing to agree that the ITF makes the *Rules of Tennis*. Cliff Drysdale responded that "the Council makes the rules but chooses to respect the ITF's study and rules on this without yielding its own sovereignty." *Once again, the players demanded that the MIPTC be the exclusive authority.*[293]

Italian Open Put On Thin Ice

In July in London, it was reported that the lack of crowd control at the Italian Open organized by Franco Bartoni prohibited many players from having a fair competition. The Italian spectators were noisy and very ill-mannered. Bartoni assured the MIPTC that measures had been adopted to ensure this did not happen again in 1979. Nevertheless, the MIPTC informed the Italian Tennis Federation that unless it appointed a referee from outside Italy and that unless there was better crowd control, the Council would reluctantly have to expel the Italian Open from the Grand Prix.

Ilie Nastase – 1978 Houston-River Oaks – Major Offense

The MIPTC received a recommendation from Houston for fines against Nastase totaling $2,900 for misconduct during the finals. This was in addition to Nastase misconduct at 1978 Palm Springs, 1978 St. Louis, 1978 Richmond, 1977 Wimbledon, 1976 U.S. Open, 1976 Wimbledon and 1976 Palm Springs. The Council conducted a hearing on July 2 at the Gloucester Hotel in London and charged Nastase with the Major Offense of Aggravated Behavior for his pattern of misconduct, fined him an additional $5,000 and suspended him for 90 days. Nastase accepted the fine and the suspension, but complained that "he was being singled out because of his reputation."

While Nastase was banned from all Colgate Grand Prix tournaments for 90 days, he was not banned from the WCT Tournament of Champions at Forest Hills staged the week after Wimbledon as a special event when his suspension was just beginning and he was not banned from his highly paid salary and participation in WTT as the player-coach of the Los Angeles Strings which he led to the 1978 WTT Championship over the summer. So, all that Nastase really missed was the 1978 U.S. Open.[294]

Pierre Darmon to Resign

Pierre Darmon stated that he planned to resign from the MIPTC after the next meeting of the MIPTC. The MIPTC agreed that the replacement of a vacancy in the last year of a term would be filled by the remaining members of that constituency rather than go to the time and expense of conducting an entirely new election. Pierre was succeeded by Arthur Ashe.[295]

WCT Philadelphia and Double Points

In September in New York, the MIPTC objected to WCT Philadelphia which was then both a Colgate Grand Prix tournament and a WCT tournament for having double WCT points for qualification for the WCT Dallas finals. The MIPTC Player Representatives stated that double WCT points gave Philadelphia an unfair advantage over other Colgate Grand Prix tournaments. Mike Davies stated that WCT was committed to double WCT points for Philadelphia by contract. Philadelphia always had a draw size double the other WCT tournaments and offered double prize money as well.[296]

Point Penalty System Adopted for 1979

In October in Tokyo, the Point Penalty System was adopted as the standard for Grand Prix use beginning in 1979. It had been experimented in 12 Grand Prix tournaments in 1978.

Huge Change in 1979 Grand Prix Player Commitment Leads To Crisis No. 18

In 1978, players were obligated to commit to play 20 tournaments as a condition of eligibility for the Bonus Pool. After extensive discussion and after receiving advice of legal counsel, the Council agreed that for 1979, the player commitment would be reduced from 20 tournaments to six designated tournaments (three Grand Slams/Super Series and three smaller tournaments), which had to be agreed *as a condition of being able to play in any Grand Prix tournament, not just eligibility for the Bonus Pool.* The six designations would be up-front so the tournaments could for the 1st time advertise them six months in advance of their tournaments instead of only after the 42-day entry deadline. The 1979 Player Commitment prohibited special events during the 28 weeks of the Super Series except for three times each year. The Council was seeking to protect as much as possible the eight weeks of the Grand Slams and the 28 weeks of the Super Series from special events by leaving 16 open weeks for special events. *Was that enough for the top players and their agents? Well, No!*[297]

Vilas Refuses to Sign – Forgoes 1978 Bonus Pool

Guillermo Vilas elected not to sign a player commitment and became ineligible for the 1978 Bonus Pool. That did not affect his eligibility to play in the Colgate Grand Prix tournaments in 1978. It was rumored that Vilas did not want to sign the affidavit that prohibited the acceptance of appearance guarantees.[298]

Suntory Cup Special Event Against WCT Houston Super Series

During the week of April 23, a $175,000 Suntory Cup special event for four players, Bjorn Borg, Jimmy Connors, Guillermo Vilas and Manuel Orantes was staged in Tokyo the same week as the $175,000 WCT Houston tournament. The week of Houston, as one of the 28 "Super Series" protected weeks, was not very protected. Houston was a WCT Super Series and had no involvement with ProServ or IMG. "This kind of exhibition tennis is absolutely abhorrent to us and damaging to the entire tournament game," Briner said to *International Tennis Weekly*. "At the start of the year, 17 free weeks were set aside in the calendar for events of this kind. We would have approved fully if this tournament had been staged in one of those free weeks."[299]

Davies Creates WCT Television Network

Masterminded by WCT Executive Director Mike Davies, WCT announced the creation of the WCT Television Network at a cost of $2 million which in 1978 planned to have 35 "super tennis" programs produced by the Mizlou Television Sports Network. The programs would include 14 one-hour and one two-hour final from the WCT Challenge Series and 14 one-hour and one two-hour final from the WCT Shakeys Tournament of Champions. Mike Davies told me that he syndicated the programs by making deals with something like 300 individual television stations in the United States for individual delivery of recorded matches. Mike believed strongly that tennis had to be exhibited on television to reach the general public. As far as I know, Mike was the first tennis executive to figure out how to create a tennis television network and syndicate tennis matches. Mike hired Cliff Drysdale as an announcer, which introduced Drysdale to his next career.[300]

The New MIPTC Grand Prix Supervisors

The MIPTC began hiring Grand Prix Supervisors in 1978. The new Grand Prix Supervisors, Dick Roberson, Franco Bartoni and Frank Smith, were introduced at the 1978 Stockholm Open. Roberson, 40, of San Diego, played football and basketball at LaVerne College in California from which he graduated with a bachelor's degree in physical education. He had been serving as WTT supervisor of officials. He was also national promotion manager for Penn Athletic Products. Frank Smith, 35, of Wilkes-Barre Pa.,

Original Grand Slam Supervisors (1979)

then residing in Vienna, VA, was a graduate of the U.S. Naval Academy. He served as a Navy carrier pilot, earned a Masters' Degree in Public Administration at University of Rhode Island and attained the rank of Lieutenant Commander. He joined KPMB Peat Marwick as a management consultant specializing in financial program management before joining the MIPTC as a Grand Prix Supervisor. Franco Bartoni, an Italian, was an economics major at University. He was a former Italian Davis Cup player and tournament director of the Italian Open in Rome. Bartoni was fluent in Italian, Spanish, French, English and

Portuguese. Briner said: "It's one of the most important steps we've taken to upgrade the quality of officiating at Grand Prix tournaments." The new Grand Prix Supervisors were to be *the final on-site authority at all Grand Prix tournaments.*[301]

Connors and Borg Did Not Qualify for 1978 Bonus Pool

Jimmy Connors and Bjorn Borg were the top two leading players in the Colgate Grand Prix Bonus Pool Standings which would have qualified them for Bonus Pool awards of $300,000 and $175,000, respectively, if they had continued to play for the Bonus Pool. However, since neither of them played the required 20 tournaments, they were both ineligible for Bonus Pool awards and thus, had no financial commitment to play in the Colgate Masters. Borg refused to play in the Masters, but Connors did.[302]

Vilas, who was ineligible for the Bonus Pool because he refused to sign the 1978 player commitment contract, was eligible for the Masters, but he also refused to play. It was embarrassing not to have Borg and Vilas in the Masters. John McEnroe defeated Arthur Ashe 6-7, 6-3, 7-5 in the final to win the event. *Not bad for McEnroe's first year as a pro.*[303]

WTT

Butch Buchholz was the WTT Commissioner and President for 1978. It was the fifth year of WTT with 10 U.S. franchises. There were no European franchises as had been proposed in 1977. However, there were some changes in the U.S. franchises. The Pennsylvania Keystones, (aka The Soviets in 1977) became the Anaheim Oranges, the Sea-port Cascades became the Seattle Cascades and the Cleveland Nets became the New Orleans Nets. Each team played 44 matches and total games won determined the winner of each match.

The leading WTT players for 1978, included Vitas Gerulaitis (New York), Ilie Nastase (Player-Coach, Los Angeles), Andrew Pattison (New Orleans), Mark Cox (Anaheim), Tom Gorman (Seattle), Chris Evert (Los Angeles), Martina Navratilova (Boston), Billie Jean King (New York), Virginia Wade (Golden Gaters) and Diane Fromholtz (Indiana). [Borg left the Cleveland Nets and WTT during the season].

EASTERN DIVISION

Team	Won	Lost	Players
Anaheim Oranges			
(formerly the Pennsylvania			
Keystones or			

The Soviets)	20	24	Coach Cliff Drysdale, Anand Amritraj, Mark Cox, Rosie Casals, Francoise Durr, Tracy Austin.
New York Apples	22	22	Coach Fred Stolle, Billie Jean King, JoAnne Russell, Vitas Gerulaitis, Ray Ruffels, Mary Carillo.
Boston Lobsters	33	11	Coach Roy Emerson, Tony Roche, Martina Navratilova, Greer Stevens, Terry Holliday, Anne Smith, Dale Collings, Mike Estep, Una Keyes.
Indiana Loves	13	31	Coach Allan Stone, Diane Fromholz, John Whitlinger, Sue Mappin, Tanya Harford, Geoff Masters.
New Orleans "Sun Belt" Nets (formerly Cleveland Nets)	20	24	Coach Marty Riessen, Renee Richards, Wendy Turnbull, Andrew Pattison, Helen Cawley, Trish Bostrom, John Lucas, Bjorn Borg (Borg left).

WESTERN DIVISION

Team	Won	Lost	Players
San Francisco/Oakland Golden Gaters	21	23	Coach Frew McMillan, Tom Dietrich, Assistant Coach, Virginia Wade, Sandy Mayer, Tom Leonard, Michael Wayman, Marise Kruger, Ilana Kloss.
Phoenix Racquets	14	30	Coach Syd Ball, Sue Barker, Butch Walts, Kristien Shaw, Rayni Fox, Dean Martin Jr.
Los Angeles Strings	27	17	Coach Ilie Nastase, Chris Evert, Vijay Amritraj, Ashok Amritraj, Stephanie

Tolleson, Ann Kiyomura.

Seattle Cascades (formerly Sea-port Cascades Or the Hawaii Leis)	20	24	Coach Tom Gorman, Marita Redondo, Sherwood Stewart, Betty Stove, Brigitte Cuypers, Chris Kachel.
San Diego Friars	30	14	Coach Rod Laver, Ross Case, Mona Guerrant, Raz Reid, Kerry Reid, Janet Young.

PLAY-OFF MATCHES

First Round: Boston d. New Orleans 2-0; New York d. Anaheim 2-0; Los Angeles d. Golden Gaters 2-0; Seattle d. San Diego 2-1.

Second Round: Boston d. Seattle 2-0, Los Angeles d. New York 2-0.

Championship Series: Los Angeles d. Boston 3-1 (24-21, 30-20, 26-27, 28-25).

After the 1979 season, WTT's franchises all folded. Thus, ended the WTT. *The Grand Prix tournaments had won after all.*

Jaime Fillol Becomes Fourth ATP President

In June, Jaime Fillol was elected as the fourth President of ATP, succeeding John Newcombe. Ray Moore was elected as Vice President, Stan Smith as Treasurer and Jim McManus as Secretary. Lito Alvarez and Ray Moore were re-elected to the ATP Board of Directors along with newcomers Victor Amaya, Colin Dibley, Richard Lewis and Charlie Pasarell, who joined Arthur Ashe, Stan Smith, Cliff Drysdale, Jaime Fillol and Bob Briner. The six new directors "at last reflected the overall membership's long expressed desire for more representation among the lower ranked players. The average ranking of the six new directors was 97, and none of them were in the top 40." In this election, the ATP also reduced the number of directors from 13 to 11 and eliminated Richard Evans and Pierre Darmon as non-player directors.[304]

During the 1977-1979 time that Bob Briner was MIPTC Chairman, Briner and Doug Tkachuk almost unilaterally ran men's professional tennis from the Texas office of the ATP. Tkachuk was overseeing the designation of players to tournaments and the enforcement of the Code of Conduct. Tkachuk hired the first four Grand Prix Supervisors and they reported to him. In 1978, Briner and Tkachuk, along with Donald Dell, supported strongly by board members Ashe and Smith, were the most powerful people in the game. However, with the election of a number of lower ranked players to the ATP Board, a new faction began led by Cliff Drysdale and Ray Moore within the ATP as a backlash by the European players against having everything run out of the ATP's Texas office.

1978 ATP JAKS AWARDS
(New York City January 1979)

Player of the Year	Bjorn Borg
Doubles Team of the Year	Bob Hewitt – Frew McMillan
Newcomer of the Year	John McEnroe
Tennis Writer of the Year	Rex Bellamy
Tennis Broadcaster of the Year	John Newcombe
Dr. R.W. Johnson Children's Award	Arthur Ashe
ATP Great Player of the Past	Jack Kramer
ATP Service Award	Jaime Fillol
Court Official of the Year	Bertie Bowron
ATP Lifetime Award	Donald Dell
President's Award	Pierre Darmon
ATP-Adidas Sportsmanship Award	Stan Smith
ATP Junior Player Award	Young Min Kwon

1978 Grand Slam Winners

French Open

Bjorn Borg d. Guillermo Vilas 6-1, 6-1, 6-3.
Gene Mayer – Hank Pfister d. Jose Higueras – Manuel Orantes 6-3, 6-2, 6-2.

Wimbledon

Bjorn Borg d. Jimmy Connors 6-2, 6-2, 6-3.
Bob Hewitt – Frew McMillan d. Peter Fleming – John McEnroe 6-1, 6-4, 6-2.

U.S. Open

[tournament moved from Forest Hills on clay to Flushing Meadow on hard courts]

Jimmy Connors d. Bjorn Borg 6-4, 6-2, 6-2.
Bob Lutz – Stan Smith d. Marty Riessen – Sherwood Stewart 1-6, 7-5, 6-3.

Australian Open

[Tournament Manager: Karen Scott (Happer)]

Guillermo Vilas d. John Marks 6-4, 6-4, 3-6, 6-3.
Wojtek Fibak – Kim Warwick d. Paul Kronk – Cliff Letcher 7-6, 7-5.

1978 Davis Cup

Davis Cup Final (Palm Springs – Hard)

United States d. Great Britain 4-1.

John McEnroe (US) d. John Lloyd (GB) 6-1, 6-2, 6-2.
Buster Mottram (GB) d. Brian Gottfried (US) 4-6, 2-6, 10-8, 6-4, 6-3.
Bob Lutz – Stan Smith (US) d. Mark Cox – David Lloyd (GB) 6-2, 6-2, 6-3.
John McEnroe (US) d. Buster Mottram (GB) 6-2, 6-2, 6-1.
Brian Gottfried (US) d. John Lloyd (GB) 6-1, 6-2, 6-4.

Nations Cup – Dusseldorf

[There was no Nations Cup in 1976-1977]

Spain d. Australia 2-1.

Jose Higueras (ES) d. John Newcombe (AU) 6-2, 6-3.
Manuel Orantes (ES) d. Phil Dent (AU) 6-3, 6-4.
Phil Dent – John Newcombe (AU) d. Jose Higueras – Manuel Orantes (ES) 7-6, 6-4.

1978 World Rankings[305]

Bud Collins

1. Jimmy Connors
2. Bjorn Borg
3. Guillermo Vilas
4. John McEnroe
5. Vitas Gerulaitis
6. Eddie Dibbs
7. Brian Gottfried
8. Raul Ramirez
9. Harold Solomon
10. Corrado Barazzutti

Lance Tingay

1. Bjorn Borg
2. Jimmy Connors
3. Vitas Gerulaitis
4. Guillermo Vilas
5. Eddie Dibbs
6. Raul Ramirez
7. Brian Gottfried
8. Corrado Barazzutti
9. Sandy Mayer
10. John McEnroe

Rino Tommasi

1. Jimmy Connors
2. Bjorn Borg
3. Guillermo Vilas
4. Vitas Gerulaitis
5. John McEnroe
6. Eddie Dibbs
7. Brian Gottfried
8. Sandy Mayer
9. Jose Higueras
10. Manuel Orantes

ATP Year End Rankings[306]

1. Jimmy Connors
2. Bjorn Borg
3. Guillermo Vilas
4. John McEnroe
5. Vitas Gerulaitis
6. Eddie Dibbs
7. Brian Gottfried
8. Raul Ramirez
9. Harold Solomon
10. Corrado Barazzutti

1978 Colgate Grand Prix Bonus Pool Top 10[307]

Singles (9th Bonus Pool)			Doubles (4th Bonus Pool)	
1.	Jimmy Connors	*	1. Wojtek Fibak	$90,000
2.	Bjorn Borg	*	2. Bob Hewitt	$60,000
3.	Eddie Dibbs	$300,000	3. Frew McMillan	$40,000
4.	Raul Ramirez	$200,000	4. Tom Okker	$28,000
5.	Harold Solomon	$150,000	5. Raul Ramirez	$20,000
6.	John McEnroe	$100,000	6. Peter Fleming	$18,000
7.	Guillermo Vilas	**	7. John McEnroe	$16,000
8.	Brian Gottfried	$ 80,000	8. Fred McNair	$14,000
9.	Corrado Barazzutti	$ 60,000	9. Sherwood Stewart	$12,000
10.	Arthur Ashe	$ 50,000	10. Hank Pfister	$10,000
**	Did not compete for Bonus Pool.			
*	Did not meet Bonus Pool eligibility requirements.			

Note: MIPTC awarded bonus pool money to some players who, because of injury could not play in the 20 required tournaments in 1978.

1978 Official Earnings Top 10[308]

1.	Eddie Dibbs	$575,273	6.	Wojtek Fibak	$384,665
2.	Bjorn Borg	$459,441	7.	Vitas Gerulaitis	$380,444
3.	Raul Ramirez	$463,868	8.	Harold Solomon	$353,234
4.	John McEnroe	$460,285	9.	Ilie Nastase	$351,843
5.	Jimmy Connors	$392,153	10.	Brian Gottfried	$349,771

1978 Tournament Calendar

Date	Tournaments	Singles Winner	Singles #2	Doubles Winners	Doubles #2
1/15/1978	Birmingham $175,000 SS	Bjorn Borg	Dick Stockton	V. Gerulaitis - S. Mayer	D. Stockton - F. McMillan
1/22/1978	Baltimore $100,000 GP	Cliff Drysdale	Tom Gorman	F. McMillan - F. McNair	A. Zugerelli - R. Taylor
1/22/1978	Boca Raton $250,000 SP	Bjorn Borg	Jimmy Connors	7-6, 3-6, 6-1	
1/29/1978	Philadelphia $250,000 SS	Jimmy Connors	Roscoe Tanner	B. Hewitt - F. McMillan	V. Gerulaitis - S. Mayer
1/29/1978	Sarasota $50,000 GP	Tomas Smid	Nick Saviano	C. Dowdswell - G. Masters	B. Bertram - B. Mitton
2/5/1978	Richmond $175,000 SS	Vitas Gerulaitis	John Newcombe	B. Hewitt - F. McMillan	V. Gerulaitis - S. Mayer
2/5/1978	Little Rock $50,000 GP	Dick Stockton	Hank Pfister	C. Dibley - G. Masters	T. Gullikson - T. Gullikson
2/5/1978	Mexico City $50,000 GP	Raul Ramirez	Pat Dupre	G. Mayer - B. Mitton	R. Ramirez - M. Lara
2/12/1978	St. Louis $175,000 SS	Sandy Mayer	Eddie Dibbs	B. Hewitt - F. McMillan	W. Fibak - T. Okker
2/12/1978	Springfield $75,000 GP	Heinz Gunthardt	Harold Solomon	S. Smith - B. Lutz	J. Kodes - M. Riessen
2/19/1978	Palm Springs $225,000 SS	Roscoe Tanner	Raul Ramirez	R. Tanner - R. Moore	B. Hewitt - F. McMillan
2/26/1978	Denver $125,000 GP	Jimmy Connors	Stan Smith	B. Hewitt - F. McMillan	F. McNair - S. Stewart
2/26/1978	Ocean City	Balazs Taroczy	Ray Moore	V. Gerulaitis - I. Nastase	Z. Franulovic - B. Taroczy
3/5/1978	Memphis $225.000 SS	Jimmy Connors	Tim Gullikson	B. Gottfried - R. Ramirez	J. Newcombe - P. Dent
3/5/1978	Miami $50,000 GP	Ilie Nastase	Tom Gullikson	Tom Gullikson - G. Mayer	B. Teacher - B. Carmichael
3/5/1978	Lagos $50,000 GP	Kjell Johansson	Robin Drysdale	G. Hardie - B. Mitton	J. Fassbender - C. Dowdeswell
3/8/1978	Stockholm $60,000 SP	Bjorn Borg	Vitas Gerulaitis	6-4, 1-6, 6-3	
3/12/1978	Cairo $38,000	Jose Higueras	Kjell Johansson	I. El Shafei - B. Fairlie	L. Alvarez - G. Hardie
3/12/1978	Madrid $175,000 Cup SP	Europe	South America	4-3,	

3/12/1978	Madrid $175,000 Cup SP	Jaime Fillol	Corrado Barazzutti	6-4, 6-3	
3/12/1978	Madrid $175,000 Cup SP			6-3, 6-3	J. Fillol - G. Vilas	I.Nastase - A. Panatta
3/12/1978	Madrid $175,000 Cup SP	Ilie Nastase	Guillermo Vilas	6-3, 6-2, 6-2	
3/12/1978	Madrid $175,000 Cup SP	Mark Cox	Thomas Koch	6-3, 6-0	
3/12/1978	Madrid $175,000 Cup SP	Ivan Molina	Adriana Panatta	6-4, 7-5	
3/12/1978	Madrid $175,000 Cup SP	Victor Pecci	Wojtek Fibak	7-6. 7-6	
3/12/1978	Madrid $175,000 Cup SP			6-7, 6-2, 6-3	M. Cox - W. Fibak	I. Molina - V. Pecci
3/19/1978	Washington $125,000 GP	Brian Gottfried	Raul Ramirez	S. Smith - B. Lutz	A. Ashe - J. McEnroe
3/26/1978	Las Vegas $200,000 TC	Bjorn Borg	Vitas Gerulaitis		
4/2/1978	Milan $175,000 SS	Bjorn Borg	Vitas Gerulaitis	J. Higueras - V. Pecci	W. Fibak - K. Warwick
4/2/1978	Dayton $75,000 GP	Brian Gottfried	Eddie Dibbs	B. Gottfried - G. Masters	H. Pfister - B. Walts
4/9/1978	Rotterdam $175,000 SS	Jimmy Connors	Raul Ramirez	F. McNair - R. Ramirez	S. Smith - B. Lutz
4/10/1978	Johannesburg $75,000 GP	Cliff Richey	Colin Dowdeswell	B. Hewitt - F. McMillan	G. Masters - C. Dibley
4/16/1978	Guadalajara $50,000 GP	Gene Mayer	John Newcombe	S. Mayer - S. Stewart	G. Mayer - B. Mitton
4/16/1978	Monte Carlo $175,000 SS	Raul Ramirez	Tomas Smid	T. Smid - P. Fleming	J. Fillol - I. Nastase
4/18/1978	Copenhagen SP	Bjorn Borg	Vitas Gerulaitis	2-6, 6-4, 6-4	
4/23/1978	Houston $175,000 SS	Brian Gottfried	Ilie Nastase	W. Fibak - T. Okker	T. Leonard - M. Machette
4/23/1978	Nice $50,000 GP	Jose Higueras	Yannick Noah	F. Jauffret - P. Donminguez	J. Kodes - T. Smid
4/23/1978	Tokyo $200,000 SP	Bjorn Borg	Jimmy Connors	6-1, 6-2	
4/24/1978	San Jose $50.000 GP	Arthur Ashe	Bernie Mitton	S. Mayer - G. Mayer	H. Pfister - B. Rowe
4/30/1978	Las Vegas $250,000 SS	Harold Solomon	Corrado Barazzutti	J. Fillol - A. Fillol	B. Hewitt - R. Ramirez
4/30/1978	Tulsa $50,000 GP				

5/8/1978	Kansas City $200,000			6-7, 6-4, 6-0, 6-3	W. Fibak - T. Okker	S. Smith - B. Lutz
5/8/1978	Dusseldorf $200,000 NC	Spain	Australia	2-1,		
5/8/1978	Dusseldorf $200,000 NC	Jose Higueras	John Newcombe	6-2, 6-3		
5/8/1978	Dusseldorf $200,000 NC	Manuel Orantes	Phil Dent	6-3, 6-4		
5/8/1978	Dusseldorf $200,000 NC			7-6, 6-4	P. Dent - J. Newcombe	J. Higueras - M. Orantes
5/12/1978	Hartford $100,000 WC	United States	Australia	6-1,		
5/12/1978	Hartford $100,000 WC	Brian Gottfried	John Newcombe	6-4, 6-4		
5/12/1978	Hartford $100,000 WC			6-2, 4-6, 6-4	B. Lutz-S. Smith	J. Alexander- P. Dent
5/12/1978	Hartford $100,000 WC	Jimmy Connors	John Newcombe	6-4, 6-4		
5/12/1978	Hartford $100,000 WC	Roscoe Tanner	Tony Roche	6-4, 6-2		
5/12/1978	Hartford $100,000 WC	Brian Gottfried	John Alexander	7-5, 6-4		
5/12/1978	Hartford $100,000 WC	Jimmy Connors	John Alexander	6-2, 6-4		
5/12/1978	Hartford $100,000 WC			7-6, 7-6	J. Newcome-T. Roche	B. Gottfried- R. Tanner
5/14/1978	Dallas $200,000 WCT Finals	Vitas Gerulaitis	Eddie Dibbs	6-3, 6-2, 6-1		
5/21/1978	Hamburg $175,000 SS	Guillermo Vilas	Wojtek Fibak		W. Fibak - T. Okker	V. Pecci - A. Munoz
5/21/1978	Florence $50,000 GP	Jose Luis Clerc	Patrice Dominguez		C. Barazzutti - A. Panatta	M. Edmondson - J. Marks
5/28/1978	Rome $175,000 SS	Bjorn Borg	Adriana Panatta		V. Pecci - B. Prajoux	J. Kodes - T. Smid
5/28/1978	Munich $75,000 GP	Guillermo Vilas	Buster Mottram		G. Vilas - I. Tiriac	T. Okker - J. Fassbender
5/29/1978	Athens NCAA Singles	John McEnroe	John Sadri	7-6, 7-6, 5-7, 7-6		
6/11/1978	French Open $400,000 GS	Bjorn Borg	Guillermo Vilas		H. Pfister - G. Mayer	M. Orantes - Jose Higueras
6/18/1978	B'ingham $125,000 GP	Jimmy Connors	Raul Ramirez		D. Stockton - E. Van Dillon	J.L. Clerc - B. Prajoux
6/18/1978	Brussels $50,000 GP	Werner Zimgibl	Ricardo Cano		A. Zugarelli - J. Haillet	O. Parun - V. Zednik

6/24/1978	London $125,000 GP	Tony Roche	John McEnroe	B. Hewitt - F. McMillan	F. McNair - R. Ramirez
6/25/1978	Berlin $50,000 GP	Vladimir Zednik	Harald Elschenbroich	C. Doddswell - J. Fassbender	Z. Franulovic - H. Gildemeister
7/8/1978	Wimbledon $269,619 GS	Bjorn Borg	Jimmy Connors	B. Hewitt - F. McMillan	P. Fleming - J. McEnroe
7/8/1978	Raleigh $25,000 Challenger	Mike Cahill	William Prinsloo	F. Gonzales - C. Sylvan	B. Csipkay - J. Sadri
7/15/1978	Gstaad $75.000 GP	Guillermo Vilas	Jose-Luis Clerc	M. Edmondson - T. Okker	B. Hewitt - K. Warwick
7/16/1978	Cincinnati $125,000 GP	Eddie Dibbs	Raul Ramirez	G. Mayer - R. Ramirez	I. El Shafei - B. Fairlie
7/16/1978	Newport $75,000 GP	Bernie Mitton	John James	T.Gullikson - T. Gullikson	C. Dibley - B. Giltinan
7/16/1978	NY $300,000 WCT SP	Vitas Gerulaitis	Ilie Nastase	J. Alexander - P. Dent	F. McNair - S. Stewart
7/23/1978	Washington $175,000 SS	Jimmy Connors	Eddie Dibbs	A. Ashe - B. Hewitt	R. Ramirez - F. McNair
7/23/1978	Bastad $75,000 GP	Bjorn Borg	Corrado Barazzutti	M. Edmonson - B. Carmichael	B. Taroczy - P. Szoke
7/23/1978	Stuttgart $50,000 GP	Uli Pinner	Kim Warwick	J. Kodes - T. Smid	B. Prajoux - C. Kirmayr
7/30/1978	Louisville $175,000 SS	Harold Solomon	John Alexander	W. Fibak - V. Pecci	V. Amaya - J. James
7/30/1978	Kitzbuhel $75,000 GP	Chris Lewis	Vladimir Zednik	M. Fishback - C. Lewis	P. Slozil - P. Hutka
7/30/1978	Hilversum $50,000 GP	Balazs Taroczy	Tom Okker	B. Taroczy - T. Okker	M. Edmondson - B. Carmichael
8/5/1978	New Orleans $75,000 GP	Roscoe Tanner	Victor Amaya	D. Stockton - E. Van Dillon	B. Aairlie - I. El Shafei
8/5/1978	So. Orange $75,000 GP	Guillermo Vilas	Jose-Luis Clerc	J. McEnroe - P. Fleming	G. Vilas - I. Tiriac
8/6/1978	No. Conway $175,000 SS	Eddie Dibbs	John Alexander	A. Drysdale - V. Winitsky	M. Fishbach - B. Mitton
8/13/1978	Indianapolis $175,000 SS	Jimmy Connors	Jose Higueras	H. Pfister - G. Mayer	C. Lewis - J. Borowiak
8/13/1978	Columbus $75,000 GP	Arthur Ashe	Bob Lutz	C. Dibley - B./ Giltinan	E. Teltscher - M. Lara
8/20/1978	Toronto $175,00 SS	Eddie Dibbs	Jose-Luis Clerc	W. Fibak - T. Okker	C. Dowdeswell - H. Gunthardt
8/20/1978	Stowe $75,000 GP	Jimmy Connors	Tim Gullikson	T. Gullikson - T. Gullikson	K. Warwick - M. Edmondson
8/20/1978	Cleveland $50,000 GP	Peter Feigl	Van Winitsky	D. Stockton - E. Van Dillon	B. Manson - R. Fisher

8/27/1978	Atlanta S $50,000 GP	Stan Smith	Eliot Teltscher	J. Alexander - B. Walts	M. Cahill - M. Lara
8/28/1978	Somers $30,000 SP	Peter Fleming	Cliff Richey	6-1, 6-1	
8/28/1978	Boston $200,000 SS	Manuel Orantes	Harold Solomon	V. Pecci - B. Taroczy	H. Gunthardt - V. Winitsky
9/10/1978	US Open $450,000 GS	Jimmy Connors	Bjorn Borg	S. Smith - B. Lutz	M. Riessen - S. Stewart
9/17/1978	Woodlands $125,000 GP			W. Fibak - T. Okker	M. Riessen - S. Stewart
9/24/1978	Los Angeles $200,000 SS	Arthur Ashe	Brian Gottfried	J. Alexander - P. Dent	F. McNair - R. Ramirez
9/24/1978	Hartford $75,000 GP	John McEnroe	Johan Kriek	M. McEnroe - B. Maze	M. Edmondson - V. Winitsky
9/24/1978	Bornemouth $50,000 GP	Jose Higueras	Paolo Bertolucci	L. Sanders - R. Thung	D. Carter - R. Frawley
9/26/1978	Buenos Aires SP	Jimmy Connors	Bjorn Borg	5-7, 6-3, 6-3	
10/1/1978	San Francisco $175,000 SS	John McEnroe	Dick Stockton	J. McEnroe - P. Fleming	S. Smith - B. Lutz
10/1/1978	Mexico City $50,000 GP	Vijay Amritraj	Raul Ramirez	V. Amritraj - A. Amritraj	R. Ramirez - F. McNair
10/1/1978	Aix-En-Provence $50,000 GP	Guillermo Vilas	Jose-Luis Clerc	G. Vilas - I. Tiriac	J. Kodes - T. Smid
10/8/1978	Madrid $100,000 GP	Jose Higueras	Tomas Smid	J. Kodes - W. Fibak	T. Smith - P. Slozil
10/8/1978	Maui $100,000 GP	Bill Scanlon	Peter Fleming	T. Gullikson - T. Gullikson	J. McEnroe - P. Fleming
10/15/1978	Barcelona $175,000 SS	Balazs Taroczy	Ilie Nastase	H. Gildemeister - Z. Franulovic	G. Morretton - J. Haillet
10/15/1978	Brisbane $50,000 GP	Mark Edmondson	John Alexander	J. Alexander - P. Dent	A. Stone - S. Ball
10/22/1978	Sydney $175,000 SS	Jimmy Connors	Geoff Masters	J. Newcombe - T. Roche	M. Edmondson - J. Marks
10/22/1978	Hamburg SP	Bjorn Borg	Wojtek Fibak	6-1, 6-1	
10/22/1978	Rotterdam SP	Guillermo Vilas	Tim Gullikson	7-5, 6-4	
10/26/1978	Kobe SP	Bjorn Borg	Vitas Gerulaitis	1-6, 6-3, 6-3	
10/29/1978	Osaka $100,000 GP	Adriano Panatta	Pat Dupre	R. Case - G. Masters	B. Mottram - Z. Franulovic
10/29/1978	Vienna $75,000 GP	Stan Smith	Balazs Taroczy	V. Pecci - B. Taroczy	B. Hewitt - F. McMillan
10/29/1978	Basle $75,000 GP	Guillermo Vilas	John McEnroe	J. McEnroe - W. Fibak	B. Manson - A. Pattison

10/29/1078	Manila SP	Bjorn Borg	Vitas Gerulaitis	6-2, 7-6	
11/5/1978	Cologne $75,000 GP	Wojtek Fibak	Vijay Amritraj	J. McEnroe - P. Fleming	B. Hewitt - F. McMillan
11/5/1978	Tokyo $200,000 GP	Bjorn Borg	Brian Teacher	R. Case - G. Masters	T. Gorman - P. DuPre
11/5/1978	Paris $50,000 GP	Bob Lutz	Tom Gullikson	B. Manson - A. Pattison	G. Vilas - I. Tiriac
11/13/1978	Stockholm $175,000 SS	John McEnroe	Tim Gullikson	W. Fibak - T. Okker	S. Smith - B. Lutz
11/13/1978	Hong Kong $75,000 GP	Eliot Teltscher	Pat Dupre	M. Edmonson - J. Marks	B. Rowe - H. Pfister
11/19/1978	London $175,000 SS	John McEnroe	Tim Gullikson	J. McEnroe - P. Fleming	B. Hewitt - F. McMillan
11/19/1978	Bogota $50,000 GP	Victor Pecci	Rolf Gehring	J. Fillol - A. Fillol	V. Pecci - H. Gildenmeister
11/19/1978	Tapei $50,000 GP	Brian Teacher	Tom Gorman	B. Walts - S. Stewart	M. Edmondson - J. Marks
11/25/1978	Buenos Aires $175,000 SS	Jose-Luis Clerc	Victor Pecci	C. Lewis - V. Winitsky	B Prajoux - J.L. Clerc
11/26/1978	Manila $75,000 GP	Yannick Noah	Peter Feigl	S. Stewart - B. Teacher	R. Case - C. Kachel
11/26/1978	Bologna $50,000 GP	Peter Fleming	Adriana Panatta	J. McEnroe - P. Fleming	J. Haillet - A. Zugarelli
11/26/1978	Kobe/ Toyko SP	Jimmy Connors	Ilie Nastase	V. Amaya - P. DuPre	J. Austin - I. Nastase
11/30/1978	Milan $100,000 SP	Vitas Gerulaitis	Adriana Panatta	6-7,, 6-2, 6-2	
12/3/1978	Jo'burg $175,000 SS	Tim Gullikson	Harold Solomon	P. Fleming - R. Moore	B. Hewitt - F. McMillan
12/3/1978	Santiago $75,000 GP	Jose-Luis Clerc	Victor Pecci	V. Pecci - H. Gildenmeister	J. Fillol - A. Fillol
12/3/1978	Calcutta $50,000 GP	Yannick Noah	Pascal Portes	S. Stewart - S. Menon	Y. Noah - G. Moretton
12/3/1978	Pontre Vedra $25,000	Bob Lutz	Dick Stockton	D. Stockton - R. Tanner	A. Ashe - B. Lutz
12/15/1978	Montego Bay $10,000 SP	Bjorn Borg	Harold Solomon	6-3, 6-2	
12/15/1978	Montego Bay $10,000 SP	Bjorn Borg	Raul Ramirez	6-1, 6-3	
12/15/1978	Montego Bay $10,000 SP	Raul Ramirez	Roscoe Tanner	3-6, 6-5, 6-1	
12/15/1978	Montego Bay $10,000 SP	Bjorn Borg	Roscoe Tanner	3-6, 6-5, 6-4	

12/15/1978	Montego Bay $10,000 SP	Raul Ramirez	Harold Solomon	6-4, 6-2	
12/15/1978	Montego Bay $10,000 SP	John McEnroe	Ilie Nastase	6-5, 3-6, 6-4	
12/15/1978	Montego Bay $10,000 SP	Roscoe Tanner	Harold Solomon	6-2, 6-4	
12/15/1978	Montego Bay $10,000 SP	Peter Fleming	Dick Stockton	2-6, 6-4, 6-4	
12/15/1978	Montego Bay $10,000 SP	Peter Fleming	John McEnroe	6-5, 4-6, 6-4	
12/15/1978	Montego Bay $10,000 SP	Ilie Nastase	Dick Stockton	6-5, 6-4	
12/15/1978	Montego Bay $10,000 SP	Ilie Nastase	Peter Fleming	4-6, 6-2, 6-4	
12/15/1978	Montego Bay $10,000 SP	Dick Stockton	John McEnroe	6-4, 6-2	
12/16/1978	Montego Bay $50,000 SP	Peter Fleming	Bjorn Borg	6-5, 6-5	
12/16/1978	Montego Bay $50,000 SP	Ilie Nastase	Raul Ramirez	6-1, 6-2	
12/17/1978	Montego Bay $100,000 SP	Ilie Nastase	Peter Fleming	2-6, 5-6, 6-2, 6-4, 6-4	
12/24/1978	Sydney $125,000 GP	Tim Wilkison	Ken Warwick	S. Stewart - H. Pfister	B. Carmichael - S. Ball
1/3/1979	Australian Open $335,000 GS	Guillermo Vilas	John Marks	W. Fibak - K. Warwick	P. Kronk - C. Letcher
1/7/1979	London $200,000 SP			J. McEnroe - P. Fleming	I. Nastase - S. Stewart
1/14/1979	NY $400,000 Colgate Masters	John McEnroe	Arthur Ashe	J. McEnroe - P. Fleming	W. Fibak - T. Okker

http://www.atpworldtour.com/en/scores/results-archive.

http://www.itftennis.com/procircuit/tournaments/men's-calendar.aspx?tour=&reg=&nat=&sur=&cate=AL&iod=&fromDate=01-01-1968&toDate=29-12-1978.

Tennis History, Jim McManus, (Canada 2010).

1979 USLTA Yearbook.

Official 1989 MTC Media Guide, (MTC 1989).

World of Tennis 1979, Edited by John Barrett and compiled by Lance Tingay, (London 1979).

CHAPTER 13:

1979: MIPTC SUPERVISORS BEGIN, PLAYERS OBJECT TO DESIGNATIONS, CRISES NOS. 18, 19

1979 Governing Bodies

The MIPTC was the governing body for men's professional tennis in 1979. WCT continued to be merged into the Colgate Grand Prix in 1979. The governance of the Davis Cup was transferred from the Davis Cup Nations to the ITF.

1979 Significant Tennis Leaders	
ITF President:	Philippe Chatrier (France)
USTA President:	W.E. "Slew Hester", then Joe Carrico
Australian LTA President:	Brian Tobin
British LTA President:	Sir Carl Aarvold
French FFT President:	Philippe Chatrier
Chairman of Wimbledon:	Sir Brian Burnett
ATP President:	Jaime Fillol
ATP Executive Director:	Bob Briner
WCT Owners:	Lamar Hunt and Al Hill, Jr.
WCT Executive Director:	Mike Davies

1979 MIPTC

ITF: Derek Hardwick, Brian Tobin and Stan Malless with David

            Gray as Joint Secretary. In September, Philippe Chatrier

            succeeded Brian Tobin and was elected Chairman to succeed

Bob Briner.

Tournaments:	Lars Myhrman (Europe), Owen Williams (Rest of the World and John Harris (North America) until September when he was succeeded by Jack Kramer.
Players:	Bob Briner, Chairman until September, Arthur Ashe and Cliff Drysdale with Doug Tkachuk as Joint Secretary.
Legal Counsel:	Roy L. Reardon, Esquire.
Grand Prix Supervisors:	Dick Roberson, Chief, Frank Smith, Franco Bartoni and Kurt Nielsen.

Two Competitions

In 1979, the 12th year of Open Tennis, there were two organized competitions for men: Colgate Grand Prix and the Davis Cup. WTT was gone. Davis Cup was open to all players and was won 5-0 by the United States over Italy.

There were 89 Colgate Grand Prix Open prize money tournaments, including the year-end Colgate Masters in Madison Square Garden in New York City. Included in the 89 tournaments were the four Grand Slams and 28 Super Series. The Colgate Masters was again staged at Madison Square Garden and was won by Bjorn Borg over Vitas Gerulaitis 6-2, 6-2 in singles and by Peter Fleming and John McEnroe over Wojtek Fibak and Tom Okker 6-3, 6-7, 6-1 in doubles.

WCT continued to be merged into the Grand Prix and again staged eight of the 28 Super Series. The eight WCT tournaments, in addition to leading as part of the 88 Grand Prix tournaments to the Colgate Grand Prix Bonus Pool and the Colgate Masters, also led as a "circuit within a circuit" to the WCT Finals in Dallas won by John McEnroe over Bjorn Borg 7-5, 4-6, 6-2, 7-6, and the WCT Braniff Airways World Doubles Finals in London won by Peter Fleming and John McEnroe over Ilie Nastase and Sherwood Stewart 3-6, 6-2, 6-3, 6-1.

In addition to the Dallas Finals and the WCT World Doubles, WCT staged four additional special events outside of the Colgate Grand Prix: (i) February 19, Puerto Rico, $200,000 Tournament of Champions won by Jimmy Connors over Vitas Gerulaitis 6-5, 6-0, 6-4, (ii) March 8, Hartford, $100,000 Aetna World Cup won by the USA over Australia 7-0, (iii) July 9, Forest Hills $300,000 WCT Invitational won by Eddie Dibbs over Harold Solomon 7-6, 6-1 in singles and by Peter Fleming and John McEnroe over Gene Mayer and Sandy Mayer 6-7, 7-6, 6-3 in doubles and (iv) December 4, Montreal $320,000 WCT Challenge Cup won by Bjorn Borg over Jimmy Connors 6-4, 6-2, 2-6, 6-4.

In 1979, the ATP was involved in seven events: (i) February 18, Palm Springs, $250,000 ATP Volvo Tennis Games, (ii) April 29, Las Vegas, $250,000 ATP Alan King Classic at Caesar's Palace, (iii) May 14, Dusseldorf, $200,000 Ambre Solaire ATP Nation's Cup, (iv) June 18, London, $125,000 Stella Artois Queens ATP Grass-Court Championships, (v) August 26, Cincinnati, $200,000 ATP Championships, (vi) September 16, Woodlands, $200,000 ATP-Lipton World Doubles and (vii) November 18, London, $175,000 ATP Benson and Hedges Championships at Wembley. All were in the Colgate Grand Prix except for the Nations Cup and the ATP Championships in Cincinnati. Cincinnati became the subject of the very bitter Crisis No. 19.

None of the other Grand Prix tournaments liked having ATP involved with tournaments since all tournaments were always competing for players and the ATP involvement with some tournaments gave them an unfair advantage. But, on the other hand, the tournaments did not want to fund the operations of the ATP (yet), so they had to accept ATP's involvement in a few tournaments.

Crisis No. 18: Six Designations Required

In 1979, the MIPTC was offering on behalf of the tournaments in the Grand Prix over $12 million in prize money plus the Bonus Pool and under the 1978 rules the tournaments had no advance assurance of a marketable player field upon which to market their tournaments. After analyzing the problem, the Council determined that if it could designate players just six times a year, it could give sponsors and promoters advance guarantees of enough stars to give all the tournaments a fighting chance for survival and it also needed to limit the number of special events staged against its major tournaments.

The new 1979 player commitment rule adopted at the October 26-28, 1978, MIPTC meeting required each player to commit to six tournaments designated by the MIPTC to provide each tournament with a balanced field in advance for the purpose of marketing. Special events were permitted in 16 open weeks and only three times per year against Super Series tournaments. Each player was required to agree to the new player commitment rule *as a condition of eligibility to play in any Grand Prix tournament, including the Grand Slams.* That new 1979 player commitment rule became Crisis No. 18 for men's professional tennis.

In January, just before the beginning of the 1979 Colgate Grand Prix, representatives for Jimmy Connors, Bjorn Borg, Guillermo Vilas, Vitas Gerulaitis and Adriano Panatta among others, objected to the 1979 Player Commitment Rule and refused to sign for the

1979 Colgate Grand Prix. Slew Hester, who was still USTA President in January, also objected to the new Rule. As reported by Neil Amdur in the *New York Times*[309], John McEnroe Sr., a lawyer and the father of John McEnroe, Jr., now one of the world's top players, termed the new rule and several regulations that require players to register for specific tournaments "'unacceptable as a matter of principle and as matter of legality. I do think they're susceptible to legal challenge,' McEnroe said last week. 'Even if they weren't, I would object to them.'" Briner said that "if the game was going to survive, mild order must be brought."[310]

The MIPTC met January 9-12,[311] in New York in conjunction of the staging of the 1978 Colgate Grand Prix Masters at Madison Square Garden. Most of the MIPTC meeting was devoted to Crisis No.18. George Gowan (USTA legal counsel), John McEnroe, Sr. (representing John McEnroe, Jr., and also being spokesman for the group of unsigned players), Bob Kain (IMG, representing Borg and Gerulaitis), Joe Rountree (representing Jimmy Connors), Slew Hester (USTA President) and Mike Burns (USTA Staff) attended the MIPTC meeting on Wednesday to formalize their objections to the 1979 Player Commitment Rules. On Thursday night, Drysdale and Hardwick met with the USTA's Slew Hester and others, but no agreement was found. The MIPTC later entered into a joint meeting with the USTA Management Committee to no avail.

Ashe and 200 other players, including Brian Gottfried, Eddie Dibbs, Raul Ramirez, Stan Smith, Ray Moore and Cliff Drysdale, said the rules were "reasonable and minimal." After lots discussions, eventually, the USTA and Wimbledon, along with the ITF, ATP and WCT backed the MIPTC rules and the MIPTC continued to negotiate with John McEnroe, Sr., who was serving as spokesman for McEnroe, Jr., Borg, Vilas, Gerulaitis and Connors.[312]

Briner said in the *New York Times*[313]: "I join Arthur Ashe in asking John McEnroe, Jimmy Connors, Bjorn Borg, Guillermo Vilas and Vitas Gerulaitis to join their fellow pros and help tennis continue to prosper."

After "both sides had cooled down," Briner and Tkachuk were able to negotiate a reasonable compromise with the top players. The compromise reached in February permitted each player the right to veto one of the six designated tournaments and special events permitted against Super Series weeks was increased from three to six. Players could always play special events in the 16 open weeks, so the limitation was solely to try to protect the big money Super Series as much as possible.[314]

On February 18, McEnroe, Sr., said to the *New York Times*[315]: "In sum, I believe that the revised rules satisfy the players' objections and assure continued success for the Grand Prix circuit. Now everyone can get back to playing tennis."

The Courage of the MIPTC Members

It took a lot of courage for the 9 members of the MIPTC with the able assistance of Roy Reardon, the new MIPTC counsel, to risk threatened anti-trust litigation to enact and support a player commitment rule that they believed was necessary to ensure the viability of the Grand Prix circuit for the tournaments and for the players for the future. Neither the MIPTC or its 9 members had any anti-trust insurance coverage and the MIPTC was just an unincorporated association as it was never incorporated. In the end, the MIPTC rules were supported by everyone involved in men's professional tennis.

The new rules did in fact make a player ineligible to play in any Grand Prix tournament, *including the Grand Slams*, if the player refused to sign the player commitment for six designations with one veto and a limit of six special events against major tournaments. The new special event restriction permitting six weeks against Super Series was frankly, not much of a restriction. While Crisis No. 18 was ended with the 1979 compromise, the difficulty of providing balanced fields for a lot of tournaments and protecting them from harmful special events would continue to be a problem faced by the MIPTC in every year.

Crisis No. 19: ATP Cincinnati vs. Boston

In 1978, all of the U.S. Summer circuit tournaments leading to the U.S. Open were on clay as the U.S. Open had been in 1975, 1976 and 1977 at Forest Hills. Upon the move to Flushing Meadows in 1978, the USTA changed the U.S. Open surface from clay to hard courts. The Canadian Open and Boston, both on clay were staged in the two weeks prior to the 1978 U.S. Open. The 1978 Boston player field consisted mainly of clay court players and it was won by Manuel Orantes over Harold Solomon. Understandingly, the ATP and the MIPTC hoped to get the Canadian Open and Boston, which were after the U.S. Clay Court Championships in Indianapolis, to change from clay to hard courts so the players would have two hard court tournaments in front of the U.S. Open. Toronto agreed to change from clay to hard courts for 1979, but the Board of the Longwood Cricket Club in Boston voted 14-1 to remain a clay court tournament.

For over 15 years the Longwood Cricket Club had hosted a professional men's tournament. On February 14, 1975, Longwood and the ATP had entered into a contract for the joint promotion of the Boston tournament for 1975-1980 which was reluctantly approved by the MIPTC. Briner erroneously claimed that approval gave ATP ownership of Boston's sanction. Longwood lost its title sponsor and on October

20, 1978, and notified the ATP that it was terminating the Longwood-ATP agreement. This action resulted in a lawsuit between Longwood and the ATP. A lot of confusing information emanated from Longwood as to whether it did or did not want to continue a Super Series tournament on clay the week before the U.S. Open. At the October 26-28, 1978, meeting of the MIPTC in Tokyo, the Council instructed Bob Briner to go to Boston along with either or both John Harris and Stan Malless to try to work out the situation; that resulted in no resolution of the issue. On January 29, 1979, Malless, Tobin, Hardwick, Myhrman and Williams confirmed to Briner that the MIPTC had not approved ATP as the owner of Boston's sanction for the week before the U.S. Open.

Briner Disregards Council Majority

Nevertheless, Briner, the ATP Executive Director and then also the Chairman of the Council, made a deal for the ATP with Cincinnati which was a $125,000 tournament in the first non-protected week after Wimbledon in 1978, to replace Boston as a Super Series tournament in the week before the 1979 U.S. Open with a new "ATP Championships" in Cincinnati. This new tournament was officially announced by the ATP on March 15, 1979. Boston objected and claimed that it "owned" the sanction for the week before the 1979 U.S. Open as a clay court tournament and was prepared to file litigation to protect its claim of ownership. This was Crisis No. 19.

5-4 Vote at Hearing for Boston

On Thursday, April 5, 1979, the MIPTC held a hearing for Longwood's Boston Super Series tournament's request to continue in 1979, in its traditional date on clay just before the 1979 U.S. Open. Under Boston's threat of litigation, the MIPTC voted 5-4 to award Boston the sanction for the week before the U.S. Open. You have to conclude that Owen Williams had "swung" back from Briner and the ATP towards the ITF.[316]

Cincinnati as a Special Event

Briner who was Chairman of the MIPTC, defied the decision of the majority and proceeded with the staging of the new ATP Championships on hard courts in Cincinnati as a $200,000 special event (non-Grand Prix tournament) in the same week against Boston. So, the week before the 1979 U.S. Open, Boston was a $175,000 Super Series Grand Prix tournament on clay with 12.5% of its prize money going to the Bonus Pool and Cincinnati was a $200,000 special event on hard courts with all of its prize money going to the players on-site and a percentage of the profits going to the ATP. The Boston Super Series was won by Jose Higueras over Hans Gildemeister, two clay court players, while Cincinnati as a special event was won by Peter Fleming over Roscoe Tanner. The MIPTC survived Crisis No. 19, but not without a lot of hard feelings. This would soon be the end of Bob Briner's Chairmanship of the MIPTC and very soon (March 1, 1980), the end of his tenure as Executive Director of ATP and the discovery by the ATP that he had left the ATP almost bankrupt.[317]

New Sanctioning Factors

The Crisis No. 18 compromise approved the new player commitment rule which required six designations and permitted up to six special events against the 28 Super Series tournaments as a condition of entry into the Grand Prix and the Grand Slams. In its ongoing effort to protect the Grand Slams and the Super Series tournaments from competing special events, the Council added to the factors to be considered in the evaluation of tournaments for sanction into the Grand Prix the "promotion of the sponsor's interest" and "whether or not the applicant promotes a special event" against Super Series tournaments. ProServ and IMG were the most likely ones affected by this rule change as they were involved in the promotion of both Grand Prix tournaments and in special events against Super Series tournaments.[318]

Grand Prix Supervisors at the Grand Slams

The Tournament Regulations provided that the Grand Prix Supervisors would "act as the final on-site arbitrator in all matters of tennis law, the Code of Conduct and the Grand Prix Rules and that the decision of the Grand Prix Supervisor on these topics is final," and that "The Grand Prix Supervisor, acting as the Council's ombudsman, shall be the final on-site authority to rule on any matters not specifically covered in the Colgate Grand Prix Rules and Regulations." *Do you think the Grand Slams liked having the Grand Prix Supervisors as the final on-site authority at their tournaments?*

MIPTC Meetings

In 1979, the MIPTC held six meetings: January 9-12 in New York, April 4-6 in London, June 21-23 in London, July 8-10 in London, September 3-5 in New York and November 5-8 in Paris.

In New York in January[319], the MIPTC approved the request of the Joint Secretaries to permit the deduction of outstanding fines from the 1978 Bonus Pool awards of players. As it turned out, just about all the fines assessed by the new Grand Prix Supervisors and actually collected were from Bonus Pool winners. Most of the other fines were appealed, the appeals never heard and the fines never paid, until I was hired as the MIPTC Administrator in 1981 and began hearing and determining appeals for over $600,000 in outstanding fines.

Italian Open

In April in London[320], at the request of Paulo Angeli, a former member of the MIPTC, the Council agreed that the Italian Open could appoint an Italian referee approved by the MIPTC. This was made possible because there was then going to be a Grand Prix Supervisor at the Italian Open. Heretofore, it was well known that the Italian fans and the Italian officials were a sort of nightmare for non-Italian players.

WCT Merger with the Grand Prix Extended though 1980

The original agreement with WCT for participation as a "circuit within a circuit" inside the Grand Prix covered 1978 and 1979. A motion to extend the agreement with WCT through 1980 was approved. Later it would be further extended to also cover 1981. The MIPTC always feared that if it did not continue with WCT inside the Grand Prix, WCT would compete with the Grand Prix and it would eventually lead to expensive anti-trust litigation. Everyone was convinced that Lamar Hunt was never going to leave tennis.

End of Terms

The July meeting in London[321] was the final meeting for Brian Tobin, who would be replaced by Philippe Chatrier. This was also the final meeting for John Harris as North American Tournament Representative, who would be succeeded by Jack Kramer, who was returning to the MIPTC even though he was still unhappy that WCT was part of the Grand Prix.

In September in New York[322], Chatrier was elected Chairman to replace Bob Briner unopposed. "The unanimous feeling of the Council was that an Executive Director should be appointed, and Owen Williams and Arthur Ashe agreed to present a job description and budget to the next meeting." *This is 1979. I was not hired until 1981.*

Colgate to Withdraw after 1979

In August, Colgate announced that it would not be exercising its option to sponsor the Grand Prix after 1979, and the January 1980 Colgate Masters. *International Tennis Weekly*[323] reported: "According to Briner, the loss of Colgate to the men's tour will not hurt the prosperity the Grand Prix has enjoyed in recent years. 'We feel confident about obtaining another sponsor for the next year's Grand Prix,' he said. 'We have been talking with other major international corporations in case Colgate did not renew for 1980, and have been very encouraged by the feedback we have received. Unlike some people in the game, I feel that major commercial sponsorship is a necessary part of the game and will be working hard to firm up a new agreement for 1980,' said Briner."

Briner always supported the sale of a title sponsorship for the Grand Prix, e.g. the "Colgate Grand Prix", whereas the ITF members of the MIPTC always hoped for "Grand Prix of Tennis" without a title sponsor. The problem, of course, was that sufficient funding could only be obtained with the "Colgate Grand Prix" format and it would not be until 1990 when the "ATP Tour" began that it was not necessary to sell the title.

Grand Prix Sponsorship and Ownership of the Masters

With the Colgate sponsorship completing at the end of 1979, the Council discussed how to obtain a new sponsor. It was obvious to everyone that the Colgate Masters at the 18,000 seat Madison Square Garden on national television was a huge financial success for Colgate and for ProServ. It was agreed that "the Council make every effort to retain complete control of the Masters and take the profit and loss" in any future sponsorship agreement. Dell who had represented Colgate and staged the Colgate Masters in Madison Square Garden for Colgate had other ideas as he was courting Volvo to become the next Grand Prix sponsor.

Grand Prix Supervisors at Wimbledon and U.S. Open

In September in New York[324], it was reported that Wimbledon and the U.S. Open had rejected the authority of the Grand Prix Supervisors, which irritated the players. It was unanimously agreed that the MIPTC Chairman, with the assistance of Stan Malless and Derek Hardwick, should discuss once more the role of the Grand Prix Supervisors with Wimbledon and the U.S. Open and try to persuade them to accept the Supervisors for next year.

Here Comes Volvo With Dell and Briner

On Tuesday, September 4, Rick Dowden, Vice President of Volvo of America Corporation, put forward an offer to sponsor the Grand Prix for three years: 1980, 1981 and 1982, on the lines similar to the sponsorship by Colgate. Volvo would own and control the Masters. When it was not immediately accepted, Volvo informed Chatrier that its offer had been withdrawn. *That caused quite a bit of stress.*

Volvo and Dell Win

In November in Paris[325], negotiations with Volvo were revived and the new sponsorship agreement between Volvo and the MIPTC was dated September 25, 1979, and was signed by Volvo and by Philippe Chatrier, Chairman, for the MIPTC. The term of the contract was three years with Volvo having an option for two additional years. The financial terms were:

Grand Prix Year	License Fee	Bonus Pool Contribution	Total
1980-81	$130,000	$750,000	$ 880,000
1981-82	$140,000	$850,000	$ 990,000
1982-83	$150,000	$950,000	$1,100,000
1983-84 Option	$160,000	$1,050,000	$1,210,000
1984-85 Option	$160,000	$1,050,000	$1,210,000

Volvo was reluctantly given all rights to the Masters tournament guaranteeing at least $250,000 in prize money with the MIPTC to consider contributing an additional $150,000 towards such prize money. The MIPTC would have two MIPTC members on the tournament committee managing the Masters Tournament, but Volvo reserved "the right to make final decisions on purely financial matters." The MIPTC was entitled to receive 50 percent of all net television revenues in excess of $1,000,000. Net television revenues were defined as "all television rights fees (worldwide) paid to Volvo, less (i) agents or other commissions (to ProServ), (ii) cost of any commercial time purchased by Volvo on such telecast and (iii) any other expenses directly related to such televising or its promotion." *There would never be any television income paid from the Volvo Masters to the MIPTC.*[326]

Point Penalties

The schedule of point penalties was approved and set as:

1st Offence	Warning
2nd Offence	Next point
3rd Offence	Next point
4th Offence	One game
5th Offence	Default

Code of Conduct Appeals

The Joint Secretaries were authorized to decide the Code of Conduct appeals from players. *They never did.*

Kurt Nielsen Hired as Fourth Grand Prix Supervisor

In January, Kurt Nielsen of Copenhagen was hired as the fourth Grand Prix Supervisor. Kurt was one of Denmark's greatest players and an experienced Davis Cup referee. He was a singles finalist at Wimbledon in 1953 and 1955.[327]

Nastase Defaulted in New Orleans

On March 20, 1979 at the WCT New Orleans $175,000 tournament, Ilie Nastase was defaulted for misconduct in a first-round match against Bob Lutz via the Point Penalty System.[328]

First MIPTC Officials School – Dallas

The first MIPTC Officials School was held May 1-5 in Dallas and 29 persons were certified as Grand Prix officials in the first officials' certification. The "ATP personnel and organization" that conducted the school was mostly Doug Tkachuk, the Players' MIPTC Joint Secretary with Grand Prix Supervisors Dick Roberson and Frank Smith.[329] The 29 officials certified at the first MIPTC Officials School were: Bruce Avery, Joe Lynch, Bob Balink, George Parker, Flo Blanchard, Zeno Pfau, Mike Blanchard, Nick Powel, Sue Cain, DeWitt Redgrave, Bob Cranor, Kenneth Slye, Roy Dance, Robert Rockwell,

Kendall Farrar, Bob Salembier, Bill Fish, Anita Shukow, Don Frydel, Jason Smith, Marvin Goldberg, Jack Stahr, Frank Hammond, J.D. Strong, Keith Johnson, Roy Wood, Norman Korff, Don Wiley and George Lord.[330]

Indianapolis Sport Center
The First Tennis Stadium Outside of the U.S. Open

In August, the 10,000 seat Indianapolis Sport Center was opened for the U.S. National Clay Courts promoted by Stan Malless, a former USTA President and member of the MIPTC. Indianapolis was the first new tennis stadium built after the new Flushing Meadows U.S. Open tennis stadium.[331]

The Famous Nastase Un-default

John McEnroe defeated Ilie Nastase 6-4, 4-6, 6-3, 6-2 on the third day of the U.S. Open on August 30-31, at 12:36 A.M. with Frank Hammond as the chair umpire before a very raucous (and well-imbibed) New York crowd of 10,549. Hammond was a famous umpire and had umpired matches for both players numerous times. Mike Blanchard was the U.S. Open Referee and Billy Talbert was the Tournament Director. At 2-2 in the fourth set, Hammond awarded a game penalty against Nastase for delays that produced loud booing from the crowd. When Hammond was unable to silence the crowd or induce Nastase to serve the next game, he finally said, "Game, set, match, McEnroe." The disqualification set off an even louder disturbance from the spectators, some of whom actually ran onto the court.

My recollection is that this raucous late-night New York crowd, who had enjoyed lots of liquid refreshments, had sided with Nastase against McEnroe and against Hammond. When Hammond announced "default" the crowd went crazy and Blanchard, Hammond, McEnroe and Nastase were all fearful that a riot was about to erupt. I do not believe any chair umpire could have controlled that crowd on that night. To avoid a feared riot, Blanchard removed the default, took over as chair umpire, ordered the match to proceed and the players happily obliged to finish the match without a riot.[332]

Ken Farrar Hired as Grand Prix Supervisor

Ken Farrar, 45, from Wayland, Mass., a graduate of Middlebury College in Vermont who was certified at the first MIPTC Officials School, was employed as the 5th Grand Prix Supervisor in November. Farrar had been a referee for WTT for three years, an official at the U.S. Open and at Grand Prix tournaments in New England and was vice president of the New England Tennis Umpires Association.[333]

Briner's Gets ATP Extension

In February of 1979, Bob Briner was probably at his peak of influence. In February, the ATP Board had given Briner a significant increase in salary and a two-year extension of his role as ATP Executive Director, with the second year to be at Briner's option. He had been a member of the ATP Board of Directors since it was founded in 1972, he had succeeded Jack Kramer as Executive Director, he had moved the ATP Headquarters from Dallas to Garland, Texas, near his home, he was Chairman of the MIPTC and he and his assistant Doug Tkachuk were leading and controlling to a large extent the administration of professional tennis. The new Grand Prix Supervisors were selected and hired by and reporting to Tkachuk, who was also handling the designation of players to the tournaments.[334]

At the beginning of the year, Jim McManus moved to Dallas to head up the road manager program, the satellite program, the endorsement maintenance program, and to serve as the ATP's overall handyman. Briner also hired Dewey Blanton as ATP Publicity Director who produced the ATP's first media guide and would become the second editor of *International Tennis Weekly*. In February, Briner hired Butch Buchholz to work towards bringing the tournament operations of ATP events in-house and establishing a merchandising division.

I visited Doug Tkachuk at the new ATP headquarters in Garland. It really was just a metal building located in what appeared to me to be a farm field. I assumed that Bob Briner lived nearby, but it seemed to be in the middle of nowhere. The building had a tennis court and a number of offices. I do not believe that either Briner or Tkachuk played tennis, but I am sure that Jim McManus probably played on that court quite a bit. Every year Briner met with me in New York City during the U.S. Open to discuss the USTA secondary circuits and various issues relating to the USTA's involvement in professional tennis. I knew that Briner was doing that at the request of Donald Dell, who for some reason wanted to help me and the USTA Secondary Circuits. At the time, it was pretty clear to me that Briner and Tkachuk were controlling men's professional tennis with Dell's support. They were also supporting our USTA Satellite and Challenger Series circuits. With their support and the help of Jim McManus, I had drafted and obtained approval for the 1978 and 1979 USTA Circuit Regulations for the USTA Satellite and Challenger Series tournaments.[335]

In June of 1979, newcomers elected to the ATP Board were Harold Solomon, Peter Fleming and Mark Cox, who joined Arthur Ashe, Cliff Drysdale, Jaime Fillol, Richard

Lewis, Lito Alvarez, Colin Dibley, Charlie Pasarell and Briner. Fleming replaced Ray Moore who had resigned. Mark Cox replaced Moore as Vice President. The officers were Jaime Fillol, President, Mark Cox, Vice President, Richard Lewis, Treasurer and Jim McManus, Secretary.

Cliff Drysdale, Arthur Ashe and Briner were re-elected to the MIPTC for new two-year terms to begin with the September 3-5 MIPTC meeting. Ray Moore, ATP Vice President, ran against Briner and lost by only two votes. Unknown at the time was that Briner had sent Dave Holms, an ATP staffer, to fly from Washington DC to London to deliver 25 votes on the July 23 deadline to provide his winning vote margin, as reported by Richard Evans in *Tennis Week*.[336]

Unbeknownst to me, Briner and Tkachuk were simultaneously involved in an internal struggle within the ATP. The players did not like being in a lawsuit with Boston and did not like the way Briner had handled the deal with Cincinnati over the objection of the members of the MIPTC. Richard Evans wrote in his book *Open Tennis*[337]: "The players demanded leadership of a higher moral tone than Briner was giving them. And they demanded, too, a greater response to their wishes concerning the way in which their affairs should be run. In the most literal sense, they were frequently ignored…The problem was that Briner was only a symptom. In my view, the real problem was Dell… Tennis players are, by nature, suspicious and Dell's apparently insatiable hunger for power and influence aroused their suspicions at every turn. Compromise was a word Dell never seemed to understand and, as he launched himself into each meeting, no matter how low-key the client or how unimportant the subject, the list of the enemies he made grew longer and longer…the battle was joined to get a Board elected that would carry a majority of anti-Dell players so that, apart from cutting the strings of the puppet (Briner), the ATP could also get rid of the puppeteer (Dell)…The new Board contained a sufficient number of players of the Drysdale/Moore persuasion to ensure that, within a year, Briner would have gone and the arrangement whereby Dell acted as the ATP's legal advisor would be terminated." Later in the year, the law firm of Dell, Craighill, Fentress and Benton resigned as legal advisors to the ATP.[338]

The JAKS Awards were again staged during the Volvo Masters in New York City:

1979 ATP JAKS AWARDS
(New York City January 1980)

Player of the Year	Bjorn Borg
Doubles Team of the Year	John McEnroe – Peter Fleming
Newcomer of the Year	Vince Van Patten

Most Improved Player of the Year	Victor Pecci
Tennis Writer of the Year	Rex Bellamy
Tennis Broadcaster of the Year	Tony Trabert
Dr. R.W. Johnson Children's Award	Vitas Gerulaitis
ATP Great Player of the Past	Don Budge
ATP Service Award	Stan Smith
Court Official of the Year	Jason Smith
ATP-Adidas Sportsmanship Award	Jaime Fillol

1979 Grand Slam Winners

French Open

Bjorn Borg d. Victor Pecci 6-3, 6-1, 6-7, 6-4.
Alex Mayer - Gene Mayer d. Ross Case – Phil Dent 6-4, 6-4, 6-4.

Wimbledon

Bjorn Borg d. Roscoe Tanner 6-7, 6-1, 3-6, 6-3, 6-4.
Peter Fleming – John McEnroe d. Brian Gottfried – Raul Ramirez 4-6, 6-4, 6-2, 6-2.

U.S. Open

John McEnroe d. Vitas Gerulaitis 7-5, 6-3 6-3.
Peter Fleming – John McEnroe d. Bob Lutz – Stan Smith 6-2, 6-4.

Australian Open

[Tournament Manager: Karen Scott (Happer)]

Guillermo Vilas d. John Sadri 7-6, 6-3, 6-2.
Peter McNamara – Paul McNamee d. Paul Kronk – Cliff Letcher 7-6, 6-2.

Colgate Masters

Bjorn Borg d. Vitas Gerulaitis 6-2, 6-2.

Peter Fleming-John McEnroe d. Wojtek Fibak-Tom Okker 6-3, 7-6, 6-1.

1979 Davis Cup (San Francisco – Indoors)

Davis Cup Final

United States d. Italy 5-0.

Vitas Gerulaitis (US) d. Corrado Barazzutti (IT) 6-3, 3-2, ret'd.
John McEnroe (US) d. Adriano Panatta (IT) 6-2, 6-3, 6-4.
Bob Lutz -Stan Smith (US) d. Paolo Bertolucci – Adriano Panatta (IT) 6-4, 12-10, 6-2.
John McEnroe (US) d. Tonino Zugarelli (IT) 6-4, 6-3, 6-1.
Vitas Gerulaitis (US) d. Adriano Panatta (IT) 6-1, 6-3, 6-3.

Nations Cup - Dusseldorf

Australia d. Italy 2-1.

John Alexander (AU) d. Corrado Barazzutti (IT) 6-2, 6-0.
Adriano Panatta (IT) d. Phil Dent (AU) 6-3, 6-3.
John Alexander – Phil Dent (AU) d. Paolo Bertolucci – Adriano Panatta (IT) 6-3, 7-6.

1979 World Rankings[339]

Bud Collins		Lance Tingay	
1.	Bjorn Borg	1.	Bjorn Borg
2.	Jimmy Connors	2.	John McEnroe
3.	John McEnroe	3.	Jimmy Connors
4.	Vitas Gerulaitis	4.	Vitas Gerulaitis
5.	Roscoe Tanner	5.	Roscoe Tanner

6.	Guillermo Vilas	
7.	Arthur Ashe	
8.	Harold Solomon	
9.	Jose Higueras	
10.	Eddie Dibbs	

6.	Guillermo Vilas
7.	Victor Pecci
8.	Jose Higueras
9.	Eddie Dibbs
10.	Harold Solomon

Rino Tommasi

1. Bjorn Borg
2. John McEnroe
3. Jimmy Connors
4. Vitas Gerulaitis
5. Roscoe Tanner
6. Victor Pecci
7. Arthur Ashe
8. Eddie Dibbs
9. Brian Gottfried
10. Harold Solomon

ATP Year End Rankings[340]

1. Bjorn Borg
2. Jimmy Connors
3. John McEnroe
4. Vitas Gerulaitis
5. Roscoe Tanner
6. Guillermo Vilas
7. Arthur Ashe
8. Harold Solomon
9. Jose Higueras
10. Eddie Dibbs

1979 Colgate Grand Prix Bonus Pool Top 10[341]

Singles (10th Bonus Pool)

1. John McEnroe — $300,000
2. Bjorn Borg — $200,000
3. Jimmy Connors — $150,000
4. Guillermo Vilas — $100,000
5. Vitas Gerulaitis — $ 80,000

Doubles (5th Bonus Pool)

1. Sherwood Stewart — $90,000
2. John McEnroe — $60,000
3. Peter Fleming — $40,000
4. Marty Riessen — $28,000
5. Gene Mayer — $20,000

6.	Rosco Tanner	$ 60,000	6.	Wojtek Fibak	$18,000
7.	Jose Higueras	$ 50,000	7.	Frew McMillan	$16,000
8.	Harold Solomon	$ 40,000	8.	Stan Smith	$14,000
9.	Eddie Dibbs	$ 35,000	9.	Tomas Smid	$12,000
10.	Victor Pecci	$ 30,000	10.	Tom Okker	$10,000

1979 Official Earnings Top 10[342]

1.	Bjorn Borg	$1,008,742	6. Peter Fleming	$ 351,778
2.	John McEnroe	$1,001,745	7. Roscoe Tanner	$ 255,551
3.	Jimmy Connors	$ 699,605	8. Eddie Dibbs	$ 249,551
4.	Vitas Gerulaitis	$ 413,578	9. Harold Solomon	$ 240,333
5.	Guillermo Vilas	$ 375,966	10. Wojtek Fibak	$ 234,694

1979 Tournament Calendar

Date	Tournaments	Singles Winner	Singles #2	Doubles Winner	Doubles #2
1/7/1979	Hobart $50,000 GP	Guillermo Vilas	Mark Edmondson	P. Dent - B. Giltinan	G. Vilas - I. Tiriac
1/8/1979	Auckland $50,000 GP	Tim Wilkison	Peter Feigl	B. Mitton - K. Warwick	A. Jarrett - J. Smith
1/21/1979	Birmingham GP SS/WCT	Jimmy Connors	Eddie Dibbs	M. Riessen - S. Stewart	I. Nastase - T. Okker
1/21/1979	Baltimore $75,000 GP	Harold Solomon	Marty Riessen	M. Riessen - S. Stewart	An Amritraj - C. Drysdale
1/28/1979	Philadelphia $250,000 GP SS/ WCT	Jimmy Connors	Arthur Ashe	W. Fibak - T. Okker	J. McEnroe - P. Fleming
2/4/1979	Richmond $175,000 GP SS/ WCT	Bjorn Borg	Guillermo Vilas	J. McEnroe - B. Gottfried	G. Vilas - I. Tiriac
2/4/1979	Little Rock $50,000 GP	Vitas Gerulaitis	Butch Walts	V. Gerulaitis - V. Zednik	P. Dent - C. Dibley
2/11/1979	Boca Raton $300,000 Pepsi Special	Bjorn Borg	Jimmy Connors	John McEnroe #3	Guillermo Vilas #4
2/18/1979	Palm Springs $250,000 GP SS/ATP	Roscoe Tanner	Brian Gottfried	S. Mayer - G. Mayer	C. Drysdale - B. Manson
2/18/1979	Sarasota $50,000 GP	Johan Kriek	Ricky Meyer	I. Nastase - S. Krulevitz	J. James - K. Richardson
2/25/1979	Denver $125,000 GP	Wojtek Fibak	Victor Amaya	S. Smith - B. Lutz	W. Fibak - T. Okker
2/25/1979	Dorado Beach $200,000 WCT TOC SP	Bjorn Borg	Vitas Gerulaitis		
3/4/1979	Memphis $250,000 US Nat'l GP SS	Jimmy Connors	Arthur Ashe	W. Fibak - T. Okker	D. Stockton - F. McMillan
3/4/1979	Lagos $50,000 Lagos Classic GP	Hans Kary	Peter Fergi	J. Bailey - B. Kleege	P. Fergi - I. El Shafei
3/7/1979	Vienna SP	Bjorn Borg	John McEnroe		
3/11/1979	New Haven $100,000 WC WCT SP	United States	Australia	7-0,	
3/11/1979	New Haven $100,000 WC WCT SP	Arthur Ashe	John Newcombe	6-0, 6-2	

3/11/1979	New Haven $100,000 WC WCT SP	Brian Gottfried	Phil Dent	6-1, 6-4	
3/11/1979	New Haven $100,000 WC WCT SP	Arthur Ashe	Phil Dent	6-4, 6-1	
3/11/1979	New Haven $100,000 WC WCT SP	Brian Gottfried	John Alexander	6-2, 6-4	
3/11/1979	New Haven $100,000 WC WCT SP	B. Lutz - S. Smith	J. Alexander - P. Dent	7-6, 6-1	
3/11/1979	New Haven $100,000 WC WCT SP		7-6, 6-3	B. Gottfried - D. Stockton	R. Case - G. Masters
3/11/1979	New Haven $100,000 WC WCT SP		7-6, 6-1	S. Smith - D. Stockton	G. Masters - A. Stone
3/18/1979	Washington $125,000 Volvo GP	Roscoe Tanner	Brian Gottfried	S. Smith - B. Lutz	B. Teacher - B. Carmichael
3/25/1979	New Orleans $175,000 GP SS & WCT	John McEnroe	Roscoe Tanner	J. McEnroe - P. Fleming	S. Smith - B. Lutz
3/25/1979	San Jose $50,000 GP	Bernie Mitton	Tom Gorman	G. Vilas - I. Tiriac	An Amritraj - C. Dibley
3/25/1979	Nancy $50,000 de Lorraine Open GP	Yannick Noah	Jean Haillet	K. Eberhard - K. Meiler	R. Drysdale - A. Jarrett
4/1/1979	Milan $200,000 GP SS & WCT	John McEnroe	John Alexander	J. McEnroe - P. Fleming	J.L. Clerc - T. Smid
4/1/1979	Dayton $75,000 GP	Butch Walts	Marty Riessen	B. Manson - C. Drysdale	R. Case - P. Dent
4/1/1979	Stuttgart $75,000 Poesche GP	Wojtek Fibak	Guillermo Vilas	W. Fibak - T. Okker	B. Teacher - B. Carmichael
4/7/1979	Buenos Aires Challenge Match	Jimmy Connors	Guillermo Vilas	7-5, 6-3, 6-3	
4/8/1979	Rotterdam $175,000 GP SS & WCT	Bjorn Borg	John McEnroe	J. McEnroe - P. Fleming	B. Mitton - H. Gunthardt
4/8/1979	Nice $50,000 GP	Victor Pecci	John Alexander	P. McNamara - P. McNamee	P. Slozil - T. Smid
4/15/1979	Monte Carlo $175,000 GP SS & WCT	Bjorn Borg	Vitas Gerulaitis	I. Nastase - R. Ramirez	V. Pecci - B. Taroczy

4/15/1979	Tulsa $50,000 GP	Jimmy Connors	Eddie Dibbs	E. Teltscher - F. Gonsalez	C. Dibley - Tom Gullikson
4/15/1979	Cairo $75,000 Egyptian Open GP	Peter Feigl	Carlos Kirmayr	P. McNamara - P. McNamee	V. Amritraj - An Amritraj
4/22/1979	Houston $175,000 GP SS & WCT	Jose Higueras	Gene Mayer	S. Stewart - G. Mayer	J. Alexander - G. Masters
4/22/1979	San Jose $50.000 Smythe GP	John McEnroe	Peter Fleming	J. McEnroe - P. Fleming	H. Pfister - B. Rowe
4/23/1979	Johannesburg $75,000 Sigma Open GP	Jose-Luis Clerc	Deon Joubert	C. Dowdeswell - H. Gunthardt	I. Nastase - R. Moore
4/29/1979	Las Vegas $250,000 GP SS & ATP	Bjorn Borg	Jimmy Connors	M. Riessen - S. Stewart	R. Ramirez - A. Panatta
5/5/1979	Dallas $200,000 WCT Finals WCT SP	John McEnroe	Bjorn Borg		
5/14/1979	Dusseldorf $250,000 NC ATP SP	Australia	Italy	2-1,	
5/14/1979	Dusseldorf $250,000 NC ATP SP	John Alexander	Corrado Barazzutti	6-2, 6-0	
5/14/1979	Dusseldorf $250,000 NC ATP SP	J. Alexander - P. Dent	P. Bertolucci -A. Panatta	6-3, 7-6	
5/14/1979	Dusseldorf $250,000 NC ATP SP	Phil Dent	Adriano Panatta	3-6, 3-6	
5/15/1979	Raleigh $25,000 Challenger	John Sadri	Charles Owens	J. Austin - B. Martin	C. Letcher - C. Lewis
5/20/1979	Hamburg $175,000 German Open GP SS	Jose Higueras	Harold Solomon	J. Kodes - T. Smid	M. Edmondson - J. Marks
5/20/1979	Florence $50,000 Alitalia Open GP	Raul Ramirez	Karl Meiler	A. Panatta - P. Bertolucci	P. Slozil - I. Lendl
5/20/1979	Kobe World Invitational SP	Victor Amaya	Dick Stockton		
5/27/1979	Rome $175,000 Italian Open GP SS	Vitas Gerulaitis	Guillermo Vilas	P. Fleming - T. Smid	J.L. Clerc - I. Nastase
5/27/1979	Munich $75,000 Romika Cup GP	Manuel Orantes	Wojtek Fibak	W. Fibak - T. Okker	J. Fassbender - J. Haillet

6/10/1979	French Open $375,000 GP GS	Bjorn Borg	Victor Pecci	S. Mayer - G. Mayer	R. Case - P. Dent
6/17/1979	Brussels $50,000 GP	Balazs Taroczy	Ivan Lendl	P. McNamara - B. Martin	C. Kimayr - B. Taroczy
6/18/1979	Queens $125,000 GP & ATP	John McEnroe	Victor Pecci	T. Gullikson - T. Gullikson	S. Stewart - M. Riessen
6/24/1979	Surbiton $50,000 LTA GP	Victor Amaya	Mark Edmondson	T. Gullikson - T. Gullikson	M. Riessen - P. DuPre
6/24/1979	Berlin $50,000 GP	Peter McNamara	Patrice Dominguez	C. Kimayr - I. Lendl	J. Andrews - S. Bimer
7/7/1979	Wimbledon $300,000 GP GS	Bjorn Borg	Roscoe Tanner	J. McEnroe - P. Fleming	S. Mayer - G. Mayer
7/15/1979	Forest Hills $300,000 WCT SP	Eddie Dibbs	Harold Solomon	J. McEnroe - P. Fleming	S. Mayer - G. Mayer
7/15/1979	Newport $100,00 Hall of Fame GP	Brian Teacher	Stan Smith	S. Smith - B. Lutz	C. Kachel - J. James
7/15/1979	Gstaad $75,000 Switzerland GP	Uli Pinner	Peter McNamara	M. Edmondson - J. Marks	G. Vilas - I. Tiriac
7/22/1979	Washington $175,000 GP SS	Guillermo Vilas	Victor Pecci	S. Stewart - M. Riessen	B. Gottfried - R. Ramirez
7/22/1979	Bastad $75,000 Swedish Open GP	Bjorn Borg	Balazs Taroczy	B. Hewitt - H. Gunthardt	M. Edmondson - J. Marks
7/22/1979	Stuttgart $75,000 Mercedes Benz GP	Tomas Smid	Uli Pinner	C. Dowdeswell - F. McMillan	W. Fibak - P. Slozil
7/29/1979	Louisville $175,000 GP SS	John Alexander	Terry Moor	M. Riessen - S. Stewart	V. Amritraj - R. Ramirez
7/29/1979	Kitzbuhel $75,000 Head Cup GP	Vitas Gerulaitis	Pavel Slozil	H. Gunthardt - Z. Franulovic	D. Crealy - A. Zugarelli
7/29/1979	Hilversum 75,000 Netherlands GP	Balazs Taroczy	Tomas Smid	B. Taroczy - T. Okker	J. Kodes - T. Smid
8/5/1979	North Conway Volvo $175,000 GP SS	Harold Solomon	Jose Higueras	G. Vilas - I. Tiriac	J. Sadri - T. Wilkison
8/5/1979	South Orange $75,000 Mutual GP	John McEnroe	John Lloyd	J. McEnroe - P. Fleming	F. Buehning - B. Nichols
8/5/1979	Lafayette $75,000 GP	Marty Riessen	Pat DuPre	M. Riessen - S. Stewart	V. Amaya - E. Friedler

8/11/1979	Indianapolis $175,000 Clay GP SS	Jimmy Connors	Guillermo Vilas	J. McEnroe - G. Mayer	J. Kodes - T. Smid
8/11/1979	Columbus $75,000 GP	Brian Gottfried	Eddie Dibbs	B. Gottfried - B. Lutz	T. Gullikson - T. Gullikson
8/19/1979	Toronto $175,000 GP SS	Bjorn Borg	John McEnroe	J. McEnroe - P. Fleming	H. Gunthardt - B. Hewitt
8/19/1979	Stowe $75,000 English Leather GP	Jimmy Connors	Mike Cahill	M. Cahill - S. Krulevitz	An Amritraj - C. Dibley
8/19/1979	Cleveland $50,000 GP	Stan Smith	Ilie Nastase	S. Smith - B. Lutz	F. Gonzalez - F. McNair
8/26/1979	Cincinnati $200,000 ATP SP	Peter Fleming	Roscoe Tanner	I. Nastase - B. Gottfried	S. Smith - B. Lutz
8/26/1979	Boston $175,000 US Pro GP SS	Jose Higueras	Hans Gildemeister	P. Slozil - H. Gunthardt	S. Ball - K. Warwick
9/9/1979	US Open $322,500 GP GS	John McEnroe	Vitas Gerulaitis	J. McEnroe - P. Fleming	S. Smith - B. Lutz
9/16/1979	Woodlands $150,000 Doubles GP ATP			M. Riessen - S. Stewart	B. Carmichael - T. Gullikson
9/16/1979	Atlanta $50,000 GP	Eliot Teltscher	John Alexander	I. Nastase - R. Moore	W. Fibak - F. McMillan
9/23/1979	Los Angeles $175,000 GP SS	Peter Fleming	John McEnroe	M. Riessen - S. Stewart	W. Fibak - F. McMillan
9/23/1979	Palermo $75,000 Palermo Open GP	Bjorn Borg	Corrado Barazzutti	P. McNamara - P. McNamee	I. El Shafei - J. Feaver
9/27/1979	Ascuncion Boqueron International	Jimmy Connors	Guillermo Vilas	7-5, 6-3	
9/30/1979	San Francisco $175,000 GP SS	John McEnroe	Peter Fleming	J. McEnroe - P. Fleming	W. Fibak - F. McMillan
9/30/1979	Madrid $75,000 GP	Yannick Noah	Manuel Orantes	C. Karayr - C. Motta	R. Drysdale - J. Feaver
9/30/1979	Marbella $200,000 European Open	Bjorn Borg	Adriano Panatta	H. Gunthardt - I. Nastase	B. Borg - M. Santana
10/6/1979	Rotterdam	Bjorn Borg	Eddie Dibbs	6-3, 6-0	
10/7/1979	Kaanapali $100,000 GP	Bill Scanlon	Peter Fleming	J. Lloyd - N. Saviano	R. Frawley - F. Gonzalez
10/7/1979	Bordeaux $50,000 Bordeaux Open GP	Yannick Noah	Harold Solomon	P. Dominquez - D. Naegelen	B. Fritz - I. Molina

10/7/1979	Bogota	Wojtek Fibak	Pat DuPre	P. DuPre - W. Fibak	D. Stockton - E. Van Dillen
10/8/1979	Buenos Aires	Jimmy Connors	Victor Pecci	Guillermo Vilas #3	Ilie Nastase #4
10/13/1979	Tel Aviv $50,000 Israel GP	Tom Okker	Per Hjertquist	I. Nastase - T. Okker	M. Cahill - C. Dibley
10/14/1979	Barcelona $175,000 GP SS	Hans Gildemeister	Eddie Dibbs	A. Panatta - P. Bertolucci	C. Kimayr - C. Motta
10/14/1979	Brisbane $50,000 GP	Phil Dent	Ross Case	R. Case - G. Masters	C. Kachel - J. James
10/21/1979	Sydney $175,000 GP SS	Vitas Gerulaitis	Guillermo Vilas	R. Frawley - F. Gonzalez	P. DuPre - V. Amritraj
10/21/1979	Basle $75,000 Swiss Indoor GP	Brian Gottfried	Johan Kriek	B. Hewitt - F. McMillan	B. Gottfried - R. Ramirez
10/28/1979	Tokyo $125,000 Japan Open GP	Terry Moor	Pat DuPre	P. Dupre - C. Dibley	R. Frawley - F. Gonzalez
10/28/1979	Vienna $75,000 Fischer Cup GP	Stan Smith	Wojtek Fibak	G. Mayer - S. Smith	H. Gunthardt - P. Slozil
11/4/1979	Cologne $75,000 European Indoor GP	Gene Mayer	Wojtek Fibak	G. Mayer - S. Smith	H. Gunthardt - P. Slozil
11/4/1979	Tokyo $300,000 Seiko GP SS	Bjorn Borg	Jimmy Connors	M. Riessen - S. Stewart	M. Cahill - T. Moor
11/4/1979	Paris $50,000 Crocodile Open GP	Harold Solomon	Corrado Barazzutti	J. Haillet - G. Moretton	J. Lloyd - T. Lloyd
11/5/1979	Canton SP	Bjorn Borg	John Alexander		
11/11/1979	Stockholm $175,000 GP SS	John McEnroe	Gene Mayer	J. McEnroe - P. Fleming	W. Fibak - T. Okker
11/11/1979	Hong Kong $75,000 Colgate GP	Jimmy Connors	Pat DuPre	P. DuPre - B. Lutz	S. Denton - M. Turpin
11/11/1979	Quito $50,000 GP	Victor Pecci	Jose Higueras	J. Fillol - A. Fillol	I. Molina - J. Velasco
11/18/1979	London $175,000 Wembley GP SS	John McEnroe	Harold Solomon	J. McEnroe - P. Fleming	S. Smith - T. Smid
11/18/1979	Bogota $50,000 GP	Victor Pecci	Jairo Velasco	E. Montano - J. Velasco	B. Nichols - C. Owens
11/18/1979	Tapei $75,000 Cathay Trust GP	Bob Lutz	Pat DuPre	M. Edmondson - J. Marks	P. DuPre - B. Lutz
11/25/1979	Buenos Aires $175,000 GP SS	Guillermo Vilas	Jose-Luis Clerc	T. Smid - S. Stewart	J. Soares - M. Hocevar
11/25/1979	Bombay $75,000 GP	Vijay Amritraj	Peter Elter	J. Delaney - C. Delaney	W. Popp - T. Furst

11/25/1979	Bologna $75,000 Italian Indoor GP	Butch Walts	Gianni Ocleppo	J. McEnroe - P. Fleming	F. Buehning - F. Taygan
11/28/1979	Milan $300,000 Masters RR SP	Bjorn Borg	John McEnroe		
12/2/1979	Johannesburg $175,000 SAB GP SS	Andrew Pattison	Victor Pecci	B. Hewitt - F. McMillan	M. Cahill - B. Mottram
12/2/1979	Santiago $50,000 GP	Hans Gildemeister	Jose Higueras	J. Higueras - J. Velasco	J. Fillol - A. Fillol
12/2/1979	Frankfurt $233,000 Frankfurt Cup SP	Bjorn Borg	Jimmy Connors		
12/9/1979	Montreal WCT 10,000 WTAll SP	Hans Gildemeister	Patrick Dupre	6-3, 6-3	
12/9/1979	Montreal WCT 10,000 WTAll SP	Hans Gildemeister	Johan Kriek	7-2, 7-5	
12/9/1979	Montreal WCT 10,000 WTAll SP	Jimmy Connors	Tim Gullikson	6-3, 6-3	
12/9/1979	Montreal WCT 10,000 WTAll SP	Jimmy Connors	Ilie Nastase	4-6, 7-6, 6-2	
12/9/1979	Montreal WCT 10,000 WTAll SP	Jimmy Connors	Peter Fleming	7-5, 6-3	
12/9/1979	Montreal WCT 10,000 WTAll SP	Ilie Nastase	Peter Fleming	6-3, 7-5	
12/9/1979	Montreal WCT 10,000 WTAll SP	Tim Gullikson	Peter Fleming	6-1, 2-6, 6-4	
12/9/1979	Montreal WCT 10,000 WTAll SP	Tim Gullikson	Ilie Nastase	6-1, 2-6, 6-4	
12/9/1979	Montreal WCT 10,000 WTAll SP	Bjorn Borg	Johan Kriek	6-4, 6-2	
12/9/1979	Montreal WCT 10,000 WTAll SP	Bjorn Borg	Patrick Dupre	6-1, 6-2	
12/9/1979	Montreal WCT 10,000 WTAll SP	Bjorn Borg	Hans Gildemeister	6-2, 6-2	
12/9/1979	Montreal WCT 10,000 WTAll SP	Johan Kriek	Patrick Dupre	6-2, 7-6	
12/9/1979	Montreal WCT 10,000 WTAll SP	Jimmy Connors	Hans Gildemeister	4-6, 6-0, 6-3	
12/9/1979	Montreal WCT 10,000 WTAll SP	Bjorn Borg	Tim Gullikson	6-3, 6-2	
12/9/1979	Montreal WCT 10,000 WTAll SP	Bjorn Borg	Jimmy Connors	6-4, 6-2, 2-6, 6-4	

12/16/1979	Adelaide $50,000 GP	Kim Warwick	Bernie Mitton	C. Dibley - C. Kachel	P. Dent - J. Alexander
12/23/1979	Sydney $100,000 NSW GP	Phil Dent	Hank Pfister	P. McNamara - P. McNamee	S. Docherty - C. Lewis
1/2/1980	Australian Open $350,000 GP GS	Guillermo Vilas	John Sadri	P. McNamara - P. McNamee	C. Letcher - P. Kronk
1/7/1980	London $200,000 Doubles WCT SP			J. McEnroe - P. Fleming	I. Nastase - S. Stewart
1/13/1980	New York 400,000 Colgate Masters GP	Bjorn Borg	Vitas Gerulaitis	J. McEnroe - P. Fleming	W. Fibak - T. Okker

http://www.atpworldtour.com/en/scores/results-archive.

http://www.itftennis.com/procircuit/tournaments/men's-calendar.aspx?tour=&reg=&nat=&sur=&cate=AL&iod=& fromDate=01-01-1968&toDate=29-12-1979.

Tennis History, Jim McManus, (Canada 2010).

1980 USTA Yearbook.

Official 1989 MTC Media Guide, (MTC 1989).

World of Tennis 1980, Edited by John Barrett and compiled by Lance Tingay, (London 1980).

CHAPTER 14:

1980: VOLVO GRAND PRIX BEGINS, GRAND SLAMS REJECT SUPERVISORS, CRISIS NO. 20

1980 Governing Bodies

The MIPTC was the governing body for men's professional tennis in 1980 when Volvo succeeded Colgate as the sponsor of the Volvo Grand Prix. WCT continued to be merged into the Volvo Grand Prix in 1980. The ITF was the governing body for the Davis Cup.

1980 Significant Tennis Leaders	
ITF President:	Philippe Chatrier (France)
USTA President:	Joe Carrico
Australian LTA President:	Brian Tobin
British LTA President:	Sir Carl Aarvold
French FFT President:	Philippe Chatrier
Chairman of Wimbledon:	Sir Brian Burnett
ATP President:	Jaime Fillol until July
ATP President:	Harold Solomon beginning in July
ATP Executive Director:	Bob Briner until March 1
ATP Executive Director:	Butch Buchholz beginning March 1
WCT Owners:	Lamar Hunt and Al Hill, Jr.
WCT Executive Director:	Mike Davies

In February of 1979, the ATP Board had given Bob Briner a significant increase in salary and a 2-year extension of his role as ATP Executive Director, with the 2nd year to be at Briner's option. In January, Bob Briner, announced that he was not going to serve for the second year of his two-year extension contract as Executive Director of the

ATP and that he was resigning as of March 1. The resignation of Donald Dell as legal advisor to the ATP in November of 1979 probably had an impact on Briner's decision. Bob Briner was quoted in *International Tennis Weekly*[343]: "'The years with the ATP have been both very rewarding and challenging. It has been a great pleasure to work with the ATP presidents whose terms have coincided with mine. Arthur Ashe, John Newcombe and Jaime Fillol have been great leaders and have contributed much to the success of the association. I have been a part of the ATP since before it was officially formed and I feel that after all these years it is time to step aside and allow new leadership to take over. I want to thank every member who has worked with me for the positive growth of the association as well as our great staff, both in Dallas and Paris. Since I have always tried to honor my commitments, I will serve out the remaining months on my Pro Council term and will continue to try to represent the best interests of the players and the game.'"

You probably would never guess that Briner started "ProServ Television" in Dallas in 1980, in business with Donald Dell and his ProServ company; Dennis Spencer, the first Editor of *ITW*, had left the ATP in late 1979 or early 1980 to work for ProServ's "Volvo Grand Prix" subsidiary. He would move to work with Briner's ProServ Television subsidiary in Dallas in 1982 and begin a long career as a professional dealing with international television rights and television production for tennis.

1980 MIPTC

ITF:	Philippe Chatrier, Chairman, Derek Hardwick and Stan Malless with David Gray as Joint Secretary.
Tournaments:	Lars Myhrman (Europe), Owen Williams (Rest of the World) and Jack Kramer (North America).
Players:	Bob Briner until November 4, Butch Buchholz beginning November 4, Arthur Ashe and Cliff Drysdale with Doug Tkachuk as Joint Secretary until July 25 and Ron Bookman as Joint Secretary beginning July 25.
Legal Counsel:	Roy L. Reardon, Esquire and John Cambria, Esquire.
Grand Prix Supervisors:	Dick Roberson, Chief, Frank Smith, Franco Bartoni and Kurt Nielsen

Two Competitions

In 1980, the 13th year of Open Tennis, there were two organized competitions for men: Volvo Grand Prix and the Davis Cup. Davis Cup was open to all players and was won 4-1 by Czechoslovakia over Argentina. There were 93 Volvo Grand Prix Open prize money tournaments, including the year-end Volvo Masters in Madison Square Garden in New York City. Included in the 93 tournaments were the four Grand Slams and 28 Super Series tournaments. The Volvo Masters was again staged at Madison Square Garden and was won by Bjorn Borg over Ivan Lendl 6-4, 6-2, 6-2 in singles and by Peter Fleming and John McEnroe over Peter McNamara and Paul McNamee 6-4, 6-3 in doubles.

WCT again staged eight of the 28 Super Series tournaments. The eight WCT tournaments, in addition to leading as part of the 92 Grand Prix tournaments to the Volvo Grand Prix Bonus Pool and the Volvo Masters, also led as a "circuit within a circuit" to the WCT Finals in Dallas won by Jimmy Connors over John McEnroe 2-6, 7-6, 6-1, 6-2 in singles and by Peter McNamara and Paul McNamee over Andy Pattison and Butch Walts 6-4, 6-4, 7-6 in doubles.

In addition to the Dallas Finals, WCT staged 5 other Special Events outside of the Volvo Grand Prix: (i) February 24, Salisbury MD, $200,000 WCT Invitational won by Bjorn Borg over Vijay Amritraj 7-5, 6-1, 6-3, (ii) March 9, Hartford, $130,000 Aetna World Cup won by the USA over Australia 5-2, (iii) May 11, Forest Hills $300,000 WCT Tournament of Champions won by Vitas Gerulaitis over John McEnroe 2-6, 6-2, 6-0 in singles and by Peter Fleming – John McEnroe over Peter McNamara – Paul McNamee 6-2, 5-7, 6-2 in doubles, (iv) December 14, Montreal, $320,000 WCT Challenge Cup won by John McEnroe over Vijay Amritraj 6-1, 6-2, 6-1 and (v) January 6, 1981, London, $200,000 WCT Braniff World Doubles won by Brian Gottfried and Raul Ramirez over Wojtek Fibak and Tom Okker 3-6, 6-4, 6-4, 3-6, 6-3.

No Significant Rule Changes

The 1980 Grand Prix Rules did not make significant changes to the 1979 Grand Prix Rules. The 1979 player commitment rule was continued, which required players to commit to six designated tournaments (with one veto) in order to be eligible to play in any of the Grand Prix tournaments, including the Grand Slams and to be eligible for a Bonus Pool award. Players could play in no more than six special events during the weeks of the 28 Super Series.[344]

Tournament Doctors Required for First Time

For the first time each tournament was required to have an official tournament doctor and the power to rule a player ineligible to compete on account of an obvious physical impairment was delegated to the Grand Prix Supervisors who were required to use that power with great discretion after seeking medical advice in all such cases.

Automatic 21-Day Suspension Threshold Increased

The threshold for the automatic 21-day suspension for the annual accumulation of fines was increased from $3,000 to $5,000. *It was just a little inflation adjustment.*

Review of Minor Offenses

The MIPTC Code provided for the hearing of player appeals from minor offense fines by a MIPTC member or Joint Secretary for each area. However, there was no listing of disciplinary officers and as I would later learn, no one ever heard any of the player minor offense fine appeals from fines levied by the Grand Prix Supervisors in 1979 and 1980.

MIPTC Meetings

In 1980, the MIPTC held seven meetings: January 8-11 in London, March 17-19 in London, April 30-May 2 in Dallas, June 17-19 in London, July 23-25 in New York, August 26-28, September 4 in New York and November 3-5 in London.

Designations

In January in London[345], the Tournament Representatives proposed and the Council agreed on the following guidelines for the 1980 designations: (i) that the top six players for their three major Super Series designations, should go to 18 separate tournaments, (ii) that those 18 tournaments should be the weakest tournaments based on the 1979 statistics of entries and (iii) that no player should be designated to a tournament where that player's agent was involved in any way with the tournament. It was agreed that the MIPTC would take over the responsibility for the player designations (instead of a designation committee) with the two Joint Secretaries to submit up-to-date designation lists every two weeks. *Good luck with that!*

U.S. Open Rejects Grand Prix Supervisors: Observers Only

Joe Carrico, USTA President, appeared and stated that the U.S. Open would only "welcome" the Grand Prix Supervisors as "observers" and not as the final authority as specified in the MIPTC Tournament Regulations. *This would create Crisis No. 20.*

Boston-Longwood, Cincinnati and Louisville

In March in London[346], Louisville submitted a letter withdrawing its application for a 1980 Super Series tournament which thankfully provided an open date to move Boston on clay to an earlier date before the USTA National Clay Courts in Indianapolis. The MIPTC agreed to sanction Cincinnati as a Super Series tournament and rearrange the U.S. summer schedule so that Canada and Cincinnati were just prior to the U.S. Open on hard courts. Thus, the withdrawal of Louisville settled Crisis No. 19 which was the extremely bitter Boston-Cincinnati and ATP vs. MIPTC dispute.

WCT Requests Extension for 1981

Mike Davies proposed a draft agreement for WCT to continue in the Grand Prix in 1981 on substantially the same terms as its agreement for 1978-1980. The MIPTC was concerned with the advantage the eight WCT Super Series tournaments had over the other Super Series tournaments in the Grand Prix by virtue of the WCT points and their "circuit within a circuit" program. The MIPTC was also concerned that the WCT Philadelphia Super Series received double WCT points. Finally, the MIPTC wanted indemnification from any claims made by WCT tournaments against the MIPTC. Some of WCT's eight Super Series were complaining about the terms upon which WCT subcontracted its MIPTC sanctions to them and also their possible claims against the MIPTC if WCT dropped them; instead of staging its own tournaments, WCT was in fact just licensing its eight Super Series sanctions.

Australian Open and Volvo Masters Dates

The MIPTC approved a change of dates for the Australian Open and the Volvo Masters: Australian Open: December 26, 1980 – January 4, 1981, Volvo Masters: January 14-18, 1981. It was noted that Ray Benton of ProServ would be the tournament director of the Volvo Masters. As long as the Masters was in January, the Australian Open would continue to have difficulty getting players to fly to Australia to play on grass in December, but Volvo and ProServ insisted on January for the Volvo Masters.

1981 Grand Prix Player Commitment

In April-May in Dallas[347], Jack Kramer proposed that players who did not agree to sign a player commitment would be required to enter all tournaments for the year via qualifying. The vote was 8-0 in favor with one abstention. This meant that contrary to the Player Commitment Rule of 1979 and 1980, which provided that players who refused the player commitment (six designations) *could not play in any Grand Prix tournament, including the Grand Slams*, players would still be able to play in 1981 if they did not agree to the player commitment, but would have to go through the qualifying of each tournament. Having to play in two or three rounds of qualifying before beginning the main draw of any tournament was an almost impossible burden and it was intentionally made so as to get players to sign the annual player commitment. Without the commitment of the players, the tournaments could not afford to offer the large amounts of prize money being offered so it was always viewed as a reasonable compromise bargain between the players and the tournaments.

1981 Special Events Limited to Six Against Super Series

By a vote of 5-4, it was agreed to keep the total special events permitted against Super Series weeks at six per year (in addition to the 16 open weeks). Naturally, the Super Series tournaments hated having any special events during their tournament weeks in which the top players would be playing instead of playing in their Super Series tournament and somehow the special events would often be in the weeks of Super Series tournament not involved with either ProServ or IMG. WCT Super Series were always a big target for special events.

Player-Agents

At almost every meeting of the MIPTC, the conflict of interest issue resulting from the involvement of agents for some players being involved in Grand Prix tournaments open to all players was discussed *ad nauseum*. "It was agreed that the Council should try to find rules to deal with abuses that might occur through the involvement of player-agents in tournament promotions. Roy Reardon, MIPTC counsel, was asked to make proposals on the matter to the next meeting."

Designations

In London in June[348], Doug Tkachuk and David Gray, the Joint Secretaries, reported on the final designations for the American Summer Circuit and the European Autumn Circuit. So even though the designations of players to tournaments was being "controlled" by the nine members of the MIPTC, the designation of players was actually being made by the Joint Secretaries and that usually meant Tkachuk. Since Tkachuk worked for the ATP and had more connection with the players, it is easy to conclude that he probably controlled the designations.

WCT Extension Through 1981 Grand Prix

Philippe Chatrier, as MIPTC Chairman, and WCT signed a letter extending WCT's participation in the Grand Prix through 1981, under essentially the same terms as the agreement covering 1978-1980. WCT did not agree to indemnify the MIPTC from claims that might be made by WCT Super Series tournaments, but WCT agreed that it would not change the site of any of the eight WCT Super Series tournaments without the prior written approval of the MIPTC, "which approval shall not be unreasonably withheld." WCT also agreed that it would not conduct any special events during Grand Prix Super Series weeks.

Administrator Proposed Finally

After years of debate, finally in July in New York[349], "The Council unanimously accepted a proposal from Arthur Ashe that they should employ an Administrator who would carry out his duties under the aegis and direction of the Council according to a job description. The Council agreed to hire a search firm to find a suitable candidate with a target date of 31st December." Arthur always was an advocate for more and more professionalism for the Council. He was instrumental in the drafting of the Tournament Regulations, the Code of Conduct and from the beginning he had pushed for an independent administration for the Council.

Six Designations

In August-September in New York[350], the Council discussed at length the various issues relating to the player commitment of 6 designations. Once again, the Council decided that a Designation Committee, with the assistance of the Joint Secretaries, should issue the player designations and inform each tournament six months in advance of its designations with the provision that if there was any disagreement among the Designation Committee, it would be settled by the Council. *This was not going to work either.* Players hated being told where to go and no one involved on the MIPTC was willing to force them to do so. Meanwhile, some tournaments were not getting representative fields – particularly those not in business with ProServ or IMG. Illegal appearance guarantees also warped the player fields.

1981 Designations

In November in London[351], Derek Hardwick, as Chairman of the Designations Committee, reported on the reluctance of the top players to accept particular designations and that he was asking them to get together among themselves and work out a solution. *Good Luck to the Chairman of the Designations Committee!*

Administrator Search

The MIPTC finalized its agreement to hire an executive search firm to find candidates for the new position of Administrator of the MIPTC and set up a new office in New York City. It was agreed that it would take a 2/3 majority for the selection of an Administrator. Phillipe Chatrier, Owen Williams and Arthur Ashe were appointed to a sub-committee with the task of screening and interviewing applicants before the next meeting of the Council in the week of January 12 during the Volvo Masters and producing a short list of candidates.

Briner Abruptly Resigns from Council

Bob Briner, who had resigned at ATP Executive Director in January and was succeeded by Butch Buchholz on March 1, did not return after lunch on November 4. Instead, he left a letter for the Chairman, saying that he had resigned from the Council. Drysdale, and Ashe who had been surprised by Briner's resignation then formally agreed on the election of Butch Buchholz to replace Briner.

Monte Carlo and Easter

Monte Carlo was one of WCT's eight Super Series tournaments in 1980. Monte Carlo was a very powerful tournament due to the fact through its connection with the Monaco government, it could and had been able to offer permanent residency to a number of top tennis players, like Bjorn Borg and Guillermo Vilas. Residency included no income taxes instead of 50+ percent in income taxes in the United States and in most European countries. Monaco residents somehow just had to play in the Monte Carlo Super Series Tournament every year. Players never had to be designated there. The problem was that Monte Carlo had only a few thousand permanent residents, but during Easter vacation more than 25,000 people poured into Monte Carlo. So, guess what? Monte Carlo was convinced that it could only have a successful tournament during Easter of each year and the date of Easter jumps all over the calendar each year, sometimes as much as a month. Easter Sunday in 1981 was April 19, 1981, so naturally, Monte Carlo would only agree to stage its tournament in that week. That was, however, the week of the Los Angeles Super Series and was outside of the WCT time period for its 8 Super Series (after the WCT Dallas Finals). Monte Carlo had a quite simple position. Unless the MIPTC somehow made Monte Carlo a Super Series tournament in the Easter week of April 12-19, 1981, Monte Carlo would stage a special event with a plan to re-apply for a WCT Super Series tournament in 1982 (if WCT continued to be in the Grand Prix). This was just about a problem without any possible solution. Finally, the solution found was that Los Angeles gave up its Super Series sanction and for 1981 only became a $75,000 tournament and Monte Carlo became a (non-WCT) Super Series in Easter week of 1981. In 1982, Easter would be in the WCT time period (if WCT remained in the Grand Prix) and Monte Carlo could then be one of the eight WCT Super Series for 1982. Los Angeles was promised that it could resume its status as a Super Series in April of 1982. The dates for Monte Carlo and Easter continued to cause a nightmare for the Grand Prix calendar every year.

Mike Davies and Ilie Nastase

Mike Davies as Executive Director of WCT contracted with players like Ilie Nastase for WCT special events outside of the Grand Prix, like the Braniff WCT World Doubles in London in January of 1980 and the WCT Invitational in Salisbury MD, in February of 1980. The MIPTC Code of Conduct did not apply to WCT special events. Mike had contractual control of the players he signed for the WCT special events and he was, in fact, the sole authority for player misconduct at those WCT events. Mike also had a low tolerance level for player misconduct. In 1980, Nastase was 34 years old, still competing at a high level and yes still misbehaving. At the Braniff WCT World Doubles in London in January of 1980, Nastase won $5,250 in prize money and was fined $5,000 by Mike for conduct detrimental to the sport of professional tennis. "I am very offended at the way he speaks to umpires and linesmen who are doing a job the best way they know how," said Davies to the *New York Times*[352]: "I am very upset also that he should speak to another human being in that way. I don't care whether there is a lot of money on the line. Offensive language, when we have children and ladies in the audience, is also something I can't tolerate. And his continued stalling shows no respect for his opponents."

At the WCT special event in Salisbury Md., on February 22, 1980, Vijay Amritraj was leading Ilie Nastase 6-3, 3-6, 1-0, when Davies halted the match on the grounds that Nastase had engaged in excessive stalling and had used abusive language. Richard Evans wrote is *Open Tennis*[353]: "Davies was in the (TV) truck directing the show which was to be sold to stations as a tape-delayed event through WCT's own television network. Finally, the antics were more than Davies could bear, so he threw down his headphones, stormed out of the truck and straight on to the court, kicked down the singles stick and said to an amazed Nastase, 'Right, that's it, you're defaulted.' The crowd were equally amazed because Davies, not expecting to be on public view that day, was dressed in a shirt and jeans and looked as if he had walked in off the street."[354]

Hamilton Jordan in 1980, Chief of Staff

In 1988, Hamilton Jordan would be the ATP Executive Director and would lead the ATP's destruction of the MIPTC, the creation of the ATP Tour and the separation of the Grand Slams from the ATP Tour in 1990. In 1980, Jordan was the Chief of Staff for President Jimmy Carter.

"In recent weeks, President Carter's 35-year-old chief of staff has flown surreptitiously to Paris, Algiers and other capitals in a new and largely unpublicized role as the President's special envoy on Iran," wrote Terence Smith on April 4, 1980, in the *New York Times*[355]. "Of all the President's aides, Mr. Jordan is both the most influential and least visible…'I don't advertise my comings and goings,' he said with a small smile. Traveling by government plane, sometimes reportedly using disguises, Mr. Jordan has met several times in Paris and elsewhere with French lawyers hired by Iran as go-between in negotiations on the hostage crisis. White House officials have acknowledged these trips reluctantly, contending that any detailed disclosure might endanger the contacts."

Ashe Retires

In 1979, Arthur Ashe suffered a mild heart attack and underwent quadruple bypass surgery. In April, Ashe, age 36, announced that he was retiring from competitive tennis.[356] Thankfully, Arthur did not retire from the MIPTC or the ATP and continued his role as a player leader. [Arthur would have a 2nd bypass operation in 1983, with a blood transfusion which infected him with HIV that eventually caused his death in 1993].

Borg Over McEnroe at Wimbledon – The Greatest Match

Bjorn Borg defeated John McEnroe 1-6, 7-5, 6-3, 6-7, 8-6 in three hours and 53-minutes in the final of Wimbledon in what many people say was the greatest major championship final ever played. "If this marathon was not the greatest major

championship final ever played – and tennis historians treasure the past with reverence – it ranked as one of the most exciting," wrote Neil Amdur in the *New York Times*[357]. "Lance Tingay of *The London Daily Telegraph*, who was watching his 43rd final here, put it at the top of his Wimbledon list."

In September, McEnroe got revenge for his Wimbledon loss by defeating Borg in 4

Bjorn Borg   John McEnroe

hours and 13 minutes in the U.S. Open final 7-6, 6-1, 6-7, 5-7, 6-4. Borg won six French Opens and five Wimbledons, but was never able to win the U.S. Open.

Nastase Suspended Again – Davis Cup 18 Months

In July, the ITF suspended Ilie Nastase for 18 months from the Davis Cup competition. In a Romania vs. Great Britain European Zone semifinal, Nastase defeated John Feaver in five sets in the deciding match, but was guilty of bad language in exchanges with spectators and the Norwegian referee Cato Vik.[358]

At the U.S. Open, Nastase lost to Harold Solomon in the second round. Nastase received $1,250 in fines at the U.S. Open: $250 for an obscene gesture, $500 for hitting a linesman with a batted ball and $500 for throwing two tennis balls at an umpire. *Ilie was consistently terrible!*[359]

Arthur Ashe Succeeds Trabert as Davis Cup Captain

Arthur Ashe was appointed U.S. Davis Cup Captain succeeding Tony Trabert.[360]

ATP

Butch Buchholz Succeeds Bob Briner

Butch Buchholz who was hired by Briner in 1979 to establish a merchandising division and bring the ATP tournament operations in-house, was selected to succeed Briner as ATP Executive Director as of March 1, 1980. Butch Buchholz had been a junior Grand Slam champion, a member of the old Kramer touring pros, a leading member of the 1st players' association, the International Professional Tennis Players Association (IPTPA), one of the original WCT pros known as the "Handsome Eight", a tournament promoter in Kansas City, tennis club owner and the Commissioner of WTT. *Butch Buchholz is one of the nicest people I have ever met and as far as I know, then or even now, I do not believe there has ever been one person who did not like Butch Buchholz.*

I should also mention and remind you that Butch Buchholz and Mike Davies were the closest of friends since they played on the Kramer Tour together, ran the IPTPA together and Butch brought Mike Davies to replace Bob Briner as the WCT Executive Director to save the then bankrupt WCT.

Dewey Blanton wrote in *World of Tennis 1981*[361]: "Butch certainly drew on this considerable experience as the head of the players' organisation with a membership in excess of 250, but even more useful was his naturally co-operative, trusting and sincere disposition. Other powerbrokers in tennis, previously loath to say anything good about the ATP, were full of praise for the style and panache of Buchholz. It was his style that was instrumental in the addition of two new names to the ATP membership rolls. The Association had long suffered the stigma of not having any top players as members (Since Drysdale, Ashe, Newcombe, Smith, etc.); an obvious handicap to strength and bargaining power. But with Bjorn Borg and John McEnroe as members, the Association can now boast representation among the top players on the ATP computer rankings. Borg joined after discussions with Buchholz during the Toronto tournament, while McEnroe signed up in San Francisco. Both men felt their allegiance lay with the players, and said they were impressed with Buchholz's leadership. Butch, having been a player himself, and therefore having an understanding of the problems players face, was of tremendous importance here."

Buchholz added to the ATP staff: Ron Bookman who had been Editor of *World Tennis Magazine* as Director of Communications, Jim Westhall, who had been Tournament Director of the North Conway Super Series tournament, as Marketing Administrator and liaison to the six official ATP events and Mike Savitt as ATP Director of Public Relations. Continuing ATP staff included Doug Tkachuk, Administrative Director, David Fechtman and Bill Norris, ATP trainers and Paul Svehlik, Director of European Operations at the

ATP Paris Office. Soon after Buchholz became the Executive Director in March, he went to Doug Tkachuk and asked to see the books and financial records of the ATP. To his dismay, Butch learned that there were no books and financial records. All Tkachuk had was a rudimentary spreadsheet showing income and expenses. Buchholz could not believe it. "To the tune of a $600,000 overdraft, the ATP was broke. Or as near as made no difference," wrote Richard Evans in *Open Tennis*[362]. After Buchholz replaced Tkachuk with Bookman on July 25, as the MIPTC Players' Joint Secretary, Buchholz fired Tkachuk who began looking for a new job. Remember that Briner had left WCT in financial ruins when he left as WCT Executive Director and now he had done the same to the ATP.

Harold Solomon Becomes Fifth ATP President

Harold Solomon was elected in July as the new ATP President to succeed Jaime Fillol, with Charlie Pasarell as Vice President, Colin Dowdeswell as Treasurer and Jim McManus again as Secretary. The other members of the ATP Board were Arthur Ashe, Cliff Drysdale, Mark Cox, Richard Lewis, Victor Amaya, Geoff Masters and Butch Buchholz. Ray Moore was not yet back on the Board.

JAKS Awards

The JAKS Awards were again staged during the Volvo Masters in New York City in January of 1981:

Player of the Year	Bjorn Borg
Doubles Team of the Year	Bob Lutz – Stan Smith
Rookie of the Year	Mel Purcell
Most Improved Player of the Year	Ivan Lendl
Media Distinguished Service Award	Barry Lorge
The Dr. R.W. Johnson ATP Award	Charlie Pasarell
Tennis Magazine Comeback Player of the Year	Bob Lutz
Cystic Fibrosis Service Award	Frank DeFord and Bob Briner
ATP Great Player of the Past	Tony Trabert

ATP Service Award   Jaime Fillol

Court Official of the Year   Frank Hammond

ATP-Adidas Sportsmanship Award   Bjorn Borg

ProServ and IMG

In 1980, the two biggest management companies were: Dell, Craighill, Fentress and Benton, a law firm, founded in 1970, upon the signing of Arthur Ashe, Stan Smith, Charles Pasarell and Bob Lutz and its service company, Pro Serv Inc.; and International Management Group (IMG), owned by Mark McCormack, which was founded in 1960 upon the signing of golfer Arnold Palmer. IMG's tennis business was handled by Bob Kain, IMG Vice President. ProServ's original emphasis was on representing tennis players, whereas IMG's original emphasis was on representing golfers. In 1980, ProServ represented about half of the top 20-30 professional tennis players, such as Roscoe Tanner, Brian Gottfried, Eddie Dibbs, Ilie Nastase, Gene Mayer, Dick Stockton, Ivan Lendl and Raul Ramirez, plus a number of top women like Tracy Austin and Pam Shriver. ProServ also represented 15 NBA players, including Moses Malone, Phil Ford, Bobby Jones and Adrian Dantley. ProServ would soon represent Michael Jordan. IMG was bigger than ProServ, but was later coming into tennis. In 1980, IMG represented Bjorn Borg and Chris Evert. Just about the only top tennis players not represented by either ProServ or IMG were John McEnroe, who was represented by his father, John P. McEnroe, Sr., Guillermo Vilas, who was represented by Ion Tiriac, and Jimmy Connors, who was represented by his mother, Gloria Connors (sometimes also by IMG and then ProServ). In addition to representing players, ProServ and IMG became more and more involved in owning or defacto owning (just owning the commercial rights for a contracted fee to the tournament owner) and staging Grand Prix tournaments and in representing tournaments for the procurement of sponsors and for the sale of television rights. Both ProServ and IMG also got into the television production of tennis events. They also promoted and/or were involved with special events (sometimes against Grand Prix tournaments). Both ProServ and IMG were constantly faced with conflict of interest issues as was the MIPTC in trying to administer and protect men's professional tennis from conflicts of interest.

Donald Dell of ProServ along with Jack Kramer and Bob Briner founded the ATP in 1972, and Dell and Frank Craighill served as the legal advisor to the ATP until 1979. Thereafter, Dell continued to represent the ATP and its seven official ATP tournaments and events for sponsorships and television. ProServ also represented Colgate during its sponsorship of the Colgate Grand Prix in the staging of the Colgate Masters at Madison

Square Garden and in 1980 was representing Volvo, not only for the staging of the Volvo Masters at Madison Square Garden, but for all of Volvo's promotion of the worldwide Volvo Grand Prix through a sort of ProServ subsidiary known as the "Volvo Grand Prix" promotion arm. ProServ's "Volvo Grand Prix" operation provided all the promotion for the Volvo Grand Prix, including the annual media guides and the media liaisons at each tournament. ProServ's representation of Volvo for the Volvo Grand Prix promotion and for the staging and promotion of the Volvo Masters was a very lucrative arrangement for ProServ. The MIPTC had no presence at any of the Volvo Grand Prix tournaments except via the Grand Prix Supervisors who were there to enforce the Grand Prix Rules and Regulations.

In addition to all kinds of conflicts of interest with players represented vs. players not represented in tournaments in which the management companies were involved, there was an inherent conflict when more than one player was represented. Which one do you pitch for the highest endorsement or appearance fee? Do you use a star player to help get an exhibition fee for a lesser player and so on? If you have control of the wild card entries for a tournament who do you give them to? An existing client or a new player you are soliciting for a client? Certainly not a new player with whom you have no current or potential business relationship!

1980 Crisis No. 20: Grand Prix Supervisors at the Grand Slams

In order to establish the authority of the Grand Prix Supervisors to ensure the uniform administration of the rules at all Grand Prix tournaments, the MIPTC provided in the 1979 and 1980 MIPTC Tournament Regulations that the Grand Prix Supervisors would be the final on-site authority at all MIPTC sanctioned tournaments. There was a simmering issue about the authority of the Grand Prix Supervisors at the Grand Slams.

Jacques Dorfmann French Referee Openly Hostile: Orantes and Vilas

The U.S. Open and Wimbledon had offered to accept the Grand Prix Supervisors only as "observers" and the French Open Referee Jacques Dorfmann was openly hostile to the Grand Prix Supervisors. Dorfmann was also known to have some favorites among the player field. At the 1980 French Open, Manuel Orantes was scheduled to play Guillermo Vilas in the quarterfinals. Matches began at 11:00 am and the Orantes vs. Vilas match was scheduled as the third match following the Barrazzutti vs. McNamee match on Court No. 1. Vilas arrived at Roland Garros at 10:00 AM, but was ill and received treatment by the official doctors and trainers. After practicing for a short while, Vilas said that he was still not very well and the doctors proposed additional treatment which required about one hour. The Barazzutti match finished early and Vilas was not available to play as Dorfmann had granted him extra time to recover. Orantes refused to accept the delay and requested a default. The Grand Prix Supervisors directed Dorfmann to default Vilas for not being available to play when the match was scheduled to begin. Dorfmann refused to default Vilas and claimed he had the unilateral authority to delay the order of play in his discretion. When Vilas finally arrived later for the match, Orantes refused to play, claiming Vilas should be defaulted. The next day Dorfmann attempted to again get Orantes to play Vilas, but when he continued to refuse, Dorfmann defaulted Orantes.[363]

Thus, we had complete and total defiance by Dorfmann of the instructions of the Grand Prix Supervisors that Vilas should be defaulted by not appearing for play at

Jacques Dorfmann

the scheduled time for his match against Orantes. Dorfmann obviously was granting his favorite player extra time to recover. Butch Buchholz, as the new Executive Director of the ATP, convinced the players not to boycott so he could pursue a fine against the French Open at the next meeting of the MIPTC. The MIPTC fined the French Open $2,800 for improperly defaulting Orantes to be paid to Orantes, less a 20 percent administrative fee to be retained by the MIPTC. Orantes was awarded a total of 70 Grand Prix points. The fine amount and the Grand Prix points were the same that Orantes would have received if he had played and defeated Vilas. Over Dorfmann's objection, Chatrier elected to accept the fine and support the MIPTC and the Grand Prix Supervisors. After all, he was the Chairman of the MIPTC and a strong supporter of the ATP since it had been created. This was the beginning of Crisis No. 20 and the struggle for the authority of the Grand Prix Supervisors at the Grand Slams.

At the June MIPTC meeting in London[364], Butch Buchholz said he had met Sir Brian Burnett, Chairman of Wimbledon, and it was apparent that Wimbledon would only accept the Supervisors in an advisory capacity. In addition, the MIPTC had received a letter from the USTA saying that the Grand Prix Supervisors would only be accepted as advisors at the U.S. Open. Cliff Drysdale reported that the ATP Board had unanimously approved a resolution supporting the authority of the Grand Prix Supervisors at the Grand Slams and that following Wimbledon, the ATP would demand that their authority be accepted by the Grand Slams. He said at the meeting: "The players have participated with good faith in the rule-making mechanism of the Grand Prix along with the tournaments directors and the ITF. Now this good faith is being repaid by selective enforcement of the rules, a double standard, which the ATP cannot condone and will resist to the fullest."

The dilemma facing the MIPTC was the need to have the four Grand Slams as part of the Grand Prix and the need to have uniform rules for all Grand Prix tournaments, including the Grand Slams. Owen Williams proposed, seconded by Jack Kramer, the following resolution: "The Supervisors will act as advisors to the Grand Slam tournament committees on all matters pertaining to the rules. The Supervisors have been appointed to ensure that tournaments are conducted in accordance with the Rules of Tennis, the Grand Prix Rules and the Code of Conduct and the uniformity of their interpretation. They will report any breaches of these rules by tournaments or players to the Council, which will, if an offence is proven, impose the appropriate penalties. These include fines or exclusion from the Grand Prix in the case of persistent or serious offences. In all cases the final authority will rest with the Council." The Resolution was approved by a vote of 6-3 *with the three Player Representatives dissenting.*

That Resolution Kept the Grand Slams in the Grand Prix

The Resolution, apparently agreed by Wimbledon and the U.S. Open, clearly established the MIPTC as the final authority while making the Grand Prix Supervisors advisors and not the final authority at the Grand Slam tournaments (during the tournaments). Dewey Blanton wrote in *World of Tennis 1981*[365]: "But still the problem was not solved by any means. When things failed to improve in the summer, the players demanded action, obviously with the U.S. Open in mind. Players began to withdraw from the tournament, vowing not to play unless the Supervisors were made solely responsible for such matters as scheduling. As the entry deadline neared, 86 of the top 100 players on the ATP computer had either withdrawn from, or not entered, the Open."

The *New York Times* reported[366]: "The top five players – Bjorn Borg, John McEnroe, Jimmy Connors, Vitas Gerulaitis and Vilas – have entered the United States Open, (Harold) Solomon said, but 'right now, 80 of the top 100 have not entered and, with withdrawals, before the deadline, I think 95 out of the top 100 won't enter.' 'I don't know if they can have a tournament with the top five and then the next guy is ranked 200th,' he said."

Subsequently, Butch Buchholz and Harold Solomon were able to work out a compromise for the 1980 U.S. Open which provided for the creation of a committee to serve as the final authority at the U.S. Open. The committee consisted of two representatives of the U.S. Open, two Grand Prix Supervisors and Col. Nick Powel, as a mutually agreed upon fifth person as an independent arbitrator. The Council noted that agreement for the

1980 U.S. Open and informed the USTA and the ATP that it would not be considered a precedent for the future "as the Council is the final authority on the rules."[367]

Wimbledon and U.S. Open Support the MIPTC

In November in London[368], the MIPTC was informed that the U.S. Open and Wimbledon were going to support the MIPTC as the governing body of men's professional tennis, support the mandatory signing by players of a player commitment or be subject to entry via qualifying only and accept the Grand Prix Supervisors as "advisors," subject to the final authority of the MIPTC. That concluded Crisis No. 20.

1980 Grand Slam Winners

French Open

Bjorn Borg d. Vitas Gerulaitis 6-4, 6-1, 6-2.
Victor Amaya – Hank Pfister d. Brian Gottfried – Raul Ramirez 1-6, 6-4, 6-4, 6-3.

Wimbledon

Bjorn Borg d. John McEnroe 1-6, 7-5, 6-3, 6-7, 8-6.
Peter McNamara – Paul McNamee d. Bob Lutz – Stan Smith 7-6, 6-3, 6-7, 6-4.

U.S. Open

John McEnroe d. Bjorn Borg 7-6, 6-1, 6-7, 5-7, 6-4.
Bob Lutz – Stan Smith d. Peter Fleming – John McEnroe 7-9, 3-6, 6-1, 3-6, 6-3.

Australian Open

Brian Teacher d. Kim Warwick 7-5, 7-6, 6-3.
Mark Edmondson – Kim Warwick d. Peter McNamara – Paul McNamee 7-5, 6-4.

Volvo Masters

Bjorn Borg d. Ivan Lendl 6-4, 6-2, 6-2.
Peter Fleming-John McEnroe d. Peter McNamara-Paul McNamee 6-4, 6-3.

1980 Davis Cup

Davis Cup Final (Prague - Indoors)

Czechoslovakia d. Italy 4-1.

Ivan Lendl (CZ) d. Corrado Barazzutti (IT) 4-6, 6-1, 6-1, 6-2.
Tomas Smid (CZ) d. Adriano Panatta (IT) 3-6, 6-3, 3-6, 6-3, 6-4.
Ivan Lendl – Tomas Smid (CZ) d. Paolo Bertolucci – Adriano Panatta (IT) 3-6, 6-3, 6-3, 6-4.
Corrado Barazzutti (IT) d. Tomas Smid (CZ) 3-6, 6-3, 6-2.
Ivan Lendl (CZ) d. Gianni Ocleppo (IT) 6-3, 6-3.

Nations Cup (Dusseldorf)

Argentina d. Italy 3-0.

Guillermo Vilas (AR) d. Corrado Barazzutti (IT) 6-3, 6-2.
Jose-Luis Clerc (AR) d. Adriano Panatta (IT) 7-6, 6-3.
Jose-Luis Clerc – Guillermo Vilas (AR) d. Paolo Bertolucci (IT) – Adriano Panatta 6-2, 6-3.

1980 World Rankings[369]

	Bud Collins		Lance Tingay
1.	Bjorn Borg	1.	Bjorn Borg
2.	John McEnroe	2.	John McEnroe
3.	Jimmy Connors	3.	Jimmy Connors
4.	Gene Mayer	4.	Guillermo Vilas
5.	Guillermo Vilas	5.	Vitas Gerulaitis
6.	Ivan Lendl	6.	Ivan Lendl
7.	Harold Solomon	7.	Harold Solomon
8.	Jose-Luis Clerc	8.	Gene Mayer
9.	Vitas Gerulaitis	9.	Eliot Teltscher
10.	Eliot Teltscher	10.	Brian Gottfried

Rino Tommasi

1. Bjorn Borg
2. John McEnroe
3. Jimmy Connors
4. Gene Mayer
5. Guillermo Vilas
6. Ivan Lendl
7. Harold Solomon
8. Vitas Gerulaitis
9. Jose-Luis Clerc
10. Vijay Amritraj

ATP Year-End Rankings[370]

1. Bjorn Borg
2. John McEnroe
3. Jimmy Connors
4. Gene Mayer
5. Guillermo Vilas
6. Ivan Lendl
7. Harold Solomon
8. Jose-Luis Clerc
9. Vitas Gerulaitis
10. Eliot Teltscher

1980 Volvo Grand Prix Bonus Pool Top 10[371]

Singles (11th Bonus Pool)

1. John McEnroe — $300,000
2. Ivan Lendl — $200,000
3. Jimmy Connors — $150,000
4. Bjorn Borg — $100,000
5. Gene Mayer — $ 80,000
6. Harold Solomon — $ 60,000
7. Guillermo Vilas — $ 50,000
8. Jose-Luis Clerc — $ 40,000
9. Eliot Teltscher — $ 35,000
10. Brian Teacher — $ 30,000

Doubles (6th Bonus Pool)

1. Stan Smith — $90,000
2. Bob Lutz — $60,000
3. Paul McNamee — $40,000
4. Brian Gottfried — $28,000
5. John McEnroe — $20,000
6. Peter Fleming — $18,000
7. Steve Denton — $16,000
8. Brian Teacher — $14,000
9. Peter McNamara — $12,000
10. Ivan Lendl — $10,000

1980 Official Earnings Top 10[372]

1.	John McEnroe	$972,369	6.	Guillermo Vilas	$378,217
2.	Bjorn Borg	$731,762	7.	Wojtek Fibak	$368,073
3.	Ivan Lendl	$583.406	8.	Vitas Gerulaitis	$340,823
4.	Jimmy Connors	$570,060	9.	Brian Gottfried	$296,800
5.	Gene Mayer	$397,156	10.	Jose-Luis Clerc	$280,697

1980 Tournament Calendar

Date	Tournaments	Singles Winner	Singles #2	Doubles Winners	Doubles #2
1/6/1980	Hobart $50,000 GP	Shlomo Glickstein	Robert Van't Hof	J. James - C. Kachel	B. Guam - P. Davies
1/7/1980	Auckland $50,000 Open	John Sadri	Tim Wilkison	F. Feigl - R. Frawley	J. Sadri - T. Wilkison
1/20/1980	Birmingham $175,000 GP SS/ WCT	Jimmy Connors	Eliot Teltscher	W. Fibak - T. Okker	J. L. Clerc - I. Nastase
1/20/1980	Baltimore $75,000 GP	Harold Solomon	Tim Gullikson	T. Gullikson - M. Riessen	B. Gottfried - F. McMillan
1/27/1980	Philadelphia $250k GP SS/ WCT	Jimmy Connors	John McEnroe	J. McEnroe - P. Fleming	B. Gottfried - R. Ramirez
2/3/1980	Richmond $175,000 GP SS/ WCT	John McEnroe	Roscoe Tanner	F. Buehning - J. Kriek	B. Gottfried - F. McMillan
2/3/1980	San Juan $75,000 GP	Raul Ramirez	Phil Dent	P. Kronk - P. McNamee	M. Turpin - R. Trologo
2/10/1980	Boca West $300,000 Pepsi GS SP	Bjorn Borg	Vitas Gerulaitis	7-5, 6-1, 6-3	
2/17/1980	Palm Springs $250k GP SS ATP	Rained out			
2/17/1980	Sarasota $50,000 GP	Eddie Dibbs	Andres Gomez	R. Ycaza - A. Gomez	D. Carter - R. Fagel
2/24/1980	Denver $125,000 GP	Gene Mayer	Victor Amaya	K. Curren - S. Denton	W. Fibak - H. Gunthardt
2/24/1980	Salisbury $200,000 WCT SP	Bjorn Borg	Vijay Amitraj		
3/2/1980	Memphis $250,000 GP SS	John McEnroe	Jimmy Connors	J. McEnroe - B. Gottfried	R. Frawley - T. Smid
3/2/1980	Lagos $50,000 GP	Peter Feigl	Harry Fritz	B. Nichols - T. Graham	K. Johansson - L. Palin
3/9/1980	Washington $125,000 GP	Victor Amaya	Ivan Lendl	B Teacher - F. Taygan	K. Curren - S. Denton
3/9/1980	Cairo $75,000 GP	Corrado Barazutti	Paolo Bertolucci	I. El Shafei - T. Okker	B. Fritz - C. Freyss
3/9/1980	Hartford $130,000 WC WCT SP	United States	Australia	5-2,	

306

3/9/1980	Hartford $130,000 WC WCT SP	Tom Gorman	Ken Rosewall	5-7, 6-2, 6-4		
3/9/1980	Hartford $130,000 WC WCT SP	Marty Riessen	John Newcombe	6-1, 2-6, 6-4		
3/9/1980	Hartford $130,000 WC WCT SP	Marty Riessen	Ken Rosewall	6-4, 6-1		
3/9/1980	Hartford $130,000 WC WCT SP	John Osborne	John Newcombe	7-5, 5-7, 6-3		
3/9/1980	Hartford $130,000 WC WCT SP			4-6, 6-2, 7-6	R. Emerson - F. Stolle	D. Ralston - M. Riessen
3/9/1980	Hartford $130,000 WC WCT SP			6-1, 5-7, 6-1	R. Laver - J. Newcombe	T. Gorman - C. Pasarell
3/9/1980	Hartford $130,000 WC WCT SP			3-6, 7-5, 6-2	C. Pasarell - D. Ralston	R. Emerson - R. Laver
3/16/1980	Rotterdam $175,000 GP SS/ WCT	Heinz Gunthardt	Gene Mayer		V. Amritraj - S. Smith	B. Scanlon - B. Teacher
3/16/1980	Stuttgart $75,000 GP	Tomas Smid	Mark Cox		W. Fibak - T. Smid	C. Mayotte - L. Stefanki
3/16/1980	San Jose $50,000 GP	Jose-Luis Clerc	Jimmy Connors		J. Fillol - A. Fillol	An. Amritraj - N. Saviano
3/23/1980	Frankfurt $175,000 GP SS/ WCT	Stan Smith	Johan Kriek		V. Amritraj - S. Smith	A. Pattison - B. Walts
3/23/1980	Metz $50,000 GP	Gene Mayer	Gianni Ocleppo		C. Dibley - G. Mayer	C. Delaney - K. Warwick
3/23/1980	Linz	Tony Graham	Onny Parum			
3/28/1980	Vienna SP	Stan Smith	Roscoe Tanner			
3/30/1980	Milan $200,000 GP SS/WCT	John McEnroe	Vijay Amritraj		J. McEnroe - P. Fleming	A. Pattison - B. Walts
3/30/1980	Dayton $50,000 GP	Wojtek Fibak	Bruce Manson		W. Fibak - G. Masters	F. Buehning - F. McNair
3/30/1980	Nice $50,000 GP	Bjorn Borg	Manuel Orantes		C. Delaney - K. Warwick	S. Bimer - J. Hrebec
4/6/1980	Monte Carlo $175,000 GP SS/ WCT	Bjorn Borg	Guillermo Vilas		P. Bertolucci - A. Paatta	V. Gerulaitis - J. McEnroe

4/6/1980	New Orleans $75,000 GP	Wojtek Fibak	Eliot Teltscher	T. Moor - E. Teltscher	R. Moore - R. Trogolo
4/6/1980	Palm Harbor. $50,000 GP	Paul McNamee	Stan Smith	P. Kronk - P. McNamee	SlDocherty - J. James
4/13/1980	Houston $175,000 GP SS/ WCT	Ivan Lendl	Eddie Dibbs	P. McNamara - P. McNamee	M. Riessen - S. Stewart
4/13/1980	Tulsa $50,000 GP	Howard Schoen-field	Trey Waltke	B. Lutz - D. Stockton	F. Gonzalez - V. Winitsky
4/13/1980	Tokyo $250,000 SP	Jimmy Connors	John McEnroe	7-5, 6-3	
4/14/1980	Johannesburg $75,000 GP	Heinz Gunthardt	Victor Amaya	B. Hewitt - F. McMillan	H. Gunthardt - C. Dowdeswell
4/20/1980	Los Angeles $175,000 GP SS	Gene Mayer	Brian Teacher	B. Teacher - B. Walts	J. Austin - An. Amritraj
4/27/1980	Las Vegas $300,000 GP SS - ATP	Bjorn Borg	Harold Solomon	S. Smith - B. Lutz	W. Fibak - G. Mayer
5/4/1980	Dallas $200,000 WCT Finals	Jimmy Connors	John McEnroe		
5/4/1980	San Paulo $175,000	Wojtek Fibak	Vince Van Patten	An. Amritraj - F. Buehning	C. Lewis - D. Carter
5/11/1980	New York $300,000 TC WCT SP	Vitas Gerulaitis	John McEnroe	P. Fleming - J. McEnroe -	P. McNamara - P. McNamee
5/12/1980	Dusseldorf $414,000 NA CP ATP SP	Argentina	Italy	3-0,	
5/12/1980	Dusseldorf $414,000 NA CP ATP SP	Guillermo Vilas	Carrado Baraz-zutti	6-3, 6-2	
5/12/1980	Dusseldorf $414,000 NA CP ATP SP	Jose-Luis Clerc	Adriano Panatta	7-6, 6-3	
5/12/1980	Dusseldorf $414,000 NA CP ATP SP	J. Clerc - G. Vilas	Bertolucci - Panat-ta	6-2, 6-3	
5/18/1980	Hamburg $200,000 GP SS	Harold Solomon	Guillermo Vilas	H. Guildemeister - A. Gomez	M. Wunshig - R. Probst
5/18/1980	Florence $50,000 GP	Adriano Panatta	Raul Ramirez	G. Mayer - R. Ramirez	P. Bertertolucci - A. Panatta
5/18/1980	Kobe $175,000 SP	John McEnroe	Victor Amaya	6-2, 6-3	
5/18/1980	Louisville $104,000 SP	Jimmy Connors	Eddie Dibbs	6-2, 6-3	

5/25/1980	Rome $200,000 GP SS	Guillermo Vilas	Yannick Noah	M. Edmondson - K. Warwick	B. Tarcozy - E. Teltscher
5/25/1980	Munich $75,000 GP	Rolf Gehring	Christophe Freyss	B. Hewitt - H. Gunthardt	C. Lewis - D. Carter
6/2/1980	Manchester $25,000	RoscoeTanner	Stan Smith	J. Sadri - T. Wilkison	
6/7/1980	Beckenham	Onny Parum	Sandy Mayer	J. Austin - V. Winitsky	T. Cain - J. DiLouie
6/8/1980	French Open $617,000 GP GS	Bjorn Borg	Vitas Gerulaitis	V. Amaya - H. Pfister	B. Gottfried - R. Ramirez
6/15/1980	London $125,000 GP-ATP	John McEnroe	Kim Warwick	R. Frawley - G. Masters	P. McNamee - S. Stewart
6/15/1980	Brussels $50,000 GP	Peter McNamara	Balazs Taroczy	S. Kruevitz - T. Stevaux	E. From - C. Leeds
6/22/1980	Surbitan $50,000 GP	Brian Gottfried	Sandy Mayer	M. Edmondson - K. Warwick	A. Pattison - B. Walts
6/22/1980	Vienna $50,000 GP	Angel Gimenez	Tomas Smid	G. Ocleppo - C. Roger-Vasselin	T. Smid - P. Slozel
7/6/1980	Wimbledon GP GS	Bjorn Borg	John McEnroe	P. McNamara - P. McNamee	S. Smith - B. Lutz
7/13/1980	Newport $100,000 GP	Vijay Amritraj	Andrew Pattison	A. Pattison - B. Walts	F. Buehning - P. Rennert
7/13/1980	Gstaad $125,000 GP	Heinz Gunthardt	Kim Warwick	C. Dowdeswell - El. Shafei	M. Edmondson - K. Warwick
7/20/1980	Boston $175,000 GP SS	Eddie Dibbs	Gene Mayer	G. Mayer - S. Mayer	H. Gildemeister - A. Gomez
7/20/1980	Bastad $75,000 GP	Balazs Taroczy	Tony Giammalva	H. Gunthardt - M. Gunthardt	J. Feaver - P. McNamara
7/20/1980	Stuttgart $75,000 GP	Vitas Gerulaitis	Wojtek Fibak	F. McMillan - C. Dowdeswell	J. Yuill - C. Lewis
7/27/1980	Washington $175,000 GP SS	Brian Gottfried	Jose-Luis Clerc	H. Gildemeister - A. Gomez	G. Mayer - S. Mayer
7/27/1980	Kitzbuhel $75,000 GP	Guillermo Vilas	Ivan Lendl	U. Marten - K. Uberhard	C. Lewis - C. Kimayr
7/27/1980	Hilversum $75,000 GP	Balazs Taroczy	Haroon Ismail	T. Okker - B. Tarozcy	T. Giammalva - B. Mottram
8/3/1980	North Conway $175,000 GP SS	Jimmy Connors	Eddie Dibbs	B. Gottfried - J. Connors	K. Curren - S. Denton
8/3/1980	South Orange $75,000 GP	Jose-Luis Clerc	John McEnroe	J. McEnroe - B. Maze	F. Buehning - V. Winitsky
8/10/1980	Indianapolis $200,000 GP SS	Jose-Luis Clerc	Mel Purcell	K. Curren - S. Denton	W. Fibak - I. Lendl

PIONEERS OF THE GAME

8/10/1980	Columbus $75,000 GP	Bob Lutz	Terry Rocavert	B. Gottfried - S. Mayer	P. Fleming - B. Teacher
8/10/1980	Zell Am See $50,000	Peter McNamara	Chris Lewis	P. Hutka - J. Hrebec	D. Siegler - W. Pascoe
8/17/1980	Toronto $175,000 GP SS	Ivan Lendl	Bjorn Borg	B. Manson - B. Teacher	H. Gunthardt - S. Mayer
8/17/1980	Stowe $75,000 GP	Bob Lutz	Johan Kriek	B. Lutz - B. Mitton	I. Nastase - F. Taygan
8/17/1980	Cleveland $75,000 GP	Gene Mayer	Victor Amaya	V. Amaya - G. Mayer	F. McNair - S. Menon
8/24/1980	Cincinnati $200,000 GP SS - ATP	Harold Solomon	Francisco Gonzalez	B. Manson - B. Teacher	W. Fibak - I. Lendl
8/24/1980	Atlanta $75,000 GP	Eliot Teltscher	Terry Moor	Tom Gullikson - B. Walts	J. Austin - An. Amitraj
9/7/1980	US Open $306,258 GP GS	John McEnroe	Bjorn Borg	S. Smith - B. Lutz	P. Fleming - J. McEnroe
9/14/1980	Sawgrass $150,000 GP - ATP			B. Gottfried - R. Ramirez	S. Smith - B. Lutz
9/14/1980	Palermo $75,000 GP	Guillermo Vilas	Paul McNamee	G. Ocleppo - R. Ycaza	V. Pecci - B. Taroczy
9/14/1980	Bournemouth $50,000 GP	Angel Gimenez	Shlomo Glickstein	E. Edwards - C. Edwards	A. Jarrett - J. Smith
9/28/1980	San Francisco $175,000 GP SS	Gene Mayer	Eliot Teltscher	P. Fleming - J. McEnroe	G. Mayer - S. Mayer
9/28/1980	Geneva $75,000 GP	Balazs Taroczy	Adriano Panatta	B. Taroczy - Z. Franulovic	H. Gunthardt - M. Gunthardt
9/28/1980	Bordeaux 75,000 GP	Mario Martinez	Gianni Ocleppo	J. Feaver - G. Moretton	G. Ocleppo - R. Ycaza
10/5/1980	Madrid $125,000 GP	Jose-Luis Clerc	Guillermo Vilas	H. Gildemeister - A. Gomez	J. Kodes - B. Taroczy
10/5/1980	Kaanapali $100,000 GP	Eliot Teltscher	Tim Wilkison	P. Fleming - J. McEnroe	G. Mayer - S. Mayer
10/12/1980	Tel Aviv $50,000 GP	Harold Solomon	Shlomo Glickstein	P. Hjertqvist - S. Krulevitz	E. From - C. Leeds
10/12/1980	Barcelona $175,000 GP SS	Ivan Lendl	Guillermo Vilas	S. Denton - I. Lendl	P. Slozil - B. Taroczy
10/12/1980	Brisbane $50,000 GP	John McEnroe	Phil Dent	J. McEnroe - Matt Mitchell	P. Dent - R. Frawley
10/19/1980	Sydney $175,000 GP SS	John McEnroe	Vitas Gerulaitis	P. Fleming - J. McEnroe	Tim Gullikson - J. Kriek
10/19/1980	Canton $50,000 GP	Jimmy Connors	Eliot Teltscher	R. Case - J. Fillol	L. Stefanki - A. Kohlberg

310

10/19/1980	Basle $75,000 GP	Ivan Lendl	Bjorn Borg	K. Curren - S. Denton	B. Hewitt - F. McMillan
10/26/1980	Tokyo $125,000 GP	Ivan Lendl	Eliot Teltscher	R. Case - J. Fillol	L. Stefanki - A. Kohlberg
10/26/1980	Vienna $100,000 GP	Brian Gottfried	Balazs Taroczy	S. Smith - B. Lutz	H. Gunthardt - P. Slozil
10/26/1980	Melbourne $125,000 GP	Vitas Gerulaitis	Peter McNamara	F. Buehning - F. Taygan	T. Wilkison - J. Sadri
11/2/1980	Cologne $75,000 GP	Bob Lutz	Nick Saviano	B. Mitton - A. Pattison	J. Kodes - T. Smid
11/2/1980	Tokyo $300,000 GP SS	Jimmy Connors	Tom Gullikson	V. Amaya - H. Pfister	M. Riessen - S. Stewart
11/2/1980	Paris $50,000 GP	Brian Gottfried	Adriano Panatta	P. Bertolucci - A. Panatta	B. Gottfried - R. Moore
11/9/1980	Stockholm $200,000 GP SS	Bjorn Borg	John McEnroe	P. McNamee - H. Gunthardt	S. Smith - B. Lutz
11/9/1980	Hong Kong $75,000 GP	Ivan Lendl	Brian Teacher	P. Fleming - F. Taygan	B. Manson - B. Teacher
11/9/1980	Quito $50,000 GP	Jose-Luis Clerc	Victor Pecci	H. Gildemeister - A. Gomez	J.L. Clerk - B. Prajoux
11/16/1980	London $175,000 GP SS - ATP	John McEnroe	Gene Mayer	J. McEnroe - P. Fleming	B. Scanlon - E. Teltscher
11/16/1980	Bogota $50,000 GP	Dominque Bedel	Carlos Kimayr	A. Fillol - C. Kimayr	A. Gomez - R. Ycazy
11/16/1980	Tapei $75,000 GP	Ivan Lendl	Brian Teacher	B. Manson - B. Teacher	J. Austin - F. Taygan
11/23/1980	Buenos Aires $175,000 GP SS	Jose-Luis Clerc	Rolf Gehring	H. Gildemeister - A. Gomez	A. Gimenez - J. Velasco
11/23/1980	Bangkok $75,000 GP	Vijay Amritraj	Brian Teacher	F. Taygan - B. Teacher	T. Okker - D. Stockton
11/23/1980	Bologna $75,000 GP	Tomas Smid	Paolo Bertolucci	B. Taroczy - B. Walts	P. McNamee - S. Denton
11/23/1980	Brisbane	Mike Estep	John Fitzgerald		
11/30/1980	Johannesburg $175,000 GP SS	Kim Warwick	Fritz Buehning	S. Smith - B. Lutz	H. Gunthardt - P. McNamee
11/30/1980	Santiago $50,000 GP	Victor Pecci	Christophe Freyss	B. Prajoux - R. Ycazy	C. Kimayr - Soares
11/30/1980	Dubai $680,000 SP	Wojtek Fibak	Ilie Nastase	B. Lutz - S. Smith	Y. Noah - J. Sadri
12/14/1980	Montreal $320,000 WCT SP	John McEnroe	Vijay Amritraj	6-1, 6-2, 6-1	
12/21/1980	Sydney $75,000 GP	Fritz Buehning	Brian Teacher	P. McNamara - P. McNamee	B. Gottfried - V. Gerulaitis

12/21/1980	Sofia $75,000 GP	Per Hjertqvist	Vadim Borisov	R. Reininger - H. Kirchhubel	V. Borisov - T. Emmrich
1/4/1981	Australian Open $350,000 GP GS	Brian Teacher	Kim Warwick	K. Warwick - M. Edmondson	P. McNamara - P. McNamee
1/6/1981	London $200,000 WCT SP			B. Gottfried - R. Ramirez	W. Fibak - T. Okker
1/18/1981	NY $400,000 Volvo Masters	Bjorn Borg	Ivan Lendl	J. McEnroe - P. Fleming	P. McNamara - P. McNamee

http://www.atpworldtour.com/en/scores/results-archive.

http://www.itftennis.com/procircuit/tournaments/men's-calendar.aspx?tour=&reg=&nat=&sur=&-cate=AL&iod=&fromDate=01-01-1968&toDate=29-12-1980.

Tennis History, Jim McManus, (Canada 2010).

1981 USTA Yearbook.

Official 1989 MTC Media Guide, (MTC 1989).

World of Tennis 1981, Edited by John Barrett and compiled by Lance Tingay, (London 1981).

CHAPTER 15:

1981: MARSHALL HAPPER AND
THE ADMINISTRATOR EXECUTIVE SEARCH

Who Was Marshall Happer?

I was a native of Kinston in eastern NC, an Eagle Scout at age 12, a member of my high school National Honor Society, North Carolina Junior Tennis Champion in 1955 and 1956, and co-captain/point guard of North Carolina State High School AA Basketball Champions in 1955 and 1956. I attended the University of North Carolina at Chapel Hill (UNC) and played on the ACC Championship tennis team. At UNC, I earned a B.A. degree and a LLB/JD degree and was admitted to practice law in North Carolina in 1963. After an active duty stint in the United States Coast Guard Reserve (6 months active duty, then 5.5 years of reserve), I began the practice of law in 1964 in Raleigh NC.

In 1980, I was 42 years-old and was practicing law in Raleigh, North Carolina, as a partner with Manning, Fulton & Skinner specializing in commercial real estate law and in real estate and construction litigation. By 1977, I had received the rating of "AV" by Martindale Hubble, the organization that rates lawyers. In 1978-1980, I also represented John Sadri as a professional player. Sadri was an All-American at NC State University in Raleigh and he turned pro in 1978 after losing in the finals of the NCAA Collegiate Championships to John McEnroe 7-6, 7-6, 5-7, 7-6. In January of 1980, Sadri reached the finals of the Australian Open which he lost to Guillermo Vilas 7-6, 6-3, 6-2.

For the North Carolina Bar Association, I was a lecturer at various continuing legal education seminars, Chairman of the Public Records Committee, and in 1980, I was Vice Chairman of the Real Property Section.

Between 1964 and 1980, I was a volunteer in tennis. In 1968, I founded the Raleigh Racquet Club, which eventually had 400 family members and 25 tennis courts, including a lighted stadium court for 2,500 spectators. At the Racquet Club, I directed the N.C State tournament in 1971, the Southern (prize money) Championships in 1972-1977, and the American Express-WRAL $25,000 Challenger Series Championships in 1978 and 1979. I served as President of the North Carolina Tennis Association in 1973-1974, President of the Southern Section of the USTA in 1976-1977 and was a member of the USTA Executive

Committee in 1978-1980. I founded the North Carolina Tennis Hall of Fame in 1975 and the Southern Tennis Hall of Fame in 1977.

How I Met Arthur Ashe, Stan Smith and Donald Dell

In 1973, Stan Smith was ranked No. 1 (co-No. 1 with Jimmy Connors) in the United States and Arthur Ashe was ranked No. 3. Both were represented by Donald Dell. In 1974, the Carolina Cougars of the American Basketball Association played their home games in Raleigh, Greensboro and Charlotte in North Carolina. Carolina was scheduled to play Denver on January 11, 1974 in the Greensboro Coliseum and before the game Stan was scheduled to play Arthur "in a $6,000 tennis challenge match" with the winner to receive $5,000 and the loser $1,000.[373]

As the President of the North Carolina Tennis Association, I was asked to serve as the Chair Umpire for this important challenge match. The local Greensboro Tennis Association provided the linesmen for the match. I drove from Raleigh to Greensboro (a little over an hour drive) excited to meet Ashe, Smith and Dell and frankly a bit nervous since the players were going to be playing for a lot of money in the 22,000 seat Greensboro Coliseum. For the ABA basketball game, the 13,594 attendance was the largest crowd in Cougar history at that time.

I met Ashe, Smith and Dell just before the match was to begin on a carpet court laid on the basketball court. I informed the players that I had no idea as to the quality of the linesmen so they could let me know if they detected any problems. Sort of to my surprise, Ashe said: "Don't worry about it. We will play to whatever they call." Then someone from the Greensboro Coliseum said, "We are going on television with the Cougars at 9:00 PM so the match has to be finished in time for the court to be removed." I understood that the court was going to be removed at that time whether the $5,000 challenge match was completed or not! *A little more anxiety.*

Then Donald Dell took the microphone from the Umpire's Chair and announced that the challenge match would be $5,000 winner-take-all. We began the match probably a little after 7 pm. I had never seen such an environment for a tennis match. I was not sure anyone could hear my announcements from the chair during the match on account of the noise in the Coliseum. During the entire match, there were hundreds and probably thousands of people arriving for the basketball game with lots of noise and continuous movement behind both ends of the court. Nevertheless, the players played on and they never questioned one call by a linesman.

Stan Smith won the first set 6-4 and Arthur Ashe won the second set 7-5. At this point we were getting closer and closer to the 9:00 pm deadline so I was quite nervous when the players began the third set with less than 20 minutes left. I could just see the nightmare of them being pushed off the court so the court could be removed before the match could be finished. Then right before my eyes I learned about exhibition tennis. To my surprise, Smith and Ashe finished that final set with very short games leading to a final tie-breaker which Ashe won just in the nick of time. So, Ashe defeated Smith 4-6, 7-5, 7-6.[374] However, the start of the Cougars game was delayed 30 minutes because of a delay in removing the tennis court.

USTA Secondary Circuits

Since 1973, I had been organizing and administering the Southern (prize money) Satellite Circuit and our fight to obtain ATP Computer Rankings points for the new up-an-coming players on the Satellite circuits was finally successful in 1976. In 1978 and 1979, Hy Zausner and Alex Aitchison of the Port Washington Tennis Academy got American Express to sponsor ten $25,000 Challenger tournaments and when we increased the $25,000 tournament draws from 32 to 48 they received the same ATP points as $50,000 tournaments. With the American Satellite and Challenger circuits, we were able to increase the number of players on the ATP Computer Rankings from 300 in 1978 to 750 in 1979. *The professional game was finally open to new players.*

In 1979, we moved the administration of the then four USA satellite circuits: Florida WATCH, Southern Spring, Southern Summer and Missouri Valley, plus the American Express Challenger Series to the USTA for the first time and I became the first Chairman of the USTA Circuits Committee. Jim Colclough was hired by the USTA as the USTA Circuits Administrator and the USTA provided professional supervisors to travel to each tournament. With the help of Jim McManus, I drafted a complete set of rules for the USA Satellite and Challenger Series tournaments to conform to the MIPTC's Grand Prix Rules, Tournament Regulations and Code of Conduct which were entitled the "USTA Circuit Regulations."[375]

Nomination for USTA Treasurer

In 1980, I finally decided that I would make myself available to become a volunteer officer of the USTA. In September after the U.S. Open, I was advised that I had been nominated to be the next USTA Treasurer as of February of 1981. Since nine of the 17 USTA Sections were represented on the Nominating Committee, there were never any additional nominations, so nomination was tantamount to election. The fastest progression through the officer chairs of the USTA *might* have been something like 1981-

1982 as Treasurer, 1983-1984 as second Vice President, 1985-1986 as First Vice President and then 1987-1988 as President. *None of that was to happen.*

Executive Search

At the November 3-5, 1980 MIPTC meeting in London, the Council announced the search for an Administrator and provided the details to all National Associations, Grand Prix tournament directors and the top 150 players. The screening committee of Phillipe Chatrier, Owen Williams and Arthur Ashe had the task of screening and interviewing applicants to provide a short list before the next meeting of the Council in the week of January 12, 1981.

The MIPTC hired Gerald J. Bump of Billington, Fox & Ellis, Inc., an executive search firm, to conduct the search. The recruitment profile stated: "This is a critical moment in the future of men's professional tennis. The right person will have a great effect on the future of the game. Accordingly, this position will yield much in the way of satisfaction to a person who is fully dedicated to the wholesome development of men's professional tennis."[376]

Sometime in November, I received a telephone call from Gerald Bump informing me about the MIPTC executive search and asking me for my recommendations. I told him that I thought it was a great idea for the MIPTC to seek professional management and I wanted to help him in any way I could. Gerald was just learning about professional tennis and the conflicting personalities and agendas of those involved were all new to him. I gave him as many suggestions as I could for possible candidates. I wanted him to be successful in his search and I wanted the MIPTC to be successful. After several calls, Gerald suggested that I consider being a candidate for the MIPTC Administrator position. He told me that if selected for an actual interview, it would be by Philippe Chatrier, Arthur Ashe and Owen Williams for the MIPTC. I thought about it for a long while and eventually concluded that while I was improbable as the candidate they might want, I thought the opportunity to just meet with Chatrier, Ashe and Williams to be too important to pass up. So, I completed and mailed an application for the job.[377]

In December, I got another call from Gerald telling me that I had been selected among some number of candidates to actually interview with Chatrier, Ashe and Williams. I was excited to get to meet with them so I flew to New York for about a 20-minute interview with each of them and flew back to Raleigh the same day. The very next day to my surprise, I received another call from Gerald informing me that I was now one of the top three candidates and I needed to return to New York for an interview with all nine members of the MIPTC. Then panic hit me. For the first time, the situation was really, really serious and if I went back to New York and got selected

I would be faced with giving up my law practice of 17 years and embarking into the unknown with the MIPTC and all of the conflicting personalities and agendas. My marriage had ended in 1977 and my three children were living with my ex-wife, but were visiting with me regularly in Raleigh at the small townhouse I had purchased in 1979. If I had still been married, I would not have considered the Administrator's job. I knew that Eastern Airlines had regular one-hour flights between Raleigh-Durham Airport and LaGuardia Airport in New York for a roundtrip fare of $99 with a "super saver – three-week in advance purchase." I reasoned that by keeping my townhouse in Raleigh and renting an apartment in New York, I could make regular trips to Raleigh to see my children and they could visit with me in New York, when I was not traveling outside of the United States. Nevertheless, it was difficult to even think about actually leaving Raleigh. I knew I should not go up for the final interviews with only three finalist candidates if I was not going to really consider taking the job if it was offered. The safest course of action was to quickly withdraw from the MIPTC Administrator search process and stay in Raleigh. Then, as I think everyone does when faced with a big crossroad decision in life, I began to wonder if I would spend the rest of my life asking myself "what if" I had been offered the job and had taken it. I telephoned a number of my closest mentor type friends for advice. I met with the members of my law firm for advice and I remember my senior partner, Howard Manning, who was the founder of Manning, Fulton & Skinner, telling me that I should go for it because it offered the unique and rare opportunity to marry my avocation with my vocation. He and I knew that the practice of law was both his avocation and his vocation. While I loved helping clients as a practicing lawyer, the practice of law wasn't my avocation. I finally decided that I had to go to the final interviews, knowing that even if I were selected, I could still decline if I became convinced that was the right thing for me to do. I also knew I could always return to the practice of law in Raleigh if selected and if the job did not work out. I flew back up to New York, interviewed all of the nine members of the MIPTC, presumably along with the other two candidates, and flew back to Raleigh the same day. No one ever told me who the other two candidates were.

Council Interview

The nine members of the MIPTC, Philippe Chatrier, Derek Hardwick, Stan Malless, Arthur Ashe, Cliff Drysdale, Butch Buchholz, Lars Myhrman, Jack Kramer and Owen Williams, were in my judgment then the most important leaders in the world for men's professional tennis and it was an honor to meet all of them. I knew that they were trying to bring order and professionalism to the administration of professional tennis, and I was convinced that it was the right thing for them to do and that it very much needed to be done. I assured them that I had no agenda or connection with any of the factions in men's professional tennis and if selected I would work for all of them. I did ask them to please not select me unless they were unanimous on my selection and willing to give me enough authority and support so I could do a good job for men's professional tennis. After meeting with them, I again flew back to Raleigh. The next day, I again received a telephone call from Gerald Bump to tell me I had been selected to be the Administrator of the MIPTC and I needed to return to New York City to discuss the terms for an employment contract and view the Volvo Masters now underway at Madison Square Garden.

Selected

I was very honored to have been selected for this important role and I was happy to have the unanimous support of the nine members of the Council, the ITF and the ATP to help me be successful. In retrospect, that may have been the first time that the MIPTC appeared to be unanimous on anything.[378]

Owen Williams, Roy Reardon and Jack Kramer

In New York, I met at length with Owen Williams and with Roy Reardon, the MIPTC legal counsel, to develop an employment contract and a preliminary budget to create a new MIPTC office and staff in New York City. I also spent a lot of time at Madison Square Garden during the Volvo Masters. I still remember sitting there with Jack Kramer watching matches. Jack was then the North American Tournament Representative on the MIPTC, but he was much more than that to me. Growing up as a junior tennis player in North Carolina and playing collegiate tennis at the University of North Carolina (1956-1960), every year I purchased and exclusively used two Jack Kramer autographed Wilson wood tennis racquets. Jack Kramer could not have been more famous with me and I was honored just to meet him, much less work for him as a member of the MIPTC.

Two-Year Employment Contract

As the "new kid on the block" being "welcomed to the fray" of men's professional tennis, I met lots of other famous and important people involved in our sport during the Volvo Masters. I signed an employment contract with Philippe Chatrier as Chairman of the Council for a term of two years, from March 1, 1981 to February 28, 1983. While I intended to give the position of Administrator everything I could be to make it successful, I knew that if it did not work out, I could easily return to Raleigh to practice law, as I had protected myself with a "leave of absence" from Manning, Fulton & Skinner. I then began to reassign my 75+ litigation and other legal matters in my law practice to other members of my law firm as I took my leave of absence as a partner in the firm. I resigned as the Vice Chair of the Real Property Section of the North Carolina Bar Association. I also withdrew as the Treasurer-elect of the USTA.

Congratulations

I was honored to receive congratulations from lots of folks in the tennis world, especially a genuinely nice letter from my friend Jim McManus of the ATP[379]: "Congratulations again on your appointment to the Pro Council," he wrote. "As I said yesterday, they couldn't have chosen a fairer more impartial person to handle all the administration and conflicts in the game. I look forward to working with you in any manner so requested. Please don't hesitate to call on me." I did call on Jim many times during my 1981-1989 tenure with the MIPTC.

Gene Scott wrote in *Tennis Week*[380]: "*Tennis Week* has often postured for Happer's ascension to the lofty parapets that govern our game, and in our 1980 Year End issue suggested the grandest Christmas prize to tennis would be Happer being picked as Administrator. The MIPTC was cagey and secretive in its selection process even going to the lengths of leaking names of four 'finalists', Richard Evans, Bob Smith, David Whitehead, and Pierre Darmon as a smokescreen in order to conceal the choice until the decision was final to avert last minute waffling or lobbying. In truth, the Council had simply run out of candidates with the requisite qualities of toughness, fairness and objectivity. Happer combines these virtues uniquely although he did not apply for the Administrator's job, but rather was summoned as the MIPTC's 'last clear chance'. He is upright, just and has no ax to grind. *Tennis Week* has at different times been on opposite sides of the political fence from Happer, but even when in vigorous disagreement, this writer respected his position."

Off into the Unknown!

I departed Raleigh for New York City to begin on March 1, 1981 as the Administrator of the MIPTC. I left Raleigh with my briefcase and the new luggage given me by my law partners and headed to New York City with no place to live, no office, no staff (except for the four Grand Prix Supervisors), no bank account, no office equipment and literally nothing else. Up to then, the MIPTC had been operating with a Joint Secretary in the ATP Texas office with a MIPTC checking account and a Joint Secretary in the ITF London office with a MIPTC checking account. The Bonus Pool deposits received from tournaments and from Volvo were in an MIPTC account in the Royal Bank of Canada in the Channel Islands controlled by the ITF. I was quite literally off into the unknown.[381]

CHAPTER 16:

1981: MIPTC ADMINSTRATION BEGINS, WCT WITHDRAWS, CRISES NOS. 21, 22

1981 Governing Bodies

The MIPTC was the governing body for men's professional tennis in 1981, except for the Davis Cup. WCT continued to be merged into the Volvo Grand Prix in 1981. The ITF was the governing body for the Davis Cup and in charge of the *Rules of Tennis*.

1981 Significant Tennis Leaders

ITF President:	Philippe Chatrier (France)
USTA President:	Marvin Richmond
Australian LTA President:	Brian Tobin
British LTA President:	Sir Carl Aarvold
French FFT President:	Philippe Chatrier
Chairman of Wimbledon:	Sir Brian Burnett
ATP President:	Harold Solomon
ATP Executive Director:	Butch Buchholz
WCT Owners:	Lamar Hunt and Al Hill, Jr.
WCT Executive Director:	Mike Davies until May 19
WCT CEO:	Owen Williams beginning in July or August

1981 MIPTC

ITF: Philippe Chatrier, Chairman, Derek Hardwick and Stan Malless with David Gray as Joint Secretary until March 1.

Tournaments: Lars Myhrman (Europe), Jack Kramer (North America) and Owen Williams until August 31.

Players: Butch Buchholz, Arthur Ashe, Cliff Drysdale until June 1 and Ray Moore beginning June 1 with Ron Bookman as Joint Secretary until March 1.

Administrator: Marshall Happer beginning March 1.

Ass't Admin. Mark Meyers beginning April 1.

Legal Counsel: Roy L. Reardon, Esquire and John Cambria, Esquire.

GP Supervisors: Dick Roberson, Chief, Frank Smith until July 15, Franco Bartoni, Kurt Nielsen, Keith Johnson and Bill Gilmour.

1981 Major Player Representatives

ProServ: Principals: Donald Dell, Frank Craighill, Lee Fentress and Ray Benton.

IMG: Principals: Mark McCormack and Bob Kain.

Others: Ion Tiriac and Thomas Betz, Esquire (Vilas).

John McEnroe, Sr., Esquire (McEnroe).

Gloria Connors and Joseph Rountree, Esquire (Connors).

Two Competitions

In 1981, the 14th year of Open Tennis, there were two organized competitions for men: Volvo Grand Prix and the Davis Cup. Davis Cup was open to all players and was won 3-1 by the United States over Argentina. There were 92 Volvo Grand Prix Open prize money tournaments, including the year-end Volvo Masters in Madison Square Garden in New York City. Included in the 92 tournaments were the four Grand Slams and 28 Super Series tournaments with $175,000+ in prize money. The Volvo Masters was again staged at Madison Square Garden and was won by Ivan Lendl over Vitas Gerulaitis 6-7, 2-6, 7-6, 6-2, 6-4 in singles and by Peter Fleming and John McEnroe over Kevin Curren and Steve Denton 6-3, 6-3 in doubles.

WCT continued to be merged into the Grand Prix and again staged eight of the 28 Super Series tournaments. The eight WCT tournaments, in addition to leading as part of the 91 Grand Prix tournaments to the Volvo Grand Prix Bonus Pool and the Volvo Masters, also led as a "circuit within a circuit" to the WCT Finals in Dallas won by John McEnroe over Johan Kriek 6-1, 6-2, 6-4. There was no doubles in Dallas in 1981.

In addition to the WCT Finals in Dallas, WCT staged 3 other special events outside of the Volvo Grand Prix: (i) March 8, Salisbury, $200,000 WCT Invitational won by Bill Scanlon over Vijay Amritraj 3-6, 6-2, 6-4, 3-6, 6-4, (ii) May 10, Forest Hills, $592,000 WCT Tournament of Champions won by Eddie Dibbs over Carlos Kirmayr 6-3, 6-2 in singles and by Peter Fleming and John McEnroe over John Fitzgerald and Andy Kohlberg 6-4, 6-4 in doubles and (iii) January 1, 1982, London, $200,000 WCT Braniff World Doubles won by Peter McNamara and Paul McNamee over Victor Amaya and Hank Pfister 6-3, 2-6, 3-6, 6-3, 6-2. The Aetna World Cup in Hartford and the WCT Challenge Cup in Montreal special events were not held and were discontinued.

In 1981, the ATP was involved in eight events: (i) February 22, La Quinta, $175,000 Grand Marnier ATP Tennis Games, (ii) April 26, Las Vegas, $300,000 Alan King Classic at Caesar's Palace, (iii) May 11, Dusseldorf, $430,000 Ambre Solaire Nation's Cup (won by Czechoslovakia over Australia 2-1), (iv) June 14, London, $125,000 Stella Artois Queens ATP Grass-Court Championships, (v) July 19, Boston, $175,000 US Pro Championships, (vi) August 23, Cincinnati, $200,000 ATP Championships, (vii) September 20, Sawgrass, $175,000 ATP-Lipton World Doubles and (viii) November 15, London, $175,000 ATP Benson and Hedges Championships at Wembley. All of the ATP tournaments were in the Grand Prix, except for the Nation's Cup.

Rules

The 1980 player commitment rule was continued, which required players to commit to six designated tournaments (with one veto) and also commit to limit special events against Super Series weeks to a total of six. In 1980, if a player refused to commit to six designations and the new special event rules, he would not be eligible to play in any Grand Prix tournaments. This was changed for 1981 to provide that if a player refused to sign the player commitment, he could still play in Grand Prix tournaments and be eligible for the Bonus Pool and the Masters, but he would have to enter through qualifying at each and every tournament – an extremely difficult alternative since most tournaments had two or three rounds of qualifying before each main draw began.[382]

The only significant change from the 1980 Tournament Regulations was that the Grand Prix Supervisors continued to be the final authority at all Grand Prix tournaments except for the Grand Slams. In the Grand Slams, while the Supervisors would be advisors only to the Grand Slam tournaments, decisions made by the Grand Slam tournaments would be subject to review by the Council. *It was finally agreed that the MIPTC would be the final authority.*

There were no significant changes to the MIPTC Code of Conduct for 1981 other than the addition of the MIPTC Administrator. There would be lots of amendments for the 1982 MIPTC Code of Conduct to provide for the role of the new Administrator.

Creation of the First New York MIPTC Office

As soon as I was hired as the new MIPTC Administrator, I began planning how to create a new MIPTC office in Manhattan and find the initial staffing that would be needed. My official start date was March 1, 1981. I figured that initially I was going to need a good legal secretary (executive assistant in New York), a good Assistant Administrator, plus another legal secretary, plus a receptionist/bookkeeper. This meant I was looking for 1500 to 2500 square feet of office space. I also needed to find an apartment. I knew that I would be traveling to Paris March 18-21, my first trip ever outside of the United States for the next MIPTC meeting and I knew that I would be traveling to another meeting in Paris in June during the French Open and in London in June during Wimbledon. This would be my first trip to the French Open and my first trip to Wimbledon. However, I would be working and not there to watch tennis. I knew that my time to find office space and set up an office was limited as I had to stay in Europe between the June 1-2 meeting of the MIPTC during the French Open and the June 15-18, MIPTC meeting during Wimbledon. During that time, I had to make time to revise and re-draft the MIPTC Code to insert the new position of Administrator into the proceedings for approval by the Council.

I was fortunate to have the help of a number of folks in New York who I could and did call on for help and for references: Roy L. Reardon, a senior partner with Simpson Thacher & Bartlett LLP, was our MIPTC legal counsel, John P. McEnroe, Sr., a senior partner with Paul, Weiss, Rifkind, Wharton & Garrison, LLP, who represented John McEnroe, Jr., George W. Gowen, a senior partner with Dunnington, Bartholow & Miller, LLP, was General Counsel of the USTA, Mike Burns, Executive Secretary of the USTA (the new Executive Director, Rick O'Shea, had already departed the USTA) and Eugene L. "Gene" Scott, Attorney and Publisher of *Tennis Week* magazine.

In March when I arrived in New York City with my trusty black briefcase, my friend Gene Scott arranged for me to rent a very small room at the River Club on 52nd Street and the East River for $60 per night for a few weeks while I looked for office space and for an apartment. For several weeks, my entire office was located in my briefcase as I moved around Manhattan looking for office space, an apartment, a bank, office equipment, stationary, etc. Philippe Chatrier, the French Chairman of the MIPTC, suggested that I should look for space in the Empire State Building, so I did. Now, if you live in Paris, the Empire State Building is iconic and sounds like a nice address to have. And since I was from North Carolina, it sounded interesting to me. However, when I went there, it looked like every shoe and garment company in the world had offices there. I did not see one professional services firm listed. The absolute clincher for me was when I got to an available office on the 84th floor and walked through the door, I could see that an outside window was actually open – yes, I mean open in case you needed to jump out. I went no further, just backed out of the office and never looked again at the Empire State Building. *That was too scary for me.*

Eventually, Gene Scott introduced me to a friend of his, Louis F. "Bo" Polk, Jr. Bo had retired as President and CEO of MGM and had purchased a toy company which was now sort of defunct. Bo had 18 months left on a five-year lease of about 2,500 square feet on the 26th floor of the Seagram's Building, one of the classiest buildings in Manhattan at 375 Park Avenue (the famous Four Seasons Restaurant was also in the Seagram's Building). Bo's rental rate was something like $25 per square foot and since the entire office space was vacant and furnished, except for his one office (he was almost never there), it was a perfect set up for me to get into business fast. So, I rented approximately 1800 square feet furnished from Bo at around $28 per square foot and we had our first MIPTC office in Manhattan. Just to show you the value of this office space, when Bo's five-year lease terminated 18 months later, the asking rent went from $25 per square foot to $90 per square foot so we moved a bit down market from the Seagram's Building for our next office location.

Then an Apartment

Next, I had to find an apartment so I could move out of the River Club as my small room there was beginning to give me claustrophobia. Gene Scott came through again. Gene had another friend, Randy Jones, who happened to be from North Carolina and was an insurance salesman in New York City. Randy rented me an apartment at 201 East 66th Street at its intersection with Third Avenue for one year for $1,200 per month. Randy was a place holder for the apartment pending the planned conversion of the apartments to a co-op. I was delighted and I was moving as soon as possible from the River Club. Soon, I would learn to my dismay that about every 20 minutes all night long, a siren comes down Third Avenue, so I will promise you that my next apartment in New York City was not facing Third Avenue.

MIPTC Staff

The next most important issue was how to get a really good Assistant Administrator. Since I only had a two-year employment contract and no one could know if the new MIPTC administration (or the MIPTC) would last any time into the future, I decided to seek as my assistant a really good young lawyer and ask for only a one-year commitment. From a young lawyer's perspective, if he could get a one-year leave of absence, he could live in New York City, travel with me around the world, help create the MIPTC office and operation for the governance of men's professional tennis worldwide and do something really important for tennis. I found the perfect candidate in Mark B. Meyers. Mark was a native of New Orleans and a 1975 graduate of Duke University with a B.A. *Cum Laude* degree. I had known Mark when he was the No. 1 tennis player at Duke as he had played in a number of my tournaments at the Raleigh Racquet Club. Mark had played some on the satellites, reached a ranking of No. 112 and had been an ATP member. Mark had forgone tennis as a profession to go to law school at Louisiana State University where he had graduated with a J.D. degree in 1979. Mark had been admitted to Louisiana Bar in 1979, and had begun the practice of law in New Orleans with a large law firm. Mark loved the idea of being an Assistant Administrator with me for a year and his law firm wisely agreed to give him a one-year leave of absence considering it to be a valuable experience.

John McEnroe, Sr., welcomed me to New York and was extremely helpful in answering questions for me. When I told John I needed to find a really good legal secretary, he knew exactly what that meant and he actually sent me Chris Fiaccavento (O'Connor) as a candidate. Chris had been working part time for his firm and was looking for a full-time job as a legal secretary. Chris was smart, liked to work hard, understood the need for legal accuracy and was one of the best pure typists I had ever seen. She easily typed 125 words a minute with absolutely no errors and with our new memory typewriters she was even faster. Chris would be my Executive Assistant for the duration of my job with the MIPTC through the end of 1989. Next, I hired Pat Wallenstein, as an executive secretary and bookkeeper. Pat had been employed by Bo Polk, so she was familiar with the office and was an experienced executive secretary. Mark found another talented legal secretary/administrative assistant, Pat Pollard, and behold, we had a professional staff. I opened a bank account for the MIPTC with Chase Manhattan and began to phase out the MIPTC checking accounts maintained by the ITF Joint Secretary, David Gray, in London and the ATP Joint Secretary, Ron Bookman, in Dallas. I initially met some resistance from David Gray of the ITF about relinquishing his control of the MIPTC account with the Royal Bank of Canada in the Channel Islands at which the Bonus Pool contributions were invested, but eventually he turned over control to me as I was now responsible for the collection and the fiduciary investing of all Bonus Pool contributions from tournaments and from our sponsor, Volvo.

Equipment

I purchased two IBM 100-page memory typewriters, a telex machine and rented a copy machine, set up utility and trade accounts, ordered new letterhead stationary and office supplies and we were in business. Remember, this is before there were personal computers and fax machines. The IBM memory typewriter was the newest and best thing available and was the first step to do away with "white-out" to cover typing errors and carbon paper (maybe you never heard of carbon paper). The only way to communicate internationally was by telephone, telex or cable and most of rest of the world still had rotary dial telephone systems. I opened the new MIPTC New York City office on April 1, 1981, just 30 days after I became the Administrator. While I was traveling in Europe, Mark, my new Assistant Administrator, finished setting up the office with Chris. Our new address was: Men's International Professional Tennis Council, Suite 2601, 375 Park Avenue, New York, New York 10152 U.S.A., Telephone (212) 838-8450, Telex: 968145 (New York), Cable Address: (GRANDPRIX NEWYORK). *We were in business!*

Our Initial 1981 Tasks

A few of the initial tasks we had to undertake were: (1) create a new manual bookkeeping system with the help of our accountants (there were no personal computers or computer bookkeeping systems then). This included all financial records, employee

withholding, tax reporting, etc., (2) create a new filing system for correspondence, tournaments, Code of Conduct cases, financial, legal, etc., (3) create application and reporting forms for tournaments and for Grand Prix Supervisors, (4) create forms for Code of Conduct cases involving players and tournaments, (5) collection of all on-site prize money from the nine U.S. summer tournaments using an experimental Merrill Lynch Cash Management Account Program for all players, including all tax withholding and reporting on non-U.S. players. The handling of tax collection and reporting would make this program untenable to continue in the future, but it took literally more than 100+ hours in 1981, mostly by Mark Meyers, (6) management of MIPTC, scheduling and organization of MIPTC meetings, development of the minute book and preparation and drafting of MIPTC minutes, communication with members of the MIPTC and the Joint Secretaries, etc., (7) management of the Grand Prix Supervisors and their certification program, (8) liaison with 90+ Grand Prix tournaments, collection of Bonus Pool contributions, administrative fees, etc., (9) revising the Code of Conduct to insert the new MIPTC Administrator position into the procedures, (10) drafting the first formal Constitution and Bylaws for the MIPTC as an international unincorporated association and application for a U.S. tax exemption, (11) disappointingly, we found that there were over $600,000 in player fines levied by the Grand Prix Supervisors in 1979 and 1980, that were unpaid and on pending appeals that had never been held. So, we had to begin the investigation and determination of each appeal and either dismiss or uphold and collect the unpaid fines. As you might have imagined, that was not welcomed by the players. However, it served to put everyone on notice that henceforth the Code would be professionally administered and enforced, (12) handling 1981 Major Offense cases, (13) drafting and printing of the 1982 Volvo Grand Prix Yearbook, which had 144 pages as compared to only 56 pages in the 1981 Volvo Grand Prix Rule Book produced by Volvo and ProServ. Our 1982 Yearbook added the 1982 tournament calendar, photos and bios for the nine members of the MIPTC, plus me as Administrator and Mark Meyers as the Assistant Administrator, List of Review Officers, Rules of Tennis, Constitution and Bylaws of the MIPTC, names and addresses of all Volvo Grand Prix tournament directors, names and addresses of all MIPTC certified officials, player medical certification certificate for medical withdrawals from tournaments and a complete index.

MIPTC Meetings

In 1981, the MIPTC held 7 meetings: January 15-17 in New York, March 18-21 in Paris, April 20-21 in New York, May 10-11 in New York, June 1-2 in Paris, June 15-18 in London and August 31 - September 3 in New York.

Crisis No. 21: WCT Withdraws

WCT was inside the Grand Prix, as "a circuit within a circuit" for 1978, 1979, 1980 and 1981 during which WCT staged eight of the 28 Super Series tournaments. WCT also staged a number of special events outside of the Grand Prix each year. Every year, the Council expressed concern that ProServ and IMG, the major player-agent companies, were becoming more and more involved with Grand Prix tournaments in varying roles ranging for outright ownership, defacto ownership, sponsorship and/or television sales agent, etc. It was generally thought that these relationships gave those tournaments an unfair advantage over the diminishing number of truly independent tournaments in attracting players as it was quite normal for ProServ player clients to just happen to enter ProServ aligned tournaments and IMG player clients to just happen to enter IMG aligned tournaments.

Since every top ranked player was authorized to play in special events in all 16 "open weeks" (non-Super Series weeks and non-Grand Slam weeks) plus six Super Series weeks, ProServ and IMG staged, consulted with, or were involved with special events to provide extra income to their player clients. Somehow, those special events were not scheduled against each other's Grand Prix tournaments (obviously afraid of retaliation), so they tended to schedule them against the few independent tournaments and the WCT tournaments.

By 1981, the Council was receiving requests from some of the eight WCT Super Series tournaments complaining to the MIPTC about the terms of their agreements with WCT and asking for independent Super Series status. The Council always responded that the eight Super Series were per the MIPTC agreement with WCT and the MIPTC would not get in the middle of a dispute between WCT and one of its Super Series tournaments. However, when WCT terminated its relationship with a tournament and moved to a new city for one of its eight Super Series, the old city would threaten legal action against both WCT and the MIPTC.

In 1981, WCT announced that it was going to open a new WCT player-agent business. WCT claimed that it needed to be in the player-agent business to protect itself and be able to compete with ProServ and IMG. So, when discussions began with WCT to continue on the Volvo Grand Prix for 1982, the MIPTC had two important issues: (i) the MIPTC wanted to be indemnified by WCT from any and all claims made against the MIPTC by WCT Super Series tournaments; and (ii) the MIPTC objected to WCT also becoming a player-agent firm since it was being sanctioned for eight of the 28 Super Series tournaments in the Volvo Grand Prix. Over and over again, the members of the Council had expressed concern about ProServ and IMG's increasing involvement in Grand Prix tournaments and they reasoned that permitting WCT to have eight of the 28 Super Series tournaments and to also enter the player-agent business would just exacerbate the problem.[383]

At my very first meeting of the MIPTC in Paris, March 18-20[384], WCT's possible continued participation in the 1982 Volvo Grand Prix was on the agenda. At the request of WCT, the discussion was postponed so that a meeting would be held in New York on April 8 between Lamar Hunt, Mike Davies, counsel for WCT, with Roy Reardon and me for the MIPTC. Surprisingly, WCT unilaterally cancelled the April 8 meeting and on April 9 sent a letter to the MIPTC withdrawing from the Volvo Grand Prix for 1982 and issued a press release about the new independent 1982 WCT circuit to be staged in competition with the Volvo Grand Prix.[385]

I knew, as everyone else knew, that WCT was supported by Lamar Hunt and Al Hill, Jr., that WCT began promoting men's professional tennis in 1967 and had been instrumental in forcing Open Tennis in 1968. From 1967 to 1981, WCT had become important promoters of men's professional tennis and provided a lot of prize money and job opportunities for players. We all knew that Hunt and Hill had significant wealth and that they could and probably would easily fund whatever was needed to promote a successful competitive circuit in 1982. You can bet that was a big jolt for me in my new job as MIPTC Administrator, then for only 40 days. Just what I needed was a war between the MIPTC's Volvo Grand Prix and WCT. *I wondered if my two-year employment contract was too short or too long.*

Involvement of Player Agents in Grand Prix Tournaments

Also in March in Paris, the Council issued a *proposed* new rule restricting the involvement of player-agents as owners, defacto owners or managers in Grand Prix tournaments, *subject to a study* to be conducted by the Administrator. The proposed limitation did not restrict tournaments from making arrangements with player-agents to handle TV rights and/or obtaining sponsorship. *Do you think ProServ and IMG hated this proposed new rule?*

1982 Super Series

In May in New York[386], 34 tournaments applied for Super Series status in 1982 to replace the eight Super Series being withdrawn by WCT.

Drysdale Resigns, Ray Moore Elected

In June in Paris[387], Butch Buchholz submitted Cliff Drysdale's resignation and announced that he and Arthur Ashe had unanimously elected Ray Moore to succeed Drysdale for the remainder of his term. The Council expressed its gratitude and appreciation to Drysdale for his numerous contributions "through his many years of diligent and faithful service on the Council." At the next meeting[388], Drysdale appeared briefly at the meeting to explain that the reason for his resignation from the MIPTC was to avoid any appearance of a conflict with respect to his representation of the players since he had contracted to be the television commentator for WCT. *Cliff stands out as maybe the first person to avoid the appearance of a conflict of interest in tennis.*

Mark McCormack and Donald Dell Object to Proposed New Player-Agent Restriction

Mark McCormack of IMG and Donald Dell of ProServ joined the June MIPTC meeting to object to the proposed new "Player-Agent Rule" under consideration. Both of them said that as player-agents they had very little to do with the selection of tournaments by a player client. *Would you like to purchase the Brooklyn Bridge?* Dell further stated that it was his understanding that a large number of tournaments in Europe were now offering players guarantees or some form of payment to induce participation. Dell's opinion was that such payments were one of the most serious problems now facing professional tennis. Both he and McCormack stated that they would support the uniform application of the Grand Prix Rules, including the rules prohibiting appearance guarantees. *Guess who was negotiating for the players for guarantees from Europe. You get a cigar if you guessed correctly.*

1981 MIPTC Election

Also in June, the Council approved the election rules for the nine members of the Council, with the nine newly elected members for two-year terms to commence at the first meeting of the MIPTC after September 8, 1981. Canada was moved from the "Rest of the World" area to the North American area. Hawaii was in the "Rest of the World" area.

New Super Series

Also in June, the Council approved nine new Super Series for 1982 to replace the eight WCT Super Series, which increased the total number of Super Series to 29 instead of 28. The nine new Super Series to replace WCT's eight Super Series were: (1) Philadelphia (formerly WCT), (2) Denver, (3) Brussels (formerly WCT), (4) Rotterdam (formerly WCT), (5) Milan (formerly WCT), (6) Frankfurt (formerly WCT), (7) Monte Carlo, (8) Madrid and (9) Sydney.

Adding Administrator to Code of Conduct for 1982: Making Justice Certain and Swift

After the completion of the French Open, I traveled to London to prepare for the MIPTC meetings during Wimbledon. I stayed at the Gloucester Hotel, which was the players' hotel and I was able to hire a talented bookkeeper from the Gloucester to help me develop a draft of the needed revisions of the MIPTC Code of Conduct for presentation to the MIPTC. At the June 15-18 London meeting of the MIPTC, the Council adopted the amendments I drafted to insert the MIPTC Administrator into the Code of Conduct procedures. To deal with the problem caused by players who were fined avoiding payment of the fines by filing appeals which were never heard and to streamline and revise the Code of Conduct procedures, the new amendments provided that: (i) henceforth, all fines levied by the Grand Prix Supervisors for Minor Offenses against players would be collected immediately from the players' prize money, (ii) players would have one appeal of Minor Offense fines to the MIPTC Administrator and if the fine was reversed the fine would be refunded and (iii) for Major Offenses, the MIPTC Administrator would investigate and make the first determination, subject to review, modification and reversal by the Council.. *Thus, justice became certain and swift.* It took more than a year to investigate and determine the appeals for the $600,000 in outstanding Minor Offense fines levied by the Supervisors in 1979 and 1980. Under the new procedure, all appeals of Minor Offense fines in the future would be determined in less than 30 days. When a Major Offense determined by the Administrator was approved by the Council, it would be prosecuted by the Administrator in a hearing before 1-3 Review Officers selected from a list of MIPTC approved Review Officers. As in the past, one Review Officer would be selected by the MIPTC Administrator, one Review Officer would be selected by the player and those two Review Officers would select a third Review Officer. In 1981, and previously, the requirement for the conviction of a Major Offense was that the decision of the three Review Officers had to be unanimous, i.e., the Review Officer selected by the player had to vote for conviction too. Beginning in 1982, the Code was changed to only require a majority vote of the Review Officers so the Review Officer selected by the player could not alone acquit the player. This amendment was made before the 1981 McEnroe Major Offense case arose.

List of Arbitrators

Also in June, the Council approved a list of 21 Arbitrators for Major Offenses: Sir Carl Aarvold, O.B.E.T.D. (GB), Lew Hoad (AU), Robert Abdesselam (FR), W. Hofer (DE), Tut Bartzen (US), Harry Hopman (US), Marcel Bernard (FR), Hon. Robert J. Kelleher (US), John Bromwich (AU), Enrique Morea (AR), Don Budge (US), Chuck McKinley (US), W.J. "Bill" Clothier (US), Adrian Quist (AU), Jaroslav Drobny (GB), Ulf Schmidt (SE), Forrest A. Hainline, Jr. (US), Frank Sedgman (AU), E. Victor Seixas, Jr. (US), Ashley J. Cooper (AU) and William Talbert (US).

Constitution and Bylaws

Heretofore, the MIPTC operated as an unincorporated association with just election rules and no formal Constitution and Bylaws. I drafted the election rules into a new Constitution and Bylaws and they were enacted by the Council. The MIPTC remained as an international unincorporated non-profit association because there was never any agreement to be incorporated in any one country.

1982 WCT World Series of Tennis Format

WCT announced its 1982 Spring schedule: eight tournaments with $300,000 in prize money (16 draws or 32 draws) with $100,000 to the winners, plus the WCT Finals in Dallas and the Tournament of Champions in Forest Hills. Qualification points for the Dallas Finals included the eight Spring tournaments plus the winners of the 1981: Tournament of Champions, French Open, Wimbledon and U.S. Open. Bonus Pool and other prizes for the WCT Spring circuit included: $10,000 Gold Ball Dallas Trophy, $290,000 in player participation bonuses for top ranked players, $500,000 for cash bonuses for the top eight, $200,000 for the Dallas eight, $467,000 in travel credits by Braniff and Hyatt and a $200,000 Bonus Pool for the Tournament of Champions. The player commitment deadline was August 10, 1981, for full Spring circuit (no 42 day per tournament entry deadline). All rules were promulgated unilaterally by WCT, including a WCT Code of Conduct.

Lamar Hunt's strategy was to offer a lot more money to the top players to play in the WCT tournaments ($300,000 vs. the Grand Prix $200,000 and $100,000 to the winner vs. $35,000 to the winner). If the WCT tournaments were only 16 draws, the prize money would be further increased as all of the Grand Prix Super Series tournaments were either 32, 48 or 64 draws. The prize money offered by the Grand Prix tournaments were usually based on market considerations, whereas the prize money offered by WCT would overpay the "market" simply because of Lamar Hunt's willingness to use his great personal wealth.[389]

New Player Commitment Rule for 1982

In June in London, faced with the expected competition from the new competing WCT circuit for 1982, the Council revised the Player Commitment Rule. Instead of just requiring six designations, the new Player Commitment Rule for 1982 required 10 designations exclusive of the French, Wimbledon and the U.S. Open. The Australian Open still needed help and was included in the player designations. The most important part of the rule was a Grand Prix player commitment was required as a condition of playing in any Grand Prix tournaments in 1982, *including the Grand Slams.* In addition, the Council clarified the definition of "special event" by exempting only special events in tournaments with minimum 32 draws in a circuit of eight or more tournaments provided entries are accepted in accordance with a recognized system of merit. This meant that if WCT staged a 16-draw tournament against a Super Series, as WCT planned to do, it would be a special event and thus subject to the six special event limitation. In addition, if entries were not accepted in accordance with a recognized system of merit (the ATP Computer being the only one in existence), then even a 32-draw WCT tournament would be a "special event." I have not even mentioned yet that ATP demanded a 42-day entry deadline instead of WCT selecting entries for the entire year at the beginning of the year. Can you see the trouble that this might cause? As a result, at the August 31-September 3 MIPTC meeting, the Council denied the request of WCT for exemption from the Special Event Rule for its 1982 tournaments. This meant that every WCT tournament in which a player competed would count as one of his six special events if during the same week as a Grand Prix Super Series tournament.[390]

In August, Lamar Hunt addressed the players through *ITW* in which he objected to new increased Grand Prix Player Commitment and the decision to declare all 22 WCT tournaments in 1982 as special events. He claimed that the Council was "carrying out a pattern of interference and obstruction that appears to be directed at impeding or destroying the competitive tournament schedule of WCT," and suggested that all players "should question the motives of those making and/or influencing Council decisions."[391]

In August, Butch Buchholz replied on behalf of the ATP Board that the ATP supports the Grand Prix because it "affords the greatest number of players the most opportunity to earn a living consistent with rules and regulations formulated with the input of players." Buchholz said to *International Tennis Weekly* that ATP was not opposed to the new WCT circuit and if WCT would agree "to generally abide by the rules and regulations for which the ATP has fought so hard since its inception" the ATP would "be glad to offer its support."[392]

1982 Bonus Pool Increased to $3,000,000

To compete with WCT, the Council approved $3,000,000 for the 1982 Bonus Pool with $2,400,00 for 32 singles players and $600,000 for 16 doubles players.

Volvo Extension Offer

The Council requested Volvo to help with the expected competition in 1982 with the new WCT circuit. Rick Dowden "presented to the Council an offer dated August 28, 1981, whereby Volvo would agree to certain increases in its sponsorship investment for 1982, 1983 and 1984 in return for a stated option for sponsorship for 1985, 1986 and 1987." Volvo obviously considered this to be a good time to obtain an extension of its sponsorship rights upon favorable terms. The Council "instructed the Administrator to review the same and offer a recommendation to the Council as soon as possible. Mr. Dowden requested a response by October 1, 1981 to his offer."[393]

ATP in Financial Difficulty

In August, Butch Buchholz reported to the Council that the ATP was in current financial difficulty and required additional sources of funds. Buchholz stated that he was requesting the players to pay two percent of their prize money to ATP and he intended to request additional funds from the tournament directors at their meeting on September 6, 1981. The Council had agreed that ATP could be involved in a limited number of Grand Prix and other tournaments like the Nations Cup, to raise funds. Obviously, ATP was not raising enough funds from its involvement in tournaments and Bob Briner had left the ATP in serious financial difficulty. Should the Council come to the rescue? *We could not have ATP go out of business!*

Owen Williams Resignation, To Become WCT CEO

Owen Williams sent a telex on August 31, 1981, stating: "Please accept my resignation from the Council. It was a pleasure working with you all for the past 6 years." The back story here was that after WCT announced it was going to withdraw from the 1982 Volvo Grand Prix and stage an independent competing circuit in competition with the Volvo Grand Prix, Mike Davies had resigned as the WCT Executive Director and Owen Williams had been hired by WCT to succeed him. Mike told me that he resigned because he felt certain that an independent WCT circuit in 1982 would be a failure. *He was right.*

Anti-Apartheid and Professional Tennis Players

Apartheid was the system of institutionalized racial segregation and discrimination in South Africa between 1948 and 1991 enforced by the South African government. All or almost all countries condemned South Africa's Apartheid. The South African Government's Apartheid policy caused an almost impossible problem for the South African professional tennis players, e.g., Cliff Drysdale, Ray Moore, Frew McMillan, Johan Kriek, Kevin Curren, Bernie Mitton, etc. Like all professional tennis players, the South African pros were sportsmen and not politicians and they were trying to earn a living. They had no control over what the South African government did.

There were a number of countries that would not permit the South African players to enter their countries and play in their tournaments. Soon the discrimination against South African tennis players was extended to all players who had ever been to South Africa. So, if a player had a South African visa stamp on his passport, it would be used to exclude that player from entry. Eventually, the South African immigration officials stopped placing a South African stamp on passports to try to protect the players. That, of course did not help the South African players who had to use their South African passports.

There were 250 athletes and officials from 22 countries, among them 63 Americans, who were included in the first United Nations Centre against Apartheid blacklist for having participated in sports exchanges in South Africa during 1980. Names on the list included Guillermo Vilas, Stan Smith, Bob Lutz, Dick Stockton, Pat DuPre and 24 other tennis players. The only way for a player to get his name removed from the "blacklist" was to write a letter promising not to return to South Africa.

The MIPTC and for that matter the entire professional tennis world refused to be intimidated by the "blacklist" and continued to designate players to South African tournaments and to threaten to withdraw the sanction of any tournament that refused entry of a professional player for political reasons.[394]

French Open Free Player Hotel Rooms

In 1981, I learned that in order to build up the French Open, Philippe Chatrier had begun some years earlier providing free hotel rooms at the Paris Sofitel for all the players entered into the French Open each year. The French Open was the first Grand Slam to provide free hotel rooms for the players and the cost exceeded $400,000 per year. Chatrier had correctly reasoned that the best way to enhance the French Open was to make sure that the players could all afford to come to Paris and participate. Eventually, all the Grand Slams and all the other tournaments would follow Chatrier's example either with free hotel rooms or per diems to cover hotel room expenses.

Nastase 21-Day Automatic Suspension

Nastase was suspended for 21 days commencing April 27, for exceeding the $5,000 maximum of Minor Offense fines in 12 months. *Not much of a surprise.*[395]

Keith Johnson Replaces Frank Smith; Bill Gilmour is Hired

Frank Smith, one of the original Grand Prix Supervisors who was hired in 1978, resigned as of July 15 to take a position with the Los Angeles Olympic Organizing Committee, which was putting together the 1984 Olympics. Keith Johnson, of Hawaii was hired to replace Smith. Keith was a native of Fremont, Nebraska and he studied Forestry at the University of Nebraska and at the University of Washington. He was commissioned into the U.S. Navy on November 22, 1944, and retired on July 1, 1975. Keith began officiating while residing in Hong Kong in 1972 and subsequently in Hawaii. He attended and was certified at the first MIPTC Officials School (1979) in Dallas. Bill Gilmour of New South Wales, Australia was hired as the fifth Grand Prix Supervisor. As a player, Bill won Open tournaments in Great Britain, Europe, Asia, Australia and New Zealand. He was the President of the Tennis Professionals Association of Australia and a well-respected MIPTC certified tennis official.

Gerulaitis 21-Day Automatic Suspension

Vitas Gerulaitis was suspended from the Volvo Grand Prix tennis circuit for 21 days for Minor-Offense fines accumulated in excess of $5,000 over the last year.[396]

Hong Kong MIPTC Officials School

In October, Grand Prix Supervisors Dick Roberson and Bill Gilmour staged the first Far East MIPTC Officials School in Hong Kong and certified 20 additional officials from Hong Kong, Australia, Japan, Taiwan and Thailand. This made 200 as the total number of MIPTC certified officials.

McEnroe 21-Day Automatic Suspension

In November, John McEnroe began a three-week suspension from Grand Prix tennis tournaments for having exceeded the $5,000 maximum for 12 months. *John tended to take a vacation near the end of each year.*[397]

McEnroe Tennis Over America Tour

John McEnroe, Sr., had only one tennis player client, John McEnroe, Jr. ProServ and IMG, which represented lots of players, were continuously arranging exhibitions with their players to create additional income. In order to create exhibition income for his son, John Sr., entered into a promotional agreement with Steven Corey of the Dallas-based Incorsel International Entertainment Consultants, Inc., a rock promoter, for the creation of what would become the very successful "John McEnroe Tennis Over America Tour" which began in September of 1981 and continued through February of 1986. Gary V. Swain, then a young professional who was just beginning in the tennis business, worked for Corey and McEnroe in the promotion and production of the tour. During those years, John played in 99 one-night exhibitions in 90 US cities against various other pros. The tour provided an opportunity for all of the cities that did not have Grand Prix tournaments to see John and some of the other great pros of that era up close and personally in fun type exhibitions. The players traveled via private jet to keep up with this hectic schedule. Each exhibition included a one set "Future Stars" match with junior talent, followed by a best-of-three set "Feature Match" and then four games of a "Celebrity Doubles" match with John and his opponent in the feature match teaming up with local media celebrities and sometimes big time celebrities.[398]

Buchholz Settled ATP vs. Boston Lawsuit

Butch Buchholz settled the lawsuit between Boston's Longwood Club and the ATP and entered into a new agreement with Boston for 1981 to "provide staff for the tournament office, professional management of the event and assistance in arranging sponsorship." No one needed to be in a lawsuit with Butch Buchholz. He was just too nice a guy. Butch also got support for moving Boston to the earlier July clay court dates being vacated by Louisville and for adding Cincinnati as a Super Series in the now hard court week before the U.S. Open.[399]

Buchholz on Player Misconduct

Buchholz took a strong position against player misconduct in *International Tennis Weekly* for the ATP Board. "Sometimes I think our sport is determined to self-destruct," he said to *ITW*. "It is always easy to tell when a tennis player has lost control of himself and violated what fans and media generally consider to be acceptable court behavior. Depending on the significance of the match and the television coverage, the telephones at ATP headquarters start ringing. Most of the callers ask what the ATP is going to do about the conduct of its members. Several weeks ago, the ATP Board spent quite a bit of time discussing the problem. The Board members are sensitive because as players they understand the intensity of emotions of a player who is disgusted with himself, his opponent, an official or with a real or imagined tournament condition. The ATP directors also feel a responsibility to the game, a call to help provide the best possible setting for ATP members to display their talents. The ATP feels strongly that all players have a mandate to give their best as role models for young people, as entertainers who seek to attract, not turn off paying customers and as human beings who recognize the rights of others not to be subjected to vulgar or offensive behavior."[400]

ATP Growth Since 1975 – Mike Davies Hired

From four full-time employees in 1975, the ATP had 20 employees by 1981. The ATP headquarters remained in Dallas with the ATP European Tennis Bureau in Paris managed by Paul Svehlik. Buchholz opened a new ATP Marketing Office on 42nd Street in New York City in 1981. Newly hired Mike Davies was the marketing director.[401]

Harold Solomon Re-Elected ATP President

Harold Solomon was re-elected as ATP President, as were Charlie Pasarell as Vice President, Richard Lewis, as Treasurer and Jim McManus as Secretary. New ATP Board members were Mark Edmondson, who replaced Geoff Masters who resigned, Alejandro Cortes and Erik Van Dillen, Stan Smith (returning after two years off the board), Victor Amaya, Arthur Ashe and Cliff Drysdale.

1981 ATP JAKS AWARDS
(New York City January 1982)

Player of the Year	John McEnroe
Doubles Team of the Year	Peter Fleming – John McEnroe
Newcomer of the Year	Tim Mayotte
Most Improved Player of the Year	Peter McNamara
Player Achievement Award	John Fitzgerald
Comeback Player of the Year	Jeff Borowiak
Media Service Award	Rino Tommasi
Broadcaster of the Year	Dan Maskell
ATP Special Award	Philippe Chatrier
The Dr. R.W. Johnson ATP Award	Arthur Ashe
ATP Lifetime Award	Billy Talbert
ATP Service Award	Jaime Fillol
Court Official of the Year	Frank Hammond
ATP-Adidas Sportsmanship Award	Jose-Luis Clerc
President's Award	Bjorn Ahlstrom

Crisis No. 22: Borg Refuses 1982 Player Commitment

Bjorn Borg lost the Wimbledon final in 1981 to John McEnroe in four sets and played only one ($75,000) tournament, on clay, in Stuttgart prior to the 1981 U.S. Open. *Borg must have needed another Mercedes from the Stuttgart tournament sponsor.* With no more preparation than that, I have no idea how Borg reached the U.S. Open final where he lost again to McEnroe.

In September, after the U.S. Open, Borg announced that he was going to take a five-month break from professional tennis and indicated that he was not going to agree to the full player commitment for the 1982 Volvo Grand Prix. The members of the Council believed that it could not insist on all the other players signing the 1982 player commitment if Borg was not also required to sign. *If Borg refused to sign, was Wimbledon going to support the MIPTC and require Borg, a five-time singles champion, to have to qualify to compete in 1982?*

1981 MIPTC Financials

The MIPTC began 1981 with a deficit of ($111,466) and after hiring an Administrator (March 1) and staff, opening the New York office (April 1) and providing $2,000,000 in Bonus Pool awards to players in the Volvo Grand Prix, the MIPTC ended 1981 with a surplus of $384,169. Volvo paid for its promotion as the Volvo Grand Prix sponsor and its promotion of the Volvo Grand Prix through a ProServ subsidiary doing business with the confusing name of the "Volvo Grand Prix." Volvo and ProServ promoted the Volvo Masters at Madison Square Garden, telecast on NBC and were responsible for all expenses and received all income. Volvo and ProServ refused to disclose to the MIPTC the financials of the Volvo Masters while seeking an extension of its Volvo sponsorship term (1980-1984) beyond 1984. The MIPTC always reimbursed the members of the Council for first class travel. However, until sometime in 1988, I always traveled around the world in coach class to save money. As long as I traveled in coach class, all of the employees of the MIPTC had to also travel coach class. We saved a lot of money for the Council on our extensive travel while we were getting some additional personal "wear and tear." *We were solvent after my first year of operation!*[402]

1981 Grand Slam Winners

French Open

Bjorn Borg d. Ivan Lendl 6-1, 4-6, 6-2, 3-6, 6-1.
Heinz Gunthardt – Balazs Taroczy d. Terry Moor – Eliot Teltscher 6-2, 7-6, 6-3.

Wimbledon

John McEnroe d. Bjorn Borg 4-6, 7-6, 7-6, 6-4.
Peter Fleming – John McEnroe d. Bob Lutz – Stan Smith 6-4, 6-4, 6-4.

U.S. Open

John McEnroe d. Bjorn Borg 4-6, 6-2, 6-4, 6-3.
Peter Fleming – John McEnroe d. Heinz Gunthardt – Peter McNamara W.O.

Australian Open

Johan Kreik d. Steve Denton 6-2, 7-6, 6-7, 6-4.
Mark Edmondson – Kim Warwick d. Hank Pfister – John Sadri 6-3, 6-7, 6-3.

Volvo Masters

Ivan Lendl d. Vitas Gerulaitis 6-7, 2-6, 7-6, 6-2, 6-4.
Peter Fleming - John McEnroe d. Kevin Curren – Steve Denton 6-3, 6-3.

1981 Davis Cup

Davis Cup Final (Cincinnati - Indoors)

United States d. Argentina 3-1

John McEnroe (US) d. Guillermo Vilas (AR) 6-3, 6-2, 6-2.
Jose-Luis Clerc (AR) d. Roscoe Tanner (US) 7-5, 6-3, 8-6.
Peter Fleming – John McEnroe (US) d. Jose-Luis Clerc – Guillermo Vilas (AR) 6-3, 4-6, 6-4, 4-6, 11-9.
John McEnroe (US) d. Jose-Luis Clerc (AR) 7-5, 5-7, 6-3, 3-6, 6-3.
Roscoe Tanner (US) vs. Guillermo Vilas (AR) 11-10 Unfinished.

Nations Cup

Czechoslovakia d. Australia 2-1.

Peter McNamara (AU) d. Ivan Lendl (CZ) 6-3, 6-4.
Tomas Smid (CZ) d. Paul McNamee (AU) 6-4, 7-6.
Ivan Lendl – Tomas Smid (CZ) d. Peter McNamara – Paul McNamee (AU) 6-4, 6-3.

1981 World Rankings[403]

Bud Collins	Lance Tingay	ATP Year-End Rankings
1. John McEnroe	1. John McEnroe	1. John McEnroe
2. Ivan Lendl	2. Bjorn Borg	2. Ivan Lendl
3. Jimmy Connors	3. Jimmy Connors	3. Jimmy Connors
4. Bjorn Borg	4. Ivan Lendl	4. Bjorn Borg
5. Jose-Luis Clerc	5. Jose-Luis Clerc	5. Jose-Luis Clerc
6. Guillermo Vilas	6. Victor Pecci	6. Guillermo Vilas
7. Gene Mayer	7. Gene Mayer	7. Gene Mayer
8. Eliot Teltscher	8. Guillermo Vilas	8. Eliot Teltscher
9. Vitas Gerulaitis	9. Vitas Gerulaitis	9. Vitas Gerulaitis
10. Peter McNamara	10. Brian Teacher	10. Peter McNamara

1981 Volvo Grand Prix Bonus Pool Top 10[404]

Singles (12th Bonus Pool)		Doubles (7th Bonus Pool)	
1. Ivan Lendl	$300,000	1. Heinz Gunthardt	$90,000
2. John McEnroe	$200,000	2. John McEnroe	$60,000
3. Jimmy Connors	$150,000	3. Ferdi Taygan	$40,000
4. Jose-Luis Clerc	$100,000	4. Peter Fleming	$28,000
5. Guillermo Vilas	$ 80,000	5. Sherwood Stewart	$20,000
6. Bjorn Borg	****	6. Peter McNamara	$18,000
7. Roscoe Tanner	$ 60,000	7. Steve Denton	$16,000
8. Eliot Teltscher	$ 50,000	8. Raul Ramirez	$14,000
9. Vitas Gerulaitis	$ 40,000	9. Kevin Curren	$12,000
10. Yannick Noah	$ 35,000	10. Mark Edmondson	$10,000

1981 Official Earnings Top 10[405]

1.	John McEnroe	$991,000		6.	Vitas Gerulaitis	$288,475
2.	Ivan Lendl	$846,037		7.	Heinz Gunthardt	$278,642
3.	Jimmy Connors	$405,872		8.	Peter McNamara	$273,066
4.	Guillermo Vilas	$402,261		9.	Eliot Teltscher	$267,630
5.	Jose-Luis Clerc	$327,375		10.	Roscoe Tanner	$245,380

1981 Tournament Calendar

Date	Tournaments	Singles Winner	Singles #2	Doubles Winners	Doubles #2
1/11/1981	Adelaide $50,000 GP	Mark Edmondson	Brad Drewett	C. Dibley - J. James	E. Edwards, - C. Edwards
1/11/1981	London $200,000 WCT SP			P. McNamara - P. McNamee	V. Amaya - H. Pfister
1/11/1981	Auckland $50,000 GP	Bill Scanlon	Tim Wilkison	F. Taygan - T. Wilkison	T. Graham - B. Scanlon
1/11/1981	Chicago $350,000 SP	John McEnroe	Jimmy Connors	6-2, 6-4, 6-1	
1/25/1981	Mont'rey $175,000 SS WCT	Johan Kriek	Vitas Gerulaitis	S. Denton - S. Curren	J. Kriek - R. Simpson
1/25/1981	San Juan $75,000 GP	Eliot Teltscher	Tim Gullikson	C. Mayotte - T. Mayotte	Tim Gullikson - E. Teltscher
1/25/1981	Guaruja $75,000 ATP CH	Carlos Kimayr	Ricardo Cano	D. Carter - P. Kronk	A. Gomez - B. Prajoux
2/1/1981	Philly $250,000 SS WCT	Roscoe Tanner	Wojtek Fibak	M. Riessen - S. Stewart	B. Gottfried - R. Ramirez
2/1/1981	Vina Del Mar $50,000 GP	Victor Pecci	Hose Higueras	D. Carter - P. Kronk	A. Gomez - B. Prajoux
2/8/1981	Richmond $175,000 SS WCT	Yannick Noah	Ivan Lendl	Tim Gullikson - B. Mitton	B. Gottfried - R. Ramirez
2/8/1981	Mar Del Plata $75,000 - GP	Guillermo Vilas	Victor Pecci	D. Carter - P. Kronk	A. Gomez - J. Velasco
2/8/1981	Toronto $500,000 SP	Vitas Gerulaitis	John McEnroe	6-4, 4-6, 6-3, 6-3	
2/8/1981	Christchurch	Onny Parun	Larry Stefanki		
2/15/1981	Boca Raton $300,000 SP	John McEnroe	Guillermo Vilas		
2/19/1981	Sydney $500,000 SP	Bjorn Borg	John McEnroe	6-0, 6-4	
2/20/1981	Sydney $500,000 SP	Bjorn Borg	John McEnroe	6-2, 6-4	
2/21/1981	Melbourne AU $500,000 SP	John McEnroe	Bjorn Borg	6-4, 1-6, 7-6, 6-4	
2/22/1981	La Quinta $175,000 SS	Jimmy Connors	Ivan Lendl	B. Manson - B. Teacher	E. Teltscher - T. Moor
3/1/1981	Memphis $200,000 SS	Gene Mayer	Roscoe Tanner	G. Mayer - S. Mayer	M. Cahill - Tom Gullikson

3/1/1981	Mexico City $75,000 - GP	Jaime Fillol	David Carter	M. Davis - C. Dunk	R. Case - J. Alexander
3/2/1981	Hong Kong - SP	Vitas Gerulaitis	Bjorn Borg	6-4, 3-6, 6-4, 7-6	
3/8/1981	Denver $125,000 GP	Gene Mayer	John Sadri	A. Pattison - B. Walts	M. Purcell - D. Stockton
3/8/1981	Salisbury $200,000 WCT SP	Bill Scanlon	Vijay Amritraj	3-6, 6-2, 6-4, 3-6, 6-4	
3/8/1981	Lagos $50,000 GP	Larry Stefanki	Peter Feigl	B. Kleege - L. Stefanki	I. Harris - C. Wittus
3/15/1981	Brussels $175,000 SS WCT	Jimmy Connors	Brian Gottfried	S. Mayer - F. McMillan	K. Curren - S. Denton
3/15/1981	Tampa $75,000 GP	Mel Purcell	Jeff Borowiak	B. Mitton - B. Walts	D. Carter - P. Kronk
3/15/1981	Cairo $75,000 GP	Guillermo Vilas	Peter Elter	I. El Shafei - B. Taroczy	P. Bertolucci - G. Ocleppo
3/22/1981	Rotterdam $175,000 SS WCT	Jimmy Connors	Gene Mayer	F. Buehning - F. Taygan	G. Mayer - S. Mayer
3/22/1981	Nancy $50,000 GP	Pavil Slozil	Ilie Nastase	I. Nastase - A. Panatta	J. Feaver - J. Hrebec
3/29/1981	Milan $175,000 SS WCT	John McEnroe	Bjorn Borg	B. Gottfried - R. Ramirez	J. McEnroe - P. Rennert
3/29/1981	Stuttgart $75,000 GP	Ivan Lendl	Chris Lewis	N. Saviano - B. Mottram	E. Edwards, - C. Edwards
3/29/1981	Napa $50,000 GP	Sammy Giammalva	Scott Davis	C. Mayotte - R. Meyer	T. Delatte - T. Hayes
4/5/1981	Frankfurt $175,000 SS WCT	John McEnroe	Tomas Smid	B. Teacher - B. Walts	V. Gerulaitis - J. McEnroe
4/5/1981	Linz $50,000 GP	Gianni Ocleppo	Mark Edmondson	A. Jarryd - H. Simonsson	B. Drewett - P. Slozil
4/12/1981	Houston $175,000 SS WCT	Guillermo Vilas	Sammy Giammalva	M. Edmondson - S. Stewart	An. Amritraj - F. McNair
4/12/1981	Nice $50,000 GP	Yannick Noah	Mario Martinez	Y. Noah - P. Portes	C. Lewis - P. Slozil
4/12/1981	Johannesburg $75,000 GP	Kevin Curren	Bernard Mitton	V. Mitton - R. Moore	S. Glickstein - D. Schneider
4/12/1981	Tokyo $250,000 SP	Jimmy Connors	John McEnroe	6-4, 7-6	
4/20/1981	Monte Carlo $250,000 SS	Jimmy Connors Rain	Guillermo Vilas Rain	H. Gunthardt - B. Taroczy	P. Slozil - T. Smid
4/20/1981	Los Angeles $75,000 GP	John McEnroe	Sandy Mayer	J. McEnroe - F. Taygan	Tom Gullikson - B. Walts
4/20/1981	Yokohama $25,000 ATP CH	Jimmy Arias	Billy Martin		

Date	Tournament	Winner	Finalist	Doubles Winners	Doubles Finalists
4/26/1981	Las Vegas $300,000 SS	Ivan Lendl	Harold Solomon	P. Fleming - J. McEnroe	T. Delatte - T. Waltke
4/26/1981	Bournemouth $75,000 GP	Victor Pecci	Balazs Taroczy	R. Cano - V. Pecci	B. Mottram - T. Smid
5/3/1981	Dallas $200,000 WCT Finals SP	John McEnroe	Johan Kriek		
5/10/1981	NY $592,000 TC - WCT SP	Eddie Dibbs	Carlos Kirmayr	P.Fleming - J. McEnroe	J. Fitzgerald - A. Kohlberg
5/11/1981	Dusseldorf $430,000 ATP SP	Czechoslovakia	Australia	2-1,	
5/11/1981	Dusseldorf $430,000 ATP SP	Peter McNamara	Ivan Lendl	6-3, 6-4	
5/11/1981	Dusseldorf $430,000 ATP SP	Tomas Smid	Paul McNamee	6-4, 7-6	
5/11/1981	Dusseldorf $430,000 ATP SP		6-4, 6-3	I. Lendl-T. Smid	P. McNamara- P. McNamee
5/17/1981	Hamburg $200,000 SS	Peter McNamara	Jimmy Connors	H. Guildemeister - A. Gomez	P. McNamara - P. McNamee
5/17/1981	Florence $50,000 GP	Jose-Luis Clerc	Raul Ramirez	R. Ramirez - P. Slozil	P. Bertolucci - A. Panatta
5/17/1981	Guadalajara $25,000 ATP CH	Joao Soares	Matt Anger	G. Holroyd - S. Sherbeck	A. Kohlberg - B. Kleege
5/17/1981	Tokyo $200,000 SP	Brian Teacher	Bill Scanlon	J. Sadri - B. Teacher	B. Scanlon - V. Van Patten
5/24/1981	Rome $200,000 SS	Jose-Luis Clerc	Victor Pecci	H. Gildemeister - A. Gomez	B. Manson - T. Smid
5/24/1981	Munich $75,000 GP	Chris Lewis	C. Roger-Vasselin	D. Carter - P. Kronk	S. Glickstein - E. Fromm
6/7/1981	French Open $450,000 GS	Bjorn Borg	Ivan Lendl	H. Gunthardt - B. Taroczy	T. Moor - E. Teltscher
6/14/1981	London $125,000 GP ATP	John McEnroe	Brian Gottfried	P. Dupre - B. Teacher	K. Curren - S. Denton
6/14/1981	Brussels $50,000 GP	Marko Ostoja	Ricardo Ycazy	R. Cano - A. Gomez	C. Motta - C. Kimayr
6/20/1981	Bristol $75,000 GP	Mark Edmondson	Roscoe Tanner	B. Martin - R. Simpson	J. Kriek - J. Austin
6/21/1981	Venice $50,000 ATP CH	Mario Martinez	Paolo Bertolucci	6-4, 6-4	
7/4/1981	Wimbledon $450,000 GS	John McEnroe	Bjorn Borg	P. Fleming - J. McEnroe	B. Lutz - S. Smith
7/12/1981	Newport US $100,000 GP	Johan Kriek	Hank Pfister	Brad Drewett - E. Van Dillon	K. Curren - B. Martin
7/12/1981	Gstaad $125,000 GP	Wojtek Fibak	Yannick Noah	H. Gunthardt - M. Gunthardt	D. Carter - P. Kronk

7/19/1981	Boston $175,000 SS ATP	Jose-Luis Clerc	Hans Gildemeister	R. Ramirez - P. Slozil	H. Gildemeister - A. Gomez
7/19/1981	Kitzbuhel $75,000 GP	John Fitzgerald	Guillermo Vilas	D. Carter - P. Kronk	M. Ostoja - L. Sanders
7/19/1981	Stuttgart $75,000 GP	Bjorn Borg	Ivan Lendl	P. McNamara - P. McNamee	M. Edmondson - M. Estep
7/26/1981	Washington $175,000 SS	Jose-Luis Clerc	Guillermo Vilas	R. Ramirez - V. Winitsky	P. Slozil - F. Taygan
7/26/1981	Hilversum $75,000 GP	Balazs Taroczy	Heinz Gunthardt	H. Gunthardt - B. Taroczy	R. Moore - A. Pattison
7/27/1981	Bastad $75,000 GP	Thierry Tulasne	Anders Jarryd	M. Edmondson - J. Fitzgerald	S. Simonsson - A. Jarryd
8/2/1981	South Orange $75,000 GP	Shlomo Glickstein	Dick Stockton	F. Buehning - A. Pattison	S. Glickstein - D. Schneider
8/2/1981	Zell Am See $50,000 ATP CH	Fernando Luna	Jiri Hrebec	R. Acuna - R. Benavides	C. Johnstone - W. Hampson
8/3/1981	North Conway $175,000 SS	Jose-Luis Clerc	Guillermo Vilas	H. Gunthardt - P. McNamara	P. Slozil - F. Taygan
8/9/1981	Indianapolis $200,000 SS	Jose-Luis Clerc	Ivan Lendl	K. Curren - S. Denton	R. Ramirez - V. Winitsky
8/9/1981	Frejus SP	John McEnroe	Thierry Tulasne	6-2, 6-3. 2-6, 6-4	
8/10/1981	Columbus $75,000 GP	Brian Teacher	John Austin	B. Manson - B. Teacher	V. Amritraj - An. Amritraj
8/16/1981	Montreal $200,000 SS	Ivan Lendl	Eliot Teltscher	R. Ramirez - F. Taygan	P. Fleming - J. McEnroe
8/16/1981	Stowe $75,000 GP	Brian Gottfried	Tony Graham	J. Kriek - L. Stefanki	B. Lutz - B. Gottfried
8/16/1981	Cleveland $75,000 GP	Gene Mayer	David Siegler	E. Van Dillon - V. Winitsky	R. Case - S. Ball
8/23/1981	Cincinnati $200,000 SS ATP	John McEnroe	Chris Lewis	J. McEnroe - F. Taygan	B. Gottfried - R. Ramirez
8/23/1981	Atlanta $75,000 GP	Mel Purcell	Giles Moreton	F. Buehning - P. Fleming	S. Giammalva - T. Giammalva
8/30/1981	Jerricho $30,000 SP	Brian Teacher	Yannick Noah	4-6, 6-3, 6-4	
9/13/1981	US Open $500,000 GS	John McEnroe	Bjorn Borg	P. Fleming - J. McEnroe	H. Gunthardt - P. McNamara
9/20/1981	Sawgrass $175,000 Dbls. GP			H. Gunthardt - P. McNamara	S. Smith - B. Lutz
9/20/1981	Palermo $75,000 - GP	Manuel Orantes	Pedro Rebolledo	J. Damiani - D. Perez	J. Fillol - B. Prajoux
9/27/1981	Geneva $75,000 GP	Bjorn Borg	Tomas Smid	H. Gunthardt - B. Taroczy	T. Smid - P. Slozil

9/27/1981	Bordeaux $50,000 GP	Andres Gomez	Thierry Tulasne	A. Gomez - B. Prajoux	J. Gurfein - A. Jarryd
9/28/1981	San Francisco $175,000 SS	Eliot Teltscher	Brian Teacher	P. Fleming - J. McEnroe	M. Edmondson - S. Stewart
10/4/1981	Madrid $75,000 GP	Ivan Lendl	Pablo Arraya	H. Gildemeister - A. Gomez	H. Gunthardt - T. Smid
10/4/1981	Maui $50,000 GP	Hank Pfister	Tim Mayotte	T. Graham - M. Mitchell	J. Alexander - C. Delaney
10/11/1981	Tel Aviv $50,000 GP	Mel Purcell	Per Hjertqvist	S. Meister - V. Winitsky	J. Feaver - S. Krulevitz
10/11/1981	Barcelona $175,000 SS	Ivan Lendl	Guillermo Vilas	A. Jarryd - H. Simonsson	H. Gildemeister - A. Gomez
10/11/1981	Brisbane $50,000 GP	Mark Edmondson	Chris Lewis	R. Frawley - C. Lewis	M. Edmondson - M. Estep
10/11/1981	Melbourne $457,000 SP	Gene Mayer	Eliot Teltscher	7-5, 6-1, 7-6	
10/13/1981	Edmonton $300,000 SP	Bjorn Borg	Jose-Luis Clerc	6-2, 6-2, 7-5	
10/18/1981	Sydney $175,000 SS	John McEnroe	Roscoe Tanner	P. Fleming - J. McEnroe	S. Stewart - F. Taygan
10/18/1981	Basle $75,000 GP	Ivan Lendl	Jose-Luis Clerc	J. L. Clerc - I. Nastase	M. Gunthardt - P. Slozil
10/18/1981	Naples $390,000 SP	Gene Mayer	Adriano Panatta	6-3, 6-2	
10/25/1981	Tokyo $125,000 GP	Balazs Taroczy	Eliot Teltscher	H. Gunthardt - B. Taroczy	L. Stefanki - R. Van't Hof
10/25/1981	Vienna $125,000 GP	Ivan Lendl	Brian Gottfried	S. Denton - T. Wilkison	F. McNair - S. Giammalva
10/25/1981	Melbourne $125,000 GP	Peter McNamara	Vitas Gerulaitis	P. McNamara - P. Kronk	S. Stewart - F. Taygan
11/1/1981	Cologne $75,000 GP	Ivan Lendl	Sandy Mayer	S. Mayer - F. McMillan	J. Kodes - K. Meiler
11/1/1981	Tokyo $300,000 SS	Vince Van Patten	Mark Edmondson	H. Pfister - V. Amaya	H. Gunthardt - B. Taroczy
11/1/1981	Paris $50,000 GP	Mark Vines	Pascal Portes	I. Nastase - Y. Noah	A. Jarrett - J. Smith
11/9/1981	Stockholm $200,000 SS	Gene Mayer	Sandy Mayer	K. Curren - S. Denton	F. Taygan - S. Stewart
11/8/1981	Hong Kong $75,000 GP	Van Winitsky	Mark Edmondson	C. Dunk - C. Mayotte	M. Davis - B. Drewett
11/8/1981	Quito $75,000 GP	Eddie Dibbs	David Carter	H. Gildemeister - A. Gomez	D. Carter - R. Ycaza
11/15/1981	London $200,000 SS ATP	Jimmy Connors	John McEnroe	S. Stewart - F. Taygan	P. Fleming - J. McEnroe

11/15/1981	Tapei $75,000 GP	Robert Van't Hof	Patrick DuPre	M. Bauer - J. Benson	J. Austin - M. Cahill
11/22/1981	Buenos Aires $175,000 SS	Ivan Lendl	Guillermo Vilas	M. Hocevar - J. Soares	A. Fillol - J. Fillol
11/22/1981	Bangkok $75,000 GP	Bill Scanlon	Mats Wilander	J. Austin - M. Cahill	L. Bourne - V. Winitsky
11/22/1981	Bologna $75,000 GP	Sandy Mayer	Illie Nastase	S. Giammalva - H. Leconte	B. Taroczy - T. Smid
11/28/1981	Johanesburg $300,000 SS	Vitas Gerulaitis	Jeff Borowiak	T. Moor - J. Yuill	F. Buehning - R. Simpson
11/29/1981	Santiago $50,000 GP	Hans Gildemeister	Andres Gomez	H. Gildemeister - A. Gomez	R. Cano - B. Prajoux
11/29/1981	Manila $75,000 GP	Ramesh Krishnan	Ivan DuPasquier	W. Bauer - J. Benson	D. Gitlin - J. Gurfein
11/29/1981	Milan $300,000 SP	Ivan Lendl	John McEnroe	6-4, 2-6, 6-4	
12/10/1981	Rosemont $200,000 SP	Jimmy Connors	John McEnroe	6-7, 7-5, 6-7, 7-5, 6-4	
12/20/1981	Sydney $125,000 GP	Tim Wilkison	Chris Lewis	P. McNamara - P. McNamee	H. Pfister - J. Sadri
12/20/1981	Sofia $50,000 GP	Ricky Meyer	Leo Palin	T. Emmrich - J. Granat	R. Meyer - I. El Shafei
1/3/1982	Australian Open $400,000 GS	Johan Kriek	Steve Denton	M. Edmonson - K. Warwick	H. Pfister - J. Sadri
1/10/1982	London $200,000 Dbles WCT			H. Gunthardt - B. Taroczy	K. Curren - S. Denton
1/17/1982	NY $400,000 Volvo Masters	Ivan Lendl	Vitas Gerulaitis	J. McEnroe - P. Fleming	K. Curren - S. Denton

http://www.atpworldtour.com/en/scores/results-archive.

http://www.itftennis.com/procircuit/tournaments/men's-calendar.aspx?tour=&reg=&nat=&sur=&cate=AL&iod=&fromDate=01-01-1968&toDate=29-12-1981.

Tennis History, Jim McManus, (Canada 2010).

1982 USLTA Yearbook.

Official 1989 MTC Media Guide, MTC (1989).

World of Tennis 1982, Edited by John Barrett and compiled by Lance Tingay, (London 1982).

CHAPTER 17:

1981: McENROE MAJOR OFFENSE CASE, "YOU CANNOT BE SERIOUS," PLUS TELTSCHER, GERULAITIS

Eliot Teltscher Player Major Offense No. 1: 1981 French Open

At the 1981 French Open, the French Open Referee Jacques Dorfmann and the FFT Committee of Management (mostly just Philippe Chatrier as FFT President) were in charge of the enforcement of the Code of Conduct with the Grand Prix Supervisors acting as advisors only. Ilie Nastase (age 34 now) upset No. 10 seed Eliot Teltscher 6-2, 6-4, 7-5 on Court No. 10. During the match, Teltscher had an altercation with the Chair Umpire, Patrick Flodrops, and he was unhappy about his loss. After the completion of the match, a lot of fans poured onto the court and as Teltscher was leaving the court, he bumped into Flodrops hard enough to knock him onto the ground. Flodrops claimed it was intentional while Teltscher claimed it was accidental.

At the June 15-18 MIPTC London Meeting, the Council charged Teltscher with the Major Offense of "Aggravated Behavior" and assessed a fine to be prosecuted by me as the new Administrator for $2,500 subject to Teltscher's right of appeal to three Review Officers. After investigation of the facts, on June 30, I issued a formal notice of the Major Offense charge to Teltscher with the $2,500 fine.[406] Teltscher elected to appeal, but later withdrew his appeal and his fine was deducted from his Bonus Pool award. Teltscher was one of the first players to learn that now that the MIPTC had a full-time Administrator, the Code of Conduct was going to be enforced. That was an important part of my new job.

John McEnroe Player Major Offense No. 2: 1981 Wimbledon

The 1981 John McEnroe Major Offense case was the first case to go the full procedural distance for a decision by three independent Review Officers under the 1981 MIPTC Code of Conduct. At Wimbledon in 1981, the Wimbledon chair umpires had the authority to issue point penalties for conduct violations subject to the five steps specified in the Code. The Wimbledon Referee and Wimbledon Committee, with the Grand Prix Supervisors as advisors only, had the authority to issue Minor Offense fines and for Aggravated Behavior to issue an immediate default. John McEnroe won his first Wimbledon singles title in 1981, finally defeating five-time Wimbledon champion Bjorn Borg 4-6, 7-6, 7-6, 6-4 in the final. Borg had defeated McEnroe in five sets to win his fifth Wimbledon the year before in one of the best matches of all time. McEnroe and Peter Fleming also won the men's doubles over Bob Lutz and Stan Smith 6-4, 6-4, 6-4.

However, en route to his titles, McEnroe had some problems. Here is a list of some of the *angry* statements or remarks charged against McEnroe that I determined most clearly constituted Verbal Abuse of Officials:

1. Why don't you call his balls out also?

2. You call all the balls for him and none for me (?) Watch the line! Watch the line!

3. Umpire, you know what a lousy job is, that is the definition of what you're doing. Did you say you were doing a lousy job? Oh, I thought I heard you say that. You only missed three balls on him and none on me (?) ….

4. The ball hit the chalk. It came up all over the place. Excuse me, look, *you can't be serious; (and then louder) you can't be serious!* The ball was on the line, chalk flew up, it was clearly in (very emphatically).

5. *You guys are the absolute pits of the world.* (Point Penalty) - ($750.00 Minor Offense Fine 1ˢᵗ round against Tom Gullikson).

6. I'm not going to have a point taken away because this guy is an incompetent fool. That's all he is, that's all he is. We're not going to have a point taken away for that. *I said he was the pits of the world, which, that is exactly what he is.* I'm not going to have a point taken away.

7. You are a Shit, you are as bad as the rest of them (to Fred Hoyles, the Wimbledon Referee). (Point Penalty) - ($750.00 Minor Offense Fine 1ˢᵗ round against Tom Gullikson).

8. That was an Indian Call. (Or worse depending on the resolution of the conflict in the facts) ($750.00 Minor Offense Fine, doubles match).

    [This was the only Minor Offense fine that McEnroe appealed to me, claiming that he had been joking. With respect to McEnroe's version of the facts, I concluded that 'if a player makes an abusive statement to an official, he must take the risk that the official will understand it in accordance with the normal meaning of his words', so I upheld the fine. Actually, the linesman, Mhajan was wearing a turban and although he was a Pakistani, he appeared to be an Indian during the Fleming-McEnroe vs. the Amritraj brothers' doubles match. Mhajan's sworn account was that McEnroe's actual statement was 'you Indians don't have to cheat' and a few games later 'fuck you.' Either way the fine was affirmed]

9.   Can you make another bad call now.

10.   I get screwed because of the umpires in this place. (Warning)

11.   You're not going to beat me. You're not going to beat me. I want you to know that right now.

12.   Everyone is against me, including you Freddie Baby. (to Referee Fred Hoyles).

Wimbledon issued three fines of $750 each against McEnroe for Verbal Abuse and recommended that he be charged with the Major Offense of Aggravated Behavior and fined an additional $10,000. Wimbledon could have defaulted McEnroe for his egregious Verbal Abuse in his 1st round match against Gullikson. However, Wimbledon was unsure whether the Code permitted immediate default for egregious misconduct so Wimbledon eventually decided to recommend that McEnroe be charged with a Major Offense and the Wimbledon officials stopped issuing point penalties and Minor Offense fines for additional statements made by McEnroe.

Welcome, Marshall to your first Wimbledon and to your new job. You have just met and been helped by John McEnroe, Sr., in staffing the new MIPTC office in New York. You were pleased to meet him as he is the only practicing senior lawyer representing a top player, and that top player, John McEnroe, Jr., is the top ranked player in the world. You have also just met the Chairman and the officials of Wimbledon. I guess it is fair to say they were all upset. Butch Buchholz had just recruited McEnroe to finally join the ATP. All of a sudden, I was thrust into the middle between the McEnroes and the Wimbledon officials. So, get on with it, you have an administrative and legal job to do for yet another Major Offense case.

On July 8, as MIPTC Administrator, I issued a formal notice of investigation to commence an investigation to determine if McEnroe should be charged with one or more Major Offenses for Aggravated Behavior as recommended by the Wimbledon Committee and McEnroe was provided the opportunity to appear and respond during my investigation. Wimbledon provided me with 75 minutes of BBC television tape showing the highlights of McEnroe's conduct during Wimbledon. The BBC tape was 2" wide so I had to have it converted to half inch video tape to play it on an American video player. I took the converted tape to John McEnroe Sr.'s law office so we could watch it together on his video machine. When the video finished playing, Mr. McEnroe turned to me and said: "That wasn't so bad was it Marshall?" To which I replied: "John, I am not sure we were watching the same video tape as I thought it was terrible!" The numerous incidents of angry verbal abuse appeared to be way over the top and Wimbledon could have actually defaulted McEnroe in his first match. While I had only recently met John McEnroe, Sr., and he had helped me find my first administrative assistant, we were both lawyers and we had a common view of laws and rules. We both also were subject to the same canons of ethics. I then and always considered that tennis was lucky to have John McEnroe, Sr., represent his son, John, who was now number No. 1 in the world. All the other top players were represented by "player-agents" and it was always refreshing to know that at least McEnroe would be required by his father to follow the rules. The other thing that I considered to be important was that John McEnroe, Jr., no matter what conduct issues he had in a match, always went to the after-match press conference to face the press. He also never refused to play Davis Cup for his country. However, my disagreement with John McEnroe, Sr., over the conduct of John McEnroe, Jr., at 1981 Wimbledon was the beginning of a sometimes tenuous relationship I was to have in the future with him. It also brought home to me quickly that my job responsibility to enforce the Code of Conduct was going to cause lots of personal unpleasantness for me.

As part of my investigation, I met with John McEnroe, Jr. and Sr., and I furnished to them the evidence that I received in my investigation. On August 21, 1981, counsel for McEnroe filed with me a 28-page memorandum on behalf of McEnroe in opposition to the recommendations of the All England Lawn Tennis and Croquet Club which I considered as part of my investigation. Under the provisions of the Code as revised, I and I alone as the Council Administrator was charged with the responsibility for making the first determination of innocence or guilt which would be subject to review, modification or reversal by the Council and subject to review by a panel of three disinterested Review Officers if McEnroe appealed. After a lot of research and soul searching, on September 1, 1981, I concluded that John's statements or remarks were abusive and a number of them were severe and aggravated. I found that together, they, along with other statements or remarks clearly and convincingly evidenced a pattern of aggressive and abusive conduct that must be considered sufficient for proof of the Major Offense of Aggravated Behavior. As a result, I issued my formal Determination of Administrator charging John McEnroe with one Major Offense of Aggravated Behavior under the Code of Conduct with an additional fine of $5,000. Wimbledon had recommended the maximum additional Major Offense fine of $10,000, but I concluded that since the misconduct was all verbal abuse without any physical abuse, that the maximum of $10,000 was inappropriate under the then existing Code provisions. The maximum additional fine for a Major Offense was being raised to $20,000 in 1982, but for 1981 it remained at $10,000. As you might have imagined John McEnroe and Wimbledon were *both* unhappy with my decision. I delivered a copy of my written determination to McEnroe on September 1 and I informed McEnroe that I was going to present it to the MIPTC the next day and would provide McEnroe an opportunity to appear before the MIPTC to oppose my determination.

At the August 31-September 3, 1981, meeting of the MIPTC, I reported on my denial of McEnroe's appeal of the third Minor Offense fine of $750 and I presented my written determination that McEnroe should be charged with the Major Offense of Aggravated Behavior and fined an additional $5,000. I had also provided the MIPTC with McEnroe's response to my investigation. Pursuant to the amendments to the Code of Conduct enacted in June, my Administrator's Determination was subject to review, modification and/or reversal by the MIPTC.[407]

At the MIPTC meeting, there were only eight members present as Owen Williams had just resigned on August 31 to become the new WCT CEO. Thus, the MIPTC members present were Philippe Chatrier (Chairman), Derek Hardwick and Stan Malless as ITF Representatives, Lars Myhrman (Europe) and Jack Kramer (US) as Tournament Representatives and Arthur Ashe, Butch Buchholz and Ray Moore as Player Representatives. The Council interviewed Kurt Nielsen, the head Grand Prix Supervisor for 1981 Wimbledon, for his observations of the facts and his opinions on them. The Council also reviewed at length the 75-minute composite video tape showing the various incidents that occurred at Wimbledon. Thereafter Martin London, Gerald Harper and John F. McEnroe, Sr., attorneys for John McEnroe, Jr., entered the meeting and presented their legal and factual arguments on behalf of McEnroe and requested the Council to overrule the Determination made by me as the Administrator.

After extensive consideration, there were motions duly made and seconded to overrule and to modify the determination made by me as the Administrator. All of those motions failed or were defeated. Consequently, my Administrator Determination was unchanged and McEnroe was charged, subject to his right to appeal. The $5,000 additional fine was trivial to McEnroe, but John, and especially his father, considered that a "conviction" for a Major Offense was the same as a "felony" and they were never going to accept a "felony" conviction for any amount of money. On September 24, 1981, McEnroe elected to contest the charge and proceed to a hearing before three Review Officers. McEnroe also requested that the hearing be closed to the public, so it was going to be private. I selected as the first Review Officer, the Honorable Robert J. Kelleher, who was now a sitting United States Federal District Judge in California, who had been the President of the USTA in 1968 and had been a champion of bringing about Open Tennis.

McEnroe selected Harry Hopman, a former famous Australian Davis Cup Captain, who had had some kind of coaching relationship with John McEnroe at the Port Washington Tennis Academy and together they selected Lawrence W. Krieger, a New York lawyer, as the third Review Officer. The burden of proof required of me as the Administrator and my Assistant Administrator, Mark Meyers, was to convince all three Review Officers of the case against McEnroe by "clear and convincing evidence." At this time, I did not consider it appropriate to employ Roy Reardon, our MIPTC counsel, to participate since the Code of Conduct clearly placed the responsibility on me as the Administrator to prosecute the case.

John McEnroe, Sr., was a senior business law partner in the large Paul, Weiss, Rifkin, Wharton & Garrison law firm in New York. To represent John McEnroe in our Major Offense case, he brought in from the Paul Weiss litigation department, Martin London and Gerald E. Harper. I soon learned that Martin London was one of the best trial lawyers in the United States and that he had represented Vice President Spiro Agnew in connection with criminal charges brought against him that led to his nolo plea and resignation. My "law firm" for the McEnroe case was me, a North Carolina licensed lawyer since 1963, and Mark Meyers, a recently licensed New Orleans lawyer.

On November 20, 1981, the hearing of the Review Officers, closed to the public at the request of McEnroe, was held in New York City. At the hearing, I introduced a number of documentary exhibits for the MIPTC, including the BBC video tape, and Dick Roberson, the Chief Grand Prix Supervisor testified in person. I detailed each and every instance of the 12-25 incidents of the alleged verbal abuse by McEnroe at Wimbledon in 1981. After I presented the case for the MIPTC against McEnroe, Martin London and his defense team presented McEnroe's case with a few surprises which always happen in any litigation context. London's first surprise was live testimony from Butch Buchholz, the Executive Director of the ATP and a Player Representative on the Council. Butch testified that as a member of the Council he participated in the Council's decision to charge McEnroe with a Major Offense. He said the Council was divided on the subject and that "the Player Representatives on the Council felt very strongly that this was not Aggravated Behavior and was not a Major Offense based on what we saw on the tapes...I am here because I honestly believe that the Code of Conduct should be enforced. We can't just arbitrarily change things as we go along because it is the number one tournament or the number two tournament in the world. I think we ought to have or start having some consistent guidelines for bad behavior and I don't think that John falls in the Major Offense category." Buchholz testified that the three Player Representatives on the Council voted against charging McEnroe with the Major Offense of Aggravated Behavior.[408]

London's second surprise was an affidavit from Arthur Ashe, another MIPTC Player Representative. At this time, Ashe had retired as an active player on the circuit and was the U.S. Davis Cup Captain. The panel agreed to accept Ashe's affidavit even though he would not be available for cross examination. Ashe said: "As a member of the Pro Council, I was involved in the discussions leading to the adoption of the player Code of Conduct including the Major Offense provision. I believe that John McEnroe's conduct at the Wimbledon tournament was not a Major Offense under the Code."[409]

The third surprise was that John McEnroe was not going to appear in person for examination and cross examination and that the panel was asked to accept his affidavit. While the panel could have held his affidavit in abeyance and delayed the proceeding so he could appear for cross examination, the panel agreed to accept his affidavit. McEnroe's affidavit said that he believed "the charge is based on a distortion" of the remarks he made at Wimbledon which overlooked the context in which they arose. McEnroe objected to the use of "selective excerpts" shown in an "hour-long videotape" when he had played in 13 matches for over 40 hours at Wimbledon. He noted that there was no videotape of the "atmosphere at Wimbledon or of the actions of the Wimbledon officials off the court." McEnroe said that "before the tournament began, the referee, Fred Hoyles, came up and warned me that the Code of Conduct would be strictly enforced against me by all officials. Mr. Hoyles made it clear that he was speaking on behalf of the whole tournament committee; it was obvious to me that the committee had met and decided to monitor my actions with special scrutiny. This had never happened to me before. To my knowledge, no other player at the tournament was singled out in this manner, even though, at that point, my total fines in the preceding year were a mere $400, well below that of many other players there."

McEnroe said further that "I knew – as anyone who has played at Wimbledon knows – that many of the officials are exceptionally poor and that the conditions of play (apart from the Centre Court and perhaps Court One) are terrible. The chair umpires, while quick to find fault with the most innocuous comment from a player, never pay attention to a player who exercises his right to question a call. They simply ignore the player, and this exacerbates the problem. The 1981 tournament did nothing to alter my views – and the views of many others – about these conditions."[410]

After the presentation of all the evidence, Martin London and I made our final arguments to the Review Officers. Thereafter Judge Kelleher closed the hearing, reserving time to make a decision later. In January, Kelleher and Krieger provided me with a 10-page "Decision" in essence finding McEnroe guilty and upholding the $5,000 fine. On January 11, Hopman provided me with his decision to "dismiss the charge." He wrote, "If the Wimbledon Committee and various Supervisors did not see fit to disqualify John

McEnroe on the spot, or even after discussion over, incidents in his matches, I cannot see clear to do so later."[411]

When I received the Hopman "opinion" to the extent it made any sense, it was apparent that he had been convinced by what might be called the "Constitutional Right to a Default Defense," which provides that since you failed to default me for my misconduct on the spot, I cannot later be penalized at all. His additional justification seemed to be that the treatment of McEnroe by the Wimbledon officials justified McEnroe's misconduct. Hopman's rambling opinion made little sense and his decision was disappointing. Nevertheless, he had ended the case in McEnroe's favor and it was time to move on. Hopman had also shown the wisdom of changing the Code in the future so that a player's Review Officer selection could not unilaterally acquit him of a Major Offense violation.

Upon receiving the written decisions of the Review Officers, I received a request from Martin London that they be maintained as confidential. I disagreed with Mr. London, but I sent copies to the members of the Council and recommended to the Council that they not be released to the press as they "will tend to precipitate a stream of statements and counter-statements that will probably serve no useful purpose and will prolong the anxiety caused to professional tennis by this case." They were never released by anyone and I am sure I have the only remaining copies.[412]

On January 26, I issued a press release concluding the matter and saying: "The Major Offense charge brought by the Men's International Professional Tennis Council concerning the conduct of John McEnroe at the 1981 Wimbledon Championships was dismissed by the independent three-man arbitration panel selected to hear the case. The $5,000 fine assessed by the Council was thereby overturned. The members of the Arbitration Panel were Larry Krieger, a New York City Attorney, the Honorable Robert J. Kelleher, a California Federal District Court Judge, and Harry Hopman, former Australian Davis Cup Captain. The vote was 2 to 1 in favor of sustaining the charge and fine, with Mr. Hopman voting for dismissal. Under the 1981 Code of Conduct a unanimous decision is necessary to sustain a charge." The decision was heavily criticized, particularly by the British press.[413]

Lessons Learned

The John McEnroe 1981 Major Offense case was very important and it taught all of us a lot. We learned a number of important lessons: (i) how the procedure for the conduct of a Major Offense case worked under the 1981 Code (which preceded my employment) and how it could and needed to be improved, (ii) the need for chair umpires to enforce the Code during each match by dealing with each instance of misconduct at the time, (iii) how players should be able to ask questions of officials in a professional and non-abusive manner (I never wanted to hear another player be able to complain that a chair umpire did not answer his question, if asked in a professional and non-abusive manner), (iv) how officials should answer players' questions professionally with as little delay in play as possible, (v) the need to teach the players all the provisions of the Code and to seek their understanding that the enforcement of the Code benefits them for fairly officiated matches and protects the public interest and the popularity of their sport, (vi) McEnroe was right in his claim that tennis officiating was not very good and that we needed to train and seek better and more professional officials and (vii) all players learned that we would prosecute them for Major Offenses they committed and the cost of hiring an expensive trial lawyer to defend them was something to avoid and the best way to avoid it was not to commit a Major Offense.

"You Cannot Be Serious"

John McEnroe's famous "You cannot be serious" rant during his first round Wimbledon match with Tom Gullikson became the title of McEnroe's 2002 book.

Vitas Gerulaitis Player Major Offenses No. 3 and No. 4: 1981 U.S. Open and 1981 Melbourne Indoors

At the 1981 U.S. Open in a 4th round match against Ivan Lendl, Gerulaitis hit a ball with anger in the direction of linesperson Nancy Epting. The ball was hit hard and traveled over Epting's head into the stands where it struck a spectator. Gerulaitis said: "See how bad my aim is. I was aiming for that bitch on the baseline…God damn you, you and your husband have been screwing up my matches for ten years." In the semifinals against McEnroe, Gerulaitis questioned a call and approached the chair umpire, Leon Lipp, and said: "Bull shit, it was a foot out you dumb son of a bitch; the ball was a fucking foot out; don't come anywhere near me off the court or I'm going to beat the shit out of you, dumb bastard."

On January 19, I issued a notice of charge for the Major Offense of Aggravated Behavior for a $5,000 fine against Gerulaitis.[414]

In October, at the Melbourne Indoors final, Peter McNamara was leading Gerulaitis 6-4, 1-6, 7-5, 5-5 when Gerulaitis disputed a call, refused to continue and was defaulted by chair umpire David Bierwirth. Gerulaitis was fined $1,990 for the on-site offenses of failing to complete a match and for verbal abuse. In addition, I issued a notice for the Major Offense of Aggravated Behavior with an additional fine of $10,000. Gerulaitis elected not to contest the $15,000 in major offense fines and paid them off.[415]

Peter McNamara Player Major Offense No. 5: 1981 Brussels

At the 1981 tournament in Brussels, Peter McNamara was entered and was the defending champion. McNamara made a late withdrawal on Wednesday or Thursday before the tournament claiming that he sprained his ankle in the preceding French Open, but he then played in an exhibition in Holland on the next Saturday and Sunday before the beginning of the Brussels tournament on the next Monday. The Brussels tournament director stated that McNamara's late withdrawal did not damage his tournament in Brussels. In my determination on January 8, I found Peter not to be guilty of the Major Offense and that the withdrawal fine of $3,000 was sufficient penalty. The MIPTC elected not to modify or reverse my Administrator's Determination and this case was closed.[416]

Lagos Tournament Offense No. 1: 1981 Lagos

Three British players, Harvey Becker, John Whiteford and John Feaver, an ATP member, were issued visas to enter Nigeria to play in three tournaments, including the Lagos Volvo Grand Prix tournament. However, they were refused entrance to Nigeria the week of February 16-22, 1981, because they had competed in South Africa in recent months (they were not South Africans, but unfortunately, they had a South African visa stamp in their passports from when they had previously competed in a South African tournament). Prior to being sent back to London, the three were detained in a locked cell for 16 hours.

According to the MIPTC Minutes of the March 18-21 meeting in Paris, "The Council regarded Nigeria's action as an attack on the right of individuals to participate freely and a breach of Grand Prix Rule 6(a) which required that all tournaments "be open to all categories of men players without discrimination." "They agreed to invite representatives of the tournament to attend the next meeting of the Council to present their case, but agreed that unless they gave assurances that all players eligible to compete would be admitted to Nigeria, they could no longer be part of the circuit."[417]

On Sunday, June 14, 1981, I met upon request with the delegation from the Lagos tournament in the conference room of Brown's hotel in London and I sat on one side of a very long conference room table while five representatives for Lagos sat on the other side. Almost amusingly, it sort of looked like one (me) vs. five (them). The representatives of Lagos included E.O. Bayagona, the Lagos tournament director, R.A. Adejumo, the Lagos Club President, the Nigerian Commissioner of Sport and others. *My impression was they all lived in London on the government payroll: Why not!* Their argument was that the Nigerian Government, over which the tournament had no control, had required that the three players be expelled from Nigeria because they had played in South Africa, had a South African stamp on their passports and were on the "blacklist." I explained to them over and over again that our Grand Prix Rules required that all qualified players must be admitted and if qualified players were denied entry by the government or anyone, the tournament could not continue to be sanctioned by the Council. I agreed to present their views to the MIPTC, and Mr. Adejumo appeared before the Council to present his views. The Lagos tournament never could provide the required guarantee of compliance, so they were not sanctioned for the 1982 Volvo Grand Prix.[418]

CHAPTER 18:

1982: VOLVO GRAND PRIX VS. WCT TOUR, BORG WAS LOST, CRISES NOS. 22, 23, 24

1982 Governing Bodies

The MIPTC was the governing body for men's professional tennis in 1982, except for the Davis Cup, the *Rules of Tennis* and the new WCT competing circuit. The ITF was the governing body for the Davis Cup and in charge of the *Rules of Tennis*. WCT governed its own separate circuit and events.

1982 Significant Tennis Leaders

ITF President:	Philippe Chatrier (France)
USTA President:	Marvin Richmond
Australian LTA President:	Brian Tobin
British LTA President:	J.R. Cockrane
French FFT President:	Philippe Chatrier
Chairman of Wimbledon:	Sir Brian Burnett
ATP President:	Harold Solomon
ATP Executive Director:	Butch Buchholz
WCT Owners:	Lamar Hunt and Al Hill, Jr.
WCT CEO:	Owen Williams

1982 MIPTC

ITF: Philippe Chatrier, Chairman, Derek Hardwick and Stan Malless.

Tournaments:	Lars Myhrman (Europe), Jack Kramer (North America) and Brian Tobin (Rest of the World).
Players:	Butch Buchholz, Arthur Ashe and Ray Moore.
Administrator:	Marshall Happer.
Ass't Admn:	Mark Meyers until August 4.
Ass't Admn:	Ted Daniel beginning August 4.
Legal Counsel:	Roy L. Reardon, Esquire and John Cambria, Esquire.
GP Supervisors:	Kurt Nielsen, Franco Bartoni, Ken Farrar, Keith Johnson and Bill Gilmour.

1982 Major Player Representatives

ProServ:	Principals: Donald Dell, Frank Craighill, Lee Fentress and Ray Benton.
IMG:	Principals: Mark McCormack and Bob Kain.
Others:	Ion Tiriac and Thomas Betz, Esquire (Vilas).
	John McEnroe, Sr., Esquire (McEnroe).
	Gloria Connors and Joseph Rountree, Esquire (Connors).

Three Competitions

In 1982, the 15th year of Open Tennis, there were three organized competitions for men: Volvo Grand Prix, WCT and the Davis Cup. Davis Cup was open to all players and was won 4-1 by the United States over France. There were 82 Volvo Grand Prix Open prize money tournaments, including the year-end Volvo Masters in Madison Square Garden in New York City. Included in the 82 tournaments were the four Grand Slams and 29 Super Series tournaments with $200,000+ in prize money. The Volvo Masters was again staged at Madison Square Garden and was won by Ivan Lendl over John McEnroe 6-4, 6-4, 6-2 in singles and by McEnroe and Peter Fleming over Sherwood Stewart and Ferdi Taygan 6-2, 6-2 in doubles.

The ATP was involved in eight events: (i) February 28, Monterrey, $300,000, Copa Monterrey ATP Tennis Games, (ii) April 25, Las Vegas, $350,000 ATP Alan King Classic at

Caesar's Palace, (iii) May 10, Dusseldorf, $450,000 Ambre Solaire ATP World Team Cup, (iv) June 13, London, $125,000 Stella Artois Queens ATP Grass-Court Championships, (v) June 20, Bristol, $100,000 Lambert and Butler Championships, (vi) August 22, Cincinnati, $300,000 ATP Championships, (vii) September 19, Sawgrass $200,000 ATP-Lipton World Doubles and (viii) November 14, London, $250,000 ATP Benson and Hedges Championships at Wembley. All of the ATP tournaments were in the Grand Prix, except for the World Team Cup. IMG replaced the ATP for Boston beginning in 1982. Philippe Chatrier complained to Butch Buchholz that the title "Nation's Cup" was a problem for the Davis Cup so Butch changed the title to "World Team Cup" in 1982.

WCT promoted 22 tournaments divided into a Spring Circuit, a Summer-Fall Circuit and a Winter Circuit, plus the 1982 Winter Finals in January of 1983 in Detroit. In an effort to qualify top ranked players, WCT awarded points for the French Open, Wimbledon and the U.S. Open. Each WCT tournament had either a 16 or 32 draw, with $300,000 in prize money and $100,000 to the winner. *Lendl, who was ranked No. 3, became a millionaire, but very few of the other top players compete in the WCT circuits.* McEnroe qualified for the 1982 WCT Finals in Dallas solely by winning Wimbledon and the U.S. Open in 1981, and he lost to Lendl. All but five of the new WCT tournaments were head-to-head in the same weeks as Grand Prix Super Series tournaments.

The ATP did not award ATP Computer Ranking points to WCT tournaments because entries were selected a year in advance and were not based on the ATP Computer Rankings at the 42-day entry deadline. WCT attempted to compete with this by creating its own Nixdorf Computer Rankings.

Ish Haley quoted Owen Williams and Lamar Hunt in *World of Tennis 1983*[419]: "'We started out with 22 cities, and we were new in 18 of them,' he (Owen Williams) said. 'We were operating in new cities, new stadiums, with a new concept, new management, new prize-money structure, our own bonus pool, our own computer, our own newspaper. All of those things add up to lot of unknowns. Our first year was very much a time of trial and error for us.'" "'The first new singles event was in the week of 19 January in Mexico City. The event was a disaster for all except (Tomas) Smid, the winner. The field was weak, and the attendance poor, with only around 500 spectators turning out for the finals." "'It was very frustrating,' said Hunt, who had just folded his professional soccer franchise in Dallas due to low fan attendance."

"WCT, throughout the year, argued behind the scenes that the Grand Prix's minimum (10) tournament rule was strangling the new circuit's opportunity to compete in the open market. It was speculated that Hunt's group was building a case for an anti-trust suit, but no legal action was then taken. WCT suffered, with seven of its tournaments won by players ranked ten or below on their Nixdorf computer."

Crisis No. 22 Continued: Bjorn Borg

In January, the Council approved Borg's request to be released from his obligation to make up three designations from 1981 upon forfeiture of his $60,000 share of the 1981 Bonus Pool. The Council denied Borg's "request for a reduced commitment of seven (7) tournaments for 1982 based on his agreement not to play in any professional event between January 1 and March 31, 1982." I was directed to offer Borg ten (10) days within which to select five (5) tournaments in the first half of the year or ten (10) tournaments for the entire year. No one expected Borg to actually refuse. *After all, he was a professional tennis player and playing tennis was not a burden.* Without a meaningful player commitment by the players, the tournaments could not afford to offer the ever-increasing amounts of on-site prize money, bonus pool contributions and ATP service fees. The members of the Council were convinced that if they did not enforce the player commitment rule against Borg, then all the other players would refuse to abide by the rule.

Borg surprised everyone by announcing that he would not sign a player commitment and instead would play in the qualifying round for any tournament he entered in 1982.[420] Since Borg had won five straight Wimbledons, the focus immediately became whether Wimbledon would support the rules and make Borg qualify. At that time, it was generally thought that if Wimbledon did not support the Council and its rules that it would be disastrous for the Council and for the Volvo Grand Prix. Wimbledon hated the idea of forcing a five-time Wimbledon champion to have to qualify to play in Wimbledon in 1982.[421]

Borg did play in qualifying in Monte Carlo and lost in the quarters to Yannick Noah 6-1, 6-2.[422] At the April 4-6 Monte Carlo Meeting of the MIPTC, Sir Brian Burnett and Mr. Bimby Holt, the Chairman and Vice Chairman of Wimbledon, appeared before the Council and reported that Borg had refused all requests for reconsideration including a Wimbledon proposal for a commitment to ten (10) tournaments between April 1, 1982 and March 31, 1983.[423] When Borg rejected the "compromise" proposed by Sir Brian Burnett, Wimbledon reluctantly agreed to support the MIPTC rules. Borg later played and lost to Dick Stockton in the qualifying in Las Vegas before he quit for the year.[424]

Borg's decision not to play in the Grand Prix in 1982 was a terrible result for Borg and for tennis. In retrospect, the Council should have tried to find a way to keep him playing; however, there may have not been anything that would have kept him playing as he had apparently lost interest. Borg played a ton of special events in 1982 and could have but did not play for WCT. The *New York Times*[425] reported that he lost five of six exhibition matches to Jimmy Connors, culminating in San Francisco in November.

Crisis No. 23: ATP Financial Difficulties

In September of 1981, ATP Executive Director Butch Buchholz sounded the alarm that the ATP was in serious financial difficulty and could not continue to provide the variety of services for the tournaments and the players without financial assistance. The services being provided by ATP included the ATP Computer Rankings, the ATP player tournament entry bureaus, ATP Road Managers and Trainers, etc. Buchholz proposed that all players would agree to have two percent of their 1982 prize money paid to the ATP provided the tournaments would also pay the ATP for its tournament services.[426]

To solve the ATP financial problem, I worked with Butch to develop a draft contract between the MIPTC and the ATP to submit to the MIPTC at its January 12-15, 1982 meeting in New York. The contract[427] was approved by the Council and was dated January 28, 1982, and provided: (i) ATP would continue to provide its ATP Computer Ranking services, acceptance and coordination of player entries in tournaments, provide a special tournament "hotline" for tournament directors, provide a road manager at each tournament, provide two ATP trainers and provide the Council with one full page in each issue of the ATP's *International Tennis Weekly*, (ii) the Council would enact new Grand Prix Rule 31A requiring tournaments to deduct and pay to the Council for the ATP two percent of each player's prize money. Since it was too late to require the tournaments to pay additional money to ATP for 1982, the MIPTC agreed to fund and pay to the ATP: $2,000 for each Regular Series tournament, $4,000 for each Super Series tournament and for the Doubles Series tournament plus $6,000 for each Grand Slam Tournament and (iii) the term of the contract was for 1982 only and either party could terminate it upon 120-days' notice. The MIPTC actually paid the ATP $236,000 in 1982 out of the Council reserves for the tournaments.

That solved this Crisis No. 23 for 1982, but the players objected big time to the deduction of two percent from their prize money. In dealing with players (even by Butch Buchholz their Executive Director), it was always true that *"You can never take anything away from the players." The players did not want to pay the ATP for its player services for them.*

Crisis No. 24: ATP Decision to Withdraw from MIPTC

After solving Crisis No. 23 on January 28, Crisis No. 24 was soon to manifest itself on February 5, whereby the ATP voted to withdraw the Player Representatives from the MIPTC in 1983.

ATP Press Release

On February 5, the ATP issued a press release[428]: "The Board of Directors of the Association of Tennis Professionals (ATP) voted unanimously to inform the Men's International Professional Tennis Council (MIPTC) that as of January 1, 1983, it would no longer have Player Representatives participate on the Council."

It looked like Lamar Hunt and Owen Williams had succeeded in getting the ATP to separate from the MIPTC. Buchholz followed the press release with a letter[429] to Philippe Chatrier as Chairman of the MIPTC dated February 5, along with a six-page draft contract asking the MIPTC to agree to require each tournament, including the Grand Slams, to pay fees to the ATP for "services" along with 15 percent of their net television revenues.

We understood that Buchholz made the same offer to WCT and there was no way that Lamar Hunt was going to agree to place WCT under the governance of the ATP. Likewise, there was no way that the Grand Slams were going to give up 15 percent of their television revenue and the rest of the tournaments felt the same way. Nevertheless, ATP was in real financial difficulty and so our Crisis No. 24 was a real nightmare. At the February 18-20 meeting[430], the members of the Council requested ATP to reconsider its withdrawal decision and asked for time to consult with its various constituencies.

On April 1, 1982, I provided the members of the MIPTC my confidential memorandum on the "existing issues confronting men's professional tennis and to develop a recommendation for 1983." I recommended the development of uniform rules and regulations for the sanctioning of Grand Prix, Challenger Series and Satellite Series tournaments under the umbrella of the MIPTC with fair funding by the tournaments for ATP's services.[431] This would be the 1st time that uniform Tournament Regulations applied to all levels of professional tournaments.

After lots of discussion with Butch between February and June, at the June 15-18 London Meeting[432], I presented a draft five-year contract between the MIPTC and ATP, which was approved with a few minor amendments, subject to final drafting and approval by counsel for the MIPTC and ATP with the further approval of the ATP Board of Directors and approval by the players at an open ATP meeting. Buchholz reported to the players in *International Tennis Weekly*[433]: "In January, the players voted to withdraw from the Council at the end of this year, but after six months of intensive negotiations that decision has been reversed…We feel this agreement will give much-needed stability to the game. It ensures that the players will have a significant voice in the operation of the sport." Philippe Chatrier, President of the ITF and the Chairman of the MIPTC said: "The ITF and the tournaments believe that the continuation of this relationship with the players is vital for the proper operation of the world-wide Grand Prix circuit. We are achieving something that is unique in any sport."

At the August 27-30, 1982, meeting of the MIPTC in New York, the Council (without the participation of the Player Representatives) approved the draft contract for execution. The final new five-year contract for 1983-1987[434], was dated August 30, 1982, and was signed by Buchholz and me on October 7 and 12, 1982. In addition to providing for uniform rules for all levels of men's professional tennis (except for the WCT events) and the funding for the ATP services, the agreement provided for ATP to establish a new two-week "Grand Slam" type tournament for men and women for the long term funding of ATP, which would be substituted for two of the existing ATP fundraising events.

On September 3, *International Tennis Weekly*[435] conducted an interview with Buchholz about the new five-year ATP-MIPTC agreement. "It means stability," he said. "For the first time in the 14-year history of open tennis, players, tournament directors, media, fans, equipment manufacturers, clubs and anyone else associated with the game know that pro tennis is looking beyond the next year. At least, there is a five-year plan."

With a lot of time and effort and the good faith of all concerned, we managed to get through Crisis No. 24 and keep the MIPTC intact. But we still had WCT declining to coordinate with us and competing with the Grand Prix tournaments for players. *Do you think that future litigation would be soon?*

Rules

In October of 1981, I published my first "1982 Volvo Grand Prix Yearbook" consisting of 144 pages as compared to the 1981 publication which was published by Volvo and ProServ and had 56 pages. The Bonus Pool was increased to $3 million with $2.4 million for singles and $600,000 for doubles. The singles awards were decreased from 50 to 32 and the doubles awards were decreased from 25 to 16, to compete with the new 1982 WCT circuit. For 1982, the player commitment rule was changed to require 10 (instead of six) "self-designations" by September 15, 1981, to tournaments other than the French Open, Wimbledon and the U.S. Open. The 10 "Self-Designations" were subject to three substitutions to balance the fields of the Grand Prix tournaments. The 1981 alternative to the player commitment was continued which provided that if a player refused to sign the player commitment, he could still play in Grand Prix tournaments and be eligible for the Bonus Pool and the Masters, but he would have to enter through qualifying at each and every tournament. No direct entries and no wild cards. It would be a nightmare to have to qualify for every tournament. Players could play in a maximum of six special events against Grand Prix Super Series weeks. WCT tournaments against Grand Prix Super Series weeks were considered as prohibited special events because entries were not "accepted by a recognizable system of merit" and some were 16-draws instead of the required 32-draws. The Volvo Masters singles and doubles draws for the 1982 Masters were increased from eight to 12.[436]

1982 MIPTC Code of Conduct

The Point Penalty Schedule was changed:

Current Point Penalty Schedule	New Point Penalty Schedule
Warning	Warning
Point	Point
Point	Game
Game	Default
Default	

This was to provide a further deterrent for player misconduct. We considered it important to curtail the player misconduct before it adversely affected the public's interest in men's professional tennis. The misconduct of one player was also always detrimental to the other player in the match. A new provision authorizing immediate default was added permitting the chair umpire or referee to declare a default for either "a single violation of this Code, or pursuant to the Point Penalty Schedule set out above, subject to an appeal to the Grand Prix Supervisor". This amendment was a result of the McEnroe Major Offense case from Wimbledon in 1981. In 1981, Wimbledon was unsure whether it had the authority to issue an immediate default for egregious misconduct. The new language eliminated any possible doubt as to the option of an immediate default when necessary and reasonable. I was a little nervous about this power being in the hands of the Grand Slam referees instead of the Grand Prix Supervisors. Major Offense fines were increased from a maximum of $10,000 to a maximum of $20,000 to try to keep up with inflation.

To aid in our policing of unauthorized appearance money, a new rule authorized me as Administrator to demand that players furnish copies of all records relating in any way to an alleged guarantee and providing for suspension if such records were not provided. The members of the Council were determined to stop the payment of appearance money to players by tournaments, so this new power was to provide a way to investigate and discover and thus try to prevent the payment of appearance money. I drafted a detailed interpretation of the guarantee rules for the Code of Conduct to clarify what was and what was not a prohibited appearance guarantee, which the Council adopted effective June 18. It outlined the distinction between payments to a player already committed to a tournament to maximize his income while there as contrasted with payments to induce a player to enter a tournament. A new Major Offense was added to the Code prohibiting "Conduct Contrary to the Integrity of the Game which was subject to a fine up to $20,000 and/or to suspension from play in the Volvo Grand Prix or any successor circuit for a period up to three (3) years."

1982 MIPTC Supplement

To deal with the problem of player misconduct, the MIPTC increased the penalties for player misconduct in the 1982 Code of Conduct. However, just as big a problem as player misconduct was the unprofessionalism of tennis officials. Quite a lot of player misconduct incidents began with poor or incompetent officiating. Players would object to calls or chair umpire rulings and the chair umpires made mistakes and responded poorly to player questions, complaints and verbal abuse. We issued a *MIPTC Supplement* containing 48 pages to provide written standards and procedures for the uniform administration of tennis officiating worldwide.[437]

Frank Hammond, the First Full-Time Tennis Umpire

In the 1970s, Frank Hammond of New York (1930-1995) was one of the best known and respected chair umpires. He was the first full-time tennis official. Frank had exceptionally good eyesight and he taught the tennis officials how to "sell" a call. Whenever Frank made a call as a linesmen, it was loud and with such demonstrable conviction that players rarely wanted to question his call.[438]

Hammond was regularly paid $5,000 per tournament to travel to events around the world and "put on a show" from the chair with a running commentary with the players and the spectators. To his credit, Frank attended and graduated from our first MIPTC Officials School in 1979 and he enthusiastically supported our efforts to change and professionalize tennis officiating and completely eliminate commentary or "a show" by chair umpires. In our view, a perfect officiating job was a match that was fairly officiated without incident and that the chair umpire and the on-court officials were barely noticed so the focus would be on the professional play of the professional players.

The Grand Prix Supervisors led the way with the MIPTC Officials Schools, the certification of officials and the evaluation of all officials at every tournament. There were 110 MIPTC International Officials in October of 1981 when the 1982 MIPTC Yearbook was printed. As time progressed, more and more tennis officials applied for and received our MIPTC certification. The MIPTC was creating a new viable profession for tennis officials.

MIPTC Meetings

In 1982, the MIPTC held six meetings: January 12-15 in New York, February 18-20 in La Quinta, April 4-6 in Monte Carlo, June 15-18 in London, August 27-30 in New York and November 9-11 in Stockholm.

MIPTC Meeting, New York January 12-15, 1982

Chairman

In January in New York, Philippe Chatrier was re-elected as Chairman by acclamation.

Volvo

The Council was concerned about the promotion of the Volvo Grand Prix against the new competing WCT circuit and had asked if Volvo would consider providing additional funds for promotion. Rick Dowden, Volvo's Executive Vice President, had indicated that Volvo was willing to consider providing additional funds for promotion of the circuit, except that if such additional funds were substantial, there should be some contractual benefit to Volvo in the way of an additional option or the like. Up to this time, Volvo had refused to provide an accounting of the finances of the Volvo Masters for 1980 and 1981 at Madison Square Garden, so the Council had not considered an extension of Volvo's sponsorship agreement.

WCT Finals to Count as Just One Special Event

The Council agreed that the 1982 WCT Finals in Dallas which ended on a Monday would count as only one special event. The 1982 WCT Finals was in the same week as the Las Vegas Alan King Super Series (also an ATP event) so it would be one of the six permitted weeks for special events against Super Series for anyone playing in Dallas. At least it would not count as two special events.

Insurance

The Council instructed me to obtain Fidelity bond insurance and professional liability insurance with the maximum coverage for the costs of litigation in anti-trust cases. Subsequently, I obtained via Lloyds of London a professional liability insurance policy for around $10,000 per year for full anti-trust coverage. The regulation of a professional sport that balances the interests of the players, tournaments and outside competitors that includes the United States, is subject to the United States anti-trust laws. That is why the Council had employed Roy Reardon, a well-respected anti-trust lawyer, to attend all MIPTC meetings to to provide legal advice to the Council at every meeting. Previously there had been an anti-trust lawsuit by Jimmy Connors and WCT had often threatened anti-trust litigation. This was the first time that the MIPTC as an unincorporated association and its members, (who were all volunteers) had ever had any insurance coverage since the creation of the MIPTC in 1974. They had all been terrified personally of anti-trust litigation which inhibited their ability to govern the sport.

Gerulaitis

Gerulaitis was suspended for twenty-one days commencing on September 21, 1981 and continuing through October 11, 1981 for exceeding the $5,000 annual accumulation of on-site misconduct fines. *Another Fall vacation for Vitas.*

McEnroe

McEnroe was suspended for twenty-one days commencing on November 16, 1981 through December 6, 1981 for exceeding the $5,000 annual accumulation of on-site misconduct fines. *Also another Fall vacation for John.*[439]

Copenhagen

In February in La Quinta[440], the Council withdrew the sanction for the proposed $150,000 tournament in Copenhagen scheduled for May 1-7, 1982, because Denmark's Ministry of Foreign Affairs told the Danish Tennis Association "that, because of South

Africa's racial policies (Apartheid), no South African players will be admitted to the country."

MIPTC Meeting, Monte Carlo April 4-6, 1982

Five-Set Finals and the "Limited Attention Span of Americans"

In April in Monte Carlo, requests for five-set singles finals were approved for Hamburg, Munich, Kitzbuhel, Stuttgart, Vienna and London. In Europe, there was great interest in having five-set finals and the European tournaments considered that it gave them increased status like the Grand Slams. At one of the Council meetings when the subject was being discussed, David Gray, the ITF General Secretary and previously a famous tennis journalist from *The Guardian*, told me that Europeans needed to have five-set finals because they have "a longer attention span than Americans." I remember distinctly saying to David that I was quite sure he believed that, but I was astonished that he said it out loud. In those days, the only television in Europe was government owned over-the-air channels (no cable channels yet) and since they did not have television commercials, sponsor signage on tennis courts was the best form of exposure for sponsors. So, the longer the match, the longer the signage exposure on public television.

French Open and Wimbledon

Requests "for the Tournament Committees (of the French Open and Wimbledon) to be the final authority for the selection of seeds were granted." This permitted these two Grand Slams to adjust the seedings to recognize some especially good "clay court" or "grass court" players in the seedings without following the computer rankings which were an average of the last 12 months on all surfaces.[441]

MIPTC Meeting, London, June 15-18, 1982.

More Five-Set Finals

In June in London, five-set finals were approved for Gstaad, Bordeaux, Hilversum and Sydney Indoors. I assumed they all had long attention spans.

1983 Player Commitment Rule:
Tournaments Increased from 10 to 12

For 1983, the player commitment for the Grand Prix would increase the number of required tournaments from 10 to 12 (plus Masters) with up to three substitutions with one veto in each half of year. The alternative to the player commitment continued to be qualifying at every tournament, except a Grand Slam could give a wild card to any player who won the event in the last three years (the "Borg Rule"). No special events were permitted within 100 miles and 30 days of a Super Series or Grand Slam; however, 8 special events could be against Super Series weeks provided that 4 of them were on another continent. Tournaments with less than 32 draws (like some of the WCT tournaments) were to be deemed as special events.

Referees Required to be MIPTC Certified Officials for the First Time

For the first time in 1983, all referees were required to be MIPTC certified officials. *This really made the MIPTC schools and the MIPTC certifications especially important for the professionalism of tennis officiating. It also aggravated some of the national associations.*[442]

MIPTC Meeting, New York, August 27-30, 1982

Volvo

In August in New York,[443] Volvo and ProServ continued to press for an extension of the Volvo sponsorship agreement of the Volvo Grand Prix and Volvo Masters after 1984. The Council directed me to commence a good faith negotiation period with Volvo, provided Volvo made full disclosure of all financial details with respect to the Volvo Masters. The Council further agreed that if a suitable agreement could not be obtained by the time of the Volvo Masters in January of 1983, then a new sponsor would be sought starting in 1985. *Volvo always claimed that if it gave us the financial information on the MIPTC's Masters tournament, it would be "negotiating against itself" in some manner.*

MIPTC Meeting, Stockholm, November 9-11, 1982

Even More Five-Set Finals Approved

In November in Stockholm,[444] five-set finals were approved for Philadelphia, Monte Carlo, Madrid, Hamburg, Rome, Barcelona, London and Johannesburg. *More long attention spans; Philadelphia must have had a special fan base with longer than usual attention spans for Americans!*

MIPTC Officials Schools

The MIPTC staged four MIPTC Officials Schools in 1982: March 23-25 in Paris, May 4-6 in Toronto, September 28-30 in Sydney and October 26-28 in Buenos Aires.

Jacques Dorfmann – Director of Competitions for French Tennis Federation

One of the reasons for the Paris school was to try to get Jacques Dorfmann, who since 1975 was the head of all tennis officials for the French Tennis Federation and the French Open Referee, to support our international certification program and to become certified himself. Dorfmann was the manager of an insurance firm and had been a volunteer tennis official since 1954. He was extremely bright and claimed to have worked 15,000 matches. Dorfmann often boasted that as a chair umpire his eyesight was so good, he never once had to get out of the chair to check a mark on a clay court. Every other chair umpire in the world often got out of the chair to inspect a mark on a clay court to confirm whether the ball was in or out. Dorfmann was also a champion bridge player "ranked first Pique series by the French Bridge Federation."[445] Dorfmann was extremely arrogant and considered himself to be greatly, and I mean greatly, superior to the Grand Prix Supervisors and any MIPTC certification. Remember that at the 1980 French Open he gave Vilas extra recovery time contrary to the rules and the advice of the Grand Prix Supervisors for which the French Open was fined $2,800. Dorfmann hated the MIPTC and the Supervisors. However, somehow the Supervisors found a way to have Dorfmann pass the certification exam and become certified as a "MIPTC International Official" as a referee and as a chair umpire.

We learned that all the French tennis officials were scared of Dorfmann because he had the authority to let them work or not let them work. It was not uncommon at the French Open for Dorfmann to station himself near the end of the center court during a match so that the chair umpire could look at him before making any decision which, of course, is the wrong thing for a chair umpire to do, because decisions and announcements should be instantaneous. Generally, Dorfmann refused to assign anyone except his French umpires as a chair umpire during the French Open, claiming that no one else could control the crowd in French, except for volatile player matches which scared him and the French officials. None of them wanted to chair a McEnroe or Gerulaitis match. Dorfmann always assigned himself to be the chair umpire for the French Open men's singles final and he would assign himself to one men's quarterfinal as practice. You can rest assured that he never assigned himself to chair a McEnroe match. Dorfmann treated the Grand Prix Supervisors with more than a little disdain. Remember at the French Open, the Supervisors were "advisors" only. The Supervisors related a lot of instances when they would make a recommendation to Dorfmann in writing for a scheduling of matches and he would summarily and publicly disregard them. At the beginning of 1982, we had 111 MIPTC certified officials. At the end of 1982, we had 188 MIPTC certified officials with another 18, pending certification.

National Associations Did Not Like the MIPTC Certification Program

Some of the national associations opposed our MIPTC certification program because they wanted to control the certification of officials in their respective countries. The political favoritism in the certification of tennis officials by the national associations had contributed greatly to the enlistment of lots of incompetent officials who could not handle the players who were now playing for large sums of prize money. *We had to have competent officials. We could not have a group of elderly officials who just wanted to strut around in blue blazers and who were afraid of the players. In Australia, an elderly linesman actually fell asleep in his chair.*

The absolute worst kind of telephone call I often received went something like this: "Marshall I am happy to let you know that I have finally gotten old enough to retire from my job and I plan to become a full-time tennis official." I always thought I should say that professional tennis officiating is better handled by young folks with really good eyes and reflexes, not retirees. I probably was too polite to bluntly say you are exactly the wrong kind of person we need for professional tennis officiating, but I certainly did not encourage them and I knew they would probably never get approved by the Grand Prix Supervisors. One of the worst tasks I had was when I had to tell an elderly certified official who could no longer handle professional matches properly that he or she was no longer going to be certified.

MIPTC National Official Certification Added

The original MIPTC certification was for "MIPTC International Official." To accommodate the national associations, the Council adopted MIPTC Standing Order Article I to provide for a "MIPTC National Official" for officials who had not yet attended a MIPTC Officials School. But they still had to meet all the other qualifications of a "MIPTC International Official" and still be "personally observed and recommended by a Grand Prix Supervisor."

ETA's Request for the Right of Prior Approval for MIPTC School Denied

In 1982, I received a request from Heinz Grimm, the President of the European Tennis Association (ETA), the association of all the European National Associations and an important part of the ITF, seeking the prior approval of all applicants for MIPTC Officials Schools in Europe. Heinz was a really good volunteer tennis leader in Europe and we wanted the ETA's recommendations and support, but we could not give the ETA the ability to reject candidates that the Grand Prix Supervisors considered to be worthy of acceptance. So, just as we were dealing with the players by enforcing the new tougher rules in the Code of Conduct to curtail player misconduct, we were also having some issues with the national associations who did not particularly like that we were conducting the international program for the certification of tennis officials. *But, the truth of the matter was that we were the only organization that could do this on an international professional basis.*

Tennis in 1984 Olympics

The ITF was successful in getting tennis approved for the 1984 Olympics through the outstanding efforts of Philippe Chatrier and David Gray. Tennis would be played as a demonstration sport at the Los Angeles Olympics before being introduced as a full medal sport in competition in the 1988 Games in Seoul, South Korea.[446] We knew that it would be challenging to create open dates for the summer Olympics in the already crowded tennis calendar, but the benefits of having tennis in the Olympics were just too important. One of the huge benefits was that every country involved in the Olympics would begin financially supporting the development of tennis in their respective countries.

Up to 1982, the MIPTC did not have a drug testing program because the players just would not agree to have one on the fear that someone would be prosecuted for use of an illegal drug like cocaine. No one suspected that there was any use of performance enhancing drugs in tennis. However, we knew that by the 1984 Olympics, we would have to develop a drug testing program acceptable to the International Olympic Committee.

Lendl Skips Wimbledon

Ivan Lendl, the world No. 3 behind John McEnroe and Jimmy Connors, announced that he was going to skip Wimbledon in 1982. In March, the *New York Times* quoted Lendl[447]: "'I trained on grass for six hours every day for a fortnight last year before Wimbledon, and that had a very bad effect on my performance,' he said in an

Ivan Lendl

interview with DPA, the West German news agency. 'This year I would like to take a break in June and prepare myself instead for the second round of the Davis Cup in July. I will not be taking part at Wimbledon."

Lendl's agent ProServ said Lendl would be abandoning the tournament schedule for the next four weeks and would play a five-set exhibition June 13 against Guillermo Vilas in Reno (Prior to Wimbledon). In the early 1980s, it was not unusual for several European and South American "clay court specialists" to skip Wimbledon's grass. Vilas probably also skipped Wimbledon because of the UK/Argentina Falkland War which began on April 2 and ended on June 14. *Skipping Wimbledon by Lendl and Vilas really, really upset Sir Brian Burnett and the Wimbledon Committee. Skipping Wimbledon was a sort of "blasphemy." Borg had already announced he was retiring and not going to defend his Wimbledon title. That had also really, really upset Sir Brian Burnett and the Wimbledon Committee.*[448]

Lunch at Wimbledon

In March, I received a telephone call at my office in Manhattan from Sir Brian Burnett, the Chairman of Wimbledon from 1974-1984. I was very honored just to meet Sir Brian, who was one of the most respected and famous people in Great Britain. Sir Brian had earned his reputation as an important leader in Great Britain. He had been a senior Royal Air Force officer who became Air Secretary and served as the last Commander-in-Chief of the Far East Command. His complete title was "Sir Brian Kenyon Burnett, Air Chief Marshall, GCB, DFC, AFC, ADC".

I remember Sir Brian saying he wanted to talk to me which naturally led me to say I am happy to talk to you right now on the telephone. Sir Brian politely suggested that he wanted to talk to me at lunch at Wimbledon in London. I called Philippe Chatrier, the Chairman of the MIPTC, who was my main "boss" at his office in Paris, and he told me that if Sir Brian wanted me to meet with him in London, I should arrange to fly from New York to London. So, I did.

I called Sir Brian and told him I had been authorized to fly to London to meet with him, so we arranged to have lunch at Wimbledon the next day. I took an evening flight from JFK Airport to London Heathrow and arrived early the next morning. I took a shower and dressed at Wimbledon and met Sir Brian for lunch. By this time in 1982, I was fairly well-acquainted with the many problems that Wimbledon had with its relationship with the players in addition to the John McEnroe 1981 Major Offense case. At that time, the Wimbledon prize money for men was $400,000, but Wimbledon was deducting $40,000 for the Wimbledon Plate tournament for the first round losers. This meant that the total prize money for the men's singles and doubles was only $360,000 and due to the then existing exchange rate, the actual U.S. Dollar amount was around $320,000. I told Sir Brian that the players were upset with the actual amount of prize money being offered, which was less than the French Open and less than the U.S. Open. Further, I told Sir Brian that the players really disliked Wimbledon's offensive attitude toward them and that Wimbledon's refusal to let the ATP staff and ATP trainers into Wimbledon along with its very restrictive policy for tickets for players had all the players angry. Sir Brian was very perceptive and was extremely interested in taking all necessary steps to remedy the problem that Wimbledon had with the players. After lunch, I took a taxi back to Heathrow and took a late afternoon flight back to Manhattan. *I cannot remember what I had for lunch.*

As a result of our meeting, Sir Brian immediately announced that the prize money for 1982 Wimbledon was being increased to $500,000 for men and that the ATP staff and trainers would be welcome at Wimbledon. He also reversed the restrictive policy for tickets for players and completely changed the attitude of Wimbledon toward the players.

Neil Amdur described Sir Brian's new actions in the *New York Times*[449]: "The 16-page brochure includes a welcoming message from the chairman, a map of the All-England Lawn Tennis and Croquet Club, important telephone numbers, how and where to find a practice court and ticket information. To the astonishment of many players here for today's start of the Wimbledon championships, the brochure is specifically designed for them - not for debenture holders, news media representatives, tennis politicos, ticket touts or spectators. Wimbledon is a tournament in transition, an institution trying to retain the dignity of its historic past while learning, sometimes painfully, that tennis now dances to a disco beat, not waltz time. The more publicized changes in this year's championships are the extra day (Sunday, July 4) for the men's singles finals, a 41 percent increase in prize money (to the equivalent of about $1.1 million), expanded catering and service facilities on the grounds and the advance sale of standing-room seats for the last four days that will probably end the customary overnight camping queues outside the club.

"To the players, however, the new informational brochure, more and better practice facilities, increased ticket allowances, and the establishment of a player liaison committee are equally significant signs of Wimbledon's sensitivity in the face of mounting criticism. 'We are making a lot of changes,' Sir Brian Burnett, the chairman of the club, said the other day. 'Last year, we spent 3 million pounds to improve Court 1 and give the players a new restaurant, lounge and quiet room. This year, we're concentrating on other areas that are equally as important to the equation of staging a successful tournament.'"

"Often accused of smugness, Wimbledon has become image-conscious enough to hire a public relations firm to represent the championships for the first time. Competition from the French and United States Opens and recent complaints from Ivan Lendl, Vitas Gerulaitis, Harold Solomon and other pros over insufficient practice time and administrative indifference have glazed the club's mauve and green roots.

So, has the aftershock of the McEnroe Affair. One year after the tempestuous American created front-page headlines on the court and then spurned the champions' dinner, Wimbledon seems willing to forgive his behavior and forget that the club bypassed him for honorary membership. Committee representatives located and rounded up the three trophies that McEnroe never received or simply forgot to pick up after his four-set victory over Borg in last year's singles final. A quiet dialogue has also begun between committee representatives and John P. McEnroe, Sr., in an effort to avoid future communication problems with the family."

"If Wimbledon has mellowed somewhat toward McEnroe, it has also belatedly again found a tender spot for Ted Tinling, the former British dress designer, whose unconventional tennis fashions frequently upstaged play on the grass courts. After 32 years in what he describes as 'the wilderness,' the 71-year-old Tinling was named to head the club's liaison committee with the players, supported by Jim McManus of the Association of Tennis professionals and Lindsey Beaven of the Women's Tennis Association."

Wimbledon is owned and operated by the All England Lawn Tennis and Croquet Club and unlike the Lawn Tennis Association of Australia, the French Tennis Federation and the United States Tennis Association, which own and operate the other three Grand Slams, Wimbledon has no other relationship with players other than its Wimbledon tournament. Wimbledon has long had an agreement with the Lawn Tennis Association of Great Britain (LTA) to make Wimbledon the official British Championships and Wimbledon annually gives its excess income to the LTA. *Nevertheless, Wimbledon probably now has the best relationship with the players, current and retired, than any of the other Grand Slams and a lot of the credit for this belongs to the change of attitude of Wimbledon towards the players begun by Sir Brian Burnett.* I remember Sir Brian saying to me at 1982 Wimbledon that he was concerned that everyone wanted him to socialize with the players at night which he couldn't do because of his responsibilities at Wimbledon. I assured him that the players did not really believe he should drink beer and socialize with them every night. *He had changed the attitude and the relationship of Wimbledon towards the players and they were very appreciative.*

Lendl – WCT Tournament of Champions vs. ATP World Team Cup: $10,000 Fine

During the week ending on May 10, Ivan Lendl was entered into both the $500,000 WCT Tournament of Champions at Forest Hills and the $450,000 ATP World Team Cup in Dusseldorf. Dusseldorf was an ATP special event, was not in the Grand Prix and was not subject to the MIPTC Code of Conduct. When Lendl learned that WCT was going to withhold his WCT bonus, Lendl withdrew from the ATP World Team Cup to play in the WCT Tournament of Champions. Dusseldorf and the ATP were furious. The ATP fined Lendl $10,000 and suspended him indefinitely from the ATP. Lendl explained that he had misunderstood his contractual commitment to WCT and he did not challenge the fine or the suspension.[450]

Gerulaitis Fined Again, Over $5,000 So Another 21-Day Suspension

At Wimbledon, Gerulaitis was fined again for misconduct which put him in excess of $5,000 in on-site fines in 12 months. When Gerulaitis elected not to appeal the Wimbledon fines, I issued the automatic suspension of 21 days from July 12 to August 1, 1982. *You might conclude that Vitas was a "repeat offender."*[451]

Wimbledon's New Rule 21 – Wimbledon's New Default Rule

At Wimbledon in 1981, the Wimbledon Committee was unsure as to whether it could default John McEnroe for misconduct, so it decided to recommend that McEnroe be charged with the Major Offense of "Aggravated Behavior" and the officials stopped issuing point penalties and additional Minor Offense fines and simply referred the matter to the MIPTC or in other words to me. The MIPTC Code was amended for 1982 to make it clear that a player could be defaulted for "either a single egregious violation of this Code, or pursuant to the Point Penalty Schedule set out above, but upon appeal by a player, the Grand Prix Supervisor shall have the discretionary authority to affirm or set aside the default." At the Grand Slams the Referee had the power of the Grand Prix Supervisors.

The MIPTC Code of Conduct was the *exclusive* disciplinary Code applicable to all players in Grand Prix tournaments and the only Code to which the players agreed to be bound so I was surprised to learn that Wimbledon had devised a new "default rule" in its entry application[452] for players which read as follows:

"21.   The Referee is empowered to take whatever measures he thinks necessary in the interest of the Championships, including defaulting a player, without the Committee or the Referee being in any way liable for redress or otherwise."

That "rule" was also included in the Wimbledon entry applications for 1983 through 1989. First of all, players rarely, if ever, received or read a Wimbledon Entry Application as entries are generally made by telephone to the ATP and delivered as a consolidated entry list by ATP to Wimbledon. Once I was told that whenever the ATP received a batch of Wimbledon Entry Applications, they were just discarded. Next, the "Rule No. 21" was not part of the MIPTC Code, which was the *exclusive* disciplinary Code applicable to players. Because of this "rule," in my pre-tournament meetings every year (1982-1989) with the Chairman of Wimbledon, the Wimbledon Referee and the Chief Grand Prix Supervisor, I politely warned and requested Wimbledon not to consider acting under that "rule." The default rules in the MIPTC Code were more than enough to deal with player misconduct and I warned Wimbledon that if it sought to default a player under its Rule 21, which was outside of the MIPTC Code that had been agreed with the players, the players would most likely want to boycott Wimbledon. Fortunately, Wimbledon never sought to use its Rule No. 21 before the MIPTC was dissolved in 1989, so that crisis was avoided. *Would you be surprised if I told you that "rule" was in the Wimbledon Entry Application in 2019?*

Davis Cup Quarterfinals, 6 Hours 32 Minutes

In the Wimbledon final, John McEnroe lost to Jimmy Connors 3-6, 6-3, 6-7, 7-6, 6-4 in 4 hours and 14 minutes. The next week, McEnroe represented the United States in defeating Sweden 3-2 in the quarterfinals of the Davis Cup, indoors in the Checker Dome in St. Louis. McEnroe defeated Anders Jarryd 10-8, 6-3, 6-3 in the opening match. McEnroe and Peter Fleming defeated Jarryd and Hans Simonsson 6-4, 6-3, 6-0 in the doubles. In the final match, which lasted 6 hours and 32 minutes, McEnroe (age 23) defeated Mats Wilander (age 17) 9-7, 6-2, 15-17, 3-6, 8-6. Wilander had won the 1982 French Open earlier by defeating Guillermo Vilas in the finals.[453]

Slew Hester Dropped as U.S. Open Chairman

USTA President Marvin Richmond dropped Slew Hester and assumed the position as Chairman of the 1982 U.S. Open. Marvin was an extremely bright tax lawyer from Kansas City with a powerful ego and he had an intense longing for power and for recognition. In a brilliant move, Marvin was responsible for getting from the IRS a 501(c)(3) charitable designation for the USTA National Tennis Center, Inc., and for finally getting a long term written lease for the USTA National Tennis Center with the City of New York. *Well, what had Slew done for the USTA lately? Once you got out of power in the USTA, you really got out of power as those who had been patiently waiting for years to obtain power just had to have all of it.*[454]

Outstanding Player Fines

In May of 1982, I notified all of the players with outstanding fines that I would accept medical certificates for late withdrawals and would hear all appeals for outstanding misconduct fines from 1979-1981, until July 12, after which I would instruct the Grand Prix Supervisors to collect them at the next tournament entered. The total of the outstanding fines then was $431,700. Ron Bookman printed the entire list of players with outstanding fines in *International Tennis Weekly*, twice. I heard and determined lots of appeals throughout Wimbledon.[455]

Our enforcement efforts and the decision to have fines immediately deducted from a player's prize money beginning in 1982 had already caused a substantial drop in misconduct fines. *We were making a meaningful impact on player misconduct.*

Ted Daniel Succeeds Mark Meyers

Mark Meyers returned to the practice of law in New Orleans and he was succeeded by Ted Daniel as Assistant MIPTC Administrator on August 4. Ted, a Tulsa native, graduated *Magna Cum Laude* from Duke University in 1978 with a business administration degree. He was like Mark, the No. 1 tennis player at Duke. He later graduated from the Southern Methodist University law school and served as editor of the Southwest Law Review, before joining the litigation section of the Dallas law firm of Jenkens and Gilchrist. Ted had played on the USTA Satellite Circuit. Mark had finished his one-year commitment with me and now Ted was beginning his one-year commitment with a leave of absence from his law firm in Dallas. I still was inside my two-year employment contract through February of 1983.

Player Misconduct Progress

With respect to player misconduct, I said in the *New York* Times in October[456]: "Professional tennis is very young. For the first 10 years of open tennis, there were no disciplinary procedures or enforcement. It was out of control. But now we are making progress. The Council determines the rules and penalties. This year fines have been increased substantially and suspension can be for as long as six months. The point-penalty system gives players fewer opportunities to protest incessantly before they are penalized and forced to forfeit. And officials are better schooled. As a result, the number of incidents has decreased. Compared with past years, the major tournaments, such as Wimbledon and the United States Open, proceeded uneventfully."

Illegal Drugs Prohibited

The Council added a new rule for 1983 that made drug-taking at a tournament an offense that can lead to instant default and a penalty of $5,000. No one believed and there was no evidence known to us that any players were using "performance enhancing" drugs in tennis. We did not believe that any drug would last long enough to help a player win a five-hour tennis match. However, there were enough "rumors" about some players making recreational use of marijuana and cocaine that the Council was concerned about the implications for the sport if a player was charged and convicted of a crime. The Player Representatives were fearful of having a player charged with an illegal drug crime. At this stage, they would not agree to having the rule applicable beyond the "precincts of a tournament," thus this rule would not apply to a player who was arrested outside of "the precincts of a tournament." However, at least this was a start towards the much more vigorous drug testing that would be required before the 1984 Los Angeles Olympics.[457]

Administrator's Five-Year Contract

When I was hired to begin a two-year employment contract as MIPTC Administrator on March 1, 1981 to create a New York office and hire a staff for the administration of the MIPTC and the Grand Prix, neither the MIPTC or I knew how it would work out. I took a two-year leave of absence from my Raleigh law firm, so I could return if necessary. At the November 9-11, 1982, MIPTC meeting in Stockholm, the Council agreed to extend my employment for five more years from January 1, 1983 to December 31, 1987. By this time, I was convinced that we were making real progress in organizing men's professional tennis. We had a five-year contract with the ATP, and except for the competing WCT circuit, we had unity. We had developed reasonable and uniform rules applicable to the Grand Prix, the Challenger Series and the Satellite Series and we were on our way to developing professional officials. The Code of Conduct and the immediate collection of fines had clamped down and begun to diminish the incidents of player misconduct. The Council had given me the necessary authority to conduct the Council's administration for the players, the tournaments, the ITF and its national associations. I was proud to accept my continuation as the MIPTC Administrator which was now a longer career commitment. As part of our agreement, the Council permitted me to move back to North Carolina with a small Raleigh office. I agreed to commute back and forth weekly to our Manhattan office and our new Paris office, while also maintaining an apartment in Manhattan. In those days, the Eastern Airline round-trip fare from Raleigh to New York was still only $99.

Neil Amdur wrote in the *New York Times*[458]: "Men's tennis has never had a commissioner, preferring to pass policy through a nine-member Council comprising players, officials and tournament directors. But by rewarding Marshall Happer with a five-year contract last week to continue as Administrator of the Men's International Professional Tennis Council, the circuit has come as close as it ever has to having a commissioner. Relatively unknown in the sport when he accepted the post in March 1981, the 44-year-old Happer has gained the respect of players and officials, expanded his role in decision making and encouraged stronger, more effective rules."

New Manhattan and Paris Offices

When our short-term sub-lease at 375 Park Avenue expired, we moved to new office space at 919 Third Avenue (the large black building just behind P.J. Clarks). In addition, on January 1, 1983, we opened our new office in Paris at Stade Roland Garros, the home of the French Open, which was being provided to the MIPTC gratis by the French Tennis Federation of which Philippe Chatrier, the Chairman of the MIPTC, was also President. He was also President of the ITF.

Our new office addresses were:

New York Office: 28th Floor, 919 Third Avenue, New York, NY 10022, Telephone: 212-838-8450, Telex: 968145 or 661643, Telecopier Telephone: 212-759-9528, Cable Address: GRANDPRIX NEWYORK.

Paris Office: Stade Roland Garros, 2 Avenue Gordon Bennett, 75016 Paris, France, Telephone: 651-21-09, Telex: 611871, Telecopier Telephone 651-02-41.

In Manhattan, before we had "telecopier" or "fax" machines, it took so long for a letter to travel by U.S. Mail to anywhere in Manhattan that we almost always had to pay $10 for a bicycle messenger to deliver each letter. All international communication was via telephone, Telex or Cable. Finally, we had a fax machine so no more bicycle messengers.

Paul Svehlik, Assistant Administrator and Opening of Paris Office

With the blessings of Butch Buchholz, I hired Paul Svehlik as a second Assistant Administrator (with Ted Daniel) to manage the new Paris Office. Paul had been the ATP Director of European Operations managing the ATP office in Paris since 1977. Paul was born in Tilbury, England to Czech parents. He was educated at Cambridge University and played on the British field hockey team. Paul was fluent in French, English, Czech and German. Prior to working with the ATP, Paul was a road manager for WCT.

Dick Roberson Retires

Dick Roberson, the Chief of Grand Prix Supervisors since October of 1978, resigned effective November 21 to resume his career with Penn Athletics. "Dick has to be credited with a large part of the successful development of professional officiating," I was quoted saying in *International Tennis Weekly*[459]: "He has proven that Supervisors are needed as we seek to apply standardized rules worldwide, enforce the Code of Conduct and train officials."

Kriek Leads In 1982 Fines

Neil Amdur noted in the *New York Times*[460]: "Johan Kriek finished eighth in the season-long Volvo Grand Prix point standings on the men's professional tennis tour. But for dubious distinction in the numbers game, Kriek appears to be the overwhelming winner for the 1982 season. According to the Men's International Professional Tennis Council, Kriek led the tour with fines from five tournaments that totaled $11,500. The latest $5,250 from a tournament last week in Australia ($500 for an obscenity, $750 for abuse of an official and $4,000 for physical abuse of an official) resulted in Kriek's second 21-day suspension of the year, which began on Monday. The physical abuse fine was for throwing a towel. By contrast, John McEnroe was fined in the same number of tournaments as Kriek – five. But McEnroe's total for the year amounts to only $2,060, well below the $5,000 limit for suspension."

John McEnroe Tennis Over America Tour

In 1982, Steve Corey and Gary Swain continued to promote the John McEnroe Over America Tour exhibitions with 15 events mostly against Guillermo Vilas.[461]

ATP

Harold Solomon President for a Third Year

Harold Solomon was re-elected as ATP President for a third year, with Stan Smith as Vice President, Jim McManus as Secretary and Mike Estep as Treasurer. New board members were Rolf Gehring, Carlos Kirmayr and Balazs Taroczy. The returning board members were Mark Edmondson, Alejandro Cortes, Cliff Drysdale and Arthur Ashe along with Butch Buchholz.[462]

1982 ATP JAKS AWARDS
(New York City, January 1983)

Player of the Year	Jimmy Connors
Doubles Team of the Year	Sherwood Stewart – Ferdi Taygan
Newcomer of the Year	Chip Hooper
Comeback Player of the Year	Butch Walts
Media Service Award	Neil Amdur
Broadcaster of the Year	Pat Summerall
ATP Special Award	Margie Smith

Buchholz as ATP Executive Director

Butch Buchholz became the ATP Executive Director in 1980. He recruited McEnroe and Borg to join the ATP which gave it credibility with the top players; he settled the Boston lawsuit and extended ATP's relationship with Boston; he found a way to bring the ATP out of its financial crisis created by Bob Briner and Doug Tkachuk; and he helped create uniform rules and provide for stability for all of men's professional tennis (except for WCT) with the new contracts with the MIPTC. However, that apparently was not enough for the ATP. I never heard of anyone then or even now who did not like Butch. He is, perhaps, the only one of the Pioneers of Tennis that never had any enemies, except perhaps Harold Solomon and Cliff Drysdale.

Solomon and Drysdale led the ATP Board to agree to seek other candidates for the position of ATP Executive Director when Buchholz's employment contract expired at the end of July of 1983. Richard Evans reported in *World of Tennis1983*: "Butch's supporters on the board insisted that he should remain as one of those considered but Buchholz, aware that he had not been fired, but that it amounted to the same thing, announced that he would continue to the end of 1982 by which time, he hoped, the ATP would have found someone to replace him."

Buchholz said in *International Tennis Weekly*[463]: "The ATP Board was unable at this time to make a decision about my future with the Association. My contract runs through July of 1983, and when the Board became split on the direction to take, I elected not to be a candidate to continue. Harold asked me to be a serious candidate, but there are other things which I want to pursue. I am fulfilling my contract and have asked the ATP staff to remain in place. I will help the new executive director in any way and intend to make the transition as smooth as possible."

Solomon credited Buchholz with bringing the ATP through a difficult period since assuming the job two and half years earlier and said, "Buchholz inherited a tough situation and brought the Association a long way. The esteem of the ATP is much higher than it was and we hope the new executive director continues along those lines."

Mike Davies Succeeds Buchholz as ATP Executive Director

Three hundred candidates applied for the job and after all was said and done, the ATP selected Mike Davies in January of 1983 to succeed Buchholz as the new ATP Executive Director. I always heard that the ATP was upset at Buchholz's hiring of his old friend, Mike Davies, as the ATP Marketing Director, so I was surprised that the ATP selected Davies to succeed Buchholz. I could only assume that of the 300 candidates that were considered, none of them were really qualified and there was, of course, no one in the game more knowledgeable or more qualified than Mike Davies.[464]

Butch Buchholz Interview

Butch Buchholz reflected in *International Tennis Weekly*[465]: "There are a lot of problems, but it is getting better. Time will prove that the decision of the players to remain as part of the Council was the proper decision…It is in the players' best interests to be a part of the system. The Council is a proper mix of tournaments, associations and players. I have been a member of the Pro Council for two years, and although it is not perfect and has problems, I am impressed that the members vote for what they feel is the best interest of pro tennis, not their particular constituencies. That takes guts. The stakes are high, but they really care about what is happening in pro tennis."

"I have believed for 24 years that the players deserve their own Grand Slam – level, two-week tournament. The players are the last entity in the game to build such an event, and my major goal is to provide them with a tournament. I am working now on sponsorships, television and marketing to make this event happen in 1985. I have negotiated this with the Pro Council. There is a lot of support for it because the idea is a good one. Everyone will gain because it builds something where there was nothing before." Mike Davies as the new ATP Executive Director had asked Butch to promote the new ATP 2 week "players' grand slam".

Stuttgart Tournament Offense No. 2

At the $75,000 tournament in Stuttgart in 1981, Bjorn Borg defeated Ivan Lendl 1-6, 7-6, 6-2, 6-4. It was the only tournament Borg played after losing in the 1981 Wimbledon final to John McEnroe and before the 1981 U.S. Open, where he also lost to McEnroe in the final. Both Borg and Lendl should have been playing in the Boston Super Series tournament that week.

The Stuttgart tournament was sponsored by Daimler-Benz, the manufacturer of the expensive Mercedes autos in Stuttgart. Obviously, everyone suspected that Stuttgart was doing something more valuable than offering $75,000 in prize money to induce these players to enter. Violation of the prohibitions against the payment of guarantees was widely suspected so I was instructed to investigate. Christopher Stokes, the financial manager of the ITF, and I traveled to meet on June 4, in Stuttgart with representatives of the Stuttgart tournament. We learned that Daimler-Benz was offering a 20 percent discount on the purchase of Mercedes to the "promotional value" players, e.g., Borg and Lendl.

After completing my investigation on August 19, I issued my "Determination of MIPTC Administrator" concluding that the discount was a prohibited appearance guarantee and I issued a $20,000 fine against the tournament and applied its $3,000 deposit for 1983 to the fine. Stuttgart refused to pay the $17,000 balance due on the fine and appealed to the MIPTC. On November 8, Stuttgart withdrew its application for the 1983 Volvo Grand Prix and asked for the return of its $3,000 deposit. We declined.[466]

1982 Stockholm Tournament Offense No. 3

The Stockholm Open in 1982 received entries from four South African players: Kevin Curren, Freddie Sauer, Danie Visser and Bernard Mitton. They were all refused visas because they were South African and the Swedish Government in its opposition to the Apartheid policy of the South African government discriminated against the individual South African players by refusing to permit them entry into Sweden. At the November 9-11, 1982, meeting of the MIPTC in Stockholm, the Council fined the Stockholm Open $25,000, but did not withdraw its sanction for 1983. However, Stockholm was informed that if "in the future any qualified player is denied the right to participate in a Grand Prix event in Sweden," its sanction would be withdrawn.[467]

Thereafter, until Apartheid was discontinued, the South African players elected not to enter tournaments in Sweden since it would cause the tournaments to lose their sanctions, which would cause the loss of player jobs for the other players. That was the nightmare that the South African professional players had to endure.

1982 MIPTC Financials

The MIPTC began 1982 with a surplus of $384,169, and after operating its New York office and providing $3,000,000 in Bonus Pool awards to players in the Volvo Grand Prix, the MIPTC ended 1982 with a surplus of $788,890. The MIPTC paid ATP $236,000 for services to Volvo Grand Prix tournaments pursuant to the 1982 agreement. Volvo continued to pay for its promotion through ProServ. Volvo and ProServ promoted the Volvo Masters at Madison Square Garden, telecast on NBC, and were responsible for all expenses and received all income. Volvo and ProServ continued to refuse to disclose to the MIPTC the financials of the Volvo Masters while seeking an extension of its Volvo sponsorship term (1980-1984) beyond 1984, upon favorable terms.[468]

1982 Grand Slam Winners

French Open

Mats Wilander d. Guillermo Vilas 1-6, 7-6, 6-0, 6-4.
Sherwood Stewart – Ferdi Taygan d. Hans Gildemeister – Belus Prajoux 7-5, 6-3, 1-1 ret'd.

Wimbledon

Jimmy Connors d. John McEnroe 3-6, 6-3, 6-7, 7-6, 6-4.
Peter McNamara – Paul McNamee d. Peter Fleming – John McEnroe 6-3, 6-2.

U.S. Open

Jimmy Connors d. Ivan Lendl 6-3, 6-2, 4-6, 6-4.
Kevin Curren – Steve Denton d. Victor Amaya -Hank Pfister 6-2, 6-7, 5-7, 6-2, 6-4.

Australian Open

Johan Kreik d. Steve Denton 6-3, 6-3, 6-2.
John Alexander – John Fitzgerald d. Andy Andrews – John Sadri 6-4, 7-6.

Volvo Masters

Ivan Lendl d. John McEnroe 6-4, 6-4, 6-2.
Peter Fleming - John McEnroe d. Sherwood Stewart – Ferdi Taygan 6-2, 6-2.

1982 Davis Cup

Davis Cup Final (Grenoble- Clay)

United States d. France 4-1

John McEnroe (US) d. Yannick Noah (FR) 12-10, 1-6, 3-6, 6-2, 6-3.
Gene Mayer (US) d. Henri Leconte (FR) 6-2, 6-2, 7-9, 6-4.
Peter Fleming – John McEnroe (US) d. Henri Leconte – Yannick Noah (FR) 6-3, 6-4, 9-7.
Yannick Noah (FR) d. Gene Mayer (US) 6-1, 6-0.
John McEnroe (US) d Henri Leconte (FR) 6-2, 6-3.

World Team Cup (Dusseldorf)

United States d. Australia 2-1.

Gene Mayer (US) d. Kim Warwick (AU) 7-6, 6-2.
Eliot Teltscher (US) d. Peter McNamara (AU) 6-4, 7-6.
Mark Edmondson – Peter McNamara (AU) d. Gene Mayer – Sherwood Stewart (US) 6-1, 6-2.

1982 World Rankings[469]

Bud Collins	Lance Tingay	ATP Year-End Rankings
1. John McEnroe	1. Jimmy Connors	1. John McEnroe
2. Jimmy Connors	2. Ivan Lendl	2. Jimmy Connors
3. Ivan Lendl	3. John McEnroe	3. Ivan Lendl
4. Guillermo Vilas	4. Mats Wilander	4. Guillermo Vilas
5. Vitas Gerulaitis	5. Guillermo Vilas	5. Vitas Gerulaitis
6. Jose-Luis Clerc	6. Victor Pecci	6. Jose-Luis Clerc
7. Mats Wilander	7. Jose Higueras	7. Mats Wilander
8. Gene Mayer	8. Andres Gomez	8. Gene Mayer
9. Yannick Noah	9. Yannick Noah	9. Yannick Noah
10. Peter McNamara	10. Eliot Teltscher	10. Peter McNamara

1982 Volvo Grand Prix Bonus Pool Top 10[470]

Singles (13th Bonus Pool)		Doubles (8th Bonus Pool)	
1. Jimmy Connors	$600,000	1. Sherwood Stewart	$150,000
2. Guillermo Vilas	$400,000	2. Ferdi Taygan	$125,000
3. Ivan Lendl	$300,000	3. Steve Denton	$ 75,000
4. John McEnroe	$200,000	4. Mark Edmondson	$ 50,000
5. Mats Wilander	$125,000	5. John McEnroe	$ 40,000

6.	Vitas Gerulaitis	$100,000	6.	Kevin Curren	$ 30,000
7.	Jose Higueras	$ 80,000	7.	Brian Gottfried	$ 25,000
8.	Johan Kriek	$ 70,000	8.	Peter Fleming	$ 20,000
9.	Andres Gomez	$ 45,000	9.	Tim Gullikson	$ 18,000
10.	Steve Denton	$ 35,000	10.	Pavel Slozil	$ 14,000

1982 Official Earnings Top 10[471]

1.	Ivan Lendl	$2,028,850	6.	Tomas Smid	$ 582,700
2.	Jimmy Connors	$1,173,850	7.	Wojtek Fibak	$ 533,626
3.	Guillermo Vilas	$ 932,150	8.	Vitas Gerulaitis	$ 450,875
4.	John McEnroe	$ 842,725	9.	Johan Kriek	$ 449,098
5.	Jose-Luis Clerc	$ 635,400	10.	Steve Denton	$ 401,079

1982 Tournament Calendar

Date	Tournaments	Singles Winner	Singles #2	Doubles Winner	Doubles #2
1/10/1982	Birmingham $200,000 WCT			H. Gunthardt - B. Taroczy	K. Curren - S. Denton
1/10/1982	Adelaide AU, $75,000 GP	Rod Frawley	Lloyd Bourne	M. Edmondson - K. Warwick	A. Jarrett - J. Smith
1/11/1982	Rosemont IL $350,000 SP	Jimmy Connors	John McEnroe	6-7, 7-5, 7-5, 6-4	
1/17/1982	Auckland NZ, $75,000 GP	Tim Wilkison	Russell Simpson	A. Jarrett - J. Smith	L. Stefanki - R. Van't Hof
1/18/1982	Guaruja BR, $100,000 CH	Van Winitsky	Carlos Kimayr		
1/24/1982	Mexico City $300,000 WCT	Tomas Smid	John Sadri	S. Stewart - F. Taygan	T. Smid - B. Taroczy
1/31/1982	Philadelphia $300,000 GP SS	John McEnroe	Jimmy Connors	P. Fleming - J. McEnroe	S. Stewart - F. Taygan
1/31/1982	Vina Del Mar $75,000 GP	Pedro Rebolledo	Raul Ramirez	M. Orantes - R. Ramirez	G. Aubone - A. Gomez
1/31/1982	Delray Beach $300,000 WCT	Ivan Lendl	Peter McNamara	M. Purcell - E. Teltscher	T. Smid - B. Taroczy
2/7/1982	Denver $250,000 SS	John Sadri	Andres Gomez	K. Curren - S. Denton	P. Dent - K. Warwick
2/7/1982	Buenos Aires $75,000 GP	Guillermo Vilas	Alejandro Ganzabal	H. Kary - Z. Kuharszky	A. Gimenez - M. Orantes
2/7/1982	Toronto CA, $350,000 SP	Ivan Lendl	John McEnroe	7-5, 3-6, 7-6, 7-5	
2/14/1982	Richmond VA $300,000 WCT	Jose-Luis Clerc	Fritz Buehning	M. Edmondson - K. Warwick	S. Ball - R. Gehring
2/14/1982	Caracas VE, $75,000 GP	Raul Ramirez	Zoltan Kuharszky	S. Meister - C. Wittus	E. Fromm - C. Lewis
2/14/1982	Memphis $225,000 GP SS	Johan Kriek	John McEnroe	K. Curren - S. Denton	P. Fleming - J. McEnroe
2/21/1982	Palm Springs $200,000 SS	Yannick Noah	Ivan Lendl	B. Gottfried - R. Ramirez	J. Lloyd - D. Stockton
2/28/1982	Monterrey $300,000 SS/ATP	Jimmy Connors	Johan Kriek	V. Amaya - H. Pfister	T. Delatte - M. Purcell
2/28/1982	Genoa IT, $300,000 WCT	Ivan Lendl	Vitas Gerulaitis	P. Slozil - T. Smid	M. Cahill - B. Mottram
2/28/1982	Cairo EG, $75,000 GP	Brad Drewett	Claudio Panatta	D. Gitlin - J. Gurfein	H. Gunthardt - M. Gunthardt
3/14/1982	Brussels BE, $250,000 SS	Vitas Gerulaitis	Mats Wilander	P. Slozil - S. Stewart	T. Delatte - C. Dunk

3/14/1982	Linz FR, $75,000 GP	Anders Jarryd	Jose Higueras	A. Jarryd - H. Simonsson	R. Frawley _ P. Kronk
3/14/1982	Munich DE, $300,000 WCT	Ivan Lendl	Tomas Smid	M. Edmondson - T. Smid	K. Curren - S. Denton
3/21/1982	Strasbourg FR $300,000 WCT	Ivan Lendl	Tim Mayotte	W. Fibak - J. Fitzgerald	S. Mayer - F. McMillan
3/21/1982	Rotterdam NE, $250,000 SS	Guillermo Vilas	Jimmy Connors	M. Edmondson - S. Stewart	F. Buehning - K. Curren
3/21/1982	Metz FR, $75,000 GP	Erick Iskersky	Steve Denton	D. Carter - P. Kronk	M. Doyle - D. Siegler
3/23/1982	Copenhagen SP	Vitas Gerulaitis	Bjorn Borg	6-2, 6-7. 6-2	
3/25/1982	Cascais, PT, $68,000 SP	Bjorn Borg	Vitas Gerulaitis	7-6, 6-1	
3/28/1982	Milan IT, $350,000 SS	Guillermo Vilas	Jimmy Connors	H. Gunthardt - P. McNamara	M. Edmondson - S. Stewart
4/4/1982	Frankfurt DE. $250,000 SS	Ivan Lendl	Peter McNamara	S. Denton - M. Edmondson	T. Giammalva - T. Mayotte
4/4/1982	Nice FR, $75,000 GP	Balazs Taroczy	Yannick Noah	H. Leconte - Y Noah	P. McNamee - B. Taroczy
4/4/1982	Zurich CH, $300,000 WCT	Bill Scanlon	Vitas Gerulaitis	S. Giammalva - T. Gullikson	W. Fibak - J. Fitzgerald
4/11/1982	Monte Carlo $300,000 SS	Guillermo Vilas	Ivan Lendl	P. McNamara - P. McNamee	M. Edmondson - S. Stewart
4/12/1982	Johannesburg $75,000 GP	Danny Visser	Van Winitski	F. Saver - S. Van Der Merwe	T. Wiljoen - D. Visser
4/18/1982	Houston TX $300,000 WCT	Ivan Lendl	Jose-Luis Clerc	K. Curren - S. Denton	M. Edmondson - P. McNamara
4/18/1982	Los Angeles CA $200,000 SS	Jimmy Connors	Mel Purcell	S. Stewart - F. Taygan	B. Manson - B. Teacher
4/18/1982	Tokyo JP, $250,000 SP	Bjorn Borg	Guillermo Vilas	6-1, 6-2	
4/25/1982	Las Vegas $350,000 SS/ATP	Jimmy Connors	Gene Mayer	S. Stewart - F. Taygan	C. Kimayr - V. Winitsky
4/25/1982	Bournemouth $100,000 GP	Manual Orantes	Angel Gimenez	P. McNamara - B. Mottram	H. Leconte - I. Nastase
4/26/1982	Dallas $1,300,000 WCT	Ivan Lendl	John McEnroe		
5/1/1982	Hilton Head $100,000 WCT	Van Winitsky	Chris Lewis	M. Edmondson - R. Frawley	A. Waldman - V. Winitsky
5/2/1982	Madrid ES, $200,000 SS	Guillermo Vilas	Ivan Lendl	P. Slozil - T. Smid	H. Gunthardt - B. Taroczy
5/2/1982	Tampa FL US, $75,000 GP	Brian Gottfried	Mike Estep	T. Gullikson - T. Gullikson	B. Gottfried - H. Pfister

5/9/1982	NY $500,000, TC - WCT	Ivan Lendl	Eddie Dibbs	T. Delatte - J. Kriek	D. Stockton - E. Van Dillon
5/10/1982	Dus'ldorf $450,000 WTC	United States	Australia	2-1,	
5/10/1982	Dus'ldorf $450,000 WTC	Gene Mayer	Kim Warwick	7-6, 6-2	
5/10/1982	Dus'ldorf $450,000 WTC	Eliot Teltscher	Peter McNamara	6-4, 7-6	
5/10/1982	Dus'ldorf $450,000 WTC		6-1, 6-2	M. Edmondson - P. McNamara	G. Mayer - S. Stewart
5/16/1982	Hamburg DE, $250,000 SS	Jose Higueras	Peter McNamara	P. Slozil - T. Smid	A. Jarryd - H. Simonsson
5/16/1982	Florence FR, $75,000 GP	Vitas Gerulaitis	Stefan Simonsson	P. Bertolucci - A. Panatta	S. Giammalva - T. Giammalva
5/16/1982	Kobe JP, $200,000 SP	Vijay Amritraj	Sandy Mayer	M. Edmondson - B. Teacher	V. Amritraj - S. Mayer
5/23/1982	Rome IT, $300,000 SS	Andres Gomez	Eliot Teltscher	H. Gunthardt - B. Taroczy	W. Fibak - J. Fitzgerald
5/23/1982	Munich DE, $75,000 GP	Gene Mayer	Peter Elter	C. Hooper - M. Purcell	T. Viljoen - D. Visser
6/6/1982	French Open $450,000 GS	Mats Wilander	Guillermo Vilas	S. Stewart - F. Taygan	H. Gildemeister - B. Prajoux
6/13/1982	London $150,000 GP/ATP	Jimmy Connors	John McEnroe	J. McEnroe - P. Rennert	V. Amaya - H. Pfister
6/13/1982	Venice IT, $75,000 GP	Jose-Luis Clerc	Peter McNamara	C. Kimayr - C. Motta	J.L. Clerc - I. Nastase
6/13/1982	Reno SP	Ivan Lendl	Guillermo Vilas		
6/20/1982	Bristol $100,000 GP/ATP	John Alexander	Tim Mayotte	T. Gullikson - T. Gullikson	M. Edmondson - K. Warwick
7/4/1982	Wimbledon $500,000 GS	Jimmy Connors	John McEnroe	P. McNamara - P. McNamee	P. Fleming - J. McEnroe
7/11/1982	Newport $100,00 GP	Hank Pfister	Mike Estep	A. Andrews - J. Sadri	S. Ball - R. Frawley
7/11/1982	Gstaad $100,000 GP	Jose-Luis Clerc	Guillermo Vilas	S. Mayer - F. Taygan	H. Gunthardt - M. Gunthardt
7/18/1982	Zell Am See $300,000 WCT	Jose-Luis Clerc	Heinz Gunthardt	W. Fibak - B. Manson	S. Giammalva - T Giammalva
7/18/1982	Boston $200,000 SS	Guillermo Vilas	Mel Purcell	S. Meister - C. Wittus	F. Sauer - S. van der Merwe
7/18/1982	Stuttgart $75,000 GP	Ramesh Krishnan	Sandy Mayer	M. Edmondson - B. Teacher	A. Maurer - W. Popp
7/18/1982	Bastad $75,000 GP	Mats Wilander	Henrik Sundstrom	A. Jarryd - H. Simonsson	J. Nystrom - M. Wilander

7/24/1982	Industry Hills $100,000 SP	Jimmy Connors	Bjorn Borg	5-7, 6-2, 6-2, 6-7, 6-2	
7/25/1982	Kitzbuhel $100,000 GP	Guillermo Vilas	Marcos Hocevar	M. Edmondson - K. Warwick	R. Frawley - Slozil
7/25/1982	Washington $200,000 SS	Ivan Lendl	Jimmy Arias	R. Ramirez - V. Winitsky	H. Gildemeister - A. Gomez
7/25/1982	Hilversum $75,000 GP	Balazs Taroczy	Buster Mottram	J. Kodes - T. Smid	H. Gunthardt - B. Taroczy
8/1/1982	Cap d Agde $300,000 WCT	Tomas Smid	Lloyd Bourne	A. Andrews - D. Gitlin	P. Slozil - T. Smid
8/2/1982	South Orange $75,000 GP	Yannick Noah	Raul Ramirez	R. Ramirez - V. Winitsky	J. DiLouie - B. Willenborg
8/2/1982	North Conway $200,000 SS	Ivan Lendl	Jose Higueras	S. Stewart - F. Taygan	P. Arraya - E. Fromm
8/8/1982	Indianapolis $200,000 SS	Jose Higueras	Jimmy Arias	S. Stewart - F. Taygan	R. Venter - B. Willenborg
8/8/1982	Columbus $100,000 GP	Jimmy Connors	Brian Gottfried	Tim Gullikson - B. Mitton	V. Amaya - H. Pfister
8/15/1982	Toronto $300,000 SS	Vitas Gerulaitis	Ivan Lendl	S. Denton - M. Edmondson	P. Fleming - J. McEnroe
8/15/1982	Cleveland $75,000 GP	Sandy Mayer	Robert Van't Hof	V. Amaya - H. Pfister	M. Mitchell - C. Wittus
8/15/1982	Carlsbad $300,000 WCT	Johan Kriek	Roscoe Tanner	F. Buehning - J. Kriek	B. Lutz - R. Ramirez
8/22/1982	Cincinnati $300,000 SS/ATP	Ivan Lendl	Steve Denton	P. Fleming - J. McEnroe	S. Denton - M. Edmondson
8/22/1982	Stowe $75,000 GP	Jay Lapidus	Eric Fromm	A. Andrews - J. Sadri	M. Fishbach - E. Fromm
8/29/1982	Summers SP	Guillermo Vilas	Eliot Teltscher	7-6, 6-3	
8/29/1982	Jericho Hamlet Cup SP	Gene Mayer	Johan Kriek	6-2, 6-3	
9/12/1982	US Open $600,000 GS	Jimmy Connors	Ivan Lendl	K. Curren - S. Denton	V. Amaya - H. Pfister
9/19/1982	Sawgrass $200,000 GP/ATP			B. Gottfried - R. Ramirez	M. Edmondson - K. Warwick
9/19/1982	Palermo $100,000 GP	Mario Martinez	John Alexander	G. Marchetti - E. Vattuone	J. Damian - D. Perez
9/19/1982	San Francisco $200,000 SS	John McEnroe	Jimmy Connors	F. Buehning - B. Teacher	C. Dunk - M. Davis
9/19/1982	San Diego SP	Ivan Lendl	Roscoe Tanner	6-2, 6-4	
9/19/1982	Houston SP	Vitas Gerulaitis	John McEnroe	6-4, 2-6, 6-3	
9/26/1982	Los Angeles $300,000 WCT	Ivan Lendl	Kevin Curren	K. Curren - H. Pfister	A. Andrews - D. Gitlin

9/26/1982	Geneva $75,000 GP	Mats Wilander	Tomas Smid	P. Slozil - T. Smid	C. Linberger - M. Myburg
9/26/1982	Bordeaux $75,000 GP	Hans Gildemeister	Pablo Arraya	H. Gildemeister - A. Gomez	A. Jarryd - H. Simonsson
9/29/1982	Ottawa SP	Bjorn Borg	Jimmy Connors	1-6, 6-3, 6-3, 4-6, 6-2	
10/3/1982	Maui $100,000 GP	John Fitzgerald	Brian Teacher	M. Cahill - E. Teltscher	F. Gonzalez - B. Mitton
10/3/1982	Montreal $250,000 SP	Jimmy Connors	Bjorn Borg	6-4, 6-3	
10/10/1982	Melbourne $100,000 GP	Vitas Gerulaitis	Eliot Teltscher	F. Gonzalez - M. Mitchell	S. Ball - R. Frawley
10/10/1982	Barcelona $200,000 SS	Mats Wilander	Guillermo Vilas	A. Jarryd - H. Simonsson	C. Kimayr - C. Motta
10/17/1982	Sydney $200,000 SS	John McEnroe	Gene Mayer	J. McEnroe - P. Rennert	S. Denton - M. Edmondson
10/17/1982	Basle $100,000 GP	Yannick Noah	Mats Wilander	H. Leconte - Y Noah	F. Buehning - P. Slozil
10/17/1982	Naples $250,000 WCT	Ivan Lendl	Wojtek Fibak		
10/24/1982	Tokyo $125,000 GP	Jimmy Arias	Dominque Bedel	S. Stewart - F. Taygan	T. Gullikson - T. Gullikson
10/24/1982	Vienna $100,000 GP	Brian Gottfried	Bill Scanlon	P. Slozil - H. Leconte	M. Dickson - T. Moor
10/24/1982	Amsterdam $300,000 WCT	Wojtek Fibak	Kevin Curren	F. Buehning - T. Smid	K. Curren - B. Mottram
10/24/1982	Melbourne $250,000 SP	Ivan Lendl	Vitas Gerulaitis	6--2, 6-2, 7-5	
10/31/1982	Cologne $75,000 GP	Kevin Curren	Shlomo Glickstein	J. Damiani - C. Kimayr	J. Lapidus - R. Meyer
10/31/1982	Tokyo $300,000 SS	John McEnroe	Peter McNamara	T. Gullikson - T. Gullikson	J. McEnroe - P. Rennert
10/31/1982	Paris $75,000 GP	Wojtek Fibak	Bill Scanlon	B. Gottfried - B. Manson	J. Lapidus - R. Meyer
11/3/1982	Perth SP	John McEnroe	Bjorn Borg	6-1, 6-4	
11/6/1982	Sydney SP	Bjorn Borg	Ivan Lendl	6-1, 6-4, 6-2	
11/7/1982	Hong Kong $100,000 GP	Pat DuPre	Morris Strode	C. Strode - M. Strode	K. Warwick - V. Winitsky
11/7/1982	Quito $75,000 GP	Andres Gomez	Loic Courteau	J. Fillol - P. Rebolledo	E. Adams - R. Royer
11/7/1982	Baltimore $300,000 WCT	Paul McNamee	Guillermo Vilas	An. Amritraj - T. Giammalva	V. Amaya - F. Stolle

11/8/1982	Stockholm $250,000 SS	Henry Leconte	Mats Wilander	M. Dickson - J. Gunnarsson	S. Stewart - F. Taygan
11/11/1982	San Francisco $100,000 SP	Jimmy Connors	Bjorn Borg	7-5, 7-6	
11/14/1982	London $250,000 SS/ATP	John McEnroe	Brian Gottfried	P. Fleming - J. McEnroe	H. Gunthardt - T. Smid
11/14/1982	Tapei $75,000 GP	Brad Gilbert	Craig Wittus	L. Stefanki - R. Van't Hof	F. McNair - T. Wilkison
11/14/1982	Houston $450,000 Mxd		6-4, 6-3, 7-6	P. McNamara - M. Navatilova	S. Stewart - J. Russell
11/15/1982	Los Angeles $125,000 SP	Jimmy Connors	Bjorn Borg	6-3, 2-6, 6-2	
11/20/1982	Vancouver - SP	Jimmy Connors	Bjorn Borg	6-2, 5-7, 6-4	
11/21/1982	Sao Paulo $200,000 SS	Jose-Luis Clerc	Marcus Hocevar	C. Kimayr - C. Motta	P. McNamara - F. Taygan
11/21/1982	Bangkok $75,000 GP	Mike Bauer	Jim Gurfein	M. Bauer - J. Benson	C. Strode - M. Strode
11/21/1982	Ancona $75,000 GP	Anders Jarryd	Mike DePalmer	A. Jarryd - H. Simonsson	Tim Gullikson - B. Mitton
11/21/1982	Dortmund $300,000 WCT	Brian Teacher	Wojtek Fibak	P. Slozil - T. Smid	M. Cahill - F. Gonzalez
11/22/1982	Itaparica $75,000 GP	Jaime Fillol	Ricardo Acuna		
11/28/1982	Johannesburg $300,000 SS	Vitas Gerulaitis	Guillermo Vilas	B. Gottfried - F. McMillan	S. Glickstein - A. Pattison
11/28/1982	Salvador BR, $75,000 GP	Jamie Fillol	Ricardo Acuna	G. Barbosa - J. Soares	T. Koch - J. Schmidt
11/29/1982	Barcelona $600,000 SP	Europe	Americas	7-5,	
11/29/1982	Barcelona $600,000 SP	Ivan Lendl	Andres Gomez	3-6, 6-3, 6-4	
11/29/1982	Barcelona $600,000 SP	Gene Mayer	Ivan Lendl	2-6, 6-0, 8-6	
11/29/1982	Barcelona $600,000 SP	Ivan Lendl	John McEnroe	2-6, 7-5, 6-2	
11/29/1982	Barcelona $600,000 SP	Bjorn Borg	Vince Van Patten	6-3, 2-6, 7-5	
11/29/1982	Barcelona $600,000 SP	John McEnroe	Bjorn Borg	6-3, 2-6, 6-4	
11/29/1982	Barcelona $600,000 SP	Gene Mayer	Bjorn Borg	6-3, 4-6, 6-3	
11/29/1982	Barcelona $600,000 SP	John McEnroe	Mats Wilander	6-4, 6-2	

11/29/1982	Barcelona $600,000 SP	Mats Wilander	Andres Gomez	6-7, 6-3, 6-2	
11/29/1982	Barcelona $600,000 SP	Mats Wilander	Vince Van Patten	6-0, 6-3	
11/29/1982	Barcelona $600,000 SP	Jose Higueras	Gene Mayer	6-3, 4-6, 7-5	
11/29/1982	Barcelona $600,000 SP	Jose Higueras	Vince Van Patten	6-1, 6-4	
11/29/1982	Barcelona $600,000 SP	Andres Gomez	Jose Higueras	3-6, 7-6, 7-5	
12/5/1982	Chicago IL $300,000 WCT	Wojtek Fibak	Bill Scanlon	An. Amritraj - V. Amritraj	M. Cahill - B. Manson
12/5/1982	Antwerp BE, $700,000 SP	Ivan Lendl	John McEnroe	3-6, 7-6, 6-3, 6-3	
12/12/1982	Australian Open $450,000 GS	Johan Kriek	Steve Denton	J. Alexander - J. Fitzgerald	A. Andrews - J. Sadri
12/12/1982	Toulouse FR, $75,000 GP	Yannick Noah	Tomas Smid	P. Slozil - T. Smid	J. Haillet - Y. Noah
12/19/1982	Sydney NSW $125,000 GP	John Alexander	John Fitzgerald	J. Alexander - J. Fitzgerald	C. Letcher - C. Miller
12/19/1982	Hartford CT $300,000 WCT	Ivan Lendl	Bill Scanlon	B. Lutz - D. Stockton	M. Cahill - T. Delatte
12/19/1982	Sydney AU, $125,000 GP	John Alexander	John Fitzgerald	J. Alexander - J. Fitzgerald	C. Letcher - C. Miller
12/20/1982	Miami Beac $300,000 SP	Jimmy Connors	Brian Teacher	6-2, 6-2	
12/28/1982	Adelaide AU, $75,000 GP	Mike Bauer	Chris Johnstone	P. Cash - C. Johnstone	B. Dyke - W. Hampson
1/2/1983	Melbourne AU, $75,000 GP	Pat Cash	Rod Frawley	E. Edwards - J. Smith	B. Dyke - W. Hampson
1/9/1983	Rosemont IL US, $250,000 SP	Ivan Lendl	Jimmy Connors	4-6, 6-4, 7-5, 6-4	
1/23/1983	NY $400,000 Volvo Masters	Ivan Lendl	John McEnroe	P. Fleming - J. McEnroe	S. Stewart - F. Taygan
1/30/1983	Detroit $250,000 Finals WCT	Ivan Lendl	Guillermo Vilas	7-5, 6-2, 2-6, 6-4	

http://www.atpworldtour.com/en/scores/results-archive.
http://www.itftennis.com/procircuit/tournaments/men's-calendar.aspx?tour=&reg=&nat=&sur=&cate=AL&iod=
&fromDate=01-01-1968&toDate=29-12-1983.
Tennis History, Jim McManus, (Canada, 2010).
1983 USLTA Yearbook.
Official 1989 MTC Media Guide, MTC (1989).
World of Tennis 1983, Edited by John Barrett and compiled by Lance Tingay, (London, 1983).

CHAPTER 19:

1983: VOLVO GRAND PRIX VS. WCT TOUR

1983 Governing Bodies

The MIPTC was the governing body for men's professional tennis in 1983, except for the Davis Cup, the *Rules of Tennis* and the WCT competing circuit. The ITF was the governing body for the Davis Cup and in charge of the *Rules of Tennis*, and WCT governed its own separate circuits and events.

1983 Significant Tennis Leaders

1983 Significant Tennis Leaders	
ITF President:	Philippe Chatrier (France)
USTA President:	Hunter Delatour
Australian LTA President:	Brian Tobin
British LTA President:	J.R. Cockrane
French FFT President:	Philippe Chatrier
Chairman of Wimbledon:	Sir Brian Burnett
ATP President:	Harold Solomon until July
ATP President:	Ray Moore, beginning in July
ATP Executive Director:	Mike Davies
WCT Owners:	Lamar Hunt and Al Hill, Jr.
WCT CEO:	Owen Williams

1983 MIPTC

ITF: Philippe Chatrier, Chairman, Derek Hardwick and Stan Malless.

Tournaments:	Lars Myhrman (Europe), Jack Kramer (North America) and Brian Tobin (Rest of World).
Players:	Mike Davies, Ray Moore, Arthur Ashe until June and Stan Smith beginning in June.
Administrator:	Marshall Happer.
Ass't Admn:	Ted Daniel until August.
Ass't Admn:	Paul Svehlik.
Ass't Admn:	Tony Eugenio beginning in April.
Ass't Admn:	David Cooper beginning in July.
Legal Counsel:	Roy L. Reardon, Esquire and John Cambria, Esquire.
GP Supervisors:	Ken Farrar, Chief, Kurt Nielsen, Franco Bartoni, Keith Johnson, Bill Gilmour and Roy Dance.

1983 Major Player Representatives

ProServ:	Principals: Donald Dell and Ray Benton.
Advantage Int'l:	Principals: Frank Craighill, Lee Fentress, Dean Smith and Peter Lawler.
IMG:	Principals: Mark McCormack and Bob Kain.
Others:	Ion Tiriac and Thomas Betz, Esquire (Vilas).
	John McEnroe, Sr., Esquire (McEnroe)
	Gloria Connors and Joseph Rountree, Esquire (Connors).

Three Competitions

In 1983, the 15th year of Open Tennis, there were three organized competitions for men: Volvo Grand Prix, WCT and the Davis Cup. Davis Cup was open to all players and was won by Australia over Sweden 3-2. There were 73 Volvo Grand Prix Open prize money tournaments, including the year-end Volvo Masters in Madison Square Garden in New York City. Included in the 73 tournaments were the four Grand Slams and 28 Super Series tournaments with $200,000+ in prize money. There were 29 Super Series in 1982, but Frankfurt withdrew for 1983. The Volvo Masters was again staged at Madison Square Garden and won by John McEnroe over Ivan Lendl 6-3, 6-4, 6-4 and the doubles was won by McEnroe and Peter Fleming over Pavel Slozil and Tomas Smid 6-2, 6-2.

In 1983, WCT staged only nine tournaments: (i) January 9, London, $200,000, Barratt World Doubles, (ii) January 30, Detroit, $250,000, WCT Winter Finals (for 1982 mini-circuit), (iii) February 13, Richmond, $300,000, United Virginia Bank Classic, (iv) February 28, Delray Beach, $300,000, Gold Coast Cup, (v) March 20, Munich, $300,000, Munich Cup, (vi) April 10, Houston, $300,000, (vii) April 17, Hilton Head, $250,000, WCT Spring Finals, (viii) May 1, Dallas, $300,000, WCT Finals and (ix) May 8, Forest Hills, $300,000, Mercedes Tournament of Champions.

In 1983, the ATP was involved in eight events: (i) January 29, Sao Paulo, $200,000 Hollywood Classic, (ii) April 10, Lisbon, (replacing 1982 Monterrey) $250,000 Lights Cup, (iii) April 24, Las Vegas, $350,000 ATP Alan King Classic at Caesar's Palace, (iv) May 9, Dusseldorf, $450,000 Ambre Solaire ATP World Team Cup in Dusseldorf, (v) June 12, London, $150,000 Stella Artois Queens ATP Grass-Court Championships, (vi) June 19, Bristol, $100,000 Lambert and Butler Championships, (vii) August 21, Cincinnati, US $300,000 ATP Championships and (viii) November 13, London, $250,000 ATP Benson and Hedges Championships at Wembley. The Sawgrass ATP-Lipton World Doubles was not staged. All of the ATP tournaments were in the Grand Prix, except for the World Team Cup.

Rules

For 1983, the player commitment was changed from 10 tournaments, not counting the French Open, Wimbledon or the U.S. Open, to 12 self-designations including the Grand Slams. To balance the tournament fields, up to three substitutions could be made by an allocation committee consisting of the Administrator and a Player Representative (which usually meant just me as "the bad guy") appointed by the MIPTC. Players could veto two substitutions, but the allocation committee could then select replacements. Players could play in eight special events in Super Series weeks, four in another continent and none within 100 miles and 30 days before or after a Super Series tournament. Players refusing to sign the player commitment could not play in any Volvo Grand Prix tournaments, even as a qualifier, except Grand Slams could offer a wild card to a 1980, 1981 or 1982 singles winner.[472]

For the first time, each tournament was required to include "one (1) full page of editorial identifying the members of the MIPTC and its staff and describing the role of the MIPTC as the governing body of the Volvo Grand Prix." I remember asking Chris Gorringe, the Chief Executive of Wimbledon, to include the MIPTC in the 1983 Wimbledon Program. Chris's response to me was "no problem, Marshall, as long as we did it last year." Trying to get Wimbledon to do anything new required a lot of persuasion. For Wimbledon to include the MIPTC for the very first time in the Wimbledon program would have been something very new and Wimbledon did not include anything until several years later.

MIPTC International Chair Umpires Required for the First Time!

In the 1983 MIPTC Yearbook, we listed the names and addresses of 188 certified MIPTC international officials and 18 officials pending certification for a total of 206. For 1983, each Volvo Grand Prix tournament was required to have a MIPTC certified referee and a minimum number of MIPTC certified chair umpires:

128	Draw	8 MIPTC International Officials
64	Draw	4 MIPTC International Officials
48	Draw	3 MIPTC International Officials
32	Draw	2 MIPTC International Officials

This was important for the development of professional officiating. It gave status to the officials who had attended the MIPTC Schools and who had earned the MIPTC certification from the Grand Prix Supervisors. It also created a market for their employment by the Volvo Grand Prix tournaments. *The importance of this action cannot be overstated. Guess who every professional tennis player wanted in the chair for his match – a MIPTC certified official is the correct answer!*

1983 Tournament Financial Commitments

The new five-year contract between the MIPTC and the ATP required the MIPTC to provide the ATP with the following: Grand Slams - $25,000 each, Super/Doubles Series - $15,000 each, Open Week/Regular Series - $3,000 each. Three maxims in professional tennis were recognized: (i) You can never reduce the current prize money levels to pay money to the ATP, (ii) Tournaments will not pay money for the ATP unless they can call it and advertise it as prize money for players and (iii) If you increase the prize money and pay the increase to the ATP, the tournaments will not object because they can call it and advertise it as prize money. As a result, for 1983, the minimum prize money levels for Super Series and the Doubles Series was increased by $15,000 and the minimum prize money levels for the Open Week and Regular Week Series was increased by $3,000 all to be paid to the ATP. And while we were at it, we permitted the tournaments to add their Bonus Pool contributions to their prize money and advertise it as "Player Compensation."

1983 MIPTC Tournament Regulations Provided for the First Time Uniform Regulations Applicable to all Professional Tournaments

For the first time, the new uniform MIPTC Tournament Regulations were applicable to all Volvo Grand Prix tournaments, all Challenger Series tournaments and all Satellite Series tournaments. The MIPTC Code was applicable to all of them and the ATP Computer Rankings System was the "system of merit" for all of them.

MIPTC Supervisors at Challenger, Satellite Series Required

Each Challenger Series tournament was required to have a certified MIPTC International Official serve as the MIPTC Supervisor and each Satellite Series tournament was required to have a certified MIPTC International Official as the MIPTC Supervisor. At the Satellites, we permitted the MIPTC Supervisor to also be the tournament referee. This is the first time that MIPTC certified officials were required at Challenger and Satellite level tournaments as part of the new uniform rules. Each MIPTC Supervisor had the power to issue on-site misconduct fines.

1983 MIPTC Code of Conduct Applies Everywhere

In 1983, for the first time, the MIPTC Code of Conduct applied to the Challenger Series and the Satellite Series in addition to the Volvo Grand Prix and also to the Davis

Cup, Kings Cup and World Team Cup. The MIPTC Code was the exclusive basis for disciplinary action against any player or MIPTC sanctioned or recognized tournament, team competition or other event.

The Point Penalty System was reduced to just four steps: Warning, Point, Game, Default.

MIPTC Meetings

In 1983, the MIPTC held six meetings: January 19-22 in New York, March 28-31 in Monte Carlo, June 6-9 in Paris, June 25-27 in London, August 25-30 and September 4 and 7 in New York and November 7-10 in Stockholm.

MIPTC Meeting, New York January 19-22, 1983

Davies Replaces Buchholz

In January in New York, Butch Buchholz submitted his resignation and Mike Davies, as successor ATP Executive Director, was duly elected to succeed him on the MIPTC.

ATP Players Championship – The Players' Grand Slam"

Per its contract dated August 30, 1982 with ATP, the Council approved a sanction to ATP for a two-week tournament for men and women to be scheduled between February 15 and April 1, commencing in 1985. This was to be the "Player's (men's and women's) grand slam" which the players were supposed to develop and use to raise their own funds, instead of seeking more funds from the Grand Slams. *Yea, for the "Players' grand slam" which they could build over the years to fund both the ATP and the WTA! Did this happen?*[473]

MIPTC Meeting, Monte Carlo March 28-31, 1983

Monte Carlo and Easter Date Finally Settled for the Future

In March in Monte Carlo,[474] the demand of Monte Carlo to be scheduled in the week of Easter continued to cause an annual scheduling nightmare. Monte Carlo requested the Easter week again for 1984. The Council voted to calendar Monte Carlo for the Easter week of April 16-22, 1984, upon condition that Monte Carlo agreed to accept a firm date for 1985 as determined by the Council to be in the best interest of the circuit and which may or may not be during the week of Easter. This action finally provided the Council with the ability to make a more reasonable and certain calendar for tournaments during this time period in 1985 and the future.

MIPTC Meeting, Paris June 6-9, 1983

Ashe Resigns – Smith Succeeds

In June in Paris, Arthur Ashe submitted his resignation and was replaced by Stan Smith. Ashe sent a brief hand-written letter[475] to Philippe Chatrier saying: "After much reflection, I feel I must resign from the MIPTC. I was simply doing a bit too much but my resignation in no way reflects a lack of interest on my part. I fervently hope the Council maintains its integrity in both body and principle. *For it may be, to paraphrase a statement concerning the U.S. Constitution, 'the last best hope for tennis' – for a while. Good Luck to all of you.*"

MIPTC Officials Program to be Independent of National Associations

I reported that the European Tennis Association and several European National Associations had objected to the selection and certification of officials by the MIPTC. The Council approved the continued policy of independence and selection of officials solely upon merit. However, as Administrator I agreed to request the recommendation of each national association for applicants for MIPTC Schools from their respective countries for consideration by the Supervisors along with other information and evaluations that the Supervisors had with respect to such officials. *This policy of independence and selection only by merit was the only way to keep tennis politics out of the MIPTC Officials' program.*[476]

MIPTC Meeting, London June 25 and 27, 1983

1983 MIPTC Election, Mike Estep Failed to File Acceptance as a Candidate

In June in London,[477] I reported on the 1983 MIPTC election which was underway. The Tournament Representative nominees were: North America: Jack Kramer and Gene Scott, Europe: Clive Bernstein, Leo Heumer and Jacques Hermenjat, Rest of World: Brian Tobin and Graham Lovett. (Lars Myhrman did not seek re-election). The Player Representative nominees were: Mike Davies, Ray Moore and Stan Smith.

Mike Estep planned to run as a Player Representative candidate, but he had failed to "file his acceptance of nomination because he did not know it was required." Estep admitted that he had received the official notice of acceptance at his official address. Mike Davies moved "that the election for Player Representatives be interrupted and that a new election procedure be commenced, and such motion was duly seconded. After extensive discussion a vote was taken, and the motion failed." So, Estep could not become a candidate for this election. My assumption was that Estep hoped to replace Mike Davies; by asking for the interruption so Estep could be a candidate, Mike was trying to support Estep who was an important member of the ATP Board; of course, it was also important that the ATP Executive Director be a member of the MIPTC.

MIPTC Meeting, New York August 25-30, September 4, and 7, 1983

MIPTC Election Results

In August in New York[478] the results of the MIPTC election were reported: Tournament Representatives: Jack Kramer (North America), Jacques Hermenjat (Europe) and Brian Tobin (Rest of World). Player Representatives: Mike Davies, Ray Moore and Stan Smith. ITF Representatives: Philippe Chatrier, Derek Hardwick and Stan Malless. Graham Lovett, the tournament director for the Sydney Indoors who was independent of the LTAA and who lost to Brian Tobin, objected to Brian being a tournament candidate since he was a Vice President of the ITF as well as the President of the LTAA; Tobin usually voted with the three ITF members on the MIPTC.

MIPTC Meeting, London November 7-10, 1983

Election of Chairman

In November in London,[479] Philippe Chatrier was re-elected MIPTC Chairman by acclamation.

Roy Dance Hired as Sixth Grand Prix Supervisor

Roy Dance of Memphis TN was hired as the sixth Grand Prix Supervisor to replace Dick Roberson, effective February 22. Roy had attended the first MIPTC Officials School in Dallas in 1979 and he was one of the few MIPTC certified officials who was certified as a chair umpire, chief of umpires and referee. Roy had followed me as President of the Southern Tennis Association in 1978 and 1979 and had served as referee for the U.S. Indoors at Memphis and the ATP Championships at Cincinnati.[480]

ProServ Splits

The ProServ management company split. Donald Dell, Ray Benton and David Falk, along with Jerry Solomon, remained with ProServ. Frank Craighill, Lee Fentress and Dean Smith, along with Peter Lawler, founded Advantage International, a new sports management firm. While the joint press release stated that "they had the utmost professional respect and personal fondness for each other," it was not quite true. The real reason for the split was that Craighill and Fentress disagreed with the conflict of interest created when ProServ was representing players and also tournaments. Dell and Benton were adamant about continuing and increasing ProServ's involvement with tournaments. Craighill and Fentress did not want that conflict of interest any longer.[481]

Borg's Finale at Monte Carlo

Borg decided to retire and play only one tournament in 1983 at Monte Carlo. After going through the qualifying, he lost in the 1st round to 19-year-old Henri Leconte 4-6, 7-5, 7-6. Jane Gross quoted Borg in the *New York Times*[482]: "'I tried my best and everything, and now it's over,' Borg said. 'I feel good. When I wake up in the morning now, I know I don't have to go out and practice four or five hours.'"[483]

Philippe Chatrier was quoted in the *New York Times*[484]: "'His (Borg's) retirement should give cause for reflection on the circuit's physical and moral constraints,' Chatrier said. 'Borg simply cracked.' Chatrier rejected suggestions that the federation's decision last year to require Borg to play qualifying rounds had led to his decision to quit. 'He had already made his decision,' he said."

Tony Eugenio Succeeds Ted Daniel

Since my first employment contract beginning March 1 was for two years, in order to get really good Assistant Administrators to work with me, I decided to seek young lawyers knowledgeable in tennis to work for me for one year. My first Assistant Administrator was Mark Meyers from 1981-1982, and after Mark returned to New Orleans to resume the practice of law, Mark and I recruited Ted Daniel, another young lawyer, for 1982-1983. In January of 1983, my employment contract was extended for five more years, so, I had more flexibility in the hiring of Assistant Administrators in the future. In January, when we opened our new Paris office at Stade Roland Garros, I hired Paul Svehlik as the MIPTC European Assistant Administrator. Ted Daniel was finishing his year in August to return to Dallas to resume the practice of law, so,

Ted and I recruited Tony Eugenio to begin April 16. Tony was born in Chicago but grew up in Abilene and Corpus Christi. He had received a tennis scholarship to the University of Oklahoma and graduated in 1978 with a B.A. in Political Science. In the summer of 1977, Tony played on the Italian and Spanish satellite circuits. Following his graduation from Oklahoma, Tony enrolled at Southern Methodist University in Dallas and earned a joint Masters of Business Administration and Law Degree in May of 1982 and was admitted to the Texas Bar in 1982. For the preceding 15 months, Tony had been working for the accounting firm of Peat, Marwick and Mitchell in Dallas with plans to take the Certified Public Accountant examination in November. Tony was fluent in Spanish. I knew that Tony was going to be a great help to my fledgling administrative team.[485]

Bad Blood: Lendl and McEnroe

I always watched Connors vs. McEnroe matches and Lendl vs. McEnroe matches because they were all great players, they played their best against each other and they really disliked each other on the court. At the 1983 WCT Tournament of Champions at Forest Hills, Lendl assailed McEnroe publicly as reported by Neil Amdur in the *New York Times*[486]: "Ivan Lendl said last night that if tennis officials declined to discipline John McEnroe in their future matches, 'I will take it into my own hands.'" *There was always plenty of adrenaline in their matches.*

McEnroe Fined $1,000

In the quarterfinals of the Tournament of Champions against Tomas Smid, McEnroe was fined $1,000 for misconduct. Neil Amdur reported in the *New York Times*: "McEnroe intentionally drove a ball at Smid from close range, just missing him. Smid hit McEnroe in the side with a backhand over the net, and McEnroe called Smid a communist amid several obscenities resulting in a $1,000 fine."[487]

McEnroe and the Non-Seeing French Officials

As I left New York on May 27 for the French Open in Paris, the newspapers were full of reports of misconduct by McEnroe in his contentious five-set win over Ben Testerman, a 21-year-old American ranked No. 84 in the world on the previous day. The press reported audible obscenities and the physical abuse of a photographer. At Roland Garros, the French have small holes in the stadium court backdrops for photographers to shoot through. Apparently, McEnroe irritated with noise from a camera shoved the camera which unfortunately fell back into the photographer's face. No fine was issued for those actions and the only fine that had been issued against McEnroe for the Testerman match was $350 for abuse of balls at another time. The news reports stated that neither the chair umpire, the linesmen on the match or the MIPTC Supervisor watching the match personally heard or saw these incidents, so no violations of the Code were charged by them at that time. However, the press had made sure that everyone in the world knew about them.

When I arrived at the French Open the next day, I called the MIPTC Supervisors into my office and instructed them to investigate these incidents and take the appropriate action. At the conclusion of the investigation, McEnroe was fined $3,000 by the MIPTC Supervisors additionally for shoving the camera into the photographer's face and for verbal abuse during the Testerman match.

I called John McEnroe, Sr., in New York to inform him about the fines and explain to him that the reason it was necessary to have an investigation after the completion of the match was that even though John did not intend physical harm, his shoving the camera into the face of a photographer was so bad, I just could not let it go uninvestigated and not acted on later by the MIPTC Supervisors. To put it mildly, John Sr., was not pleased, but he did not file an appeal of the fines to me as the Administrator.[488]

30 Second Rule and Time for a Serious Player Inquiry

Everyone was unhappy with the slowness of tennis matches because of the abuse of the 30 seconds between points rule, which was more often than not misunderstood, misinterpreted and violated by players and chair umpires. So, I wrote an article for *International Tennis Weekly*[489] to clarify the rule for everyone once and for all. The most important point emphasized was that "the ball must actually be *struck* for the next point within the maximum of 30 seconds between points." Instructions were provided for short delays for a player to ask a question in a professional manner and for a chair umpire to respond.

CBS, Inc. vs. French Tennis Federation and National Broadcasting Company, Inc., Bad Faith in Negotiations

CBS had a contract to broadcast the French Open in 1980, 1981 and 1982. The French Open television rights (managed by FFT President Philippe Chatrier) were represented by Donald Dell of ProServ. When the FFT entered into a contract with NBC for 1983, CBS sued the FFT and NBC and obtained a preliminary injunction prohibiting the enforcement of the new NBC contract upon CBS's claim that ProServ had negotiated with NBC during CBS's exclusive negotiating period and ProServ had included a requirement in the first refusal offer to CBS that CBS promote NBC's telecast of Wimbledon, which was an unreasonable and bad faith requirement.[490] ProServ denied the charges, and a settlement was quietly reached before the matter became too messy. William Taafe reported in *Sports Illustrated*[491] that CBS was paid $117,000 in the settlement.

This Octopus Embraces All

William Taafe's article in *Sports Illustrated* was entitled "This Octopus Embraces All" and he remarked about Dell's conflicts of interest as a television commentator, player agent, etc.: "Now that Donald Dell has chalked up the French Open and set his sights on Wimbledon, his next commentating gig for NBC, the time is ripe for the TV question nobody seems willing to ask: Inasmuch as Dell serves as the agent for many of the players he covers for NBC, and recently delivered the French Open TV rights to the very network that employs him as an analyst, how can viewers be expected to buy a used commentary from this man? Let's put it another way. However insightful and articulate Dell may be – and he scores brilliantly on those counts, - is he credible? After all, he admits to having as many conflicts of interest as John McEnroe has disposable razors.

Dell's Washington, D.C. – based firm, ProServ Inc., handles the business affairs of Yannick Noah, Jimmy Connors, Tracy Austin and about half the remainder of the ATP printout sheets. He's the octopus of tennis, his tentacles reaching everywhere. ProServ administers the Grand Prix tour, the TV rights of which Dell peddles to the USA Cable Network, where he's also a commentator. He still appears on telecasts of events he sells to PBS. And yet we're supposed to believe that he can promote a tournament's interests, his players' interest, his own interests and the interests of unwitting viewers all at the same time.

Dell, the former Davis Cup Captain whose organizing talents helped usher in the age of Open tennis in the late 1960s, says the crucial point about such conflicts is disclosure. 'Tell 'em and forget it' is his motto. He doesn't worry if a player is (1) his, (2) somebody he'd like to have or (3) some ingrate who just crawled into another agent's embrace. Dell says, 'I try to call the match exactly as I see it.'"

Code of Conduct at Wimbledon

Before Wimbledon began, Sir Brian Burnett, Chairman of Wimbledon, Alan Mills, the new Wimbledon Referee, Kurt Nielsen, Grand Prix Supervisor and I met with 200 umpires and linesmen to discuss the enforcement of the Code of Conduct. Wimbledon had 20 MIPTC certified chair umpires and they were given priority for the officiating of the men's matches. We had six Grand Prix Supervisors at Wimbledon.[492]

Jimmy Connors $10,000 Fine

On April 4, 1983 Jimmy Connors was designated to play in Stockholm, but Connors instead played in a mixed doubles special event in Houston that week with Chris Evert. They won the mixed doubles tournament by defeating Andrea Jaeger and Roscoe Tanner 6-4, 6-2, 6-4 in the final. Connors was fined $10,000.[493]

Sun City Bophuthatswana Blockbuster

Jimmy Connors defeated Ivan Lendl, 7-5, 7-6 to win the $400,000 first prize in the four-player Sun City tennis exhibition on July 10. Lendl received $300,000. In the consolation match, Johan Kriek beat Kevin Curren 6-2, 6-0 and received $200,000. Curren's prize was $100,000. The Czechoslovak tennis authorities fined Lendl and suspended him from its Davis Cup team for playing this exhibition. Just picture that you are promoting a 64 draw Volvo Grand Prix Super Series with $300,000 in prize money ($75,000 to the winner) and someone promotes a 4 man special event like this in the same week with $400,000 to the winner in which wins or losses do not count against rankings. That is why there was always a big effort to try to limit the number of special events against Super Series weeks.[494]

David Cooper Hired as Assistant Administrator

I hired David Cooper so that when Ted Daniel left in August, I would have three Assistant Administrators, Paul Svehlik in Europe, plus Tony Eugenio and David Cooper in New York. David had earned a Bachelor of Arts degree in Environmental Studies/ Biology from Columbia University in 1980, where he was the captain of the Columbia tennis team. He had played on the French pro satellite circuit in the summers of 1980 and 1981, so he knew tennis. David graduated in May from the Indiana University School of Law and was scheduled to take the New York Bar Exam in July, after which he would work full time for the MIPTC in New York. I was delighted to now have three really good Assistant Administrators to take on the increasing work load of the Administrator's office.[495]

Decertification of 41 Officials

The requirements for the MIPTC certification of officials as a "MIPTC International Official" required attendance and passing of a MIPTC Officials School and working as a tennis official sufficiently to be evaluated by and recommended by the MIPTC Supervisors for certification. Upon certification, every MIPTC International Official was evaluated at every match at which he or she officiated. And every official had to take and pass a MIPTC officials' examination every year. In 1983, 41 MIPTC certified officials failed their new examinations so I had to withdraw their certifications. "I hated to do it," I was quoted saying in *International Tennis Weekly*[496]. "But we owe it to the players and the game to have the best officiating possible. The test is not easy, but we give everyone two chances and it's taken with the rule book open. Officials who have lost their certification can take the test again next year."

Mike Davies on the MIPTC Officials Program

Mike Davies wrote a long article in *International Tennis Weekly*[497] praising the MIPTC Officials Program and explaining to the players ATP's role in supporting it. "One of the by-products of the certification program was to remove control of court officials working Grand Prix tournaments from associations and local umpire groups with their attendant politics, a blow to the 'old boy network' and its resultant mediocrity," he wrote. "Another goal was to encourage tournament promoters to use qualified referees, umpires and linesmen, when the natural incentive is to get by as economically as possible. I think that all will agree that progress is being made toward those goals, but now a challenge is being mounted by those officials who either cannot pass the rigid tests required or those who perceive the certification program as a loss of their personal authority. Their egos simply will not let them admit that anyone else can judge whether they are competent officials…One Grand Prix Supervisor actually sees more tennis in a year than many officials see in a lifetime…We are making some headway in the battle for good officiating."

McEnroe at the U.S. Open

At the U.S. Open, John McEnroe defeated Trey Waltke 6-3, 5-7, 4-6, 6-0, 6-1 in 3 hours and 10 minutes and was fined $350 for ball abuse, $500 for verbal abuse and $1,000 for throwing sawdust at a spectator for a total of $1,850.[498]

David Gray Dies

Sadly, on September 3, 1983, David Gray, General Secretary of the ITF, died of cancer at age 55. David had just flown back to London from New York where he had been at the August 25-29 meetings of the MIPTC. David was one of the world's leading tennis writers with the *Guardian*, one of Britain's national newspapers, from 1956 to 1976. In 1976, David left the *Guardian* and was appointed general secretary of the ITF. David also served as the ITF Joint Secretary of the MIPTC until I was hired as MIPTC Administrator in 1981. He was inducted into the International Tennis Hall of Fame as a contributor in 1985.[499]

U.S. Open Fines

Jimmy Connors earned $120,000 for winning his fifth U.S. Open singles title in 1983, but he was fined $1,000 for one verbal obscenity during his four-set victory over Ivan Lendl in the final. There were 19 fines totaling $8,200 at the U.S. Open assessed against 13 male players during the qualifying and main draws. (five violations involving fines of $100 each, occurred alone in the qualifying rounds.) In 1982, six fines totaling $6,650 were levied and in 1981, there were nine fines for $3,600. I told the *New York Times*[500] that the increase in fines reflected an increased scrutiny being applied to the Code of Conduct: "I'll bet most people weren't even aware of the violations." "But our Supervisors were there and saw them." "The pendulum has swung." "And the enforcement is a lot better."

[Note: I would not learn about a secret injection into Connors foot during the match that permitted him to continue playing and winning the 1983 U.S. Open against Lendl until many years later].

Connors Wins U.S. Open with Secret Injection

At age 31, Jimmy Connors defeated Ivan Lendl 6-3, 6-7, 7-5, 6-0 to win the 1983 U.S. Open. At one set each Lendl double faulted leading 5-4 in the 3rd set and then choked losing the next nine games.

Donald Dell, Connors' agent at the time, described Jimmy's illegal injection in his 2009 book *"Never Make the First Offer"*. When Dell was informed that Jimmy wanted to default to Lendl in the final on account of a blood blister on his foot, he contacted a New York Jets' team trainer and persuaded Jimmy to play with a shot of Xylocaine (a souped up version of Novocaine) to deaden the pain in his foot. The problem was that the shot only lasted 1½ hours so Dell had to arrange for the trainer to provide a second shot during the match. At 2-1 in the third set, Connors was given a short bathroom break and

Dell had the trainer secretly meet him in the rest room and administer the second shot. Afterwards, Jimmy went on to win the match after Lendl choked. Connors confirmed this story in his 2012 book *The Outsider*.[501]

The second "secret" injection during a "bathroom break" for a faked upset stomach, was not allowed by any of the rules. At the 1983 U.S. Open, the MIPTC Supervisors were "advisors" to the U.S. Open Referee Bob Howe and the tournament committee headed by Tournament Chairman Bill Talbert. The "secret" injection was known only by Connors, Dell and the New York Jet trainer. According to Dell, Talbert "nodded" to permit the injection. It is unclear if Ken Farrar, one of my MIPTC Supervisors, actually knew what was happening. U.S. Open Referee Bob Howe was not mentioned. Dr. Irving Glick, the head U.S. Open doctor, apparently did not want to know about it. I did not learn about this secret injection until many years later when I read about it in Dell's 2009 book. It should not have been allowed.

Now guess who Lendl's agent was at the time. You guessed it... Donald Dell and ProServ, although Jerry Solomon of ProServ personally handled Lendl's representation. Lendl apparently never knew about Dell's actions for Connors until I told Jerry about in during my research for this book. It was not mentioned in later litigation between Lendl and ProServ.[502]

McEnroe Exceeds $7,500 Fine Limit and is Suspended

At the Sydney Indoors, John McEnroe defeated Henri Leconte 6-1, 6-4, 7-5 in the final. McEnroe was fined $1,500 for verbal abuse which brought his total for the year over $7,500 resulting in an automatic suspension of 21 days. *October of each year was always a favorite vacation time for John.*[503]

John McEnroe Tennis Over America Tour

In 1983, Steve Corey and Gary Swain continued to promote the John McEnroe Tennis Over America Tour with 18 matches mostly against Guillermo Vilas.[504]

ATP

ATP Members

At the end of 1983, the ATP had 330 members, 200 in its First Division.[505] All the world's leading players were members except four: Jimmy Connors, Guillermo Vilas, Vitas Gerulaitis and Jose-Luis Clerc.

Jaime Fillol ATP Pension Fund

"The Jaime Fillol Pension Fund" for ATP members was launched by Mike Davies with an initial contribution of $225,902 from the ATP Championships (Cincinnati) and scheduled for $80,000 per year through 1995. The pension plan was a first in professional tennis and was named in honor of Chile's Jaime Fillol, a founder and past president of the ATP.[506]

Ray Moore Succeeds Harold Solomon as ATP President

At the June ATP Annual Meeting in London during Wimbledon, Ray Moore, age 37, and a leading advocate of player rights throughout the Open Era, was elected to succeed Harold Solomon, who was retiring after three years as president. Mike Estep (current Treasurer and Chair of Computer Committee) was elected Vice President and re-elected as Treasurer. Jim McManus was re-elected as Secretary. Three new Board members elected were Paul McNamee, Ferdi Taygan and Jose Higueras to serve with Mark Edmondson, Stan Smith, Balazs Taroczy, Carlos Kirmayr and Rolf Gehring, plus Mike Davies as Executive Director.[507]

New Computer Rule

The ATP added a new computer rule that required that eligible tournaments had to be played under tournament regulations and a code of conduct approved by the ATP. This was obviously aimed at WCT which had created its own tournament regulations and code of conduct without the agreement or approval of the ATP.

Ray Moore Interviews

Moore spoke to *International Tennis Weekly*[508] about his goals with the ATP and his views on the professional tennis landscape. "My No. 1 goal is to make the ATP as powerful as possible," he said. "In order to do that, you have to unify the players...I think the majority of the membership would like us to leave (the Council), but that is mainly because the majority of the membership doesn't understand how the Council works. The Council works fairly well right now. The ATP has a lot of input into the decisions and there are very few votes that the players have lost over the last couple of years. That is what the general membership doesn't quite understand. Emotionally, the players just don't want to be allied or tied to the International Tennis Federation. That goes back to their weaning days. When you start off in tennis, the ITF is always there.

Players feel opposition toward the ITF. The ITF represents authority throughout their lives. It's a kind of rebellion against that authority."

"Something has to be done about the guarantee situation. The ATP officially can in no way, shape or form endorse guarantees paid under the table. The credibility of the game is at stake. Once you have a player receiving more money than the first prize to show, you have a real credibility problem with the public because even if a losing player does try 100 percent, you will never convince the public of that."

"I would like to see WCT back in the game. WCT brought with it a certain amount of expertise and professionalism. WCT has something to offer the game of tennis and we are sadder with it out of the game. I would like to see the sides sit down and talk about it."

1983 ATP JAKS AWARDS
(New York City January 1984)

Player of the Year	John McEnroe
Doubles Team of the Year	Peter Fleming – John McEnroe
Newcomer of the Year	Scott Davis
Most Improved Player of the Year	Jimmy Arias
ATP Sportsmanship Award	Jose Higueras
Great Player of the Past	Rod Laver
Media Service Award	Russ Adams
ATP Service Award	Paul Flory
Humanitarian Award	Alan King

Tennis's Sheriff

To emphasize the importance of curbing player misconduct for the new enforcement of the Code of Conduct, Dave Anderson interviewed me and wrote an article in the *New York Times*[509] about my role on behalf of the Council for the new enforcement of the Code of Conduct: "The most important person in tennis is not competing in the United States Open this week. The most important person in tennis

419

is a rangy 45-year-old North Carolina attorney with a soft Southern accent and a soft button-down shirt. M. Marshall Happer 3rd is the Administrator of the Men's International Professional Tennis Council, the closest thing to a commissioner that this fragmented and footloose sport has had in its 15 years of open tournaments. To some tennis people, Marshall Happer is known as 'Sheriff,' for the same reason Wyatt Earp was known as Marshal. Just as Dodge City attracted the gun-slinging outlaws of the old West, the boom of open tennis attracted racquet-slinging outlaws who have held up tournament promoters, abused officials and ripped off spectators. But now, with a new five-year contract that denotes not only the Council's support, but also his own commitment, Marshall Happer is slowly restoring law and order. 'The thing we're looking for,' he was saying yesterday in his midtown office, 'is reasonable order with a system that will last for a few hundred years. 'The top players think we're being too tough and the public feels we're being too lenient.'"

"'Appearance money is bad for the integrity of the sport,'" Marshall Happer said. 'If a guy is being paid $100,000 to show up for a tournament where the first prize is $32,000, it's wrong. I don't mind a player being paid big prize money, but I do mind a player being paid under the table and just for showing up. Instead of providing appearance money, a tournament should add that money to the prize money.'"

"Tennis has always had rules, but Marshall Happer appears to be the first administrator with the power, as well as the courage and the independence, to enforce those rules, whether the top players like it or not." "'In the past, the men's game was ruled part-time by the International Tennis Federation and part-time by the Association of Tennis Professionals, which created conflicts of interest,'. 'Needless to say, a lot of things were never done. But now it's a full-time effort by the total game rather than a portion of it. And the Council has been extremely good in backing me." "'I really think misbehavior is slowly coming under control. Two years ago, it was common to see misbehavior on almost every court at a big tournament. But that no longer happens. Now it's only a small number who have problems, but the public is more aware of that minority than it is of the overall change. What happened this year is that all the fines were collected out of a player's prize money immediately. The younger players quit misbehaving because they can't afford it. The top players, of course, can afford it.'"

"'For the last 10 years, the top players have been getting away with murder,' Marshall Happer said. 'So, this comes as shock to them. But our enforcement of the conduct code is really a long-term investment for the younger players' benefit. In the next generation we'll have a healthy sport.'"

Anderson concluded his story writing, "That's as close as the 'Sheriff' would come to acknowledging that tennis isn't healthy now, and won't be until the top players and the tournaments support him completely."

MIPTC Financials

The MIPTC began 1983 with a surplus of $788,890 and, after operating its New York and Paris offices and providing $3,000,000 in Bonus Pool awards to players in the Volvo Grand Prix, the MIPTC ended 1983 with a surplus of $674,388. The MIPTC collected and paid ATP prize money to the ATP of $535,000 for services to Volvo Grand Prix tournaments pursuant to its 1982 agreement covering 1983 to 1987. Volvo paid for its promotion as the Volvo Grand Prix sponsor and its promotion of the Volvo Grand Prix through ProServ. Volvo and ProServ promoted the Volvo Masters at Madison Square Garden, again telecast on NBC, and were responsible for all expenses and received all income. The operating expense included $442,367 in legal expenses of which $300,000 was paid to the ITF as a contribution towards the ITF and ATP legal expenses for the WCT lawsuit, thus creating a $114,502 deficit for the year. The MIPTC legal expenses for the WCT lawsuit were covered by insurance.[510]

1983 Grand Slam Winners

French Open

Yannick Noah d. Mats Wilander 6-2, 7-5, 7-6.
Anders Jarryd – Hans Simonsson d. Mark Edmondson – Sherwood Stewart 7-6, 6-4, 6-2.

Wimbledon

John McEnroe d. Chris Lewis 6-2, 6-2, 6-2.
Peter Fleming – John McEnroe d. Tim Gullikson – Tom Gullikson 6-4, 6-3, 6-4.

U.S. Open

Jimmy Connors d. Ivan Lendl 6-3, 6-7, 7-5, 6-0.
Peter Fleming – John McEnroe d. Fritz Buehning – Van Winitsky 6-3, 6-4, 6-2.

Australian Open

Mats Wilander d. Ivan Lendl 6-1, 6-4, 6-4.
Mark Edmonson – Paul McNamee d. Steve Denton – Sherwood Stewart 6-3, 7-6.

Volvo Masters

John McEnroe d. Ivan Lendl 6-3, 6-4, 6-4.
Peter Fleming - John McEnroe d. Pavel Slozil – Tomas Smid 6-2, 6-2.

1983 Davis Cup

Davis Cup Final (Melbourne - Grass)

Australia d. Sweden 3-2

Mats Wilander (SE) d. Pat Cash (AU) 6-3, 4-6, 9-7, 6-3.
John Fitzgerald (AU) d. Joakim Nystrom (SE) 6-4, 6-2, 4-6, 6-4.
Mark Edmondson – Paul McNamee (AU) d. Anders Jarryd – Hans Simonsson (SE) 6-4,
6-4 6-2.
Pat Cash (AU) d. Joakim Nystrom (SE) 6-4, 6-1, 6-1.
Mats Wilander (SE) d. John Fitzgerald (AU) 6-8, 6-1, 6-0.

1983 World Team Cup

Spain d. Australia 2-1.

Jose Higueras (ES) d. Mark Edmondson (AU) 6-2, 6-4.
Manual Orantes(ES) d. Pat Cash (AU) 6-3, 6-2.
Pat Cash – Mark Edmondson (AU) d. Angel Gimenez – Jose Higueras (ES) 7-5, 4-6, 6-1.

1983 World Rankings[511]

Bud Collins	Lance Tingay	
1. John McEnroe	1. John McEnroe	1. John McEnroe
2. Ivan Lendl	2. Jimmy Connors	2. Ivan Lendl
3. Jimmy Connors	3. Ivan Lendl	3. Jimmy Connors
4. Mats Wilander	4. Mats Wilander	4. Mats Wilander
5. Yannick Noah	5. Yannick Noah	5. Yannick Noah

6. Jimmy Arias	6. Jimmy Arias	6. Jimmy Arias
7. Jose Higueras	7. Jose Higueras	7. Jose Higueras
8. Jose-Luis Clerc	8. Guillermo Vilas	8. Jose-Luis Clerc
9. Kevin Curren	9. Jose-Luis Clerc	9. Kevin Curren
10. Gene Mayer	10. Vitas Gerulaitis	10. Gene Mayer

1983 Volvo Grand Prix Bonus Pool Top 10[512]

Singles (14th Bonus Pool)			Doubles (9th Bonus Pool)		
1.	Mats Wilander	$600,000	1.	Peter Fleming	$150,000
2.	Ivan Lendl	$400,000	2.	Sherwood Stewart	$100,000
3.	John McEnroe	$300,000	3.	Mark Edmondson	$ 75,000
4.	Jimmy Connors	$200,000	4.	John McEnroe	$ 60,000
5.	Yannick Noah	$100,000	5.	Tim Gullikson	$ 45,000
6.	Jimmy Arias	$ 80,000	6.	Steve Denton	$ 35,000
7.	Jose Higueras	$ 65,000	7.	Tom Gullikson	$ 25,000
8.	Andres Gomez	$ 55,000	8.	Hans Simonsson	$ 20,000
9.	Jose-Luis Clerc	$ 45,000	9.	Anders Jarryd	$ 17,000
10.	Eliot Teltscher	$ 37,000	10.	Pavel Slozil	$ 15,000

1983 Official Earnings Top 10[513]

1.	Ivan Lendl	$ 1,747,128	6.	Tomas Smid	$ 457,886
2.	John McEnroe	$ 1,206,844	7.	Yannick Noah	$ 378,394
3.	Mats Wilander	$ 1,119,650	8.	Jimmy Arias	$ 340,033
4.	Guillermo Vilas	$ 677,035	9.	Brian Teacher	$ 332,948
5.	Jimmy Connors	$ 598,047	10.	Kevin Curren	$ 306,852

1983 Tournament Calendar

Date	Tournaments	Singles Winner	Singles #2	Doubles Winners	Doubles #2
1/9/1983	London $300,000 WCT			H. Gunthardt - B. Taroczy	B. Gottfried - R. Ramirez
1/16/1983	Auckland $75,000 GP	John Alexander	Russell Simpson	C. Lewis - R. Simpson	D. Graham - L. Warder
1/29/1983	Sao Paulo $200,000 SS	Jose-Luis Clerc	Mats Wilander	Tim Gullikson - T. Smid	S. Glickstein - V. Winitsky
1/30/1983	Detroit $250,000 WCT	Ivan Lendl	Guillermo Vilas	7-5, 6-2, 2-6, 6-4	
2/6/1983	Philadelphia $300,000 SS	John McEnroe	Ivan Lendl	K. Curren - S. Denton	P. Fleming - J. McEnroe
2/6/1983	Caracas $75,000 GP	Raul Ramirez	Morris Strode	J. Fillol - S. Smith	A. Gomez - I. Nastase
2/13/1983	Richmond $300,000 WCT	Guillermo Vilas	Steve Denton	P. Slozil - T. Smid	F. Buehning - B. Teacher
2/13/1983	Toronto $250,000 SP	Jimmy Connors	Jose Higueras	6-2, 6-0, 5-7, 6-0	
2/20/1983	Memphis $300,000 SS	Jimmy Connors	Gene Mayer	P. McNamara - P. McNamee	T. Gullikson - T. Gullikson
2/20/1983	Vina Del Mar $75,000 GP	Victor Pecci	Jaime Fillol	H. Gildemeister - B. Prajoux	J. Goes - N. Keller
2/27/1983	Palm Springs $200,000 SS	Jose Higueras	Eliot Teltscher	B. Gottfried - R. Ramirez	T. Viljoen - D. Visser
2/27/1983	Delray Beach $300k WCT	Guillermo Vilas	Pavel Slozil	P. Slozil - T. Smid	An. Amritraj - J. Kriek
2/27/1983	Kuwait City $75,000 GP	Vitas Gerulaitis	Heinz Gunthardt	V. Amritraj - I. Nastase	B. Dyke - R. Frawley
3/6/1983	Monterey $75,000 GP	Sammy Giammalva	Ben Testerman	D. Dowlen - N. Odizor	A. Andrews - J. Sadri
3/13/1983	Brussels $250,000 SS	Peter McNamara	Ivan Lendl	H. Gunthardt - B. Taroczy	H. Simonsson - M. Wilander
3/13/1983	Nancy $75,000 GP	Nick Saviano	Chip Hooper	J. Gunnarsson - A. Jarryd	R. Acuna - B. Prajoux
3/20/1983	Rotterdam $250,000 SS	Gene Mayer	Guillermo Vilas	F. Buehning - Tom Gullikson	P. Fleming - P. Slozil
3/20/1983	Munich $300,000 WCT	Brian Teacher	Mark Dickson	K. Curren - S. Denton	H. Gunthardt - B. Taroczy
3/27/1983	Milan $250,000 SS	Ivan Lendl	Kevin Curren	P. Slozil - T. Smid	F. Buehning - P. Fleming

3/27/1983	Nice $75,000 GP	Henrix Sundstrom	Manuel Orantes	B. Boileau - L. Pimek	B. Fritz - J. Hallet
4/3/1983	Monte Carlo $300,000 SS	Mats Wilander	Mel Purcell	H. Gunthardt - B. Taroczy	H. Leconte - Y. Noah
4/10/1983	Lisbon $250,000 SS/ATP	Mats Wilander	Yannick Noah	C. Kirmayr - C. Motta	P. Slozil - F. Taygan
4/10/1983	Houston $300,000 WCT	Ivan Lendl	Paul McNamee	K. Curren - S. Denton	M. Dickson - T. Smid
4/11/1983	Tokyo $300,000 SP	Jimmy Connors	Bjorn Borg	6-3, 6-4	
4/17/1983	Los Angeles $200,000 SS	Gene Mayer	Johan Kriek	P. Fleming _ J. McEnroe	S. Mayer - F. Taygan
4/17/1983	Aix-en-Prov. $75,000 GP	Mats Wilander	Sergio Casal	H. Leconte - G. Moretton	I. Camus - S. Casal
4/17/1983	Hilton Head $250,000 WCT	Ivan Lendl	Guillermo Vilas		
4/24/1983	Las Veg. $350,000 SS/ATP	Jimmy Connors	Mark Edmondson	K. Curren - S. Denton	T. Delatte - J. Kriek
4/24/1983	Bournemouth $125,000 GP	Jose Higueras	Tomas Smid	T. Smid - S. Stewart	H. Gunthardt - B. Taroczy
5/1/1983	Madrid ES $200,000 SS	Yannick Noah	Hendrix Sundstrom	H. Gunthardt - P. Slozil	M. Gunthardt - Z. Kuharszky
5/1/1983	Tampa $100,000 GP	Johan Kriek	Bob Lutz	T. Giammalva - S. Meister	E. Fromm - D. Gitlin
5/1/1983	Dallas $300,000 WCT Finals	John McEnroe	Ivan Lendl	6-2, 4-6, 6-3, 6-7, 7-6	
5/8/1983	NY $300,000 TC WCT	John McEnroe	Vitas Gerulaitis	T. Delatte - J. Kriek	K. Curren - S. Denton
5/9/1983	D'dorf $450,000 WTC ATP	Spain	Australia	2-1,	
5/9/1983	D'dorf $450,000 WTC ATP	Jose Higueras	Mark Edmondson	6-2, 6-4	
5/9/1983	D'dorf $450,000 WTC ATP	Manuel Orantes	Pat Cash	6-3, 6-2	
5/9/1983	D'dorf $450,000 WTC ATP		7-5, 4-6, 6-1	P. Cash - M. Edmondson	A. Gimenez - J. Higueras
5/15/1983	Hamburg $250,000 SS	Yannick Noah	Jose Higueras	H. Gunthardt - B. Taroczy	M. Edmondson - B. Gottfried
5/15/1983	Florence $75,000 GP	Jimmy Arias	Francesco Cancellotti	F. Gonzalez - V. Pecci	D. Bedel - B. Fritz
5/15/1983	Tulsa US RR SP	Jimmy Connors	Roscoe Tanner		
5/22/1983	Rome $300,000 SS	Jimmy Arias	Jose Higueras	F. Gonzalez - V. Pecci	J. Gunnarsson - M. Leach

5/22/1983	Munich $75,000 GP	Tomas Smid	Joakim Nystrom	C. Lewis - P. Slozil	A. Jarryd - T. Smid
6/5/1983	French Open 4,382,812 FF GS	Yannick Noah	Mats Wilander	A. Jarryd - H. Simonsson	M. Edmondson - S. Stewart
6/5/1983	Beckenham	Steve Dentorn	Pat Cash		
6/12/1983	London $150,000 GP/ATP	Jimmy Connors	John McEnroe	B. Gottfried - P. McNamee	K. Curren - S. Denton
6/12/1983	Venice $75,000 GP	Roberto Arguello	Jimmy Brown	F. Gonzalez - V. Pecci	S. Krulevitz - Z. Kuharszky
6/19/1983	Bristol $100,000 GP/ATP	Johan Kriek	Tom Gullikson	J. Alexander - J. Fitzgerald	Tom Gullikson - J. Kriek
7/3/1983	Wimbledon 443,806£ GS	John McEnroe	Chris Lewis	P. Fleming - J. McEnroe	T. Gullikson - T. Gullikson
7/10/1983	Newport $100,000 GP	John Fitzgerald	Scott Davis	V. Amritraj - J. Fitzgerald	T. Gullikson - T. Gullikson
7/10/1983	Gstaad $100,000 GP	Sandy Mayer	Tomas Smid	P. Slozil - T. Smid	C. Dowdeswell - W. Fibak
7/10/1983	Sun City $1,000,000 RR SP	Jimmy Connors	Johan Kriek	Kevin Curren	Ivan Lendl
7/17/1983	Bastad $75,000 GP	Mats Wilander	Anders Jarryd	J. Nystrom - M. Wilander	A. Jarryd - H. Simonsson
7/17/1983	Boston $200,000 SS	Jose-Luis Clerc	Jimmy Arias	M. Dickson - C. Motta	H. Gildemeister - B. Prajoux
7/17/1983	Stuttgart $100,000 SP	Jose Higueras	Heinz Gunthardt	A. Amritraj - M. Bauer	P. Slozil - T. Smid
7/24/1983	Kitzbuhel $100,000 GP	Guillermo Vilas	Henri Leconte	W. Fibak - P. Slozil	C. Dowdeswell - Z. Kuharszky
7/24/1983	Hilversum $75,000 GP	Tomas Smid	Balazs Taroczy	H. Gunthardt - B. Taroczy	J. Kodes - T. Smid
7/25/1983	Washington $200,000 SS	Jose-Luis Clerc	Jimmy Arias	M. Dickson - C. Motta	P. McNamee - F. Taygan
7/31/1983	South Orange $75,000 GP	Brad Drewett	John Alexander	F. Buehning - T. Cain	J. Lloyd - D. Stockton
7/31/1983	Beaver Creek SP	Jimmy Connors	Mats Wilander	7-6, 6+-2	
8/1/1983	North Conway $200,000 SS	Jose-Luis Clerc	Andres Gomez	M. Edmondson - S. Stewart	C. Motta - F. Taygan
8/7/1983	Indianapolis $300,000 SS	Jimmy Arias	Andres Gomez	M. Edmondson - S. Stewart	C. Kimayr - C. Motta
8/7/1983	Columbus $100,000 GP	Brian Teacher	Bill Scanlon	S. Davis - B. Teacher	V. Amritraj - J. Fitzgerald
8/7/1983	Newport Beach SP	Jimmy Connors	Tim Mayotte	6-3, 6-4, 6-2	

8/15/1983	Montreal $450,000 SS	Ivan Lendl	Anders Jarryd	S. Mayer - F. Taygan	T. Gullikson - T. Gullikson
8/21/1983	Cincy $300,000 SS/ATP	Mats Wilander	John McEnroe	V. Amaya - Tom Gullikson	C. Kimayr - C. Motta
8/21/1983	Stowe US $75,000 GP	John Fitzgerald	Vijay Amritraj	B. Drewett - K. Warwick	F. Buehning - T. Gullikson
8/27/1983	Rye $50,000 SP	Vitas Gerulaitis	Jimmy Arias		
8/28/1983	Jericho SP	Gene Mayer	Heinz Gunthardt	6-7, 6-4, 6-0	
9/11/1983	US Open $800,000 GS	Jimmy Connors	Ivan Lendl	P. Fleming - J. McEnroe	F. Buehning - V. Winitsky
9/18/1983	Dallas $250,000 SS	Andres Gomez	Brian Teacher	N. Odizor - V. Winitsky	S. Denton - S. Stewart
9/18/1983	Palermo $100,000 GP	Jimmy Arias	Jose-Luis Clerc	P. Arraya - J. L. Clerc	T. Viljoen - D. Visser
9/25/1983	San Francisco $200,000 SS	Ivan Lendl	John McEnroe	P. Fleming - J. McEnroe	I. Lendl - V. Van Patten
9/25/1983	Geneva $75,000 GP	Mats Wilander	Henrix Sundstrom	S. Bimer - B. Willenborg	J. Nystrom - M. Wilander
9/25/1983	Bordeaux $75,000 GP	Pablo Arraya	Juan Aguilera	S. Simonsson - M. Tideman	C. Castellan - M. Jaite
10/2/1983	Maui $100,000 GP	Scott Davis	Vince Van Patten	T. Giammalva - S. Meister	M. Bauer - S. Davis
10/9/1983	Brisbane $100,000 GP	Pat Cash	Paul McNamee	P. Cash - P. McNamee	M. Edmondson - K. Warwick
10/9/1983	Barcelona $200,000 SS	Mats Wilander	Guillermo Vilas	A. Jarryd - H. Simonsson	J. Gurfein - E. Iskersky
10/16/1983	Sydney $200,000 SS	John McEnroe	Henri Leconte	M. Edmondson - S. Stewart	J. McEnroe - P. Rennert
10/16/1983	Basle $100,000 GP	Vitas Gerulaitis	Wojtek Fibak	P. Slozil - T. Smid	S. Edberg - F. Segarceanu
10/16/1983	Tel Aviv IS $75,000 GP	Aaron Krickstein	Christophe Zipf	C. Dowdeswell - Z. Kuharszky	P. Elter - P. Feigl
10/23/1983	Vienna $100,000 GP	Brian Gottfried	Mel Purcell	M. Purcell - S. Smith	M. Hocevar - C. Motta
10/23/1983	Tokyo $125,000 GP	Eliot Teltscher	Andres Gomez	S. Giammalva - S. Meister	T. Gullikson - T. Gullikson
10/23/1983	Sydney Non GP	Simon Youl	Rod Frawley	M. Fancutt - W. Masur	P. Carter - M. Kratzmann
10/30/1983	Tokyo $300,000 SS	Ivan Lendl	Scott Davis	M. Edmondson - S. Stewart	S. Denton - J. Fitgerald
10/30/1983	Cologne $75,000 GP	Matt Doyle	Hans-Dieter Beutel	N. Saviano - F. Segarceanu	P. Annacone - E. Korita

11/6/1983	Stockholm $250,000 SS	Mats Wilander	Tomas Smid	A. Jarryd - H. Simonsson	P. Fleming - J. Kriek
11/6/1983	Hong Kong $100,000 GP	Wally Masur	Sammy Giammal-va	D. Gitlin - C. Miller	S. Giammalva - S. Meister
11/13/1983	London $250,000 SS/ATP	John McEnroe	Jimmy Connors	P. Fleming - J. McEnroe	S. Denton - S. Stewart
11/13/1983	Tapei $75,000 GP	Nduka Odisor	Scott Davis	W. Masur - K. Warwick	K. Flach - R. Seguso
11/20/1983	Ferrara $75,000 GP	Thomas Hogstedt	Butch Walts	B. Mitton - B. Walts	S. Bimer - S. Simonsson
11/20/1983	Antwerp $750,000 SP	John McEnroe	Gene Mayer	6-4, 6-3, 6-4	
11/27/1983	Johannesburg $300,000 SS	Johan Kriek	Colin Dowdeswell	S. Meister - B. Teacher	A. Gomez - S. Stewart
11/27/1983	Toulouse $100,000 GP	Heinz Gunthardt	Pablo Arraya	H. Gunthardt - P. Slozil	B. Mitton - B. Walts
11/27/1983	Bahia $75,000 GP	Pedro Rebolledo	Julio Goes	P. Barbosa - J. Soares	J. Goes - N. Keller
12/11/1983	Australian Open $502,400 GS	Mats Wilander	Ivan Lendl	M. Edmondson - P. McNamee	S. Denton - S. Stewart
12/18/1983	Sydney $125,000 GP	Joakim Nystrom	Mike Bauer	P. Cash - M. Bauer	B. Dyke - R. Frawley
12/19/1983	Miami Nastase SP	Jimmy Connors	Ivan Lendl	6-3, 7-6, 6-1	
1/1/1984	Melbourne $75,000 GP	Pat Cash	Rod Frawley		
1/4/1984	Adelaide $75,000 GP	Mike Bauer	Miloslav Mecir	C. Miller - E. Sherbeck	B. Dyke - R. Frawley
1/15/1984	NY $400,000 Volvo Masters	John McEnroe	Ivan Lendl	P. Fleming - J. McEnroe	P. Slozil - T. Smid

http://www.atpworldtour.com/en/scores/results-archive.

http://www.itftennis.com/procircuit/tournaments/men's-calendar.aspx?tour=&reg=&nat=&sur=&cate=AL&iod=&-fromDate=01-01-1968&toDate=29-12-1983.

Tennis History, Jim McManus, (Canada 2010).

1984 USLTA Yearbook.

Official 1989 MTC Media Guide, (MTC 1989).

World of Tennis 1984, Edited by John Barrett and compiled by Lance Tingay, (London 1984).

CHAPTER 20:

1983: NOAH, NASTASE AND VILAS MAJOR OFFENSE CASES

Tournament Offense No. 2: Stuttgart Continued

Stuttgart requested approval for the week of July 11-17, but had an outstanding fine of $17,000. At the January 19-22 meeting of the MIPTC in New York, the Council agreed to approve Stuttgart for the week of July 11-17, 1983, provided that it paid a reduced fine of $10,000 and reorganized its Mercedes offers for the benefit of all players, whether of not they played in Stuttgart. Stuttgart rejected that compromise offer and its proposed sanction for 1983 was withdrawn.[514]

Major Offense No. 6: Van Winitsky, 1983 Antigua

Van Winitsky, then ranked No. 35 in the world, had signed a Player Commitment and was participating in the 1983 Volvo Grand Prix. During the week of January 4-8, Winitsky was one of 12 professional tennis players who participated in the non-MIPTC sanctioned $14,000 prize money tournament known as the "Circle Line Tournament" staged at the Half Moon Bay Hotel on the Island of Antigua in the Caribbean Sea as part of "Antigua Tennis Week" promoted by Gene Scott and *Tennis Week*. Winitsky got into an altercation with one of the 500 fans at the tournament. He, as documented by Richard Evans in *Tennis Week*[515], "jumped the courtside railing with his racquet and began swinging it at that spectator. Although he missed the spectator who had thrown the ball, Winitsky did hit another spectator before he was physically restrained, led from the court and defaulted."

My Determination dated March 23, 1983[516] was that Winitsky was guilty of the Major Offense of "Conduct Contrary to the Integrity of Game" and I suspended him "from all MIPTC sanctioned or recognized events for a period of thirty-five days." On April 11, Winitsky waived his right to appeal my Determination and the suspension began. This was the first and only Code of Conduct case I ever had to apply the Code at a non-MIPTC sanctioned tournament. I concluded that since Winitsky had signed the 1983 Player Commitment for the Volvo Grand Prix on September 7, 1982, he had agreed to be subject to the Code as a tennis professional. The incident had been widely reported in the press and throughout the tennis community.

Tournament Offense No. 4: 1982 Johannesburg

The 1982 Johannesburg Super Series tournament was known as the Altech South African Open and was owned and controlled by the South African Tennis Union (SATU). The week before the 1982 Johannesburg tournament, the SATU promoted a "Standard Bank Cup" special event by paying appearance fees to teams from the United States, Spain, Great Britain and South Africa. The players in the special event also played in the 1982 Johannesburg Super Series. The Standard Bank Cup had been staged by the SATU on other dates as a special event since 1979, but in 1982 it was obviously being used to get players for the Johannesburg Super Series. On July 28, I issued my Determination[517] that "the operation of this special event under the circumstances described herein is an inducement in violation of Section V.A. (prohibition against the payment of guarantees) of the Code" and I issued a fine of $20,000. Obviously, if a tournament could stage an exhibition or other special event and pay huge amounts to its top players to compete in both the special event and the Grand Prix tournament, the prohibition against guarantees would be subverted. At the November 7-10 meeting in London[518], the Council heard Johannesburg's appeal and reduced the fine from $20,000 to $5,000. The members of the Council knew how difficult it was for Johannesburg to get any players to travel to South Africa to play in their tournament on account of the South African racial policy of Apartheid and the blacklisting of players by countries opposed to Apartheid.

Major Offense No. 7: Yannick Noah, 1983 World Team Cup

The 1983 ATP-Ambre Solaire World Team Cup held in Dusseldorf, West Germany, on May 2-9 was an international team event organized by the ATP and played by eight teams from different countries throughout the world. Included among the eight participant teams was France, whose individual members were Yannick Noah, Dominique Bedel and Bernard Fritz. The total compensation potentially available at the World Team Cup was $1,001,000, consisting of $420,000 in prize money, individual prize money of $30,000 and potential ATP ranking bonus payments in the amount of $464,000. Each individual player, including Noah, signed an official entry form, agreeing among other things, to be available to compete in the event beginning May 2, and continuing for eight consecutive days through Monday, May 9. This was the first year that the World

Team Cup was subject to the MIPTC Code of Conduct and Noah agreed in his entry form to be subject to the Code. Noah's agent at the time was Pierre Darmon of ProServ.

On Thursday evening, May 5, after his match against Jose Higueras in the France-Spain tie, Noah returned to Paris without notifying the tournament committee. However, Noah's agent confirmed that Noah would be in Dusseldorf in time for his scheduled 1:00 PM Saturday match against Damir Keretic of West Germany on court No. 1. The Noah-Keretic match was programmed and advertised for a live broadcast on national television and approximately 7,000 paid spectators were present at court No. 1 expecting to watch Noah-Keretic, together with an undeterminable number of television spectators. Noah failed to return from Paris to Dusseldorf and failed to show for his match which was defaulted. Noah did not even let Dusseldorf know he was not going to show. Probably the worst thing a professional tennis player or any professional athlete for that matter can do is fail to show for the paying fans.

Noah was, in addition to being a famous French tennis player, one of the nicest players in tennis. I could not ever remember issuing a fine against him for misconduct and his agent, Pierre Darmon, was also a famous retired French player and a well-respected participant in the founding and success of the ATP. But we had a Code of Conduct approved by the players and it was my job to enforce it. In my Administrator's Determination dated June 7[519], I concluded that Noah was guilty of the Major Offense of Aggravated Behavior in that his failure to appear in Dusseldorf was "flagrant and particularly injurious to the success of a tournament and was singularly egregious." I issued a fine of $20,000 and suspended Noah from play in all MIPTC sanctioned or recognized events for a period of 42 days, commencing on Monday after the expiration of the time within which an appeal may be filed, or, in the case of an appeal, commencing on the Monday after a final decision on appeal.

At the June 5-9, MIPTC meeting in Paris, held just after the conclusion of the 1983 French Open, which was won by Yannick Noah in a magnificent performance, the Council affirmed my Determination, fine and suspension[520]. So, as Noah was celebrating his historic French Open win, we had to deliver him the bad news. Noah waived an appeal of the Determination and began the 42-day suspension on June 13, which, of course, kept him from playing at Wimbledon. Noah and his agent, Pierre Darmon, were upset about this penalty and I do not believe either of them spoke to Philippe Chatrier, the Chairman of the MIPTC, President of the ITF and President of the French Tennis Federation for a couple of years. Noah was, except for this incident, a superb gentleman, which made this case very unpleasant for all of us. However, it was unfortunately unavoidable. Noah resigned from the ATP for a while, but he eventually rejoined.[521]

At the January 16-19, 1984, MIPTC meeting in New York, the Council agreed to reduce Noah's fine from $20,000 to $7,400, since the Council had been previously erroneously advised that Noah had received $12,600 in prize money.[522]

Major Offense No. 8: Ilie Nastase, 1983 Stowe

Even in the twilight of his career, Ilie Nastase could still get into trouble. At the Volvo Grand Prix tournament in Stowe, August 15-21, Frank Hammond was the referee and sometimes when he served as a chair umpire, he appointed a substitute referee. Nastase lost in the first round of singles to Danny Salz 7-6, 6-4. During that match he was fined: $500 for racquet abuse (smashed racquet) and $1,500 for verbal abuse (called a female line umpire "a fucking bitch" and "a bitch" (4 or 5 times), "goddamned woman" and "watch the fucking line" and "fuck the linesman" and "the bitch cost me the match." Nastase and Wojtek Fibak lost to Brad Drewett and Kim Warwick in the doubles semifinals 6-4, 6-3. In that match, Nastase was fined: $500 for racquet abuse (he beat his racquet against the fence and an advertising banner over and over again until the banner tore) and $1,000 for verbal abuse (called chair umpire "a fucking pig").

Immediately after losing the doubles semifinal match, Nastase picked up his racquets and as he was leaving the court with the tournament security guard, he abruptly turned away for the exit and accelerated through the crowd towards the walkway at the center of the stands where Frank Hammond, the referee, and Ken Farrar, the MIPTC Supervisor, stood. Nastase was yelling, on the way to Hammond, "you fucking fat pig" and "you bastard" and "you fucking bastard" and "you've been out to get me for four years." As Nastase approached Hammond, he pushed Farrar out of his way and kicked Joe Lynch, in the calf of his right leg. Lynch, who was a very strong line umpire, had put himself between Nastase and Hammond the instant just before the kick to keep Nastase from reaching Hammond. Nastase was physically restrained and removed by the security guard. The MIPTC Supervisor Farrar issued additional fines for that incident: $2,000 for verbal abuse (of referee) and $5,000 for physical abuse (of official).

I commenced an official investigation and Determined[523] that in addition to the foregoing mentioned fines, Nastase was also guilty of the Major Offense of Aggravated Behavior and I issued an additional fine of $10,000 and a suspension for 126 days, subject to reduction to 63 days if there was no play in any professional tennis event. Nastase did not appeal and he paid the fines and honored the suspension.

Tournament Offense No. 5: 1983 Rotterdam

Since the beginning of the MIPTC in 1974, the MIPTC and especially the ATP had struggled with finding a way to investigate and stop the payment of under-the-table guarantees to players to induce their appearance at tournaments. Article VII. B. of the MIPTC Code of Conduct made it an offense for a tournament pay an appearance guarantee and the penalty was a fine up to $20,000 and loss of sanction.

The 1983 Rotterdam Super Series tournament (ABN-Wereldtennistoernooi) was staged March 14-20 with $250,000 in prize money at the Sportpalace Ahoy indoor arena. The tournament was owned by the City of Rotterdam and Peter Bonthuis was the tournament director. Wim Buitendijk was the manager of the Sportpalace Ahoy. Just prior to noon on Friday before the tournament, I received notice in my New York office that Jimmy Connors had just withdrawn claiming an injury, which left the tournament without a star attraction as Bjorn Borg, who had retired, had also withdrawn previously. The tournament was immediately in a panic mode and I agreed to try to help. My only leverage with the top players was my administration of the 12 "self-designations" committed each year and when a player missed a "designation," I could usually find an agreement for a make-up "designation." After checking all the scheduling and calling around, I found that the only possible top player who might be available was Guillermo Vilas, so I called Ion Tiriac, who was his coach, manager, agent and boss. The only thing I could offer was to count Rotterdam as a make-up "designation," which would probably be needed before the end of 1983. Tiriac promised to talk to Vilas and to contact me. I notified Rotterdam of this possibility, which was my only possibility. On Saturday at 6 p.m. Europe time, I received a telephone call from Tiriac informing me that Vilas was going to Rotterdam and that he had notified Rotterdam. I was delighted. Vilas played in and "saved" the Rotterdam tournament even though he lost in the final to Gene Mayer 6-1, 7-6.

Subsequently, the MIPTC met in Monte Carlo March 28-31 during the Monte Carlo Super Series. During the Monte Carlo tournament, the rumors were "flying" to the effect that Vilas had received a cash money guarantee from Rotterdam. I saw Tiriac in Monte Carlo and told him about the rumors and that I was going to have to commence an investigation of both Vilas and the Rotterdam tournament. Tiriac said something like "no problem, go ahead and investigate." On April 28, I issued a formal Notice of Investigation[524] to the Municipality of Rotterdam and Wim Buitendijk of Sportpalace Ahoy and to Guillermo Vilas to determine if they had violated the prohibition against guarantees. In my Notice of Investigation, I demanded that I be furnished on or before May 30, all documents which related in any way to any payments to Vilas. I made a similar demand for "all documents" from Vilas relating to 1983 Rotterdam. My demand for documents from 1983 Rotterdam directed to the Municipality of Rotterdam was delivered to Dr. C. Hoekwater, Managing Director of the Sports and Exhibition Center Ahoy, who was a City Official.

During the 1983 French Open (May 23-June 5), I worked at our new Paris Office at Stade Roland Garros with Paul Svehlik, our European Assistant Administrator. Among other things, I was preparing for the MIPTC meeting scheduled for June 6-9. On May 30, Dr. C. Hoekwater visited me in our MIPTC office at Roland Garros and delivered me his letter dated May 30[525], in which he admitted *in writing* that Rotterdam had paid Tiriac the $60,000 cash appearance fee he demanded for Vilas' participation in the tournament.

Hoekwater's letter said: "Mr. Happer advised us to contact Mr. Tiriac, the manager/ trainer of Mr. Vilas. In connection herewith, he provided Mr. Tiriac's telephone number. After this telephone call we made an evaluation of the situation. We arrived at the conclusion that we had to do something because of our obligations to our sponsor and to the already more than 40,000 ticket-holders. Furthermore, Dutch television was already considering to reduce the number of broadcasting hours because of these withdrawals, which in its turn would have caused very big problems with our sponsor. Receiving no more support from the administrative office, except for declaring Rotterdam an emergency situation and the willingness to regard Rotterdam as one of the 10 qualified tournaments for Vilas, we felt, contacting Mr. Tiriac would be our only feasible solution, knowing beforehand that the appearance of Mr. Vilas would not be for free on such short notice. As was to be expected, Mr. Tiriac was not so willing to have Mr. Vilas play in Rotterdam, because at that moment he was on the plane from Buenos Aires to Paris and could be expected to be tired. Mr. Tiriac, however, indicated that Mr. Vilas might be willing to play in case we would be willing to pay appearance money to an amount of $75,000. On Saturday, March 12th, after long telephone negotiations, the matter was settled for $60,000. As Managing Director of Ahoy, I authorized our former tournament director Peter Bonthuis to pay $60,000. A cash payment was made Monday night, the 14th, to Mr. Tiriac. As a result of these arrangements, Mr. Vilas appeared and played the finals. By doing so, Mr. Vilas saved our tournament for the public, the sponsor and the press, although the tournament resulted for Ahoy Rotterdam in a big financial loss of about Df 1,200,000."

The Hoekwater letter was the proverbial "smoking gun" in that it was a written admission that the Rotterdam tournament had paid a prohibited appearance guarantee of $60,000 which had been solicited and received by Ion Tiriac for Guillermo Vilas. It also meant, of course, the Tiriac and Vilas were also guilty and that would be a separate Code of Conduct case. At the June 6-9 Paris meeting of the MIPTC, I presented my Determination, dated June 7[526], with respect to the 1983 Rotterdam tournament in which I issued a fine of $10,000, but did not withdraw Rotterdam's sanction. We all had a great deal of sympathy for the tournament, but we could not ignore the violation of the guarantee rule by the tournament. The MIPTC affirmed my Determination.[527]

For some number of years after 1983, I learned that all of the top players sought to just boycott the Rotterdam tournament by either not selecting it as a "self-designation" or trying to use "vetoes" to avoid going to Rotterdam. Every year, I had to use all the administrative leverage I had to ensure that Rotterdam received as good of a marketable field as our system would allow. We just could not let the tournament be destroyed because it confessed to the violation during its emergency.

Major Offense No. 9: Guillermo Vilas, 1983 Rotterdam

Richard Evans wrote in *Open Tennis*[528]: "Guillermo (Vilas) was, at his own request, totally controlled by Ion Tiriac" his agent and coach. Neither Vilas or his agent, Tiriac, furnished anything pursuant to my demand for documents. While there were rumors of the solicitation and payment of prohibited appearance guarantees for numerous years, the May 30 Rotterdam letter was the first written admission (confession) of the demand for a cash appearance fee from a player and the payment of a cash appearance fee by a tournament that we had ever received. There was no reason to question the veracity of this letter or Dr. Hoekwater's admission-confession as there was no conceivable reason for him to make a false admission-confession.

Guillermo Vilas

As soon as my meeting with Dr. Hoekwater was concluded, I immediately asked Tiriac to meet me in my office at Roland Garros. When Tiriac came to my office I showed him a copy of the May 30 Rotterdam letter which stated that he had demanded and received a $60,000 cash appearance fee for the participation of Vilas in the Rotterdam tournament. It was obvious that Tiriac had not been truthful with me when he told me in Monte Carlo that no guarantee was sought or paid. However, Tiriac, who is smarter in his fourth language than most people are in their native language, was careful not to formally admit that he had solicited and been paid the cash appearance fee of $60,000.

I informed Tiriac that: (i) Neither, he and Vilas, nor I, could disregard this letter, (ii) This May 30 letter was clear and convincing evidence that Vilas had violated the prohibition against guarantees, which under the Code of Conduct was a Major Offense and Vilas was subject to a fine up to $20,000 and a suspension up to three years and (iii) I was duty bound to make a Determination that Vilas was guilty of the Major Offense. I then told Tiriac that I was concerned about Vilas being penalized for soliciting and taking a guarantee if other players were doing the same thing and I asked Tiriac to consider getting all the other player agents who may have been obtaining guarantees for their clients (if there were any as rumored), to join with him and place the entire issue of the payment of guarantees to players on the table at the upcoming MIPTC meeting for consideration and perhaps, a different resolution. I told Tiriac that if he did not pursue such an alternative course of action and get back to me before the MIPTC meeting, I would have to issue a Determination of guilt against Vilas. Tiriac not only did not bother to get back to me before the MIPTC meeting, he immediately after leaving my office went into the players' locker room and began attacking the Rotterdam tournament and the MIPTC.

Therefore, when Vilas later complained that he was being singled out as the only player violating the guarantee rules, he was wrong and his agent and manager could have opened the entire issue up with the MIPTC, but Tiriac elected to try to "stonewall" the case instead on his behalf. Consequently, I issued my Determination that Vilas was guilty of the Major Offense of soliciting and accepting a cash guarantee to participate in 1983 Rotterdam and I set out a penalty of a $20,000 fine and a one-year suspension. My hope was that the severe one-year suspension would encourage Vilas and especially Tiriac to come forward and present the entire picture of the illegal payment of guarantees to other players on the Grand Prix. *That did not happen.* At the June 6-9 MIPTC Paris meeting, the MIPTC affirmed my Determination, which was, of course, subject to appeal by Vilas.[529]

Apparently, Tiriac had not informed Vilas of the opportunity he had to bring the matter of the payment of guarantees before the Council because Vilas believed he had been unfairly singled out. In addition, 20 players including John McEnroe, Ivan Lendl and Vitas Gerulaitis signed a statement of support for Vilas incorrectly believing that somehow Vilas had been singled out unfairly.[530]

Vilas elected to appeal to three Review Officers. I selected Forrest Hainline, then the General Counsel for American Motors and the Chairman of the USTA Grievance Committee. Vilas selected Billy Talbert, the U.S. Open Tournament Director, and the third Review Officer selected was Vic Sexias. Roy Reardon, represented the MIPTC along with Nolst Trenite Hoogenraad and Van Velzen of Rotterdam. I had to have Roy handle this case because I was going to be a witness. Martin London and Gerard E. Harper of Paul Weiss Rifkind Wharton & Garrison of New York represented Vilas along with Tom Betz of Guy Cromwell Betz & Lustig of Virginia Beach. Remember that the Paul Weiss law firm, was the law firm of John McEnroe, Sr., and that Martin London and Gerard Harper represented John McEnroe Jr., in his 1981 Major Offense case. The case was tried for two days in Rotterdam on December 8-9, and then three days in New York City December 12-14, before the three Review Officers.

The representatives of the Rotterdam tournament and the City of Rotterdam testified under oath that that they negotiated a $60,000 cash appearance fee as a condition of Vilas' participation in the Rotterdam tournament, withdrew $60,000 in cash, gave it to the Peter Bonthuis, the tournament director, who personally delivered it to Tiriac. Vilas and Tiriac testified *under oath* that they did not solicit or receive any appearance money. It is quite possible that Vilas may not have had any idea then or now what Tiriac actually did.

Finally, on just about the final cross examination question by Roy Reardon to Tiriac, Tiriac reluctantly admitted that he had recorded a telephone conversation with Bonthuis, the tournament director, on Saturday, March 12, before the tournament. And, just like magic, Martin London, Esquire, reached into the bottom of his legal briefcase and produced *for the first time* a Paul Weiss typed transcript of that telephone conversation. *The existence of that tape recording and its transcript had inexplicably been kept secret by London and Tiriac until that moment.* London told the Review Officers that the decision to keep that recording secret was his *trial tactic* and that he expected it would be discovered on cross examination. *The truth is, it was only inadvertently discovered on cross examination, so if it had not been discovered, we would have never known about it.* Neither Tiriac or London could explain why it had not been produced upon my initial investigation and demand for documents and records or any time previously to this moment on cross examination.

The pertinent part of the Paul Weiss transcript[531] of the telephone conversation in which Tiriac negotiated the appearance fee was:

"B: This is Peter Bonthuis.

T: Yes, Peter.

B: Yeah, I've spoken with, well, a lot of firms this evening.

T: Yes

B: I really think that the maximum we can, we can pick up will be $50,000, and I really think that this will be the maximum.

T: Yeah

B: So that, the, the question is, ah, ok, will you accept that or

T: I don't know, I, ah, I don't know, Peter. I didn't consider that because I didn't want to negotiate anything.

B: Pardon?

T: I didn't consider that because I didn't want to negotiate anything.

B: No, well, the thing is not that I want to negotiate but if I promise something, you know, I, ah, it is necessary, of course, that I can keep that promise.

T: Uh, Un.

B: And I, I can assure that, that – well, but that's not the most important thing - that also I've put in also the money that I'm earning on the tournament.

T: Uh, Uh.

B: I'm putting that in, and, you know, but that's not another thing to tell him, of course, it's only that I would like to show how much I would try, try to do for it, and, you know, well, I've phoned almost everybody.

T: Uh. Uh.

B: And, uh, I think that really will be the maximum I can get.

T: Uh, Uh. Okay, I'll, uh, I'll think about it and I'll call you back. Okay?

B: Okay, and, uh, Mr. Tiriac, I'm, uh, in the _____ Center, can I give you the number?

T: Where is the qualifying?

B: It's the qualifying, yes.

T: Yeah, have you talked to Marshall Happer?

B: Un, I tried to call him, but I haven't spoken to him.

T: Uh, uh. Okay, I'll call you back in, in a while.

B: Okay, that's fine.

T: Okay, thank you, bye.

B: Okay, bye, bye."

Since we only had a transcript and not the original audio, you could not hear the obvious pleading by Bonthuis for Tiriac to bring Vilas to Rotterdam to save the tournament. The most logical conclusion was that Tiriac had demanded $75,000 and Bonthuis had offered $50,000, and on the follow up conversation an agreement was reached on $60,000 for the appearance guarantee. Tiriac telephoned me on Saturday around noon EST (6:00 p.m. in Paris) to inform me that Vilas was going to Rotterdam. As you might guess, Tiriac did not tell me he had obtained a cash appearance guarantee of $60,000. It was my belief that in 1983, Tiriac had a telephone with a recording-tape device and he had a practice of recording his telephone conversations as a record. Fortunately, I believe he was afraid not to tell his lawyer, Martin London, about it and when he did, London was bound by legal ethics not to destroy it. *However, he had it transcribed and kept it secret never to be found, unless Roy Reardon uncovered it on cross examination.*

Reardon said in his closing argument: "The Vilas position on this issue is clear: 'Bonthuis is lying' (Bonthuis stole the $60,000). We submit that this position is at odds with common sense and is contrary to the credible evidence introduced in this proceeding, including Tiriac's own tape recording of his conversation with Bonthuis on March 12. That recording leaves little doubt where the truth lies." Without the payment, Tiriac would not have brought Vilas to Rotterdam!

Forrest Hainline, Bill Talbert and Vic Sexias, the three Review Officers, unanimously concluded on January 17, 1984[532]: "The record establishes that $60,000 was withdrawn from the Ahoy account at the ABN Bank on March 14, that the money was given to then Rotterdam tournament director Peter Bonthuis and that the Ahoy representatives believed that Bonthuis was to give the money to (Ion) Tiriac as appearance money. The record consists of 1,220 pages of testimony. We believe that the credible evidence offered by the Council outweighs the credible evidence offered by Vilas." The Review Officers affirmed the $20,000 fine, but they terminated the proposed one-year suspension.[533]

The suspension had been stayed pending the appeal to the Review Officers, so Vilas never had a day of suspension. Nevertheless, he claimed for a long time that this case had ruined his career. The panel said Vilas' suspension should be terminated effective immediately, because: "It is believable that Vilas' tennis has been adversely affected for a least nine months by the pendency of the charge. During his 14 years as a professional the conduct of Vilas has been exemplary.'"

Because Tiriac elected to "stonewall" and deny he received the $60,000 appearance guarantee instead of opening up the issue of appearance guarantees being paid by other tournaments to other players, this case did not solve for all time the issue of the solicitation and payment of appearance guarantees for MIPTC sanctioned tournaments. However, it did show that the MIPTC was serious and would prosecute violations of the guarantee rules. It was clear to the Review Officers and everyone in the tennis community that

Vilas had incurred significant legal fees for the defense of the case with two days in Rotterdam and three days in New York. The cost of defending such a case became an important deterrent to future violations of the guarantee rules. None of them wanted to test us as the Vilas case had shown how much trouble and expense it was.

I still believe that one-day Ion Tiriac is going to come up to me and tell me, "yes" I got the $60,000 cash. If he does, I will ask him if Vilas ever got any of it?

Vilas was inducted into the International Tennis Hall of Fame in 1991 and Tiriac was inducted in 2013. Tiriac went on to own and promote the ATP Tour 1000 Series tournament in Madrid and is reputed to be the first tennis billionaire.

CHAPTER 21:

1983: WCT SUES MIPTC, ITF AND ATP,
COST OF DEFENSE PANIC, CRISIS NO. 25

The 1982 WCT circuit of 22 tournaments was not successful as all of the players committed to the Volvo Grand Prix and only some also played in the WCT tournaments. None of the top players really participated except for Ivan Lendl who became a millionaire as he won most of them. Owen Williams later disclosed in his book *Ahead of the Game*[534] that the ever-increasing demands of ProServ and IMG for greater and greater appearance money for their player clients to play in the 1982 WCT tournaments soon even "had the rank and file players asking for appearance money."

On January 21, 1983, WCT filed an anti-trust lawsuit against the ITF, ATP and the MIPTC in the United States District Court for the Southern District of New York.[535] A number of high-priced lawyers were hired by the various parties and it was clear that the case was going to be expensive. Thankfully, we had previously obtained anti-trust insurance coverage for the MIPTC via Lloyds of London for something like $10,000 per year in premiums. I believe that the ITF also may have had anti-trust insurance coverage, but the ATP did not have any insurance coverage so the cost of defense could very well exceed the net worth of the ATP, which was always on shaky financial ground.

WCT's Complaint

WCT's complaint alleged that the defendants had violated the anti-trust laws of the United States (Sections 1 and 2 of the Sherman Act and Section 4 and 16 of the Clayton Act) and that the nine members of the MIPTC "form an interlocking directorate that exerts control over all aspects of the conduct of men's professional tennis." The complaint alleged that the co-conspirators, "include, among others, the USTA, the Lawn Tennis Association of Great Britain (LTA), FFT (French Tennis Federation) and LTAA (Lawn Tennis Association of Australia), which have permitted the Tennis Council to make participation in a minimum number of other Volvo Grand Prix tournaments and conformity to the Tennis Council's rules, including those penalizing players who agree to compete in WCT's tournaments, a condition of participation in the prestigious Grand Slam tennis tournaments, which they, respectively, administer." For some reason, the

All England Lawn Tennis and Croquet Club, which owned Wimbledon under sanction with the LTA, was not included. I guessed that WCT did not want to offend Wimbledon.

WCT requested the court: (1) To award WCT treble its damages "resulting from defendants' unlawful acts," plus "reasonable attorneys' fees and cost of this suit," (2) To enjoin ATP from: (i) "promoting or conducting any tennis tournaments," and (ii) "Entering into any contractual or other arrangement to sponsor, approve, sanction or otherwise provide endorsements or services to the Volvo Grand Prix tournament series," (3) To enjoin all the defendants from establishing a long list of "eligibility requirements," establishing a ranking system, foreclosing WCT from an equal opportunity to compete for players or making any rules that inhibited WCT's ability to compete for players, etc.

Needless to say, if the injunctions requested were to be granted, then the MIPTC, ITF and ATP would not be able to govern the sport and it probably would not make much difference as all of them would be bankrupted by the treble damages. If the "co-conspirators" were ultimately brought into the lawsuit as additional defendants and subjected to treble damages, perhaps the four Grand Slams would have been destroyed. The result of the WCT lawsuit could have been that men's professional tennis would have become an ungoverned free-for-all with no structure and with lots of bankruptcies.

Mike Davies, who was appointed ATP Executive Director six days before the suit was filed, said to *International Tennis Weekly*[536]: "The players are shocked that Lamar Hunt is suing them. Every top player in the game today has, at one time or another, supported Lamar's circuit. The ATP is an association of international athletes and our interest is in serving our members and all tournaments. We are mystified as to what Lamar has to gain by this suit against the game. I personally feel it is a very sad day for the sport with which I have been involved all my life." "Since WCT filed a lawsuit against the ATP, members have been calling the Paris, Garland and New York offices asking, 'What does it mean?' My answer: It means that if there ever was a time when players should stick together, it is now. The tremendous cost to defend against the complex suit brought by Lamar Hunt will be an extreme burden on the ATP. At a time when the association's financial situation was easing, and the two percent prize money deduction eliminated, Lamar's action now threatens the only organization to speak only for players. The ATP attorney cannot even give us a guess as to how much it will cost the players to defend this suit."

"If you are a professional tennis player and you plan to be around for five years or so, you need to think of what it would be like if the ATP were not around to represent you." "Ask some of the guys who started it all. Ask them how much of a voice an individual player had with WCT or with the ITF. Ask me what it was like when I used to go to war monthly with the British LTA over what I felt were my rights, not just as a tennis player, but as an individual. The conditions were not by any stretch of the imagination like they are today with the ATP to represent you and only you. When Ben Franklin told John Hancock on July 4, 1776, at the signing of the American Declaration of Independence, 'We must all hang together, else we all shall hang separately,' he certainly said a mouthful. Now more than ever, the players must rise above narrow individual interests for the good of the association. The ATP needs you. My job is to lead the ATP in this fight. Give me the weapon that can't be overcome – unity."

Lamar Hunt wrote to the players in *International Tennis Weekly*[537]: "First and foremost, I want to make it clear that WCT has no intention or desire to seek monetary damages from any individual player. I am concerned by rumors that your ATP leadership may be telling you that you may be called upon to support a legal defense fund on the theory that you are being sued individually. That notion is totally false. It was never, and is not now, our intention that any individual player should suffer any personal expense. The facts are that inasmuch as the ATP is part of the membership and administration of the men's Pro Council, WCT had to sue the ATP. It was the choice last year of the ATP leadership to relinquish the ATP's independence and to align the group with the Pro Council in what many consider to be its monopolistic practices. This relationship, we think, puts the association in a very awkward position. WCT's lawsuit seeks, among other things, to require that the players' association take an independent stance and give the players the freedom of choice deciding when, where and how often they play."

ITF Agrees to Fund ATP Legal Fees

The ITF volunteered to pay ATP's legal fees incurred in the WCT lawsuit. Davies said in *International Tennis Weekly*[538]: "Fortunately, the ITF recognized the threat to the players by the huge lawyers' bills the ATP is incurring in defending itself…This money was earmarked for other tennis needs such as junior programs in underdeveloped countries, but Philippe Chatrier and Derek Hardwick feel that it is important to protect the investment which the ITF has made toward a worldwide game. The ATP and the ITF disagree over issues, but one thing we definitely agree on is the importance of a strong player association to represent the needs of all players."

Was a Settlement Possible?

By August of 1983, the parties had incurred significant legal expense and thus far the case was still just beginning in the discovery phase with interrogatories and the production of documents and I do not think one actual deposition had been taken. I could not think of any outcome of the case that would be good for men's professional tennis. I did not want the MIPTC, ATP and ITF to be destroyed and it made no sense to me to try to get WCT out of professional tennis. I respected the contributions of WCT to men's professional tennis, which in some ways it instigated in 1967, and I hoped we could find a solution that would satisfy everyone at least enough to settle the litigation. On August 15, with the approval of MIPTC Chairman Philippe Chatrier, Roy Reardon and I met in Dallas with Lamar Hunt and Owen Williams "to discuss the possibility of commencing confidential discussions relating to the possible settlement of the pending civil action." The U.S. Open was staged in New York, August 29 – September 11. At the August 25-30, September 4 and 7 MIPTC meeting in New York, Roy and I reported on our meeting in Dallas and, we "recommended that such discussions be commenced." On August 25, the Council authorized the commencement of settlement discussions with WCT on a confidential basis with Mike Davies, Brian Tobin, Stan Malless and me appointed as a committee to conduct such discussions, along with Roy Reardon. On Monday, August 29, the negotiating committee met with Lamar Hunt and Owen Williams of WCT and reported back to the MIPTC late on August 29. Thereafter the secret settlement discussions were continued by Davies, Reardon and me with Hunt and Williams all-day, for many, many hours, on August 30, 31, September 1 and 3.

In 1981, when WCT was part of the Grand Prix, WCT had eight of 28 Super Series tournaments, plus it had the WCT Finals in Dallas, Tournament of Champions at Forest Hills and the London World Doubles. For 1982, the MIPTC had approved nine new Super Series tournaments for a total of 29 Super Series. Consequently, since we could not just throw out some of the new Super Series to accommodate WCT, the solution to merge WCT back into the Grand Prix was not going to be easy. Thankfully, the Frankfurt Super Series had withdrawn for 1983, so we only had 28 Super Series in 1983, instead of the 29 we had in 1982. We knew that Hunt had been responsible for the creation of the NFL Super Bowl for the champions of the AFL and the NFL and that he always wanted to create a "tennis super bowl" for the winners of the Dallas WCT Finals and the Grand Prix Masters. We also knew that was probably impossible. The meetings went on for so long, I remember Lamar Hunt bringing a basket of fruit for snacks and Lamar actually doing push-ups and other exercises from time to time to stay refreshed. While Lamar Hunt had lots of lawyers involved in the WCT anti-trust action, he did not bring any of them to these settlement negotiations. That was probably the first indication that maybe he really wanted to settle the case. I, of course, had Roy Reardon, one of the best lawyers in the United States, with me. During that time, we went through all the possible issues between WCT, MIPTC, ATP, ITF and Volvo Grand Prix, one by one by one. Our negotiating format was to place all the issues readily agreeable in one imaginary basket and all the issues not-readily agreeable in another imaginary basket.

Sometime during our meetings, Lamar related to me the negotiation in which he was involved for the merger of the NFL with the AFL. Lamar told me that when they finished their negotiations, there was also one imaginary basket with all the issues readily agreeable and another much larger imaginary basket with all the issues not-readily agreeable. Then Lamar told me something that was especially important and revealing. He said that the NFL and the AFL knew they had to complete the merger, so they just proceeded with the merger and left it for the business operations people to deal with the not-readily agreeable issues in the much larger imaginary basket. As you might have guessed, when we finished our last marathon session on Saturday, September 3, we had one imaginary basket with all the issues readily agreeable and another much, much larger imaginary basket with all the issues not readily agreeable. We had agreed to report back to the Council on Sunday, September 4, at a continuation of the MIPTC meeting. On Sunday morning, September 4, I telephoned Owen Williams and I went through with him each of the issues in the not-readily agreeable imaginary basket and I told him how I planned to propose a resolution for each issue. While Owen was in no position without Lamar to agree to my resolutions of those issues, he gave me some indication on each issue, particularly if it was a deal breaker.

To deal with the issues that just could not be resolved, I created a contract section entitled "Matters Subject to Study" which provided for a future good faith study without any obligation for either party to agree on any of them. I then drafted a proposed Settlement Agreement containing a resolution of all the issues and presented it to the MIPTC later, on Sunday, September 4. The Council considered my draft, made some modifications to it and authorized me to deliver a revised draft to Lamar Hunt and Owen Williams for review; then the MIPTC meeting was adjourned until September 7. Council members, Jack Kramer, Lars Myhrman and Derek Hardwick had left New York so I provided them with a copy of the Settlement draft, so they could participate on any discussions on September 7 by telephone. "On September 7, the representatives of WCT submitted an alternative draft agreement unacceptable to the six (6) members of the Council present in person and further consideration of this matter was deferred until after the U.S. Open and/or the November 7-10, meeting of the Council."

After lots of additional discussions, we developed a Settlement Agreement dated October 31, which was approved by WCT and approved by the Council at its November 7-10, meeting in London. In addition to the Settlement Agreement, the parties executed a Mutual Release between WCT, Lamar Hunt, Al Hill, Jr., Owen Williams, MIPTC, ITF, ATP, the nine individual members of the MIPTC and me as the MIPTC Administrator. There was also a side Agreement between the ATP and WCT that guaranteed ATP Computer Ranking points for the WCT Tournament of Champions that selected its entries from tournament winners instead of current computer rankings. The ATP agreed to consider that method of selection of entries as an acceptable "system of merit."

The 18-page Settlement Agreement[539] provided for WCT to rejoin the Grand Prix in 1985-1989. The term would continue beyond 1989, unless either party gave two years written notice of termination. If for example it was to be terminated at the end of 1989 (after five years), the notice of termination would have to be given by January 1, 1988. It was agreed that there would be four official Grand Prix Championship events: Grand Prix Masters, WCT Finals, WCT Tournament of Champions and WCT World Doubles. If the MIPTC decided to create a separate Grand Prix Doubles Masters, then there would be five official Grand Prix Championship events. All tournaments would be staged under the uniform Grand Prix Rules, MIPTC Tournament Regulations and MIPTC Code. The WCT Finals in Dallas would have 12 players "selected based on the results of all Grand Slam and Super Series tournaments for the preceding 12 months and would be in a "protected week." Participation would be mandatory under the Grand Prix Rules. Prize money would be the same as the Grand Prix Masters. Lamar insisted over and over that the Dallas Finals should be equal to the Grand Prix Masters. For the WCT Finals, WCT agreed to pay $25,000 in ATP Prize Money, a Bonus Pool contribution of $200,000 and a MIPTC administrative fee of $25,000.

The WCT Tournament of Champions at Forest Hills would be the only Grand Prix "All Star" event with entries selected from the champions of all MIPTC sanctioned tournaments with on-site prize money of $10,000 and above during the preceding 12 months. It would have a maximum draw of 64 singles and 32 doubles. The Tournament of Champions would be in a protected week with a minimum of $300,000 in prize money and could be one of each player's "self-designations" under the Grand Prix Player Commitment, but no player could be substituted out of the Tournament of Champions. For the WCT Tournament of Champions, WCT agreed to pay $25,000 in ATP prize money, a Bonus Pool contribution of $100,000 and a MIPTC administrative fee of $15,000. The WCT World Doubles in London would have eight doubles teams and $200,000 in minimum prize money with entries selected on a system of merit on a voluntary entry basis. The WCT World Doubles would be in a protected week and would be equal to any Grand Prix Masters doubles that may be created later. For the WCT World Doubles, WCT agreed to pay $25,000 in ATP prize money, a Bonus Pool contribution of $100,000 and a MIPTC administrative fee of $15,000. In addition, WCT was to receive sanctions for four Super Series: (i) a first and second Super Series in 1985, (ii) a third Super Series in 1986 and (iii) a fourth Super Series in 1987. In 1983, the Grand Prix had 28 Super Series. The maximum number of Super Series going forward were: 1985: 31 Super Series, 1986: 32 Super Series and 1987: 33 Super Series. WCT was permitted to retain its player management business, but agreed to terminate it if the MIPTC adopted a rule "which prohibited player management companies or player agents from directly or indirectly owning or operating MIPTC sanctioned events." WCT had been forced to enter into appearance guarantee player contracts with respect to its 1982-1984 WCT tournaments. WCT informed us that all existing player contracts WCT had entered into in 1982-1984 would expire by the end of 1986, and no new ones would be added as those expired. In the Settlement Agreement, WCT was required to disclose those contracts only to me as the MIPTC Administrator on a confidential basis. I could and did take that into account when I allocated the player "self-designations" among the Super Series in 1985 and 1986. To accommodate the increase in the number of tournaments, we agreed to increase the minimum player commitment to 13 "self-designations," including the Grand Slams, Tournament of Champions and Super Series.

WCT was permitted to have a non-voting member at all MIPTC meetings, except when the relationship between the MIPTC and WCT was to be discussed in private. For the issues that just could not be solved, now or maybe forever, that were identified as the "Matters Subject to Study," the MIPTC and WCT agreed to promptly consider and review from time to time as appropriate without limitation: (i) a new bonus award for the player who achieves the best record in the combined Masters, WCT Finals and Tournament of Champions and a higher award for any player who wins all three of those tournaments, (ii) establishment of a new event owned jointly by the MIPTC and WCT with the players to be selected from the results of the Masters, WCT Finals and Tournament of Champions (this was Lamar's "Super Bowl" idea), (iii) establish the pooling of television rights for marketing, (iv) establish two bonus pools with separate sponsors for singles and doubles, (v) review tournament ownership by national associations, private individuals, the players' association, player management groups and tennis promotional organizations and (vi) establish a "traditional date" year-long schedule of tournaments for schedule continuity.

All parties agreed to cooperate to assure the credibility of all Grand Prix events to focus on public trust in relation to player compensation. The MIPTC and WCT agreed to use best efforts to encourage the fullest possible player participation in both the 1984 MIPTC and WCT tournaments. We agreed that if WCT could not provide its Houston and Richmond tournaments with Super Series franchises in 1985, the MIPTC would offer them Open Week or Regular Series sanctions if dates were available. In addition, we agreed that two-week tournaments would be limited to the four Grand Slams and the approved new ATP two-week tournament. If a fifth tournament for two weeks were to be approved, the WCT Tournament of Champions would have first option.

My recollection is that in a case that began in January and ended in November, the parties incurred legal fees in these incredibly high approximate amounts: MIPTC: $90,000, ITF: $500,000 and ATP: $300,000 (agreed to be paid by the ITF). The MIPTC legal fees were covered by our professional liability insurance and I believe that the ITF may have also had anti-trust insurance coverage, but it had also agreed to fund the ATP legal expenses since ATP had no insurance (and no money). We had budgeted $300,000 in the MIPTC budget for legal fees, so, I recommended, and the Council approved the payment of $300,000 to the ITF as partial reimbursement for legal expenses paid by the ITF for ATP and the ITF.

During our settlement negotiations, Lamar Hunt told me that WCT had incurred $400,000 in legal expenses. We specially and emphatically did not agree for the MIPTC to cover WCT's legal expenses and it was not mentioned in the Settlement Agreement. However, the next time I visited the WCT Dallas Finals, Lamar asked me once again (maybe just for fun, but maybe seriously) to reimburse WCT's $400,000 in legal expenses. *I politely declined once again.*

As you can see, this Crisis No. 25, which was the WCT anti-trust lawsuit, was at the time the biggest threat ever to the structure of men's professional tennis, the MIPTC, ITF and ATP, and while this five-year Settlement Agreement wasn't liked by everyone and certainly wasn't perfect, it stopped this nightmare legal case, provided for the merger of WCT back into the Grand Prix with added prize money and events for the players and guaranteed peace for at least five years, as the MIPTC also had a five-year agreement with ATP for 1982-1987. *So, was this the last crisis for men's professional tennis?*

CHAPTER 22:

1983: STRESSFUL VOLVO TO NABISCO SPONSORSHIP, CRISIS NO. 26

Volvo and ProServ

The negotiations with Volvo, which were conducted mainly by Rick Dowden, a Volvo Senior Vice President and lawyer, and with ProServ's Donald Dell and Ray Benton, proved to be some of the most stressful activities I undertook during my nine years as the MIPTC Administrator. Volvo was a terrific sponsor for men's professional tennis and professional tennis gave Volvo a unique new upmarket image for its association with the sport of tennis throughout the world as sponsor of the Volvo Grand Prix and the Volvo Masters. Rick Dowden attended lots of MIPTC meetings and supported the MIPTC and I was especially happy to have his support for my Administrator's job. Rick, however, was an American in a Swedish company and as he often told me, the Swedes always had the final decision for the company. Rick's boss was Bjorn Ahlstrom, President of Volvo USA, a very strong-minded Swedish executive.

In support of its sponsorship, Volvo provided worldwide promotion of the circuit significantly greater than Colgate or any of the prior sponsors. Volvo provided the media support for the circuit with media guides, player biographies, tournament calendars and Volvo/ProServ press liaisons at every tournament. All of the promotion was provided by Volvo through ProServ doing business as the "Volvo Grand Prix" so there was a ProServ employee working for the Volvo funded ProServ operation at every tournament. ProServ also promoted and staged the Volvo Masters at Madison Square Garden for Volvo. ProServ doing business as the "Volvo Grand Prix" caused significant confusion since the MIPTC was the governing body of the Volvo Grand Prix, not ProServ or Volvo. Naturally, all Volvo's promotion was weighted heavily for the promotion of Volvo first and then the Volvo Grand Prix. The MIPTC had no budget for promotion of the Volvo Grand Prix so, there was no budget for the promotion of the MIPTC, the governing body of men's professional tennis, the ITF or the ATP. The MIPTC was only barely mentioned in the Volvo Grand Prix Rule Book.

The Volvo sponsorship contract[540] dated September 25, 1979, was for three years of 1980, 1981 and 1982, with options which had been exercised for 1983 and 1984 at the following fees: 1980: $880,000, 1981: $990,000, 1982: $1,100,000, 1983: $1,210,000 and 1984: $1,210,000. Volvo (with ProServ) had control of and was entitled to all the income of the Volvo Masters, except that the Council was to receive 50 percent of the "net television revenue". Nothing was ever paid to the MIPTC from the Masters' television "net television revenue." It was clear to everyone that Volvo was making a lot of money from the Volvo Masters and that the Volvo sponsorship was an exceptionally good deal for Volvo and for ProServ.

With respect to sponsorship of the Grand Prix after 1984, it was my responsibility try to professionally determine the fair market value of any future sponsorship in conjunction with the then current needs of the MIPTC, the tournaments and the players and provide the members of the Council with recommendations based on my best professional analysis. Over and over again, the members of the MIPTC insisted that after the term of Volvo's sponsorship, the MIPTC wanted to own and control the Masters and not just give it to the sponsor.

Donald Dell had earned the reputation of being one of most successful negotiators in professional tennis because he was so single minded and relentless that many folks just got so tired, gave in and agreed with him. Donald was a master at using every possible way to exert pressure that he thought would force the result he desired. Dell was literally involved in every aspect of men's professional tennis, representing players, tournaments, television as well as Volvo. Then and now, I have always considered Donald Dell to be both a really tough professional colleague and a personal friend. As lawyers, we both had learned how to separate professional disagreements from personal relationships. But, stay tuned, and I will describe a few of our "professional disagreements" over Volvo's sponsorship of the Volvo Grand Prix and the Volvo Masters.

I eventually learned that a typical negotiation or "discussion" with Donald would generally have three phases: (i) Phase I would begin with Donald telling me how wonderful I was, how important I was to the sport of tennis, etc., etc., (ii) Phase II would follow with his "reasonable" proposal for agreement and why it was wonderful and how the sport would fall apart if it were not accepted and (iii) Phase III when I disagreed, or refused to agree with him, Donald would become agitated and sometime yell as he informed me that if I did not accept and support his proposal, I would soon be out of a job. That apparently worked for him with a lot of people. In especially long sessions with Donald, sometimes after Phase III, he would return to Phase I, then Phase II and Phase III, all over again, and again.

Once, I flew to Washington to meet for several hours with Donald in his office during which he wanted my agreement and support for his current proposal to extend Volvo's sponsorship of the Grand Prix with Volvo and ProServ owning the Volvo Masters. Upon finishing those several hours without any agreement, I made the mistake of letting Donald and his driver, drive me to the DC airport for my Piedmont Jet flight. As a result, Donald had the opportunity to continue with Phase I, Phase II and Phase III again all the way to the airport and then he actually followed me onto the airplane, sat next to me and continued until the plane was ready for take-off, when, thankfully, the Piedmont stewardess forced him to deplane. So here comes the MIPTC-Volvo saga and solicitation of replacement sponsors, which ultimately led to Nabisco.

On May 21, 1981, I wrote to Rick Dowden to request copies of the television contracts and financials for the Volvo Masters and to ascertain Volvo's interest in renegotiating the sponsorship contract. On June 29, 1981, Rick responded by declining to furnish financial reports on the Volvo Masters saying that there were "no secrets within the tennis community and we do not wish the details of our financial arrangements made public....In any future negotiations we would in effect be negotiating against ourselves."[541]

On August 28, 1981, Volvo requested an option for 1985-1987 at $1.8 million per year with Volvo continuing to own and control the Volvo Masters. I told Rick that my recommendation to the Council was that the Volvo offer not be accepted. Rick and Donald attempted to cast my recommendation as purely my "personal recommendation" and seek approval of the Council. However, after surveying the members of the Council, Volvo apparently concluded that upon a forced vote by the members, the Volvo proposal would not be agreed so on December 17, Volvo withdrew its offer.[542]

Finally, Rick delivered a letter dated January 11, 1982, exercising Volvo's option to extend its sponsorship contract for 1983 and 1984, while continuing to refuse to provide any financial information on the Volvo Masters, which was, of course, owned by the MIPTC. Additional negotiations continued in 1983. Volvo submitted yet another revised offer on May 23 for 1985-1989 providing that Volvo would still own and control the Volvo Masters, but that the MIPTC would get 50 percent of the net profits or losses with Volvo's television buy being a tournament expense. The proposed sponsorship fees for 1985-1989 ranged from $1.8 million to $2.6 million. Volvo included in its revised offer $200,000 per year to ATP "for its pension fund, payment of legal fees or payment of other of its expenses."[543] This was the first time that a direct payment to ATP had been proposed, an obvious attempt to lure the Player Representatives who were struggling with the WCT lawsuit and other financial issues.

The 1983 French Open was staged May 23 – June 5, with the MIPTC meeting beginning on June 6. On June 6, Rick Dowden, Donald Dell and Ray Benton of ProServ formally presented Volvo's revised offer for the sponsorship of the Grand Prix and the Masters for 1985-1989, dated May 23. *Dowden said that the financial terms of the offer, the control of the promotion of the Grand Prix and the control of the operation of the Volvo Masters were not negotiable.* After extensive discussions and consideration, the Council voted 8-1 to reject the Volvo offer without regard to the issue as to whether it might be proper or improper for money to be paid to ATP in a Grand Prix sponsorship contract. Mike Davies was the only dissenting vote. After the 8-1 vote, Rick Dowden left the MIPTC meeting and said the matter was concluded.

On June 7, Rick sent a letter withdrawing the Volvo offer which said: "Following our various discussions of the past two days, Volvo no longer feels it to be appropriate to continue its offer for continued sponsorship of the Grand Prix circuit. We therefore respectfully withdraw our offer with our thanks to the members of the Council for their consideration." *Volvo never made another offer for sponsorship of the Grand Prix after June 7, 1983.*[544] Bjorn Ahlstrom, President of Volvo North America, said in the press, "That's it, it's over, it's done…This is a divorce that will take place in January 1985, after we complete the 1984 schedule."[545]

Subsequently, I had a number of marathon meetings with Mike Davies and Donald Dell as Dell attempted to formulate a proposed offer for the MIPTC to make to Volvo. In October, Dell sent letters to all of the Volvo Grand Prix tournaments claiming that Volvo had offered $25 million over five years which had been rejected by the Council.[546] The letter was blatantly untrue. I considered the letter to be an attempt to try to get the Grand Prix tournament directors to put pressure on the MIPTC to make a new offer to Volvo. I informed Dell what I thought of his letter and informed him that I was not going to waste any more time trying to help him formulate an acceptable offer to Volvo. I advised him to make whatever offer he wanted to make directly to the Council. While Donald would continue to make proposals for a possible offer by the MIPTC to Volvo, he was never able to provide another actual offer by Volvo because Volvo refused to authorize another offer.

In June, I received a letter from Frank Craighill saying that he had a company "seriously interested" in the sponsorship of the Grand Prix. Craighill's idea was to maintain the title of the circuit as the "Grand Prix of Tennis" and then sell the title to the Bonus Pool and the title to the Masters separately, along with lots of official suppliers, etc., e.g., the format of the current ATP Tour.[547] The ITF members of the MIPTC had always hated having a commercial title in front of the name of the Grand Prix of Tennis. I subsequently learned that Craighill's prospective sponsor was Seiko and he was working with Yoicho Hattori of Dentsu, the large and powerful Japanese advertising agency. At Frank's request, he and I flew to Tokyo (13 hours each way) to meet with Dentsu and Seiko about sponsorship of the Grand Prix. We left on October 18 and returned on October 20 – a long and brief trip. On October 20, at our meeting in Tokyo, we learned that Seiko appeared to be agreeable to offer to sponsor the Masters for $1.25 million per year, but had reservations about the sponsorship of the Bonus Pool. Japanese companies are extraordinarily careful to avoid embarrassment of any kind. I have been told that usually decisions are made from the bottom of a company to the top, so by the time the top officer has to make the final decision, there is a huge consensus already provided in support.

August 4 Dentsu Telex Mistake

On August 4, Dentsu, in communicating with Frank Craighill about their joint efforts to get Seiko as a Grand Prix sponsor, by mistake sent a telex to Craighill at the old ProServ telex address. As a result, Dell probably learned that his former partner, Craighill, had some real interest from Seiko and was working on a competitive bid for the Grand Prix sponsorship.[548]

Unfortunately, by virtue of its sponsorship of the Seiko Super Series tournament in Tokyo, Seiko received a copy of the ProServ letter touting a phony $25 million offer by Volvo for renewal of its sponsorship of the Grand Prix and Masters. On November 4, Craighill received a telex[549] from Yoichi Hattori of Dentsu saying: The Proserv letter "ruined all our efforts." In addition, on November 24, Yoichi Hattori of Dentsu sent a telex[550] to Frank Craighill informing him of a communication Dentsu had received from Dell saying "Volvo definitely wants to renew its sponsorship of the Grand Prix circuit," and "I would appreciate hearing from you if it is true that Dentsu is out looking for a new sponsor of the Grand Prix. If this is true, this could cause great problems between Volvo and ProServ and also Proserv and Dentsu." Frank Craighill tried desperately to try to revive Seiko's interest in sponsoring the Masters to no avail.

In May of 1982, Ohlmeyer Communications Corporation, which provided entertainment, sport and general programming was founded as a joint venture with Nabisco Brands, Inc., by Don Ohlmeyer, previously head of sports programming of NBC. In October, John Martin, vice president of ABC Sports was named president of Ohlmeyer Communications with Don Ohlmeyer as chairman.

Butch Buchholz learned that Nabisco might be interested in sponsoring the Grand Prix. On November 2, I met in New York with Buchholz, Fred Kovaleski (of Nabisco), Don Ohlmeyer and John Martin of Ohlmeyer Communications. The approach of Buchholz and later Nabisco was they understood the problems caused by the MIPTC having no promotion and they understood the MIPTC's desire to control the Masters. They were interested to help the sport. I had to explain that the MIPTC had not been offered $25 million by Volvo and that the Volvo final offer had been rejected and withdrawn, although Dell was still trying to put something together. I was informed that Buchholz would be sent to the November 7-10 meeting of the MIPTC in London for Nabisco and because of the lack of time to formulate a proper bid, Nabisco would offer to match anything Dell/ Volvo offered so the MIPTC would not be pressured into making a decision out of fear of not having another offer. *Wow!* Nabisco was an important multi-national company with a huge advertising budget, the sponsor of the famous Nabisco-Dinah Shore Golf Tournament and Nabisco had a cadre of famous athletes, including Rod Laver, who Nabisco used for various promotions.

At the November 7-9, 1983, MIPTC London meeting, various proposals for sponsorship in 1985 and beyond were presented. Dell and Ray Benton of ProServ presented a proposal that they "believed" would be acceptable to Volvo if approved by the Council. Donald emphasized that if the Council decided to approve his proposal, he would need seven to ten days to try to obtain approval from Volvo. Buchholz requested that Nabisco, Inc., have the opportunity to negotiate a sponsorship agreement for 1985 and beyond. In connection with Buchholz's appearance, I received a telex[551] from Fred Kovaleski of Nabisco saying: "The sponsorship came to our attention just two weeks ago, thus time constraints prevent presentation of a fully detailed proposal at this time. I want you to know, however, Nabisco is prepared at the very least to meet the conditions, as we understand them, offered by Volvo. We recognize the Council's reservations and concerns related to sponsorship of the Grand Prix and assure you of our sensitivity to them and willingness to accommodate to them. Nabisco subscribes to the logic of separate functional roles of the Sponsor and Administration/Management of the Grand Prix. I suggest the Council's and Professional Tennis interest would be best served if the Council would defer final decision on sponsorship until Nabisco has had an opportunity to present a detailed proposal. We are prepared to meet with the Council or a select sub-committee last half November or first part December either in New York or Europe, whichever is convenient to you."

The Council took those proposals under advisement for further study until the next meeting in January and instructed me to meet with representatives of Nabisco to determine what offer Nabisco may desire to present to the Council. There was, of course, no offer from Volvo, just proposals by Dell.

On November 14, I received a telephone call from Fred Kovaleski of Nabisco to inform me that Donald Dell had visited with him and asked that (i) Nabisco not get involved, (ii) if Nabisco wanted to get involved, then it should get involved as a partner with Volvo and (iii) Nabisco should hire ProServ. I was genuinely concerned because I knew that Nabisco was a really good company and I doubted that Nabisco wanted to get involved in a contentious fight in professional tennis. I was quite sure that Dell hoped that Nabisco would elect to not get involved. On November 17, I wrote to Donald and told him that I considered his action with Nabisco to be improper. I copied Bjorn Ahlstrom and Rick Dowden of Volvo and the members of the MIPTC with this letter.[552]

On December 30, Dell responded denying that he asked Nabisco to remove its company as a proposed sponsor (which Kovaleski had verified to me) and confirmed that Volvo was "fully aware of what I did suggest." Dell then went on to admit that he asked if Nabisco would "consider the possibility of a joint sponsorship of the Grand Prix" with Volvo in 1985.[553]

Disappointingly, on November 21, Fred Kovaleski called me to inform me that Nabisco was no longer interested in pursuing the sponsorship of the Grand Prix. *All of a sudden, we had no offer from Volvo, no offer from Seiko and now no offer from Nabisco!* Thereafter, I had several telephone conversations with John Martin of Ohlmeyer Communications and John expressed an interest in resurrecting's Nabisco's offer. He told me that Nabisco had been turned off by the thought of $25 million being required at a time when it was engaged in a big "cookie war."

As the negotiations progressed, I knew that some members of the Council really wanted the "Grand Prix of Tennis" concept with no commercial title in front of the name of the circuit, but with title sponsors for the Masters and the Bonus Pool. Other members of the Council believed that the "Volvo Grand Prix" and "Volvo Masters" concept was necessary in order to attract a sponsor. Eventually, I presented both concepts to the various interested parties with suggested "ballpark" values of $3.0 to $3.5 million for the "Grand Prix of Tennis" concept and $4 million for the "Volvo Grand Prix" concept, both with the Council owning and controlling the Masters. On December 14, I met with Fred Kovaleski and John Martin in New York and we discussed the general parameters for an offer. They seemed to be interested in both sponsorship concepts and I gave them my "ballpark" estimates of value $3-$3.5 million for the "Grand Prix of Tennis" concept and $4 million for the "Nabisco Grand Prix" concept: with $500,000 included in each for "pure tennis" promotion and an additional expense of $500,000 for a media buy on the telecast of the Masters, plus Nabisco's own promotion. I had learned that Nabisco had a $350 million advertising budget.

On January 11, 1984, I met in New York with Bob Kain of IMG and a representative of West Nally who advised me that they were joining together to make a joint proposal at the January MIPTC meeting. In addition, on January 12, I received a letter[554] from Rey Olsen of World Sports Group for a sponsorship by an unnamed company of the "Grand Prix of Tennis presented by XYZ" for three years for $3,325,000 plus a $500,000 ad purchase on the telecast of the Masters. On January 15, I received a telex[555] from Jeffry B. Franklin, Director of Marketing, McDonalds System of Europe, confirming that it had requested World Sports Group to bring them a sponsorship opportunity with the Grand Prix to be discussed in Frankfurt on February 6. Obviously, this would be after the January MIPTC meeting and thus too late to be considered.

On January 13, I met with Fred Kovaleski and John Martin in New York. They advised me that if they could be assured that a Nabisco offer could be made, not shopped and a prompt decision made thereon by the MIPTC that they planned to make a firm offer for the sponsorship. I was advised for the first time that they were only interested in the "Nabisco Grand Prix" concept. They indicated they planned to make an offer of $3 million and I told them that was too low in my opinion as I had given them a value of $4 million for the "Nabisco Grand Prix" concept. I encouraged them to consider the matter further and make their best offer to the MIPTC. Martin asked if I would review confidentially the form of a proposal if he got it to me over the weekend and I agreed to do so.

I received a proposal dated January 13 from Bob Kain of IMG and Patrick Nally of West Nally, for a commission agency for the "Grand Prix of Tennis" concept with a 30 percent sales commission after the MIPTC receives: $3.0 million, $3.5 million and $4.0 million in 1985, 1986 and 1987. I was never quite sure how much was actually being guaranteed and when they presented this later to the MIPTC, the guarantee was limited to $1.7 million per year so it would not be acceptable.[556]

At around 5:00 pm on January 13, during the Volvo Masters, I met Rick Dowden briefly at the Felt Forum. Rick told me confidentially, that if it would help, he might be able to get Volvo to continue one more year (1985) for the same contract terms ($1,210,000). He told me that he had no idea if what Dell was proposing could get approval from Volvo/Sweden even if offered by the MIPTC. Later on January 15, at Madison Square Garden, Rick handed me a letter[557] typed on plain white paper, obviously typed at the Garden, to Philippe Chatrier as Chairman with copies to Davies, Kramer and Happer saying: "We understand that the Council is entertaining this week several new sponsorship proposals for the Grand Prix circuit. Therefore, we wanted to assure you that Volvo North America Corporation will certainly be open to receive and evaluate any proposal or offer *from the Council* for the continued sponsorship of the Volvo Grand Prix beginning in 1985." *I discussed briefly with Rick Dowden at the time the problem that would arise if there was a firm offer from someone else and there was no actual offer from Volvo. Rick said he understood.*

On January 15, John Martin had delivered to my New York apartment a draft sponsorship proposal for my review as to the format for a draft offer. The proposal was for the "Nabisco Grand Prix" concept for an annual fee of $3 million. After discussing the format and the need to guarantee a minimum amount for promotional expenditures, I again urged him to consider the $4 million value I had given him for the "Nabisco Grand Prix" concept. John said he would reconsider the amount of his offer and asked me to discard his letter and keep it confidential. He said he would make-up his mind and make an offer to the MIPTC. I told him I did not want to know his final decision and I would try to schedule him last to eliminate any possibility of his offer being disclosed prior to the time the MIPTC was called upon to make a decision. I did not talk to him again about his offer and I did not know what his offer was going to be until he made it to the MIPTC.

January 16-19, 1984 MIPTC New York Meeting

At the January 16-19, 1984 MIPTC meeting in New York, the members of the MIPTC were: ITF: Philippe Chatrier, Chairman, Derek Hardwick and Stan Malless; Tournaments: Jack Kramer (North America), Jacques Hermenjat (Europe) and Brian Tobin (Rest of the World); Players: Mike Davies, Stan Smith and Ray Moore. Donald Dell's relationship with the members of the Council at that time was strong. Kramer was like a father figure to Dell and always supported both him and Volvo. Dell represented Chatrier's French Open for television rights and Stan Smith as a player. I thought that Dell may have recently guaranteed sponsorship of Hardwick's tournament at Bournemouth. Dell represented the ATP for endorsements, tournament television and World Team Cup and Davies was the ATP Executive Director. I thought also that Dell had just found JC Penny to sponsor Malless' Indianapolis Super Series. I understood that Dell and Moore had been enemies and there was some rumor that Dell had kept him out of the 35 circuit for some time and had held up $25,000 in a split fee for a special in South Africa for at least six months, which I was informed was paid just prior to the meeting.[558]

Dell had openly claimed he had evidence to convict Tobin and Hermenjat of violating the guarantee Rule for the Australian Open and for Gstaad. My assumption was that Dell would have had such information because he had probably negotiated appearance money for his player clients at their tournaments.

I scheduled the sponsorship presentations as follows: (1st) Bob Kain of IMG and J. Triggle of West Nally, (2nd) Donald Dell and Ray Benton of ProServ for a possible offer to be made by the MIPTC to Volvo with 7-10 days for Volvo to review and accept or reject and (3rd) John Martin and Ray Volpe of Ohlmeyer Communications for Nabisco. I had several telephone calls with Donald Dell, who wanted to be scheduled last. I had promised Nabisco that its offer would not be shopped and the only way I could guarantee that was by scheduling John Martin's presentation for Nabisco last.

West Nally and IMG proposed to be 25 percent sales commission agents for the "Grand Prix of Tennis" concept but with only a $1.7 million guarantee per year. The ProServ proposal was another solicitation of an offer from the MIPTC to Volvo with Volvo to have 7-10 days to review and accept and, of course, with no guarantee of acceptance. Remember that just three days earlier at the Volvo Masters in Madison Square Garden, Rick had told me that "he had no idea if what Dell was proposing could get approval from Volvo/Sweden even if offered by the MIPTC." ProServ proposed the "Volvo Grand Prix" concept with the MIPTC getting 50 percent of the profits of the Volvo Masters and no losses which would still be controlled by Volvo/ProServ. ProServ proposed license fees of $2.6 million to $3.4 million for 1985-1989, but required that Volvo could sell a presenting sponsor e.g., "Volvo Grand Prix Presented by Budweiser."

ProServ also proposed a guarantee of $200,000 to $600,000 per year for official product sponsors of the Volvo Grand Prix for a 25 percent sales commission. The proposed sale of another sponsorship category for a presenting sponsor for Volvo's account and additional sponsorship categories for official product sponsors could never have been agreed by the MIPTC as it would have taken all those sponsorship categories away from the tournaments. *Dell was at a big disadvantage because he could not make a firm offer for Volvo of any amount. Donald was obviously scrambling hard to try to keep the door open for Volvo even though Volvo had refused to consider giving up the Masters or submitting an increased actual financial offer.*

The Nabisco offer was a firm offer, as long as it was accepted immediately. Otherwise, it would be withdrawn. Nabisco proposed the "Nabisco Grand Prix" concept with the MIPTC having full ownership and control of the Nabisco Masters. Nabisco would promote its sponsorship and the MIPTC would provide the "pure tennis" promotion. The term was for three years with two one-year options at $3.5 million per year. I was pleasantly surprised to learn that John Martin had in fact decided to increase the proposed Nabisco annual fee from $3 million to $3.5 million per year for $17,500,000 over five years. It is interesting to note that even if Nabisco had only offered $3 million per year, it still would have been a better offer than the ProServ "non-offer" because there would have been no presenting sponsors or official suppliers and the MIPTC would own, control and receive all of the profits from the Nabisco Masters. Nabisco's offer was a firm offer that had to be accepted immediately or it was going to be withdrawn and ProServ did not have any firm offer for Volvo. All ProServ had was an inferior proposal, which if the MIPTC wanted to use it to make an offer to Volvo, Volvo would have 7-10 days to decide to accept or reject during which time Nabisco would be lost.

After the last presentation, the Player Representatives appeared to be under stress. I knew they had been worked on during the Volvo Masters by Dell. They asked to caucus and left the room. Upon their return, they inquired if the Nabisco offer could be shopped with Volvo. Answer "No." If the Nabisco offer was shopped or not accepted immediately, it would be withdrawn. We did some comparisons on the blackboard. Kramer, Volvo's biggest supporter, stated that Nabisco's offer "was just too good." The vote was 9-0 for Nabisco.

Philippe Chatrier called Bjorn Ahlstrom of Volvo to inform him about the selection of Nabisco's offer and I called Donald Dell to inform him that the Nabisco offer was superior to his non-offer proposal and that it included the ownership of the Masters for the MIPTC. Donald said something like: "Congratulations, you got what you wanted." *There was no point in telling him that I personally got nothing.* Donald then asked me if he could run the Masters for the MIPTC. I told him that would be a MIPTC decision, but I planned to recommend that we do it in-house. On January 30, 1984,

I signed a sponsorship contract[559] with Nabisco for 1985, 1986 and 1987 for $3.5 million per year with the MIPTC having full ownership of the Nabisco Masters and with two one-year options at $3.5 million per year. In 1984, Volvo would be paying $1,210,000 and have all the income from the Volvo Masters. In 1985, Nabisco would be paying $3,500,000 and the MIPTC would have all the income from the Nabisco Masters.

In 1985 for the first time, the MIPTC would have enough money to develop its own promotion and public relations staff for the pure tennis promotion of the tournaments and players, while Nabisco added its own promotions as well. By 1989, the MIPTC would be netting over $1 million per year from the Nabisco Masters. *While the negotiations for the Grand Prix sponsorship were stressful and tested all of us, the Council did the right thing in holding out for ownership and control of the Nabisco Masters and for its own "pure tennis" promotion of the circuit.*

Now in summary, I had an extended five-year employment contract, the MIPTC had a five-year contract with the ATP, a five-year contract with WCT, a three to five-year contract with Nabisco and the Vilas case had established an important precedent against appearance guarantees. *Did we finally have a stable environment for the governing of men's professional tennis? Problems with Dell and Volvo, unfortunately, were not over. We also had the continuing problem of the involvement of player-agents in the Grand Prix tournaments.*

Just to show you how long memories are in tennis and how feisty my friend and colleague Donald Dell remains, in March of 2017, I talked to Donald at the BNP Showdown at Madison Square Garden. Donald just had to tell me that tennis would be better off today, if I had just agreed with and supported him with Volvo in 1983. That was 34 years later when we were both 79! *You gotta love Donald!*

CHAPTER 23:

1984: CONFLICTS OF INTEREST, VOLVO GRABS MADISON SQUARE GARDEN, CRISES NOS. 27, 28

1984 Governing Bodies

The MIPTC was the governing body for men's professional tennis in 1984, except for the Davis Cup, the *Rules of Tennis* and the WCT competing circuit. The ITF was the governing body for the Davis Cup and in charge of the *Rules of Tennis*, and WCT governed its own small separate circuit and events.

```
┌─────────────────────────────────────────────────────────────┐
│              1984 Significant Tennis Leaders                  │
│                                                               │
│  ITF President:              Philippe Chatrier (France)       │
│  USTA President:             Hunter Delatour                  │
│  Australian LTA President:   Brian Tobin                      │
│  British LTA President:      J.R. Cockrane                    │
│  French FFT President:       Philippe Chatrier                │
│  Chairman of Wimbledon:      Buzzer Hadingham                 │
│  ATP President:              Ray Moore                        │
│  ATP Executive Director:     Mike Davies                      │
│  WCT Owners:                 Lamar Hunt and Al Hill, Jr.      │
│  WCT CEO:                    Owen Williams                    │
└─────────────────────────────────────────────────────────────┘
```

1984 MIPTC

ITF: Philippe Chatrier, Chairman, Derek Hardwick and Stan Malless.

Tournaments:	Kobi Hermenjat (Europe), Brian Tobin (Rest of the World), Jack Kramer (North America) until May 4 and Ray Benton (North America) after May 4.
Players:	Mike Davies, Stan Smith and Ray Moore.
Administrator:	Marshall Happer.
Ass't Admn:	Paul Svehlik.
Asst Admn:	Tony Eugenio.
Asst Admn:	David Cooper.
Legal Counsel:	Roy L. Reardon, Esquire and John Cambria, Esquire.
GP Supervisors:	Ken Farrar, Chief, Kurt Nielsen until September, Franco Bartoni, Keith Johnson, Bill Gilmour and Roy Dance until February 15.

1984 Major Player Representatives

ProServ:	Principals: Donald Dell, Ray Benton and Jerry Solomon.
Advantage Int'l:	Principals: Frank Craighill, Lee Fentress, Dean Smith and Peter Lawler.
IMG:	Principals: Mark McCormack and Bob Kain.
Others:	Ion Tiriac and Thomas Betz, Esquire (Vilas).
	John McEnroe, Sr., Esquire (McEnroe).
	Gloria Connors and Joseph Rountree, Esquire (Connors).

Three Competitions

In 1984, the 16th year of Open Tennis, there were three organized competitions for men: Volvo Grand Prix, WCT and the Davis Cup. Davis Cup was open to all players and was won 4-1 by Sweden over the United States. There were 67 Volvo Grand Prix Open prize money tournaments, including the year-end Volvo Masters in Madison Square Garden in New York City. Included in the 67 tournaments were the four Grand Slams and 26 Super Series tournaments with $200,000+ in prize money. The Volvo Masters was again staged at Madison Square Garden and was won again by John McEnroe over Ivan Lendl 7-5, 6-0, 6-4, and the doubles was won by McEnroe and Peter Fleming over Mark Edmondson and Sherwood Stewart 6-3, 6-1. There were 28 Super Series in 1983. Dallas moved to Boca West. Sao Paulo, Lisbon and Las Vegas dropped out and Luxembourg was added for a total of 26.

ATP was involved in five events: (i) May 27, Dusseldorf, $531,000 Ambre Solaire ATP World Team Cup, (ii) June 17, London, $200,000 Stella Artois Queens ATP Grass-Court Championships, (iii) June 23, Bristol, $100,000 Lambert and Butler Championships, (iv) August 26, Cincinnati, $300,000 ATP Championships and (v) November 11, London, $250,000 ATP Benson and Hedges Championships at Wembley. Lisbon and the Las Vegas Alan King Classic were not included in 1984. All of the ATP tournaments were in the Grand Prix, except for the World Team Cup.

In 1984, WCT staged only six tournaments: (i) January 8, London, $200,000, Barratt World Doubles won by Pavel Slozil and Tomas Smid over Anders Jarryd and Hans Simonsson 1-6, 6-3, 3-6, 6-4, 6-3, (ii) February 5, Richmond, $100,000 won by John McEnroe over Steve Denton 6-3, 7-6 in singles and by John McEnroe and Patrick McEnroe over Kevin Curren and Steve Denton 7-6, 6-2 in doubles, (iii) April 8, Houston, River Oaks $250,000 won by Mark Dickson over Sammy Giammalva 6-3, 6-2 in singles and by Pat Cash and Paul McNamee over David Dowlen and Nduka Odizor 7-5, 4-6, 6-3 in doubles, (iv) April 30, Dallas, $500,000, WCT Finals won by John McEnroe over Jimmy Connors 6-1. 6-2, 6-3, (v) May 13, Forest Hills, $500,000, Mercedes Tournament of Champions won by John McEnroe over Ivan Lendl 6-4, 6-2 in singles and by David Dowlen and Nduka Odizor over Ernie Fernandez and David Pate 7-6, 7-5 in doubles, and (vi) January 6, 1985 , London, $200,000, WCT World Doubles won by Ken Flach and Robert Seguso over Heinz Gunthardt and Balazs Taroczy 6-3, 3-6, 6-3, 6-0. *You can guess that WCT was paying huge guarantees for star players to participate.*

Ian Barnes wrote in *World of Tennis 1985*[560]: "After 1982, when World Championship Tennis made Ivan Lendl very rich, and 1983, when it was the lawyers' turn to collect the big cheques, 1984 turned out to be a quiet year in Dallas. Heads were kept well below the parapet as legal actions were dropped and peace settled once more over Lamar Hunt's relationship with the rest of tennis. Few could doubt that the new arrangements, restoring Hunt's innovative and energetic organisation to respectability and acceptability - particularly as part of the men's Grand Prix - was in the best interests of the game. The two-year trend of staff cut-backs was reversed, and a mood of confidence once again prevailed in the Texas office where excellence had always been a watchword."

Rules

The 1984 Rules were essentially the same as in 1983.[561]

MIPTC Meetings

In 1984, the MIPTC held six meetings: January 16-19 in New York, March 14 in New York, April 17-20 and May 6-7 in Monte Carlo and New York, June 18-21, 30, July 6 in London, August 23-26, September 3 in New York and October 29 - November 1 in Paris.

MIPTC Meeting, New York January 16-19, 1984

Stuttgart

In January in New York, Stuttgart was approved to rejoin the 1984 Volvo Grand Prix, subject to: (i) Payment of the $17,000 balance due on the fine from its 1983 Tournament Offense case; and (ii) Receipt of adequate assurance that any car discounts offered by the tournament sponsor to players would be solely on the basis of objective rankings and without condition of any kind for entry to the Stuttgart tournament.

Jack Kramer Resignation

Jack Kramer announced that for "personal reasons" he would be resigning from the Council at the conclusion of the April 17-20 meeting in Monte Carlo. The Council decided to immediately commence a special election so his successor could be elected and could also attend the Monte Carlo meeting with Kramer. Roy Reardon was appointed as the "election agent" for this special election which was scheduled to conclude on April 3.

Jack Kramer and Lamar Hunt were two of the most important "Pioneers of the Game" for the development of men's professional tennis and to say they were competitive with each other would be a profound understatement. Kramer wanted a world-wide game without Lamar Hunt and WCT. Lamar Hunt wanted to promote WCT as his own championship tour as an artistic and business success. The merging of WCT with the Nabisco Grand Prix for 1985-1989, was a compromise that was unacceptable to Kramer.

However, that compromise had settled the expensive and dangerous WCT anti-trust lawsuit against the MIPTC, ITF and the ATP. *Ray Benton of ProServ, Kramer's replacement in 1984, would create yet another huge problem for the Council.*[562]

MIPTC Meeting, New York March 14, 1984

Nabisco Masters Television Rights

In March in New York,[563] the Council selected Ohlmeyer Communications to represent the marketing of the Nabisco Masters television rights. Therefore, 1985 would be the first time in many years that Donald Dell and ProServ did not represent or control the television rights of the Masters.

MIPTC Meeting, Monte Carlo April 17-20, 1984 and New York May 6-7

[The meeting agenda was not completed in Monte Carlo and the meeting was recessed on April 20 and reconvened on May 6 in New York to complete the agenda]

Election of Ray Benton to Succeed Jack Kramer

Ray Benton, President of ProServ, Tournament Director of Boca West, Charlie Pasarell, Tournament Director of La Quinta and Gene Scott, Tournament Director of South Orange, were all candidates to replace Kramer as the North American Tournament Representative on the Council. Reardon, who was the election agent, advised me that the vote of the USTA National Indoor Championships staged at the Memphis Racquet Club owned by Billy Dunavant was going to be determinative of this close election. Dunavant and the USTA each claimed the right to cast the vote for this tournament. While the actual ballots were still confidential, it was clear that Dunavant had voted for Ray Benton and the USTA had voted for Charles Pasarell. Both Dunavant and Pasarell were clients of ProServ.

Lawyers for Benton and Dunavant demanded that Dunavant had the right to cast the vote for Memphis and that Ray Benton be declared as elected. George Gowen, Esquire, General Counsel for the USTA, demanded the MIPTC declare that the USTA had the right to cast the vote for Memphis and that Charlie Pasarell be declared as elected. All the lawyers appeared before the Council to present their views. The MIPTC decided that the Memphis Racquet Club (Billy Dunavant) had the right to cast the ballot in this election and Ray Benton was elected to Kramer's unexpired term to begin after May 7, 1984 and expire in September or October of 1985.

Ray Benton's Conflicts of Interest

On April 18, the Council reviewed the agenda of the meeting and ascertained that Benton had a potential and serious conflict of interest as to many, if not most, of the items on the agenda. At the conclusion of that discussion, Kramer announced that he was withdrawing his invitation for Benton to be present as an observer at the meeting and said that he intended to ask Benton and the North American tournaments to reconsider the situation. The April 17-20 meeting in Monte Carlo was extended to May 6-7 in New York with Benton not invited to be an observer.

Amendment to Bylaws

The Council immediately amended the MIPTC Bylaws to prohibit player agents from becoming members of the Council (in the future) and requiring that in all future elections, only tournaments in good standing with the MIPTC would be permitted to vote. The vote on prohibiting player agents from membership on the MIPTC was 9-0, which meant that Jack Kramer also voted for it.

Nabisco Masters

The first Nabisco Masters was scheduled for the week of January 13-19 in 1986 in New York. Having fought so hard to finally gain control of the Masters, it was unanimous that operation and promotion of the Nabisco Masters should be done in-house by new MIPTC staff and I was so instructed.

Travel Expenses for Tournament Working Groups

The MIPTC had always paid the travel and living expenses of the members of the MIPTC and it was recognized that the Grand Prix tournaments, along with the Grand Prix sponsor, provided the income of the MIPTC. Beginning in 1985, with the extra income from Nabisco over what Volvo had been paying and with income from the Nabisco Masters, the MIPTC could for the first time provide some traveling expense reimbursements for a small group of tournament representatives from each geographical area. As a result, we included tournament group traveling expenses in the 1985 budget. When this budget got in place in 1985 and subsequent years, it gave the three Tournament Representatives on the MIPTC lots of power as they got to decide which tournament directors in their geographical areas received travel reimbursements. This tended to guarantee their continued re-elections to the MIPTC.

ATP 'Players' Grand Slam

The new ATP two-week tournament was approved for the weeks of February 4 and 11, 1985, in Delray Beach, Florida.[564]

MIPTC Meeting, London June 18-21, 30, July 6, 1984

Request for Observer Status by IMG and Advantage International Because of Ray Benton's Election

In June and July in London,[565] representatives of IMG and Advantage International petitioned the Council for permission to observe the meetings of the Council as long as Ray Benton was a member. The Council denied that request but agreed to provide them an opportunity to address the Council when appropriate. Ray Benton participated in the discussion but abstained on the vote. It *was his first conflict of interest as a member of the Council.*

Hawaii

The Bylaws were amended to move Hawaii from the Rest of the World to North America.

MIPTC Meeting, New York, August 23-26, September 3, 1984

New MIPTC Office 437 Madison

In August-September in New York, I reviewed the termination of the lease at 919 Third Avenue and the leasing of additional office space at 437 Madison Avenue (between 49th and 50th streets) as of December 1, 1984, for a new Manhattan New York Office. *This would be our third office in Manhattan.*[566]

Television Highlights Show

I informed the Council that it appeared that all of the Grand Prix tournaments would agree to provide excerpts for the proposed television highlights show, except for Wimbledon, the U.S. Open and the Australian Open and that if all the Grand Slams did not participate there could be no highlights show. *There was to be no highlights show!*

MIPTC Meeting, Paris October 29 – November 1, 1984

Nabisco Purchased 20 Percent of ESPN, Ohlmeyer Resigns as Television Agent

In October-November in Paris, John Martin, President of Ohlmeyer Communications, (a joint venture with Nabisco), reported that since Nabisco had just purchased 20 percent of ESPN, he had a conflict of interest and was withdrawing as television agent for the domestic television rights of the Nabisco Masters, but would continue with respect to the marketing of the international rights. *Recognizing a conflict of interest was a new concept for folks in the tennis community.*

January 1986 Nabisco Masters, Then December 1986 Nabisco Masters

The Council confirmed the week of January 13-20, 1986, for the first Nabisco Masters (for the 1985 Grand Prix Year), and then agreed to move the Nabisco Masters to the week beginning December 1, 1986, for the 1986 Grand Prix Year, subject to obtaining the agreement of Madison Square Garden for the change of date and subject to obtaining a suitable domestic television rights deal. It was known that staging the Nabisco Masters in New York during December was one of the busiest times of the year in New York and would be somewhat risky. However, the goal of ending the Grand Prix Year within the calendar year and permitting the Australian Open and its lead-up tournaments to move into January was important. Ever since the Masters was moved to January, the players were all reluctant to travel the long distance to Australia to play on grass and then return to New York in January for the Masters indoors. As a result, lots of the top players had elected for years to skip the Australian Open. After we explained the importance of the move to December for the game, Nabisco was fully supportive. They were going to be a great sponsor us. We just had to make sure they received good value for their sponsorship. John Martin helped us get ESPN to televise the Nabisco Masters which permitted us to move it into December of 1986.[567]

We Discovered the IBM PC

Tony Eugenio, who was my Assistant Administrator from 1983-1985, was in addition to being a fine young lawyer and a certified public accountant, an early expert on the developing technology via the IBM Personal Computer. First, IBM used a 5¼ disc, then 3½" discs, then modest hard drives with black and white displays. Tony introduced us to *Visiword,* one of the earlier word processing programs, and as soon as we learned that you could make corrections on the computer screen, our 100-page IBM memory typewriters became obsolete. I found that I could purchase IBM PCs cheaper at the 47ᵗʰ Street photo company in Manhattan than I could from IBM so, we began using them. Tony introduced me to the spreadsheet program, *Lotus123,* and I was hooked. Every day we had to maintain a 52-week tournament calendar that changed daily and had to be retyped daily. *Lotus123* immediately changed all that. We loved it. We also were able to find an accounting software program to convert our bookkeeping system from a handwritten system to a computer data backed system. Tony even wrote a rudimentary DOS database program to manage the player designations to all of the Grand Prix tournaments. Through Tony's expertise, we all embraced this new technology early in its development.

New "Playing Fair" Column for *ITW*

In February we introduced a new monthly column entitled "Playing Fair" for the ATP's *International Tennis Weekly*[568] in which I said: "How many times have you heard it said that 'There are too many rules' or 'Tennis was better when there were not so many rules?' If you stop to analyze these statements, you find that tennis was less complicated when there were fewer rules because there was always one rule that provided that someone (not the players) had unilateral discretion to change or add any necessary rule as required by the circumstances. That situation was not popular with or fair to the players then and it certainly would not be accepted now. Once the *discretion rule* was abolished, it naturally became important to spell out in as much detail as possible the rights and duties of the players, tournaments and officials. Clear and detailed rules do not create problems; they eliminate problems. The MIPTC Grand Prix Rules, Tournament Regulations and Code have been developed in large part by players and with the agreement and approval of tournaments and national associations. It is vital to the future of our sport that this body of rules protect an open and fair system for advancement by merit of all players in every level of professional tennis. The Players, Tournaments and ITF Representatives on the MIPTC are dedicated to the continuous review and improvement of these rules. Now having made our speech in support of clear and detailed rules, we have to admit that this necessarily means the rules are lengthy and somewhat complex. As professional athletes, it is imperative that each player know and understand the rules." The new Playing Fair monthly column was designed to help educate the players.

1984 Rotterdam

During the final between Ivan Lendl and Jimmy Connors at Rotterdam in 1984, with Lendl having won the first set 6-0 and being up a service break in the second set, the match was stopped because of a bomb threat and the Ahoy Sports Hall was evacuated and searched. When no bomb was found, Lendl refused to resume play because he "was not prepared to take any risks." The $50,000 winner's prize money and the $25,000 runner-up prize money was placed in escrow for a possible completion of the match. However, the MIPTC declined to permit the match to be completed at a later date as it would conflict with other tournaments, etc.[569]

New Two Week Tournament – The Players "Grand Slam"

On April 25, Ray Moore, ATP President and Chris Evert, WTA President, announced the creation of the new $1.8 million ATP/WTA two-week event with 128 singles draws for men and women, plus doubles and mixed doubles, scheduled to be played in Delray Beach, Florida.[570] However, the tournament was not immediately accepted by the top players. Gene Scott pointed out in *Tennis Week* that John McEnroe and Jimmy Connors both exercised their vetoes of their designations to the tournament, called the Lipton Championships.[571]

Los Angeles Permanent Tennis Stadium

On May 20, the Los Angeles Tennis Center on the campus of UCLA was opened in time for the 1984 Olympics in which tennis was returning as a demonstration sport. It had 5,800 seats. Los Angeles followed the 1979 Indianapolis Tennis Stadium that would lead the way for permanent tennis stadiums to be constructed later in Cincinnati, Indian Wells, Washington D.C., Key Biscayne and New Haven, etc.[572]

McCormack Threat

On May 31, Philippe Chatrier and I met with Mark McCormack and Bob Kain of IMG. At the time, IMG and ProServ were representing both players and were heavily involved in tournaments as owners, defacto owners, marketing and television agents, etc. IMG was solely owned by McCormack and the IMG tennis division headed by Bob Kain (USA) and Eric Drossart (IMG Europe) were usually the only persons we saw from IMG, so McCormack was pretty much of an unknown to me personally. McCormack asked for the meeting and it was held at a penthouse apartment in an old hotel in Paris that he apparently always had when in Paris for the French Open. Eventually, we learned that the purpose of the meeting was for McCormack to deliver a threat to Chatrier and to me for the MIPTC to the effect that if the MIPTC threatened or did anything to threaten IMG's tournament business, IMG would join with ProServ to fight the MIPTC. The implication was that he was threatening litigation, although litigation was not generally McCormack's style. I chalked the meeting up to just another threat – by this stage I had received lots of threats. However, McCormack would eventually join in litigation against the MIPTC.

Retired Bjorn Borg Plays Stuttgart Again

On July 17, Bjorn Borg lost 6-3, 6-1, to Henri Leconte in the first round of Stuttgart, which was reinstated into the Grand Prix for 1984. He came out of retirement to go to Stuttgart. *He must have needed a new Mercedes!*[573]

ATP-WTA Two-Week Tournament

Mike Davies appointed Butch Buchholz to head up the ATP two week tournament – the Lipton Championships – in Delray Beach. Buchholz said the ATP and WTA would get 20 percent of the gross ticket sales, less taxes and commissions and 20 percent of the television revenue less commissions. ABC was committed to televise the men's and women's singles finals and 10-12 foreign countries were going to carry the telecasts. The ITF representatives and the four Grand Slams supported the development of this "Players' grand slam" to provide a source of income for the ATP and the WTA and with the unwritten agreement that they would not ever seek the profits of the Grand Slams, which had been developed by hundreds and thousands of hours of volunteer contributions and which were used to fund the extensive cost of their facilities and their national associations.[574]

John Hewig Hired as MIPTC Director of Communications

I hired John A. Hewig as the first MIPTC Director of Communications. The development of a MIPTC communications and promotion staff was made possible by the new sponsorship contract with Nabisco. Hewig was 36 and a native of Battlecreek, Michigan. He was formerly Director of Communications for the New York Knickerbockers of the NBA and had similar positions with the LPGA and the Harford Whalers of the NHL. Beginning in 1985, the MIPTC would be responsible for the promotion of the

Nabisco Grand Prix and Nabisco Masters, while Nabisco would be responsible for the promotion of Nabisco.

McEnroe Fined $2,100

In the semifinals of Stockholm, John McEnroe was fined $2,100 for three Code violations in a match in which he defeated Anders Jarryd 1-6, 7-6, 6-2. McEnroe hit a spectator with a ball he "boomed away in anger," he shouted at the umpire "Answer my question jerk!" and he smashed a can on the court. These fines made McEnroe's total for 12 months $8,500 so he was over the $7,500 limit for a 21 to 42-day suspension. After McEnroe defeated Mats Wilander in the final 6-2, 3-6, 6-2, he announced he was not going to appeal these fines so he could begin his suspension immediately, which would let him finish his suspension in time to play Davis Cup, while being ineligible for the Australian Open. *It was exceptionally good vacation planning!*[575]

Jack Diller Hired as Nabisco Masters Tournament Director

In keeping with the mandate to stage the Nabisco Masters with in-house personnel, I hired Jack Diller, age 46, as our first Senior Marketing Executive and Tournament Director for the Nabisco Masters. Jack was a Yale Law graduate and had originally been with Roy Reardon's New York firm of Simpson Thacher. He had been executive vice president of RCTV, a joint venture of RCA Corporation and Rockefeller Center, in the cable TV programing industry and was previously vice president of legal affairs at Madison Square Garden. I was delighted to find someone so qualified who had a great relationship with Madison Square Garden. Jack had the responsibility to direct the Nabisco Masters at Madison Square Garden, to identify marketing opportunities for the MIPTC and the Nabisco Grand Prix and to develop the Nabisco Masters' television potential.[576]

John McEnroe Tennis Over America Tour

In 1984, Steve Corey and Gary Swain continued to promote the John McEnroe Tennis Over America Tour with 23 more exhibitions against Guillermo Vilas and Vitas Gerulaitis.[577]

ATP

At the end of 1984, ATP had 450 members with 350 in its First Division. Ray Moore was re-elected president, John McEnroe was elected Vice President, Mike Estep was re-elected as Treasurer and Jim McManus was re-elected as Secretary. McEnroe, Mats Wilander and Matt Doyle were the three new board members elected to replace Stan Smith, Balazs Taroczy and Rolf Gehring. The addition of McEnroe and Wilander was the first time since the beginning of the ATP in 1972, when the ATP Board was led by Arthur Ashe, Stan Smith and John Newcombe, that top players joined the board. Mark Edmondson resigned and was replaced by Colin Dowdeswell. The other board members were Paul McNamee, Jose Higueras, Ferdi Taygan and Mike Davies as Executive Director.

Another Political Use of ATP Computer Rankings

To encourage and reward players for playing in more than 13 tournaments each year, the ATP agreed to use a smaller divisor to determine average points on which the ATP ranking was based. If a player played in 14 tournaments, the divisor remained at 13, instead of being 14, etc. This was another "political use" of the ATP Computer Rankings System. Every time this was done, the rankings got a little bit warped.

Mike Estep's Brilliant Move

In one of the most brilliant moves for the ATP, Mike Estep, the ATP Computer Chairman, added a new computer rule (Rule XV "Hospitality Credit") beginning in 1984, giving tournaments credit for providing free hotel rooms ("hospitality") for players. This was another "political use" of the rankings system. The new rule required seven nights of hotel accommodations for all singles and doubles main draw players. Estep reasoned that the tournaments were in a better position to negotiate hotel accommodations than the players. First, a few tournaments began to take advantage of the hospitality credit to gain more points for players in their tournaments – a small advantage over other tournaments. Soon, all the tournaments began to participate so none of them actually got any more computer points than any other tournament, but the players got free rooms. *Every player owes a debt of gratitude to Mike Estep for this brilliant move. The beauty of Estep's plan was it actually cost the ATP nothing, but it created a huge financial benefit for the players.*

New Dallas Headquarters

The ATP broke ground for a new world headquarters building at a site near the expressway linking Dallas and Fort Worth, Texas, on the other side of Dallas from the current Garland office, which was a metal building in a farm field constructed by Bob

Briner when he was the ATP Executive Director. The new building was at the EastChase Sports Club in Fort Worth.[578]

1984 ATP JAKS AWARDS
(New York City January 1985)

Player of the Year	John McEnroe
Doubles Team of the Year	Peter Fleming – John McEnroe
Newcomer of the Year	Robert Green
Player of the Decade	Bjorn Borg
ATP Sportsmanship Award	Brian Gottfried
Media Service Award	Bob Briner

Crisis No. 27: Volvo/ProServ and Madison Square Garden

The 1984 Grand Prix was the last year of Volvo's sponsorship of the Volvo Grand Prix and the Volvo Masters, which would be staged in January of 1985. So, what does Volvo and ProServ do to help in the transition to Nabisco's new sponsorship of the Nabisco Grand Prix and the Nabisco Masters beginning in 1985?

Volvo Leases Madison Square Garden for Proposed Nabisco Masters Dates

At the April 17-20, May 6-7, 1984, MIPTC meetings in New York[579], Rick Dowden appeared and informed the Council that Volvo on the last day of the Volvo option had leased Madison Square Garden for the traditional Masters' dates in January of 1986, 1987 and 1988. Dowden also acknowledged that Volvo had entered into a contract through ProServ with NBC for televising of the Volvo Masters in January, 1984, and January, 1985, and for a new 'first class tennis event' in January of 1986. Dowden stated that it was Volvo's current intention to run its own "really major indoor" event in January 1986 in Madison Square Garden during the traditional dates of the Masters, i.e. during the first Nabisco Masters dates. The members of the Council were appalled and objected to the actions of Volvo and clearly reiterated their position that Volvo had no right to appropriate the venue for the Masters or use the Volvo Masters to leverage a television contract for its own use after the end of its sponsorship agreement. We offered to meet with representatives of Volvo to ascertain if the matter could be settled amicably.

On May 2, I had a lunch meeting with Rick Dowden in which Rick suggested to me that while discussions were possible, Volvo was interested in having its special event in Madison Square Garden in January of 1986, perhaps creating a alternative circuit to compete with the Nabisco Grand Prix, or as a "circuit within the Nabisco Grand Prix circuit." I told him that none of that was acceptable to the MIPTC.

On May 7, Ahlstrom wrote to Chatrier and contended that the MIPTC had no rights to Volvo's contract with Madison Square Garden or the television contract between Volvo and NBC. Ahlstrom said, "We would consider any attempts to force us out of our tournament plans to be part of a conspiracy among the Council, the constituent members, its administrator, its Counsel and Nabisco to monopolize the sport of professional tennis and would respond in whatever manner is necessary to fully and completely protect Volvo's interests."[580]

On May 10, Roy Reardon and I met with Rick Dowden and Bjorn Ahlstrom at the Volvo headquarters in New Jersey. Ahlstrom said he didn't want to settle anything, just wanted to have the "World Championships" at Madison Square Garden. He acted as if he could not understand that the MIPTC had any position. I believed he planned to take that posture on purpose as Rick had mentioned that he wanted us to hear it from Ahlstrom so we wouldn't think it was just him. After Ahlstrom departed the meeting, we talked with Rick who did not have quite the same hard line as Ahlstrom. My impression was that Ahlstrom wanted to be seen as a "tough guy" as Ray Benton later described him; he was after all the top Volvo Swede in North America; *I wondered how tough he would be under questioning by Roy Reardon before a Judge or Jury.*

On May 18, I wrote to Ahlstrom in response to his May 7 letter and our meeting on May 10 saying: "I do not favor extended debate in correspondence and therefore will not detail the Council's serious disagreement with the facts and conclusions in your letter. I think our respective positions are clear. Unfortunately, time does not permit us to let our dispute remain unresolved. The Council must proceed promptly to finalize its plans for the January 1986 (Nabisco) Masters. Accordingly, unless we are able to resolve this situation by June 1, 1984, we will have to proceed in accordance with the various alternatives available to us."[581]

The next meetings of the MIPTC was scheduled for June 18-21, 30 and July 7, 1984 in London in conjunction with Wimbledon. On June 16, I had a lengthy telephone conversation with Jerry Solomon of ProServ in which he surprisingly agreed to settle the

Volvo claim to Madison Square Garden and the NBC television contract in return for a new open week series tournament for Volvo, the week before the first Nabisco Masters. Roy Reardon and I discussed the fact that Volvo and ProServ seemed to be caving fast for some reason by retreating from its planned "World Championships" at Madison Square Garden the same week as the first Nabisco Masters. Our guess was that NBC had refused to televise such a Volvo special event staged in the same week as the Nabisco Masters. Also, I did not believe that Volvo, even with ProServ's muscle, was going to be able to steal the players away from the Nabisco Masters and the Nabisco Grand Prix Bonus Pool. Ray Benton, who was Jerry Solomon's boss, enjoyed telling me later that he was directing Solomon's conversations with me "because he did not have the patience to deal with me."

On the next day, June 17, Benton informed me that the Solomon proposal was wrong and that Volvo would have to be given a new Super Series to settle the matter. I was against adding any new Super Series on account of the dilution it would cause to the fields of all the existing Super Series. We were not going to get the top players to commit to any more than 14 tournaments plus the Nabisco Masters and the WCT Finals so adding another Super Series would hurt all of the other Super Series, particularly those not represented by ProServ or IMG.

Ray Benton replaced Jack Kramer as the North American Tournament Representative on the MIPTC beginning with the June 17 meeting - conflicts of interest and all. At the meeting, the MIPTC was presented with a resolution of the North American tournaments asking Benton to disregard his conflict of interest and to vote in favor of giving Volvo a new Super Series. Since ProServ represented most of the North American tournaments for the marketing of their television rights and had provided sponsors for some of them, it was easy to understand why those tournaments supported the Volvo/ProServ request for a new Super Series. The Tournament Representatives for Europe (Hermenjat) and the Rest of the World (Tobin) hated the idea of giving the United States another Super Series. At the meeting, the Council reluctantly voted 6-3 for the sake of protecting Nabisco's first Nabisco Masters event at Madison Square Garden, to give Volvo a new Super Series for three years in a non-Grand Prix city approved by the MIPTC. The terms of the agreed settlement were to require the delivery of the Madison Square Garden and NBC agreements to the MIPTC, the agreement of Volvo not to stage special events against other Grand Prix tournaments and finally that Volvo and ProServ deliver information to the MIPTC on the promotion of the circuit by Volvo and ProServ and the operation and finances of the Volvo Masters, all of which had been continuously withheld by them. *The only good thing about this agreement which was agreed under duress was that it only had a three-year term.* The MIPTC agreed to cooperate with Volvo's reasonable promotional activities and Volvo agreed to cooperate with the MIPTC's reasonable promotion activities.[582]

Jacques Hermenjat and Brian Tobin put the MIPTC on notice that the next Super Series to be awarded, if any, would be either in Europe or the Rest of the World and not in North America. At the August MIPTC meeting, the MIPTC agreed that the next two Super Series, if any, would be in Europe and/or the Rest of the World.

It took several months to renegotiate the agreements with Madison Square Garden and with NBC. The final settlement contract with Volvo and ProServ was dated January 14, 1985, and was authorized at the January meeting of the MIPTC in New York.

Having finally settled with Volvo and ProServ, we all wanted to enjoy and celebrate the final Volvo Masters at Madison Square Garden with a hope once again for a future of peace and prosperity for men's professional tennis. *How do you think Volvo and ProServ intended to "support and cooperate" with the MIPTC and Nabisco's sponsorship of the Nabisco Grand Prix and Nabisco Masters? Stay tuned for Crises No. 28 and 29.*

17,955 Spectators for Last Volvo Masters

At the January 13, 1985, last Volvo Masters, John McEnroe defeated Ivan Lendl 7-5, 6-0, 6-4, before 17,955 spectators at Madison Square Garden, which was telecast nationally by NBC and covered internationally. That is why the MIPTC wanted to own and control the Nabisco Masters going forward. Also, that is why Volvo/ProServ had wanted to retain the control and income from the Masters. Eventually, the MIPTC began to make over $1 million per year from the Nabisco Masters.[583]

Crisis No. 28: WBC Lawsuit

In November of 1984, we were surprised to receive a Federal court Complaint filed by WBC Productions against ProServ, Steve Disson and Ray Benton of ProServ plus Volvo, MIPTC and Nabisco.[584] The case included allegations of dealings with Steve Disson of ProServ and had nothing to do with the MIPTC or Nabisco, and probably nothing to do with Volvo, except to the extent that ProServ was Volvo's agent. Apparently, Steve Disson, who I believed was sort of a "loose cannon" salesman with ProServ, had made some highly questionable representations to WBC, which had a planned special event scheduled in Chicago for the week of March 11-17, 1985. Presumably when Volvo obtained its new Super Series to be known as the Volvo Classic scheduled in Chicago of the week April 1-7, 1985, WBC felt deceived by Disson and filed a lawsuit against everyone. The Council demanded that Benton and ProServ obtain the dismissal of the

WBC case immediately. The MIPTC quickly agreed to indemnify Nabisco of all costs and expenses to be incurred and demanded that ProServ indemnify Nabisco and the MIPTC for all costs and expenses to be incurred. I guessed that ProServ also had to indemnify its client, Volvo.

Finally, at the April 15-18, 1985, MIPTC meeting it was announced that the WBC lawsuit had been dismissed without prejudice. ProServ reluctantly reimbursed both Nabisco and the MIPTC for their litigation expenses in the WBC case which was caused solely by ProServ.[585] *This was just another conflict of interest issue with Ray Benton's membership on the MIPTC.*

MIPTC Financials

The MIPTC began 1984 with a surplus of $674,388, and after operating its New York and Paris offices and providing $3,000,000 in Bonus Pool awards to players in the Volvo Grand Prix, the MIPTC ended 1984 with a surplus of $614,538. The MIPTC collected and paid ATP prize money to the ATP of $525,000 for services to Volvo Grand Prix tournaments pursuant to its 1982 agreement covering 1983-1987. Volvo paid for its promotion as the Volvo Grand Prix sponsor and its promotion of the Volvo Grand Prix through ProServ. Volvo and ProServ promoted the Volvo Masters at Madison Square Garden, telecast on NBC, and were responsible for all expenses and received all income. On September 29, 1984, the MIPTC entered into a nine-year lease for office space at fourth floor, 437 Madison Avenue, New York, New York 10022. The lease provided for termination by either party upon 11-months-notice, commencing October 1, 1987.[586]

1984 Grand Slam Winners

French Open

Ivan Lendl d. John McEnroe 3-6, 2-6, 6-4, 7-5, 7-5.
Henri Leconte - Yannick Noah d. Pavel Slozil - Tomas Smid 6-4, 2-6, 3-6, 6-3, 6-2.

Wimbledon

John McEnroe d. Jimmy Connors 6-1, 6-1, 6-2.
Peter Fleming – John McEnroe d. Pat Cash - Paul McNamee 6-2, 5-7, 6-2, 3-6, 6-3.

U.S. Open

John McEnroe d. Ivan Lendl 6-3, 6-4, 6-1.
John Fitzgerald - Tomas Smid d. Stefan Edberg - Anders Jarryd 7-6, 6-3, 6-3.

Australian Open

Mats Wilander d. Kevin Curren 6-7, 6-4, 7-6, 6-2.
Mark Edmonson – Sherwood Stewart d. Joakim Nystrom - Mats Wilander 6-2, 6-2, 7-5.

Volvo Masters

John McEnroe d. Ivan Lendl 7-5, 6-0, 6-4.
Peter Fleming - John McEnroe d. Mark Edmondson - Sherwood Stewart 6-3, 6-1.

1984 Davis Cup

Davis Cup Final (Gothenburg - Clay)

Sweden d. United States 4-1.

Mats Wilander (SE) d. Jimmy Connors (US) 6-1, 6-3, 6-3.
Henrik Sundstrom (SE) d. John McEnroe (US) 13-11, 6-4, 6-3.
Stefan Edberg - Anders Jarryd (SE) d. Peter Fleming - John McEnroe (US) 7-5, 5-7, 6-2, 7-5.
John McEnroe (US) d. Mats Wilander (SE) 6-3, 6-7, 6-3.
Hendrik Sundstrom (SE) d. Jimmy Arias (US) 3-6, 8-6, 6-3.

World Team Cup

United States d. Czechoslovakia 2-1.

John McEnroe (US) d. Ivan Lendl (CZ) 6-2, 6-2.
Tomas Smid (CZ) d. Jimmy Arias (US) 4-6, 7-6, 6-4.
Peter Fleming – John McEnroe (US) d. Ivan Lendl – Tomas Smid (CZ) 6-1, 6-2.

1984 World Rankings[587]

Bud Collins	Lance Tingay	ATP Year-End Rankings
1. John McEnroe	1. John McEnroe	1. John McEnroe
2. Jimmy Connors	2. Ivan Lendl	2. Jimmy Connors
3. Ivan Lendl	3. Mats Wilander	3. Ivan Lendl
4. Mats Wilander	4. Jimmy Connors	4. Mats Wilander
5. Andres Gomez	5. Andres Gomez	5. Andres Gomez
6. Anders Jarryd	6. Pat Cash	6. Anders Jarryd
7. Henrik Sundstrom	7. Henrik Sundstrom	7. Henrik Sundstrom
8. Pat Cash	8. Kevin Curren	8. Pat Cash
9. Eliot Teltscher	9. Juan Aguilera	9. Eliot Teltscher
10. Yannick Noah	10. Aaron Krickstein	10. Yannick Noah

1984 Volvo Grand Prix Bonus Pool Top 10[588]

Singles (15th Bonus Pool)			Doubles (10th Doubles Bonus Pool)		
1.	John McEnroe	$600,000	1.	Tomas Smid	$150,000
2.	Jimmy Connors	$400,000	2.	Mark Edmondson	$100,000
3.	Ivan Lendl	$300,000	3.	Sherwood Stewart	$ 75,000
4.	Mats Wilander	$200,000	4.	Peter Fleming	$ 60,000
5.	Andres Gomez	$100,000	5.	Pavel Slozil	$ 45,000
6.	Joakim Nystrom	$ 80,000	6.	Anders Jarryd	$ 35,000
7.	Henrik Sundstrom	$ 65,000	7.	Heinz Gunthardt	$ 25,000
8.	Eliot Teltscher	$ 50,000	8.	John McEnroe	$ 20,000
9.	Anders Jarryd	$ 40,000	9.	Robert Seguso	$ 17,000
10.	Tomas Smid	$ 32,000	10.	Ken Flach	$ 15,000

PIONEERS OF THE GAME

1984 Official Earnings Top 10[589]

1.	John McEnroe	$2,026,109	6.	Andres Gomez	$ 444,143
2.	Ivan Lendl	$1,060,196	7.	Jimmy Arias	$ 364,176
3.	Jimmy Connors	$ 974,400	8.	Anders Jarryd	$ 359,162
4.	Mats Wilander	$ 671,256	9.	Joakim Nystrom	$ 326,478
5.	Tomas Smid	$ 591.037	10.	Henrik Sundstrom	$ 320,412

\multicolumn{6}{c}{**1984 Tournament Calendar**}					
Date	**Tournaments**	**Singles Winner**	**Singles #2**	**Doubles Winners**	**Doubles #2**
1/8/1984	London $200,000 WCT			K. Flach - R. Seguso	H. Gunthardt - B. Taroczy
1/15/1984	Auckland $75,000 GP	Danny Saltz	Chip Hooper	B. Levine - J. Van Nostrand	D. Graham - L. Warder
1/29/1984	Phiadelphia $300,000 SS	John McEnroe	Ivan Lendl	P. Fleming - J. McEnroe	H. Leconte - Y. Noah
2/5/1984	Toronto $250,000 SP		Ivan Lendl	Yannick Noah	6-0, 6-2, 6-4
2/6/1984	Richmond $100,000 WCT	John McEnroe	Steve Denton	J. McEnroe - P. McEnroe	K. Curren - S. Denton
2/12/1984	Memphis $250,000 SS	Jimmy Connors	Henri Leconte	F. Buehning - P. Fleming	H. Gunthardt - T. Smid
2/18/1984	Sydney $400,000 4 man SP	John McEnroe	Guillermo Vilas	6-3, 6-3, 6-3	
2/19/1984	Palm Springs $200,000 SS	Jimmy Connors	Yannick Noah	B. Mitton - B. Walts	S. Davis - F. Taygan
2/19/1984	Auckland $100,000 SP	Ivan Lendl	John McEnroe	2-6, 6-4, 6-2, 7-6	
3/4/1984	Madrid $200,000 SS	John McEnroe	Tomas Smid	P. Fleming - J. McEnroe	F. Buehning - F. Taygan
3/11/1984	Brussels $250,000 SS	John McEnroe	Ivan Lendl	T. Gullikson - T. Gullikson	K. Curren - S. Denton
3/18/1984	Metz $75,000 GP	Ramesh Krishnan	Jan Gunnarsson	E. Edwards - D. Visser	W. Hampsòn - W. Masur
3/18/1984	Rotterdam $250,000 SS	Jimmy Connors	Ivan Lendl	K. Curren - W. Fibak	F. Buehning - F. Taygan
3/25/1984	Milan $365,000 SS	Stefan Edberg	Mats Wilander	P. Slozil - T. Smid	K. Curren - S. Denton
4/1/1984	Boca West $250,000 SS	Jimmy Connors	Johan Kriek	M. Edmondson - S. Stewart	D. Dowlen - N. Odizor
4/5/1984	Osaka Suntory Cup SP	John McEnroe	Yannick Noah	7-6, 0-6, 6-3	
4/8/1984	Bari $75,000 GP	Henrix Sundstrom	Pedro Rebolledo	S. Bimer - L. Pimek	M. Freeman - T. Wilkison
4/8/1984	Houston $250,000 WCT	Mark Dickson	Sammy Giammal-va	P. Cash - P. McNamee	D. Dowlen - N. Odizor
4/8/1984	Tokyo $250,000 SP	Ivan Lendl	John McEnroe	6-4, 3-6, 6-2	

4/15/1984	Luxembourg $200,000 SS	Ivan Lendl	Tomas Smid	A. Jarryd - T. Smid	M. Edmondson - S. Stewart
4/15/1984	Nice $75,000 GP	Andres Gomez	Henrix Sundstrom	J. Gunnarsson - M. Mortensen	H. Gildemeister - A. Gomez
4/22/1984	Monte Carlo $325,000 SS	Henrix Sundstrom	Mats Wilander	M. Edmondson - S. Stewart	J. Gunnarsson - M. Wilander
4/29/1984	Aix-en-Prov. $75,000 GP	Juan Aguilera	Fernando Luna	P. Cash - P. McNamee	C. Lewis - W. Masur
4/29/1984	Dallas $500,000 WCT	John McEnroe	Jimmy Connors	6-1, 6-2, 6-3	
5/13/1984	NY $500,000 TC WCT	John McEnroe	Ivan Lendl	D. Dowlen - N. Odizor	K. Curren - S. Denton
5/13/1984	Hamburg $250,000 SS	Juan Aguilera	Henrix Sundstrom	S. Edberg - A. Jarryd	H. Gunthardt - B. Taroczy
5/13/1984	Florence $75,000 GP	Francisco Gonzalez	Jimmy Brown	M. Dickson - C. Hopper	B. Mitton - B. Walts
5/20/1984	Rome $300,000 SS	Andres Gomez	Aaron Krickstein	K. Flach - R. Seguso	J. Alexander - M. Leach
5/20/1984	Munich $75,000 GP	Libor Pimek	Gene Mayer	B. Becker - W. Fibak	E. Fromm - F. Segarceanu
5/27/1984	Dusseldorf $531,000 WTC	USA	Czechoslovakia	2-1,	
5/27/1984	Dusseldorf $531,000 WTC	John McEnroe	Ivan Lendl	6-2, 6-2	
5/27/1984	Dusseldorf $531,000 WTC	Tomas Smid	Jimmy Arias	4-6, 7-6, 6-4	
5/27/1984	Dusseldorf $531,000 WTC		6-1, 6-2	P. Fleming - J. McEnroe	I. Lend - T. Smid
6/10/1984	French Open 7.1 m FF GS	Ivan Lendl	John McEnroe	H. Leconte - Y. Noah	P. Slozil - T. Smid
6/17/1984	London $200,000 GP	John McEnroe	Lief Shiras	P. Cash - P. McNamee	B. Mitton - B. Walts
6/23/1984	Bristol $100,000 GP	Johan Kriek	Brian Teacher	L. Stefanki - R. Van't Hof	J. Alexander - J. Fitzgerald
7/8/1984	Wimbledon £666,712 GS	John McEnroe	Jimmy Connors	P. Fleming - J. McEnroe	P. Cash - P. McNamee
7/15/1984	Newport $100,000 GP	Vijay Amritraj	Tim Mayotte	D. Graham - L. Warder	K. Flach - R. Seguso
7/15/1984	Gstaad $00,000 GP	Joakim Nystrom	Brian Teacher	H. Gunthardt - M. Gunthardt	G. Barboso - J. Soares
7/22/1984	Bastad $100,000 GP	Henrix Sundstrom	Anders Jarryd	J. Gunnarsson - M. Mortensen	J. Avendano - F. Roese
7/22/1984	Stuttgart $100,000 GP	Henri Leconte	Gene Mayer	S. Mayer - A. Maurer	F. Buehning - F. Taygan

7/23/1984	Boston $200,000 SS	Aaron Krickstein	Jose-Luis Clerc	K. Flach - R. Seguso	G. Donnelly - E. Fernandez
7/29/1984	Kitzbuhel $100,000 GP	Jose Higueras	Victor Pecci	H. Leconte - P. Portes	C. Dowdeswell - W. Fibak
7/29/1984	Hilversum $75,000 GP	Anders Jarryd	Tomas Smid	A. Jarryd - T. Smid	B. Dyke - M. Fancutt
7/29/1984	Washington $200,000 SS	Andres Gomez	Aaron Krickstein	P. Slozil - F. Taygan	D. Gitlin - B. Willenborg
8/5/1984	N'th Conway $200,000 SS	Joakim Nystrom	Tim Wilkison	B. Gottfried - T. Smid	C. Motta - B. Willenborg
8/5/1984	Livingston $75,000 GP	Johan Kriek	Michael Westphal	S. Davis - B. Testerman	P. Annacone - G. Michibata
8/11/1984	Los Angeles Olympics	Stefan Edberg	Francisco Maciel	6-1, 7-6	
8/12/1984	Indianapolis $300,000 SS	Andres Gomez	Balazs Taroczy	K. Flach - R. Seguso	H. Gunthardt - B. Taroczy
8/12/1984	Cleveland $100,000 GP	Terry Moor	Marty Davis	F. Gonzalez - M. Mitchell	S. Mayer - B. Taroczy
8/19/1984	Columbus $100,000 GP	Brad Gilbert	Hank Pfister	S. Mayer - S. Smith	B. Cox - T. Moor
8/19/1984	Toronto $300,000 SS	John McEnroe	Vitas Gerulaitis	P. Fleming - J. McEnroe	J. Fitzgerald - K. Warwick
8/26/1984	Cincinnati $375,000 SS	Mats Wilander	Anders Jarryd	F. Gonzalez - M. Mitchell	M. Davis - C. Dunk
8/26/1984	Rye Brook SP	Vitas Gerulaitis	Chip Hooper	7-6, 6-3	
8/26/1984	Jericho $150,000 SP	Ivan Lendl	Andres Gomez	6-2. 6-4	
9/9/1984	US Open $1,066,676 GS	John McEnroe	Ivan Lendl	J. Fitzgerald - T. Smid	S. Edberg - A. Jarryd
9/11/1984	Syracuse McEnroe SP	John McEnroe	Bjorn Borg		
9/16/1984	Los Angeles $200,000 SS	Jimmy Connors	Eliot Teltscher	K. Flach - R. Seguso	W. Fibak - S. Mayer
9/16/1984	Palermo $75,000 GP	Francesco Cancellotti	Miloslav Mecir	T. Smid - B. Willenborg	C. Panatta - H. Sundstrom
9/16/1984	Tel Aviv $75,000 GP	Aaron Krickstein	Shahar Perkiss	P. Doohan - B. Levine	C. Dowdeswell - J. Hlasek
9/23/1984	San Francisco $200,000 SS	John McEnroe	Brad Gilbert	P. Fleming - J. McEnroe	S. Giammalva - M. DePalmer
9/23/1984	Geneva $75,000 GP	Aaron Krickstein	Henrix Sundstrom	M. Mortensen - M. Wilander	L. Pimek - T. Smid
9/23/1984	Bordeaux $75,000 GP	Jose Higueras	Francisco Gonzalez	P. Slozil - B. Willenborg	L. Courteau - G. Forget

9/30/1984	Honolulu $100,000 GP	Marty Davis	David Pate	G. Donnelly - B. Walts	M. Dickson - M. Leach
10/7/1984	Brisbane $100,000 GP	Eliot Teltscher	Francisco Gonzalez	F. Gonzalez - M. Mitchell	B. Dyke - W. Masur
10/7/1984	Barcelona $200,000 SS	Mats Wilander	Joakim Nystrom	P. Slozil - T. Smid	M. Jaite - V. Pecci
10/14/1984	Sydney $225,000 SS	Anders Jarryd	Ivan Lendl	A. Jarryd - H. Simonsson	M. Edmondson - S. Stewart
10/14/1984	Basle $125,000 GP	Joakim Nystrom	Tim Wilkison	P. Slozil - T. Smid	S. Edberg - T. Wilkison
10/14/1984	Tokyo $125,000 GP	David Pate	Terry Moor	B. Dowlen - N. Odizor	M. Dickson - S. Meister
10/21/1984	Tokyo $375,000 SS	Jimmy Connors	Ivan Lendl	S. Giammalva - T. Giammalva	M. Edmondson - S. Stewart
10/21/1984	Cologne $75,000 GP	Joakim Nystrom	Miloslav Mecir	W. Fibak - S. Mayer	J. Gunnarsson - J. Nystrom
10/21/1984	Melbourne $150,000 GP	Matt Mitchell	Pat Cash	B. Dyke - W. Masur	J. McCurdy - P. Johnston
10/28/1984	Hong Kong $200,000 GP	Andres Gomez	Tomas Smid	K. Flach - R. Seguso	M. Edmondson - P. McNamee
10/28/1984	Vienna $100,000 GP	Tim Wilkison	Pavel Slozil	W. Fibak - S. Mayer	H. Gunthardt - B. Taroczy
11/4/1984	Stockholm $315,000 SS	John McEnroe	Mats Wilander	H. Leconte - T. Smid	V. Amritraj - I. Nastase
11/4/1984	Tapei $75,000 GP	Brad Gilbert	Wally Masur	K. Flach - R. Seguso	D. Gitlin - H. Pfister
11/11/1984	London $250,000 SS	Ivan Lendl	Andres Gomez	A. Gomez - I. Lendl	P. Slozil - T. Smid
11/18/1984	Treviso $75,000 GP	Vitas Gerulaitis	Tarik Benhabiles	P. Slozil - T. Wilkison	J. Gunnarsson - S. Stewart
11/25/1984	Johannesburg $200,000 SS	Eliot Teltscher	Vitas Gerulaitis	T. Delatte - F. Gonzalez	E. Meister - E. Teltscher
11/25/1984	Toulouse $100,000 GP	Hark Dickson	Heinz Gunthardt	J. Gunnarsson - S. Stewart	B. Mitton - B. Walts
12/9/1984	Aussie Open $645,000 GS	Mats Wilander	Kevin Curren	M. Edmondson - S. Stewart	J. Nystrom - M. Wilander
12/16/1984	Sydney $125,000 GP	John Fitzgerald	Sammy Giammalva	P. Annacone - C. van Rensburg	Tom Gullikson - S. McCain
12/23/1984	Adelaide $75,000 GP	Peter Doohan	Huub van Boeckel	B. Dyke - W. Masur	P. Doohan - B. Levine
1/1/1985	Melbourne $75,000 GP	Dan Cassidy	John Fitzgerald	B. Dyke - W. Masur	M. Bauer - S. McCain
1/5/1985	Las Vegas $1.3 Million SP	John McEnroe	Guillermo Vilas	7-5, 6-0	

1/6/1985	London $200,000 WCT Db.		6-3, 3-6, 6-3, 6-0	K. Flach - R. Seguso	H. Gunthardt - B.Taroczy
1/13/1985	NY $400,000 Volvo Masters				

http://www.atpworldtour.com/en/scores/results-archive

http://www.itftennis.com/procircuit/tournaments/men's-calendar.aspx?tour=&reg=&nat=&sur=&cate=AL&iod=&-fromDate=01-01-1968&toDate=29-12-1984

Tennis History, Jim McManus, (Canada 2010).

1985 USLTA Yearbook.

Official 1989 MTC Media Guide, (MTC 1989).

World of Tennis 1985, Edited by John Barrett and compiled by Lance Tingay, (London 1985).

CHAPTER 24

1985: NABISCO GRAND PRIX BEGINS WITH WCT INSIDE, VOLVO TENNIS SCHEME, CRISIS NO. 29

1985 Governing Bodies

The MIPTC was the governing body for men's professional tennis in 1985, except for the Davis Cup and the *Rules of Tennis*. The ITF was the governing body for the Davis Cup and in charge of the *Rules of Tennis*.

1985 Significant Tennis Leaders

ITF:	Philippe Chatrier (France)
USTA:	Randy Gregson
Tennis Australia President:	Brian Tobin
British LTA President:	G.B. Brown
French FFT President:	Philippe Chatrier
Chairman of Wimbledon:	Buzzer Hadingham
ATP President:	Ray Moore until July
ATP President:	Matt Doyle beginning in July
ATP Executive Director:	Mike Davies
WCT Owners:	Lamar Hunt and Al Hill, Jr.
WCT CEO:	Owen Williams

1985 MIPTC

ITF: Philippe Chatrier, Chairman until September, Derek Hardwick, Stan Malless until September and Forest Hainline beginning in September.

Tournaments:	Kobi Hermenjat (Europe) until September, Franco Bartoni (Europe) beginning in September, Ray Benton (North America until September and Charles Pasarell (North America) beginning in September, Brian Tobin (Rest of the World).
Players:	Mike Davies, Chairman beginning in September, Stan Smith until September, Harold Solomon beginning in September and Ray Moore.
Administrator:	Marshall Happer.
Asst Admn:	Tony Eugenio until October.
Asst Admn:	Bill Babcock beginning in October.
Asst Admn:	Paul Svehlik.
Asst Admn:	David Cooper.
Legal Counsel:	Roy L. Reardon, Esquire.
GP Supervisors:	Ken Farrar, Chief, Franco Bartoni until September, Keith Johnson, Bill Gilmour, Thomas Karlberg, John Heiss III, appointed part time in February, Tony Gathercole appointed part time in March.
Chair Umpires:	Rich Kaufman and Jeremy Shales, beginning after Wimbledon.
Communications:	John Hewig, Director of Communications, Reg Lansberry, Assistant Director of Communications.
Tour Liaisons:	Sandra "Sandy" Genelius, Jennifer Proud and Marieke van der Drift.

Nabisco Masters:	Jack Diller, Tournament Director until June, Eugene "Gene" Scott, Tournament Director beginning in June, Sue "Suzie" Rothstein, Tournament Manager.

1985 Major Player Representatives

ProServ:	Principals: Donald Dell, Ray Benton, Jerry Solomon and Ivan Blumberg.
Advantage Int'l:	Principals: Frank Craighill, Lee Fentress, Dean Smith and Peter Lawler.
IMG:	Principals: Mark McCormack and Bob Kain.
Others:	Ion Tiriac and Thomas Betz, Esquire (Vilas). John McEnroe, Sr., Esquire (McEnroe). Gloria Connors and Joseph Rountree, Esquire (Connors).

Two Competitions

In 1985, the 17th year of Open Tennis, there were two organized competitions for men: Nabisco Grand Prix and the Davis Cup as WCT was merged into the Nabisco Grand Prix. Davis Cup was open to all players and was won 3-2 by Sweden over Germany.

There were 72 Nabisco Grand Prix Open prize money tournaments, including the year end Nabisco Masters in Madison Square Garden in New York City. Included in the 72 tournaments were: four Grand Slams, the ATP two-week Lipton International Players Championships, 29 Super Series tournaments (including two WCT Super Series in Houston and Atlanta), 34 Regular and Open Week Series tournaments and four Nabisco Grand Prix Circuit Championships: Buick WCT Finals in Dallas, WCT Tournament of Champions in Forest Hills, Nabisco Masters at Madison Square Garden and the WCT World Doubles in London.

In 1985, in addition to the 3 Circuit Championships, WCT had 3 other tournaments: (i) January 6, London, $200,000, Fuji Film WCT World Doubles won by Ken Flach-Robert Seguso over Heinz Gunthardt – Balazs Taroczy 6-3, 3-6, 6-3, 6-0 [The January 1985 World Doubles was the end of the 1984 WCT non-Grand Prix circuit]; (ii)

March 3, Houston $300,000 River Oaks WCT Super Series won by John McEnroe over Kevin Curren 7-5, 6-1, 7-6 in singles and won by Peter Fleming and John McEnroe over Hank Pfister and Ben Testerman 6-3, 6-2 in doubles; (iii) April 28, Atlanta, $300,000 WCT Super Series won by John McEnroe over Paul Annacone 7-6 (7-2), 7-6 (7-5), 6-2 in singles and Paul Annacone and Christo van Rensburg over Steve Denton and Tomas Smid 6-4, 6-3 in doubles. In 1986, WCT would add a new Super Series in Phoenix and in 1987 another Super Series could be added.[590]

There were 27 Challenger Series with prize money of $25,000-$75,000 and 179 Satellite Series with prize money of $25,000-$50,000.

In 1985, the ATP was involved in six events: (i) February 17-Delray Beach, $300,000, Lipton International Players' Championships, (ii) May 26, Dusseldorf, $500,000 ATP Ambre Solaire World Team Cup, (iii) June 17, London, $200,000 Stella Artois Queens ATP Grass-Court Championships, (iv) June 23, Bristol, $100,000 Lambert and Butler Championships, (v) August 25, Cincinnati, $300,000 ATP Championships and (vi) November 17, London, $300,000 ATP Benson and Hedges Championships at Wembley. All of the ATP tournaments were in the Grand Prix, except for the World Team Cup.

Rules

The *1985 Official MIPTC Yearbook* combined for the first time the MIPTC Media Guide, Rules, Regulations and Code in a 609-page book. The book proved to be too cumbersome and the combined book was discontinued after 1985, back to two separate publications. The *Yearbook* included 208 MIPTC International Officials and 27 MIPTC National Officials.[591]

Bonus Pool

The Grand Prix Bonus Pool was increased from $3 million to $4 million with $3,250,000 for 64 singles players and $750,000 for 24 doubles players.

Bonus Prize Money for Small Tournaments

New for 1985 was an additional series of bonuses for players who played in the smaller Grand Prix tournaments: Winner - $8,000, Runner-Up - $4,000 and Losing Semifinalists - $2,000.

Player Commitment

In 1985, the number of self-designations for the top 100 players was increased from 12 to 14, plus the Nabisco Masters and the WCT Finals in Dallas, if qualified. The 14 included the Grand Slams, Super Series and the WCT Tournament of Champions. As MIPTC Administrator, I was authorized to make up to two substitutions.

The Balancing of Player Fields for the Tournaments

The most our player commitment system could provide to the ATP-2 Week Lipton tournament, Tournament of Champions and the 29 Super Series was approximately 3.2 players each in the top 10. Those designations gave the tournaments some players they could advertise and promote well in advance of their tournaments. As each year progressed, many players elected to play in a lot more than 14 tournaments, but we would not know about that until the 42-day entry deadline, so it was just about too late to use them in advertising. However, as you might imagine, there was no such thing as enough good players for a tournament director, so they were always dissatisfied and asking for more. All tournaments were always in competition with each other for the best players and the best dates.

Confidential Help from the Player Agents

As a matter of practice every year, I hosted a meeting of the main player agents, i.e., Bob Kain of IMG, Peter Lawler of Advantage International, Jerry Solomon and Ivan Blumberg of ProServ, John McEnroe, Sr., and Ion Tiriac, to confidentially disclose all the self-designations received for the next year and seek their cooperation for the moving of players among the various tournaments to ensure that each tournament had as much of a balanced field as our system could provide. My goal was, always, to avoid having to force a substitution on a player, unless absolutely necessary, as every player hated that. My characterization was that the player agents cooperated and tried to help. Jerry Solomon's characterization was that each year they had a war with me over the movement of players to balance the fields and then they would have a war with their player clients about what we had worked out. Sometimes, when their clients just would not agree voluntarily, I would have to require one or more substitutions. Somehow, working together with the player agents, we made the system work every year and our tournaments continued to be successful. I doubt if many of the professional players and, for that matter, members of the MIPTC, were aware of the confidential help the player agents provided to me every year. As you will learn a little later, they were suing me and the MIPTC and I was suing them. *In Tennis, all of our friends and enemies were the same folks.*

Special Events Restriction

The Special Events restriction on the top 100 players was revised to: (i) Prohibit special events during the calendar weeks of the Grand Slams, the Nabisco Masters, the WCT Dallas Finals and any week in which there were two Super Series tournaments scheduled; (ii) Prohibit special events within 100 miles and 30 days before or after a Grand Slam, Nabisco Masters, WCT Dallas Finals, the WCT Tournament of Champions or any Super Series tournament; and (iii) Prohibit special events on the same continent during the week of the WCT Tournament of Champions or the week of any Super Series more than four times per year.

Alternative to Commitment

The alternative to the Player Commitment Rule was revised to permit players to enter via the qualifying of every tournament or agree to six "hard" designations. Faced with that nightmare alternative effectively persuaded all players to sign the full 14 tournament player commitment. However, we still had at the insistence of the Grand Slams their right to offer a wild card to a 1982, 1983 or 1984 singles winner, who refused to sign for the full 14 tournament player commitment. (The "Borg" Rule.)

MIPTC Certified Officials

In addition to the referee, each tournament was required to provide the following increased minimum numbers of certified MIPTC International Chair Umpires:

Draw Size	1985 Minimum No.	1984 Minimum No.
128	10	8
96	8	6
64	6	4
56	6	4
48	5	3
32	4	2

Thus, as the MIPTC Officials Schools and the MIPTC evaluation of on-site officials improved, so did the requirement for the tournaments to provide more of them to provide the best officiating for the players and the tournaments. Without exception, every player supported the professionalization of the officials.

MIPTC Identification

As in 1983 and 1984, each tournament was required to include "one (1) full page of editorial identifying the members of the MIPTC and its staff and describing the role of the MIPTC with respect to the Nabisco Grand Prix." Finally, Wimbledon devoted a half page to the Nabisco Grand Prix on page 37 of its 1985 tournament program. Remember the statement by Chris Gorringe, the Wimbledon executive, to me in effect: "Marshall we can do anything for you as long as we did it last year." *We had made some important progress with Wimbledon!*[592]

Crisis No. 29: 1985 Volvo Tennis Promotion Scheme

The members of the MIPTC and I were excited and pleased to have a first-class international company like Nabisco join in the sponsorship of the Nabisco Grand Prix and Nabisco Masters to support men's professional tennis. Nabisco was a great company and it was managed by some really nice and very smart executives. At the conclusion of the January 1985 final Volvo Masters, Ed Redding, Executive Vice President of Nabisco, wrote a nice letter to Rick Dowden, Volvo's Senior Vice President, saying "I can assure you that Nabisco will strive to continue the same high level relationship that you have developed" with the Pro Council and the people who really count in the tennis world."[593]

Neither Ed Redding or Nabisco had any idea that they might soon be embroiled in a distasteful professional tennis war. Unbeknownst to the members of the MIPTC or to me during the final Volvo Masters and the January 1985 meeting of the MIPTC in New York at the time of the final settlement agreement was signed for the Volvo/ProServ new Super Series tournament for Volvo in Chicago, Volvo and ProServ already had a then secret plan underway that was not designed to "support and cooperate" with the MIPTC and Nabisco's sponsorship of the Nabisco Grand Prix and Nabisco Masters. The new promotion would be known as "Volvo Tennis," which we would later allege in our Counterclaim to the Volvo lawsuit, was "a deliberate, conscious and fraudulent program to use their power in the tennis world to damage the MIPTC, to undermine and destroy Nabisco's sponsorship rights, and to confuse the public into believing that Volvo still remained the overall sponsor of the Grand Prix. The central device for achieving these ends was a scheme called "Volvo Tennis." "Volvo Tennis" is not a company, a sport, a competition, nor any form of legal or physical entity whatsoever, but was a fictional concept designed, publicized, marketed and promoted by Volvo, ProServ, Dell and Benton solely in order to make the public think, in Benton's own words, that "everything in tennis is Volvo."[594]

During its sponsorship of the Volvo Grand Prix and Volvo Masters for 1980-1984, Volvo developed a Volvo Grand Prix logo which was often marketed with the slogan "linking the world's official tennis tournaments." The "Volvo Tennis" scheme used the same logo by just changing the name from "Volvo Grand Prix" to "Volvo Tennis" and using the similar slogan: "Linking the world's great tennis tournaments through television."

If Nabisco's sponsorship rights could be undermined and damaged enough so that Nabisco walked away from its sponsorship of the Nabisco Grand Prix and Nabisco Masters, the MIPTC, the Grand Prix tournaments and the players would be left pretty much at the mercy of Volvo and ProServ. *If you did not think that professional tennis in those years was a tough business before, I'll bet you do now.*

ProServ, Volvo, WCT Meeting

Owen Williams of WCT was at the January 1985 MIPTC meeting. After the meeting, he told Roy Reardon that "Ray Benton (and probably Donald Dell also) had a meeting (in the summer of 1984) with Dowden (Rick Dowden of Volvo) and with Lamar (Lamar Hunt of WCT) and me (Owen Williams) and tried to enlist us to become part of the Volvo team and said that if he could link Volvo and WCT together they could 'kill Nabisco.'" When Williams raised the question of whether Volvo was not seeking to create a circuit within a circuit in violation of the Grand Prix Rules, Benton stated "damned right we are going to have a circuit within a circuit. Volvo put $25 million into tennis and it's not going to walk away; that Ahlstrom is a tough guy." When Williams asked again "Isn't that contrary to your agreement? (with the Council), Benton responded 'Williams, grow up – for the next year or two, the public is going to think everything in tennis is Volvo. If Philippe thought he could just insult Ahlstrom and that Ahlstrom would walk away from tennis he's mistaken.'" WCT elected not to join with Volvo.[595]

When the first Nabisco Grand Prix began, the Volvo/ProServ "Volvo Tennis" promotion became obvious to everyone. Volvo and ProServ had merely changed the name of the "Volvo Grand Prix" promotional staff to the "Volvo Tennis" staff with essentially the same personnel promoting "Volvo Tennis." Volvo became the title sponsor of the tournaments at Newport, Livingston, Washington (Dell's tournament) and Los Angeles (Kramer's tournament) and each was required to use the words "Volvo Tennis" in their titles: "Volvo Tennis Hall of Fame" for Newport, "Volvo Tennis Livingston," "Volvo

Tennis Washington" and "Volvo Tennis Los Angeles." That was in addition to the new Super Series, "Volvo Tennis Chicago" and the existing "Volvo Tennis North Conway" in New Hampshire.

ProServ organized the telecasts of the North American tournaments on PBS and USA Network and the commentary was provided by Donald Dell, who spent a lot of time talking about "Volvo Tennis" and no time mentioning the "Nabisco Grand Prix." Each telecast would begin with "Volvo Tennis presents the singles finals" and would include promotional announcements such as "This program is made possible by grants from Volvo, sponsors of Volvo Tennis, linking the world's great tennis events through television." During the telecast of the LaQuinta Super Series, Dell attempted to place a "Volvo Tennis" banner on the back of the center court. Ken Farrar, our MIPTC Supervisor called me about the banner and informed me that the Nabisco representatives were terribly upset about it. I ordered the banner to be removed, but Dell sent me a message that he intended to erect a banner at all of his telecasts.

To say that the Nabisco representatives were upset with the new "Volvo Tennis" promotion would be putting it mildly. Nabisco had not agreed to become embroiled in a nasty tennis war and I feared that the MIPTC could lose Nabisco if the Volvo Tennis promotion continued. I consulted with Roy Reardon about what we could do to try to stop Volvo and ProServ from using the Volvo Tennis promotion to ruin our sponsorship with Nabisco and at my request, Roy provided me with recommended draft letters to Volvo, the Grand Prix tournaments and to the television networks.

After talking further to Roy Reardon, MIPTC Chairman Philippe Chatrier and several of the other members of the MIPTC (except Ray Benton), I was convinced that in advance of the April 15 MIPTC meeting, immediate and firm action was necessary to protect the rights of the Council and our contractual relationship with our sponsor.[596]

As stated in our Counterclaim later we said: "By letters dated March 13, 1985, Happer wrote to Volvo as well as to the networks involved in the recent broadcasts described above, to protest Volvo's violations of the Grand Prix Rules and of its agreement, as well as the attempts to pass itself off as the continuing Grand Prix sponsor. Representatives of the MIPTC also made numerous attempts in person, by telephone, by letter and by telex, to have Volvo and ProServ cease the improper, illegal and misleading actions described above and have their literature, graphics and tournament insignia conform to the Grand Prix Rules and to Volvo and ProServ's contractual commitments."[597]

Crisis No. 29 involving the Volvo Tennis promotional scheme led to the new Crisis No. 30, the Volvo lawsuit.

MIPTC Meetings

In 1985, the MIPTC held five meetings: January 14-17 in New York, April 15-18 in Dallas, June 10-13 in Paris, September 10-12 in New York and November 4-7 in London.

MIPTC Meeting, New York January 14-17, 1985

Canadian Open Chairman's Day Prohibited

In January in New York, I reported on the Canadian Open's promotion of a sponsor's "Chairman's Day" in which top players were paid a fee to participate just prior to the beginning of the Canadian Open each year. As Administrator, I advised the Canadian Open that the "Chairman's Day" event staged in connection with tournament could no longer be held in the same manner as in the past without violating the MIPTC Code. The tournament appealed to the MIPTC, but the MIPTC voted 8-1 (Benton voting against) to affirm my Determination.

Employment of Two Professional Chair Umpires

After extensive discussion, the Council, by a 6-3 vote, authorized me to employ two professional chair umpires to work year-round on an experimental basis. We asked each tournament to reimburse the MIPTC on a voluntary basis for the costs of providing them since it would count as their required minimum MIPTC certified officials. *This was a huge step forward for professional officiating.*

Paris Super Series

Philippe Chatrier departed the meeting for the consideration and voting on the approval of a new Super Series in Paris. By a vote of 4-3 with one abstention (Malless), Paris was granted the sanction for a new Super Series, which became the Paris Indoors.

Player's Request for Removal of an Official Eliminated

The Council amended the MIPTC Tournament Regulations to eliminate the right of players to request removal of any on-court officials.

Madison Square Garden

I reported on the new MIPTC agreement for the renting of Madison Square Garden for five years for the Nabisco Masters, assuming Nabisco opted to exercise its option to extend its sponsorship from three to five years. The base "turn-key" rent for Madison Square Garden was:

1985 Nabisco Masters	$600,000	[January of 1986]
1986 Nabisco Masters	$650,000	[December of 1986]
1987 Nabisco Masters	$675,000	[December]
1988 Nabisco Masters	$675,000	[December]
1989 Nabisco Masters	$700,000	[December]

ESPN

ESPN became the exclusive broadcaster of the Nabisco Masters in the United States in December of 1986, 1987 and 1988 for rights fees of $550,000, $625,000 and $700,000, respectively. NBC was covering the January 1986 Nabisco Masters; it helped a lot that Nabisco at the time owned 20 percent of ESPN. We could not have moved the Nabisco Masters into December without this ESPN contract.[598]

MIPTC Meeting, Dallas April 15-18, 1985

Player-Agent Prohibition Bylaw

In April in Dallas,[599] Ray Benton (ProServ President) reported (reluctantly) that the North American tournaments had voted on April 14 "not to seek a repeal of the Bylaw that prohibited player-agents from becoming members of the MIPTC.

MIPTC Meeting, London June 15-18, 1985

Ray Benton Refuses To Resign

In June in London, Ray Benton stated that he had decided not to resign as a member of the MIPTC, notwithstanding his numerous conflicts of interest. The other members of the MIPTC felt that a player-agent with a personal financial interest in numerous players and numerous tournaments could not be impartial or appear to be impartial on enough of the issues before the MIPTC for decision to offer credibility to the MIPTC. Membership by a player-agent on the MIPTC also affected the balance of the three constituent groups as many issues were "player vs. tournament" issues. The Council considered and rejected Ray Benton's request that it rescind the new Bylaw amendment prohibiting player-agents from being members of the MIPTC.

Malless and Smith Did Not Run For Re-Election

ITF Representative Stan Malless and Player Representative Stan Smith each announced that they were retiring from the MIPTC and would not be running for re-election. As captured in the MIPTC Meeting Minutes: "Both spoke on their general views of the game and gave their ideas for improvement in the future," "The Council thanked each of them for their service to the Council and their many contributions to the sport."[600]

MIPTC Meeting, New York September 10-12, 1985

Hermenjat and Malless Attended

In September in New York, Kobi Hermenjat attended the meeting to assist his successor, Franco Bartoni. It would soon be evident that Franco had no interest in Kobi's advice. Stan Malless attended the meeting to assist his successor, Forrest Hainline.

Election of Chairman

Philippe Chatrier and Mike Davies were nominated for the office of MIPTC Chairman. When Lars Myhrman and then Kobi Hermenjat represented the European tournaments, they always voted with the ITF Representatives and Brian Tobin as the Rest of World Tournament Representative (who was also a Vice President of the ITF and President of Tennis Australia (LTAA) to elect Philippe Chatrier as the MIPTC Chairman. When Franco Bartoni replaced Kobi Hermenjat as the European Tournament Representative, he began always voting against the ITF so he, along with Charles Pasarell, the North American Tournament Representative and a long-time ATP member, joined with the Player Representatives to make it a 5-4 vote for Mike Davies as the new MIPTC Chairman.

Prior to this election, I had learned of Franco Bartoni's intention to "defeat" Chatrier and I wondered if, somehow, I should have tried to get the ITF members to support Mike Davies so as to avoid the 5-4 voting "defeat," which shocked and upset

Chatrier. The disaster of having Bob Briner as MIPTC Chairman when he was the ATP Executive Director had been long forgotten and everyone respected Mike Davies.

Franco Bartoni had been one of the original MIPTC Supervisors hired in 1978, and from 1978 until 1985, he had mainly worked at his assigned tournaments each day and then returned to his hotel room, I was told, to watch movies. No one heard much from Franco outside of his work as a Supervisor. In any event, after resigning as a MIPTC Supervisor, Franco became the tournament director of Rome and was elected to the MIPTC to represent the European tournaments replacing Kobi Hermenjat. Even though Rome was the Italian Open owned by the Italian Tennis Federation which was an important member of the ITF, Bartoni was able to get the Italian Tennis Federation to permit him not to support the ITF on the MIPTC. Franco immediately sought to and did change the character of the Council as he became an adversary of the ITF, the North American tournaments and the Rest of the World Tournaments. He constantly sought to make any deal he could with the Player Representatives to gain favorable treatment for the European tournaments. Franco was fluent in many languages and brilliant in all of them. I learned how dangerous he would be as he pursued the "best interest of Franco and the European tournaments" more than the "best interest of the game."

In a side note, I later learned that Mike Davies did not even know he was going to be nominated for the Chairmanship or that the ATP had a deal with Franco to secure his election, even though in January, his contract as the ATP Executive Director had been extended for two additional years. I heard that the ATP Board decided to have Mike become the MIPTC Chairman in executive session while they were discussing whether to fire Mike or not as the ATP Executive Director.

Mike said in *International Tennis Weekly*[601]: "'Professional tennis has many challenges ahead, and I hope I can contribute in helping the game in all aspects. Philippe Chatrier has been a great teacher for me and has led the sport through many difficult years. I hope that I can achieve a little of the success Philippe has had."

Rotation of MIPTC Chairmanship

I was directed to prepare for consideration a draft Bylaw providing for the rotation of the office of MIPTC Chairman among the three constituencies of the Council. This would eventually be enacted but never utilized because the Player Representatives controlled the Chairmanship until the Council was liquidated after 1989.

Connors Automatic Suspension

As of September 8, Jimmy Connors had reached $7,500 in on-site fines. Since he waived his right to appeal the fines assessed at the Canadian Open and the U.S. Open, he began a 42-day suspension on September 9, to be reduced to 21 days if he did not play at all. *Another scheduled vacation!*

By now it should be obvious that the 21-day suspension was somewhere between ineffective and meaningless as the players just picked a vacation time when they did not want to play Grand Prix tournaments.

Age Eligibility Restrictions

The Council adopted the following age restrictions: age 14 and under: not eligible for any tournaments. Age 14-15: eligible for a maximum of eight tournaments and age 15-16: eligible for a maximum of 12 tournaments. Players on the computer rankings as of September 16, 1985, were exempted from these age restrictions. Any player could petition the MIPTC for exemption from this restriction.

Minimum Seating Requirements

For the first time, the Council adopted minimum seating requirements for MIPTC sanctioned tournaments: Super Series required 5,000 seats, Regular/Open Week Series required 3,500 for outdoor and 2,500 for indoor.

Five-Set Doubles Final

A tournament whose singles final was 60 minutes of less, could have a five-set doubles final.

Grass Court Shoes

No one actually markets grass court shoes. The shoe companies, as a matter of courtesy, make a few pairs and distribute them to the players at the French Open just in advance of the small grass court season leading to Wimbledon. After two years of research by Wimbledon with the shoe manufacturers and the players, the Council accepted Wimbledon's recommendation for the specifications for grass court shoes. Long ago spikes were rejected due to the damage to the grass courts and now rubber knobs and rubber spikes on the bottoms and sides of the shoes were prohibited. Even so, the Wimbledon Centre Court continued to show its wear and tear by the finals each year, but it was not as bad as before.

Inquiry of Linesman Prohibited

The provision permitting a player to make an inquiry of a linesman's call was deleted.

No Press Conferences For Officials

To avoid actions that might be considered to affect the impartiality of officials, on-court tennis officials were prohibited from participation in press conferences. If something needed to be clarified for the press, we would have it done by the MIPTC Supervisor, not an on-court official. This also protected the on-court officials from the press.[602]

MIPTC Meeting, London November 4-7, 1985

Rotation of Chairmanship Tabled

In November in London,[603] after consideration of several drafts for a Bylaw amendment providing for the rotation of the MIPTC Chairmanship, the matter was tabled by a vote of 5-3-1. Do *you want to guess how the three Player Representatives, Franco Bartoni and Charlie Pasarell voted now that Mike Davies was the new Chairman?*

Masters Television Rights Beyond
Volvo's Sponsorship Term Previously Sold

On June 5, I was advised by Richard Bunn of the European Broadcasting Union (EBU) who represented all of the over-the-air government television channels in Europe that he had a contract signed by Bob Briner of ProServ purportedly giving EBU the television rights to the Masters for 1984, 1985, 1986 and 1987. I had to tell him that ProServ had no authority to sell EBU the rights for the Nabisco Masters in 1986 and 1987 and we would have to negotiate a new agreement. He was upset. However, subsequently, we did make another agreement with him for the Nabisco Masters as EBU still had a monopoly of all the public over-the-air networks in Europe and Europe was yet to get cable channels.

New MIPTC Staff and 437 Madison Avenue

Beginning in 1985, with our new sponsorship contract with Nabisco, Nabisco was paying the MIPTC $3.5 million per year and, for the first time, the MIPTC owned and controlled the Nabisco Masters. As a result, the MIPTC would have the capability to and be responsible for the promotion of the Nabisco Grand Prix and the Nabisco Masters. Nabisco was providing the separate promotion of Nabisco's sponsorship. In late 1984, I hired Jack Diller as the Senior Marketing Executive and Tournament Director for the Nabisco Masters and I hired John Hewig as the Director of Communications to begin building the necessary MIPTC staff. In November of 1984, we moved the MIPTC to new expanded offices at the fourth floor of 437 Madison Avenue in Manhattan to accommodate the increased staff. We continued our Paris office at Stade Roland Garros courtesy of the French Tennis Federation.

Susie Rothstein, Tournament Manager

Jack Diller recruited the absolute best possible person to be his Nabisco Masters Tournament Manager and on January 1, we hired Suzie Rothstein. Suzie was a native of San Marino, CA, a 1977 graduate of UCLA, and had for seven years been with ProServ as the Tournament Manager at Madison Square Garden for the Colgate Masters and the Volvo Masters and previously was involved with the Avon Championships and the Westchester Golf Classic.

Diller Resigns, Gene Scott Hired

Diller began with some really good plans for the first Nabisco Masters. One of his important innovations was to purchase and cover a large part of the Madison Square Garden rotunda with indoor outdoor carpet to create a brand new corporate entertainment area just off of and close to the floor entrances to the court. However, sometime around June or July, about six months before our first Nabisco Masters was scheduled for January of 1986, Jack came to me and said he was resigning as the Tournament Director. I remember he told me something like "I don't like this job and I am not good at it." I was fortunate to get my friend Gene Scott to immediately take over as Tournament Director. Gene was a graduate of Yale in 1960 with a B.A. and University of Virginia School of Law 1964. He was a New York attorney, a former U.S. Davis Cup team member and previously had a world ranking of No. 11 in 1965. Gene was the publisher and founder of *Tennis Week*, vice president of the International Tennis Hall of Fame and the president of the U.S. International Lawn Tennis Club. He had been the tournament director of the Grand Prix tournament in South Orange through 1983 and had a great relationship with all the leading players. Gene worked as an independent contractor and he did a great job for five years. Gene was inducted into the International Tennis Hall of Fame in 2008 after passing away in in 2006. Jack Diller would eventually find his calling as the long time Chief Executive Officer of the San Antonio Spurs of the NBA.

Reg Lansberry, Jennifer Proud (Mearns), Marieke van der Drift and Sandy Genelius

John Hewig recruited, and we were fortunate to hire, Reg Lansberry, formerly of Rowayton, CT, as the assistant director of communications for the MIPTC. Reg had spent almost six years as a senior writer for *World Tennis* magazine. Reg's responsibilities included all MIPTC publications, including the Nabisco Masters programs and press articles and releases, in addition to assisting with the day-to-day operation of the Council's public relations activities. Hewig also recruited, and we hired three really capable tour liaisons: Jennifer Proud (Mearns), Marieke van der Drift and Sandy Genelius to travel the worldwide Nabisco Grand Prix to represent the MIPTC with the tournaments and the players, provide the press with bios on the players, tournament results, rankings and other important information, help the tournaments and the players with the press, conduct player press conferences, and provide public relations for the MIPTC, etc. Jennifer had earned a B.S. in Business Administration from Bryant University and had worked for the previous two years for the public relations staff at Madison Square Garden. She had been involved in the publicity efforts of many major sporting and entertainment events, including the Volvo Masters and the Virginia Slims Championships. Jennifer was assigned to work out of our New York office. Marieke was a native of the Netherlands and was fluent in Dutch, English, German, French and Italian. She had earned a Masters in Germanic languages from the University of Brussels and a Masters from the School for Interpreters (Marie Haps). She had been a freelance journalist and publicist for Grand Prix motor racing and skiing. Marieke was assigned to work out of our Paris office. Sandy had worked with IMG for five years on the promotion, public relations and operations of various tennis tournaments throughout North America. Sandy was assigned to work out of our New York office. These three Tour Liaisons did a terrific job and for the first time provided pure tennis promotion for the tournaments and the players instead of having ProServ provide "Volvo oriented" promotion as had been done in the past. At last, the "Game" was represented by the democratically-elected MIPTC and had a promotional voice.

Thomas Karlberg, John Heiss, Tony Gathercole, Rich Kaufman and Jeremy Shales

To replace Kurt Nielsen, who had resigned in 1984, Ken Farrar recruited Thomas Karlberg, age 36 of Stockholm, as his replacement beginning January 1. Ken also recruited, and we hired John Heiss and Tony Gathercole to work as part-time MIPTC Supervisors in 1985. Thomas was the former head coordinator of the European Kings Cup tournament and referee of the Grand Prix tournaments in Stockholm and Bastad. Col. John Heiss III, age 53 of Cocoa Beach, Fla., was hired in February as a part-time MIPTC Supervisor. John was a graduate of Millikin University in 1953 and captain of his tennis team for four years. John had been two years with the USTA, working satellite circuits and serving as an assistant referee at the U.S. Open. Tony Gathercole of Surrey, England, was hired in March as a part time MIPTC Supervisor. Tony was an assistant referee at Wimbledon. We hired Rich Kaufman and Jeremy Shales as our first two full-time MIPTC Chair Umpires on an experimental one-year basis to begin after 1985 Wimbledon. By 1985, the MIPTC Officials Program had trained and certified a number of chair umpires and now the MIPTC Rules required each tournament to provide a minimum number of them. However, the one weakness of the system was simply on account of the geographical movement of the Grand Prix from country to country and continent to continent, individual certified chair umpires could not afford to travel the circuit, so their work was limited to part time when the circuit was in their geographical area. The decision to employ two chair umpires to work every week on the circuit meant that they would be officiating in around 300 matches per year and the players would be seeing them on a regular basis. This was the beginning of real professional officiating for men's tennis and the end of player misconduct. This would also be the end of a player like John McEnroe having to look up at the chair and see a chair umpire he had never seen before or one who was not an expert on the rules. It would also be the last time a chair umpire refused to answer any player's questions providing they were professionally stated. John McEnroe would henceforth always have one of these two chair umpires for his matches as would other players who needed their expertise. These two chair umpires had our full backing.

Jeremy Shales

Jeremy Shales, born in Fulmer, Buckinghamshire, England, began officiating age 17. He was certified as a MIPTC International Official, having graduated from the 1981 MIPTC Officials School in Madrid. Jeremy was a graduate of St. Paul's School in England and a former member of the Bank of England.

Rich Kaufman

Rich Kaufman's trials and tribulations were both typical and untypical of what a professional tennis official had to go through to make it with the national tennis associations control of tennis officiating. Rich was born in Buffalo, grew up in State College, Pa., and received his B.A. from Hiram (Ohio) College in 1972. In June of 1977, he earned his Masters in International Relations from University of Southern California, which was taught in London for USC by the faculty of the London School of Economics. In 1977, while in London, Rich went to the local Cumberland Club, which was two blocks from his apartment, to help with a local tennis tournament. There he met some tennis officials from the British Professional Tennis Umpires Federation (PTUF) who gave him his first training as a tennis official. At the time he had no knowledge that the PTUF was a "splinter" group of professional tennis officials who had broken away from and were in competition with the "official" Lawn Tennis Umpires Association (LTUA). The PTUF officials also provided umpires for the Queens tournament before Wimbledon and the LTUA provided umpires for Wimbledon. The LTUA disliked the PTUF and would not let any of them officiate at Wimbledon.

In 1977, Kaufman was invited by the PTUF to work at Queens as a linesman, but when he arrived, a flu epidemic had sidelined a lot of the PTUF officials and he was all of a sudden given chair assignments at Queens, a Grand Prix tournament. He was given no linesmen, so at his first professional tournament as a chair umpire, he became a solo chair umpire. At Queens, Kaufman happened to meet George Armstrong, one of the most respected British tennis officials who had been the chair umpire for the famous 1975 Wimbledon final won by Arthur Ashe over Jimmy Connors. Armstrong was a LTUA official, so he was not working at Queens. Armstrong told Kaufman he could get him into Wimbledon in 1977, but he should not mention that he worked at Queens because of the war between the LTUA and the PTUF. Armstrong was successful in getting Kaufman invited by the LTUA and Rich worked as a linesman for 1977 Wimbledon (for little or no pay but that "didn't matter" to him).

In August of 1977, Kaufman moved to Seattle, joined the Pacific Southwest Section of the USTA and in 1978 obtained his USTA certification as a tennis official. He may have been the only first-time candidate who had already worked as a chair umpire for Queens, a Grand Prix tournament. The USTA certification permitted Kaufman to begin working in USTA tournaments and the U.S. Open, which was then controlled by the Eastern Tennis Umpires Association (ETA). During those years, if you were not a member of the ETA, you did not get to be a chair umpire for main draw matches at the U.S. Open. You were either a linesman or maybe the chair for some junior matches or qualifying matches. The ETA pretty much controlled the U.S. Open until Bob Rockwell became the U.S. Open

Chief of Umpires in 1983-1984, followed by Woody Sublett (Walker) in 1985. So slowly, officials like Kaufman began to get main draw chair umpire assignments instead of all of them always going to ETA members.

Kaufman, as an independent tennis official from the United States, continued to travel to London to work with the PTUF at the Grand Prix tournaments at Queens and at the London Indoors at Wembley and with the LTUA at Wimbledon until 1981 when the LTUA discovered that he had worked at Queens for the PTUF. Notwithstanding that he was an independent American tennis official, the LTUA summarily "disinvited" him from working at Wimbledon in 1981. However, in 1982, Wimbledon had a shortage of umpires and largely through the efforts of David Lloyd, then an official with the British Lawn Tennis Association, umpires were brought in from the PTUF to help. Lloyd knew that the PTUF officials were good tennis officials and they were needed for Wimbledon. However, the PTUF officials were pretty much relegated to the field courts and were not given the special clothing provided to the LTUA officials as the LTUA continued its petty war against them. Finally, in 1983, Wimbledon demanded that the PTUF and the LTUA merge into the LTUA. That finally ended the LTUA vs. PTUF war.

In 1985, Kaufman was hired to train officials as a traveling supervisor for the USTA with the USTA's secondary circuits. Then, at age 34, he was recruited by David Cooper to become the first American full time chair umpire for the MIPTC along with Jeremy Shales. Kaufman continued as a leader of professional chair umpires from 1985 until the end of the MIPTC on December 31, 1989.

During his tenure with the MIPTC, Kaufman and his fellow professional chair umpires were assigned to almost every match involving "volatile" or "difficult" players. This at first created a significant amount of resentment by the local national umpires, but we backed the MIPTC Supervisors to use our new professionals as much as possible and necessary. As they were scrutinized by the players and our MIPTC Supervisors (and all the local umpires) they got better and better and by their example the local umpires also got better.

Kaufman and his colleagues developed a written matrix and learned how to call matches, handle crowd control, recognize curse words and obscene gestures in French, Italian, Hebrew, Spanish (including Catalan), German, Czech, Russian and Belgium's various languages. Jacques Dorfmann, the French Open Referee, tried to use the French language and the need to control the crowd in French as an excuse not to use the MIPTC Chair Umpires (except, of course for "volatile" type players which scared him) until the MIPTC pros proved that they could handle matches at the French Open in fluent French. Kaufman's French was once even featured in a Perrier ad on French television to the dismay of Dorfmann.

In preparation for this book, I interviewed Rich and asked him how he learned as a full-time professional Chair Umpire to best deal with the "volatile" players, like McEnroe, Connors, Nastase, Kriek, etc. At one Stockholm Open, Kaufman was assigned to umpire every McEnroe match. Kaufman did not consider Lendl a "volatile" player. He said: "Lendl was very intelligent and was just really good at putting pressure on the officials all the time, " and that "Lendl was similar to all American athletes who grow up learning to test their sports officials during a game."

Kaufman said that no player was looking for any umpire to "suck up" to them. Some were just more "volatile" than others. Kaufman said that with every player's rant, it was important to try to determine what the real problem was which maybe had nothing to what he was ranting. Kaufman found that if he communicated with the player, a relationship was established and if he identified the real problem, he could deal with it directly and if he acted professionally, the player would tend to also act professionally. On the other hand, Kaufman learned when he started officiating at Queens, that the British officials were horrified by the language of some players against officials. However, Kaufman knew a lot of that was only normal reactions by athletes as in all sports. Shales unfortunately exhumed some British arrogance in communicating with the players and the players resented it.

Kaufman said that "it took a while for the players to learn that we were not intimidated by them." McEnroe and Connors eventually wanted the pros. Lendl got comfortable with Kaufman and Shales. Lendl said he did want to have an umpire that he had never seen before. Kaufman said that once a match started, Connors was against all officials simply as just a fierce competitor. One time at the Lipton tournament, Kaufman got out of chair and told Connors privately: "I am out of patience." Rich said that Connors never looked at him but heard him and never said anything else in the match which he lost. Kaufman said he never tried to show up a player and he never went after a player or tried to get in the last word with a player. Kaufman said that if a player was "shown up" or "embarrassed" publicly during a match, there were no penalty (fine or suspension) that would stop him from reacting badly, so he always avoided it. Rich said, "After I got used to them and they got used to me, I never got close to having to default a player. I would tell a player verbally or non-verbally: "I have had it, that's enough." Kaufman described that private interchange as *"preventative officiating."*

Rich Kaufman's struggle to get involved in tennis officiating, often without compensation and always without adequate compensation, is pretty much typical of what happened with all tennis officials, all of whom had an enduring love for the sport of tennis and wanted to contribute. Kaufman, like his fellow professional chair umpires, never got rich following their dream to participate in men's professional tennis as officials. In the beginning of his career, Kaufman rarely got enough compensation to even cover his traveling expenses and it was not until he was hired by the MTC in 1985, that he received year-round compensation as a professional official. However, the role they played in developing professional officiating to assist the players in having the best and fairest conditions as they competed around the world for prize money was invaluable and very much appreciated by everyone involved in tennis, especially the players.

Kaufman learned as did all of the professional officials, that a perfect job as a chair umpire was a match that was conducted fairly for both players, with most of the questionable calls by linesman being corrected and which at the end of the match no one even noticed who the chair umpire was except when the players shook his hand at the end of the match. The players were the "show" not the chair umpire, so it was not uncommon for chair umpires to be unknown and almost incognito with the public. *However, inside of professional tennis, Rich Kaufman, during his time, was one of the most famous respected tennis officials in the world.*

Bill Babcock Succeeds Tony Eugenio as Assistant MIPTC Administrator

In October, I hired Bill Babcock as Assistant MIPTC Administrator in New York to succeed Tony Eugenio, who resigned to return to private law practice in Texas. Bill joined Paul Svehlik, Assistant Administrator in Paris, and David Cooper, Assistant Administrator in New York. Bill was 35 and had an undergraduate degree from Harvard University and a law degree from Hastings College in San Francisco. He had been a member of the law firm of Oppenheimer, Wolff, Foster, Shepard & Donnelly in Minneapolis, MN, specializing in commercial litigation. Bill was vice president and a member of the board of directors of the Northwestern Tennis Association (a USTA Section) and a member of the board of directors of the Northwestern Tennis Patrons, Inc. From 1973-1977, Bill had competed on the Grand Prix circuit.[604]

Officials Schools Toughened

In 1985, we took steps to improve our officiating schools to raise the quality of officiating at all sanctioned tournaments as it had become obvious to us that our school curriculum needed a complete overhaul and that our on-site evaluations and recertification procedure were a bit too lax. I said in the February 1, 1985 edition of *International Tennis Weekly*[605]: "In the past our on-site evaluations have too often graded marginal or poor officiating as 'average' based on a poor international standard. In 1985, marginal performances will be rated as 'unacceptable' and if continued will lead to withdrawal of certification. We certainly do not intend to upset anyone with our new policy, but if the MIPTC certification is to be meaningful for our best officials, the standards must be high." *The players always supported better and better officiating. Every time a player stepped on court in a Nabisco Grand Prix event, he was under pressure, with ranking and prize money and contract bonuses at stake. All on-court officials were also evaluated by the MIPTC Supervisors in each match they worked.*

Lendl Plays $100,000 Stuttgart

Immediately after defeating John McEnroe in the finals of the 1985 U.S. Open on hard courts, Lendl, the then No. 1 player in the world flew on Wednesday to compete in the Mercedes Cup in Stuttgart on clay. Lendl defeated Brad Gilbert 6-4, 6-0 in the singles finals and Lendl and Tomas Smid defeated Andy Kohlberg and Joao Soares 3-6, 6-4, 6-2 in the doubles finals.[606] *You could guess, but could not prove, that Lendl probably needed another Mercedes as there was no good professional tennis reason for the No. 1 player in the world playing in Stuttgart on clay in a $100,000 tournament the week after the U.S. Open.*

Las Vegas Withdraws Over Suntory Cup

On September 21, the Alan King Caesar's Palace Classic in Las Vegas withdrew its application for its 1986 Nabisco Grand Prix Super Series tournament, which was to have a 32 draw and pay $495,000 in total player compensation. The tournament was cancelled because of the scheduling of the Suntory eight-man special event in Japan during the same week for four of the top six players. The Suntory Cup special event destroyed a big Grand Prix tournament opportunity for the players.[607]

Arthur Ashe Replaced by Tom Gorman as Davis Cup Captain

Randy Gregson, USTA President, dropped Arthur Ashe as Davis Cup Captain. Gregson overlooked Stan Smith and replaced Ashe with Tom Gorman. Gregson personally denied Gorman the authority to invite John McEnroe to play Davis Cup for the United States during his 1985-1986 presidency.[608]

Yellow Balls at Wimbledon – Finally

On November 27, 1985, Wimbledon Chairman Buzzer Hadingham announced that after 108 years, beginning in 1986, yellow tennis balls would be used at Wimbledon.[609]

McEnroe: Another Automatic Suspension

John McEnroe was fined $1,250 for audible obscenity during his first-round match against Dannie Visser at the 1985 Australian Open being played on grass at Kooyong in Melbourne. He was then fined $1,500 for verbal abuse in the fourth round against Henri Leconte, which put him over the $7,500 annual limit which subjected him to another 21-day suspension beginning immediately after the Australian Open.[610] *Another vacation for John!*

Lendl Suspended Too

At the 1985 Australian Open, Ivan Lendl was fined $1,000 for a dress and equipment violation, $500 for audible obscenity and $350 for ball abuse which took him over the $7,500 annual limit. *He also got a vacation!*[611]

John McEnroe Tennis Over America Tour

In 1985, Steve Corey and Gary Swain continued to promote the John McEnroe Tennis Over America Tour with 26 events against Vitas Gerulaitis and Bjorn Borg. Even though Borg had been retired since 1982, the McEnroe vs. Borg six-city tour on November 12-17, 1985, set big-time attendance records. "Box office records set by Frank Sinatra, Elvis Pressley and Kenny Rogers fell during a six-night blitz exhibition tour November 12-17 (1985) by tennis superstars Bjorn Borg and John McEnroe, "wrote Doug Graves in *Amusement Business.*[612] "Combined box office figures for the appearances in Milwaukee, Nashville, Bloomington, Minn, St. Louis, Des Moines, Iowa and Richmond, Va., showed attendance of 54,382 and a gross of $1,177,701."

Steve Corey, president of Tennis Over American Tours, Inc., told Graves that the run was a "once-in-a-lifetime event," but even he didn't know that demand would be that great. "Nobody – not me, not the people at the facilities, not even the players themselves – expected what happened," he said. With merchandise figures added to the box office numbers, the tour made in excess of $1.5 million, Graves reported. In addition, corporate cash sponsorship for the six appearances was $454,000. "the media blowout was 10 times what it would be, on the average, for a rock concert," Corey said to Graves.[613]

ATP

Mike Davies Gets Two-Year Contract Extension

In January,[614] Mike Davies received a two-year extension on his employment contract as the ATP Executive Director through 1987. "'The ATP wanted to recognize the outstanding job Mike has done for the players,' said ATP President, Ray Moore in *International Tennis Weekly*. 'As a player, he understands the problems and needs of the guys on the tour. As a salesman for tennis he knows the importance of sponsors and tournament organizers.' Said the 49-year-old Davies, 'I'm happy that the board has extended my contract. I see this as adding more stability to the ATP's position in the game, and it gives me the opportunity for some long-term planning for the future of the Association.'"

Hewlett-Packard ATP Computer Rankings

Hewlett-Packard became the new sponsor of the ATP Computer Rankings in July and provided an advanced computer system to the ATP that was designed and installed to provide a totally integrated program to track entries, collate results and spew out the weekly rankings.

Matt Doyle Elected ATP President

During Wimbledon, Matt Doyle, a 27-year-old Yale graduate from Menlo Park, CA, the 1983 winner of the Cologne, Germany tournament and who was ranked No. 138 at the end of 1984, was elected ATP President in July to succeed Ray Moore, who had been president since 1983. Alexander McNab wrote in *World of Tennis 1986*: "Word among the players was that they wanted a president who was in the locker room and an active tour player while Moore, aged 39, was around the tournaments, but competed mainly on the over 35s tour." Mats Wilander, was elected to replace John McEnroe as Vice President, Mike Estep continued as Treasurer and Jim McManus, continued as Secretary. The other board members were Ray Moore, Colin Dowdeswell, Carlos Kirmayr, John McEnroe and Paul McNamee, plus Brian Gottfried and Harold Solomon who replaced Ferdi Taygan and Jose Higueras.

ATP Moves to Arlington Texas

After the U.S. Open, the ATP moved its offices into a new brown tower just north of the Dallas-Fort Worth expressway in Arlington.[615]

1985 ATP JAKS AWARDS
(New York City January 1986)

Player of the Year	Ivan Lendl
Doubles Team of the Year	Ken Flach – Robert Seguso
Newcomer of the Year	Jaime Yzaga
Most Improved Player of the Year	Boris Becker
ATP Sportsmanship Award	Mats Wilander
Hewlett-Packard Computer Award	John McEnroe
Nabisco Grand Prix Points Trophy	Ivan Lendl
CF Humanitarian Award	Mrs. Kay McEnroe
ATP Lifetime Achievement Award	Ted Tinling
ATP Media Service Award	Richard Evans

Drug Testing Rule for 1986

Tennis was part of the Olympics from 1896 through 1924, when it was dropped. The ITF fought for years to get tennis back into the Olympics knowing that if tennis got back in the Olympics, immediately the governments of every country would begin supporting tennis which would significantly expand tennis worldwide. Finally, after many years and extensive effort, Philippe Chatrier, the ITF President, and David Gray, the ITF General Secretary, were able to convince the IOC to invite tennis back into the Olympics. Tennis was a demonstration sport in Los Angeles in 1984 and its success guaranteed the re-introduction of tennis beginning in 1988. The ITF knew, and frankly everyone knew, that tennis would only be permitted to actually join the Olympics in 1988, if it had a drug testing program. No one, including me, believed that there was a "drug enhancing" problem in tennis. We knew of nothing that could possibly help a player in a four-hour match and at that time there was not much information on the effects of steroids. We, however, all suspected that there was some use of recreational drugs like marijuana and cocaine by some players outside of tournaments.

So, every time the need for a drug testing rule by the MIPTC was brought up, the MIPTC Player Representatives and the ATP opposed it as an invasion of privacy and a fear that we might create a criminal charge against a player for the use of recreational drugs. As a result, there was a dilemma: The ITF members of the MIPTC believed that the MIPTC could not afford to enact a drug testing rule opposed by the MIPTC Player Representatives and the ATP and if that opposition continued, tennis would reluctantly have to be removed from the 1988 Olympics. So, at every meeting of the MIPTC for several years, the matter was discussed and no showdown was suggested in the hopes that the MIPTC Player Representatives and the ATP would eventually do the right thing to protect the Sport with some kind of reasonable drug testing that would be acceptable to the IOC. It was going to be necessary to keep tennis in the Olympics so as to gain the worldwide government support of tennis that followed tennis being in the Olympics. Drug testing would also help guarantee to the players that drugs would not be used to enhance the performance of any of their opponents on the court.

At the September 10-12 MIPTC meeting in New York[616], I provided a draft drug testing rule for discussion by the Council. At the request of the MIPTC Player Representatives, the Council once again deferred taking any action on the adoption of a new drug testing rule. Finally, at the November 4-7 MIPTC meeting in London[617], the MIPTC Player Representatives presented a drug-testing provision for the MIPTC Code of Conduct that they could support and it was adopted to be effective January 1, 1986. The provision prohibited the "possession, use or distribution of heroin, cocaine or amphetamines by players, members of the MIPTC, MIPTC staff and members of ATP and ATP staff with provision for mandatory testing by an independent expert approved by the ATP at any two (2) of the following tournaments: Boca West (ATP Lipton), French Open, Wimbledon, U.S. Open or Australian Open." My staff and I were going to be tested too along with the ATP staff. *We were going to test everyone, so no one would feel left out!*

Mike Davies said to *International Tennis Weekly*[618]: "Although tennis does not have a so-called problem like some other sports, the players recognize that they are role models and that they owe it to themselves, tournament sponsors, and fans to take the lead in ensuring that the game continues to be clean." We all believed that it was important to give the credit for the adoption of the drug testing rule to the players, so we confirmed and reconfirmed that it was the players' idea.

MIPTC Financials

The MIPTC began 1985 with a surplus of $614,538, and after operating its New York and Paris offices and providing $4,000,000 in Bonus Pool awards and $466,000 in Bonus Prize Money to players in the Nabisco Grand Prix, the MIPTC ended 1985 with a surplus of $1,648,465. The MIPTC collected and paid to ATP, pursuant to the 1982 agreement covering 1983-1987: $693,000 in ATP prize money for services to Nabisco Grand Prix tournaments, $65,672 in ATP entry fees and $32,775 in ATP Challenger and Satellite sanction fees.

Nabisco paid for its promotion as the Nabisco Grand Prix sponsor and for the first time, the MIPTC provided the promotion of the Nabisco Grand Prix via MIPTC staff. The MIPTC promoted the Nabisco Masters in January of 1986 at Madison Square Garden, telecast on NBC, and was responsible for all expenses and received all income. The first Nabisco Masters would be in January of 1986 and the second Nabisco Masters would be in December of 1986 and they would both be reported in the 1986 financials.[619]

1985 Grand Slam Winners

French Open

Mats Wilander d. Ivan Lendl 3-6, 6-4, 6-2, 6-2.
Mark Edmondson – Kim Warwick d. Shlomo Glickstein – Hans Simonsson 6-3, 6-4, 6-7, 6-3.

Wimbledon

Boris Becker d. Kevin Curren 6-3, 6-7, 7-6, 6-4.
Heinz Gunthardt – Balazs Taroczy d. Pat Cash – John Fitzgerald 6-4, 6-3, 4-6, 6-3.

U.S. Open

Ivan Lendl d. John McEnroe 7-6, 6-3, 6-4.
Ken Flach – Robert Seguso d. Henri Leconte – Yannick Noah 7-6, 6-7, 7-6, 6-0.

Australian Open

Stefan Edberg d. Mats Wilander 6-4, 6-3, 6-3.

Paul Annacone – Christo Van Rensburg d. Mark Edmondson – Kim Warwick 3-6, 7-6, 6-4, 6-4.

Lipton International Players Championships

Tim Mayotte d. Scott Davis 4-6, 4-6, 6-3, 6-2, 6-4.
Paul Annacone – Christo Van Rensburg d. Sherwood Stewart – Kim Warwick 7-6, 7-5, 6-4.

Nabisco Grand Prix Circuit Championships

Buick WCT Finals

Ivan Lendl d. Tim Mayotte 7-6, 6-4 6-1.

WCT Tournament of Champions (Forest Hills)

Ivan Lendl d. John McEnroe 6-3, 6-3.
Ken Flach – Robert Seguso d. Gustavo Barbosa – Ivan Kley 7-6, 6-2.

Nabisco Masters (New York)

Ivan Lendl d. Boris Becker 6-2, 7-6, 6-3.
Stefan Edberg – Anders Jarryd d. Joakim Nystrom – Mats Wilander 6-1, 7-6.

WCT Mazda World Doubles (London)

Heinz Gunthardt – Balazs Taroczy d. Paul Annacone – Christo Van Rensburg 6-4, 1-6, 7-6, 6-7, 6-4.

1985 Davis Cup

Davis Cup Final (Munich – Carpet)

Sweden d. Germany 3-2.

Mats Wilander (SE) d. Michael Westphal (DE) 6-3, 6-4,10-8.

Boris Becker (DE) d. Stefan Edberg (SE) 6-3, 3-6, 7-5, 8-6.
Joakim Nystrom – Mats Wilander (SE) d. Boris Becker – Andreas Maurer (DE) 6-4, 6-2, 6-1.
Boris Becker (DE) d. Mats Wilander (SE) 6-3, 2-6, 6-3, 6-3.
Stefan Edberg (SE) d. Michael Westphal (DE) 3-6, 7-5, 6-4, 6-3.

World Team Cup

United States d. Czechoslovakia 2-1.

Ivan Lendl (CZ) d. John McEnroe (US) 6-7, 7-6, 6-3.
Jimmy Connors (US) d. Miloslav Mecir (CZ) 6-3, 3-6, 7-5.
Ken Flach – Robert Seguso (US) d. Ivan Lendl – Tomas Smid (CZ) 6-4, 7-6.

1985 World Rankings[620]

Bud Collins	Lance Tingay	ATP Year-End Rankings
1. Ivan Lendl	1. Ivan Lendl	1. Ivan Lendl
2. John McEnroe	2. Mats Wilander	2. John McEnroe
3. Mats Wilander	3. John McEnroe	3. Mats Wilander
4. Jimmy Connors	4. Boris Becker	4. Jimmy Connors
5. Stefan Edberg	5. Stefan Edberg	5. Stefan Edberg
6. Boris Becker	6. Jimmy Connors	6. Boris Becker
7. Yannick Noah	7. Anders Jarryd	7. Yannick Noah
8. Anders Jarryd	8. Keven Curren	8. Anders Jarryd
9. Miloslav Mecir	9. Yannick Noah	9. Miloslav Mecir
10. Kevin Curren	10. Joakim Nystrom	10. Kevin Curren

1985 Nabisco Grand Prix Bonus Pool Top 10[621]

Singles (16th Bonus Pool)

1.	Ivan Lendl	$ 800,000
2.	John McEnroe	$ 550,000
3.	Mats Wilander	$ 400,000
4.	Stefan Edberg	$ 250,000
5.	Boris Becker	$ 150,000
6.	Jimmy Connors	$ 100,000
7.	Yannick Noah	$ 75,000
8.	Anders Jarryd	$ 55,000
9.	Johan Kriek	$ 45,000
10.	Joakim Nystrom	$ 40,000

Doubles (11th Bonus Pool)

1.	Robert Seguso	$ 165,000
2.	Ken Flach	$ 120,000
3.	Christo v Rensburg	$ 90,000
4.	Kim Warwick	$ 70,000
5.	Paul Annacone	$ 50,000
6.	Anders Jarryd	$ 40,000
7.	Tomas Smid	$ 30,000
8.	Mats Wilander	$ 25,000
9.	Pavel Slozil	$ 20,000
10.	John Fitzgerald	$ 17,000

1985 Official Earnings Top 10[622]

1.	Ivan Lendl	$ 1,971,074	6.	Jimmy Connors	$ 562,336
2.	John McEnroe	$ 1,455,611	7.	Anders Jarryd	$ 534,822
3.	Mats Wilander	$ 1,081,697	8.	Yannick Noah	$ 406,881
4.	Stefan Edberg	$ 731,152	9.	Tomas Smid	$ 404,460
5.	Boris Becker	$ 625,757	10.	Robert Seguso	$ 394,908

1985 Tournament Calendar

Date	Tournaments	Singles Winner	Singles #2	Doubles Winner	Doubles #2
1/6/1985	London $200,000 WCT Dbls.			K. Flach - R. Seguso	H. Gunthardt - B. Taroczy
1/6/1985	Las Vegas $1,000,000 SP	John McEnroe	Guellermo Vilas	7-6, 6-0	
1/13/1985	Auckland $80,000 GP	Chris Lewis	Wally Masur	J. Fitzgerald - C. Lewis	B. Dyke - W. Masur
1/26/1985	Philadelphia $300,000 SS	John McEnroe	Miloslav Mecir	J. Nystrom - M. Wilander	W. Fibak - S. Mayer
2/3/1985	Memphis $250,000 SS	Stefan Edberg	Yannick Noah	P. Slozil - T. Smid	K. Curren - S. Denton
2/17/1985	Del. Beach $300,000 SS/ATP	Tim Mayotte	Scott Davis	P. Annacone - Van Rensburg	S. Stewart - K. Warwick
2/24/1985	LaQuinta $300,000 SS	Larry Stefanki	David Pate	H. Gunthardt - B. Tarcozy	K. Flach - R. Seguso
2/24/1985	Toronto $125,000 GP	Kevin Curren	Anders Jarryd	P. Fleming - A. Jarryd	G. Layendecker - G. Michibata
3/2/1985	Houston $300,000 WCT/SS	John McEnroe	Kevin Curren	P. Fleming - J. McEnroe	H. Pfister - B. Testerman
3/2/1985	Buenos Aires $80,000 GP	Martin Jaite	Diego Perez	M. Jaite - C. Miniussi	D. Perez - E. Bengoechea
3/17/1985	Brussels $210,000 SS	Anders Jarryd	Mats Wilander	S. Edberg - A. Jarryd	K. Curren - W. Fibak
3/24/1985	Rotterdam $250,000 SS	Miloslav Mecir	Jacob Hlasek	P. Slozil- T. Smid	V. Gerulaitis - P. McNamee
3/24/1985	Nancy $80,000 GP	Tim Wilkison	Slobodan Zivojinovic	M. Freeman - R. Harmon	J. Navratil - J. B. Svensson
3/31/1985	Milan $300,000 SS	John McEnroe	Anders Jarryd	M. Gunthardt - A. Jarryd	B. Dyke - W. Masur
3/31/1985	Ft. Myers $315,000 SS	Ivan Lendl	Jimmy Connors	K. Flach - R. Seguso	S. Giammalva - D. Pate
4/7/1985	Monte Carlo $325,000 SS	Ivan Lendl	Mats Wilander	P. Slozil - T. Smid	S. Glickstein - S. Perkins
4/7/1985	Chicago Volvo SS	John McEnroe	Jimmy Connors	J. Kriek - Y. Noah	K. Flach - R. Seguso
4/14/1985	Dallas $500,000 WCT/GP	Ivan Lendl	Tim Mayotte		
4/14/1985	Nice $80,000 GP	Henri Leconte	Victor Pecci	C. Panatta - P. Slozil	L. Courtneau - M. Schapers
4/21/1985	Bari $80,000 GP	Claudio Panatta	Lawson Duncan	A. Ganzabal - C. Panatta	M. Freeman - L. Warder

4/28/1985	Atlanta $300,000 SS/WCT	John McEnroe	Paul Annacone	P. Annacone - Van Rensburg	S. Denton - T. Smid
4/28/1985	Marbella $100,000 GP	Horacio de la Pena	Lawson Duncan	A. Gomez - C. Motta	L. Courtneau - M. Schapers
4/28/1985	Tulsa SP	Jimmy Connors	Yannick Noah	6-4, 6-4	
5/5/1985	Las Vegas $400,000 SS	Johan Kriek	Jimmy Arias	P. Cash - J. Fitzgerald	P. Annacone - Van Rensburg
5/5/1985	Hamburg $250,000 SS	Miloslav Mecir	Henrik Sundstrom	H. Gildemeister - A. Gomez	H. Gunthardt - B. Taroczy
5/12/1985	NY $500,000 TC WCT/GP	Ivan Lendl	John McEnroe	K. Flach - R. Seguso	G. Barbosa - I. Kley
5/12/1985	Munich 100,000 GP	Joakim Nystrom	Hans Schwaier	M. Edmondson - K. Warwick	S. Casal - E. Sanchez
5/12/1985	Tokyo $250,000 Suntory SP	Bjorn Borg	Anders Jarryd	6-4, 6-3	
5/19/1985	Rome $350,000 SS	Yannick Noah	Miloslav Mecir	A. Jarryd - M. Wilander	K. Flach - R. Seguso
5/19/1985	Madrid $80,000 GP	Andreas Maurer	Lawson Duncan	G. Barbosa - I. Kley	J. Bardou - A. Tous
5/26/1985	Florence $80,000 GP	Sergio Casal	Jimmy Arias	D. Graham - L. Warder	B. Derlin - C. Limberger
5/26/1985	Dusseldorf $500,000 WTC/SP	United States	Czechoslovakia	2-1,	
5/26/1985	Dusseldorf $500,000 WTC/SP	Ivan Lendl	John McEnroe	6-7, 7-6, 6-3	
5/26/1985	Dusseldorf $500,000 WTC/SP	Jimmy Connors	Miloslav Mecir	6-3, 3-6, 7-5	
5/26/1985	Dusseldorf $500,000 WTC/SP		6-4, 7-6	K. Flack - R. Seguso	I. Lendl - T. Smid
6/9/1985	French Open GS	Mats Wilander	Ivan Lendl	M. Edmondson - K. Warrick	S. Glickstein - H. Simonsson
6/17/1985	London $200,000 GP/ATP	Boris Becker	Johan Kriek	K. Flach - R. Seguso	P. Cane - J. Fitzgerald
6/17/1985	Bologna $80,000 GP	Thierry Tulasne	Claudio Panatta	P. Cane - S. Colombo	J. Arrese - A. Tous
6/23/1985	Bristol $100,000 GP/ATP	Marty Davis	Glen Layendecker	E. Edwards - D. Visser	J. Alexander - R. Simpson
7/7/1985	Wimbledon GS	Boris Becker	Kevin Curren	H. Gunthardt - B. Taroczy	P. Cash - J. Fitzgerald

7/14/1985	Boston $210,000 SS	Mats Wilander	Martin Jaite	L. Pimek - S. Zivojinovic	P. McNamara - P. McNamee
7/14/1985	Gstaad $150,000 GP	Joakim Nystrom	Andreas Mauer	W. Fibak - T. Smid	B. Drewett - M. Edmondson
7/14/1985	Newport $100,000 GP	Tom Gullikson	John Sadri	P. Doohan - S. Giammalva	P. Annacone - Van Rensburg
7/21/1985	Bastad $80,000 GP	Mats Wilander	Stefan Edberg	S. Edberg - A. Jarryd	S. Casal - E. Sanchez
7/21/1985	Washington $210,000 SS	Yannick Noah	Martin Jaite	H. Gildemeister - V. Pecci	D. Graham - B. Taroczy
7/28/1985	Indianapolis $300,000 SS	Ivan Lendl	Andres Gomez	K. Flach - R. Seguso	P. Slozil - K. Warwick
7/28/1985	Livingston GP	Brad Gilbert	Brian Teacher	M. DePalmer - P. Doohan	E. Edwards - D. Visser
7/28/1985	Hilversum $80,000 GP	Ricki Osterthun	Kent Carlsson	H. Simonsson - S. Simonsson	C. Linberger - M. Woodforde
8/11/1985	Stratton Mtn. $250,000 SS	John McEnroe	Ivan Lendl	S. Davis - D. Pate	K. Flach - R. Seguso
8/11/1985	Kitzbuhel $100,000 GP	Pavel Slozil	Michael Westphal	S. Casal - E. Sanchez	P. Cane - C. Panatta
8/18/1985	Cleveland $80,000 GP	Brad Gilbert	Brad Drewett	L. Palin - D. Rahnasto	H. Pfister - B. Testerman
8/18/1985	Montreal $300,000 SS	John McEnroe	Ivan Lendl	K. Flach - R. Seguso	S. Edberg - A. Jarryd
8/25/1985	Cincinnati $300,000 SS/ATP	Boris Becker	Mats Wilander	S. Edberg - A. Jarryd	J. Nystrom - M. Wilander
8/26/1985	Jerrico $150,000 Hamlet SP			H. Gunthardt - B. Tarcozy	W. Fibak - T. Smid
9/8/1985	US Open GS	Ivan Lendl	John McEnroe	K. Flach - R. Seguso	H. Leconte - Y. Noah
9/15/1985	Stuttgart $100,000 GP	Ivan Lendl	Brad Gilbert	I. Lendl - T. Smid	A. Kohlberg - J. Soares
9/15/1985	Palermo $80,000 GP	Thierry Tulasne	Joakim Nystrom	C. Dowdeswell - J. Nystrom	S. Casal - E. Sanchez
9/24/1985	Los Angeles $210,000 SS	Paul Annacone	Stefan Edberg	S. Davis - R. Van't Hof	P. Annacone - van Rnsburg
9/24/1985	Geneva $100,000 GP	Tomas Smid	Mats Wilander	S. Casal - E. Sanchez	C. Kirmayr - C. Motta
9/24/1985	Bordeaux $80,000 GP	Diego Perez	Jimmy Brown	D. Felgate - S. Shaw	L. Pimek - S. Willenborg
9/29/1985	San Francisco $210,000 SS	Stefan Edberg	Johan Kriek	P. Annacone - Van Rensburg	B. Gilbert - S. Mayer
9/29/1985	Barcelona $210,000 SS	Thierry Tulasne	Mats Wilander	S. Casal - E. Sanchez	J. Gunnarsson - M. Mortensen

10/13/1985	Johannesburg $210,000 SS	Matt Anger	Brad Gilbert	C. Dowdeswell - Van Rensburg	J. Mansdorf - S. Perkiss
10/13/1985	Brisbane $80,000 GP	Paul Annacone	Kelly Evanden	M. Davis - B. Drewett	B. Schultz - B. Testerman
10/13/1985	Toulouse $125,000 GP	Yannick Noah	Tomas Smid	R. Acuna - J. Hlasek	P. Slozil - T. Smid
10/20/1985	Sydney $225,000 SS	Ivan Lendl	Henri Leconte	J. Fitzgerald - A. Jarryd	M. Edmondson - K. Warwick
10/20/1985	Basle $150,000 GP	Stefan Edberg	Yannick Noah	T. Gullikson - T. Gullikson	M. Dickson - T. Wilkison
10/20/1985	Tokyo $125,000 GP	Scott Davis	Jimmy Arias	S. Davis - D. Pate	S. Giammalva - G. Holmes
10/27/1985	Tel Aviv $80,000 GP	Brad Gilbert	Amos Mansdorf	B. Gilbert - I. Nastase	M. Robertson - F. Segarceanu
10/27/1985	Tokyo $300,000 SS	Ivan Lendl	Mats Wilander	K. Flach - R. Seguso	S. Davis - D. Pate
10/27/1985	Melbourne $100,000 GP	Marty Davis	Paul Annacone	B. Drewett - M. Mitchell	D. Dowlen - N. Odizor
10/27/1985	Cologne $80,000 GP	Peter Lundgren	Ramesh Krishnan	A. Antonitsch - M. Schapers	J. Gunnarsson - P. Lundgren
11/3/1985	Antwerp $850,000 SP	Ivan Lendl	John McEnroe	1-6, 7-6, 6-2, 6-2	
11/10/1985	Stockholm $250,000 SS	John McEnroe	Anders Jarryd	G. Forget - A. Gomez	M. DePalmer - G. Donnelly
11/17/1985	London $300,000 SS/ATP	Ivan Lendl	Boris Becker	G. Forget - A. Jarryd	B. Becker - S. Zivojinovic
11/24/1985	Hong Kong $200,000 GP	Andres Gomez	Aaron Krickstein	B. Drewett - K. Warwick	J. Hlasek - T. Smid
11/24/1985	Vienna $100,000 GP	Jan Gunnarsson	Libor Pimek	M. DePalmer - G. Donnelly	S. Casal - E. Sanchez
12/8/1985	Australian Open GS	Stefan Edberg	Mats Wilander	P. Annacone - Van Rensburg	M. Edmondson - K. Warwick
12/15/1985	Sydney $125,000 GP	Henri Leconte	Kelly Everden	D. Dowlen - N. Odizor	B. Dyke - W. Masur
12/20/1985	Adelaide $80,000 GP	Eddie Edwards	Peter Doohan	M. Edmondson - K. Warwick	N. Aerts - T. Wameke
12/29/1985	Melbourne $80,000 GP	Jonathan Canter	Peter Doohan	D. Cahill - P. Carter	B. Dickinson - R. Saad
1/11/1986	Las Vegas $500,000 AT&T SP	Ivan Lendl	Jimmy Connors	6-2, 6-3	
1/12/1986	London $200,000 WCT GP			H. Gunthardt -B. Taroczy	P. Annacone - Van Rensburg

1/19/1986	NY $500,000 Nabisco Masters	Ivan Lendl	Boris Becker	S. Edberg - A. Jarryd	J. Nystrom - M. Wilander

http://www.atpworldtour.com/en/scores/results-archive

http://www.itftennis.com/procircuit/tournaments/men's-calendar.aspx?tour=&reg=&nat=&sur=&cate=AL&iod=&-fromDate=01-01-1968&toDate=31-01-1986

Tennis History, Jim McManus, (Canada 2010).

1986 USLTA Yearbook.

Official 1989 MTC Media Guide, (MTC 1989).

World of Tennis 1986, Edited by John Barrett and compiled by Lance Tingay, (London 1986).

CHAPTER 25:

1985: VOLVO, PROSERV, IMG VS. MIPTC, CHATRIER AND HAPPER, CRISIS NO. 30, PART I

Anti-Trust Counsel

Every governing body of a sport has by necessity some type of monopolistic power as required to actually provide governance. However, rules that provide for the enhancement of the sport and its participants, if reasonable and necessary, are generally not subject to anti-trust challenge. Beginning in 1978, the MIPTC had the foresight to employ Roy L. Reardon, Esquire, of Simpson Thacher & Bartlett of New York, an accomplished and well-respected anti-trust lawyer, to attend almost all of the MIPTC meetings to advise the members of the Council on anti-trust concerns with respect to the rules proposed and enacted by the MIPTC for the governance of the sport of tennis.

Proposed Rule to Deal with Player-Agent Conflicts of Interest in Tournaments

For years and almost at every meeting of the MIPTC, the problem of the player agents' involvement in tournaments was discussed and finally the Council decided to try to deal with the issue. At the January 14-17 MIPTC meeting in New York[623], the Council adopted a *proposed rule* amendment that would restrict the actions of any player agent company with respect to MIPTC sanctioned tournaments "to be circulated by the Administrator for written comment by April 1, 1985, by any interested party." The Council agreed to adopt such amendment at the April 15-18, 1985 meeting, subject to consideration of the comments received. The *proposed* effective date for the amendment was to be the 1987 Grand Prix Year.

At my invitation, Rick Dowden of Volvo appeared at the April 15-18 MIPTC meeting in Dallas presumably to discuss the objections of the Council and Nabisco to the new Volvo Tennis promotion which we and Nabisco believed was undermining Nabisco's sponsorship. The MIPTC minutes say: "Mr. Dowden entered the meeting and expressed his anger at the Administrator's letters (about the Volvo Tennis promotion) to Volvo, various television networks and the tournaments. Mr. Dowden 'challenged' the

Council to look into the bidding process for the Grand Prix sponsorship and 'promised' the Council that an anti-trust Complaint would be filed in the federal court in New York within a few days. Mr. Dowden said that Volvo of North America was a company with about $3 Billion in sales in the United States and further 'promised' that the Administrator's letters were going to be 'the most expensive letters ever written in the history of the world.' Thereupon Mr. Dowden abruptly departed the meeting without entertaining any opportunity for discussion."[624]

Anti-Trust Complaint Filed April 17

As promised by Rick Dowden, the original anti-trust Complaint was filed by Volvo on April 17, 1985, in the United States District Court for the Southern District of New York by Volvo against the MIPTC, plus M. Marshall Happer III and Philippe Chatrier, personally. The case was assigned to U.S. District Judge, Kevin Thomas Duffy. The original Complaint alleged violations of the anti-trust laws by the MIPTC, defamation of Volvo, breach of its sponsorship and other rights, etc. The original Complaint would soon be superseded by a First Amended Complaint in which ProServ and IMG would join as plaintiffs with Volvo.

I believe that Volvo was unpleasantly surprised to learn that we had obtained anti-trust insurance coverage for the MIPTC, so the mere filing of an expensive anti-trust lawsuit was not going to bankrupt the MIPTC. However, as soon as the Volvo lawsuit was filed, our insurance carrier, Calvert Insurance Company, issued a cancellation of our insurance policy as of April 25, but it could not cancel the coverage of the pre-existing Volvo lawsuit. So, to the dismay of Volvo, and later to ProServ and IMG, the MIPTC had insurance coverage for the Volvo lawsuit. I did not believe that either Volvo, ProServ or IMG had any insurance coverage for their legal expenses.

Volvo asked or demanded that ProServ join as a Plaintiff in the case and Donald Dell began to solicit Mark McCormack of IMG to also join to fight the proposed new rule to restrict their involvement with tournaments. So, Volvo was mad, Dell and Benton were mad and now McCormack and IMG were mad. *Nice job I had.* Nabisco appreciated our attempts to deal with the "Volvo Tennis" issue that was undermining Nabisco's sponsorship. On April 12, Roy Reardon and I met with John Martin of Ohlmeyer Communications and Nabisco lawyers, Brodie and Dunnington. *At the meeting, Martin said that if it hadn't been for our relationship, Nabisco would have put us on notice that we were in breach if we didn't stop the "Volvo Tennis" scheme.*

Settlement Explorations

On May 3, Steve Umin, attorney for ProServ, met with Roy Reardon for two hours in New York. Umin presented five demands to settle the lawsuit with Volvo and avoid having ProServ and IMG join in the lawsuit. Those demands were: (i) The Council must abandon the "pending" rules restricting player agents control of tournaments, (ii) The Council must be restructured to remove the ITF domination of the MIPTC and either make ProServ and IMG as members or at least as "Trusted Advisors" (The ITF only had three of the nine votes on the MIPTC and it was definitely not dominant); (iii) There must be an impartial lawyer or law firm retained by the Council to make a factual investigation and legal analysis to determine if there was any impropriety involved in the bidding for the sponsorship of the Grand Prix, (iv) That Volvo and Nabisco meet and agree on a peaceful co-existence, and (v) That the Council pay Volvo's legal fees. The meeting ended with no resolution and no explanation how Volvo who had refused to make an offer in the final bidding process for the sponsorship of the Grand Prix could have any legal complaint.[625] If the case ever went to trial, Volvo and ProServ were going to have a very uncomfortable time on cross examination by Roy Reardon as they tried to explain their claim since Volvo had refused in writing to make any offer for the sponsorship at the time the cash, take-it-or-leave it $3.5 million offer with the full ownership of the Masters with the MIPTC was made by Nabisco and accepted by the MIPTC.

On May 7, Bob Briner met with Roy Reardon to talk about a possible settlement to no avail. On May 8, Reardon proceeded as required to file a Motion to Dismiss Volvo's Complaint. On May 10, Reardon told Jim Maloney, Volvo's lawyer, that he was "confident that there had been nothing done that was improper in the bidding process and that Volvo was way off base in the things it alleged in the Complaint."[626]

On May 16, Rick Dowden told Reardon that Volvo wanted to force a restructuring of the Council "so that the influence which the ITF has over the game of men's professional tennis is reduced or eliminated so that commercial interests can act in a free market. In particular, he said that he didn't want people like (Philippe) Chatrier and (Derek) Hardwick calling the shots in men's tennis." Chatrier and Hardwick were two of the nine members of the Council so they could not "call the shots in men's tennis."[627]

ProServ and IMG Letter Demand

On June 9, ProServ and IMG wrote a letter to the MIPTC demanding that the proposed rules out for comment that would restrict their ownership of tournaments be permanently withdrawn, that the prohibition against player agents being members of the MIPTC be repealed, along with other demands, which if not done would result in their joining in the Volvo lawsuit.[628]

At the June 10-13 meeting, the MIPTC did not agree to the ProServ/IMG demands. However, the MIPTC did: (i) decide to continue the Bylaw prohibition against player-agents being members of the MIPTC and (ii) decided not to then enact the proposed rule restricting player agent ownership in tournaments. The Council referred those proposed rules to the Administrator for further study.[629] *Thus, the proposed rules objected to in the Volvo Complaint were not then enacted.*

Dell Meeting with Chatrier

I met with Philippe Chatrier on July 1. Philippe told me about a recent meeting he had with Donald Dell at the Westbury Hotel in London. Dell had for some years been representing the French Open via Chatrier in the marketing of its television rights. With Volvo's lawsuit having included Philippe (and me) personally as a defendant and ProServ threatening to join the lawsuit, their relationship was in jeopardy. Philippe told me that he declined a television meeting proposed by Dell and he told Dell he did not like doing business with him. Dell struggled with his conflict between representing his client, Volvo, who was suing his client Chatrier.

Meetings with Bob Kain

On June 29, at Bob Kain's request, I agreed to an "off-the-record" meeting with him at the IMG Wimbledon tent from 6-7:30 PM. Bob said he wanted our conversation to be strictly confidential as the Dell people did not want him talking to me. He said Benton had said to him: "He (Happer) is the enemy." Bob said he wanted to avoid IMG from joining the Volvo lawsuit. I always kept our counsel, Roy Reardon, up to date on all my meetings. On July 3, I received a call from Bob Kain saying that Mark McCormack was enthusiastic about some of the ideas we had discussed as a solution and he wanted to deliver me today a handwritten letter outlining some points for my consideration.[630] He said he "thought" they had filed (an Amended Complaint adding ProServ and IMG to the Volvo lawsuit) yesterday. He said they did it because Mark had "promised" Dell to do it, but if any agreement could be reached they would withdraw. Kain said Dell does know he has talked to me. Kain proposed various ideas for a settlement of the lawsuit.

When I reported on my conversations and the handwritten settlement proposal I received from Bob Kain, Roy Reardon instructed me to tell Bob Kain that he was "outraged" if IMG was filing the Amended Complaint at the same time some sort of settlement was being discussed.

First Amended Complaint Filed July 3

The First Amended Complaint in which ProServ and IMG joined the Volvo lawsuit was actually filed on July 3, 1985.[631] We later heard that Volvo had agreed to fund the litigation costs of IMG in order to induce them to join the lawsuit, and perhaps Volvo was also funding ProServ's litigation expenses. Dell and ProServ, of course, were still representing Volvo and had no choice. McCormack sort of reluctantly was convinced by Dell and Volvo to also join the lawsuit.

IMG issued a press release about its joining the Volvo lawsuit in which it cited its involvement with the tournaments at Hamburg, Rome, Boston, Australian Open (TV only), Wimbledon (TV and merchandising only), U.S. Open (TV only), Geneva, Cleveland, Palermo, Bari and Bologna as being positive for the game. IMG did not mention that it used the players it represented to support those tournaments, while staging special events against other tournaments. IMG and ProServ avoided scheduling special events involving the top players against each other's tournaments because there were plenty of WCT and other independent tournaments available for that purpose. *That, of course, was the problem!*

In addition to naming the MIPTC, Philippe Chatrier and myself as defendants, the First Amended Complaint also named the ITF as a co-conspirator along with other un-named co-conspirators. It contained 119 allegations of purported facts and 13 counts. The 13 counts were: five anti-trust claims, plus interference with prospective business relationships, breach of contract, fraud, defamation and product disparagement claims. The prayers for relief asked for treble damages and injunctions against just about all of the MIPTC rules for the orderly organization of the Grand Prix for the players and the tournaments.

In general, the plaintiffs were asking for massive, treble compensatory and punitive damages from the MIPTC, Chatrier and me, and to enjoin the scheduling of tournaments, the classification of tournaments, the prize money limits on the various classification of tournaments, the contract between the MIPTC and WCT, the Grand Prix Bonus Pool, the Player Commitment Rules, any prohibition on special events, any restrictions on the conflicts of interest of player-agents owning and managing tournaments, any restrictions on the awarding of wild cards and any restrictions on player-agents being members of the MIPTC. The last one was kind of funny, because if the Plaintiffs were successful, there would be no MIPTC to be members of. Needless to say, the MIPTC, Philippe Chatrier and I would all be bankrupt. I considered it to be sad that Volvo, ProServ, IMG, Dell, Benton and McCormack were apparently asking in their Complaint for the literal destruction of the organization of men's professional tennis that had been painfully developed successfully over a number of years for the tournaments and the players *and them.*

Trial By Jury

It is interesting to note that Volvo, ProServ and IMG did not request a trial by jury with respect to their massive allegations and large number of claims, which if successful would have destroyed the MIPTC and the fabric of men's professional tennis. I believed that the last thing they wanted was to have a jury trial. However, that was just their preference as when we filed our Answer and Counterclaim against the plaintiffs, we did demand a jury trial, so the determination of the actual facts in this case would be decided a jury and not just a federal judge.

Cliff Drysdale's Commentary:
The Bitter Assault that Threatens the Men's Game

In August of 1985, Cliff Drysdale, Contributing Editor of *Tennis Magazine* wrote[632]: "We all make mistakes and when I was a member of the Pro Council, the group that governs men's pro tennis, I made a serious one. I should have fought harder to prevent the Council from letting Volvo North America Corp., sponsor the Grand Prix tour, permit its representative, ProServ, to run the tour and the Masters tournament for the automaker. Why? Because that has now led to a landmark antitrust lawsuit by Volvo against the Pro Council and its Administrator, M. Marshall Happer, that threatens to seriously undermine the professional game. I agree with Happer that the suit is nothing less than an attempt 'to destroy the fabric of the sport through intimidation.' Volvo was the sponsor of the tour from 1980 through the 1985 Masters tournament, after which the Pro Council shifted the sponsorship to Nabisco. But Volvo has employed various devices that make it appear it is still the sponsor. The Pro Council cracked down on those practices and Volvo retaliated with its lawsuit that accused the Council of monopoly."

"I hope the Pro Council wins the suit and that the victory leads to the successful implementation of Happer's objectives – principally the restriction or elimination of player agents from running Grand Prix tournaments, brokering TV rights and serving as representatives of tournament sponsors. I view the suit as an effort by Volvo and ProServ to challenge Nabisco's sponsorship of the Grand Prix and Happer's efforts to bring order to men's pro tennis. ProServ – the Washington, D.C. – based player management firm whose clients include Jimmy Connors and Ivan Lendl – has always represented Volvo's interests in tennis. To me, any suggestion that Volvo is acting alone in this case – without ProServ's consultation – is naïve."

"After Volvo lost the sponsorship of the Grand Prix to Nabisco last winter, it developed a new program to keep its name in the game. It worked out participating sponsorship deals with individual Grand Prix tournaments that are being marketed under the banner of Volvo Tennis. In fact, the Volvo Tennis banners at tournaments use virtually the same logo Volvo employed when it was Grand Prix sponsor. ProServ, of course, is representing Volvo in that part of its current tennis involvement. You may say that, from Volvo's standpoint, that's an intelligent redirection of its tennis investment. But in my opinion, it is morally questionable, and is being done at the expense of Nabisco. For example, you can tune into a telecast of a Nabisco Grand Prix tournament on TV, and, in the opening credits, it is labeled as part of Volvo Tennis. But there is no mention that it is part of the Nabisco Grand Prix. I think Volvo Tennis is a deceptive promotional vehicle."

"The conflicting interests of Volvo's representative in tennis, ProServ, are staggering. On the same Volvo Tennis telecast, the chances are good that one of the commentators is Donald Dell, ProServ's chairman, or else a ProServ client. It's likely that ProServ has sold the rights to the tournament and possibly that ProServ is running the tournament. Then, there's the distinct possibility that at least one of the players on the court is a ProServ client. Companies that run tournaments represent sponsors and sell TV rights to events should not also be representing the players in those tournaments. It's a fundamental conflict of interest. Happer is trying to get player agents out of the Grand Prix tournament business. I think he is doing the right thing."

"When one organization controls so many aspects of pro tennis, fair market competition is stifled. And fair market competition is what will help the game grow and prospect. The irony, of course, is that it is Volvo that is suing the Pro Council for trying to monopolize the game. Nabisco, for its part, has been a good sponsor. It has brought more money into the tour than ever before. It has no entangling alliances with firms that have conflicts of interest. And under Nabisco, the Masters will be controlled and run by the Pro Council itself."

"The Volvo-Pro Council lawsuit may ultimately decide who controls the sport. I believe that if Volvo wins, the sport will continue to flounder without strong central authority, which I think it still desperately needs. Happer is trying to assert that strong authority for the Pro Council. A victory for the Pro Council is the best thing that can happen for the long-term health and growth of the men's pro game."

On September 9, we the defendants filed our motion to dismiss the plaintiffs' First Amended Complaint and filed a memorandum of law in support of the motion.[633]

October Settlement Exploratory

On October 9, Mike Davies arranged an "off the record without prejudice" meeting at the Waldorf Astoria to determine if there was any reasonable possibility of a settlement of the lawsuit. Attendees at the meeting were Mike Davies (ATP and MIPTC Chairman), Donald Dell (ProServ), Bill Carpenter (IMG Lawyer), Marshall Happer (MIPTC), Forrest Hainline (ITF Representative), Michael Coyne and Jim Maloney (Volvo Lawyers), Ray Benton (ProServ), Steve Umin (ProServ Lawyer), Bob Kain (IMG), Rick Dowden (Volvo) and Roy Reardon (MIPTC Lawyer). At the meeting, the plaintiffs submitted 10 settlement demands to no avail.[634]

ATP Backs Council

The ATP Board of Directors met on November 1 during the Antwerp special event and voted to support the Council in its lawsuit with Volvo, ProServ and IMG. IMG had attended the meeting to try to split the players from the Council.

Answer and Counterclaim Filed November 6

Our Answer to the allegations of the First Amended Complaint and our Counterclaim was filed on November 6, 1985.[635] The defendants, MIPTC, Happer and Chatrier, answered the allegations in the First Amended Complaint by denying the significant allegations made by the plaintiffs. That means, we believed that they could never prove their allegations to be actually true when the evidence was finally presented.

A Counterclaim is a statement of specific affirmative claims being made by the Counterclaimants against Counterclaim Defendants and it was filed with the Answer to the First Amended Complaint. It was in fact our antitrust lawsuit against the plaintiffs and a few new folks. Since it involved the plaintiffs and the defendants, along with the new folks, the claims in the First Amended Complaint and the claims made in the Counterclaims were to be litigated all together in one action. The Counterclaimants were the MIPTC and M. Marshall Happer III against the Counterclaim Defendants who were: Volvo, ProServ and IMG, and several additional Counterclaim defendants: Donald L. Dell, Raymond S. Benton, Dell Benton and Falk (Dell law firm), Mark H. McCormack, International Merchandising Group, International Management, Inc., Transworld International, Inc., and A.B. Volvo (the Swedish parent of Volvo North America). Now, all of the Volvo companies, all of the ProServ and IMG companies and all of the key individuals were personally involved in the lawsuit. *Just like one big tennis family!*

The Counterclaim contained 117 allegations of facts relating to ProServ and IMG's domination of the world-wide markets for professional tennis players, tournaments and tennis on television, including "extensive power over players from 'the cradle to the grave' – that is, over junior, world-class and senior men's professional tennis players." Allegation No. 46 said: "ProServ and IMG also represent the majority of the world's leading men's professional tennis players. As of the filing of the Complaint herein, they represented nine of the top 10 ranked players in the world; 14 of the top 15, and 16 of the top 20:

1.	McEnroe	Other [John McEnroe, Sr.]
2.	Connors	ProServ
3.	Lendl*	ProServ
4.	Wilander	IMG
5.	Gomez	ProServ
6.	Jarryd	IMG
7.	Sundstrom	IMG
8.	Curren	IMG
9.	Cash	IMG
10.	Krickstein	ProServ
11.	Teltscher	ProServ
12.	Nystrom	IMG
13.	Smid	Other
14.	Noah	ProServ
15.	Mayotte	IMG
16.	Kriek	Other
17.	Davis	Other
18.	Edberg	Other
19.	Gerulaitis	IMG
20.	Mayer	ProServ"

"On information and belief, they also represent a majority of the players who have the potential to achieve either a high enough ranking or a high enough public recognition factor to become a 'tennis property' that can produce significant income and further entrench and perpetuate ProServ's and IMG's dominance of men's tennis."

The Counterclaim contained three anti-trust claims and numerous claims for breach of contract and defamation. The prayers for relief asked for treble actual compensatory damages, costs and attorneys fees, plus injunctions to prohibit ProServ and IMG from representing both players and tournaments and to prohibit the Volvo Tennis scheme.

The MIPTC Press Release issued November 7[636] said: "Tennis agents Mark McCormack, Donald Dell and Raymond Benton have been charged by the governing body of men's professional tennis with holding the game hostage and seeking to strangle it in an illegal web of pervasive conflicts, intimidation, fraud and corruption. Illegal restraint of trade, conspiracy to monopolize and unfair competition are charged against the agents, their firms, International Management Group and ProServ, and Swedish auto maker Volvo in a suit filed in U.S. Federal District Court in New York on Wednesday by the Men's International Professional Tennis Council."

"In addition to the illegal conspiracy, Volvo, the embittered former sponsor of the Grand Prix, is charged with illegal use of a marketing scheme known as 'Volvo Tennis' created by Dell, Benton, ProServ and Volvo which unfairly restricts the players, tournaments and national federations represented by the MIPTC of their rights to sell the sponsorship of the $23 million Grand Prix. The MIPTC also charges that the 'Volvo Tennis' scheme misleads and confuses the public."[637]

Pleadings, Allegations and Evidence

The "pleadings" in this civil case consisted of the plaintiffs' First Amended Complaint and the defendants' Answer and Counterclaimants' Counterclaim. The Complaint contained "allegations" of facts made by the plaintiffs and it is improper to submit "allegations" that are false and untrue. Whenever a party is unsure of the facts of an allegation, if they believe them to be true they usually allege them "on information and belief." The same principle applies to "allegations" in the Counterclaims. The purpose of the "allegations" in the pleadings is for the parties to put each other on notice as to what to expect at trial. Until trial on the merits, the only thing before the court are the allegations contained in the pleadings and when the court considers a dismissal motion by either party with respect to the sufficiency of the "allegations," the court gives the party making the "allegations" the benefit of the doubt by considering them in the most favorable light possible. It is also an accepted practice by the court to permit the parties to freely amend their pleadings.

Eventually, the "allegations" in the pleadings would be completely replaced and superseded by the evidence presented at the trial which would be by live testimony from witnesses, documentary evidence and other types of evidence. Since the defendants in this case demanded trial by jury, a jury would be empaneled to evaluate the credibility of the witnesses and the evidence presented and determine the facts, while the trial judge would determine and instruct the jury on the applicable law to be applied.

Volvo's "Bidding Process" Claim

Volvo was still angry that I had not supported its last offer to the Council which was rejected by an 8-1 vote and withdrawn on June 7, 1983. Surprisingly, Volvo's Complaint contained allegations that Volvo had an agreement with the MIPTC permitting it to match any proposal by anyone else for the sponsorship of the Grand Prix and the Masters and that Volvo had made a proposal for the sponsorship in January of 1984. I had never heard any of that and I could not imagine how Volvo was going to deal with that upon cross examination at trial by Roy Reardon. Volvo knew that it withdrew its last and final offer on June 7 and never made another offer for the sponsorship of the Grand Prix and the Masters.

Nevertheless, Volvo discovered an internal memo written by John Martin of Ohlmeyer Communications touting his negotiation abilities and claiming that he got some "last minute intelligence" to justify the increase of the Nabisco cash offer from $3 million to $3.5 million for the Nabisco sponsorship. Volvo disregarded the fact that a $3 million offer from Nabisco with the MIPTC owning the Masters was far superior to even the ProServ proposed non-offer soliciting an offer to Volvo with Volvo selling a presenting sponsorship and appointing official suppliers and with Volvo controlling the Masters. Nevertheless, Volvo and ProServ jumped to the conclusion that I must have given John Martin information on the inferior ProServ proposal and that I should be fired.

When I learned about the internal Martin memo, I demanded that he clarify the matter with Volvo which he did in person with officers of Nabisco and in writing. Nevertheless, Volvo and ProServ communicated the claim against me with the members of the Council and throughout the tennis community and sought to have me fired. It is my belief that Volvo and Dell thought that if they could get me fired that somehow they could get the members of the Council to somehow reinstate Volvo as the sponsor of the Grand Prix and the Masters. It was disappointing to me that any of them would think I was dishonest or that I would violate the legal canons of ethics under which I have always been subject or jeopardize my law license. Thankfully, the members of the Council supported me.

The only deposition ever taken in the Volvo/ProServ/IMG lawsuit was by Volvo of John Martin on September 18, 1985.[638] In summary, John Martin testified under oath that his "last minute intelligence" was from Frank Craighill of Advantage International, a former partner of Dell, to the effect that Dell and ProServ were making so much money on Volvo and the Volvo Masters that they could not afford to give up the Masters to the MIPTC. He further testified that he obtained approval from Jim Welch, the Senior officer of Nabisco, on Tuesday, January 17, the day before Dell made his presentation to the MIPTC so neither he or anyone knew what Dell was going to present and everyone, including Volvo, knew that Dell was not authorized to and was not going to present an actual offer for Volvo. Martin testified that he had no idea what Dell was planned to proposed or what he actually did propose.

Volvo's bidding process claim failed to get me fired and was eventually abandoned when the case was settled later.

Discovery and the Massive Production of Documents

At the end of 1985, the issues were before the court via the First Amended Complaint, Answer and Counterclaim and the parties began discovery via the extensive production of documents as permitted. Almost all of the relevant documents of the MIPTC were already public documents as it was always operated with full transparency to all its various constituents. The relevant documents the MIPTC demanded to be produced by Volvo, ProServ and IMG were their private documents. As discovery progressed, the number of documents being produced was massive. To protect the sensitivity of the documents being produced in discovery prior to trial, a confidentially order was issued by the court requiring that they remain confidential to the parties until trial.

CHAPTER 26:

1986: PLAYERS CONSOLIDATE POWER,
DRUG TESTING FINALLY, CONNORS MAJOR OFFENSE

1986 Governing Bodies

The MIPTC was the governing body for men's professional tennis in 1986, except for the Davis Cup and the *Rules of Tennis*. The ITF was the governing body for the Davis Cup and in charge of the *Rules of Tennis*.

1986 Significant Tennis Leaders

ITF President:	Philippe Chatrier (France)
USTA President:	Randy Gregson
Tennis Australia President:	Brian Tobin
British LTA President:	G.B. Brown
French FFT President:	Philippe Chatrier
Chairman of Wimbledon:	Buzzer Hadingham
WCT Owners:	Lamar Hunt and Al Hill, Jr.
WCT CEO:	Owen Williams
ATP President:	Matt Doyle
ATP Executive Director:	Mike Davies until August

1986 MIPTC

ITF:	Philippe Chatrier, Derek Hardwick and Forrest Hainline
Tournaments:	Franco Bartoni (Europe), Charles Pasarell (North America) and Brian Tobin (Rest of the World).

Players:	Mike Davies, Chairman until September, Ray Moore, Chairman beginning in September, Harold Solomon and Weller Evans, beginning in September.
Administrator:	Marshall Happer.
Asst Admn:	Bill Babcock.
Asst Admn:	Paul Svehlik.
Asst Admn:	David Cooper.
Legal Counsel:	Roy L. Reardon, Esquire.
GP Supervisors:	Ken Farrar, Chief, Keith Johnson, Bill Gilmour, Thomas Karlberg, John Heiss III and Charlie Beck.
Chair Umpires:	Rich Kaufman, Jeremy Shales and Richard Ings, beginning in July.
Communications:	John Hewig, Director of Communications, Reg Lansberry, Assistant Director of Communications.
Tour Liaisons:	Sandra "Sandy" Genelius, Jennifer Proud and Marieke van der Drift.
Nabisco Masters:	Eugene "Gene" Scott, Tournament Director, Sue "Suzie" Rothstein, Tournament Manager.

1986 Major Player Representatives

ProServ:	Principals: Donald Dell, Ray Benton, Jerry Solomon and Ivan Blumberg.
Advantage Int'l:	Principals: Frank Craighill, Lee Fentress, Dean Smith and Peter Lawler.
IMG:	Principals: Mark McCormack and Bob Kain.
Others:	Ion Tiriac and Thomas Betz, Esquire (Vilas).
	John McEnroe, Sr., Esquire (McEnroe).
	Gloria Connors and Joseph Rountree, Esquire (Connors).

Two Competitions

In 1986, the 18th year of Open Tennis, there were two major organized competitions for men: Nabisco Grand Prix and the Davis Cup, as WCT continued to be merged into the Nabisco Grand Prix. In addition to the Nabisco Grand Prix, which was the major circuit of professional tournaments for men, the MIPTC also sanctioned smaller Challenger tournaments (68+) and Satellite Series tournaments (195+), all to be conducted under the uniform MIPTC Tournament Regulations and MIPTC Code. Davis Cup was open to all players and was won 3-2 by Australia over Sweden.

There were 69 Nabisco Grand Prix tournaments which included three Grand Slams [There was no Australian Open in 1986 as it moved from December of 1985 to January of 1987], ATP two-week Lipton International Players Championships at Boca West in Florida, 29 Super Series tournaments (including two WCT Super Series in Houston and Atlanta), 32 Regular and Open Week Series tournaments, four Circuit Championships: Buick WCT Finals in Dallas, WCT Tournament of Champions in Forest Hills, Nabisco Masters at Madison Square Garden and the Nabisco Masters Doubles in London.

In 1986, the ATP was involved in six events: (i) February 23, Boca Raton, Boca West, $725,000, Lipton International Players' Championships, (ii) May 25, Dusseldorf, $500,000 Ambre Solaire ATP World Team Cup, (iii) June 15, London, $200,000 Stella Artois Queens ATP Grass-Court Championships, (iv) June 22, Bristol, $100,000 Lambert and Butler Championships, (v) August 24, Cincinnati, $300,000 ATP Championships and (vi) November 17, London, $300,000 ATP Benson and Hedges Championships at Wembley. All of the ATP tournaments were in the Grand Prix, except for the World Team Cup.

Rules

The *Official 1986 MIPTC Yearbook* (279 pages) and the *Official 1986 Media Guide* (413 pages) were split into two publications. The Grand Prix Rules for 1986 were essentially unchanged from 1985. The player commitment remained at 14 self-designations, plus the WCT Dallas Finals and the Nabisco Masters with up to two substitutions and the Bonus Pool continued to be $4 million for 64 singles players and 24 doubles players. The Bonus Prize money for the smaller tournaments was continued: Winner - $8,000, Runner-Up - $4,000 and Losing Semifinalists - $2,000. I again had to continue to protect Rotterdam with substitutions as none of the top players again selected it as one of their contract tournaments.

Player Injury

Tennis purists always believed that the only medical help a player could have was in the event of an accidental injury. I had been advocating for some time the need to provide medical treatment for players during matches so as to avoid defaults and keep a match going for the paying spectators. This was difficult for the "tennis purists" who believed that if a player was not able to continue to play without treatment he must be defaulted. Finally, with this rule change for 1986, the MIPTC recognized the necessity of protecting the spectators from avoidable defaulted matches. The new rule read: "A player may within any ninety (90) second changeover receive treatment, consultation and supplies from a medical doctor or trainer when necessary and appropriate upon the approval of the Supervisor." Assuming that there would always be paying spectators for the match, the MIPTC for the first time provided for medical treatment so the players could continue to play rather than have to default. *This was especially important for professional tennis.*

32 Seeds

Grand Slams and the ATP two-week tournaments with 128 draws were given the option to have 32 seeds. As soon as this was adopted it protected the top 32 players from ever having to play each other until the round of 32 and made it more difficult for new players to break into the top 32.

Unreasonable Delays

The Point Penalty for time violations was changed to "warning" and thereafter one point for each violation. However, refusal to play, delay for natural loss of physical condition or injury delays, after being ordered to resume play, time violations continued to be under the Point Penalty Schedule of "warning" and then "point", "game" and "default."

Drug Offenses and Drug Testing

The 1985 rule which merely prohibited "Illegal Drugs" was deleted and replaced by the new drug testing rule which prohibited cocaine, heroin and amphetamines and provided for testing at no more than two of the following tournaments: four Grand Slams and the ATP two-week Lipton International Players tournament. Urinalysis testing included all players plus random testing of the MIPTC and its staff, ATP

Board of Directors and its staff, the tournament committees, all certified and other court officials. The players insisted that if they were going to be tested, everyone had to be tested, so we were all tested. If anyone tested positive during drug testing, then there was no penalty if counseling and treatment was agreed confidentially. If counseling and treatment was not agreed, then the penalty was suspension and disqualification. Dr. Joseph Pursch, a nationally recognized authority in the field of alcohol and drug-related abuse, was named the independent expert responsible for overseeing mandatory and confidential drug testing of men's professional tennis players by the MIPTC along with the confidential counseling and treatment of any players testing positive.

Coaching

In addition to the prohibition of coaching during matches, the Code now required players to prohibit their coaches from: using audible obscenities, making obscene gestures, verbally abusing any official and physically abusing any official, opponent, spectator or other person, "within the precincts of the tournament site." This made the players responsible for the actions of their coaches. The penalty was the Point Penalty Schedule plus a fine of $5,000 per violation.[639]

MIPTC Meetings

In 1986, the MIPTC held five meetings: January 20-23 in New York, April 21-24 in Monte Carlo, June 17-18 in London, September 8-10 in New York and December 5-8 in New York.

MIPTC Meeting, New York January 20-23, 1986

Chair Umpires

The Council reviewed[640] the experimental program with the two full-time Chair Umpires (Rich Kaufman and Jeremy Shales) and due to the success of the program decided to authorize the addition of a third Chair Umpire for the second half of 1986 (Richard Ings), plus a further addition of two more Chair Umpires to begin in 1987, which would make a total of five full-time MIPTC Chair Umpires.

Nabisco Masters Doubles – WCT World Doubles

The Council agreed to combine the WCT World Doubles and the Nabisco Masters Doubles in December of each year in return for WCT relinquishing its contracted right for a fourth Super Series.

MIPTC Meeting, Monte Carlo, April 21-24, 1986

Nabisco Extension for 1988 and 1989 Plus New Option for 1990 and Nabisco Masters Doubles

In April in Monte Carlo,[641] it was obvious that our actions against the Volvo Tennis scheme had saved our relationship with Nabisco. Ed Redding, Senior Vice President of Nabisco, said, "Nabisco has seen the value of its involvement with the Grand Prix grow with each passing month. We have been very impressed with the support we have received from the tennis community and feel that the time has arrived to extend our commitment to tennis."

The Council agreed to Nabisco's exercise of its options to extend its sponsorship of the Nabisco Grand Prix and Nabisco Masters through 1988-1989 and to provide Nabisco with an option for 1990, on the same terms (no increase in the $3.5 million rights fee) "to compensate for Nabisco's loss by virtue of the negative impact caused by the actions taken by Volvo." For the combining of the WCT World Doubles with the Nabisco Masters Doubles, Nabisco and the MIPTC agreed to pay WCT $100,000 each for the 1986 and 1987 Nabisco Masters Doubles. Nabisco agreed to pay WCT $225,000 for 1988 and $225,000 for 1989 with WCT providing a minimum of $200,000 in prize money each year.

Maximum Aggravated Behavior Fines for 1987 Increased to $25,000

For 1987, the Council increased the maximum fine for the Major Offense of Aggravated Behavior "from $20,000 to $25,000 or the amount of prize money won at the tournament, whichever is greater."

WCT Atlanta to Tokyo

The Council approved WCT's request to move its Atlanta Super Series to Tokyo during the week of April 13, 1987, as the Japan Open with the Japanese National Tennis Association. Apparently, the "Suntory Japan Open" would be sponsored by Suntory and it was represented that the Suntory Cup special event would be discontinued. But a Suntory special event was held anyway.[642]

MIPTC Meeting, London, June 17-18, 1986

Exemption of Special Events

In June in London,[643] the Council agreed to exempt the Suntory Cup four-man special event (April 4-5, 1987) and the Gunze Cup special event (May 6-10, 1987), which were within 30 days of the Japan Open Super Series, from the special event prohibition rules. The Council also exempted the 16-player Hamlet Cup on Long Island (week of August 18, 1986), which was within 30 days and 100 miles of the U.S. Open.

MIPTC Meeting, New York, September 8-10, 1986

Mike Davies Fired as ATP Executive Director, Ray Moore Becomes Chairman

In January of 1985, Mike Davies received a two-year extension on his employment contract as the ATP Executive Director through 1987. At the September 10-12, 1985, MIPTC meeting in New York,[644] Mike was elected as a Player Representative for a two-year term for 1986 and 1987, and he was also elected as the MIPTC Chairman succeeding Philippe Chatrier, who had been Chairman for six years.

At the ATP Championships in Cincinnati staged the week ending August 24, 1986, the ATP Board voted to fire Mike Davies and terminate his employment contract which continued through December 31, 1987. When Davies asked the ATP to honor the terms of his employment contract by paying him through December 31, 1987, the ATP refused, concocting a claim that he was terminated for "cause" and thus had breached his employment contract. ATP's refusal to honor Mike's employment contract created a large amount of unnecessary ill will and forced him to hire a lawyer to sue the ATP for breach of his employment contract.

The next meeting of the MIPTC was scheduled for September 8-10 in New York at which Davies was Chairman of the MIPTC and his term on the MIPTC as a Player Representative (not an ATP Representative) was for two years of 1986 and 1987. As the MIPTC meeting began on September 8, the ATP wanted Mike to resign from the MIPTC, but the ATP did not want to pay him the balance due on his employment contract which was now in litigation and costing Mike legal fees. I overheard Derek Hardwick, one of the brightest members of the MIPTC and one of the ITF Representatives, advising Mike to refuse to resign until he got paid in full. Mike refused to resign on September 8 and he chaired the MIPTC meeting that day. When the MIPTC meeting resumed on September 9, we were advised that the ATP and Mike Davies had settled their controversary and Mike tendered a written resignation to the MIPTC and as its Chairman. My impression was that Ray Moore had become personally concerned with the way Mike had been treated by the ATP.

Weller Evans, a well-respected and popular ATP Road Manager, was elected by Ray Moore and Harold Solomon (the other two Player Representatives) to succeed Davies on the MIPTC. Moore was elected as the new Chairman of the MIPTC by acclamation on September 9.

John Barrett wrote in *World of Tennis 1987*[645]: "To uninformed outsiders, it would appear that the Association in 1986 had taken a sidestep towards the left and militancy. The 'resignation' of Michael Davies, who had not only proved an able administrator at domestic level but had also become an international tennis politician of some stature, was a total surprise. It had appeared that Davies's skill in becoming Chairman of the Men's International Professional Tennis Council in succession to the long-serving Establishment figure, Philippe Chatrier, was much appreciated by the ATP membership. It was no longer the case that the players were second-class citizens."

1987 Lipton

Permission was granted to move 1987 Lipton to Key Biscayne FL, instead of the previously proposed Weston Fla.

McEnroe's Extended Rest

The intensity of professional tennis got to John McEnroe and he was replaced as world No. 1 by Ivan Lendl in 1985 and he lost in the January 1986 Nabisco Masters to Brad Gilbert 5-7, 6-4, 6-1. At the January 20-23, 1986, meeting of the MIPTC in New York, the Council agreed to let McEnroe withdraw for extended rest from the 1986 Nabisco Grand Prix and "upon his return to make a reduction in his 1986 contract tournament commitment based on the then existing circumstances." The Council had learned from its handling of Bjorn Borg's similar request in 1982, which may have resulted in losing Borg to men's professional tennis. The Council hoped that giving McEnroe an extended rest would keep him in the game – and it worked. The Council later agreed on McEnroe's request for a reduced player commitment for 1986 consisting of seven tournaments:

Stratton Mountain, Canadian Open, U.S. Open, Los Angeles, San Francisco, Scottsdale and Houston.

John McEnroe Tennis Over America Tour

In January of 1986, the MIPTC granted McEnroe's request for an extended period of rest from the Nabisco Grand Prix and he did not begin play until August of 1986. Steve Corey and Gary Swain continued to promote the John McEnroe Tennis Over America Tour and McEnroe was permitted to satisfy his obligation to his tour through February 9, even though he was in his period of extended rest. This was the final year of the tour and included 11 exhibition matches with Mats Wilander and Yannick Noah.

In 1986, Gary Swain joined IMG as a professional agent and in 1991 he began representing John McEnroe. Their relationship had, of course begun with the "John McEnroe Tennis Over America Tour." After John retired in 1993 from the ATP Tour, Gary, who went to become a very respected Senior Vice President with IMG, became his exclusive agent at IMG during his very successful post active career, that included being the world's leading television commentator, a senior tournament and exhibition player and for endorsements and personal appearances among other projects. I heard it said once that John McEnroe had earned worldwide name identification similar to that of Mohammed Ali.

Proposed Exception of Promotional Rights for Four Grand Slams

The Administrator reported that he had been informed that the ATP was requesting the top 100 players to "except the grant of promotion rights to the 4 Grand Slams" in their Player Commitment contracts for the 1987 Nabisco Grand Prix. *If it happened it would be a declaration of War…just what we needed.* The Council directed that any Player Commitment contracts containing such an exception were to be rejected. Ray Moore, the new Chairman of the Council was able to obtain the removal of all the proposed exceptions from the 1987 player commitment contracts.

1988 Format

The Council adopted a proposed 1988 Format, which for the first time provided for two classes of Super Series, which was controversial since no one wanted to be 2nd class. The proposal was for 15 (1st Class) Super Series and 13 (2nd Class) Super Series.

MIPTC Meeting, New York, December 5-8, 1986[646]

Ray Benton of ProServ Threat and Leave of Absence

In December in New York, Ray Benton of ProServ told Nabisco that if the Council went forward with the new 1988 format (two classes of Super Series), Nabisco would not get the value of its sponsorship contract as Volvo and ProServ would start a new competing circuit. A motion to rescind the 1988 format failed and further consideration of the 1988 format was deferred until the next meeting. Benton announced that he would be taking a leave of absence as President of ProServ in January.

Lendl Saves Philadelphia at the Very Last Minute

The Ebel U.S. Pro Championships in Philadelphia was scheduled for January 27 – February 2, 1986 indoors at the Spectrum. Philadelphia was considered one of the most important tournaments in the world and it usually had around 14,000 fans for the final. Marilyn Fernberger and her husband Edward were a famous husband-wife team and they had been co-tournament directors since founding the tournament in 1969 as the first really big indoor tennis tournament. In the early years of the tournament, Marilyn and Edward hosted a number of the players at their home during the tournament. Marilyn and Edward raised a lot of prize money for professional players through the years and they staged a great tournament.

McEnroe had been designated as the lead marketing star for 1986 Philadelphia, but he had now been permitted to withdraw for his leave of absence and Marilyn, to put it mildly, was extremely panicked. While Marilyn was always panicked and seemingly close to hysteria, this time the MIPTC, by granting McEnroe his requested leave of absence, was involved in creating the problem for Philadelphia with McEnroe's last-minute withdrawal. I had completed all of my possible substitutions of players in October with the assistance of the player agents so that process had been completed. However, afterwards I, from time to time, had to assign players who missed a designated tournament for an injury to a replacement designation which I always attempted to do by agreement with the players instead of trying to force a replacement which I could do under the rules and only occasionally had to do. All of the players, including Ivan Lendl hated the designation system with a passion and every year threatened a boycott of the Grand Prix.

On Saturday, January 20, Marilyn had her scheduled official draw scheduled for something like noon or 2 PM and she was on her car telephone (then a fairly new invention) to me constantly in panic mode as she was in her car driving to the Spectrum for the official draw. Marilyn was begging us to get Lendl to "save" Philadelphia. Somehow, I got a message to Jerry Solomon, Lendl's agent, who was with Lendl and they were about to take off on a flight from somewhere out west back to the east coast. Jerry called me on an airplane telephone (there were no cell phones yet). Lendl did not like to play Philadelphia and he did not like Marilyn, which is why he had not entered it in the first place, so it was uphill to try to get him to agree to play in Philadelphia in two days. I was asking Jerry to get Lendl to play Philadelphia in two days, and I was offering to count Philadelphia as a future make-up designation for any designated tournament that Lendl might miss during the remainder of 1986, and I was agreeing not to force him to go anywhere all year. To make a long story short, after a number of telephone calls, Jerry convinced Lendl to play Philadelphia, so I confirmed that to Marilyn on her car phone. Marilyn arrived at the draw ceremony a few minutes later and entered Lendl as a late entry wild card. Lendl was seeded No. 1 in Philadelphia and won the tournament when Tim Mayotte defaulted the final on account of an injury he sustained in his semifinal win over Yannick Noah.

While this situation was extremely unusual, it demonstrated how everyone had to work together to make men's professional tennis successful, sometimes under serious time pressures, and it was our use of new car phone technology and an airplane telephone that made it possible for us to communicate under this kind of time pressure. Remember Jerry Solomon was with ProServ who was suing me personally and trying to get me fired for its client Volvo. *Nothing personal!* We all worked together, notwithstanding the pending lawsuit and other competitive disagreements. Solomon demonstrated on that day the importance of having really good player agents in the game and likewise, Lendl demonstrated his commitment to making professional tennis successful. *Lendl agreed to enter a tournament he did not like to play and "saved" Philadelphia.*

IBM PC Convertible

By 1986, we were deeply into using IBM PC's in our offices in New York and in Paris. I had actually smuggled an American keyboard into Paris since the French keyboard, just to be "French," had various letters in different positions which caused a kind of nightmare for an American. On April 3, 1986, IBM issued the IBM PC Convertible, which was the first laptop computer released by IBM. It had two 3.5" floppy disc drives. As soon as I saw it, I purchased four of them so that I could carry one around the world with me as I traveled and so each of our three Tour Liaisons could also travel with one. The attachable printers permitted them to update player records on the road, daily and really modernized their ability to provide the press with up-to-date biographical and other information on the players. For reference, the USTA staff would not even have IBM PC's until I became the USTA Executive Director in 1990.

MIPTC Office at Wimbledon

In addition to working in our Manhattan and Paris offices, Wimbledon also furnished us an office for three weeks each year before and during Wimbledon. The windowless office was located on the third top floor of the Wimbledon Centre Court building. In those days, the United Kingdom still had a rotary telephone system and when we began to use our new IBM convertible PCs which had a United States telephone jack, we learned with the help of British Telecom how to rewire our telephone jacks to the British telephones. To slow down our digital computer modems for the slower rotary system we had to insert a number of commas with each number dialed.

Drug Testing at Wimbledon

We had our first drug testing at Wimbledon in 1986. Under the new Code provision, we had to take a urine sample from every male singles and doubles player, along with the MIPTC members and MIPTC staff, ATP board members and staffs (including me and the Chairman of Wimbledon) and all the MIPTC certified officials. I rented a large suite at the Gloucester Hotel, which was the official hotel for the players, and the testing was done by a professional drug testing company from New Jersey (TDLA Testing Laboratories) under the supervision of Dr. Joseph Pursch, our official independent expert. We provided lots of fruit juices and soft drinks for the players to help them provide the urine samples which were stored on ice to be taken back to the United States for testing.

Our testing suite became extremely popular with the Russian players who were traveling with a female KGB agent. Instead of being locked in their rooms every night by the agent, they loved the freedom to sit in our testing suite, visit with other players and get free soft drinks and juice. I remember Andrei Chesnokov, the most famous of the Russian players at the time, asking if he could return for testing every night. Anything to get free of the KGB lady and get free soft drinks.

Our new drug testing rule, which only tested for cocaine, heroin and amphetamines, was focused on intervention and treatment. We did not think that performance enhancing drugs were an issue in men's professional tennis and no professional sport had ventured into drug testing. We all knew that the IOC drug testing for performance enhancing drugs was much more elaborate, but the Olympics were still limited to amateurs.

There was an official IOC testing lab in London and the British press was incensed that we were using a New Jersey testing company and that all of the urine samples were going to be flown back to New Jersey for testing. Someone in the press actually accused us of keeping evidence (urine samples) of criminal substances secret and shipping them out of Great Britain. Nevertheless, we followed our testing protocol which had been approved by the players and sent all of the urine samples to our professional testing service in New Jersey. If there were any positive tests, they were dealt with confidentially by our independent expert, Dr. Joseph Pursch. This type of drug testing rule for tennis was permitted by the IOC for the 1988 Olympics and it was continued through the destruction of the MIPTC at the end of 1989. When the ATP and the players started the new ATP Tour in 1990, Hamilton Jordan convinced them to agree for the first time to IOC testing for performance enhancing drugs in an effort to show how responsible they were becoming.

Pat Cash Verbal Abuse at 1986 Wimbledon:
Persecution Claims by Pat Cash, Sr., Esquire

At Wimbledon in 1986, Pat Cash was fined for verbal abuse of Rich Kaufman, one of our first two full time MIPTC Chair Umpires during a second round match with Russell Simpson. I agreed that Cash's remarks were intended to be and were abusive and I upheld the fine on appeal. On July 29, I wrote to Pat Cash Sr. (Pat's father who was an Australian lawyer) to confirm to him that our full-time chair umpires were instructed not to accept verbal abuse from players. I agreed to meet with Pat Jr. to assure him that we had nothing against him and that we were only going to enforce the provisions of the Code of Conduct.[647]

Micky den Tuinder (Lawler):
New MIPTC Media Liaison

In July, we hired Micky den Tuinder as the replacement for Marieke van der Drift, joining Sandy Genelius and Jennifer Proud and their titles were changed from MIPTC Tour Liaisons to MIPTC Media Liaisons. Micky was a native of Holland and was residing in Paris. She had resided in Latin America, Africa, Europe and the United States and was fluent in Dutch, English, Spanish, French and German. She had attended the University of Delaware where she obtained a M.A. degree in Applied Linguistics. Before joining the MIPTC in July 1986, Micky served as a research assistant and language interpreter in the United States. *Today Micky den Tuinder Lawler, is President of the WTA.*

Drug Testing at U.S. Open: CBS Praises New Rule

The MIPTC tested all the players at the 1986 U.S. Open in the same manner that was done at Wimbledon. As reported in *International Tennis Weekly*[648]: "CBS reporter Anne Butler introduced a segment on the ATP/MIPTC drug testing by saying, 'The spectre of drugs hangs heavily over virtually every arena of sports, yet the image of tennis is relatively clean-cut and drug-free. While other groups of professional athletes are actively resisting the trend toward drug testing, the men's tennis players' union has voluntarily decided to create a screening program of its own. The program is designed to protect, rather than penalize, the players… So, credit men's tennis. The sport faced up to a situation that no one even accused it of having…The plan has been well thought out. It has a carrot: the promise of a clean life and continued career through rehab. And it has a stick: the threat of suspension. It protects a player's right to privacy, while assuring the public that the players can be caught since the testing has an element of surprise. And the plan itself has no penal implication, no assumed guilt…Men's tennis now has a reasonable and, it is hoped effective anti-drug operation in place. The players did it themselves. They have shown foresight and not a little courage. They deserve Applause.'"

Richard Ings Hired as MIPTC Full-Time Chair Umpire No. 3

Richard Ings, age 20 and a graduate of the University of Sydney with a B.S. in Applied Mathematics and Computer Sciences, began his officiating career at age 16 when he volunteered to become a linesman at the White City Grand Prix tournament in Sydney. At the 1984 Australian Open, at age 18, Richard was assigned a center court match simply because no other chair umpires were available. In that first round match Bill Scanlon defeated John Fitzgerald 3-6, 7-5, 7-5, 6-7, 6-2. In 1985 at the Australia Open, he was assigned as the chair umpire for the center court semifinal where Stefan Edberg defeated Ivan Lendl 6-7, 7-5, 6-1, 4-6, 9-7. Richard attended the MIPTC Officials' School in Sydney in November 1985, and upon graduation, was certified as a MIPTC International Official. Richard was hired to begin after Wimbledon in 1986 joining Rich Kaufman and Jeremy Shales as MIPTC full-time Chair Umpires.

McEnroe and Fleming Disqualified at U.S. Open

John McEnroe and Peter Fleming "got stuck in traffic" traveling from McEnroe's parents' home in Cove Neck, (Oyster Bay) Long Island and failed to arrive on time for their first round match at the U.S. Open. The match was called at 2:00 PM and since they were not present by 2:15 PM, they were disqualified by Gayle Bradshaw the U.S. Open Referee as specified in the tournament regulations.

Soon after arrival at the U.S. Open site, McEnroe and Fleming were informed in the players' lounge that they had been defaulted. McEnroe went into a tirade and verbally abused Bradshaw. Ken Farrar, our MIPTC Supervisor, fined McEnroe $4,000 for verbal abuse and McEnroe Sr. appealed to me as the MIPTC Administrator claiming that John's abusive statements were "essentially private conversations" and should not be the subject of any penalty under the Code. On September 25, I upheld the fine because the MIPTC Code of Conduct prohibits verbal abuse "within the precincts of the tournament site." When I sent my decision to McEnroe's agent, John McEnroe, Sr., I reminded him that fines had been issued for verbal abuse within the "precincts of the tournament site" against John for 1984 Toronto for verbal abuse in a press tent of a female reporter, against Pat Cash at the 1984 Australian Open for verbal abuse of the tournament director in the official tournament office and against Eliot Teltscher at 1985 Toronto for verbal abuse of a Supervisor at 2:00 AM.

McEnroe and Shales and Another Suspension

At the 1986 Paris Indoors, John McEnroe lost 6-3, 7-6 to Sergio Casal of Spain, a qualifier. McEnroe said to Jeremy Shales, the Chair Umpire "You are the worst umpire I've seen in my life." McEnroe was fined $3,000, which made his total for the year exceed $7,500 forcing another 21-42-day automatic suspension. *Another Fall vacation.*

Gerry Armstrong and Paulo Periera Hired as MIPTC Full-Time Chair Umpires

In October, we hired Gerry Armstrong and Paulo Periera as our No. 4 and No. 5 MIPTC full-time Chair Umpires, to join with Rick Kaufman, Jeremy Shales and Richard Ings. Armstrong, age 31, was born and resided in Eastbourne, England. He had started his officiating career in 1973 and was certified as an MIPTC International Official at the 1986 International Officials School in Paris. In 1981, Gerry earned an Honors Degree in Physical Education from the University of Sussex (England). He was a member of the British Tennis Umpires Association (BTUA) and had officiated at a total of 12 Wimbledons. *When Gerry became a paid MIPTC Chair Umpire, the volunteers at the BTUA dropped him from its membership, but said he could be reinstated if in the future he became a volunteer again. In 2020, Gerry was appointed to be the new Referee of Wimbledon.*

From Sao Paulo, Brazil, Paulo Periera, age 37 who was fluent in five languages, began officiating in 1982 and was certified as an MIPTC International Official at the 1984 Johannesburg school. He had a degree in civil engineering from Mackenzie University in Sao Paulo. He had served both as an international chair umpire and as a referee in Davis Cup competition.

ATP
Matt Doyle Re-Elected ATP President

During Wimbledon, Matt Doyle was re-elected ATP President in July by a ballot of the ATP[649] members and not just the board as had been done in the past. Brian Gottfried was elected Vice President and Mike Estep and Jim McManus, continued as Treasurer and Secretary, respectively. The other board members were Ray Moore, Colin Dowdeswell, Carlos Kirmayr, Paul McNamee, Harold Solomon, Yannick Noah and Ricardo Acuna, so John McEnroe and Mats Wilander departed the Board.

JAKS AWARDS (New York City December 1986)

Player of the Year	Ivan Lendl
Doubles Team of the Year	Hans Gildemeister – Andres Gomez
Newcomer of the Year	Ulf Stenlund
Most Improved Player of the Year	Mikael Pernfors
ATP Adidas Sportsmanship Award	Yannick Noah
Great Player of the Past	Ken Rosewall
ATP Super Series Tournament of the Year	Cincinnati
ATP Regular Series Tournament of the Year	Mercedes Cup, Stuttgart

Major Offense No. 9: Jimmy Connors, 1986 Lipton

Jimmy Connors competed in the 1986 Lipton International Players Championships in Boca Raton, Florida, staged February 10-23, 1986. On Friday, February 21, Connors played Ivan Lendl in the semifinals of the tournament before a standing room only packed audience of about 10,000 fans. Jeremy Shales, one of the two full-time MIPTC Chair Umpires was the Chair Umpire for the match. Ken Farrar was the MIPTC Supervisor at the tournament and Alan Mills of Great Britain was the Referee (Mills was also the

Referee at Wimbledon). The match was covered live by a national television audience on ESPN and taped and replayed by ABC the next day.

After three hours and 40 minutes, with Lendl serving and leading 3-2, 30-0 in the fifth set, Lendl hit a volley that landed on or near the baseline on Connors' side of the net. The linesman signaled the ball as "good" and Connors failed to make a good return, which made the score 40-0. Connors disputed the call and refused to continue play. Arthur Ashe said on the ABC coverage of the match: "The ball looked good to me. If it was out, it was the tiniest bit out, not enough to tell." Connors argued with Shales, but Shales thought the "good call" was correct so he did not and actually could not change the call. Connors refused to continue play.

Shales announced: "Time violation. Warning, Mr. Connors." When Connors continued to refuse to play, Shales announced: "Code violation. Delay of game. "Point". "Game Mr. Lendl." This made the score 4-2 Lendl in the fifth set. When Connors continued to refuse to play, Shales announced: "Code violation. Delay of game. "Game". "Lendl leads 5 games to 2." MIPTC Supervisor Ken Farrar came on court and told Connors that neither he, the Referee or the Chair Umpire could change a "good" line call as it was a question of fact and the call was final.

Shales said: "I'm going to call the match; I'm going to call the default." Farrar said to Connors: "Don't go out this way." Connors said: "I can't play under circumstances like that." Shales said to Farrar: "The clock's on. Default is coming up now OK? OK? Default is coming up now; OK?" Farrar said: "You've already given him a game penalty?" Shales answered: "Yes." Farrar turned to Connors with his hands to indicate that default was imminent. Connors said one last time to Farrar: "I refuse to play under conditions like that." Farrar said to Shales: "Then default him." Shales announced: "Game, Set and Match, Lendl, by default." Connors "shook" Shales' hand and left the court. The crowd booed Shales, as they had been hoping that Connors would come back and win the fifth set! Lendl won the match by the final score of 1-6, 6-1, 6-2, 2-6, 5-2 (default).

Farrar fined Connors $5,000 for the on-site offense of "Failure to complete a match." As a semifinalist, Connors won $28,125 in prize money and the $5,000 on-site offense fine was deducted and paid to the MIPTC.[650]

On February 25, I commenced my investigation into whether to also charge Connors with the Major Offense of "Aggravated Behavior" and served notice on Connors via his attorney, Ivan Blumberg of ProServ. On February 26, Connors appealed the $5,000 on-site fine and I agreed to consider that appeal at the same time as I considered the Major Offense case. On March 12, Connors presented his appeal and response to my Major Offense investigation through Ivan Blumberg, video tape replays and Connors' own testimony by telephone with Mike Davies, Roy Reardon and me.

In arriving at my decision, which was subject to review by the MIPTC and subject to appeal to three Review Officers, I explained that the "good" call made by the linesman during the Lendl match was a determination of fact and could not be changed by the Chair Umpire, the Referee or the Supervisor. The only way a Chair Umpire can ever change a linesman's call is by the overrule which is limited to a "clear mistake" that is corrected promptly and immediately. Shales not only did not consider an overrule in this case, he actually told Connors he saw the ball as "good" just as did the linesman. No matter how much Connors wanted to dispute the call, it could not be changed by anyone.

In my opinion, one of the worst things a professional athlete can do is cheat the paying fans by failing to complete a match. In this case, about 10,000 fans were cheated along with a live television audience. However, strangely, they apparently applauded Connors when he refused to play and was defaulted. I guess they just did not like Lendl or our Chair Umpire Shales. My decision was to deny Connors' appeal of the $5,000 on-site offense fine and to find him guilty of the Major Offense of "Aggravated Behavior" for which I assessed an additional fine of $20,000 and a suspension of 10 weeks. The MIPTC Council agreed with my Determination.[651]

Connors elected to waive his right to appeal, paid the additional $20,000 and began his 10-week suspension, which prevented him from playing in the 1986 French Open. If he had appealed, which he surely would have lost, he could have been prevented from playing in Wimbledon as well, depending on when the appeal would have been completed.[652]

Apparently, during his suspension, Connors played in special event exhibitions in Tulsa, Tokyo and New Orleans. Connors wrote in his book The Outsider[653]: "The Lipton default cost me $25,000 in fines and a 10-week ban. How did I feel about that? The things you have to do to get some time off, right? Anyway, the suspension I received was an opportunity for me to play a couple of special events and half a dozen exhibitions. I made a hell of a lot more money that I would have playing the tournaments." When I was asked by Neil Amdur of the New York Times if I was bothered by Connors cashing in so lucratively while on suspension, I said, "A little bit. It doesn't devastate me. What he's not doing is playing in official tournaments to get the ranking points he needs."[654]

Major Offense No.10: Libor Pimek, 1986 Stockholm

Libor Pimek of Czechoslovakia was ranked No. 47 and he competed in 26 Nabisco Grand Prix tournaments in 1986. Pimek was entered by designation as one of his contract tournaments for 1986 into the Stockholm Open, scheduled for the week of November 3-9. Instead of playing in Stockholm, Pimek participated in a special event in Antwerp, Belgium, known as the "European Champions Championships" and failed to show for Stockholm. Pimek received $5,000 for his participation in the Antwerp special event. I concluded that Pimek's "decision to participate in the Antwerp special event was singularly egregious and injurious to the success of the Stockholm Open, and therefore he was "guilty of the Major Offense of "Aggravated Behavior." I specified a penalty of a $5,000 fine and a 21-day suspension. The Council approved my Administrator's Determination and penalty at its December 5-8, 1986 meeting in New York. Pimek elected not to appeal, accepted and paid the fine and served the 21-day suspension.

MIPTC Financials

The MIPTC began 1986 with a surplus of $1,648,465 and after operating its New York and Paris offices and providing $4,000,000 in Bonus Pool awards and $452,000 in Bonus Prize Money to players in the Nabisco Grand Prix, the MIPTC ended 1986 with a surplus of $3,529,829. In addition, the MIPTC collected and paid to ATP, pursuant to a 1982 agreement covering 1983-1987, $685,110 in ATP prize money for services to Nabisco Grand Prix tournaments, $54,663 in ATP entry fees and $56,005 in ATP Challenger and Satellite sanction fees.[655]

Nabisco paid for its promotion as the Nabisco Grand Prix sponsor and the MIPTC provided the promotion of the Nabisco Grand Prix. The MIPTC, via MIPTC staff, promoted the Nabisco Masters in January of 1986 and in December of 1986 at Madison Square Garden. The January 1986 Nabisco Masters (for the 1985 Nabisco Grand Prix) was telecast by NBC. The December 1986 Nabisco Masters (for the 1986 Nabisco Grand Prix) was telecast by ESPN.

Nabisco and the MIPTC each contributed $100,000 for the $200,000 in prize money for the Nabisco Masters' Doubles to be promoted and operated by WCT at the Royal Albert Hall in London. The gross income for the two Nabisco Masters tournaments in 1986 was $5,828,589 and the gross expense was $4,238,228, so the MIPTC net for the two tournaments was $1,590,361. That is why the MIPTC wisely insisted on owning and operating the Nabisco Masters. Also, the ownership and control of the Nabisco Masters permitted the MIPTC for the first time to move the tournament from January into December, thus permitting the Australian Open to move into January. *That move permitted the Australian Open to flourish instead of always having to beg players to come to Australia in December and play on grass just before the Masters and the U.S. Indoor tournaments.*

1986 Grand Slam Winners

French Open

Ivan Lendl d. Mikael Pernfors 6-3, 6-2, 6-4.
John Fitzgerald – Tomas Smid d. Stefan Edberg – Anders Jarryd 6-3, 4-6, 6-3, 6-7, 14-12.

Wimbledon

Boris Becker d. Ivan Lendl 6-4, 6-3, 7-5.
Joakim Nystrom – Mats Wilander d. Gary Donnelly – Peter Fleming 7-6, 6-3, 6-3.

U.S. Open

Ivan Lendl d. Miloslav Mecir 6-4, 6-2, 6-0.
Andres Gomez – Slobodan Zivojinovic d. Joakim Nystrom – Mats Wilander 4-6, 6-3, 6-3, 4-6, 6-3.

Australian Open

[There was no Australian Open in 1986 as with the Nabisco Masters moving from January to December, the Australian Open moved from December to be the first Grand Slam in January of 1987]

Lipton International Players' Championships (Boca Raton)

Ivan Lendl d. Mats Wilander 3-6, 6-1, 7-6, 6-4.
Brad Gilbert – Vince Van Patten d. Stefan Edberg – Anders Jarryd w.o.

Nabisco Grand Prix Circuit Championships

Buick WCT Finals (Dallas)

Anders Jarryd d. Boris Becker 6-7, 6-1, 6-1, 6-4.

WCT Tournament of Champions (Forest Hills)

Yannick Noah d. Guillermo Vilas 7-6, 6-0.
Hans Gildemeister – Andres Gomez d. Boris Becker - Slobodan Zivojinovic 7-6, 7-6.

Nabisco Masters (New York)

Ivan Lendl d. Boris Becker 6-4, 6-4, 6-4.

Nabisco Masters Doubles (London)

Stefan Edberg - Anders Jarryd d. Guy Forget – Yannick Noah 6-3, 7-6, 6-3.

1986 Davis Cup

Davis Cup Final (Melbourne-Grass)

Australia d. Sweden 3-2.

Pat Cash (AU) d. Stefan Edberg (SE) 13-11, 13-11, 6-4.
Mikael Pernfors (SE) d. Paul McNamee (AU) 6-3, 6-1, 6-3.
Pat Cash – John Fitzgerald (AU) d. Stefan Edberg – Anders Jarryd (SE) 6-3, 6-4, 4-6, 6-1.
Pat Cash (AU) d. Mikael Pernfors (SE) 2-6, 4-6, 6-3, 6-4, 6-3.
Stefan Edberg (SE) d. Paul McNamee (AU) 10-8, 6-4.

1986 World Team Cup

France d. Sweden 2-1.

Henri Leconte (FR) d. Anders Jarryd (SE) 6-3, 3-6, 6-1.
Mats Wilander (SE) d. Thierry Tulasne (FR) 6-1, 6-4.
Guy Forget – Henri Leconte (FR) d. Anders Jarryd – Mats Wilander (SE) 6-3, 2-6, 6-2.

1986 World Rankings[656]

Bud Collins	Lance Tingay	ATP Year-End Rankings
1. Ivan Lendl	1. Ivan Lendl	1. Ivan Lendl
2. Boris Becker	2. Boris Becker	2. Boris Becker
3. Mats Wilander	3. Henri Leconte	3. Mats Wilander
4. Yannick Noah	4. Miloslav Mecir	4. Yannick Noah
5. Stefan Edberg	5. Stefan Edberg	5. Stefan Edberg
6. Henri Leconte	6. Mats Wilander	6. Henri Leconte
7. Joakim Nystrom	7. Joakim Nystrom	7. Joakim Nystrom
8. Jimmy Connors	8. Andres Gomez	8. Jimmy Connors
9. Miloslav Mecir	9. Yannick Noah	9. Miloslav Mecir
10. Andres Gomez	10. Anders Jarryd	10. Andres Gomez

1986 Nabisco Grand Prix Bonus Pool Top 10[657]

Singles (17th Bonus Pool)		Doubles (12th Bonus Pool)	
1. Ivan Lendl	$ 800,000	1. Guy Forget	$ 165,000
2. Boris Becker	$ 550,000	2. Andres Gomez	$ 120,000
3. Stefan Edberg	$ 400,000	3. Sherwood Stewart	$ 90,000
4. Joakim Nystrom	$ 250,000	4. Slobodan Zivojinovic	$ 70,000
5. Yannick Noah	$ 150,000	5. Peter Fleming	$ 50,000
6. Mats Wilander	$ 100,000	6. Joakim Nystrom	$ 40,000
7. Henri Leconte	$ 75,000	7. Gary Donnelly	$ 30,000
8. Andres Gomez	$ 55,000	8. Tomas Smid	$ 25,000
9. Jimmy Connors	$ 45,000	9. Yannick Noah	$ 20,000
10. Miloslav Mecir	$ 40,000	10. Stefan Edberg	$ 17,000

1986 Official Earnings Top 10[658]

1.	Ivan Lendl	$ 1,987,537	6.	Andres Gomez	$ 610,121
2.	Boris Becker	$ 1,434,324	7.	Yannick Noah	$ 575,015
3.	Stefan Edberg	$ 1,028,906	8.	Guy Forget	$ 504,820
4.	Joakim Nystrom	$ 841,242	9.	Henri Leconte	$ 449,422
5.	Mats Wilander	$ 653,652	10.	Anders Jarryd	$ 442,036

1986 Tournament Calendar

Date	Tournaments	Singles Winner	Singles #2	Doubles Winners	Doubles #2
1/11/1986	Atlanta $500,000SP	Ivan Lendl	Jimmy Connors		
1/12/1986	London $200,000 WCT Dbls. GP			H. Gunthardt - B. Taroczy	P. Annacone - Van Rensburg
1/12/1986	Auckland $85,000 GP	Mark Wood-forde	Bud Schultz	B. Dyke - W. Masur	K. Richter - R. Rudeen
2/2/1986	Philadelphia $375,000 SS	Ivan Lendl	Tim Mayotte	S. Davis - D. Pate	S. Edberg - A. Jarryd
2/9/1986	Memphis $250,000 SS	Brad Gilbert	Stefan Edberg	K. Flach - R. Seguso	G. Forget - A. Jarryd
2/10/1986	Toronto $125,000 GP	Joakim Nystrom	Milan Srejber	W. Fibak - J. Nystrom	C. Steyn - D. Visser
2/23/1986	Boca West $725,000 ATP 2-WK	Ivan Lendl	Mats Wilander	B. Gilbert - V. Van Patten	S. Edberg - A. Jarryd
3/2/1986	LaQuinta $325,000 SS	Joakim Nystrom	Yannick Noah	P. Fleming - G. Forget	Y. Noah - S. Stewart
3/16/1986	Milan $300,000 SS	Ivan Lendl	Joakim Nystrom	C. Dowdeswell - C. Steyn	B. Levine - L. Warder
3/16/1986	Metz $85,000 GP	Thierry Tulasne	Broderick Dyke	W. Fibak - G. Forget	F. Gonzalez - M. Schapers
3/23/1986	Brussels $250,000 SS	Mats Wilander	Broderick Dyke	B. Becker - S. Zivojinovic	J. Fitzgerald - T. Smid
3/30/1986	Rotterdam $250,000 SS	Joakim Nystrom	Anders Jarryd	S. Edberg - S. Zivojinovic	W. Fibak - M. Mitchell
3/30/1986	Chicago $250,000 Volvo SS	Boris Becker	Ivan Lendl	K. Flach - R. Seguso	E. Edwards - F. Gonzalez
4/6/1986	Ft. Myers $250,000 SS	Ivan Lendl	Jimmy Connors	A. Gomez - I. Lendl	P. Doohan - P. McNamee
4/6/1986	Atlanta $220,000 WCT/SS	Kevin Curren	Tim Wilkison	A. Kohlberg - R. Van't Hof	D. Steyn - D. Visser
4/6/1986	Cologne $100,000 GP	Jonas Svensson	Stefan Eriksson	K. Evernden - C. Hooper	J. Gunnarsson - P. Lundgren
4/13/1986	Dallas $500,000 WCT Finals GP	Anders Jarryd	Boris Becker		
4/13/1986	Bari $85,000 GP	Kent Carlsson	Horacio de la Pena	G. Donnelly - T. Smid	S. Casal - E. Sanchez
4/20/1986	Nice $85,000 GP	Emilio Sanchez	Paul McNamee	J. Hlasek - P. Slozil	G. Donnelly - C. Dowdeswell
4/20/1986	Tokyo $250,000 Suntory SP	Jimmy Connors	Mats Wilander	6-4, 6-0	

4/27/1986	Monte Carlo $325,000 SS	Joakim Nystrom	Yannick Noah	G. Forget - Y. Noah	J. Nystrom - M. Wilander
5/4/1986	Indianapolis $300,000 SS	Andres Gomez	Thierry Tulasne	H. Gildemeister - A. Gomez	J. Fitzgerald - S. Stewart
5/4/1986	Madrid $85,000 GP	Joakim Nystrom	Kent Carlsson	A. Jarryd - J. Nystrom	J. Colas - D. de Miguel
5/11/1986	NY $515,000 WCT TC GP	Yannick Noah	Guillermo Vilas	H. Gildemeister - A. Gomez	B. Becker - S. Zivojinovic
5/11/1986	Munich $100,000 GP	Emilio Sanchez	Ricki Osterthun	S. Casal - E. Sanchez	B. Dyke - W. Masur
5/18/1986	Rome $$350,000 SS	Ivan Lendl	Emilio Sanchez	G. Forget - Y. Noah	M. Edmondson - S. Stewart
5/25/1986	Florence $85,000 GP	Andres Gomez	Henrik Sundstrom	S. Casal - E. Sanchez	M. DePalmer - S. Donnelly
5/26/1986	Dusseldorf $500,000 WTC SP ATP	France	Sweden	2-1,	
5/26/1986	Dusseldorf $500,000 WTC SP ATP	Henri Leconte	Anders Jarryd	6-3, 3-6, 6-1	
5/26/1986	Dusseldorf $500,000 WTC SP ATP	Mats Wilander	Thierry Tulasne	6-1, 6-4	
5/26/1986	Dusseldorf $500,000 WTC SP ATP		6-3, 2-6, 6-2	G. Forget -H. Leconte	A. Jarryd - M. Wilander
6/8/1986	French Open 9,315,000 FF GS	Ivan Lendl	Mikael Pernfors	J. Fitzgerald - T. Smid	S. Edberg - A. Jarryd
6/15/1986	London $200,000 GP/ATP	Tim Mayotte	Jimmy Connors	K. Curren - G. Forget	D. Cahill - M. Kratzmann
6/15/1986	Bologna $85,000 GP	Martin Jaite	Paolo Cane	P. Cane - S. Colombo	C. Panatta - B. Willenborg
6/22/1986	Bristol $100,000 GP/ATP	Vijay Amritraj	Henri Leconte	C. Steyn - D. Visser	M. Edmondson - W. Masur
6/22/1986	Athens $100,000 GP	Henrik Sund-strom	Francisco Maciel	L. Pimek - B. Willenborg	C. DiLaura - C. Panatta
7/6/1986	Wimbledon £933,350 GS	Boris Becker	Ivan Lendl	J. Nystrom - M. Wilander	G. Donnelly - P. Fleming
7/13/1986	Gstaad $200,000 GP	Stefan Edberg	Roland Stadler	S. Casal - E. Sanchez	S. Edberg - J. Nystrom
7/13/1986	Bordeaux $125,000 GP	Paulo Cane	Kent Carlsson	J. Arrese - D. de Miguel	R. Agenor - M. Bahrami
7/13/1986	Newport $100,000 GP	Bill Scanlon	Tim Wilkison	V. Amritraj - T. Wilkison	E. Edwards - F. Gonzalez
7/27/1986	Boston $220,000 SS	Andres Gomez	Martin Jaite	H. Gildemeister - A. Gomez	D. Cassidy - M. Purcell

7/27/1986	Livingston $85,000 GP	Brad Gilbert	Mike Leach	B. Green - W. Masur	S. Giammalva - G. Holmes
7/27/1986	Bastad $125,000 GP	Emilio Sanchez	Mats Wilander	S. Casal - E. Sanchez	D. Campbell - J. Rive
8/3/1986	Washington $220,000 SS	Karel Novacek	Thierry Tulasne	H. Gildemeister - A. Gomez	R. Acioly - C. Kist
8/3/1986	Hilversum $100,000 GP	Thomas Muster	Jaco Hlasek	M. Mecir - T. Smid	T. Nijsson - J. Vekemans
8/10/1986	Stratton Mountain $250,000 SS	Ivan Lendl	Boris Becker	P. Fleming - J. McEnroe	P. Annacone - Van Rensburg
8/10/1986	Kitzbuhel $150,000 GP	Miloslav Mecir	Andres Gomez	H. Gunthardt - T Smid	H. Gildemeister - A. Gomez
8/17/1986	Toronto $300,000 SS	Boris Becker	Stefan Edberg	C. Hooper - M. Leach	B. Becker - S. Zivojinovic
8/17/1986	St. Vincent $85,000 GP	Simone Colombo	Paul McNamee	L. Pimek - P. Slozil	B. Cox - M. Fancutt
8/24/1986	Cincinnati $300,000 SS/ATP	Mats Wilander	Jimmy Connors	M. Kratzmann - K. Warwick	C. Steyn - D. Visser
8/24/1986	Rye World Invitational SP	Mileslav Mecir?	Vitas Gerulaitis?	Guillermo Vilas?	Andrei Chesnokov?
8/24/1986	Jericho $150,000 Hamlet SP	Ivan Lendl	John McEnroe	6-2, 6-4	
9/7/1986	US Open $1,400,000 GS	Ivan Lendl	Miloslav Mecir	A. Gomez - S. Zivojinovic	J. Nystrom - M. Wilander
9/14/1986	Geneva $200,000 GP	Henri Leconte	Thierry Tulasne	A. Maurer - J. Windahl	G. Luza - G. Tiberti
9/14/1986	Stuttgart $162,500 GP	Martin Jaite	Jonas Svensson	H. Gildemeister - A. Gomez	M. Bahrami - D. Perez
9/21/1986	Hamburg $315,000 SS	Henri Leconte	Miloslav Mecir	S. Casal - E. Sanchez	B. Becker - E. Jelen
9/21/1986	Los Angeles $250,000 SS	John McEnroe	Stefan Edberg	S. Edberg - A. Jarryd	P. Fleming - J. McEnroe
9/28/1986	San Francisco $220,000 SS	John McEnroe	Jimmy Connors	P. Fleming - J. McEnroe	M. DePalmer - G. Donnelly
9/28/1986	Barcelona $220,000 SS	Kent Carlsson	Andreas Maurer	J. Gunnarsson - J. Nystrom	C. DiLaura - C. Panatta
10/5/1986	Palermo $100,000 GP	Uli Stenlund	Pablo Arraya	P. Cane - S. Colombo	C. Mezzadri - G. Ocleppo
10/12/1986	Scottsdale $250,000 SS	John McEnroe	Kevin Curren	L. Lavalle - M. Leach	S. Davis - D. Pate
10/12/1986	Toulouse $150,000 SS	Guy Forget	Jan Gunnarsson	M. Mecir - T. Smid	J. Hlasek - P. Slozil
10/12/1986	Tel Aviv $85,000 GP	Brad Gilbert	Aaron Krickstein	J. Letts - P. Lungren	C. Steyn - D. Visser

10/19/1986	Sydney $275,000 SS	Boris Becker	Ivan Lendl	B. Becker - J. Fitzgerald	P. McNamara - P. McNamee
10/19/1986	Basle $175,000 GP	Stefan Edberg	Yannick Noah	G. Forget - Y. Noah	J. Gunnarsson - T. Smid
10/19/1986	Tokyo $121,500 GP	Ramesh Krishnan	Johan Carlsson	M. Anger - K. Flach	J. Arias - G. Holmes
10/26/1986	Tokyo $300,000 SS	Boris Becker	Stefan Edberg	M. DePalmer - G. Donnelly	A. Gomez - I. Lendl
10/26/1986	Vienna $125,000 GP	Brad Gilbert	Karel Novacek	R. Acioly - W. Fibak	B. Gilbert - S. Zivojinovic
11/2/1986	Paris $500,000 SS	Boris Becker	Sergio Casal	P. Fleming - J. McEnroe	M. Bahrami - D. Perez
11/2/1986	Hong Kong $200,000 GP	Ramesh Krishnan	Andres Gomez	M. DePalmer - G. Donnelly	P. Cash - M. Kratzmann
11/9/1986	Stockholm $350,000 SS	Stefan Edberg	Mats Wilander	S. Stewart - K. Warwick	P. Cash - S. Zivojinovic
11/17/1986	London $300,000 SS/ ATP	Yannick Noah	Jonas Svensson	P. Fleming - J. McEnroe	S. Stewart - K. Warwick
11/17/1986	Buenos Aires $85,000 GP	Jay Berger	Franco Davin	L. Courteau - H. Skoff	G. Luza - G. Tiberti
11/20/1986	Atlanta AT& T Challenge SP	Boris Becker	John McEnroe	3-6, 6-3, 7-5	
11/23/1986	Johannesburg $300,000 SS	Amos Mansdorf	Matt Anger	M. DePalmer - Van Rensburg	A. Gomez - S. Stewart
11/23/1986	Houston $220,000 WCT/ SS	Slobodan Zivojinovic	Scott Davis	R. Acuna - B. Pearce	C. Hooper - M. Leach
11/30/1986	Itaparica $125,000 GP	Andres Gomez	Jean Fleurian	C. Hooper - M. Leach	L. Courteau - G. Forget
12/8/1986	NY $500,000 Nabisco Masters	Ivan Lendl	Boris Becker	S. Edberg - A. Jarryd	J. Nystrom - M. Wilander
12/14/1986	London $200,000 Masters Dbls.			S. Edberg - A. Jarryd	G. Forget - Y. Noah
12/14/1986	Stuttgart $150,000 Young Masters SP	Boris Becker	Jonas Svensson	7-6, 7-6, 6-3	

http://www.atpworldtour.com/en/scores/results-archive.

http://www.itftennis.com/procircuit/tournaments/men's-calendar.aspx?tour=&reg=&nat=&sur=&cate=AL&iod=&-fromDate=01-01-1968&toDate=31-01-1987.

Tennis History, Jim McManus, (Canada 2010).

1987 USLTA Yearbook.

Official 1989 MTC Media Guide, (MTC 1989).

World of Tennis 1987, Edited by John Barrett and compiled by Lance Tingay, (London 1987).

CHAPTER 27:

1986: VOLVO, PROSERV, IMG VS. MIPTC, CHATRIER AND HAPPER, CRISIS NO. 30, PART II

The Lawsuit Continued Throughout 1986

In 1986, the massive number of documents being produced by the parties continued. I believed that ProServ and IMG began to understand how bad it was going to be before a jury with written evidence of what they had been doing in men's professional tennis. "Dirty Laundry" would have been a mild description in my opinion. During January 15-17, conversations originated by Bob Kain of IMG with Ray Moore, Roy Reardon and me, led to a meeting between Roy Reardon and Bill Carpenter, IMG's in-house lawyer about the possibility of settlement. Kain volunteered that IMG wanted to settle and get out of the Volvo lawsuit and would be willing to get out of the business of owning and running tournaments as long as IMG could continue to sell television rights, sponsorships and merchandising on a commission basis for tournaments. IMG was willing to forego running special events against Super Series if a reasonable number of free weeks were provided in the calendar. The issue that evaded a solution was how to avoid IMG from procuring its players for tournaments it represented on a commission basis for television, etc., which we referred to as the "player procurement" issue.

Bob Kain told Roy Reardon on January 21 that he had made a presentation to the ATP Board claiming that in 1985, IMG had been very ineffective in getting its players to play in its tournaments because the players were now very independent and that "the designations system was working and that Happer was getting players to go where they didn't want to go and that all of this was cutting into guarantees."[659]

Kain and Carpenter made it clear that ProServ was unaware of their talks and that IMG was prepared to enter into a separate settlement agreement if one could be agreed. At the January 20-23 MIPTC meeting, Roy Reardon reported in executive session on his talks with Bill Carpenter when the Council meeting began on January 20. The Council appointed a committee consisting of Ray Moore, Derek Hardwick, Roy Reardon and myself to continue settlement conversations with Bob Kain and Bill Carpenter of IMG. At the end of that meeting, the parties concluded with an agreement to continue to seek a solution to the elusive "player procurement" issue.[660]

Grudge Match: Big Tennis Has Turned Against Big Operator and He Returns Favor

Teri Agins wrote in the *Wall Street Journal*[661]: "Tennis has been very good to Donald Dell. The former captain of the U.S. Davis Cup team got in on the ground floor when tennis shed its amateur status in 1968 with highly promoted tournaments open to professionals and amateurs alike. For a tennis player who was also a Yale-educated Washington lawyer, the opportunities were many and ripe.

Rules needed writing, tournaments needed organizing, sponsors had to be found and broadcast rights had to be auctioned off. Players, sniffing money in big tournament prizes and fees, needed agents and financial advisers. There was new work for television producers and announcers. Mr. Dell happily met the demand for all these services, dipping his fingers into every pie that came his way. Eventually he founded ProServ, Inc., a sports marketing agency that today represents 150 athletes in nine sports and brings in an estimated $25 million a year in revenues.

But Big Tennis has turned on its most powerful operator with a vengeance. The only question some tennis people have is why it took so long. The 'octopus of tennis' and the 'unquestioned heavyweight king of conflicts of interest' are some of the terms sportswriters have used to describe Mr. Dell over the years. The 47-year-old Mr. Dell's various and interlocking tennis interests have landed him at the center of a bitter dispute over control of the game. The sport's official governing body, the Men's International Professional Tennis Council, has filed a civil suit against ProServ and another big sports agency, International Management Group (IMG), alleging that the two agencies have conspired to monopolize men's professional tennis in violation of antitrust law and the Racketeer Influenced and Corrupt Organization Act."

At the June 17-18 MIPTC meeting in London[662]: Roy Reardon reported on the status of the case including pending motions and the progress of discovery and that pursuant to the confidentiality order issued by the court only three members of the Council would have access to confidential documents obtained during discovery. The members of the Council not included objected and it was agreed that Mr. Reardon should as soon as advisable ask the court to permit each member access to such documents so that they could provide assistance to counsel in the prosecution and defense of the case and better represent their constituent groups. *Everyone wanted access to the "explosive" documents being produced.*

September 8-10, 1986 MIPTC New York Meeting

At the September 8-10 MIPTC meeting,[663] Roy Reardon again reported on the status of pending lawsuit and the progress of discovery. Ray Moore replaced Mike Davies on the current list of those authorized to review discovery documents pending the filing of a motion at the appropriate time to authorize all members access to such documents. Since Philippe Chatrier and I were also individual defendants, we were authorized to see the documents being produced. *Philippe never looked at one document.*

Volvo Chicago Date Change Denied

At its September 8-10, 1986 meeting, the MIPTC Council denied Volvo's request to change the date of its Chicago Super Series tournament to accommodate a possible NBC television contract which would have upset the schedule of other Grand Prix tournaments. Volvo sought an order from Judge Duffy of the USDC to overrule the Council and mandate the Council to approve the change of date. Judge Duffy summarily denied Volvo's request.[664]

First Wave of Discovery Documents

On September 25, Roy Reardon reported that the "first wave" of the production of documents was still underway. He said we were producing documents from our New York and Paris offices and that as of June 30, we had produced approximately 140,000 pages of documents and made available many hours of audio tapes. Reardon reported that we should be able to complete all of our "first wave" and "second wave" documents by November 30, 1986.

Only one box of documents, containing less than 3,400 pages was produced by Volvo who claimed that it had a 15 month "retention policy" so many of its relevant documents had been destroyed. Reardon suspected that Volvo's short "retention policy" was due in part to try to relieve it of the burden of producing documents in litigation. He had asked for and received assurance from Volvo that no additional documents would be destroyed while this litigation was pending. Reardon reported that we had received approximately 19,000 pages of documents from IMG and 32 boxes of documents from ProServ. IMG and ProServ represented that the "first wave" of documents would be completed by early summer. Documents created between January 1, 1973, and January ᵀ 1979, were to be produced as part of a "second wave" of document production. *We w literally in "document hell."*[665]

October 1, 1986 Settlement Meeting

On October 1, at the request of Volvo's lawyer Jim Maloney, Roy Reardon met with Rick Dowden of Volvo and Maloney to discuss the possibility of having settlement negotiations. Dowden denied that Volvo was paying IMG's litigation expenses (contrary to what Bob Kain had said) but he said that Volvo was paying for the litigation of "common" claims. Dowden made it clear that Volvo wanted to restart settlement negotiations, but there would have to be a "global settlement" of all parties. Reardon reported the results of his meeting to Ray Moore and to me concluding that he did not think the settlement negotiations would go anywhere as there was no solution to the "player procurement" issue with ProServ and IMG and Volvo wanted a permanent long-term sanction for its Chicago Super Series tournament which only had a three-year sanction. Reardon observed that he thought Dowden and Maloney wanted to see the case settled remarking that *"Dowden had changed his tone considerably from 'fight to the death,' to 'any case can be settled.'"*[666]

Barry Lorge on Dell

Barry Lorge wrote in *Tennis Magazine*[667]: "Donald Dell – lawyer, agent, promoter, TV producer and commentator, entrepreneur and power broker who for years has had finger in nearly every pro tennis pie – onetime-good-naturedly threatened me with a libel action for referring to him as the King of Conflict of Interest. I told him that if he sued, I'd retain him to defend me. If anybody could find a way to represent both sides in a suit, 'Donald Deal' would. So, what if he's the plaintiff? One of his partners could argue for the defendant. For 15 percent, the fellow on the bench also could become a client: 'Your Honor, we could make you the next Judge Wapner.' They'd sell book and movie rights and produce the spinoff TV series, *Tennis Court*. Dell would get a finder's fee if the program is scheduled opposite rival Mark McCormack's new show, *The Racket*. Modesty would not prevent Dell from portraying himself."

"Dell's firm, a multinational conglomerate called ProServ, represents players, tournaments, sponsors and television - the labor, management and independent contractors of the pro tournament game. It also promotes its own tournaments, exhibitions and special events – some of which conflicted with the Grand Prix circuit when Dell & Co. represented it, too. McCormack's International Management Group (IMG) and subsidiaries similarly take multiple bits of the game's succulent apple. The two firms represent the majority of ranking men players, compete fiercely to sign promising juniors and run separate senior tournaments for oldie-but-goodie stars. Both promote their own events, and sell services – publicity, promotion, TV packages, product licensing – to pro tournaments."

"There are other agent-promoters, but ProServ and IMG are the super powers. They have become strange bedfellows in litigation originally brought by the Swedish automaker Volvo – a ProServ client and former sponsor of the Grand Prix circuit – against the Men's International Professional Tennis Council, which governs the Grand Prix. Each side accuses the other of attempting to monopolize pro tennis in restraint of free trade. Most everybody who is anybody in the power structure has overlapping interests, but the agent-promoters lead the league. They manage players' endorsements, appearances, investments and finances, usually for a percentage of total income. If those players are also featured in the events the agents run, or the ones they help promote for a fee, is that anybody else's business? Well, yes. The agent-promoters who embrace so may stars, suppliers and sponsors have enormous economic leverage. They say they don't tell their clients when or where to play or not to play, but you'd have to be naive to think they don't have an influence."

"IMG and ProServ don't have to go to a tournament director and say, 'Unless we get a bite of the apple, you won't get any of our players – or maybe we'll do a televised eight-man event your week and bite the apple two ways.' As a savvy promoter once said of Dell: 'He has never overtly threatened or bullied me, but he doesn't have to. I know how many ways he could hurt me if he was so inclined.' The agent-promoters argue that the game has prospered under the current system, and as long as their conflicts are disclosed, no one should be concerned. That is a self-serving rationalization. For the most part, they have acted to maximize short-term profits for themselves and their clients, which has fragmented the pro game and possibly stunted its growth. Nobody can represent all constituencies effectively. A strong world circuit would best be served by separation of economic powers. It is time the courts decided how many ways the agent-promoters can bite the apple without turning tennis into a core of its former self."

As 1986 ended, the Volvo, ProServ and IMC lawsuit was continuing mainly with the discovery and production of documents pursuant to a confidentially order issued by the court. *The documents being produced were going to be in my opinion explosive if we ever got to a trial.*

CHAPTER 28:

1987: CONFLICT OF INTEREST RULE FINALLY, HAMILTON JORDAN JOINS FRAY

1987 Governing Bodies

The MIPTC was the governing body for men's professional tennis in 1987, except for the Davis Cup and the *Rules of Tennis*. The ITF was the governing body for the Davis Cup and in charge of the *Rules of Tennis*.

1987 Significant Tennis Leaders	
ITF President:	Philippe Chatrier (France)
USTA President:	Gordon Jorgensen
Tennis Australia President:	Brian Tobin
British LTA President:	G.B. Brown
French FFT President:	Philippe Chatrier
Chairman of Wimbledon:	Buzzer Hadingham
WCT Owners:	Lamar Hunt and Al Hill, Jr.
WCT CEO:	Owen Williams
ATP President:	Matt Doyle until July
ATP President:	Brian Gottfried beginning in July
ATP Executive Director:	Hamilton Jordan beginning in February

1987 MIPTC

ITF   Philippe Chatrier, Derek Hardwick until May, Thomas Hallberg in the June-September interim, Brian Tobin in September, Forrest Hainline until September and David Markin beginning in September.

Tournaments:	Franco Bartoni (Europe), Charles Pasarell (North America), Brian Tobin (Rest of the World) until September and Graham Lovett beginning in September.
Players:	Ray Moore, Chairman, Weller Evans, Harold Solomon until July and Hamilton Jordan beginning in July.
Administrator:	Marshall Happer.
Asst Admn:	Bill Babcock.
Asst Admn:	Paul Svehlik.
Asst Admn:	David Cooper.
Legal Counsel:	Roy L. Reardon, Esquire and John Cambria, Esquire.
GP Supervisors:	Ken Farrar, Chief, Keith Johnson, Bill Gilmour, Thomas Karlberg, Charlie Beck and Stefan Fransson.
Chair Umpires:	Rich Kaufman, Jeremy Shales until July, Richard Ings, Gerry Armstrong, Paula Pereira and Rudy Berger beginning in July.
Communications:	John Hewig, Director of Communications until August, Reg Lansberry, Director of Media Relations.
Tour Liaisons:	Micky den Tuinder, Jennifer Proud until February, Lori Stukes beginning in February, Sandy Genelius until August and Catalina Cox beginning in August.
Nabisco Masters:	Eugene "Gene" Scott, Tournament Director, Sue "Suzie" Rothstein, Tournament Manager.

1987 Major Player Representatives

ProServ:	Principals: Donald Dell, Ray Benton, Jerry Solomon and Ivan Blumberg.

Advantage Int'l:	Principals: Frank Craighill, Lee Fentress, Dean Smith and Peter Lawler.
IMG:	Principals: Mark McCormack and Bob Kain.
Others:	Ion Tiriac and Thomas Betz, Esquire (Vilas).
	John McEnroe, Sr., Esquire (McEnroe).
	Gloria Connors and Joseph Rountree, Esquire (Connors).

Derek Hardwick Passed Away

Derek Hardwick was the only member of the MIPTC who passed away during the existence of the MIPTC. Derek was born on January 30, 1921, in London, England and died on May 28, 1987, in Dorchester. Derek was a retired farmer from Dorset who gave a lifetime of voluntary service to the Sport of Tennis. "It takes perseverance, fortitude, vision, and conviction to create change and Derek Hardwick had all of those traits," is how Derek is described by the International Tennis Hall of Fame: "Hardwick was instrumental – and a true champion – in perhaps the greatest modification to the game in history: The creation of Open Tennis in 1968. Few sports have made such a sweeping deviation from established tradition, and Hardwick was a leading advocate. Hardwick was amongst a group of three visionaries, including fellow Englishman, Herman David (Chairman of Wimbledon) and American Bob Kelleher (President of the USLTA), all Hall of Famers, who fought the International Tennis Federation to introduce Open Tennis, involving both amateurs and professionals. The staid and provincial tennis hierarchy in Europe and the United States had long abhorred the notion of Open Tennis, and Hardwick lobbied diligently for this major reform."[668]

I first met Derek Hardwick after I was employed in 1981 as the first MIPTC Administrator. In my judgment, Derek was one of the brightest and wisest people ever to be involved in tennis. Derek was not only a visionary but he was many ways the thought leader of the establishment. After the 1973 boycott of Wimbledon by the ATP, he, along with Philippe Chatrier, convinced the ITF to open the governance of men's professional tennis to the participation by professional players with the ITF's Grand Slam Committee in 1974, which soon became the independent MIPTC in September of 1974. I was never quite sure how Derek, even though he was a staunch ITF advocate, had earned the enduring respect of the professional players, but he had. Maybe it was because of his successful advocacy for the players for "Open Tennis" or for his standing up against hostile Davis Cup crowds to protect players as a Davis Cup Referee. Derek supported the governance by the MIPTC of men's professional tennis which always tried to balance the needs of the players, the tournaments, the ITF and its national associations. Philippe Chatrier said, "The game has lost probably its greatest fighter. He was happiest in the trenches as he fought for tradition, the official game, especially the Davis Cup, and his beloved Wimbledon. He had an unrivaled knowledge of the game. We will never see another character like Derek again. He was very special."[669]

I sadly remember traveling on Thursday, June 4th from Paris to Bournemouth for Derek's funeral with Philippe Chatrier, Roy Reardon and other members of the MIPTC at the St. Martin's Church Cheselbourne. Derek's death was a huge loss for the MIPTC. If Derek had been alive a year and a half later when the existence of the MIPTC as an institution was destroyed, he might have been able to save it because of his special relationship and respect of the players. Derek Hardwick was posthumously inducted into the International Tennis Hall of Fame in 2010.

Two Competitions

In 1987, the 19th year of Open Tennis, there were two major organized competitions for men: Nabisco Grand Prix and the Davis Cup, as WCT continued to be merged into the Nabisco Grand Prix. In addition to the Nabisco Grand Prix, which was the major circuit of professional tournaments for men, the MIPTC also sanctioned smaller Challenger and Satellite Series tournaments, all to be conducted under the uniform MIPTC Tournament Regulations and MIPTC Code. Davis Cup was open to all players and was won 5-0 by Sweden over India.

There were 77 Nabisco Grand Prix tournaments consisting of the four Grand Slams, ATP two-week Lipton International Players Championships in Key Biscayne, 27 Super Series tournaments (including two WCT Super Series in Tokyo and Scottsdale – Houston was cancelled), 41 Regular and Open Week Series tournaments and four Circuit Championships: Buick WCT Finals in Dallas, WCT Tournament of Champions in Forest Hills, Nabisco Masters at Madison Square Garden and the Nabisco Masters Doubles in London.

In 1987, the ATP was involved in six events: (i) March 8, Key Biscayne, $925,000, Lipton International Players' Championships, (ii) May 24, Dusseldorf, $500,000 Ambre Solaire ATP World Team Cup, (iii) June 15, London, $250,000 Stella Artois Queens ATP Grass-Court Championships, (iv) June 21, Bristol, $100,000 Lambert and Butler Championships, (v) August 23, Cincinnati, $300,000 ATP Championships and (vi) November 15, London, $375,000 ATP Benson and Hedges Championships at Wembley. All of the ATP tournaments were in the Grand Prix except for the World Team Cup.

Rules

The *Official 1987 MIPTC Yearbook* (271 pages) and the *Official 1987 Media Guide* (480 pages) were again split into two publications. The tournament classifications, bonus pool and bonus prize money and Player Commitment (14 tournaments) were the same as in 1986.[670]

Conflicts of Interest

Notwithstanding the pending Volvo, ProServ, IMG lawsuit, by a vote of 9-0, the MIPTC voted to amend the Grand Prix Rules, effective for the 1989 Nabisco Grand Prix, to prohibit the sanctioning of tournaments in which player agents were involved as the owner, defacto owner or tournament manager-director. Ray Moore said in *International Tennis Weekly*[671]: "The rule reflects the Council's deep concern with the influence on the game by player agents which also own or operate tournaments…It is in the interest of all players that the agents do not own, operate or manage tournaments."

The *New York Times*[672] reported: "To the Men's International Professional Tennis Council, it's a long-overdue reform to assure fair and equitable competition among more than 70 tournaments on the Grand Prix circuit. To ProServ and the International Management Group, which represent a number of big-name players on the tour, it's a threat to financial well-being. Given such incompatible views, the matter would seem to be headed to court. In this case, however, the two sides have rushed things a bit. They had already filed lawsuits against each other well before the Council took its latest action." The Council contends that the two management companies steer the players they represent to the tournaments they own or operate, a practice the Council believes is distinctly unfair to the other tourneys, especially since tour players are required to play only 14 Grand Prix events a year. The agents deny applying any such pressure."

Challenger Series MIPTC Official Required

In addition to having a MIPTC International Referee for the first time, each Challenger and Satellite Series tournament was also required, per the Tournament Regulations, to provide certified MIPTC International Chair Umpires at their events. For Challenger Series events, two were required and one was required for each Satellite Series.

Cumulative On-Site Offenses

By this time, we had witnessed a number of players who each year exceeded $7,500 in on-site offense fines and were given a 42-21 day "automatic suspension," which they could usually time for a needed vacation. To deal with this issue, the MIPTC amended the Code to add a new penalty for "cumulative" offenders. This new provision would not be retroactive and would begin "cumulating" as of January 1, 1987.

The new provision stated: "Any player who has accumulated $7,500 in fines for any combination of Player On-Site Offenses in MIPTC sanctioned or recognized events during any twelve (12) month period, beginning on and after January 1, 1987, shall have committed for each such $7,500 in fines a Cumulative Offense and shall be _additionally_ penalized as follows:

1st Cumulative Offense	$10,000 Fine
2nd Cumulative Offense	$10,000 Fine and Two (2) Months Suspension
3rd Cumulative Offense	$10,000 Fine and Four (4) Months Suspension
4th and Each Subsequent	$10,000 Fine and Six (6) Months Suspension

If this new provision had been in effect for many years previously, the players who incurred on-site misconduct fines in excess every year would have stopped incurring them or faced significant additional fines and suspensions. Guess who the first player was to get a two-months suspension?

Rotation of Chairmanship of MIPTC Bylaw Amendment

The MIPTC Bylaws were amended to provide for the rotation of the Chairmanship of the MIPTC every two years with a Tournament Representative to be Chairman in 1991 and an ITF Representative to be Chairman in 1993. Ray Moore as a Player Representative was Chairman until the demise of the MIPTC after 1989, so no rotations ever occurred.

MIPTC Meetings

In 1987, the MIPTC held six meetings: February 3-6 in Indian Wells, April 21-23 in Monte Carlo, June 8-11 in Paris, July 21 in New York, September 14-16 in New York and December 3-7 in New York.

MIPTC Meeting, Indian Wells February 3-6

In February in Indian Wells,[673] the MIPTC voted to repeal the previously adopted 1988 format and replace it with a continuation of the 1987 format for 1988. This deleted the controversial proposal for two classes of Super Series in 1988. *So no 2nd class Super Series in 1988.*

Volvo Chicago Not to Be Extended Beyond Three Years

In the settlement agreement with Volvo to obtain the lease for Madison Square Garden for the Nabisco Masters, the MIPTC was forced to give Volvo a Super Series sanction for Volvo Chicago for three years: 1985, 1986 and 1987, ahead of all the other existing tournaments that had been applying for Super Series for years. The only good thing about a bad agreement is its expiration after its three-year term. Don't forget the Volvo lawsuit against the MIPTC was still pending and running up legal fees for everyone. Volvo attempted to claim that the three-year expiration date did not exist. At this meeting, Volvo requested a Super Series sanction for Volvo Chicago for 1988. By a vote of 7-0-2, the request was denied. Volvo renewed that request at just about every meeting and it was denied each time. The closest it got was a 5-4 denial. Volvo elected to stage unsanctioned tournaments in Chicago in 1988 and 1989. The 1988 tournament was won by Tim Mayotte over Paul Annacone as Jimmy Connors lost in the semis. The 1989 tournament was won by Ivan Lendl over Brad Gilbert, who had defeated John McEnroe in the quarters. *Wonder what it cost to get those players?*

New York Office Space

I reported on the need for additional office space in New York greater than our current office on the fourth floor of 437 Madison Avenue. The Council authorized me to obtain additional office space as long as the initial rent did not exceed $250,000 per year.

MIPTC Meeting, Monaco April 21-23

WCT Houston Super Series

In April in Monte Carlo,[674] WCT was permitted to cancel WCT Houston for 1987. WCT had three "Circuit Championships" and three Super Series. Here WCT cancelled one of its three Super Series.

Additional MIPTC Supervisor and Additional MIPTC Chair Umpire

The Council approved the addition of one new MIPTC Supervisor so there would be seven MIPTC Supervisors in 1988, one of whom could cover some Challenger Series tournaments. In addition, the Council approved the addition of one new full-time MIPTC Chair Umpire so there would be six MIPTC Chair Umpires in 1988.

MIPTC Meeting, Paris, June 8-11

Election of Thomas Hallberg to Replace Derek Hardwick

In June in Paris, Philippe Chatrier announced that the ITF had voted to appoint Thomas Hallberg, the ITF Manager of Men's Tennis, to replace Derek Hardwick, who had passed away, as a member of the Council for the completion of his unexpired term of office. Hallberg was welcomed and accepted as a member of the MIPTC (he was succeeded in September by Brian Tobin).

Administrator's New Five-Year Employment Contract

When I began with the MIPTC in 1981, I left my law practice in Raleigh, N.C., for a two-year (March 1981-March 1983) employment contract to become the first (and only) Administrator of the MIPTC, to create and open an MIPTC office in New York City. Thereafter, my employment contract was extended for 1983-1987 and we opened our Paris office in 1983. By 1987, we were looking for larger office space in New York City and the seventh and final year of my employment contract was expiring December 31, 1987. It was my seventh year away from my law practice and it was becoming more and more difficult, but certainly not impossible, to return to the practice of law in Raleigh. After lots of discussion by the Council in executive session, I agreed with Roy Reardon and Ray Moore, as MIPTC Chairman, on a new five-year employment contract (1988-1992), with extensions from year to year after 1992. The contract provided for early termination in the event of the dissolution of the MIPTC. The contract also provided for me to continue the MIPTC offices in New York City and Paris, or in any "other cities as may be selected by the MIPTC."

John McEnroe – 1987 World Team Cup Major Offense Investigation

On the final day of the World Team Cup, Miloslav Mecir was leading John McEnroe 7-5, 2-6, 2-1, when McEnroe left the court and was disqualified and defaulted.

I investigated his disqualification as a possible Major Offense and when I received medical evidence from Dr. Hartmut Krahl concluding that McEnroe left the match on account of an injury that justified his discontinuation of the match, I reversed the $1,000 fine assessed by the MIPTC Supervisor for his default. The Council concurred with my decision.[675, 676]

Hamilton Jordan Becomes ATP Executive Director

After Mike Davies was fired the previous August, the ATP hired the executive search firm of Russell Reynolds Associates to search for a new Executive Director. Hamilton Jordan, age 42, was hired on February 26. Said ATP President Matt Doyle in *International Tennis Weekly*[677]: "Jordan gained international prominence as a campaign manager and key aide to President Jimmy Carter. The players are extremely pleased that a man with Hamilton Jordan's abilities and experience has agreed to join the ATP as executive director. We know Hamilton will bring outstanding leadership to our organization." Said Jordan in his press release, "I am honored that the ATP has given me this exciting opportunity. I have a strong interest in tennis. I pledge to the ATP that I will work to enhance pro tennis and to make a meaningful contribution to the continued growth of the sport."

President Jimmy Carter wrote the Foreword to Jordan's book *A Boy From Georgia*[678], that Hamilton started before his death in 2008 which was finished by his daughter, Kathleen Jordan, and published in 2015. Carter wrote, "Hamilton had the ability to make people want to do the right thing and to sacrifice their own egos and agendas for a greater good. We began a form of communication where in addition to frequent conversations he would produce correspondence in thoughtful memos on a variety of subjects, both political and about policy. He could distill a cross section of opinions and research into an objective, brief document that expressed the pros and cons of a decision. Hamilton devised a strategy that became famous, to solve one of the most intricate political riddles on Earth – how do you get a relatively unknown Georgia peanut farmer elected president of the United States of America? We did what Hamilton proposed, and we went to the White House together. Although he initially rejected any formal title as Chief of Staff, he was naturally recognized by others as their leader. Hamilton was a driving force behind the Panama Canal Treaties, the Middle East peace process, the safe return of the hostages from Iran, and every other good thing that we attempted or accomplished while in Washington. His political skills were legendary – and so was his character. His charisma and sense of humor kept us afloat during the darkest times."

Ray Moore said of Jordan in *International Tennis Weekly*[679]: "What we were looking for was a capable person. Certainly, Hamilton's background in politics was considered, but that was not a prime quality of his, that you have to be in politics to be involved with the ATP. What we're looking for is an inspirational leader, someone who can devise a master plan for the ATP and take us up a level or two in the sport and enhance professional tennis."

Peter Alfano reported in the *New York Times*[680]: "'I told the A.T.P. that I was looking for an opportunity, not a job.' Jordan said. 'I did not want a job in politics or business. This challenge is totally different, and it came at the right time in my life.'

'When the A.T.P. called, it sounded crazy,' Jordan said. 'but then I thought it would be exciting trying to understand the sport, defining some long-term goals and objectives. If you said, 'Are you going to do this for 10 or 15 years?' I'd say, 'I don't think so.' But I think it will take four or five years to make an impact. I've got a lot to learn.' Jordan said he is a casual tennis fan. He also plays some and has a court in the backyard of his home in suburban Atlanta. He had become bored, he said, with pursuing real estate investments and serving as a strategic planner for corporations since leaving the White house, even though he had done well.

'This,' he said, 'is an entirely new puzzle. I suspect that having had success in another arena makes a good impression but just because I worked in the White House doesn't mean I'll be successful here. I'll be looking out not only for the interests of the players, but for the game too. We want to enhance tennis. I wouldn't be interested in just being a figurehead.'" "'I'm going to be visible,' Jordan said. 'I'm going to have to prove myself to the players. I think, though, I will be successful.'"

I Welcomed Hamilton

I welcomed having Hamilton Jordan join us for the promotion and management of men's professional tennis. Hamilton was the first ATP Executive Director to begin without any real knowledge or involvement in professional tennis and I pledged to help him in any way I could as he learned about our Sport. Hamilton was one of the most astute communicators I ever met. The day after I met him at the ATP press conference at the Lipton introducing him as the new Executive Director of the ATP, I received a FedEx delivery of a short personal handwritten note from Hamilton[681]: "Marshall, I have a lot to learn about professional tennis and hope that I can learn from you. While our respective organizations may occasionally have different interests, it would seem to me that we have overwhelming mutual interests that rest ultimately on enhancing the Sport of Tennis. When I get through with my tour of duty with the ATP, I would be very pleased if I had done as good a job for the ATP as you have already done for the Pro Council."

MIPTC Meeting, New York, July 21

Harold Solomon Retires; Hamilton Jordan is Elected

Harold Solomon announced that he had "after much soul-searching" decided to withdraw his nomination for another term on the MIPTC and that he would be retiring from the MIPTC at the conclusion of his current term. In New York in July, [682] a letter of resignation was received from Harold. Player Representatives Ray Moore and Weller Evans elected Hamilton Jordan to fulfill the remainder of Harold Solomon's term.

MIPTC Meeting, New York, September 14-16

MIPTC Election Results – Players Gain Control

In September in New York, [683] the results of the MIPTC election were approved:

ITF: Philippe Chatrier, David Markin and Brian Tobin. David Markin, First Vice President of the USTA replaced Forrest Hainline and Brian Tobin (President of Tennis Australia and Vice President of the ITF) replaced Thomas Hallberg, who had been the interim replacement for Derek Hardwick. This opened the slot for a new Rest of the World Tournament Representative.

Players: Ray Moore, Chairman, Weller Evans and Hamilton Jordan were re-elected.

Tournaments: Charles Pasarell, (North America), Franco Bartoni, (Europe) and Graham Lovett, (Rest of the World). Lovett replaced Brian Tobin. Pasarell had defeated Gene Scott by a vote of 47-3. Graham Lovett had defeated Max Camilletti by a vote of 23-10 and Franco Bartoni had been unopposed and was thus re-elected. The effect of this election was a realignment of the general voting strength to give the players usually a 6-3 majority with Pasarell, Bartoni and Lovett voting with the Player Representatives. It began an unhealthy shift of voting from "the overall best interests of the game" to voting for "what was best for me and my constituency." Franco Bartoni hated the American tournaments and often traded "deals" with the Player constituency for votes favorable to Europe. Graham Lovett's apparent sole interest was what he could get for himself and for his Sydney Indoor Super Series event. I could never prove it, but I suspected that Lovett offered prohibited appearance money to two top players each year to play in Sydney. Sometime later, I learned that contrary to the MIPTC rules, Lovett had secretly sold the Sydney Indoor tournament to Television Channel 10 in Australia.

While the ITF Representatives could and usually would be out voted by the three Player Representatives and the three Tournament Representatives, sometimes when the player demands were too much, two of the Tournament Representatives might side with the ITF Representatives. *In retrospect, this realignment of the membership of the Council was probably the beginning of its destruction.*

Election of Chairman

At the September MIPTC meeting both Ray Moore and Philippe Chatrier were nominated for Chairman. After discussion, and before a formal vote, there was a "straw vote" in which Moore won by a vote of 5-3-1. After the "straw vote" Chatrier withdrew his nomination in support of Moore who was elected by acclamation.

Ray Moore Statement

Ray Moore read a statement to the MIPTC presented on behalf of the ATP "relating to proposed ATP Player Schools, a proposed reduction in the number of Super Series tournaments, the relations of the ITF and the MIPTC, the conduct of the Grand Slams, the scheduling of the Davis Cup by the ITF, the conflicts of interest caused by the involvement of player agents in tournaments, the formation of a more cohesive calendar, the relations of the MIPTC and WCT and the marketing and promotion of tennis." The Council discussed all of the issues raised in Moore's statement. *This probably was the beginning of ATP's idea to destroy the Council if it could.*

Designation Committee

It was an unpopular task to make substitutions of player designations to balance the fields of all the tournaments, which would force a player to go to a tournament he did not select. Just about every year the Council proposed the creation of a designation committee for contract tournament substitutions, consisting of a Player Representative, a Tournament Representative and me as the Administrator. Every year that designation committee proposal would be deleted leaving me as the Administrator to make all required substitutions. No Player Representative and no Tournament Representative really wanted to have to ask or force a player to play in a tournament that they did not want to play. *However, this was part of my job and it had to be done to try to balance the fields among the tournaments.*

MIPTC-WCT Contract

The contract for the settlement of the WCT anti-trust lawsuit against the MIPTC was for five years – 1985-1989. After considering the WCT contract in executive session, the Council had Roy Reardon inform Owen Williams (WCT Executive Director) that no vote had been taken, "but in the interest of fairness, the MIPTC wanted WCT to know that the MIPTC had a strongly held view that it would not continue with WCT beyond 1989 *under the present contractual terms.* Mr. Reardon further stated that the MIPTC would like to have further discussions with WCT as to the future. Messrs. Moore and Happer were thereafter designated by the Council to participate in such discussions as may be requested by WCT."

Mats Wilander Fine Reduced to $5,000 for Missing Dallas Press Conference

Mats Wilander qualified and was entered into the Buick WCT Finals in Dallas, which had its pre-tournament media conference scheduled for Monday April 7. The MIPTC Rules provided that "failure to appear at such a media conference shall result in a fifteen percent (15%) reduction in all Bonus Pool and Bonus Prize Money awards(s) of such player." Wilander and several other players requested permission to be excused from attending the WCT press conference and all of such requests were denied. The Buick WCT Finals was an official Nabisco Grand Prix Championship event showcasing eight players and offering $500,000 in prize money. Wilander elected to not appear at the press conference claiming he had an important meeting with an architect in New York. Under the provisions of the Grand Prix Rules and MIPTC Code, I investigated the matter and issued the required Determination dated May 8, 1987, finding that Wilander had intentionally failed to attend the press conference and as required I specified the penalty as a 15 percent reduction in all Bonus Pool and Bonus Prize Money awards. Wilander appealed to the MIPTC and appeared via his agent, Chuck Bennett of IMG, who admitted the facts and the violation, but requested relief from the fine on basis of Wilander's prior good conduct and contributions and his perceived need to attend the meeting in New York with his architect, since he would not be able to return to New York until July. The Council agreed to reduce the prescribed fine to $5,000.

MIPTC Office Space

In 1987, the MIPTC had a New York office on the fourth floor of 437 Madison Avenue (between 49th and 50th Streets) and a Paris office at Stade Roland Garros furnished gratis by the French Tennis Federation. We needed more office space than we had on the fourth floor of 437 Madison Avenue and I had found an available space for half of the 17th floor. At the meeting, I presented to the MIPTC a proposed 12-year lease for a half of the 17th floor of 437 Madison Avenue containing approximately 7,800 square feet at an annual rental of $306,150 for the first seven years and $321,750 for the remaining five years. The proposed lease permitted subletting "in the event that the MIPTC should ever decide to move its offices." I was authorized to make the decision whether or not to execute the proposed lease.

During the discussion on the proposed new lease on the 17th floor of 437 Madison Avenue, the Council discussed the feasibility of maintaining offices in Manhattan or moving the administrative operation to Raleigh NC and maintaining offices in New York City solely for the Nabisco Masters' staff. A straw vote was taken and the results of which indicated that the office did not have to be in New York City. After a full discussion, a motion was duly made, seconded and passed authorizing and directing me as the Administrator to study the matter in detail and to make the decision as to the best location for the MIPTC and either to complete and execute the lease for 437 Madison Avenue or seek alternative arrangement for reduced space in New York City and enlarged space in Raleigh NC.

Now, I had a big decision to make. I could lease a small office for Gene Scott and Suzie Rothstein for the Nabisco Masters and move the main administrative office for the MIPTC to Raleigh, my home town and the home town of my three children. The cost of office space in Raleigh would be significantly less for the MIPTC, perhaps as much as $100,000 per year less. On other hand, all of our employees in New York lived in New York and they obviously hoped the office would remain in New York. Further, New York was familiar and better suited for folks involved in international tennis for travel and being in New York enhanced the international image of the MIPTC as the governing body of men's professional tennis. At the end of the day, I decided that, although it would not be as convenient for me to keep the office in Manhattan, that it was better to do so for the MIPTC, our international visitors and for our staff. So, I signed the 12-year lease for half (7,800 square feet) of the 17th floor at 437 Madison Avenue. Before the space could be upfitted, we had to pay to remove the asbestos in the ceiling which would be disturbed in the upfitting construction. That was a typical landlord shifting of upfitting expenses to tenants in New York City, but at least I had a financial cap on it.

MIPTC Meeting, New York, December 3-7

In December in New York,[684] I reported that I had decided "that it was in the best interest of the MIPTC to remain in New York City." I reported on the status of the leasing of half of the 17th floor at 437 Madison Avenue and the Council approved my plan to stay in New York City.

MIPTC / WCT Contract

Ray Moore, Roy Reardon and I reported on our meeting in Dallas on October 13 with Lamar Hunt, Owen Williams and Bill Adams, WCT's attorney. At that meeting, we had discussed the objections that the European tournaments had to the favoritism provided WCT in the settlement of its 1983 lawsuit, the resistance of the players being forced to play in the WCT Finals in Dallas and the conflict of the dates of the WCT Tournament of Champions in May in the middle of the European tournaments in Monte Carlo, Hamburg and Rome leading up to the French Open. We told WCT that in our opinion there was no support among the members of the Council to continue the contract after 1989.

Almost as if Owen and Lamar Hunt had not heard what we told them, they sent a letter to the Council dated November 30[685], outlining WCT's request for a minimum five-year extension of the MIPTC/WCT contract with essentially the same terms of the 1985-1989 agreement. The members of the Council considered the matter in executive session but made no decision at this meeting. However, there was little or no interest by the members of the Council in continuing with WCT under the requested terms. I never knew if WCT just did not listen to us or whether WCT had decided that it would not want to continue in the Grand Prix without all the same terms.

Stefan Fransson, New MIPTC Supervisor

Effective January 1, 1987, Stefan Fransson of Landskkrona, Sweden, was hired as a full-time MIPTC Supervisor. Stefan was a 1979 graduate of the University of Luna in Sweden and was a teacher before joining the MIPTC. Fransson was certified as a MIPTC International Official in 1985. [*After the demise of the MIPTC at the end of 1989, Stefan continued as the Chief Supervisor for the Grand Slams and the Davis Cup through 2020*].

Lori Stukes Replaces Jennifer Proud as MIPTC Media Liaison

Effective February 2, Lori Stukes of Hillside, NJ was appointed as a MIPTC Media Liaison replacing Jennifer Proud, who left to accept the position of manager of marketing with Ohlmeyer Communications Company in New York. Lori had been a member of the MIPTC communications office team for the previous 18 months. Stukes, age 23, graduated from the University of Massachusetts in 1985 with a Bachelor of Science in Sports Marketing. While at UMass, Lori competed on the women's soccer team for four years and was a 1983 and 1984 NCAA All-America and four-time All-New England selection. That followed a stellar athletic career at Hillside High School in New Jersey, where she competed on the basketball, soccer and softball teams, earning four varsity letters in each. Upon graduation, Stukes interned with the U.S. Olympic volleyball team and the Virginia Slims Championships before joining the MIPTC staff in September, 1985.

RJR Nabisco Major Changes

Nabisco stands for the "National Biscuit Company." Prior to the sponsorship by Nabisco of the Nabisco Grand Prix and the Nabisco Masters beginning in 1985, Nabisco also had since 1982 been the sponsor of the Nabisco-Dinah Shore Golf Championships at Mission Hills Country Club in California. Soon after the 1984 sponsorship contract between the MIPTC and Nabisco for the sponsorship of the Nabisco Grand Prix in 1985-1989, RJR Nabisco was formed in 1985 with the merger of Nabisco Brands and R.J. Reynolds Tobacco Company. F. Ross Johnson, the CEO of Nabisco Brands, became the CEO of the merged RJR Nabisco. After the merger, in addition to the new tobacco business, Nabisco continued as an international company manufacturing and selling cookies and various food brands worldwide. The various cookie and food brands manufactured and sold by Nabisco all had separate brand names and some of the same ones had different names in different countries, e.g., Del Monte, Saltines, Oreos, Lorna Doone, Wheat Thins, Ritz, Chips Ahoy, Fleishman Yeast, Nilla, Milk Bone, Belin (in France), etc. Under Ross Johnson's tenure, Nabisco focused on promotion of the "Nabisco" umbrella name. Nabisco used its sponsorship of the Nabisco Grand Prix and the Nabisco Masters to entertain and get close to the owners of grocery chains around the world to sell its various brands and also to obtain favorable placements in the grocery stores. Nabisco was successful in getting to some customers that were not ordinarily available, when Nabisco could invite the owners and their families to professional tennis tournaments, including the Grand Slams. In June, as reported in the *New York Times*[686], "H. John Greeniaus, an energetic 42-year-old executive vice president at Nabisco Brands, Inc., was named as president and chief executive of the big foods company, which is a unit of RJR Nabisco, Inc." *We would soon learn the impact that Mr. Greeniaus would have on us.*

John Hewig Resigns, Reg Lansberry Promoted

On April 1, John Hewig resigned as MIPTC Director of Communications and Reg Lansberry, who had been the Assistant Director of Communications since

September of 1984, was promoted to succeed him with the title of Director of Media Relations to manage our servicing of the media. *Our original plan of having a Director of Communications to represent the MIPTC with the media just did not work as no one in that position could really speak for the MIPTC or for me for that matter.*

Sandy Genelius Succeeded by Catalina Cox

In August, after 2½ years traveling the Nabisco Grand Prix, Sandy Genelius resigned as a Media Liaison to follow Jennifer Proud for a new job with Ohlmeyer Communications in New York. On August 10, Catalina Cox, age 24, replaced Genelius as a Media Liaison. Catalina received her Bachelor of Arts in Political Science and Foreign Languages from Principia College in Eleah, Illinois in 1985, and was named its Alfred Gertsch Freedom Award recipient. The following year, she received a certificate of language in French civilization from the Sorbonne in Paris. Catalina was a citizen of Chile and had been with the Cuban American National Foundation in Washington, DC as a research assistant.

Ray Benton Resigns as ProServ President

Ray Benton took a leave of absence beginning in January and in August announced he was resigning as President of ProServ but would remain a shareholder and a member of the board of directors. Donald Dell remained as Chairman and Jerry Solomon was appointed to succeed Benton as President of ProServ. However, Ray Benton could not resign as a personal counterclaim defendant in the Volvo lawsuit which was still pending.[687]

McEnroe, MIPTC Chair Umpire, Richard Ings, Fines and Suspension

John McEnroe defeated Slobodan Zivojinovic of Yugoslavia 6-4, 5-7, 6-7, 6-4, 6-3 in the round of 16 of the U.S. Open. "Three times during the match, McEnroe drew code-violation warnings from the chair umpire, Richard Ings of Australia," wrote Peter Alfano in the *New York Times*[688]. "The first was just a warning, the second cost him a point and the third resulted in the loss of a game. One more and McEnroe would have been disqualified." Richard Ings handled McEnroe's match exactly as he should have with professionalism and that is exactly what we were seeking to achieve with our full-time MIPTC Chair Umpires. "Within the specific rules, he was within his rights," McEnroe said. "I used obscene language. I do feel like I made it more difficult for myself, but I usually make it as difficult as possible. I reacted badly…I knew I was one bad call away from being defaulted…I thought I owed it to myself not to go out that way. I cooled off. I don't want a reputation as a quitter."

Ken Farrar, the Chief of MIPTC Supervisors, fined McEnroe $7,500 for the three Code violations during the match, in addition to the point penalties assessed by Richard Ings. This would be the second time that McEnroe incurred over $7,500 in on-site fines in 1987. So, under the new cumulative on-site offense provision of the Code effective January 1, 1987, McEnroe would be automatically fined an additional $10,000 and given a two-month suspension, subject to his right to appeal to me as the MIPTC Administrator.

Peter Alfano reported in the *New York Times*[689]: "The third warning cost McEnroe the 12th game of the second set. It came when he shouted an obscenity at a man holding a microphone. McEnroe has long objected to courtside microphones because he believes they are used to eavesdrop on his discussions with officials. Farrar was sympathetic, but felt the reason was unwarranted. 'From a personal point of view,' Farrar said, 'I question having a microphone on the court. I question whether it is valid or worthwhile and I think that it is an issue that should be addressed by the Council.'"

"'It's pretty hard to say that professional athletes playing for money in front of the public should be protected from what they do or say,' said Marshall Happer, the Administrator of the Men's International Professional Tennis Council, which will rule on any appeal. 'But on the other side,' Happer said, 'there are no microphones in a football huddle. First of all, we'd like not to have said what was said. Second, we'd like not to hear it.'"

McEnroe through his agent, Peter Lawler of Advantage International, appealed the fine and suspension to me as the MIPTC Administrator. I upheld the fines and suspension so McEnroe was fined $7,500 plus another $10,000 and his two-month suspension began on November 27, which ended the season for him. McEnroe was not in the top eight for the year and was not qualified for the 1987 Nabisco Masters. If McEnroe exceeded $7,500 again in on-site offense fines, he would have faced an additional $10,000 in fines and a four-month suspension under the new cumulative on-site offense penalties designed to stop player misconduct. *Thankfully, that never happened.*

September 8, 1987 Registration of "Masters®"

On September 8, we obtained the Registration of the Service Mark "Masters®" "for organizing and conducting an annual tennis tournament in Class 41: Registration #1,456,875. The Registration was cancelled March 14, 1994.[690]

MIPTC Position on South Africa, Apartheid and Discrimination

The MIPTC reaffirmed its long-standing position against discrimination via a press statement[691] after its December 3-7 meeting. I was quoted as saying, "There have been numerous recent suggestions that the MIPTC should discriminate against the Johannesburg Super Series tournament by denying its sanction as a protest against the policy of Apartheid of the government of South Africa. While individual members of the MIPTC do not in any way approve or condone Apartheid, the MIPTC as an institution cannot and does not engage in government-level political matters. The MIPTC is a sports-based organization and is non-political."

"The tournaments sanctioned by the MIPTC in 23 countries on the worldwide Nabisco Grand Prix are independent of the governments of their respective countries as are the individual players who compete in them as professionals. The tournaments staged, and the players competing in them, fall under the jurisdiction of international, uniform Rules promulgated by the MIPTC which prohibit discrimination."

The MIPTC would prefer that governments and politicians seek to settle their differences other than by penalizing individual sportsmen or sporting events," I said in the press release."

Edwardo Menga and Edward Hardisty Become MIPTC Supervisors

Effective, January 1, 1988, Edwardo Menga, age 35 of Sao Paulo, Brazil, and Dr. Edward Hardisty, age 48 of Great Britain, were hired as full-time MIPTC Supervisors. Menga was a graduate of the Faculdade de Engenharia Industrial in Sao Paulo. He was a tennis instructor since 1978 and began his officiating career in 1981. He attended the 1985 MIPTC Officials School in Sao Paulo, where he was certified as an MIPTC International Official. Edwardo was fluent in four languages. Hardisty began his officiating career in 1973 and had officiated at Davis Cup ties for seven years. He had been Secretary of the Hong Kong Tennis Association since 1975. Edward attended the 1981 MIPTC Officials School in Sydney at which he was certified as an MIPTC International Official.

Mike Davies to General Manager of the ITF

In 1987, to everyone's surprise, Philippe Chatrier, President of the ITF hired Mike Davies as the new General Manager of the ITF, so Mike moved to London. Mike had now been a player, Executive Director of WCT, Executive Director of the ATP and now the General Manager of the ITF. The only top job he never had was a job with the women's tour although he later became the chief executive of the WTA tournament in Connecticut.

Rudy Berger Replaces Shales as Full-Time Chair Umpire

Rudolf E. Berger, age 35 of Munich, was employed as a full-time MIPTC Chair Umpire to replace Jeremy Shales. Rudy began his officiating career in 1980. He was the holder of an administration degree and was a government official at the German Patent Office in Munich. He graduated from the 1984 MTC Officials School in Basel, Switzerland.

ATP Election

In July of 1987, Brian Gottfried was elected ATP President succeeding Matt Doyle who then became the Vice President. Colin Dowdeswell was Treasurer and Jim McManus continued as Secretary. The Board of Directors were: Ricardo Acuna, Marty Davis, Colin Dowdeswell, Matt Doyle, Mike Estep, Brian Gottfried, Carlos Kirmayr, Paul McNamee, Ray Moore and Yannick Noah. Hamilton Jordan was Executive Director and Ron Bookman was the Deputy Executive Director.[692]

1987 ATP JAKS Awards.

The JAKS Awards was held on December 1 at the New York Hilton:

Player of the Year	Ivan Lendl
Doubles Team of the Year	Stefan Edberg and Anders Jarryd
Newcomer of the Year	Richey Reneberg
Most Improved Player of the Year	Peter Lundgren
Sportsmanship Award	Miloslav Mecir
ATP Super Series Tournament of the Year	Stratton Mountain
ATP Open/Regular Series Tourney of the year	Stuttgart
CF Humanitarian Award	Bob Finkelstein

Would there be a contract deal between the MIPTC and the ATP for 1988-1992 to provide further stability for the Grand Prix? Stay Tuned.

MIPTC Full-Time Chair Umpires

In 1987, the MIPTC had six Supervisors: Ken Farrar (Chief), Charles Beck, Bill Gilmour, Stefan Fransson, Keith Johnson and Thomas Karlberg and five Chair Umpires: Rich Kaufman, Richard Ings, Gerald Armstrong, Paulo Pereira and Rudi Berger. Ken Farrar's summary of the chair assignments for the finals of the singles and doubles at the 1987 Nabisco Grand Prix tournaments showed:

Kaufman:	12 singles finals and 2 doubles finals.
Armstrong:	11 singles finals and 7 doubles finals.
Ings:	15 singles finals and 4 doubles finals.
Pereira:	12 singles finals and 5 doubles finals.
Berger:	2 singles finals and 2 doubles finals.
Others:	18 singles finals and 53 doubles finals.

Farrar calculated that the grand total was 150 finals with the MIPTC Chair Umpires doing 79 and all others doing 71 for a 52.6 percent vs. 47.4 percent ratio. These figures did not include the number of matches also officiated before the finals in the tournaments or the fact that they officiated in most of the matches in which "difficult" or "volatile" players competed. John McEnroe saw a lot of Rich Kaufman and then all of them. Our full-time professional chair umpires averaged around 300 matches per year, which were more than the players were playing. They soon were accepted by the players as fellow traveling pros doing an important job for the players. Our MIPTC Chair Umpires had the full support and backing of the Supervisors as well as me and my administrative staff and the ATP. The players knew that they knew the rules and that they were obligated to enforce them evenly. They also set a good example for all the local MIPTC certified International Officials who were at each tournament.

Bruno Rebeuh Added as Sixth Full-Time Chair Umpire

We added Bruno Rebeuh from Nice, France, who had been a chair umpire since 1978, to begin as our sixth full-time MIPTC Chair Umpire beginning in 1988. Bruno had graduated from our MIPTC Officials School in Paris in 1987. Now, we also had a real Frenchman and happily, 1988 was going to be the last year that the antagonistic Jacques Dorfmann was to be the French Open Referee.

Nabisco to Discontinue Sponsorship

Soon after the completion of the Nabisco Masters at Madison Square Garden on December 5, I was invited to the Nabisco Offices in Manhattan to meet with Mr. John Greeniaus, who had been appointed in June as President and Chief Executive of Nabisco Brands. Ed Redding, Senior Vice President of Nabisco, and probably John Martin, President of Ohlmeyer Communications (Nabisco's tennis promotion vehicle), were also present. After I was introduced to Mr. Greeniaus, he got directly to the point of the meeting. Nabisco was changing its marketing strategy immediately, and in the future would be concentrating on the marketing the brands of its various food and cracker brands and not on the marketing of the umbrella "Nabisco" name. As a result, Nabisco would not exercise its option to sponsor the Nabisco Grand Prix and Nabisco Masters for 1990 and in fact, Nabisco would like to withdraw immediately from the sponsorship, if possible, but would continue its sponsorship contract through its term that ends with 1989. I could only say that I was disappointed and we would begin to seek a new sponsor as soon as possible. I told him I believed that if the MIPTC found a new sponsor that agreed to begin in 1988 or 1989, the MIPTC would certainly agree to terminate our agreement with Nabisco early. However, if no replacement sponsor could be found, we would have to continue through 1989.

On account of the gigantic impact that this decision and action would have on MIPTC, the tournaments and players, we agreed to keep this information confidential until the upcoming January 25-28, 1988, MIPTC meeting in Melbourne, when Ed Redding could inform the members of the MIPTC personally of Nabisco's change of marketing strategy and its decision to withdraw from tennis. I shared this information on a confidential basis with Roy Reardon who agreed that it should remain confidential until the MIPTC meeting in Melbourne. *Just when you think, the future is bright, it rains.*

1987 MIPTC Financials

The MIPTC began 1987 with a surplus of $3,529,829 and after operating its New York, Paris and Raleigh offices and providing $4,000,000 in Bonus Pool awards and $542,000 in Bonus Prize Money to players in the Nabisco Grand Prix, the MIPTC ended 1987 with a surplus of $5,506,897. In addition, the MIPTC collected and paid to ATP, pursuant to a 1982 agreement covering 1983-1987: $719,806 in ATP prize money for services to Nabisco Grand Prix tournaments, $60,658 in ATP entry fees and $58,554 in ATP Challenger and Satellite sanction fees.[693]

Nabisco paid for its promotion as the Nabisco Grand Prix sponsor and the MIPTC provided the promotion of the Nabisco Grand Prix. The MIPTC promoted the Nabisco Masters in December of 1987 at Madison Square Garden telecast by ESPN.

Nabisco and the MIPTC each contributed $100,000 for the $200,000 in prize money for the Nabisco Masters' Doubles to be promoted and operated by WCT at the Royal Albert Hall in London. The gross income for the 1987 Nabisco Masters at Madison Square Garden was $3,797,558 and the gross expenses were $2,267,489, so the MIPTC net was $1,530,069, almost double that for the two tournaments in 1986. Again, that is why the MIPTC wisely insisted on owning and operating the Nabisco Masters.

On September 29, 1984, the MIPTC had entered into a nine-year lease for office space at the fourth floor, 437 Madison Avenue, for $146,970 per year. The lease provided for termination by either party upon 11-months-notice, commencing October 1, 1987. That lease was terminated in April of 1988, when a new 12-year lease for 7,800 square feet (half of the floor) office space on the 17th floor was to begin after the completion of renovations, estimated to be May of 1988. The new annual rent would be $306,150 per year. We continued to let our fund balance increase pending the disposition of the Volvo/ProServ/IMG lawsuit since its final expenses were still unknown.

1987 Grand Slams

Australian Open

Stefan Edberg d. Pat Cash 6-3, 6-4, 3-6, 5-7, 6-3.
Stefan Edberg – Anders Jarryd d. Peter Doohan – Laurie Warder 6-4, 6-4, 7-6.

French Open

Ivan Lendl d. Mats Wilander 7-5, 6-2, 3-6, 7-6.
Anders Jarryd – Robert Seguso d. Guy Forget – Yannick Noah 6-7, 6-7, 6-3, 6-4, 6-2.

Wimbledon

Pat Cash d. Ivan Lendl 7-6, 6-2, 7-5.
Ken Flach – Robert Seguso d. Sergio Casal – Emilio Sanchez 3-6, 6-7, 7-6, 6-1, 6-4.

U.S. Open

Ivan Lendl d. Mats Wilander 6-7, 6-0, 7-6, 6-4.
Stefan Edberg – Anders Jarryd d. Ken Flach – Robert Seguso 7-6, 6-2, 4-6, 5-7, 7-6.

Lipton International Players' Championships

Miloslav Mecir d. Ivan Lendl 7-5, 6-2, 7-5.
Paul Annacone – Christo Van Rensburg d. Ken Flach – Robert Seguso 6-2, 6-4, 6-4.

Nabisco Grand Prix Circuit Championships

Buick WCT Finals (Dallas)

Miloslav Mecir d. John McEnroe 6-0, 3-6, 6-2, 6-2.

WCT Tournament of Champions
(Forest Hills, New York)

Andres Gomez d. Yannick Noah 6-4, 7-6, 7-6.
Guy Forget – Yannick Noah d. Gary Donnelly – Peter Fleming 4-6, 6-4, 6-1.

Nabisco Masters (Singles)
(Madison Square Garden New York)

Ivan Lendl d. Mats Wilander 6-2, 6-2, 6-3.

Nabisco Masters Doubles WCT (London)

Miloslav Mecir – Tomas Smid d. Ken Flach – Robert Seguso 6-4, 7-5, 6-7, 6-3.

1987 Davis Cup

Davis Cup Final (Gothenburg – Clay)

Sweden d. India 5-0.

Mats Wilander (SE) d. Ramesh Krishnan (IN) 6-4, 6-1, 6-3.

Anders Jarryd (SE) d. Vijay Amritraj (IN) 6-2, 6-3, 6-1.
Joakim Nystrom – Mats Wilander (SE) d. Anand Amritraj – Vijay Amritraj (IN) 6-2, 3-6, 6-1, 6-2.
Anders Jarryd (SE) d. Ramesh Krishnan (IN) 6-4, 6-3.
Mats Wilander (SE) d. Vijay Amritraj (IN) 6-2, 6-0.

World Team Cup

Czechoslovakia d. United States 2-1.

Miloslav Mecir (CZ) d. John McEnroe (US) 7-5, 2-6, 2-1 Disqualified(Injury).
Brad Gilbert (US) d. Milan Srejber (CZ) 6-4, 5-7, 6-4.
Miloslav Mecir – Tomas Smid (CZ) d. Brad Gilbert – Robert Seguso (US) 6-3, 6-1.

1987 World Rankings[694]

Bud Collins	Lance Tingay	ATP Year-End Rankings
1. Ivan Lendl	1. Ivan Lendl	1. Ivan Lendl
2. Stefan Edberg	2. Pat Cash	2. Stefan Edberg
3. Mats Wilander	3. Stefan Edberg	3. Mats Wilander
4. Jimmy Connors	4. Mats Wilander	4. Jimmy Connors
5. Boris Becker	5. Miloslav Mecir	5. Boris Becker
6. Miloslav Mecir	6. Boris Becker	6. Miloslav Mecir
7. Pat Cash	7. Jimmy Connors	7. Pat Cash
8. Yannick Noah	8. Andres Gomez	8. Yannick Noah
9. Tim Mayotte	9. Yannick Noah	9. Tim Mayotte
10. John McEnroe	10. John McEnroe	10. John McEnroe

1987 Nabisco Grand Prix Bonus Pool Top 10[695]

Singles (18th Bonus Pool)

1.	Ivan Lendl	$ 800,000
2.	Stefan Edberg	$ 550,000
3.	Mats Wilander	$ 400,000
4.	Miloslav Mecir	$ 250,000
5.	Boris Becker	$ 150,000
6.	Jimmy Connors	$ 100,000
7.	Pat Cash	$ 75,000
8.	Brad Gilbert	$ 55,000
9.	Tim Mayotte	$ 45,000
10.	Andres Gomez	$ 40,000

Doubles (13th Bonus Pool)

1.	Anders Jarryd	$ 165,000
2.	Robert Seguso	$ 120,000
3.	Emilio Sanchez	$ 90,000
4.	Sergio Casal	$ 70,000
5.	Ken Flach	$ 50,000
6.	Tomas Smid	$ 40,000
7.	Paul Annacone	$ 30,000
8.	Guy Forget	$ 25,000
9.	Stefan Edberg	$ 20,000
10.	Yannick Noah	$ 17,000

1987 Official Earnings Top 10[696]

1.	Ivan Lendl	$ 2,003,656	6.	Anders Jarryd	$ 558,979
2.	Stefan Edberg	$ 1,587,467	7.	Boris Becker	$ 575,015
3.	Miloslav Mecir	$ 1,205,326	8.	Emilio Sanchez	$ 538,158
4.	Mats Wilander	$ 1,164,674	9.	Brad Gilbert	$ 507,187
5.	Pat Cash	$ 565,934	10.	Tim Mayotte	$ 458,821

1987 Tournament Calendar

Date	Tournaments	Singles Winner	Singles #2	Doubles Winners	Doubles #2
1/4/1987	Adelaide AU $89,400 GP	Wally Masur	Bill Scanlon	I. Lendl - B. Scanlon	P. Doohan - L. Warder
1/11/1987	Auckland NZ $89,400 GP	Miloslav Mecir	Michiel Schapers	K. Jones - B. Pearce	C. Linberger - M. Woodforde
1/25/1987	Australian Open $670,161 GS	Stefan Edberg	Pat Cash	S. Edberg - A. Jarryd	P. Doohan - L. Warder
2/1/1987	Guaruja $89,400 GP	Luiz Mattar	Cassio Motta	L. Mattar - C. Motta	M. Hipp - T. Meinecke
2/1/1987	Sydney $89,400 GP	Miloslav Mecir	Peter Doohan	B. Drewett - M. Edmondson	P. Doohan - L. Warder
2/8/1987	Philadelphia $375,000 SS	Tim Mayotte	John McEnroe	S. Casal - E. Sanchez	C. Steyn - D. Visser
2/8/1987	Lyon $150,000 GP	Yannick Noah	Joakim Nystrom	G. Forget - Y. Noah	K. Jones - D. Pate
2/15/1987	Memphis $250,000 SS	Stefan Edberg	Jimmy Connors	A. Jarryd - J. Svensson	S. Casal - E. Sanchez
2/22/1987	Indian Wells $350,000 SS	Boris Becker	Stefan Edberg	G. Forget - Y. Noah	B. Becker - E. Jelen
3/8/1987	Key Biscayne $925,000 ATP	Miloslav Mecir	Ivan Lendl	P. Annacone - Van Rensburg	K. Flach - R. Seguso
3/22/1987	Rotterdam $250,000 SS	Stefan Edberg	John McEnroe	S. Edberg - A. Jarryd	C. Hooper - M. Leach
3/22/1987	Orlando $250,000 SS	Van Rensburg	Jimmy Connors	S. Stewart - K. Warwick	P. Annacone - Van Rensburg
3/29/1987	Brussels $250,000 SS	Mats Wilander	John McEnroe	B. Becker - S. Zivojinovic	C. Hooper - M. Leach
3/29/1987	Nancy $89,400 GP	Pat Cash	Wally Masur	R. Krishnan - C. Mezzadri	G. Connell - L. Scott
4/5/1987	Milan $300,000 SS	Boris Becker	Miloslav Mecir	B. Becker - S. Zivojinovic	S. Casal - E. Sanchez
4/5/1987	Chicago $300,000 Volvo SS	Tim Mayotte	David Pate	P. Annacone - C. van Rensburg	M. DePalmer - G. Donnelly
4/12/1987	Dallas $500,000 WCT Finals	Miloslav Mecir	John McEnroe		
4/12/1987	Bari $89,400 GP	Claudio Pistolesi	Francesco Cancellotti	C. Allgardh - U. Stenlund	R. Azar - M. Ingaramo
4/19/1987	Tokyo $400,000 WCT/SS	Stefan Edberg	David Pate	P. Annacone - K. Curren	A. Gomez - A. Jarryd

4/19/1987	Nice $89,400 GP	Kent Carlsson	Emilio Sanchez	S. Casal - E. Sanchez	C. Mezzadri - G. Ocleppo
4/26/1987	Monte Carlo $415,000 SS	Mats Wilander	Jimmy Arias	H. Gildemeister - A. Gomez	M. Bahrami - M. Mortensen
4/26/1987	Seoul $89,400 GP	Jim Grabb	Andre Agassi	E. Korita - M. Leach	K. Flach - J. Grabb
5/3/1987	Hamburg $300,000 SS	Ivan Lendl	Miloslav Mecir	M. Mecir - T. Smid	C. Mezzadri - J. Pugh
5/10/1987	NY $500,000 WCT TC	Andres Gomez	Yannick Noah	G. Forget - Y. Noah	G. Donnelly - P. Fleming
5/10/1987	Munich 125,000 GP	Guillermo Perez-Roldan	Marian Vajda	J. Pugh - B. Willenborg	S. Casal - E. Sanchez
5/17/1987	Rome $400,000 SS	Mats Wilander	Martin Jaite	G. Forget - Y. Noah	M. Mecir - T. Smid
5/24/1987	Dusseldorf $750,000 WTC	Czechoslovakia	USA	2-1,	
5/24/1987	Dusseldorf $750,000 WTC	Miloslav Mecir	John McEnroe	7-5, 2-6, 2-1 Disqualified	
5/24/1987	Dusseldorf $750,000 WTC	Brad Gilbert	Milan Srejber	6-4, 5-7, 6-4	
5/24/1987	Dusseldorf $750,000 WTC		6-3, 6-1	Miloslav Mecir-Tomas Smid	Brad Gilbert - Robert Seguso
5/24/1987	Florence $89,400 GP	Andre Chesnokov	Alessandro D. Minicis	W. Popp - U. Riglewski	P. Cane - G. Ocleppo
6/7/1987	French Open $1,325,000 GS	Ivan Lendl	Mats Wilander	A. Jarryd - R. Seguso	G. Forget - Y. Noah
6/14/1987	Bologna $89,400 GP	Kent Carlsson	Emilio Sanchez	S. Casal - E. Sanchez	C. Panatta - B. Willenborg
6/14/1987	Edinburgh SP	Anders Jarryd	Andres Gomez	Rain	
6/15/1987	London $250,000 GP	Boris Becker	Jimmy Connors	G. Forget - Y. Noah	R. Leach - T. Pawsat
6/21/1987	Athens $100,000 GP	Guillermo Perez-Roldan	Tore Meinecke	T Meinecke - R. Osterthun	J. Navratil - T. Nijssen
6/21/1987	Bristol $100,000 GP	Kelly Evernden	Tim Wilkison	Rain	Rain
7/5/1987	Wimbledon $1,577,592 GS	Pat Cash	Ivan Lendl	K. Flach - R. Seguso	S. Casal - E. Sanchez
7/12/1987	Boston $232,000 SS	Mats Wilander	Kent Carlsson	H. Gildemeister - A. Gomez	J. Nystrom - M. Wilander
7/12/1987	Gstaad $200,000 GP	Emilio Sanchez	Ronald Agenor	J. Gunnarsson - T. Smid	L. Courteau - G. Forget
7/12/1987	Newport $100,000 GP	Dan Goldie	Sammy Giammalva	D. Goldie - L. Scott	C. Hooper - M. Leach

7/19/1987	Indianapolis $300,000 SS	Mats Wilander	Kent Carlsson	L. Warder - B. Willenborg	J. Nystrom - M. Wilander
7/19/1987	Bordeaux $125,000 GP	Emilio Sanchez	Ronald Agenor	S. Casal - E. Sanchez	D. Cahill - M. Woodforde
7/19/1987	Livingston $89,400 GP	Johan Kriek	Christian Saceanu	G. Donnelly - G. Holmes	K. Flach - R. Seguso
7/19/1987	Stuttgart $200,000 GP	Miloslav Mecir	Jan Gunnarsson	R. Leach - T. Pawsat	M. Pernfors - M. Tideman
7/26/1987	Schenectady $89,400 GP	Jaime Yzaga	Jim Pugh	G. Donnelly - G. Muller	B. Pearce - J. Pugh
8/2/1987	Washington $232,000 SS	Ivan Lendl	Brad Gilbert	G. Donnelly - P. Fleming	L. Warder - B. Willenborg
8/2/1987	Bastad $175,000 GP	Joakim Nystrom	Stefan Edberg	S. Edberg - A. Jarryd	E. Sanchez - J. Sanchez
8/2/1987	Hilversum $150,000 GP	Miloslav Mecir	Guillermo Perez-Roldan	W. Fibak - Mecir	T. Nijssen - J. Vekemans
8/9/1987	Stratton Mountain $250,000 SS	John McEnroe	Ivan Lendl	P. Annacone - C. van Rensburg	R. Flach - R. Seguso
8/9/1987	Kitzbuhel $175,000 GP	Emilio Sanchez	Miloslav Mecir	S. Casal - E. Sanchez	M. Mecir - T. Smid
8/16/1987	Montreal $300,000 SS	Ivan Lendl	Stefan Edberg	P. Cash - S. Edberg	P. Doohan - L. Warder
8/16/1987	Prague $150,000 GP	Marian Vajda	Tomas Smid	M. Mecir - T. Smid	S. Birner - J. Navratil
8/16/1987	St. Vincent $100,000 GP	Pedro Rebolledo	Francesco Cancellotti	B. Cox - M. Fancutt	M. Cierro - A. De Minicis
8/23/1987	Cincinnati $300,000 ATP/SS	Stefan Edberg	Boris Becker	K. Flach - R. Seguso	S. Denton - J. Fitzgerald
8/30/1987	Rye Brook $89,400 GP	Peter Lundgren	John Ross	L. Bourne - J. Klaparda	C. Limberger - M. Woodforde
8/30/1987	Jerrico $150,000 Hamlet SP	Jonas Svensson	David Pate		
9/14/1987	US Open $1,666,667 GS	Ivan Lendl	Mats Wilander	S. Edberg - A. Jarryd	K. Flach - R. Seguso
9/20/1987	Geneva $200,000 GP	Claudio Mezzadri	Tomas Smid	R. Acioly - L. Mattar	M. Bahrami - D. Perez
9/20/1987	Madrid $89,400 GP	Emilio Sanchez	Javier Sanchez	C. DiLaura - J. Sanchez	S. Casal - E. Sanchez
9/27/1987	Los Angeles $250,000 SS	David Pate	Stefan Edberg	K. Curren - D. Pate	B. Gilbert - T. Wilkison
9/27/1987	Barcelona $232,000 SS	Martin Jaite	Mats Wilander	M. Mecir - T. Smid	J. Frana - C Miniussi

10/4/1987	San Francisco $232,000 SS	Peter Lundgren	Jim Pugh	J. Grabb - P. McEnroe	G. Layendecker - T. Witsken
10/4/1987	Palermo $100,000 GP	Martin Jaite	Karel Novacek	L. Lavalle - C. Panatta	P. Korda - T. Smid
10/11/1987	Scottsdale $232,000 WCT/ SS	Brad Gilbert	Eliot Teltscher	R. Leach - J. Pugh	D. Goldie - M. Purcell
10/11/1987	Basle $200,000 GP	Yannick Noah	Ronald Agenor	A. Jarryd - T. Smid	S. Birner - J. Navratil
10/11/1987	Brisbane $150,000 GP	Kelly Evernden	Eric Jelen	M. Anger - K. Evernden	B. Dyke - W. Masur
10/11/1987	Atlanta AT&T SP	John McEnroe	Paul Annacone	6-4, 7-6	
10/18/1987	Tel Aviv $89,400 GP	Amos Mansdorf	Brad Gilbert	M. Purcell - T. Wilkison	E. Sanchez - J. Sanchez
10/18/1987	Sydney $275,000 SS	Ivan Lendl	Pat Cash	D. Cahill - M. Kratzmann	B. Becker - R. Seguso
10/18/1987	Toulouse $175,000 GP	Tim Mayotte	Ricki Osterthun	W. Fibak - M. Schapers	K. Jones - P. Kuhnen
10/25/1987	Tokyo $300,000 SS	Stefan Edberg	Ivan Lendl	B. Dyke - T. Nijssen	S. Giammalva - J. Grabb
10/25/1987	Vienna $125,000 GP	Jonas Svensson	Amos Mansdorf	M. Purcell - T. Wilkison	E. Sanchez - J. Sanchez
10/31/1987	Antwerp $923,000 ECC SP	Ivan Lendl	Miloslav Mecir	5-7, 6-1, 6-4, 6-3	
11/1/1987	Hong Kong $200,000 GP	Eliot Teltscher	John Fitzgerald	M. Kratzmann - J. Pugh	M. Davis - B. Drewett
11/8/1987	Paris $700,000 SS	Tim Mayotte	Brad Gilbert	J. Hlasek - C. Mezzadri	S. Davis - D. Pate
11/8/1987	Stockholm $425,000 SS	Stefan Edberg	Jonas Svensson	S. Edberg - A. Jarryd	J. Grabb - J. Pugh
11/15/1987	London 375,000 SS	Ivan Lendl	Anders Jarryd	M. Mecir - T. Smid	K. Flach - R. Seguso
11/15/1987	Frankfurt $150,000 GP	Tim Mayotte	Andres Gomez	B. Becker - P. Kuhnen	S. Davis - D. Pate
11/15/1987	Sao Paulo $89,400 GP	Jaime Yzaga	Luiz Mattar	G. Bloom - J. Sanchez	T. Carbonell - S. Casal
11/21/1987	Friedrichshafen $150,000 SP	Tomas Muster	Jonas Svensson	6-4, 4-6, 7-5, 6-2	
11/22/1987	Johannesburg $232,000 SS	Pat Cash	Brad Gilbert	K. Curren - D. Pate	E. Korita - B. Pearce
11/22/1987	Buenos Aires $89,400 GP	Guillermo Perez-Roldan	Jay Berger	T. Carbonell - S. Casal	J. Berger - H. de la Pena

11/29/1987	Itaparica $125,000 GP	Andre Agasse	Luiz Mattar	S. Casal - E. Sanchez	J. Lozano - D. Perez
12/7/1987	NY $500,000 Nabisco Masters	Ivan Lendl	Mats Wilander		
12/13/1987	London $200,000 Masters Db.			M. Mecir - T. Smid	K. Flach - R. Seguso

http://www.atpworldtour.com/en/scores/results-archive.

http://www.itftennis.com/procircuit/tournaments/men's-calendar.aspx?tour=&reg=&nat=&sur=&cate=AL&iod=&-fromDate=01-01-1968&toDate=31-12-1987.

Tennis History, Jim McManus, (Canada 2010).

1988 USTA Yearbook.

Official 1989 MTC Media Guide, (MTC 1989).

World of Tennis 1988, Edited by John Barrett and compiled by Lance Tingay, (London 1988).

CHAPTER 29:

1987: VOLVO, PROSERV, IMG VS. MIPTC, CHATRIER AND HAPPER, CRISIS NO. 30, PART III

The Volvo, ProServ, IMG Lawsuit Continued in 1987

During 1987, the massive number of documents being produced by the parties continued for the Volvo, ProServ, IMG lawsuit. Roy Reardon and his firm were reviewing the documents as they came in for us. However, Graham Lovett, Rest of the World Tournament Representative, made a special visit to look at the documents. I assumed he feared that the documents would show his appearance fee deals for players for his Sydney Indoors tournament. *They would, of course.*

Council Provides Answers On New Conflict of Interest Rule

The problem of having the player agents owning and operating tournaments had gotten so serious, that the Council had decided not to wait on the conclusion of the lawsuit to deal with it and in February the Council had voted 9-0 to prohibit the sanctioning of tournaments in which player agents were involved as the owner, defacto owner or tournament manager-director beginning with the 1989 Nabisco Grand Prix.

Official Memo

We provided in a Memo[697], our official answers for questions about the new Conflict of Interest Rule:

"Q: What is the real effect of the new rule?

A: Beginning in December of 1988, the beginning of the 1989 Nabisco Grand Prix, the more blatant conflicts of interest heretofore existing in professional tennis will be eliminated. Those blatant conflicts of interest are when a Player Agent representing some of the players competing in a prize money tournament is also the owner or manager of the tournament.

Q: Why is this conflict of interest so bad?

A: The Owner/Manager of a tournament controls the conduct of the tournament for all of the professional competitors including the employment of most of the officials. When the Player Agent for some of the players, who is paid a percentage of the prize money won by his clients, is the owner/manager, the situation is unacceptable. The MIPTC is interested in preventing the appearance of abusive situations as well as preventing the opportunity for actual abuses so that the integrity of a prize money sport played before the public will be protected.

Q: Why did the MIPTC pass this rule now instead of waiting for the conclusion of the lawsuit?

A: First of all, there is no way to estimate when the lawsuit will be completed; secondly there is some evidence that the Player Agents have continued to attempt to gobble up additional tournaments during the lawsuit; finally as the MIPTC has continued to study the problem, it has become clear that the conflict of interest outlawed in the new rule is so bad as to necessitate immediate action.

Q: Under the new rule, will tournaments be denied a sanction?

A: Yes. Applicants for the 1989 Nabisco Grand Prix will have to comply with the new Conflicts of Interest Rule. A specific tournament that will be affected is the ProServ Super Series tournament in Orlando since ProServ is a Player Agent, if ProServ is in the same conflicting relationship in 1989.

Q: Will any tournaments be grandfathered in for 1989?

A: No. We are giving the tennis tournaments almost two years notice to eliminate these serious and disabling conflicts of interest. A Grandfather clause that would permit these conflicts to continue in the numerous instances that they now exist would defeat the purpose of the Rule.

Q: What about the conflict of interest caused when a Player Agent represents a tournament as agent for the sale of sponsorships, merchandising or television rights?

A: These are also conflict of interest areas that are being further studied by the MIPTC for possible future action if we find that such relationships create the same problems encountered when a Player Agent is the owner or manager of the tournament. It appears that often the control or agency for the sale of these assets is so important to the financial success of the tournament, that the status of the agent becomes important in the tournament organizations. The MIPTC is continuing to study these areas."

Blumberg of ProServ Objects

Not surprisingly, Ivan Blumberg of ProServ objected and wrote to me on April 21[698]: "The so-called 'Conflict of Interest' Rule adopted in February is a further attempt by the Council to cement its monopoly hold over men's professional tennis and to damage ProServ's legitimate business without justification...It is the sort of anticompetitive behavior reflected in these new rules that forced us to sue; it is the Council's continued intransigence that is forcing tennis to endure a lawsuit that neutral observers believe will harm the sport." Then he said: "We are prepared to sit down with you at any time to discuss these matters." *That was a good indication that ProServ might be willing to accept our new conflict of interest rule.*

Surprise Compliance

As tournament applications for the 1989 Nabisco Grand Prix were solicited, inquiry was made of each tournament with respect to its involvement with Player Agents as sanctions would not be granted to tournaments involved with Player Agents as owners, defacto owners or managers. Player Agents as commission agents for the sale of sponsorships, merchandising and television rights would continue to be permitted in 1989. *To everyone's surprise, the tournaments and the Player Agents began to revise their agreements for 1989 to comply with the rule and ensure Council sanctioning, except for ProServ's Orlando Super Series tournament which could not be modified since it was owned by ProServ.*

Motions to Dismiss for "Failure to State a Claim Defense"

Every party in a civil lawsuit always makes a motion to dismiss the other parties' case on the technical legal grounds that the complaint or the counterclaim "fails to state a claim upon which relief can be granted." We had filed a motion to dismiss the Plaintiffs' claims on September 9, 1985, and the Plaintiffs had filed a motion to dismiss our Counterclaims on February 3, 1986. As required, all parties had filed memorandums of law in support of the motions to dismiss. *It is extremely rare when a case is actually dismissed at an early stage "for failing to state a claim upon which relief can be granted" and it is almost never done without a Judge entertaining oral argument by the parties involved – except in this case.*

District Court Dismissal of Claims in First Amended Complaint August 10

To the utter surprise of all the parties to the lawsuit, U.S. District Judge Kevin Thomas Duffy, on August 10, without notice to anyone, issued an Order[699] saying "counts one through seven and thirteen of plaintiffs' complaint are dismissed. Counts eight through twelve are dismissed with leave to replead." That Order was a disaster to Volvo, ProServ and IMG's side of the case.

Plaintiffs Appeal Dismissal to Second Circuit Court of Appeals

The Plaintiffs appealed to the Second Circuit Court of Appeals and the appeal was briefed and argued on October 20, 1987, so at the end of 1987, the parties were awaiting a decision from the Court of Appeals, while discovery was continuing.

CHAPTER 30:

1988: DRUG TESTING EXPANDED, NABISCO TO WITHDRAW, PLAYERS' PENSION PLAN BEGINS

[Note: Chapter 30 covers the 1988 Year exclusive of Crisis No. 31: MTC-ATP Five Year Contract 1988-1992, Crisis No. 30, Part IV: 1988 Volvo, Proserv, IMG Lawsuit Conclusion and Crisis No. 32: Coup D' Etat: The Final Crisis which are covered separately in Chapter 31.]

1988 Governing Bodies

The Men's Tennis Council (MTC, name changed from Men's International Professional Tennis Council in 1988) was the governing body for men's professional tennis in 1988, except for the Davis Cup and the *Rules of Tennis*. The ITF was the governing body for the Davis Cup and in charge of the *Rules of Tennis*.

1988 Significant Tennis Leaders	
ITF President:	Philippe Chatrier (France)
USTA President:	Gordon Jorgensen
Tennis Australia President:	Brian Tobin
British LTA President:	Ron Pressly
French FFT President:	Philippe Chatrier
Chairman of Wimbledon:	Buzzer Hadingham
WCT Owners:	Lamar Hunt and Al Hill, Jr.
WCT CEO:	Owen Williams
ATP President:	Brian Gottfried
ATP Executive Director:	Hamilton Jordan

1988 MTC

ITF:	Philippe Chatrier, Brian Tobin and David Markin.
Tournaments:	Franco Bartoni (Europe), Charles Pasarell (North America), Graham Lovett (Rest of the World).
Players:	Ray Moore, Chairman, Weller Evans, Hamilton Jordan until November and Marty Davis beginning in November.
Administrator:	Marshall Happer.
Asst Admn:	Bill Babcock.
Asst Admn:	Paul Svehlik.
Asst Admn:	David Cooper.
Legal Counsel:	Roy L. Reardon, Esquire.
GP Supervisors:	Ken Farrar, Chief, Bill Gilmour, Thomas Karlberg, Stefan Fransson, John Heiss, Edwardo Menga and Edward Hardisty.
Chair Umpires:	Rich Kaufman, Richard Ings, Gerry Armstrong, Paula Pereira, Rudy Berger and Bruno Rebeuh.
Communications:	Reg Lansberry, Director of Media Relations and Barbara Travers, Assistant Director of Media Relations.
Tour Liaisons:	Micky den Tuinder, Lori Stukes, Catalina Cox and Wendy Miller beginning in April.
Nabisco Masters:	Eugene "Gene" Scott, Tournament Director, Sue "Suzie" Rothstein, Tournament Manager.

1988 Major Player Representatives

ProServ: Principals: Donald Dell, Jerry Solomon and Ivan

Blumberg.

Advantage Int'l: Principals: Frank Craighill, Lee Fentress, Dean Smith and

Peter Lawler.

IMG: Principals: Mark McCormack and Bob Kain.

Others: Ion Tiriac and Thomas Betz, Esquire (Vilas).

John McEnroe, Sr., Esquire (McEnroe).

Gloria Connors and Joseph Rountree, Esquire (Connors).

Two Competitions

In 1988, the 20th year of Open Tennis, there were two major organized competitions for men: Nabisco Grand Prix and the Davis Cup, as WCT continued to be merged into the Nabisco Grand Prix. In addition to the Nabisco Grand Prix, which was the major circuit of professional tournaments for men, the MTC also sanctioned 41 smaller Challenger tournaments and 40 Satellite Series, all to be conducted under the uniform MTC Tournament Regulations and MTC Code of Conduct. Davis Cup was open to all players and was won 4-1 by Germany over Sweden in Gothenburg.

There were 78 Nabisco Grand Prix tournaments consisting of: four Grand Slams, the ATP two-week Lipton International Players Championships in Key Biscayne, 27 Super Series tournaments (including three WCT Super Series in Tokyo, Scottsdale and Detroit), 40 Regular and Open Week Series tournaments and four Circuit Championships: Buick WCT Finals in Dallas, WCT Tournament of Champions in Forest Hills, Nabisco Masters at Madison Square Garden and the Nabisco Masters Doubles in London.

In 1988, the ATP was involved in six events: (i) March 27 in Key Biscayne $725,000, Lipton International Players' Championships, (ii) May 22 in Dusseldorf $750,000 Peugeot ATP World Team Cup, (iii) June 12 in London, $290,000 Stella Artois Queens ATP Grass-Court Championships, (iv) June 18 in Bristol, $93,400 Lambert and Butler Championships, (v) August 21 in Cincinnati, $425,000 ATP Championships and (vi) November 13 in London, $335,000 ATP Benson and Hedges Championships at Wembley. All of the ATP tournaments were in the Grand Prix, except for the World Team Cup.

Rules

The 1988 year was the fourth year of Nabisco's sponsorship of the Nabisco Grand Prix and Nabisco Masters and the fourth year of a five-year agreement combining WCT into the Nabisco Grand Prix. The MIPTC-ATP 1983-1987 five-year agreement was supposedly being extended with a new 1988-1992 MIPTC-ATP agreement which had been negotiated and drafted, but not yet signed pending a few legal review issues relating to the formation of the ATP Deferred Compensation Plan. The *Official 1988 MIPTC Yearbook* (288 pages) and the *Official 1988 Media Guide* (555 pages) were again split into two publications.

The tournament classifications, bonus pool and bonus prize money and player commitment (14 tournaments, plus the WCT Dallas Finals and Nabisco Masters) were the same as in 1987. There was only one class of Super Series events in 1988.

Player Compensation Included
New Deferred Compensation Contributions

In 1988, "Player Compensation" included on-site prize money, optional Bonus Pool prize money, ATP prize money, Bonus Pool contributions and deferred compensation.

Acting as Player Agents for other Active Players Prohibited

On March 20, the Council amended the conflict of interest rules to prohibit an active player acting as the player agent for another active player.

Drug Testing Extended to All Tournaments

The Code increased the tournaments at which drug testing could be scheduled from just the Grand Slams and the Lipton ATP 2-week tournament to "any MTC sanctioned Grand Prix tournament as arranged by the Independent Expert."[700]

MTC Meetings

In 1988, the MTC held six meetings: January 25-28 in Melbourne, March 17-20 in Key Biscayne, June 15-18, 27, 30 in London, August 26-29 in New York, November 2-3, 1988 in London, and November 29 - December 1 in New York.

MIPTC Meeting, Melbourne January 25-28

Name Change to Men's Tennis Council (MTC)

At the January 25-28 meeting in Melbourne, the Council approved the amendment of the MIPTC Constitution and Bylaws to change its name from the "catchy name" of Men's International Professional Tennis Council (MIPTC) to the Men's Tennis Council. (MTC)

Nabisco's Bad News

In January in Melbourne, Ed Redding, Senior Vice President of Nabisco appeared at the meeting on behalf of Nabisco and said: "Since our initial commitment was made, we have conducted a major reorganization of our corporate structure and have made significant changes in our marketing strategies. We have moved our Planters (Peanut) and Life Saver Division from Nabisco to RJR Tobacco. A decision was made to shift emphasis away from the Nabisco Brands corporate umbrella and focus more directly on our major trademarks such as Del Monte and Fleishman's, etc. Given this change in strategy, we have concluded that continuing sponsorship beyond 1989 would be inappropriate and we must decline the option to renew."

Roy Reardon told me: "It was clear that Redding was very quietly annoyed in general about the way the Grand Prix had treated Nabisco and that attitude was at the bottom of the decision by Nabisco to walk away. While they clearly had other objectives in golf and while there was certainly a change of personalities at the Nabisco management level, I got the impression that the Grand Prix could have survived if Nabisco had been more successful in the promotion of its name. Part of the problem, and Redding was very clear about this, was the fact that Volvo made it difficult in the beginning and has been hanging in there causing a dilution of the value of Nabisco's Grand Prix sponsorship."[701]

Our press release[702] put the best face on the Nabisco decision to withdraw: "Nabisco Brands, Inc., will continue its sponsorship of the worldwide Nabisco Grand Prix circuit for two more years, and will then phase out its circuit sponsorship in 1990." *Obviously, our strategy was to emphasize the positive that the sponsorship was continuing for two more years to try to alleviate any panic among the tournaments and the players.*

1988 Tournament Sanction Applications and Conflicts of Interest

Notwithstanding the claims in the pending lawsuit, the Conflict of Interest Committee consisting of Hamilton Jordan, David Markin, Charles Pasarell and

Franco Bartoni reviewed the tournament sanction applications for 1989 and the various disclosed involvement of tournaments with Player Agents. When the sanction applications were received for the 1989 Nabisco Grand Prix, the following involvements with Player Agents were documented for 32 tournaments:

(1)   Australian Open – Player Agent Tournament Director, IMG for TV.

(2)   Barcelona – IMG for television and sponsorships.

(3)   Bari- IMG is defacto owner.

(4)   Bologna – IMG is defacto owner.

(5)   Boston – IMG is defacto owner.

(6)   Brussels – IMG is defacto owner.

(7)   Chicago Proposed – ProServ and Volvo are owners.

(8)   Cincinnati – ProServ for TV.

(9)   Florence – ProServ is defacto owner.

(10)   Geneva – IMG is defacto owner.

(11)   Hamburg – IMG is defacto owner.

(12)   Indian Wells – ProServ is agent for TV and sponsorships.

(13)   Lipton – IMG is agent for TV and sponsorships.

(14)   London – ProServ is agent for TV.

(15)   Los Angeles – Volvo and ProServ are defacto owners.

(16)   Memphis – ProServ is agent for TV and sponsorships.

(17)   Milan – IMG is defacto owner.

(18)   Montreal – IMG is defacto owner.

(19)   Newport – ProServ is agent for TV and sponsorships.

(20)   Nice – No agent relationship.

(21)   Orlando – ProServ is owner.

(22)   Palermo – IMG is defacto owner.

(23)   Philadelphia – ProServ is agent for TV and sponsorships.

(24)   Queens – ProServ is agent for TV.

(25)   Rome – ProServ is agent for TV and IMG is agent for sponsorships.

(26)   San Francisco – ProServ is agent for TV.

(27)   Stratton – ProServ is agent for TV.

(28)   St. Vincent -   ProServ is Tournament Director.

(29)   Tokyo Seiko – ProServ is agent for TV.

(30)   U.S. Open – IMG is agent for TV.

(31)   Washington – ProServ is 50% defacto owner.

(32)   Wimbledon – IMG is agent for TV and merchandising.

On account of the demise of the MTC, the final determinations on these conflicts of interest were never made. However, before the demise of the MTC, a few preliminary decisions were made with respect to a few tournaments:

(i)   Barcelona. Barcelona had an exclusive agency agreement with IMG for the sale of sponsorship and television rights. The MTC determined that Barcelona was in compliance with the Conflict of Interest Rule.

(ii)   Australian Open. The MTC agreed to grandfather the agreement appointing Colin Stubs, a Player Agent, as tournament director pursuant to pre-existing agreement on condition that the agreement would expire after the 1991 tournament.

(iii)   Los Angeles. The MTC agreed to grandfather the agreement with Volvo and ProServ on condition that it would expire after the 1990 tournament.

(iv)   Washington: The Super Series sanction for 1989 was approved for the Washington Area Tennis Patrons Foundation "subject to written confirmation of the intention to comply with the Conflict of Interest Rule." This meant that the joint ownership with ProServ would be terminated.

(v)   Boston: The Super Series sanction for 1989 was denied "subject to resubmission on or before March 31, 1988, in compliance with the Conflict of Interest Rule." IMG had all the tournament rights so it was the "defacto owner" and ProServ was the television sales agent.

(vi)   Orlando: The Super Series application for 1989 was denied because the tournament was owned by ProServ.

No Substitutions for Johannesburg

There was a continuing problem with the players being blacklisted by various Olympic and allied opponents of South Africa's Apartheid racial policy. The Council voted that no players should be forced by a "hard" substitution to play in Johannesburg in 1988 or 1989.[703]

MTC Meeting, Miami March 17-20

Jacques Dorfmann – French Open Referee

In March in Miami,[704] it was reported that Jacques Dorfmann, the French Open Referee for many years, refused to take the MTC annual re-certification test to comply with the MTC Officials Program. He had always exhibited a very French arrogant attitude that he was superior to all of the MIPTC Supervisors and he insulted them at every French Open, where under the rules he, as the Grand Slam Referee, was in charge and the MTC Supervisors were merely his advisors to be disregarded at will and upon his whim. Dorfmann also liked to assign himself as the chair umpire for one "non-controversial" men's quarterfinal and then assign himself to the men's singles final. He was one of those old school tennis officials "who believed he had a royal type prerogative to disregard the rules when he deemed it appropriate to do so." He also had demonstrated a personal favoritism to some players over other players. Even though Dorfmann's certification as an MTC Referee was being withdrawn since he refused to take the annual exam, a motion was made by Philippe Chatrier, who was also the President of the French Tennis Federation, to approve Dorfmann as the Referee of the French Open for 1988. Ray Moore and the other Player Representatives were adamantly opposed to having Dorfmann continue. *No one liked Dorfmann.*

So, what did the Council do with this hot potato? They deferred the matter to me as the Administrator to deal with it. After a long private discussion, Chatrier promised that he would replace Dorfmann in 1989, if I would just let him continue for 1988 in respect of his many years of service so as to avoid embarrassment to the French Tennis Federation. Reluctantly, I agreed to approve Dorfmann for the 1988 French Open. *Ray Moore, the MTC Chairman, was upset with my decision and, of course, Dorfmann was upset that he would be replaced in 1989.*

After he was retired, Dorfmann wrote a book that was published in France. In it he devoted a chapter to "Marshall Happer" and said: "His character is very typical of how the system works. There is no possible discussion with him. Whenever he deigns talking to you, the only thing he talks about are rules. His face is impenetrable, and he has a blind judgment. He follows the rules very strictly and has never had a sense of the tennis spirit. An excellent civil servant who enforces the law with no compromise. I often exchanged mails with the administrator of the Professional Council; the latest one was the letter I received informing me that I had lost my license. I had been fired after 35 years of duty. I have been a trouble maker for the last ten years." *Would you conclude that Dorfmann was angry?*

WCT Tournament of Champions and Hamburg

In the 1988 calendar, the schedule was:

April 11-17	Suntory Japan Open Super Series - Hard
April 11-17	Madrid Regular Series - Clay
April 11-17	Nice Regular Series - Clay
April 18-24	Monte Carlo Super Series - Clay
April 18-24	Seoul Regular Series - Hard
April 25-May 1	Hamburg Super Series - Clay
April 25 -May 1	Charleston Regular Series - Clay
May 1-8	WCT Tournament of Champions – New York - Clay
May 1-8	Munich Regular Series - Clay
May 9-15	Rome Super Series - Clay
May 16-22	World Team Cup – Dusseldorf - Clay
May 16-22	Florence Open Week Series - Clay
My 23 -June 5	French Open - Clay

This was the so-called "high clay court season" leading to the French Open. As you can see, all of the clay court tournaments were in Europe except for Charleston and the WCT Tournament of Champions in Forest Hills. The Europeans, especially Hamburg, hated having the American tournaments compete with them as the American players tended to stay in America until after the WCT Tournament of Champions before traveling to Europe for the European clay season and the European grass court season through Wimbledon. To attempt to deal with that problem, the Council moved the WCT Tournament of Champions into the week before Hamburg in the proposed 1989 calendar.

Having the WCT Tournament of Champions earlier was difficult because the weather in New York was still cold in early May. Hamburg's weather was also not good in early May. My suggestion every year that Hamburg and Rome, which was further south, switch dates was always rejected by Rome, now represented by Franco Bartoni, a member of the Council. In the 1982 lawsuit settlement agreement with WCT, the WCT Tournament of Champions was made a Circuit Championship with scheduling priority. The contract also provided that WCT events could not be doubled up with other events, without WCT's approval. Thus, we could not double up the Tournament of Champions with Hamburg.[705]

WCT requested that the WCT Tournament of Champions be scheduled a week later in 1989. The Council refused, but it offered WCT the option to agree to double-up with Hamburg on the week of May 8-14, 1989. The result was that WCT was mad and claiming breach of contract. The Europeans were just a little less mad than they were before. No tournament was ever fully satisfied with its dates or its field of players. This was one of the problems that caused the Council to want to terminate its contract with WCT after 1989. When the ATP sought to entice Monte Carlo, Hamburg and Rome to join the 1990 ATP Tour, it did so by eliminating any competing clay court tournament (like the WCT Tournament of Champions) in the United States.

Competing Circuits

Ray Moore and Franco Bartoni informed the Council about various solicitations and discussions directed at them by undisclosed third parties relative to the development of a competing circuit or circuits. Roy Reardon reminded each member of the MTC of his fiduciary obligation to the MTC and the Grand Prix Circuit and told them that any member of the MTC who violated their fiduciary duty to the MTC by participating in a competing circuit would be subject to being sued by the MTC. *At this point, neither Reardon or I had any idea of what was to happen at the August meeting.*[706]

1990 Format

The MTC extensively discussed proposals for a new 1990 format and the various options available in an effort to develop principles which would enhance the image of and secure a healthy future for the sport. Included among the various principles agreed to was the MTC intention to proceed in 1990 with a coordinated Grand Prix television package and to provide up-front contracts for the top players for the first time. At the conclusion of this discussion, the MTC prepared, reviewed and approved the issuance of a press release to that effect.[707][708]

MTC Meeting, London June 15-18, 27, 30

Ron Bookman Killed in Bicycle Accident

Ron Bookman, Deputy Executive Director of the ATP, was accidentally killed when he and his bicycle collided with a car in Dallas on April 12. The members of the MTC[709] observed a moment of silence in memory of Ron whose "tireless dedication and numerous contributions to tennis were recognized by all present." Ron and I had worked together to jointly provide the administration necessary for the Grand Prix. Ron was supportive of the MTC and what we were doing and his untimely death deprived Hamilton Jordan of a wealth of information and understanding about professional tennis and the importance of the MTC. I attended Ron's funeral in Dallas.

Rex Bellamy said: "Tennis has lost one of its most widely experienced and appreciated administrators. Moreover, Bookman spread more goodwill around him in every role he tried. Few men had such diversity of experience in professional tennis during the era of open competition and none inspired more affection." Ray Moore said: "Everyone associated with the men's professional game knew Ron as an extremely capable and multi-talented man. Not only was he an unwavering friend, he was also a key part of the fabric of tennis, always going the extra step to get things accomplished without drawing attention to himself, and able to lighten an issue with his knowledge."

MTC/WCT Contract to be Terminated

Since the Council was unable to agree on terms with WCT for a more reduced schedule, for a resolution of the scheduling problem between the WCT Tournament of Champions and Hamburg and the objections of the players in being forced to play in the Dallas Finals, the Council voted to terminate its contract with WCT at the end of the 1989 Grand Prix year. WCT responded by saying that WCT would continue "Business as Usual" through 1989. Owen Williams told Peter Alfano of the *New York Times*[710]: "As of today, we're looking for the ways and means to continue the five events we have and to build on them. We're thinking of having eight or nine major events of our own in 1990." *I fully expected WCT to compete with the Grand Prix again in 1990 which probably would lead to another anti-trust lawsuit. Lamar Hunt was not a quitter.*[711]

MTC Meeting, New York August 26-29

Ron Bookman Family Fund

I supported and the Council agreed to join with ATP by contributing $50,000 to a Ron Bookman Family Fund in memory of Ron Bookman, the Deputy Executive Director of the ATP.

No ETA Sanction to be Required

The European Tennis Association (ETA) always was trying to obtain control of men's professional tennis in Europe over the MTC. At the request of the ETA, a motion was made to require an ETA sanction for all Challengers and Satellites in Europe as a condition of a MTC sanction. The motion failed as did an earlier request by the ETA for prior approval of all officials for MTC Officials schools.[712]

MTC Meeting, London, November 2-3

Wendy Miller Becomes MTC Media Liaison

Wendy Miller, who started substituting for Lori Stukes while she had knee surgery in the fall of 1987, was promoted to a full-time Media Liaison in 1988. Wendy was a native of New Rochelle, NY. She was a graduate of Lafayette College with a B.A. in Psychology and had earned a M.B.A. from Pace University in Marketing and Finance. The other two Media Liaisons continuing were Catalina Cox and Micky den Tuinder, who was then the senior member of the group.[713]

J. Wayne Richmond Hired by ATP

On April 27, Hamilton Jordan announced in *International Tennis Weekly*[714] the hiring of J. Wayne Richmond, age 36, as Senior Vice President of Marketing for the ATP, to begin at the end of May. "Richmond had worked with Adidas since July 1979, serving as a field promotion representative for two years in baseball, football and basketball on the west coast before being named National Promotion Director in April 1981. He developed and directed Adidas' tennis promotions programs in the United States, then moved to Adidas USA in New Jersey in January of 1986 to reorganize the company's overall athletic promotions department. A native of Tennessee, Richmond was a 1973 graduate of Belmont College in Nashville where he played varsity tennis."

Washington Scheduling Nightmare

The Washington Super Series was scheduled to begin on Monday, July 18 and end on Sunday July 24. The tournament was scheduled in the same week as the second round of Davis Cup, so the available player field had been limited. The second semifinal between Jimmy Connors and Aaron Krickstein was scheduled for Saturday night at 7:00 pm on live television with 7,000 spectators. It was raining and the forecast was for continuing rain throughout Saturday night. The scheduling committee, consisting of the Tournament Director, Referee, MIPTC Supervisor and Player Representative, was deadlocked on whether to: (i) Wait as long as necessary on Saturday night (probably in the middle of the night) for the rain to hopefully stop and try to get the match played before morning (with no television and no spectators), or (ii) Cancel the Saturday night session and reschedule the Connors v. Krickstein semifinal for Sunday afternoon with the finals to be played at 7:00 pm on Sunday night, which could require the winner to play two matches in the same day, or (iii) Cancel the Saturday night session, reschedule the Connors v. Krickstein semifinal for Sunday afternoon and permit the final to be played on Monday afternoon.

Since the scheduling committee was deadlocked, they called me at 5:00 pm on Saturday, agreeing that a decision had to be made by 6:00 pm so the players, fans and television would know what to do. It was my responsibility to break the deadlock one way or the other. A few *irrelevant* factors were: (i) Connors had refused to join the ATP, so the ATP members did not like him and they always wanted to make sure he got no extra favorable treatment, (ii) The rank-and-file ATP members all believed that the top ranked players like Connors got extra favorable treatment, (iii) Donald Dell and ProServ, who were Player Agents, were the defacto owners and managers of the Washington tournament contrary to the Council's stand against conflicts of interest, (iv) Donald Dell and ProServ were suing the Council and me personally and were actively trying to get me fired and (v) The Washington tournament was in the process of trying to raise $10 million to build a permanent tennis stadium at Rock Creek Park for the tournament.

My decision was to cancel the Saturday night scheduled semifinal on account of the rain, reschedule that semifinal for Sunday afternoon and schedule the final for Monday afternoon, as the players, the fans and television needed an immediate decision by 6:00 pm. That ensured that neither player (Krickstein or Connors) would have to play two matches on Sunday and the tournament could have a Sunday semifinal for its fans and television and a Monday final for its fans and television. The rank and file ATP members objected big time to my decision claiming that I had given extra favorable treatment to Connors. It was in fact favorable to Connors or Krickstein, whichever one won the second semifinal because they would not be faced with two matches on Sunday. It was also favorable to professional tennis as it accommodated the fans and television which was good for the tournament and ultimately good for all the players. To counter some of the players' criticism of my decision, I flew to Stratton Mountain to attend the first meeting of the ATP Player Council on Tuesday of the next week to face them and explain the reasons for my decision. While the rank and file ATP members appreciated my meeting with them, they continued to object to my decision. ATP Road Manager Weller Evans said, "It was not the right decision. I disagree with the decision because

I feel like Connors should have had to play according to schedule. You can't grant the Monday final when the tournament can possibly be completed on Sunday." It could have only been completed on Sunday if the Connors v. Krickstein semis were played after midnight on Friday or the winner had played the semifinal and the final on Sunday.[715]

Now, as I write this in 2021, I still believe my decision was in the best interest of the tournament, the fans, the players, television and the Grand Prix. The players wanted to find an irrevocable rule that would penalize Connors (also Krickstein) without regard to the best interests of the tournament, the fans, television or the Grand Prix. *I could never have agreed to that.*

Barbara Travers Hired

In September, Barbara Travers, a native of St. Louis, was hired as the Assistant Director of Communications. Barbara was a graduate of the University of Missouri - St. Louis with a degree in English Literature. She had been Manager of Network Production with USA Network for seven years. She had also been five years with WCT in Dallas and in New York.

Nabisco Buyout

On October 19, Ross Johnson, the CEO of RJR Nabisco, set in motion "the deal that forever changed Reynolds and Winston-Salem – the leveraged buyout of RJR Nabisco." Johnson's group offered $75.00 per share, which started the process which ultimately ended on November 30 when the board approved a sale to Kohlberg Kravis Roberts & Co., for $109.00 a share or $25.4 billion guaranteed. The Ross Johnson team which included Ed Redding were all retired.[716]

ATP Ponte Vedra Office To Open February 1, 1989

In December, the ATP announced that its new Ponte Vedra office would open on February 1, 1989, and the Arlington Texas office would close. Hamilton Jordan announced that ATP was purchasing a 11.2 acre tract of land in St. John's County, Ponte Vedra, Florida, for a new world headquarters for the ATP. It was to include a newly constructed office building, a clubhouse with fully equipped training room and initially, eight tennis courts – two grass courts, two European clay courts, two American clay courts and two hardcourts, with more courts planned for the future. Ground breaking was November 15 with planned occupancy by January 1, 1989.[717]

Grand Prix Continues to Boom

On December 30, the ATP reported on the progress of the Grand Prix between 1976 and 1988 in *International Tennis Weekly*[718]:

	Total Compensation in Millions Prize Money and Bonuses	Progress of No. 100 Ranked Player
1976	$ 5.5	
1977	$ 9.5	$23,610
1978	$12.5	$29,248
1979	$12.5	$26,723
1980	$13.2	$30,466
1981	$13.0	$38,589
1982	$15.9	$53,575
1983	$16.4	$40,994
1984	$16.7	$47,915
1985	$21.4	$50,284
1986	$22.5	$52,918
1987	$26.1	$63,384
1988	$31.8	$79,751

ATP

In 1988, Brian Gottfried was re-elected ATP President. Larry Scott was elected as Vice President. Colin Dowdeswell was re-elected Treasurer and Jim McManus continued as Secretary. Brian Gottfried would be the last president of the ATP as a pure player association. The Board of Directors were: Ricardo Acuna, Marty Davis, Colin Dowdeswell, Brad Drewett, Mike Estep, Brian Gottfried, Bill Scanlon, Michiel Schapers, Ray Moore and Larry Scott. Hamilton Jordan was Executive Director, Ron Bookman was the Deputy Executive Director until his untimely death and J. Wayne Richmond was Senior Vice President Marketing.[719]

1988 ATP Awards

Jack Kramer had supported the continuation of the MTC instead of the proposed new ATP Tour. As a result, the ATP changed the name of the "JAKS" awards, named after Kramer, the founder of the ATP to the "ATP Awards". The 14th annual ATP Awards was held on November 29 at the New York Hilton:

Player of the Year	Mats Wilander
Doubles Team of the Year	Sergio Casal – Emilio Sanchez
Newcomer of the Year	Michael Chang
Most Improved Player of the Year	Andre Agassi
Comeback Player of the Year	Kent Carlsson
Sportsmanship Award	Stefan Edberg
ATP Super Series Tournament of the Year	Indianapolis
ATP Open/ Regular Series Tourney of the Year	Stuttgart
CF Humanitarian Award	Bob Sullivan

Note how much the players loved the Stuttgart tournament!

1988 MTC Financials

The MTC began 1988 with a surplus of $5,506,897 and after operating its administrative offices, providing $4,000,000 in Bonus Pool awards and $478,000 in Bonus prize money to players in the Nabisco Grand Prix, the MTC ended 1988 with a surplus of $6,687,904. In addition, the MTC collected and paid to ATP, pursuant to the "agreed" but never signed 1988-1992 agreement: $867,994 in ATP prize money for services to Nabisco Grand Prix tournaments and $97,856 in ATP Challenger and Satellite sanction fees.

Nabisco paid for its promotion as the Nabisco Grand Prix sponsor and the MTC provided the promotion of the Nabisco Grand Prix. The MTC promoted the Nabisco Masters in December of 1988 at Madison Square Garden telecast by ESPN.

Nabisco paid the $225,000 for WCT for the Nabisco Masters Doubles to be promoted and operated by WCT at the Royal Albert Hall in London with $200,000 in prize money. The MTC promoted the Nabisco Masters at Madison Square Garden in December of 1988. The gross income for the 1988 Nabisco Masters was $4,016,227 and the gross expenses were $2,633,042, so the MTC net was $1,383,185. Again, that is why the MTC wisely insisted on owning and operating the Nabisco Masters.

The new 12-year lease for 7,800 square foot (half of the floor) office space on the 17th floor began after the completion of renovations, in May of 1988. The new annual rent was $306,150 per year. The relocation costs were $35,823. The office space for the MTC's Paris office at Stade Roland Garros was furnished free of charge by the French Tennis Federation.

Included in the operating expense were the MTC's legal expenses:

	1985	1986	1987	1988	Total
General	$116,324	$ 71,362	$232,079	$122,164	$ 541,929
Lawsuit	$ 32,752	$208,925	$108,859	$328,416	$ 678,952
Totals	$149,076	$280,287	$340,938	$450,580	$1,220,881

Prior to 1988, 80 percent of the legal fees charged to the Council were paid by two insurance companies under full reservation of rights. Beginning in 1988, payments were not made due to the settlement of the lawsuit and the Council paid 100 percent of all legal fees during the year. Final resolution of the responsibility of the insurance companies relating to these legal fees had not yet been determined or agreed upon at the end of 1988.[720]

Grand Slam Winners

Australian Open

Mats Wilander d. Pat Cash 6-3, 6-7, 3-6, 6-1, 8-6.
Rick Leach – Jim Pugh d. Jeremy Bates – Peter Lundgren 6-3, 6-2, 6-3.

French Open

Mats Wilander d. Henri Leconte 7-5, 6-2, 6-1.
Andres Gomez – Emilio Sanchez d. John Fitzgerald – Anders Jarryd 6-3, 6-7, 6-4, 6-3.

Wimbledon

Stefan Edberg d. Boris Becker 4-6, 7-6, 6-4, 6-2.
Ken Flach – Robert Seguso d. John Fitzgerald – Anders Jarryd 6-4, 2-6, 6-4, 7-6.

U.S. Open

Mats Wilander d. Ivan Lendl 6-4, 4-6, 6-3, 5-7, 6-4.
Sergio Casal – Emilio Sanchez d. Rick Leach – Jim Pugh WO.

Nabisco Grand Prix Circuit Championships

Buick WCT Finals (Dallas)

Boris Becker d. Stefan Edberg 6-4, 1-6, 7-5, 6-2.

WCT Eagle Tournament of Champions

Andre Agassi d. Slobodan Zivojinovic 7-5, 7-6, 7-5.
J. Lozano – Todd Witsken d Peter Aldrich – Danie Visser 6-4, 7-6.

Nabisco Masters (New York)

Boris Becker d. Ivan Lendl 5-7, 7-6, 6-2, 7-6.

Nabisco Masters Doubles (London)

Rick Leach – Jim Pugh d. Sergio Casal – Emilio Sanchez 6-4, 6-3, 2-6, 6-0.

Davis Cup

Davis Cup Final (Gothenburg – Clay)

Germany d. Sweden 4-1.

Carl-Uwe Steeb (DE) d. Mats Wilander (SE) 8-10, 1-6, 6-2, 6-4, 8-6.
Boris Becker (DE) d. Stefan Edberg (SE) 6-3, 6-1, 6-4.
Boris Becker – Eric Jelen (DE) d. Stefan Edberg – Anders Jarryd (SE) 3-6, 2-6, 7-5, 6-3, 6-2.

Stefan Edberg (SE) d. Carl-Uwe Steeb (DE) 6-4, 8-6.
Patrik Kuhnen (DE) d. Kent Carlsson (SE) WO

World Team Cup

Sweden d. United States 2-1.

Stefan Edberg (SE) d. Tim Mayotte (US) 6-4, 6-2.
Kent Carlsson (SE) d. Aaron Krickstein (US) 6-4, 6-3.
Ken Flach – Robert Seguso (US) d. Stefan Edberg – Anders Jarryd (SE) 6-7, 6-3, 7-6.

1988 World Rankings[721]

Bud Collins	Lance Tingay	ATP Year-End Rankings
1. Mats Wilander	1. Mats Wilander	1. Mats Wilander
2. Ivan Lendl	2. Stefan Edberg	2. Ivan Lendl
3. Andre Agassi	3. Boris Becker	3. Andre Agassi
4. Boris Becker	4. Ivan Lendl	4. Boris Becker
5. Stefan Edberg	5. Miloslav Mecir	5. Stefan Edberg
6. Kent Carlsson	6. Andre Agassi	6. Kent Carlsson
7. Jimmy Connors	7. Henri Leconte	7. Jimmy Connors
8. Jakob Hlasek	8. Jimmy Connors	8. Jacob Hlasek
9. Henri Leconte	9. Emilio Sanchez	9. Henri Leconte
10. Tim Mayotte	10. Pat Cash	10. Tim Mayotte

1988 Nabisco Grand Prix Bonus Pool Top 10[722]

Singles (19th Bonus Pool)			Doubles (14th Bonus Pool)		
1.	Mats Wilander	$ 800,000	1.	Rich Leach	$ 165,000
2.	Boris Becker	$ 550,000	2.	Jim Pugh	$ 120,000
3.	Stefan Edberg	$ 400,000	3.	John Fitzgerald	$ 90,000
4.	Ivan Lendl	$ 250,000	4.	Emilio Sanchez	$ 70,000
5.	Andre Agassi	$ 150,000	5T.	Ken Flach	$ 45,000
6.	Jakob Hlasek	$ 100,000	5T.	Robert Seguso	$ 45,000
7.	Henri Leconte	$ 75,000	7.	Jorge Lozano	$ 30,000
8.	Tim Mayotte	$ 55,000	8.	Todd Witsken	$ 25,000
9.	Jimmy Connors	$ 45,000	9.	Sergio Casal	$ 20,000
10.	Kent Carlsson	$ 40,000	10.	Anders Jarryd	$ 17,000

1988 Official Earnings Top 10[723]

1.	Mats Wilander	$ 1,726,731	6.	Jakob Hlasek	$ 624,716
2.	Boris Becker	$ 1,696,953	7.	Emilio Sanchez	$ 555,146
3.	Stefan Edberg	$ 1,402,802	8.	Henri Leconte	$ 554,491
4.	Ivan Lendl	$ 983,938	9.	Kent Carlsson	$ 546,539
5.	Andre Agassi	$ 822,062	10.	Tim Mayotte	$ 505,754

1988 Tournament Calendar

Date	Tournaments	Singles Winner	Singles #2	Doubles Winners	Doubles #2
1/3/1988	Wellington $115,000 GP	Ramesh Krishnan	Andrei Chesnokov	D. Goldie - R. Leach	B. Dyke - G. Michibata
1/3/1988	Adelaide $93,400 GP	Mark Woodforde	Wally Masur	D. Cahill - M. Kratzmann	C. Limberger - M. Woodforde
1/3/1988	Auckland $93,400 GP	Amos Mansdorf	Ramesh Krishnan	M. Davis - T. Pawsat	S. Giammalva - J. Grabb
1/10/1988	Sydney $93,400 GP	John Fitzgerald	Andrei Chesnokov	D. Cahill - M. Kratzmann	J. Rive - B. Schultz
1/24/1988	Aussie Open $1,054,984 GS	Mats Wilander	Pat Cash	R. Leach - J. Pugh	J. Bates - P. Lundgren
1/31/1988	Guaruja $100,000 GP	Luiz Mattar	Eliot Teltscher	R. Acuna - L. Jensen	J. Frana - D. Perez
2/14/1988	Rotterdam $375,000 SS	Stefan Edberg	Miloslav Mecir	P. Kuhnen - T. Meinecke	M. Gustafsson - D. Nargiso
2/14/1988	Lyon $240,000 GP	Yahiya Doumbia	Todd Nelson	B. Drewett - B. Dyke	M. Mortensen - B. Willenborg
2/21/1988	Memphis $297,500 SS	Andre Agassi	Mikael Pernfors	K. Curren - D. Pate	P. Lundgren - M. Pernfors
2/21/1988	Milan $372,500 SS	Yannick Noah	Jimmy Connors	B. Becker - E. Jelen	M. Mecir - T. Smid
2/28/1988	Philadelphia $485,000 SS	Tim Mayotte	John Fitzgerald	K. Evernden - J. Kriek	K. Curren - D. Visser
2/28/1988	Metz $93,400 GP	Jonas Svensson	Michiel Schapers	J. Navratil - T. Nijssen	R. Baxter - N. Odisor
3/6/1988	Indian Wells 585,000 SS	Boris Becker	Emilio Sanchez	B. Becker - G. Forget	J. Lozano - T. Witsken
3/12/1988	Orlando $297,500 SS	Andrei Chesnokov	Miloslav Mecir	G. Forget - Y. Noah	S. Stewart - K. Warwick
3/27/1988	Key Biscayne $745,000 ATP	Mats Wilander	Jimmy Connors	J. Fitzgerald - A. Jarryd	K. Flach - R. Seguso
4/2/1988	Dallas $500,000 WCT Finals	Boris Becker	Stefan Edberg		
4/10/1988	Chicago $315,000 Volvo SP	Tim Mayotte	Paul Annacone		
4/17/1988	Tokyo $500,000 WCT/SS	John McEnroe	Stefan Edberg	J. Fitzgerald - J. Kriek	S. Denton - D. Pate
4/17/1988	Nice $115,000 GP	Henri Leconte	Jerome Potier	G. Forget - Y. Noah	H. Gunthardt - D. Nargiso

4/17/1988	Madrid $93,400 GP	Kent Carlsson	Fernando Luna	S. Casal - E. Sanchez	J. Stoltenberg - T. Woodbridge
4/24/1988	Monte Carlo $375,000 SS	Ivan Lendl	Martin Jaite	S. Casal - E. Sanchez	H. Leconte - I. Lendl
4/24/1988	Seoul $93,400 GP	Dan Goldie	Andrew Castle	A. Castle - R. Saad	G. Donnelly - J. Grabb
4/30/1988	Atlanta $500,000 SP	Ivan Lendl	Stefan Edberg	2-6, 6-1, 6-3	
5/1/1988	Hamburg $410,000 SS	Kent Carlsson	Henri Leconte	D. Cahill - L. Warder	R. Leach - J. Pugh
5/1/1988	Charleston $190,000 GP	Andre Agassi	Jimmy Arias	P. Aldrich - D. Visser	R. Leach - J. Pugh
5/8/1988	NY $560,000 WCT/TC	Andres Gomez	Yannick Noah	G. Forget - Y. Noah	G. Donnelly - P. Fleming
5/8/1988	Munich $165,000 GP	Guillermo Perez-Roldan	Jonas Svensson	R. Leach - J. Pugh	A. Mancini - C. Miniussi
5/15/1988	Rome $595,000 SS	Ivan Lendl	Guillermo Perez-Roldan	J. Lozano - T. Witsken	A. Jarryd - T. Smid
5/22/1988	Florence $93,400 SS	Massimiliano Narducci	Claudio Panatta	J. Frana - C. Miniussi	C. Pistolesi - H. Skoff
5/22/1988	Dusseldorf $750k WTC/ATP	Sweden	USA	2-1.	
5/22/1988	Dusseldorf $750k WTC/ATP	Stefan Edberg	Tim Mayotte	6-4, 6-2	
5/22/1988	Dusseldorf $750k WTC/ATP	Kent Carlsson	Aaron Krickstein	6-4, 6-3	
5/22/1988	Dusseldorf $750k WTC/ATP		6-7, 6-3, 7-6	K.Flach - R. Seguso	S.Edberg - A. Jarryd
6/6/1988	French Open GS	Mats Wilander	Henri Leconte	A. Gomez - E. Sanchez	J. Fitzgerald - A. Jarryd
6/12/1988	Bologna $93,400 GP	Alberto Mancini	Emilio Sanchez	E. Sanchez - J. Sanchez	R. Hertzog - M. Walder
6/12/1988	London $290,000 GP	Boris Becker	Stefan Edberg	K. Flach - R. Seguso	P. Aldrich - D. Visser
6/12/1988	Edinburgh SP	Jacob Hlasek	Peter Lundgren		
6/18/1988	Bristol $93,400 GP	Christian Saceanu	Ramesh Krishnan	P. Doohan - L. Warder	M. Davis - T. Pawsat
6/19/1988	Athens $93,400 GP	Horst Skoff	Bruno Oresar	R. Bergh - P. Henricsson	P. Arraya - K. Novacek
7/4/1988	Wimbledon GS	Stefan Edberg	Boris Becker	K. Flach - R. Seguso	J. Fitzgerald - A. Jarryd
7/10/1988	Boston $297,500 SS	Thomas Muster	Lawson Duncan	J. Lozano - T. Witsken	B. Oresar - J. Yzaga

7/10/1988	Gstaad $215,000 GP	Darren Cahill	Jakob Hlasek	P. Korda - M. Srejber	A. Gomez - E. Sanchez
7/10/1988	Newport $115,000 GP	Wally Masur	Brad Drewett	K. Jones - P. Lundgren	S. Davis - D. Goldie
7/17/1988	Stuttgart $275,000 GP	Andre Agassi	Andres Gomez	S. Casal - E. Sanchez	A. Jarryd - M. Mortensen
7/17/1988	Bastad $215,000 GP	Marcelo Filippini	Francesco Candellotti	P. Baur - U. Riglewski	S. Edberg - N. Kroon
7/25/1988	Washington $297,500 SS	Jimmy Connors	Andres Gomez	R. Leach - J. Pugh	J. Lozano - T. Witsken
7/25/1988	Schenectady $93,400 GP	Tim Mayotte	Johan Kriek	A. Mronz - G. VanEmburgh	P. Annacone - P. McEnroe
7/31/1988	Stratton Mt. $475k SS	Andre Agassi	Paul Annacone	P. Aldrich - D. Visser	J. Lozano - T. Witsken
7/31/1988	Bordeaux $215,000 GP	Thomas Muster	Ronald Agenor	J. Nystrom - C. Panatta	C. Miniussi - N. Nargiso
7/31/1988	Hilversum $93,400 GP	Emilio Sanchez	Guillermo Perez-Roldan	S. Casal - E. Sanchez	M. Gustafsson - G. Perez
8/7/1988	Indianapolis $297,500 SS	Boris Becker	John McEnroe	R. Leach - J. Pugh	K. Flach - R. Seguso
8/7/1988	Kitzbuhel $240,000 GP	Kent Carlsson	Emilio Sanchez	S. Casal - E. Sanchez	J. Nystrom - C. Panatta
8/14/1988	Toronto $485,000 SS	Ivan Lendl	Kevin Curren	K. Flach - R. Seguso	A. Castle - T. Wilkison
8/14/1988	Prague $140,000 GP	Thomas Muster	Guillermo Perez-Roldan	P. Korda - J. Navratil	T. Muster - H. Skoff
8/14/1988	St. Vincent $125,000 GP	Kent Carlsson	Thierry Champion	A. Mancini - C. Minissi	P. Cane - B. Taroczy
8/21/1988	Cincinnati $485,000 SS	Mats Wilander	Stefan Edberg	R. Leach - J. Pugh	J. Grabb - P. McEnroe
8/21/1988	Livingston $93,400 GP	Andre Agassi	Jeff Tarango	G. Connell - G. Michibata	W. Flur - S. Giammalva
8/28/1988	Rye Brook GP	Milan Srejber	Ramesh Krishnan	A. Castle - T. Wilkison	J. Bates - M. Mortensen
9/11/1988	US Open GS	Mats Wilander	Ivan Lendl	S. Casal - E. Sanchez	R. Leach - J. Pugh
9/18/1988	Barcelona $372,500 SS	Kent Carlsson	Thomas Muster	S. Casal - E. Sanchez	C. Mezzadri - D. Perez
9/25/1988	Los Angeles $297,500 SS	Mikael Pernfors	Andre Agassi	J. McEnroe - M. Woodforde	P. Doohan - J. Grabb
9/25/1988	Geneva $190,000 GP	Marian Vajda	Kent Carlsson	M. Bahrami - T. Smid	G. Luza - G. Perez-Roldan
9/25/1988	Bari $93,400 GP	Thomas Muster	Marcelo Filippini	T. Muster - C. Panatta	F. Cancellotti - S. Colombo

Date	Tournament	Winner	Runner-up		
10/1/1988	Seoul Olympic Games	Miloslave Mecir	Tim Mayotte	K. Flach - R. Seguso	S. Casal - E. Sanchez
10/2/1988	San Francisco $297,500 SS	Michael Chang	Johan Kriek	J. McEnroe - M. Woodforde	S. Davis - T. Wilkison
10/2/1988	Palermo $93,400 GP	Mats Wilander	Kent Carlsson	C. DiLaura - M. Filippini	A. Mancini - C. Miniussi
10/9/1988	Scottsdale $297,500 SS	Mikael Pernfors	Glenn Layendecker	S. Davis - T. Wilkison	R. Leach - J. Pugh
10/9/1988	Basle $240,000 GP	Stefan Edberg	Jacob Hlasek	J. Hlasek - T. Smid	J. Bates - P. Lundgren
10/9/1988	Brisbane $165,000 GP	Tim Mayotte	Marty Davis	E. Jelen - C. Steeb	G. Connell - G. Michibata
10/16/1988	Tel Aviv $95,000 GP	Brad Gilbert	Aaron Krickstein	R. Smith P. Wekesa	P. Baur - A. Mronz
10/16/1988	Sydney $392,500 SS	Slobodan Zivojinovic	Richard Matuszewski	D. Cahill - J. Fitzgerald	M. Davis - B. Drewett
10/16/1988	Toulouse $225,000 GP	Jimmy Connors	Andrei Chesnokov	T. Nijssen - R. Osterthun	M. Bahrami - G. Forget
10/23/1988	Tokyo $$500,000 Seiko SS	Boris Becker	John Fitzgerald	A. Gomez - S. Zivojinovic	B. Becker - E. Jelen
10/23/1988	Vienna $140,000 GP	Horst Skoff	Thomas Muster	A. Antonitsch - B. Taroczy	K. Curren - T. Smid
10/23/1988	Frankfurt $140,000 GP	Tim Mayotte	Leonardo Lavalle	R. Haas - G. Ivanisevic	J. Bates - T. Nijssen
10/30/1988	Paris $960,000 SS	Amos Mansdorf	Brad Gilbert	P. Annacone - J. Fitzgerald	J. Grabb - C. van Rensburg
11/5/1988	Antwerp $1,000,000 SP	John McEnroe	Andrei Chesnokov	6-1, 7-5, 6-2	
11/6/1988	Stockholm $525,000 SS	Boris Becker	Peter Lundgren	K. Curren - J. Grabb	P. Annacone - J. Fitzgerald
11/6/1988	Sao Paulo $100,000 GP	Jay Berger	Horacio de la Pena	Berger - de la Pena	R. Acuna - J. Sanchez
11/10/1988	Stuttgart $350,000 SP	John McEnroe	Ivan Lendl		
11/13/1988	London $$335,000 SS	Jacob Hlasek	Jonas Svensson	K. Flach - R. Seguso	M. Davis - Brad Drewett
11/13/1988	Buenos Aires $89,400 GP	Javier Sanchez	Guillermo Perez-Roldan	C. Costa - J. Sanchez	E. Bengoechea - J. Clerc
11/20/1988	Johannesburg $472,500 SS	Jacob Hlasek	Christo van Rensburg	K. Curren - D. Pate	G. Muller - T. Wilkison
11/20/1988	Detroit $297,500 WCT/SS	John McEnroe	Aaron Krickstein	R. Leach - J. Pugh	K. Flach - R. Seguso
11/27/1988	Brussels $372,500 SS	Henri Leconte	Jacob Hlasek	W. Masur - T. Nijssen	J. Fitzgerald - T. Smid

11/28/1988	Itaparica $275,000 GP	Jaime Yzaga	Javier Frana	S. Casal - E. Sanchez	J. Lozano - T. Witsken
12/5/1988	NY $750k Nabisco Masters	Boris Becker	Ivan Lendl		
12/11/1988	London $200,000 Masters Dbls.			R. Leach - J. Pugh	S. Casal - E. Sanchez

http://www.atpworldtour.com/en/scores/results-archive.

http://www.itftennis.com/procircuit/tournaments/men's-calendar.aspx?tour=&reg=&nat=&sur=&cate=AL&iod=&fromDate=01-01-1968&toDate=31-12-1988.

Tennis History, Jim McManus, (Canada 2010).

1989 USTA Yearbook.

Official 1989 MTC Media Guide, (MTC 1989).

World of Tennis 1989, Edited by John Barrett and compiled by Lance Tingay, (London 1989).

CHAPTER 31:

1988: LAWSUIT SETTLEMENT, DESTRUCTION OF MTC IN COUP D' ÉTAT, CRISES NOS. 30 PART IV, 31, 32

CRISIS NO. 31: MTC-ATP FIVE-YEAR CONTRACT 1988-1992,

CRISIS NO. 30, PART IV: 1988 VOLVO, PROSERV, IMG LAWSUIT CONCLUSION

CRISIS NO. 32: COUP D' ÉTAT: THE FINAL CRISIS

Crisis No. 31: MTC-ATP Five Year Contract 1988-1992

At ATP's request, the MTC began requiring the tournaments to provide funding for ATP in 1982 and then in a five-year agreement for 1983-1987. As discussions began at the February 3-6, 1987, MTC meeting for a new five-year agreement for 1988-1992, the ATP threatened once again to withdraw from the Council unless a player pension plan was funded.

At the April 21-23, 1987, MIPTC Monaco Meeting, Dick Barovick, the ATP's legal counsel, presented an "ATP Player Benefit Plan" and asked that it be approved to begin in 1988, and funded with a commitment of 10 percent of the on-site and major tournament bonus prize money offered by sanctioned tournaments. When it was not immediately approved, the Player Representatives again threatened to withdraw from the Council.[724]

The proposed 1988-1992 MIPTC-ATP contract was discussed and debated at every subsequent meeting. Eventually, it was agreed that the new contract would require in the 1988 Grand Prix Rules for the funding of the ATP prize money for ATP's services and funding for the a new ATP deferred compensation plan. The ATP prize money and deferred compensation agreed was:

	1988 ATP Prize Money	1988 Deferred Compensation
Australian Open	$30,000	$100,000
French Open	$30,000	$125,000
Wimbledon	$30,000	$150,000
U.S. Open	$30,000	$150,000
Lipton 2-Week Tournament	$30,000	$100,000
Tournament of Champions, Super Series	$17,500	$ 40,000
Regular/Open Week Series	$ 4,000	$ 10,000
Buick WCT Finals	$30,000	
Masters Singles		
Masters Doubles	$17,500	

It never occurred to me or to any of the ITF Representatives and the Tournament Representatives and probably also the then Player Representatives, that the MIPTC-ATP contract might not and would not ever be signed. Throughout 1988, I collected the agreed ATP prize money and paid it to ATP when collected. I also collected the ATP deferred compensation contributions and held them pending the signing of the MIPTC-ATP contract. The reason for the delay in signing was supposed to be related to "legal issues" relating to the creation of Tennis Players Promotions B.V., a special Dutch entity to receive, invest, hold and distribute the deferred compensation funds received.

At the January 25-28, 1988 MTC Melbourne Meeting, Ron Bookman, Deputy Executive Director of ATP, said "that the final technical and legal details were near completion." In good faith, the MTC had already begun collection of the required contributions for the ATP Deferred Compensation Plan from all 1988 Grand Prix tournaments.[725] At the March 17-20, 1988, MTC Miami Meeting, Ron Bookman again reported that the final contract was nearly completed "subject to the final legal and technical details."[726]

On June 18, Dick Barovick, counsel for ATP "advised that the MTC/ATP contract was completed except for certain legal and technical details and would be submitted to the MTC for approval as soon as possible."[727]

At the time of the August MTC New York Meeting in New York, the ITF Representatives and the Tournament Representatives were unaware of any problem relating to the signing of the "agreed" MTC-ATP 1988-1992 Contract. The fact that it was not yet signed was just a pending Crisis No. 31, which would soon be superseded by Crisis No. 32: Coup D' État: The Final Crisis and the end of the MTC.

Crisis No. 30, Part IV: 1988 Volvo, ProServ, IMG Lawsuit Conclusion and Crisis No. 32: Coup D' État: The Final Crisis Occurred Simultaneously in 1988

Lawsuit Discovery Continues During 1988

During 1988, the massive number of documents being produced by the parties in the Volvo, ProServ, IMG lawsuit continued pursuant to the agreed confidentiality order.

2nd Circuit Court of Appeals Reversing Dismissal of First Amended Complaint: February 8, 1988

The Plaintiffs appeal of the dismissal of the Volvo, ProServ, IMG Complaint by District Court Judge Duffy was heard and determined by the 2nd Circuit Court of Appeals. The Appeal was argued on October 20, 1987, and decided on February 8, 1988.[728] The Court's Opinion said: *"We conclude that the district court erred by granting the motion to dismiss on grounds neither raised nor briefed by the parties."* The Opinion concluded that the *allegations of the Amended Complaint satisfied various technical requirements for anti-trust claims, but then said: "We express no opinion at this time as to whether appellees' conduct should be condemned as per se unlawful or, instead, should be analyzed under the Rule of Reason.... Moreover, we recognize that professional sporting events cannot exist unless the producers of such events agree to cooperate with one another to a certain extent, and that the antitrust laws do not condemn such agreements when coordination is essential if the activity is to be carried out at all." "Thus, on remand, the district court should carefully consider whatever arguments appellees may offer in support of their practices relating to player compensation before deciding whether the per se rule or the Rule of Reason should apply."*

Effect of 2nd Circuit Reversal and the Rule of Reason

While the 2nd Circuit reversed the dismissal of the Plaintiffs' claims, it decided nothing because it was only dealing with the "allegations" in the complaint which were subject to evidentiary proof at the eventual trial and it purposely did not deal with the most certain applicability of the Rule of Reason to the administration and rules of the MTC.

I do not pretend to understand the nuances of the Rule of Reason, but I understand that the Rule of Reason is generally applicable to anti-trust claims involving sporting bodies and that it requires a careful balancing of the pro-competitive aspects of various rules and practices with their likely harmful effects, if any, to determine if there is or is not an anti-trust violation. In other words, a "reasonable" restriction would not be a violation whereas an "unreasonable" restriction would be a violation. That was the essence of the legal opinion we received from Roy Reardon on the Rule of Reason and its applicability to the rules of the Council. Reardon, our attorney, was an accomplished anti-trust lawyer, so we would have been well represented at trial.

Without the assurance of specific dates for tournaments, specific classification of tournaments, limitation on the number of Super Series and numbers of other tournaments based on the number of tournaments that the players were willing to support and the specified prize money limits and distribution formulas, the tournaments would have not been able to continue to raise prize money for players, build tennis stadia, etc. Without the prize money minimums and the Grand Prix Bonus Pool, the professional tennis players would not have agreed to the player commitment rules and without the player commitment rules the tournaments would not have agreed to pay the prize money and Bonus Pool contributions. Without some reasonable restrictions on special events, the tournaments could not afford to put up the prize money and Bonus Pool money for players.

It was always my opinion that a fair application of the Rule of Reason would find that the rules of the MIPTC adopted over a period of years with the participation of the ITF, the ATP and the tournaments, would find them to be reasonable and not a violation of any anti-trust laws. On the other hand, I did not see how ProServ and IMG, with their new friend Volvo, could possibly justify their misuse of their monopoly power obtained from representing players and owning and managing the tournaments, while also staging special events against tournaments with which they were not involved.

Nevertheless, the ultimate outcome of this case, like all cases, was uncertain and therefore dangerous for all parties. What was certain was that it would be expensive for all parties to prosecute this case to trial and at trial it was quite possible that a lot of embarrassing information would be entered into evidence for the application of the Rule of Reason. All parties could also anticipate the cost of the probable additional appeals that would follow any trial. I was extremely glad we had insurance coverage; at least we were not intimidated by the cost of defense.

District Court Dismissal of Counterclaims
May 18, 1988

Likewise, to the utter surprise of all the parties to the Volvo lawsuit, Judge Kevin Thomas Duffy, on May 18, 1988, without notice to anyone, issued an Order saying: "counterclaims 1 through 4, 6, 13 and 14 are dismissed. Counterclaims 5 and 7 through 12 are dismissed with leave to replead granted." That effectively gutted our Counterclaim case.[729]

The Defendants and Counterclaimants (us) likewise appealed to the 2nd Circuit Court of Appeals. We were anticipating a similar reversal of Judge Duffy's 2nd hasty and defective dismissal. We believed that Judge Duffy was just intent on trying to get rid of our case.

Meanwhile, lots of interesting documents were being produced by Volvo, ProServ and IMG. I was told numerous times that Mark McCormack realized that he had made a mistake letting Donald Dell talk him into joining the Volvo lawsuit, but like all of us, he and his companies could not be removed from its entanglement in the lawsuit in which McCormack was now also an individual party as were Dell and Benton. So far, the only deposition taken was in 1985, of John Martin.

ATP/NATD Proposal for
Grand Prix Marketing for their (not the MTC's) Account

Sometime before the June meeting of the MIPTC in London, I received a visit in New York by Hamilton Jordan and Charlie Pasarell in which they sought my approval for ATP to be the marketing agent for the Grand Prix for the North American tournaments (NATD), obviously to seek to make money for the ATP and the NATD. I had to explain to them that I had no authority to approve such a proposal as it could only be done by the MTC. I was the COO and not the CEO of the MTC. They seemed to be upset that I could not approve their request. I further told them, I did not see how one part of the MTC could sell the assets of the MTC for their own account without the approval of the other parts of the MTC. Roy Reardon, after discussing the ATP-North American tournaments proposal, provided me with a written legal opinion dated June 23, 1988, to that effect.[730]

Disastrous Personal Relationship Between
Hamilton Jordan and Philippe Chatrier

At some point I learned that Hamilton Jordan had a sincere and serious personal dislike of Philippe Chatrier. It was so severe he almost did not want to be in Philippe's presence. I had no idea what could possibly have caused that but I along with a few others finally persuaded Hamilton to have a one-on-one lunch with Philippe in the hopes that the situation could be salvaged. Well it didn't and if anything, the situation got worse. Since Hamilton had no background in professional tennis he probably did not know and certainly did not appreciate Philippe's long history of support for the ATP and the players inside of the ITF. I think that Philippe probably resented the fact that Hamilton had no background and knowledge about the Sport of Tennis which somehow led Hamilton to consider Philippe to be an arrogant Frenchman. After lunch on June 17, Hamilton Jordan handed me a personal handwritten note and summarily departed the Council meeting. In the note, he apologized for leaving, but said something to the effect that he considered the MTC to be a flawed organization and that he was going to withdraw from it. *There was absolutely nothing I could do about that.*

Tim Smith Hired

During the summer, Hamilton Jordan hired Tim Smith, former Deputy Commissioner and Chief Operating Office of the PGA Tour, as a consultant "to the ATP on organization and marketing strategy." Hamilton had no background in tennis but he was enamored by the PGA Tour organization. "Our members and others who are closely involved in professional tennis have long admired the job done by the PGA Tour in structuring and promoting tournament golf," Jordan said in a press release. "We are fortunate to obtain someone of Tim Smith's experience and credibility in helping to advise us and formulate the ATP's long-range strategy for the future."[731] *The employment of Tim Smith signaled that a problem was brewing with Hamilton and the ATP.*

Settlement Negotiations

I had become of the opinion that the lawsuit was not going to accomplish anything as had many of the Plaintiffs. Between January 6 and August 25, 1988, there were lots of meetings to discuss the possible settlement of the case. In consultation with Jerry Solomon and Ivan Blumberg of ProServ, on August 16, I prepared drafts of a revised settlement agreement that upheld the Council rule prohibiting player agents from owning, defacto owning or managing tournaments, but permitted them to be commission agents for the sale of sponsorship, merchandising and television rights.

My Wedding August 23, 1988

I married my lovely new wife, Karen Scott of Sydney, Australia, on August 23, at the River Club on East 52nd Street in Manhattan. Karen had been the Managing Director of Donald Dell's ProServ management company in Australia for eight years managing the ProServ players, ProServ tournaments and exhibitions in Australia and Asia and ProServ's representation of Volvo, the sponsor of the Volvo Grand Prix and Volvo Masters from 1980-1984. Previously Karen has been the Tournament Manager for the Australian Open in 1978 and 1979, and she was then the only female to ever run a Grand Slam tournament. She had resigned from ProServ and was immigrating to the USA to marry me.

Happer-Scott Wedding, August 23, 1988
LR Bill Babcock, Pam Shriver, Marshall Happer, Karen Scott Happer, Gene Scott and Sara Fornaciari

At that moment, the Volvo, ProServ and IMG major anti-trust lawsuit against the MTC, and also against Philippe Chatrier, the former MTC Chairman, and me personally was pending. I have to say it is very unpleasant to personally be sued by a multi-billion-dollar company for doing my job. Karen and I both were scheduled to be witnesses if the case went to trial. She would be a witness for ProServ, and I was, of course, a major witness for the MTC and a personal defendant in the case. However, we were then engaged in settlement discussions and were close to a *possible* settlement of this complicated and expensive lawsuit.

On account of the adversarial relationship between ProServ and the MTC and me, professionally, we kept our relationship secret until we decided to get married. *Some people still say that this was the only secret ever kept in tennis.* It is not difficult to imagine the surprise reaction I received when I personally notified the members of the MTC of our relationship and planned wedding or the reaction Karen received from her bosses at ProServ. Donald Dell, Karen's former boss was more than a little perturbed when he found out Karen was going to marry me since he considered me to be an "enemy" of ProServ. He was, of course, also suing me personally and we were suing him and Mark McCormack of IMG personally as well.

Soon everyone in the tennis world accepted and supported our decision and wedding plans as we all were able to separate business issues from personal issues.

However, when Donald called Karen to offer to give her away at our wedding, we politely declined as I remarked to her at the time: "I am not ready to turn my back on Donald!" For our wedding reception at the River Club, we invited all the members of the MTC

Happer-Scott Wedding,
August 23, 1988
Ilie Nastase breaks in bridal dance
with Karen Scott Happer

and everyone from ProServ, plus officers of ATP, IMG, Advantage International and the USTA. We intended to have and actually did have one happy night for all the professionals in the game who were available in New York City at that time, in spite of the competing agendas and the pending lawsuit. Karen's bridesmaids were her close friends, Sara Fornaciari of ProServ and JoAnn Cella, Director of Women's Tennis for the USTA. Attendees included Philippe Chatrier, David Markin and Ray Moore of the MTC, Roy Reardon, the MTC's Legal Counsel, Gene Scott, ProServ's Donald Dell, Ray Benton, Jerry Solomon, Ivan Blumberg and Heather MacLachlan, IMG's Bob Kain (Mark McCormack had planned to attend and could not make it because of an unexpected flight delay), Frank Craighill, Lee Fentress and Peter Lawler from Advantage International, Gordon Jorgenson, President of the USTA and Marylyn and Ed Fernberger of Philadelphia plus a lot of old friends from North Carolina and Australia.

Karen had also invited her friend, Alexandria Nastase and her husband, Ilie, the former No. 1 ranked player in the world. Ilie is one of the funniest and nicest of the great professional players personally, but more than a nightmare on the court. As part of my job as MTC Administrator, I had been required to fine and suspend Ilie who was then in the twilight of his career numerous times for on-court misconduct. So, to everyone's surprise, as I began my bridal first dance with Karen, Ilie cut in and finished the dance with her with his joking remark, we both fondly remember: "This is one thing you can't fine me for M***F***". Everyone had a great time at our wedding reception as we had great food, great music and lots of Australian beer and wine. After our wedding on August 23, we did not have time for any honeymoon as the U.S. Open was about to begin and I had MTC meetings scheduled for August 26-29 in Manhattan. *I had no idea what was about to happen to the MTC and to the governance of men's professional tennis.*

Lawsuit Settlement Almost Agreed

On August 25 (two days after my wedding), I met in New York with Ray Moore (MTC Chairman), Ivan Blumberg, Jerry Solomon and Bill Babcock to discuss settlement. This meeting lasted all day and at the end of the day we were in general agreement on a settlement agreement draft *except for the mandatory pooling of television rights*. I prepared another revision of the draft settlement agreement dated August 25. We agreed to meet for one hour at 8:00 am on August 26, just prior to the beginning of the MTC meeting to try to finish the television issues.

Confidential Pre-War Telephone Call

After meeting all day on August 25 with Ray Moore relative to the settlement of the lawsuit, on the evening of August 25, Ray telephoned to inform me of ATP's intention to withdraw from the MTC on condition that I maintain it in confidence until he informed the MTC on August 27 during the August 26-29 schedule MTC meeting. Also, before the meeting, Hamilton Jordan had delivered to me a personal and confidential letter[732]: "Finally, on a personal note, I regret that this difficult decision that I have reached on behalf of the players will probably put you and I on a collision course. I have never doubted for a minute your good intentions for the game. I hope that you will not doubt my motivations which are heartfelt and sincere. While some will be tempted to think that my decision is only a reaction to being rebuffed by the Council on our marketing plans, please know that this was just another good example of the problem that we must now address. Marshall, you and I agree that authority and responsibility in the game must be centralized. You think that centralization can *only* be achieved under the umbrella of the MTC. I think it can only the achieved with the adequate *player representation and support* which the current system does not enjoy." Hamilton and I also had a personal telephone call.

August 26

On August 26, I again revised the draft settlement agreement and I met for one hour with Ray Moore, Jerry Solomon, Ivan Blumberg and Bill Babcock to discuss the final television pooling issues. *We were literally about one hour away from reaching an agreed settlement of the lawsuit.* While I could not tell Solomon and Blumberg the problem, I made sure that nothing further was then accomplished, and we concluded the meeting at 9:00 am just prior to the beginning of the MTC meeting. When the Council meeting began, I reported on the status of the settlement discussions to the Council and distributed and reviewed a marked up draft settlement agreement.

Hamilton had prepared a seven-page document entitled "Tennis at the Crossroads" to support his position for the ATP:

Tennis at the Crossroads

A Critique of the Opportunities and Problems Facing Men's Professional Tennis

Prepared by The Association of Tennis Professionals

Introduction

"It appears to us that men's professional tennis is at the crossroads. Those people with responsibility for the current 'system' must address a variety of major issues in the next few months that will have a long-term impact on the nature and scope of our sport. As the players are the central, indispensable element of the professional game, no group has a greater stake in the outcome nor a greater responsibility to provide the leadership in addressing these problems.

Some of the questions to be addressed are: (i) Will the Council continue to add tournaments to an already crowded global calendar? Will the schedule be 'streamlined' or will professional tennis continue to be the only major sport in the world without even a brief off-season? (ii) Will professional tennis be centrally marketed by one entity or will we continue to be the only major professional sport in the world that has no circuit marketing? (iii) Will the suit between the Men's Tennis Council, two management companies and a sponsor be settled, or will the image of our sport continue to be tarnished by court battles and lawsuits? (iv) Should the television rights of the Grand Prix tournaments be pooled? If so, how and by whom? Will the Grand Slams agree to contribute their television rights, or any portion thereof, to that pool?

Simply put, will tennis 'get its act together' and become a well-organized modern professional sport, or are we going to continue to be a highly fragmented, poorly organized sport that fails to realize its tremendous potential around the world? Properly addressed, these and other questions can be resolved in favor of a stronger game and system. Ignored, we must fear an eventual erosion of popular support for our sport as tennis competes in an increasingly competitive global sports and entertainment marketplace.

Unfortunately, the recent history of the Men's Tennis Council – of which we are an integral and important part – in addressing these basic problems is not good. Despite the best intentions and efforts of the Council and its membership, these basic questions persist. We are not confident that the present system can or will resolve these issues in a manner that earns the full support of the various constituencies represented on the Council. As this critique is largely an exercise in examining the problems facing professional tennis and the Council's role in addressing them, it is necessary first that we put this into historical context through a review of the accomplishments since the advent of 'open tennis' in 1968.

Our Progress

Since the advent of 'open tennis in 1968, the professional game has prospered by any objective standard.

(i) The professional game is well established. (ii) A system of rules for governing the sport – including a Code of Conduct and a drug testing program advocated and supported by the players – has evolved and is widely accepted by every element of the game. (iii) A system for sanctioning and scheduling tournaments (imperfect as it is) is in place as is a system for administering the Nabisco Grand Prix. (iv) A system of tournaments (which comprise the Nabisco Grand Prix) is well established and managed by a sophisticated group of sports administrators and entrepreneurs. (v) Revenues for the tournaments and the players has increased at a good pace. (vi) The official game has achieved both integrity and credibility under the leadership of Marshall Happer and through the development of a professional officiating program that is supported by the players. (vii) The popularity of our sport – spearheaded by the professional game – has spread throughout the world. (viii) The Grand Slams, the pillars of our sport, have earned a special place as global sporting events viewed and admired around the world by millions of fans. (ix) Professional tennis has made enormous strides around the world, gaining new popular support in Europe, Asia and Australia in recent years. (x) Critical to the success and progress of tennis in every respect, the players and the Association of Tennis Professionals has been loyal to and supportive of the system.

It is one of the many paradoxes of our sport that despite this overall progress, almost every element of the professional game today – the tournaments, the players and many sponsors – is broadly dissatisfied with our current system.

Our Problems

1. <u>Professional Tennis is Not Well Organized.</u> The great appeal of professional tennis is that it is an exciting international sport played on different surfaces on every continent. Our inherent weakness is that our sport is organized in a way that defies public understanding. Who runs professional tennis? Is it the MTC or the ITF or the ATP or the WCT or the USTA or the WITA? What is the official game? Is it the Davis Cup or the AT&T Challenge or the Grand Slams or the tournament in my city? What is important

– the ATP computer points or Nabisco Grand Prix Points or bonus pool points? Most importantly, how well does the governing body (the Men's Tennis Council) manage this international sport? In the opinion of the players, many tournament directors and many sponsors, *not very well.* It is not the fault of any particular individual or constituency – the inherent weakness of our system is the lack of a central structure.

2.   <u>Because Professional Tennis is Poorly Organized and Confusing to the Sports Consumer, It has not Realized its Potential.</u> For the very reason that sports consumers have to sort through the 'alphabet soup' of professional tennis to try to understand the 'official game', companies looking to invest sports marketing dollars are often confused by professional tennis and discouraged by the fragmentation. If I sponsor an event, which players do I get? If I want to sponsor a season-long promotion covering several events, or all events, to whom do I go? Must I go through a player agent? Am I prohibited from going through a player agent? What role does the ATP have?

The demographics of professional tennis are excellent for those companies wanting to reach certain target groups, and some companies have tolerated the fragmentation and found a way to make tennis work through a series of small direct investments in tournaments and players. But our sport – as currently organized – discourages overall investment and our single largest sponsor (Nabisco) is leaving, sending a signal to large companies around the world that tennis not a good buy. The condition of tennis today is not bad – it is simply that with proper organization and promotion, the overall administration, economic condition and image of our sport could be greatly enhanced.

3.   <u>No One Markets The Professional Circuit.</u> No one markets the professional tennis circuit. We are the only major professional sport in the world that does not have circuit marketing which packages the 'official game' for maximum exposure and sponsorship dollars. We are also the only major sport in the world that does not sell its sport to the consumer. Hundreds of millions of dollars are poured into product advertising but no one markets the circuit or the game to the sports consumer. Many attribute the growth of golf around the world to the fact that millions of dollars have been spent selling the game and values of golf to the sports consumers.

To its credit, the Men's Tennis Council – reflecting its concern over the departure of Nabisco as the circuit sponsor in 1990 and the resulting revenue shortfall – has focused in the past few months on marketing the game through a pooling of television rights. Unfortunately, this has been in reaction to short term problems instead of recognition of a basic need of a modern international sport. Our fragmented system makes the prospects of effective circuit marketing through the Council structure unlikely.

4.   <u>The Players Must Assume More Responsibility for their Game.</u> The players – due in part to the feeling of alienation from a system over which they have so little

control – must assume greater responsibility for every area of the game. We must hone our commitments to the tournaments and more actively support the tournaments and their sponsors. We must become more directly involved in the promotion of our sport. We must foster a more cooperative relationship between the players and the working press. If we are not generally available and accessible to the media, we undermine the coverage of our sport and contribute to an image of our players that is not attractive. *We must in short, produce a better informed, more responsible player who understands and accepts his obligations to the game and to the system.*

The ATP recognizes its responsibility on behalf of the players to take a leadership role in educating the players. Two new programs have been developed for this purpose. Our 'Player Services Program' which was initiated this summer at several tournaments is dedicated to the direct support and promotion of the individual tournaments and its sponsors. The ATP University – which will be mandatory for all new members of the ATP – will educate our young players about the off-court game: the economics of the tournaments, how to deal with the media; how to handle their finances; life on the tour; etc. Our responsibilities and obligations to the game are clear to us and will be met.

5.   <u>The Players are not Fairly Represented in the Current System.</u> Professional tennis players are in a weaker relative position in their sport than professional athletes in any other major sport. In some sports (like golf), the players' organization has responsibility for regulating the sport, sanctioning the tournaments, disciplining the players and marketing the circuit. At worst, players in most team sports have a labor-management relationship.

In professional tennis, the players are three of nine votes on the Council. The players are the one indispensable element of the sport and are the part of the game most directly affected by the decisions of the Council on format and schedule, yet they have only one-third of the votes in *their* sport. The result is that the players feel alienated from 'the system' and lack confidence that their voice has been heard on tennis issues which affect their livelihoods and careers. Without a strong central organization in which players feel a real involvement and stake, it is not surprising that some leading players have adopted a 'go-it-alone' attitude, with minimal or grudging support of the Grand Prix, passive involvement with the ATP and alienation from the Council. The current system is simply not fair to the players. We will no longer be satisfied to be mere 'junior partners' in running *our* sport. By freezing the players out of any meaningful responsibility, the administration, promotion and structure of the game is less effective for everyone: contestants, sponsors, media and fans alike.

6.   <u>The International Tennis Federation has Disproportionate Influence in the Current System.</u> The International Tennis Federation is the father of our sport and deserves the respect of the tennis world for its contribution to the amateur and

professional game. The Grand Slams are the 'crown jewels' of our sport; the Davis Cup has earned a special place in the 'sports world' and the ITF provided strong leadership in establishing tennis as an official sport in the 1988 Olympics. Yet, their historic and current contribution to our game should *not* give the ITF the privileged position and weight in the official system that they enjoy today.

The ITF has three of the nine seats on the Council which governs the official circuit. And although they sit on the Council, the ITF does *not* submit those elements of the sport in their domain – the Grand Slams and the Davis Cup – to the same authority and judgment that governs every other professional tournament. The Grand Slams participate in our system on their own terms, scheduling their tournaments whenever they choose and selecting which regulations they will or will not follow. In the past year, there have been striking contradictions in what the ITF representatives on the Council have demanded of the non-Grand Slam tournaments as opposed to what they themselves were willing to do.

(i)   The ITF representatives on the Council were the strongest advocates of limiting the role of management companies in the operation of tournaments, yet, they refused to terminate the relationship that several of the Grand Slams have with these same companies.

(ii)   The ITF representatives on the Council were strong supporters of efforts to pool the television rights of the Grand Prix tournaments. Yet, when it was suggested that they might contribute *some* of their rights to greatly strengthen that pool, they reacted negatively and with indignation.

(iii)   The ITF has always strongly supported the enforcement of player commitments and the right of the Administrator to designate players to tournaments that lack representative fields. Yet, when some top players were committed to play tournaments that conflicted with the 1988 Olympics, the ITF took the leadership in getting these players released from their commitments.

There is certainly nothing wrong about what the ITF representatives have done as they were simply advocating their own interests just as the other constituencies on the Council pursue their interests, but these examples illustrate that the ITF interests and needs differ so greatly from the non-Grand Slam tournaments that it calls into question the fairness of their role on the Council equal to that of the players and the non-Grand Slam tournament directors.

7.   <u>Other Problems.</u> *The role of the management companies in our sport should be better defined.* We believe that they have a role to play in the professional game and a contribution to make. We also believe that their role is excessive in some areas and should be limited. They have a right to make a profit just as others do in a professional sport. We believe that some way can be found for the management companies to

contribute to and support 'the system' while allowing these companies and their clients (our top players) economic opportunities outside of 'the system' that are not disruptive.

The entire system is excessively dependent on a handful of top players. Because we have not effectively marketed the game and our top 100-200 players as 'the best in the world', the entire system – and particularly the tournaments – are dependent on a few very top players to service an expanding number of tournaments. This problem is manifest in the crowded schedule and is the result of not having a strong, centralized system.

The 'super series' tournaments – the cornerstones of the system – have the most at risk and are vulnerable to factors beyond their control. Exhibitions, the Olympics, changes in the Davis Cup schedule, player injuries and outright violations of player commitments deny the tournaments the predictability and stability they need and deserve. A better system would provide the tournaments a multi-year schedule and format.

A bias against non-American tournaments exists in the system today. Because the United States was the dominant tennis market for so long and because so many of the organizations (the ATP and the MTC) are located in the USA and staffed by Americans, non-American tournaments do not always receive equal treatment and consideration. The booming tennis markets – particularly Europe and Australia – deserve to be recognized and judged fairly.

Tennis should have a stronger identification with charity. Association with charities are attractive to the fans and to the sponsors and increase volunteer support. Most importantly, a professional sport generating millions of dollars should invest some of its proceeds in worthwhile projects in the communities which support our game.

Summary

The Men's Tennis Council is struggling now to deal with these problems that are the consequence of a poorly organized, fragmented system. The Council is seeking – in our opinion – short-term piecemeal solutions to problems that demand a major reorganization of the official game and the system. The players do not believe that the Men's Tennis Council – as presently constituted – is capable of the bold leadership and structural change necessary to make global professional tennis a truly modern, well-organized sport.

There are three options for the players. First, we can support the current system. This is totally unacceptable to us. Secondly, we could support a new, reorganized Council which gives players a voice and responsibility in the system commensurate with their contribution to the sport. Finally, if the changes that we desire in the structure of the Council are not accomplished, we could seriously consider the organization of an ATP international circuit in

1990 in conjunction with the tournament directors who share our hopes for the game. While we await a formal response from the Council, we will be examining our options through a series of discussions with our players, the tournament directors, sponsors and others. We will make our final decisions and announce our plans by early December. Whatever our ultimate decision, in fairness to those with a need to plan for the future, it is our firm intention to honor our commitments to the Council and to the Nabisco Grand Prix through 1989. Whatever system we support for 1990 will be predicated on our membership honoring their player commitments to the tournaments in 1989."

My Immediate Observation: A Big Mistake

I had just spent almost eight years trying to keep the Grand Slams in the Grand Prix, so I told both Ray and Hamilton that I considered it to be a huge mistake to throw them out. In 1988, the Grand Slams, as part of the Nabisco Grand Prix, were played under the MTC Tournament Regulations and the MTC Code of Conduct upon which the players had a lot of influence – especially with the players' current 6-3 voting majority. In addition to losing the players' influence on the rules for the Grand Slams and losing having the Grand Slams under the governance of the MTC, which had the involvement of the players, the ATP would be losing their significant financial contributions. In 1988, the Grand Slams were contributing $600,000 to the Bonus Pool, $120,000 to ATP prize money, $525,000 to the ATP deferred compensation and $100,000 to MTC administration. Further, requiring the needed player commitment as a condition of participation in the Grand Slams provided the MTC, as the governing body, its most important leverage over the players for support of the tournament game. Without the Grand Slams, the tournaments would not be able to stand up to the players when they were unreasonable. Without the Grand Slams, the ATP Tour would have great difficulty competing against an ITF-Grand Slam competing tour or a WCT Tour, whose players would not have to also commit to the ATP tour to play in the Grand Slams. *I believed giving all that up was a big mistake.*

Nevertheless, as the MTC meeting began on August 26, I was braced for all hell to break loose, and it did. I was faced with having three members of the Council making demands of the other six members of the Council, which, if not agreed, threatened the existence of the Council. I was convinced that the MTC was now a valuable institution and I was disappointed that it might be destroyed. I also had just signed a new 5 year employment contract and a new 12-year lease for new Manhattan office space and still had some new furniture on order for delivery. *All I could do at the meeting was listen and take the minutes as my board members began a profoundly serious internal struggle – essentially a "Coup D' État."*

August 26-29 MTC New York Meeting

Marty Davis Approved as Proxy for Hamilton Jordan

On August 26 at the beginning of the MTC meeting,[733] Ray Moore requested and the Council agreed that Marty Davis could "vote on behalf of" Hamilton during the meeting.

The Offer Than Could Never Be Accepted

On August 27, at 9:00 am, the Player Representatives delivered to each member of the MTC the document entitled "Tennis at the Crossroads, a Critique of the Opportunities and Problems Facing Men's Professional Tennis" prepared by Hamilton Jordan. It was delivered with an offer that could not possibly be accepted by the ITF Representatives or the Grand Slams. "Mr. Moore stated that the Player Representatives and the ATP would not continue to participate and support the MTC in 1990 and the future under the current structure and that continuation would be agreed only if: (i) the Grand Slams agreed to pool their television rights, (ii) the ITF Representatives withdrew as voting members of the MTC with the ITF permitted as observers at MTC meetings, and (iii) the MTC was restructured to consist of four (4) ATP Representatives, three (3) Tournament Representatives and two (2) Independent Business Men." The players seemed to have forgotten that the Grand Slams and the ITF supported ATP's request for a "Players' Grand Slam", the Lipton International Players Tournament, begun in 1985, in return for the players not seeking the television rights income of the Grand Slams.

Thereafter, Ray Moore discussed briefly the issues presented in the ATP document. At 10:10 am, the meeting was recessed so that separate caucuses among the three constituencies could be held. At 2:00 pm, the meeting reconvened and a general discussion ensued with respect to the negotiations and status of the proposed MTC/ATP five year contract for 1988-1992, which should have begun on January 1, 1988, with the collection of ATP prize money and ATP deferred compensation from the tournaments by the MTC. I was directed to pay the ATP prize money collected for 1988 to the ATP. The contributions to the proposed ATP pension plan were to be held pending completion of the 1988-1992 MTC-ATP contract. At 3:30 pm, the meeting was recessed until Monday, August 29, at which time an additional discussion ensued with respect to the ATP position paper. During the discussion Moore stated that "well over 100 players have signed a document ...backing our present stance..., the 4-3-2 structure is negotiable... but the players will require at least 50% of the voting..." Thereafter, the MTC recessed for constituent caucuses for 15 minutes and then reconvened. At that time Philippe

Chatrier delivered a written statement entitled: 'Response of ITF Council Members to ATP Ultimatum.' Such Response 'rejected' the proposal presented by ATP on August 27.

The ITF response presented to the players on Saturday (August 27) called the document presented by the players, *Tennis at the Crossroads*, an "ultimatum and a blatant attempt to take over men's tennis." The response prepared by Buzzer Hadingham, Gordon Jorgensen, Philippe Chatrier and Brian Tobin stated, "If the present structure of the Men's Tennis Council (MTC) is no longer acceptable to ATP's management, then the undersigned representatives of Wimbledon, the U.S. Open, the French Championships and the Australian Open will ask the ITF, the governing body of tennis for the past 75 years, to form a new structure to carry on the worldwide work for the game."

I was sure this release was prepared by Mike Davies, the ITF General Manager, and that the response was exactly what Hamilton had predicted and hoped for as it gave him a way to go to the players and the media and claim that ATP's "perfectly reasonable" request for part of the television income of the Grand Slams and the removal of the ITF from representation on the MTC had been unfairly and "harshly rejected". Ray Moore then said that the ATP and the Player Representatives "are going to examine our options." The Council then deferred all proposed restructuring for 1990 pending further developments.[734]

Parking Lot Press Conference

After the meeting on August 29, Hamilton Jordan asked David Markin for permission to use the U.S. Open press room to present ATP's position to the media. When Markin later told me he had summarily refused the request, I told him that was a mistake and this is why: "In a surprise move, the ATP was blocked Monday from using the U.S. Open press facilities by USTA President Gordon Jorgensen and Vice President

Hamilton Jordan (1988 Press Conference)

David Markin," reported *International Tennis Weekly*[735]. "The ATP was seeking a forum to respond to the harsh statement issued by the Grand Slams rejecting the players' request for a greater voice." Said Jordan, "It is unbelievable that while our players are the featured attraction at the U.S. Open that the players' association was not given the simple privilege of meeting the international press."

The next day, Tuesday, August 30, in a really effective move, Hamilton Jordan staged a press conference in the parking lot outside the front gates of the U.S. Open. With Mats Wilander, Brad Gilbert, Tim Mayotte and Yannick Noah by his side, Hamilton Jordan, stated that the players will organize their own international tour in 1990 because of the inability of the Men's Tennis Council to effectively govern the men's game.[736]

On Thursday, September 1, the ITF and the Grand Slams held their press conference to respond in the U.S. Open press facilities. They said the ITF and the Grand Slams supported the governance by the MTC because it gave everyone who had a stake in the game a voice. In addition, they confirmed that "this power struggle for control of the men's game will probably not result in a lockout of players from the Grand Slam events."[737]

I had no idea what I was supposed to do or could do in this situation. "Happer, who is caught in the middle in his role as Administrator, said he would prefer not to comment on the situation at this time. Obviously, it will further complicate the M.T.C.'s own plans to restructure the game," wrote Peter Alfano in the *New York Times*[738].

Restructuring Proposed

Peter Alfano reported in the *New York Times*[739]: "Hamilton Jordan, the chief executive officer of the association, charged, however, that the Council was too fragmented, the members concerned only for their own interests and not the good of the game. Backed by the top ranked players in the world – among them Mats Wilander, Stefan Edberg, Yannick Noah, Boris Becker and John McEnroe – the association proposed that the Council be restructured to give the players more power. In a restructured Council, the association (ATP) would have a voting plurality and the federation, which runs the Grand Slams and Davis Cup and presides over Olympic tennis would be eliminated. 'The I.T.F. will not relinquish its rights,' Markin said."

I Had to Get Involved

I had a long talk with Roy Reardon who recommended that I get actively involved to try to save the MTC, so I did. On September 4, I prepared and sent to all members of the MTC, plus Hamilton Jordan, a document entitled "Issues for Discussion."

Chatrier Almost Conceded On September 9

I left the U.S. Open on Friday, September 9, to fly to Raleigh to attend an important event with my daughter. Just as the event was about to begin, I received a telephone call from Mike Davies (ITF General Manager) who was with Philippe Chatrier in New York. Mike read me a draft letter he had prepared at Philippe's request in which Philippe was conceding to the ATP the governance of men's professional tennis. *I was flabbergasted to put it mildly.* The ATP started the controversy on August 27, the ITF and the Grand Slams issued a unified rejection on August 27, and held a press conference on September 1 to explain their rejection. Now, just a few days later, Chatrier was offering to give up? That would mean the end of the institution of the MTC in just a few days without any meaningful discussion or thought. I implored Mike to ask Philippe to not send that letter and give me a chance to try to save the MTC. Mike was successful in stopping Philippe from giving up then. I would never be able to adequately explain to my daughter why I was late to her event.

Hamilton's Response

Hamilton responded to my September 4 suggestions for possibly resolving the issues between the ATP and the ITF. Hamilton said: "I want you to know that I have called an emergency meeting of the ATP Board for September 27th and 28th in San Francisco. At that time, we will make some final decisions about our plans for the future. As I told you in our telephone conversation on September 5th, we have had no choice but to proceed to make plans for our own tour in 1990 based on the harsh and negative public reaction of the ITF to our proposal…I believe that our San Francisco meeting will be the point of no return for the ATP. Beyond that point, our commitment to organizing our own tour in 1990 will be firm and irrevocable. Again, thank you for your good efforts on behalf of the ITF and the ATP to resolve these problems."[740]

ITF Tour in 1990?

To further incite the situation, Hamilton advised the ATP members that the ITF was planning a new ITF tour in 1990 saying in *International Tennis Weekly*[741]: "The ITF now controls amateur tennis, the Olympics, the Davis Cup and the Slams. Now, they are prepared to use their considerable resources and monies, (obtained) from professional tennis, to stop the players from starting their own tour." *While an ITF Tour was an option, I did not think it was then being considered. However, Hamilton used the threat of an ITF Tour to further his plan for a new ATP Tour and create more opposition to the ITF.*

My Call for an Urgent Meeting of MTC Members

On September 20, I sent a letter[742] via fax to all of the members of the MTC, plus Hamilton Jordan requesting an unofficial meeting of representatives of the various constituencies of the MTC at the MTC New York Office on October 4, beginning at 9:00 am to ascertain if any agreement could be reached between the Player Representatives, Tournament Representatives and ITF Representatives on behalf of all constituencies for a continuation of a unified sport and of the MTC after 1989. I said: "I have and will continue to offer suggestions to you for consideration, but only you can agree on a solution for these issues or determine that no solution is possible. If a solution is not found that is acceptable to everyone, then I assume that the MTC will be dissolved after 1989. If you feel that it will be necessary to have separate meetings of your constituent groups such as the ATP Board of Directors, ITF Committee of Management, Tournament Working Groups or others, I urge you to have them meet simultaneously or otherwise be available. *It is my request that each of you consider carefully the value of unity in professional tennis, including the important contributions that each of you make, and that your Representatives come to the meeting prepared to seek a good faith accommodation to achieve unity and correction of whatever flaws that exist in our current system.*"

My September 22 Discussion Alternatives

In preparation for the October 4 meeting on September 22, I sent a letter[743] to the members of the MTC and to Hamilton Jordan, containing suggested discussion alternatives for a possible unified governance with suggested fixes for a number of the perceived "flaws." I said: "On Tuesday, October 4, 1988, representatives of the various constituencies of the MTC will have an opportunity, *perhaps the last opportunity*, to find common ground so as to maintain a unified sport in 1990 and the future. I am hopeful that the enclosed information will be of some assistance to you.

"The current crisis in professional tennis begins with the Grand Prix Calendar which has proven increasingly unsatisfactory each year as political, legal, and individual business considerations have driven the MTC decision-making process rather than good planning. The structure of the MTC, while by no means unanswerable, has been incidental to the creation and resolution of the problems we now face together. These problems stem primarily from other causes and have been difficult to resolve while being fair to everyone. The time has now come to deal forthrightly with the critical issues and stop trying to be everything to everyone. No matter what restructuring, if any, is agreed for the future, the most important issues relate to the establishment of a sensible calendar and format for professional tennis that fairly balances the interests of the players, the tournaments and the national federations."

"I respectfully submit that some of the advantages of unity are as follows: (i) Professional Tennis from the Grand Prix down through the Satellites can be played under uniform rules that every constituency will understand and respect, i.e., one set of *Grand Prix Rules* and *Tournament Regulations*, one *Code of Conduct*, one recognized certification for officials, etc., (ii) All the major tournaments can be included and marketed together by one organization serving all interests. Professional tennis can obtain maximum cooperation in the scheduling of all major tournaments and other events such as the Davis Cup and World Team Cup, (iii) The huge financial contributions of the Grand Slams in Bonus Money, ATP Prize Money, Pension Funds, Administrative Fees, etc., as well as use of entertainment marquees can be retained and utilized for the benefit of a unified system, (iv) Those countries and governments that only recognize the ITF as the governing body for men's professional tennis will continue to recognize the MTC on behalf of all constituents, (v) We can avoid another lawsuit contesting ATP's ability to act as both labor and management so as to eliminate competitive circuits or events and (vi) The investment in the MTC of hundreds of thousands of dollars in furniture, equipment, recruiting and training of the 33 full-time employees and world-wide identification and good will can be maintained and improved instead of being discarded and replaced at great new expense to the constituents of the game.

"There has never been a more challenging time for professional tennis. In my opinion, the players are right in demanding a change. It does not however, follow that total destruction should be inflicted and fragmented circuits begun just to obtain change if all constituents acting responsibly can effectively address and correct the flaws within the system while preserving its achievements. It is my wish that all parties be flexible enough to see the value of unity and to make it work. I will be available to discuss any of these issues with any of you at your convenience."

Volvo Supports ATP Tour

On September 25, Volvo announced that it supported the proposed ATP Tour. Since Volvo was mad at the MTC and was suing the MTC, it was not surprising to me that Volvo would support a proposed new ATP Tour.[744]

October 4 Meeting

Attending my October 4 "unofficial" meeting in New York, were ITF: David Markin, ATP: Ray Moore, Hamilton Jordan, Bob Green, Jim McManus, Dick Barovic, Esquire, ATP Legal Counsel, and Tournaments: Graham Lovett (Rest of World), Charles Pasarell (North America), Franco Bartoni (Europe), Mike Cardoza, Esquire, North American Tournaments Legal Counsel, plus Bill Babcock, Assistant Administrator, Roy Reardon, MTC Legal Counsel and me.

The meeting began at 9:00 am and every possible issue was discussed in some detail at the meeting. Probably the most promising idea coming from the meeting was the possible establishment of a 50-50 Player-ITF committee to deal with Grand Slam matters and a 50-50 Player-Non-Grand Slam Tournament committee to deal with non-Grand Slam matters. Various alternatives for the breaking of ties were discussed. My suggestion that each of the Grand Slams provide a free two-week marquee for Grand Prix marketing was considered very valuable and important and David Markin promised to take that up with the Grand Slams and he said he thought it was "doable." Hamilton Jordan requested that a comprehensive proposal be provided in writing. Hamilton said that he was "proceeding on the hope that this works out, but he will also proceed on preparation of the 1990 tour." Eventually, even though the parties could not articulate the specifics of what might be agreed, I was asked to draft a proposal and submit it to all the parties by October 11, for review.

Near the end of the meeting, Hamilton inquired about the funds being collected by the MTC for the ATP deferred compensation plan which were agreed as part of the proposed new five-year MTC-ATP agreement. When David Markin said that his position was that "these funds were dependent upon an MTC/ATP five-year agreement that is no longer in effect," Hamilton sort of went ballistic and said that he wanted "to tell my Board the pension plan is in jeopardy." *You have to admire Hamilton's logic.* The MTC in good faith in reliance on an "agreed" new 1988-1992 contract with the ATP required and collected funds from the tournaments for a new ATP deferred compensation plan. The ATP was now refusing to execute the contract and was seeking to destroy the Council and get all the funds collected from the tournaments. *He was actually going to be successful!* The meeting ended at 4:15 pm and I provided 11 pages of detailed minutes of the meeting to all attendees.[745]

Hamilton Demands Deferred Compensation Funds

On October 9, Hamilton sent a letter[746] to the MTC demanding that the funds collected by the MTC for the ATP deferred compensation plan be delivered immediately to the Dutch BV that was the proposed administrator of the plan. He said: "We will not allow these monies to be utilized as potential leverage against us in the current dispute. The only way to avoid this happening is to have a clear understanding from the MTC on this subject in advance of any decision the ATP might make about return to the MTC or starting a new tour in 1990...I would like to know if it is the belief or intention of any member of the Council that our ATP fund should not receive these monies for either 1988 or 1989. I will ask the Chairman of the Council, Ray Moore, to request an immediate telex vote on this subject. Due to the significant influence that both our Administrator and General Counsel exert on the decisions of the Council, I would also like for both Marshall and Roy to express their opinion on this subject. If Roy has legal concerns about this, I would like for them to be stated now."

October 11 Drafts for a Proposed Solution Per the October 4 Meeting

On October 11, I sent to the members of the MTC drafts[747] based on the *positive* suggestions made on October 4 to hopefully settle the issues and provide for the continued unification of the game with the MTC. The drafts included a written agreement for 1988-1995 to settle all the issues between the parties (as "tentatively" agreed on October 4.) Without going into extensive detail, it contained the format of two classes of Super Series desired by ATP and just about everything ATP had suggested. It also provided for a continued nine-member Council, but with a 3-3 ITF/ATP Committee to decide together all Grand Slam matters with the Administrator who votes only in case of tie and a 3-3 Tournament/ATP Committee to decide all non-Grand Slam matters with the Administrator who votes only in case of a tie. All nine members of the Council would vote on all other matters. With Ray Moore as MTC Chairman, the Player Representatives were regularly winning all Council votes 6-3 so Hamilton Jordan's distressful claim for 50 percent of the voting power was disingenuous. Nevertheless, I proposed, with the blessing of David Markin, for the ITF and the Grand Slams to give the ATP 50 percent of the voting on all Grand Slam matters. In addition, I proposed, with Markin's blessing, that the Grand Slams would contribute: $30,000 each for ATP prize money for a total of $120,000 per year; $400,000 each for Bonus Pool for a total of $1,600,000 per year; A total of $525,000 per year for the ATP deferred compensation plan; and a free two-week entertainment marquee at each Grand Slam for circuit sponsors. In my fax transmittal, I said: "Needless to say, there are numerous issues and to the extent that I have not in these drafts solved them to everyone's satisfaction, I hope that I have at least raised all of the issues. I will await your review, questions, agreement, disagreement and suggestions for improvement. It is, of course, important that everyone analyze these documents carefully and let all members of the MTC know what changes are required."

October 13 London Meeting

Almost simultaneously with receipt of my October 11 proposed and what I believed were "tentatively agreed" settlement documents, on October 13, Hamilton Jordan, Ray Moore and Colin Dowdeswell met in London with Buzzer Hadingham and some members of the Wimbledon Committee to discuss the proposed 1990 ATP Tour.

Recently, Ray Moore re-confirmed to me that the ATP representatives left the meeting with a clear understanding that Wimbledon would not oppose a new proposed ATP Tour. If I had known that and that the Grand Slams would never be able to stand together as a group, I would have given up then and just gone fishing.

Tournament Representatives Did Not Agree

Graham Lovett, Franco Bartoni and Charles Pasarell disappointingly informed me that they did not agree with my October 11 proposal for settlement.[748] On October 25, I sent a copy of my October 11 draft compromise and proposed contract and other documents to all tournament directors.[749]

ATP Board Rejects Compromise

On October 27, I received a letter[750] from Hamilton Jordan informing me that the ATP Board had rejected the compromise proposal I prepared, dated October 11. Hamilton said: "First, there is a genuine appreciation of the efforts that you, your staff and the other members of the Council have made to accommodate the concerns that were originally expressed in our critique, 'Tennis at the Crossroads'. Despite the initial harsh, negative public reaction of the ITF to our analysis, we appreciate the time that the ITF generally and David Markin specifically has devoted to trying to find a way to resolve our differences. Secondly, all of the members of my Board, except one, believe that the proposal (My October 11 draft compromise) represents a considerable improvement for the players over the current system. But ultimately the ATP Board's reaction to this proposal was not a negative expression about the Council's efforts as much as it was a strong and unanimous endorsement for a new system. No one in professional tennis has spent as much time in the past ninety days as I have in meetings with a variety of players. The degree of alienation felt by the players from the current system is enormous. I think it is difficult if not impossible to restore player confidence in the current system."

Also, on October 27, Hamilton sent me a "Personal" letter[751]: "I know that you will be disappointed in the action of our Board in rejecting the tentative proposal. They made this decision without any advice or encouragement from me. However, I believe they made the correct decision. When the dust settles, I would like to come see you and have a candid conversation. I know that you think we have made a mistake and are not capable of organizing a better system. Only time will tell. No one should be surprised at our ultimate decision as we stated from the outset our desire to start our own tour."

Happer Response

On October 28, I responded to Hamilton's letter of rejection[752]: "Needless to say, I was disappointed with your decision since, at the meeting of the constituencies of the MTC on October 4 when the proposal was developed, you stated that it was 'very constructive and positive' and asked that I prepare a draft for presentation to the ATP Board...Hamilton, I recognize and appreciate the fact that you and the members of the ATP Board of Directors are sincere in wanting to bring about constructive change for the sport. At the same time, I also recognize and agree that there is a strong sense of alienation felt by many players towards the MTC and our system. In large part, the alienation of the top players has been caused by our efforts, mainly at the demand of ATP, to approve too many tournaments in a desire to create more and more player jobs and then to ask or demand that the top players support them. As you know, I have been more or less in the middle between the players, the tournaments and the ITF as constituents of the MTC as this disagreement has developed. I have heretofore stated that I agreed that improvements were necessary, and I have supported your efforts toward meaningful change. I cannot, however, support your present efforts because while your plan may seem good for ATP in the short term, it is, in my opinion, bad for the tournaments, national associations and the players in both the short term and the long term. The substantive changes that you may effect unilaterally, even if you are successful in taking over the game as you have proposed, are not significantly different from the changes you could effect within the MTC via compromise. In all likelihood, your actions will result, as indicated above, in more litigation and in the fragmentation of our sport and will lead to substantial chaos that is unnecessary.

"If it wasn't so serious, it might be humorous to consider that the biggest weakness of the MTC has been the approval of too many tournaments at the demand of the players to create more jobs. And today you want to disband the MTC and reduce the number of tournaments and player jobs. Another weakness of the MTC has been to try to be fair to all the tournaments and recognize their strong representation whereas today you want to totally eliminate the effective representation of the tournaments as well as the ITF. (The ATP proposal then was for a board of 4 ATP, 3 tournament representatives and 2 independent business men, which would effectively give total control to the ATP). I am going to ask the non-Player Representatives on the MTC to maintain an open mind with the hope that, next week at the November 2-3, 1988 meetings in London, you will change your position. I respectfully request you and the members of the ATP Board of Directors to reconsider this matter in an effort to find the best solution for our sport. Each constituent group has a significant contribution to make and the value of all those contributions can only be maximized by working together."

Hamilton Signing Players for 1990 ATP Tour

At this time, I still had no idea that Wimbledon may not be supporting the other three Grand Slams in opposition to the creation of a new ATP Tour. Meanwhile, Hamilton was signing players for a 1990 ATP Tour.[753]

Lawsuit Settlement Discussions Resumed on October 28

Eventually settlement discussions resumed and on October 28, when I received a draft Settlement Agreement dated October 26 from Ivan Blumberg represented as "approved: by all the plaintiffs." On November 1, I met with Ray Moore, Donald Dell, Ivan Blumberg and Bill Babcock in London (prior to the November 2-3 MTC London meeting). There was a general discussion of Ray Moore's status relative to representing the MTC in settlement discussions, but there was no discussion of the October 26 draft Settlement Agreement. At that time, I informed Ray Moore that I did not think it remotely proper for him to conduct or be involved in settlement negotiations. He was Chairman of the MTC, but he and Hamilton Jordan were leading the ATP to undermine and destroy the MTC and threating a new ATP Tour to replace the Grand Prix. On November 2, at the MTC meeting in London, I reported on the status of the settlement discussions and summarized the October 26 draft Settlement Agreement and the minor differences between the MTC position and the plaintiff's position. Thereafter, Ray Moore and the other Player Representatives (Weller Evans and Marty Davis) withdrew from the meeting.

MTC Meeting, London, November 2-3

Marty Davis Succeeds Hamilton Jordan

In November in London,[754] Ray Moore announced the resignation of Hamilton Jordan as a Player Representative and Marty Davis was elected to succeed him.

Report and Discussions

At the November MTC London meeting, I reported on the negotiations held on October 4 in New York to seek a compromise solution between the MTC and ATP, the provisions of the draft compromise agreement dated October 11 and its rejection by ATP. The members of the MTC discussed the various aspects of the situation and Ray Moore confirmed that ATP planned to go forward with an ATP Tour in 1990. Then, the Player Representatives withdrew from the meeting, declining to participate in any discussions relating to 1990 and the future. Jim Westhall, the tournament director of Stratton Mountain, and Jeff Mishkin, the legal counsel for the North American tournaments, were permitted to join the remainder of the meeting. The remaining members of the MTC discussed, in the absence of the Player Representatives, the current situation facing the MTC.

LTA-Wimbledon British Plan

In the midst of the discussion, Ron Presley said that "the Lawn Tennis Association of Great Britain and Wimbledon had worked on a proposed reorganization for professional tennis which they planned to present on Friday, November 4. Presley was asked to present that proposal to the meeting and he along with LTA Chief Executive Ian Peacock presented the general principles of a proposed "British Plan" which involved the possible division of the Grand Prix into three regional tours. Splitting the Grand Prix into three regional tours was neither feasible or of interest.

1990 Tournament Application Deadline Extended

After lunch on November 3, the MTC resumed discussions of a new format for the 1990 Grand Prix, but nothing could be agreed since the Player Representatives were not present and the Tournament Representatives refused to vote on any format for 1990. The tournament application deadline for 1990 was extended to December 31, 1988.

Europe Backs New ATP Tour

In November it was reported that Europe backed the proposed new ATP Tour.[755] The three biggest and most important tournaments in Europe outside the Grand Slams were Rome, owned by the Italian Tennis Federation, Hamburg owned by the German Tennis Federation, and Stockholm, owned by the Swedish Federation, all major members of the ITF. When Rome, Hamburg and Sweden deserted the ITF and agreed to go with the ATP Tour that pretty much forced the rest of Europe to do the same. Hamilton and Ray had carefully organized the proposed new ATP calendar to give Hamburg and Rome the prime dates in front of the French Open with no interference from the WCT Tournament of Champions and with only one small clay court tournament left in the United States in Charleston, SC.

November 7

On November 7, Ray Moore told me on the telephone that Hamilton Jordan has changed his proposal to now offer 50 percent voting rights to the tournaments on the proposed ATP Tour to begin in 1990. Ray said: *"For the record: I am desirous for a better tennis system in a restructured MTC. As that appears not to be attainable, I am committed to an ATP Tour in 1990. I will devote all of my energies in making the transition as smooth as possible, particularly the governance of the 1989 Grand Prix."*[756]

Happer Letter to Tournaments

On November 9, I wrote[757] to all of the proposed 1990 Grand Prix tournaments and said: "As I see it, you have three options: (i) Join together to operate the Grand Prix through the MTC and negotiate a solution as a single unit just as the players are doing; and/or (ii) Commence litigation to determine if the actions of ATP are legal and proper; or (iii) Capitulate and seek to join the ATP Tour…While it will be difficult and somewhat unpleasant to oppose ATP with respect to its proposed 'ATP Tour,' I am convinced that it will be better for the players and the tournaments in the long term if the tennis family stays together and by standing together you can achieve that result. If the ATP and the players begin to understand all that has already been offered to them by the tournaments and the ITF, and that continued cooperation and unified representation through the 'new and improved' MTC is the only demand, then I still believe we can all return to the table as partners rather than opponents."

Friction with Ray Moore

As you might imagine, I am the COO of the MTC and I am trying to save it from being destroyed, while at the same time Ray Moore is the CEO of the MTC and is leading its destruction. I wrote to Ray: "We are involved in an unbelievable professional and legal problem that will probably only get worse. Until otherwise instructed, I feel compelled as an employee of the institution of the MTC to seek to preserve the MTC and the Grand Prix. As Chairman and as a member of the MTC you have, in my view, a fiduciary duty to do the same. I have no idea how you can possibly justify the course you are on with that duty. I do not believe that you can decide that the MTC is to be dissolved at the end of 1989 and that as an employee of the MTC, I should just standby to 'make the transition as smooth as possible.' In any event, if that is to be the legal decision of the MTC, I would very much appreciate being so informed so that I can avoid all of the friction I am having with you and others in the sport as it is surely unpleasant. If on the other hand you are interested in a compromise solution to this crisis through a restructured MTC, and you can persuade ATP likewise, then you could find an agreement with the tournaments and the ITF."[758]

Buzzer Hadingham to the Rescue by Concorde

On November 9, Buzzer Hadingham and Ian Peacock traveled by Concorde and met 3½ hours with Hamilton Jordan in New York to present the LTA-Wimbledon British Plan for splitting the world into three areas: the American, the European and the Pacific (including Australia) which would each have its own circuit under an area commissioner. Buzzer reported that Hamilton said that this idea was even more revolutionary than he had in mind and that Hamilton said he would need time to examine it and then talk it over with the ATP Board while stressing that it might be difficult to get such an organization in place in time for 1990. Hamilton's strategic goal in his discussions with Buzzer was to keep Wimbledon from joining the other three Grand Slams to oppose the proposed new ATP Tour. To that end it was understandable that Hamilton would appear to maybe agree with what Buzzer was proposing when he had no intention of actually doing so. In a recent discussion with Ray Moore, he agreed with me that Hamilton Jordan was a masterful politician with the ability to leave a meeting with everyone thinking he was in complete agreement with them when it just wasn't so. I tried to no avail to get Hamilton to correct Buzzer's misunderstandings with him.[759]

November 10 Telephone Call with Ray Moore

On November 10, Ray Moore telephoned to see if I was available for a meeting with him and the Volvo lawsuit plaintiffs to discuss possible settlement issues on November 27. I told Ray that "I cannot understand your position in wanting to deal with the lawsuit and its possible settlement given your current position with respect to the MTC. I am advised by counsel that this is definitely inappropriate. Since August, you have refused to discuss any MTC business relating to 1990 and the future of the MTC. If we applied *your* standard to the Settlement Agreement proposed by the plaintiffs which includes a term of eight years into the future, it should be dealt with likewise. There should be some resolution of this issue prior to your conducting any further settlement discussions."[760]

November 15

On November 15, I wrote to the Grand Slam Chairmen[761]: "I am sure that each of you is aware of the fast-moving development with respect to the Grand Prix and the proposed '1990 ATP Tour.' There is *no chance* that ATP is going to consider anything other than its own tour unless forced to do so. Hamilton Jordan reconfirmed that position to me again last night. If ATP is successful with the '1990 ATP Tour,' the Grand Slams will not be part of the Tour and will become isolated, independent tournaments. In one last effort to try to bring ATP back to the negotiating table, I have prepared a format to compete if necessary, with the 'ATP Tour,' a copy of which is enclosed on a confidential basis. This format is based on the fact that the top players are not legally committed to the 'ATP Tour' and my belief that the Grand Prix under the enclosed format is more attractive to them."

Buzzer Rejects

On November 18, Buzzer Hadingham rejected my suggestion of a proposed ITF Tour to try to get ATP back to the bargaining table. Buzzer continued to believe that Hamilton would agree to the creation of a Men's International Tennis Board (MITB) consisting of four ATP members, two from the ITF and three from the Grand Slams, which would act as an umbrella organization responsible for liaison with an ATP Tour Board for the Grand Slams, Davis Cup and Olympics, matters of strategy and also decisions affecting the international game with meeting two to three times a year. *Hamilton Jordan never seriously considered this proposal.* Buzzer was still believing that if the Grand Slams supported the new ATP Tour and the dissolution of the MTC, that Hamilton Jordan and the ATP would agree to the creation of a new MITB above the new ATP Tour, which would have one token ITF member on its board. Hamilton Jordan and the ATP never agreed to this type of organization except maybe as a discussion group. *If I had not known it before, I now knew that Wimbledon was now clearly going to support the new ATP Tour, contrary to the positions of the other three Grand Slams.*

November 23: "War Will be Over in 10 Days"

On November 23, Ray Moore met with Roy Reardon and told him that ATP's "War" with the MTC and the ITF would be "all over in 10 days." I am quite sure that Reardon advised Moore that he had a conflict of interest and a violation of fiduciary duty to the MTC issue that made it inappropriate for him to be involved in the settlement of the Volvo lawsuit.

November 28

Dell Wanted to Save MTC

If you had to guess who became the biggest advocate for settling the Volvo lawsuit and "saving" the MTC, the last person you would guess would be my friend Donald Dell of ProServ. I remember his plea to me to please recommend the proposed settlement of the lawsuit so I can "take the gloves off" and work to stop the ATP Tour. On November 28, Donald telephoned me and asked me to specify what changes would be necessary to the Plaintiffs' October 26 draft settlement agreement to obtain my recommendation for approval. I told him I would consult with Roy Reardon and call him back. On November 29, I consulted with Roy and we agreed on changes to the October 26 draft that we could recommend to the MTC. I telephoned those changes to Ivan Blumberg in the morning. On the evening of November 29, Ivan telephoned me just prior to the ATP Awards Dinner to discuss a few changes and clarifications for the Settlement Agreement and stated that Jerry Solomon wanted to personally inform Ray Moore of the various positions on the proposed Settlement Agreement. Ivan faxed a revised Settlement Agreement to my office early on the morning of November 30.

New 1990 Grand Prix Format Proposal

After we finally got the terms Roy Reardon and I needed to recommend the draft settlement agreement to the MTC, Donald assigned Jerry Solomon and Ivan Blumberg to work with me to develop another proposal for a 1990 Grand Prix format that they thought might have a chance to compete with the proposed ATP Tour format for 1990. So, I spent a number of hours with Jerry and Ivan developing one last 1990 Grand Prix format to present to the MTC for competition to the proposed new ATP Tour.

MTC Meeting, New York, November 29 - December 1

Prior to the beginning of the November meeting,[762] Ray Moore informed me that he had talked with Jerry Solomon and was upset that I had conducted any settlement negotiations without him. I told him that I had received a draft Settlement Agreement and that the Plaintiffs had requested that it be considered as the first matter of business. He told me that he did not want it considered until the next day.

Fiduciary Duties of MTC Members Explained

On November 30, the nine members of the MTC met from approximately 9:00 am until Noon. At the meeting in executive session, Roy Reardon provided the members of the MTC with legal advice on their fiduciary duties to the MTC which concluded that the Player Representatives support of the proposed 1990 ATP Tour and the intended destruction of the MTC had violated their duties to the MTC and they should not be permitted to serve as members of the MTC. Reardon's opinion was articulated in his lengthy letter of November 16 to me which concluded with: "Legally, directors are fiduciaries of the corporation and its shareholders, and a corporation's directors and officers may not pursue personal endeavors that are inconsistent with their duty of undivided loyalty to the corporation. Until recently, the Player Representatives have been in the position of serving two masters – MTC and ATP. Since ATP has announced its clear intention to proceed with its own tour, and in so doing to appropriate MTC's pre-existing business opportunity, the Player Representatives (as evidenced by their statements at the recent Council meeting) have chosen to be dominated by ATP and to neglect their duty to MTC. No director who acted in this fashion would be allowed to remain on a corporation's board."

"To summarize, the issue is really quite simple; it is a matter of loyalty and duty. The Player Representatives, through ATP, have, at least since the U.S. Open, vigorously and selfishly appropriated to themselves the business opportunities of MTC, an organization to which they legally owe the most uncompromising honor and loyalty. Instead of scrupulously protecting MTC's interests, the Player Representatives have abandoned their duty to the Council, the tournaments and the ITF, all for ATP's own gain. In so doing, the players have disqualified themselves from further active participation in the decisions and activities of the Council which they have strived to undermine."[763]

Player Representatives Refuse to Withdraw Except as to 1990 Issues and Lawsuit Settlement

The three Player Representatives, Ray Moore, Weller Evans and Marty Davis, did not accept that they were disqualified to serve on the MTC as a result of the violation of their fiduciary duties to the MTC. However, they apparently finally received some legal advice and in a November 30 letter[764] said: "As you know, as of December 31, 1989, the Player Representatives and the ATP will cease to participate on the Council and the undersigned will withdraw therefrom. Beginning in 1990, ATP and its members intend to participate in a new men's professional tennis tour which will not involve the Council. Until such time, we intend to fully perform our obligations to the Council to the extent that those obligations are proper and consistent with our obligations to the players. In light of the above, we believe that it would be improper for the Council to make, or even to discuss making, any commitments beyond December 31, 1989, as has been previously suggested by you and others, which in any way may affect the ATP, its members and/ or the above-mentioned new tennis tour or which may be misleading to any third party, including the parties to the litigation referred to below. In the event that the Council makes any such commitments, the undersigned, the ATP, its members and the new tour will not be bound thereby. Please be advised that in the event there are any discussions or votes at today's Council meeting or any subsequent meetings of the Council which relate in any way to Council actions or commitments after December 31, 1989, including, without limitation, discussions or votes relating to the resolution of the litigation entitled *Volvo North America Corporation, at al., v. Men's International Professional Tennis Council, et al., Index No. 85 Civ. 2959 (KTD)*, we shall withdraw, and thereby shall be deemed to have withdrawn, from such Council meetings for all purposes."

1990 Format

Thereafter, the remaining six members began discussing what they wanted to do with respect to a 1990 Grand Prix format and after some discussion I was asked to present another revision of the 1990 format for their consideration. After a lengthy discussion it was clear that the three ITF Representatives wanted to adopt the new proposed format. Jim Westhall, who was sitting in for Charles Pasarell, wanted it adopted so the North American tournaments could have an alternative but was afraid to vote. Franco Bartoni and Graham Lovett did not want to consider any format or adopt anything that would jeopardize their positions with the ATP. After the matter was discussed and upon motion duly made and seconded, the proposal that I had developed with Jerry Solomon and Ivan Blumberg of ProServ was adopted. Jim Westhall abstained, and Bartoni and Lovett asked to be recorded as neither voting in favor or against the motion or as abstaining; accordingly, their position was recorded as "Not Voting."

At the conclusion of the meeting on November 30, it was my clear understanding and it was my stated intention to release the new format as soon as possible so that the players and the tournaments had an alternative to consider in advance of ATP's press conference.

I contemplated staging a press conference on the evening of November 30, but since it was difficult to get the press release complete and to properly notify the journalists, I postponed the press conference until 4:30 pm on Thursday, December 1. On Wednesday, November 30, we began notifying journalists of the time for the press conference for the next day. Sometime during the evening, John Parsons of Britain's *Daily Telegraph* came to me and asked that he and some of the non-American journalists be given an advance on the press release as their deadlines were before 4:30 pm New York time. I agreed to provide the advance sometime early on December 1. I prepared the press release materials on the afternoon and evening of November 30 for release on December 1. I did however provide copies of the format to several player agents on November 30, so they could discuss it with their player-clients. As soon as the MTC meeting recessed at approximately 2:00 pm on November 30, most of the "Tennis Family,' of course, knew about the new format. There are almost "no secrets in tennis."

During Wednesday evening, November 30, I was advised that a meeting between Hamilton Jordan, Brian Tobin and David Markin had been held in the afternoon after the MTC had recessed and Jordan had declined to offer suitable representation to the ITF on the new ATP Tour Board.

Thursday, December 1

On Thursday morning before the MTC meeting began, Buzzer Hadingham sent another letter to the Grand Slam Chairmen asking them to join in a press release with Hamilton Jordon on the new 1990 ATP Tour. *Hamilton had done a masterful job on Buzzer by saying a few positive things about his wishful British MITB proposal. Buzzer thought that Hamilton had agreed that the MITB could have authority over the ATP Tour Board, but we all knew that was never the case. The other three Grand Slam Chairmen knew that Hamilton Jordan had no interest in Buzzer's 12-year plan, no interest in Buzzer's proposed MITB, which would have no power, and Buzzer's belief that Hamilton had agreed to have ITF Representatives on the ATP Board was just not correct. I thought Buzzer had been misled or had misunderstood what Hamilton had told him.* The ITF members of the MTC had asked me to provide one final proposal for a 1990 Grand Prix format, which I had done and it had been adopted at the meeting.

Buzzer Disagreed with My Holding a Press Conference to Offer the Council's 1990 Grand Prix Format as an Alternative to the New ATP Tour Format

On December 1, Buzzer sent me a telex[765] expressing his disagreement: "I must tell you that I totally disagree with your apparent intention to hold a press conference this afternoon to announce a new plan for a MTC Tour. You will force Wimbledon to disassociate with any such plan, although I would very much regret having to do this when the Grand Slams should be seen to be standing together both now and especially in any possible future problems. If you go ahead, Wimbledon does not support your plan and would refuse to co-operate." *Buzzer's agreement to support the new ATP Tour contrary to the positions of the other three Grand Slams had doomed the MTC from the start. Hamilton Jordan and Ray Moore knew that without Wimbledon, the ITF and the other three Grand Slams would not be able to offer a meaningful alternative to the proposed new ATP Tour.*

Resumption of Meeting on Thursday, December 1

Before the meeting began on Thursday, I gave Buzzer's telex to Roy Reardon and he informed me that each of the ITF Representatives had a copy and I should wait for whatever was going to transpire during the meeting. The meeting resumed on Thursday with all nine members present. During the meeting, no one made any suggestion that I should not proceed with the planned press conference. Tennis Players Promotions BV was the new company being created in the Netherlands to receive and manage the ATP Deferred Compensation Plan. During 1988, I had collected contributions to the plan from the Grand Prix tournaments by the MTC pursuant to the terms of the "agreed" 1998-1992 MTC-ATP contract, which was still unsigned and in fact would never be signed. Subject to receipt of an indemnification agreement protecting the MTC from any claims with respect to funds delivered to the BV and receipt of an acceptable legal opinion from Dutch counsel, I was authorized to pay over the funds collected to the BV. The vote was 7-0-2. Thereafter, the Player Representatives again withdrew from the meeting. *You have to love the logic of tennis folks. ATP got the funding for the Deferred Compensation Plan as part of the consideration for ATP entering into a contract with the MTC for 1988-1992, which, of course, the ATP would not be doing.*

Approval of Lawsuit Settlement

On December 1, after the conclusion by the Council of general business and the departure of Ray Moore and the other two Player Representatives, the remaining six members considered the new revised "final" proposed Settlement Agreement dated December 1 for the settlement of the Volvo/ProServ/IMG lawsuit. After explaining the terms of the proposed Settlement Agreement, I recommended the settlement because I thought it was the best deal the MTC could get under the circumstances and I hoped that concluding the lawsuit would be positive for professional tennis. I then departed while the matter was considered in a separate caucus between Roy Reardon and the ITF Representatives. Ian Peacock, the Executive Director of the British LTA was also present and this caucus continued for more than one hour. Roy also met separately with Graham Lovett and I am not sure if Roy met with the three Tournament Representatives as a group. The Tournament Representatives definitely met together in private caucus to discuss the matter.

When the meeting reconvened at 2:00 pm, the Settlement Agreement was approved with four votes in favor with Chatrier, Tobin, Markin and Pasarell voting in favor and Bartoni and Lovett asking to be recorded as "not voting." Bartoni said he did not want to participate as he continued his dislike of American law.

Settlement Agreement Terms

The terms of the Settlement Agreement,[766] in addition to settling all claims and counterclaims in the Volvo lawsuit were:

(1) Term. Eight-year term through December 31, 1997.

(2) Conflicts of Interest. ProServ, IMG and Volvo agreed not to contest the MTC Grand Prix Rule IV prohibiting conflicts of interest.

(3) Player Representation. MTC will not require registration of player-agents and will not interfere with the representation of players.

(4) Wild Cards. Any rule restricting "wild cards" had to be objective and of general application and not just targeted at Player Agents.

(5) No Pooling of Sponsorship Rights. MTC agrees not to require the pooling of tournament sponsorship rights, but MTC can market the umbrella rights of the Grand Prix.

(6) Orlando. Orlando, owned by ProServ would be sanctioned for 1989, 1990 and 1991 as a Super Series tournament and ProServ could sell Orlando or the MTC could purchase Orlando for $300,000.

(7) Washington. ProServ could continue as owner/manager of Washington for 1989.

(8) Boston. IMG could continue as defacto owner of Boston for 1989.

(9) Special Events. IMG and ProServ will not challenge the Grand Prix Rules prohibiting special events against major tournaments. The MTC agrees

that there will be a minimum of 14 open weeks between the Australian Open and the Masters for special events.

(10) <u>No Mandatory Television Pooling.</u> MTC agrees that there will be no mandatory television rights pooling.

(11) <u>Chicago.</u> The MTC agrees to sanction Volvo for an Open Week Series tournament in 1989 and if there is a future opening in North America for a new Super Series, to approve it for Volvo.

(12) <u>Volvo Tennis.</u> Volvo can use "Volvo Tennis" provided that the tournaments are clearly identified as part of the Grand Prix and Volvo is not to be portrayed in a sponsorship capacity other than the actual capacity of such sponsorship.

The so-called Volvo bidding process claim used to try to get me fired was abandoned.

Advised to Proceed with Press Conference

After the meeting adjourned, I again consulted with Roy Reardon with respect to whether I should do anything about Buzzer's telex and Roy advised that since no action had been taken at the meeting that I should proceed with my press conference. I then authorized my staff to provide the advance release of the press release to the British journalist John Parsons et al.

ITF Conference

Later, the ITF Representatives (Chatrier, Markin, Tobin) plus Gordon Jorgensen and Ian Peacock continued to meet together in the conference room for over an hour. When I was asked to meet with them, I was asked about the press conference and I told them that I had just released the press release to John Parsons, et al. *I reviewed the entire procedure leading to its release and informed them I planned to present it as a format for a compromise produced by the MTC in satisfaction of its fiduciary duty to offer a constructive 1990 program as an alternative to the proposed new ATP Tour. I assured those present that I had no intention of suggesting that the format had been approved by the ITF, the Grand Slams or anyone other than the MTC.* At the request of Brian Tobin and Ian Peacock, I was able to add a new paragraph to the press release to clarify those issues even more.

Press Conference on the Settlement of the Lawsuit and the Proposed 1990 Grand Prix Format

On December 1, at the 4:30 pm I held a press conference at Madison Square Garden to announce the settlement of the Volvo/ProServ/IMG lawsuit and the new proposed 1990 Format for the Grand Prix.

The lawsuit press release stated[767]: "The settlement establishes by agreement the boundaries for participation by Player-Agent/Management Companies in tournaments by prohibiting them from owning or managing tournaments, while permitting independently owned and managed tournaments to employ them as commission agents for the solicitation of sponsorship and the sale of television rights and merchandising rights. IMG and ProServ will be permitted to gradually phase out of ownership and management of tournaments over the next three years as existing contracts expire. 'It is a positive development for professional tennis to have this lawsuit concluded on a basis that is good for the future of the sport,' Happer said. 'The line drawn with respect to the activities of the management companies is sensible and settles finally the conflict of interest problem that professional tennis has lived with for years. With this troublesome matter now concluded, we can again concentrate fully on moving forward with the growth and prosperity of professional tennis which continues to be the most successful international sport.'"

I then presented the new 1990 Grand Prix Format approved by the MTC and stated that in my opinion it was better for the players, tournaments and the national federations than anything we have had proposed in the past and it was better than what the ATP was proposing. I specifically stated that it was not approved by Wimbledon or any of the other Grand Slams. The press release was dated December 1 and included the highlights of the new proposed 1990 Grand Prix Format: (i) The structure of the MTC will be revised to provide for 50 percent voting strength for the Player Representatives as well as representation for the tournaments and the International Tennis Federation, (ii) Streamlining of the circuit featuring the Grand Slams – Australian Open, French Open, Wimbledon and the U.S. Open – new class of 14 $1,000,000 World Series tournaments just under the Grand Slams, up to 13 Super Series – plus the Regular and Open Week Series. The new World Series tournaments will provide a new 'mini-grand slam' level for professional tennis, (iii) Signing Bonuses will be offered to the players to commit to the circuit totaling $3.9 million, plus other bonuses for additional participation, thus bringing professional tennis in line with other professional sports in compensation of its top athletes. Players would be given more freedom and responsibility to control their own destiny than ever before; The Doubles Bonus Pool will be increased to $1,000,000, (iv) A new circuit-wide marketing strategy will feature entertainment marquees at every tournament for use by circuit sponsors, endorsers and for the promotion of the sport. The new marketing effort will increase the income to tournaments and indirectly the compensation to the players, (v) Existing Super Series will be guaranteed a franchise and a place in the Grand Prix calendar, (vi) All tournaments in the 1990 Grand Prix will be offered for the first time six-year franchises with calendar stability so they may better plan for the future with long term sponsorships and facilities, (vii) An 'Off-Season' of approximately two months between the end of the Masters and the beginning of the Australian Open will be provided for the first time and (viii) We will protect the numerous professional player jobs now existing without placing unreasonable demands on the top players.[768]

Reaction of Players to New 1990 Grand Prix Format

Peter Alfano reported on the reaction of the players in the *New York Times*,[769] stating that Ion Tiriac, the former player and the manager of Boris Becker, said that Men's Tennis Council "made a very generous offer" to the ATP but "it was a few months too late." Alfano also quoted Ray Moore saying, "Now, they make concessions. Now, they have a better schedule and signing bonuses. Why do they come up with this now?" *Perhaps, Ray Moore forgot for a moment that he was the Chairman of the MTC and a member of the "They".* At the Grand Prix tournament meeting on December 2, I explained to the tournaments the details of the new 1990 Grand Prix format.

ATP Press Conference

At 2:30 pm on December 2, Hamilton Jordan staged his press conference announcing he had the "finest players in the world and the finest tournaments in the world" for the 1990 ATP Tour. Present for the press conference were Mats Wilander, Stefan Edberg, Boris Becker, Andre Agassi, Ray Moore, Marty Davis, Larry Scott, Jakob Hlasek, Tim Mayotte, J. Wayne Richmond and Bill Norris. He detailed a 4-4 "ATP Tour Board" consisting of four players and four tournament directors with a CEO to break the ties. Disappointingly, he stated that Open Week Series tournaments would be able to pay appearance fees to players and that tournament applications would be accepted from Player Agents.

After all of the time and expense by the MTC to stop the conflicts of interest caused when Player Agents own or run tournaments, the first announcement made by Hamilton Jordan for the new ATP Tour on December 2, was that the ATP would accept and approve tournament applications for sanction from Player Agents. Go Figure!

The ATP press release contained the following statement about Wimbledon: "'I would like to express my personal gratitude and the profound appreciation of the players to 'Buzzer' Hadingham, Chairman of Wimbledon, for his untiring efforts to find a fair and peaceful solution to the problems that have separated the players and the ITF. Once again, Wimbledon has proven it is the friend of the players and the leader of our sport.'" *Hamilton really owed a debt of gratitude to Buzzer. He had succeeded in separating Wimbledon from the other three Grand Slams.*[770]

Chances of Compromise Ended For All Practical Purposes

On December 3, Peter Alfano reported in the *New York Times*[771]: "For all practical purposes, this ended chances for a compromise between the players and the Men's Tennis Council, which runs the existing Grand Prix circuit…Jordan said that although the Council's proposal, which incorporated many of the players' suggestions, was generous, but it was too late.' 'Marshall Happer is an honest, decent man presiding over a badly flawed system,' said Jordan, who was chief of staff under former President Carter."

Transition Period – Selection of New CEO for ATP Tour

Peter Alfano wrote on December 12 in the *New York Times*[772]: "In the men's game, 1989 will be noteworthy because it is a lame-duck year for Nabisco, the tour sponsor, and most likely, the Men's Tennis Council, the game's governing body. The Association of Tennis Professionals has staged the first coup d' ètat with a transition period. The players have decided to run their own tour beginning in 1990, but it will be business as usual next year under the council's grand prix format. Thus, the A.T.P. will have the best of all worlds: time to organize and implement its own plan while continuing to reap the benefits of playing under an imperfect system it says does not work."

My Response to Buzzer

Buzzer claimed that the proposed 1990 MTC format I presented was not properly approved by the Council, because it had only four votes.[773] On December 19, I responded to Buzzer[774]: "With respect to the voting on the MTC there is a black letter principle of law, inherited I believe from English law, that the members of the Board of Directors and the employees of an organization have a fiduciary duty to act in a manner consistent with the preservation of the organization. In our case, we have three Player Representatives who clearly are acting contrary to the best interests of the MTC as they have designed and are seeking through the '1990 ATP Tour' to take over men's professional tennis and put the MTC out of business or liquidate the MTC and seek to obtain a distribution of its assets. In addition, we have at least two Tournament Representatives who claim to have made 'deals' with ATP. I am quite certain that under American and English law as well as common sense, no one would seriously contend that those five members can or should control the business of the MTC. As long as any member of the MTC wants to continue its business, then it should be continued. It continues to be the case that the three ITF members and possibly the North American Tournament Representative desire that the MTC continue in business in 1990. So yes, the voting of the 'loyal' members of the MTC should be quite enough to constitute approval of the 1990 Grand Prix format and that is the legal advice that we received.

"I will always respect and admire you and the position you hold as Chairman of Wimbledon. I know that you have always sought what you believe to be best for tennis and I know that was your motive during these negotiations. However, I respectfully suggest that the ATP has utilized the negotiations with you to neutralize Wimbledon and to seek to keep the Grand Slams from unifying at a critical moment in tennis history. I telephoned you before you met with Hamilton Jordan, Ray Moore and Colin Dowdeswell on October 13 to impress on you the importance of letting them know that the Grand Slams would fight to the extent necessary to maintain an effective voice in the governing of the sport for the ITF. However, the ATP Representatives left their meeting with you on October 13 with the clear understanding that Wimbledon would not upset the '1990 ATP Tour.' When Ray Moore and Hamilton Jordan each told me that Wimbledon would not fight, I simply did not believe them. It now seems that they were correct – at least up to the present time. The October 13 meeting was critical as Hamilton and Ray boarded the plane for London, they had just received the October 11 draft compromise documents which included the provisions they tentatively agreed at my office on October 4. *I am absolutely convinced that when the history of this event is written, it will be clearly shown that the indication received from Wimbledon on October 13 was the single most important factor in the ATP decision to reject the compromise tentatively agreed on October 4 and to go forward with a separate ATP Tour.*

The subsequent proposal you developed with Hamilton Jordan was never remotely agreed by Hamilton or the ATP. My analysis of your proposal was that you were by 'agreement' delivering the sport to ATP for observer status on the ATP Tour Board, for the founding of a 'discussion' group known as the 'Men's International Tennis Board' and for 12 years of date (not even financial) protection for the Grand Slams. Your colleagues representing the ITF and the other three Grand Slams thought your proposal was not acceptable and that the ITF and Grand Slams would be better off to be completely independent than to proceed with that deal."

On December 22, Buzzer responded by letter saying[775]: "When we agreed to meet Hamilton at Wimbledon (October 13), I was extremely careful at that time to emphasize that we would listen to what he had to say. He tried to get me to give a reaction, but I repeated that I could say nothing until I had had the opportunity to discuss the whole question with the Committee of Management of The Championships." Nevertheless, Ray Moore and Hamilton Jordan left the meeting convinced that Wimbledon would not join with the other 3 Grand Slams to fight against the creation of the ATP Tour and the destruction of the MTC as the unified governing body for men's professional tennis.

My Offer to Resign

On December 19, I wrote to Hamilton and offered to resign and let the ATP take over the MTC to keep the tennis family together and to avoid the expense of creating a new company for the ATP Tour recommending that: "The Men's Tennis Council be reorganized with 50 percent ATP, 25 percent Tournaments and 25 percent ITF with an ATP/Tournament Committee for Non-Grand Slam matters and an ATP/ITF Committee for Grand Slam matters. This way you can take advantage of the considerable assets of the MTC instead of losing many of them in liquidation just to set up a new Council. The MTC would be reorganized to be run by a new CEO-Commissioner, who is neutral to each of the representative factions and has the authority to run the game."[776] Hamilton replied, saying to *International Tennis Weekly*[777]: "To his credit, Mr. Happer made the generous offer to step aside personally if that gesture would facilitate some resolution of the current conflict."[778]

On December 19, I wrote to each of the MTC Tournaments Representatives, Franco Bartoni, Graham Lovett and Charlie Pasarell as one last effort to request them to support the MTC and the 1990 Grand Prix format with their respective tournaments. The tournaments were faced with having to decide to file applications for the 1990 Grand Prix and/or the 1990 ATP Tour at the end of the year (December 31 for the Grand Prix and January 2 for the ATP Tour). I explained that the Grand Prix format was better for the tournaments and the players and that with the Grand Prix, none of their tournaments would be demoted or rejected. The ATP was proposing a reduction in the number of Super Series and those that were demoted would be faced with bidding with the payment of guarantees to attract players.[779]

Official End of Volvo/ProServ/IMG Lawsuit with its Formal Dismissal

On December 19, a stipulation of withdrawal of appeal was signed by all the attorneys for all the parties and the MTC appeal of the District Court Dismissal of the

Counterclaims was duly withdrawn. On December 28, the Stipulation of Dismissal *with prejudice* for all Claims and all Counterclaims was filed in the United States District Court for the Southern District of New York. *Thus, the Volvo litigation which was Crisis No. 30, Parts I, II, III and IV was fully and finally completed.*

The End of the Final Crisis No. 32: The Successful Coup D' État

At the end of 1988, a few tournaments filed applications with both the MTC and the ATP, but the rest of them only filed with the ATP. They were naturally afraid that if they did not apply to the ATP Tour they would not be able to get any players. *That is when I finally gave up trying to save the MTC. From that time forward, I began to help Hamilton as much as I could in the transition, while continuing the 1989 Nabisco Grand Prix to its conclusion, after which I had to liquidate the MTC.*

The End of the MTC and the ATP as a Player Association

Crisis No. 32 was the "Final Crisis" for the MTC and it was fatal, a real Coup d'Etat. It was also fatal for the ATP as a player organization as it would be replaced by a revised Delaware corporation known as the ATP Tour, Inc., which would be a "tour organization" and neither a player association or a tournament association. I would be the first and last Administrator of the MTC. Ray Moore would be the last Chairman of the MTC. Hamilton Jordan would be the last Executive Director of the ATP, as a player association, and Brian Gottfried would be the last President of the ATP as a player association.

Lame Duck 1989 and Cleaning Up the Damage

So then, all I had to do was run the 1989 Nabisco Grand Prix and figure out a way to deal with our new 12-year lease of half of the 17th floor at 437 Madison Avenue, our existing furniture and equipment and our new furniture in transit for delivery along with dealing with the termination of our 33 employees. We had been proud of our new large windowed conference room in the southwestern corner of the building facing onto Madison Avenue and 50th Street. We had a brand-new long conference table for MTC meetings and David Cooper had found a friend who built a custom wall cabinet in the conference room to store the many video tapes we were now making of all televised matches.

What had the ITF and the Grand Slams Actually Done for the ATP?

Before closing this Chapter and the "War" won by the ATP over the ITF, in which the ITF and the Grand Slams were separated from and forced to become independent of the non-Grand Slam tournaments and the players, it is worth looking at just what the ITF, the Grand Slams and the MTC had actually done for the ATP. Without the ITF, the MTC and the Grand Slams, the ATP, which was created by Jack Kramer and Donald Dell in 1972, could never have lasted.

1.   Creation of MTC. In 1974, the ITF, in lieu of treating the ATP as a player union to be dealt with via collective bargaining agreements as is done with lots of other professional sports, elected to share the governance of men's professional tennis with the ATP through the creation of the MTC. Originally, the ITF wanted the governing body to be an ITF Committee, but in 1974, they agreed that it would be an independent governing body, independent of the ITF. Since 1974, the ITF and the Grand Slams had concurred with the governing rules of the MTC.

2.   ATP Tournaments. The MTC agreed from the outset that the ATP could be involved in a limited number of Grand Prix tournaments through the years to provide funding for its operations.

3.   World Team Cup. Even though the ITF did not like to have the ATP World Team Cup, which was ATP's competition with the Davis Cup, the ITF supported it as an additional fund raiser.

4.   Lipton Two-Week Player's Grand Slam. The ITF and the Grand Slams supported the ATP's request for the Lipton two-week player's "Grand Slam." The agreement was that it could never be called a "Grand Slam," but in effect it would be the player's Grand Slam and be a big fund raiser for the ATP and the WTA and it would eliminate any need or desire for the ATP or the WTA to try to get into the television rights income of the Grand Slams which had been developed by the contributions of time and efforts of thousands of volunteers over a 100 years, had all incurred significant debt to provide better and better facilities for the players and were used to support their national associations.

5.   ATP Tournaments. By 1988 and 1989, ATP owned the Lipton two-week tournament in Key Biscayne, World Team Cup, part of the Cincinnati Super Series, and had participation deals with Bristol, Queens and the London Wembley Super Series.

6.   ATP was Bankrupt in 1982. When Butch Buchholz followed Bob Briner as the Executive Director of the ATP, he discovered that the ATP was bankrupt. In 1982, Butch asked and collected two percent of each player's on-site prize money for the ATP and encountered significant objection from the players. In 1982, the MTC paid $236,000 from its reserves to the ATP to assist with its immediate financial problems.

7.   <u>WCT Anti-Trust Lawsuit Would Have Bankrupted the ATP.</u> In 1983, WCT filed an anti-trust lawsuit against the MTC, ITF and ATP. The ATP did not have sufficient funds to pay for its defense of the lawsuit and would have been bankrupted by the lawsuit if the ITF had not come to ATP's rescue and agreed to fund all of ATP's legal expenses.

8.   <u>1983-1987 MTC-ATP Contract and ATP Prize Money.</u> The MTC entered into a five-year contract with the ATP for 1983-1987 to charge the tournaments to pay ATP for the services it was providing to its members and to the tournaments. Since this charge was going to be from additional new money paid by the tournaments, it did not require any reduction of the on-site prize money for the players, so the players did not object. In order for the tournaments to be able to claim some credit for these additional payments, it was called "ATP Prize Money." The actual amounts of ATP Prize Money collected by the MTC and paid to the ATP for 1983-1987 was: 1983 - $535,000, 1984 - $525,000, 1985 - $693,000, 1986 - $685,110. 1987 - $719,806.

9.   <u>1988-1992 Proposed MTC-ATP Contract for Increased ATP Prize Money and for Additional Contributions for a new ATP Deferred Compensation Plan.</u> The MTC and the ATP agreed to a new five-year contract for 1988-1992 for an increase and continuation of the ATP Prize Money and for the addition of a deferred compensation payment required of each tournament, which could also be advertised as "Player Compensation." In good faith that the new five-year agreement would be executed by the ATP as agreed, the MTC enacted the rules for the ATP Prize Money and Deferred Compensation payments by tournaments beginning in 1988. However, the proposed and agreed 1988-1992 MTC-ATP agreement was put on hold and *never signed* as ATP began the "war" in August of 1988 to create a new ATP Tour for 1990 and destroy the MTC.

In good faith, the MTC collected, and subsequently paid to ATP the ATP Prize Money and Deferred Compensation contributions received from tournaments for 1988 and 1989 as follows: ATP Prize Money - $867,994 and $836,877, Deferred Compensation - $2,255,985 and $1,932,805.

10.   <u>ATP Actually Had A 6-3 Voting Majority on the MTC.</u> In 1988, as the "War" began claiming the need for the players to obtain 50 percent of the voting strength on the MTC for the ATP, the ITF Representatives attempted in vain to point out that with Ray Moore, as the MTC Chairman, and with the three Tournament Representatives regularly voting with the Player Representatives, the ITF was effectively out numbered 6-3 in voting, yet they continued to support the Council.

It is hard not to believe that the ATP was actually saying to the ITF: "Why haven't you done more for me lately?"

CHAPTER 32:

1989: THE FINAL LAME DUCK YEAR, MTC LIQUIDATION, $2,025,033 LOST

1989 Governing Bodies

The MTC was the governing body for men's professional tennis in 1989, except for the Davis Cup and the *Rules of Tennis*. The ITF was the governing body for the Davis Cup and in charge of the *Rules of Tennis*.

1989 Significant Tennis Leaders

ITF President:	Philippe Chatrier (France)
USTA President:	Gordon Jorgensen
Tennis Australia President:	Brian Tobin
British LTA President:	Ron Pressly
French FFT President:	Philippe Chatrier
Chairman of Wimbledon:	Buzzer Hadingham
WCT Owners:	Lamar Hunt and Al Hill, Jr.
WCT CEO:	Owen Williams
ATP President:	Brian Gottfried
ATP Executive Director:	Hamilton Jordan

1989 MTC

ITF:	Philippe Chatrier, Brian Tobin and David Markin.
Tournaments:	Franco Bartoni (Europe), Charles Pasarell (North America), Graham Lovett (Rest of the World).

Players:	Ray Moore, Chairman, Weller Evans and Marty Davis.
Administrator:	Marshall Happer.
Asst Admn:	Bill Babcock until August.
Asst Admn:	David Cooper until June.
Legal Counsel:	Roy L. Reardon, Esquire.
GP Supervisors:	Ken Farrar, Chief, Bill Gilmour, Thomas Karlberg, Stefan Fransson, John Heiss, Edwardo Menga and Edward Hardisty.
Chair Umpires:	Rich Kaufman, Richard Ings, Gerry Amstrong, Paula Pereira, Rudy Berger and Bruno Rebeuh.
Communications:	Reg Lansberry, Director of Media Relations and Barbara Travers, Assistant Director of Media Relations.
Tour Liaisons:	Lori Stukes, Catalina Cox, Wendy Miller and Camille Guthrie.
Nabisco Masters:	Eugene "Gene" Scott, Tournament Director, Sue "Suzie" Rothstein, Tournament Manager.

1989 Major Player Representatives

ProServ:	Principals: Donald Dell, Jerry Solomon and Ivan Blumberg.
Advantage Int'l:	Principals: Frank Craighill, Lee Fentress, Dean Smith and Peter Lawler.
IMG:	Principals: Mark McCormack and Bob Kain.
Others:	Ion Tiriac and Thomas Betz, Esquire (Vilas).
	John McEnroe, Sr., Esquire (McEnroe).
	Gloria Connors and Joseph Rountree, Esquire (Connors).

Two Competitions

In 1989, the 21st year of Open Tennis and the last year of the Grand Prix, there were two major organized competitions for men: Nabisco Grand Prix and the Davis Cup, as WCT continued to be merged into the Nabisco Grand Prix for one more year. In addition to the Nabisco Grand Prix, which was the major circuit of professional tournaments for men, the MTC also sanctioned smaller Challenger and Satellite Series tournaments, all to be conducted under the uniform MTC Tournament Regulations and MTC Code of Conduct.

1989 Nabisco Grand Prix – 76 Tournaments in 1989

There were 76 tournaments in the Nabisco Grand Prix consisting of four Grand Slams, the ATP two-week Lipton International Players Championships in Key Biscayne, 26 Super Series tournaments (including two WCT Super Series in Tokyo and Scottsdale; WCT Super Series in Detroit was cancelled) and 41 Regular and Open Week Series tournaments, plus four Circuit Championships: Buick WCT Finals in Dallas, WCT Tournament of Champions at Forest Hills, Nabisco Masters at Madison Square Garden and Nabisco Masters Doubles in London. There were 94 Challenger Series tournaments and 51 Satellite Series.

Rules

The *Official 1989 MIPTC Yearbook* (286 pages) and the *Official 1989 Media Guide* (525 pages) were again split into two publications. These would be the last editions to ever be produced by the MTC which would be dissolved after December 31, 1989. My Administrator's welcoming letter, which was obviously written before the fate of the MTC had been decided, stated: "In 1989, as we enter into the third decade of 'Open Tennis,' I am pleased to report on the continuing growth and prosperity of our sport throughout the world, etc." The Grand Prix Rules, Tournament Regulations and Code of Conduct for 1989 were the same as in 1988.[780]

Camille Guthrie Tour Liaison

Camille Guthrie joined the MTC Communications Department in November of 1986, and in 1989, she became a MTC Tour Liaison along with Wendy Miller and Lori Stukes to service the Nabisco Grand Prix Tournaments. Camille was a graduate of Trinity College in Hartford, Connecticut with a degree in History and had studied at the Institute of European Studies in Vienna, Austria.

Paul Svehlik Resigns as Assistant MTC Administrator and Moves to European Tournaments

In December of 1988 or early January of 1989, I accepted Paul Svehlik's resignation as an Assistant MTC Administrator and I bid him farewell as Franco Bartoni hired him to work for the European tournaments. I closed the MTC Paris Office upon the dissolution of the MTC. Paul would serve on the new ATP Tour tournament application selection committee on behalf of the European tournaments to select the tournaments for the new 1990 ATP Tour. It was easy to accommodate Monte Carlo, Hamburg and Rome without a WCT Tournament of Champions in New York being in between Hamburg and Rome.

Hamilton Jordan's Nice Tribute to the MTC and the MTC Staff

In the January 27 issue of *International Tennis Weekly*[781], Hamilton Jordan said: "'Finally…a personal word of thanks to the leadership and to the staff of the Men's Tennis Council. For the past four months, we have had a lively discussion with the MTC over the future organization of the sport. Some members of the MTC felt that the current system was adequate. Many tournament directors shared the ATP view that drastic change was required. There is no argument that the game is better off today due to the hard work and efforts of Marshall Happer and his staff at the MTC over the past six years. They have brought integrity to the game and the system of professional officiating that has been, and is currently in place, is considered to be excellent by all involved in the sport. When tennis history is written, we believe that it will be said that the MTC, under Marshall Happer's leadership, took professional tennis to a new level of achievement. The challenge of the new ATP Tour is to build on that progress and to attempt in the next decade to take our sport to even greater levels of accomplishment. That is our challenge.'"

Reconciliation with Ray Moore

Ray Moore, MTC Chairman, had led the effort with Hamilton Jordan to create the new ATP Tour in 1990, which resulted in the dissolution of the MTC. I had fought to save the Council so naturally some friction occurred between us. On January 29, Ray wrote me a nice and friendly letter[782] "now that the dust has settled, and the war is seemingly over." Ray was concerned with the conflict of interest position he had been placed in as the MTC Chairman on opposite sides from me during the "war" and he said he regretted that I would be a casualty of the ATP Tour. I very much appreciated Ray's letter and I told him so. Ray Moore was (and is) one of the smartest professional tennis players I have ever met. Even though Hamilton Jordan had led the promotion effort for the creation of the new ATP Tour, Ray was the "tennis mastermind." As the necessary tennis mastermind of the creation of the ATP Tour and the destruction of the MTC, Ray had been required to forgo his "fiduciary duty" as Chairman and a member of the MTC. I believed that Ray was uncomfortable in that role. He could, of course, have been sued by the MTC. My sense then was that Ray had some second thoughts and maybe even some regrets that the MTC would be destroyed in the process. He had been a highly effective and successful MTC Chairman and he was going to be the last MTC Chairman.

David Cooper Moves to ATP Tour

I hired David Cooper as an Assistant MTC Administrator in June of 1983 and his primary job was to administer the MTC Officials Program and work daily with the MTC Supervisors and MTC Chair Umpires. Together, we had created a well-respected professional program to train and certify tennis officials and we had developed a cadre of talented professional Supervisors and Chair Umpires. I received a call from Hamilton Jordan asking me about David and I recommended him highly to Hamilton for the ATP Tour. David was extremely popular with the Supervisors and Chair Umpires and was a good choice for the ATP Tour. When David came to me and told me he had been offered a job with the new ATP Tour, I congratulated him and made arrangements, so he could move to Ponte Vedra Beach, Florida and begin work with the ATP Tour as soon as he wished. Hamilton hired David to begin in June as the "Administrator of Regulations and Director of Research."[783]

MTC Chair Umpire Richard Ings Receives Death Threat

At the 1989 French Open, Richard Ings was assigned as the chair umpire for the fourth round of 16 match between Ivan Lendl, the three-time French Open champion and the tournament favorite, and 17-year-old Michael Chang. Ings handled the match in perfect French. Lendl won the first two sets and then Chang, despite severe cramping, came back to win the last three sets, so the final score was 4-6, 4-6, 6-3, 6-3, 6-3. Chang went on to become the youngest player ever to win a Grand Slam title after he beat Stefan Edberg in the final. Soon after the French Open, Richard received a death threat from someone claiming to be a supporter of Lendl. Richard received the death threat at the Queens Grand Prix tournament just before Wimbledon and since it had been mailed from the United States, it was decided for him to avoid the U.S. summer tournaments except for the U.S. Open. We reported the death threat to the FBI and during the 1989 U.S. Open, Richard was provided with personal security. The FBI was not able to ever determine the identity of the person who made the threat.

Bill Babcock Hired by ITF and Grand Slams

Mike Davies, as General Manager of the ITF, called me to ask for my suggestions for the ITF to hire someone to administer the ITF's involvement in professional tennis via the Davis Cup and Olympics and also for the Grand Slams. I recommended that he hire Bill Babcock and Bill accepted his offer and moved from New York to London to work for both the ITF and the Grand Slam Committee, consisting of the four Grand Slams and the ITF. Bill began his new job in August. By this time, I no longer had any Assistant MTC Administrators, but with only the 1989 Nabisco Grand Prix to complete and nothing to do for a 1990 Grand Prix, I no longer needed their assistance. Bill would continue to work for the Grand Slams through 2020 and the 2021 Australian Open.

Happer Hired by USTA

John Fogarty was hired as the Executive Director of the USTA in 1986 and resigned in 1988, so the USTA only had an acting Executive Director in 1989. In August of 1989, David Markin, who was then President of the USTA, offered me the job of Executive Director and Chief Operating Officer of the USTA, effective January 1, 1990, with the understanding that I would be able to also complete the dissolution of the MTC which was finally completed on April 30, 1990. I accepted and David Markin announced my employment on September 8.

On September 19, Hamilton Jordan sent me a personal note[784]: "I want to offer my congratulations on your new position with the USTA. I think my reaction has been the same as that of the entire tennis community – 'It is good for Marshall and good for the USTA.' I am confident that you will bring the USTA the strong leadership and continuity that it has lacked in recent years. Marshall, we have both been through a lot this past year. Only time will tell who is right, but please know that my respect for your integrity and ability was not diminished by all of the fights and arguments. Hope this new position fully utilizes your many talents. I look forward to working with you for a more normal relationship between the USTA and ATP."

MTC Meetings

In 1989, the MIPTC held four meetings: February 15 in Milan, June 26-27 in London, August 27 in New York and December 1 in New York.

MTC Meeting, Milan February 15, 1989

Deferred Compensation

In February in Milan, the Council authorized and directed the payment of all funds received in 1988 and 1989, plus any accrued interest thereon, for the ATP players deferred compensation plan to Tennis Players Promotions, B.V. (TPP) pursuant to the full indemnity provided to the Council, except: "Nabisco Grand Prix Tournaments who objected to the payment of the deferred compensation funds they contributed by February 28, 1989, shall be retained by the MTC pending the further determination and instruction of the Council."

Chairman's Statement

Ray Moore, the MTC Chairman "made a statement commending the conduct of the Administrator in his efforts to try to keep the constituencies of the MTC together and requested that such statement be included in these minutes."

Proposal for Dissolution

"A proposal was made on behalf of the Player Representatives to dissolve the MTC after the conclusion of the 1989 Nabisco Grand Prix. Such proposal was supported by the Tournament Representatives. The ITF Representatives proposed at that time to continue the operation of the MTC after 1989. Thereafter a general discussion ensued, and the matter was deferred pending further study." There was no way legally that the three Player Representatives and the three Tournament Representatives could force the dissolution of the MTC without the consent of the ITF Representatives. If at the end of 1989, the Player Representatives and the Tournament Representatives all resigned or were removed for breach of their fiduciary duties, the ITF Representatives could have continued the MTC with replacement Representatives or with a restructuring of the MTC to something like four ITF Representatives and four Grand Slam Representatives. If they had done that, the MTC would have had the benefit of the approximate $8 million that was in the MTC assets.

The ITF Representatives debated among themselves their two options: "peaceful co-existence" with the ATP Tour or create a competing circuit and go to war or at least make a threat to do so enough to try to force a compromise. Since Buzzer Hadingham and Wimbledon were not going to stand with the ITF and the other three Grand Slams, they elected to select "peaceful co-existence" and remain independent of the ATP Tour.

They agreed to the dissolution of the MTC and the division of its assets 1/3 to the ITF and 2/3 to the ATP Tour for the players and the tournaments.[785]

MTC Meeting, London June 26-27, 1989

Deferred Compensation

In June in London, "The ATP Deferred Compensation Plan dated January 1, 1989 for Tennis Players Promotions B.V., submitted on March 13, 1989 was approved."

Refund of Deferred Compensation Contributions by Some Tournaments

The Council approved the refund of deferred compensation contributions to the following tournaments: Livingston, Los Angeles, WCT Scottsdale, WCT Tokyo, WCT Forest Hills and WCT Detroit. Since the MTC-ATP Agreement was never signed, any tournament that objected to the payment for the ATP Deferred Compensation Plan was entitled to a refund, so the tournaments that did not plan to join the new ATP Tour all requested a refund.

Dissolution

"Upon motion duly made and seconded, the MTC adopted the following resolution with respect to dissolution:

WHEREAS the members of the Men's Tennis Council ('MTC') have determined that they wish to wind up the affairs of the MTC after completion of the 1989 year and at that time to dissolve the MTC; and

WHEREAS, in connection with such dissolution, the MTC will discharge its liabilities and distribute any remaining assets to successor organizations, in accordance with its Constitution;

NOW, THEREFORE, IT IS HEREBY RESOLVED that the Chief Operating Officer of the MTC is hereby instructed to develop a plan of liquidation and to proceed, in accordance with the attached set of principles and the MTC Constitution, towards a dissolution of the MTC as soon as practicable after the end of 1989.

The 'Set of Principles' which were attached to the Resolution and above referred to were as follows:

(i)   Dissolution. At the conclusion of the 1989 Nabisco Grand Prix, the MTC shall cease operations and the MTC shall be dissolved. The dissolution shall be effective upon the completion of the MTC's business and the liquidation process.

(ii)   <u>Liquidation and Distribution.</u> All of the net assets (cash and in-kind) of the MTC (including names, logos, trademarks and copyrights) shall be distributed to a successor or successors in accordance with the Article VI of the MTC Constitution and shall be distributed 2/3 to the Association of Tennis Professionals, Inc. ('ATP') for the benefit of the players and the tournaments, and 1/3 to the International Tennis Federation ('ITF').

(iii)   <u>Joint Ownership.</u> Subsequent to such distribution the, ATP and ITF shall have joint ownership (2/3 and 1/3) of all codes, rules, regulations, files, books and records, etc. of the MTC and prior to and subsequent to such distribution each shall have access to and the right to use the same.

(iv)   <u>Names(s), Logo(s) and Trademark(s).</u> The names(s), logo(s) and trademark(s) of the MTC shall, subsequent to the distribution, be jointly owned as provided in the paragraph 3 above, and neither party shall be entitled to use or license the use thereof without the consent of the other.

(v)   <u>Principles/Details.</u> The dissolution, liquidation and distribution of the assets of the MTC (and the details thereof) shall be implemented promptly in good faith and in accordance with the foregoing.

(vi)   <u>Advance Payments.</u> Advance payment from cash assets may be made in the ratio referred to in Paragraph 2, provided cash flow and legal liabilities allow.

New York 12-Year Office Lease

"Upon motion duly made and seconded the MTC authorized and directed the Administrator to proceed as soon as possible to find a subtenant or successor tenant for the MTC offices in New York upon the best terms available."

Severance Pay for Employees

The Council approved a schedule of severance pay for employees in the Administration, Communication and permanent Masters departments as recommended by the Administrator, who do not receive a new job with either the ITF or the ATP. It was assumed that all of the Supervisors and Chair Umpires would receive a new job with either the ITF or the ATP.

Liquidation Committee

The Council appointed Franco Bartoni, David Markin and Ray Moore as the Liquidation Committee to work with the Administrator in effecting the completion of the dissolution.[786]

MTC Meeting, New York August 27, 1989

WCT Requested a Share of the MTC Dissolution Distribution

In New York in August, Owen Williams requested that WCT be given a portion of the distribution of proceeds for the MTC upon dissolution. After considering the matter in executive session, Roy Reardon informed Williams that no distribution could be made to WCT under the MTC Constitution.

Plan of Dissolution

The Council considered a draft plan of dissolution prepared by Roy Reardon. The plan was approved with various directed changes, which when completed was to be provided at the MTC office for the signature of each member of the Council. On September 12, 1989, I distributed to each member of the Council a copy of the final Plan of Dissolution as approved.[787]

MTC Meeting, New York December 1, 1989

WCT

In December in New York,[788] the Council approved the refunding of $160,000 to WCT "in settlement of all claims against the MTC."

New York Office 12-Year Lease

The Council authorized the payment up to $600,000 if required to settle the 12-year lease of office space on the 17th Floor of 437 Madison Avenue. In lieu of having to sublease the office space, the landlord ultimately agreed to a termination of the lease for $500,000.

Furniture and Equipment

The Council approved a sale of all of the furniture and equipment of the Council, except for the file cabinets, to the USTA for $25,000.

Council Files

The Council approved my recommendation for the storage of the filing cabinets and Council files at a storage facility in Princeton, New Jersey, along with the payment for such storage for five years with each constituent to have access thereto. It was further agreed that neither party would remove original files or records from such storage facility without the consent of the other party. I provided a key to the storage facility to both the ATP and the ITF. Some of those files contained important financial information on the payment of Bonus Pool etc., monies by the MTC and needed to be consulted with respect to some tax issues after the liquidation of the MTC. After 5 years, the old MTC files were moved to the ATP office in Pontre Vedra FL.

Amendment to Plan of Dissolution

The Plan of Dissolution was amended and signed by all members of the Council to clarify that the only assets that could not be used without the approval of all parties would be the "names, logos or the trademarks of the MTC" so all parties would be able to use the MTC rules, regulations, codes, etc.[789] In fact, the new ATP Tour would use the MTC Grand Prix Rules, MTC Tournament Regulations and MTC Code as the basis for its new rules as would the Grand Slam Committee on behalf of the Grand Slams. The problem, of course, was that the ATP Tour rules, regulations and code would only apply to non-Grand Slam tournaments, and the Grand Slam Committee rules, regulations and code would only apply to the Grand Slams. The Code of Conduct enforcement for the new ATP Tour would be by an employee of the ATP Tour and the enforcement of the Code of Conduct for the now independent Grand Slams would be by an employee of the Grand Slams. *I do not think that bothered any of them.*[790]

Masters of Tennis Trophy

When the MTC finally got control of the Nabisco Masters in 1985, we obtained a new permanent trophy from Tiffany entitled: "Masters of Tennis, Men's Singles" and we inscribed it with the winners of the Masters from 1970 – 1989. Each of the winners in 1985-1989 received a replica as a permanent gift. Upon the dissolution of the MTC, the Masters of Tennis Trophy was donated to the International Tennis Hall of Fame.

1989 MTC Financials

The MTC began 1989 with a surplus of $6,687,904, and after operating its administrative offices and providing $4,000,000 in Bonus Pool awards and $672,000 in bonus prize money to players in the Nabisco Grand Prix, the MTC ended 1989, after payment of $2,025,933 in liquidation expenses, with a surplus of $6,833,350. In addition, the MTC collected and paid to ATP, pursuant to a proposed agreement covering 1988-1992, which was never signed:

$836,877	ATP Prize Money for services to Nabisco Grand Prix tournaments.
$ 0	ATP Entry Fees
$ 99,334	ATP Challenger and Satellite Sanction Fees

Nabisco paid for its promotion as the Nabisco Grand Prix sponsor and the MTC provided the promotion of the Nabisco Grand Prix. The MTC promoted the Nabisco Masters in December of 1989 at Madison Square Garden telecast by ESPN. The MTC was responsible the promotion and operation of the Nabisco Masters and for all expenses and received all income.

The MTC promoted the Nabisco Masters at Madison Square Garden in December of 1989. The gross income for 1989 was $3,595,419 and the gross expenses were $2,561,251, so the MTC net was $1,034,169. In April of 1988, the MTC entered into a new 12-year lease for 7,800 square feet (half of the floor) office space on the 17th floor at an annual rent is $306,150 per year. In liquidation, the MTC paid $500,000 to terminate the lease. The office space for the MTC's Paris office at Stade Roland Garros was furnished free of charge by the French Tennis Federation and the office was closed in 1989. Included in the operating expense were the MTC's legal expenses:

	1985	1986	1987	1988	Total
General	$116,324	$ 71,362	$232,079	$122,164	$ 541,929
Lawsuit	$ 32,752	$208,925	$108,859	$328,416	$ 678,952
Totals	$149,076	$280,287	$340,938	$450,580	$1,220,881

In a final settlement with the two insurance companies, the MTC received $393,680 in 1989 to fully resolve all claims. On April 25, 1990, there was $109,073 in outstanding and uncashed checks to players. The MTC stopped payment on those checks and issued one certified check to the ATP for $109,073, to cover those checks for the players. Upon dissolution, the MTC had $133,399 in receivables due from Brussels, Buenos Aires, EGI, Itaparica, Nabisco Lifesavers, Palermo, San Francisco and Sao Paulo. Those receivables were distributed to the ATP and the ITF with the agreement that upon collection they be divided 2/3 to ATP and 1/3 to the ITF.

Total 1989 MTC Revenues	$15,603,701
Total 1989 MTC Expenses	$13,432,322
1989 MTC Excess	$ 2,171,379
MTC Fund Balance End of 1988	$ 6,687,904
MTC Fund Balance End of 1989	$ 8,859,283
Liquidation Expenses	$ 2,025,933
Fund Balance After Liquidation	$ 6,833,350
Additional Interest (1990)	$ 157,071
Final Fund Balance (1990)	$ 6,990,421
Distribution to ATP (1990)	$ 4,660,281
Distribution to ITF (1990)	$ 2,330,140
Final Balance April 30, 1990	$ 0

On April 30, 1990, the Council concluded the winding down of its operations and fully liquidated. The net assets of $6,990,471 were distributed as follows:

$4,660,261 to the ATP

$2,330,140 to the ITF

So, the Game lost $2,025,933 by dissolving the MTC.[791]

1989 Grand Slam Winners

Australian Open

Ivan Lendl d. Miloslav Mecir 6-2, 6-2, 6-2.
Rick Leach – Jim Pugh d. Darren Cahill – Mark Kratzmann 6-4, 6-4, 6-4.

French Open

Michael Chang d. Stefan Edberg 6-1, 3-6, 4-6, 6-4, 6-2.
Jim Grabb – Patrick McEnroe d. Mansour Bahrami – Eric Winogradsky 6-4, 2-6, 6-4, 7-6.

Wimbledon

Boris Becker d. Stefan Edberg 6-0, 7-6, 6-4.
John Fitzgerald – Anders Jarryd d. Rick Leach – Jim Pugh 3-6, 7-6, 6-4, 7-6.

U.S. Open

Boris Becker d. Ivan Lendl 7-6, 1-6, 6-3, 7-6.
John McEnroe – Mark Woodforde d. Ken Flach – Robert Seguso 6-4, 4-6, 6-3, 6-3.

Nabisco Grand Prix Circuit Championships

Buick WCT Finals (Dallas)

John McEnroe d. Brad Gilbert 6-3, 6-3, 7-6.

WCT Eagle Tournament of Champions (Forest Hills)

Ivan Lendl d. Jaime Yzaga 6-2, 6-1.
Rick Leach – Jim Pugh d. Jim Courier – Pete Sampras 6-4, 6-2.

Nabisco Masters (New York)

Stefan Edberg d. Boris Becker 4-6, 7-6, 6-3, 6-1.

Nabisco Masters Doubles (London)

Jim Grabb – Patrick McEnroe d. John Fitzgerald – Anders Jarryd 6-4, 6-1, 6-3.

1989 Davis Cup

Davis Cup Final (Stuttgart – Indoor Carpet)

Germany d. Sweden 3-2.

Mats Wilander (SE) d. Carl-Uwe Steeb (DE) 5-7, 7-6, 6-2, 6-3.
Boris Becker (DE) d. Stefan Edberg (SE) 6-2, 6-2, 6-4.
Boris Becker – Eric Jelen (DE) d. Jonas Gunnarsson (SE) -Anders Jarryd 7-6, 6-4, 3-6, 6-7, 6-4.
Boris Becker (DE) d. Mats Wilander (SE) 6-2, 6-0, 6-2.
Stefan Edberg (SE) d. Carl-Uwe Steeb (DE) 6-2, 6-4.

World Team Cup

Germany d. Argentina 2-1.

Boris Becker (DE) d. Guillermo Perez-Roldan (AR) 6-0, 2-6, 6-2.
Martin Jaite (AR) d. Carl-UWE Steeb (DE) 6-4, 6-3.
Boris Becker – Eric Jelen (DE) d. Javier Frana – Gustavo Luza (AR) 6-4, 7-5.

1989 World Rankings[792]

Bud Collins	Lance Tingay	ATP Year-End Rankings
1. Ivan Lendl	1. Boris Becker	1. Ivan Lendl
2. Boris Becker	2. Ivan Lendl	2. Boris Becker
3. Stefan Edberg	3. Michael Chang	3. Stefan Edberg
4. John McEnroe	4. Stefan Edberg	4. John McEnroe
5. Michael Chang	5. John McEnroe	5. Michael Chang
6. Brad Gilbert	6. Tim Mayotte	6. Brad Gilbert
7. Andre Agassi	7. Andre Agassi	7. Andre Agassi
8. Aaron Krickstein	8. Brad Gilbert	8. Aaron Krickstein
9. Alberto Mancini	9. Jimmy Connors	9. Alberto Mancini
10. Jay Berger	10. Yannick Noah	10. Jay Berger

1989 Nabisco Grand Prix Bonus Pool Top 10[793]

Singles (20th Bonus Pool)			Doubles (15th Bonus Pool)		
1.	Ivan Lendl	$ 800,000	1.	Rich Leach	$165,000
2.	Boris Becker	$ 550,000	2.	Jim Pugh	$120,000
3.	Stefan Edberg	$ 400,000	3.	Anders Jarryd	$ 90,000
4.	Brad Gilbert	$ 250,000	4T.	Pieter Aldrich	$ 60,000
5.	John McEnroe	$ 150,000	4T.	Danie Visser	$ 60,000
6.	Michael Chang	$ 100,000	6.	Jim Grabb	$ 45,000
7.	Andre Agassi	$ 75,000	7.	John Fitzgerald	$ 30,000
8.	Aaron Krickstein	$ 55,000	8.	Todd Witsken	$ 25,000
9.	Alberto Mancini	$ 45,000	9.	Patrick McEnroe	$ 20,000
10.	Jay Berger	$ 40,000	10.	John McEnroe	$ 17,000

1989 Official Earnings Top 10[794]

1.	Ivan Lendl	$ 2,334,367	6.	Michael Chang	$ 682,130
2.	Boris Becker	$ 2,216,823	7.	Aaron Krickstein	$ 582,651
3.	Stefan Edberg	$ 1,661,491	8.	Alberto Mancini	$ 510,430
4.	John McEnroe	$ 946,023	9.	Anders Jarryd	$ 485,873
5.	Brad Gilbert	$ 900,848	10.	Andre Agassi	$ 478,901

1989 Tournament Calendar

Date	Tournaments	Singles Winner	Singles #2	Doubles Winners	Doubles #2
1/8/1989	Wellington $115,000 GP	Kelly Evernden	Shuzo Matsuoka	P. Doohan - L. Warder	R. Baxter - G. Michibata
1/8/1989	Adelaide $93,400 GP	Mark Woodforde	Patrick Kuhnen	N. Broad - S. Kruger	M. Kratzmann - G. Layendecker
1/15/1989	Auckland $115,000 GP	Ramesh Krishnan	Amos Mansdorf	S. Guy - S. Matsuoka	J. Letts - B. Man Song Hing
1/15/1989	Sydney $115,000 GP	Aaron Krickstein	Andrei Cherkasov	D. Cahill - W. Masur	P. Aldrich - D. Visser
1/29/1989	Aussie Open $1.2M GS	Mats Wilander	Pat Cash	R. Leach - J. Pugh	J. Bates - P. Lundgren
2/12/1989	Rotterdam $325,000 SS	Jakob Hlasek	Anders Jarryd	M. Mecir -M. Sjreber	J. Gunnarsson - M. Gustafsson
2/12/1989	Guaruja $100,000 GP	Luiz Mattar	Jimmy Brown	R. Acioly - D Campos	C. .Kist - M. Menezes
2/12/1989	Chicago $350,000 SP	Ivan Lendl	Brad Gilbert		
2/19/1989	Memphis $297,000 SS	Brad Gilbert	Johan Kriek	P. Annacone - Van Rensburg	S. Davis - T. Wilkison
2/19/1989	Milan $375,000 SS	Boris Becker	Alexander Volkov	J. Hlasek - J. McEnroe	H. Gunthardt - B. Taroczy
2/26/1989	Philadelphia $410,000 SS	Boris Becker	Tim Mayotte	P. Annacone - Van Rensburg	R. Leach - J. Pugh
2/26/1989	Lyon $261,000 GP	John McEnroe	Jacob Hlasek	E. Jelen - M. Mortensen	J. Hlasek - J. McEnroe
3/5/1989	Nancy $100,000 GP	Guy Forget	Michiel Schapers	U. Riglewski - T. Svantessan	J. Silva - E. Masso
3/5/1989	Dallas $500,000 WCT	John McEnroe	Brad Gilbert		
3/12/1989	Scottsdale $297,000 SS	Ivan Lendl	Stefan Edberg	R. Leach - J. Pugh	P. Annacone - Van Rensburg
3/19/1989	Indian Wells $510,000 SS	Miloslav Mecir	Yannick Noah	B. Becker - J. Hlasek	K. Curren - D. Pate
4/2/1989	Key Biscayne $745,000 SS	Ivan Lendl	Thomas Muster	J. Hlasek - A. Jarryd	J. Grabb - P. McEnroe
4/10/1989	Beijing $123,400 GP	Kelly Jones	Amos Mansdorf	R. Leach - J. Pugh	P. Chamberlin - P. Wekesa
4/16/1989	Seoul $93,400 GP	Robert Van't Hof	Brad Drewett	S. Davis - P. Wekesa	J. Letts - B. Man Song Hing

4/16/1989	Rio de Jan. $200,000 GP	Mauricio Hadad	Guillermo Minutella	J. Lorzano - T. Witsken	P. McEnroe - T. Wilkison
4/16/1989	Athens $93,400 GP	Ronald Agenor	Kent Carlsson	C. Panatta - T. Smid	G. Giussani - G. Mirad
4/23/1989	Tokyo $425,000 SS	Stefan Edberg	Ivan Lendl	K. Flach - R. Seguso	K. Curren - D. Pate
4/23/1989	Nice $140,000	Andrei Chesnokov	Jerome Potier	R. Osterthun - U. Riglewsky	H. Gunthardt - B. Taroczy
4/30/1989	Monte Carlo $405,000 SS	Alberto Mancini	Boris Becker	T. Smid - M. Woodforde	P. Cane - D. Nargiso
4/30/1989	Singapore $93,400 GP	Kelly Jones	Amos Mansdorf	R. Leach - J. Pugh	P. Chamberlin - P. Wekesa
5/8/1989	NY $485,000 WCT TC	Ivan Lendl	Jaime Yzaga	J. Leach - J. Pugh	J. Courier - P. Sampras
5/7/1989	Munich $175,000 GP	Andrei Chesnokov	Martin Strelba	J. Sanchez - B. Taroczy	P. Doohan - L. Warder
5/14/1989	Hamburg $500,000 SS	Ivan Lendl	Horst Skoff	E. Sanchez - J. Sanchez	B. Becker - E. Jelen
5/14/1989	Charleston $190,000 GP	Jay Berger	Lawson Duncan	M. Pernfors - T. Svantesson	A. Moreno - J. Yzaga
5/21/1989	Rome $807,500 SS	Alberto Mancini	Andre Agassi	J. Courier - P. Sampras	D. Marcelino - M. Menezes
5/28/1989	Florence $93,400 GP	Horacio De La Pena	Goran Ivanisevic	M. DePalmer - B. Willenborg	P. Pennisi - S. Restelli
5/28/1989	Dus'ldorf $750,000 WTC	Germany	Argentina	2-1,	
5/28/1989	Dus'ldorf $750,000 WTC	Boris Becker	G. Perez-Roldan	6-0, 2-6, 6-2	
5/28/1989	Dus'ldorf $750,000 WTC	Martin Jaite	Carl-UWE Steeb	6-4, 6-3	
5/28/1989	Dus'ldorf $750,000 WTC		6-4, 7-5	B. Becker- E. Jelen	J Frana-G. Luza
6/11/1989	French Open $4.5 M GS	Michael Chang	Stefan Edberg	J. Grabb - P. McEnroe	M. Bahrami - E. Einogradsky
6/18/1989	Bologna $93,400 GP	Javier Sanchez	Franco Davin	S. Casal - J. Sanchez	T. Nydahl - J. Windahl
6/18/1989	London $350,000 GP	Ivan Lendl	Christo Van Rensburg	D. Cahill - M. Kratzmann	T. Pawsat - L. Warder
6/18/1989	Edinburg SP	John McEnroe	Jimmy Connors		
6/25/1989	Bristol $100,000 GP	Eric Jelen	Nick Brown	P. Chamberlin - T. Wilkison	M DePalmer - G. Donnelly
6/25/1989	Bari $93,400 GP	Juan Aguilera	Marian Vajda	S. Colombo - C. Mezzadri	S. Casal - J. Sanchez

7/9/1989	Wimbledon GS	Boris Becker	Stefan Edberg	J. Fitzgerald - A. Jarryd	R. Leach - J. Pugh
7/16/1989	Boston $415,000 SS	Andres Gomez	Mats Wilander	A. Gomez - A. Mancini	T. Nelson - P. Williamson
7/16/1989	Gstaad $275,000 GP	Carl-Uwe Steeb	Magnus Gustafsson	C. Motta - T. Witsken	P. Korda - M. Srejber
7/16/1989	Newport $125,000 GP	Jim Pugh	Peter Lundgren	P. Galbraith - B. Garrow	N. Broad - S. Kruger
7/23/1989	Schenectady $100,000 GP	Simon Youl	Scott Davis	S. Davis - B. Dyke	B. Pearce - B. Talbot
7/30/1989	Washington $297,500 SS	Tim Mayotte	Brad Gilbert	N. Broad - G. Muller	J. Grabb - P. McEnroe
7/30/1989	Stuttgart $275,000 GP	Martin Jaite	Goran Prpic	P. Korda - T. Smid	F. Segarceanu - C. Suk
7/30/1989	Hilversum $150,000 GP	Karel Novacek	Emilio Sanchez	T. Carbonell - D. Perez	P. Haarhuis - M. Koevermans
8/6/1989	Stratton Mtn. $602,500 SS	Brad Gilbert	Jim Pugh	M. Kratzmann - W. Masur	P. Aldrich - D. Visser
8/6/1989	Bastad $275,000 - GP	Paolo Cane	Bruno Oresar	P. Henricsson - N. Utgren	J. Cihak - K. Novacek
8/6/1989	Kitzbuhel $300,000 GP	Emilio Sanchez	Martin Jaite	E. Sanchez - J. Sanchez	P. Korda - T. Smid
8/13/1989	Indianapolis $300,000 SS	John McEnroe	Jay Berger	P. Aldrich - D. Visser	P. Doohan - L. Warder
8/13/1989	Prague $140,000 GP	Marcelo Filippini	Horst Skoff	J. Arrese - H. Skoff	P. Korda - T. Smid
8/13/1989	Livingston $93,400 GP	Brad Gilbert	Jason Stoltenberg	T. Pawsat - T. Wilkison	K. Evernden - S. Giammalva
8/20/1989	Montreal $742,500 SS	Ivan Lendl	John McEnroe	K. Evernden - T. Witsken	C. Beckman - S. Cannon
8/21/1989	Cincinnati $485,000 SS	Brad Gilbert	Stefan Edberg	K. Flach - R. Seguso	P. Aldrich - D. Visser
8/20/1989	St. Vincent $125,000 GP	Franco Davin	Juan Agilera	J. Cihak - C. Suk	M. Cierro - A. De Minicis
8/27/1989	San Marino $93,400 GP	Jose Francisco Altur	Roberto Azar	S. Colombo - C. Mezzadri	P. Albano - G. Luza
8/27/1989	Jericho Hamlet SP	Ivan Lendl	Mikael Pernfors		
9/10/1989	US Open GS	Boris Becker	Ivan Lendl	J. McEnroe - M. Woodforde	K. Flach - R. Seguso
9/15/1989	London SP	John McEnroe	Stefan Edberg		
9/17/1989	Geneva $190,000 GP	Marc Rosset	Guillermo Perez-Roldan	A. Gomez - A. Mancini	M. Bahrami - G. Perez-Roldan

9/17/1989	Madrid $175,000 GP	Andres Gomez	Marc Rosset	T. Carbonell - C. Costa	F. Clavet - T. Smid
9/24/1989	Barcelona $375,000 SS	Andres Gomez	Horst Skoff	G. Luza - C. Miniussi	S. Casal - T. Smid
9/24/1989	Los Angeles $297,000 SS	Aaron Krickstein	Michael Chang	M. Davis - T. Pawsat	J. Fitzgerald - A. Jarryd
10/1/1989	San Francisco $297,000 SS	Brad Gilbert	Anders Jarryd	P. Aldrich - D. Visser	P. Annacone - Van Rensburg
10/1/1989	Palermo $225,000 GP	Guillermo Perez-Roldan	Pablo Cane	P. Ballauff - R. Haas	G. Ivansevic - D. Nargiso
10/1/1989	Bordeaux $225,000 GP	Ivan Lendl	Emilio Sanchez	T. Carbonell - C. Di Laura	A. Moreno - J. Yzaga
10/8/1989	Orlando $297,500 SS	Andre Agassi	Brad Gilbert	S. Davis - T. Pawset	K. Flach - R. Seguso
10/8/1989	Basle $361,000 GP	Jim Courier	Stefan Edberg	U. Riglewski - M. Stich	O. Camporese - C. Mezzadri
10/8/1989	Brisbane $150,000 GP	Nicklas Kroon	Mark Woodforde	D. Cahill - M. Kratzmann	B. Dyke - S. Youl
10/15/1989	Sydney $375,000 SS	Ivan Lendl	Lars Wahlgren	D. Pate - W. Warner	C. Cahill - M. Kratzmann
10/15/1989	Toulouse $225,000 GP	Jimmy Connors	John McEnroe	M. Bahrami - E. Winogradsky	T. Nijssen - R. Smith
10/22/1989	Vienna $225,000 GP	Paul Annacone	Kelly Evernden	J/ Gunnarsson - A. Jarryd	P. annacone - K. Evernden
10/22/1989	Tokyo $500,000 SS	Aaron Krickstein	Carl-Uwe Steeb	K. Curren - D. Pate	A. Gomez - S. Zinojinovic
10/22/1989	Tel Aviv $100,000 GP	Jimmy Connors	Gilab Bloom	J. Bates - P. Baur	R. Bergh - Per Henricsson
10/29/1989	Frankfurt $175,000 GP	Kevin Curren	Petr Korda	P. Aldrich - D. Visser	K. Curren - P. Galbraith
11/5/1989	Paris $1,000,000 SS	Boris Becker	Stefan Edberg	J. Fitzgerald - A. Jarryd	J. Hlasek - E. Winogradsky
11/5/1989	Antwerp $1M ECC SP	John McEnroe	Andrei Cherkasov		
11/10/1989	Stuttgart $350,000 SP	John McEnroe	Ivan Lendl		
11/10/1989	Stockholm $832,500 SS	Ivan Lendl	Magnus Gustafsson	J. Lorzano - T. Witsken	R. Leach - J. Pugh
11/12/1989	London $400,000 SS	Michael Chang	Guy Forget	J. Hlasek - J. McEnroe	J. Bates - K. Curren
11/12/1989	Sao Paulo $100,000 GP	Martin Jaite	Javier Sanchez	cancelled	R. Acuna - J. Sanchez

11/19/1989	Johannesburg $297,000 SS	Christo van Rensburg	Paul Chamberlin	L. Jensen - R. Reneberg	K. Jones - J. Rive
11/19/1989	Detroit Little Caesars SP	John McEnroe	Aaron Krickstein		
11/25/1989	Edinburgh SP				
12/3/1989	NY $750,000 Nabisco Masters	Stefan Edberg	Boris Becker		
12/10/1989	London $200,000 Nabisco Masters			J. Grabb - P. McEnroe	J. Fitzgerald - A. Jarryd

http://www.atpworldtour.com/en/scores/results-archive.

http://www.itftennis.com/procircuit/tournaments/men's-calendar.aspx?tour=&reg=&nat=&sur=&cate=AL&iod=&-fromDate=01-01-1968&toDate=31-12-1989.

Tennis History, Jim McManus, (Canada 2010).

1990 USTA Yearbook.

Official 1989 MTC Media Guide, (MTC 1989).

World of Tennis 1990, Edited by John Barrett and compiled by Marijke Volger, (London 1990).

CHAPTER 33:

1989: CADRE OF MEN'S TENNIS COUNCIL CERTIFIED TENNIS OFFICIALS[795]

Just as important as curtailing the player misconduct that was prevalent before the creation of the MTC in 1974, the MTC pioneered the development of professional tennis officiating through its official's schools, its certification program and its Code for officials. The MTC employed the first full-time professional Supervisors and the first full-time professional Chair Umpires and provided evaluations of all on-court officials in its sanctioned tournaments. The MTC provided men's professional tennis with a trained, tested and certified cadre of referees, chiefs of umpires and chair umpires to lead tennis officiating for many years. The 1989 MTC certified officials were:

MTC Certified Referees

1. Leonard S. Allard, Mississauga, Canada
2. Thomas C. Barnes, Fresno, Calif., USA
3. William John Barry, Auckland, New Zealand
4. Ian Morris Basey, Blair Athol, Australia
5. Peter Bellenger, Glen Waverly, Australia
6. Andre Binet, St. Eustache, Canada
7. Vincenzo Bottone, Rome, Italy
8. Gayle Bradshaw, Evans, Georgia, USA
9. Luigi Brambilla, Pomezia, Italy
10. Pedro Bravo, Vina Del Mar, Chile

29. Thomas J. Johnston, Brisbane, Australia
30. Kosei Kamo, Tokyo, Japan
31. Henk C. D. Korvinus, Rotterdam, Netherlands
32. Herbert Kosten, Memphis, Tenn., USA
33. Michael J. Lugg, Lymington, Great Britain
34. Peter Madl, Vienna, Austria
35. Giuseppe Martini, Rieti, Italy
36. Alan Ronald Mills, Surrey, Great Britain
37. James Moore, Brisbane, Australia
38. Warwick Guy Nash, Auckland, New Zealand

11. Dr. Benny J.Y. Chen, Taiwan

12. Georgia Clark, Banbury, Great Britain

13. Mark Darby, Schenectady, NY, USA

14. Peter B. Duncan North Rocks, Australia

15. Brian Early, Charlotte, NC, USA

16. Dr. Peter Eder, Kitzbuhel, Austria

17. Dr. Hans Gaber, Vienna, Austria

18. Dr. Sultan H. Ganji, London, Great Britain

19. Tony Gathercole, Surrey, Great Britain

20. Daniel Gelley, Ashkelon, Ill., USA

21. Claudio Grether, Steffsburg, Switzerland

22. Charles Guillemot, Pornichet, France

23. Frank Hammond, Jr., New York, NY, USA

24. James G. Haslam, Greensboro, NC, USA

25. John L. Heiss, Cocoa Beach, Fla., USA

26. John Walter Holsinger, Pokfulam, Hong Kong

27. Robert N. Howe, Irving, Calif., USA

28. Keith Johnson, Honolulu, Hi., USA

39. Kurt Nielsen, Lynghy, Denmark

40. Lars Nordenhoek, Stockholm, Sweden

41. Lars Pawli, ESBO FI

42. Norbert Peick, Munich, Germany

43. Zeno J. Pfau, Jr., Richardson, Texas, USA

44. Marcel Poelmans, Brussels, Belgium

45. Javier Sansierra, Madrid, Spain

46. E. Victor Seixas, Jr., Mandeville, La., USA

47. Jeremy Shales, Middlesex, Great Britain

48. Didier Simonnet, Didonne, France

49. Sean Sloane, Williamstown, Mass., USA

50. Juan M. Tintore, Barcelona, Spain

51. Isao Watanabe, Tokyo, Japan

52. Anders G. Wennberg, Helsingborg, Sweden

53. Donald J. Wiley, Santa Barbara, Calif., USA

54. Dr. Jochen Wulff, Pittsburgh, Pa., USA

55. Gilbert Ysern, Tounan en Brie, France

56. James Zimmerman, Cupertino, Calif., USA

MTC Certified Chief of Umpires

1. Karl Allison, New Market, Canada

2. William H. Barber, Brandywine, Md., USA

3. Thomas C. Barnes, Fresno, Calif, USA

4. B. Sue Benson, Greenbelt, Md., USA

5. Davie Bierwirth, East Malvern, Australia

34. Bo Harling, Vasteras Sweden

35. Donald G. Harmon, Cincinnati, Ohio, USA

36. Toh-Itsu Hasagawa, Achi-Ken, Japan

37. Thomas J. Johnson, Brisbane, Australia

38. Henk C.D. Korvinus, Rotterdam, Netherlands

6. John V. Blaze, Osterville , Mass., USA

7. Kevin R. Bolton, S. Blackburn, Australia

8. Norris B. Bond, Wellesley, Mass., USA

9. Gayle Bradshaw, Evans, Georgia, USA

10. Luigi Brambilla, Pomezia, Italy

11. Jurgen Buttkus, Geneva, Switzerland

12. D. Emma Catalini, Londonberry, NH, USA

13. Georgina Clark, Banbury, Great Britain

14. Manuel Costa, Barcelona, Spain

15. Robert E. Cranor, Panorama City, Calif., USA

16. Keith Crossland, Chicago, Ill., USA

17. David F. Crymble, Auckland, New Zealand

18. Robert B. Da Viega, Sao Paulo, Brazil

19. Thomas I. Earl, Memphis, Tenn., USA

20. Brian Earley, Charlotte, NC, USA

21. Peter Eder, Kitzbuhel, Austria

22. Ronald C. Eick, Devon, Pa., USA

23. Ingvar Emmertz, Lund, Sweden

24. Jacques Fargo, Forest Hills, NY, US

25. John G. Frame, Midlothian, Great Britain

26. Don G. Frydell, Indianapolis, Ind., USA

39. Phillip John Leek, Chadstone, Australia

40. Ove Lindh, Gothenburg, Sweden

41. Michael John Lugg, Lymington, Great Britain

42. Richard John Lumb, Wiltshire, Great Britain

43. Les Maddock, Hants, Great Britain

44. Kenji Masuda, Tokyo, Japan

45. David H. Munro, Christchurch, New Zealand

46. Martin Parker, Briarcliff Manor, Md., USA

47. David L. Parker, Parsonburg Md. USA

48. John Parry, Derbyshire, Great Britain

49. Thomas Patterson, Chicago Ill., USA

50. Zeno J. Pfau, Jr., Richardson, Texas, USA

51. Janet Ryan, Huntington Beach, Calif., USA

52. Javier Sansierra, Madrid, Spain

53. Stewart Samphire, Silver Spring, Md., USA

54. Jeff Shafer, Johannesburg, South Africa

55. Joyce Siegel, Hollywood, Fla., USA

56. Kenneth M. Slye, Alexandria, Va., USA

57. Roger B. Smith, Bucks, Great Britain

58. Joseph Snyder, Hummelstown, Pa., USA

59. Woodie Sublett, Evansville, Ind., USA

27. Dr. Hans Gaber, Vienna, Austria

28. Dr. Sultan H. Ganji, London, Great Britain

29. Dr. Wolfgang Gnettner, Munich, Germany

30. Heinz Grueter, Basel, Switzerland

31. Charles Guillemot, Pornichet, France

32. Jim Handly, Tampa, Fla., USA

33. John E. Hansen, Orange Park, Fla., USA

60. Roy Van Brunt, Jr., Columbia, Md. USA

61. Joan Vormbaum, San Jose, Calif., USA

62. Patricia Walker, Carlingford, Australia

63. Christopher F. Webster, Brisbane, Australia

64. Lt. Col. Peter B. Webster, Wiltshire, Great Britain

65. Donald J. Wiley, Santa Barbara, Calif, USA

66. Michel Willems, Loverval, Belgium

MTC Certified Chair Umpires

1. Jorge Amilibia, Barcelona, Spain

2. Gerald Armstrong, East Sussex, Great Britain

3. William H. Barber, Brandywine, Md., USA

4. Thomas C. Barnes, Fresno, Calif., USA

5. William John Barry, Auckland, New Zealand

6. Ronnie L. Bennett, San Diego, Calif., USA

7. Sue Benson, Greenbelt, Md. USA

8. Rudolf Berger, Munich, Germany

9. Alan Bezzant, Kent, Great Britain

10. David Bierwirth, East Malvern, Australia

11. Andre Binet, Quebec, Canada

59. David Johnson, Bromley, Great Britain

60. Thomas J. Johnston, Brisbane, Australia

61. Jean Jonret, Knesselare-Ured, Belgium

62. Lars Karlsson, Stockholm, Sweden

63. Peter C. Kasavage, San Ramone, Calif, USA

64. Richard Kaufman, New York, NY US

65. William A. Kempffer, Ontario, Canada

66. Mike C. Lai, Taipei, Taiwan

67. Lionel Laskar, Nice, France

68. Walter Leeman, Brasschant, Belgium

69. Stephen K.T. Leung, Queensway, Hong Kong

12. John V. Blaze, Osterville, Mass., USA

13. Zoltan Bognar, Stuttgart, Germany

14. Philippe Boivin, Cergy, France

15. Norris B. Bond, Wellesley, Mass., USA

16. Vincenzo Bottone, Rome, Italy

17. Luigi Brambilla, Pomezia, Italy

18. Pedro Bravo, Vina Del Mar, Chile

19. Ian Gregory Bray, Leumeah, Australia

20. John D. Bryson, Essex, Great Britain

21. Dean C.D. Chan, Taipei, Taiwan

22. Norm Chryst, Martinez, Calif., USA

23. Brett D. Clarke, Chesapeake, Va., USA

24. David V. Cotton, East Kilara, Australia

25. Lindsey Cox, Unley, Australia

26. Robert E. Cranor, Panorama City, Calif., USA

27. Keith Crosland, Chicago, Ill., USA

28. David F. Crymble, Auckland, New Zealand

29. Jorge Dias, Lisbon, Portugal

70. David Littlefield, Lakeworth, Fla., USA

71. Dana Loconto, Gadsden, Ala., USA

72. Michael C. Loo, Walnut Creek, Calif., USA

73. Michael John Lugg, Lymington, Great Britain

74. Richard John Lumb, Wilshire Great Britain

75. William MacDonald, Perth Scotland

76. Peter Madl, Vienna, Austria

77. Kurt Magnusson, Vaxjo, Sweden

78. Youssef Makar, Lausanne, Switzerland

79. Dr. David John Martin, Auckland, New Zealand

80. Sergio Massetti, Geneva, Switzerland

81. Gabriel Mato, Madrid, Spain

82. Fran McDowell, Mt. Vernon, Wash., USA

83. James A. McKnight, Longwood, Fla., USA

84. Jean-Philippe Merlet, Cagnes Sur Mer, France

85. Javier Moreno, Barcelona, Spain

86. Kazuo Mukai, Taipei, Taiwan

87. David H. Munro, Christchurch, New Zealand

30. Guiseppe DiStefano, Capri, Italy

31. Raymond Dombrecht, Brussels, Belgium

32. Dr. Peter Dunovic, Basking Ridge, NJ, USA

33. Peter B. Duncan, North Rocks, Australia

34. Andreas Egli, Weggis, Switzerland

35. Jacques Fargo, Forest Hills, NY, USA

36. Dr. Peter Foltyn, Parramatta, Australia

37. John G. Frame, Midlothian, Great Britain

38. Dr. Sultan H. Gangji, London, Great Britain

39. Daniel Gelley, Ashekelon Ill., USA

40. Brunello Giglio, Rome, Italy

41. Ove Glamheden, Sandared, Sweden

42. Marvin A. Goldberg, Fremont, Calif., USA

43. Knut A. Graebner, Krefeld, Germany

44. Lars Graff, Stockholm, Sweden

45. Herbert Granierer, Ramat Gan, Ill., USA

46. Marco Grether, Basel, Switzerland

47. George H. Grime, Wegberg, German

88. Stephen T. Nash, Auckland, New Zealand

89. Warwick Guy Nash, Auckland, New Zealand

90. Leif Ake Nilsson, Malmo, Sweden

91. Syuya Oyama, Hirosaki City, Japan

92. Christian Parigger, Tirol, Austria

93. John Parry, Derbyshire Great Britain

94. Paulo Pereira, Sao Paulo, Brazil

95. Ross T. Perkinson, Auckland, New Zealand

96. Michel Perrot, Aix-en-Provence, France

97. Zeno J. Pfau, Jr., Richardson, Texas, USA

98. Stefan Rauth, Bregenz, Austria

99. Bruno Rebeuh, Nice, France

100. Michael A. Rice, Johannesburg, South Africa

101. Claude Richard, Noisy le Sec, France

102. Erich Rottinger, Tulin, Austria

103. William Ruhle, Balboa Island, Calif., USA

104. George Rustscheff, Ontario, Canada

105. Goran Sandstrom, Saltsjo-Boo, Sweden

48. Heinz Grueter, Basel, Switzerland

49. Walter Hahne, Riedstadt, Germany

50. Jeff Hall, Sydney, Australia

51. Toh-Itsu Hasegawa, Aichi-ken, Japan

52. Koichi Hiraki, Chiba, Japan

53. John Walter Holsinger, Pokfulam, Hong Kong

54. David C. Howie, London, Great Britain

55. Malcolm Huntington, York, Great Britain

56. Richard L. Ings, N. Epping, Australia

57. Shyen Ming Jang, Taipei, Taiwan

58. Philip Jankelevitch, Hasseh, Belgium

117. Kenyon T. Stubbs, St. Louis, Mo., USA

118. Stuart Super, Southwest Africa

119. Jane Tabor, Dorset, Great Britain Calif., USA

120. Alberto Tintore, Barcelona, Spain

121. Steve Ullrich, Tampa, Fla., USA

122. Fabricio Valdivieso, Guayaquil, Ecuador

123. Roy Van Brunt, Jr., Columbia, Md., USA

106. Salvador Sans, Barcelona, Spain

107. Javier Sansierra, Madrid, Spain

108. Stewart Saphier, Silver Spring, Md. USA

109. Ronnie Sender, Ramat Hasharon Ill., USA

110. Jeremy Shales, Middlesex, Great Britain

111. David K. Y. Siu, Hong Kong

112. Kenneth M. Slye, Alexandria, Va., USA

113. Roger B. Smith, Bucks, Great Britain

114. Joseph Snyder, Hummelstown, Pa., USA

115. Stanley Sperber, Ramat Aviv Ill., USA

116. John H. Sternbach, Denver, Colo., USA

125. Joan Vormbaum, San Jose, Calif., USA

126. Maxwell C. Ward, Carlingford, Australia

127. Donald Wiley, Santa Barbara,

128. Lars Wingard, Jarfalla, Sweden

129. Stephen Winyard, West Yorkshire, Great Britain

130. Nicolas Wolff, Ontario, Canada

131. Juergen H. Wuerzner, Hamburg, German

124. Marleen van Noortwijk, Breda New Zealand

132. James Zimmerman, Cupertino, Calif., USA

MTC Certified National Referees

1. Don Andrews, Mililani Twn, Hawaii, USA

2. Mrs. J. Angus, Buckingham, Great Britain

3. Cees A.M. Beerepoot, Eindhoven, Netherlands

4. B. Sue Benson, Greenbelt, Md., USA

5. Peter Cap, Prague Czech Republic

6. Sr. Miguel Crespo, Valencia, Spain

7. Jorge Dias, Lisbon, Portugal

8. Peter Dose, Rufenacht, Switzerland

9. Ingvar Emmertz, Lund, Sweden

10. Andrea Fabri, Rome, Italy

11. Patrick Flodrops, Boulogne, France

12. Don G. Frydell, Indianapolis, Ind., USA

13. Jean Fyfe, London, Great Britain

14. Renzo Gambi, Ravenna, Italy

15. Patrick Grahn, Helsinki, Finland

16. Herbert Granierer, Ramat Gan, Ill., USA

17. George H. Grime, Wegberg, German y

18. Gabriel Guix, Barcelona, Spain

19. James C. Handly, Tampa, Fla., USA

20. Toh-Itsu Hasegawa, Aichi-ken, Japan

21. Carl-Edward Hedelund, Hojbjerg, Denmark

22. Vesselin Houbaunov, Sofia, Bulgaria

27. Henry Lappin, Dublin, Ireland

28. Jacek Luba, Warsaw, Poland

29. Richard John Lumb, Wiltshire, Great Britain

30. Rolf-Dieter Madlindl, Gauting, German

31. Peter S. Malik, New Delhi, India

32. Leonard Markwart, Urbach, Germany

33. Gabriel Mato, Madrid, Spain

34. Javier Moreno, Barcelona, Spain

35. Peter Nader, Vienna, Austria

36. Leif Ake Nilsson, Malmo, Sweden

37. Laszlo Nyiro, Budapest, Hungary

38. Michel Perrot, Aix-en-Provence, France

39. Claude Richard, Nosy de Sec, France

40. Roland Schmid, Linz, Austria

41. Antonio Segueira, Liston, Portugal

42. J. M. Sexton London, Great Britain

43. Thomas Stubenbock, Tirol, Austria

44. Woodie Sublett, Evansville, Ind., USA

45. Franco Vivona, Rome, Italy

46. Maxwell C. Ward, Carlingford, Australia

47. Michel Willems, Loverval, Belgium

48. Stephen Winyard, West Yorkshire, Great Britain

23. Fred W. Hoyles, Spalding Lanes, Great Britain

24. Daxuan Huang, Shanghai, China

25. Lauri Julin, Tampere Fla., USA

26. Eugene Lapierre, Quebec, Canada

49. Lucien Zadelaar, Apeldoorn, New Zealand

50. Baoen Zhou, Beijing China

51. Mr. Ziesak, Prague Czech Republic

CHAPTER 34:

1989: A ROCKY BEGINNING FOR THE NEW ATP TOUR

ATP Tournament Application Committee

In January of 1989, the ATP announced that its ATP Tournament Application Committee that would select the tournaments for the 1990 ATP Tour would consist of player representatives Jaime Fillol, Harold Solomon and Zeljko Franolovic and tournament representatives Paul Svehlik, Stan Smith and Ross Case.[796]

One big advantage the new ATP Tour had with respect to dealing with tournament applications and developing a 1990 calendar was that no tournament had any history or any rights they could claim. ATP was not subject to the settlement of the Volvo lawsuit or the WCT lawsuit and ATP had no pre-existing agreements. *Put another way, the tournaments were completely at the mercy of the ATP Tournament Application Committee, bidding against each other and a number of proposed new tournaments.* In addition to the four Grand Slams, the 1989 Grand Prix had 26 Super Series, plus the Lipton and the WCT Tournament of Champions and the 1990 ATP Tour was going to have only 21 "Championship Series" events, 11 of which would be single weeks and 10 of which would be double-up weeks. WCT was not requested to and did not apply for any tournament sanctions from the new ATP Tour. Based on prior history, it was then assumed that WCT would create a new WCT circuit for 1990 or 1991, as Lamar Hunt still had plenty of money and had never accepted being left out since WCT began in 1967.

ATP Tour World Championship

On January 27, the ATP announced that its 1990 year-end finals event replacing the Nabisco Masters would be called the ATP Tour World Championship and moved from New York City to Frankfurt, Germany, with prize money of $2 million. The 1989 Nabisco Masters had only $750,000. However, in 1990 due to the explosion of satellite television in Europe, the German satellite "SAT.1" would pay a whopping $5 million for the television rights to just Germany, Austria and Switzerland for the new ATP Finals. The new Grand Slam Cup which also began in 1990 would also receive another $5 million from SAT.1. The most we could obtain for the 1985 television rights for the Nabisco Masters from the European Broadcasting Union (EBU) which represented all of the public over-the-air television networks in Europe (before the advent of European cable networks) was only $75,000.

1990 ATP Tournaments Selected

On January 27, the ATP Tour reported that the Application Committee had selected 75 tournaments for the new ATP Tour. The 1990 Tour included for the first time two levels of "Championship Series" events: 11 single-week tournaments and 10 double-up week tournaments and 54 "World Series" tournaments, plus the year-end ATP Tour Singles Finals and the ATP Tour Doubles Finals. Contrast that with the MTC's 1989 calendar which, in addition to the Grand Slams, included the Lipton two-week ATP tournament and 26 Super Series, WCT Tournament of Champions, WCT Finals, Nabisco Masters and Nabisco Masters Doubles.

First Class: 11 Single-Week Championship Series - $1 Million Minimum

There were 11 single-week Championship Series tournaments ($1 million minimum) that would receive designations of six of the top 10. Selected were:

Tournament	Week Of	Player Compensation
1. Indian Wells	March 5-11	$1 million

[Charles Pasarell TD].

2. Key Biscayne	March 16-25	$1.5 million

[reduced from 2 weeks to 10 days and now owned by Butch Buchholz with no ATP involvement: *Goodbye to the "Players' Grand Slam."*]

3. Monte Carlo	April 23-29	$1 million
4. Hamburg	May 7-13	$1 million
5. Rome	May 14-20	$1 million

[Franco Bartoni TD]. [There was no longer a WCT Tournament of Champions in New York in between Hamburg & Rome].

6. Canada	July 23-29	$1.2 million

| 7. | Cincinnati | August 6-12 | $1.3 million |

[now owned by Paul Flory's company with no ATP involvement].

| 8. | Sydney | October 1-7 | $1 million |

[Graham Lovett TD, now owned by Channel 10].

| 9. | Tokyo Seiko | October 8-14 | $1 million |
| 10. | Paris | October 29 – Nov. 4 | $2 million |

[Note that Pasarell, Bartoni and Lovett, former members of the MTC and also now on the new ATP Tour Board, each got one of the select single-week tournaments. The Paris Indoors was owned by the French Tennis Federation, Philippe Chatrier, President, and he was always fearful that the ATP would retaliate against the Paris Indoors, thus the $2 million offer].

| 11. | Stockholm | October 22-28 | $1.1 million |

Second Class: 10 Double-Up Week Championship Tournaments, $500,000 Minimum

There were 10 double up or second class Championship Series tournaments ($500,000 minimum) that would receive designations of three of the top 10. Selected were:

1.	Toronto	February 12-18	$1.2 million
2.	Brussels	February 12-18	$ 600,000
3.	Philadelphia	February 19-25	$1 million
4.	Stuttgart [new Tiriac Indoors]	February 19-25	$1 million
5.	Japan Open [No longer with WCT]	April 9-15	$1 million
6.	Barcelona	April 9-15	$ 500,000
7.	Stuttgart (outdoors)	July 16-22	$ 900,000

[Moved up from Grand Prix Regular Series, still "selling" Mercedes]

8.	Washington	July 16-22	$ 550,000
9.	Stratton	August 13-19	$ 625,000
10.	Indianapolis	August 13-19	$ 650,000

Note: Even though the minimum for the second class tournaments was $500,000, several tournaments offered $1,000,000 because they wanted to claim there were just as important as the first class tournaments even though their designations were to be only three of the top 10 instead of six of the top 10; *that provided a big first step towards bankruptcy.*

The following Grand Prix Super Series were demoted from Grand Prix Super Series to ATP Tour World Series:

1.	Rotterdam	$250,000
2.	Memphis	$250,000
3.	Scottsdale [No longer WCT]	$250,000
4.	Los Angeles	$250,000
5.	San Francisco	$250,000
6.	Orlando [ProServ]	$250,000
7.	Johannesburg	$250,000
8.	London	$500,000

In addition to the financial commitment, each tournament was also required to provide free housing ("hospitality") for all singles and doubles players and pay appearance fees to attract some players.

In addition to the four Grand Slams, the following major Grand Prix tournaments were not included in the 1990 ATP Tour:

1. Boston Super Series

2. WCT Dallas Finals

3. WCT Forest Hills Tournament of Champions

4. Nabisco Masters (Singles) [replaced by ATP Tour Singles Finals in Frankfurt]

5. Nabisco Masters Doubles [replaced by ATP Tour Doubles Finals in Gold Coast, Australia

Meeting with Philip Galloway

On March 8 at Hamilton's request, I met with Philip Galloway of Ernst & Whinney and provided him confidentially with as much information as I could on the costs of operation of the MTC, including the salary information for our current employees. I also agreed at Hamilton's request to provide him with "my evaluation and comments on our current employees who I would like to possibly place with the ATP Tour." Philip "Flip" Galloway would soon be hired away from Ernst & Whinney by Hamilton to become the outstanding career financial officer of the ATP Tour.[797]

ATP Tour – ITF/Grand Slam Crisis No. 1: Davis Cup I Schedule

In 1989, the ITF had scheduled Davis Cup I (Davis Cup, round of 16), the first round of Davis Cup, for the week of February 3-5, 1989, the week immediately after the 1989 Australian Open. When ATP issued its first calendar for the 1990 ATP Tour, it "scheduled or left open" a week for Davis Cup No. 1 for the comparable week of February 2-4, 1990, the week immediately after the Australian Open. The ATP Tour then scheduled Milan ($600,000), San Francisco ($250,000) and (Guaruja $150,000) for the next week of February 5-11, 1990. On February 17, the ITF scheduled Davis Cup I for the week of February 9-11, 1990, the second week after the Australian Open and in the same week that the ATP had scheduled Milan, San Francisco and Guaruja.

Hamilton Jordan immediately objected to the change of the Davis Cup I date to conflict with three ATP Tour tournaments and threatened that if the ITF and the Grand Slams do not respect the dates wanted by the ATP Tour then the ATP Tour would no longer "protect" dates for the Davis Cup and the Grand Slams, i.e., the ATP might schedule ATP Tour tournaments during the weeks of the Davis Cup and during the weeks of the Grand Slams. Not mentioned, was the significant anti-trust issues that would be presented if the ATP attempted to use its "monopoly" with the players to compete with or destroy the Davis Cup and the Grand Slams. The ITF ultimately relented and 1990 Davis Cup I was re-scheduled for the week after the Australian Open on February 2-4, 1990.[798]

IMG Hired for ATP Tour

At a press conference on March 27 at Key Biscayne, Hamilton Jordan announced that the ATP Tour had hired IMG as its exclusive marketing agent for the sale of the ATP Tour presenting sponsor rights, international television rights and ATP Tour Finals rights, which contained a minimum guarantee of $56.1 million over three years: $17.2 million in 1990, $16.7 million for 1991 and $20.2 million for 1992. *Television rights were pooled after all!*[799]

Voluntary Pools of Marketing and Television Rights

On April 14, 1989, Hamilton Jordan explained that the new contract with IMG made possible the voluntary pooling of individual tournament marketing and television rights. Hamilton Jordan reported to the new ATP Tour Board: "Simply stated, the $56.1 million guarantee from IMG means that the financial future of the ATP Tour is secure in its early years. It also means that we will have the necessary resources that we need to organize the new Tour, staff it properly, develop a television package and market the Tour and our sport centrally and aggressively. It also means that the ATP Tour will have sufficient resources to provide direct funding to the individual tournaments to support the Tour sponsor and to assemble an international television package."[800]

Wimbledon: "The Leaders of Our Sport"

After saluting Wimbledon's increase in 1989 prize money, Hamilton Jordan wrote in *International Tennis Weekly*[801]: "In addition, R.E. H. 'Buzzer' Hadingham and the Committee of Management at the All England Club have also demonstrated their leadership in the game and their sensitivity to player concerns by acting as an intermediary between the new ATP Tour and the ITF. Although they shared the ITF's initial concerns about the ATP Tour, once the new ATP Tour had demonstrated broad player and tournament support and had proven its viability, our friends at Wimbledon have been at the forefront of trying to find a peaceful solution to the problems which continue to divide the ITF and the ATP Tour. For their continuing leadership and help, the players salute our friends at the All England Club. They are truly, the 'Leaders of Our Sport.'" *I had to smile at Hamilton's effectiveness.*

ITF/Grand Slam Crisis No. 2: ATP Objects to ITF Challenger and Satellite Governance

On June 13, the ITF announced the creation of the ITF Challenger and Satellite Committee to sanction, schedule and administer the 1990 challenger and satellite circuits. ATP was invited to join the committee. In the second new dispute between the ATP Tour and the ITF, on June 15, Hamilton Jordan refused to agree with the ITF providing the governance for the challenger and satellite circuits. As long as the ATP Computer Rankings were used for entrance into the ATP Tour, challengers and satellites, the ATP had the dominant position.[802]

ITF Grand Slam Committee Formed

On June 15, the ITF issued its press release for the formation of the ITF Grand Slam Committee to form a harmonizing committee to maintain a uniform policy for Grand Slam tournaments on such matters as rules and regulations, code of conduct, supervisors and officials and liaison with the ATP, the Women's International Tennis Association, and the Women's International Professional Tennis Council.[803]

ProServ et al. Wimbledon Meeting with ITF

The ATP accused Donald Dell and ProServ of plotting strategy against the ATP Tour with the ITF and the Grand Slams at an ad hoc meeting on July 4, in London during Wimbledon. Attendees included Mike Davies and Bill Babcock of the ITF staff, Jerry Solomon, Bob Briner and Donald Dell of ProServ, Rick Dowden of Volvo North America, Mr. Saigo of Dentsu, Jack Kramer, Brian Tobin, David Markin, Gordon Jorgensen and Owen Williams. There were a lot of issues discussed at the meeting, but no conclusions drawn.

Hamilton also reported in *International Tennis Weekly*[804]: "Wimbledon was also criticized at the meeting. ITF President Philippe Chatrier blamed Wimbledon for 'surrendering' to the players last Fall. Chatrier said that if Wimbledon had not broken ranks with the other Grand Slams, the ATP Tour would never have been created. Hadingham was not present to hear that comment but was represented by LTA President Ron Presley." Buzzer Hadingham responded: "We're not isolationists. We judged it to be impossible to organize a separate tour, which might not have any players anyway."[805]

ProServ responded to Hamilton's attack saying: "ProServ is rather perplexed at the hysterical reaction to what was basically an informational meeting in London with representatives of the Grand Slams." "We are businessmen, in the business of professional sports. We have meetings all the time, just as the ATP has frequent meetings."[806]

ATP Shuns Grand Slams,
Then Wonders Why There is No Agreement with Them

Hamilton Jordan began his new plan to seek $1 million from each of the Grand Slams for ATP to provide its ATP supervisors, ATP chair umpires, ATP road managers and ATP trainers, ATP rankings, ATP entry services and ATP press data bases. As preparation for that, he published a piece in *International Tennis Weekly*[807], informing the players that they may not have any ATP services at the Grand Slams because the Grand Slams have not entered into any agreements with the ATP Tour for them. ATP claimed that instead of the ATP professional supervisors and chair umpires, the Grand Slams would have "a mixture of essentially part-time ITF officials and local umpires." *You have to admire the irony of Hamilton convincing the Grand Slams he did not want to do business with them and then turn around and seek to do business with them – actually "blackmail" them for an outrageous fee.*

Bill Babcock responded for the Grand Slam Committee[808] saying that ATP's "portrayal of Ken Farrar, Stefan Fransson, Bill Gilmour, Bruno Rebeuh and Stephen Winyard, and the ITF/Grand Slam Officiating Programme as 'part-time ITF officials and local umpires' is completely inaccurate and offensive to those professionals." Babcock said the ITF/Grand Slam officials were all independent contractors and were free to contract with the ATP Tour and he hoped that the ATP Tour officials were likewise independent contractors and available to contract with the ITF/Grand Slams. With respect to the ATP trainers and ATP road managers, he made it clear that "the Grand Slams have never expressed any objection to their presence at these events and *ITW*'s suggestions to the contrary again misinforms the players."

J. Wayne Richmond ATP Tour Commissioner for North America

J. Wayne Richmond, ATP's Senior Vice President/Marketing, was named ATP Commissioner for North America. Hamilton Jordan said to *International Tennis Weekly*: "In the current system, the MTC has a major office in New York City, a two-person office in Europe and no presence in the 'Rest of the World.' As a result, all communications and decision-making had to come from New York. While the ATP Tour will be centrally organized for the purpose of implementing the policies and directions of the ATP Tour Board, we will vest the day-to-day decision-making in our regional leadership on the theory that people close to the individual regions and tournaments will have a better knowledge and ability to make on the spot decisions than we can here in Ponte Vedra. We see our regional leaders as the key link in our management of the new tour. These offices will provide an important link between the tour, the tournaments and the players and will also have an important marketing, press and administrative function."[809]

ATP Tour Adopts and Expands MTC Drug Testing and Finally Agrees to Olympic Testing

The ATP announced that it had adopted the MTC's drug testing rule and had agreed to expand it in 1990 to also include performance enhancing drugs such as steroids. "The ATP was one of the very first player organizations to develop its own drug testing program and the decision to expand the program signals the continuing desire of the players to be at the forefront of professional sports," said ATP Player Council President Vijay Amritraj to *International Tennis Weekly*.[810]

Heretofore, the MTC Player Representatives and the ATP had refused to expand the MTC drug testing program. I was quite sure that Hamilton Jordan had convinced the players that as part of their taking the responsibility for the 1990 ATP Tour, they needed to step up and agree to expanded drug testing. This was a good thing.

ITF/Grand Slam Crisis No. 3: Grand Slam Cup and ATP

Mike Davies, General Manager of the ITF, made a $8 million deal with Axel Meyer-Wölden of Munich for the creation in 1990 of the Grand Slam Cup as a year-end finals event for the four Grand Slams with $6 million in prize money for 16 players selected based on their results at the Grand Slams ($2 million to the winner) and $2 million to the ITF for worldwide player development. The Grand Slam Cup was to be staged in Munich, annually. Bill Dennis of Salisbury, Maryland, a protégé of Bill Riordan, was the tournament director in partnership with Meyer-Wölden. The Grand Slam Cup was owned by the four Grand Slams (22.5% each) and the ITF (10%) and their agreement was with Axel Meyer-Wölden via his company, Teviri B.V., for the promotion and staging of the Grand Slam Cup. Compaq became the title sponsor and it was known as the Compaq Grand Slam Cup.

The ATP had previously announced that the "ATP World Finals," was being moved from Madison Square Garden in New York to Frankfurt in 1990 with prize money of $2 million.

In the November 3 issue of *International Tennis Weekly*, Hamilton attacked the ITF and the Grand Slams: "Perhaps life's greatest disappointment is when one's heroes behave in a manner that diminishes the very qualities that earned our admiration and respect. That disappointment described the feeling of the ATP Tour as we struggle to try to understand the announcement by the Grand Slams that they would host a $6 million exhibition in Germany only weeks after the new ATP Tour World Championship, which will be staged in Frankfurt and will highlight the end of the season."[811] *Think about it. Hamilton and the ATP Tour were asking the Grand Slams and the ITF not to let the Grand Slam Cup promoter offer the players another $6 million after completion of the ATP Tour year; entry was voluntary.*

Ivan Lendl was the only top 10 player to speak in favor of the Grand Slam Cup. Lendl told Robin Finn of the *New York Times*[812]: "I know I'll catch flak for this, but this is like G.M. saying isn't it terrible that Toyota sells cars in the U.S." "The ATP says the competition from the ITF is terrible; I say it's better, and are monopolies legal? Just ask AT&T." *You could have never guessed that Lendl, who was born and raised in a Communist country, would have to teach the Americans about the valuable attributes of capitalism and the importance of the American Anti-Trust laws.*

ESPN Roundtable November 15

On November 15, just prior to the 1989 final Nabisco Masters, Cliff Drysdale, one or the original 1967 WCT "Handsome 8," the ATP's first President and respected ESPN sportscaster, hosted a nationally-televised roundtable discussion on ESPN between Hamilton Jordon, CEO of the ATP Tour, David Markin, President of the USTA, Jack Kramer the founder of the Grand Prix, founder of ATP and ATP's first Executive Director, Lamar Hunt of WCT, Frank Craighill of Advantage International and me. This would be the first and only time that this group of people would ever sit down together in one room. Cliff Drysdale, Frank Craighill and I are the only survivors in 2021.

Hamilton Jordan expressed over and over again his objection to the creation of the $8 million Grand Slam Cup in 1990, which was offering $6 million to players in Munich, in the same market as Frankfurt, the location of the new $2 million ATP Tour Finals. Hamilton liked to call the Grand Slam Cup an "exhibition" and claimed that it distorted the market. David Markin, who was a very astute business man in his own right, defended the creation of the Grand Slam Cup to be played weeks after the completion of the ATP Tour as a reasonable year ending event for the Grand Slams provided on a real market basis (a commercial promoter was funding the $8 million). Markin told Hamilton that the Grand Slam Cup was not a declaration of war and it was scheduled later than the ATP finals in the open season. Markin said the ITF and the Grand Slams do not understand what the controversy is all about. Markin said he was very much in favor of the Grand Slam Cup.

My comment was that if the market provided an $8 million event for the players, then it would be inappropriate for a group of administrators to say the players could not have it. At this time in November of 1989, I said that with the unfortunate fragmentation of the governance, it was likely that in 1990 there would be three "Masters" type events: ATP Tour Finals, Grand Slam Cup and the WCT Finals (assuming there would also be a 1990 WCT Tour).

The panel discussed the impact of the reduction in the number of major events on the new ATP Tour from 26 Grand Prix Super Series, Lipton and Tournament of Champions to 21 ATP Tour Championship events, including the loss of major event status for a number of American tournaments such as Los Angeles, San Francisco, Boston, Memphis, WCT Tournament of Champions, WCT Finals, etc. The United States was left with a small tournament in Charleston as the only clay court tournament in the United States. Hamilton responded by saying the big money was now in Europe and tennis, as a global sport had to recognize and accommodate that. The panel discussed the significance of the ATP Tour permitting guarantees to be paid by its World Series tournaments which offered the least amount of prize money. There was no answer given as to how to explain how a tournament could pay more money in appearance fees than its on-site prize money and how that would be received by the players and the public.

When David Markin asked Hamilton Jordan how he was explaining to the players on the 1990 ATP Tour that there was no Bonus Pool, no up-front contracts and no other bonuses in 1990, Hamilton claimed that bonuses were not important to the players and that there had been a massive increase in tournament prize money (less the 25% fee charged by the ATP Tour).

Jack Kramer explained that Los Angeles, which had been dropped from a Grand Prix Super Series in 1989 to a $250,000 World Series ATP tournament in 1990, was facing having to pay something like $450,000 in appearance fees to just get three top ranked players. Kramer said he did not think that was going to work. Lamar Hunt said that WCT was going to have a limited schedule in 1990, and that the Dallas Finals was going to be a doubles only event. WCT planned to wait and see what happened in 1990. In fact, WCT did not stage the WCT Finals in 1990, and its only 1990 tournament was the WCT Tournament of Champions at Forest Hills just prior to the 1990 U.S. Open.

Kramer pointed out that now that the players had a 4-3 majority over the tournaments they could make some bad decisions favoring themselves that were bad for the game and that it would have been better to have the ITF/Grand Slams involved to make sure they did not damage the game. *Hamilton Jordan said that the players only had a 3-3 vote and while he had the tie-breaking vote, he only had to use it once. Hamilton said that he did not consider the ATP Tour to be a players' organization. It was a Tour business organization. "I voted one time and I regret that I voted," said Jordan. "I am trying to balance the interests of the tournaments and the players."*

The panel discussed the new "Best 14" ATP Computer Ranking rule. I pointed out that letting a player drop a bad Grand Slam result to be replaced by a better result in a smaller tournament was unfair to the players and that it diminished the integrity of the ranking system. Hamilton said that he had received no objections from the players.[813]

Crisis No. 4 between the ATP Tour and the ITF/Grand Slams: ATP Computer Rankings for 1990 and Best of 14

On December 1, the ATP announced that beginning in 1990, only the best 14 tournament results would be counted in the ATP Computer Rankings so that players could drop all results in tournaments over 14. The hope was that it would encourage players to play more tournaments, play smaller tournaments and play on a variety of tournament surfaces.

Two criticisms were: (i) Players could conceivably drop bad results in Grand Slams and (ii) There would be less incentive to win when the result could be dropped and this coupled with the now authorized receipt of appearance fees from World Series tournaments offered the possibility that a player could collect a guarantee and intentionally lose early since the result would not count. The points for the Grand Slams were capped at 400 for Grand Slams with $2 million or more in prize money (French Open, Wimbledon and U.S. Open) and 360 for Grand Slams with $1 million or more in prize money (Australian Open). The points for the ATP single week Championship Series ranged from 230 for $1 million in prize money to 300 for $2 million in prize money. *That diminished the ranking value of wins in the Grand Slams on purpose!*[814]

David Markin's Letter to the USTA

On December 6, David Markin reported to the USTA Executive Committee and the USTA Sectional Presidents on his policy as President of the USTA with respect to the ATP Tour[815]: "For the past two years, various elements of the ITF have been holding meetings with the ATP," Markin wrote. "These meeting have taken place at semi-public forums such as the MTC and later with the Grand Slam Committee. What is the purpose of these meetings? What does the ATP want from the ITF and most important from the Grand Slams? The answer is ultimate control of the game partially through control of the TV rights and income of the Grand Slams. In addition to this, further eroding of the rule making rights of the ITF and control of the Davis Cup through scheduling power and the threat of a player boycott. If you couple this with their demand to exclusively use their official package of officials at an extortionate price (over $1 million each), you get an idea of ATP motivation."

Markin then responded with nine points with his thoughts on what was the best policy for the ITF and the Grand Slams.

1.   Absolute independence of the ATP Circuit.

2.   Make no further concessions to the ATP as to their official position vis-à-vis the Grand Slams. The ATP has stated they will not schedule opposite the Grand Slams recognizing the adverse public relations resulting from such action. All conversation about lack of communication between the ITF and ATP simply means that the ITF has not capitulated to the ATP's excessive demands. In summation, I recommend that we emphasize that we will not be part of the ATP Tour and wish to remain independent. We should continue with projects such as the Grand Slam finals which reinforce our commitment to independence. We should also increase prize money for the second

and third round losers as well as continue to increase prize money every year, market conditions permitting. An additional benefit to the players could be tournament hospitality in the form of hotel allowances and nursery accommodations for players' children.

3.   Promotion of the Grand Slam Cup which forces the ATP to do the one thing they fear more than anything else – compete with another tennis force.

4.   Development of a Grand Slam computer as part of the Grand Slam Championships to measure performance in the Grand Slams.

5.   Continue communication with Lamar Hunt and Donald Dell and others – who represent market forces not included in the ATP Circuit.

6.   Continued communication with the players – informing them that the Grand Slams and the ITF are working for their benefit.

7.   Observe 1990 ATP Tour and research player response.

8.   Continued discounting of any threat of a player boycott of the Grand Slams.

9.   Continued increase in prize money for Davis Cup.

1989 ended with a relative "peaceful co-existence" between the ATP Tour, the ITF and the independent Grand Slams.

CHAPTER 35:

1990: ATP TOUR BEGINS, GRAND SLAM COMMITTEE BEGINS, NO MORE UNIFIED GOVERNANCE

Hamilton Jordan Memo

We completed the dissolution of the Men's Tennis Council on April 30, 1990, and made the final distribution of its remaining assets. On May 3 Hamilton Jordan wrote to me and said: "I just wanted to express our appreciation to you for the orderly, efficient and professional job that you have done in the last six months in 'winding down' the MTC. Given the history and disagreements over substantive issues, a lesser man might have behaved differently. You have been fair, objective and effective throughout. On behalf of the constituencies that we represent, I wanted to express our thanks for both your good efforts and your professional attitude performing this thankless task."[816]

Thus, the Men's Tennis Council became history!

ATP Becomes ATP Tour, Inc

The Association of Tennis Professionals was originally an unincorporated players association. On June 1, 1987, the Association of Tennis Professionals, Inc., was incorporated in the State of Delaware. In 1989, the name was changed to ATP Tour, Inc., and an Amended and Restated Articles of Incorporation was filed changing the ATP from a players' association to an ATP Tour organization of players and non-Grand Slam tournaments.

Thus by 1990, there was no longer an ATP player association.

1990 ATP Tour Board

The initial ATP Tour Board consisted of Marty Davis, Colin Dowdeswell and Larry Scott as Player Representatives and Franco Bartoni, Graham Lovett and Charles Pasarell as Tournament Representatives. Hamilton Jordan was the Chief Executive Officer and could vote as a member of the ATP Tour Board only in the case of a tie vote.

MTC Supervisors and MTC Chair Umpires Split Between ATP Tour and ITF Davis Cup and Grand Slams

One of the many downsides of the split between the ATP Tour and the ITF and the demise of the MTC was the splitting of the professional officiating programs into two competing programs, instead of one unified program under the MTC. As to the MTC Supervisors, Edwardo Menga, Ed Hardisty, Thomas Karlberg and John Heiss went with the ATP Tour in 1990, while Ken Farrar, Stefan Fransson and Bill Gilmour went with the ITF/Grand Slams in 1990. As to the MTC Chair Umpires, Richard Kaufman, Richard Ings, Gerry Armstrong, Paula Pereira and Rudy Berger went with the ATP Tour and Bruno Rebeuh went with the ITF and the Grand Slams. When Gayle Bradshaw the U.S. Open Referee joined the ATP Tour, I recruited former MTC Supervisor, Keith Johnson, to come out of retirement to become the new U.S. Open Referee in 1990.

McEnroe Defaulted at 1990 Australian Open

John McEnroe was leading Mikael Pernfors 6-1, 4-6, 7-5, 2-4 in the 1990 Australian Open with Gerry Armstrong of the ATP Tour as the chair umpire and being played under the new Grand Slam Committee Code of Conduct which provided for three steps of Point Penalties for misconduct: "Warning, Point, Default." McEnroe was given a warning for unsportsmanlike conduct for "bouncing a ball on his racquet and glaring at her (lineman) in intimidating fashion." Later McEnroe smashed his racquet on the court and was given a point penalty. McEnroe then swore at Armstrong, demanded to see Ken Farrar, now the Grand Slam Supervisor, but continued complaining and swearing, his words clearly audible to nearby fans and television viewers." Armstrong with Farrar's approval called, 'Code violation. Verbal Abuse. Default Mr. McEnroe, Game. Set. Match.' Farrar later described McEnroe's harangue as "the most vile language he had ever heard in a tennis match." "If I'd known the rules, I would probably have still broken my racquet, but I probably wouldn't have said what I said to the guy," McEnroe said. "I let things rattle me and then also he was playing tougher and I wasn't happy with my own game."[817]

San Francisco and Appearance Money

San Francisco had been a Grand Prix Super Series in 1989, but in 1990 was demoted to an ATP Tour Championship Series Free (meaning authorized to pay appearance fees), which meant it had a minimum prize money of $250,000, which after deducting the $25,000 ATP fee, offered $225,000 in on-site prize money to players, plus free hotel rooms, costing approximately $40,000. Barry Mackay, the tournament director, had apparently agreed to pay Andre Agassi, Brad Gilbert and Michael Chang $200,000 each in appearance money. Do the math: $225,000 in on-site prize money and $600,000 in appearance fees for three players. Chang withdrew with an injury. Brad Gilbert lost in the first round to Gary Muller 6-4, 7-6. Andre Agassi defeated Todd Witsken 6-1, 6-3 in the final. Wrote Robin Finn in the *New York Times*[818] of the circumstance: "Just as the tournament director, Barry MacKay, suspected it would, the issue of the $200,000 in player contract money paid to Brad Gilbert, the defending champion, and Agassi to guarantee their participation in the San Francisco event created controversy all week....Todd Witsken, runner-up to Agassi and already irritable because of a trio of painful blisters on his right hand, was less than elated about the lion's share of the payout going to Gilbert. 'To know that Brad Gilbert made more money than I made even if I win the tournament is kind of alarming,' said Witsken, who picked up $19,090 for making his first career final."

Players Attack Hamilton Jordan

In the new tournament in Toronto, both John McEnroe and Ivan Lendl expressed their displeasure about the new ATP Tour. The *New York Times*[819] reported on February 17: "upon leaving the court after a victory Thursday night, McEnroe opened up with a stream of invective at Hamilton Jordan, chief executive of the Association of Tennis Professionals Tour. McEnroe said the new tour was being run for administrators rather than the players. He said Jordan had hoodwinked the players into supporting a system that forces them to play too often and does not respect their right to retire from a match when injured. 'This isn't the players' tour,' said McEnroe, who was one of the ATP's biggest boosters when it displaced the Men's Tennis Council. 'This is a tour for guys like Hamilton Jordan. He doesn't know what tennis is about and he's the guy representing us. He's a politician. He does know how to take advantage of us and that's just what he's done.'"

Lendl defeated McEnroe 6-3, 6-2 in the Toronto final. Robin Finn reported in the *New York Times*: "After the match, the two players, who in the past have clashed nearly as often about tour issues as they have on courts, also re-emphasized their displeasure with the new Association of Tennis Professionals Tour."[820]

Search for Hamilton Jordan Replacement

At the ATP board meeting in May of 1989 in Dusseldorf, Hamilton Jordan said he was not "interested in their proposal of a long-term contract as the chief executive officer." Hamilton's employment agreement was going to expire in June 1992, and he said that he intended to honor it but would take advantage of a clause that allowed him to convert to an active chairman of the board. In November of 1989, Russell Reynolds

Associates, Inc., was hired to search for Jordan's successor. Henry de Montebello, managing director of Russell Reynolds said to the *New York Times*[821], "I don't think the ATP board is critical of Hamilton, but realizes he wants to move up and do other things…Hamilton was the right answer at the time he came in, now the board feels it's time not to duplicate Hamilton Jordan, but bring in somebody who will perhaps be a little closer to some of the players."

IBM Sponsorship

The ATP Tour signed a title sponsorship agreement with IBM on February 8.[822]

Bob Briner Critiques ATP Tour

Bob Briner, President of ProServ Television, criticized the ATP Tour writing in the *New York Times*[823] on March 4: "Only three weeks into the new 'player-owned, player-run' Association of Tennis Professionals Tour we are already hearing loud cries of anguish and stories of major dissension in the ranks. Where are the complaints coming from? Naturally, from the players who supposedly own and run the tour. And the loudest complaints are coming from the top players. Why am I not surprised? I am not surprised because for me, as Yogi Berra said, 'It is Deja-vu all over again.' The complaints of the tennis players are the same ones they have been voicing for at least the last 20 years. I've heard them all before, many times. Basically, tennis players want more and more money for playing less and less tennis. They also want to play only where they want to play. And, by the way, they don't want the rules enforced too strictly, either."

Ray Moore Responds to Briner

Ray Moore responded in the *New York Times*[824] on March 25 to Briner's article: "The hypocrisy, self-promotion and general conflicts of interest that abound throughout the article boggle the mind. It's akin to the chief executive officer of Coca-Cola promoting his product and goals at the expense of his major competitor, Pepsi-Cola. Bob Briner is a major competitor of the Association of Tennis Professionals Tour. ProServ bid for almost every entity in the makeup of the A.T.P. Tour, came up empty-handed and now seems to be throwing all its weight behind the only major competitor of the A.T.P. Tour, the International Tennis Federation….He talks of the 'new breed' of bottom-line men running the A.T.P. Heavens above! When he left the A.T.P. 10 years ago after several years as its C.E.O., he left the A.T.P. in a total state of bankruptcy. Perhaps the years have eroded his memory."

Mark Miles Hired to Succeed Hamilton Jordan

On March 15, the ATP Tour announced that after "a long and exhaustive search and consideration of people inside and outside of tennis,' Mark Miles of Indianapolis was unanimously selected" as the new chief executive officer of the ATP Tour to replace Hamilton Jordan, "who will become chairman of the board." The 36-year-old Miles had been director of corporate relations for Eli Lilly and served as the Tournament Director of the Indianapolis Grand Prix Super Series tournament.[825]

Hamilton apparently had some sort of falling out with the ATP Board in August and left the ATP Tour effective in December of 1990. Previous ATP Executive Directors, Bob Briner, Butch Buchholz and Mike Davies also ended their tenures after a falling out with the players. "Falling out with the players" would continue to plague future ATP Tour Executive Directors, including Mark Miles in 2005.

ATP Tour Fines Edberg, Lendl and Agassi

Under the new ATP Tour rule that fines players 10 percent of their earnings for each of the 11 contract tournaments they fail to play during the year,[826] fines were issued for:

Stefan Edberg	$115,496
Ivan Lendl	$95,443
Andre Agassi	$85,042

WCT

To everyone's surprise, WCT only staged one tournament in 1990, the WCT Tournament of Champions at Forest Hills during the week ending August 26, and won by Ivan Lendl over Aaron Krickstein 6-4, 6-7, 6-3. Everyone expected WCT to begin again in 1991 as an independent circuit in competition with the ATP Tour, which would probably require another anti-trust lawsuit against the ATP Tour for access to the players. Owen Williams, WCT's CEO, cited in his book *Ahead of the Game*[827] the ever-increasing demands of ProServ and IMG for greater and greater appearance money for their player clients made it impossible for WCT to survive as an independent circuit so he suggested to Lamar Hunt and Al Hill, Jr. that "we pack it in."

On August 28, the *New York Times*[828] reported: "The decision to terminate operations was a business judgment based on the realities of the economics in sports marketing as well as the difficult circumstances of an independent company operating a group of high-quality tennis tournament events on a financially viable basis…Tournaments scheduled for London in December, Scottsdale, Ariz., in March and Dallas in April, have been cancelled."

That was a lucky day for the new ATP Tour. Not having any commercial competition gave the ATP Tour a free rein without the threat of any antitrust issues.

Grand Slam Cup

To the consternation of the ATP Tour, the ITF and the Grand Slams staged their first Compaq Grand Slam Cup in December of 1990, won by Pete Sampras over Brad Gilbert 6-3, 6-4, 6-2. The rest of the 16-player field was: Michael Chang, Stefan Edberg, Yannick Noah, David Wheaton, Ivan Lendl, Goran Ivanisevic, Henri Leconte, Aaron Krickstein, Andres Gomez, Christian Bergstrom, Kevin Curren, Jonas Svensson, Andrei Cherkasov and Thomas Muster. In 1998 and 1999, the Grand Slam Cup also had eight women and was therefore, the first and only year-end event for men and women. In 1999, Greg Rusedski defeated Tommy Hass 6-3, 6-4, 6-7, 7-6 and Serena Williams defeated Venus Williams 6-1, 3-6, 6-3.[829]

CHAPTER 36:

1990-2021: PEACEFUL CO-EXISTENCE AND COOPERATION WITH ARMS-LENGTH CONTRACTS

My detailed research for this book concluded at the end of the 1989 Nabisco Grand Prix and the dissolution of the Men's Tennis Council finally on April 30, 1990. However, from my now outside vantage point, it is obvious that the sky did not fall in and while there were a number of challenges and crises, there was no serious disaster for men's professional tennis as a result of the demise of the MTC and the demise of the ATP as a player association upon the creation of the ATP Tour and the split of the Grand Slams and ITF from the ATP Tour and the non-Grand Slam tournaments. As a matter of fact, it appears to me that the ATP Tour has been very successful as have the independent Grand Slams and the ITF's Davis Cup competition with their policies of "peaceful co-existence," even though relationships may have sometimes been somewhat strained.

1990 ATP Tour Board

The 1990 ATP Tour Board after the departure of Hamilton Jordan was: Player Representatives: Marty Davis, Colin Dowdeswell and Larry Scott. Tournament Representatives: Franco Bartoni, Graham Lovett and Charles Pasarell with Mark Miles as CEO with the tiebreaking vote.

I always wondered why Ray Moore, who was the "tennis mastermind" for the creation of the new ATP Tour and who got more than a little bloodied working for the players, was not included. After all, he was a retired player and no longer the volunteer Chairman of the Men's Tennis Council. Ray told me years later that he did not want to be involved in the new ATP Tour and in fact had wanted to retire for some time from tennis. Well, he had stayed to be the "tennis mastermind" to create the ATP Tour.

When I asked Hamilton Jordan what he planned to do for Ray, he told me that the ATP was honoring Ray with the naming of a "Ray Moore Room" at the new ATP Tour Headquarters located at 200 Tournament Players Road, Ponte Vedra, Florida. I never knew if he was joking or not, but Ray confirmed to me years later that there was a Ray Moore Room in the first ATP Tour Headquarters building in Ponte Vedra. When I visited the new ATP Tour Headquarters located at 201 ATP Tour Boulevard in 2018,

I asked about the "Ray Moore Room" and no one had any idea what I was talking about. So, the "Ray Moore Room" that was apparently located in the first headquarters building of the ATP Tour was apparently deleted when the ATP Tour moved into its new headquarters building. *I wonder if today's players even know Ray was an important player leader.*

1990 ITF and Grand Slam Leaders

In 1990, Philippe Chatrier was President of the ITF and the French FFT and the Grand Slams were represented by:

Australian Open	Geoff Pollard, Tennis Australia President
French Open	Philippe Chatrier, French FFT President
Wimbledon	John Curry, Chairman
British LTA	Ron Presly, President
U.S. Open	David Markin, USTA President

Bill Babcock was the Administrator for the Grand Slam Committee and head of professional tennis for the ITF and Davis Cup reporting to Mike Davies, the ITF General Manager.

John Curry, New Chairman of Wimbledon

The succession of John Curry to Buzzer Hadingham as Chairman of Wimbledon in 1990 was especially important. I found John Curry to be one of the smartest and toughest leaders to join the world of international tennis. When he succeeded Buzzer Hadingham in 1990, that was the end of Wimbledon being some kind of "patsy" for Hamilton Jordan and the new ATP Tour. David Markin of the USTA was just as smart and just as tough. They supported the policy of "peaceful co-existence" with the ATP Tour, and insisted on the independence of the Grand Slams.

Curry, along with David Markin (U.S. Open), Philippe Chatrier (French Open and ITF) and Geoff Pollard (Australian Open), was a big supporter of the Compaq Grand Slam Cup. John Curry would be an important Chairman of Wimbledon for 10 years and the architect of most of the new construction and modernization of the Wimbledon grounds, including the roof over Centre Court. Andrew Longmore wrote an excellent description of John Curry in Britain's *The Independent*[830] and his 10-year tenure as Chairman: "This is typical John Curry. A bit of bluster, a pinch of 'like it or lump it,' all part of the kick and cuddle style of management which has characterised

his 10-year reign as chairman of Wimbledon. He has the four- square build of a bulldog and much the same level of toleration. 'If conflict is required, I'm a front row forward,' he laughs....The AEC, in the manner of so many treasured English institutions, had an instinctive understanding of the man they needed to guide them to the verge of

new millennium. Curry had proven commercial acumen, clear vision and the courage to ruffle a few exotic feathers. A decade on, his success can be measured in the balance sheet which shows a rise in the Wimbledon surplus to the Lawn Tennis Association from pounds 9.2m in 1989 to just over pounds 33m last year and in the smooth upgrading of Wimbledon's image. 'An agent for change,' Curry calls himself, a description confirmed by a wander around the pristine food courts, the bright new gardens planted in Wimbledon colours and the new No 1 Court, all part of a radical

John Curry

redevelopment programme."

"'Besides the grass, the core of Wimbledon is that we address the parties in completely the reverse order from everyone else,' he says. 'We put the players first, the fans second and television and the media third. Every other tournament has the media first, the fans second and the players third.'"

If my list of the Pioneers of the Game had not been cut off as of December 31, 1989, for this book, I would have easily included John Curry as one of my most influential Pioneers of the Game.

Mark Miles 1990-2005

Mark Miles was the ATP CEO from 1990-2005. Richard Evans wrote in *Tennis Week*[831]: "There is no question that Miles' greatest achievement was preventing the ship he was given from breaking up. The HMS ATP Tour was a vessel built to capsize. Not even Admiral Nelson could have saved this ship if half the crew had been Royal Navy and half mercenaries from the Spanish Main. But that was the task Miles was given: to balance and maintain a board made up of three tournament directors and three player representatives. It was a lovely idea back in 1990, but as Vijay Amritraj, then a very influential president of the ATP (ATP Tour Players' Council), told the tournament directors mischievously at the time, 'This 50-50 partnership will work just as long as you realize that our 50 is bigger than your 50'. They thought he was joking, and only a politician of Miles' skill could have allowed the humor while manipulating egos and ambitions in such a way as to ensure the inherent balance would not spring holes in the hull. It is inevitable that players hold the upper hand because they always have the extra card to deal in extremis – 'We will not play' but somehow, Miles spent 14 years ensuring that he would never have to cast the deciding vote at board level, a remarkable achievement."

ATP Tour CEOs 1990-2021

1990
Hamilton Jordan

2012-2014
Brad Drewett

1990-2005
Mark Miles

2014-2019
Chris Kermode

2005-2009
Etienne de Villiers

2020+
Andrea Gaudenzi,
Chairman

2009-2012
Adam Helfant

2020+
Massimo Calvelli,
Chief Executive
Officer

It is my understanding that Jordan, Miles, de Villiers, Helfant and Kermode all departed because they were no longer supported by the players. Drewitt tragically contracted ALS and passed away. Being an ATP Tour CEO has not been a particularly good career opportunity.

ITF/Grand Slam Leaders 1990-2021

These are the important ITF and Grand Slam leaders responsible for men's professional tennis between 1990 and 2021:

ITF Presidents

1977-1991	Philippe Chatrier	France
1991-1999	Brian Tobin	Australia
1999-2015	Francesco Ricci Bitti	Italy
2016+	Dave Haggerty	United States

Chairmen of Wimbledon

1990-1999	John Curry
2000-2010	Tim Phillips
2011-2019	Philip G. H. Brook
2020+	Ian Hewitt

Tennis Australia Presidents

1989-2010	Geoff N. Pollard AM
2010-2017	Steve Healy
2017+	Jayne Hrdlicka

French Tennis Federation Presidents

1973-1993	Philippe Chatrier
1993-2008	Christian Bimes
2009-2017	Jean Gachassin
2017-2020	Bernard Giudicelli
2021+	Giles Moretton

USTA Presidents

1989-1990	David R. Markin	Kalamazoo
1991-1992	Bob Cookson	San Francisco
1993-1994	J. Howard Frazer	Cincinnati
1995-1996	Lester M. Snyder, Jr.	Tempe
1997-1998	Harry Marmion	Southhampton
1999-2000	Judy Levering	Lancaster
2001-2002	Merv Heller, Jr.	Reading
2003-2004	Alan Schwartz	Chicago
2005-2006	Franklin Johnson	Los Angeles
2007-2008	Jane Brown Grimes	New York
2009-2010	Lucy S. Garvin	Greenville SC
2011-2012	Jon Vegosen	Chicago
2013-2014	David Haggerty	Pennington
2015-2018	Katrina Adams	New York
2019-2020	Patrick J. Galbraith	Tacoma
2021+	Mike McNulty	New Orleans

British LTA Presidents

1988-1990	R.J. Presley	2006-2008	S.G. Smith
1991-1993	I.A. King	2009-2010	Derek Howorth
1994-1996	J.C. Robbins	2011-2013	Peter Bretherton
1997-1999	Geoffrey Cass	2014-2016	Cathie Sabin
2000-2002	J.M. Gracie	2017-2019	Martin Corrie
2003-2006	C.R. Trippe	2020+	David Rawlinson

Tournament Regulations and Code of Conduct Use
MTC Regulations and Code

The ATP Tour Tournament Regulations and Code of Conduct incorporated the provisions and often the verbatim language of the MTC's Tournament Regulations and Code. The separate Tournament Regulations and Code of Conduct for the independent Grand Slams promulgated by the Grand Slam Committee or Grand Slam Board likewise incorporated the provisions, and often the verbatim language, of the MTC's Tournament Regulations and Code. As you might guess, as the new Executive Director of the USTA in 1990, and also the Tournament Director of the 1990 U.S. Open, I was significantly involved in the drafting of the new Grand Slam Committee Tournament Regulations and Code of Conduct with Bill Babcock, which were based on the MTC rules that had been developed over many years with the participation and agreement of the players.

Separate Codes of Conduct and Separate Suspensions

There are, however, separate Codes of Conduct for the ATP Tour and for the Grand Slams, both based on the MTC Code of Conduct. For the ATP Tour, on-site offense appeals are heard by the Executive Vice President of Rules and Regulations (David Cooper, then Gayle Bradshaw, now Miro Bratoev) instead of the Administrator of the MTC, and the appeal of major offenses are heard solely by the President of the ATP Tour and not by a MTC style independent review panel. For the Grand Slams, on-site offense fines are issued by the Grand Slam Referee in consultation with the Grand Slam Supervisors and appeals are heard by the Director of the Grand Slam Board (Bill Babcock through 2020 then Ugo Valensi in 2021) while the appeal of a major offense is heard by the Grand Slam Board. Player suspensions under the ATP Tour Code only apply to ATP non-Grand Slam tournaments and player suspensions under the Grand Slam Code only apply to the Grand Slams. However, the Grand Slam Code of Conduct (Article IV.B.) now contains a provision whereby a player convicted of a major offense by the ATP Tour "may" also be suspended from the Grand Slams.[832] *Query: is this provision legally enforceable?*

If during the existence of the Men's Tennis Council a proposal was ever made to eliminate the safety valve of having three independent review officers decide Major Offense appeals and have them heard solely by the four Grand Slam Chairmen or the Chairman of the MTC, the resistance would have been significant. I cannot imagine John McEnroe, Sr., Bob Kain, Donald Dell or Ion Tiriac every agreeing. However, I am advised that since 1990, there has never been a contested major offense case appeal to and determined in a formal appeal to either the Grand Slam Board or the ATP President. *Apparently, no one has become concerned, and the new system has worked. Go figure.*

Grand Slam Prize Money, Funding of ATP Tour, Etc.

Instead of the Grand Slams contributing to the administration of the Men's Tennis Council, the administration of the ATP and the ATP Deferred Compensation Plan as they did before the end of 1989, the independent Grand Slams began to pay for their own separate administration and put all their money directly into prize money, per diems and other benefits for the players competing in the Grand Slams each year. The non-Grand Slam tournaments then provided *all of the money* for the ATP Tour administration and the ATP Deferred Compensation Plan. *The ATP Tour began without any Bonus Pool or any "up-front contracts" for the top players, surprisingly without objection from the players. However, I suspect that the newly permitted appearance money guarantees more than made up for them.*

Appearance Money Was Prohibited by the MIPTC Through 1989

In 1983, Cliff Drysdale wrote in *World Tennis* magazine[833]: "I find the guarantee debate one of economics as well as ethics. I oppose guarantees because I think they can lead to a lowering of the total prize money purse in tournaments. The reason is simple: any tournament director given the choice between putting on a $400,000 tournament in which he takes his chances with the field, or a $50,000 tournament where he pays $350,000 in guarantees to the leading players, would inevitably choose the latter. Why? A tournament director who wants to have a successful tournament must get the top players: paying guarantees ensures their entry…The theory behind playing for prize money is that the better you perform in the tournament, the more money you make. The integrity of the tournament game is based on this principle. Those in favor of guarantees argue that the players are going to get them whether we like it or not, so why not accept that truth and make these payments legal? Many informed people in tennis say you simply can't enforce the rule against guarantees. We can't always stop robbery, but does it follow that we should accept it?"

Also in 1983, Ray Moore said to *International Tennis Weekly*[834]: "Something has to be done about the guarantee situation. The ATP officially can in no way, shape or form endorse guarantees paid under the table. The credibility of the game is at stake. Once you have a player receiving more money than the first prize to show, you have a real credibility problem with the public because even if a losing player does try 100 percent, you will never convince the public of that."

Paul Fein quoted[835] Arthur Ashe: "When guarantees dwarf even the tournament winners' prize money, it has to affect players' incentive." "Whenever the public suspects an athlete isn't giving his honest, all-out best, that perception inevitably besmirches the sport. The public should know that if so-and-so misses a volley at 40-40 it's going to cost him the match and maybe $30,000. If things do reach bottom, tennis will lose its credibility. Then one of two things will happen. Either there's a serious attempt to clean it up, or it will follow the dishonest lines of boxing until a clean champion revives it."

Jack Kramer: "I predict the continued growth of guarantees will drive more and more tournaments out of business because only the richest 12 or 13 can afford guarantees and they'll get all the best players." "What I'm afraid of is we're going to lose legitimate tournaments and come up with even more 4- and 8-man specials where the big guys will skim the money off the top, where the agents will control the television and where they're staged, and the legitimate circuit will slowly disappear."

Steve Goldstein wrote in *World Tennis* magazine[836], "The chief objection to guarantees is that they reduce the player's incentive to win. Presumably, once a player has some money in his pocket, he may not go all-out in every match of the tournament. Happer is fearful of tournament tennis catching that dreaded disease: exhibitions. 'The reason we have guarantee rules is we want players who are playing in public tennis tournaments to be playing for prize money and paid commensurate with their performance,' says Happer. 'If players are competing honestly then the competition is clean and the spectators and public are getting a clean sport. Whereas if players are getting money, whether they win or lose, you have a different thing. You have something like professional wrestling, which I think would be disastrous to tennis.'…'I don't like the idea that this is not disclosed to the public if this is going to be done,' says Happer. 'I don't want to see a match where McEnroe is playing for $32,000 and getting $100,000 on the side, and then wonder about it.'"

Appearance Fees Permitted by the ATP Tour Since 1990

In 1990, the new ATP Tour permitted the payment of appearance guarantees only for the World Series events without designations. Beginning in 2009, all non-ATP 1000 were permitted to offer "promotional fees." Thus, appearance money, once called by Harold Solomon as the "cancer in the game" became permissible and so 53 tournaments are allowed to bid against each other for whatever number of additional tournaments players wish to play after their 13 ATP Tour tournaments (eight Masters 1000 tournaments, four 500 Series tournaments, plus the ATP Finals), four Grand Slams and Davis Cup and/or the new ATP Team Cup.

I fear that sooner or later some enterprising investigative reporter will find out the amounts being paid for the appearance of players which is now a secret and report it in the press. When it shows that the appearance money exceeds the prize money, I believe it will be a big problem.

ATP Deferred Compensation Program

At the request of ATP, the Men's Tennis Council organized the creation of the ATP Deferred Compensation Program in 1988 and taxed the tournaments for contributions of $2,255,984 in 1988 and $1,932,805 in 1989, which were paid to the ATP Tour upon the dissolution of the MTC. The ATP Tour formalized the program after the dissolution of the MTC. Philip Galloway, the Chief Financial Officer of the ATP Tour, told me that the ATP Tour continued to enhance the program through the years and by 2020, the assets in the plan exceeded $150 million and had approximately 800 current participants. The ATP Tour was then contributing between $9 and $10 million annually. In 2019, there were 270 participants currently receiving benefit payments and approximately 100 former players had received and been fully paid their benefits.

Annually, 125 singles players and 40 doubles players who are in the main draw of 11 ATP Tour tournaments (not Grand Slams, Challenger or Futures tournaments) are qualified. In the case of ties, ATP ranking points are used to break the ties. Players are fully vested after qualifying for five years, although they partially vest with 3-4 years of credit. The average balance per player in the plan is around $220,000 which is paid out between ages 50-70, although most players defer the beginning of the payments until later.[837]

Needless to say, this is a tremendous benefit to professional tennis players, especially the rank-and-file lower ranked players as it provides a respectable retirement fund after they complete their careers. It also provides a huge incentive for all players to commit to and to complete their player commitments to the ATP Tour each year.

ATP Tour Masters 1000 Series

During Mark Miles' tenure as CEO of the ATP Tour, the original 11 ATP single week Championship Series were:

1.	Indian Wells	7.	Cincinnati
2.	Key Biscayne	8.	Sydney
3.	Monte Carlo	9.	Tokyo
4.	Hamburg	10.	Paris

5.	Rome	11.	Stockholm
6.	Canada		

In 1995, Sydney was cancelled and in 2000, Tokyo was cancelled. Stockholm was sold to Ion Tiriac who then moved the Stuttgart Indoors to Essen in 1995 as a single week Championship Series. It was later moved from Essen to the Madrid Indoors in 2002. The top tier was then renamed "the Super 9."

1.	Indian Wells	6.	Canada
2.	Key Biscayne	7.	Cincinnati
3.	Monte Carlo	8.	Paris
4.	Hamburg	9.	Madrid
5.	Rome		

ISL Marketing Disaster

In 1999, Mark Miles executed a 10-year agreement with ISL Marketing led by Daniel Beauvois for $1.2 billion for the rights to market the television rights and all on-court signage for the "Super 9" ATP tournaments. Every tournament except for Key Biscayne had to give up its tournament sponsor and provide a "clean court" for ISL to sell on-court signage. ISL was unsuccessful in marketing the ATP Tour television and sponsorship rights and defaulted. On May 21, 2001, ISL went bankrupt and left the ATP Tour tournaments scrambling to try to entice back their local sponsors or find new ones. It was a disaster for the tournaments and the players on the ATP Tour. Afterwards, the Super 9 tournaments created Tennis Properties Ltd.(TPL) to take over the marketing of their TV Rights from the ATP Tour, which is now handled through ATP media.[838]

Indianapolis and Washington vs. Mark Miles and the ATP Tour 2002

On February 4, 2002, the Indianapolis and Washington double-up (2nd class) Championship Series tournaments filed an anti-trust complaint against Mark Miles as Chief Executive Officer of the ATP Tour, Inc., and the ATP Tour in the Federal Court in Indianapolis[839]. My recollection is that the ATP Tour had doubled-up Indianapolis and Washington in the week after the Canadian and Cincinnati single week Championship Series tournaments, which made it difficult to get players to play three consecutive weeks. The case was settled and while I do not know anything about the settlement agreement, the ATP Tour calendar was changed so that Washington and Indianapolis were doubled-up with European tournaments instead of each other in 2003 and neither one was scheduled immediately after Canada and Cincinnati. I suspect there was a multi-year agreement in this regard with respect to Washington, but the Indianapolis tournament eventually disappeared and Washington has now been sold to a new owner.

International Men's Tennis Association (IMTA)

In 2003, Wayne Ferreira, with the support of Lleyton Hewitt and Henri-James Tieleman, attempted to create a new player association, the International Men's Tennis Association (IMTA) to represent the professional players.[840] They wanted access to the financial records of the ATP Tour, especially the salaries of the officers and they wanted more money from the Grand Slams. Apparently the IMTA fizzled out, but in 2003, Mark Miles, as described by Charlie Bricker in the *South Florida Sun-Sentinel*[841]: "walked into the conference room at Roland Garros and requested a 50 percent increase ($50 million) in the amount of money the Grand Slams contributed to the men's tour. Of course, he didn't get it. And of course, one of the points of this request was to show the band of renegade ATP players, led by Wayne Ferreira that their demands for significantly more money isn't going to happen because everyone is strapped."

Wrote Richard Evans in *Tennis Week*[842]: "Amazingly for such an astute strategist, Miles led his players up a blind alley with no escape routes. It would be invidious to make a glib comparison with something as serious as the Iraq war, but Miles, like the Bush administration, went into battle with no exit strategy. Happily, there was no blood spilled in the tennis confrontation, but the bruises left on Miles' reputation were real." Miles left the ATP Tour in 2005.

Adidas Lawsuit 2006

For many years, Adidas had an "Adidas Logo" on all of its clothing, plus what it called a "distinctive design element known as the "adidas 3-stripes" which utilized three equally spaced stripes from the top to the bottom of its clothes. Up until 2005, manufacturer's logos were limited for two square inches in size, but nothing was done about the "adidas 3-stripes." The Grand Slams and ITF became concerned that if Adidas was permitted to continue the massive "adidas 3-stripes" then all the other clothing manufacturers would create their own massive "design elements." The Grand Slams and the ITF increased the permitted size of manufacturer's logos from two to four square inches and advised Adidas that beginning June 26, 2006, the "adidas 3 stripes" would be considered a manufacturer's logo and limited in size.

On April 5, 2006, Adidas filed a complaint against the Grand Slams and the ITF in the British High Court of Justice, Chancery Division[843] to enjoin the enforcement of the new limitations on its clothing. Nike joined in the case to support the Grand Slams' position. After extensive and expensive legal proceedings, the case was eventually settled with an amendment permitting manufacturer's logos, including the Adidas "3 stripes" to a maximum of eight square inches. This would be the first time that Adidas had ever agreed that its "3 stripes" was a logo. The ATP Tour was quite happy not to be included in the Adidas lawsuit which probably cost millions of dollars in litigation expenses.

"Brave New World Plan"

In 2005, Etienne de Villiers succeeded Mark Miles as the CEO of the ATP Tour. In 2007, de Villiers developed a reorganization of the ATP Tour known as the "Brave New World Plan" that was "designed to revitalize its popularity, enabling it to better compete with other sports and entertainment events." Etienne's innovations were the most significant ones since the founding of the ATP Tour in 1990. The crux of the plan was to create eight super-duper tournaments (renamed the "Masters 1000 Series") in which all the highest ranked players would be mandated to enter so as to create the toughest and most exciting competition possible. *If you were one of the eight anointed tournaments, the "Brave New World Plan" was great, but if you were one of the other ATP Tournaments, the plan was not very good for you.* The ATP Tour attempted to make up for the loss of designations to the double-up Series 500 tournaments by now permitting them to pay appearance fees in competition with all the other non-Masters 1000 tournaments. The plan also provided for the downgrading of Monte Carlo and Hamburg from the new "Masters 1000" top tier category, and the addition of Shanghai as a new top tier tournament.

Tiriac had purchased the Stratton Mountain (then New Haven, CT) double up week series from Butch Buchholz in 1999 and moved it to Kitzbuhel, which he promoted in Kitzbuhel through 2008. Apparently, Tiriac either sold his Kitzbuhel double-up week franchise to the ATP Tour or just gave it up as part of getting Hamburg's May date, as he did not operate the Kitzbuhel tournament after 2008. Hamburg, as a demoted ATP 500 category tournament, was moved to a less attractive date in July. In summary, Shanghai received Hamburg's Masters 1000 franchise and Madrid changed from indoors to clay and got Hamburg's May date on the calendar in front of the French Open. As you might have guessed, both Hamburg and Monte Carlo filed anti-trust lawsuits against the ATP Tour.

Monte Carlo Lawsuit 2007

On April 9, 2007, Monte Carlo filed a complaint[844], demanding a jury trial, against the ATP Tour, Inc., Etienne de Villiers and Charles Pasarell, as a member of the ATP Tour Board and an owner of the Indian Wells Masters 1000 Series tournament. This case was settled upon an agreement to permit Monte Carlo to remain as a Masters 1000 tournament, but without any mandatory entry from players.

Hamburg Lawsuit 2007

On March 28, 2007, Hamburg filed a complaint[845], against the ATP Tour, Inc., ATP CEO Etienne de Villiers, and ATP Board members Charles Pasarell, Graham Pearce, Jacco Eltingh, Perry Rogers and Iggy Jovanovic, demanding a jury trial, in the United States District Court for the District of Delaware. The Qatar Tennis Federation (a 25 percent owner of the tournament) was added as an additional plaintiff. Rob McGill, of Barnes and Thornburg in Indianapolis, the Tournament Director of Indianapolis, was the lead attorney for the plaintiffs and Bradley Ruskin of Proskauer Rose of New York, was the lead attorney for the ATP Tour. The claims against the individual defendants were based on their voting for the "Brave New World Plan," which required a "super majority" of at least two of the three Player Representatives and two of the three Tournament Representatives on the ATP Tour Board. Charles Pasarell was a part owner of Indian Wells and its tournament director so, the plaintiffs claimed he had a conflict of interest in voting for the new plan because Indian Wells would benefit tremendously by the "Brave New World Plan."

The jury trial began on July 21, 2008, and ended on August 5, 2008. The trial judge dismissed all of the claims against the individual defendants determining that they were entitled to vote as members of the ATP Tour Board and that therefore they did not violate their fiduciary duty as a matter of law. The plaintiffs' evidence on anti-trust violations was incomplete and not very convincing. Strangely, the plaintiffs made no claim for breach of contract for the sale of the Hamburg franchise by ATP to Shanghai for a lot of money or the sale of Hamburg's May calendar date to Madrid on clay in front of the French Open. The trial judge instructed the jury on the application of the Rule of Reason on the plaintiffs' anti-trust claims and the jury rendered a verdict for the ATP Tour on all claims.

Hamburg appealed to the Third Circuit Court of Appeals[846], which affirmed the trial judge's dismissal of the claims against the individual defendants and the verdict of the jury and the Supreme Court refused to permit a further appeal.

Subsequently, the ATP Tour requested the USDC to order the reimbursement of the legal fees of the ATP Tour, Inc., and the individual defendants pursuant to an ATP Bylaw that provided for reimbursement of legal expenses if the ATP Tour was sued unsuccessfully. On May 8, 2014, the Delaware Supreme Court answered four questions certified by the USDC by concluding that the ATP Tour Bylaw requiring reimbursement of litigation expenses was valid and enforceable under Delaware law if enacted properly with regard to the litigation expenses of the ATP Tour, Inc., but not the individual defendants.[847] Probably this matter was then settled by the parties.

Etienne de Villiers Replaced

After creating the Brave New World Plan and navigating the ATP Tour through the two biggest anti-trust cases in its history, the ATP Tour players had *some kind of falling out* with Etienne de Villiers and he resigned and was replaced by Adam Helfant, who would after 3 years also have a "falling out" with the players.

Nine Masters 1000 Series Beginning in 2009

So, beginning in 2009, there have been nine "Masters 1000 Series" tournaments, only eight of which are mandatory for all eligible players, since Monte Carlo is not mandatory:

1. Indian Wells
2. Key Biscayne
3. Monte Carlo
4. Rome
5. Madrid
6. Canada
7. Cincinnati
8. Paris
9. Shanghai

Before you cry for Monte Carlo, you should remember that Monte Carlo has a fabulous professional tennis player inducement program which is citizenship in Monaco where there is no personal income tax. You would not be surprised to learn how many top ranked professional tennis players are residents of Monaco or that somehow, they always voluntarily choose to play in the Monte Carlo Masters 1000 tournament each year. An American professional tennis player, as long as he is a United States citizen, would gain no tax advantage by becoming a resident of Monaco as he would always have to also pay United States income taxes (unless he renounced his American citizenship). European players apparently can however, completely avoid income taxes in their home countries by becoming a resident of Monaco. Tennis players cannot however, avoid taxes deducted from prize money winnings in other countries. The USA withholds 30% of prize money as do a lot of countries now.

ATP Tour 500 Series

The 2019 original 10 double-up week Championship Series tournaments were:

1.	Toronto	February 12-18	$1.2 million
2.	Brussels	February 12-18	$ 600,000
3.	Philadelphia	February 19-25	$1 million
4.	Stuttgart	February 19-25	$1 million
5.	Japan Open	April 9-15	$1 million
6.	Barcelona	April 9-15	$ 500,000
7.	Stuttgart (outdoors)	July 16-22	$ 900,000
8.	Washington	July 16-22	$ 550,000
9.	Stratton MT.	August 13-19	$ 625,000
10.	Indianapolis	August 13-19	$ 650,000

In 2019, the ATP Tour had thirteen 500 Series tournaments (only eight were actually doubled-up) were:

1.	Rotterdam	February 12
2.	Rio de Janeiro	February 19
3.	Acapulco	February 26
4.	Dubai	February 26
5.	Barcelona	April 23
6.	Halle	June 18
7.	London (Queens)	June 18
8.	Hamburg	July 23
9.	Washington	July 30
10.	Beijing	October 1
11.	Tokyo	October 1
12.	Vienna	October 22
13.	Basel	October 22

2019 ATP World Tour 250 Series Tournaments

In 2019, there were 40 ATP World Tour 250 Series Tournaments.
For 2020, on account of the Covid-19 Pandemic, the entire tennis calendar was turned upside down with lots of tournaments cancelled for the year.

Player Commitment

In 1990, the player commitment plan for the ATP Tour was for the top 10 players to commit to 11 non-Grand Slam tournaments: eight single week championship tournaments and three double-up week championship tournaments. The ATP Tour Designation Committee had the power to substitute up to two tournaments to balance the fields with a goal to provide each of the 11 single week championship tournaments with a minimum of six in the top 10 and each of the double-up week championship tournaments with a minimum of three in the top 10.

The ATP Player Commitment for 2019 was the ATP Tour Finals, if qualified, plus eight of the nine Masters 1000 Series tournaments (not including Monte Carlo) and four ATP World 500 Series tournaments selected by each player without substitutions, which could include Monte Carlo. This meant that each player was committed to 13 ATP Tour tournaments, not including the Grand Slams or Davis Cup. Players with 12 years of service and 600 matches qualified for a reduction in the commitment.

There are no rules for substitutions to try to balance the fields of the ATP World 500 Series tournaments. Apparently, the ATP World 500 Series tournaments made no complaint or fuss about losing the three of the top 10 as designations beginning in 2009 – maybe because the designation system wasn't working very well and maybe they liked to now be able to pay appearance guarantees legally. However, they must compete with all the other ATP Tour tournaments, outside of the 1000 Series tournaments, with their appearance fees. *I think it must be a lucrative players' market.*

Chris Kermode

After the creation of the "Brave New World Plan" in 2009 by Etienne De Villars, the next innovations for the ATP Tour were by Chris Kermode, who created the Next Generation ATP Finals in 2017 and the revival of the World Team Cup as the ATP Cup in 2020.

The Next Generation ATP Finals features the eight best 21-and-under players and has been staged in Milan since 2017.[848] The ATP World Team Cup was cancelled after the 2012 event, but it was reinvented as the ATP Cup in January of 2020 in Australia.

The new ATP Cup event is in competition with the newly reorganized ITF Davis Cup 18-nation team event which began in November of 2019 in Spain.

First, I would have thought that having the player's "Grand Slam" would have been a better investment for the ATP Tour and the WTA Tour than any new ATP Cup event. I have included the results of the ATP World Team Cup events through 1989 in this book, but I doubt that anyone remembers any of them. I often hear who is the current "Davis Cup Nation" but I have never heard who is the "World Team Cup Nation." I suspect that the new ATP Cup, like the relatively new Laver Cup, consisting of Europe vs. the Rest of the World, will, as long as they are supported by marketable players, be successes during their respective weeks. *However, the Davis Cup with all of its history and tradition will in my opinion continue to be a success when it is held and will be discussed year-round as truly representing all countries with unmatched tradition.* A player who plays Davis Cup for his country, even players relatively low on the computer rankings, become national heroes and gain important marketability in their home countries. I do not believe that the Laver Cup or the ATP Cup will offer the same benefits to the players as they are only singular events and without an international stature.

On December 12, 2020, Chris Kermode, the former CEO of the ATP Tour who was responsible for reviving the ATP Cup which began in 2020, recommended that the new ATP Cup be merged with the Davis Cup as the first event of each year when all the players would be fresh and eager to begin. Kermode did not mention the Laver Cup.[849]

ATP Gross Revenue 2013 – 2018

On December 17, 2020, Chris Kermode said that the gross revenue of the ATP Tour rose from $97 million in 2013 to $115 million in 2018. The total prize money ballooned from $85 million in 2013 to $135 million in 2018. From 2013 to 2018 there was a 90 percent increase of players winning over $1 million. Players ranked 50-100 increased by 69 percent and players 150-200 increased by 65 percent.[850]

35 of 76 of the 1989 Grand Prix Tournaments Survived in 2019

The surviving 1989 Grand Prix tournaments still going include the four Grand Slams and 31 ATP Tour tournaments which are:

1.	1/9/1989	Brisbane (formerly Adelaide)	ATP 250
2.	1/16/1989	Auckland	ATP 250

3.	1/16/1989	Sydney	ATP 250
4.	1/29/1989	Australian Open	Grand Slam
5.	2/13/1989	Rotterdam	ATP 500
6.	2/20/1989	Long Island (formerly Memphis)	ATP 250
7.	2/27/1989	Lyon	ATP 500
8.	3/20/1989	Indian Wells	ATP 1000
9.	4/2/1989	Key Biscayne	ATP 1000
10.	4/17/1989	Athens (now Valencia)	ATP 250
11.	4/24/1989	Tokyo Japan Open	ATP 500
12.	4/30/1989	Monte Carlo	ATP 1000
13.	5/7/1989	Munich	ATP 250
14.	5/14/1989	Hamburg	ATP 500
15.	5/14/1989	Houston (formerly Charleston)	ATP 500
16	5/21/1989	Rome	ATP 1000
17.	6/11/1989	Paris French Open	Grand Slam
18.	6/18/1989	London Queens	ATP 500
19.	7/9/1989	London Wimbledon	Grand Slam
20.	7/16/1989	Gstaad	ATP 250
21.	7/16/1989	Newport	ATP 250
22.	7/30/1989	Washington	ATP 500
23.	7/30/1989	Stuttgart	ATP250
24.	8/6/1989	Bastad	ATP 250
25.	8/21/1989	Canada	ATP 1000
26.	8/21/1989	Cincinnati	ATP 1000
27.	9/10/1989	New York U.S. Open	Grand Slam
28.	9/24/1989	Barcelona	ATP 500
29.	10/8/1989	Basel	ATP 500
30.	10/8/1989	Brisbane	ATP 250
31.	10/8/1989	Buenos Aires (formerly Orlando)	ATP 250
32.	10/15/1989	Metz (formerly Toulouse)	ATP 250

33.	10/22/1989	Vienna	ATP 500
34.	11/5/1989	Paris	ATP 1000
35.	11/12/1989	Madrid (formerly Stockholm)	ATP 1000

Tournaments Lost Forever

Every tournament is subject to going bankrupt whenever it has a tournament without a title sponsor as the prize money offered to players and the other expenses for the promotion and production of a professional tournament always exceed the gate, food and beverage, merchandising and television rights income. Further, as Jack Kramer predicted in 1989, the difficulty of ATP Tour tournaments, not a part of the Masters 1000 tournaments, to obtain marketable player fields, even with the payment of appearance money, made a lot of tournaments like Los Angeles bankrupt. It happened to the U.S. Pro Indoors in Philadelphia, once the most important indoor tournament in the world and Stratton Mountain, which moved from Vermont to New Haven in Connecticut in a huge new public financed stadium before becoming bankrupt. So, it is no surprise that 41 of the 76 tournaments that existed in 1989, the last year of the Nabisco Grand Prix, are no longer alive. Those tournaments raised a lot of money for professional players through the years and provided a lot of promotion for our sport. *They should not be completely forgotten*:

1. Wellington
2. Guaruja
3. Milan Super Series
4. Philadelphia Super Series
5. Nancy
6. Dallas WCT Finals Grand Prix Circuit Championship
7. Scottsdale WCT Super Series
8. Beijing
9. Seoul
10. Rio de Janeiro
11. Nice
12. Singapore
13. New York WCT Tournament of Champions
14. Florence
15. Bologna
16. Bristol
17. Bari
18. Boston Super Series
19. Schenectady
20. Hilversum
21. Hartford Super Series
22. Kitzbuhel
23. Indianapolis Super Series
24. Prague

25.	Livingston	34.	Sydney Super Series
26.	St. Vincent	35.	Tokyo Super Series
27.	San Marino	36.	Tel Aviv
28.	Geneva	37.	Frankfurt
29.	Madrid	38.	London Super Series
30.	Los Angeles Super Series	39.	Sao Paulo
31.	San Francisco Super Series	40.	Johannesburg
32.	Palermo	41.	London WCT Doubles
33.	Bordeaux		

Linesmen, Radar and Finally Hawkeye

By the end of 1989, the MTC had trained and certified 56 international referees, 66 international chief of umpires, 132 international chair umpires and 51 national referees. This resulted in a significant improvement on tennis officiating. However, it was impossible to develop an international certification program for tennis line-umpires as too many were required at each tournament and it was never going to be feasible to fund professional line-umpires to travel the worldwide tennis circuit. As a result, all tournaments had to use local line-umpires; some were good and some were not so good depending on the local recruitment and training provided.

Cyclops

Commercially, the most successful system to emerge in the early experimental period of electronic officiating was the "Cyclops." Cyclops was a device used only for service line calls but functioned reliably and was used around the world for many years until superseded by video and television technology. The Cyclops system consisted of a series of infrared laser light beams projected, at a centimeter above the ground, to a receiver device across the court and then to a computer. The series of beams were aligned to accurately determine if the ball hit behind the service line. Balls landing outside of the narrow beams still had to be called by a service linesman.[851]

TEL Magnetic System

In 1993, Stan Malless, a former MTC member, a Mensa and the owner of the Permanent Magnet Company in Indianapolis, convinced the USTA to experiment with the TEL new electro-magnetic system developed by the Australian company, Tel

Proprietary Ltd. The TEL system required embedded sensors under each line and tennis balls with embedded iron particles for magnetic detection. Unfortunately, Tel Proprietary Ltd., became bankrupt so the TEL system, after an expensive installation by the USTA for the 1993 U.S. Open was not used and was scrapped.[852]

Hawk-Eye Finally

The Sony-owned Hawk-Eye system was developed in the United Kingdom by Paul Hawkins. The system uses six (sometimes seven) high-performance cameras, positioned on the underside of the stadium roof, which track the ball from different angles. The video from the six cameras is then triangulated and combined to create a three-dimensional representation of the ball's trajectory. Hawk-Eye is not infallible, but is accurate to within 3.6 millimeters and generally trusted because of its consistency.[853]

In late 2005, Hawk-Eye was tested by the ITF in New York City and was passed for professional use. In March 2006, at the Nasdaq-100 Open in Key Biscayne, Hawk-Eye was used officially for the first time at a tennis tour event. Later that year, the U.S. Open became the first Grand Slam to use the system. Since 2006, the Hawk-Eye system has been used exclusively as it has been added to more and more tournament courts and the three unsuccessful challenges per player per set has relieved the pressure on line-persons, chair umpires and players as they seek to have the most accurate line calls possible.

Hawk-Eye Live

Hawk-Eye Live added additional cameras mounted behind the court and looking across the baseline to detect foot faults. The ATP Tour tested Hawk-Eye Live at its 2017 Next-Gen Finals to call all lines.[854] Gayle David Bradshaw, ATP's executive vice-president said to Cindy Shmerler in the *New York Times*[855]: "I understand that this may kill officiating, especially because our eventual chair umpires are almost always linespersons first. We're also taking away some of the entertainment value with the challenges because fans like to debate whether they think the call was right or not. But we can replace that by showing close calls on the big screens so the fans can see them as replays at the same time the players and officials are seeing them. As far as the players, they no longer have to worry about bad calls; they can just play the game. And if we have a system out there that's better, don't we owe it to our athletes to have access to it?" John McEnroe said that he may have been a better player without line judges to argue with "but I would have been more boring."

During the 2020 Pandemic Covid-19 year when matches were played at the USTA National Tennis Center for the Cincinnati ATP 1000 and the U.S. Open without fans, Hawk-Eye Live was used successfully on the outside courts. It was again used successfully at the 2021 Australian Open and is going to be used more and more.

Tennis Channel

One of the most important developments for professional tennis was the creation of the Tennis Channel in 2003. A digital cable and satellite television network, it was purchased by the Sinclair Television Group, a subsidiary of the Sinclair Broadcast Group, in 2016. As of January of 2019, the Tennis Channel had 61.2 million households as subscribers (66.4 percent of those with cable). The Tennis Channel is headquartered in Culver City, California. Ken Solomon has steered the network as its Chief Executive Officer since 2005.

In 2014, Tennis Channel Plus, a direct-to-consumer subscription service, was launched to include coverage of additional events not seen on television. In March of 2017, Sinclair acquired *Tennis Magazine* and www.tennis.com to increase its cross-platform presence. In October of 2020, the Tennis Channel became the exclusive U.S. broadcaster of all ATP Masters 1000 tournaments beginning in 2021. In addition, the Tennis Channel provides television coverage for lots of professional and some amateur tennis tournaments worldwide.[856]

In my opinion, the Tennis Channel is so important to the future of professional tennis that it should be purchased by the tennis family consisting of the ITF, the Grand Slams, ATP Tour and WTA Tour to ensure that it stays in business permanently. I hope that the Tennis Channel will become the primary broadcaster of all professional tournaments and even if a tournament is covered by another network, I hope all rights holders will insist that the Tennis Channel be given the rights to cover matches not otherwise covered as well as repeats of primary coverage. Hopefully, it will eventually be available worldwide to ensure that professional tennis is promoted everywhere.

ATP Tour Leaders 2021

In 2021, the ATP Tour Board consists of: Massimo Calvelli, CEO and Andrea Gaudenzi, Chairman, plus:

Player Representatives: Alex Inglot (Europe), David Egdes (Rest of the World) and Mark Knowles, (North America). Alex Inglot of London is the Director of Communications and Public Affairs at Sportradar, a global leader in sports data, David Egdes of South Africa is Senior Vice President of Tennis Industry Relations at the Tennis Channel and Mark Knowles of Nassau in the Bahamas was ranked No. 1 in Doubles in 2002.

Tournament Representatives: Gavin Forbes, Charles Smith and Herwig Straka. Gavin Forbes is employed by IMG, the owner of the Masters 1000 tournament in Miami and IMG also represents lots of professional men players. There is no prohibition against player agents serving as a Tournament Representative. We did fight a lawsuit for the right to exclude player agents from membership on the Men's Tennis Council on account of their obvious conflicts of interest. *Strangely, the ATP Tour has not seen that as a problem. I wonder who gets the Wild Cards at the Miami Open?* Charles Smith, an American, is the tournament director of the Masters 1000 tournament in Shanghai. He has lived in China for many years now and is very well respected by the Chinese government and throughout the tennis industry. Herwig Straka is the tournament director of the Masters 500 tournament in Vienna.

I understand that each member of the ATP Tour Board is paid $100,000 per year and that the members of the ATP Tournament Council and ATP Player Council are unpaid. All the members of the MTC served as unpaid volunteers.

Tournament Council

The 2021 ATP Tournament Council members are: Europe (5): Giorgio DiPalermo, Stephen Farrow, Christer Hult, Richard Krajicek and Herwig Straka, International (4): Allon Khakshouri, Cameron Pearson, Salah Tahlak and Charles Smith, Americas (4): Bronwyn Greer, Eugene Lapierro, Raul Zurutuza and Gavin Forbes.

Player Council

The 2021 ATP Player Council members are: 1-50 Singles: Felix Auger-Aliassime, John Millman, Rafael Nadal, Roger Federer, 51-100 Singles: Pablo Andujar, Gilles Simon, 1-100 Doubles: Marcus Daniell, Bruno Soares, At Large: Kevin Anderson, Andy Murray, Alumni: Colin Dowdeswell and Coach: Daniel Vallverdu.

ITF & Grand Slam Leaders 2021

In 2021, the President of the ITF is David Haggerty.

In 2021, the Grand Slam Board included:

Wimbledon: Ian Hewitt, Chairman

Australian Open: Jayne Hrdlicka, President of Tennis Australia

French Open: Giles Moretton, President of the French Tennis Federation

U.S. Open: Mike McNulty Chairman of the USTA

Bill Babcock was the Director of the Grand Slam Board, retired at the end of 2020

and was succeeded by Ugo Valensi

Arms-Length Negotiated Agreements

While the Grand Slams and the ITF no longer had any say in the organization of the non-grand slam ATP Tour circuit and the players, the non-grand slam tournaments and the ATP Tour no longer had any say with the Grand Slams, the parties found a new way to live together. *It had always been the case that all parties in the sport of tennis had to work together and so now instead of debating issues together in a Men's Tennis Council democratically elected single organization, the parties learned to work together through a series of arms-length negotiated agreements. Each organization jealously protected its turf, but when reasonable and necessary, cooperation was apparently found. In this connection, there have been a number of such contracts:*

1.   Rankings. The Grand Slams agreed to use the ATP Computer Rankings (instead of an independent ITF-Grand Slam developed computer ranking system) for the Grand Slams and the ATP Tour agreed that the Grand Slams would always have computer points double the number of computer points for the highest level of ATP Tour events, e.g., computer points awarded for the U.S. Open would always be double the computer points awarded for Indian Wells. The Grand Slams have a similar agreement with the WTA Tour with respect to the WTA Tour Computer Rankings. This agreement also included the mandatory entry into each of the Grand Slams of all players who were qualified by their computer rankings.

2.   Year End Event. The Grand Slams agreed to discontinue the Grand Slam Cup year-end event after 1999 as it was somehow merged into the ATP Tour Finals with both parties having some kind of ownership in the ATP Tour Finals for 10 years. It is unclear to what extent, if any, that the Grand Slams continue to have an interest in the ATP Finals.

3.   Officials Training & Certification. Beginning in 1990, there were two competing programs for the training and certification of tennis officials - one by the ITF and Grand Slams and one by the ATP Tour. In 1990, there was a cadre of professional supervisors and chair umpires employed by the ATP Tour (mostly from the MTC), and also a cadre of professional supervisors and chair umpires employed by the ITF for the

Grand Slams and the Davis Cup (also mostly from the MTC). Eventually, the parties got together and agreed to have one training and certification program jointly administered.

4. <u>Anti-Doping.</u> The Grand Slams, ATP Tour and WTA Tour agreed to consolidate the administration and enforcement of the Olympic drug testing first with the ITF and now it has been being merged into the Tennis Integrity Unit which on January 1, 2021, became the independent International Tennis Integrity Agency (ITIA) which is jointly funded.

5. <u>Anti-Corruption.</u> The Grand Slams, ATP Tour and WTA Tour agreed to a consolidated administration and enforcement of an anti-corruption program beginning in 2008, originally housed in the ITF, which as of January 1, 2021, was moved into the new ITIA.

6. <u>Integrity of Sport.</u> The Grand Slams, ATP Tour and WTA Tour jointly agreed to and did fund the employment of an internationally respected Independent Review Panel for a two-year study of integrity issues in tennis and for recommendations on how to protect the integrity of the sport. Some insiders complain that this study was an excessively expensive study which was unnecessary on account of the ongoing good work of the Tennis Anti-Corruption Unit. Nevertheless, it was funded and supported jointly and found no serious problems with the Sport.

7. <u>Player Relief Fund.</u> The Grand Slams, ATP Tour and WTA Tour jointly agreed to fund a Player Relief Fund to help the lower ranked professional players survive the COVID-19 global Pandemic crisis of 2020.

Representatives of the ATP Tour and the WTA Tour regularly are invited to and do make appearances at Grand Slam Board meetings to discuss matters of mutual interest. Perhaps a more formal meeting of all of the various independent constituencies a few times each year would be helpful. *It is sort of like the old Men's Tennis Council except every agreement has to be unanimous or put another way, each party has a veto.*

ATP Tour Board Structure Problems

My belief is that there is a wide range of agendas among the various classes of tournaments and the individual tournaments within each class so the tournaments are never particularly unified. During the tenure of the MTC, the rank-and-file players more or less dominated the ATP as a player association and their agenda was to support the development or more and more player jobs. There is always a wide range of agendas among the players in various levels of the rankings so the players are also never particularly unified; however, it appears to me that *today* the player interests on the ATP Tour are dominated more by the top players and the emphasis is not for more and more player jobs. I was told that in the early years of the ATP Tour when Miles was CEO there was a spirit of cooperation between the Tournament Representatives and the Player Representatives, except at one point Graham Lovett was asked to resign for a conflict of interest. Mark Miles claimed that he never voted to break a tie.

Apparently, the spirit of cooperation that existed in the early years does not *now* continue. Recently, the Player Representatives seem to be trying to dominate the ATP Tour Board. During the existence of the MTC, the non-grand slam tournaments always had the support of the ITF/Grand Slams if the players became unreasonable and the players always had the support of the ITF/Grand Slams if the non-grand slam tournaments became unreasonable. Now that the ITF/Grand Slams are independent, the non-grand slams and the players do not have the same protection.

Justin Gimelstob served as the U.S. Player Representative on the ATP Board from 2008-2019 and during his tenure he was a very aggressive advocate for the players against the tournaments and the players loved it. Gimelstob also had a coaching relationship with John Isner, one of the members of the ATP Tour Player Council on which Novak Djokovic led as President until 2020. *Gimelstob apparently believed that the players' 50 percent was greater than the tournaments' 50 percent.*

When ATP CEO Brad Drewett passed away on May 3, 2013, the three Tournament Representatives and the three Player Representatives were unable to reach an immediate agreement on Drewett's replacement until Chris Kermode was finally hired on November 20 to begin a three-year term on January 1, 2014, which was subsequently extended to December 31, 2019. In 2019, when Roger Rasheed was a "Rest of the World" Player Representative on the ATP Tour Board and he voted a small compromise with the Tournament Representatives, he was summarily terminated by the Player Council led by Djokovic and replaced by David Egdes on an interim basis. Egdes was re-elected for a full term at the next election. In 2019, the Player Council voted not to extend Chris Kermode's employment beyond December 31, 2019, reportedly hoping to find someone who would "always" side with the players on tie-break votes. Gimelstob was known to be interested in replacing Kermode as CEO.

On October 31, 2018, Gimelstob was involved in a physical altercation with Randall Kaplan, a friend of his ex-wife, in West Los Angeles. Gimelstob was charged with felony battery in California and he refused to take a leave of absence from the ATP Tour Board while his criminal charge was pending with the public support of Djokovic and Isner to the consternation and objection of lots of other players. On April 22, 2019, Gimelstob pleaded "no contest" and the judge reduced the charge to a misdemeanor and sentenced Gimelstob to three years probation and 60 days of community labor. Gimelstob finally agreed to step down from the ATP Tour Board on May 1 after even more backlash from the players. Weller Evans a retiree of ATP and a former member of the MTC was elected to replace Gimelstob for a while until he was succeeded by Mark Knowles.[857]

Many people considered that the ATP Tour might literally be ungovernable as it then stood and that it was facing the possibility of having the players and the non-Grand Slam tournaments seek to split and deal with each other via a collective bargaining agreement. *Splitting the ATP Tour with all its assets around the world including the Deferred Compensation Plan would be a nightmare.* Presumably, the ATP Tour Board found a solution with the employment of two new executives instead of one to lead the ATP Tour in 2020, which was apparently supported by the Player Council and the Tournament Council. Andrea Gaudenzi began a four-year term as the Chairman of the ATP Board to serve as the tie-breaking vote and Massimo Calvelli began a four-year term as the Chief Executive Officer of the ATP Tour without a vote on the Tour Board. *But what did Djokovic do next?*

2020 Professional Tennis Players' Association (PTPA)

At the 2020 U.S. Open, Novak Djokovic and Vasek Pospisil (co-presidents) announced the formation of player association No. 5, the Professional Tennis Players' Association (PTPA) to represent the top 500 singles players and the top 200 doubles players with the assistance of the Canadian (global) law firm of Norton Rose Fullbright. They claimed that 150+ players signed up during the U.S. Open. The PTPA was said to be also open for membership by women. Djokovic, Pospisil, John Isner and Sam Querry resigned from the ATP Tour Players' Council to join the PTPA. Djokovic and Pospisil claimed that "it is very difficult, if not impossible, to have any significant impact on any major decisions made by our tour." Pospisil said to Ben Rothenberg in the *New York Times*[858] that the PTPA will have "essentially the same function as a union" but with more flexibility. He said, "Our voices will finally be heard and we will soon have an impact on decisions that affect our lives and livelihoods."

Former ATP Player Council President Tim Mayotte said to *Sportico*[859] that "by agreeing to share control over the tour with non-grand slam tournament directors, the players – who are not represented by a union – limited their ability to negotiate directly with the Grand Slams and the Davis Cup." Said Mayotte, "Grand Slam tournament revenues have exploded since 1988, but because the players have been unable to negotiate directly with organizers over the last 30+ years, they believe they're not receiving a fair share of that money. Despite the widespread belief amongst players that they are being short-changed, Djokovic has struggled to get enough support to threaten the status quo."

Comparing Tennis Majors to Golf Majors

Comparing the majors of professional tennis to the majors of professional golf shows that the Grand Slams of tennis are much, much more lucrative for professional tennis players than are the majors of professional golf for the professional golfers. For example, in 2021, the Masters in Augusta offered $11.5 million for 50 men golfers. The U.S. Open (golf) offers $12.5 million and The Players (golf) offers $15 million for around 50-60 players.

In 2019, the U.S. Open (tennis) offered $57+ million and Wimbledon offered £28.49 million for 128 men in singles, 128 men in doubles, 128 women in singles and 128 women in doubles, plus up to another 128 in the singles and doubles qualifying, plus various per diems for traveling expenses. The winner of the Augusta Masters received $2 million whereas the men and women's winner of the U.S. Open each receive $3-$3.85 million. *By almost any measure, it seems clear that the Grand Slam tennis tournaments are much more lucrative for the professional tennis players than are the major golf tournaments for the golfers.*

When the players seek to demand even more from the Grand Slams they disregard that those tournaments support tennis in their countries and worldwide, that they have achieved their success from the efforts and contributions of 1000s of volunteers over 100+ years and that they all have significant loan and bond debts which financed their world-class facilities for the players. Since 1986, the Grand Slams have contributed over $50 million to the ITF's Grand Slam Development Fund to develop competitive tennis worldwide. The Fund is designed to assist players directly, through touring teams or travel grants (now known as Grand Slam Player Grants), to gain international competitive experience.

When the ATP Tour was created in 1990, it attempted to replicate the PGA Tour for golf. I don't believe the individual golfers ever attempted to form a separate players' association. *Now, we have the ATP Players Council representing the players on the ATP Tour and a new PTPA that wants to represent all the players on everything. That is an obvious conflict.* It may literally be impossible for Pospisil and Djokovic or anyone for that matter to represent all the players on everything and they most certainly could not represent the women pros. At this moment, it is unknown what effect this conflict will have on the ATP Tour, the ATP Tour Player Council, the Grand Slams and the Davis Cup. *Could Pospisil and Djokovic be planning to threaten to boycott the Grand Slams if the players are not paid more prize money?*

In October of 2020, the ATP Tour Board unanimously amended its Certificate of Incorporation to prohibit membership on the Player Council and the Tournament Council by anyone who is a member of another entity that is involved in similar functions. The obvious purpose was to prohibit members with a conflicting interest in another organization like the PTPA. That same restriction had previously applied to the tournament and player members on the ATP Tour Board.

In December of 2020, when Pospisil and Djokovic wanted to run for election back on the ATP Player Council, they were informed that it was prohibited because of their involvement with the PTPA. *It looks like a lot of new legal work will be required before all this is resolved. Does anyone remember Wayne Ferreira's proposed 2003 International Men's Tennis Association?*

COVID-19

The COVID-19 Pandemic, which began soon after the 2020 Australian Open, caused extensive interruption of men's professional tennis in 2020 and 2021. It *did, however, cause all the stakeholders in professional tennis to continue to work together.*

Would the 1988 Unified Governance Deal be Rejected today?

In the 1988 final Crisis No. 32, the ATP, as a pure players' association executed the Coup D' État that forced the dissolution of the Men's Tennis Council as the unified governing body of men's professional tennis and created the ATP Tour as a partnership between the ATP and the non-Grand Slam tournaments. As a result, the Grand Slams became completely independent and the ATP as a pure player association was terminated.

Here, again, is what the five-year offer was in 1988, and I wonder if it were offered today, if it would be rejected again:

1.   The Men's Tennis Council would have continued with nine members, three from the ITF, three from the ATP and three from the tournaments. The name of the Grand Prix Tour could have been changed to "ATP Tour." The Grand Slams would have continued to be part of the ATP Tour, continued to be the major contributors to the ATP and to the ATP Pension Plan. In 1988, the Grand Slams were, I believe, also willing to provide free marquees to support sponsorships of the Tour.

2.   The ATP would continue as a pure player association and would have been financed by payments from the Grand Slams and the non-grand slams and the ATP would continue its private ownership of the two-week "Players' grand slam" in Key Biscayne/Miami, the World Team Cup (ATP Cup) and half ownership of the ATP Championships in Cincinnati.

3.   The three ATP members would have 50-50 voting on all non-grand slam matters with the three tournament representatives, similar to what now exists in the ATP Tour, with a mutually agreed person to vote to break any ties.

4.   The three ATP members would have 50-50 voting on all Grand Slam matters with the three ITF representatives, with a mutually agreed person to vote to break any ties. Today, the ATP has no vote on any Grand Slam matters and the Grand Slams do not contribute anything to the ATP or the ATP Pension Plan, having elected to put all their money into prize money and expense money for participating players in each Grand Slam.

Would men's professional tennis be stronger with a unified governing body? In my opinion, then it should have been an easy decision for the ATP and the non-grand slam tournaments. All constituents would have benefited quite a bit by having the ITF and the Grand Slams involved. While, then the Grand Slams were amenable as the deal offered was approved by the presidents of the ITF, USTA, Tennis Australia and the French Tennis Federation with the knowledge and at least the initial support of Wimbledon, today with the success of the Grand Slams independent of the ATP Tour, I doubt that they would now be amenable to such a deal. Perhaps the non-grand slam tournaments or the players would not like it either.

Today, it appears to me that with the Grand Slam Board, the ATP Tour, the WTA Tour and the ITF all being separate, independent governing bodies, they are quite happy to be able to each protect their respective properties and deal with each other in good faith for the betterment of the Sport through a series of arms-length negotiated contracts. It is now really like they can do anything together that is unanimous and each party reserves the full right to veto anything. Mike Davies told me once that putting tennis governance back together in a unified governing body would be just about as difficult as "putting the ivory from a piano's keys back into an elephant's trunk!" Regardless, whether the governance of men's professional tennis is ever unified again, the principals of the Sport will always have to work together because the real competition for tennis is all the other sports and entertainment events, not competition among the various tennis constituencies.

T7 Gets Down to the Business of Evolution

On March 10, 2021, Sudipto Ganguly of Reuters reported on an interview with the ATP's Andrea Gaudenzi: "Tennis could be set for a radical overhaul as the game's main stakeholders come together in an unprecedented effort to chart a roadmap for streamlining the governance of the sport. A 'T7 working group,' which involves the ATP, WTA, the four Grand Slams and the International Tennis Federation, will start work later this month examining areas such as a unified calendar, shared commercial offerings, sponsorships and TV deals."

"I'm excited to go through that process because it's never been done before," Gaudenzi told Reuters. "I don't know the outcome, but I look forward to exploring all options. We committed to start after the Australian Open to work together on our project with the help of a consultant from March. Governance, calendar rules, synergies in commercial media data rights, sponsorship …everything is on the table."

Ganguly wrote, "Tennis enjoys a massive worldwide following, but its governance is fractured with the seven organisations running different parts of the game."[860]

Unified Goverance

There are different ranking systems, different logos, different websites and viewers need different pay TV platforms to watch matches. Unifed governance could simplify television contracts and sponsorship deals.

The unprecedented challenge of the pandemic helped forge closer links between the bodies - they united to raise more than $6 million in May to help lower level players, for example - and laid the foundations for the T7 group."

"Gaudenzi said the process could take six to nine months of bi-weekly meetings to thrash out ideas that will enable tennis to better meet the challenges of a changing marketplace. 'We are in the entertainment industry,' the Italian said."

"I would like to have a different governance structure moving forward and we've shown we can all work together. That's important.'"

Just maybe the elephant tusks can be united again with the elephant!

CHAPTER 37:

1990+: MARSHALL HAPPER AFTER THE DEMISE OF THE MEN'S TENNIS COUNCIL

USTA Executive Director 1990-1995

I could, if I had time, write another book about what happened next, but I am going to provide just some of the highlights. I did become the Executive Director of the USTA on January 1, 1990, and Karen and I moved to Stamford Connecticut from which I learned how to commute daily by train to Manhattan and the USTA Office on 6th Avenue and 48th Street. All commuters sort of learn to lie to themselves about how short a time their commute is. I usually left home just after 6 am and returned around 9 pm each day. Notwithstanding my long relationship with the USTA, I found that the USTA was significantly dysfunctional and that the USTA staff, many of whom had been there over 25 years, were not accustomed to and resisted to being managed. Being Executive Director presented a number of different challenges from the ones I had just lived through with the Men's Tennis Council.

David Markin, USTA President/CEO, wrote in the *1990 USTA Yearbook*[861]: "No book can express the intrinsic value of our organization. This value lies in the vast network of volunteers who strive to promote the game and are the backbone of our Association." I would soon learn that David and the other volunteers of the USTA were intent on controlling and operating the USTA using the professional staff merely to assist them. They made the staff extremely difficult to manage.

During my tenure as Executive Director, in addition to managing the USTA staff of 100-150 people and the business of the USTA, I was also the only in-house legal counsel as I was not permitted to hire additional help. In those years, we were able to generate an annual surplus of $11-$31 million so by 1995, the USTA had a fund balance of $182 million. The USTA's goal was to have one year's operating cost in reserve plus a $100 million for investment in the new U.S. Open Project.

1991-1996 U.S. Open Television Rights

In 1990, David Markin appointed Donald Dell and ProServ as the exclusive worldwide marketing agents for the U.S. Open television rights for 1991-1996 and Donald did a great job for the USTA. I worked with Donald on the marketing of the U.S. Open television rights worldwide as I had to draft and sign all the contracts for some 66 countries. When ABC and NBC pulled out of the bidding for the U.S. Open for 1991-1996, CBS had taken advantage of the USTA and only offered a reduced rights fee contract for the U.S. Open that required the USTA to provide $2 million in additional revenue for CBS each year or suffer a $2 million reduction. Every year Donald had to try to find that $2 million in additional revenue for CBS. Between 1991-1996, CBS continued to require that the USTA have no back court signage and no signage on the west side of the stadium court when CBS was on the air. It would not be until 1997-2002 after CBS loss the NFL and NBC also bid for the U.S. Open that the USTA would obtain the control of the signage on its stadium court from CBS.

USTA Headquarters Building - 70 Red Oak Lane, White Plains NY

In 1992, I found a vacant 110,000 square foot four story building at 70 West Red Oak Lane in Harrison/White Plains and convinced the USTA to purchase it to consolidate the Manhattan, Princeton and Jericho USTA offices and move the Player Development and Sport's Science headquarters to the Key Biscayne tournament site. We purchased the building for $3.25 million, spent $6.6 million upgrading it, occupied the 1st and 2nd floors for the consolidated USTA offices and rented out the 3rd and 4th floors for $1 million per year. We moved in our new USTA Headquarters in early 1993. As the USTA is now transitioning its headquarters to Orlando Fla, this building will probably be sold hopefully at a large profit for the USTA.[862]

Expansion of USTA National Tennis Center – New Arthur Ashe Stadium

David Markin was the president of the USTA for 1989 and 1990 and David began in 1989 to plan for the redevelopment of the home of the U.S. Open in Flushing-Meadows Queens.

The LaGuardia Runway #13 Take-Off Nuisance

The main drawback to having the U.S. Open at Flushing Meadows, beginning in 1978, was understood later when it was discovered that when the wind was coming from the South, airplanes from the nearby LaGuardia runway #13 (130 degrees) had adopted a "noise abatement" procedure that redirected all the planes taking off to make a right turn to fly over Flushing Meadows at just over 1,000 feet in the air. Actually, a direct takeoff from runway #13 would send the planes at 130 degrees directly over Great Neck, Long Island. Apparently, the rich folks at Great Neck were successful some time previously in getting the FAA to order a "noise abatement" right turn at 1000' to go over Flushing Meadows before circling back at a much higher altitude over Great Neck. When the planes started taking off on runway #13, the noise every few minutes was terrible for the players and the fans.

Robert McG Thomas, Jr., wrote in the *New York* Times[863]: "Complaints about the noise of La Guardia takeoffs have been almost as incessant as the takeoffs themselves (about 500 a day) ever since the Open moved from its former home at the West Side Tennis Club in Forest Hills in 1978." "Players often gripe about the distraction of departing aircraft, although few quite as forcefully as Kevin Curren, who once expressed the wish that the low-flying planes should be used to bomb the stadium."

In late 1989, I attended a meeting between David Markin, President of the USTA, with Mr. Daniel Peterson, the Regional Commissioner of the FAA, Deputy Mayor Robert Eznard (Mayor Ed Koch's administration), Nick Garaufis, then Legal Counsel to Queens Borough President Claire Shulman, and the then New York City Parks Commissioner, Henry Stern. Markin was beginning discussions with New York City for an extension of the U.S. Open lease for Flushing Meadows and the possible expenditure of millions of dollars to build a new (Arthur Ashe) Stadium and make other renovations to the USTA National Tennis Center for the U.S. Open. We knew that unless the planes taking off from LaGuardia were diverted away from the U.S. Open, the U.S. Open could not continue at this site in New York City.

FAA's Mr. Peterson: "I don't like you"

To everyone's surprise, Mr. Peterson said at the meeting something to the effect "I don't like you (tennis) people and last year even when the wind was not from the south, just for good measure, I sent some extra planes over Flushing Meadows during the U.S. Open. I assure you, the 'noise abatement' procedure that sends planes over Flushing Meadows will never, ever be changed." We were flabbergasted. I remember saying something like, "I can't believe you care which direction the planes take off if no safety issue is involved and New York City representing its citizens wants you to change it." *To say that Mr. Peterson of the FAA was arrogant would be an understatement.*

Mayor Ed Koch had no interest in tennis or any sports for that matter and so we were delighted with the election of David Dinkins in 1990, since he was a tennis player and an avid tennis fan. Markin informed Mayor Dinkins that if the planes continued to take off over Flushing Meadows, the USTA would have to move the U.S. Open out of Flushing Meadows in the 1990s, because the fans and the players just would not continue to support the tournament with that kind of nuisance and therefore the USTA could not justify any additional financial investment there.

Nick Garaufis Saved the U.S. Open for Queens

With the support of David Dinkins and Claire Shulman, Nick Garaufis, Shulman's brilliant lawyer, was able to persuade the FAA to agree to change the take-off pattern for runway #13 for 2 weeks (and only 2 weeks) of each year during the matches of the U.S. Open. I can still remember the *irony* of Mr. Peterson at the eventual press conference explaining "how happy he was" to be able to accommodate New York City, the Borough of Queens and the U.S. Open. The air traffic over Flushing Meadows was diverted each year from the actual beginning of matches in the morning until the actual end of the last night match via direct communication between the U.S. Open Referee and the LaGuardia tower.

Before every U.S. Open in every year while I was the Executive Director, Nick Garaufis and I would attend a meeting at an FAA office at JFK at which along a huge conference table would be representatives of the FAA, the airlines, the LaGuardia tower and a number of other folks we did not know. Each time, someone would open the meeting with a statement like: "Ok, we all know what we are going to do" and the meeting would then be summarily concluded and someone would give me the secret telephone number for the LaGuardia tower for the use of the U.S. Open Referee to keep the tower informed when matches would begin and end each day.

The change made to accommodate the U.S. Open was much safer that the "noise abatement" right turn over Flushing Meadows as it just sent the runway #13 planes straight out at 130 degrees, which was the first established take-off pattern, and yes, directly over Great Neck.

Experimental Fanning as a Permanent Solution Rebuked by Great Neck and D'Amato

Lindsey Gruson later reported in the *New York Times*[864] that Nick Garaufis had been successful in having the FAA experiment with a proposed year-round "fanning" of take-off directions from Runway #13 so the "take-off noise" would be dispersed to different areas instead of being concentrated in just one area. However, when the rich folks at Great Neck heard about it, they insisted and obtained the assistance of Senator Alfonse M. D'Amato to have the flight paths restored over Queens and Flushing Meadows "because an experimental diversion to more affluent areas of Long Island (Kings Point, Great Neck's million dollar homes) had failed to reduce noise pollution."

"Claire Shulman, the Queens Borough President, disputed that finding and attacked the Senator, who acknowledged he had not seen the data. She said that the decision was made to buy off wealthy Long Islanders and that there was a great deal of evidence that noise pollution was reduced (by the experimental fanning of take-offs) for tens of thousands of residents of Kew Gardens, Forest Hills, Corona and Elmhurst."

Flights are Still Diverted Thanks to
Nick Garaufis, Claire Schulman and David Dinkins

However, the diversion of LaGuardia flights from runway #13 during the U.S. Open each year has continued to the shagreen of the rich folks in Great Neck. Everyone in tennis should thank David Dinkins, Claire Schulman and *especially Nicholas Garaufis* for diverting the planes from LaGuardia from flying low over Flushing Meadows during the U.S. Open matches. Otherwise, the U.S. Open would be located somewhere else.

Subsequently, Nick Garaufis became general counsel for the FAA in Washington and later a Senior United States Federal Judge for the Eastern District of New York. I never knew what happened to our "friendly" Mr. Peterson of the FAA, but I doubt he became a tennis fan.

Planning, Approvals & Construction

In 1990, David Markin was in his second and last year as president of the USTA and he initially believed that he could complete the construction of several new tennis stadiums in Flushing Meadows before he went out of office since Nick Garaufis had obtained the agreement of the FAA to stop the aggravating overflights from La Guardia during the two weeks of the U.S. Open each year. However, the U.S. Open Project that resulted in the construction of the new Arthur Ashe Stadium and renovation of the Louis Armstrong Stadium along with other improvements would not be completed until 1997 as it took two years and around $10 million to deal with the architectural, environmental, permitting and construction issues. Flushing Meadows – Corona Park had been a big landfill and so very expensive boring studies had to be completed to learn that all pilings for the new stadium would have to be over 130 feet deep before they hit bedrock.

Gino Rossetti was selected as the architect because he had been the first architect to design luxury suites in the middle of a stadium instead on the top of a stadium when he designed the Palace at Auburn Hills for the Detroit Pistons. The new Arthur Ashe Stadium would at about 20 rows up be interrupted with two rings of luxury suites with 45 luxury suites on each ring, before the seating rows would resume above.

Markin assembled a team consisting of an architect, structural engineer, environmental lawyer, a real estate lawyer, a Queens lobbyist, a Queens public relations firm and a Republican and a Democratic lobbyist to the New York State Legislature. Eventually, Lehrer McGovern was hired as the project manager and after the project was bid, the large Turner Construction Company became the general contractor.

To obtain the approval for the new 99-year lease for the expansion of the USTA National Tennis Center property and for the construction of the new tennis stadium and related facilities, it was necessary to provide an Environmental Impact Study and obtain the approval of the New York City Planning Commission, New York City Council and the New York State Legislature

Arthur Ashe Went to 15 Neighborhood Associations for USTA

Before the proposed new U.S. Open Project could even be presented to the New York City Planning Commission, it had to be submitted individually to each of the 15 Neighborhood Associations adjoining the 1200 acre Flushing-Meadows-Corona Park. I had worked with and for Arthur Ashe on the Men's Tennis Council and I have never known a finer person. Arthur was one of the most important and famous Pioneers of the Game.

In September of 1988, Arthur learned that as a result of a blood transfusion in an earlier heart operation he had contracted the H.I.V. "AIDs" virus. On April 9, 1992, I attended Arthur's press conference in Manhattan where he informed the public that he indeed had AIDS. Arthur knew that the dreaded disease was going to take his life and he passed away on February 6, 1993, at age 49. I attended Arthur's Memorial Service in Richmond and also his Memorial Service in New York City.

Notwithstanding that Arthur knew he was dying, I want you to know that he went to every one of the 15 Neighborhood Associations adjoining Flushing-Meadows-Corona Park and helped convince each of them to support the new U.S. Open Project. That permitted the project to proceed to the New York City Planning Commission, the New York City Council and the New York State Legislature.

After obtaining approvals from the Planning Commission, City Council and the State Legislature, one additional New York City condition was required and that was the approval of the New York City Art Commission. If the Art Commission had not approved, the U.S. Open Project, all the millions of dollars and time invested in the planning and design would have been loss. Fortunately, the only requirement of the Art Commission was the alignment of the new Stadium bowl with the axis of the 1964-1965 World's Fair Unisphere in Flushing Meadows – Corona Park.

As Executive Director I went with David to lots and lots of meetings for the negotiation of a new 99-year lease (100+ pages) with New York City and to develop architectural and construction plans for the new Arthur Ashe stadium and related improvements to the USTA National Tennis Center. I actually signed the new 99-year lease and the construction contracts for the Project. The initial plan was for the USTA to invest its special U.S. Open Project Reserve which was then $100 million and then borrow $150 million from tax free New York City bonds for a total outlay of $250 million. I think the final tab got to something like $285 million.

After David Markin went out of office as the USTA president at the end of 1990, he continued in charge of the new U.S. Open Project until its completion in 1997. The improvements made to the Billie Jean King USTA National Tennis Center with the construction of the new Arthur Ashe Stadium and its 90 luxury suites enabled the U.S. Open to more than double or triple its income from the U.S. Open.

No Roof

I tried in vain to get David and the USTA to install a roof on the new Arthur Ashe Stadium so it could be used year-round or at least install substantial enough pilings to accommodate a future roof. David was in a hurry to get the project finished and he told me that the U.S. Open would always be an outdoor tournament so no roof would ever be needed. I did not agree and I was certain that since the airplanes were not stopped after the U.S. Open that the new stadium could not be used even for a rock concert. I thought that was a huge waste. I actually had a meeting with representatives of Madison Square Garden to see if some arrangement could be made to have a NBA team join with the USTA and use the stadium year-round. I had no luck with that.

I understand that, because the USTA did not provide sufficient pilings in the original Arthur Ashe Stadium construction to support a roof that in 2016, the USTA had to spend something like $150 million to install additional new pilings to add a roof over Arthur Ashe Stadium and it is still not good enough so the stadium can be used as an indoor arena year-round.[865]

Problems with USTA Presidents

In addition to my difficulty in managing the USTA staff with the interference of the volunteers, I had some problems with the USTA presidents who were, of course, my bosses.

HRH Construction as General Contractor, Supervised by HRH Construction?

Sometime in 1992, David Markin became impatient with the slowness of progress and he came to me and told me he planned to hire immediately HRH Construction Company to be both the general contractor and the project manager for the U.S. Open Project. I objected to having the same company in both jobs since the project manager had to supervise the general contractor for the USTA. This irritated Markin, but Bob Cookson who was then the USTA President agreed to appoint a committee to review the matter and wanted me to be on the committee. I respectfully asked not to be on the committee as I had irritated my bosses enough. The committee eventually rejected Markin's plan and rightfully required that the project manager be separate.

Seven Luxury Suites for President's Dining Room?

The agreed plan for the new Arthur Ashe Stadium was to have two rings of luxury suits about 20 rows up from the court with 45 luxury suites on each ring for a total of 90 luxury suites. When Bumpy Frazer was USTA President, he insisted that the President's dining room use seven luxury suites on the top ring so diners could see the court. In the beginning, we planned to charge $100,000 per year to rent luxury suites (they are now around $300,000+). I objected at a USTA Board meeting pointing out that using seven luxury suites for the USTA President's dining room would then cost the USTA $700,000 per year in income. At the Board meeting, Bumpy told me to "shut up" and not one member of the Board joined in my objection. So, the original construction contract for Arthur Ashe Stadium used seven luxury suites on the upper ring for the President's dining room. Bumpy was succeeded by Les Snyder as USTA President and Les was, of course, aware that I knew about the seven luxury suites and that I had objected to the loss of income for the USTA. Snyder, who had not objected when Bumpy was in charge, very quietly had the President's dining room moved behind the second ring luxury suites for something like a $2 million change order that was never mentioned to the volunteers, thus making the seven luxury suites rentable.

Reunion with Hamilton Jordan at Southern Tennis Hall of Fame

In January of 1995, while I was still the USTA Executive Director, I was inducted into the Southern Tennis Hall of Fame. I was proud to have Hamilton Jordan who was long retired from the ATP Tour and professional tennis to be my Presenter for the induction ceremony in Atlanta. Hamilton was very gracious in his presentation again saying that "only history will show whether he or I was right" about the destruction of the MTC and the creation of the ATP Tour. I very much enjoyed visiting with Hamilton and his beautiful wife, Dorothy, in Atlanta and that was the last time I saw him as his cancer returned and he passed away on May 20, 2008, at age 69.[866]

USTA Presidents as CEO

As Executive Director of the USTA, I was the Chief Operating Officer and the volunteer USTA President was the Chief Executive Officer. The USTA is an organization of 17 geographical Sections engaged mainly in grass roots tennis and as a result, the USTA President as well as the officers and directors in those years came mainly from the grass roots which did not provide them with a background on professional tennis. In those years, the "long term" policy of the USTA was just the two years of a USTA Presidency as each President made up his on plan. Also at that time, the members of USTA Board mostly agreed with whatever the President wanted to do because the only way a member of the Board could be re-elected or become an officer required a positive recommendation of the outgoing President to the USTA Nominating Committee. So, the USTA had several significant flaws: (i) each CEO had little or no expertise in professional tennis that was the main source of revenue for the USTA and (ii) each volunteer President could as the CEO get involved in the management of the staff and the business of the USTA.

During my tenure as USTA Executive Director, the USTA Presidents were David Markin, 1989-1990, Bob Cookson 1991-1992, Bumpy Frazer 1993-1994 and Les Snyder 1995-1996. Bob Cookson was the only one of my USTA Presidents who acted as a Chairman of the Board and not as a CEO. Markin, Cookson and Frazer were all accomplished business CEOs. Snyder was a psychology professor at Arizona State University with no business experience. In those years, the officers of the USTA were intent on maintaining control of the USTA by the volunteers and they considered the ATP and the tennis industry as "enemies." I remember going before the USTA Nominating Committee to ask them to consider the nomination of Arthur Ashe and Stan Smith to the USTA Board, but the volunteers would not consider them. This was before the U.S. Olympic Committee required some token player representation on the Board.

Les Snyder Was a Problem

When Les Snyder became the USTA President in 1995, it was immediately clear to me that he had no business experience, no information about professional tennis and that he was going to be a big problem for the USTA. Les did have a gigantic ego and a yearning to be important in professional tennis. As President, he became a member of the Grand Slam Committee for the Grand Slams and he was the Grand Slam representative on the WTA Board. Les told me once how much he really loved being involved in professional tennis and that he might consider it as a new profession. I remember telling him that it would probably take him 10 years to understand all the nuances of the people involved in professional tennis. Nevertheless, Les began having secret meetings with television executives, agents and sponsors and he also began having secret meetings with members of my senior staff, especially those who hated being managed. At that time, Brian Tobin had become a paid Executive President of the ITF and Geoff Pollard had become a paid Executive President of the Australian LTA. I was convinced that Les wanted to be a paid Executive President of the USTA for more than his two-year term.

1997-2002 U.S. Open Television Rights

With respect to the U.S. Open television rights for 1997+, at the request of the USTA, Donald Dell who had very ably represented the USTA for the marketing of the 1991-1996 worldwide television rights of the U.S. Open reported to the USTA as follows[867]: "The new incoming President, Mr. Les Snyder, changed the entire television negotiating representation. He selected TWI (IMG) to negotiate the domestic network rights with CBS. The Board then overruled Mr. Snyder and selected ProServ Television to continue negotiating the domestic cable rights. In addition, Mr. Snyder unilaterally terminated relations with the German company, Ufa, a subsidiary of the Bertlesmann Company, despite the fact the Ufa had paid $66 million to the USTA over the previous 5 year contract period. Mr. Snyder put out bids to various groups and ultimately he alone surprisingly accepted a $15 million per year guarantee for 4 years from another German television group known as ISPR - more than $2 million less than ProServ Television generated for the USTA in 1996." Les sought to accept an ISPR offer at a surprise press conference in London without any notice to me as the Executive Director. The problem was all he had was an incomplete proposal from ISPR and it took me months to clean up the mess he created between ISPR and the USTA. Of course, the relationship between the USTA and Ufa was permanently destroyed.

My Resignation as Executive Director

In August of 1995, Les came to me and told me that he wanted to replace me as the "manager" of the USTA and move me to another position in the USTA to oversee the business and legal affairs of the USTA. I was convinced that Les planned to try to become the paid Executive President of the USTA with me looking after the business for him so I declined and resigned as Executive Director. Subsequently, Les discovered that he could not actually become the paid Executive President of the USTA and so a committee of the Board after months of delay hired Rick Ferman, a teaching pro/coach who was a member of the Board, to succeed me as Executive Director. In the interim, Les asked and I agreed to become an outside business affairs attorney for the USTA with an agreed retainer that was extended in different forms through the years. I did not mind being an outside lawyer for the USTA, but I vowed never to again be an employee for the USTA. Les acted as CEO and signed all the new television contracts for the U.S. Open in 1996 and he actually signed television contracts for Japan and Australia on December 31, 1996, the last day of his presidency before he was succeeded by Harry Marmion. Les had refused to let me provide any information on the television contracts or any USTA business to Harry during Les's presidency and immediately after becoming president, Harry instructed me to never provide Les with any information again. *Just a little bad blood!*

Les Snyder and the 1996 U.S. Open Draw

In August of 1996, Les Snyder called me in my capacity as outside business affairs counsel. In summary, he admitted that he had disregarded the ATP Computer Rankings in making the U.S. Open draw on the previous day and had moved the seeds "in his judgment" which resulted in more favorable draws for Americans, Andre Agassi and Michael Chang. Les had just received a letter from Mark Miles, ATP Tour CEO, threatening a boycott of the U.S. Open. Les asked for my advice. I told him "you should have called me yesterday before you made the draw." I recommended that he immediately announce a remake of the draw, which he reluctantly did.[868]

USTA Today

Slowly through the years, the USTA Board began long range planning so that its plans would not be in merely two-year presidential increments and, as the business of the USTA became more and more complex, additional professional administrative and legal staff was added and with whom I worked as an outside business affairs counsel. However, It would take until 2018 for the USTA to finally decide to make the Executive Director the CEO.

Eventually, the USTA elected members of the tennis industry as Presidents with Alan Schwartz in 2003-2004 and Dave Haggerty in 2013-2014. Haggerty was also elected President of the ITF in 2015. For the first time, the USTA elected professional players as President with Katrina Adams in 2015-2018 and Pat Galbraith in 2019-2020. In 2021, Mike McNulty, a talented New Orleans litigation attorney, became President with Dr. Brian Hainline, Chief Medical Officer of the NCAA, (son of Pioneer Forrest Hainline) as his projected successor. In the 1990s, I recruited Brian, a Neurologist and expert in Sports Science, to completely professionalize the medical services for the players at the U.S. Open. The 2021 members of the USTA Board of Directors includes the most educated and professional group I have ever seen at the USTA and the new Executive Director and CEO, Michael Dowse, the first Executive Director from the tennis industry, appears to have the ability to lead and manage the USTA. The USTA in 2021 is an entirely different and much more professional organization than it was in 1995.

Outside Business Affairs Counsel for USTA and Back to NC to Practice Law

From 1995 to 2009, I served as an outside business affairs counsel for the USTA during which time I was involved in the negotiation and drafting of all U.S. Open sponsorship, television, food service and merchandising contracts. In 1998, I moved back to Raleigh with my law firm of Manning, Fulton & Skinner and in addition to my outside counsel work for the USTA, I returned to litigation and commercial real estate law and now added sports and entertainment law. During that time, I represented a variety of real estate and litigation clients plus some clients in the sports and entertainment industry, e.g., the Capital Area Soccer League in 2002 for the construction of the new professional soccer stadium in Cary NC (SAS Stadium), the location of the Women's Courage professional soccer team to Cary in 2002 and 2003 and the Carolina Cobras of the Arena Football League.

Sports and Entertainment Law for the New Millennium

On October 21-22, 1999, I was the Program Planner for the first sports law forum in North Carolina for the North Carolina Bar Association: "Sports and Entertainment Law for the New Millennium" and we had 200 attendees from 25 states and a dynamite list of nationally recognized and respected speakers. The entire Live presentation was taped and shown to lots more lawyers via video after the Live presentation. In addition to serving as the Program Planner, I spoke on the negotiation and drafting of sports television contracts. At my request, Ivan Blumberg (Washington DC), Executive Vice President and General Counsel for ProServ spoke about representing professional tennis players. Also, at my request, Mark McCormack sent Alan Fuente (Cleveland OH), Associate Counsel, International Management Group (IMG) to speak on representing professional baseball players. Mark S. Levinstein, Esquire (Washington DC) of Williams & Connolly, spoke on "The Role of the Antitrust Laws in Sports; Monopolies, Boycotts, the Rule of Reason; and Ethical Considerations." Mark Levinstein was the lawyer for ProServ in the Volvo, ProServ, IMG lawsuit which also included me personally that we settled in 1988. Mark and I had never met before and he made a terrific presentation at our seminar. Mark was the co-author of an important book on anti-trust law: *Sports Law: Cases and Materials* (2d. ed. 2007). The success of our conference led to the creation by the NC Bar Association of the first full Sports and Entertainment Law Section and I agreed to serve as its first Chairman.

Donald Dell Speaks in Raleigh

In 2001, I held a special meeting in Raleigh of our new Sports and Entertainment Law Section and at my request, Donald Dell, flew to Raleigh to make a really good presentation that was very well received by our Section lawyers. Donald flew in and out of Raleigh in one day at his own expense as a favor to me.

So, you see, in spite of all the wars and lawsuits and controversies, we all ended our years in professional tennis together with respect for each other so we could work together again when it was appropriate. We all sort of chuckle together when we see each other occasionally now and reminisce about our younger years.

I am proud that I had the opportunity to work for and with the Pioneers of the Game!

CHAPTER 38:

1926-1989: THE PIONEERS OF THE GAME

If you have made it this far in this book, you have read about the relatively small number of people who created the format and governance for the development of men's professional tennis from 1926-1989. As I told you at the outset, many of them were bitter rivals with competing agendas and yet, somehow, they were able to lead the development of our Sport through 1989, to provide the platform for men's professional tennis to reach for the next levels of growth beginning in 1990. The growth of men's professional tennis from 1990-2021 and the future is the direct result of their efforts and accomplishments. *Everyone in the Sport today is standing on their shoulders.*

It has always been true and still is, that even the biggest rivals always had to work together, sometimes in strained cooperation, to keep the Sport growing. And they did it! Here are my selections for the Pioneers of the Game. Remember, this is based on what occurred *prior to 1990.* See if you agree and don't worry too much about my numbering as it is impossible to accurately rank the Pioneers. Every time I look at the list of Pioneers, I change my ranking numbers.

My Most Important Pioneers of the Game

Jack Kramer No. 1 (United States)

Hall of Fame: 1968
[D: September 12, 2009, age 88]

Jack Kramer won Wimbledon and the US Championships in 1947, turned pro and ran the Kramer Pro Tour until 1962. Lots of tennis players, including me grew up playing with Jack Kramer wood Wilson tennis racquets. He was instrumental in bringing about Open Tennis in 1968. He founded the Grand Prix of Tennis in 1970 to compete with WCT, founded the ATP in 1972 and served as its 1st ATP Executive Director from 1972-1975 for a salary of $1 per year. Jack and Cliff Drysdale led the 1973 ATP Boycott of Wimbledon which established the ATP as a force in the Game. Jack was one of the founders of the 1973 ILTF Grand Prix Committee and the Men's Tennis Council (MTC) in 1974. Jack served first as a Player Representative and then as a Tournament Representative on the Men's Tennis Council. He was a Player Representative in 1974-1976 and a Tournament Representative for the North American Tournaments in 1976-1977 and 1979-1984. *Jack is without doubt the most important person and contributor in the history of men's professional tennis.*

Philippe Chatrier No. 2 (France)

Hall of Fame 1992
[D: June 22, 2000, age 74]

Philippe Chatrier retired as a French Davis Cup Player in 1960, founded *Tennis de France* magazine in 1953 and became life-long personal friends with Jack Kramer and later with Donald Dell. He was Vice President of the French Tennis Federation (FFT) from 1968-1973, French Davis Cup Captain in 1969, President of the FFT in 1973-1993 and President of the ITF in 1977-1991. He directed the resurgence of the French Open as FFT President. Chatrier, Kramer and Dell devoted a lot of time together as they sought to structure and restructure men's professional tennis through the years. Chatrier supported the ATP Boycott of Wimbledon. Philippe was one of the founders of the ILTF Grand Prix Committee and the Men's Tennis Council (MTC) in 1974. He was an ITF Representative on the Men's Tennis Council in 1974-1977 and 1979-1989, and was the MTC Chairman in 1979-1985. Philippe was briefly succeeded on the MTC by Brian Tobin for 1977-1978.

Lamar Hunt No. 3 (United States)

Hall of Fame 1993
[D: December 13, 2006, age 74]

Lamar Hunt, along with Dave Dixon and Al Hill, Jr., founded World Championship Tennis (WCT) in 1967, began contracting with the best players and created the WCT professional tour culminating with the Dallas Finals each year. WCT introduced professional tennis to indoor venues and television and was responsible for many innovations for professional tennis. Lamar promoted WCT as an independent tour from 1967-1977, then as a "circuit within a circuit" as part of the Grand Prix in 1978-1981, then as an independent tour in 1982-1984, and finally as part of the Grand Prix in 1985-1989. Lamar closed WCT in 1990.

Herman F. David No. 4 (Great Britain)

Hall of Fame 1998
[D: February 25, 1984, age 68]

Herman David was the Chairman of Wimbledon in 1959-1973. Wimbledon was an amateur tournament through 1967, while the actual best players in the world (e.g., Don Budge, Jack Kramer, Pancho Gonzales, Frank Sedgman, Tony Trabert, Ken Rosewall, Lew Hoad, Rod Laver, etc.) were ineligible because they had turned professional. John Newcombe won 1967 (Amateur) Wimbledon over Wilhelm Bungert 6-3, 6-1, 6-1. Herman David and Jack Kramer promoted an 8-man professional tournament at Wimbledon in 1967 after (Amateur) Wimbledon, won by Rod Laver over Ken Rosewall and televised by the BBC which proved that professional tennis would be very popular with the public. *As a result, Herman David declared that "shamateur tennis" was a "living lie" and decided to open Wimbledon in 1968 to the professionals. That decision forced the ILTF to ultimately agree to Open Tennis in 1968.*

Derek N. Hardwick No. 5 (Great Britain)

Hall of Fame 2010
[D: May 28, 1987, age 66]

Derek Hardwick was a retired farmer and a British doubles champion from Bournemouth. He was instrumental in leading the fight for Open Tennis in 1968 as Chairman of the British Lawn Tennis Association (LTA) and he hosted the first Open tournament in Bournemouth in 1968. He was President of the ILTF in 1975-1977. He was one of the founding members of the 1973 ILTF Grand Prix Committee which was created after the 1973 ATP Boycott of Wimbledon and which was the predecessor to the creation of the independent Men's Tennis Council in 1974. He was a founder of the Men's Tennis Council and a member until his death in 1987. Derek was the thought leader of the ITF for many, many years and was very well respected by the professional players.

Judge Robert J. Kelleher No. 6 (United States)

Hall of Fame 2000
[D: June 20, 2012, age 99]

Robert Kelleher was an amateur New England tennis player. He graduated from Harvard Law School in 1938 and practiced law in New York and Los Angeles before becoming a United States District Judge in 1970. He was President of the USLTA in 1967 and 1968 and he successfully led the USLTA to support Open Tennis in 1968, and was instrumental in obtaining approval of the ILTF for Open Tennis to begin in 1968.

Donald L. Dell No. 7 (United States)

Hall of Fame: 2009

Donald Dell graduated from Yale and the University of Virginia law school. He was ranked No. 5 in the US and was a member of the US Davis Cup team. With his close friend, Jack Kramer, Donald became a leading advocate for Open Tennis. He was the US Davis Cup Captain in 1968 and 1969. Dell founded the ProServ management company (with Frank Craighill, Lee Fentress and Ray Benton), representing many of the top players, top tournaments and the sponsors of the Grand Prix. In addition to representing lots of professional tennis players, ProServ also was heavily involved in the ownership, defacto ownership and representation of Grand Prix tournaments and special events. He and Jack Kramer founded the Association of Tennis Professionals in 1972 and for many years he served as its legal counsel, marketing and television agent. Donald participated with Kramer as a leader of 1973 ATP Boycott of Wimbledon that established the new ATP as a force in the Game. He was a member of the 1973 ILTF Grand Prix Committee created after the Wimbledon Boycott and he was an advocate for the creation of the Men's Tennis Council in 1974, which gave the players a voice in the administration of the sport.

Michael G. Davies No. 8 (Great Britain)

Hall of Fame 2012
[D: November 3, 2015, age 79]

Mike Davies was Britain's No. 1 player in 1958-1960. Mike signed as a pro in 1960 with the Kramer Tour and after Kramer terminated the tour at the end of 1962, Mike became a leader of the International Professional Tennis Players Association (IPTPA), the 1st Players Association (1963-1967) to keep professional tennis going with Tony Trabert, Ken Rosewall, Rod Laver, Lew Hoad, Butch Buchholz, Barry MacKay, Pancho Gonzales, etc. Mike became the Associate Director of WCT with Bob Briner in 1967-1968 and the 2nd Executive Director of WCT, succeeding Briner, for 1969-1981. For WCT,

Mike instituted a tie-breaker system, colored clothing for players, yellow tennis balls, 30 seconds between points and 90 seconds on changeovers to accommodate television commercials so tennis could be televised. This led to having chairs for the players on the court during changeovers for the first time. Mike led the promotion of tennis indoors and on national television and he created the first syndication of tennis on television in the United States. Later Mike became the 4th Executive Director of ATP for 1983-1986, succeeding Butch Buchholz. Mike succeeded Butch Buchholz as a Player Representative on the Men's Tennis Council in 1983-1986 and was the MTC Chairman in 1985-1986. In 1988-1993, Mike became the General Manager of the ITF; the only top job in tennis Mike never had was one with the women's WTA Tour. Mike also negotiated for the ITF the creation of the Grand Slam Cup event in Munich 1990-1999, which provided $6 million per year for players and $2 million per year for the ITF worldwide Development Fund.

Allan Heyman No. 9 (Denmark)

[D: September 1988, age 77]

Allan Heyman, a native of Denmark, was a Queens Court Barrister in London and was the ILTF President in 1971-1974. He negotiated and signed the 1972 "Peace Agreement" for the ILTF with WCT that gave WCT a monopoly for 16 weeks in the first part of each year for 1973-1975 and the ILTF (and later the MTC) a monopoly for the rest of the year for the Grand Prix. He led the ILTF ban that forced the ATP Boycott of Wimbledon in 1973, which led to bringing in the ATP into the governance of men's professional tennis with the ILTF Grand Prix Committee in 1973 and the independent Men's Tennis Council in 1974.

Tony Trabert No. 10 United States)

Hall of Fame 1970
[D: February 3, 2021, age 90]

Tony Trabert was a No. 1 in the World in 1953 and the winner of 5 Grand Slams including Wimbledon, 2 U.S. Opens and 2 French Opens. He turned pro in 1955 and played on the Kramer Tour. Tony was the original acting promoter for the International Professional Tennis Players Association (IPTPA) tour in 1963-1967 which kept professional tennis going after the demise of the Kramer Tour. The IPTPA professional players, consisted mainly of Trabert (until he retired), Frank Sedgman (mostly retired), Rosewall, Hoad (when he was well), Laver, Gonzales (retired, then unretired), Luis Ayala, Andres Gimeno, Barry MacKay, Butch Buchholz, Pancho Segura, Mike Davies (until he retired) and Alex Olmedo. Fred Stolle and Dennis Ralston joined in January of 1967. Trabert was succeeded as promoter of the IPTPA tour by Wally Dill and later by Mike Davies, Butch Buchholz and Barry Mackay.

E. Cliff Drysdale No. 11 (South Africa)

Hall of Fame 2013

Cliff Drysdale was a South African Davis Cup Player and was one of the 1967 "Handsome Eight" of WCT that forced the ILTF to vote for Open Tennis in 1968. Cliff was the 1st president of ATP in 1972-1974, and he led the 1973 Boycott of Wimbledon which established the ATP as a force in the Game. He was a Player Representative on the Men's Tennis Council in 1976-1981. When Mike Davies as Executive Director of WCT created the first television syndication of tennis in the United States, he hired Cliff to be the television commentator which led Cliff into a new career as a famous ESPN commentator.

Arthur Ashe No. 12 (United States)

Hall of Fame 1985
[D: February 5, 1993, age 49]

Arthur Ashe was a great American Davis Cup player and Captain. He won the first U.S. Open in 1968 as an amateur followed by an extensive professional career, also winning Wimbledon and the Australian Open. Arthur was the 2nd president of the ATP in 1974-1976. Arthur wrote the first MIPTC Code of Conduct and pushed hard for a professional administration for the MIPTC. He was a Player Representative on the Men's Tennis Council in 1974-1976 and 1979-1983.

Robert A. Briner No. 13 (United States)

[D: June 18, 1999, age 63]

Bob Briner was the 1st Executive Director of WCT in 1967-1968 until he was succeeded by Mike Davies. He was a founding member of the ATP in 1972, the Associate Director of ATP for 1972-

1975 with Jack Kramer and he succeeded Kramer as the 2nd Executive Director of ATP in 1975-1980. Bob was the ATP Joint Secretary to the Men's Tennis Council in 1974-1976. He succeeded Jack Kramer as a Player Representative on the MTC in 1976-1979 and he was MTC Chairman in 1977-1978.

Earl "Butch" Buchholz No. 14 (United States)

Hall of Fame: 2005

Butch Buchholz won the Australian, Wimbledon and U.S. Open junior championships in 1958 and 1959 and was ranked No. 5 in the World in 1960. Butch became a Kramer Tour pro in 1960, an IPTPA pro in 1963-1967, and a member of the 1967 "Handsome Eight" of WCT that forced the ITF to vote for Open Tennis in 1968. In 1977-1978, Butch was the Commissioner of World Team Tennis. In 1979-1980, Butch was an assistant to Bob Briner at the ATP and Butch succeeded Briner as the 3rd Executive Director of ATP in 1980-1983, and saved the ATP from bankruptcy. Butch succeeded Briner as a Player Representative on the Men's Tennis Council in 1980-1983. In 1985, he created the 2-week Lipton International Players Tennis Championships for the ATP and the WTA, the "players' grand slam".

John Newcombe No. 15 (Australia)

Hall of Fame: 1986

John Newcombe was a World No. 1 ranked player and winner of 7 Grand Slams: 3 Wimbledons, 2 Australian Opens and 2 U.S. Opens. He was the President of the 2nd player association formed in 1969 as the International Tennis Players Association (ITPA) and he was the 3rd ATP President in 1977-1978.

Frank Craighill No. 16 (United States)

Frank Craighill was a partner with the law firm of Dell, Craighill, Fentress and Benton, and their ProServ management company until 1983. He and Donald Dell served as the ATP Legal Counsel from 1972-1980. In 1983, Frank and Lee Fentress withdrew from ProServ and created Advantage International to represent professional players. They refrained from getting involved with tournaments and agreed with the MTC that it was a conflict of interest for a player agent who represented some players to also own or promote a tournament involving other players.

Bill Riordan No. 17 (United States)

[D: January 20, 1991, age 71]

Bill Riordan represented the Mid-Atlantic Section of the USLTA for many years and was the tournament director of the US National Indoor Championships in Salisbury MD in 1964-1976. Bill founded the Independent Players' Association (IPA) for the independent pros (not under contract with WCT or the NTL) who were not members of the ATP. He was the promoter of the USLTA Indoor Circuit ("Riordan-IPA Circuit") against WCT in the January-May WCT "exclusive" time frame in 1970-1976, featuring Jimmy Connors and Ilie Nastase, etc. Riordan represented Connors for many years and he created and promoted the "World Heavyweight Championship of Tennis" challenge matches featuring Jimmy Connors against Rod Laver, John Newcombe, Guillermo Vilas and Ilie Nastase.

Air Chief Marshall, Sir Brian Burnett No. 18 (Great Britain)

[D: September 16, 2011, age 98]

Sir Brian Burnett became Chairman of Wimbledon in 1974-1983, after the 1973 ATP Boycott of Wimbledon. Sir Brian earned his reputation as an important leader in Great Britain. He had been a senior Royal Air Force officer who became Air Secretary and served as the last Commander-in-Chief of the Far East Command. His complete title was "Sir Brian Kenyon Burnett, Air Chief Marshall, GCB, DFC, AFC, ADC". Sir Brian changed the attitude of Wimbledon to become more respectful and accommodating to the professional players.

Eugene L. "Gene" Scott No. 19 (United States)

Hall of Fame 2008
[D: March 20, 2006, age 68]

Gene Scott was ranked No. 4 in the US in 1963 before Open tennis. Gene was Donald Dell's roommate at Yale and he graduated from law school at the University of Virginia in 1964. Gene was a lawyer and he became a tennis agent for professional players, the tournament director of the Grand Prix tournament in Orange NJ, Publisher of *Tennis Week* beginning in 1974 providing editorial critique of everyone and everything in men's professional tennis. Gene was a confidential consultant and advisor to most of the important Presidents and leaders through the years. He was the Nabisco Masters Tournament Director in 1985-1989.

Raymond "Ray" Moore No. 20 (South Africa)

Ray Moore was a South African Davis Cup player and was a successful professional player beginning with the first Open Tennis tournament in 1968 at Bournemouth. He was the first Chairman of the powerful ATP Computer Committee when the computer ranking began in 1973. Ray was President of the ATP for 1983-1985. Ray was a long-time member of the ATP Board of Directors. Ray was one of the smartest tennis players I ever met and even after his retirement as an active player, he spent a tireless number of volunteer hours to improve things for his fellow players. He was probably the most important "thought-leader" for the rank-and-file players. Ray succeeded Drysdale on the MTC as a Player Representative in 1981-1989 and was MTC Chairman in 1986-1989. Ray had a powerful ethical conscience that tormented him as he struggled with his fiduciary duty to the Men's Tennis Council as its Chairman, while leading the charge as the "Tennis Mastermind" for the ATP, which resulted in a Coup d' État that destroyed the Men's Tennis Council at the end of 1989. It also ended the ATP as a pure player association. In 2021, Ray Moore is the respected "Mastermind" behind the ATP Tour Masters 1000 tournament (BNP Paribas Open) for men and women in Indian Wells.

Harold Solomon No. 21 (United States)

Harold Solomon was a graduate of Rice University and as a professional player he achieved a World ranking of No. 5 in 1980. Harold was a 3 year President of ATP for 1980-1983 and a long-time member of the Board of Directors. He was one of the serious thought leaders of the ATP. He once wrote an article saying that guarantees were "a cancer on the game". He succeeded Stan Smith and served as a Player Representative on the Men's Tennis Council in 1985-1987.

James Henry "Jim" McManus No. 22 (United States)

[D: January 18, 2011, age 70]

Jim McManus was a retired professional tennis player. He was a founding member of the ATP in 1972 and served as its Secretary from its beginning until it ended in 1989. He was personally responsible for finding a way to have the ATP Computer rankings recognize the Satellite tournaments beginning in 1976, which opened up the rankings to the new up-and-coming players for the first time. Jim did just about everything for the ATP and Jim McManus's *Tennis History* (August 2010) is one of the most important research books ever written and was invaluable for the research for this book.

Stanley "Stan" Malless No. 23 (United States)

[D: January 19, 2012, age 97]

Stan Malless played college tennis at Perdue University. He was an engineer and a Mensa and was the founder and president of the Permanent Magnet Company of Indianapolis. Stan was Chairman of USLTA Sanction and Schedules Committee for US Summer Circuit tournaments and before the ATP Rankings he was responsible for the selection of player entries for all the US Summer Circuit tournaments. He directed the US National Claycourt Championships in Indianapolis for many years and was instrumental in building the Indy tennis stadium in 1979 which was the first permanent stadium outside of the U.S. Open built in the United States. He was President of the USTA in 1974-1976, and was a member of the original 1973 ILTF Grand Prix Committee that preceded the founding of the Men's Tennis Council in 1974. Stan was an ITF Representative on the Men's Tennis Council in 1974-1985.

Owen Williams No. 24 (South Africa)

At one time Owen Williams considered himself the "highest paid (shamateur) tennis player in the world". Owen became the very successful tournament director of the South African Championships in Johannesburg and also for a tournament in Atlanta. He was the Tournament Representative for the Rest of World Tournaments on the Men's Tennis Council in 1976-1981. He resigned from the MTC in 1981 to succeed Mike Davies as the CEO of the WCT, a job he continued until WCT went out of business in 1990.

Brian Tobin No. 25 (Australia)

Hall of Fame 2003

Brian Tobin was a top 10 Aussie player in 1956-1962. He was President of Tennis Australia in 1977-1989 and had the responsibility for the Australian Open and several other Australian tournaments. He was also a Vice President of the ITF. Brian served first as an ITF Representative on the Men's Tennis Council in 1977-1978, then as a Rest of the World Tournament Representative in 1982-1988, and finally as an ITF Representative in 1988-1989. If my list of Pioneers were not cut off at the end of 1989, Brian would be much higher since he succeeded Philippe Chatrier for 1991-1999, as the important president of the ITF.

William Hamilton McWhorter Jordan No. 26 (United States)

[D: May 20, 2008, age 63]

Hamilton Jordan graduated from the University of Georgia in 1967 majoring in Political Science. Hamilton was the key advisor and strategist for Jimmy Carter's 1976 presidential campaign, and he served as Chief of Staff for President Jimmy Carter in 1979 and 1980. He succeeded Mike Davies as the 5th and last Executive Director of the ATP for 1987-1990 and succeeded Harold Solomon as a Player Representative on the Men's Tennis Council in 1987-1988. Hamilton resigned from the MTC and devised a plan with Ray Moore in 1988 to lead the Coup d' État that destroyed the Men's Tennis Council at the end of 1989 and created the ATP Tour beginning in 1990. That action terminated the unified governance of men's professional tennis by the Men's Tennis Council and forced the ITF and the Grand Slams to become independent.

Pierre Darmon No. 27 (France)

Pierre Darmon was a great French Davis Cup player ranking No. 8 in the World in 1963. He was an original founding member of the ATP and an original member of the ATP Board. He developed and administered the 1st ATP's European Tournament Bureau in Paris. Pierre was a Player Representative on the Men's Tennis Council in 1974-1978.

Paolo Angeli No. 28 (Italy)

[D: May 8, 2012, age 71]

Paolo Angeli was the first president of the European Tennis Association in 1975-1978, which included all the national tennis associations in Europe, and he was an ITF Representative on the Men's Tennis Council in 1975-1977.

Lars Myhrman No. 29 (Sweden)

Lars Myhrman was a retired Swedish Davis Cup player and the Tournament Director of the popular Grand Prix tournament in Bastad. He was the Tournament Representative on the Men's Tennis Council for the European Tournaments in 1976-1983.

John A. Harris No. 30 (United States)

John Harris was a real estate developer and was a co-owner and co-director with Donald Dell of the Washington DC Super Series Tournament. He was the Tournament Representative for the North American Tournaments on the Men's Tennis Council in 1977-1978.

Stanley "Stan" Smith No. 31 (United States)

Hall of Fame: 1987

Stan Smith was a great American Davis Cup player and former World No. 1 wining the U.S. Open in 1971 and Wimbledon in 1972. He would have been seeded No. 1 for 1973 Wimbledon, but for the ATP Boycott. He was one of the founding members of the ATP and was a long-time member of the Board of Directors. Stan succeeded Arthur Ashe as a Player Representative on the Men's Tennis Council in 1983-1985. Stan became the President of the International Tennis Hall of Fame.

Jacques "Kobi" Hermenjat No. 32 (Switzerland)

Kobi Hermenjat was the Tournament Director of the popular Grand Prix clay court tournament after Wimbledon in Gstaad. Kobi succeeded Lars Myhrman as the Tournament Representative for the European Tournaments on the Men's Tennis Council in 1983-1985.

Ray Benton No. 33 (United States)

Ray Benton was a partner in the law firm of Dell, Craighill, Fentress and Benton and was an owner and president of the ProServ management company which represented a large number of professional players and Grand Prix tournaments. ProServ also represented Colgate and Volvo as Grand Prix sponsors and Ray was the tournament director of the Colgate Masters and the Volvo Masters at Madison Square Garden. Ray succeeded Jack Kramer as the Tournament Representative for the North American Tournaments on the Men's Tennis Council in 1984-1985. Ray became the CEO of the Junior Tennis Championship Center in College Park, MD.

Franco Bartoni No. 34 (Italy)

[D: August 14, 2005, age 56]

Franco Bartoni was a retired Italian Davis Cup player. He had been one of the first MTC Supervisors hired in 1978 and he had been traveling the Grand Prix in 1978- 1984. Franco became the Tournament Director of the Italian Championships in Rome and Milan and he succeeded Kobi Hermenjat as the Tournament Representative on the Men's Tennis Council for the European Tournaments in 1985-1989.

Charles M. Pasarell No. 35 (United States)

Hall of Fame: 2013

Charlie Pasarell was a former US Davis Cup player, a successful professional player, a founding member and alumnus of ATP. He was the founder and tournament director of the Grand Prix tournament originally in La Quinta which became a Super Series in 1982 and eventually moved to Indian Wells and became an ATP Tour 1000 tournament. Charlie succeeded Ray Benton as the Tournament Representative for the North American tournaments on the Men's Tennis Council in 1985-1989.

Graham G. Lovett No. 36 (Australia)

[D: September 2, 1999, age 63]

Graham Lovett was a retired player and had been the managing director of Dunlop Slazenger. He founded the Australian Indoors Championship in Sydney AU and served as its tournament director from 1973-1994. He was involved in Sydney's successful Olympic bid for the 2000 Olympics. Graham succeeded Brian Tobin as the Tournament Representative for the Rest of World Tournaments on the Men's Tennis Council in 1988-1989.

David Markin No. 37 (United States)

[D: May 30, 2013, age 82]

David Markin was president-elect of the USTA in 1987 and 1988 and was president in 1989 and 1990. For the USTA, he also served as Chairman of the US Davis Cup Committee, Chairman of the Junior Tennis Council, and, for many years, was the official referee for the National 16-18 Boys' Championships in Kalamazoo. He succeeded Forrest Hainline as an ITF Representative on the Men's Tennis Council in 1988-1989. David later chaired the U.S. Open Project committee in 1990-1997 for the USTA and was the leader of the revitalization of the Billie Jean National Tennis Center, which included the construction of the new Arthur Ashe Stadium and the renovation and refurbishment of the Louis Armstrong stadium. In 1990, David was successful in getting the LaGuardia air traffic take-off pattern diverted away from the USTA National Tennis Center during the U.S. Open.

Forrest Hainline No. 38 (United States)

[D: March 3, 1993, age 74]

Forrest Hainline was the retired General Counsel of American Motors. He was Chairman of the USTA Grievance Committee for 1970-1985, USTA Constitution and Rules Committee 1983-

1986, and the ITF Rules Committee in 1987-1990. He succeeded Stan Malless as an ITF Representative on the Men's Tennis Council in 1985-1988.

Weller B. Evans, Jr. No. 39 (United States)

Weller Evans graduated from Princeton in 1976, and was a career employee of the ATP and for many years he was an "ATP Road Manager" working every week at a professional tournament directly with the players entered. Weller's position was the closest to the players of any position in the ATP. He was one of the few people who knew all of the players personally and he had their respect. Weller succeeded Mike Davies as a Player Representative on the Men's Tennis Council in 1986-1989.

Thomas Hallberg No. 40 (Sweden)

Thomas was a retired Swedish Davis Cup Player and was ITF's Director of Men's Tennis. Derek Hardwick died in 1987 and was succeeded by Thomas as an ITF Representative in 1987 on an interim basis until he was succeeded by Brian Tobin in 1988.

Martin "Marty" Davis No. 41 (United States)

Marty Davis was a professional player and was ranked No. 29 in 1988. He was very active in the ATP and when Hamilton Jordan resigned from the MTC in 1988 to lead the fight to dissolve the MTC and start the new ATP Tour, Marty became his replacement on the MTC. Marty succeeded Hamilton as a Player Representative on the Men's Tennis Council in 1988-1989.

Basil Reay No. 42 (Great Britain)

[D: November 7, 1987, age 78]

Basil Reay was the General Secretary of the ILTF/ITF from 1973-1976. He was the first ILTF Joint Secretary for the Men's Tennis Council in 1974-1976.

David Gray No. 43 (Great Britain)

Hall of Fame 1985
[D: September 6, 1983, age 56]

David Gray was a famous tennis journalist with the *Guardian* before he succeeded Basil Reay as the General Secretary of the ILTF in 1976. He also succeeded Basil Reay as the ILTF Joint Secretary of the Men's Tennis Council for 1976-1981.

Doug Tkachuk No. 44 (United States)

[D: August 15, 1987, age 41]

Doug Tkachuk was the ATP Administrative Director, during 1978-1979 when Bob Briner was Chairman of the MTC and Executive Director of the ATP. Doug literally ran the Grand Prix in those years. He hired and trained the Grand Prix Supervisors, organized the Officials' schools, made the player designations to the tournaments, oversaw the Code of Conduct and just about everything else. The Europeans complained that he favored the US tournaments. Doug succeeded Briner as the ATP Joint Secretary of the Men's Tennis Council in 1976-1980.

Ron Bookman No. 45 (United States)

[D: April 12, 1988, age 46]

Ron Bookman was the first public relations professional for World Championship Tennis in 1967 when Bob Briner was the WCT Executive Director. Ron went on to become the Editor and Associate Publisher of *World Tennis* in 1971-1980. In 1980, when Butch Buchholz became Executive Director of the ATP he hired Ron as the ATP Director of Communications. Ron succeeded Doug Tkachuk as the ATP Joint Secretary of the Men's Tennis Council in 1980-1981. Ron developed the 1st ATP Press System database and served as Acting ATP Executive Director and then ATP Deputy Executive Director in 1986-1988 until his untimely accidental death in 1988.

Roy L. Reardon, Esquire No 46 (United States)

Roy Reardon was a graduate of St. Johns University School of Law in 1954 and he was a senior partner with Simpson Thacher & Bartlett in New York. He was an outstanding anti-trust lawyer, advisor and litigator and was recognized as A Fellow of the American College of Trial Lawyers. Roy attended most meetings of the MTC to advise on the legal "reasonableness" of its governance rules and he represented the MTC in the two big anti-trust cases against the MTC, one brought by WCT and another brought by Volvo, ProServ and IMG. He also represented the MTC in the Guillermo Vilas Major Offense Code of Conduct case in 1983. Roy was so well respected that he could have at any time received 100% approval to become the Czar of men's professional tennis, but it unfortunately would have required him to give up his beloved work as a practicing lawyer. Roy served as Legal Counsel for the Men's Tennis Council in 1978-1989.

Reginald Edward Hawke "Buzzer" Hadingham No. 47 (Great Britain)

[D: December 27, 2004, age 89]

Buzzer Hadingham was the Chairman of Wimbledon in 1983-1989. He supported the creation of the Lipton International 2-week "players' grand slam" and he also supported the creation of the new ATP Tour in 1990.

Larry King No. 48 (United States)

Larry King was an attorney, real estate broker, promoter, bridge player and ex-husband of Billie Jean King. He was one of the founders and owners of World Team Tennis during 1974-1978, when WTT competed heavily with the Grand Prix tournaments for the best men and women players for its intercity league within the United States.

Mark Hume McCormack No. 49 (United States)

Hall of Fame 2008
[D: May 16, 2003, age 72]

Mark McCormack was a graduate of William & Mary and Yale Law School. He was the founder and sole owner of International Management Group (IMG), the international sports management firm representing lots of famous athletes (originally in Golf with Arnold Palmer, Jack Nicklaus and Gary Player) and including Bjorn Borg, Billie Jean King and lots of famous professional tennis players. IMG also was heavily involved in the ownership, defacto ownership and representation of Grand Prix tournaments and special events. Mark maintained a strong personal relationship with all of IMG's top player clients. When you attended an "IMG Player Party", there would always be an appearance of IMG's player clients as a personal tribute to Mark.

Robert D. "Bob" Kain No. 50 (United States)

Bob Kain joined Mark McCormack's International Management Group in 1976 and by 1983 he was Head of the IMG's Tennis Division and was an agent for lots of the top ranked men and women players. Bob worked confidentially with the other player agents and me each year to help balance the fields for the Grand Prix tournaments.

Ion Tiriac No. 51 (Romania)

Hall of Fame 2013

Ion Tiriac was a promoter and entrepreneur and was the coach and agent for Ilie Nastase, Guillermo Vilas and numerous other top ranked players. He owns and promotes the ATP Tour 1000 tournament in Madrid on clay in front of the French Open and is said to be the first entrepreneur billionaire from the tennis world.

John McEnroe, Sr., Esquire No. 52 (United States)

[D: February 18, 2017, age 81]

John McEnroe, Sr., was a senior partner in the New York law firm of Paul, Weiss, Rifkin, Wharton & Garrison. He served as agent for John McEnroe, Jr., and was often the spokesman for all the top players.

Peter Lawler, Esquire No. 53 (United States)

Peter Lawler began as an attorney-agent for ProServ and in 1983 he left ProServ and became one of the founders of Advantage International. He was the agent for lots of top players and for several years John McEnroe, Sr., enlisted his assistance in representing John McEnroe, Jr. Peter, along with Bob Kain, Jerry Solomon and Ivan Blumberg worked with me each year to help balance the fields for the Grand Prix tournaments.

Jerry Solomon No. 54 (United States)

Jerry Solomon began working for the Colgate Grand Prix and then he became a player agent with ProServ. Soon he became the President of ProServ. His most famous personal client was Ivan Lendl, who he still represents as he promotes various events under his new company, Star Games. Jerry, along with Ivan Blumberg, Bob Kain and Peter Lawler worked with me each year to help balance the fields for the Grand Prix Tournaments.

Ivan Blumberg, Esquire No. 55 (United States)

Ivan was a 1980 graduate of Hobart College and a 1983 Graduate of Washington University School of Law. In 1983, he began as the special Assistant to Donald Dell, and soon became a player agent and eventually the Senior Vice President & General Counsel of ProServ. Ivan also worked with me to help balance the fields for the Grand Prix tournaments each year. Since 2007, Ivan has been the CEO of Athletes for Hope, a nonprofit organization that works to educate professional athletes about philanthropy. It has amassed a collection of over 6,000 professional, Olympic and collegiate athletes who are committed to using their platform to make the world a better place.

Eric Drossart No. 56 (Belgium)

Eric was a retired professional, three-time Belgian champion and Davis Cup Player. He joined IMG in 1974 and he became the Head of IMG in Europe. He represented IMG's player clients in Europe and was the tournament director of the European tournaments either owned or defacto owned by IMG.

Additional Selections for Pioneers of the Game

These are additional Pioneers for whom I could not decide on a numerical ranking so you will have to insert them as you determine your own rankings.

Charles C. "Cash and Carry" Pyle (United States)

[D: February 3, 1939, age 57]

Promoter of the 1st recorded professional tour featuring Suzanne Lenglen vs. Mary K. Brown in the United States, Canada, Cuba and Mexico during 1926.

Jack Harris (United States)

[D: August 9, 1997, age 98]

Promoter of "Jack Harris Pro Tours", before World War II, with Ellsworth Vines, Don Budge, Fred Perry, et al. Also promoted a 1946-1947 professional tour after World War II with Bobby Riggs vs. Don Budge, et al., and a 1947-1948 professional tour with Bobby Riggs vs. Jack Kramer et al.

Bobby Riggs (United States)

Hall of Fame 1967
[D: October 25, 1995, age 77]

Promoter of 1949-1950 "Bobby Riggs Professional Tour" with Jack Kramer vs. Pancho Gonzalez. Riggs also promoted the famous "Battle of the Sexes" against Margaret Court and Billie Jean King in 1973.

George MacCall (United States)

[D: December 24, 2008, age 90]

George MacCall was the founder and promoter of the National Tennis League (NTL) professional tour in 1967 with 7 men and 4 women featuring: Ken Rosewall, Rod Laver, Fred Stolle, Pancho Gonzales, Roy Emerson, Andres Gimeno, Pancho Seguro, Billie Jean King, Ann Jones, Francoise Durr and Rosie Casals. MacCall also was the Commissioner of World Team Tennis before Butch Buchholz.

David Frank "Dave" Dixon (US)

[D: August 8, 2010, age 87]

Dave Dixon and Al Hill, Jr., along with Lamar Hunt, were the founders and promoters of World Championship Tennis (WCT)

Al G. Hill, Jr., (United States)

[D: December 2, 2017, age 72]

in 1967, featuring Butch Buchholz, Cliff Drysdale, Roger Taylor, John Newcombe, Tony Roche, Nikki Pilic, Dennis Ralston and Pierre Barthes marketed as the "Handsome Eight". Dixon dropped out in 1968. Lamar Hunt and Al Hill, Jr. continued WCT until 1990.

Derek Victor Penman (Great Britain)

[D: July 3, 2004, age 89]

Derek Penman partnered with Derek Hardwick to lead the British LTA to approve Open Tennis for Great Britain in 1968. They traveled to Australia and the United States to persuade the rest of the world to follow suit. He was one of the heroes for the approval of Open Tennis by the ILTF.

Dr. Giorgio de Stefani (Italy)

[D: October 22, 1992, age 88]

Giorgio Stefani was the ILTF President in 1967-1969. He vehemently opposed Open Tennis, but had no problem engaging in "Shamateurism" to keep Italy's Davis Cup players like Nicola Pietrangeli as amateurs.

Ben A. Barnett (Australia)

[D: June 29, 1979, age 71]

Ben Barnett was the ILTF President in 1969-1971. He was a famous Australian Cricketer who represented the Australian LTA with the ILTF to save on travel expenses because he happened to reside in London. Maybe he was the only Cricketer to get elected President of the ILTF.

Walter E. Elcock (United States)

[D: October 9, 2003, age 81]

Walter Elcock was President of the USTA in 1973-1974, and President of the ILTF in 1974-1975. He resigned from the USTA Presidency and USTA Committee of Management in 1974 to avoid a conflict of interest with being also the President of the ITF and was succeeded as USTA President by Stan Malless in 1974; thus, Malless got a 3-year term as the USTA President from 1974-1976. Walter was mainly a ceremonial Chairman of the MTC in 1974. Interestingly, after he resigned from the USTA, the ILTF determined that he could not continue as President of the ILTF because he was no longer on the USTA Committee of Management. He was then succeeded by Derek Hardwick.

Important Additional ATP Officers and Key Professional Staff

There were a number of additional ATP Officers and Key Professional ATP Staff that should also be included in the Pioneers of the Game.

Jaime Fillol (Chile)

ATP President
1979-1980

Larry Davidson (United States)

ATP Director of
European Operations

Matt Doyle (United States)

ATP President
1985-1987

Dennis Spencer (United States)

ATP's 1st *ITW* Editor

Brian Gottfried (United States)

ATP President
1987-1989

Dewey Blanton (United States)

ATP's 2nd *ITW* Editor
[D: February 14,
2021, age 63]

Richard Evans (Great Britain)

2nd European ATP
Bureau Director

Temple Pouncey (United States)

ATP's 3rd *ITW* Editor.

David Arnott
(United States)

ATP Publicity
Director

Vittorio Selmi
(Italy)

ATP Road Manager

George Pharr
(United States)

ATP Public Relations
Director

Benjy Robbins
(United States)

ATP Road Manager

Michael Savitt
(United States)

ATP Public Relations
Director

David Fechtman
(United States)

ATP Trainer,
Marketing Manager

Greg Sharko
(United States)

Ranking
Coordinator, Director
of Public Relations
(1986-2021+)

Bill Norris
(United States)

ATP Trainer

Men's Tennis Council Professional Staff (1974-1989)

In 1981, I was hired as MTC Administrator to develop a MTC office in New York City and in Paris and to develop a professional staff for the MTC to replace the Joint Secretaries. I was privileged to find and work with an extraordinary group of professionals for the MTC. Our professional staff did a great job between 1981 and 1990, so I want to add them to my list of Pioneers of the Game.

MTC Administrators

Marshall Happer, Esquire (United States)

MTC Administrator, 1981-1989

After MTC: USTA Executive Director for 1990-1995, then outside business affairs counsel for the USTA from 1996-2009 and private practice in Raleigh NC for 1998-2005.

Christine Fiaccavento (O'Connor) (United States)

MTC Executive Assistant 1981-1989

After the MTC: Executive Assistant at the USTA.

Mark B. Meyers, Esquire (United States)

MTC Assistant Administrator, 1981-1982

After MTC: returned to the practice of law in New Orleans, then became Associate Counsel for the Shell Oil Company for 27+ years in The Hague, NL and later in Houston.

Theodore "Ted" W. Daniel, Esquire (United States)

Assistant Administrator, 1982-1983

After MTC: returned to Dallas to resume the practice of law. Partner in Norton Rose Fulbright (NRF) specializing in business litigation.

Paul J. T. Svehlik (Great Britain)

MTC Assistant Administrator, 1983-1988

After MTC: General Manager of the Royal Wimbledon Golf Club, then Director General of the International Boxing Association in Lausanne before retiring in the UK.

Anthony W. "Tony" Eugenio, Esquire (United States)

MTC Assistant Administrator 1983-1985

After MTC: returned to Texas to practice real estate law and become a real estate Broker. Developed numerous master planned subdivisions in the San Antonio metropolitan area. Syndicates and represents international clients in the purchase of office and service center buildings across the southern United States.

David R. Cooper, Esquire (United States)

MTC Assistant Administrator 1985-1989

After MTC: joined ATP Tour in 1989 as Director of Regulations and Research to oversee the ATP Tour professional officials' program and to administer the ATP Tour Code of Conduct. Retired from the ATP Tour on June 15, 1999.

William L. Babcock, Esquire (United States)

MTC Assistant Administrator, 1985-1989

After MTC: moved to London in 1989 and joined the ITF and the Grand Slams as Administrator and then the Executive Director of Men's Tennis and the Davis Cup for the ITF and the Administrator, then Director for the Grand Slam Committee, which later became the Grand Slam Board through 2020. Worked approximately 140 Grand Slams and 20 Davis Cup Finals.

MTC Grand Prix Supervisors

[Not including Franco Bartoni who became a member of the MTC and is listed with the MTC members]

Dick Roberson (United States)

Chief Grand Prix Supervisor 1978-1982

After MTC: returned to a career with Penn Athletics.

Frank Smith (United States)

Grand Prix Supervisor 1978-1981

After MTC: joined the Los Angeles Olympic Organizing Committee, serving as Vice President/Chief Administrative Officer of the Olympic Village at UCLA followed by an extensive business career in California.

Kurt Nielsen (Denmark)

[D: June 11, 2011, age 80]

Grand Prix Supervisor 1979-1984 [D: June 11, 2011, age 80]

After MTC: retired in Copenhagen.

Ken Farrar (United States)

Grand Prix Supervisor 1979-1983,
Chief Grand Prix Supervisor 1983-1989

After MTC: Chief Supervisor for the Grand Slams and the Davis Cup until retirement in 1997.

Bill Gilmour (Australia)

Grand Prix Supervisor 1979-1989
After MTC: worked for the ITF and the Grand Slams as a Supervisor for the Grand Slams and the Davis Cup until retirement.

Keith V. Johnson (United States)

[D: August 14, 2021, age 97]

Grand Prix Supervisor 1981-1989 [D: August 14, 2021, age 97]

After MTC: Referee for the 1990 U.S. Open.

Roy Dance (United States)

Grand Prix Supervisor 1983

After MTC: became a business consultant and moved to Texas.

Thomas Karlberg (Sweden)

Grand Prix Supervisor 1985-1989

After MTC: joined ATP Tour as a career Supervisor.

Charles F. Beck (United States)

Grand Prix Supervisor 1986-1987. [D: July 4, 2012 age 89]

After MTC: joined ATP Tour as a career Supervisor.

John L. Heiss III (United States)

Grand Prix Supervisor 1985-1989. [D: January 4, 2013]

After MTC: joined ATP Tour as a career Supervisor.

Stefan Fransson (Sweden)

Grand Prix Supervisor 1987-1989

After MTC: joined ITF and Grand Slams through 2020, officiating at over 20 Davis Cup Finals and over 140 Grand Slams.

Eduardo Menga (Brazil)

Grand Prix Supervisor 1988-1989

After MTC, joined ATP Tour as a career Supervisor

Edward W. Hardisty (Great Britain)

Grand Prix Supervisor 1988-1989

After MTC: joined ATP Tour as a career Supervisor

MTC Chair Umpires

Rich Kaufman (United States)

MTC Chair Umpire 1985-1989
After MTC: joined ATP Tour as a Chair Umpire through 1996. Then Director of Officials for the USTA and Chief of Umpires for the U.S. Open until his retirement in 2014. Grand Slam Finals: U.S. Open Singles 1983, 1987, 1996; Australian Open Singles 1985, Wimbledon Doubles 1987 and French Open Doubles 1988.

Jeremy Shales (Great Britain)

[D: September 8, 2005 age 62]

MTC Chair Umpire 1985-1987.

After MTC: continued to work in Great Britain and at Wimbledon as a professional chair umpire.

Richard I. Ings (Australia)

MTC Chair Umpire 1987-1989
After MTC: joined ATP Tour as a chair umpire until 1993, then worked for Coca-Cola and PepsiCo before rejoining the ATP Tour in 2000 as Executive Vice President of Rules and Competition

until 2005. Now runs a small software company in Canberra and on the side does sports integrity and anti-doping commentary, consulting and expert witness work.

Gerald Armstrong (Great Britain)

MTC Chair Umpire 1987-1989

After MTC: joined ATP Tour as a Chair Umpire through 2014, then as an ATP Tour Supervisor through 2019. 14 Wimbledon finals: 4 Men's Singles, 4 Women's Singles, 4 Men's Doubles and 2 Women's Doubles. Became Referee of Wimbledon in 2020 before Covid 19 forced the cancellation of the tournament.

Paulo Pereira (Brazil)

MTC Chair Umpire 1987-1989

After MTC: joined ATP Tour as a career Chair Umpire.

Rudy E. Berger (Germany)

[D: August 15, 2007, age 55]

MTC Chair Umpire 1988-1989. [D: August 15, 2007 age 55]

After MTC: joined ATP Tour as a career Chair Umpire.

Bruno Rebeuh (France)

MTC Chair Umpire 1988-1989

After MTC: joined ITF and the Grand Slams until 2001 as a Chair Umpire for Grand Slam and Davis Cup matches. Worked for Lacoste as worldwide sponsorship manager and now runs the golf business for the Amaury Sports Organisation (ASO) and provides consulting in tennis.

MTC Masters, Communications, Media and Public Relations Staff (not including Gene Scott who is listed above)

Sue M. Rothstein (Boyer) (United States)

Nabisco Masters Tournament Manager 1985-1989.

After MTC: Susie worked on initial Kremlin Cup in Moscow, then moved to Pasadena, CA and worked on professional soccer events at the Rose Bowl.

John Hewig (United States)

MTC Director of Communications 1985-1987

After MTC: continued to work as a public relations professional.

Reg Lansberry (United States)

MTC Assistant Director of Communications and then Director of Media Relations 1984-1989

After MTC: pursued a new career with the State of Georgia. Also became the author of "9 Goals" the "New York Rangers Once-in-a-lifetime Miracle Finish".

Jennifer L. Proud (Mearns) (United States)

MTC Tour Liaison 1985-1987

After MTC: joined Ohlmeyer Communications, Spectrum Sports (Ivan Lendl's company) and International Sports & Entertainment Strategies (ISES), then executive recruiting with TeamWork Consulting and now has her own recruiting firm working with corporate clients.

Sandra M. Genelius (United States)

MTC Tour Liaison 1985-1987

After MTC: joined Ohlmeyer Communications, then CBS News Communications, then Sony Corp. of America. Now is Chief Communications Officer of Amherst College.

Marieke van der Drift (Belgium)

MTC Tour Liaison 1985-1986

After MTC: became an international event organiser based in London, Montreal, Paris and Brussels, then a college teacher of French and Dutch in Brussels and now is a guidance counselor in the Brussels area for university students.

Micky den Tuinder (Lawler) (Netherlands)

MTC Tour Liaison 1987-1988

After MTC: became a player agent with Advantage International in Paris, later moved to Washington DC with Advantage International which later became Octagon and became the leader of women's and men's tennis. Became President of the WTA in 2015.

Lori M. Stukes (Derkay) (United States)

MTC Tour Liaison 1985-1989

After MTC: worked for the *Golf Digest*, then became an account representative for Carlson Marketing Group and worked on 2 Goodwill Games and 6 Olympics.

Catalina A. Cox (Agars) (United States)

MTC Tour Liaison 1988

After MTC: managed a joint business with husband, Graeme Agars, reporting on major golf and tennis tournaments around the world. Developed special curriculum to teach the Spanish language and Hispanic culture to university students and adults.

Barbara Travers (United States)

MTC Assistant Director of Media Relations 1988-1989

After MTC: worked freelance for Grand Slams, Barcelona Olympics and some television. In 1993, joined ITF in London as Communications Administrator and then Head of Communications for the ITF, retiring at the end of 2016. Provided communication services for 7 Olympics, 25 Davis Cup Finals, 21 Fed Cup Finals and 27 years of Grand Slams missing only 3 for a total of 105 Grand Slams and that did not include 5 U.S. Opens and 1 French Open with USA Network before joining the ITF.

Wendy Miller (Hart) (United States)

MTC Tour Liaison 1986-1989

After MTC: joined Prince Sports Group as the Manager of Professional Tennis, then as a consultant with Prince, ATP Tour, Synergy Sports, and NYC Parks and Recreation. Later became an executive search professional.

Camille Guthrie (United States)

MTC Tour Liaison 1986-1989

After MTC: continued to work in tennis in various communications roles at Grand Slam and Olympic events and as the Director of Sports Research for the USA Network cable television. Followed by working in television production for ESPN, NBC, and CBS at a myriad of events, including figure skating, golf and football. Later became a project manager at a top hedge fund. Now, directs operations for two nonprofit organizations in Connecticut.

Important National Association Presidents Prior to 1990

I would be remiss if we did not also add as Pioneers of the Game the important Grand Slam national association presidents, some of whom are already included:

USLTA/USTA

1967-1968	Robert J. Kelleher	Los Angeles, CA	[D: June 20, 2012, age 99]
1969-1970	Alastair B. Martin	New York City, NY	[D: January 12, 2010, age 94]
1971-1972	Robert B. Colwell	Seattle, WA	[D: October 25, 1988, age 82]
1973-1974	Walter E. Elcock	Brookline, MA	[D: October 9, 2003, age 81]
1974-1976	Stanley Malless	Indianapolis, IN	[D: January 19, 2012, age 97]
1977-1978	W.E. Slew Hester, Jr.	Jackson, MS	[D: February 8, 1993, age 88]
1979-1980	Joseph E. Carrico	Chicago, IL	[D: October 27, 1971, age 52]
1981-1982	Marvin Richmond	Kansas City, MO	[D: December 18, 2009, age 96]
1983-1984	Hunter L. Delatour	Portola Valley, CA	[D: January 17, 2013, age 96]
1985-1986	J. R. "Randy" Gregson	New Orleans, LA	[D: May 23, 2010, age 92]
1987-1988	Gordon D. Jorgensen	Phoenix, AZ	[D: June 10, 2007, age 86]
1989-1990	David R. Markin	Kalamazoo, MI	[D: May 30, 2013, age 82]

French Tennis Federation (FFT)

1968-1973	Marcel Benard	[D: April 29, 1994, age 79]
1973-1993	Philippe Chatrier	[D: June 22, 2000, age 74]

Vice Presidents

1930-1968	Jean Borotra	[D: July 17, 1994, age 95]
1969-1972	Philippe Chatrier	[D: June 22, 2000, age 74]

Tennis Australia (LTAA)

1965-1969	C.A. Edwards OBE	[D: August 8,1990]
1969-1977	Wayne V. Reid OBE	
1977-1989	Brian Tobin AM	

Lawn Tennis Association of Great Britain (LTA)

LTA Presidents

1963-1981	Sir Carl Aarvold	[D: March 17, 1991, age 83]
1982-1984	J. R. "Jim" Cochrane	[D: November 6, 2007, age 82]
1985-1987	Geoffrey B. Brown	[D: November 1, 2015, age 83]
1988-1990	R. "Ron" J. Presley	[D: December 9, 2009, age 78]

CHAPTER 39

A FEW REMEMBRANCES

1967 World Championship Tennis

Handsome Eight

1st Row LR: John Newcombe, Nikki Pilic, Butch Buchholz, Cliff Drysdale

2nd Row LR: Dennis Ralston, Roger Taylor, Tony Roche, Pierre Barthes

THE 1971 WORLD CHAMPIONSHIP OF TENNIS

Front Row LR: Roy Emerson, Dennis Ralston, Tom Okker, Tony Roche, Ken Rosewall, Rod Laver, Arthur Ashe, John Newcome, Ismail El Shafei, Brian Fairlie;

2nd Row LR: Mike Davies, Lamar Hunt, Owen Davidson, Charles Pasarell, Fred Stolle, Andres Gimeno, Nikola Pilic, John Alexander, Bob Lutz, Marty Riessen, Dick Crealy, Torben Ulrich, Ray Ruffels, Steve Freyer, Al Hill, Jr.;

3rd Row LR: Wayne Henry, Ron Bookman, Allan Stone, Bill Bowrey, Phil Dent, Bob Carmichael, Roger Taylor, Cliff Drysdale, Frew McMillan, Mark Cox, Rob Maud, Roy Barth, Graham Stilwell, John McDonald Bob Shytles.

1977 USTA Executive Committee

LaCosta Country Club & Spa, Carlsbad, CA

February 12, 1977

1st Row LR: Les Fitzgibbon (Treasurer), Hunter Delatour (Secretary), Slew Hester (President), Joe Carrico (1st Vice President), Marvin Richmond (2nd Vice President);

2nd Row LR: Judge Robert Kelleher, Ed Turville, Robert Colwell, Jack Blair;

3rd Row LR: Lloyd Bridges, Nancy Jeffett, Dick Botsch, Ron Fisher, Gordon Jorgensen, Carl Simonie, Randy Gregson, Victor Denny;

4th Row LR: Tony Trabert, Tony Bull, Don Gardner, Ned Weld, James Moulton, Rolla Anderson, Warren Brown, Les Jenkins;

5th Row LR: Ed Kenehan, Marshall Happer, Bob Dane, Bill Clothier, Ruben Velez, James Fought, Julie Hoyt, Darren Eden;

Not Present: Bumpy Frazer, Jack Kramer, Paul Cranis, Walter Hall, Lawrence Baker, George Barnes, Alastair Martin, Walter Elcock, Stan Malless.

1978 Japan MTC Meeting

Tokyo Meeting October 26-28, 1978

LR Seated: Arthur Ashe, John Harris and Cliff Drysdale

LR Standing: Bob Briner, Brian Tobin, Stan Malless, Derek Hardwick, Doug Tkachuk, David Gray, Owen Williams and Lars Myhrman

Paul McNamee, Lew Hoad, Peter McNamara & Karen Scott

1981 Volvo Masters

Jack Kramer & Marshall Happer

1981 Volvo Masters

Marshall Happer, Don Budge, Arthur Ashe, Lew Hoad & Jack Kramer

1981 World Champions Dinner – Paris

January 12-15, 1982 MIPTC Meeting

Seated LR: Philippe Chatrier, Jack Kramer, Stan Malless, Arthur Ashe

Standing LR: Brian Tobin, Lars Myhrman, David Gray, Marshall Happer, Ray Moore, Butch Buchholz, Ron Bookman. (Derek Hardwick not present)

Tony Trabert, Fred Perry, Lew Hoad, Don Budge, Frank Sedgman

Lew Hoad & Mike Davies

LR: ATP Road Managers: Weller Evans, Benji Robbins, Vittorio Selmi, Jim McManus & Trainer:
David Fechtman

Hamilton Jordan &
Marshall Happer

1986 Lipton (Key Biscayne)

Marshall Happer

1987 French Open

Frank Hammond

First Full-Time Professional
Official

Ted Tinling

Hall of Fame 1986

Marshall Happer, Ron Bookman & Brian Gottfried

Tennis Sheriff Caricature, Tennis Magazine 1985

Russ Adams

Dean of Tennis Photographers

Bud Collins

Dean of Tennis Writers

Vitas Gerulaitis

August 27, 1995 Vitas Gerulaitis Foundation Fundraiser Dinner, Plaza Hotel, New York:
American (Carbon Monoxide) Sensors Sponsor Representative, Tracy Austin, Pete Sampras,
Alan King, Guillermo Vilas, Ruta Gerulaitis (Vitas' Sister), Aldona Gerulaitis (Vitas' Mother,
Karen Scott Happer, Event Organizer

US Open Plaque

Men's Tennis Council Logo

Masters of Tennis Trophy

Sine die!

Endnotes

Chapter 1

1   *Ahead of the Game*, Owen Williams, (USA 2013), 30.

2   *Ibid*, 97.

3   *Open Tennis*, Richard Evans, (London 1993), 13-14.

4   *We Have Come A Long Way*, Billie Jean King with Cynthia Starr, (New York 1988), 40-41.

5   *The Bud Collins, History of Tennis*, Bud Collins, (Canada 2008), Chapter "1931: The Wimbledon Final That Was Never Played", 43.

6   *The Game, My 40 Years in Tennis*, Jack Kramer with Frank Deford, (New York 1979), 236.

7   *The Encyclopedia of Tennis*, Edited by Max Robertson, Advisory Editor Jack Kramer, (New York 1974), 63.

8   *The History of Professional Tennis*, Joe McCauley, (Great Britain 2000, 2003), 57-58.

9   *The Encyclopedia of Tennis*, Edited by Max Robertson, Advisory Editor Jack Kramer, (New York 1974), 64.

10   *The Game, My 40 Years in Tennis*, Jack Kramer with Frank Deford, (New York 1979), 233-235.

11   *Man with a Racket*, the autobiography of Pancho Gonzales as told to Cy Rice, (New York 1959), 192, 209.

12   *Shades of Gray, Tennis Writings of David Gray*, edited by Lance Tingay, (London 1988), 187.
       The Game, My 40 Years in Tennis, Jack Kramer with Frank Deford, (New York 1979), 253-255.

13   *Ibid*, 241-242.

14   *Ibid*, 257-258

15   *The History of Professional Tennis*, Joe McCauley, (Great Britain 2000, 2003), 136.

16   *Tennis Rebel, Mike Davies*, (London 1962), 137.

17   *The Game, My 40 Years in Tennis*, Jack Kramer with Frank Deford (New York 1979),245.

18   *Tennis Down Under*, Fred Stolle & Kenneth Wydro, (Bethesda MD 1985), 97-99.

19   *The Game, My 40 Years in Tennis*, Jack Kramer with Frank Deford, (New York 1979), 260.

20   *Open Tennis*, Richard Evans, (London 1993), 13.

21   *The Bud Collins, History of Tennis*, Bud Collins, (Canada 2008), 141.

22   *Shades of Gray, Tennis Writings of David Gray*, edited by Lance Tingay, (London 1988), 188-189.

Chapter 2

23   *Open Tennis*, Richard Evans, (London 1993), 22-24.

24   *The Bud Collins, History of Tennis*, Bud Collins, (Canada 2008), 896-898.
       Shades of Gray, Tennis Writings of David Gray, edited by Lance Tingay, (London 1988), 190-192.

25   *Open Tennis*, Richard Evans, (London 1993), 24-25.
       London Times, Rex Bellamy, April 1, 1968, "LTA's Initiative Pays Off."
       The Bud Collins, History of Tennis, Bud Collins, (Canada 2008), 144-145.

26   *New York Times*, Neil Amdur, February 9, 1969, "U.S.L.T.A. Creates A New Category Called 'Player'."

27   *The Game, My 40 Years in Tennis*, Jack Kramer with Frank Deford, (New York 1979), 63-66).

28   *Open Tennis*, Richard Evans, (London 1993), 4.

29   *New York Times*, Eugene L. Scott, July 7, 1968, "Open Tennis: The Pros Now Respect the Amateurs".

30   *New York Times*, July 5, 1968, "Pros Barred from Davis Cup; Rosewall calls it a 'Lockout'.

31   *Open Tennis*, Richard Evans, (London 1993), 17.
       The Tennis Bubble, Rich Koster, (New York 1976), 53, 62.

32   *Ibid*, 63-66

33   *Open Tennis*, Richard Evans, (London 1993), 17.

         The Tennis Bubble, Rich Koster, (New York 1976), 53.

         New York Times, Neil Amdur, March 7, 1968, "Pro Tennis Tour $100,000 in Red, Hill replaces Dixon and New Format is Set Up."

34   *The Encyclopedia of Tennis,* Edited by Max Robertson, Advisory Editor Jack Kramer, (New York 1974), 74.

         New York Times, October 9, 1968, "Pro Tennis Groups Warn of a Boycott".

         New York Times, Neil Amdur, November 6, 1968, "US Tennis Officials Planning Seven Opens Worth $400,000".

         New York Times, October 22, 1968, "Australia Cancels Open Tennis Tournaments in Dispute on Purses".

         New York Times, Dave Anderson, February 19, 1969, "Tennis Pros Accept Truce; Will Participate in U.S. Opens."

         New York Times, February 18, 1969, "Boycott Threat in Tennis Lifted".

35   *The Bud Collins, History of Tennis,* Bud Collins, (Canada 2008), 698.

         BP Year Book of World Tennis 1969, edited by John Barrett, compiled by Peter West, (London 1969), 83.

36   *Official 1989 MTC Media Guide,* (MTC 1989), 370.

Chapter 3

37   *New York Times,* July 4, 1969, "Davis Cup Group Rejects Open Bid, French Proposal to Permit Entry of Pros Vetoed."

38   *New York Times,* Neil Amdur, January 19, 1969, "Martin, New Tennis Chief, Seeks Twin Goal of Unity, Expansion."

39   *New York Times,* Fred Tupper, February 24, 1969, "Tennis Powers Reach Accord With U.S. Pro Promoters".

40   *The Game, My 40 Years in Tennis,* Jack Kramer with Frank Deford, (New York 1979), 262-264, 266, 267-268.

41   *Open Tennis*, Richard Evans, (London 1993), 32-33.

         The Game, My 40 Years in Tennis, Jack Kramer with Frank Deford, (New York 1979), 262-264, 266, 267-268.

         Minding Other People's Business, Donald L. Dell, (New York 1989), 6-7, 10.

42   *New York Times*, Neil Amdur, February 25, 1969, "Ashe, Out of Army, Stays Independent".

         New York Times, Arthur Daley, March 21, 1969, "What's in a Name?"

         New York Times, Neil Amdur, February 13, 1969, "Non-Open Tennis Events to Offer Prize Money.

43   *New York Times*, Neil Amdur, "Pro Tennis Gets $200,000 Tourney".

44   *The Encyclopedia of Tennis,* Edited by Max Robertson, Advisory Editor Jack Kramer, (New York 1974), 77.

45   *London Times*, Rex Bellamy, September 5, 1969, "Top Tennis Job for Davies".

         Open Tennis, Richard Evans, (London 1993), 47.

         New York Times, Neil Amdur, September 14, 1969, "Briner Serves His Tennis Philosophy".

46   *Open Tennis*, Richard Evans, (London 1993), 142.

         The Tennis Bubble, Rich Koster, (New York 1976), 66.

47   *London Times*, Rex Bellamy, February 28, 1970, "Welshman Rules from Dallas, Davies – Potatoes to Power."

48   *New York Times*, April 1, 1969, "Cullman Will Direct U.S. Open Tennis Here".

         New York Times, Neil Amdur, May 9, 1969, "Williams Appointed Director of U.S. Open Tennis Tourney."

49   *New York Times*, Eugene L. Scott, August 24, 1969, "Slow on the Serve".

         New York Times, Parton Keese, September 9, 1969, "Except For Rain, Twas Fine Tennis".

New York Times, September 30, 1969, "Williams Proposes Change at U.S. Open."

50   *New York Times*, Neil Amdur, November 4, 1969, "Tennis Factions Embroiled Anew".
New York Times, Neil Amdur, December 17, 1969, "U.S.L.T.A. Pushing Accord with Pros".
New York Times, Eugene L. Scott, January 11, 1970, "Tennis Suicide Stride".

51   *The Bud Collins, History of Tennis*, Bud Collins, (Canada 2008), 698.
BP Year Book of World Tennis 1970, edited by John Barrett, compiled by Lance Tingay, (London 1971), 94.

52   *Official 1989 MTC Media Guide*, (MTC 1989), 370.
BP Year Book of World Tennis 1970, edited by John Barrett, compiled by Lance Tingay, (London 1970), 134.

Chapter 4

53   *1970 Experimental Grand Prix Rules*, (ILTF 1970).

54   *New York Times*, Neil Amdur, February 7, 1970, "Tennis Dispute Flares Anew Over Structure for Opens, Boycott Likely at Forest Hills, Pros Consider Scheduling Major Tournament Here at Time of U.S. Open".
New York Times, Neil Amdur, February 8, 1970, "Disorder on the Court, When Tennis Factions Fumble a Truce, It's the Fan Who Faces Consequences."

55   *New York Times*, Dave Anderson, January 24, 1970, "Gonzales Defeats Laver Before 14,761."

56   *New York Times*, Eugene L. Scott, March 8, 1970, "Independent Net Pros Form New Unit".

57   *New York Times*, May 6, 1970, "Dell Manages U.S. Quartet."

58   *New York Times*, Neil Amdur, July 26, 1970, "U.S. Open Adopts Sudden-Death Set".

59   *New York Times*, Neil Amdur, July 29, 1970, "Top Tennis Pros Join Hunt's Unit, Texan Acquires Contracts of Laver, Gonzales, 4 Others."

60   *New York Times*, September 4, 1970, "$1-Million Tennis Series Listed For Top 32 Players Next Year."

61   *The Game, My 40 Years in Tennis*, Jack Kramer with Frank Deford, (New York 1979), 277-278.
Open Tennis, Richard Evans, (London 1993), 45.
New York Times, Neil Amdur, September 17, 1970, "Deal Estimated at $1.5 Million, Hunt Scores Coup in Battle with World Federation and Now Controls 27 Stars."

62   *New York Times*, Neil Amdur, November 6, 1970, "Committee Vote is Due Thursday, Approval Would Keep Ashe, Laver and Rosewall Out of National Open Here".

63   *The Bud Collins, History of Tennis*, Bud Collins, (Canada 2008), 633-634.
Tennis Rebel, Mike Davies, (London 1962), 65-66.

64   *New York Times*, Fred Tupper, November 14, 1970, "Peace Plan Offered World Tennis Unit."
London Times, Rex Bellamy, November 14, 1970, "Tinling move can give ILTF hope of decisive voice."
New York Times, Fred Tupper, November 18, 1970, "Major Tennis Tourneys Decide To Bargain With Contract pros."

65   *New York Times*, Neil Amdur, December 6, 1970, "Order on the Court?, Tennis Pros, Amateur Groups Believed Near Accord After Five-Day Meeting."
New York Times, December 9, 1970, "ACCORD REACHED IN TENNIS DISPUTE, Contract Pros Will Play in 3 Major World Tourneys."

66   *The Bud Collins, History of Tennis*, Bud Collins, (Canada 2008), 698.
World of Tennis '71, edited by John Barrett, compiled by Lance Tingay, (London 1971), 182.

67   *Official 1989 MTC Media Guide*, (MTC 1989), 356.

68   *Ibid*, 370.

Chapter 5

69   *World of Tennis 1972*, edited by John Barrett, compiled by Lance Tingay, Rex Bellamy, "World Championship of Tennis Finals", (London 1972), 147-148.

70   *1971 Pepsi Grand Prix Rules,* (ILTF 1971).
71   *New York Times,* January 19, 1971, "93-Year-Old Wimbledon Adopts 12-Point Tiebreak in First Scoring Change."
72   *New York Times,* February 14, 1971, "Contract Pros in Net Rankings, U.S.L.T.A. Includes Them for First Time – Richey No. 1."
      1971 U.S.L.T.A. Yearbook, 90-105.
73   *New York Times,* November 4, 1971, "8 Champion Tennis Tourneys To Be Shown on N.B.C. in '72."
74   *World of Tennis 1972,* Edited by John Barrett, Compiled by Lance Tingay, Lamar Hunt, "WCT Looking Forward", (London 1972), 145.
75   *New York Times,* November 13, 1971, "Grand Prix Loses Backer".
76   *New York Times,* July 8, 1971, "Either Them or Us."
      New York Times, July 8, 1971, "Tennis Federation Bans Contract pros."
      New York Times, Charles Friedman, July 11, 1971, "More Tennis Turmoil, Dollar Factor Inspires World Group To Bar Hunt's Pros From Open Events."
77   *New York Times,* August 18, 1971, "Rosewall, 4 Others Say They'll Bypass Open Tennis Here."
      New York Times, Gerald Eskenazi, August 25, 1971, "Laver Joins Five Others In Passing Up U.S. Open."
      New York Times, September 8, 1971, "Tennis Sponsor Enters Dispute, Cullman Threatens to End TV Contract for Open if Top Pros are Banned."
78   *New York Times,* November 16, 1971, "U.S.L.T.A. Will Offer Plan On Ending Tennis Dispute."
79   *World of Tennis 1972,* edited by John Barrett, compiled by Lance Tingay, Lamar Hunt, "WCT Looking Forward", (London 1972), 145-146.
80   *The Bud Collins, History of Tennis,* Bud Collins, (Canada 2008), 699.
      World of Tennis '72, edited by John Barrett, compiled by Lance Tingay, (London 1972), 187.
81   *World of Tennis '72,* edited by John Barrett, compiled by Lance Tingay, (London 1972), 143-144.
82   *Official 1989 MTC Media Guide,* (MTC 1989), 370-371.

Chapter 6

83   *New York Times,* May 15, 1972, "Rosewall Topples Laver In $50,000 Tennis Final."
      https://www.tennis.com/pro-game/2015/03/1972-rod-laver-vs-ken-rose II-wct-final-dallas/54333/ accessed July 22, 2020, Steve Tignor, March 12, 2015, u1972: the Rod Laver vs. Ken Rosewall Final in Dallas".
84   *Tennis Confidential,* Paul Fein, (USA 2002), 284.
85   *1972 Commercial Union Grand Prix Rules,* (ILTF 1972).
86   *New York Times,* January 16, 1972, "Storm Over Courts", Reinstatement of South Africa and Feud Between 2 Groups Stir Tennis World."
87   *New York Times,* Neil Amdur, February 13, 1972, "What Price Peace?, There Are Profits in Tennis War, Too, And Most Pro Players Are Cashing In."
88   *New York Times,* April 16, 1972, "Net Talks Completed: No Solution."
89   *New York Times,* Fred Tupper, April 27, 1972, "Tennis Factions Reach Agreement, Wimbledon" Won't Get Hunt's Pros This Year, Forest Hills Probably Will, Accord Reached In Tennis Dispute."
90   *New York Times,* Fred Tupper, April 27, 1972, "Tennis Factions Reach Agreement."
91   *The Game, My 40 Years in Tennis,* Jack Kramer with Frank Deford, (New York 1979), 278.
92   *New York Times,* April 30, 1972, "U.S.L.T.A. Votes to Support Tennis 'Peace' Agreement."
93   *New York Times,* July 13, 1972, "SO. Africa Wins Davis Cup Entry, Reinstated to Compete Next Year – I.L.T.F. Ratifies Pact Ending Tennis War."
94   *New York Times,* Neil Amdur, April 12, 1972, "Richey Goes Over To Hunt's Group with 4-year Pact, Richey Becomes A Contract Pro."
95   *The Tennis Bubble,* Rich Koster, (New York 1976), 28-29, 34, 43.
96   *https://en.wikipedia.org/wiki/Mike_Davies_(tennis),* accessed December 2, 2018.

97   *New York Times*, June 26, 1972, "Pro Tennis Players Planning To Unite."

98   *The Game, My 40 Years in Tennis*, Jack Kramer with Frank Deford, (New York 1979), 106.

99   *London Times*, Rex Bellamy, November 25, 1972, "Players devise prize money scales."

100   *New York Times*, November 28, 1972, "U.S. Indoor Tennis Circuit Set."

101   *London Times*, Rex Bellamy, June 23, 1972, "Setback for Smith at hands of Paish."

102   *The Bud Collins, History of Tennis*, Bud Collins (Canada 2008), 699.
      World of Tennis '73, edited by John Barrett, compiled by Lance Tingay, (London 1974), 199.

103   *Official 1989 MTC Media Guide*, (MTC 1989), 356.

104   *Ibid*, 371.

Chapter 7

105   *New York Times*, Neil Amdur, May 21, 1973, "Gottfried Takes Las Vegas Tennis, Earns $30,000
      With 6-1, 6-3 Rout of Ashe, Runner-Up 5th Time in 6 Events."

106   *1973 Commercial Union Grand Prix Rules* (ILTF 1973).

107   *New York Times*, February 24, 1973, "Nastase Is Fined By Players' Unit, Star is Penalized $500 for
      Behavior at Salisbury."

108   *New York Times*, August 13, 1973, "Nastase Gets Title, No Money."
      New York Times, Gerald Eskenazi, August 23, 1973, "Nastase's New Image: Just Call Him 'Nicely."
      New York Times, September 11, 1973, "Nastase Is Fined $5,500 For Antics in 2 Tourneys."

109   *The Game, My 40 Years in Tennis*, Jack Kramer with Frank Deford, (New York 1979), 105.

110   *Ibid*, 106-107.

111   *New York Times*, June 6, 1973, "Nastase Routs Pilic in French Final, Wins by 6-3, 6-3, 6-0 –
      Yugoslav Is Suspended."
      New York Times, June 14, 1973. "Wimbledon is Facing Loss of Top Players."
      London Times, Rex Bellamy, June 14, 1973, "Wimbledon singles may be weaker through absence
      of leading men."

112   *The Game, My 40 Years in Tennis*, Jack Kramer with Frank Deford, (New York 1979), 107.

113   *World of Tennis '74*, edited by John Barrett, compiled by Lance Tingay (London 1974), David
      Gray "Year of Dispute", 15.

114   *The Game, My 40 Years in Tennis*, Jack Kramer with Frank Deford, (New York 1979), 108.

115   *Ibid*, 109.

116   *London Times*, June 13, 1973, "Suspension of Pilic Defended by ILTF."

117   *London Times*, Rex Bellamy, June 15, 1973, "Men's titles at Wimbledon in the balance at another
      court."

118   *The Game, My 40 Years in Tennis*, Jack Kramer with Frank Deford, (New York 1979), 110.

119   *Ibid*, 111-112.
      New York Times, Fred Tupper, June 20, 1973, "Wimbledon Boycotted By Top Tennis Players,
      Player Boycott Hits Wimbledon."
      London Times, Rex Bellamy, June 21, 1973, "35 Withdraw, but Nastase will play."

120   *The Game, My 40 Years in Tennis*, Jack Kramer with Frank Deford, (New York 1979), 116-118.

121   *New York Times*, June 24, 1973, "Wimbledon's Dropout Total Is At 82."

122   *The Game, My 40 Years in Tennis*, Jack Kramer with Frank Deford, (New York 1979), 120.

123   *Ibid*, 118, 120.

124   *London Times*, Rex Bellamy, June 23, 1973, "Taylor will give his prize money to professional group."

125   *London Times*, Rex Bellamy, June 26, 1973, "Borg blasts his way to centre court climax."

126   *London Times*, Rex Bellamy, July 9, 1973, "Give peace a chance, says Kodes."

127   *New York Times*, June 30, 1973, "Italy Bans Its Davis Cup Stars."
      London Times, July 2, 1973, "Banned Britons may switch from Newport to Dublin."
      New York Times, July 3, 1973, "Spain Suspends Three For Wimbledon Boycott."
      London Times, September 26, 1973, "LTA lift bans on Britons."

128   *The Game, My 40 Years in Tennis*, Jack Kramer with Frank Deford, (New York 1979), 115.
129   *Ibid*, 119.
130   https://en.wikipedia.org/wiki/Novak_Djokovic, accessed May 29, 2020.
131   *The Game, My 40 Years in Tennis*, Jack Kramer with Frank Deford, (New York 1979), 120.
132   *London Times*, Rex Bellamy, October 18, 1973, "Council of Peace a step towards world harmony."
133   *The Art of World Team Tennis*, Greg Hoffman, (San Francisco 1977), 11-13.
134   Ibid, 15.
135   Ibid, 17.
       London Times, July 12, 1973, "ILTF move against militants."
136   *The Art of World Team Tennis*, Greg Hoffman, (San Francisco 1977), 18-19.
       New York Times, September 10, 1973, "Peace Agreement Reached in Tennis."
       London Times, Rex Bellamy, September 12, 1973, "Expulsion incompatible with principle."
137   *New York Times*, Neil Amdur, September 18, 1973, "Goolagong Signs With Net League, Miss Goolagong Signs With New Tennis Loop."
       New York Times, October 12, 1973, "People in Sports: Kerry Melville Signs With Boston Net Team."
       New York Times, Charles Friedman, November 11, 1973, "W.T.T. Causing Stir in Tennis World."
       New York Times, November 17, 1973, "People in Sports."
       New York Times, December 12, 1973, "Rosewall Will Play In W.T.T."
138   *London Times*, Rex Bellamy, November 26, 1973, "WTT offer large fees to gain sanction."
       London Times, November 27, 1973, "Heyman gives WTT little encouragement."
       The Art of World Team Tennis, Greg Hoffman, (San Francisco 1977), 18-19.
139   *London Times*, November 30, 1973, "Wimbledon's £97,100 owes nothing to sponsors."
       The Art of World Team Tennis, Greg Hoffman, (San Francisco 1977), 18-19.
140   *London Times*, December 15, 1973, "European nations call meeting to discuss WTT."
141   *London Times*, November 6, 1973, "French threaten to leave."
142   *New York Times*, Neil Amdur, June 3, 1973, "U.S. to Weigh Quitting International Tennis Unit."
143   *New York Times*, Dave Anderson, July 3, 1973, "Ashe Outlines A.T.P.'s Format For Condensed Davis Cup Play."
144   *The Story of the Davis* Cup, Alan Trengove, (London 1985), 249-250.
145   *New York Times*, May 14, 1973, Neil Amdur "Riggs Defeats Mrs. Court 6-2, 6-1.
       New York Times, March 8, 1973, "Mrs. Court Takes Riggs Challenge, She'll Play Former Star in $10,000 Match April 28."
       New York Times, March 4, 1973, "Riggs vs Margaret Court: A Mismatch?"
       New York Times, May 14, 1973, "Riggs Files an Entry For Women's Tourney."
146   *New York Times*, Neil Amdur, May 14, 1973, "Riggs Defeats Mrs. Court, 6-2, 6-1."
147   *New York Times*, Gerald Eskenazi, July 12, 1973, "$100,000 Tennis Match: Bobby Riggs vs. Mrs. King, Its's Mrs. King Against Riggs for $100,000."
148   *Ibid*
149   *New York Times*, Grace Lichtenstein, September 21, 1973, "Mrs. King Calls Victory 'Culmination' of Career."
       New York Times, Neil Amdur, September 22, 1973, "'She Played too Well,' Says Riggs of Mrs. King, Mrs. King Is Lauded By Riggs."
       New York Times, September 22, 1973, "Leaders in Senate acclaim Mrs. King."
       New York Times, Grace Lichtenstein, September 23, 1973, "Film Study of Riggs Aided Billie Jean."
       New York Times, November 15, 1973, "Mrs. Court Bombards King, Riggs."
150   *The Bud Collins, History of Tennis*, Bud Collins, (Canada 2008), 699.
       World of Tennis '74, edited by John Barrett, compiled by Lance Tingay, (London 1974), 219.
151   *Ibid*, 332.
152   *Official 1989 MTC Media Guide*, (MTC 1989), 357.
153   *Ibid*, 371.

Chapter 8

154   *World of Tennis '75*, edited by John Barrett, compiled by Lance Tingay, (London 1975), Rex Bellamy, "The World Championship of Tennis 1974", 135-137.

155   *1974 Commercial Union Grand Prix Rules, (MIPTC 1974).*

156   *Ibid.*

157   *MIPTC Minutes*, September 4, 1974, New York Meeting.

158   *MIPTC Minutes*, October 31-November 2, 1974, Paris Meeting.

159   *MIPTC Minutes*, December 12-14, 1974, Melbourne Meeting.

160   *The Art of World Team Tennis*, Greg Hoffman, (San Francisco 1977), 27, 30-33.
       World of Tennis '75, edited by John Barrett and compiled by Lance Tingay, (London 1975), 170-171.

161   *New York Times*, Neil Amdur, August 20, 1974, "First, Serve Is In."

162   *New York Times*, Charles Friedman, October 31, 1974, "Clay-Courts Plan Approved for Open."

163   *New York Times*, January 25, 1974, "Pro Tennis Group Cuts USLTA Link, Pro Players Break with U.S.L.T.A."

164   *New York Times*, Fred Tupper, January 27, 1974, "I.L.T.F. Lists Conditions For Team Tennis League."

165   *New York Times*, January 25, 1974, "Pro Tennis Group Cuts USLTA Link, Pro Players Break with U.S.L.T.A."

166   *The Tennis Bubble*, Rich Koster, (New York 1976), 28-29.

167   *New York Times*, May 23, 1974, "Italians Insist Connors Is Barred From Tourney."

168   *London Times*, May 29, 1974, "French want to be sued."

169   *London Times*, May 31, 1974, "Court action lost by Miss Goolagong and Connors."

170   *The Outsider*, Jimmy Connors, (New York 2013), 115.

171   *New York Times*, September 5, 1974, "Connors, Miss Goolagong File Suit."

172   *New York Times*, June 24, 1974, "Tennis Ban Spurs Suit By W.T.T., Kramer Target of Suit By W.T.T. for $10-Million."

173   *Connors v. Kramer et al.*, USDC, Southern District of NY, Amended and Supplemental Complaint, dated December 20, 1974, Civil Action File No. 74 CIV 2894.

174   *New York Times*, November 4, 1974, "French to Lift Ban On W.T.T. Players."
       New York Times, November 6, 1974, "Elcock, Head, Healing Wounds in International Tennis."
       London Times, Rex Bellamy, November 14, 1974, "A maverick essential to the health of the game."

175   *The Bud Collins, History of Tennis*, Bud Collins, (Canada 2008), 699.
       World of Tennis '75, edited by John Barrett, compiled by Lance Tingay, (London 1975), 209, 221.

176   *Official 1989 MTC Media Guide*, (MTC 1989), 357.

177   *Ibid*, 371-372.

Chapter 9

178   *New York Times*, February 16, 1975, "U.S.L.T.A. Drops 'Lawn' in Name."

179   *New York Times*, Robin Herman, July 11, 1975, "Nations Cup Put Up for Men's Team Tennis."

180   *New York Times*, Leonard Koppett, May 19, 1975, "Tanner is Victor in Final."

181   *1975 Commercial Union Grand Prix Rules, (MIPTC 1975).*

182   *Ibid.*

183   *1975 USLTA Yearbook*, 482-483.

184   *Ibid*, 476.
       London Times, Rex Bellamy, May 21, 1975, "Conflict over rule will bring lively LTA meeting."

185   *Kramer v. Riordan and Connors*, USDC, SD Indiana, Indianapolis Division, Civil Action File No. IP 75-241-C, Exhibit attached to Complaint for defamation.

186   *MIPTC Minutes*, February 7-9, 1975 Bermuda Meeting.

187   *MIPTC Minutes*, June 19, 1975, London Meeting.

188 *MIPTC Minutes*, August 31-September 2, 1975, New York Meeting.
189 *Minutes*, ILTF Committee of Management, April 18-19, 1975.
190 *Minutes*, ILTF Committee of Management, July 2-4, 1975.
191 *New York Times*, Charles Friedman, December 31, 1975, "W.C.T. Cuts Draws, Adds a Pair of Aces."
192 *MIPTC Minutes*, November 2-5, 1975, Paris Meeting.
193 *World of Tennis '76*, edited by John Barrett, compiled by Lance Tingay, (London 1976), Richard Evans "ATP's Year", 218-221.
194 *The Art of World Team Tennis*, Greg Hoffman, (San Francisco 1977), 40-41.
195 *Ibid*, 40, 127-135.
196 *The Outsider*, Jimmy Connors, (New York 2013), 137-139.
     The Tennis Bubble, Rich Koster, (New York 1976), 41-42.
     New York Times, Charles Friedman, October 22, 1974, "Connors vs. Laver for $100,000.
     New York Times, October 24, 1974, "Laver Battles Connors In Las Vegas On Feb."
     New York Times, January 15, 1975, "Connors Declines Berth on Cup Team."
     New York Times, Dave Anderson, January 21, 1975, "Special to the New York Times."
197 *New York Times*, February 2, 1975, "Laver, Connors Play for $100,000 Today."
     The Outsider, Jimmy Connors, (New York 2013), 139.
198 *New York Times*, February 3, 1975, "Connors Triumphs."
     The Outsider, Jimmy Connors, (New York 2013), 139-140, 142.
199 *New York Times*, December 3, 1974, "Newcombe Mocking Connors For Dropping Out of Tourney."
     New York Times, January 2, 1975, "Newcombe Vanquishes Connors."
200 *New York Times*, Gerald Eskenazi, February 27, 1975, "Newcombe vs. Connors: Winner to Get $250,000."
201 *New York Times*, Leonard Koppett, April 27. 1975, "Connors Downs Newcombe."
202 *The Tennis Bubble*, Rich Koster, (New York 1976), 42.
203 *New York Times*, Leonard Koppett, April 6, 1975, "Nastase Acts Up, Defeats Rosewall."
204 *New York Times*, Leonard Koppett, April 7, 1975, "Alexander Captures Final As Nastase Sulks at End."
205 *New York Times*, June 1, 1975, "2d Italian Title for Miss Evert."
206 *New York Times*, July 27, 1975, "Solomon Beats Ashe."
207 *New York Times*, September 1, 1975, "Nastase's Case Put Off by Council."
208 *New York Times*, September 4, 1975, "Nastase is Fined $8,000 for Outburst."
209 *New York Times*, Bernard Kirsch, December 2, 1975, "Ashe Ruled Victor in Dispute."
     New York Times, Ed Meyer, December 7, 1975, "Mixed-Up Tennis World Needs a Czar."
     New York Times, December 9, 1975, "Tennis Sets Fines for Misconduct."
210 *MIPTC Minutes*, December 3-7, 1975, Stockholm Meeting.
211 *Complaint*, April 10, 1975, United States District Court Southern District of Indiana, Indianapolis Division (Case No. TP 75-251-C.
212 *New York Times*, June 22, 1975, "Connors Sues Ashe."
213 *The Outsider*, Jimmy Connors, (New York 2013), 155.
     Days of Grace, Arthur Ashe, (New York 1993), 72.
214 *New York Times*, August 23, 1975, "Sports News Briefs."
215 *The Outsider*, Jimmy Connors (New York 2013), 165-166.
216 *Ibid*, 169.
217 *The Tennis Bubble*, Rich Koster, (New York 1976), 52.
218 *The Game, My 40 Years in Tennis*, Jack Kramer with Frank Deford, (New York 1979), 283-285.
219 *Ibid*.
220 *The Bud Collins, History of Tennis*, Bud Collins, (Canada 2008), 699.
     World of Tennis '76, edited by John Barrett, compiled by Lance Tingay, (London 1976), 209.

221   *Ibid*, 211, 221.
222   *Official 1989 MTC Media Guide*, (MTC 1989), 357-358.
223   *Ibid*, 372.

Chapter 10

224   *New York Times*, February 28, 1976, "Borg Beats Laver In $100,000 Match.
225   *New York Times*, Leonard Koppett, February 29, 1976, "Connors Crushes Orantes."
226   *1976 Commercial Union Grand Prix Rules,* (MIPTC 1976).
227   *MIPTC Minutes*, January 8-10, 1976, Dominican Republic Meeting.
228   *MIPTC Minutes*, March 9-10, 1976, London Meeting.
229   *MIPTC Minutes*, April 12, 1976, Majorca Meeting.
230   *MIPTC Minutes*, May 25, 1976, New York Meeting.
231   *MIPTC Minutes*, June 19-20, 22, 26, 29, 1976, New York Meeting.
232   *MIPTC Minutes*, August 30-31, 1976, New York Meeting.
233   *MIPTC Minutes*, September 3, 1976, New York Meeting.
234   *Contract*, October 20, 1976, Colgate Palmolive and MIPTC with approval by ATP.
235   *MIPTC Minutes*, October 25-27, 1976, London Meeting.
236   *MIPTC Minutes*, December 8-9, 11-12, 1976, Houston Meeting.
237   *The Art of World Team Tennis*, Greg Hoffman, (San Francisco 1977), 61.
238   *Open Tennis*, Richard Evans, (London 1993), 144.
239   *New York Times*, March 27, 1976, "Nastase Ousted From Tourney For Behavior in Tanner Match."
240   *New York Times*, August 26, 1976, "Nastase, Dibley in Flareup, Dibley Bows to Nastase In Flareup."
        New York Times, Parton Reese, September 4, 1976, "Nastase Angers Crowd While Beating Pohmann, Nastase Riles Fans In Tennis Victory."
        New York Times, Parton Reese, September 5, 1976, "Nastase Debate Rages."
        New York Times, Dave Anderson, September 9, 1976, "The Nastase Phenomenon."
        New York Times, Neil Amdur, October 6, 1976, "Nastase Plays, Wins Purses Despite Ban, Nastase Keeps Playing, Winning While Under a 21-Day Suspension."
        New York Times. November 15, 1976, "Rosewall Captures Final From an Angry Nastase."
241   *MIPTC Minutes*, March 9-10, 1976, London Meeting.
242   *MIPTC Minutes*, April 12, 1976, Majorca Meeting.
243   *MIPTC Minutes*, May 25, 1976, New York Meeting.
244   *MIPTC Minutes*, June 19-20, 22, 26, 29, 1976, New York Meeting.
245   *Letter*, September 10, 1976, WCT to all members of the MIPTC.
246   *Letter*, September 30, 1976, Bob Briner, Cliff Drysdale, Jack Kramer and Stan Malless to WCT, which was endorsed by a cable dated October 4, 1976, from Paulo Angeli, Pierre Darmon Derek Hardwick and Lars Myhrman to WCT.
247   *Letter*, October 26, 1976, WCT to the Chairman of the MIPTC.
        MIPTC Minutes, October 25-27, 1976, London Meeting.
248   *MIPTC Minutes*, December 8-9, 11-12, 1976, Houston Meeting.
249   *The Bud Collins, History of Tennis*, Bud Collins, (Canada 2008), 699.
        World of Tennis 1977, edited by John Barrett, compiled by Lance Tingay, (London 1977), 206, 238.
250   *Official 1989 MTC Media Guide*, MTC (1989), 358-359.
251   *Ibid*, 372-373.

Chapter 11

252   *The Game, My 40 Years in Tennis*, Jack Kramer with Frank Deford, (New York 1979), 279.
253   *MIPTC Minutes*, March 21-23, 1977, Paris Meeting.

254   *MIPTC Minutes*, June 15-16, 1977, Eastbourne Meeting.

255   *MIPTC Minutes*, June 26, 1977, London Meeting.

256   *MIPTC Minutes*, August 26-28, 1977, Boston Meeting.

257   *The Game, My 40 Years in Tennis*, Jack Kramer with Frank Deford, (New York 1979), 279-281.

258   *1977 Colgate Grand Prix Rules and Regulations*, (MIPTC 1977).

259   *MIPTC Minutes*, January 20-22, 1977, Paris Meeting.

260   *MIPTC Minutes*, June 15-16, 1977, Eastbourne Meeting.

261   *MIPTC Minutes*, August 26-28, 1977, Boston Meeting.

262   *New York Times*, Neil Amdur, November 17, 1977, "Tennis Curbs Secret Payoffs and Money Guarantees."

263   *MIPTC Minutes*, October 28-30, 1977, London Meeting.

264   *New York Times*, February 5, 1977, "W.C.T. Sues Borg and Colgate, Alleging a Breach of Contract."

265   *New York Times*, Neil Amdur, June 8, 1977, "Americanization of Pro Tennis Feared and Criticized in Europe."

266   *The Tennis Bubble*, Rich Koster, (New York 1976), 196.

267   *Ibid* 194-197.

268   *New York Times*, Rich Koster, March 13, 1977, "The Future of Tennis: Order Is Needed."

269   *New York Times*, Neil Amdur, September 29, 1977, "'Spaghetti' Tennis Racquet Faces a Ban."
         New York Times, October 1, 1977, "Vilas, Behind, Quits in Final Over Racquet."
         New York Times, Charles Friedman, October 9, 1977, "Controversy Boils on 'Spaghetti' Racquet."
         New York Times, October 20, 1977, "U.S.T.A. Joins Double-Strung Racquet Ban."

270   *New York Times*, October 4, 1977, "People in Sports."

271   *New York Times*, April 24, 1977, "Soviet Union Joins Team Tennis This Week."

272   *World of Tennis 1978*, edited by John Barrett, compiled by Lance Tingay, (London 1988), Mike Lupica, "World Team Tennis", 187.

273   *World of Tennis 1978*, edited by John Barrett, compiled by Lance Tingay, (London 1988), Richard Evans "The ATP Year Tennis", 263.

274   *New York Times*, Neil Amdur, March 20, 1977, "Deep South's Slew Hester: A Canny Tennis Maverick."

275   *New York Times*, Charles Friedman, February 22, 1977, "U.S.T.A. Seeks Purchase Of West Side Tennis Club."

276   *Tennis Week*, David Kenneth Specter, February 20, 1997, "A Stadium is Born."

277   *The United States Tennis Association: Raising The Game*, Warren F. Kimball, Lincoln: Univ. of Nebraska Press, (2017), 209-210.

278   *Ibid*, 213.

279   *New York Times*, Neil Amdur, December 21, 1977, "Pro Tennis Slated at Forest Hills."

280   *The Tennis Bubble*, Rich Koster, (New York 1976), 42.

281   *New York Times*, Neil Amdur, May 7, 1977, "Winner-Take-All Tennis Match on TV Called a Ruse."

282   *New York Times*, Neil Amdur, August 7, 1977, 'CBS Winner-Take-All' Illusion Leads to an F.C.C. Investigation."

283   *New York Times*, Neil Amdur, November 2, 1977, "Tennis Series Is Called Deceptive."
         New York Times, Les Brown, November 2, 1977, "House Inquiry Looking Into Network Responsibility."

284   *New York Times*, Neil Amdur, November 4, 1977, "CBS: No Tennis Deceit."

285   *New York Times*, Les Brown, March 16, 1978, "Robert Wussler, President of CBS Sports, Resigns."

286   *New York Times*, Les Brown, March 17, 1978, "F.C.C. Censures CBS Over Sports."
         New York Times, April 10, 1978, "CBS Admits Deception On Tennis."
         New York Times, Les Brown, July 21, 1978, "F.C.C. to Take Action Against CBS."

287   *The Bud Collins, History of Tennis*, Bud Collins, (Canada 2008), 699.
         World of Tennis 1978, edited by John Barrett, compiled by Lance Tingay, (London 1978), 232.

288   *Ibid*, 242, 265.
289   *Official 1989 MTC Media Guide,* (MTC 1989), 359.
290   *Ibid,* 373-374.

Chapter 12

291   *1978 Colgate Grand Prix Rules and Regulations,* (MIPTC 1978).
292   *MIPTC Minutes,* January 5-7, 1978, New York Meeting.
293   *MIPTC Minutes,* April 17-19, 1978, Nice Meeting.
294   *New York Times,* July 7, 1978, "Sports New Briefs."
295   *MIPTC Minutes,* July 23-24, 1978, London Meeting.
296   *MIPTC Minutes,* September 1-2, 1978, New York Meeting.
297   *MIPTC Minutes,* October 26-28, 1978, Tokyo Meeting.
298   *New York Times,* January 4, 1978, "Vilas Will Not Compete for Prix Bonus."
299   *International Tennis Weekly,* May 5, 1978, "Council to Fight Exhibitions."
300   *Tennis Week,* Murray Janoff, April 15, 1978, "Tennis On TV."
301   *New York Times,* Neil Amdur, November 10, 1978, "Tennis Moves to Improve Officiating."
302   *New York Times,* Neil Amdur, November 11, 1978, "No Masters for Connors, Borg"
303   *New York Times,* December 9, 1978, "Tennis Stars to Bypass Masters."
        New York Times, Neil Amdur, January 4, 1979, "Bolsters Event Here."
        New York Times, Neil Amdur, January 12, 1979, "McEnroe Is Victor On Connors Default."
        New York Times, Neil Amdur, January 14, 1979, "The Masters: A Showcase With Problems."
        New York Times, Neil Amdur, January 15, 1979, "McEnroe Tops Ashe, 6-7, 6-3, 7-5."
304   *World of Tennis 1979,* edited by John Barrett, compiled by Lance Tingay, (London 1979), Dennis Spencer "The ATP Year", 253-256.
305   *The Bud Collins, History of Tennis*, Bud Collins, (Canada 2008), 699.
        World of Tennis 1979, edited by John Barrett, compiled by Lance Tingay, (London 1979), 230.
306   *Ibid,* 239, 257.
307   *Official 1989 MTC Media Guide,* (MTC 1989), 359-360.
308   *Ibid,* 374-375.

Chapter 13

309   *New York Times,* Neil Amdur, January 8, 1979, "New Rule Brings a Crisis To Men's Tennis Tour."
310   *New York Times,* Dave Anderson, January 13, 1979, "In Tennis, Trust Is a Fault."
311   *MIPTC Minutes,* January 9-12, 1979, New York Meeting.
312   *International Tennis Weekly,* January 1979.
        New York Times, January 29, 1979, "I.T.F. Backs Rule Changes."
313   *New York Times,* Bob Briner, February 11, 1979, "Holdouts Endanger Future of Tennis."
314   *International Tennis Weekly,* February 23, 1979, "MIPTC, Top Five Reach Accord on '79 Grand Prix Revision."
        New York Times, James Tuite, February 12, 1979, "Tennis: Borg Beats Connors, Tennis Compromise Quells Top-5 Threat."
        World of Tennis 1980, edited by John Barrett, compiled by Lance Tingay, (London 1980), Dennis Spencer "The ATP Year", 283.
315   *New York Times,* John P. McEnroe (Sr.) February 18, 1979, "Laissez-Faire And Pro Tennis."
316   *MIPTC Minutes,* April 4-6, 1979, London Meeting.
317   *International Tennis Weekly,* Bob Briner, May 25, 1979, "Open Letter on ATP Championships."
        Tennis Week, July 26, 1979, "Tennis Politics."
        Letter, Robert A. Briner, July 1979, to the 'Fabulous Five'.

New York Times, Ed Hickey, July 22, 1979, "Is Pro Tennis Turning Its Back on an Early Supporter?"
World of Tennis 1980, edited by John Barrett, compiled by Lance Tingay, (London 1980), David Gray, "The Year in Review", 13.

318 *1979 Colgate Grand Prix Rules and Regulations,* (MIPTC 1979).
319 *MIPTC Minutes,* January 9-12, 1979, New York Meeting.
320 *MIPTC Minutes,* April 4-6, 1979, London Meeting.
321 *MIPTC Minutes,* July 8-10, 1979, London Meeting.
322 *MIPTC Minutes,* September 3-5, 1979, New York Meeting.
323 *International Tennis Weekly,* August 24, 1979, "Colgate Passes On Option Years."
324 *MIPTC Minutes,* September 3-5, 1979, New York Meeting.
325 *MIPTC Minutes,* November 5-8, 1979, Paris Meeting.
326 *New York Times,* James Tuite, October 11, 1979, "Volvo Will Sponsor Grand Prix of Tennis."
Contract, September 25, 1979, Volvo of America Corporation and MIPTC.
327 *International Tennis Weekly,* January 1979, "Pro Council Adds Nielsen."
328 *New York Times,* March 21, 1979, "Nastase Is Disqualified."
329 *International Tennis Weekly,* May 18, 1979, "First GP Certification School Pleases Participants."
330 *International Tennis Weekly,* June 15, 1979, "Grand Prix Officials Certification School."
331 *Tennis Week,* Eugene L. Scott, August 30, 1979, "Vantage Point."
332 *New York Times,* Neil Amdur, August 31, 1979, "McEnroe Captures Tumultuous Match."
New York Times, Jane Gross, September 1, 1979, "Hammond Concedes He Lost Control."
333 *International Tennis Weekly,* November 1979, "Farrar Joins Supervisors."
334 *World of Tennis 1979,* edited by John Barrett, compiled by Lance Tingay, (London 1979), Dennis Spencer, "The ATP Year", 253-256.
335 *1978 USTA Circuit Regulations,* (USTA 1978).
1979 USTA Circuit Regulations, (USTA 1979).
336 *Tennis Week,* Richard Evans, September 20, 1979, "How Briner Beat the Ballot, a Tennis Week Exclusive."
337 *Open Tennis,* Richard Evans, (London 1993), 185-187.
338 *International Tennis Weekly,* 1979, "Open Letter to ATP Membership from Dell, Craighill, Fentress and Benton."
339 *The Bud Collins, History of Tennis,* Bud Collins, (Canada 2008), 699.
World of Tennis 1980, edited by John Barrett, compiled by Lance Tingay, (London 1980), 258.
340 *Ibid,* 267, 286.
341 *Official 1989 MTC Media Guide,* (MTC 1989), 360-361.
342 *Ibid,* 375-376.

Chapter 14

343 *International Tennis Weekly,* January 18, 1980, "Briner Passes on ATP Option."
344 *1980 Volvo Grand Prix Rules and Regulations,* (MIPTC 1980).
345 *MIPTC Minutes,* January 8-11, 1980, London Meeting.
346 *MIPTC Minutes,* March 17-19, 1980, London Meeting.
347 *MIPTC Minutes,* April 30 – May 2, 1980, Dallas Meeting.
348 *MIPTC Minutes,* June 17-19, 1980, London Meeting.
349 *MIPTC Minutes,* July 23-25, 1980, New York Meeting.
350 *MIPTC Minutes,* August 26-28, September 4, 1980, New York Meeting.
351 *MIPTC Minutes,* November 3-5, 1980, London Meeting.
352 *New York Times,* January 7, 1980, "Nastase Gets a $5,000 Fine."
353 *Open Tennis,* Richard Evans, (London 1993), 180.
354 *New York Times,* February 23, 1980, "Borg Defeats Connors; Nastase Defaults Match."

355   *New York Times*, Terence Smith, April 4, 1980, "Hamilton Jordan Emerges as Envoy on Iran."

356   *New York Times*, April 17, 1980, "Ashe Retires From Tennis."

357   *New York Times*, Neil Amdur, July 6, 1980, "Beats McEnroe In Four-Hour, 5-Set Struggle," "Borg Beats McEnroe in 5 Sets For 5th Wimbledon Title in Row."

358   *New York Times*, July 6, 1980, "Nastase Given 18-Month Ban."

359   *New York Times*, Jane Gross, August 30, 1980, "Nastase Penalized And Out."

360   *New York Times*, September 8, 1980, "Ashe Will Coach Davis Cup Team."

361   *World of Tennis 1981*, edited by John Barrett, compiled by Lance Tingay, (London 1981), Dewey Blanton, "The ATP Year," 269-270.

362   *Open Tennis*, Richard Evans, (London 1993), 184.

363   *New York Times*, June 4, 1980, "Connors, Gerulaitis Move to Semifinals; Orantes Defaults."

364   *MIPTC Minutes*, June 17-19, 1980, London Meeting.

365   *World of Tennis 1981*, edited by John Barrett, compiled by Lance Tingay, (London 1981), Dewey Blanton, "The ATP Year," 270.

366   *New York Times*, July 13, 1980, "Tennis Players Warn of U.S. Open Boycott."

367   *New York Times*, July 17, 1980, "Agreement Ends Threat of U.S. Open Boycott."
        MIPTC Minutes, July 23-25, 1980, New York Meeting.

368   *MIPTC Minutes*, November 3-5, 1980, London Meeting.

369   *The Bud Collins, History of Tennis*, Bud Collins, (Canada 2008), 699.
        World of Tennis 1981, edited by John Barrett, compiled by Lance Tingay, (London 1981), 254.

370   *Ibid*, 259, 272.

371   *Official 1989 MTC Media Guide*, (MTC 1989), 361-362.

372   *Ibid*, 376.

Chapter 15

373   *New York Times*, January 2, 1974, "People in Sports".

374   *High Point Enterprise*, Paul Shinn, January 12, 1974, "Exhibition Season Winds Up, Ashe Takes Tiebreak Win."

375   *1978 USTA Circuit Regulations* (USTA 1978).
        1979 USTA Circuit Regulations (USTA 1979).

376   *Recruitment Profile for the position of Administrator for the Men's International Professional Tennis Council*, (1980).

377   *Letter*, Gerald J. Bump, December 30, 1980.

378   *Ahead of the Game*, Owen Williams (USA 2013), 214-216.
        International Tennis Weekly, February 6, 1981, "A Well-Kept Secret."
        Tennis Week, Eugene Scott, January, 1981, "Down The Publisher's Alley."

379   *Letter*, Jim McManus, January 22, 1981.

380   *Tennis Week*, Eugene Scott, January, 1981, "Down The Publisher's Alley."

381   *International Tennis Weekly*, February, 1981, "Marshall Happer: Man on the Tennis Hot Seat", "Happer Brings Clean Slate to New Post."

Chapter 16

382   *1981 Volvo Grand Prix Rules and Regulations*, (MIPTC 1981).

383   *MIPTC Minutes*, January 15-17, 1981, New York Meeting.

384   *MIPTC Minutes*, March 18-21, 1981, Paris Meeting.

385   *MIPTC Minutes*, April 20-21, 1981, New York Meeting.

386   *MIPTC Minutes*, May 10-11, 1981, New York Meeting.

387   *MIPTC Minutes*, June 1-2, 1981, Paris Meeting.

388   *MIPTC Minutes*, June 15-18, 1981, London Meeting.

389   *New York Times*, May 1, 1981, "Tennis Prizes to Rise In Battle for Players."

390   *MIPTC Minutes*, August 31 – September 3, 1981, New York Meeting.

391   *International Tennis Weekly*, August 7, 1981, "Hunt Addresses Players on WCT Circuit."
        International Tennis Weekly, August 14, 1981, "WCT Tells Players Association to Face 'Realities.'".

392   *International Tennis Weekly*, September 4, 1981, ATP Board Issues Statements on WCT Plans."
        International Tennis Weekly, August 14, 1981, "Buchholz Outlines ATP Position to Hunt."

393   *MIPTC Minutes*, August 31 – September 3, 1981, New York Meeting.

394   *New York Times*, Neil Amdur, April 26, 1981, "Sports-Apartheid Moves Build."
        New York Times, Neil Amdur, May 16, 1981, "Anti-Apartheid Unit Publishes Sports List."
        New York Times, November 14, 1981, "Connors on Blacklist."
        New York Times, November 18, 1981, "Connors Withdraws."
        New York Times, November 20, 1981, "Gerulaitis to Play."

395   *International Tennis Weekly*, May 1, 1981, "Council Moves on '82, Nastase Suspended."

396   *New York Times*, September 23, 1981, "Gerulaitis Suspended."

397   *New York Times*, Neil Amdur, November 17, 1981, "McEnroe Suspended; Still in Cup."

398   *Emails*, August 2, 2019, Gary V. Swain to Marshall Happer.

399   *International Tennis Weekly*, February 1981, "ATP, Longwood Sign Pact on U.S. Pro."

400   *International Tennis Weekly*, Earl "Butch" Buchholz, February 27, 1981, "Mandate for the ATP: End Court Misconduct," "Players Strongly Support GP Rules."

401   *World of Tennis 1982*, edited by John Barrett, compiled by Lance Tingay, (London 1982), Dewey Blanton, "The ATP Year", 266.

402   *Audited Financial Statements*, Ernst & Whinney, December 31, 1982, "Men's International Professional Tennis Council."

403   *The Bud Collins, History of Tennis*, Bud Collins, (Canada 2008), 699.
        World of Tennis 1982, edited by John Barrett, compiled by Lance Tingay, (London 1982), 254, 268.

404   *Official 1989 MTC Media Guide*, (MTC 1989), 362-363.

405   *Ibid*, 377.

Chapter 17

406   *Notice of Charge for a Major Offense, To Mr. Eliot Teltscher*, June 30, 1981.

407   *Determination of Major Offense Investigation and Minor Offense Appeal*, September 1, 1981 (19 pages).

408   *Transcript of McEnroe Major Offense Hearing*, Newrock Reporting Service, September 20, 1981, New York City Bar Association Offices.

409   *Affidavit*, Arthur Ashe, November 18, 1981.

410   *Affidavit*, John McEnroe, Jr., November 18, 1981.

411   *Decision of the Arbitrators Together with Factual Findings and Reasons for Decision*, Lawrence W. Krieger and Robert J. Kelleher, McEnroe Arbitration Proceeding, September 20, 1981.
        Letter, Harry Hopman to Lawrence W. Krieger and The Honorable Robert J. Kelleher, January 11, 1982.
        Opinion John McEnroe Case "Player Code of Conduct," Harry Hopman, January 27, 1982.

412   *Letter,* M. Marshall Happer III to Philippe Chatrier, Chairman and Members of the Council, January 27, 1982.

413   *MIPTC Press Release*, January 26, 1982.
        London Daily Mail, Laurie Pignon, January 27, 1982, "McEnroe – the great escape!"

414   *Notice of Charge for a Major Offense,* MIPTC vs. Vitas Gerulaitis, 1981 U.S. Open, January 19, 1982.

415   *MIPTC Minutes*, January 12-15, 1982, New York Meeting.
        Notice of Charge for a Major Offense, MIPTC vs. Vitas Gerulaitis, 1981 Melbourne Indoor, January 19, 1982.

New York Times, Neil Amdur, January 21, 1982, "Gerulaitis Is Fined $15,000 for Conduct."

416   *MIPTC Minutes*, January 12-15, 1982, New York Meeting.
417   *MIPTC Minutes*, March 18-21, 1981, Paris Meeting.
418   *MIPTC Minutes*, June 15-18, London Meeting.

Chapter 18

419   *World of Tennis 1983*, edited by John Barrett, compiled by Lance Tingay, (London 1983), Ish Haley, "The WCT Year", 158, 161.
420   *New York Times*, January 20, 1982, "Borg Joins Qualifiers."
421   *New York Times*, Neil Amdur, March 31, 1982, "Wimbledon Sifts Borg's Case."
422   *New York Times*, April 7, 1982, "Borg Status Unresolved."
       New York Times, April 12, 1982, "Borg Won't Play in French Open."
423   *International Tennis Weekly*, April 16, 1982, "Borg Issue Mulled."
       MIPTC Minutes, April 4-6, 1982, Monte Carlo Meeting.
       New York Times, April 7, 1982, "Borg Status Unresolved."
424   *International Tennis Weekly*, April 20, 1982, "Borg Rejects Offer, Will Skip Wimbledon.
       New York Times, Neil Amdur, April 25, 1982, "For Borg Choices to Be Made."
       International Tennis Weekly, February 19, 1982, "Council Cites Equality in Upholding Rule."
       New York Times, April 21, 1982, "Borg Toppled in Qualifying."
425   *New York Times*, November 22, 1982, "Connors Turns Back Borg 7-5, 7-6 in Series Finale."
426   *Letter*, November 12, 1981, Earl "Butch" Buchholz, Executive Director to Tournament Directors.
427   *Contract*, January 28, 1982, MIPTC and ATP for Player and Tournament Service Fees.
428   *International Tennis Weekly*, February 12, 1982, "Players to Withdraw Reps from MIPTC."
429   *Letter*, February 5, 1982, Earl "Butch" Buchholz to Philippe Chatrier.
430   *MIPTC Minutes*, February 18-20, 1982, La Quinta Meeting.
431   *Memorandum*, April 1, 1982, M. Marshall Happer to MIPTC, "ATP Finances."
432   *MIPTC Minutes*, June 15-18, 1982, London Meeting.
433   *International Tennis Weekly*, May 7, 1982, "Buchholz Hopeful As Talks Continue."
       International Tennis Weekly, July 16, 1982, "ATP, MIPTC Announce Five-Year Agreement."
434   *Contract*, August 30, 1982, MIPTC and ATP.
435   *International Tennis Weekly*, September 3, 1982, "Buchholz: Agreement Gives Tennis Stability."
436   *1982 Volvo Grand Prix Yearbook*, (MIPTC 1982).
437   *1982 MIPTC Supplement*, (MIPTC 1982).
438   *New York Times*, Norimitsu Onishi, November 27, 1995, "Frank Hammond Tennis Umpire with Style and a Sure Eye, 66."
439   *MIPTC Minutes*, January 12-15, 1982, New York Meeting.
440   *MIPTC Minutes*, February 18-20, 1982, La Quinta Meeting.
       New York Times, February 11, 1982, "Tennis Group Threatens Cancellation Over Ban."
441   *MIPTC Minutes*, April 4-6, 1982, Monte Carlo Meeting.
442   *MIPTC Minutes*, June 15-18, 1982, London Meeting.
443   *MIPTC Minutes*, August 27-30, 1982, New York Meeting.
444   *MIPTC Minutes*, November 9-11, 1982, Stockholm Meeting.
445   *https://fr.wikipedia.org/wiki/Jacques_Dorfmann_(arbitre)*, accessed March 31, 2019.
446   *New York Times*, February 10, 1982, "Tempest in Tennis."
447   *New York Times*, March 3, 1982, "Lendl to Skip Wimbledon."
448   *New York Times*, June 5, 1982, "Lendl Passing On Wimbledon."
449   *New York Times*, Neil Amdur, June 21, 1982, "Wimbledon Takes Heed."
450   *New York Times*, Neil Amdur, April 30, 1982, "Lendl Facing Penalties."
       New York Times, May 1, 1982, "Lendl Rejects Contest on Fine."

451   *New York Times*, May 30, 1982, "Gerulaitis Fined $2,500."
452   *1982 Wimbledon Entry Application.*
453   *New York Times*, Neil Amdur, July 13, 1982, "Davis Cup Tennis is Special to McEnroe."
454   *New York Times*, Neil Amdur and Lawrie Mifflin, July 15, 1982, "Tennis Feuding."
455   *International Tennis Weekly*, May 28, 1982, "Pro Council Notified Players of Fines."
       International Tennis Weekly, July 16, 1982, "Pro Council Lists Outstanding Player Fines."
       New York Times, Thomas Rogers, July 19, 1982, "Netting Errant Fines."
456   *New York Times*, October 27, 1982, "Tennis No Longer a Sport of Decorum."
457   *New York Times*, December 14, 1982, "Drug Alert in Tennis."
458   *New York Times*, Neil Amdur, November 18, 1982, "Tennis Stalwart."
459   *International Tennis Weekly*, November 21, 1982, "Supervisor Roberson Leaves Post, GP
       Supervisor Roberson Retires."
460   *New York Times*, Neil Amdur, December 23, 1982, "No. 1 on the list of Tennis Fines."
461   *Emails*, August 2, 2019, Gary V. Swain to Marshall Happer.
462   *World of Tennis 1983*, edited by John Barrett, compiled by Lance Tingay, (London 1983), Richard
       Evans, "The ATP Year," 257-259.
463   *International Tennis Weekly*, September 13, 1982, "ATP Begins Search For New Director, ATP
       Looks for Director."
464   *International Tennis Weekly*, January 28, 1983, "Davies Named ATP Director."
465   *International Tennis Weekly*, February, 1983, "Buchholz Reflects on Term as ATP Executive Director."
466   *Administrator's Determination*, August 19, 1982, Tournament Offense No. 2, 1982 Stuttgart.
       Appeal, September ___, 1982, Tennis Club Weissenhof E.V. Stuttgart Appeal of Administrator's
       Determination.
       Letter, December 7, 1982, M. Marshall Happer III to Bernd Nusch of Stuttgart.
467   *International Tennis Weekly*, November, 1982, "Pro Council Fines Stockholm $25,000."
       New York Times, November 12, 1982, "Tennis Unit Fines Event Organizers."
468   *Audited Financial Statements*, Ernst & Whinney, December 31, 1982, "Men's International
       Professional Tennis Council."
469   *The Bud Collins, History of Tennis*, Bud Collins, (Canada 2008), 699.
       World of Tennis 1983, edited by John Barrett, compiled by Lance Tingay, (London 1982), 240, 258.
470   *Official 1989 MTC Media Guide*, (MTC 1989), 363.
471   *Ibid*, 377-378.

Chapter 19

472   *1983 Official Professional Tennis Yearbook,* (MIPTC 1983).
473   *MIPTC Minutes*, January 19-22, 1983, New York Meeting.
474   *MIPTC Minutes*, March 28-31, 1983, Monte Carlo Meeting.
475   *MIPTC Minutes*, June 6-9, 1983, Paris Meeting.
476   *Letter*, June 5, 1983, Arthur Ashe to Philippe Chatrier.
477   *MIPTC Minutes*, June 25 and 27, 1983, London Meeting.
478   *MIPTC Minutes*, August 25-30, September 4 and 7, 1983, New York Meeting.
479   *MIPTC Minutes*, November 7-10, 1983, London Meeting.
480   *International Tennis Weekly*, February 1983, "Happer Hires Supervisor."
481   *New York Times*, Neil Amdur, March 10, 1983, "Split Discussed."
       Joint Press Release, March 12, 1983, Dissolution of Dell, Craighill, Fentress & Benton.
482   *New York Times*, Jane Gross, April 1, 1983, "Borg Loses and Says Goodbye."
483   *New York Times*, March 27, 1983, "Borg's Finale in Monaco."
       New York Times, Jane Gross, March 31, 1983, "Borg Starts His Last Tourney A Winner."
484   *New York Times*, April 2, 1983, "A Borg Epilogue."
485   *International Tennis Weekly*, April 16, 1983, "Pro Council Hires Eugenio as Assistant

Administrator."

486 *New York Times*. Neil Amdur, May 4, 1983, "Lendl Assails McEnroe."
487 *New York Times*, Neil Amdur, May 7, 1983, "McEnroe Beats Smid in Fiery Two Sets."
488 *New York Times*, Jane Gross, May 28, 1983, "McEnroe Tirade Under Inquiry."
    New York Times, Jane Gross, May 29, 1983, "McEnroe is Fined $3,000."
489 *International Tennis Weekly*, May 6, 1983, "Happer Details 30-Second Rule."
490 *New York Times*, Neil Amdur, June 7, 1983, "NBC Bids to Revive Appeal of Tennis."
491 *Sports Illustrated*, William Taaffe, June 1983, "This Octopus Embraces All."
492 *New York Times*, June 20, 1983, "No-Nonsense Code of Conduct Stressed."
493 *International Tennis Weekly*, November 18, 1983, "Connors Penalized for Skipping Rotterdam."
494 *New York Times*, July 11, 1983, "Connors Beats Lendl."
    New York Times, July 16, 1983, "Lendl Suspended."
495 *International Tennis Weekly*, July, 1983, "Cooper Joins Pro Council Staff."
496 *International Tennis Weekly*, July, August 26, 1983, "Officials Lose Certification."
497 *International Tennis Weekly*, August 22, 1983, "ATP, MIPTC Strive to Improve Officiating."
498 *New York Times*, Neil Amdur, August 31, 1983, "McEnroe Wins in Sets, is Fined."
499 *International Tennis Weekly*, September 23, 1983, "ITF General Secretary Gray Dies."
500 *New York Times*, Thomas Rogers, September 13, 1983, "Price They Pay: 19 Fines at Open."
501 *Never Make The First Offer*, Donald Dell with John Boswell, (New York 2009), 95-98.
    The Outsider, Jimmy Connors, (New York 2013), 277-279.
502 *Complaint, United States District Court, District of Connecticut, Ivan Lendl and Taconic Enterprises, Inc., Plaintiffs vs. Proserv, Inc., Donald L. Dell, Jerry Solomon and Alonzo Monk, Defendants filed May 5, 1988.*
503 *New York Times*, October 17, 1983, "McEnroe Takes Final, is Suspended 21 Days."
504 *Emails*, August 2, 2019, Gary V. Swain to Marshall Happer.
505 *World of Tennis 1984*, edited by John Barrett, compiled by Lance Tingay, (London 1984), Geoffrey Miller, "The ATP Year," 221-222.
506 *International Tennis Weekly*, October 28, 1983, "ATP Launches Tennis' First Pension Plan."
507 *International Tennis Weekly*, July 1, 1983, "Moore Succeeds Solomon as President of ATP."
508 *International Tennis Weekly*, July 29, 1983, "Moore seeks Unity, Independence."
    International Tennis Weekly, August 5, 1983, "Moore has Open Mind about Pro Council Issue."
509 *New York Times*, Dave Anderson, September 8, 1983, "'Tennis's Sheriff' Enforces the Law."
510 *Audited Financial Statements*, Ernst & Whinney, December 31, 1983, "Men's International Professional Tennis Council."
511 *The Bud Collins, History of Tennis*, Bud Collins, (Canada 2008), 699.
    World of Tennis 1984, edited by John Barrett, compiled by Lance Tingay, (London 1984), 216, 223.
512 *Official 1989 MTC Media Guide*, (MTC 1989), 364.
513 *Ibid*, 378-379.

Chapter 20

514 *MIPTC Minutes*, January 19-22, 1983, New York Meeting.
    MIPTC Minutes, March 28-31, 1983, Monte Carlo Meeting.
515 *Tennis Week*, Richard Evans, January 20, 1983, "Winitsky Invades The Stands."
516 *Determination of the MIPTC Administrator "In the Matter of Van Winitsky*, March 23, 1983.
517 *Determination of the MIPTC Administrator "In the Matter of the 1982 Altech/South African Open, Johannesburg, South Africa*, July 28, 1983.
518 *MIPTC Minutes*, November 7-10, 1983, London Meeting.
519 *Determination of the MIPTC Administrator "In the Matter of Yannick Noah, 1983 World Team* Cup, June 7, 1983.

520 *MIPTC Minutes*, June 6-9, 1983, Paris Meeting.
521 *New York Times*, June 27, 1983, "Noah Resigns from the ATP."
522 MIPTC *Minutes*, January 16-19, 1984, New York Meeting.
523 *Determination of the MIPTC Administrator "In the Matter of Ilie Nastase"*, September 9, 1983.
     Letter, Peter C. Lawler to M. Marshall Happer III, September 23, 1983.
524 *Notice of Investigation, In the Matter of 1983 A.B.N – Wereldtennistoernooi, Rotterdam, Netherlands*, April 28, 1983.
525 *Letter*, May 30, 1983, Hoekwater to Marshall Happer.
526 *Determination of MIPTC Administrator, In the Matter of 1983 A.B.N – Wereldtennistoernooi, Rotterdam, Netherlands*, June 7, 1983.
527 *MIPTC Minutes*, June 6-9, 1983, Paris Meeting.
528 *Open Tennis*, Richard Evans, (London 1993), 140.
529 *New York Times*, Neil Amdur, June 10, 1983, "Vilas Penalty a Warning to Top Players."
530 *New York Times*, June 22, 1983, "20 Top Players Support Vilas."
531 *Transcript of Telephone Conversation Between Peter Bonthuis and Ion Tiriac*, March 14, 1983.
     Transcript of Tiriac Testimony, December 13, 1983, 932.
532 *Opinion and Order, In the Matter of Guillermo Vilas*, Review Panel Decision.
533 *International Tennis Weekly*, December 30, 1983, "Vilas Decision Affirmed But Suspension Voided."
     MIPTC *Minutes*, January 16-19, 1984, New York Meeting.
     International Tennis Weekly, February 3, 1984, "Decision Leaves Vilas 'Terribly Disappointed."

Chapter 21

534 *Ahead of the Game*, Owen Williams, (USA 2013), 241.
535 *Complaint*, January 21, 1983, United States District Court, Southern District of New York, World Championship Tennis Inc, Plaintiff vs. International Tennis Federation, Association of Tennis Professionals and Men's International Professional Tennis Council, Defendants, Case No. 83 Civil 636 (VLV).
536 *International Tennis Weekly*, February 4, 1983, "Why Did WCT Sue ATP?"
     International Tennis Weekly, Mike Davies, February 11, 1983, Davies Urges Player Unity to Fight Lawsuit."
537 *International Tennis Weekly*, April 15, 1983, "WCT Director Explains Suit", "Hunt Addresses Players," "Hunt: It is WCT's Intention to Protect Right to do Business."
538 *International Tennis Weekly*, April 15, 1983, "ITF to Fund ATP Legal Defense."
539 *Settlement Agreement*, October 11, 1983, MIPTC and WCT et al.

Chapter 22

540 *Contract*, September 25, 1979, Volvo of America Corporation and MIPTC.
541 *Letter*, May 21, 1981, Marshall Happer to Rick Dowden.
     Letter, June 29, 1981, Rick Dowden to Marshall Happer.
542 *Letter*, October 15, 1981, Marshall Happer to Rick Dowden.
     Letter, October 21, 1981, Rick Dowden to Marshall Happer.
     Telex, December 17, 1981, Rick Dowden to Philippe Chatrier and MIPTC.
543 *Letter*, May 23, 1983, Rick Dowden to Philippe Chatrier, MIPTC Chairman.
     Letter, May 23, 1983, Bjorn Ahlstrom to Philippe Chatrier, MIPTC Chairman.
544 *Letter*, June 7, 1983, Rick Dowden to Philippe Chatrier, MIPTC Chairman.
545 *New York Times*, July 28, 1983, "Volvo Quits as Sponsor of Tennis Grand Prix."
546 *Letter*, October 7, 1983, Richard Adler to Volvo Grand Prix tournament directors.
547 *Letter*, June 2, 1983, Frank Craighill to Marshall Happer.

548   *Telex*, August 4, 1983, Yoichi Hattori to Frank Craighill.

549   *Telex*, November 4, 1983, Yoichi Hattori to Frank Craighill.

550   *Telex*, November 24, 1983, Yoichi Hattori to Frank Craighill.

551   *Telex*, November 7, 1983, Fred Kovaleski to Marshall Happer in London.

552   *Letter*, November 17, 1983, Marshall Happer to Donald Dell.

553   *Letter*, December 30, 1983, Donald Dell to Marshall Happer.

554   *Letter*, January 12, 1984, Rey Olsen of World Sports Group to Marshall Happer.

555   *Telex*, January 15, 1984, Jeffry Franklin to Marshall Happer.

556   *Letter*, January 13, 1983, Bob Kain and Patrick Nally to Marshall Happer.

557   *Letter*, January 15, 1983, Rick Dowden to Philippe Chatrier, MIPTC Chairman.

558   MIPTC *Minutes*, January 16-19, 1984, New York Meeting.

559   *Contract*, January 30, 1984, MIPTC and Nabisco Brands, Inc.

Chapter 23

560   *World of Tennis 1985*, edited by John Barrett, compiled by Lance Tingay, (London 1985), Ian Barnes, "The WCT Year," 189-190.

561   *1984 Official Professional Tennis Yearbook*, (MIPTC 1984).

562   MIPTC *Minutes*, January 16-19, 1984, New York Meeting.

563   MIPTC *Minutes*, March 14, 1984, New York Meeting.

564   MIPTC *Minutes*, Meeting April 17-20, 1984 Monte Carlo & May 6-7, 1984, New York City.

565   MIPTC *Minutes*, June 18-21, 30, July 6, 1984, London Meeting.

566   MIPTC *Minutes*, August 23-26, September 3, 1984, New York Meeting.

567   MIPTC *Minutes*, October 29 – November 1, 1984, Paris Meeting.

568   *International Tennis Weekly*, February 1984, "Playing Fair."

569   *New York Times*, March 19, 1984, "Bomb Scare Ends Rotterdam Final."

570   *New York Times*, April 26, 1984, "Joint Tennis Effort."

571   *International Tennis Weekly*, Eugene L. Scott, December 27, 1984, "Viewpoint" "ATP's Challenge: Being all Things to all Players," reprinted from *Tennis Week*.

572   *https://en.wikipedia.org/wiki/Los_Angeles_Tennis_Center*, accessed May 8, 2019.

573   *New York Times*, July 18, 1984, "Borg Loses, 6-3, 6-1, In Limited Return."

574   *International Tennis Weekly*, October 29, 1984, "Q & A, Butch Buchholz."

575   *New York Times*, November 4, 1984, "McEnroe is Fined $2,100."
       New York Times, November 5, 1984, "McEnroe Remains Eligible for Davis."

576   *International Tennis Weekly*, November 30, 1984, "Diller Named to Run Masters."

577   *Emails*, August 2, 2019, Gary V. Swain to Marshall Happer.

578   *World of Tennis 1985*, edited by John Barrett, compiled by Lance Tingay, (London 1985), Alexander McNab, "The ATP Year," 268-270.

579   MIPTC *Minutes*, April 17-20, 1984, Monte Carlo Meeting, May 6-7, 1984, MIPTC New York continuation Meeting.

580   *Letter*, May 7, 1984, Bjorn Ahlstrom to Philippe Chatrier.

581   *Letter*, May 18, 1984, Marshall Happer to Bjorn Ahlstrom.

582   *Contract*, January 14, 1985, MIPTC with Volvo of America Corporation and Volvo North America Corporation with the agreement and confirmation of ProServ, Inc., as agent for Volvo. MIPTC *Minutes*, January 14-17, 1985, New York Meeting.

583   *New York Times*, Peter Alfano, January 14, 1985, "McEnroe Takes 3D Masters Title."

584   *Complaint*, November, 1984, WBC Productions LTD vs. ProServ, Steve Disson, Ray Benton, Volvo, MIPTC and Nabisco In the United States District Ccout for the Northern District of Illinois, Eastern Division (No. 84 C. 8532).

585   MIPTC *Minutes*, April 15-18,1985, Dallas Meeting.

586   *Audited Financial Statements*, Ernst & Whinney, December 31, 1984, "Men's International Professional Tennis Council."

587   *The Bud Collins, History of Tennis*, Bud Collins, (Canada 2008), 699.
        World of Tennis 1985, edited by John Barrett, compiled by Lance Tingay, (1985), 262, 271.

588   *Official 1989 MTC Media Guide*, (MTC 1989), 364-365.

589   *Ibid*, 379-380.

Chapter 24

590   *World of Tennis 1986*, edited by John Barrett, compiled by Lance Tingay, (1986), Peter Blackman, "The WCT Year," 189-190.

591   *1985 Official MIPTC Yearbook,* (MIPTC 1985).

592   *Wimbledon '85 Program*, Tuesday, 2nd July, Eighth Day, 37.

593   *Letter*, E. P. Redding to Rick Dowden, January 15, 1985.

594   *MIPTC Counterclaim*, Volvo et al. v. MIPTC et al, USDC, Southern District of New York, 85 CIV. 2959, filed November 6, 1985, 48-51.

595   *Memo*, March 29, 1985, Roy Reardon "Conversation with Owen Williams."

596   *Letter*, Marshall Happer to members of MIPTC (except Ray Benton), dated March 13, 1985.

597   *MIPTC Counterclaim*, Volvo et al. v. MIPTC et al, USDC, Southern District of New York, 85 CIV. 2959, filed November 6, 1985, 54.

598   MIPTC *Minutes*, January 14-17, 1985, New York Meeting.

599   MIPTC *Minutes*, April 15-18,1985, Dallas Meeting.

600   *Minutes*, June 15-18,1985, MIPTC London Meeting.

601   *International Tennis Weekly*, September 10, 1985, "Davies Elected MIPTC Chairman."
        International Tennis Weekly, October 18, 1985, "Davies, MIPTC Chairman Addresses Blockbusters."

602   *Minutes*, September 10-12, 1985, MIPTC New York Meeting.

603   *Minutes*, November 4-7, 1985, MIPTC London Meeting.

604   *International Tennis Weekly*, November 1, 1985, "Short Circuits."

605   *International Tennis Weekly*, March 15, 1985, "Officials Graded, Too, in Supervisor Reports."

606   *International Tennis Weekly*, September 27, 1985, "Lendl Keeps Momentum, Wins Twice at Stuttgart."

607   *International Tennis Weekly*, October 4, 1985, "Vegas Withdraws 1986 Application."

608   *New York Times*, October 22, 1985, "Ashe to be Dropped as Davis Captain."

609   *New York Times*, November 28, 1985, "Change at Wimbledon."

610   *New York Times*, November 30, 1985, "McEnroe Fined for Outburst."
        New York Times, December 3, 1985, "Wilander Advances; McEnroe is Fined."

611   *New York Times*, December 10, 1985, "Lendl Suspended."

612   *Amusement Business*, Doug Graves, December 14, 1985, "Borg-McEnroe Tennis Exhibition Sets Box Office Marks on 6-City Tour."

613   *Emails*, August 2, 2019, Gary V. Swain to Marshall Happer.

614   *International Tennis Weekly*, January 25, 1985, "Board Gives Davies Two-Year Extension."

615   *World of Tennis 1986*, edited by John Barrett, compiled by Lance Tingay, (London 1986), Alexander McNab, "The ATP Year," 266-267.

616   *Minutes*, September 10-12,1985, MIPTC New York Meeting.

617   *Minutes*, November 4-7, 1985, MIPTC London Meeting.

618   *International Tennis Weekly*, November 15, 1985, "Council Passes ATP Drug Test Proposal."

619   *Audited Financial Statements*, Ernst & Whinney, December 31, 1985, "Men's International Professional Tennis Council."
        Audited Financial Statements, Ernst & Whinney, December 31, 1985, "Men's International Professional Tennis Council."

620   *The Bud Collins, History of Tennis*, Bud Collins, (Canada 2008), 699.
        World of Tennis 1986, edited by John Barrett, compiled by Lance Tingay, (London 1986), 260, 269.

621   *Official 1989 MTC Media Guide*, (MTC 1989), 365-366.
622   *Ibid*, 380-381.

Chapter 25

623   *MIPTC Minutes*, January 14-17, 1985, New York Meeting.
624   *Minutes*, April 15-18,1985, MIPTC Dallas Meeting.
625   *Memo*, May 22, 1985, Roy Reardon.
626   *Memo*, May 13, 1985, Roy Reardon.
627   *Memo*, May 17, 1985, Roy Reardon.
       Memo, May 21, 1985, Roy Reardon.
       Letter, June 5, 1985, Rick Dowden to MIPTC.
628   *Letter*, June 9, 1985, ProServ, Inc., and International Merchandising Corporation to MIPTC.
629   *MIPTC Minutes*, June 15-18,1985, MIPTC London Meeting.
630   *Handwritten Letter*, prepared by Bob Kain, Copied by Marshall Happer, July 3, 1985.
631   *First Amended Complaint*, Volvo et al. v. MIPTC et al, USDC, Southern District of New York, 85 CIV. 2959, filed July 3, 1985.
632   *Tennis Magazine*, August, 1985, "The Bitter Assault that Threatens the Men's Game", 20.
633   *Memorandum in Support of Motion to Dismiss by Defendants*, September 9, 1985.
634   *Demands*, October 9, 1985, "Plaintiffs' Settlement Demands."
635   *MIPTC Counterclaim*, Volvo et al. v. MIPTC et al, USDC, Southern District of New York, 85 CIV. 2959, filed November 6, 1985, 42-86.
636   *MIPTC Press Release 1985-No. 68*, November 7, 1985, "Agents McCormack, Dell, Benton and Volvo Charged in Suit by MIPTC".
       Press Statement, Mike Davies, November 7, 1985.
637   *Press Statement*, Philippe Chatrier, November 7, 1985.
       New York Times, Peter Alfano, November 10, 1985, "Control of Men's Tennis at Issue in Suits."
638   *John Martin Deposition Transcript*, September 18, 1985.

Chapter 26

639   *1986 Official MIPTC Yearbook*, (MIPTC 1985).
640   MIPTC *Minutes*, January 20-23, 1986, New York Meeting.
641   *International Tennis Weekly*, May 16, 1986, "Nabisco Adds to Sponsorship."
642   MIPTC *Minutes*, April 21-24, 1986, Monte Carlo York Meeting.
643   MIPTC *Minutes*, June 17-18, 1986, London Meeting.
644   MIPTC *Minutes*, September 8-10, 1986, New York Meeting.
645   *World of Tennis 1987*, edited by John Barrett, compiled by Lance Tingay, (London 1987), "ATP", 255.
646   MIPTC *Minutes*, December 5-8, 1986, New York Meeting.
647   *Letter*, July 29, 1986, Marshall Happer to Patrick C. Cash, Sr.
       Telex, September 17, 1986, Pat Cash Senior to Marshall Happer.
       Telex, September 17, 1986, Marshall Happer to Pat Cash Senior.
648   *International Tennis Weekly*, September 19, 1986, "ATP's Drug Testing Program Earns Praise."
649   *World of Tennis 1987*, edited by John Barrett, compiled by Lance Tingay, (London 1987), "ATP", 255-256.
650   *International Tennis Weekly*, March 7, 1986, "Connors Fined $5,000 after Default."
651   *Determination of the MIPTC Administrator "In the Matter of Jimmy Connors, 1986 Lipton Boca Raton*, March 24, 1986.
       MIPTC Minutes, April 21-24, 1986, Monte Carlo Meeting.

652   *New York Times*, April 1, 1986, "Connors Accepts Ban."
653   *The Outsider*, Jimmy Connors (New York 2013), 300-301.
654   *New York Times*, Neil Amdur, May 25, 1986, "What's the Point and Penalty of Tennis Suspension?"
655   *Audited Financial Statements*, Ernst & Whinney, December 31, 1986, "Men's International Professional Tennis Council."
656   *The Bud Collins, History of Tennis*, Bud Collins, (Canada 2008), 699.
       World of Tennis 1987, edited by John Barrett, compiled by Lance Tingay. (London 1987), 250, 257.
657   *Official 1989 MTC Media Guide*, (MTC 1989), 366-367.
658   *Ibid*, 381.

Chapter 27

659   *Memo*, January 24, 1986, Roy Reardon.
660   *MIPTC Minutes*, January 20-23, 1986, New York Meeting.
661   *Wall Street Journal*, Teri Agins, March 25, 1986, "Grudge Match: Big Tennis Has Turned Against Big Operator, and He Returns Favor."
662   *MIPTC Minutes*, June 17-18, 1986, London Meeting.
663   *MIPTC Minutes*, September 8-10, 1986, New York Meeting.
664   *Transcript*, September 24, 1986, Hearing Before Judge Kevin Thomas Duffy, 85 Civ. 2959.
665   *Letter*, September 25, 1986, Roy Reardon to the Honorable Naomi Reice Buchwald, United States Magistrate.
666   *Memo*, October 1, 1986, Roy Reardon.
667   *Tennis Magazine*, Barry Lorge, July, 1986, "Let's Stop the Agents from Eating away at the Game."

Chapter 28

668   *https://www.tennisfame.com/hall-of-famers/inductees/derek-hardwick/*, Accessed July 18, 2018.
669   *International Tennis Weekly*, June 1987, "Derek Hardwick's Death was a Great Loss for Tennis."
670   *1987 Official MIPTC Yearbook,* (MIPTC 1987).
671   *International Tennis Weekly*, February, 1987, "MIPTC Rules Out Conflicts of Interest."
672   *New York Times*, April 2, 1987, "Rules, Roles and Court Time."
673   *MIPTC Minutes*, February 3-6, 1987, Indian Wells Meeting.
674   *MIPTC Minutes*, April 21-23, 1987, Monaco Meeting.
675   *MIPTC Minutes*, June 8-11, 1987, Paris Meeting.
676   *New York Times*, June 12, 1987, "McEnroe in the Clear."
677   *International Tennis Weekly*, February 1987, "Jordan Brings While House Skills to ATP."
678   *Foreword, A Boy from Georgia*, President Jimmy Carter, (Athens GA 2015), ix-x.
679   *International Tennis Weekly*, 1987, "Jordan Begins New Job: 'A Lot to Learn'."
680   *New York Times*, Peter Alfano, March 10, 1987, "Players Hamilton Jordan is Now in Different Center Court."
681   *Personal Note*, March 10, 1987, Hamilton Jordan to Marshall Happer.
682   *MIPTC Minutes*, July 21, 1987, New York Meeting.
683   *MIPTC Minutes*, September 14-16, 1987, New York Meeting.
684   *MIPTC Minutes*, December 3-7, 1987, New York Meeting.
685   *Letter*, November 30, 1987, Owen Williams to Marshall Happer.
686   *New York Times*, Daniel F. Cuff, June 19, 1987, "Major Shifts Made at Nabisco Brands."
687   *Sports Marketing News*, August 17, 1987, "ProServ's Benton Resigns."
688   *New York Times*, Peter Alfano, September 6, 1987, "McEnroe Wins Noisily."
689   *New York Times*, Peter Alfano, September 7, 1987, "McEnroe Draws Fine, Suspension."
690   *Certificate of Registration*, September 8, 1987, United States Patent and Trademark Office.

691   *MIPTC Press Release*, December 4, 1987, "MIPTC Confirms Position Regarding South Africa."

692   *World of Tennis 1988,* edited by John Barrett, compiled by Lance Tingay, (London 1988), 276.

693   *Audited Financial Statements*, Ernst & Whinney, December 31, 1987, "Men's Tennis Council."

694   *The Bud Collins, History of Tennis*, Bud Collins, (Canada 2008), 700.
          World of Tennis 1988, edited by John Barrett, compiled by Lance Tingay, (London 1988), 265, 269.

695   *Official 1989 MTC Media Guide*, (MTC 1989), 367-368.

696   *Ibid*, 382.

Chapter 29

697   *Memo*, February 6, 1987, MIPTC's New Conflicts of Interest Rule.

698   *Letter*, April 21, 1987, Ivan Blumberg to Marshall Happer.

699   *Volvo N. America v. Men's Intern. Pro. Tennis Coun.*, Dismissal of First Amended Complaint, 678 F. Supp. 1035 August 10, 1987.

Chapter 30

700   *1988 Official MIPTC Yearbook,* (MIPTC 1988).

701   *Memo*, February 24, 1988, Roy Reardon.

702   *MIPTC Press Release*, January 28, 1988, "Nabisco Brands, Inc., to Continue Sponsorship of Grand Prix Until 1990.*Memo*, February 24, 1988, Roy Reardon.

703   *MTC Minutes*, January 25-28, 1988, Melbourne Meeting.

704   *Jacques Dorfmann Book Excerpt*, provided by Pierre Darmon of Paris FR.

705   *Contract*, August 30, 1982, MIPTC and WCT.

706   *Memo*, March 21, 1988, Roy Reardon.

707   *International Tennis Weekly*, April 8, 1988, "Council To Contract Players in 1990."

708   *MTC Minutes*, March 17-20, 1988, Miami Meeting.

709   *International Tennis Weekly*, April 29, 1988, "Tennis World is Saddened by Bookman's Sudden Death.

710   *New York Times*, Peter Alfano, August 9, 1988, "W.C.T. to Maintain Business as Usual."

711   *MTC Minutes*, June 15-18, 27, 30, 1988, London Meeting.

712   *MTC Minutes*, August 26-29, 1988, New York Meeting.

713   *Minutes*, November 2-3, 1988, MTC London Meeting.

714   *International Tennis Weekly*, May 13, 1988, "J. Wayne Richmond Joins ATP Staff."

715   *International Tennis Weekly*, August 12, 1988, "Happer Addresses Players on Washington Decision."

716   *https://en.wikipedia.org/wiki/RJR_Nabisco*, accessed August 2, 2018.
          https://en.wikipedia.org/wiki/F._Ross_Johnson, accessed August 2, 2018.
          Barbarians At The Gate, Bryan Burrough and John Helyar, (USA 1990, 2003, 2008).

717   *International Tennis Weekly*, November 18, 1988, "ATP Breaks Ground as New Home Construction Begins."

718   *International Tennis Weekly*, December 30, 1988, "The Grand Prix Tour: Still Booming."

719   *World of Tennis 1989*, edited by John Barrett, compiled by Lance Tingay, (London 1989), 256.

720   *Audited Financial Statements*, Ernst & Whinney, December 31, 1988, "Men's Tennis Council."

721   *The Bud Collins, History of Tennis*, Bud Collins, (Canada 2008), 700.
          World of Tennis 1989, edited by John Barrett, compiled by Lance Tingay, (London 1989), 245, 248.

722   *Official 1989 MTC Media Guide*, (MTC 1989), 368-369.

723   *Ibid*, 383.

Chapter 31

724   MIPTC *Minutes*, April 21-23, 1987, Monaco Meeting.

725   MTC *Minutes*, January 25-28, 1988, Melbourne Meeting.

726   MTC *Minutes*, March 17-20, 1988, Miami Meeting.

727   *Minutes*, June 15-18, 27, 30, 1988, MTC London Meeting.

728   *Volvo N. America v. Men's Intern. Pro. Tennis Coun.*, Reversal of Dismissal of Complaint, 839 F. 2d 69 (2ⁿᵈ Cir. 1988), February 8, 1988.

729   *Volvo N. America v. Men's Intern. Pro. Tennis Coun.*, Dismissal of Counterclaims, 687 F. Supp. 800, May 18, 1988.

730   *Letter*, June 23, 1988, Roy Reardon to Marshall Happer.

731   *International Tennis Weekly*, August 26, 1988, "Former Top PGA Tour Official Joins ATP as Key Advisor."
       New York Times, Peter Alfano, August 30, 1988, "Tennis; Pros May Design Tour Similar to Golf's."

732   *Letter*, Hamilton Jordan to Marshall Happer, August 26, 1988, Personal and Confidential.

733   *MTC Minutes*, August 26-29, 1988, New York Meeting.

734   *International Tennis Weekly*, September 9, 1988, "ITF Harshly Rejects Players' Request for Stronger Voice in the Game."

735   *International Tennis Weekly*, September 9, 1988, "U.S. Open Blocks ATP Press Conference On-Site."

736   *New York Times*, August 31, 1988, "A.T.P. Plans Tour in '90."

737   *New York Times*, Peter Alfano, September 2, 1988, "Tennis Federation Rejects Tour Plan."

738   *New York Times*, Peter Alfano, August 30, 1988, "Tennis; Pros May Design Tour Similar to Golf's."

739   *New York Times*, Peter Alfano, September 2, 1988, "Tennis Federation Rejects Tour Plan."

740   *Letter*, September 15, 1988, Hamilton Jordan to Marshall Happer.

741   *International Tennis Weekly*, September 30, 1988, "Former ATP Leaders Davies, Fechtman Work to Form ITF Tour."

742   *Letter*, September 20, 1988, Marshall Happer to the Members of the MTC and Hamilton Jordan.

743   *Letter*, September 22, 1988, Marshall Happer to Members of the MTC and Hamilton Jordan.

744   *International Tennis Weekly*, October, 1988, "Volvo Supports ATP Tour."

745   *Memo*, Marshall Happer, October 4, 1988, Meeting.

746   *Letter*, October 9, 1988, Hamilton Jordan to MTC.

747   *Letter*, October 11, 1988, Marshall Happer to MTC and Hamilton Jordan.
       Copies were also faxed to Buzzer Hadingham.

748   *Letter*, October 14, 1988, Graham Lovett to Marshall Happer.
       Telex, October 14, 1988, Franco Bartoni to Marshall Happer.
       Letter, October 18, 1988, Charles Pasarell to Marshall Happer.
       Letter, October 20, 1988, Michael Cardozo to Marshall Happer.
       Letter, October 23, 1988, Franco Bartoni to "Dear Sir".

749   *Letter*, October 25, 1988, Marshall Happer to all tournaments.

750   *Letter*, October 27, 1988, Hamilton Jordan to Marshall Happer.

751   *Letter*, October 27, 1988, Hamilton Jordan to Marshall Happer marked "Personal".

752   *Letter*, October 28, 1988, Marshall Happer to Hamilton Jordan.

753   *Letter*, October 30, 1988, Hamilton Jordan to Gene Scott.

754   MTC *Minutes*, November 2-3, 1988, London Meeting.

755   *Sports Inc.*, November 7, 1988, "Europe Backs ATP Tour."
       International Tennis Weekly, November 25, 1988, "Battle is Won, ATP Tour on the Way."

756   *Letter*, November 7, 1988, Marshall Happer to Ray Moore.
       Letter, November 9, 1988, Ray Moore to Marshall Happer.

757   *Letter*, November 9, 1988, Marshall Happer to all proposed 1990 Grand Prix tournaments.

758   *Letter*, November 10, 1988, Marshall Happer to Ray Moore."

759   *Letter*, November 17, 1988, Hamilton Jordan to Marshall Happer.
       Letter, November 18, 1988, Marshall Happer to Hamilton Jordan.

760   *Letter*, November 10, 1988, Marshall Happer to Ray Moore.

761   *Letter*, November 15, 1988, Marshall Happer to Grand Slam Chairmen.
762   MTC *Minutes*, November 29 – December 1, 1988, New York Meeting.
763   *Letter*, November 16, 1988, Roy Reardon to Marshall Happer.
764   *Letter*, November 30, 1988, Ray Moore, Marty Davis and Weller Evans to Marshall Happer.
765   *Telex*, December 1, 1988, Buzzer Hadingham to Marshall Happer.
766   *Settlement Agreement*, December 1, 1988, MTC and Volvo, ProServ and IMG.
767   *Press Release*, December 1, 1988, "Lawsuit Settlement Announced."
768   *Press Release*, December 1, 1988, "Men's Tennis Council Announces 1990 Format."
769   *New York Times*, Peter Alfano, December 2, 1988, "Tennis Council Modifies Tour."
770   *Letter*, December 7, 1988, Marshall Happer to Buzzer Hadingham.
771   *New York Times*, Peter Alfano, December 3, 1988, "Tennis Players Set Plans for New Tour."
772   *New York Times*, Peter Alfano, December 12, 1988, "Players Get Set for Season of Transition."
773   *Letter*, December 8, 1988, Buzzer Hadingham to Marshall Happer.
774   *Letter*, December 19, 1988, Marshall Happer to Buzzer Hadingham.
775   *Letter*, December 22, 1988, Buzzer Hadingham to Marshall Happer.
776   *Letter*, December 19, 1988, Marshall Happer to Hamilton Jordan with a copy to all Players, Tournaments and Other Interested Parties.
777   *International Tennis Weekly*, January 13, 1989, "ATP Responds to Latest Happer Proposal."
778   *Letter*, January 3, 1989, Hamilton Jordan to Marshall Happer.
779   *Letter*, December 19, 1988, Marshall Happer to Franco Bartoni.
       Letter, December 19, 1988, Marshall Happer to Graham Lovett.
       Letter, December 19, 1988, Marshall Happer to Charles Pasarell.

Chapter 32

780   *1989 Official MIPTC Yearbook*, (MIPTC 1988).
781   *International Tennis Weekly*, January 27, 1989, "ATP Officially Announces Tour for 1990."
782   *Letter*, January 29, 1989, Ray Moore to Marshall Happer.
783   *International Tennis Weekly*, May 5, 1989, "David Cooper Joins ATP Tour Staff in Key Position."
784   *Note*, September 19, 1989, Hamilton Jordan to Marshall Happer.
785   MTC *Minutes*, February 15, 1989, Milan Meeting.
786   MTC *Minutes*, June 26-27, 1989, London Meeting.
787   *Plan of Liquidation*, signed in September of 1989 by all 9 members of the Council.
788   MTC *Minutes*, December 1, 1989, New York Meeting.
789   *Amendment to Plan of Liquidation*, signed in December of 1989 and January of 1990 by all 9 members of the Council.
790   *MTC Minutes*, December 1, 1989, New York Meeting.
791   *Audited Financial Statements*, Ernst & Whinney, December 31, 1989, "Men's Tennis Council."
792   *The Bud Collins, History of Tennis*, Bud Collins, (Canada 2008), 700.
       World of Tennis 1990, edited by John Barrett, compiled by Marijke Volger, (London 1990), 235, 239.
793   *Ibid*, 107.
794   Ibid, 243.

Chapter 33

795   Official 1989 MTC Yearbook, (MTC 1989), 270-279.

Chapter 34

796   *International Tennis Weekly*, January 13, 1989, "Tournament Application Committee Appointed by Players and Tournaments."

797   *Confidential Fax*, dated February 23, 1989, Hamilton Jordan to Marshall Happer.
798   *International Tennis Weekly*, March 10, 1989, "Davis Cup Dates."
       International Tennis Weekly, March 10, 1989, "ITF Schedules Davis Cup Conflict with ATP Tour."
       Letter, April 14, 1989, Hamilton Jordan to all ATP Tour tournaments.
799   *International Tennis Weekly*, April 14, 1989, "ATP Tour selects IMG for Certain Marketing Rights: Presenting Sponsor, International TV Package and ATP Finals."
800   *Report No. 1 From ATP Tour Board Meeting*, April 14, 1989, "To All ATP Tour Tournaments."
801   *International Tennis Weekly*, May 5, 1989, "Wimbledon: 'The Leaders of Our Sport.'"
802   *Fax*, June 13, 1989, Philippe Chatrier to all National Associations and Regional Associations.
       Fax, June 15, 1989, Hamilton Jordan to All National Federations, National Associations and Tournament Organizers of Future Challenger Series tournaments and Satellite Series Circuits.
803   *Press Release*, June 15, 1989, "ITF Grand Slam Committee Formed."
804   *International Tennis Weekly*, July 21, 1989, "ProServ Plots Strategy Against ATP Tour."
805   *International Tennis Weekly*, August 11, 1989, "ProServ Executive Directs Criticism at Wimbledon and ATP Tour."
806   *International Tennis Weekly*, August 4, 1989, "ProServ Responds to ITW Article on Meeting in London."
807   *International Tennis Weekly*, August 4, 1989, "Grand Slams to Enter Twilight Zone Era."
808   *International Tennis Weekly*, September, 1989, "Babcock Responds on Behalf of Grand Slams."
809   *International Tennis Weekly*, August 4, 1989, "J. Wayne Richmond Named ATP Tour Commissioner for North America."
       International Tennis Weekly, August 4, 1989, "ATP Tour will Rely on Regional Leadership."
810   *International Tennis Weekly*, August 25, 1989, "ATP Tour Announces Plan to Expand Drug Testing Program."
811   *International Tennis Weekly*, Hamilton Jordan, November 3, 1989, "Grand Slams' Action Difficult to Comprehend."
       International Tennis Weekly, November 10, 1989, "ATP Tour Board meeting in special session to respond to Grand Slam Exhibition."
812   *New York Times*, December 8, 1989, Robin Finn, "No End Seen to Power Struggle in Men's Game."
813   *ESPN*, November 15, 1989, "Tennis Round Table."
814   *International Tennis Weekly*, December 1, 1989, "'Best of 12' Ranking System to Begin with ATP Tour."
815   *Letter*, December 6, 1989, David Markin to Executive Committee Members and Section Presidents.

Chapter 35

816   *Memorandum*, May 3, 1990, Hamilton Jordan to Marshall Happer.
817   *New York Times*, January 22, 1990, "Boom! McEnroe is Ejected."
       New York Times, February 24, 1990, "McEnroe Loses Appeal."
818   *New York Times*, Robin Finn, February 16, 1990, "A.T.P.'s Payoff Plan Emerges as Hot Issue."
819   *New York Times*, February 17, 1990, "McEnroe Assails Tour."
820   *New York Times*, Robin Finn, February 18, 1990, "Lendl Eliminates McEnroe Easily."
       New York Times, February 20, 1990, "McEnroe Doesn't Go Gently Onto Tour."
821   *New York Times*, February 27, 1990, "Notebook: A.T.P. Executive Switches Courts."
822   *Ibid.*
823   *New York Times*, Bob Briner, March 4, 1990, "The A.T.P. Tour is a Mess: Big Surprise!"
824   *New York Times*, March 25, 1990, "Former A.T.P. President Cries Foul."
825   *New York Times*, March 16, 1990, "New A.T.P. Chief."
826   *New York Times*, October 26, 1990, "A.T.P. Fines Edberg, Lendl and Agassi."
827   *Ahead of the Game*, Owen Williams, (USA 2013), 241.
828   *New York Times*, August 28, 1990, "W.C.T. Out of Business."

829   *https://en.wikipedia.org/wiki/Grand_Slam_Cup*, accessed October 23, 2020

Chapter 36

830   *The Independent*, October 22, 2011, Andrew Longmore, "Wimbledon '99: Break point for people's chairman."
831   *Tennis Week*, Richard Evans, September 2004, "Mark Miles is jumping ship. Can Tennis shape up?",18-21.
832   *https://www.itftennis.com/media/2495/grand-slam-rulebook-2020-f.pdf*, accessed July 3, 2020.
833   *World Tennis*, Cliff Drysdale, October 1983, 'Should Guarantees Be Legalized, No."
834   *International Tennis Weekly*, August 5, 1983, "Moore Has 'Open Mind' About Pro Council Issues."
835   *Tennis Biggest Racket: Guarantees*, Paul Fein Essay (1983).
836   *World Tennis*, Steve Goldstein, October 1983, "Policing Payola," 34, 37.
837   *Email*, July 19, 2019, Philip Galloway, ATP Chief Financial Officer.
838   *"The fall of ISL*, Jakob Staun, 02.06.2006.
        https://www.playthegame.org/news/news-articles/2006/the-fall-of-isl/
839   *Complaint*, February 4, 2002, USDC Southern District of Indiana, Indianapolis Division entitled: Indianapolis Tennis Championships, Inc. and Washington Tennis and Education Foundation, Inc. v. Mark Miles as Chief Executive Officer of the ATP Tour, Inc., and the ATP Tour in the United States District Court, Southern District of Indiana, Indianapolis Division (Case No. IP 02-0196 C-H/K".
840   *https://www.tennisforum.com/threads/world-1-supports-the-imta.60437/*, accessed April 14, 2021.
841   *South Florida Sun-Sentinel*, Charles Bricker, June 15, 2003, "ATP Money Bid Slammed."
842   *Tennis Week*, Richard Evans, September 2004, "Mark Miles is jumping ship. Can Tennis shape Up?," 18-21.
843   *Claim*, April 5, 2006, British High Court of Justice, Chancery Division, Adidas-Salomon AG v. Roger Draper and Derek Paul Howorth sued on behalf of themselves and the members of the Lawn Tennis Association, Timothy Dewe Phillips and Martin Guntrip sued on behalf of themselves and the members of the All England Lawn Tennis and Croquet Club, Lawn Tennis Association of Australia, Limited, trading as Tennis Australia, Federation Francaise de Tennis, United States Tennis Association Incorporated and ITF Limited, trading as International Tennis Federation.
844   *Complaint*, Monte-Carlo Country Club and Société Monégasque Pour L'Exploitation Du Tournoi De Tennis, Plaintiffs v. ATP Tour, Inc, Etienne de Villiers and Charles Pasarell, Defendants, USDC for the District of Delaware, April 9, 2007, Docket #07-198.
845   *Complaint*, March 28, 2007, Duetscher Tennis Bund (German Tennis Federation) and Rothembaum Sports GMBH, Plaintiffs v. ATP Tour, Inc., and John Does 1-10, Docket #07-178.
846   *Bund v. ATP Tour, Inc.*, Argued November 2, 2009, Filed June 25, 2010, 610 F. 3d 820; Cert. Denied November 29, 2010, 562 U.S. 1064.
847   *ATP Tour, Inc. et al. v Deutscher Tennis Bund, Rothenbaum Sport GMBH and Qatar Tennis Federation*, No. 534.2013, May 8, 2014.
848   https://en.wikipedia.org/wiki/Next_Generation_ATP_Finals, accessed April 14, 2021.
849   *Essentially Sports*, Bhivashya Mittal, December 12, 2020, "Former ATP President Calls for the Merger of ATP Cup and Davis Cup." https://www.essentiallysports.com/former-atp-president-calls-for-the-merger-of-atp-cup-and-davis-cup-tennis-news/, accessed January 2, 2021.
850   *https://www.essentiallysports.com/tennis-news-atp-records-significant-growth-in-gross-revenue-from-2013-to-2018/*, accessed January 2, 2021.
851   *https://en.wikipedia.org/wiki/Electronic_line_judge*, accessed August 6, 2019.
852   *New York Times*, Joshua Shapiro, March 21, 1993, "Technology; The Electronic Umpire That'll

Call the Shots at the U.S. Open."

853 *https://en.wikipedia.org/wiki/Hawk-Eye,* accessed August 6, 2019.

854 Tennis World USA, Luigi Gatto, March 3, 2018, "Hawk-Eye Live Could Be Introduced in the ATP Tour."

855 New York Times, Cindy Shmerler, March 1, 2018, "Tennis Moves Toward Taking the Human Element Out of Line Calls."

856 *https://en.wikipedia.org/wiki/Tennis_Channel,* accessed October 23, 2020.

857 *New York Times,* Cindy Shmerler, April 23, 2019, "Justin GameStop's Criminal Case Is Settled. Now He Awaits a Verdict from His Tennis Peers."
New York Times, Cindy Boren, May 1, 2019, "Justin Gimelstob resigns from ATP board after assault plea and player backlash."

858 *New York Times,* Ben Rothenberg, August 28, 2020, "Djokovic and Other top Men Are Creating a Players' Association."

859 *Sportico,* John Wallstreet, September 3, 2020, "Djokovic Forms New Professional Tennis Players Association, Lacks Support to Command Change."

860 *https://www.reuters.com/article/us-tennis-overhaul-exclusive/exclusive-tennis-t7-gets-down-to-the-business-of-evolution-atp-chief-gaudenzi-idUSKBN2B21DC,* accessed April 15, 2021.

Chapter 37

861 *1990 USTA Yearbook,* 15.

862 *New York Times,* Elsa Brenner, August 9, 1992, "Tennis Group's Move Cheers Realtors."

863 *New York Times,* Robert McG Thomas, Jr., August 17, 1990, "TENNIS: Quiet, Please! Air Traffic rerouted From U.S."

864 *New York Times,* Lindsey Gruson, May 22, 1992, "F.A.A. Returns La Guardia Flight Path to Queens."

865 *https://en.wikipedia.org/wiki/Arthur_Ashe_Stadium,* accessed May 8, 2019.

866 *https://en.wikipedia.org/wiki/Hamilton_Jordan,* accessed May 8, 2019.

867 *U.S. Open Television Report,* April 13, 1998, ProServ Television.

868 *New York Times,* Selena Roberts, August 23, 1996, "Officials Draw Criticism and Redo Men's Open."

Bibliography

1959	*Man with a Racket*, the autobiography of Pancho Gonzales as told to Cy Rice, (New York 1959).
1962	*Tennis Rebel*, Mike Davies, (London 1962).
1968	*World Tennis Magazine*, December 1968.
1969	*1969 USLTA Yearbook.*
1969	*BP Year Book of World Tennis 1969*, edited by John Barrett, compiled by Peter West, (London 1969).
1970	*1970 USLTA Yearbook.*
1970	*1970 Experimental Grand Prix Rules*, (ILTF 1970).
1970	*BP Year Book of World Tennis 1970*, edited by John Barrett, compiled by Lance Tingay, (London 1971).
1971	*1971 USLTA Yearbook.*
1971	*World of Tennis '71*, edited by John Barrett, compiled by Lance Tingay, (London 1971).
1971	*1971 Pepsi Grand Prix Rules*, (ILTF 1971).
1971	*The Education of a Tennis Player*, Rod Laver with Bud Collins, (Canada 1971, 2009).
1972	*1972 USLTA Yearbook.*
1972	*World of Tennis '72*, edited by John Barrett, compiled by Lance Tingay, (London 1972).
1972	*Wimbledon, A Celebration*, John McPhee, (New York 1972).
1972	*1972 Commercial Union Grand Prix Rules*, (ILTF 1972).
1972	*The Fireside Book of Tennis*, edited by Allison Danzig and Peter Schwed, (New York 1972).
1973	*1973 USLTA Yearbook.*
1973	*World of Tennis '73*, edited by John Barrett, compiled by Lance Tingay, (London 1973).
1973	*1973 Commercial Union Grand Prix Rules*, (ILTF 1973).

1974	*The Encyclopedia of Tennis* Edited by Max Robertson, Advisory Editor Jack Kramer, (New York 1974).
1974	*World of Tennis '74*, edited by John Barrett, compiled by Lance Tingay, (London 1974).
1974	*1974 USLTA Yearbook.*
1974	*1974 Commercial Union Grand Prix Rules*, (ILTF 1974).
1975	*1975 USLTA Yearbook.*
1975	*World of Tennis '75*, edited by John Barrett, compiled by Lance Tingay, (London 1975).
1975	*1975 Commercial Union Grand Prix Rules, (MIPTC 1975).*
1975	*Big Bill Tilden*, Frank Deford, (USA 1975).
1976	*1976 Commercial Union Grand Prix Rules*, (MIPTC 1976).
1976	*The Tennis Bubble*, Rich Koster, (New York 1976).
1976	*World of Tennis '76*, edited by John Barrett, compiled by Lance Tingay, (London 1976).
1976	*1976 USTA Yearbook.*
1977	*The Art of World Team Tennis*, Greg Hoffman, (San Francisco 1977).
1977	*World of Tennis 1977*, edited by John Barrett, compiled by Lance Tingay, (London 1977).
1977	*1977 USTA Yearbook.*
1977	*1977 Colgate Grand Prix Rules and Regulations*, (MIPTC 1977).
1978	1978 USTA Yearbook.
1978	*World of Tennis 1978*, edited by John Barrett, compiled by Lance Tingay, (London 1978).
1978	*1978 Colgate Grand Prix Rules and Regulations,*(MIPTC 1978).
1978	*1978 USTA Circuit Regulations*, (USTA 1978).
1979	*The Game, My 40 Years in Tennis*, Jack Kramer with Frank Deford , (New York 1979).
1979	*World of Tennis 1979*, edited by John Barrett, compiled by Lance Tingay, (London 1979).
1979	*1979 USTA Yearbook.*
1979	*1979 Colgate Grand Prix Rules and Regulations*, (MIPTC 1979).

1979   *1979 USTA Circuit Regulations* (USTA 1979*)*.

1980   *1980 USTA Yearbook.*

1980   *World of Tennis 1980,* edited by John Barrett, compiled by Lance Tingay, (London 1980).

1980   *1980 Volvo Grand Prix Rules and Regulations,* (MIPTC 1980).

1980   *Bud Collins Tennis Encyclopedia,* edited by Bud Collins and Zander Hollander, (USA 1980, 1994, 1997).

1981   *World of Tennis 1981,* edited by John Barrett, compiled by Lance Tingay, (London 1981).

1981   *1981 USTA Yearbook.*

1981   *1981 Volvo Grand Prix Rules and Regulations,* (MIPTC 1981).

1981   *Wimbledon, Centre Court of the Game,* Max Robertson , (Great Britain 1981).

1982   *1982 USTA Yearbook.*

1982   *World of Tennis 1982,* edited by John Barrett, compiled by Lance Tingay, (London 1982).

1982   *1982 Volvo Grand Prix Yearbook,* (MIPTC 1982).

1982   *1982 MIPTC Supplement,* (MIPTC 1982).

1982   *Wimbledon '82 Tournament Program,* All England Club Wimbledon.

1983   *World of Tennis 1983,* edited by John Barrett, compiled by Lance Tingay, (London 1983).

1983   *1983 Official Professional Tennis Yearbook,* (MIPTC 1983).

1983   *Supplement No.1, Amendments to the 1983 Official MIPTC Professional Tennis Yearbook,* (MIPTC January 22, 1983).

1983   *Supplement No.2, Amendments to the 1983 Official MIPTC Professional Tennis Yearbook,* (MIPTC March 31, 1983).

1983   *Supplement No.3, Amendments to the 1983 Official MIPTC Professional Tennis Yearbook,* (MIPTC June 10, 1983).

1983   *1983 USTA Yearbook.*

1983   *Wimbledon '83 Tournament Program,* All England Club Wimbledon.

1984   *World of Tennis 1984,* edited by John Barrett, compiled by Lance Tingay, (London 1984).

1984   *1984 Official Professional Tennis Yearbook,* (MIPTC 1984).

1984   *1984 USTA Yearbook.*

1984   *Wimbledon '84 Tournament Program*, All England Club Wimbledon.

1985   *Tennis Down Under*, Fred Stolle & Kenneth Wydro, (Bethesda MD 1985).

1985   *The Story of the Davis Cup*, Alan Trengove, (London 1985).

1985   *1985 Official MIPTC Yearbook*, (MIPTC 1985).

1985   *World of Tennis 1985*, Edited by John Barrett and compiled by Lance Tingay, (London 1985).

1985   *John Martin Deposition Transcript*, September 18, 1985.

1985   *1985 USTA Yearbook*

1985   *Wimbledon '85 Tournament Program*, All England Club Wimbledon.

1985   *Tennis Magazine*, June 1985, Peter Bodo, "Is Marshall Happer The Lawman Who'll Really Clean Up Men's Tennis", 60.

1986   *World of Tennis 1986*, edited by John Barrett, compiled by Lance Tingay, (London 1986).

1986   *1986 Official MIPTC Yearbook*, (MIPTC 1986).

1986   *1986 USTA Yearbook*

1986   *Wimbledon 1986 Tournament Program*, All England Club Wimbledon.

1987   *World of Tennis 1987*, edited by John Barrett, compiled by Lance Tingay, (London 1987).

1987   *1987 USTA Yearbook*.

1987   *1987 Official MIPTC Yearbook*, (MIPTC 1987).

1987   *Supplement No. 1 to the 1987 MIPTC Yearbook, (MIPTC February 6, 1987).*

1987   *Supplement No. 2 to the 1987 MIPTC Yearbook, (MIPTC January 1, 1987).*

1987   *Supplement No. 3 to the 1987 MIPTC Yearbook, (MIPTC April 15, 1987).*

1987   *Cumulative Supplement No. 1 to the 1987 MIPTC Yearbook, (MIPTC April 23, 1987).*

1987   *Supplement No. 4 to the 1987 MIPTC Yearbook, (MIPTC June 11, 1987).*

1987   *Wimbledon 1987 Tournament Program*, All England Club Wimbledon.

1988   *We Have Come A long Way*, Billie Jean King with Cynthia Starr, (New York 1988).

1988   *Shades of Gray, Tennis Writings of David Gray*, edited by Lance Tingay, (London 1988).

1988   *75 Years Of The International Tennis Federation 1913-1988*, edited by Dennis Cunnington, (Great Britain 1988).

1988   *World of Tennis 1988*, edited by John Barrett, compiled by Lance Tingay, (London 1988).

1988   *1988 USTA Yearbook.*

1988   *1988 Official MIPTC Yearbook*, (MIPTC 1988).

1988   *Supplement No. 6 to the 1987 MIPTC Yearbook*, (MIPTC January 4, 1988).

1988   *Trabert on Tennis*. Tony Trabert with Gerald Secor Couzens, (USA 1988).

1988   *Wimbledon 1988 Tournament Program*, All England Club Wimbledon.

1989   *Official 1989 MTC Media Guide*, (MTC 1989).

1989   *Minding Other People's Business*, Donald L. Dell, (New York 1989).

1989   *World of Tennis 1989*, edited by John Barrett , compiled by Lance Tingay, (London 1989).

1989   *1989 Official MIPTC Yearbook*, (MIPTC 1988).

1989   *1989 USTA Yearbook*

1989   *Wimbledon 1989 Tournament Program*, All England Club Wimbledon.

1990   The *1990 Official Rulebook of The ATP Tour*, (ATP Tour 1990).

1990   *World of Tennis 1990*, edited by John Barrett, compiled by Marijke Volger, (London 1990).

1990   *ATP Player Guide 1990.*

1990   *1990 USTA Yearbook.*

1990   *Barbarians At The Gate*, Bryan Burrough and John Helyar, (USA 1990, 2003, 2008).

1993   *Open Tennis*, Richard Evans, (London 1993).

1993   *Days of Grace*, Arthur Ashe, (New York 1993).

2000   *The History of Professional Tennis*, Joe McCauley, (Great Britain 2000, 2003).

2000   *No Such Thing as a Bad Day*, Hamilton Jordan, (Marietta GA 2000).

2002   *You Cannot Be Serious*, John McEnroe with James Kaplan, (New York 2002).

2002   *Tennis Confidential*, Paul Fein, (USA 2002).

2002   *Autobiography of Pat Cash*, Pat Cash, (Great Britain 2002).

2002   *Frank Parker, Champion in the Golden Age of Tennis*, (Singapore 2002).

2002   *Newk*, John Newcombe and Larry Writer, (Australia 2002).

2004   *Nonsense at the Net*, Jim Westhall, (USA 2004).

2004   *Bad News for McEnroe*, Bill Scanlon with Sonny Long and Cathy Long, (New York 2004).

2005   *You Can Quote Me on That*, Paul Fein, (USA 2005).

2006   *A Tennis Experience and All That...*, Alex B. Aitchison, (New York 2006).

2008   *The Bud Collins, History of Tennis*, Bud Collins, (Canada 2008).

2008   *Tennis Confidential II*, Paul Fein, (USA 2008).

2009   *Never Make The First Offer*, Donald Dell with John Boswell ,(New York 2009).

2009   *Holding Court*, Chris Gorringe, (United Kingdom 2009).

2009   *A Pilot at Wimbledon*, Air Chief Marshal Sir Brian Burnett GCB, DFC, AFC, (Great Britain 2009).

2009   *As it Was*, Gardnar P. Mulloy, (USA 2009).

2010   *Tennis History*, Jim McManus, (Canada 2010).

2010   *Grand Slam Record Book, Volumes 1 & 2*, Alessandro Albiero and Andrea Carta (Italy 2010).

2010   *The Grand Slam Record Book, Volume 1*, edited by Alessandro Albiero and Andrea Carta, (Monte Porzio Catone 2010).

2010   *The Grand Slam Record Book, Volume 2*, edited by Alessandro Albiero and Andrea Carta, (Monte Porzio Catone 2010).

2011   *High Strung*, Stephen Tignor, (New York, 2011).

2012   *Lamar Hunt, A Life in Sports*, Michael MacCambridge, (USA 2012).

2013   *Ahead of the Game*, Owen Williams, (USA 2013).

2013   *The Outsider*, Jimmy Connors, (New York 2013).

2013   *The International Tennis Federation, A Century of Contribution to Tennis*, Chris Bowers, edited by Emily Forder-White, (Italy 2013).

2014   *Rod Laver, An Autobiography* (Australia 2013, Great Britain 2014).

2015   *A Boy from Georgia*, Edited by Kathleen Jordan, forwood by President Jimmy Carter, (Athens GA 2015).

2017   *The United States Tennis Association: Raising The Game*, Warren F. Kimball, (Lincoln Univ. of Nebraska Press, 2017).

2018   *Arthus Ashe, A Life*, Raymond Arsenault, (USA 2018).

2021   *The History of Tennis*, Richard Evans, (USA 2021).

Photo Credits

Covers

Jack Kramer	Russ Adams Photo
Philippe Chatrier:	ITHOF/John Russell Photo
Lamar Hunt	Russ Adams Photo
Herman David	AELTC/Michael Cole Photo
Marshall Happer	Russ Adams Photo

Book

Chapter 1

Page 3:	Owen Williams as a Shamateur	Williams Photo
Page 13:	Pancho Gonzales	Russ Adams Photo
Page 13:	Lew Hoad	Ern McQuillan, Public Domain

Chapter 6

Page 100:	Ken Rosewall	Public Domain
Page 100:	Rod Laver	Russ Adams Photo

Chapter 7

Page 116:	Ilie Nastase	Russ Adams Photo
Page 117:	Nikki Pilic	Russ Adams Photo

Chapter 8

Page 146:	Jimmy Connors	ITHF/John Russell Photo

Chapter 11

Page 224:	Slew Hester	ITHF/John Russell Photo

Chapter 12

Page 244:	Grand Prix Supervisors	Russ Adams Photo

Chapter 14

Page 295:	John McEnroe	ITHF/John Russell Photo
Page 295:	Bjorn Borg	ITHF/John Russell Photo
Page 300:	Jacques Dorfman, French Open Referee	Creative Commons Attribution

Chapter 18

Page 378	Ivan Lendl	ITHF/John Russell Photo

Page 777:	Hamilton Jordan	ATP Tour Photo
Page 777:	Pierre Darmon	ATP Tour Photo
Page 778:	Paolo Angeli	ITF Photo
Page 778	Lars Myhrman	Russ Adams Photo
Page 778:	John Harris	Harris Photo
Page 778:	Stan Smith	Russ Adams Photo
Page 779:	Kobi Hermenjat	Russ Adams Photo
Page 779:	Ray Benton	Russ Adams Photo
Page 779:	Franco Bartoni	Russ Adams Photo
Page 779:	Charles Pasarell	ATP Tour Photo
Page 780:	Graham Lovett	Unknown Photographer
Page 780:	David Markin	Russ Adams Photo
Page 780:	Forrest Hainline	Hainline Photo
Page 781:	Weller Evans	ATP Tour Photo
Page 781:	Thomas Hallberg	Hallberg Photo
Page 781:	Marty Davis	Russ Adams Photo
Page 781:	Basil Reay	ITF Photo
Page 782:	David Gray	AELTC/Michael Cole Photo
Page 782:	Doug Tkachuk	Spencer Photo
Page 782:	Ron Bookman	Russ Adams Photo
Page 783:	Roy Reardon	Reardon Photo
Page 783:	Buzzer Hadingham	AELTC/Michael Cole Photo
Page 783:	Larry King	Ron Galella, Getty Images
Page 784:	Mark McCormack	Russ Adams Photo
Page 784:	Bob Kain	Russ Adams Photo
Page 784:	Ion Tiriac	Russ Adams Photo
Page 785:	John McEnroe, Sr.	Russ Adams Photo
Page 785:	Peter Lawler	Lawler Photo
Page 785:	Jerry Solomon	Solomon Photo
Page 785:	Ivan Blumberg	Blumberg Photo
Page 786:	Eric Drossart	Drossart Photo
Page 786:	Charles Pyle	George Winhart, Getty Images
Page 786:	Jack Harris	Bettman, Getty Images
Page 787:	Bobby Riggs	Public Domain
Page 787:	Georg MacCall	Photographer Unknown
Page 787:	Dave Dixon	Fairfax Media, Getty Images
Page 787:	Al Hill, Jr.	Russ Adams Photo
Page 788:	Derek Penman	AELTC/Michael Cole Photo
Page 788:	Giorgio de Stefani	ITF Photo
Page 788:	Ben Barnett	ITF Photo
Page 788:	Walter Elcock	Russ Adams Photo
Page 789:	Jaime Fillol	ATP Tour Photo
Page 789:	Matt Doyle	ATP Tour Photo
Page 789:	Brian Gottfried	Russ Adams Photo
Page 789:	Richard Evans	Art Seitz Photo
Page 789:	Larry Davidson	ATP Tour Photo
Page 789:	Dennis Spencer	Spencer Photo
Page 789:	Dewey Blanton	ATP Tour Photo
Page 789:	Temple Pouncey	Russ Adams Photo
Page 790:	David Arnott	Spencer Photo

Chapter 39: Remembrances

Page 802:	Handsome Eight	Photographer Unknown
Page 803:	1971 WCT	Russ Adams Photo
Page 804:	1977 USTA Executive Committee	Russ Adams Photo
Page 805:	1978 MIPTC Tokyo Meeting	Photographer Unknown
Page 805:	McNamee, Hoad, McNamara, Scott	Photographer Unknown
Page 806	1981 Volvo Masters, Kramer/Happer	Russ Adams Photo
Page 806:	1981 Happer, Budge, Ashe, Hoad, Kramer	Russ Adams Photo
Page 807:	1982 MIPTC New York Meeting	Russ Adams Photo
Page 807:	Trabert, Perry, Hoad, Budge, Sedgman	Russ Adams Photo
Page 808:	Hoad and Davies	Russ Adams Photo
Page 808:	Evans, Robbins, Selmi, McManus, Fechtman	ATP Tour Photo
Page 809:	Jordan and Happer	Russ Adams Photo
Page 809:	Marshall Happer	Russ Adams Photo
Page 810:	Frank Hammond	ITHOF/John Russell Photo
Page 810:	Ted Tinling	ITHOF/John Russell Photo
Page 811:	Happer, Bookman and Gottfried	Photographer Unknown
Page 811:	Tennis Sheriff Caricature	Tennis Magazine 1985
Page 812:	Russ Adams	ITHOF/John Russell Photo
Page 812:	Bud Collins	ITHOF/John Russell Photo
Page 812:	Vitas Gerulaitis	ITHOF/John Russell Photo
Page 813:	Vitas Gerulaitis Foundation Dinner	Photographer Unknown
Page 814:	US Open Commemorative Plaque	USTA National Tennis Center
Page 814:	MTC Logo	
Page 814:	Masters of Tennis Trophy	